AN ENCYCLO-
PAEDIA OF
OCCULTISM

The Reign of Antichrist

After an engraving by Michael Volgemuth in the *Liber Chronicorum*, 1493

(Cabinet of Engravings, Bibliothèque Nationale, Paris)

ANTICHRIST

Group of Arabian magicians repenting of their sorceries

Old astrological chart of the planets

Marriage is Honorable in all. Hebrews, Chap 13. Verse 4.

Astrological Idea of Marriage

ASTROLOGICAL ALLEGORIES

A Babylonian demon
(British Museum, No. 22458)

Types of Babylonian demons

The demon was a very real presence in Babylonian life. Extraordinary care was taken not to offend the beings of the unseen world and nowhere did the art of exorcism reach a higher state of evolution than in Babylonia and Assyria. The prototypes of European demonology can be traced in these figures.

Clay model of a sheep's liver
used in divination (Babylon, c. 2,000 B.C.)

Exorcizing demons of disease (Babylon)

BABYLONIAN MAGICAL OBJECTS

EMMANUEL SWEDENBORG

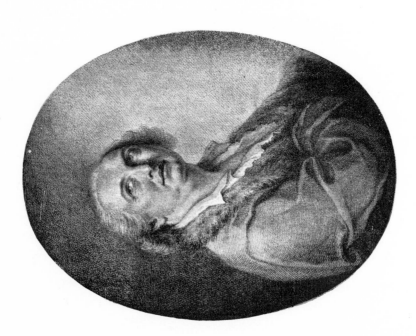

Count Cagliostro

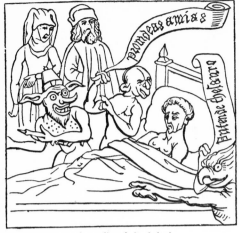

A mediæval death bed

Condemned souls carried to their place of punishment

Satan in bonds

The Demon of the Treasure

The Trumpeter of Evil

The witch and the demon

MEDIÆVAL CONCEPTIONS OF DEMONS

The Devil attempting to seize a magician who had
formed a pact with him, is prevented by a Lay Brother.
Facsimile of a miniature in the *Chroniques de Saint-
Denis* (13th cent. MS., Bibl. Nat., Paris)

The Prince of Darkness. After a miniature of the Holy
Grail (15th cent. MS., Bibl. Nat., Paris)

The Angel, holding the keys of Hell, enchains the Devil, in the shape of a dragon,
in the Pit. Miniature from a Commentary on the Apocalypse (12th cent. MS., in
the library of M. Ambrose Firmin-Didot)

MEDIÆVAL CONCEPTIONS OF THE DEVIL

Set

Amulets of Hathor

Divining Cup

The scribe Ani passing through the door of the tomb.
Outside are his shadow and his soul in the form of a
human-headed bird. (From the *Papyrus of Ani*, plate 18)

Cord with seven knots and two labels with magic spells (Berlin, 10826)

EGYPT : MAGICAL PICTURES AND OBJECTS

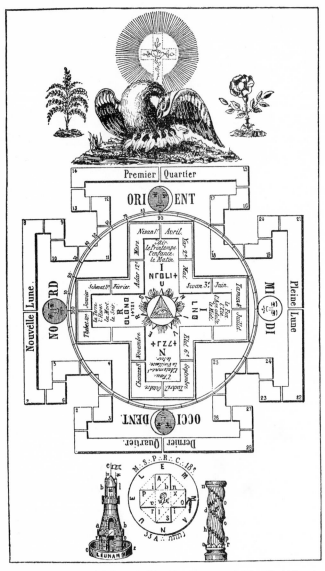

Mystical diagram of Solomon's Temple, as prophesied by Ezekiel and planned in the building scheme of the Knights Templar

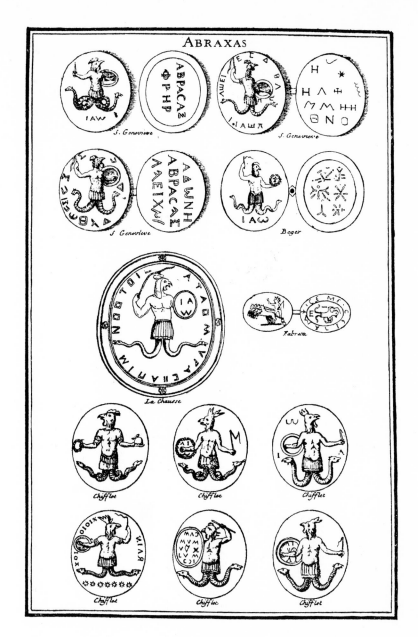

GNOSTIC GEMS

Talismans, magical charms, and invocations of the Gnostic sect. Illustrative of the mysteries of the Gnostics: it shows Abraxas, the chief Deity, in his manifestations.

Pantacle of Kabalistic letters

The diagram below illustrates the doctrine of Emanotinos, and has also an alchemistical significance in its metallurgical nomerclature of the several circles.

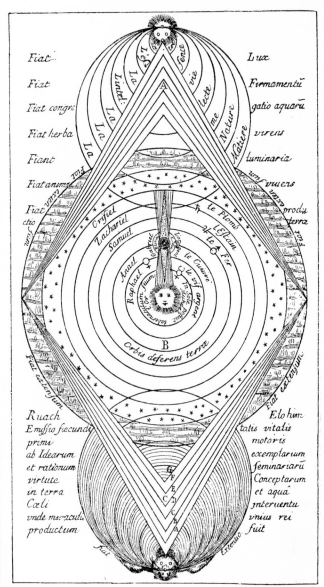

General plan of Kabalistic doctrine

The Magical Head of Zohar

KABALISTIC DIAGRAMS AND SYMBOLS

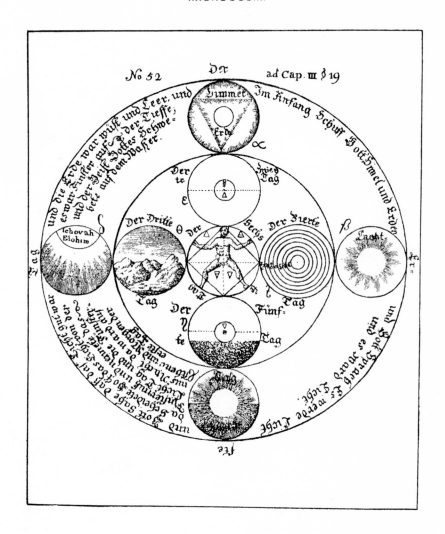

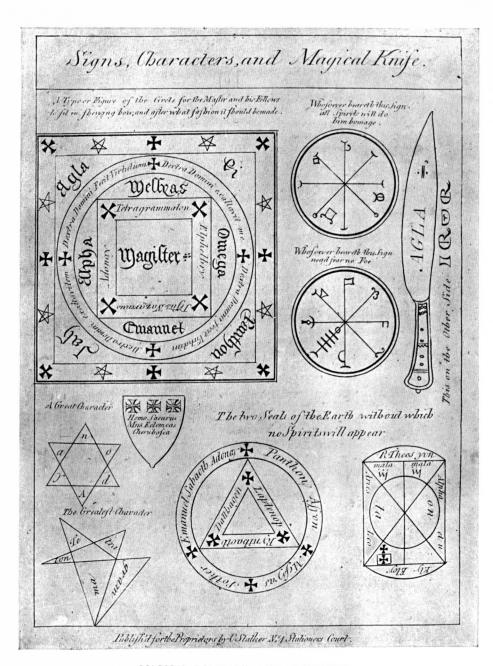

MAGICAL DIAGRAMS AND REQUISITES

Basket used in the Mithraic mysteries
to carry sacred serpents

Mithra

Mithraic temple

Inlaid pavement, showing Eleusinian neophyte carrying a
sheaf of corn and fire

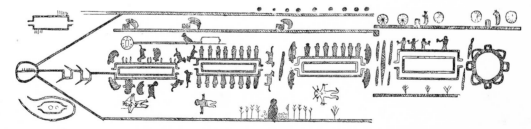

American-Indian drawing of the initiation ceremony of the Midiwiwin

ANCIENT MYSTERIES

INITIATE INTO THE ELEUSINIAN MYSTERIES,
accompanied by Demeter and Persephone
From Michael's, *Century of Archæological Discovery*
(with permission from the publisher, Mr. John Murray)

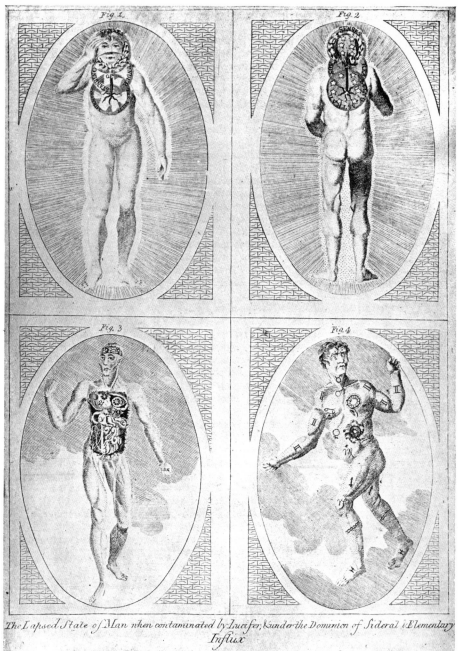

The Lapsed State of Man when contaminated by Lucifer, & under the Dominion of Sideral & Elementary Influx

Man in his lapsed and primeval states, as invested with power by his Creator to rule and govern gross elements

THE BROTHERS IRA & W^M DAVENPORT.

These were the earliest exponents of manifestations, but their methods were later exposed as of the nature of trickery.

CHA^S FOSTER AND A SPIRIT

One of the earliest spirit-photographs in existence, bearing but little resemblance to the later type of photographic materializations.

LEAH.　　　　KATE.　　　　MARGARETTA.

The three Fox Sisters, the first exponents of 'Table-tapping'

EARLY HISTORY OF SPIRITUALISM

A snap-shot photo of a child as seen clairvoyantly
by Dr. Hooper

The first spirit-photo of Archdeacon Colley, with a few
lines addressed to the Crewe 'circle' at Mr. Hope's house

A psychograph (negative, i.e, reversed). A portion of the
outermost line is erased: this was probably due to the 'tablet'
being too broad for 'precipitating' on to the photographic
plate. The dots below are meaningless additions.

A typical spirit-photograph.   Two ladies sitting; one almost entirely obscured by a
spirit-cloud.

PHOTOGRAPHS OF SPIRITUALISTIC MATERIALIZATIONS
(from Rev. G. Henslow's *The Proofs of the Truths of Spiritualism*)

Sibly del.   Ames, Sculp.

EDW^D. KELLY, A MAGICIAN.
in the Act of invoking the Spirit of a Desceased Person.
Dr Dees Werks.

THE SABBATH   St. James the Elder combating the diabolical enchantments of a magician.   Composed by Brueghel the Elder; engraved by Cock
(16th Century)

THE ROUND TABLE OF KING ARTHUR.

From the Original, preserved in the Court-House of the Castle at Winchester
"SANGREALE"— or "HOLY GRAIL."

LUNATIONS.

13 Lunations.

$\dfrac{2 = \text{"Sun—Moon."} \quad (\text{"Light—Dark."})}{26 \text{ Knights.}}$

Royal Seat.
SUN.
"PHALLOS."

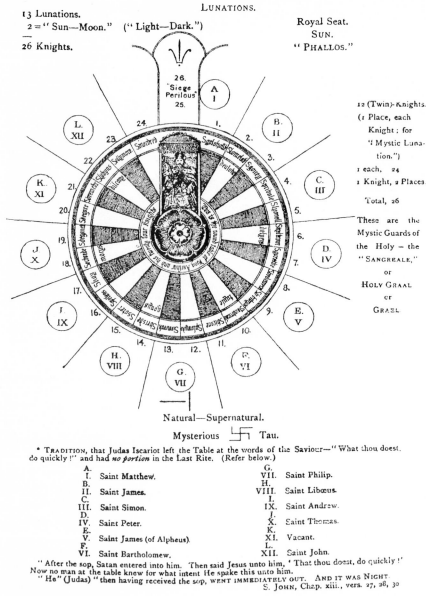

12 (Twin)-Knights.
(1 Place, each
Knight ; for
1 Mystic Luna-
tion.")
1 each, 24
1 Knight, 2 Places.

Total, 26

These are the
Mystic Guards of
the Holy — the
"SANGREALE,"
or
HOLY GRAAL
or
GRAEL.

Natural—Supernatural.

Mysterious ⌐Ⴈ Tau.

* TRADITION, that Judas Iscariot left the Table at the words of the Saviour—"What thou doest,
do quickly !" and had *no portion* in the Last Rite. (Refer below.)

A.		G.	
I.	Saint Matthew.	VII.	Saint Philip.
B.		H.	
II.	Saint James.	VIII.	Saint Libœus.
C.		I.	
III.	Saint Simon.	IX.	Saint Andrew.
D.		J.	
IV.	Saint Peter.	X.	Saint Thomas.
E.		K.	
V.	Saint James (of Alpheus).	XI.	Vacant.
F.		L.	
VI.	Saint Bartholomew.	XII.	Saint John.

"After the sop, Satan entered into him. Then said Jesus unto him, ' That thou doest, do quickly !'
Now no man at the table knew for what intent He spake this unto him.
"He" (Judas) "then having received the sop, WENT IMMEDIATELY OUT. AND IT WAS NIGHT.
S. JOHN, Chap. xiii., vers. 27, 28, 30

SEAT OF THE HOLY GRAIL AT THE ROUND TABLE

OLD-MAID WITCH.   Facsimile of a wood-engraving attributed to Holbein, taken from the
German translation of Boethius' *De Consolatione Philosophiae*, Augsburg edition, 1537.

APPOLON͏ᵗ TYANEUS in Domitians Time.

MAHOMET receives his Law by Inspiration.

ROGER BACON an Inglishman.

EDWᵈ KELLY Prophet or Seer to Dᵈ DEE.

Dᵈ DEE avoucheth his Stone is brought by Angelical Ministry.

PARACELSUS Receivs from the Inspiration of Spirits.

Ames sculp Bristol.

THE ORDER OF THE ILLUMINATI

AN ENCYCLO-PAEDIA OF OCCULTISM

A COMPENDIUM OF INFORMATION ON THE OCCULT

SCIENCES, OCCULT PERSONALITIES, PSYCHIC

SCIENCE, MAGIC, DEMONOLOGY, SPIRITISM,

MYSTICISM AND METAPHYSICS

BY LEWIS SPENCE

The Citadel Press   Secaucus, New Jersey

Library of Congress Catalog Number 59-15875

ISBN 8065-0427-7

First Paperbound Printing 1974

The Citadel Press
120 Enterprise Ave., Secaucus, N.J. 07094

Printed in U.S.A. by
NOBLE OFFSET PRINTERS, INC.
New York, N.Y. 10003

TO MY WIFE,

WHO BELIEVES IN ME RATHER THAN IN MY BELIEFS.

PUBLISHER'S PREFACE

THIS book was originally published in 1920. To reprint it now verbatim, except for an occasional correction of a misprint, calls for an explanation.

The explanation is quite simple. No book published in the past forty years has replaced this one or come near replacing it. Regardless of date of publication, this one remains the best encyclopaedia available.

It was written and published under extraordinary circumstances which have not repeated themselves. Its publisher was the London house of George Routledge & Sons, Ltd., whose leading figures had a profound interest in occult and metaphysical subjects. Their editor in this field was the late Arthur Edward Waite, himself one of the greatest scholars who ever turned to these subjects. The author, Lewis Spence, if less profound and knowledgeable than his editor, had the good fortune to be a much better writer and popularizer, with a knack for summarizing with admirable conciseness the deeper work of others. Ironically enough, there is a very great deal of A. E. Waite in these pages (properly credited) and it may well be that (except for THE PICTORIAL KEY TO THE TAROT), Waite will be remembered by posterity primarily through these pages.

A number of eminent authorities in this field, consulted on the advisability of reprinting this book, praised it as the best of its kind, but asked if no way might be found to bring it up to date. A letter from Dr. J. B. Rhine pleads eloquently for the need and value of bridging the gap between 1920 and 1960. We should have been happy to do so but the task was beyond our powers. Our editorial staff estimated that the minimum outlay necessary would be $100,000. The plain truth of the matter is that the occult and metaphysical audience has first to be brought together before an outlay like this can be risked. Consider the simple fact that for most of the forty years since the original publication of this book, it has not been in print. For twenty years it has been hard to come by and for ten years it has been as scarce as hen's teeth. In the face of these facts, we consider it a sufficient achievement for the present to reprint it and to make it available.

Here are 2500 detailed entries, many of which run to several pages. The best way to enjoy them is to make up a short list of those occult and metaphysical words which come immediately to your mind, which you know something about but not precisely enough to be sure that you know what you are talking about, look them up and see how what you do know falls into place now. One of the best tests of this great encyclopaedia is to look up the biography of one of the most famous names in this field—Paracelsus, Cagliostro, Agrippa, Appollonius of Tyana, the Comte de Saint Germain —surprises are in store for you! Finally, turn back again to the Index and run your eye down column after column. You think you know something about the subject, you are certainly interested in it, yet see how many of the entries are completely unknown to you. This is what a book should be but so seldom is—a voyage to the unknown. This time you have achieved it.

NOVEMBER 15, 1959

PREFACE

In attempting to compile a volume which might serve as a handbook or work of reference to the several occult sciences, I have not lost sight of the extensive character of the subject, which, now that I have completed my task, is more than ever painfully perceptible. Excursions into the literature of the occult, of a somewhat extensive kind, led me to the belief that popular misconceptions concerning its several branches were many and varied. Regarding definitions there did not appear to be any substantial agreement, and application to encyclopædias and ordinary works of reference generally resulted in disappointment. That a department of human thought so pregnant with interest and so abounding in vitality should not hitherto have been reduced to presentation in reference form struck me as singular; and I resolved to do what I could to supply what seemed to me a very real literary and scientific necessity. That I have been entirely successful is too much to hope. But I have made a beginning, and this volume may inspire a more worthy hand to the compilation of a more perfect handbook of the subject.

The science of Anthropology has of late years done much to elucidate questions relating to the origins of magic, and in writing this volume I have freely applied its principles. I have not, however, permitted scientific considerations to blind me to the marvellous and romantic character of the material in which I have laboured. Indeed, I am convinced that had I in any way attempted to subvert this innate quality of the occult to purely scientific considerations—however worthy of statement—the romance inherent in it would, by reason of its very native force have defeated such an intention, and, even if arrayed in the poorest of verbiage, would still retain its marvellous powers of attraction, no estimate of which can be too high.

I have relegated the subject of methods and theories to the introduction. It remains to thank the many kind friends who have assisted me actively and by advice in the compilation of this volume. My assistants, Miss Mavie Jack and Miss K. Nixey, have placed me under a deep debt of obligation by their careful collection, arrangement and independent work upon the extensive literature relative to psychic science. To Mr. David MacRitchie, F.S.A. (Scot.), F.R.A.I., late President of the Gypsy Lore Society, I owe thanks for the article "Gypsies." The late Lieut. William Begg collected much Theosophical matter; and Mr. W. G. Blaikie Murdoch has rendered me the greatest assistance with difficult biographical material. My lamented friend, the late Mr. A. J. B. Graham, greatly smoothed my path by throwing light on legal questions.

I have not burdened the articles with references, but have supplied a bibliographical appendix.

L. S.

66, Arden Street,
    EDINBURGH.

INTRODUCTION

THE sciences known as " occult " may with every reason be regarded as the culture-grounds of the science of to-day. As everyone knows, alchemy was the forerunner of chemistry, astrology the direct ancestor of astronomy, and magnetism of hypnotism. But these subjects and their kindred arts have another claim upon our attention and interest, for in their evolution we can trace many of the beginnings of philosophic and ethical processes, the recovery of which renders their examination and study as important to the whole understanding of the history of man as that of theology or the new mythology.

A generation ago it was the fashion to sneer at the occult sciences. But to-day, men of science in the foremost files of thought have placed them on the dissecting slab as fit subjects for careful examination. The result of their analysis during the past twenty years, if it has not permitted us to pierce the veil which divides man and the " supernatural," has, at all events, served to purge our sight sufficiently to enable us to see things on this side of it with a clearer vision, and to regard such researches with a more tolerant eye than hitherto. For example the *fact* of ghostly appearances is proven, whatever may be their nature, hallucinatory or otherwise, gold has been manufactured, if in small quantities, the theory of thought transference is justified, and hypnotism is utilised in ordinary medical practice.

It is perhaps necessary that in introducing such a work as this, the author should express his own beliefs regarding the subject. Concerning psychical science I firmly believe that there are " more things in heaven and earth " than our philosophy dreams of, but the vast mass of evidential matter I have perused leads me to the conclusion that as yet we have merely touched the fringes of the extra-terrestrial, and that we must rely upon psychology rather than so-called material proof to bring us further enlightenment.

As regards magic, it will be seen that I have paid considerable attention to the scientific or anthropological theories concerning it. But let not the lover of that wondrous manifestation of the human imagination dread that he has been robbed of the mystery which clings to it as darkness cleaves to night. I have amply provided for him in a hundred places, and if I have attempted to summarise current scientific hypotheses concerning magic, I have done so principally for the sake of completeness.

I may perhaps be pardoned if at this juncture I touch briefly upon a suspicion which I have refrained from including in the article on Magic, for the reason that it has not as yet blossomed into a theory.   I have for some time been of the opinion that what is known as "sympathetic" and "mimetic" magic is not of the magical species—that in short it does not partake of the nature of magic at all.   When the savage performs an act of sympathetic "magic," "rain-making" for instance, he does not regard it as magical—that is, it does not contain any element of wonder to his way of thinking.   He regards it as a cause which is certain to bring about an effect.   Now the true magic of wonder argues from effect to cause, so it would appear as if sympathetic magic were merely a species of proto-science, due to mental processes entirely similar to those by which scientific laws are produced, and scientific acts are performed—that there is an odour of certainty about it which is not found, for example, in the magic of evocation.

Although in every way in sympathy with the spirit of the esoteric societies, I have ventured to express my disbelief in the occult knowledge of the generality of their members. I am afraid, too, that I fail to grasp the arguments advanced by students of the secret tradition which plead for a belief in the "church existing before the foundations of the world," and the "inner sanctuaries" of Christianity.   I fancy most readers will agree with me that it would be extremely difficult to raise anything like a respectable membership for such an institution, and as for its prehistoric existence, that is obviously a matter for the student of mythology. That both are the product of mystical foppery and vanity is only too painfully apparent. A church which is alien to the bulk of humanity can possess little of the true spirit of Christianity.   But I must not be conceived as deriding genuine mysticism and in this connection I would advise all interested in the Grand Quest, advanced as well as neophyte, to peruse a recent admirable article by Mr. A. E. Waite, which appeared in "The Occult Review" for September, 1919, which seems to me to define the aims of the mystic once and for all.

In closing my task I feel deeply impressed by the vastness of the themes which I have so unworthily and inadequately handled during the compilation of this volume.   My attempt has been to present to the general reader a conspectus of the Occult Sciences as a whole ; and if experts in any one of those sciences observe any inaccuracy which calls for correction, I will be deeply obliged to them if they will bring it to my notice.

L.S.

66, Arden Street,
    EDINBURGH.

INDEX

PAGE

Mountain Cove Community (The) . 280
Muscle-Reading 280
Myers (Frederic William Henry) . 281
Myomancy 281
Mysteries 281
Mysteries of the Pentateuch . . 283
Mystic City of God 283
Mysticism. 283

N

" N " Rays 285
Nagualism 285
Names (Magical) 285
Napellus 285
Napper (Dr.) 285
Naströnd 285
Nat 285
Nativities 285
Natsaw. 285
Nature Spirits or Elementals . 285
Navarez (Senor) 285
Naylor (James) 285
Ndembo 286
Necromancy 286
Neoplatonism 290
Neptesh 293
Nervaura 293
Nervengeist 293
Neuhusens (Henrichus) . . 293
Nevill (William) 293
New Existence of Man upon the
    Earth 293
New Motor (The) 293
Newstead Abbey 293
New Thought 293
New Zealand 294
Ngai 296
Nganga 296
Ngembi 296
Nichusch 296
Nick, or Old Nick 296
Nicolai (Christoph Friedrich) . 296
Nif 297
Nifelheim 297
Night (Mystical of the Sufis) . 297
Nightmare 297
Nirvanic, or Atmic Plane . . 298
Norfolk (Duke of) 298
Norton (Thomas) 298
Noualli 298
Nuan 298
Numbers (Magical) 298

O

Oak Apples 298
Oak-Tree 298
Obambo (The) 299
Obeah 299
Obercit (Johann Hermann) . 299
Oberion 299
Obsession and Possession . . 299
Od Force 306
Odyle 306
Oil (Magical) 306
Ointment (Witches') . . . 306
Okey Sisters 306
Olcott (Colonel Henry Steel) . 306
Old Hat Used for Raising the Devil. 307
Old Man of the Mountain . . 307

PAGE

"Old Scratch " 307
Olympian Spirits 307
Olympic Spirits 307
Om 307
Omar Khayyam 307
Onimancy 307
Onion 307
Onomancy 307
Onychomancy 307
Onyx 307
Ooscopy and Oomantia . . 307
Opal 308
Ophites 308
Oracles 308
Orbas 311
Orchis (The Root of the) . . 311
Ordinale of Alchemy (The) . 311
Orenda 311
Orleans (Duchess of) . . . 311
Orleans (Duke of) 311
Ornithomancy 311
Oromase (Society) 311
Orphic Magic 311
Orton 311
Ostiaks 312
Oupnekhat (The) 312
Owen (Robert) 312

P

Paigoels (The) 312
Palingenesy 312
Palladino (Eusapia) 314
Palladium 314
Palladium (Order of) . . . 314
Palmistry 314
Papaloi (An Obeah Priest) . . 315
Papyri (Magical) 315
Para Brahm 315
Paracelsus 315
Paradise 318
Parama-Hamsas 320
Paraskeva (Saint) 320
Pasqually (Martinez de) . . 320
Path (The) 321
Paulicians 321
Pauline Art 321
Pawang 321
Pazzani 321
Pearls 321
Pedro de Valentia 321
Peliades 321
Pentagram 321
Perfect Sermon 321
Pernety (Antoine Joseph) . . 321
Persia 321
Peter of Apono 321
Petétin 321
Petra Philosophorum . . . 321
Phantasmagoria 321
Philadelphian Society . . . 321
Philalethes (Eirenæus) . . . 321
Philosopher's Stone . . . 322
Philosophic Summary (The) . 323
Phreno-Magnet 323
Phreno-Mesmerism . . . 323
Phrygian Cap 323
Phyllorhodomancy 324
Physical World 324

PAGE

Pierart (Z. T.) 324
Pierre (La) 324
Pinto (Grand Master of Malta) . 324
Piper (Mrs.) 324
Planchette 324
Planet 325
Planetary Logos 325
Planetary Spirits 325
Planets 325
Podovne Vile 325
Poe (Edgar Allen) 325
Poinandres 325
Polong 325
Poltergeist 325
Polynesia 326
Polytrix 328
Pontica 328
Poppy Seeds 328
Pordage 328
Porka 328
Port of Fortune 328
Postel (Guillaume) 328
Posthumous Letters . . . 328
Powder of Projection . . . 328
Powder of Sympathy . . . 328
Pozenne Vile 328
Pratyshara 328
Precipitation of Matter . . 328
Prelati 329
Premonition 329
Prenestine Lots (The) . . . 329
Pretu 329
Prophecy 329
Prophecy of Count Bombast . 330
Prophetic Books 330
Prout (Dr.) 330
Psychic 330
Psychic Body 330
Psychical Research 330
Psychograph 332
Psychography 332
Psychological Society (The) . 332
Psychomancy 333
Psychometry 333
Psylli 333
Purgatory of St. Patrick . . 333
Purrah (The) 333
Puységur 334
Pyromancy 334
Pythagoras 334
Pythia 334

Q

Quimby (Dr. Phineas) . . . 334
Quindecem Viri 334
Quirardelli (Corneille) . . . 334
Quirinus 334

R

Races (Branch) 334
Races (Root) 334
Races (Sub-) 334
Rahat 334
Rahū 334
Rakshasa 334
Randolph (P. B.) 335
Raphael (The Angel) . . . 335
Rapping 335

SELECT BIBLIOGRAPHY

THE works comprised in the following Bibliography have been selected on account of their suitability to supply the reader with a general view of the several branches of occult science. Modern works in English have, for the most part, been preferred to ancient or to foreign authorities, in an endeavour to render the list of service to those approaching the subject for the first time. In many cases Bibliographies have already been appended to the more exhaustive articles, and where this has been done, reference has been made to the article in question.

ALCHEMY. *See article* " Alchemy."

ASTROLOGY. W. LILLY [1602-81], Introduction to Astrology, edited by ' Zadkiel ' (Lt. R. J. Morrison). Bohn's Library, 1852 ; new edition, 1893.
Alan LEO, Practical Astrology. New edition. Wooderson, 1911.
H. T. WAITE, Compendium of Natal Astrology and Universal Ephemeris. Kegan Paul, 1917. (*See also article* " Astrology.")

DEMONOLOGY. A. E. WAITE, Devil Worship in France. Kegan Paul, 1896.
Sir Walter SCOTT, Letters on Demonology and Witchcraft [1830]. Routledge, *n. d.*
J. BEAUMONT, Treatise on Spirits, Apparitions, and Witchcraft, 1705.
A. CALMET, The Phantom World [1751], translated with notes by H. Christmas, 2 vols., Bentley, 1850.
BECKER, Le Monde Enchanté.

MAGIC. ' Eliphas LEVI ' [L. A. CONSTANT], History of Magic [1860], translated by A. E. Waite. Rider, 1913.
' Eliphas LEVI ' The Mysteries of Magic [1861], translated by A. E. Waite. Kegan Paul, 1886.
„   „   Transcendental Magic, translated by A. E. Waite..
A. E. WAITE, Book of Black Magic and of Pacts. Kegan Paul, 1898.
W. H. Davenport ADAMS, Witch, Warlock, and Magician : historical sketches. Chatto, 1889.
W. GODWIN, Lives of the Necromancers (1834). New edition. Chatto, 1876.
E. SALVERTE, The Philosophy of Magic, Prodigies, and Apparent Miracles, [translation of his *Des Sciences Occultes*]. 2 vols. Bentley, 1846.
F. HARTMANN, Magic, Black and White [*Madras, n. d.*] New edition. Kegan Paul, 1893.
Francis BARRETT, The Magus, or Celestial Intelligencer [1801]. New edition. Theosophical Pub. Soc., 1896.
F. LENORMANT, Chaldean Magic ; translated [by W. R. Cooper]. Bagster, *n. d.* [1877].
Lewis SPENCE, Myths of Ancient Egypt. Harrap, 1915.
„   „   Myths of Babylonia and Assyria. Harrap, 1916.
(Both the above include chapters on Magic.)
D. L. Macgregor MATHERS, The Key of Solomon the King (*Clavicula Solomonis*) [1888]. New edition, Kegan Paul, 1909.
J. A. S. COLLIN DE PLANCY, Dictionnaire Infernal. 6th edition. *Paris*, 1863.
J. P. MIGNE [ed.], Dictionnaire des Sciences Occultes, forming vols. xlviii-ix. of the First Series of the Encyclopédie Théologique.

MYSTICISM ; MYSTERIES. A. E. WAITE, New Light of Mysteries : Azoth, or the Star in the East. Theosophical Pub. Soc., 1893.
A. E. WAITE, The Hidden Church of the Holy Grail, its Legends and Symbolism. Rebman, 1909.
„   „   Studies in Mysticism and Certain Aspects of the Secret Tradition. Hodder, 1906.
„   „   The Real History of the Rosicrucians. Kegan Paul, 1887.
„   „   The Doctrine and Literature of the Kabalah. 1902.
F. CUMONT, The Mysteries of Mithra ; translated by T. J. McCormack. Open Court Pub. Co., *Chicago*, 1903.
G. R. S. MEAD, Fragments of a Faith Forgotten [Gnosticism]. Theosophical Pub. Soc., 1900.
„   „   Thrice-Greatest Hermes : Studies in Hellenistic Theosophy and Gnosis. 3 vols. 1906.
„   „   Introduction to Plotinus. Theosophical Pub. Soc., 1899.
„   „   Echoes from the Gnosis.
Evelyn UNDERHILL [Mrs. STUART-MOORE], Mysticism : a study in the nature and development of man's spiritual consciousness. Methuen, *n. d.* [1911].
Evelyn UNDERHILL, The Mystic Way : a psychological study in Christian Origins. Dent, 1913.
IAMBLICHUS (4th cent., A.D.], Theurgia, or the Mysteries of the Egyptians, Chaldeans, and Assyrians ; translated by T. Taylor. 2nd edition. Dobell, 1895.
Hargrave JENNINGS, The Rosicrucians, their Rites and Mysteries [1870]. 4th edition. Routledge, 1907.
Jacob BOEHME [1575-1624], Works ; translated. *Glasgow*, 1886.
I. de STEIGER, On a Gold Basis : a Treatise on Mysticism. Wellby, 1907.
Carl Du PREL, The Philosophy of Mysticism ; translated by C. C. Massey, 2 vols. Kegan Paul, 1889.
Em. SWEDENBORG, Treatise concerning Heaven and Hell (*De Coelo et de Inferno*] ; translated by J. W. Hancock. Swedenborg Society, 1850.

SPIRITUALISM. E. GURNAY, F. W. H. MYERS, and F. PODMORE, Phantasms of the Living [1886].   Edited and abridged by Mrs. Henry Sidgwick. Kegan Paul (Dutton, *New York*), 1918.

F. PODMORE, Modern Spiritualism : a history and a criticism, 2 vols. Methuen, 1902.

„   „   The Newer Spiritualism. Unwin, 1910.

Allan KARDEC, The Book of Spirits. Kegan Paul, 1898.

J. Arthur HILL, New Evidences in Psychical Research. Rider, 1911.

„   „   Spiritualism : its History, Phenomena, and Doctrine. Cassell, 1918.

„   „   Man is a Spirit : a collection of spontaneous cases of dream, vision, and ecstasy. Cassell, 1918.

Sir W. BARRETT, The Threshold of the Unseen [1917]. Kegan Paul, 1919

F. MYERS, Human Personality and its Survival of Bodily Death, 2 vols., Longman, 1903. Abridged by L. H. Myers [his son], 1907.

Sir O. LODGE, Raymond, or Life and Death. Methuen, 1916.

J. W. FRINGS, Life Everlasting and Psychic Evolution.

J. H. HYSLOP, Life after Death. Dutton, *New York* (Kegan Paul), 1919.

SOCIETY OF PSYCHICAL RESEARCH. Proceedings ; *and* Journal. 1882 *sqq.*

THEOSOPHY. Lilian EDGE, Elements of Theosophy. Theosophical Pub. Soc. 1903.

Annie BESANT, Popular Lectures on Theosophy. Theosophical Pub. Soc., 1910.

„   „   Evolution of Life and Form. Theosophical Pub. Soc.

Ethel MALLET, First Steps in Theosophy. *Lotus Journal* Office, 1905.

H. P. BLAVATSKY, Isis Unveiled : the Master Key to Ancient and Modern Mysteries, 2 vols. [1877]. *New York*, 1891.

„   „   The Key to Theosophy [1889]. 3rd edition. Theosophical Pub. Soc., 1893.

A. P. SINNETT, The Occult World [1881]. 4th edition. Theosophical Pub. Soc., 1885.

„   „   Expanded Theosophical Knowledge. Theosophical Book Shop. 1918.

WITCHCRAFT. Thos. WRIGHT, Narratives of Sorcery and Magic. 2 vols. Bentley, 1851.

C. G. Leland, Aradia, or the Gospel of the Witches of Italy. Scribner, *New York*, 1899.

„   „   Gypsy Sorcery and Fortune-Telling. Unwin, 1891.

F. T. ELWORTHY, The Evil Eye. Murray, 1895.

R. C. THOMPSON, Semitic Magic, its Origins and Development. Luzac, 1908.

J. GLANVIL, Saducismus Triumphatus : Evidences concerning Witches, Apparitions, and Witchcraft [1681], 4th edition, 1726.

C. Kirkpatrick SHARPE, Historical Account of Belief in Witchcraft in Scotland [1819] Morison, *Glasgow*, 1884.

W. G. SOLDAN, Geschichte der Hexenprocesse [1843], herausgegeben von H. Heppe. 2 vols. Cotta, *Stuttgart*, 1880.

AN ENCYCLOPÆDIA OF OCCULTISM

A

Ab : (Semitic magical month). Crossing a river on the 20th of that month was supposed to bring sickness. In ancient texts it states that if a man should eat the flesh of swine on the 30th of *Ab*, he will be plagued with boils.

Abaddon : (The Destroyer). Chief of the demons of the seventh hierarchy. *Abaddon* is the name given by St. John in the Apocalypse to the king of the grasshoppers. He is sometimes regarded as the destroying angel.

Abadie (Jeannette) : A young sorceress of the village of Sibourre, in Gascony. She was sleeping one day in her father's house while high mass was being said. A demon, profiting by the opportunity, carried her off to the Devil's Sabbath, where she soon awoke to find herself in the midst of a large company. She observed that the principal demon had on his head two faces, like Janus. She did not participate in the revelry, and was transported to her home by the same means as she had been conveyed thence. On the threshold she found her amulet, which the demon had taken the precaution to remove from her bosom before carrying her off. She made a confession of all that had happened, renounced her sorcery, and thus saved herself from the common fate of witches and sorcerers—the stake.

Abaris : A Scythian, high priest of Apollo, and renowned magician. In so flattering a manner did he chant the praises of Apollo, his master, that the god gave him a golden arrow, on which he could ride through the air like a bird, so that the Greeks called him the Aerobate. Pythagoras, his pupil, stole this arrow from him, and accomplished many wonderful feats by its aid. *Abaris* foretold the future, pacified storms, banished disease, and lived without eating or drinking. He made with the bones of Pelops, a statue of Minerva, which he sold to the Trojans as a talisman descended from heaven. This was the famous Palladium, which protected and rendered impregnable the town wherein it was lodged.

Abdelazys : An Arabian astrologer of the tenth century, generally known in Europe by his Latin name of Alchabitius. His treatise on astrology was so much prized that it was translated into Latin and printed in 1473. Other editions have since appeared, the best being that of Venice (1503) entitled *Alchabitius cum commento*. Translated by John of Seville. (Hispalensis.)

Aben-Ragel : An Arabian astrologer, born at Cordova, at the beginning of the fifth century. He was the author of a book of horoscopes according to the inspection of the stars, a Latin translation of which was published at Venice, 1485, under the title of *De Judiciis seu fatis stellarum*. It was said that his predictions were fulfilled in a remarkable manner.

Abigor : According to Wierius (q.v.), Grand Duke of Hades. He is shown in the form of a handsome knight, bearing lance, standard, or sceptre. He is a demon of the superior order, and responds readily to questions concerning war. He can foretell the future, and instructs the leaders how to make themselves respected by the soldiers. Sixty of the infernal regions are at his command.

Abishai : (*See* **Devil.**)

Abou-Ryhan : An Arabian astrologer whose real name was Mohammed-ben-Ahmed, to whom is ascribed the introduction of *Judicial Astrology* (q.v.) Many stories were told of him in the East, to show that he possessed in an extraordinary degree the power to read the future.

Abra Melin : (*See* **Abraham the Jew.**)

Abracadabra : A magical word said to be formed from the letters of the *abraxas*, and written thus :

A
A B
A B R
A B R A
A B R A C
A B R A C A
A B R A C A D
A B R A C A D A
A B R A C A D A B
A B R A C A D A B R
A B R A C A D A B R A

or the reverse way. The pronunciation of this word, according to Julius Africanus, was equally efficacious either way. By Serenus Sammonicus it was used as a spell to cure asthma. *Abracalan* or *aracalan* is another form of the word, and is said to have been regarded as the name of a god in Syria and as a magical symbol by the Jews. But it seems doubtful whether the *abracadabra*, or its synonyms, was really the name of a deity or not. (*See* **Abraxas.**)

Abraham, The Jew : (Alchemist and magician, circa, 1400). Comparatively few biographical facts are forthcoming concerning this German Jew, who was at once alchemist, magician and philosopher ; and these few facts are mostly derived from a very curious manuscript, now domiciled in the Archives of the Bibliotheque de l'Arsenal, Paris, an institution rich in occult documents. This manuscript is couched throughout in French, but purports to be literally translated from Hebrew, and the style of the handwriting indicates that the scribe lived at the beginning of the eighteenth century, or possibly somewhat earlier. A distinct illiteracy characterises the French script, the punctuation being inaccurate, indeed frequently conspicuous by its absence, but an actual description of the document must be waived till later. *Abraham* was probably a native of Mayence, and appears to have been born in 1362. We find that his father, Simon by name, was something of a seer and magician, and that the boy accordingly commenced his occult studies under the parental guidance, while at a later date he studied under one, Moses, whom he himself describes as " indeed a good man, but entirely ignorant of The True Mystery, and of The Veritable Magic." Leaving this preceptor, *Abraham* decided to glean knowledge by travelling, and along with a friend called Samuel, a Bohemian by birth, he wandered through Austria and Hungary into Greece, and thence penetrated to Constantinople, where he remained fully two years. He is found next in Arabia, in those days a veritable centre of mystic learning ; and from Arabia he went to Palestine, whence betimes he proceeded to Egypt. Here he had the good fortune to make the acquaintance of Abra-Melin, the famous Egyptian philosopher, who, besides entrusting to him certain documents, confided in him by word of mouth a number of invaluable secrets ; and armed thus, *Abraham* left Egypt for Europe, where eventually he settled at Wurzburg in Germany. Soon he was deep in alchemistic researches, but these did not prevent him from espousing a wife, who appears to have been his cousin ; and by her he had three daughters and also two sons, the elder named Joseph and the younger Lamech. He took great pains to instruct both of them in occult affairs, while, on each of his three daughters, he settled a dowry of a hundred thousand golden florins. This considerable sum, together with other vast wealth, he claims to have gained by travelling as an alchemist ; and whatever the truth of this statement, he certainly won great fame, being summoned to perform acts of magic before many rich and influential people, notably the Emperor Sigismund of Germany, the Bishop of Wurzburg, King Henry VI. of England, the Duke of Bavaria, and Pope John XXIII. The remainder of *Abraham's* career is shrouded in mystery, while even the date of his death is uncertain, but it is commonly supposed to have occurred about 1460.

The curious manuscript cited above, and from which the foregoing facts have been culled, is entitled *The Book of the Sacred Magic of Abra-Melin, as delivered by Abraham the Jew unto his son Lamech.* This title, however, is rather misleading, and not strictly accurate, for Abra-Melin had absolutely no hand in the opening part of the work, this consisting of some account of *Abraham's* own youth and early travels in search of wisdom, along with advice to the young man aspiring to become skilled in occult arts. The second part, on the other hand, is based on the documents which the Egyptian sage handed to the Jew, or at least on the confidences wherewith the former favoured the latter ; and it may be fairly accurately defined as dealing with the first principles of magic in general, the titles of some of the more important chapters being as follows : " How Many, and what are the Classes of Veritable Magic ? " " What we Ought to Take into Consideration before the Undertaking of the Operation," " Concerning the Convocation of the Spirits," and " In what Manner we ought to Carry out the Operations." Passing to the third and last part, this likewise is mostly derived straight from Abra-Melin ; and here the author, eschewing theoretical matter as far as possible, gives information about the actual practice of magic. In the first place he tells how " To procure divers Visions," " How one may retain the Familiar Spirits, bound or free, in whatsoever form," and how " To excite Tempests," while in one chapter he treats of raising the dead, another he devotes to the topic of transforming oneself into " divers shapes and forms," and in further pages he descants on flying in the air, on demolishing buildings, on discovering thefts, and on walking under the water. Then he dilates on the Thaumaturgic healing of leprosy, dropsy, paralysis, and various more common ailments such as fever and sea-sickness, while he offers intelligence on " How to be beloved by a Woman," and this he supplements by directions for commanding the favour of popes, emperors, and other influential people. Finally, he reverts to the question of summoning visions, and his penultimate chapter is entitled, " How to cause Armed Men to Appear," while his concluding pages treat of evoking " Comedies, Operas, and all kinds of Music and Dances."

It is by employing Kabalistic squares of letters that all these things are to be achieved, or at least, almost all of them, and lack of space makes it impossible to deal with the many different signs of this sort, whose use the seer counsels. But it behoves to ask what manner of personality exhales from these curious pages ? What kind of temperament ? And the answer is that *Abraham* is shown as a man of singularly narrow mind, heaping scorn on most other magicians, and speaking with great derision of nearly all mystical writings save his own and those of his

hero, Abra-Melin. Moreover, he inveighs fiercely against all those who recant the religion in which they were bred, and contends that no one guilty of this will ever attain skill in magic ; yet it should be said, in justice to the seer, that he manifests little selfishness, and seems to have striven after success in his craft with a view to using it for the benefit of mankind in general. His writings reflect besides, a firm belief in that higher self existing in every man, and a keen desire to develop it. (*See* **Flamel.**)

Abraxas : (or Abracax). The Basilidian (q.v.,) sect of Gnostics, of the second century, claimed *Abraxas* as their supreme god, and said that Jesus Christ was only a phantom sent to earth by him. They believed that his name contained great mysteries, as it was composed of the seven Greek letters which form the number 365, which is also the number of days in a year. *Abraxas*, they thought, had under his command 365 gods, to whom they attributed 365 virtues, one for each day. The older Mythologists placed him among the number of Egyptian gods, and demonologists have described him as a demon, with the head of a king and with serpents forming his feet. He is represented on ancient amulets, with a whip in his hand. It is from his name that the mystic word, Abracadabra (q.v.) is taken. Many stones and gems cut in various symbolic forms, such as the head of a fowl, a serpent, and so forth, were worn by the Basilidians as amulets.

Abred : The innermost of three concentric circles representing the totality of being in the British Celtic cosmogony. (*See* **Celts.**) The stage of struggle and evolution against Cythrawl, the power of evil. (*See also* **Barddas.**)

Absolute (Theosophist) : Of the Absolute, the Logos, the Word of God, Theosophists profess to know nothing further than that it exists. The universes with their solar systems are but the manifestations of this Being, which man is capable of perceiving, and all of them are instinct with him, but what man can perceive is not the loftier manifestations but the lower. Man himself is an emanation from the Absolute with which he will ultimately be re-united.

Abyssum : A herb used in the ceremony of exorcising a haunted house. It is signed with the sign of the cross, and hung up at the four corners of the house.

Acherat : (*See* **Cagliostro.**)

Achmet : An Arabian soothsayer of the ninth century. He wrote a book on *The Interpretation of Dreams,* following the doctrines of the East. The original is lost, but the Greek and Latin translations were printed at Paris, in 1603.

Aconce (Jacques) : Curate of the diocese of Trent, who became a Calvinist in 1557, and came to England, While there he dedicated to Queen Elizabeth his famous work, on *The Stratagems of Satan.* This book, however, is not, as its title might indicate, a dissertation on demonology, but a spirited attack on intolerance.

Adalbert : A French pseudo-mystic of the eighth century. He boasted that an angel had brought him relics of extraordinary sanctity from all parts of the earth. He claimed to be able to foretell the future, and to read thoughts. " I know what you have done," he would say to the people, " there is no need for confession. Go in peace, your sins are forgiven." His so-called " miracles " gained for him the awe of the multitude, and he was in the habit of giving away parings of his nails and locks of his hair as powerful amulets. He is even said to have set up an altar in his own name. In his history of his life, of which only a fragment remains, he tells us of miraculous powers bestowed by an angel at his birth. He showed to his disciples a letter which he declared had been brought to him from Jesus Christ by the hand of St. Michael. These, and similar blasphemies were put an end to by his being cast into prison, where he died.

Adam, Book of the Penitence of : A manuscript in the Library of the Arsenal at Paris, which deals with Kabalistic tradition. It recounts how the sons of Adam, Cain and Abel, typifying brute force and intelligence, slew each other, and that *Adam's* inheritance passed to his third son, Seth. Seth, it is stated, was permitted to advance as far as the gate of the Earthly Paradise without being threatened by the guardian angel with his flaming sword, which is to say that he was an initiate of occult science. He beheld the Tree of Life and the Tree of Knowledge, which had become grafted upon each other so that they formed one tree. This is supposed by some to have symbolised the harmony of science and religion in the Kabala. The guardian angel presented Seth with three seeds from this tree, directing him to place them within the mouth of his father, *Adam*, when he expired. From this planting arose the burning bush out of which God communicated to Moses his holy name, and from a part of which Moses made his magic wand. This was placed in the Ark of the Covenant, and was planted by King David on Mount Zion, grew into a triple tree and was cut down by Solomon to form the pillars, Jachin and Boaz, which were placed at the entrance to the Temple. A third portion was inserted in the threshold of the great gate, and acted as a talisman, permitting no unclean thing to enter the sanctuary. Certain wicked priests removed it however for purposes of their own, weighted it with stones, and cast it into the Temple reservoir, where it was guarded by an angel, who kept it from the sight of men. During the lifetime of Christ the reservoir was drained and the beam of wood discovered and thrown across the brook Kedron, over which our Saviour passed after his apprehension in the Garden of Olives. It was taken by his executioners and made into the cross. In this legend we can see a marked similarity to those from which the conception of the Holy Grail arose. Man is restored by the wood through the instrumentality of which *Adam*, the first man, fell. The idea that the Cross was a cutting of the Tree of Knowledge was widespread in the middle ages, and may be found in the twelfth century *Quete del St. Graal*, ascribed to Walter Map, but probably only redacted by him. All the Kabalistic traditions are embodied in the allegory contained in the *Book of the Penitence of Adam*, and it undoubtedly supplements and throws considerable light on the entire Kabalistic literature.

Adam, (L'Abbe) : About the time that the Templars were being driven from France, the Devil appeared, under various guises, to the *Abbé Adam*, who was journeying, attended by one of the servants from his convent, to a certain part of his abbacy of the Vaux de Cernay. The evil spriit first opposed the progress of the worthy Abbé under the form of a tree white with frost, which rushed towards him with inconceivable swiftness. The Abbé's horse trembled with fear, as did the servant, but the Abbé himself made the sign of the Cross, and the tree disappeared. The good man concluded that he had seen the Devil, and called upon the Virgin to protect him. Nevertheless, the fiend shortly reappeared in the shape of a furious black knight. " Begone," said the Abbé. " Why do you attack me far from my brothers ? " The Devil once more left him, only to return in the shape of a tall man, with a long, thin neck. *Adam*, to get rid of him, struck him a blow with his fist. The evil spirit shrank and took the stature and countenance of a little cloaked monk, with a glittering weapon under his dress. His little eyes could be seen darting and glancing under his cowl. He tried hard to strike the Abbé with the sword he held, but the latter repulsed the strokes with the sign of the Cross. The demon became in turn a pig and a long-eared ass. The Abbé, impatient to be gone, made a circle on the ground with a cross in the centre. The fiend was then obliged to withdraw to a little distance. He changed his long ears into horns, which

did not hinder the Abbé from boldly addressing him. Offended by his plain-speaking, the Devil changed himself into a barrel and rolled into an adjoining field. In a short time he returned in the form of a cart-wheel, and, without giving the brother time to put himself on the defensive, rolled heavily over his body, without, however, doing him any injury. After that he left him to pursue his journey in peace. (See Gaguin, *Regne de Philippe le Bel*, *and* Gerinet, *Hist. de la Magie en France*, *p.* 82.)

Adamantius : A Jewish doctor, who became a Catholic at Constantinople in the time of Constantine, to whom he dedicated his two books on *Physiognomy*, or, the art of judging people by their faces. This book, full of contradictions and fantasies, was printed in the *Scriptores Physiognomoniae veteres*, of Franzius, at Attembourg, in 1780.

Adamnan : (*See* **Scotland.**)

Addanc of the Lake : A monster that figures in the Mabinogi legend of *Peredur*. Peredur obtains a magic stone which renders him invisible, and he thus succeeds in slaying this monster, which had daily killed the inhabitants of the palace of the King of Tortures.

Adelung, (Jean Christophe) : A German author, born in 1732, who has left a work entitled, *Histoire des folies humaines, on Biographie des plus celebres necromanciens, alchimistes, devins, etc.* (Leipsic, 1785-1789.) *Adelung* died at Dresden in 1806.

Adepts are men who after stern self-denial and by means of consistent self-development, have fitted themselves to assist in the ruling of the world. The means by which this position is attained is said to be long and arduous, but in the end the successful one has fulfilled the purpose for which he was created and transcends his fellows. The activities of *Adepts* are multifarious, being concerned with the direction and guidance of the activities of the rest of mankind. Their knowledge, like their powers, say Theosophists, far exceeds that of man, and they can control forces both in the spiritual and the physical realm, and are said to be able to prolong their lives for centuries. They are also known as the Great White Brotherhood, Rishis, Rahats, or Mahatmas. Those who earnestly desire to work for the betterment of the world may become apprentices or *chelas* to *Adepts*, in which case the latter are known as " masters," but the apprentice must first have practised self-denial and self-development in order to become sufficiently worthy. The master imparts teaching and wisdom otherwise unattainable, and helps the apprentice by communion and inspiration. Madame Blavatsky (q.v.) alleged that she was the apprentice of these masters, and claimed that they dwelt in the Tibetan Mountains. The term *Adept* was also employed by mediaeval magicians and alchemists to denote a master of their sciences.

Adhab-Algal : The Mohammedan purgatory, where the wicked are tormented by the dark angels Munkir and Nekir.

Adjuration : A formula of exorcism by which the evil spirit is commanded, in the name of God, to do or say what the exorcist requires of him.

Adonai : A Hebrew word signifying " the Lord," and used by the Hebrews when speaking or writing of Jehovah, the awful and ineffable name of the God of Israel. The Jews entertained the deepest awe for this incommunicable and mysterious name, and this feeling led them to avoid pronouncing it and to the substitution of the word *Adonai* for " Jehovah " in their sacred text. This custom still prevails among the Jews, who attribute to the pronouncement of the Holy Name the power of working miracles. The Jehovah of the Israelites was their invisible protector and king, and no image of him was made. He was worshipped according to his commandments, with an observance of the ritual instituted through Moses. The term " Jehovah " means the revealed Absolute Deity, the Manifest, Only, Personal, Holy Creator and Redeemer. (*See* **Magic, God, Egypt, Kabala.**)

Adoptive Masonry : Masonic societies which adopt women as members. Early in the eighteenth century such societies were established in France, and speedily spread to other countries. One of the first to " adopt " women were the Mopses. The Felicitaries existed in 1742. The Fendeurs or Woodcutters were instituted in 1763 by Bauchaine, Master of a Parisian Lodge. It was modelled on the Carbonari, and its popularity led to the establishment of other lodges, notably the Fidelity, the Hatchet, etc. In 1774 the Grand Orient Lodge of France established a system of three degrees called the Rite of Adoption, and elected the Duchess of Bourbon as Grand Mistress of France. The rite has been generally adopted into Freemasonry, and various degrees added from time to time, to the number of about twelve in all. Latin and Greek mysteries were added to the rite by the Ladies' Hospitallers of Mount Tabor. The greatest ladies in France joined the French lodges of adoption. The Rite of Mizraim created lodges for both sexes in 1819, 1821, 1838 and 1853, and the Rite of Memphis in 1839. America founded the Rite of the Eastern Star in five points. In these systems admission is generally confined to the female relations of Masons. The Order of the Eastern Star and that of *Adoptive Masonry* were attempted in Scotland, but without success.

Adramelech : According to Wierius (q.v.,) Chancellor of the infernal regions, Keeper of the Wardrobe of the Demon King, and President of the High Council of the Devils. He was worshipped at Sepharvaim, an Assyrian town, where children were burned on his altar. The rabbis say that he shows himself in the form of a mule, or sometimes, of a peacock.

Adventists : (*See* **America, U.S. of.**)

Aeromancy : The art of foretelling future events by the observation of atmospheric phenomena, as, for example, when the death of a great man is presaged by the appearance of a comet. François de la Tour Blanche says that aeromancy is the art of fortune-telling by means of spectres which are made to appear in the air, or the representation by the aid of demons, of future events, which are projected on the clouds as if by a magic lantern. " As for thunder and lightning," he adds, " these are concerned with auguries, and the aspect of the sky and of the planets belong to the science of astrology."

Aetites or Aquilaeus : A precious stone of magical properties, composed of oxide of iron with a little silex and alumina, and said to be found in the stomach or neck of the eagle. It is supposed to heal falling sickness, and prevent untimely birth. It should be worn bound on the arm to prevent abortion, and on the thigh to aid parturition.

Africa : (*See* **Arabs, Egypt, Semites.** The north of Africa is Mohammedan. This applies also to the Sudan and the Sahara. For Moorish Magic and Alchemy see **Arabs.** Instances of Arabic sorcery will also be found in the article " Semites." In West Africa Obeah is practised, for which see **West Indies.**)

Magic in savage Africa is of the lower cultus, and chiefly of the kind known as " sympathetic." (*See* **Magic.**) But spiritualistic influence shows itself in fetishism, the cult of the dead, *ju-ju* or witchcraft, and the cult of the witch-doctor.

Bantu Tribes. Among the Zulu and other Bantu tribes the cult of witchcraft was practised, but in secret, for the results of detection were terrible. For the tracking of the witch, a caste of witch-finders was instituted, called " witch-doctors," whose duty it was to " smell out " the offenders. These were nearly all women.

" It is not difficult to understand," says Lady Barker, " bearing in mind the superstition and cruelty which existed in remote parts of England not so very long ago ; how powerful such women become among a savage people, or how tempting an opportunity they could furnish of getting rid of an enemy. Of course they are exceptional individuals ; more observant, more shrewd, and more dauntless than the average fat, hard-working Kaffir women, besides possessing the contradictory mixture of great physical powers and strong hysterical tendencies. They work themselves up to a pitch of frenzy, and get to believe as firmly in their own supernatural discernment as any individual among the trembling circle of Zulus to whom a touch from the whisk they carry is a sentence of instant death."

The Zulu witch-finders are attended by a circle of black girls and women, who, like a Greek chorus, clap their hands together, and drone through a low monotonous chant, the measure and rhythm of which change at times with a stamp and a swing. Not less necessary is a ceremonial dress ; for such things appeal directly to the imagination of the crowd, and prepare them to be readily influenced by the necromancer's devices. The " Isinyanga," " Abangoma " or " witch-finders," whom Lady Barker describes for us, were attired with an eye for effect which would have done credit to a London theatre. It will suffice to depict one of them, by name Nozinyanga. Her fierce face, spotted with gouts of red paint on cheek and brow, was partly overshadowed by a helmet-like plume of the tall feathers of the sakabula bird. In her right hand she carried a light sheaf of assegais or lances, and on her left arm was slung a small and pretty shield of dappled ox-hide. Her petticoat, made of a couple of large gay handkerchiefs, was worn kilt-wise. But if there were little decoration in her skirts, the deficiency was more than compensated by the bravery of the bead-necklaces, the goat's-hair fringes, and the scarlet tassels which covered her from coat to waist. Her ample chest rose and fell beneath the baldric of leopard skin, fastened across it with huge brazen knobs, while down her back hung a beautifully dried and flattened skin of an enormous boa-constrictor.

When the community had resolved that a certain misfortune was due to the witches, the next step obviously would be to detect and punish them. For this purpose the king would summon a great meeting, and cause his subjects to sit on the ground in a ring or circle for four or five days. The witch-finders took their places in the centre, and as they gradually worked themselves up to a frantic state of frenzy, resembling demoniacal possession, they lightly switched with their quagga-tail one or other of the trembling spectators, who was immediately dragged away and butchered on the spot. And not only he, but all the living things in his hut—wives and children, dogs and cats—not one was left alive, nor was a stick left standing. Sometimes a whole kraal would be exterminated in this way, and the reader will perceive how terrible the cruel custom could be made to gratify private revenge or to work the king's tyrannical inclinations.

A terrible little sorceress is described by Lady Barker under the name of Nozilwane, whose weird wistful glance had in it something uncanny and uncomfortable. She was dressed beautifully for her part, in lynx skins folded over and over from waist to knee, the upper part of her body being covered by strings of wild beasts' teeth and fangs, beads, skeins of gaily-coloured yarn, strips of snake's skin, and fringes of Angora goat fleece. This, as a decoration, was both graceful and effective ; it was worn round the body and above each elbow, and fell in soft white flakes among the brilliant colouring and against the dusky skin. Lynx-tails depended like lappets on each side of her face, which was over-shadowed and almost hidden by a profusion of sakabula feathers. " This bird," says Lady Barker, " has a very beautiful plumage, and is sufficiently rare for the natives to attach a peculiar value and charm to the tail-feathers ; they are like those of a young cock, curved and slender, and of a dark chesnut colour, with a white eye at the extreme tip of each feather." Among all this thick, floating plumage were interspersed small bladders, and skewers or pins wrought out of tusks. Each witch-finder wore her own hair, or rather wool, highly greased and twisted up with twine until it ceases to wear the appearance of hair, and hangs around the face like a thick fringe, dyed deep red.

Bent double, and with a creeping, cat-like gait, as if seeking a trail, out stepped Nozilwane. Every movement of her undulating body kept time to the beat of the girls' hands and their low crooning chant. Presently she pretended to find the thing she sought, and with a series of wild pirouettes, leaped into the air, shaking her spears and brandishing her little shield like a Bacchante. Nowamso, another of the party, was determined that her companion should not carry off all the applause, and she too, with a yell and a leap, sprang into the dance to the sound of louder grunts and harder hand-claps. Nowamso showed much anxiety to display her back, where a magnificent snake skin, studded in a regular pattern with brass-headed nails, floated like a stream. She was attired also in a splendid kilt of leopard skins, decorated with red rosettes, and her toilet was considered more careful and artistic than any of the others. Brighter her bangles, whiter her goat-fringes, and more elaborately painted her face. Nozilwane, however, had youth and a wonderful self-reliance on her side. The others, though they all joined in and hunted out an imaginary enemy, and in turn exulted over his discovery, soon became breathless and spent, and were glad when their attendants led them away to be anointed and to drink water.

Central Africa. The magical beliefs of Central and Eastern Africa are but little known. They are for the most part connected with the cult of the dead and that of the fetish. As regards the first :—

When the dead are weary of staying in the bush, they come for one of their people whom they most affect. And the spirit will say to the man : " I am tired of dwelling in the bush, please to build for me in the town a little house as close as possible to your own." And he tells him to dance and sing too, and accordingly the man assembles the women at night to join in dance and song.

Then, next day, the people repair to the grave of the *Obambo*, or ghost, and make a rude idol, after which the bamboo bier, on which the body is conveyed to the grave, and some of the dust of the ground, are carried into a little hut erected near the house of the visited, and a white cloth is draped over the door.

It is a curious fact, which seems to show that these people have a legend something like the old Greek myth of Charon and the Styx, that in one of the songs chanted during this ceremony occurs the following line : " You are well dressed, but you have no canoe to carry you across to the other side."

Possession. Epileptic diseases, in almost all uncivilised countries, are assumed to be the result of demoniac possession. In Central Africa the sufferer is supposed to be possessed by Mbwiri, and he can be relieved only by the intervention of the medicine-man or fetish. In the middle of the street a hut is built for his accommodation, and there he resides until cured, or maddened, along with the priest and his disciples. There for ten days or a fortnight a continuous revel is held ; much eating and drinking at the expense of the patient's relatives, and unending dances

to the sound of flute and drum. For obvious reasons the fetish gives out that Mbwiri regards good living with aversion. The patient dances, usually shamming madness, until the epileptic attack comes on, with all its dreadful concomitants—the frenzied stare, the convulsed limbs, the gnashing teeth, and the foam-flecked lips. The man's actions at this period are not ascribed to himself, but to the demon which has control of him. When a cure has been effected, real or pretended, the patient builds a little fetish-house, avoids certain kinds of food, and performs certain duties. Sometimes the process terminates in the patient's insanity ; he has been known to run away to the bush, hide from all human beings, and live on the roots and berries of the forest.

" These fetish-men," says Read, " are priest doctors, like those of the ancient Germans. They have a profound knowledge of herbs, and also of human nature, for they always monopolise the real power in the state. But it is very doubtful whether they possess any secrets save that of extracting virtue and poison from plants. During the first trip which I made into the bush I sent for one of these doctors. At that time I was staying among the Shekani, who are celebrated for their fetish. He came attended by half-a-dozen disciples. He was a tall man dressed in white, with a girdle of leopard's skin, from which hung an iron bell, of the same shape as our sheep bells. He had two chalk marks over his eyes. I took some of my own hair, frizzled it with a burning glass, and gave it to him. He popped it with alacrity into his little grass bag ; for white man's hair is fetish of the first order. Then I poured out some raspberry vinegar into a glass, drank a little of it first, country fashion, and offered it to him, telling him that it was blood from the brains of great doctors. Upon this he received it with great reverence, and dipping his fingers into it as if it was snap-dragon, sprinkled with it his forehead, both feet between the two first toes, and the ground behind his back. He then handed his glass to a disciple, who emptied it, and smacked his lips afterwards in a very secular manner. I then desired to see a little of his fetish. He drew on the ground with red chalk some hieroglyphics, among which I distinguished the circle, the cross, and the crescent. He said that if I would give him a fine ' dush,' he would tell me all about it. But as he would not take anything in reason, and as I knew that he would tell me nothing of very great importance in public, negotiations were suspended."

The fetish-man seldom finds a native disposed to question his claim of supernatural powers. He is not only a doctor and a priest—two capacities in which his influence is necessarily very powerful—he is also a witch-finder, and this is an office which invests him with a truly formidable authority. When a man of worth dies, his death is invariably ascribed to witchcraft, and the aid of the fetish-man is invoked to discover the witch.

When a man is sick a long time, they call *Ngembi*, and if she cannot make him well, the fetish-man. He comes at night, in a white dress, with cock's feathers on his head, and having his bell and little glass. He calls two or three relations together into a room. He does not speak, but always looks in his glass. Then he tells them that the sickness is not of Mbwiri, nor of Obambo, nor of God, but that it comes from a witch. They say to him, " What shall we do ? " He goes out and says, " I have told you. I have no more to say." They give him a dollar's worth of cloth, and every night they gather together in the street, and they cry, " I know that man who bewitched my brother. It is good for you to make him well." Then the witch makes him well. But if the man do not recover they call the bush doctor from the Shekani country. He sings in the language of the bush. At night he goes into the street ;

all the people flock about him. With a tiger-cat skin in his hand, he walks to and fro, until, singing all the while, he lays the tiger-skin at the feet of the witch. At the conclusion of his song the people seize the witch, and put him or her in chains, saying, " If you don't restore our brother to health, we will kill you."

African Builders' Architects : A mystical association founded by one, C. F. Koffen, a German official (1734-1797). Its ostensible object was that of literary culture and intellectual study, but masonic qualifications were required of its members, and it attracted to itself some of the most distinguished Continental literati of the period. It had branches at Worms, Cologne and Paris. It is asserted that it was affiliated with the Society of Alethophilas or Lovers of Truth, which, indeed, is the name of one of its grades, the designations of which were as follow : Inferior Grades : (1) Apprentice of Egyptian Secrets ; (2) Initiate into Egyptian Secrets ; (3) Cosmopolitan ; (4) Christian Philosopher ; (5) Alethophilos. Higher Grades : (1) Esquire ; (2) Soldier ; (3) Knight—thus supplying Egyptian, Christian and Templar mysteries to the initiate. In 1806 there was published at Berlin a pamphlet entitled *A Discovery Concerning the System of the Order of African Architects.*

Ag : A red flower used by the natives of Hindustan to propitiate their god, Sanee. It is made into a wreath with *jasoon,* also a red-coloured flower, which is hung round the neck of the god, who is of a congenial nature. This ceremony is performed by night.

Agaberte : Daughter of a certain giant called Vagnoste, dwelling in Scandinavia. She was a powerful enchantress, and was rarely seen in her true shape. Sometimes she would take the form of an old woman, wrinkled and bent, and hardly able to move about. At one time she would appear weak and ill, and at another tall and strong, so that her head seemed to touch the clouds. These transformations she effected without the smallest effort or trouble. People were so struck with her marvels that they believed her capable of overthrowing the mountains, tearing up the trees, drying up the rivers with the greatest of ease. They held that nothing less than a legion of demons must be at her command for the accomplishment of her magic feats. She seems to be like the Scottish Cailleach Bheur, a nature hag.

Agapis : This is a yellow stone, so called because it promotes love or charity. It cures stings and venomous bites, by being dipped in water and rubbed over the wound.

Agares : According to Wierius (q.v.) Grand Duke of the eastern region of Hades. He is shown under the form of a benevolent lord mounted on a crocodile, and carrying a hawk on his fist. The army he protects in battle is indeed fortunate, for he disperses their enemies, and puts new courage into the hearts of the cowards who fly before superior numbers. He distributes place and power, titles and prelacies, teaches all languages, and has other equally remarkable powers. Thirty-one legions are under his command.

Agate, or Achates : Good against the biting of scorpions or serpents, soothes the mind, drives away contagious air, and puts a stop to thunder and lightning. It is said also to dispose to solitude, promote eloquence, and secure the favour of princes. It gives victory over their enemies to those who wear it.

Agathion : A familiar spirit which appears only at mid-day. It takes the shape of a man or a beast, or even encloses itself in a talisman, bottle, or magic ring.

Agathodemon : A good demon, worshipped by the Egyptians under the shape of a serpent with a human head. The dragons or flying serpents venerated by the ancients were also called *Agathodemons,* or good genies.

Agla : A kabalistic word used by the rabbis for the exorcisms of the evil spirit. It is made up of the initial letters of the Hebrew words, *Athah gabor leolam, Adonai,* meaning, " Thou art powerful and eternal, Lord." Not only among the Jews was this word employed, but among the more superstitious Christians it was a favourite weapon with which to combat the evil one, even so late as the sixteenth century. It is also to be found in many books on magic, notably in the *Enchiridion* of Pope Leo III.

Aglaophotis : A kind of herb which grows in the deserts of Arabia, and which was much used by sorcerers for the evocation of demons. Other plants were then employed to retain the evil spirits so long as the sorcerer required them.

Agreda (Marie of) : A Spanish nun, who published about the middle of the seventeenth century a work entitled, *The Mystic City of God, a Miracle of the All-powerful, the Abyss of Grace : Divine History of the Life of the Most Holy Virgin Mary, Mother of God, our Queen and Mistress, manifested in these last times by the Holy Virgin to the Sister Marie of Jesus, Abbess of the Convent of the Immaculate Conception of the town of Agreda, and written by that same Sister by order of her Superiors and Confessors.*

This work, which was condemned by the Sorbonne, is a pretended account of many strange and miraculous happenings which befell the Virgin from her birth onwards, including a visit to Heaven in her early years, when she was given a guard of nine hundred angels.

Agrippa von Nettesheim, Henry Cornelius (1486-1535) : A German soldier and physician, and an adept in alchemy, astrology and magic. He was born at Cologne on the 14th of September, 1486, and educated at the University of Cologne. While still a youth he served under Maximilian I. of Germany. In 1509 he lectured at the University of Dole, but a charge of heresy brought against him by a monk named Catilinet compelled him to leave Dole, and he resumed his former occupation of soldier. In the following year he was sent on a diplomatic mission to England, and on his return followed Maximilian to Italy, where he passed seven years, now serving one noble patron, now another. Thereafter he held a post at Metz, returned to Cologne, practised medicine at Geneva, and was appointed physician to Louise of Savoy, mother of Francis I. ; but, on being given some task which he found irksome, he left the service of his patroness and denounced her bitterly. He then accepted a post offered him by Margaret, Duchess of Savoy, Regent of the Netherlands. On her death in 1830, he repaired to Cologne and Bonn, and thence to France, where he was arrested for some slighting mention of the Queen-Mother, Louise of Savoy. He was soon released, however, and died at Grenoble in 1535. *Agrippa* was a man of great talent and varied attainments. He was acquainted with eight languages, and was evidently a physician of no mean ability, as well as a soldier and a theologian. He had, moreover, many noble patrons. Yet, notwithstanding these advantages, he never seemed to be free from misfortune ; persecution and financial difficulties dogged his footsteps, and in Brussels he suffered imprisonment for debt. He himself was in a measure responsible for his troubles. He was, in fact, an adept in the gentle art of making enemies, and the persecution of the monks with whom he frequently came into conflict was bitter and increasing. His principal works were a defence of magic, entitled *De occulta philosophia,* which was not published until 1531, though it was written some twenty years earlier, and a satirical attack on the scientific pretensions of his day, *De incertitudine et Vanitate Scientiarum et Artium atque Excellentia Verbi Dei Declamatio,* also published at Antwerp in 1531. His other works included a treatise *De Nobilitate et Praecellentia Feminu Sexus,* dedicated to

Margaret of Burgundy out of gratitude for her patronage.

His interest in alchemy and magic dated from an early period of his life, and gave rise to many tales of his occult powers. It was said that he was always accompanied by a familiar in the shape of a large black dog. On his death he renounced his magical works and addressed his familiar thus: " Begone, wretched animal, the entire cause of my destruction ! " The animal fled from the room and straightway plunged into the Saom, where it perished. At the inns where he stayed, *Agrippa* paid his bills with money that appeared genuine enough at the time, but which afterwards turned to worthless horn or shell, like the fairy money which turned to earth after sunset. He is said to have summoned Tully to pronounce his oration for Roscius, in the presence of John George, elector of Saxony, the Earl of Surrey, Erasmus, and other eminent people. Tully duly appeared, delivered his famous oration, and left his audience deeply moved. *Agrippa* had a magic glass, wherein it was possible to see objects distant in time or place. On one occasion Surrey saw therein his mistress, the beautiful Geraldine, lamenting the absence of her noble lover.

One other story concerning the magician is worthy of record. Once when about to leave home for a short time, he entrusted to his wife the key of his museum, warning her on no account to permit anyone to enter. But the curiosity of a boarder in their house prompted him to beg for the key, till at length the harrassed hostess gave it to him. The first thing that caught the student's attention was a book of spells, from which he began to read. A knock sounded on the door. The student took no notice, but went on reading, and the knock was repeated. A moment later a demon entered, demanding to know why he had been summoned. The student was too terrified to make reply, and the angry demon seized him by the throat and strangled him. At the same moment *Agrippa* entered, having returned unexpectedly from his journey. Fearing that he would be charged with the murder of the youth, he persuaded the demon to restore him to life for a little while, and walk him up and down the market place. The demon consented ; the people saw the student apparently alive and in good health, and when the demon allowed the semblance of life to leave the body, they thought the young man had died a natural death. However, an examination clearly showed that he had been strangled. The true state of affairs leaked out, and *Agrippa* was forced to flee for his life.

These fabrications of the popular imagination were probably encouraged rather than suppressed by *Agrippa*, who loved to surround his comparatively harmless pursuits of alchemy and astrology with an air of mystery calculated to inspire awe and terror in the minds of the ignorant. It is known that he had correspondents in all parts of the world, and that from their letters, which he received in his retirement, he gleaned the knowledge which he was popu· larly believed to obtain from his familiars.

Ahazu-Demon : (The Seizer). Practically nothing is known of this Semitic demon unless it is the same *ahazie* told of in medical texts, where a man can be stricken by a disease bearing this name.

Ahi : (*See* **Devil.**)

Ahrimanes : The name given to the Chief of the Cacodaemons, or fallen angels, by the Persians and Chaldeans. These Cacodaemons were believed to have been expelled from Heaven for their sins ; they endeavoured to settle down in various parts of the earth, but were always rejected, and out of revenge they find their pleasure in injuring the inhabitants. Xenocritus thought that penance and self-mortification, though not agreeable to the gods, pacified the malice of the Cacodaemons. *Ahrimanes* and his

followers finally took up their abode in all the space between the earth and the fixed stars, and there established their domain, which is called Arhiman-abad. As *Ahrimanes* was the spirit of evil his counterpart in Persian dualism was Ormuzd, the creative and benevolent being. (*See* **Persia.**)

Ainsarii : An Ishmaelite sect of the Assassins (q.v.) who continued to exist after the stronghold of that society was destroyed. They held secret meetings for receptions, and possessed signs, words, and a catechism. (*See The Asian Mystery, Rev. C. L. Lyde.*)

Air Assisting Ghosts to become Visible : It was formerly believed by some authorities that a ghost was wrapped in air, by which means it became visible. Thus a spectre might appear wherever there was air.

Akasa, or Soniferous Ether : One of the five elementary principles of nature, mentioned in *The Science of Breath*, a Hindu Yoga. It is the first of these principles ; is given by " The Great Power," and out of it the others are created. These ethers may be likened to the five senses of man. In order to hear distinct sounds, the Hindu theosophist " concentrates " himself upon *Akasa*.

Akathaso : Evil spirits inhabiting trees. (*See* **Burma.**)

Akhnim : A town of Middle Thebais, which at one time possessed the reputation of being the habitation of the greatest magicians. Paul Lucas, in his *Second Voyage*, speaks of the wonderful Serpent of *Akhnim*, which was worshipped by the Mussulmans as an angel, and by the Christians believed to be the demon Asmodeus.

Akiba : A Jewish rabbi of the first century, who, from being a simple shepherd, became a learned scholar, spurred by the hope of winning the hand of a young lady he greatly admired. The Jews say that he was taught by the elemental spirits, that he was a conjurer, and that, in his best days, he had as many as 24,000 disciples. He is said to be the author of a famous work, entitled, *Yetzirah* (q.v., On the Creation), which is by some ascribed to Abraham, and even to Adam. It was first printed at Paris in 1552.

Aksakof, (Alexandre) : A Russian statesman, whose name stands high in the spiritualistic annals of his country. Born in 1832, he was educated at the Imperial Lyceum of St. Petersburg, and afterwards became Councillor of State to the Emperor of Russia. He made his first acquaintance with spiritualism through the writings of Swedenborg, some of which he afterwards translated. Later, he studied the works of other spiritualistic writers. He was instrumental in bringing many mediums to Russia, and identified himself with Horne, Slade, and other well-known mediums, and later with Eusapia Palladino. Mainly at the instance of *M. Aksakof*, a Russian Scientific Committee was appointed in 1877 to enquire into spiritualism, but its enquiry was conducted in a very half-hearted manner. *M. Aksakof* was for many years compelled to publish his psychic works and journals in Germany and other countries, on account of the prohibition of the Russian Government. (*See* **Russia.**)

Al : Part of inscription on a pantacle which forms a frontis· piece to the grimoire doctrine. Along with other inscriptions, it denotes the name of God.

Alain of Lisle : It has been said by some writers that there were two men to whom was given the name of Alanus Insulensis, one of whom was Bernardine, Bishop of Auxerre, and author of a *Commentary on the Prophecies of Merlin ;* the other, that " Universal Doctor," whose brilliant career at the Paris University was followed by his withdrawal to a cloister, where he devoted himself entirely to the study of philosophy. Others again maintain that the Bishop of Auxerre and the " Universal Doctor " were one and the same. Even the date when they lived is very uncertain, being variously placed in the twelfth and thirteenth centuries. In the year 1600 a treatise on alchemy, entitled

Dicta de Lapide Philosophico was published at Leyden, bearing on its title-page the name of Alanus Insulensis. It was thus ascribed to Bernardine, to the " Universal Doctor," and, by still others, to a German named Alanus. Supposing the two first-mentioned to be separate and distinct persons, we have nevertheless no proof that either was interested in alchemy ; and as for the third, there is no proof that he existed at all. On the other hand, we know that it was customary at that time to ascribe works of a very inferior nature to illustrious persons who had died, and were thus unable to deny them. The *Dicta de Lapide Philosophico*, a work of no great alchemistical value, on account of its vague and indefinite nature, may be, and probably is, a spurious work, wrongly ascribed to *Alain*.

Alamut : A mountain in Persia. (*See* **Assassins.**)

Alary (François) : A visionary, who had printed at Rouen in 1701, *The Prophecy of Count Bombaste*, (*Chevalier de la Rose-Croix*), *nephew of Paracelsus*, (published in 1609 on the birth of Louis the Great.)

Alastor : A cruel demon, who, according to Wierius, filled the post of chief executioner to the monarch of Hades. The conception of him somewhat resembles that of Nemesis. Zoroaster is said to have called him " The Executioner." Others confound him with the destroying angel. Evil genies were formerly called *Alastors*. Plutarch says that Cicero, who bore a grudge against Augustus, conceived the plan of committing suicide on the emperor's hearth, and thus becoming his *Alastor*.

Albertus Magnus : No fewer than twenty-one folio volumes are attributed to this alchemist, and though it is highly improbable that all of them are really his, the ascription in several cases resting on but slender evidence, those others which are incontestably from his pen, are sufficiently numerous to constitute him a surprisingly voluminous writer. It is noteworthy, moreover, that according to tradition, he was the inventor of the pistol and the cannon ; but, while it is unlikely that the credit is due to him for this, the mere fact that he was thus acknowledged indicates that his scientific skill was recognised by a few, if only a few, of the men of his own time.

Albertus was born at Larvingen, on the Danube, in the year 1205, and the term *Magnus*, which is usually applied to him, is not the result of his reputation, but is the Latin equivalent of his family name, de Groot. Like many another man destined to become famous, he was distinctly stupid as a boy, but from the outset he showed a predilection for religion, and so it came about that one night the blessed Virgin appeared to him, whereupon his intellect suddenly became metamorphosed, acquiring extraordinary vitality. *Albertus* therefore decided that he must show his gratitude to the Madonna by espousing holy orders, and eventually he won eminence in the clerical profession, and was made Bishop of Ratisbon ; but he held this office for only a little while, resigning it that he might give his entire time to scientific researches. Thenceforth, until his death, the exact date whereof is uncertain, he lived chiefly at a pleasant retreat in Cologne ; and it is reported that here his mental vigour gradually forsook him, being replaced by the dullness which characterised him as a youth.

Albertus was repeatedly charged by some of his unfriendly contemporaries with holding communications with the devil, and practising the craft of magic ; while *apropos* of his reputed leanings in this particular, a curious story is recounted in an early history of the University of Paris. The alchemist, it seems, had invited some friends to his house at Cologne, among them being William, Count of Holland, and when the guests arrived they were amazed to find that, though the season was mid-winter and the ground was covered with snow, they were expected to partake of a repast outside in the garden. Great chagrin

was manifested by everybody, while some even declared themselves insulted ; but their host bade them be seated, assuring them that all would be well. They continued to be dubious withal, yet they took their places, and hardly had they began to eat and drink ere their annoyance vanished, for lo ! the snow around them melted away, the sun shone brightly, the birds sang, and summer appeared to be reigning indeed.

Michael Maier, the author of *Museum Chimicum* and numerous other alchemistic works, declares that *Albertus* succeeded in evolving the philosopher's stone, and that ere his death he handed it over to his distinguished pupil, St. Thomas Aquinas, who subsequently destroyed the precious article, suspecting it to be a contrivance of the devil. The alleged discoverer himself says nothing on this subject, but, in his *De Rebus Metallicis et Mineralibus*, he tells how he had personally tested some gold which had been manufactured by an alchemist, and which resisted many searching fusions. And, be this story true or not, *Albertus* was certainly an able scientist, while it is clear that his learning ultimately gained wide recognition, for a collected edition of his vast writings was issued at Leyden so late as 1653.

Albigenses : A sect which originated in the south of France in the twelfth century. They were so called from one of their territorial centres, that of Albi. It is probable that their heresy came originally from Eastern Europe, and they were often designated Bulgarians, and undoubtedly kept up intercourse with certain secretaries of Thrace, the Bogomils ; and they are sometimes connected with the Paulicians. It is difficult to form any exact idea of their doctrines, as Albigensian texts are rare, and contain little concerning their ethics, but we know that they were strongly opposed to the Roman Catholic Church, and protested against the corruption of its clergy. But it is not as a religious body that we have to deal with the *Albigenses* here, but to consider whether or not their cult possessed any occult significance. It has been claimed by their opponents that they admitted two fundamental principles, good and bad, saying that God had produced Lucifer from Himself ; that indeed Lucifer was the son of God who revolted against Him ; that he had carried with him a rebellious party of angels, who were driven from Heaven along with him ; that Lucifer in his exile had created this world with its inhabitants, where he reigned, and where all was evil. It is alleged that they further believed that God for the re-establishment of order had produced a second son, who was Jesus Christ. Furthermore the Catholic writers on the *Albigenses* charged them with believing that the souls of men were demons lodged in mortal bodies in punishment of their crimes.

All this is, of course, mere tradition, and we may be sure that the dislike of the *Albigenses* for the irregularities then current in the Roman Church, brought such charges on their heads. They were indeed the lineal ancestors of Protestantism. A crusade was brought against them by Pope Innocent III., and wholesale massacres took place. The Inquisition was also let loose upon them, and they were driven to hide in the forests and among the mountains, where, like the Covenanters of Scotland, they held surreptitious meetings. The Inquisition terrorised the district in which they had dwelt so thoroughly that the very name of *Albigenses* was practically blotted out, and by the year 1330, the records of the Holy Office show no further writs issued against the heretics.

Albigerius : A Carthaginian soothsayer mentioned by St. Augustine. He would fall into strange ecstacies in which his soul, separated from his body, would travel abroad and find out what was taking place in distant parts. He could read people's inmost thoughts, and discover anything he wished to learn. These wonders were ascribed to the agency of the Devil. St. Augustine also speaks of another case, in which the possessed man was ill of a fever. Though not in a trance, but wide awake, he saw the priest who was coming to visit him while he was yet six leagues away, and told the company assembled round his couch the exact moment when the good man would arrive.

Albumazar : An astrologer of the ninth century, born in Korassan, known principally by his astrological treatise, entitled, *Thousands of Years*, in which he declares that the world could only have been created when the seven planets were in conjunction in the first degree of the ram, and that the end of the world would take place when these seven planets (the number has now risen to twelve) will be together in the last degree of the fish. Several of *Albumazar's* treatises on astrology have been printed in Germany, of which one was his *Tractus Florum Astrologiæ*, Augsburg, 1488. (*See* **Astrology.**)

Alcahest : The universal solvent. (*See* **Alchemy.**)

Alchemist, A Modern Egyptian : A correspondent writing to the *Liverpool Post* of Saturday, November 28th, 1907, gives an interesting description of a veritable Egyptian alchemist whom he had encountered in Cairo not long before, as follows : " I was not slow in seizing an opportunity of making the acquaintance of the real alchemist living in Cairo, which the winds of chance had blown in my direction. He received me in his private house in the native quarter, and I was delighted to observe that the appearance of the man was in every way in keeping with my notions of what an alchemist should be. Clad in the flowing robes of a graduate of Al Azhar, his long grey beard giving him a truly venerable aspect, the sage by the eager, far-away expression of his eyes, betrayed the mind of the dreamer, of the man lost to the meaner comforts of the world in his devotion to the secret mysteries of the universe. After the customary salaams, the learned man informed me that he was seeking three things—the philosopher's stone, at whose touch all metal should become gold—the elixir of life, and the universal solvent which would dissolve all substances as water dissolves sugar ; the last, he assured me, he had indeed discovered a short time since. I was well aware of the reluctance of the mediaeval alchemists to divulge their secrets, believing as they did that the possession of them by the vulgar would bring about ruin of states and the fall of divinely constituted princes ; and I feared that the reluctance of the modern alchemist to divulge any secrets to a stranger and a foreigner would be no less. However, I drew from my pocket Sir William Crookes's spinthariscope—a small box containing a particle of radium highly magnified—and showed it to the sheikh. When he applied it to his eye and beheld the wonderful phenomenon of this dark speck flashing out its fiery needles on all sides, he was lost in wonder, and when I assured him that it would retain this property for a thousand years, he hailed me as a fellow-worker, and as one who had indeed penetrated into the secrets of the world. His reticence disappeared at once, and he began to tell me the aims and methods of alchemical research, which were indeed the same as those of the ancient alchemists of yore. His universal solvent he would not show me, but assured me of its efficacy. I asked him in what he kept it if it dissolved all things. He replied ' In wax,' this being the one exception. I suspected that he had found some hydrofluoric acid, which dissolves glass, and so has to be kept in wax bottles, but said nothing to dispel his illusion.

" The next day I was granted the unusual privilege of inspecting the sheikh's laboratory, and duly presented myself at the appointed time. My highest expectations were fulfilled ; everything was exactly what an alchemist's laboratory should be. Yes, there was the sage, surrounded by his retorts, alembics, crucibles, furnace, and bellows, and, best of all, supported by familiars of gnome-like appearance, squatting on the ground, one blowing the fire (a task to be performed daily for six hours continuously), one pounding substances in a mortar, and another seemingly engaged in doing odd jobs. Involuntarily my eyes sought the pentacle inscribed with the mystic word ' Abracadabra,' but here I was disappointed, for the black arts had no place in this laboratory. One of the familiars had been on a voyage of discovery to London, where he bought a few alchemical materials ; another had explored Spain and Morocco, without finding any alchemists, and the third had indeed found alchemists in Algeria, though they had steadily guarded their secrets. After satisfying my curiosity in a general way, I asked the sage to explain the principles of his researches and to tell me on what his theories were based. I was delighted to find that his ideas were precisely those of the mediæval alchemists namely, that all metals are debased forms of the original gold, which is the only pure, non-composite metal ; all nature strives to return to its original purity, and all metals would return to gold if they could ; nature is simple and not complex, and works upon one principle, namely, that of sexual reproduction. It was not easy, as will readily be believed, to follow the mystical explanations of the sheikh. Air was referred to by him as the ' vulture,' fire as the ' scorpion,' water as the ' serpent,' and earth as 'calacant' ; and only after considerable cross-questioning and confusion of mind was I able to disentangle his arguments. Finding his notions so entirely mediæval, I was anxious to discover whether he was familiar with the phlogistic theory of the seventeenth century. The alchemists of old had noticed that the earthy matter which remains when a metal is calcined is heavier than the metal itself, and they explained this by the hypothesis, that the metal contained a spirit known as ' phlogiston,' which becomes visible when it escapes from the metal or combustible substance in the form of flame ; thus the presence of the phlogiston lightened the body just as gas does, and on its being expelled, the body gained weight. I accordingly asked the chemist whether he had found that iron gains weight when it rusts, an experiment he had ample means of making. But no, he had not yet reached the seventeenth century ; he had not observed the fact, but was none the less ready with his answer ; the rust of iron was an impurity proceeding from within, and which did not effect the weight of the body in that way. He declared that a few days would bring the realisation of his hopes, and that he would shortly send me a sample of the philosopher's stone and of the divine elixir ; but although his promise was made some weeks since, I have not yet seen the fateful discoveries."

Alchemy : The science by aid of which the chemical philosophers of mediæval times attempted to transmute the baser metals into gold and silver. There is considerable divergence of opinion as to the etymology of the word, but it would seem to be derived from the Arabic *al*=the, and *kimya*=chemistry, which in turn derives from late Greek *chemeia*=chemistry, from *chumeia* a mingling, or *cheein* " to pour out," or " mix," Aryan root *ghu*, to pour, whence the word " gush." Mr. A. Wallis Budge in his *Egyptian Magic*, however, states that it is possible that it may be derived from the Egyptian word *khemeia*, that is to say " the preparation of the black ore," or " powder," which was regarded as the active principle in the transmutation of metals. To this name the Arabs affixed the article *al*, thus giving *al-khemeia*, or alchemy.

History of Alchemy.—From an early period the Egyptians possessed the reputation of being skilful workers in metals, and, according to Greek writers, they were conversant with their transmutation, employing quicksilver in the process of separating gold and silver from the native matrix. The resulting oxide was supposed to possess marvellous powers, and it was thought that there resided within it the individualities of the various metals—that in it their various substances were incorporated. This black powder was mystically identified with the underworld form of the god Osiris, and consequently was credited with magical properties. Thus there grew up in Egypt the belief that magical powers existed in fluxes and alloys. Probably such a belief existed throughout Europe in connection with the bronze-working castes of its several races. (*See* **Shelta Thari.**) It was probably in the Byzantium of the fourth century, however, that alchemical science received embryonic form. There is little doubt that Egyptian tradition, filtering through Alexandrian Hellenic sources was the foundation upon which the infant science was built, and this is borne out by the circumstance that the art was attributed to Hermes Trismegistus (q.v.) and supposed to be contained in its entirety in his works. The Arabs, after their conquest of Egypt in the seventh century, carried on the researches of the Alexandrian school, and through their instrumentality the art was brought to Morocco and thus in the eighth century to Spain, where it flourished exceedingly. Indeed, Spain from the ninth to the eleventh century became the repository of alchemical science, and the colleges of Seville, Cordova, and Granada were the centres from which this science radiated throughout Europe. The first practical alchemist may be said to have been the Arabian Geber (q.v.), who flourished 720-750. From his *Summa Perfectionis*, we may be justified in assuming that alchemical science was already matured in his day, and that he drew his inspiration from a still older unbroken line of adepts. He was followed by Avicenna, Mesna and Rhasis (q.v.), and in France by Alain of Lisle, Arnold de Villanova and Jean de Meung (q.v.) the troubadour; in England by Roger Bac n and in Spain itself by Raymond Lully. Later, in French alchemy the most illustrious names are those of Flamel (b. ca. 1330), and Bernard Trévisan (b. ca. 1406) after which the centre of interest changes to Germany and in some measure to England, in which countries Paracelsus (ca. 1560), Khunrath (ca. 1568), Böhme, Van Helmont, the Brabanter (1553), Ripley, Norton, Dalton, Charnock, and Fludd kept the alchemical flame burning brightly. It is surprising how little alteration we find throughout the period between the seventh and the seventeenth centuries, the heyday of alchemy, in the theory and practice of the art. The same sentiments and processes are found expressed in the later alchemical authorities as in the earliest, and a wonderful unanimity as regards the basic canons of the great art is evinced by the hermetic students of all time. On the introduction of chemistry as a practical art, alchemical science fell into desuetude and disrepute, owing chiefly to the number of charlatans practising it, and by the beginning of the eighteenth century, as a school, it may be said to have become defunct. Here and there, however, a solitary student of the art lingered, and the department of this article on "Modern Alchemy" will demonstrate that the science has to a great extent revived during modern times, although it has never been quite extinct.

The Quests of Alchemy. The grand objects of alchemy were (1) the discovery of a process by which the baser metals might be transmuted into gold and silver; (2), the discovery of an elixir by which life might be prolonged indefinitely; and there may perhaps be added (3), the manufacture of an artificial process of human life. (*For the latter see* **"Homunculus."**)

The Theory and Philosophy of Alchemy. The first objects were to be achieved as follows : The transmutation of metals was to be accomplished by a powder, stone, or elixir often called the Philosopher's Stone, the application of which would effect the transmutation of the baser metals into gold or silver, depending upon the length of time of its application. Basing their conclusions on a profound examination of natural processes and research into the secrets of nature, the alchemists arrived at the axiom that nature was divided philosophically into four principal regions, the dry, the moist, the warm, the cold, whence all that exists must be derived. Nature is also divisible into the male and the female. She is the divine breath, the central fire, invisible yet ever active, and is typified by sulphur, which is the mercury of the sages, which slowly fructifies under the genial warmth of nature. The alchemist must be ingenuous, of a truthful disposition, and gifted with patience and prudence, following nature in every alchemical performance. He must recollect that like draws to like, and must know how to obtain the seed of metals, which is produced by the four elements through the will of the Supreme Being and the Imagination of Nature. We are told that the original matter of metals is double in its essence, being a dry heat combined with a warm moisture, and that air is water coagulated by fire, capable of producing a universal dissolvent. These terms the neophyte must be cautious of interpreting in their literal sense. Great confusion exists in alchemical nomenclature, and the gibberish employed by the scores of charlatans who in later times pretended to a knowledge of alchemical matters did not tend to make things any more clear. The beginner must also acquire a thorough knowledge of the manner in which metals grow in the bowels of the earth. These are engendered by sulphur, which is male, and mercury, which is female, and the crux of alchemy is to obtain their seed—a process which the alchemistical philosophers have not described with any degree of clarity. The physical theory of transmutation is based on the composite character of metals, and on the presumed existence of a substance which, applied to matter, exalts and perfects it. This, Eugenius Philalethes and others call "The Light." The elements of all metals are similar, differing only in purity and proportion. The entire trend of the metallic kingdom is towards the natural manufacture of gold, and the production of the baser metals is only accidental as the result of an unfavourable environment. The Philosopher's Stone is the combination of the male and female seeds which beget gold. The composition of these is so veiled by symbolism as to make their identification a matter of impossibility. Waite, summarising the alchemical process once the secret of the stone is unveiled, says :

"Given the matter of the stone and also the necessary vessel, the processes which must be then undertaken to accomplish the *magnum opus* are described with moderate perspicuity. There is the calcination or purgation of the stone, in which kind is worked with kind for the space of a philosophical year. There is dissolution which prepares the way for congelation, and which is performed during the black state of the mysterious matter. It is accomplished by water which does not wet the hand. There is the separation of the subtle and the gross, which is to be performed by means of heat. In the conjunction which follows, the elements are duly and scrupulously combined. Putrefaction afterwards takes place,

'Without which pole no seed may multiply.'

"Then, in the subsequent congelation the white colour appears, which is one of the signs of success. It becomes more pronounced in cibation. In sublimation the body is spiritualised, the spirit made corporeal, and again a more glittering whiteness is apparent. Fermentation afterwards fixes together the alchemical earth and water, and causes the mystic medicine to flow like wax. The matter is then augmented with the alchemical spirit of life, and the exaltation of the philosophic earth is accomplished by the natural rectification of its elements. When these processes have been successfully completed, the mystic stone will have passed through three chief stages characterised by different colours, black, white, and red, after which it is capable of infinite multication, and when projected on mercury, it will absolutely transmute it, the resulting gold bearing every test. The base metals made use of must be purified to insure the success of the operation. The process for the manufacture of silver is essentially similar, but the resources of the matter are not carried to so high a degree.

" According to the *Commentary on the Ancient War of the Knights* the transmutations performed by the perfect stone are so absolute that no trace remains of the original metal. It cannot, however, destroy gold, nor exalt it into a more perfect metallic substance ; it, therefore, transmutes it into a medicine a thousand times superior to any virtues which can be extracted from it in its vulgar state. This medicine becomes a most potent agent in the exaltation of base metals."

There are not wanting authorities who deny that the transmutation of metals was the grand object of alchemy, and who infer from the alchemistical writings that the end of the art was the spiritual regeneration of man. Mrs. Atwood, author of *A Suggestive Inquiry into the Hermetic Mystery*, and an American writer named Hitchcock are perhaps the chief protagonists of the belief that by spiritual processes akin to those of the chemical processes of alchemy, the soul of man may be purified and exalted. But both commit the radical error of stating that the alchemical writers did not aver that the transmutation of base metal into gold was their grand end. None of the passages they quote, is inconsistent with the physical object of alchemy, and in a work, *The Marrow of Alchemy*, stated to be by Eugenius Philalethes, it is laid down that the real quest is for gold. It is constantly impressed upon the reader, however, in the perusal of esteemed alchemical works, that only those who are instructed by God can achieve the grand secret. Others, again, state that a tyro may possibly stumble upon it, but that unless he is guided by an adept he has small chance of achieving the grand arcanum. It will be obvious to the tyro, however, that nothing can ever be achieved by trusting to the allegories of the adepts or the many charlatans who crowded the ranks of the art. Gold may have been made, or it may not, but the truth or fallacy of the alchemical method lies with modern chemistry. The transcendental view of alchemy, however, is rapidly gaining ground, and probably originated in the comprehensive nature of the Hermetic theory and the consciousness in the alchemical mind that what might with success be applied to nature could also be applied to man with similar results. Says Mr. Waite : " The gold of the philosopher is not a metal, on the other hand, man is a being who possesses within himself the seeds of a perfection which he has never realised, and that he therefore corresponds to those metals which the Hermetic theory supposes to be capable of development. It has been constantly advanced that the conversion of lead into gold was only the assumed object of alchemy, and that it was in reality in search of a process for developing the latent possibilities in the subject man." At the same time, it must be admitted that the cryptic character of alchemical language was probably occasioned by a fear on the part of the alchemical mystic that he might lay himself open through his magical opinions to the rigours of the law.

The Elixir of Life has been specially treated elsewhere.

Records of Alleged Actual Transmutation. Several records of alleged transmutations of base metals into gold are in existence. These were achieved by Nicholas Flamel, Van Helmont, Martini, Richthausen, and Sethon. For a detailed account of the methods employed the reader is referred to the several articles on these hermetists. In nearly every case the transmuting element was a mysterious powder or the " Philosophers' Stone."

Modern Alchemy. That alchemy has been studied in modern times there can be no doubt. M. Figuier in his *L'Alchimie et les Alchimistes*, dealing with the subject of modern alchemy, as expressed by the initiates of the first half of the nineteenth century, states that many French alchemists of his time regarded the discoveries of modern science as merely so many evidences of the truth of the doctrines they embraced. Throughout Europe, he says, the positive alchemical doctrine had many adherents at the end of the eighteenth century and the beginning of the nineteenth. Thus a " vast association of alchemists," founded in Westphalia in 1790, continued to flourish in the year 1819, under the name of the " Hermetic Society." In 1837, an alchemist of Thuringia presented to the Société Industrielle of Weimar a tincture which he averred would effect metallic transmutation. About the same time several French journals announced a public course of lectures on hermetic philosophy by a professor of the University of Munich. He further states that many Hanoverian and Bavarian families pursued in common the search for the grand arcanum. Paris, however, was regarded as the alchemistical Mecca. There dwelt many theoretical alchemists and " empirical adepts." The first pursued the arcanum through the medium of books, the others engaged in practical efforts to effect transmutation. M. Figuier states that in the forties of last century he frequented the laboratory of a certain Monsieur L., which was the rendezvous of the alchemists of Paris. When Monsieur L's pupils left the laboratory for the day the modern adepts dropped in one by one, and Figuier relates how deeply impressed he was by the appearance and costumes of these strange men. In the daytime he frequently encountered them in the public libraries, buried in gigantic folios, and in the evening they might be seen pacing the solitary bridges with eyes fixed in vague contemplation upon the first pale stars of night. A long cloak usually covered their meagre limbs, and their untrimmed beards and matted locks lent them a wild appearance. They walked with a solemn and measured gait, and used the figures of speech employed by the mediæval illuminés. Their expression was generally a mixture of the most ardent hope and a fixed despair.

Among the adepts who sought the laboratory of Monsieur L., Figuier remarked especially a young man, in whose habits and language he could see nothing in common with those of his strange companions. He confounded the wisdom of the alchemical adept with the tenets of the modern scientist in the most singular fashion, and meeting him one day at the gate of the Observatory, M. Figuier renewed the subject of their last discussion, deploring that " a man of his gifts could pursue the semblance of a chimera." Without replying, the young adept led him into the Observatory garden, and proceeded to reveal to him the mysteries of modern alchemical science.

The young man proceeded to fix a limit to the researches of the modern alchemists. Gold, he said, according to the ancient authors, has three distinct properties : (1) that of resolving the baser metals into itself, and interchanging and metamorphosing all metals into one another ; (2) the curing of afflictions and the prolongation of life ; (3), as a *spiritus mundi* to bring mankind into rapport with the supermundane spheres. Modern alchemists, he continued, reject the greater part of these ideas, especially those connected with spiritual contact. The object of modern alchemy might be reduced to the search for a substance having the power to transform and transmute all other substances one into another—in short, to discover that medium so well known to the alchemists of old and lost to us. This was a perfectly feasible proposition. In the four principal substances of oxygen, hydrogen, carbon, and azote, we have the *tetractus* of Pythagoras and the *tetragram* of the Chaldeans and Egyptians. All the sixty elements are referable to these original four. The ancient alchemical theory established the fact that all the metals are the same in their composition, that all are formed from sulphur and mercury, and that the difference between them is according to the proportion of these substances in their composition. Further, all the products of minerals present in their composition complete identity with those substances most opposed to them. Thus fulminating acid contains precisely the same quantity of carbon, oxygen, and azote as cyanic acid, and " cyanhydric " acid does not differ from formate ammoniac. This new property of matter is known as " isomerism." M. Figuier's friend then proceeds to quote in support of his thesis and operations and experiments of M. Dumas, a celebrated French savant, as well as those of Prout, and other English chemists of standing.

Passing to consider the possibility of isomerism in elementary as well as in compound substances, he points out to M. Figuier that if the theory of isomerism can apply to such bodies, the transmutation of metals ceases to be a wild, unpractical dream, and becomes a scientific possibility, the transformation being brought about by a molecular rearrangement. Isomerism can be established in the case of compound substances by chemical analysis, showing the identity of their constituent parts. In the case of metals it can be proved by the comparison of the properties of isomeric bodies with the properties of metals, in order to discover whether they have any common characteristics. Such experiments, he continued, had been conducted by M. Dumas, with the result that isomeric substances were found to have equal equivalents, or equivalents which were exact multiples one of another. This characteristic is also a feature of metals. Gold and osmium have identical equivalents, as have platinum and iridium. The equivalent of cobalt is almost the same as that of nickel, and the semi-equivalent of tin is equal to the equivalent of the two preceding metals.

M. Dumas, speaking before the British Association, had shown that when three simple bodies displayed great analogies in their properties, such as chlorine, bromide, and iodine, barium, strontium, and calcium, the chemical equivalent of the intermediate body is represented by the arithmetical mean between the equivalents of the other two. Such a statement well showed the isomerism of elementary substances, and proved that metals, however dissimilar in outward appearance, were composed of the same matter differently arranged and proportioned. This theory successfully demolishes the difficulties in the way of transmutation. Again, Dr. Prout says that the chemical equivalents of nearly all elementary substances are the multiples of one among them. Thus, if the equivalent of hydrogen be taken for the unit, the equivalent of every other substance will be an exact multiple of it—carbon will be represented by six, azote by fourteen, oxygen by sixteen, zinc by thirty-two. But, pointed out M. Figuier's friend, if the molecular masses in compound substances have so simple a connection, does it not go to prove that all natural bodies are formed of one principle, differently arranged and condensed to produce all known compounds ?

If transmutation is thus theoretically possible, it only remains to show by practical experiment that it is strictly in accordance with chemical laws, and by no means inclines to the supernatural. At this juncture the young alchemist proceeded to liken the action of the Philosophers' Stone on metals to that of a ferment on organic matter. When metals are melted and brought to red heat, a molecular change may be produced analogous to fermentation. Just as sugar, under the influence of a ferment, may be changed into lactic acid without altering its constituents, so metals can alter their character under the influence of the Philosophers' Stone. The explanation of the latter case is no more difficult than that of the former. The ferment does not take any part in the chemical changes it brings about, and no satisfactory explanation of its effects can be found either in the laws of affinity or in the forces of electricity, light, or heat. As with the ferment, the required quantity of the Philosophers' Stone is infinitesimal. Medicine, philosophy, every modern science was at one time a source of such errors and extravagances as are associated with mediæval alchemy, but they are not therefore neglected and despised. Wherefore, then, should we be blind to the scientific nature of transmutation ?

One of the foundations of alchemical theories was that minerals grew and developed in the earth, like organic things. It was always the aim of nature to produce gold, the most precious metal, but when circumstances were not favourable the baser metals resulted. The desire of the old alchemists was to surprise nature's secrets, and thus attain the ability to do in a short period what nature takes years to accomplish. Nevertheless, the mediæval alchemists appreciated the value of time in their experiments as modern alchemists never do. M. Figuier's friend urged him not to condemn these exponents of the hermetic philosophy for their metaphysical tendencies, for, he said, there are facts in our sciences which can only be explained in that light. If, for instance, copper be placed in air or water, there will be no result, but if a touch of some acid be added, it will oxidise. The explanation is that " the acid provokes oxidation of the metal, because it has an affinity for the oxide which tends to form "—a material fact almost metaphysical in its production, and only explicable thereby.

He concluded his argument with an appeal for tolerance towards the mediæval alchemists, whose work is underrated because it is not properly understood. (*See also* **Elixir of Life, Homunculus,** and the many lives of the alchemists throughout this book.)

LITERATURE. Atwood, *A Suggestive Inquiry into the Hermetic Mystery,* 1850 ; Hitchcock, *Remarks on Alchemy and the Alchemists,* Boston, 1857 ; Waite, *Lives of the Alchemystical Philosophers,* London, 1888 ; *The Occult Sciences,* London, 1891 ; Bacon, *Mirror of Alchemy,* 1597 ; The works of the Hon. Robert Boyle ; S. le Doux, *Dictionnaire Hermetique,* 1695 ; Langlet de Fresnoy, *Histoire de la Philosophie Hermetique,* 1792 ; *Theatrum Chemicum,* (Essays by many great alchemists), 1662 ; Valentine, *Triumphal Chariot of Antimony,* 1656 ; Redgrove, *Alchemy Ancient and Modern* ; Figuier, *L'Alchimie et les Alchimistes,* Paris, 1857.

Alchindi : (*See* **Arabs.**)

Alchindus : An Arabian doctor of the eleventh century, placed by some authorities among the number of magicians, but regarded by others as merely a superstitious writer. He used charmed words and combinations of figures in order to cure his patients. Demonologists maintained that the devil was responsible for his power, and based their statements on the fact that he had written a work entitled *The Theory of the Magic Arts.* He was probably, however, nothing more formidable than a natural philosopher at a time when all matter of science and philosophy were held in suspicion. Some of his theories were of a magical nature, it is true, as when he essayed to explain the phenomena of dreams by saying that they were the work of the elementals, who acted their strange fantasies before the mind of the sleeper as actors play in a theatre. But on the whole there is little to connect him with the practice of magic.

Aldinach : An Egyptian demon, whom the demonologists picture as presiding over the tempests, earthquakes, rain-storms, hail-storms, etc. It is he, also, who sinks ships. When he appears in visible form he takes the shape of a woman.

Alectorius : This stone is about the size of a bean, clear as crystal, sometimes with veins the colour of flesh. It is said to be taken from the cock's stomach. It renders its owner courageous and invincible, brings him wealth, assuages thirst, and makes the husband love his wife, or, as another author has it, " makes the woman agreeable to her husband." But its most wonderful property is, that it helps to regain a lost kingdom and acquire a foreign one.

Alectryomancy, or Alectormancy : An ancient method of divination with a cock. In practising it, a circle must be made in a good close place, and this must be divided equally into as many parts as there are letters in the alphabet. Then a wheat-corn must be placed on every letter, beginning with A, during which the depositor must repeat a certain verse. This must be done when the sun or moon is in Aries or Leo. A young cock, all white, should then be taken, his claws should be cut off, and these he should be forced to swallow with a little scroll of parchment made of lamb-skin upon which has been previously written certain words. Then the diviner holding the cock should repeat a form of incantation. Next, on placing the cock within the circle, he must repeat two verses of the Psalms, which are exactly the midmost of the seventy-two verses mentioned under the head of " Onimancy," and it is to be noted on the authority of an ancient Rabbi, that there is nothing in these seventy-two which is not of some use in the kaba-listical secret. The cock being within the circle, it must be observed from which letters he pecks the grains, and upon these others must be placed, because some names and words contain the same letters twice or thrice. These letters should be written down and put together, and they will infallibly reveal the name of the person concerning whom inquiry has been made ; it is said, though the story is doubted, that the magician Iamblicus used this art to discover the person who should succeed Valens Caesar in the empire, but the bird picking up but four of the grains, those which lay on the letters T h e o, left it uncertain whether Theodosius, Theodotus, Theodorus, or Theodectes, was the person designed. Valens, however, learning what had been done, put to death several individuals whose names unhappily began with those letters, and the magician, to avoid the effects of his resentment, took a draught of poison. A kind of *Alectromancy* was also some-times practised upon the crowing of the cock, and the periods at which it was heard.

Ammianus Marcellinus describes the ritual which ac-companied this act rather differently. The sorcerers commenced by placing a basin made of different metals on the ground and drawing around it at equal distances the letters of the alphabet. Then he who possessed the deepest occult knowledge, advanced, en-veloped in a long veil, holding in his hand branches of vervain, and emitting dreadful cries, accompanied by hideous convulsions. He stopped all at once before the magic basin, and became rigid and motionless. He struck on a letter several times with the branch in his hand, and then upon another, until he had selected sufficient letters to form a heroic verse, which was then given out to

the assembly. The Emperor Valens, informed of this circumstance, was ill-pleased that the infernal powers should have been consulted regarding his destiny. Indeed, he went further, for with unexampled severity, he pro-scribed not only all the sorcerers, but all the philosophers in Rome, and punished them so severely that many per-ished.

In the fourth song of the *Caquet Bonbec*, of Jonquieres, a poet of the fourteenth century, the details of an operation in *Alectryomancy* are exactly and curiously set forth.

Aleuromancy : A species of divination practised with flour. Sentences were written on slips of paper, each of which was rolled up in a little ball of flour. These were thoroughly mixed up nine times, and divided amongst the curious, who were waiting to learn their fate. Apollo, who was supposed to preside over this form of divination, was surnamed Aleuromantis. So late as the nineteenth century the custom lingered in remoter districts.

Alexander ab Alexandro : (Alessandro Alessandri.) A Neapolitan lawyer, who died in 1523. He published a dissertation on the marvellous, entitled *De Rebus Admira-bilibus*, in which he recounts prodigies which happened in Italy, dreams which were verified, the circumstances connected with many apparitions and phantoms, which he says that he beheld himself. He followed this dissertation with his celebrated work *Genialium Dierum*, in which he recounts with much credulity many prodigious happenings. He tells how one evening he set out to join a party of several friends at a house in Rome which had been haunted for a long time by spectres and demons. In the middle of the night, when all of them were assembled in one chamber with many lights, there appeared to them a dreadful spectre, who called to them in a loud voice, and threw about the ornaments in the room. One of the most intrepid of the company advanced in front of the spectre bearing a light, on which it disappeared. Several times afterwards the same apparition re-entered through the door. *Alexander*, who had been lying on a couch, found that the demon had slid underneath it, and on rising from it, he beheld a great black arm appear on a table in front of him. By this time several of the company had retired to rest, and the lights were out, but torches were brought in answer to their cries of alarm, on which the spectre opened the door, slid past the advancing domestics, and disappeared. *Alexander* visited many other haunted houses, but he appears to have been easily duped, and by no means the sort of person to undertake psychical research. (*See* **Avicenna**.)

Alexander of Tralles : A physician born at Tralles in Asia Minor, in the sixth century, very learned, and with a leaning towards medico-magical practice. He prescribed for his patients amulets and charmed words, as, for instance, when he says in his *Practice of Medicine* that the figure of Hercules strangling the Nemean lion, graven on a stone and set in a ring, was an excellent cure for colic. He also claimed that charms and philacteries were efficacious remedies for gout, fevers, etc.

Alexander the Paphlagonian : The oracle of Abonotica, an obscure Paphlagonian town, who for nearly twenty years held absolute supremacy in the empirical art. Born about the end of the second century, a native of Abonotica, he possessed but little in the way of worldly wealth. His sole capital consisted in his good looks, fine presence, exquisite voice, and a certain talent for fraud, which he was soon to turn to account in an extraordinary manner. His idea was to institute a new oracle, and he fixed upon Chalcedon as a suitable place to commence operations. Finding no great encouragement there he made a fresh start by setting afoot a rumour to the effect that Apollo and his son Æscula-pius intended shortly to take up residence at Abonotica. Naturally, the rumour at length reached the ears of his fellow-townsmen, who promptly set to work on a temple meet for the reception of the gods. The way was thus prepared for *Alexander*, who proceeded to Abonotica, diligently advertising his skill as a prophet, so that on his arrival people from many neighbouring towns applied to him, and ere long his fame had spread as far as Rome. We are told that the Emperor Aurelius himself consulted *Alexander* before undertaking an important military enterprise.

Lucian gives a suppositious explanation of the Paphlagonian prophet's remarkable popularity. *Alexander*, he says, came in the course of his early travels to Pella, in Macedon, where he found a unique breed of serpents, large, beautiful, and so tame and harmless that they were allowed by the inhabitants to enter their houses and play with children. A plan took shape in his brain which was to help him to attain the fame he craved. Selecting the largest and finest specimen of the Macedonian snakes that he could find, he carried it secretly to his destination. The temple which the credulous natives of Abonotica had raised to Apollo was surrounded by a moat, and *Alexander*, ever ready to seize an opportunity wherever it presented itself, emptied a goose-egg of its contents, placed within the shell a newly-hatched serpent, and sunk it in the moat. He then impressively informed the people that Apollo had arrived. Making for the moat with all speed, followed by a curious multitude, he scooped up the egg, and in full view of the people, broke the shell and exposed to their admiring eyes a little, wriggling serpent. When a few days had elapsed he judged the time ripe for a second demonstration. Gathering together a huge crowd from every part of Paphlagonia, he emerged from the temple with the large Macedonian snake coiled about his neck. By an ingenious arrangement the head of the serpent was concealed under the prophet's arm, and an artificial head, somewhat resembling that of a human being, allowed to protrude. The assembly was much astonished to find that the tiny serpent of a few days ago had already attained such remarkable proportions and possessed the face of a human being, and they appeared to have little doubt that it was indeed Apollo come to Abonotica.

By means of ingenious mechanical contrivances the serpent was apparently made to reply to questions put to it. In other cases sealed rolls containing the questions were handed to the oracle and returned with the seals intact and an appropriate answer written inside.

His audacity and ready invention enabled *Alexander* to impose at will upon the credulous people of his time, and these, combined with a strong and attractive personality, won, and preserved for him his remarkable popularity, as they have done for other " prophets " before and since.

Alfarabi : (d. 954.) An adept of remarkable gifts and an extensive knowledge of all the sciences ; born at Othrar (or, as it was then called, Faral), in Asia Minor. His name was Abou-Nasr-Mohammed-Ibn-Tarkaw, but he received, from the town of his birth, his better-known appellation of Farabi, or *Alfarabi*. Though he was of Turkish extraction, a desire to perfect himself in Arabic, led him to Bagdad, where he assiduously studied the Greek philosophers under Abou Bachar Maltey. He next stayed for a time in Hanan, where he learned logic from a Christian physician. Having far surpassed his fellow-scholars, he left Hanan and drifted at last to Egypt. During his wanderings he came in contact with all the most learned philosophers of his time, and himself wrote books on philosophy, mathematics, astromony, and other sciences, besides acquiring proficiency in seventy languages. His treatise on music, proving the connection of sound with atmospheric vibrations, and mocking the Pythagorean theory of the music of the spheres, attained some celebrity.

He gained the good-will and patronage of the Sultan of Syria in a somewhat curious fashion. While passing through Syria he visited the court of the Sultan, who was at that moment surrounded by grave doctors and astrologers, who were discussing abstruse scientific points with the potentate. *Alfarabi* entered the presence of the Sultan in his stained and dusty travelling attire (he had been on a pilgrimage to Mecca), and when the prince bade him be seated, he, either unaware of, or indifferent to the etiquette of court life, sat down boldly on a corner of the royal sofa. The monarch, unused to such an informal proceeding, spoke in a little-known tongue to a courtier, and bade him remove the presumptuous philosopher. The latter, however, astonished him by replying in the same language : " Sire, he who acts hastily, in haste repents." The Sultan, becoming interested in his unconventional guest, questioned him curiously, and learned of the seventy languages and other accomplishments of *Alfarabi*. The sages who were present were also astounded at his wide learning. When the prince called at length for some music, *Alfarabi* accompanied the musicians on a lute with such marvellous skill and grace that the entire company was charmed. When he struck up a lively measure, the gravest sages could not but dance to it. When he changed the melody to a softer lilt, tears sparkled in every eye, and at last, with a gentle lullaby, he put the court to sleep. The Sultan wished to keep such a valuable philosopher about his court, and some say that *Alfarabi* accepted his patronage and died peacefully in Syria. Others, again, maintain that he informed the Sultan that he would never rest till he had discovered the secret of the Philosophers' stone, which he believed himself on the point of finding. These say that he set out, but was attacked and killed by robbers in the woods of Syria.

Alfragenus : (*See* **Astrology**.)

Alfragius : (*See* **Astrology**.)

Alfridarya : A science resembling astrology, which lays down that all the planets, in turn influence the life of man, each one governing a certain number of years.

Alis de Telieux : In 1528, there was published in Paris a curious book, entitled, *La merveilleuse histoire de l'esprit qui, depuis naguère, s'est apparu au monastère des religieuses de Saint Pierre de Lyon, laquelle est pleine de grande admiration, comme on pourra vois par la lecture de ce présent livre, par Adrien de Montalembert, aumonier du roi François Ier*. This work dealt with the appearance in the monastery of the spirit of *Alis de Telieux*, a nun who had lived there before the reformation of the monastery in 1513. *Alis*, it seems, had led rather a worldly life, following pleasure and enjoyment in a manner unbecoming to a nun, finally stealing the ornaments from the altar and selling them. After this last enormity, she, of course, left the monastery, and for a time continued her disgraceful career outside, but before she died she repented of her sins, and through the intercession of the Virgin, received pardon. This, however, did not gain for her Christian burial, and she was interred without the usual prayers and funeral rites. A number of years afterwards, when the monastery was occupied by other and better nuns, one of their number, a girl of about eighteen years, was aroused from her sleep by the apparition of *Sister Alis*. For some time afterwards the spirit haunted her wherever she went, continually rapping on the ground near where she stood, and even communicating with the interested nuns. From all indications, it was a good and devout spirit who thus entered the monastery, but the good sisters, well versed in the wiles of the devil, had their doubts on the subject. The services of the Bishop of Lyons and of the narrator, Adrien de Montalembert, were called in to adjure the evil spirit. After many prayers and formalities, the spirit of *Alis* was found to be an innocent one, attended by a guardian angel. She answered a number of questions regarding her present state and her desire for Christian burial, and confirmed the doctrines of the Catholic Church, notably that of purgatory, which latter spirit-revelation the author advances triumphantly for the confusion of the Lutherans. The remains of *Sister Alis* were conveyed to consecrated ground, and prayers made for the release of her soul from purgatory, but for some reason or other she continued to follow the young nun for a time, teaching her, on her last visit, five secret prayers composed by St. John the Evangelist.

All Hallow's Eve : One of the former four great Fire festivals in Britain, is supposed to have taken place on the 1st of November, when all fires, save those of the Druids, were extinguished, from whose altars only the holy fire must be purchased by the householders for a certain price. The festival is still known in Ireland as Samhein, or La Samon, *i.e.,* the Feast of the Sun , while in Scotland, it has assumed the name of Hallowe'en. *All Hallow's Eve*, as observed in the Church of Rome, corresponds with the Feralia of the ancient Romans, when they sacrificed in honour of the dead, offered up prayers for them, and made oblations to them. In ancient times, this festival was celebrated on the twenty-first of February, but the Roman Church transferred it in her calendar to the first of November. It was originally designed to give rest and peace to the souls of the departed. In some parts of Scotland, it is still customary for young people to kindle fires on the tops of hills and rising grounds, and fire of this description goes by the name of a " Hallowe'en bleeze." Formerly it was customary to surround these bonfires with a circular trench symbolical of the sun. Sheriff Barclay tells us that about seventy years ago, while travelling from Dunkeld to Aberfeldy on Hallowe'en, he counted thirty fires blazing on the hill tops, with the phantom figures of persons dancing round the flames.

In Perthshire, the " Hallowe'en bleeze " is made in the following picturesque fashion. Heath, broom, and dressings of flax are tied upon a pole. The faggot is then kindled ; a youth takes it upon his shoulders and carries it about. When the faggot is burned out a second is tied to the pole and kindled in the same manner as the former one. Several of these blazing faggots are often carried through the villages at the same time.

" Hallowe'en " is believed by the superstitious in Scotland to be a night on which the invisible world has peculiar power. His Satanic Majesty is supposed to have great latitude allowed him on this anniversary, in common with that malignant class of beings known as witches, some of whom, it is said, may be seen cleaving the air on broomsticks, in a manner wondrous to behold. Others again, less aerially disposed, jog comfortably along over by-road and heath, seated on the back of such sleek tabby cats as have kindly allowed themselves to be transformed into coal-black steeds for their accommodation. The greenrobed fays are also said to hold special festive meetings at their favourite haunts. The ignorant believe that there is no such night in all the year for obtaining an insight into futurity. The following are the customs pertaining to this eve of mystic ceremonies : The youths and maidens, who engage in the ceremony of Pulling the Green Kail, go handin-hand, with shut eyes, into a bachelor's or spinster's garden, and pull up the first " kail stalks " which come in their way. Should the stalks thus secured prove to be of stately growth, straight in stem, and with a goodly supply of earth at their roots, the future husbands (or wives) will be young, goodlooking and rich in proportion. But if the stalks be stunted, crooked, and have little or no earth at their roots, the future spouses will be found lacking in good looks and fortune. According as the heart or stem proves sweet or sour to the taste, so will be the temper of the future partner. The stalks thus tasted are afterwards placed above the doors of the respective houses, and the christian names of those persons who first pass underneath will correspond with those of the future husbands or wives.

There is also the custom of Eating the Apple at the Glass. Provide yourself with an apple, and, as the clock strikes twelve, go alone into a room where there is a looking glass. Cut the apple into small pieces, throw one of them over your left shoulder, and advancing to the mirror without looking back, proceed to eat the remainder, combing your hair carefully the while before the glass. While thus engaged, it is said that the face of the person you are to marry will be seen peeping over your left shoulder. This " Hallowe'en " game is supposed to be a relic of that form of divination with mirrors which was condemned as sorcery by the former Popes.

The Burning Nuts. Take two nuts and place them in the fire, bestowing on one of them your own name ; on the other that of the object of your affections. Should they burn quietly away, side by side, then the issue of your love affair will be prosperous ; but if one starts away from the other, the result will be unfavourable.

And for the Sowing Hemp Seed, steal forth alone towards midnight and sow a handful of hemp seed, repeating the following rhyme :
" Hemp seed, I sow thee, hemp seed, I sow thee ;
And he that is my true love, come behind and harrow me."
Then look over your left shoulder and you will see the person thus adjured in the act of harrowing.

The ceremony of Winnowing Corn must also be gone through in solitude. Go to the barn and open both doors, taking them off the hinges if possible, lest the being you expect to appear, may close them and do you some injury. Then take the instrument used in winnowing corn, and go through all the attitudes of letting it down against the wind. Repeat the operation three times, and the figure of your future partner will appear passing in at one door and out at the other. Should those engaging in this ceremony be fated to die young, it is believed that a coffin, followed by mourners, will enter and pursue the too adventurous youth or maiden, who thus wishes to pry into the hidden things of the future, round the barn.

Another is Measuring the Bean Stack. Go three times round a bean stack with outstretched arms, as if measuring it, and the third time you will clasp in your arms the shade of your future partner.

Eating the Herring. Just before retiring to rest eat a raw or roasted salt herring, and in your dreams your husband (or wife) that is to be, will come and offer you a drink of water to quench your thirst.

Dipping the Shirt Sleeve. Go alone, or in company with others, to a stream where " three lairds' lands meet," and dip in the left sleeve of a shirt ; after this is done not one word must be spoken, otherwise the spell is broken. Then put your sleeve to dry before your bedroom fire. Go to bed, but be careful to remain awake, and you will see the form of your future helpmate enter and turn the sleeve in order that the other side may get dried.

The Three Plates. Place three plates in a row on a table. In one of these put clean water, in another foul, and leave the third empty. Blindfold the person wishing to try his or her fortune, and lead them up to the table. The left hand must be put forward. Should it come in contact with the clean water, then the future spouse will be young, handsome, and a bachelor or maid. The foul signifies a widower or a widow ; and the empty dish, single blessedness. This ceremony is repeated three times, and the plates must be differently arranged after each attempt.

Throwing the Clue. Steal forth alone and at night, to

the nearest lime-kiln, and throw in a clue of blue yarn, winding it off on to a fresh clue. As you come near the end, someone will grasp hold of the thread lying in the kiln. You then ask, " Who holds ? " when the name of your future partner will be uttered from beneath.

Allantara : (*See* **Spain.**)

Allat : Wife of Allah, and joint ruler with him over the Chaldean Hell. M. Maspero describes her as " the lady of the great country where all go after death who have breathed here below," and as their terrible judge.

Allen Kardec : (*See* **Spiritualism.**)

Alli Allahis : A continuation of the old sect of the Persian Magi, (q.v.).

Allmuseri : An African secret society with secret rites akin to those of the Cabiric and Orphic Mysteries. Their reception takes place once a year in a wood, and the candidate is supposed to die. The Initiates surround the Neophyte and chant funereal songs. He is then brought to the temple erected for the purpose, and anointed with palm oil. After forty days of probation, he is said to have obtained a new soul, is greeted with hymns of joy, and conducted home. (*See* Heckethorn, *Secret Societies.*)

Alludels : (*See* **Arabs.**)

Almadel : (*See* **Key of Solomon.**)

Almagest : (*See* **Astrology.**)

Almanach du Diable : An almanac containing some very curious predictions for the years 1737 and 1738, which purported to be published in the infernal regions. It is a satire against the Jansenists, which was suppressed on account of some over-bold predictions, and which has become very rare. The authorship was ascribed to Quesnel, an ironmonger at Dijon. The Jansenists replied with a pamphlet directed against the Jesuits, which was also suppressed. It was entitled *Almanac de Dieu*, dedicated to M. Carré de Montgeron, for the year 1738, and, in contra-distinction to the other, claimed satirically to be printed in heaven.

Almoganenses : The name given by the Spaniards to certain people who, by the flight and song of birds, meetings with wild animals, and various other means, foretold coming events, whether good or evil. " They carefully preserve among themselves," says Laurent Valla, " books which treat of this science, where they find rules of all sorts of prognostications and predictions. The soothsayers are divided into two classes, one, the masters or principals, the other the disciples and aspirants."

Another kind of knowledge is also attributed to them, that of being able to indicate not only the way taken by horses and other beasts of burden which are lost, but even the road followed by one or more persons. They can specify the kind and shape of the ground, whether the earth is hard or soft, covered with sand or grass, whether it is a broad road, paved or sanded, or narrow, twisting paths, and tell also how many passengers are on the road. They can thus follow the track of anyone, and cause thieves to be pursued and apprehended. Those writers who mention the *Almoganenses*, however, do not specify either the period when they flourished, or the country or province they occupied, but it seems possible from their name and other considerations that they were Moorish.

Alocer : A powerful demon, according to Wierius, Grand Duke of Hades. He appears in the shape of a knight mounted on an enormous horse. His face has leonine characteristics ; he has a ruddy complexion and burning eyes ; and he speaks with much gravity. He is said to give family happiness to those whom he takes under his protection, and to teach astronomy and liberal arts. Thirty-six legions are controlled by him.

Alomancy : Divination by means of salt, of which process little is known. It is this science which justifies people in

saying that misfortune is about to fall on the household when the salt cellar is overturned.

Alopecy : A species of charm by the aid of which one can fascinate an enemy against whom he has a grudge, and whom he wishes to harm.

Alphabet, Magical : (*See* **Kabala.**)

Alphabet of the Magi : (*See* **Tarot.**)

Alphitomancy : A method of divination carried out with the help of a loaf of barley, which has been practised since the earliest days. It was used to prove the guilt or innocence of a suspected person. When many persons were accused of a crime, and it was desired to find the true culprit, a loaf of barley was made and a portion given to each of the suspected ones. The innocent people suffered no ill-effects, while the criminal betrayed himself by an attack of indigestion. This practice gave rise to a popular imprecation : " If I am deceiving you, may this piece of bread choke me." By means of it a lover might know if his mistress was faithful to him, or a wife, her husband. The procedure was as follows : A quantity of pure barley flour was kneaded with milk and a little salt, and without any leaven. It was then rolled up in greased paper, and cooked among the cinders. It was afterwards taken out and rubbed with verbena leaves, and given to the person suspected of deceit, who, if the suspicion was justified, would be unable to digest it.

There was said to be near Lavinium a sacred wood, where *Alphitomancy* was practised in order to test the purity of the women. The priests kept a serpent, or, as some say, a dragon, in a cavern in the wood. On certain days of the year the young women were sent thither, blind-folded, and carrying a cake made of barley flour and honey. The devil, we are told, led them by the right road. Those who were innocent had their cakes eaten by the serpent, while the cakes of the others were refused.

Alpiel : An angel or demon, who, according to the Talmud, presides over fruit-trees.

Alraun : Images made of the roots of the ash tree, which are sometimes mistakenly called mandrakes, (q.v.)

Alrunes : Female demons or sorceresses, the mothers of the Huns. They took all sorts of shapes, but without changing their sex. The name was given by the Germans to little statues of old sorceresses, about a foot high. To these they attributed great virtues, honouring them as the negroes honour their fetishes ; clothing them richly, housing them comfortably, and serving them with food and drink at every meal. They believed that if these little images were neglected they would cry out, a catastrophe which was to be avoided at all costs, as it brought dire misfortunes upon the household. They may have been mandrakes, and it was claimed for them that they could foretell the future, answering by means of motions of the head, or unintelligible words. They are still consulted in Norway.

Alruy, David : A Jewish magician, mentioned in his *Voyages* by Benjamin the Jew. *Alruy* boasted himself a descendant of King David. He was educated in Bagdad, receiving instruction in the magic arts to such good purpose that he came to be more proficient than his masters. His false miracles gained so much popularity for him that some of the Jews believed him to be that prophet who was to restore their nation to Jerusalem. The King of Persia caused him to be cast into prison, but no bolts and bars could hold for long so redoubtable a magician. He escaped from his prison and appeared before the eyes of the astonished king, though the courtiers standing round saw nothing, and only heard his voice. In vain the king called angrily for someone to arrest the imposter. No one could see him, and while they groped in search of him, like men blindfolded, he slipped from the palace, with the king in pursuit, all the amazed assembly running after their prince. At length they reached the sea shore, and *Alruy* turned and showed himself to all the people. Then, spreading a scarf on the surface of the water, he walked over it lightly, before the boats which were to pursue him were ready. This adventure confirmed his reputation as the greatest magician who had lived within the memory of man. But at last a Turkish prince, a subject of the Persian king, bribed the father-in-law of the sorcerer to kill him, and one night, when *Alruy* was sleeping peacefully in his bed, a dagger thrust put an end to his existence.

Althotas : The presumed "master" and companion of Cagliostro. Considerable doubt has been expressed regarding his existence. Figuier states that he was no imaginary character; that the Roman Inquisition collected many proofs of his existence, but none as regards his origin or end, as he vanished like a meteor. "But," states the French author, "he was a magician and doctor as well, possessed divinatory abilities of a high order, was in possession of several Arabic manuscripts, and had great skill in chemistry." His connection with Cagliostro will be found detailed in the article on that adept. Eliphas Levi states that the name *Althotas* is composed of the word "thot" with the syllables "al" and "as," which if read cabalistically are *sala*, meaning messenger or envoy; the name as a whole therefore signifies "Thot, the Messenger of the Egyptians," and such, says Levi, in effect he was. *Althotas* has been sometimes identified with Kolmer, the instructor of Weishaupt in magic, and at other times with the Comte de Sainte-Germain (both of whom see). It would indeed be difficult to say with any definiteness whether or not *Althotas* was merely a figment of Cagliostro's brain. The accounts concerning him are certainly conflicting, for whereas Cagliostro stated at his trial in Paris that *Althotas* had been his lifelong preceptor, another account says that he met him first on the quay at Messina, and the likelihood is that this character is purely fictitious, as there does not appear to be any exact evidence that he was ever encountered in the flesh by anyone.

Alu-Demon : This Semitic demon owes his parentage to a human being; he hides himself in caverns and corners, and slinks through the streets at night. He also lies in wait for the unwary, and at night enters bed-chambers and terrorises folks, threatening to pounce upon them if they shut their eyes.

Amadeus : A visionary who experienced an apocalypse and revelations, in one of which he learned the two psalms composed by Adam, one a mark of joy at the creation of Eve, and the other the dialogue he held with her after they had sinned. Both psalms are printed in Fabricius' *Codex Pseudepigraphus Veteris Testamenti*.

Amaimon : One of the four spirits who preside over the four parts of the universe. *Amaimon*, according to the magicians, was the governor of the eastern part.

Amandinus : A variously coloured stone, which enables the wearer of it to solve any question concerning dreams or enigmas.

Amaranth : A flower which is one of the symbols of immortality. It has been said by magicians that a crown made with this flower has supernatural properties, and will bring fame and favour to those who wear it.

Ambassadors, Demon : (*See* **Demonology**.)

Amduscias : Grand Duke of Hades. He has, according to Wierius (q.v.), the form of a unicorn, but when evoked, appears in human shape. He gives concerts, at the command of men, where one hears the sound of all the musical instruments but can see nothing. It is said that the trees themselves incline to his voice. He commands twenty-nine legions.

America, United States of : Occultism amongst the aboriginal tribes of America will be found dealt with under the article "North-American Indians." The occult history of the European races which occupy the territory now known as the United States of America does not commence until some little time after their entrance into the North American continent. It is probable that the early English and Dutch settlers carried with them the germs of the practice of witchcraft, but it is certain that they brought with them an active belief in witchcraft and sorcery. It is significant, however, that no outbreak of fanaticism occurred in connection with this belief until nearly the end of the seventeenth century, in 1692, when an alarm of witchcraft was raised in the family of the Minister of Salem, and several black servants were charged with the supposed crime. It is quite likely that these negroes practised voodoo or obeah (q.v.), but, however this may be, the charges did not stop at them. The alarm spread rapidly, and in a brief space numerous persons fell under suspicion on the most frivolous pretexts. The new Governor of the Colony, Sir William Phipps, appears to have been carried away with the excitement, and authorised judicial prosecutions. The first person tried, a woman named Bridget Bishop, was hanged, and the Governor feeling himself embarassed among the extraordinary number of charges made after this, called in the assistance of the clergy of Boston. As events proved, this was a fatal thing to do. Boston, at this time, possessed a distinguished family of puritanical ministers of the name of Mather. The original Mather had settled in Dorchester in 1636, and three years later had a son born to him, whom he called Increase Mather. He became a clergyman, as did his son, Cotton Mather, born in 1663. Increase was President of Harvard College, and his son occupied a distinguished position therein, and also preached at Boston. The fanaticism and diabolical cruelty of these two men has probably never been equalled in the history of human persecution. Relying implicitly upon the scriptural injunction : "Thou shalt not suffer a witch to live," and blinded by their fanatic zeal, they cost the colony many precious lives. Indeed, beside their régime, the rigours of Sprenger (q.v.) and Bodin (q.v.), pale into insignificance. That ministers professing to preach a gospel of charity and love could have so far descended as to torture and condemn thousands of human beings to the gallows and the stake, can only be regarded as astounding. In 1688 an Irish washer woman, named Glover, was employed by a mason of Boston, one Goodwin, to look after his children, and these shortly afterwards displayed symptoms which Cotton Mather, on examination, stated were those of diabolical possession. The wretched washerwoman was brought to trial, found guilty, and hanged; and Cotton Mather launched into print upon the case under the title of *Late Memorable Providences Relating to Witchcraft and Possession* which displayed an extraordinary amount of ingenuity and an equally great lack of anything like sound judgment. As was the case with the works of the European writers on witchcraft and sorcery, this book fanned the flame of credulity, and thousands of the ignorant throughout the colony began to cast about for similar examples of witchcraft. Five other persons were brought to trial and executed, and a similar number shortly met the same fate, among them a minister of the Gospel, by name George Borroughs, who disbelieved in witchcraft. This was sufficient, and he was executed forthwith. Popular sentiment was on his side, but the fiendish Cotton Mather appeared at the place of execution on horseback, denounced Borroughs as an impostor, and upheld the action of his judges. Another man, called Willard, who had been employed to arrest suspected witches, refused to continue in his office, and was himself arrested. He attempted to save himself by flight, but was pursued and overtaken, and duly executed. Even dogs accused of witchcraft were put to death, but the magistrates who had undertaken the proceedings, ignorant as they were, began to have some suspicion that the course they had adopted was a violent and dangerous one, and popular sentiment rose so high that the Governor requested Cotton Mather to write a treatise in defence of what had been done. The result was the famous volume, *Wonders of the Invisible World*, in which the author gives an account of several of the trials at Salem, compares the doings of witches in New England with those in other parts of the world, and discourses elaborately on witchcraft generally. The witch mania now spread throughout the whole colony. One of the first checks it received was the accusation of the wife of Mr. Hale, a minister. Her husband had been a zealous promotor of the prosecutions, but this accusation altered his views, and he became convinced of the injustice of the whole movement. But certain persons raised the question as to whether the Devil could not assume the shape of an innocent and pious person as well as a wicked one for his own purposes, and the assistance of Increase Mather, President of Harvard College, was called in to decide this. He wrote a book, *A Further Account of the Trials of the New England Witches*, and added many cases concerning witchcraft and evil spirits personating men, in the course of which he unhesitatingly affirmed that it was possible for the enemy of mankind to assume the guise of a person in whom there was no guile. A new scene of agitation was the town of Andover, where a great many persons were accused of witchcraft and thrown into prison, until a certain justice of the peace, named Bradstreet, who deserves special mention for his enlightened policy, refused to grant any more warrants for arrest. The accusers immediately fastened upon him, and declared that he had killed several people by means of sorcery, and so alarmed was he that he fled from the town. But the fanatics who made it their business to accuse, became bolder, and aimed at persons of rank, until at last they had the audacity to impeach the wife of Governor Phipps himself. This withdrew from them the countenance of the Governor, and a certain Bostonian who was accused, brought an action of damages against his accusers for defamation of character. After this, the whole agitation died down, and scores of persons who had made confessions retracted; but the Mathers obstinately persisted in the opinions they had published, and regarded the reactionary feeling as a triumph of Satan. A Boston girl, named Margaret Rule, was seized with convulsions, and when visited by Cotton Mather, was found by him to be suffering from a diabolical attack of obsession. He did his best to renew the agitation, but to no purpose, for a certain Robert Calif, an influential merchant of the town, also examined the girl, and satisfied himself that the whole thing was a delusion. He penned an account of his examination exposing the theories of the Mathers, which is published under the title of *More Wonders of the Invisible World*. This book was publicly burned by the partisans of the fanatical clergy, but the eyes of the public were now opened, and opinion generally was steadfastly against the accusation and prosecution of reputed witches. The people of Salem drove from their midst the minister, Paris, with whom the prosecution had begun, and a deep remorse settled down upon the community. Indeed, most of the persons concerned in the judicial proceedings proclaimed their regret; the jurors signed a paper stating their repentance and pleading delusion. But even all this failed to convince the Mathers, and Cotton wrote his *Magnalia*, an ecclesiastical history of New England, published 1700, which repeats his original view of the power of Satan at Salem, and evinces no regret for the part he had taken in the matter. In 1723, he edited *The Remarkables* of his father, in which he took occasion to repeat his theories.

Increase Mather died in 1723, at the age of eighty-five, and Cotton lived on to 1728. It has been claimed that they acted according to their lights and conscience, but there is no doubt that their vanity would not permit them to retract what they had once set down regarding witchcraft, and their names will go down to posterity with those of the inquisitors and torturers of the middle ages, as men, who with less excuse than these, tormented and bereft of life hundreds of totally innocent people.

For the history of Spiritualism in America, *See* **Spiritualism,** where a full summary of the subject will be found.

Apart from the doings at Salem, colonial America has little to offer in the way of occult history; but the modern United States of America is extremely rich in occult history. This, however, is a history of outstanding individuals—Thomas Lake Harris, Brigham Young, the Foxes, Andrew Jackson Davis, and so on, biographies of whom will be found scattered throughout this work. But that is not to say that various occult movements have not from time to time either originated in, or found a home in the United States. Indeed, the number of occult or semi-occult sects which have originated there, is exceedingly great, and the foundation of occult communities has been frequent. Such were the Mountain Cove community of Harris; the Society of Hopedale, founded by Ballou; and so on. The notorious community, or rather nation of Mormons had undoubtedly a semi-occult origin. Its founder, Joseph Smith, and its first great prophet, Brigham Young, both had occult ideas, which rather remind us of those of Blake (q.v.), and were decidedly of biblical origin. Smith purported to discover tablets of brass upon which was engraved the new law. This was the germ of the *Book of Morman the Prophet*, and a certain pseudo-mysticism was associated with the Mormon movement. This, however, wore off after a while. More fresh in the recollection are the blasphemous absurdities of the prophet Dowie, who purported to be a prophet of the new Christianity, and succeeded in amassing very considerable wealth. Later, however, he became discredited, and many of his disciples seceded from him. Sects of Adventists have also been fairly numerous. These persons at the call of their leaders have met in cemeteries and elsewhere arrayed in white robes, in the belief that the Last Day had arrived; but finding themselves duped, they invariably turned upon the charlatans who had aroused these false hopes. There is an instance on record, however, where one such person succeeded in bringing about the repetition of such a scene.

Theosophy, as will be seen in the central article on that subject, owes much to America, for it may be said that in the United States it received an almost novel interpretation at the hands of William Q. Judge, and Katherine B. Tingley, the founder of the theosophic colony at Point Loma, California.

The United States is frequently alluded to as the home and birth-place of " queer " religions *par excellence.* If Paris be excepted this charge holds good, for nowhere is pseudo-occultism so rife. It would indeed be difficult to account for this state of things. Shrewd as the average American is, there is no question that he is prone to extremes, and the temper of the nation as a whole is not a little hysterical. Such sects are often founded by unscrupulous foreign adventurers, and worshippers of Isis, diabolical societies and such-like abound in the larger cities, and even in some of the lesser communities. But on the other hand many such cults, the names of which for obvious reasons we cannot mention here, are of native American origin. In course of time these duly invade Europe, with varying fortunes. There exist, however, in America, numbers of cultured persons who make a serious study of the higher branches of mysticism and occultism, and who compare favourably in erudition and character with advanced European mystics. It might indeed with truth be said that America has produced the greatest occult leaders of the last quarter of a century.

American Indians. Among the various native races of the American continent, the supernatural has ever flourished as universally as among peoples in an analogous condition of civilisation in other parts of the world. They will be treated in the present article according to their geographical situation. Mexico, Central America and Peru have been noticed in separate articles.

North American Indians. The oldest writers on the North American Indians agree that they practised sorcery and the magic arts, and often attributed this power of the Indians to Satan. The Rev. Peter Jones, writing as late as the first decade of the nineteenth century, says : " I have sometimes been inclined to think that if witchcraft still exists in the world, it is to be found among the aborigines of America." The early French settlers called the Nipissing *Jongleurs* because of the surprising expertness in magic of their medicine men. Carver and Fletcher observed the use of hypnotic suggestion among the Menominee and Sioux about the middle of last century, and it is generally admitted that this art, which is known to modern Americanists as *orenda*, is known among most Indian tribes as Mooney has proved in his *Ghost Dance Religion.* Brinton, alluding to Indian medicine-men and their connection with the occult arts, says : " They were also adepts in tricks of sleight of hand, and had no mean acquaintance with what is called natural magic. They would allow themselves to be tied hand and foot with knots innumerable, and at a sign would shake them loose as so many wisps of straw ; they would spit fire and swallow hot coals, pick glowing stones from the flames, walk with naked feet over live ashes, and plunge their arms to the shoulder in kettles of boiling water with apparent impunity.

" Nor was this all. With a skill not inferior to that of the jugglers of India, they could plunge knives into vital parts, vomit blood, or kill one another out and out to all appearances, and yet in a few minutes be as well as ever ; they could set fire to articles of clothing and even houses, and by a touch of their magic restore them instantly as perfect as before. Says Father Bautista : ' They can make a stick look like a serpent, a mat like a centipede, and a piece of stone like a scorpion.' If it were not within our power to see most of these miracles performed any night in our great cities by a well-dressed professional, we should at once deny their possibility. As it is they astonish us but little.

" One of the most peculiar and characteristic exhibitions of their power, was to summon a spirit to answer inquiries concerning the future and the absent. A great similarity marked this proceeding in all northern tribes, from the Eskimos to the Mexicans. A circular or conical lodge of stout poles, four or eight in number, planted firmly in the ground was covered with skins or mats, a small aperture only being left for the seer to enter. Once in, he carefully closed the hole and commenced his incantations. Soon the lodge trembles, the strong poles shake and bend as with the united strength of a dozen men, and strange, unearthly sounds, now far aloft in the air, now deep in the ground, anon approaching near and nearer, reach the ears of the spectators.

" At length the priest announces that the spirit is present, and is prepared to answer questions. An indispensable preliminary to any inquiry is to insert a handful of tobacco, or a string of beads, or some such douceur under the skins, ostensibly for the behoof of the celestial visitor, who would seem not to be above earthly wants and vanities. The replies received, though occasionally singularly clear and

correct, are usually of that profoundly ambiguous purport which leaves the anxious inquirer little wiser than he was before.

" For all this, ventriloquism, trickery, and shrewd knavery are sufficient explanations. Nor does it materially interfere with this view, that converted Indians, on whose veracity we can implicitly rely, have repeatedly averred that in performing this rite they themselves did not move the medicine lodge ; for nothing is easier than in the state of nervous excitement they were then in to be self-deceived, as the now familiar phenomenon of table-turning illustrates.

" But there is something more than these vulgar arts now and then to be perceived. There are statements supported by unquestionable testimony, which ought not to be passed over in silence, and yet I cannot but approach them with hesitation. They are so revolting to the laws of exact science, so alien, I had almost said, to the experience of our lives. Yet is this true, or are such experiences only ignored and put aside without serious consideration ? Are there not in the history of each of us passages which strike our retrospective thought with awe, almost with terror ? Are there not in nearly every community individuals who possess a mysterious power, concerning whose origin, mode of action, and limits, we and they are alike, in the dark ?

" I refer to such organic forces as are popularly summed up under the words clairvoyance, mesmerism, rhabdomancy, animal magnetism, physical spiritualism. Civilised thousands stake their faith and hope here and hereafter, on the truth of these manifestations ; rational medicine recognises their existence, and while she attributes them to morbid and exceptional influences, confesses her want of more exact knowledge, and refrains from barren theorising. Let us follow her example, and hold it enough to show that such powers, whatever they are, were known to the native priesthood as well as the modern spiritualists and the miracle mongers of the Middle Ages.

" Their highest development is what our ancestors called ' second sight.' That under certain conditions knowledge can pass from one mind to another otherwise than through the ordinary channels of the senses, is shown by the examples of persons *en rapport.* The limit to this we do not know, but it is not unlikely that clairvoyance or second sight is based upon it."

In his autobiography, the celebrated Sac chief, Black Hawk, relates that his great grandfather " was inspired by a belief that at the end of four years he should see a white man, who would be to him a father." Under the direction of this vision he travelled eastward to a certain spot, and there, as he was forewarned, met a Frenchman, through whom the nation was brought into alliance with France.

No one at all versed in the Indian character will doubt the implicit faith with which this legend was told and heard. But we may be pardoned our scepticism, seeing there are so many chances of error. It is not so with an anecdote related by Captain Jonathan Carver, a cool-headed English trader, whose little book of travels is an unquestioned authority. In 1767 he was among the Killistenoes at a time when they were in great straits for food, and depending upon the arrival of the traders to rescue them from starvation. They persuaded the chief priest to consult the divinities as to when the relief would arrive. After the usual preliminaries, their magnate announced that the next day precisely, when the sun reached the zenith, a canoe would arrive with further tidings. At the appointed hour, the whole vilage, together with the incredulous Englishman, was on the beach, and sure enough, at the minute specified, a canoe swung round a distant point of land, and rapidly approaching the shore, brought the expected news. Charlevoix is nearly as trustworthy a writer as Carver. Yet he deliberately relates an equally singular instance.

But these examples are surpassed by one described in the *Atlantic Monthly*, of July, 1866, the author of which, the late Col. John Mason Brown, has testified to its accuracy in every particular. Some years since at the head of a party of voyageurs, he set forth in search of a band of Indians somewhere on the vast plains along the tributaries of the Copper-mine and Mackenzie rivers. Danger, disappointment, and the fatigues of the road, induced one after another to turn back, until of the original ten only three remained. They also were on the point of giving up the apparently hopeless quest, when they were met by some warriors of the very band they were seeking. These had been sent out by one of their medicine men to find three whites, whose horses, arms, attire, and personal appearance he minutely described, which description was repeated to Col. Brown by the warriors before they saw his two companions. When afterwards, the priest, a frank and simple-minded man, was asked to explain this extraordinary occurrence, he could offer no other explanation than that " he saw them coming, and heard them talk on their journey."

Many tales such as these have been recorded by travellers, and however much they may shock our sense of probability, as well-authenticated exhibitions of a power which sways the Indian mind, and which has ever prejudiced it so unchangeably against Christianity and civilisation, they cannot be disregarded. Whether they too are but specimens of refined knavery, whether they are instigations of the devil, or whether they must be classed with other facts as illustrating certain obscure and curious mental faculties, each may decide as the bent of his mind inclines him, for science makes no decision.

Those nervous conditions associated with the name of Mesmer were nothing new to the Indian magicians. Rubbing and stroking the sick, and the laying on of hands, were very common parts of their clinical procedures, and at the initiations to their societies they were frequently exhibited. Observers have related that among the Nez Percés of Oregon, the novice was put to sleep by songs, incantations, and " certain passes of the hand," and that with the Dakotas he would be struck lightly on the breast at a preconcerted moment, and instantly " would drop prostrate on his face, his muscles rigid and quivering in every fibre."

There is no occasion to suppose deceit in this. It finds its parallel in every race and every age, and rests on a characteristic trait of certain epochs and certain men, which leads them to seek the divine, not in thoughtful contemplation on the laws of the universe and the facts of self-consciousness, but in an entire immolation of the latter, a sinking of their own individuality in that of the spirits whose alliance they seek.

The late Washington Mathews, writing in Bulletin 30 of the Bureau of American Ethnology, says:

" Sleight-of-hand was not only much employed in the treatment of disease, but was used on many other occasions. A very common trick among Indian charlatans was to pretend to suck foreign bodies, such as stones, out of the persons of their patients. Records of this are found among many tribes, from the lowest in culture to the highest, even among the Aztecs. Of course, such trickery was not without some therapeutic efficacy, for, like many other proceedings of the shamans, it was designed to cure disease by influence on the imagination. A Hidatsa, residing in Dakota, in 1865, was known by the name of Cherry-in-the-mouth, because he had a trick of producing from his mouth, at any season, what seemed to be fresh wild cherries. He

had found some way of preserving cherries, perhaps in whisky, and it was easy for him to hide them in his mouth before intending to play the trick; but many of the Indians considered it wonderful magic.

" The most astonishing tricks of the Indians were displayed in their fire ceremonies and in handling hot substances, accounts of which performances pertain to various tribes. It is said that Chippewa sorcerers could handle with impunity red-hot stones and burning brands, and could bathe the hands in boiling water or syrup; such magicians were called ' fire-dealers ' and ' fire-handlers.' There are authentic accounts from various parts of the world of fire-dancers and fire-walks among barbarous races, and extraordinary fire acts are performed also among widely separated Indian tribes. Among the Arikara of what is now North Dakota, in the autumn of 1865, when a large fire in the centre of the medicine lodge had died down until it became a bed of glowing embers, and the light in the lodge was dim, the performers ran with apparently bare feet among the hot coals and threw these around in the lodge with their bare hands, causing the spectators to flee. Among the Nahavo, performers, naked except for breechcloth and moccasins, and having their bodies daubed with a white infusorial clay, run at high speed around a fire, holding in their hands great faggots of flaming cedar bark, which they apply to the bare backs of those in front of them and to their own persons. Their wild race around the fire is continued until the faggots are nearly all consumed, but they are never injured by the flame. This immunity may be accounted for by supposing that the cedar bark does not make a very hot fire, and that the clay coating protects the body. Menominee shamans are said to handle fire, as also are the female sorcerers of Honduras.

" Indians know well how to handle venomous serpents with impunity. If they can not avoid being bitten, as they usually can, they seem to be able to avert the fatal consequences of the bite. The wonderful acts performed in the Snake Dance of the Hopi have often been described.

" A trick of Navaho dancers, in the ceremony of the mountain chant, is to pretend to thrust an arrow far down the throat. In this feat an arrow with a telescopic shaft is used; the point is held between the teeth; the hollow part of the handle, covered with plumes, is forced down toward the lips, and thus the arrow appears to be swallowed. There is an account of an arrow of similar construction used early in the eighteenth century by Indians of Canada, who pretended a man was wounded by it and healed instantly. The Navaho also pretend to swallow sticks, which their neighbours of the peublo of Zuñi actually do in sacred rites, occasionally rupturing the œsophagus in the ordeal of forcing a stick into the stomach. Special societies which practise magic, having for their chief object rain-making and the cure of disease, exist among the southwestern tribes. Swallowing sticks, arrows, etc., eating and walking on fire, and trampling on cactus, are performed by members of the same fraternity.

" Magicians are usually men; but among the aborigines of the Mosquito Coast in Central America, they are often women who are called *sukias*, and are said to exercise great power. According to Hewitt, Iroquois women are reported traditionally to have been magicians.

" A trick of the juggler among many tribes of the North was to cause himself to be bound hand and foot and then, without visible assistance or effort on his part to release himself from the bonds. Civilised conjurers who perform a similar trick are hidden in a cabinet, and claim supernatural aid; but some Indian jugglers performed this feat under observation. It was common for Indian magicians to pretend they could bring rain, but the trick consisted simply of keeping up ceremonies until rain fell, the last ceremony being the one credited with success. Catlin describes this among the Mandan, in 1832, and the practice is still common among the Pueblo tribes of the arid region. The rain-maker was a special functionary among the Menominee.

" To cause a large plant to grow to maturity in a few moments and out of season is another Indian trick. The Navaho plant the root stalk of a yucca in the ground in the middle of the winter, and apparently cause it to grow, blossom, and bear fruit in a few moments. This is done by the use of artificial flowers and fruit carried under the blankets of the performers ; the dimness of the firelight and the motion of the surrounding dancers hide from the spectators the operations of the shaman when he exchanges one artificial object for another. In this way the Hopi grow beans, and the Zuñi corn, the latter using a large cooking pot to cover the growing plant."

South American Indians. Throughout South America the magician caste analogous to the medicine men or shamans of North America are known as *piajes* or *piaes*. Of those of British Guiana, Brett writes :

" They are each furnished with a large gourd or calabash, which has been emptied of its seeds and spongy contents, and has a round stick run through the middle of it by means of two holes. The ends of this stick project—one form the handle of the instrument, and the other has a long string to which beautiful feathers are attached, wound round it in spiral circles. Within the calabash are a few small white stones, which rattle when it is shaken or turned round. The calabash itself is usually painted red. It is regarded with great awe by the heathen Indians, who fear to touch it, or even to approach the place where it is kept.

" When attacked by sickness, the Indians cause themselves to be conveyed to some friendly sorcerer, to whom a present of more or less value must be made. Death is sometimes occasioned by those removals, cold being taken from wet or the damp of the river. If the patient cannot be removed, the sorcerer is sent for to visit him. The females are all sent away from the place, and the men must keep at a respectful distance, as he does not like his proceedings to be closely inspected. He then commences his exorcisms, turning, and shaking his *marakka*, or rattle and chanting an address to the *yauhahu*. This is continued for hours, until about midnight the spirit is supposed to be present, and a conversation to take place, which is unintelligible to the Indians, who may overhear it. These ceremonies are kept up for successive nights.

" If the patient be strong enough to endure the disease, the excitement, the noise, and the fumes of tobacco in which he is at times enveloped, and the sorcerer observe signs of recovery he will pretend to extract the cause of the complaint by sucking the part affected. After many ceremonies he will produce from his mouth some strange substance, such as a thorn or gravel-stone, a fish-bone or bird's claw, a snake's tooth, or a piece of wire, which some malicious *yauhahu* is supposed to have inserted in the affected part. As soon as the patient fancies himself rid of this cause of his illness his recovery is generally rapid, and the fame of the sorcerer greatly increased. Should death, however, ensue, the blame is laid upon the evil spirit, whose power and malignity have prevailed over the counteracting charms. Some rival sorcerer will at times come in for a share of the blame, whom the sufferer has unhappily made his enemy, and who is supposed to have employed the *yauhahu* in destroying him. The sorcerers being supposed to have the power of causing, as well as of curing diseases, are much dreaded by the common people, who never wilfully offend them. So deeply rooted in the Indian's bosom is this belief concerning the origin of

diseases, that they have little idea of sickness arising from other causes. Death may arise from a wound or a contusion, or be brought on by want of food, but in other cases it is the work of the *yauhahu*.

" I once came upon a Warau practising his art upon a woman inflicted with a severe internal complaint. He was, when I first saw him, blowing violently into his hands and rubbing them upon the affected part. He very candidly acknowledged his imposture when I taxed him with it, put up his implements, and went away. The fate of the poor woman, as it was related to me some time afterwards, was very sad. Though a Venezuelan half-breed, and of the Church of Rome, she was wedded to the Indian superstitions, and after trying the most noted sorcerers without relief, she inflicted on herself a mortal wound with a razor in the vain attempt to cut out the imaginary cause of her internal pain.

" Some have imagined that those men have faith in the power of their own incantations from their performing them over their own children, and even causing them to be acted over themselves when sick. This practice it is indeed difficult to account for. The juggling part of their business is such a gross imposture as could only succeed with a very ignorant and credulous people ; but it is perhaps in their case, as in some others, difficult to tell the precise point where credulity ends and imposture begins. It is certain that they are excited during their incantations in a most extraordinary way, and positively affirm that they hold intercourse with spirits ; nor will they allow themselves to be laughed out of the assertion however ridiculous it may appear to us.

" The Waraus, in many points the most degraded of the tribes, are the most renowned as sorcerers. The huts which they set apart for the performance of their superstitious rites are regarded with great veneration.

" Mr. Nowers, on visiting a Warau settlement, entered one of those huts, not being aware of the offence he was committing, and found it perfectly empty, with the exception of the gourd, or *mataro*, as it is called by the tribe. There was, in the centre of the hut, a small raised place about eighteen inches high, on which the fire had been made for burning tobacco. The sorcerer being asked to give up the gourd, peremptorily refused, saying that if he did so his ' two children would die the same night.' "

Keller, in his *Amazon and Madeira Rivers*, says : " As with the shamans of the North Asiatic nations, the influence a Pajé may secure over his tribe depends entirely on the success of his cures and his more or less imposing personal qualities. Woe to him if by some unlucky ministration or fatal advice he forfeits his prestige. The hate of the whole tribe turns against him, as if to indemnify them for the fear and awe felt by them until then ; and often he pays for his envied position with his life.

" And an influential and powerful position it is. His advice is first heard in war and peace. He has to mark the boundaries of the hunting-grounds ; and, when quarrels arise, he has to decide in concert with the chieftain, sometimes even against the latter's wishes. By a majestically distant demeanour, and by the affectation of severe fasting and of nightly meetings with the spirits of another world, these augurs have succeeded in giving such an appearance of holiness to the whole caste, that their influence is a mighty one to the present day, even with the Indians of the Aldeamentos, where contact with the white race is sure by-and-by to produce a certain degree of scepticism.

" When I was at the Aldeamento of San Ignacio, on the Paranapanema, Cuyaba, chieftain and Pajé of an independent horde of Cayowa Indians made his appearance, and I had the honour of being introduced to this magnificent sample of a conjurer. He was a man of about fifty, with large well-cut features, framed within a dense, streaming mane of long black hair. The long *xerimbita* on his under lip (a long, thin, cylinder of a resin resembling amber), a great number of black and white beads covering his chest in regular rows like a cuirass, and a broad girdle holding his *cherapi* (sort of apron), which was fringed all round with rich, woven ornaments, gave him quite a stately, majestic appearance."

Their magicians were called by the Chilians *gligua* or *dugol*, and were subdivided into *guenguenu, genpugnu* and *genpiru*, meaning respectively " masters of the heavens," " of epidemics," and " of insects *or* worms." There was also a sect called *calcu*, or " sorcerers," who dwelt in caves, and who were served by *ivunches*, or " man-animals," to whom they taught their terrible arts. The Araucanians believed that these wizards had the power to transform themselves at night into nocturnal birds, to fly through the air, and to shoot invisible arrows at their enemies, besides indulging in the malicious mischief with which folklore credits the wizards of all countries. Their priests proper they believed to possess numerous familiars who were attached to them after death—the belief of the " magicians " of the Middle Ages. These priests or diviners were celibate, and led an existence apart from the tribe, in some communities being garbed as women. Many tales are told of their magical prowess, which lead us to believe that they were either natural epileptics or ecstatics, or that disturbing mental influences were brought about in their case by the aid of drugs. The Araucanians also held that to mention their real personal names gave magic power over them, which might be turned to evil ends. Regarding the wizards of the inhabitants of the territory around the River Chaco, in Paraguay, Mr. Barbrooke-Grubb in his book, *An Unknown People in an Unknown Land*, says :

" The training necessary to qualify an Indian to become a witch-doctor consists, in the first place, in severe fastings, and especially in abstention from fluid. They carry this fasting to such an excess as to affect the nervous system and brain. Certain herbs are eaten to hasten this stage. They pass days in solitude, and, when thoroughly worked up to an hysterical condition, they see spirits and ghosts, and have strange visions. It is necessary, furthermore, that they should eat a few live toads and some kinds of snakes. Certain little birds are plucked alive and then devoured, their power of whistling being supposed to be thus communicated to the witch-doctor. There are other features in the preliminary training which need not be mentioned, and when the initiatory stage has been satisfactorily passed, they are instructed in the mysteries under pledge of secrecy. After that their future depends upon themselves.

" It is unquestionable that a few of these wizards understand to a slight degree the power of hypnotism. They appear at times to throw themselves into a hypnotic state by sitting in a strained position for hours, fixing their gaze upon some distant object. In this condition they are believed to be able to throw their souls out—that is, in order to make them wander. It seems that occasionally, when in this state, they see visions which are quite the opposite of those they had desired. At other times they content themselves with concentrating their attention for a while upon one of their charms, and I have no doubt that occasionally they are sincere in desiring to solve some perplexing problems.

" One of the chief duties of the wizard is to arrange the weather to suit his clansmen. If they want rain it is to him they apply. His sorceries are of such a kind that they may be extended over a long period. He is never lacking in excuses, and so, while apparently busy in combating the opposing forces which are hindering the rain, he gains time to study weather signs. He will never or rarely venture an opinion as to the expected change until he is nearly certain of a satisfactory result. Any other Indian could foretell rain were he to observe signs as closely as does the wizard. The killing of a certain kind of duck, and the sprinkling of its blood upwards, is his chief charm. When he is able to procure this bird he is sure that rain cannot be far off, because these ducks do not migrate southwards until they know that there is going to be water in the swamps. These swamps are filled by the overflowing of the rivers as much as by the local rainfalls, and the presence of water in the rivers and swamps soon attracts rain-clouds.

" The wizards also observe plants and animals, study the sky and take note of other phenomena, and by these means can arrive at fairly safe conclusions. They are supposed to be able to foretell events, and to a certain extent they succeed so far as these events concern local interests. By judicious questioning and observation, the astute wizard is able to judge with some amount of exactitude how certain matters are likely to turn out.

" After we had introduced bullock-carts into their country, the people were naturally interested in the return of the carts from their periodical journeys to the river. When the wizards had calculated carefully the watering-places, and had taken into consideration the state of the roads, the character of the drivers, and the condition and number of the bullocks, all that they then required to know was the weight of the loads and the day on which it was expected that the carts would leave the river on their return journey. The last two items they had to obtain from us. When they had these data, by a simple calculation they could make a very shrewd guess, not only at the time when they might be expected to arrive at the village, but also at what particular part of the road they might happen to be on any given day. A great impression was made upon the simple people by this exhibition of power, but when we discovered what they were doing, we withheld the information, or only gave them part, with the result that their prophecies either failed ignominiously or proved very erroneous. Their reputation accordingly began to wane.

" The wizards appear to be authorities on agricultural matters, and when application to the garden spirit has failed, the witch-doctor is called in. He examines the crop, and if he thinks it is likely to be a poor one, he says it is being blighted by an evil spirit, but that he will use what sorceries he can to preserve it. If, on the other hand, he has reason to believe that the crop will be a good one, he spits upon it here and there, and then assures the people that now they may expect a good harvest.

" Some of the chief duties of the witch-doctor consist in laying ghosts, driving off spirits, exorcising *kilyikhama* in cases of possession assisting wandering souls back to their bodies, and generally in the recognising of spirits. When a ghost is supposed to haunt a village, the wizard and his assistants have sometimes an hour's arduous chanting, in order to induce the restless one to leave. When he considers that he has accomplished this, he assures the people that it is done, and this quiets their fears. Evil spirits frequenting a neighbourhood have also to be driven off by somewhat similar chanting."

Amethyst : " This gem," says Camillus Leonardus, " is reckoned among the purple and transparent stones, mixed with a violet colour, emitting rosy sparkles." The Indian variety is the most precious. When made into drinking cups or bound on the navel, it prevented drunkenness. It is also held to sharpen the wit, turn away evil thoughts, and give a knowledge of the future in dreams. Drunk in a potion, it was thought to expel poison and render the barren fruitful. It was frequently engraved with the head of Bacchus, and was a favourite with the Roman ladies.

Amiante : A species of fire-proof stone, which Pliny and the demonologists recommended as an excellent specific against the charms of magic.

Amniomancy : Divination by means of the caul, or membrane which sometimes envelopes the head of a child at birth. From an inspection of this caul, the wise women predict the sort of future the baby will have. If it be red, happy days are in store for the child, or if lead-coloured, he will have misfortunes.

Amon : A great and powerful marquis of the infernal empire. He is represented as a wolf with a serpent's tail, vomiting flame. When he appears in human form, his head resembles that of a large owl with canine teeth. He is the strongest of the princes of the demons, knows the past and the future, and can reconcile, when he will, friends who have quarelled. He commands forty legions.

Amoymon : One of the four kings of Hades, of which the eastern part falls to his share. He may be invoked in the morning from nine o'clock till midday, and in the evening from three o'clock till six. He has been identified with Amaimon (q.v.) Asmodeus (q.v.) is his lieutenant, and the first prince of his dominions.

Amphiaraus : A famous soothsayer of ancient times, who hid himself so that he might not have to go to the war of Thebes, because he had foreseen that he should die there. This, indeed happened, but he came to life again. A temple was raised to him in Attica, near a sacred fountain by which he had left Hades. He healed the sick by showing them in a dream the remedies they must use. He also founded many oracles. After sacrifice, those who consulted the oracle slept under a sheep skin, and dreamed a dream which usually found plenty of interpreters after the event. *Amphiaraus* himself was an adept in the art of explaining dreams. Some prophecies in verse, which are no longer extant, are attributed to him.

Amulets : The charm, amulet, or mascot, is, of course, directly derived from the conception of the fetish (q.v.), which was believed by savage and semi-barbarous people to contain a spirit. Amulets may be said to be of two classes : those which are worn as (1) fetishes, that is the dwelling-place of spiritual entities, who are active on behalf of the wearer ; or (2), mascots to ward off bad luck or such influences as the evil eye.

That charms were worn by prehistoric man there is little room for doubt, as objects which in many cases partake of the appearance and general description of amulets are discovered in neolithic tombs. The ancient Egyptians possessed a bewildering variety of amulets, which were worn both by the living and the dead. Indeed, among the latter, every part of the body had an amulet sacred to itself. These were, as a rule, evolved from various organs of the gods : as, for example, the eye of Isis, the backbone of Osiris, and so forth. Among the savage and semi-civilised peoples, the amulet usually takes the form of a necklace, bracelets, or anklets, and where belief in witchcraft and the evil eye is strong, the faith in these, and in charms, is always most intense. Among civilised races it has been observed that it is usually the ignorant classes who adopt the use of amulets : such as sailors, miners, beggars, Gypsies, and criminals. But amulets are also to be found in use among educated persons, although, of course, the superstitious part of the practice has in these cases often disappeared. Universally speaking, stones, teeth, claws, shells, coral and symbolic emblems, are favoured amulets. The reason for the wearing of these is exceedingly difficult to arrive at, but a kind of doctrine of correspondences may be at the root of the belief—the idea that like produces like, or that an effect resembles its cause, or that things which have once been in contact but have ceased to be so, continue to act on each other by magical means. For example, the desert goat is a sure-footed animal ; accordingly, its tongue is carried as a powerful amulet against falling by certain Malay tribes. Beads resembling teeth, are discovered are hung round the necks of Kaffir children in Africa to assist them in teething, and the incisor teeth of the beaver are frequently placed round the necks of little American-Indian girls to render them industrious, like that animal. Again, certain plants and minerals indicate by their external character the diseases for which nature intended them as remedies. Thus the euphrasia, or eyebright, was supposed to be good for the eyes because it contains a black pupil-like spot ; and the blood-stone was employed for stopping the flow of blood from a wound.

It is strange that wherever prehistoric implements, such as arrowheads and celts, are discovered, they are thought by the peasantry of the locality in which they are found to be of great virtue as amulets. Some light is cast on this custom by the fact that stone arrowheads were certainly in use among mediæval British witches. But in most countries they are thought to descend from the sky, and are therefore kept to preserve people and cattle from lightning. This does not, however, explain away the reason why water poured over a prehistoric arrowhead is given to cure cows in Ireland. Certain roots, which have the shape of snakes, are kept by the Malays to ensure them against snake-bite ; and instances of this description of correspondence, known as the doctrine of signatures, could be multiplied *ad infinitum.* Among the Celts a great many kinds of amulets were used : such as the symbolic wheel of the sun god, found so numerously in France and Great Britain ; pebbles, amulets of the teeth of the wild boar, and pieces of amber. The well-known serpent's egg of the Druids was also in all probability an amulet of the priestly class. Indian amulets are numerous, and in Buddhist countries their use is universal, especially where that religion has become degraded, or has in any way degenerated. In Northern Buddhist countries almost everyone constantly wears an amulet round the neck. These generally represent the leaf of the sacred fig-tree, and are made in the form of a box which contains a scrap of sacred writing, prayer, or a little picture. Women of position in Tibet wear a chatelaine containing a charm or charms, and the universal amulet of the Buddhist priests in that country is the thunderbolt, supposed to have fallen direct from Indra's heaven. This is usually imitated in bronze or other metal, and is used for exorcising evil spirits. Amulet types are for the most part very ancient, and present much the same characteristics in all parts of the world.

Amy : Grand President of Hades, and one of the princes of the infernal monarchy. He appears there enveloped with flame, but on earth, in human form. He teaches the secrets of astrology and of the liberal arts, and gives faithful servants. He reveals to those who possess his favour, the hiding-place of treasures guarded by demons. Thirty-six of the infernal legions are under his command. The fallen angels acknowledge his orders, and he hopes that at the end of 200,000 years, he shall return to heaven to occupy the seventh throne.

Anachitis : Used in divination to call up spirits from water ; another stone, called synochitis, obliged them to remain while they were interrogated.

Anamelech : An obscure demon, bearer of ill news. He was worshipped at Sepharvaün, a town of the Assyrians. He always reveals himself in the figure of a quail. His name, we are told, signifies a " good king," and some authorities declare that this demon is the moon, as Andramelech is the sun.

Anancithidus : Leonardus describes this as " a necromantic stone, whose virtue is to call up evil spirits and ghosts."

Anania, or Agnany (Jean d') : A lawyer of the fifteenth century, who wrote four books, entitled, *De Naturà Dæmonum*, (On the Nature of Demons), and a treatise on Magic and Witchcraft, neither of which works are well known. He died in Italy in 1458.

Ananisapta : A Kabbalistic word made up from the initial letters of the prayer : *Antidotum Nazareni Auferat Necene Intoxicationis ; Sanctificet Alimenta, Poculaque Trinitas Alma.* When written on virgin parchment, it is a powerful talisman to protect against disease.

Anarazel : One of the demons charged with the guardianship of subterranean treasure, which he carries about from one place to another, to hide them from men. It is he who, with his companions Gaziel and Fécor, shakes the foundations of houses, raises the tempests, rings the bells at midnight, causes spectres to appear, and inspires a thousand terrors.

Anathema : The name was given by the ancients to certain classes of votive offerings, to the nets that the fisherman lays on the altar of the sea-nymphs, to the mirror that Laïs consecrated to Venus ; to offerings of vessels, garments, instruments, and various other articles. The word was also applied to the victim devoted to the infernal gods, and it is in this sense that it is found among Jews and Christians, referring either to the curse or its object. The man who is anathematized is denied communication with the faithful, and delivered to the demon if he dies without absolution. The Church has often lavished *anathemas* upon its enemies, though St. John Chrysostom has said that it is well to anathematize false doctrine, but that men who have strayed should be pardoned and prayed for. Formerly, magicians and sorcerers employed a sort of *anathema* to discover thieves and witches. Some limpid water was brought, and in it were boiled as many pebbles as there were persons suspected. The pebbles were then buried under the door-step over which the thief or the sorcerer was to pass, and a plate of tin attached to it, on which was written the words : " Christ is conqueror ; Christ is king ; Christ is master." Every pebble must bear the name of one of the suspected persons. The stones are removed at sunrise, and that representing the guilty person is hot and glowing. But, as the devil is malicious, that is not enough. The seven penitential psalms must then be recited, with the Litanies of the Saints, and the prayers of exorcism pronounced against the thief or the sorcerer. His name must be written in a circular figure, and a triangular brass nail driven in above it with a hammer, the handle of which is of cypress wood, the exorcist saying meanwhile : " Thou art just, Lord, and just are Thy judgments." At this, the thief would betray himself by a loud cry. If the *anathema* has been pronounced by a sorcerer, and one wishes merely to escape the effects of it and cause it to return to him who has cast it, one must take, on Saturday, before sunrise, the branch of a hazel tree of one year, and recite the following prayer : " I cut thee, branch of this year, in the name of him whom I wish to wound as I wound thee." The branch is then laid on the table and other prayers said, ending with " Holy Trinity, punish him who has done this evil, and take him from among us by Thy great justice, that the sorcerer or sorceress may be *anathema*, and we safe." Harrison Ainsworth's famous novel, *The Lancashire Witches*, deals with the subject and the Pendleton locality.

Ancient War of the Knights, Commentary on the : (*See* Alchemy.)

Andre, Francoise : (*See* France.)

Andrews, Mrs. : (*See* Materialisation.)

Androdamas : *Androdamas* resembles the diamond, and is said to be found in the sands of the Red Sea, in squares or dies. Its name denotes the virtue belonging to it, namely, to restrain anger, mitigate lunacy, and lessen the gravity of the body.

Android : A man made by other means than the natural mode of reproduction. The automaton attributed to Albertus Magnus, which St. Thomas destroyed with his stick because its answers to his questions puzzled him, was such an *android*. Some have attempted to humanize a root called the mandrake, which bears a fantastic resemblance to a human being. (*See* **Mandragora**.)

Angekok, Eskimo Shamans : (*See* **Eskimos**.)

Angelic Brethren : (*See* **Visions**.)

Angels : The word *angel*, " angelos " in Greek, " malak " in Hebrew, literally signifies a " person sent " or a " messenger." It is a name, not of nature but of office, and is applied also to men in the world, as ambassadors or representatives. In a lower sense, *angel* denotes a spiritual being employed in occasional offices ; and lastly, men in office as priests or bishops. .The " *angel* of the congregation," among the Jews, was the chief of the synagogue. Such is the scriptural usage of a term, which, in common parlance, is now limited to its principal meaning, and denotes only the inhabitants of heaven.

The apostle of the Gentiles speaks of the *angels* as " ministering spirits, sent forth to minister for them who shall be heirs of salvation," in strict keeping with the import of the term itself. In Mark i., 2, it is applied to John the Baptist : " Behold I send my messenger (' *angel* ') before my face," and the word is the same (" malak ") in the corresponding prophecy of Malachi. In Hebrews xii., 22, 24, we read : " Ye have come to an innumerable company of *angels*, to the spirits of the just," etc., and this idea of their great number is sustained by the words of our Lord himself, where, for example, he declares that " twelve legions " of them were ready upon His demand. In the Revelation of St. John, a vast idea of their number is given. They are called the " armies " of heaven. Their song of praise is described as " the voice of a great multitude, and as the voice of many waters, and as the voice of mighty thunderings." In fine, the sense of number is overwhelmed in the effort to compute them.

As to their nature, it is essentially the same as that of man, for not only are understanding and will attributed to them, but they have been mistaken for men when they appeared, and Paul represents them as capable of disobedience (Heb. ii., 7, 16.) The latter possibility is exhibited in its greatest extent by Jude, who speaks of the " *angels* which kept not their first estate, but left their own habitation," and upon this belief is founded the whole system of tradition concerning *angels* and demons. The former term was gradually limited to mean only the obedient ministers of the will of the Almighty, and the influence of evil *angels* was concentrated into the office of the great adversary of all good, the devil or Satan. These ideas were common to the whole Eastern world, and were probably derived by the Jewish people from the Assyrians. The Pharisees charged the Saviour with casting out devils " by Beelzebub the prince of the devils." But that evil spirits acted in multitudes under one person, appears from Mark v., 9, where the evil spirit being asked his name, answered : " My name is ' Legion ' for we are many."

It is generally held that two orders are mentioned in scripture, " angels " and " archangels " ; but the latter word only occurs twice, namely, in Jude, where Michael is called " an archangel," and in I. Thess. iv., 16, where it is written : " the Lord shall descend from heaven with a shout, with the voice of the archangel, and with the trump of God." This is a slender foundation to build a theory upon. The prefix simply denotes rank, not another order of intelligence. There is nothing in the whole of Scripture, therefore, to show that intelligent beings exist who have other than human attributes. Gabriel and Michael are certainly mentioned by name, but they appeared to Daniel, Zacharias, and the Virgin Mary, in fulfilment of a function, correspondent to the high purpose of which, may be the greater power, wisdom, and goodness, we should attribute to them ; and hence the fuller representation of the angelic hosts, as chief *angels*.

The mention of Michael by name occurs five times in Scripture, and always in the character of a chief militant :— In Daniel, he is the champion of the Jewish church against Persia ; in the Revelation, he overcomes the dragon ; and in Jude he is mentioned in personal conflict with the devil about the body of Moses. He is called by Gabriel, " Michael, your prince," meaning of the Jewish church. In the alleged prophecy of Enoch, he is styled : " Michael, one of the holy *angels*, who, presiding over human virtue, commands the nations " ; while Raphael, it says, " presides oper the spirits of men " ; Uriel, " over clamour and terror " ; and Gabriel, " over Paradise, and over the cherubims." In the Catholic services, St. Michael is invoked as a " most glorious and warlike prince," " the receiver of souls," and " the vanquisher of evil spirits." His design, according to Randle Holme, is a banner hanging on a cross ; and he is armed as representing victory, with a dart in one hand and a cross on his forehead. Bishop Horsley and others considered Michael only another designation for the Son of God. We may add as a certain biblical truth, that the Lord Himself is always meant, in an eminent sense, by any *angel* named as His minister ; and he is called the *angel* of the Covenant, because he embodied in his own person the whole power and representation of the angelic kingdom, as the messenger, not of separate and temporary commands, but of the whole Word in its fulness.

Paul speaks of a " third heaven," which must be understood not as a distinct order of created intelligences, but in the same sense as the Lord's declaration : " In my Father's house are many mansions." For Jesus Christ always speaks of His kingdom as essentially one, even in both worlds, the spiritual and natural.

Dionysius, or St. Denis, the supposed Areopagite, describes three hierarchies of *angels* in nine choirs, thus : Seraphim, Cherubim, Thrones, Dominions, Principalities, Powers, Virtues, *Angels*, Archangels. And Vartan, or Vertabied, the Armenian poet and historian, who flourished in the thirteenth century, describes them under the same terms, but expressly states : " these orders differ from one another in situation and degree of glory, just as there are different ranks among men, though they are all of one nature." He also remarks that the first order are attracted to the Deity by love, and hardly attributes place to them, but states of desire and love, while the heaven which contains the whole host is above the *primum mobile*, which, again is superior to the starry firmament. This description, and all others resembling it, the twelve heavenly worlds of Plato, and the heaven succeeding it, the heaven of the Chinese, for example, are but as landmarks serving to denote the heights which the restless waves of human intelligence have reached at various times in the attempt to represent the eternal and infinite in precise terms. Boeheme recognises the " whole deep between the stars," as the heaven of one of the three hierarchies, and places the other two above it ; " in the midst of all which," he says, " is the Son of God ; no part of either is farther or nearer to him, yet are the three kingdoms circular about him." The Revelations of Swedenborg date a century later, and begin all these subjects *de novo*, but his works are accessible to all, and therefore we do not further allude to them.

The Jewish rabbi's hold the doctrine of another hierarchy superior to these three, and some of them, as Bechai and Joshua, teach that " every day ministering *angels* are created out of the river Dinor, or fiery stream, and they sing an anthem and cease to exist ; as it is written, they are new every morning." This, however, is only a misunderstanding, for to be " renewed " or " created " in the scriptural sense, is to be regenerated ; and to be renewed every morning is to be kept in a regenerate state ; the fiery stream is the baptism by fire or divine love.

The following represent the angelic hierarchies answering to the ten divine names :—

1. Jehovah, attributed to God the Father, being the pure and simple essence of the divinity, flowing through *Hajoth Hakados* to the *angel* Metratton and to the ministering spirit, *Reschith Hajalalim*, who guides the *primum mobile*, and bestows the gift of being on all. These names are to be understood as pure essences, or as spheres of *angels* and blessed spirits, by whose agency the divine providence extends to all his words.

2. Jah, attributed to the person of the Messiah or Logos, whose power and influence descends through the *angel* Masleh into the sphere of the Zodiac. This is the spirit or word that actuated the chaos, and ultimately produced the four elements, and all creatures that inherit them, by the agency of a spirit named Raziel, who was the ruler of Adam.

3. Ehjeh, attributed to the Holy Spirit, whose divine light is received by the *angel* Sabbathi, and communicated from him through the sphere of Saturn. It denotes the beginning of the supernatural generation, and hence of all living souls.

The ancient Jews considered the three superior names which are those above, to be attributed to the divine essence as personal or proper names, while the seven following denote the measures (*middoth*) or attributes which are visible in the works of God. But the modern Jews, in opposition to the tripersonalists, consider the whole as attributes. Maurice makes the higher three denote the heavens, and the succeeding the seven planets or worlds, to each of which a presiding *angel* was assigned.

4. El, strength, power, light, through which flow grace, goodness, mercy, piety, and munificence to the *angel* Zadkiel, and passing through the sphere of Jupiter fashioneth the images of all bodies, bestowing clemency, benevolence and justice on all.

5. Elohi, the upholder of the sword and left hand of God. Its influence penetrates the *angel* Geburah (or Gamaliel) and descends through the sphere of Mars. It imparts fortitude in times of war and affliction.

6. Tsebaoth, the title of God as Lord of hosts. The *angel* is Raphael, through whom its mighty power passes into the sphere of the sun, giving motion, heat and brightness to it.

7. Elion, the title of God as the highest. The *angel* is Michael. The sphere to which he imparts its influence is Mercury, giving benignity, motion, and intelligence, with elegance and consonance of speech.

8. Adonai, master or lord, governing the *angel* Haniel, and the sphere of Venus.

9. Shaddai, the virtue of this name is conveyed by Cherubim to the *angel* Gabriel, and influences the sphere of the moon. It causes increase and decrease, and rules the jinn and protecting spirits.

10. Elohim, the source of knowledge, understanding and wisdom, received by the *angel* Jesodoth, and imparted to the sphere of the earth.

The division of *angels* into nine orders or three hierarchies, as derived from Dionysius Areopagus, was held in the Middle Ages, and gave the prevalent character to much of their symbolism. With it was held the doctrine of their separate creation, and the tradition of the rebellious hierarchy, headed by Lucifer, the whole of which was rendered familiar to the popular mind by the Epic of Milton. Another leading tradition, not so much interwoven with the popular theology, was that of their intercourse with women, producing the race of giants. It was supposed to be authorised by Gen. vi. 2 in the adoption of which the Christian fathers seem to have followed the opinion of Philo-Judæus, and Josephus. A particular account of the circumstances is given in the book of Enoch, already mentioned, which makes the *angels*, Uriel, Gabriel, and Michael, the chief instruments in the subjugation of the adulterers and their formidable off-spring. The classic writers have perpetuated similar traditions of the " hero " race, all of them born either from the love of the gods for women, or of the preference shown for a goddess by some mortal man.

The Persian, Jewish, and Mohammedan accounts of *angels* all evince a common origin, and they alike admit a difference of sex. In the latter, the name of Azazil is given to the hierarchy nearest the throne of God, to which the Mohammedan Satan (Eblis or Haris) is supposed to have belonged ; also Azreal, the *angel* of death, and Asrafil (probably the same as Israfil), the *angel* of the resurrection. The examiners, Moukir and Nakir, are subordinate *angels* of terrible aspect, armed with whips of iron and fire, who interrogate recently deceased souls as to their lives. The parallel to this tradition in the Talmud is an account of seven *angels* who beset the paths of death. The Koran also assigns two *angels* to every man, one to record his good, and the other his evil actions ; they are so merciful that if an evil action has been done, it is not recorded till the man has slept, and if in that interval he repents, they place on the record that God has pardoned him. The Siamese, beside holding the difference of sex, imagine that *angels* have offspring ; but their traditions concerning the government of the world and the guardianship of man are similar to those of other nations.

The Christian fathers, for the most part, believed that *angels* possessed bodies of heavenly substance (Tertullian calls it " angelified flesh "), and, if not, that they could assume a corporeal presence at their pleasure. In fact, all the actions recorded of them in Scripture, suppose human members and attributes. It is not only so in the historic portions, but in the prophetic, even in the Apocalypse, the most replete with symbolic figures. (*See* **Magic.**)

Anglieri : A Sicilian younger brother of the seventeenth century, who is known by a work of which he published two volumes and promised twenty-four, and which was entitled *Magic Light*, or, the origin, order, and government of all things celestial, terrestial, and infernal, etc. Mongitore mentions it in his *Sicilian Library*.

Anglo-Saxons : (*See* **England.**)

Angurvadel : The sword, possessing magical properties, which was inherited by Frithjof, the hero of an Icelandic *saga*. It had a golden hilt, and shone like the Northern Lights. In times of peace certain characters on its blade were dull and pale ; but during a battle they became red, like fire.

Anima Mundi : The soul of the world ; a pure ethereal spirit which was said by some ancient philosophers to be diffused throughout all nature. Plato is considered by some to be the originator of this idea ; but it is of more ancient origin, and prevailed in the systems of certain eastern philosophers. By the Stoics it was believed to be the only vital force in the universe ; it has been entertained by many philosophical sects in a variety of forms, and in more modern times by Paracelsus and others. It is also incorporated in the philosophy of Schelling. Rich says : " The *anima mundi*, or heaven of this world, in which the stars are fixed, is understood to be a receptivity of the empyrean or heaven in which God dwells, so that the forms or seminal conceptions of the one correspond to the divine ideas of the other."

Animal Magnetism : (*See* **Hypnotism** *and* **Spiritualism.**)

Animism : The doctrine of spiritual beings, or the concept that a great part, if not the whole, of inanimate nature, as well as of animate beings, are endowed with reason and volition identical with that of man. It is difficult to distinguish this conception from that of personalisation, but the difference exists. The savage hears the wind whistle past him, and thinks that in it he can distinguish voices. He sees movement in streams, trees, and other objects, which he believes to be inhabited by spirits. The idea of a soul probably arose through dreams, apparitions, or clairvoyance, hallucinations and shadows, and perhaps through the return to life after periods of unconsciousness. Movement, therefore, argued life. The cult of fetishism well instances the belief in animism, for it posits the entrance into an inanimate body of a separate spiritual entity deliberately come to inhabit it. There is no necessity in this place to go into the question whether or not animism is at the basis of religious belief ; but it is distinctly at the root of magical belief and practice.

Annali Dello Spiritismo : (*See* **Italy.**)

Anneberg : A demon of the mines, known principally in Germany. On one occasion he killed with his breath twelve miners who were working in a silver mine of which he had charge. He is a wicked and terrible demon, represented under the figure of a horse, with an immense neck and frightful eyes.

Annie Eva Fay : Medium. (*See* **Spiritualism.**)

Annius de Viterbo : A learned ecclesiastic, born at Viterbo in 1432, who, either deceived himself, or a deceiver of others, published a collection of manuscripts full of fables and absurdities, falsely attributed to Berosus, Fabius Victor, Cato, Manettio and others, and known under the name of *The Antiquities of Annius*. He was also responsible for a treatise on *The Empire of the Turks*, and a book on the *Future Triumphs of the Christians over the Turks and the Saracens*, etc. These two works are explanations of the *Apocalypse*. The author claims that Mahomet is the Antichrist, and that the end of the world will take place when the Christians will have overcome the Jews and the Mohammedans, which event did not appear to him to be far distant.

Annwyl : The Celtic Other-world. (*See* **Heil.**)

Anonymous Adept (fl. 1750) : A noted German jesuit of the eighteenth century, known to his clerical *confrères* and his flock as Athanasius the Churchman. He composed two folio volumes of semi-alchemistic writing, which were published at Amsterdam in 1768. In the course of these voluminous works, he alludes to an alchemist whose name he refrains from revealing, and who is usually hailed in consequence by the elusive title heading this article. Athanasius, we find, having long endeavoured to discover the Philosopher's Stone, and having met with no success, chanced one day to encounter a venerable personage, who addressed him thus : " I see by these glasses and this furnace that you are engaged in search after something very great in chemistry, but, believe me, you will never attain your object by working as you are doing." Pondering on these words, the shrewd Jesuit suspected that his interlocutor was truly learned in alchemy, wherefore he besought him to display his erudition, and thereupon our *Anonymous Adept* took a quill, and wrote down a receipt for the making of transmutatory powder, together with specific directions for using the same. " Let us proceed together," said the great unknown ; nor were the hopes of Athanasias frustrated, for in a little while a fragment of gold was duly made, the wise pedagogue disappearing immediately afterwards. The Jesuit now fancied himself on the verge of a dazzling fortune, and he proceeded straightway to try and manufacture nuggets ; but, alas ! Try as he might, his attempts all proved futile. Much enraged, he went to the inn where the *Anonymous Adept* was staying, but it need scarcely be said, perhaps, that the bird was flown. " We see by this true history," remarks Athanasius, by way of pointing a moral, " how the devil seeks to deceive men who are led by a lust of riches " ; while he relates further, that having been duped in this wise, he destroyed his scientific appliances, to renounce alchemy for ever.

Anpiel : One of the angels charged by the rabbis with the government of the birds, for every known species was put under the protection of one or more angels.

Anselm de Parma : An astrologer, born at Parma, where he died in 1440. He wrote *Astrological Institutions*, a work which has never been printed. Wierius, and some other demonologists, classed him with the sorcerers, because certain charlatans, who healed sores by means of mysterious words, had taken the name of " Anselmites." But Naudé observes that they boasted that they had obtained their gift of healing, not from *Anselm of Parma*, but from St. Anselm of Canterbury, just as the Salutadores in Spain recognised in Catherine, their patron saint, and those who healed snake-bites in Italy, St. Paul.

Ansitif : A little known demon, who, during the possession of the nuns of Louviers, in 1643, occupied the body of Sister Barbara of St. Michael.

Answerer, or Fragarach : A magical sword belonging to the Irish Sea-God, Lir. It was brought from the Celtic Otherworld by Lugh, the Irish Sun-God, and it was believed that it could pierce any armour.

Anthony St. : A great demon of enormous stature one day approached St. Anthony to offer his services. By way of response the saint looked at him sideways and spat in his face. The demon took the repulse so much to heart that he vanished without a word, and did not dare to appear on earth for a long time afterwards. It is hardly conceivable that St. Anthony could have treated the devil so rudely, if one did not know how many temptations he had suffered from him, though it is difficult to admit that he was the object of so many attacks on the part of the devil, when he himself said : " I fear the demon no more than I fear a fly, and with the sign of the cross I can at once put him to flight." St. Athanasius, who wrote the life of *St. Anthony*, mingled with his hero's adventures with the devil, certain incidents which contrast strangely enough with these. Some philosophers, astonished at the great wisdom of *Anthony*, asked him in what book he had discovered so fine a doctrine. The saint pointed with one hand to the earth, with the other to the sky. " There are my books," said he, " I have no others. If men will design to study as I do the marvels of creation, they will find wisdom enough there. Their spirit will soon soar from the creation to the Creator." And certainly these were not the words of a man who trafficked with the devil.

Anthropomancy : Divination by the entrails of men or women. This horrible usage is very ancient. Herodotus said that Menelaus, detained in Egypt by contrary winds, sacrificed to his barbarous curiosity, two children of the country, and sought to discover his destiny by means of *anthropomancy*. Heliogabalus practised this means of divination. Julian the Apostate, in his magical operations, during his nocturnal sacrifices, caused, it is said, a large number of children to be killed, so that he might consult their entrails. In his last expedition, being at Carra, in Mesopotamia, he shut himself in the Temple of the Moon, and having done all manner of evil there, he sealed the

doors and posted a guard, whose duty it was to see that they were not opened until his return. However, he was killed in battle with the Persians, and those who entered the Temple of Carra, in the reign of Julian's successor, found there a woman hanging by her hair, with her liver torn out. It is probable that Gilles de Retz (q.v.) also practised this dreadful species of divination.

Antichrist : The universal enemy of mankind, who will in the latter days be sent to scourge the world for its wickedness. According to the Abbot Bergier, *Antichrist* is regarded as a tyrant, impious and excessively cruel, the arch enemy of Christ, and the last ruler of the earth. The persecutions he will inflict on the elect will be the last and most severe ordeal which they will have to undergo. Christ, himself, according to several commentators, foretold that they would have succumbed to it if its duration had not been shortened on their behalf. He will pose as the Messiah, and will perform things wonderful enough to mislead the elect themselves. The thunder will obey him, according to St. John, and Leloyer asserts that the demons below watch over hidden treasures by means of which he will be able to tempt many. It is on account of the miracles that he will perform, that Boguet calls him the " Ape of God," and it is through this scourge that God will proclaim the final judgment and the vengeance to be meted out to wrong-doers.

Antichrist will have a great number of forerunners, and will appear just before the end of the world. St. Jerome claims that he will be a man begotten by a demon ; others, a demon in the flesh, visible and fantastical, or an incarnate demon. But, following St. Ireneus, St. Ambrose, St. Augustine, and almost all the fathers, *Antichrist* will be a man similar to, and conceived in the same way as all others, differing from them only in a malice and an impiety more worthy of a demon than of a man. Cardinal Bellarmin, at a later date, and contrary to their authority, asserts however, that *Antichrist* will be the son of a demon incubus and a sorceress.

He will be a Jew of the tribe of Dan, according to Malvenda, who supports his view by the words of the dying Jacob to his sons : " Dan shall be a serpent by the way— an adder in the path ; "—by those of Jeremiah :—" The armies of Dan will devour the earth " ; and by the seventh chapter of the Apocalypse, where St. John has omitted the tribe of Dan in his enumeration of the other tribes.

Antichrist will be always at war, and will astonish the earth with his miracles. He will persecute the upright, and will mark his own by a sign on the face or the hand.

Elijah and Enoch will come at length and convert the Jews and will meet death at last by order of *Antichrist*, Then will Christ descend from the heavens, kill *Antichrist* with the two-edged sword, which will issue from His mouth, and reign on the earth for a thousand years, according to some ; an indefinite time, according to others.

It is claimed by some that the reign of *Antichrist* will last fifty years : the opinion of the majority is that his reign will last but three and a-half years, after which the angels will sound the trumpets of the day of judgment, and Christ will come and judge the world. The watchword of *Antichrist*, says Boguet, will be : " I abjure baptism." Many commentators have foreseen the return of Elijah in these words of Malachi : " I will send Elijah, the prophet, before the coming of the great and dreadful day of the Lord." But it is not certain that Malachi referred to this ancient prophet, since Christ applied this prediction to John the Baptist, when he said : " Elias is come already, and they knew him not ; " and when the angel foretold to Zacharias the birth of his son, he said to him : " And he shall go forth before the Lord in the spirit and power of Elias."

By *Antichrist* may probably be meant the persecutors of the Church. Again, the Protestants give the name to the Pope and the Catholics to all their enemies. Napoleon even has been called *Antichrist*.

The third treatise in the *Histoire Véritable et Mémorable des Trois Possédées de Flandre*, by Father Sebastien Michalies, dominican friar, throws much light in the words of exorcised demons, on *Antichrist*. "Conceived through the medium of a devil, he will be as malicious as a madman, with such wickedness as was never seen on earth. An inhuman martyr rather than a human one, he will treat Christians as souls are treated in hell. He will have a multitude of synagogue names, and he will be able to fly when he wishes. Beelzebub will be his father, Lucifer his grandfather."

The revelations of exorcised demons show that *Antichrist* was alive in 1613. It appears that he has not yet attained his growth. "He was baptised on the Sabbath of the sorcerers, before his mother, a Jewess, called La Belle-Fleur. He was three years old in 1613. Louis Gaufridi is said to have baptised him, in a field near Paris. An exorcised sorceress claimed to have held the little *Antichrist* on her knees. She said that his bearing was proud, and that even then he spoke many divers languages. But he had talons in the place of feet, and he wore no slippers. He will do much harm, but there will be comforters, for the Holy Ghost still lives." (*See* **Merlin**.) His father is shown in the figure of a bird, with four feet, a tail, a bull's head much flattened, horns and black shaggy hair. He will mark his own with a seal representing this in miniature. Michaelis adds that things execrable will be around him. He will destroy Rome on account of the Pope, and the Jews will help him. He will resuscitate the dead, and, when thirty, will reign with Lucifer, the seven-headed dragon, and, after a reign of three years, Christ will slay him.

Many such details might be quoted of *Antichrist*, whose appearance has long been threatened, but with as yet no fulfilment. (*See* **End of the World**.) We must mention, however, a volume published many years ago at Lyons, by Rusand, called, *Les Précurseurs de l' Antechrist*. This work shows that the reign of *Antichrist*, if it has not begun, is drawing near; that the philosophers, encyclopedists and revolutionaries of the eighteenth century were naught but demons incarnated to precede and prepare the way for *Antichrist*. In our own time it has frequently been averred that *Antichrist* is none other than the ex-Kaiser of Germany.

Antipathy : The old astrologers, who wished to explain everything, claimed that the dislike which one feels for a person or thing is caused by the stars. Thus two persons born under the same aspect, will be mutually attracted one to the other, and will love without knowing why. Others, again, born under opposite conjunctions, will feel an unreasoning hate for each other. But how can that *antipathy* be explained which great men sometimes have for the commonest things ? There have been many such cases, and all are inexplicable. Lamothe-Levayer could not bear to hear the sound of any instrument, and displayed the liveliest pleasure at the noise of thunder. Cæsar could not hear the crowing of a cock without shuddering ; Lord Bacon fell into despondency during the eclipse of the moon ; Marie de Medicis could not bear to look on a rose, even in a painting, though she loved all other flowers. Cardinal Henry of Cardonne had the same *antipathy*, and fell into a swoon when he felt the odour of roses ; Marshal d'Albret became ill at dinner when a young wild boar or a sucking-pig was served ; Henry III. of France could not remain in a chamber where there was a cat ; Marshal de Schomberg had the same weakness ; Ladislas, King of Poland, was much disturbed at the sight of apples ; Scaliger trembled in every limb at the sight of cress ; Erasmus

could not taste fish without having the fever ; Tycho-Brahé felt his knees give way when he met a hare or a fox ; the Duke of Epernon fainted at the sight of a leveret ; Cardan could not suffer eggs ; Ariosto, baths ; the son of Crœsus, bread ; Cæsar of Lescalle, the sound of the vielle or violin.

The causes of these *antipathies* are sometimes to be found in childish impressions. A lady who was very fond of pictures and engravings, fainted away when she found them in a book. She explained her terror thus : When she was a child her father had one day seen her turning over the leaves of the books in his library, in search of pictures. He had roughly taken the book from her hand, telling her in terrible tones that there were devils in these books, who would strangle her if she dared to touch them. These absurd threats occasionally have baneful effects that cannot be overcome. Pliny, who was fairly credulous, assures us that there is such an *antipathy* between the wolf and the horse, that if a horse pass by the way a wolf has gone, he feels his legs become so numbed that he cannot walk. But the instinct of animals does not err. A horse in America could detect the presence of a puma, and obstinately refused to go through a forest where his keen sense of smell announced to him that the enemy was at hand. Dogs also can tell when a wolf is near. Perhaps, on the whole, human beings would be wiser if they followed the dictates of these sympathetic or antipathetic impressions.

Antiphates : A shining black stone, used as a defence against witchcraft.

Antracites, or Antrachas, or Anthrax : A stone, sparkling like fire, supposed by Albertus Magnus to be the carbuncle. It cures "imposthumes." It is girdled with a white vein. If smeared with oil it loses its colour, but sparkles the more for being dipped in water.

Anupadaka Plane : (*See* **Monadic World**.)

Aonbarr : A horse belonging to Manaanan, son of the Irish Sea-God, Lir. It was believed to possess magical gifts, and could gallop on land or sea.

Apantomancy : Divination by means of any objects which happen to present themselves. To this class belong the omens drawn from chance meetings with a hare, an eagle, etc.

Apepi, Book of Overthrowing of : An Egyptian work which forms a considerable portion of the funerary papyrus of Nesi-Amsu. It deals with the diurnal combat between Ra, the Sun-God, and *Apepi*, the great serpent, the impersonation of spiritual evil, and several of the chapters, notably 31, 33, and 35 to 39 are obviously borrowed from the *Book of the Dead* (q.v.). It contains fifteen chapters, in which there is a great deal of repetition, and details the various methods for the destruction of *Apepi*, including many magical directions. It is set forth that the name of *Apepi* must be written in green on a papyrus and then burnt. Wax figures of his attendant fiends were to be made, mutilated, and burnt, in the hope that through the agency of sympathetic magic their prototypes might be injured or destroyed. Another portion of the work details the creative process and describes how men and women were formed from the tears of the god Khepera. This portion is known as *The Book of Knowing the Evolutions of Ra*. The work is evidently of high antiquity, as is shown by the circumstance that many variant readings occur. Only one copy, however, is known. The funeral papyrus in which it is contained was discovered at Thebes in 1860, was purchased by Rhind, and sold to the trustees of the British Museum by Mr. David Bremner. The linen on which it is written is of very fine texture, measures 19 feet by 9½ inches, and it has been translated by Mr. Wallis Budge in *Archaeologia*, Vol. 52, Part II.

Apollonius of Tyana : A Neo-Pythagorean philosopher of Greece, who had a great reputation for magical powers.

Born at Tyana, in Asia Minor, *Apollonius* was contemporary with Christ. He was educated at Tarsus and at the Temple of Æsculapius, at Ægae, where he became an adherent of the sect of Pythagoras, to whose strict discipline he submitted himself throughout his life. In his desire for knowledge he travelled widely in Eastern countries, and is said to have performed miracles wherever he went. At Ephesus, for instance, he warned the people of the approach of a terrible plague, but they gave no heed to him until the pestilence was actually in their midst, when they bethought them of the warning, and summoned the potent magician who had uttered it. *Apollonius* pointed out to the people a poor, maimed beggar, whom he denounced as the cause of the pestilence and an enemy of the gods, bidding them stone the unfortunate wretch to death. The citizens were at first reluctant to comply with so cruel an injunction, but something in the expression of the beggar confirmed the prophet's accusation, and the wretch was soon covered with a mound of stones. When the stones were removed no man was visible, but a huge black dog, the cause of the plague, which had come upon the Ephesians. At Rome he raised from death—or apparent death—his biographer does not seem to know which—a young lady of consular family, who had been betrothed, and was lamented by the entire city. Yet another story relates how *Apollonius* saved a friend of his, Menippus of Corinth, from marrying a vampire. The youth neglected all the earlier warnings of his counsellor, and the preparations for the wedding proceeded till finally all was in readiness for the ceremony. At this juncture *Apollonius* appeared on the scene, caused the wedding feast, the guests, and all the evidences of wealth, which were but illusion to vanish, and wrung from the bride the confession that she was a vampire. Many other similar tales are told of the philosopher's clairvoyant and magical powers.

The manner of his death is wrapped in mystery, though he is known to have lived to be nearly a hundred years of age. His disciples did not hesitate to say that he had not died at all, but had been caught up to heaven, and his biographer casts a doubt upon the matter. At all events, when he had vanished from the terrestial sphere, the inhabitants of his native Tyana built a temple in his honour, and statues were raised to him in various other temples.

A life of *Apollonius*, written by Philostratus at the instance of Julia, mother of the Emperor Severus, is the only extant source of information concerning the sage, though other lives, now lost, are known to have existed. The account given by Philostratus purports to have been compiled from the memoirs of " Damis the Assyrian," a disciple of *Apollonius*, but it has been suggested that Damis is but a literary fiction. The work is largely a romance ; fictitious stories are often introduced, and the whole account is mystical and symbolical. Nevertheless it is possible to get a glimpse of the real character of *Apollonius* beyond the literary artifices of the writer. The purpose of the philosopher of Tyana seems to have been to infuse into paganism a morality more practical combined with a more transcendental doctrine. He himself practised a very severe asceticism, and supplemented his own knowledge by revelations from the gods. Because of his claim to divine enlightenment, some would have refused him a place among the philosophers, but Philostratus holds that this in no wise detracts from his philosophic reputation. Pythagoras and Plato and Democritus he points out, were wont to visit Eastern sages, even as *Apollonius* had done, and they were not charged with dabbling in magic. Divine revelations had been given to earlier philosophers ; why not also to the Philosopher of Tyana? It is probable that *Apollonius* borrowed considerably from Oriental

sources, and that his doctrines were more Brahminical than magical.

Apparel, Phantom : (*See* **Phantom Dress.**)

Apparitions : An *apparition* (from Latin *apparere*, to appear) is in its literal sense merely an appearance, that is, a sense-percept of any kind, but in every-day usage the word has a more restricted meaning and is used only to denote an abnormal or superabnormal appearance or percept, which cannot be referred to any natural objective cause. Taken in this sense the word covers all visionary appearances, hallucinations, clairvoyance, and similar unusual perceptions. " *Apparition* " and " ghost " are frequently used as synonymous terms, though the former is, of course, of much wider significance. A ghost is a visual *apparition* of a deceased human being, and the term implies that it is the spirit of the person it represents. *Apparitions* of animals and of inanimate objects are also sufficiently frequent. All *apparitions* do not take the form of visual images ; auditory and tactile false perceptions, though less common, are not unknown, and there is record of a house that was " haunted " with the perpetual odour of violets.

Evolution of the Belief in Apparitions.—There is no doubt that the belief which identifies an *apparition* with the spirit of the creature it represents—a belief widely current in all nations and all times—is directly traceable to the ancient doctrine of animism, which endowed everything in nature, from man himself to the smallest insect, from the heavenly bodies to an insignificant plant or stone, with a separable soul. It is not difficult to understand how the conception of souls may have arisen. Sir J. Frazer, in his *Golden Bough*, says : " As the savage commonly explains the processes of inanimate nature by supposing that they are produced by living beings working in or behind the phenomena, so he explains the phenomena of life itself. If an animal lives and moves, it can only be, he thinks, because there is a little animal inside which moves it. If a man lives and moves, it can only be because he has a little man or animal inside, who moves him. The animal inside the animal, the man inside the man, is the soul. And as the activity of an animal or man is explained by the presence of the soul, so the repose of sleep or death is explained by its absence ; sleep or trance being the temporary, death being the permanent absence of the soul." Sometimes the human soul was represented as a bird—an eagle, a dove, a raven—or as an animal of some sort, just as the soul of a river might be in the form of a horse or a serpent, or the soul of a tree in human shape ; but among most peoples the belief was that the soul was an exact reproduction of the body resembling it in every feature, even to details of dress, etc. Thus, when a man saw another in dream, it was thought either that the soul of the dreamer had visited the person dreamed of, or that the soul of the latter had visited the dreamer. By an easy process of reasoning, the theory was extended to include dreams of animals and inanimate things, which also were endowed with souls. And thus it is quite probable that the hallucinations with which primitive peoples as well as those at a later stage of culture were at times visited, and which they doubtless knew well how to induce, should be regarded as the souls of the things they represent. If it be granted that telepathy and clairvoyance operate sometimes at the present day, and among civilised peoples, it may be conceded on still more abundant testimony that they were known to primitive races. And it is obvious that these faculties would have a powerful effect in the development of a belief in *apparitions*. The *apparition* of a deceased person, again, would inevitably suggest the continuance of the soul's existence beyond the grave, and the *apparition* of a sick person, or one in some other grave crisis—such as might now-a-days be accounted for telepathically—would also be regarded as the soul, which at such times was absent from the body. There is a widely diffused opinion that ghosts are of a filmy, unsubstantial nature, and this also would seem to have taken its rise in the first animistic concepts of primitive man. At a very early stage of culture we find *spirit* and *breath* confused—they are identified in the Latin *spiritus* and the Greek *pneuma*, as well as in other languages. How natural it is, therefore, that the breath, condensed in the cold air to a white mist, should be regarded as the stuff that ghosts are made of. On another hypothesis, the shadowy nature of the ghost may have resulted from an early confusion of the soul with the shadow. Thus animistic ideas of the soul have given rise to the belief in *apparitions*. But animism has a further contribution to make towards this belief in the host of spirits which have not, and never have had, bodies, true supernatural beings, as distinct from souls—gods, elementary spirits, and those evil spirits to which were attributed disease, disaster, possession, and bewitchment. This class of beings has evolved into the fairies, elves, brownies, bogies, and goblins of popular folklore, of which many *apparitions* are recorded.

Savage Instances of Apparitions. In classic and mediæval times the concept of the ghost was practically identical with that of savage peoples. It is only within the last two generations that scientific investigation was deemed necessary, as the result of the birth of a scepticism hitherto confined to the few, and in the general mind weak or non-existent. (For details of such research *see* **Spiritualism and Psychical Research.**) One of the most noteworthy features of ghosts in savage lands is the fear and antagonism with which they are regarded. Almost invariably the spirits of the deceased are thought to be unfriendly towards the living, desirous of drawing the souls of the latter, or their shadows, into the spirit-world. Sometimes, as with the Australian aborigines, they are represented as malignant demons. Naturally, everything possible is done to keep the ghost at a distance from the habitation of the living. With some peoples thorn bushes are planted round the beds of the surviving relatives. Persons returning from a funeral pass through a cleft tree, or other narrow aperture, to free themselves from the ghost of him whom they have buried. Others plunge into water to achieve the same purpose. The custom of closing the eyes of the dead is said to have arisen from the fear that the ghost would find its way back again, and the same reason is given for the practice, common among Hottentots, Hindus, North American Indians, and many other peoples, of carrying the dead out through a hole in the wall, the aperture being immediately afterwards closed. The Mayas of Yucatan, however, draw a line with chalk from the tomb to the hearth, so that the soul may return if it desires to do so. Among uncultured races, the names of the departed, in some mysterious manner bound up with the soul, if not identified with it, are not mentioned by the survivors, and any among them possessing the same name, changes it for another. The shape in which *apparitions* appear among savages may be the human form, or the form of a beast, bird, or fish. Animal ghosts are common among the Indians of North and South America. Certain African tribes believe that the souls of evil-doers become jackals on the death of the body. The Tapuya Indians of Brazil think that the souls of the good enter into birds, and this belief is of rather wide diffusion. When the *apparition* is in human shape it is generally an exact counterpart of the person it represents, and, like the *apparitions* of more civilised countries, its dress is that worn by the deceased in his lifetime. This last feature, of course, implies the doctrine of object-souls, which has its roots in animism. Though it is generally accepted by savage peoples that the shades of the departed mingle with the living, coming and

going with no particular object in view, yet the *revenant* may on occasion have a special purpose in visiting the scene of his earthly life. It may be that the spirit desires that its body be buried with the proper ceremonial rites, if these have been omitted. In savage, as in civilised countries, it is believed that the spirits of those who have not been buried at all, cannot have any rest till the rite has been duly performed. In China, the commonest ghost is that of a person who has been murdered, and who seeks to be avenged on his murderer. The spirit of one who has been murdered, or has died a violent death, is considered in Australia also to be especially likely to walk abroad, while in many barbarous or semi-barbarous lands the souls of women who have died in childbirth, are supposed to become spirits of a particularly malignant type, dwelling in trees, tormenting and molesting passers-by. There is another reason for which *apparitions* sometimes appear : to reveal the site of hidden treasure. The guardians of buried hoards are, however, supernatural beings rather than human souls, and the shapes they take are often grotesque or terrible. It is customary for ghosts to haunt certain localities. The favourite spot seems to be the burial-place, of which there is an almost universal superstitious dread ; but the Indians of Guiana go a step farther in maintaining that every place where anyone has died is haunted. Among the Kaffirs and the Maoris of New Zealand a hut wherein a death has occurred is taboo, and is often burnt or deserted. Sometimes, even a whole village is abandoned on account of a death—a practice, this, which must be attended with some inconvenience. There is one point on which the *apparitions* of primitive peoples differ from those of more advanced races—the former seldom attain to the dignity of articulate human speech. They chirp like crickets, for instance, among the Algonquin Indians, and their " voices " are only intelligible to the trained ear of the shaman. The ghosts of the Zulus and New Zealanders, again, speak to the magicians in thin, whistling tones. This idea of the semi-articulate nature of ghosts is not confined to savage concepts ; Shakespeare speaks of " the sheeted dead," who, " did squeak and gibber in the streets of Rome," and the " gibbering " ghost appears in other connections. Naturally the articulate *apparition* is doubly convincing, since it appeals to two separate senses. Dr. Tylor says : " Men who perceive evidently that souls do talk when they present themselves in dream or vision, naturally take for granted at once the objective reality of the ghostly voice, and of the ghostly form from which it proceeds." Spirits which are generally invisible may appear to certain persons and under certain circumstances. Thus in the Antilles, it is believed that one person travelling alone may see a ghost which would be invisible to a number of people. The shamans, or medicine-men, and magicians are able to perceive *apparitions* which none but they can see. The induction of hallucinations by means of fasts, rigid asceticism, solitude, the use of narcotics and intoxicants, dances, and the performing of elaborate ceremonial rites, is known all over the world, and among uncultured as well as cultured peoples. Coincidental *apparitions*, it may be remarked *en passant*, are comparatively rare in savage countries. Naturally, a great many savage instances of *apparitions* are concerned with supernatural beings other than human souls, but such cases are dealt with elsewhere.

Ancient and Modern Ideas Concerning Apparitions. The belief in *apparitions* was very vivid among ancient Oriental peoples. The early Hebrews attributed them to angels, demons, or the souls of the dead, as is shown in the numerous Scriptural instances of *apparitions*. Dreams were regarded as *apparitions* if the predictions made in them were fulfilled, or if the dream-figure revealed anything unknown to the dreamer which afterwards proved to be true. That the Hebrews believed in the possibility of the souls of the dead returning, is evident from the tale of the Witch of Endor. Calmet says, in this connection : " Whether Samuel was raised up or not, whether his soul, or only a shadow, or even nothing at all appeared to the woman, it is still certain that Saul and his attendants, with the generality of the Hebrews, believed the thing to be possible." Similar beliefs were held by other Eastern nations. Among the Greeks and Romans of the classic period *apparitions* of gods and men would seem to have been fairly common. Calmet, in his *Dissertation on Apparitions*, says :

" The ancient Greeks, who had derived their religion and theology from the Egyptians and Eastern nations, and the Latins, who had borrowed theirs from the Greeks, were all firmly persuaded that the souls of the dead appeared sometimes to the living—that they could be called up by necromancers, that they answered questions, and gave notice of future events ; that Apollo gave oracles, and that the priestess, filled with his spirit, and transported with a holy enthusiasm, uttered infallible predictions of things to come. Homer, the most ancient of all the Greek writers, and their greatest divine, relates several *apparitions*, not only of gods, but of dead men and heroes. In the Odyssey, he introduces Ulysses consulting Teresias, who, having prepared a pit full of blood, in order to call up the Manes, Ulysses draws his sword to hinder them from drinking the blood for which they were very thirsty, till they had answered the questions proposed to them. It was also a prevailing opinion, that the souls of men enjoyed no repose, but wandered about near their carcases as long as they continued unburied. Even after they were buried, it was a custom to offer them something to eat, especially honey, upon the supposition that after having left their graves, they came to feed upon what was brought them. They believed also, that the demons were fond of the smoke of sacrifices, of music, of the blood of victims, and the commerce of women ; and that they were confined for a determinate time to certain houses or other places, which they haunted, and in which they appeared.

" They held that souls, when separated from their gross and terrestial bodies, still retained a finer and more subtile body, of the same form with that which they had quitted ; that these bodies were luminous like the stars ; that they retained an inclination for the things which they had loved in their life-time, and frequently appeared about their graves. When the soul of Patroclus appeared to Achilles, it had his voice, his shape, his eyes, and his dress, but not the same tangible body. Ulysses relates, that when he went down into hell, he saw the *divine Hercules*, that is, adds he, *his image : for he himself is admitted to the banquets of the immortal gods*. Dido says, that after death she, that is, her image bigger than the life, shall go down to the infernal regions.

" '*Et mine magna mei sub terras ibit imago.*'

" And Æneas knew his wife Creusa, who appeared to him in her usual shape, but of a taller and nobler stature than when she was alive.

" *Infelix simulacrum, atque ipsius umbra Creusæ,*
Visa mihi ante oculos, et nota major imago

" In the speech which Titus made to his soldiers, to persuade them to mount to the assault of the Tower Antonia at Jerusalem, he uses this argument : ' Who knows not that the souls of those who bravely expose themselves to danger, and die in war, are exalted to the stars, are there received into the highest region of heaven, and appear as good genii to their relations ; while they who die of sickness, though they have lived good lives, are plunged into oblivion and darkness under earth, and are no more remembered after death, than if they had never existed."

Again he says ·

" We find that Origen, Tertullian, and St. Irenaus, were clearly of this opinion. Origen, in his second book against Celsus, relates and subscribes to the opinion of Plato, who says, that the shadows and images of the dead, which are seen near sepulchres, are nothing but the soul disengaged from its gross body, but not yet entirely freed from matter ; that these souls become in time luminous, transparent, and subtile, or rather are carried in luminous and transparent bodies, as in a vehicle, in which they appeal to the living. . . . Tertullian, in his book concerning the soul, asserts that it is corporeal, and of a certain figure, and appeals to the experience of those who have seen *apparitions* of departed souls, and to whom they have appeared as corporeal and tangible, though of an aerial colour and consistence. He defines the soul to be a breath from God, immortal, corporeal, and of a certain figure."

It is interesting to note that some of these classic spectres are nearly akin to the melodramatic conceptions of more modern times. The younger Pliny tells of haunted houses whose main features correspond with those of later hauntings—houses haunted by dismal, chained spectres, the ghosts of murdered men who could not rest till their mortal remains had been properly buried.

In the early centuries of the Christian era there was no diminution in the number of *apparitions* witnessed. Visions of saints were frequently seen, and were doubtless induced by the fasts, rigid asceticism, and severe penances practiced in the name of religion. The saints themselves saw visions, and were attended by guardian angels, and harassed by the unwelcome attentions of demons, or of their master, the devil. These beliefs continued into the Middle Ages, when, without undergoing any abatement in vigour, they began to take on a more romantic aspect. The witch and wer-wolf superstitions were responsible for many tales of animal *apparitions*. The poltergeist flourished in a congenial atmosphere. Vampires were terribly familiar in Slavonic lands, and nowhere in Europe were they quite unknown. The malignant demons, known as incubi and succubi, were no less common. In the northern countries familiar spirits or goblins, approximating to the Roman *lares*, or the wicked and more mischievous *lemures*, haunted the domestic hearth, and bestowed well-meant, but not always desirable, attentions on the families to which they attached themselves. These beings were accountable for a vast number of *apparitions*, but the spirits of the dead also walked abroad in the Dark Ages. Generally they wished to unburden their minds of some weighty secret which hindered them from resting in their graves. The criminal came to confess his guilt, the miser to reveal the spot where he had hidden his gold. The cowled monk walked the dim aisles of a monastery, or haunted the passages of some Rhenish castle, till the prayers of the devout had won release for his tortured soul. Perchance, a maiden in white flitted through the corridor of some old mansion, moaning and wringing her hands, enacting in pantomime some long-forgotten tragedy. At the cross-roads lingered the ghost of the poor suicide, uncertain which way to take. The old belief in the dread potency of the unburied dead continued to exercise sway. There is, for example, the German story of the Bleeding Nun. Many and ghastly had been her crimes during her lifetime, and finally she was murdered by one of her paramours, her body being left unburied. The castle wherein she was slain became the scene of her nocturnal wanderings. It is related that a young woman who wished to elope with her lover decided to disguise herself as this ghostly spectre in order to facilitate their escape. But the unfortunate lover eloped with the veritable Bleeding Nun herself, mistaking her for his mistress. This, and other traditional *apparitions*, such as the Wild Huntsman, the

Phantom Coach, the Flying Dutchman, which were not confined to any one locality, either originated in this period or acquired in it a wildly romantic character which lent itself to treatment by ballad-writers, and it is in ballad form that many of them have come down to us.

This hey-day of the *apparition* passed, however, at length, and in the eighteenth century we find among the cultured classes a scepticism as regards the objective nature of *apparitions*, which was destined two centuries later to become almost universal. Hallucination, though not yet very well understood, began to be called the " power of imagination." Many *apparitions*, too, were attributed to illusion. Nevertheless, the belief in *apparitions* was sustained and strengthened by the clairvoyant powers of magnetic subjects and somnambules. Swedenborg, who had, and still has many disciples, did much to encourage the idea that *apparitions* were objective and supernatural. To explain the fact that only the seer saw these beings and heard their voices, he says :

" The speech of an angel or of a spirit with man is heard as sonorously as the speech of one man with another : yet it is not heard by others who stand near, but by the man himself alone. The reason is, the speech of an angel or of a spirit flows in first into the man's thought, and by an internal way into the organ of hearing, and thus actuates it from within, whereas the speech of man flows first into the air, and by an external way into the organ of hearing which it actuates from without. Hence, it is evident, that the speech of an angel and of a spirit with man is heard in man, and, since it equally affects the organ of hearing, that it is equally sonorous."

Thus it will be seen that ancient and modern ideas on *apparitions* differ very little in essential particulars, though they take colour from the race and time to which they belong. Now they are thin, gibbering shadows ; now they are solid, full-bodied creatures, hardly to be distinguished from real flesh and blood ; again they are rich in romantic accessories ; but the laws which govern their appearance are the same, and the beliefs concerning them are not greatly different, in whatever race or age they may be found.

Present-Day Theories Concerning Apparitions.—At the present time *apparitions* are generally, though by no means universally, referred to hallucination (q.v.) Even those who advance a spiritualistic theory of *apparitions* frequently incline to this view, for it is argued that the discarnate intelligence may, by psychical energy alone, produce in the brain of a living person a definite hallucination, corresponding perhaps to the agent's appearance in life. Hallucinations may be either coincidental or non-coincidental. The former, also known as *telepathic hallucinations*, are those which coincide with a death, or with some other crisis in the life of the person represented by the hallucination. The Society for Psychical Research has been instrumental in collecting numerous instances of coincidental hallucinations, many of which are recorded in *Phantasms of the Living*, by Messrs. Myers, Podmore and Gurney. Mr. Podmore was indeed the chief exponent of the telepathic theory of ghosts (*for which see also* **Telepathy**) which he had adopted after many years of research and experiment. He suggested that *apparitions* result from a telepathic impression conveyed from the mind of one living person to that of another, an impression which may be doubly intense in time of stress or exalted emotion, or at the moment of dissolution. *Apparitions* of the dead he would account for by a theory of *latent impressions*, conveyed to the mind of the percipient during the agent's lifetime, but remaining dormant until some particular train of thought rouses them to activity. This view is largely

supported at the present day. Hallucinations, whether coincidental or otherwise, may, and do present themselves to persons who are perfectly sane and normal, but they are also a feature of insanity, hypnotism and hysteria, and of certain pathological conditions of brain, nerves, and sense-organs. The late Mr. Myers was of opinion that an *apparition* represented an actual " psychic invasion," that it was a projection of some of the agent's psychic force. Such a doctrine is, as Mr. Myers himself admitted, a reversion to animism. There is another modern theory of *apparitions*, particularly applicable to haunted houses. This is the theory of psychometry (q.v.). Sir Oliver Lodge, in his *Man and the Universe*, says :

" Occasionally a person appears able to respond to stimuli embededd, as it were among psycho-physical surroundings in a manner at present ill understood and almost incredible :—as if strong emotions could be unconsciously recorded in matter, so that the deposit shall thereafter affect a sufficiently sensitive organism, and cause similar emotions to reproduce themselves in its sub-consciousness, in a manner analogous to the customary conscious interpretation of photographic or phonographic records, and indeed of pictures or music and artistic embodiment generally."

Take, for example, a haunted house of the traditional Christmas-number type, wherein some one room is the scene of a ghostly representation of some long past tragedy. On a psychometric hypothesis the original tragedy has been literally *photographed* on its material surroundings, nay, even on the ether itself, by reason of the intensity of emotion felt by those who enacted it ; and thenceforth in certain persons an hallucinatory effect is experienced corresponding to such impression. It is this theory which is made to account for the feeling one has on entering certain rooms, that there is an alien presence therein, though it be invisible and inaudible to mortal sense. The doctrine of psychometry in its connection with *apparitions* is of considerable interest because of its wide possibilities, but it belongs to the region of romance rather than to that of science, and is hardly to be considered as a serious theory of *apparitions* at least, until it is supported by better evidence than its protagonists can show at present.

Spiritualistic theories of *apparitions* also vary, though they agree in referring such appearances to discarnate intelligences, generally to the spirits of the dead. The opinion of some spiritualistic authorities is, as has been said, that the surviving spirit produces in the mind of the percipient, by purely psychic means, an hallucination representing his (the agent's) former bodily appearance. Others believe that the discarnate spirit can *materialise* by taking to itself ethereal particles from the external world, and thus build up a temporary physical organism through which it can communicate with the living. Still others consider that the materialised spirit borrows such temporary physical organism from that of the medium, and experiments have been made to prove that the medium loses weight during the materialisation. (*See* **Materialisation.**) The animistic belief that the soul should become visible is not now generally credited, since it is thought that pure spirit cannot be perceptible to the physical senses. But a compromise has been made in the ' psychic body,' (q.v.), midway between soul and body, which some spiritualists consider clothes the soul at the dissolution of the physical body. The psychic body is composed of material particles, very fine and subtle, and perceptible as a rule, only to the eye of the clairvoyant. It is this, and not the spirit, which is seen as an *apparition*. We must not overlook the theory held by some Continental investigators, that " spirit materialisations " so-called are manifestations of psychic force emanating from the medium.

Different Classes of Apparitions.—Many of the various classes of *apparitions* having been considered above, and others being dealt with under their separate headings, it is hardly necessary to do more than enumerate them here. *Apparitions* may be divided broadly into two classes—induced and spontaneous. To the former class belong hypnotic and post-hypnotic hallucinations (*see* **Hypnotism**) and visions (q.v.) induced by the use of narcotics and intoxicants, fasts, ascetic practices, incense, narcotic salves, and auto-hypnotisation. The hallucinatory appearances seen in the mediumistic or somnambulistic trance are, of course, allied to those of hypnotism, but usually arise spontaneously, and are often associated with clairvoyance (q.v.). Crystallomancy (q.v.) or crystal vision is a form of *apparition* which is stated to be frequently clairvoyant, and in this case the theory of telepathy is especially applicable. Crystal visions fall under the heading of induced *apparitions*, since gazing in a crystal globe induces in some persons a species of hypnotism, a more or less slight dissociation of consciousness, without which hallucination is impossible. Another form of clairvoyance is second sight (q.v.), a faculty common among the Scottish Highlanders. Persons gifted with the second sight often see symbolical *apparitions*, as, for instance, the vision of a funeral or a coffin when a death is about to occur in the community. Symbolical appearances are indeed a feature of clairvoyance and visions generally. Clairvoyance includes retrocognition and premonition—visions of the past and the future respectively—as well as *apparitions* of contemporary events happening at a distance. Clairvoyant powers are often attributed to the dying. Dreams are, strictly speaking, *apparitions*, but in ordinary usage the term is applied only to coincidental or veridical dreams, or to those " visions of the night," which are of peculiar vividness.

From these subjective *apparitions* let us turn to the ghost proper. The belief in ghosts has come to us, as has been indicated, from the remotest antiquity, and innumerable theories have been formulated to account for it, from the primitive animistic conception of the *apparition* as an actual soul to the modern theories enumerated above, of which the chief are telepathy and spirit materialisation. *Apparitions* of the living also offer a wide field for research, perhaps the most favoured hypothesis at the present day being that of the telepathic hallucination. A peculiarly weird type of *apparition* is the wraith (q.v.) or double, of which the Irish fetch is a variant. The wraith is an exact facsimile of a living person, who may himself see it; Goethe, Shelley, and other famous men are said to have seen their own wraiths. The fetch makes its appearance shortly before the death of the person it represents, either to himself or his friends, or both. Another Irish spirit which foretells death is the banshee (q.v.), a being which attaches itself to certain ancient families, and is regularly seen or heard before the death of one of its members. To the same class belong the omens of death, in the form of certain animals or birds, which follow some families. Hauntings or localised *apparitions* are dealt with under the heading " Haunted Houses." The poltergeist (q.v.), whose playful manifestations must certainly be included among *apparitions*, suggests another classification of these as visual, auditory, tactile, etc., since poltergeist hauntings—or indeed hauntings of any kind—are not confined to *apparitions* touching any one sense. For *apparitions* of fairies, brownies, and others of the creatures of folk-lore, *see* **Fairies**.

In this article an attempt has been made to show as briefly as possible the universality of the belief in *apparitions*, and the varied forms under which this belief exhibits itself in various times and countries among savage and civilised peoples ; and to indicate the basic principles on which it rests—namely, the existence of a spiritual world capable of manifesting itself in the sphere of matter, and the survival of the human soul after the dissolution of the body. While the beliefs in this connection of savage races and of Europeans in early and mediæval times may arouse interest and curiosity for their own sakes, the scientific investigator of the present day values them chiefly as throwing light on modern beliefs. The belief in *apparitions* is a root principle of spiritualism. Many who are not spiritualists in the accepted sense have had experiences which render the belief in *apparitions* almost inevitable. A subject which touches so nearly a considerable percentage of the community, including many people of culture and education, and concerning which there is a vast quantity of evidence extending back into antiquity, cannot be a matter of indifference to science, and the investigations made by scientific men within recent years arouse surprise that such investigation has been so long delayed. The Society for Psychical Research has gathered many well attested instances of coincidental *apparitions*, clairvoyance, and *apparitions* of the dead. As yet, however, the problem remains unsolved, and the various hypotheses advanced are conflicting and sometimes obscure. The theory of telepathic hallucination offered by Mr. Podmore seems on the whole to be the most conformable to known natural laws, while at the same time covering the ground with fair completeness. But perhaps the best course to take at the present stage of our knowledge is to suspend judgment in the meanwhile, until further light has been cast on the subject.

Apports : The name given to various objects, such as flowers, jewellery, and even live animals, materialised in the presence of a medium. The production of these *apports* have always been, and still are, one of the most prominent and effective features of spiritualistic séances. Sometimes they fly through the air and strike the faces of the sitters ; sometimes they appear on the table, or in the laps of those present. A favourite form is the scattering of perfume on the company. Recent systematic experiments conducted in a purely scientific spirit have exposed fraud in numerous instances where ordinary precautions would not have sufficed for its detection. Frequently it has been found that the medium had skilfully concealed the *apports* in the room or about her person. Nevertheless, though the result is often produced by obviously unscrupulous means, it does not follow that all materialisations are performed with fraudulent intent. In cases where, so far as can be judged, the character of the medium is beyond reproach, as in the case of Hélene Smith, the idea has been advanced that any preparations made beforehand, such as the secreting of flowers, etc., must result from a process of activity of the subliminal consciousness. Other explanations are, that the *apports* are actually conveyed to the séance by spirits, or that they are drawn thither by magnetic power. Branches of trees, armfuls of fruit and flowers, money, jewels, and live lobsters are among the more extraordinary *apports*.

Apprentice : (*See* **Adept.**)

Apuleius : (*See* **Greece.**)

Aquin (Mardochee d') : A learned rabbi of Carpentras, who died in 1650. He became a Christian, and changed his name of *Mardochee* into Philip. He was the author of an *Interpretation of the Tree of the Hebrew Kabala*.

Aquinas (Thomas) who has been under the imputation of magic, was one of the profoundest scholars and subtlest logicians of his day. He was a youth of illustrious birth, and received the rudiments of his education under the monks of Monte Cassino, and in the University of Naples.

But, not contented with these advantages, he secretly entered himself in the Society of Preaching Friars, or Dominicans, at seventeen years of age. His mother, being indignant that he should thus take the vow of poverty, and sequester himself from the world for life, employed every means in her power to induce him to alter his purpose, but all in vain. The friars, to deliver him from her importunities, removed him from Naples to Terracina, from Terracina to Anagnia, and from Anagnia to Rome. His mother followed him in all these changes of residence, but was not permitted so much as to see him. At length she induced his two elder brothers to seize him by force. They waylaid him on his road to Paris, whether he was sent to complete his course of instruction, and carried him off to the castle of Aquino, where he had been born. Here he was confined for two years, but he found a way to correspond with the superiors of his order, and finally escaped from a window in the castle. *St. Thomas Aquinas* (for he was canonised after his death) exceeded perhaps all men that ever existed in the severity and strictness of his metaphysical disquisitions, and thus acquired the name of the Seraphic Doctor.

It was to be expected that a man, who thus immersed himself in the depths of thought, should be an enemy to noise and interruption. He dashed to pieces an artificial man of brass that Albertus Magnus, who was his tutor, had spent thirty years in bringing to perfection, being impelled to this violence by its perpetual and unceasing garrulity. It is further said, that his study being placed in a great thoroughfare, where the grooms were all day long exercising their horses, he found it necessary to apply a remedy to this nuisance. He made by the laws of magic a small horse of brass, which he buried two or three feet under ground in the midst of this highway, and, having done so, no horse would any longer pass along the road. It was in vain that the grooms with whip and spur sought to conquer the animals' repugnance. They were finally compelled to give up the attempt, and to choose another place for their daily exercises.

It has further been sought to fix the imputation of magic upon *Thomas Aquinas* by referring to him certain books written on that science; but these are now acknowledged to be spurious.

Arabs : The heyday of occultism among the Arab race was reached at the epoch when that division of them known as the Moors established their empire in the Spanish peninsula.

We first emerge from cloud and shadow into a precise and definite region in the eighth century, when an Arabian mystic revived the dreams and speculations of the alchemists, and discovered some important secrets. Geber (q.v.), who flourished about 720-750, is reputed to have written upwards of five hundred works upon the Philosophers' Stone and *elixir vitæ*. His researches after these desiderata proved fruitless, but if he did not bestow upon mankind immortal life and boundless wealth, he gave them nitrate of silver, corrosive sublimate, red oxide of mercury, and nitric acid.

Among his tenets were a belief that a preparation of gold would heal all diseases in animals and plants, as well as in human beings; that the metals were affected with maladies, except the pure, supreme, and precious one of gold; and that the Philsophers' Stone had often been discovered, but that its fortunate discoverers would not reveal the secret to blind, incredulous, and unworthy man.

His *Summa Perfectionis*—a manual for the alchemical student—has been frequently translated. A curious English version, of which there is a copy in the British Museum, was published by an English enthusiast, one Richard Russell, at " the Star, in New Market, in Wapping,

near the Dock," in 1686. Geber's true name was Abou Moussah Djafar, to which was added Al Sofi, or " The Wise," and he was a native of Houran, in Mesopotamia.

He was followed by Avicenna (q.v.), Averroes (q.v.) and others equally gifted and fortunate.

According to Geber and his successors the metals were not only compound creatures, but they were also all composed of the same two substances. Both Prout and Davy lent their names to ideas not unlike this. " The improvements," says the latter, " taking place in the methods of examining bodies, are constantly changing the opinions of chemists with respect to their nature, and there is no reason to suppose that any real indestructible principle has yet been discovered. Matter may ultimately be found to be the same in essence, differing only in the arrangement of its particles; or two or three simple substances may produce all the varieties of compound bodies." The ancient ideas, therefore, of Demetrius the Greek physicist, and of Geber, the Arabian polypharmist, are still hovering about the horizon of chemistry.

The Arabians taught, in the third place, that the metals are composed of mercury and sulphur in different proportions. They toiled away at the art of making many medicines out of the various mixtures and reactions of the few chemicals at their command. They believed in transmutation, but they did not strive to effect it. It belonged to their creed rather than to their practice. They were a race of hard-working, scientific artisans, with their pestles and mortars, their crucibles and furnaces, their alembics and aludels, their vessels for infusion, for decoction, for cohobation, sublimation, fixation, lixiviation, filtration and coagulation. They believed in transmutation, in the first matter, and in the correspondence of the metals with the planets, to say nothing of potable gold.

Whence the Arabians derived the sublimer articles of their scientific faith, is not known to any European historian. Perhaps they were the conjectures of their ancestors according to the faith. Perhaps they had them from the Fatimites of Northern Africa, among whose local predecessors it has been seen that it is just possible the doctrine of the four elements and their mutual convertibility may have arisen. Perhaps they drew them from Greece, modifying and adapting them to their own specific forms of matter, mercury, sulphur and arsenic.

Astrology.—Astrology was also employed by the oracles of Spain. *Albatgni* was celebrated for his astronomical science, as were many others; and in geometry, arithmetic, algebraical calculations and the theory of music, we have a long list, Asiatic and Spanish, but only known by their lives and principal writings. The works of Ptolemy also exercised the ingenuity of the Arabians; while Alchindi, as far as we may be allowed to judge from his multifarious volumes, traversed the whole circle of the sublimer sciences. But judicial astrology, or the art of foretelling future events from the position and influences of the stars, was with them a favourite pursuit; and many of their philosophers, incited by various motives, dedicated all their labours to this futile but lucrative inquiry. They often speak with high commendation of the iatro-mathematical discipline, which could control the disorders to which man was subject, and regulate the events of life.

The tenets of Islamism, which inculcate an unreserved submission to the over-ruling destinies of heaven, are evidently adverse to the lessons of astrology; but this by no means hindered the practitioners of old *Spain* and *Arabia* from attaining a high standard of perfection in the art, which they perhaps first learned from the peoples of *Chaldæa*, the past masters of the ancient world in astronomical science, in divination, and the secrets of prophecy. But in Arab Spain, where the tenets of Islam, were perhaps more lightly esteemed than in their original home, magic unquestionably reached a higher if not more thoughtful standard.

From the Greeks, still in search of science, the *Arabs* turned their attention to the books of the sages who are esteemed the primitive instructors of mankind, among whom Hermes was deemed the first. They mention the works written by him, or rather by them, as they suppose, like other authors, that there were three of the name. To one the imposing appellation of Trismegistus has been given; and the Arabians, from some ancient records, we may presume, minutely describe his character and person. They also published, as illustrative of their astrological discipline, some writings ascribed to the Persian Zoroaster.

For Sorcery, etc., see **Semites.**

Aradia, or the Gospel of the Witches of Italy : (*See* **Italy.**)

Arael : One of the spirits which the rabbis of the Talmud made princes and governors over the people of the birds.

Arariel : An angel who, according to the rabbis of the Talmud, takes charge of the waters of the earth. Fishermen invoke him so that they may take large fish.

Ararita : The *verbum inenarrabile* of the sages of the Alexandrian School, " which Hebrew Kabalists wrote *Javeh,* and interpreted by the sound *Ararita,* thus expressing the triplicity of the secondary kabalistic principle, the dualism of the means and the equal unity of the first and final principle, as well as the alliance between the triad and the triad and the tetrad in a word composed of four letters, which form seven by means of a triple and double repetition."

Arbatel : A magical ritual published at Basle in 1575. The text is in Latin, and it appears to have been influenced by Paracelsus. It is of Christian, not Jewish origin, and although the authorship is unknown it is probably the work of an Italian. Only one of its nine volumes has come down to us. It deals with the institutions of magic, and is entitled *Isagoge,* which means essential or necessary instruction. In it we are introduced to the ritual of the Olympic spirits dwelling in the air and among the stars, who govern the world. There are, we are told, one hundred and ninety-six Olympic provinces in the universe : thus Aratron has forty-nine, Bethor forty-two, Phaleg thirty-five, Och twenty-eight, Hagith twenty-one, Ophiel fourteen, and Phul seven. Each of the Olympic spirits rule alternately for four hundred and ninety years. They have natural sway over certain departments of the material world, but outside these departments they perform the same operations magically. Thus Och, the ruler of solar affairs, presides over the preparation of gold naturally in the soil. At the same time, he presides magically over the preparation of that metal by means of alchemy. The *Arbatel* proceeds to say that the sources of occult wisdom are to be found in God, spiritual essences and corporeal creatures, as well as in nature, but also in the apostate spirits and in the ministers of punishment in Hell and the elementary spirits. The secrets of all magic reside in these, but magicians are born, not made, although they are assisted by contemplation and the love of God. It will be sufficient to describe the powers and offices of one of these spirits. Aratron governs those things which are ascribed astrologically to Saturn. He can convert any living thing into stone, can change coals into treasure, gives familiar spirits to men, teaches alchemy, magic and medicine, the secret of invisibility, and long life. He should be invoked on a Saturday in the first hour of the day. The *Arbatel* is one of the best authorities extant on spiritual essences, their powers and degrees.

Arcanum, Great : The great secret which was supposed to lie behind all alchemical and magical striving. " God

and Nature," says Eliphas Levi (q.v.), " alike, have closed the Sanctuary of Transcendent Science. . . . so that the revelation of the great magical secret is happily impossible." Elsewhere he states that it makes the magician " master of gold and light."

Ardat-Lile : (Semitic Spirit). She is a female spirit or demon who weds human beings and works great harm in the dwellings of men.

Argentum, Potabile : A marvellous remedy for which the alchemists had a recipe. It was composed of sulphur, spirits of wine, and other ingredients, prepared according to specified direction, and was (if we credit these authorities) a sovereign remedy for all manner of ailments.

Ariel : A spirit. (*See* **Beaumont, John.**)

Arignote : Lucian relates that at Corinth, in the Cranaüs quarter, there was a certain house which no one would inhabit, because it was haunted by a spectre. A man named *Arignote,* well versed in the lore of the Egyptian magical books, shut himself in the house to pass the night and began to read peacefully in the court. Soon the spectre made its appearance, and in order to frighten *Arignote,* it first of all took the form of a dog, then that of a bull, and finally that of a lion. But *Arignote* was not at all disturbed. He conjured the spectre in formulæ which he found in his books, and obliged it to retire to a corner of the court, where it disappeared. On the following day the spot to which the spectre had retreated was dug up, and a skeleton was found. When it was properly buried, the ghost was not seen again. This anecdote is an adaptation of the adventure of Athenodorus, which Lucian had read in Pliny.

Arioch : Demon of vengeance, according to some demonologists. He is different from Alastor, and occupies himself only with vengeance in particular cases where he is employed for that purpose.

Ariolists : Ancient diviners, whose special occupation was called *ariolatio,* because they divined by means of the altars. They consulted demons on their altars, says Dangis ; they observed whether the altar trembled or performed any marvel, and predicted what the Devil inspired them with. According to François de la Tour Blanche, these people ought to have been put to death as idolators. He based his opinion on Deuteronomy, chap. xviii., and on Revelation, chap. xxi., where it is said that idolators and liars shall be cast into the lake of fire and sulphur, which will be their second death. Deuteronomy orders only the first.

Aristæus : A charlatan who lived in the time of Crœsus. He said that his soul would leave his body whenever he wished, and then return to it. Some maintain that it escaped in the sight of his wife and children in the figure of a stag. Wierius said that it took the shape of a crow. However that may be, Herodotus relates in his fourth book that *Aristæus* entering one day into a fuller's shop, fell dead therein, that the fuller ran to break the news to his parents, who came to bury him. But no corpse was to be found. The whole town was astonished, when some men returning from a voyage assured them that they had met *Aristæus* on the way to Crotona. It appeared that he was a species of vampire. Herodotus adds that he reappeared at the end of seven years, composed a poem and died anew. Leloyer, who regarded *Aristæus* as a sorcerer or ecstatic, quoted a certain Apollonius, who said that at the same hour as the vampire disappeared for the second time, he was transported to Sicily, where he became a schoolmaster. He is again heard of three hundred and forty years afterwards in the town of Metapontus, where he caused to be raised certain monuments which were to be seen in the time of Herodotus. So many wonderful happenings inspired the Sicilians with awe, and they raised a temple to him and worshipped him as a demi-god.

Arithmancy : (Sometimes called wrongly *Arithmomancy*). Divination by means of numbers. The Greeks examined the number and value of the letters in the names of two combatants, and predicted that he whose name contained most letters, or letters of the greatest value, would be the victor. It was by means of this science that some diviners foretold that Hector would be overcome by Achilles. The Chaldeans, who also practised it, divided their alphabet into three parts, each composed of seven letters, which they attributed to the seven planets, in order to make predictions from them. The Platonists and the Pythagoreans were also strongly addicted to this method of divination, which comprehends also a part of the Jewish Kabala.

Armida : The episode of *Armida*, in Tasso, is founded on a popular tradition related by Pierre Delancre. This skilful enchantress was the daughter of Arbilan, King of Damascus. She was brought up by an uncle, a great magician, who taught his niece to become a powerful sorceress. Nature had so well endowed her that for personal attractions she far surpassed the most beautiful women of the East. Her uncle sent her as a worthy foe against the powerful Christian army that Pope Urban XI. had collected under the leadership of Godfrey de Bouillon. And there, says Delancre, she made such havoc with her beautiful eyes, and so charmed the principal leaders of the crusaders, that she almost ruined the hopes of the Christians. She kept the valiant knight Renaud for a long time in an enchanted castle, and it was not without great difficulty that he was disenchanted.

Armomancy : A method of divination which is effected by the inspection of the shoulders. The ancients judged by this means whether a victim was suitable for sacrifice to the gods.

Arnaud, Guillaume : (*See* **France.**)

Arnoux : Author of a volume published at Rouen, in 1630, with the title of *On the Wonders of the Other World*, a work written in a bizarre style, and calculated to disturb feeble imaginations with its tales of visions and apparitions.

Arnuphis : An Egyptian sorcerer who, seeing Marcus Aurelius and his army engaged in a pass whose entrance had been closed by their enemies, and dying of thirst under a burning sky, caused a miraculous rain to fall, which allowed the Romans to quench their thirst, while the thunder and hail obliged the enemy to give up their arms.

Arphaxat : A Persian sorcerer, who was killed by a thunderbolt, according to Abdias of Babylon, at the same hour as the martyrdom of St. Simon and St. Jude. In the account of the possession of the nuns of Loudun there is a demon *Arphaxat*, who took possession of the body of Louise de Pinterville.

Ars Aurifera : (*See* **Avicenna.**)

Ars Chimica : (*See* **Avicenna.**)

Ars Notoria : The science of the Tarot (q.v.) signs and their application to the divination of all secrets, whether of nature, of philosophy, or even of the future.

Art Transmutatoire : (*See* **Pope John XXII.**)

Artephius : A well-known exponent of the hermetic philosophy, who died in the twelfth century, and is said to have lived more than a thousand years by means of alchemical secrets. François Pic mentions the opinion of certain savants who affirm that *Artephius* is identical with Appolonius of Tyana, who was born in the first century under that name, and who died in the twelfth century under that of *Artephius*. Many extravagant and curious works are attributed to him : *De Vita Propaganda* (The Art of Prolonging Life) which he claims, in the preface, to have written at the age of a thousand and twenty-five years ; *The Key to Supreme Wisdom ;* and a work on the character of the planets, on the significance of the songs of birds, on things past and future, and on the Pilhosophers' Stone. Cardan spoke

of these books, and believed that they were composed by some practical joker who wished to play on the credulity of the partisans of alchemy.

Arthur, King : The character of *Arthur* is strongly identified with the occult. Not only do we find his Court a veritable centre of happenings more or less supernatural, but his mysterious origin and the subsequent events of his career have in them matter of considerable interest from an occult standpoint. This is not the place to dispute regarding his reality, but merely to deal with the romances which cluster around him, and their contents from the supernatural point of view. We find him first of all connected with one of the greatest magical names of early times—that of Merlin the Enchanter. The possibilities are that Merlin was originally a British deity, who in later times degenerated from his high'position in the popular imagination. We possess many accounts concerning him, one of which states that he was the direct offspring of Satan himself, but that a zealous priest succeeded in baptising him before his infernal parent could carry him off. From Merlin, *Arthur* received much good advice both magical and rational. He was present when the King was gifted with his magic sword Excalibur, which endowed him with practical invulnerability, and all through his career was deep in his counsels. His tragic imprisonment by the Lady Viviana, who shut him up eternally in a rock through the agency of one of his own spells, removed him from his sphere of activity at the Arthurian Court, and from that time the shadows may be seen to gather swiftly around *Arthur's* head. Innumerable are the tales concerning the Knights of his Court who met with magical adventures, and as the stories grew older in the popular mind, additions to these naturally became the rule. Notably is this the case in that off-shoot of the Arthurian epic, which is known as the Holy Grail (q.v.), in which we find the knights who go in quest of it constantly encountered by every description of sorcery for the purpose of retarding their progress. *Arthur's* end is as strange as his origin, for we find him wafted away by faery hands, or at least by invisible agency, to the Isle of Avillion, which probably is one and the same place with the Celtic other-world across the ocean. As a legend and a tradition, that of *Arthur* is undoubtedly the most powerful and persistent in the British imagination. It has employed the pens and enhanced the dreams of many of the giants in English literature from the time of Geoffrey of Monmouth, to the present day ; and with the echoes of the poetry of Tennyson and Swinburne still ringing in their ears, the present generation is quite as justified in regarding the history of *Arthur* as a living reality as were the Britons of the twelfth century.

Artois, Countess of : (*See* **France.**)

Asal : Known as the King of the Golden Pillars, in Irish Celtic Myth. He was the owner of seven swine, which might be killed and eaten every night, yet were found alive every morning.

Asbestos : *Asbestos* is so called from being inextinguishable even by showers and storms, if once set on fire. The Pagans made use of it for lights in their temples. It is of woolly texture, and is sometimes called the Salamander's feather. Leonardus says : " Its fire is nourished by an inseparable unctuous humid flowing from its substance ; therefore, being once kindled, it preserves a constant light without feeding it with any moisture."

Asclepius : A hermetic book. (*See* **Hermes Trismegistus.**)

Ash Tree : The *Ash* had a wonderful influence. The old Christmas log was of *ash* wood, and the use of it at this time was helpful to the future prosperity of the family. Venomous animals, it was said, would not take shelter under its branches. A carriage with its axles made of *ash* wood was believed to go faster than a carriage with its axles made of any other wood ; and tools with handles made of this wood were supposed to enable a man to do more work than he could do with tools whose handles were not of *ash*. Hence the reason that *ash* wood is generally used for tool handles. It was upon *ash* branches that witches were enabled to ride through the air ; and those who ate on St. John's eve the red buds of the tree, were rendered invulnerable to witches' influence.

Ashipu : (*See* **Babylonia.**)

Ashtabula Poltergeist, The : The supposed cause of the extraordinary disturbances which took place about the middle of the nineteenth century in the presence of a lady of Ashtabula County, Ohio. First of all she became a medium on the death of her husband, and produced spirit-rappings and other manifestations. Then for a time she studied anatomy in Marlborough, and afterwards returned to her home in Austinburg. where an alarming outbreak of weird manifestations occurred. Stair-rods moved after her when she went to her room, light articles flew about the house, and uncanny sounds were heard. At Marlborough, when she resumed her anatomical studies, the disturbances increased in violence, and she and her room-mate had a ghastly vision of a corpse they had been dissecting in the day-time. Dr. Richmond, a sceptic of the day, maintained that these phenomena were the result of magneto-odylic emanations from the medium.

Asiah : According to the Kabala, the first of the three classes or natural ranks among the spirits of men, who must advance from the lower to the higher.

Asipu : Caste of priests. (*See* **Semites.**)

Aspects, Planetary : (*See* **Astrology.**)

Aspidomancy : A little known form of divination practised in the Indies, as we are told by some travellers. Delancre says that the diviner or sorcerer traces a circle, takes up his position therein seated on a buckler, and mutters certain conjurations. He becomes entranced and falls into an ecstasy, from which he only emerges to tell things that his client wishes to know, and which the devil has revealed to him.

Aspilette (Marie d') : Witch of Andaye, in the country of Labour, who lived in the reign of Henry IV. She was arrested at the age of nineteen years, and confessed that she had been led to the " sabbath," and there made to perform divers horrible rites.

Ass : The Egyptians traced his image on the cakes they offered to Typhon, god of evil. The Romans regarded the meeting of an *ass* as an evil omen, but the animal was honoured in Arabia and Judea, and it was in Arabia that the *ass* of Silanus spoke to his master. Other talking *asses* were Balaam's *ass*, which Mahomet placed in his paradise with Alborack ; the *ass* of Aasis, Queen of Sheba ; and the *ass* on which Jesus Christ rode into Jerusalem.

Some people have found something sacred and mysterious in the innocent beast, and there was practised formerly a species of divination in which the head of an *ass* was employed.

At one time a special festival was held for the *ass*, during which he was led into the church while mass was sung. This reverence in which he was held by Christians was doubtless due to the black cross which he wears on his back, and which, it is said, was given him because of the *ass* of Bethphage, who carried Christ into Jerusalem. But Pliny, who was almost contemporary with that *ass*, and who has carefully gathered all that related to the animal, has made no mention concerning the colour of its coat ! So we can only believe that the *ass* of to-day is as he always was.

It is not only the devout who respect the *ass*, for the wise Agrippa offered him an apology in his book, *On the Vanity of the Sciences*. Among the Indians of Madras,

one of the principal castes, that of the Cavaravadonques, claim to be descended from an *ass*. These Indians treat the *ass* as a brother, take his part, and prosecute those who over-burden or ill-treat him in any way. In rainy weather they will often give him shelter when they deny it to his driver.

An old fable gives us but a poor idea of the *ass*. Jupiter had just taken possession of Olympus. On his coming, men asked of him an eternal springtime, which he accordingly granted, charging the *ass* of Silenus to bear the precious treasure to earth. The *ass* became thirsty, and approached a fountain guarded by a snake, who refused to let the *ass* drink unless he parted with the treasure. The stupid animal thereupon bartered the gift of heaven for a skin of water, and since that time snakes, when they grow old, can change their skin and become young again, for they have the gift of perpetual spring-time.

But all *asses* were not so stupid as that. In a village about half a league from Cairo, there dwelt a mountebank, who possessed a highly trained *ass*, so clever that the country people took it to be a demon in disguise. One day the mountebank mentioned in the *ass's* hearing that the Soldan wished to construct a beautiful building, and had resolved to employ all the *asses* in Cairo to carry the lime, mortar and stones. The *ass* immediately lay down and pretended to be dead, and his master begged for money to buy another. When he had collected some he returned to his old *ass*. " He is not dead," he said, " he only pretended to die because he knew I had not the wherewithal to buy him food." Still the *ass* refused to rise, and the mountebank addressed the company, telling them that the Soldan had sent out the criers commanding the people to assemble on the morrow outside Cairo to see the most wonderful sights in the world. He further desired that the most gracious ladies and the most beautiful girls should be mounted on *asses*. The *ass* raised himself and pricked up his ears. " The governor of my quarter," added the mountebank, " has begged me to lend my *ass* for his wife, who is old and toothless, and very ugly." The *ass* began to limp as though he were old and lame. " Ah, you like beautiful ladies ? " said his master. The animal bowed his head. " Oh, well," said the man. " there are many present ; show me the most beautiful." Which command the *ass* obeyed with judgment and discretion.

These marvellous *asses*, said the demonologists, were, if not demons, at least men metamorphosed, like Apuleius, who was, it is said, transformed into an *ass*. Vincent de Beauvais speaks of two women who kept a little inn near Rome, and who sold their guests at the market, after having changed them into pigs, fowls, or sheep. One of them, he adds, changed a certain comedian into an *ass*, and as he retained his talents under his new skin, she led him to the fairs on the outskirts of the city, gaining much money thereby. A neighbour bought this wise *ass* at a good price, and in handing it over the sorcerers felt obliged to warn the purchaser not to let the *ass* enter water. Its new master attended to the warning for some time, but one day the poor *ass* managed to get free and cast itself into a lake, when it regained its natural shape, to the great surprise of its driver. The matter was brought to the ears of the Pope. who had the two witches punished. while the comedian returned to the exercise of his profession.

Many stories are told of the *ass* which carried Jesus Christ into Jerusalem, and which is said to have died at Verona, where its remains are still honoured. The rabbis make quite as much ado over Balaam's *ass*, which has already been mentioned. It is, they say, a privileged animal whom God formed at the end of the sixth day. Abraham employed it to carry the wood for the sacrifice of Isaac ; it also carried the wife and son of Moses in the desert. They also maintain that Balaam's ass is carefully nourished and kept in a secret place until the coming of the Jewish Messiah, who will mount it when He subdues all the earth.

Assassins : (*Hashishin*, so-called from their use of the drug *hashish*, distilled from the hemp plant). A branch of that sect of Mahomedans known as Ismaelites, founded in the latter part of the eleventh century by Hassan Sabah, in Syria and Persia. Driven from Cairo, Hassan spread a modified form of the Ismaelite doctrine throughout Syria, and in 1090 he became master of the mountain stronghold, Alamut, in Persia, where he founded a society known as the *Assassins*, and from which he ostensibly promulgated the principles of the Ismaelite sect. The difference, however, between the *Assassins* and other Ismaelites, was that they employed secret assassination against all the enemies of the sect. Their organisation was founded upon that of the Western Lodge at Cairo, and at the head of their sect was the Sheik-Al-Gebel, or " Old Man of the Mountain," as the name has been rather absurdly translated by Europeans authors, the more correct translation being " Chief of the mountain." The other officers of the society were the grand priors, lesser priors, initiates, associates, and the *fedavi* or " devoted ones," who were the *assassins* proper. These latter were young men from whose ranks those who were selected for the various deeds of blood for which the *Assassins* became notorious, were chosen. They were not initiated into the secret circle of the cult, and blind obedience was expected from them. When their services were required they were intoxicated with hashish, and in this condition were taken into the magnificent gardens of the Sheik, where they were surrounded by every pleasure. This they were told was a foretaste of what they might expect in Paradise, to which they would instantly proceed were they to lose their lives in the Sheik's service. Consequently these young men, for the most part ignorant peasants, displayed a degree of fanaticism which made them the fitting instruments of Hassan's policy. But the initiated amongst the *Assassins* were convinced of the worthlessness of religion and morality, held no belief, and sneered covertly at the Prophet and his religion.

The early history of the society is one of romantic and absorbing interest. Hassan had been a member of a secret Ismaelite society at Cairo, the head of which was the Caliph, " and of which the object was the dissemination of the doctrines of the sect of the Ismaelites. . . .

" This society, we are told, comprised both men and women, who met in separate assemblies, for the common supposition of the insignificance of the latter sex in the east. is erroneous. It was presided over by the Chief Missionary (*Dai-al-Doat*) who was always a person of importance in the state, and not infrequently Supreme Judge (*Kadhi-al-Kodhat*). Their assemblies, called Societies of Wisdom (*Mejalis-al-Hiemet*), were held twice a week, on Mondays and Wednesdays. All the members appeared clad in white. The president. having first waited on the Caliph, and read to him the intended lecture, or, if that could not be done, having got his signature on the back of it. proceeded to the assembly and delivered a written discourse. At the conclusion of it, those present kissed his hand and reverently touched with their forehead the handwriting of the Caliph. In this state the society continued till the reign of that extraordinary madman, the Caliph Haken-bi-emr-illah (Judge by the Command of God), who determined to place it on a splendid footing. He erected for it a stately edifice, styled the House of Wisdom (*Dar-al-hicmet*), abundantly furnished with books and mathematical instruments. Its doors were open to all, and paper, pens. and ink were profusely supplied for the use of those who chose to frequent it. Professors of

law, mathematics, logic, and medicine were appointed to give instructions ; and at the learned disputations which were frequently held in presence of the Caliph, these professors appeared in their state caftans (*Khalaa*), which it is said, exactly resembled the robes worn at the English universities. The income assigned to this establishment by the munificence of the Caliph, was 257,000 ducats annually, arising from the tenths paid to the crown.

" The course of instruction in this university proceeded, according to Macrisi, by the following nine degrees. (1) The object of the first, which was long and tedious, was to infuse doubts and difficulties into the mind of the aspirant, and to lead him to repose a blind confidence in the knowledge and wisdom of his teacher. To this end he was perplexed with captious questions ; the absurdities of the literal sense of the Koran and its repugnance to reason, were studiously pointed out, and dark hints were given that beneath this shell lay a kernel sweet to the taste and nutritive to the soul. But all further information was most rigorously withheld till he had consented to bind himself by a most solemn oath to absolute faith and blind obedience to his instructor. (2) When he had taken the oath he was admitted to the second degree, which inculcated the acknowledgement of the imams appointed by God as the sources of all knowledge. (3) The third degree informed him what was the number of these blessed and holy imams ; and this was the mystic seven ; for, as God had made seven heavens, seven earths, seas, planets, metals, tones, and colours, so seven was the number of these noblest of God's creatures. (4) In the fourth degree the pupil learned that God had sent seven lawgivers into the world, each of whom was commissioned to alter and improve the system of his predecessor ; that each of these had seven helpers, who appeared in the interval between him and his successor ; these helpers, as they did not appear as public teachers, were called the mute (*samit*), in contradistinction to the speaking lawgivers. The seven lawgivers were Adam, Noah, Abraham, Moses, Jesus, Mohammed, and Ismael, the son of Jaaffer ; the seven principal helpers, called Seats (*soos*) were Seth. Shem. Ishmael (the son of Abraham), Aaron, Simon, Ali, and Mohammed, the son of Ismael. It is justly observed that, as this last personage was not more than a century dead, the teacher had it in his power to fix on whom he would as the mute prophet of the present time, and inculcate the belief in, and obedience to, him of all who had not got beyond this degree. (5) The fifth degree taught that each of the seven mute prophets had twelve apostles for the dissemination of his faith. The suitableness of this number was also proved by analogy. There are twelve signs of the Zodiac, twelve months, twelve tribes of Israel, twelve joints in the four fingers of each hand, and so forth. (6) The pupil being led thus far, and having shown no symptoms of restiveness, the precepts of the Koran were once more brought under consideration, and he was told that all the positive portions of religion must be subordinate to philosophy. He was consequently instructed in the systems of Plato and Aristotle during the long space of time ; and (7) when esteemed fully qualified, he was admitted to the seventh degree, when instruction was communicated in that mystic Pantheism, which is held and taught by the sect of the Soofees. (8) The positive precepts of religion were again considered, the veil was torn from the eyes of the aspirant, all that had preceded was now declared to have been merely scaffolding to raise the edifice of knowledge, and was to be flung down. Prophets and teachers, heaven and hell, all were nothing ; future bliss and misery were idle dreams ; all actions were permitted. (9) The ninth degree had only to inculcate that nought was to be believed, everything might be done."

It is worthy of mention that one of Hassan's early intimates was the famous Omar Khayyam, with whom he and another friend contracted a bargain that the most successful of the three would share his good fortune with the others. It is likely that the practical mystic and the astrologer would feel drawn to each other by many common tastes, but we do not learn that Omar profited much from the bargain so far as Hassan was concerned. The third of the friends, Nizam-al-Melk, achieved an exalted position as vizier to the second of the Seljuk monarchs, and calling to mind his promise offered Omar a post under the government, but the author of the *Rubaiyat* was too addicted to pleasure to accept active employment, and in lieu of the dazzling position offered him, was content with a pension of 1,200 ducats, with which he went into retirement.

Hassan clearly perceived that the plan of the society at Cairo was defective as a means of acquiring temporal power. The Dais might exert themselves and proselytes might be gained, but till possession was obtained of some strongholds, and a mode of striking terror into princes devised, nothing effectual could be achieved.

With this object in view he instituted the *Fedavi*, who unhesitatingly obeyed their chief, and, without inquiry or hesitation, plunge their daggers into the bosom of whatever victim was pointed out to them, even though their own lives should be the immediate sacrifice. The ordinary dress of the *Fedavi* was (like that of all the sects opposed to the house of Abbas) white ; their caps, girdles, or boots, were red. Hence they were named the White (*Mubeiyazah*), and the Red (*Muhammere*) ; but they could with ease assume any guise, even that of the Christian monk, to accomplish their murderous designs.

Hassan was perfectly aware that without the compressing power of positive religion, no society can well be held together. Whatever, therefore, his private opinions may have been, he resolved to impose on the bulk of his followers the most rigid obedience to the positive precepts of Islam, and, actually put his own son to death for a breach of one of them.

Hassan is said to have rejected two of the degrees of the Ismaelite society at Cairo, and to have reduced them to seven, the original number in the plan of Abdallah Maimoon, the first projector of this secret society Besides these seven degrees, through which the aspirants gradually rose to knowledge, Hassan, in what Hammer terms the breviary of the order, drew up seven regulations or rules for the conduct of the teachers in his society. (1) The first of these, named Ashinai-Risk (Knowledge of Duty), inculcated the requisite knowledge of human nature for selecting fit persons for admission. To this belong the proverbial expressions said to have been current among the Dais, similar to those used by the ancient Pythagoreans, such as " Sow not on barren ground " (that is, " Waste not your labour on incapable persons), " Speak not in a house where there is a lamp " (that is, " Be silent in the presence of a lawyer "). (2) The second rule was called Teênis (Gaining of Confidence), and taught to win the candidates by flattering their passions and inclinations. (3) The third, of which the name is not given, taught to involve them in doubts and difficulties by pointing out the absurdities of the Koran, and of positive religion. (4) When the aspirant had gone thus far, the solemn oath of silence and obedience, and of communicating his doubts to his teacher alone was to be imposed on the disciple ; and then (5) he was to be informed that the doctrines and opinions of the society were those of the greatest men in church and state. (6) The Tessees (Confirmation) directed to put the pupil again through all he had learned, and to confirm him in it. And, (7) finally,

the Teêvil (Instruction in Allegory) gave the allegorical mode of interpreting the Koran, and drawing whatever sense might suit their purposes from its pages. Any one who had gone through this course of instruction, and was thus become perfectly imbued with the spirit of the society, was regarded as an accomplished Dai, and employed in the important office of making proselytes and extending its influence.

Soofeism, a doctrine of this society, which is a kind of mystic Pantheism, viewing God in all and all in God, may produce, like fatalism, piety or its opposite. In the eyes of one who thus views God, all the distinctions between vice and virtue become fleeting and uncertain, and crime may gradually lose its atrocity, and be regarded as only a means for the production of a good end. That the Ismaelite *Fedavi* murdered innocent persons without compunction, when ordered so to do by his superiors, is an undoubted fact, and there is no absurdity in supposing that he and they may have thought that in so doing they were acting rightly and promoting the cause of truth.

The followers of Hassan Sabah were called the Eastern Ismaelites, to distinguish them from those of Africa. They were also named the *Batiniyeh* (Internal or Secret), from the secret meaning which they drew from the text of the Koran, and Moolhad, or Moolahid (Impious) on account of the imputed impiety of their doctrines—names common to them with most of the preceding sects. It is under this last appellation that they were known to Marco Polo, the Venetian traveller. The name, however, by which they are best known in Europe, and which we employ, is that of *Assassins*. This name is very generally derived from that of the founder of their society ; but M. De Sacy has made it probable that the Oriental term *Hashishin*, of which the Crusaders made *Assassins*, comes (as already noted) from Hashish, a species of hemp, from which intoxicating opiates were made, which the *Fedavi* were in the habit of taking previously to engaging in their daring enterprises, or employed as a medium of procuring delicious visions of the paradise promised to them by the Sheikh-al-Gebel.

It is a curious question how Hassan contrived to infuse into the *Fedavi* the recklessness of life, joined with the spirit of implicit obedience to the commands of their superiors, which they so invariably displayed. We are told that the system adopted for this purpose was to obtain, by purchasing or otherwise, from their parents, stout and healthy children. These were reared up in implicit obedience to the will of the Sheik, and, to fit them for their future office, carefully instructed in various languages.

The *Assassins* soon began to make themselves felt as a power in Persia and Syria. Their first victim was that very Nizam with whom Hassan and Omar had completed their youthful bargain. His son speedily followed him, as did the Sultan of Persia. That monarch's successor made war with them, but was so terror-stricken by their murderous tactics, that he speedily cemented a peace. Hassan died at an advanced age in 1124, having assassinated both his sons, and left as his successor his chief prior, Hia-busurg-Omid, during the reign of whom the *Assassins* were far from fortunate. The list of their victims had by this time become a long and illustrious one. The fourth Sheik of the Mountain—another Hassan—made public the secret doctrines of the society, announcing that the religion of Islam was abolished and that the people might give themselves up to feasting and pleasure. He further stated that he was the promised Caliph of God upon earth ; but some four years after this announcement he was assassinated and succeeded by his son, Mahomed II. whose rule of forty-six years was marked by deeds of revolting cruelty. But he had several implacable enemies, one of whom was the famous Saladin, and the Syrian branch of the society seceded from his sway, and became independent. This branch it was with whom the Crusaders came so much into contact, and whose emissaries slew Raymond of Tripoli, and Conrad of Montferrat. Mahomed's son, Hassan III., restored the old form of doctrine—that is, the people were strictly confined to the practice of Islam, whilst the initiates were as before, superior and agnostic. His was the only reign in which no assassinations occurred and he was regarded with friendship by his neighbours. But after a reign of twelve years, he was poisoned, and during the minority of his son assassination was greatly in vogue. After a reign of thirty years, Mahomed III., the son in question, was slain by his successor, Rukneddin ; but vengeance quickly followed, for only a year later the Tartars swept into Persia, took Alamut and other *Assassin* strongholds, and captured the reigning monarch, who was slain because of his treachery. Over 12,000 *Assassins* were massacred, and their power was completely broken. The like fate overtook the Syrian branch, which was nearly extirpated by the Egyptian Mamelukes. But in the more isolated valleys of Syria, many of them lingered on and are believed still to exist there. At all events, doctrines similar in character to theirs are occasionally to be met with in Northern Syria. An account of the manner in which the *Assassins* aroused the lust of slaughter in the *Fedavis* is given in *Siret-al-Haken, or Memoirs of Hakim*—an Arabic historic romance, as follows :—

"Our narrative now returns to Ismael the chief of the Ismaelites. He took with him his people laden with gold, silver, pearls, and other effects, taken away from the inhabitants of the coasts, and which he had received in the island of Cyprus, and on the part of the King of Egypt, Dhaher, the son of Hakem-biemr-Illah. Having bidden farewell to the Sultan of Egypt at Tripolis, they proceeded to Massyat, when the inhabitants of the castles and fortresses assembled to enjoy themselves, along with the chief Ismael and his people. They put on the rich dresses with which the Sultan had supplied them, and adorned the castle of Massyat with everything that was good and fine. Ismael made his entry into Massyat with the Devoted (*Fedavi*), as no one has ever done at Massyat before him or after him. He stopped there some time to take into his service some more persons whom he might make devoted both in heart and body.

"With this view he had caused to be made a vast garden, into which he had water conducted. In the middle of this garden he built a kiosk raised to the height of four stories. On each of the four sides were richly-ornamented windows joined by four arches, in which were painted stars of gold and silver. He put into it roses, porcelain. glasses, and drinking-vessels of gold and silver. He had with him Mamlooks (i.e., slaves), ten males and ten females, who were come with him from the region of the Nile, and who had scarcely attained the age of puberty. He clothed them in silks and in the finest stuffs, and he gave unto them bracelets of gold and of silver. The columns were overlaid with musk, and with amber, and in the four arches of the windows he set four caskets, in which was the purest musk. The columns were polished, and this place was the retreat of the slaves. He divided the garden into four parts. In the first of these were pear-trees, apple-trees, vines, cherries, mulberries, plums, and other kinds of fruit-trees. In the second were oranges. lemons, olives, pomegranates, and other fruits. In the third were cucumbers, melons, leguminous plants, etc. In the fourth were roses, jessamine, tamarinds, narcissi, violets, lilies, anemonies, etc., etc.

"The garden was divided by canals of water, and the kiosk was surrounded with ponds and reservoirs. There were groves in which were seen antelopes, ostriches, asses, and wild cows. Issuing from the ponds, one met ducks, geese, partridges, quails, hares, foxes, and other animals. Around the kiosk the chief Ismael planted walks of tall trees, terminating in the different parts of the garden. He built there a great house, divided into two apartments, the upper and the lower. From the latter covered walks led out into the garden, which was all enclosed with walls, so that no one could see into it, for these walks and buildings were all void of inhabitants. He made a gallery of coolness, which ran from this apartment to the cellar, which was behind. This apartment served as a place of assembly for the men. Having placed himself on a sofa there opposite the door, the chief made his men sit down, and gave them to eat and drink during the whole length of the day until evening. At nightfall he looked around him, and, selecting those whose firmness pleased him, said to them, ' Ho ! such-a-one, come and seat thyself near me.' It is thus that Ismael made those whom he had chosen sit near him on the sofa and drink. He then spoke to them of the great and excellent qualities of the imam Ali, of his bravery, his nobleness, and his generosity, until they fell asleep, overcome by the power of the *benjeh* which he had given them, and which never failed to produce its effects in less than a quarter of an hour, so that they fell down as if they were inanimate. As soon as the man had fallen the chief Ismael arose, and, taking him up, brought him into a dormitory, and then, shutting the door, carried him on his shoulders into the gallery of coolness, which was in the garden, and thence into the kiosk, where he committed him to the care of the male and female slaves, directing them to comply with all the desires of the candidate, on whom they flung vinegar till he awoke. When he was come to himself the youths and maidens said to him. ' We are only waiting for thy death, for this place is destined for thee. This is one of the pavilions of Paradise, and we are the houries and the children of Paradise. If thou wert dead thou wouldest be for ever with us, but thou art only dreaming, and wilt soon awake.' Meanwhile, the chief Ismael had returned to the company as soon as he had witnessed the awakening of the candidate, who now perceived nothing but youths and maidens of the greatest beauty. and adorned in the most magnificent manner.

"He looked around the place, inhaled the fragrance of musk and frankincense, and drew near to the garden, where he saw the beasts and the birds, the running water, and the trees. He gazed on the beauty of the kiosk, and the vases of gold and silver, while the youths and maidens kept him in converse. In this way he remained confounded, not knowing whether he was awake or only dreaming. When two hours of the night had gone by, the chief Ismael returned to the dormitory, closed to the door, and thence proceeded to the garden, where his slaves came around him and rose before him. When the candidate perceived him, he said unto him, ' O, chief Ismael, do I dream, or am I awake ? ' The chief Ismael then made answer to him . ' O, such-a-one beware of relating this vision to any one who is a stranger to this place ! Know that the Lord Ali has shown thee the place which is destined for thee in Paradise. Know that at this moment the Lord Ali and I have been sitting together in the regions of the empyrean. So do not hesitate a moment in the service of the imam who has given thee to know his felicity.' Then the chief Ismael ordered supper to be served. It was brought in vessels of gold and of silver, and consisted of boiled meats and roast meats, with other dishes. While the candidate ate, he was sprinkled with rose-water ; when he called for drink there were brought to him vessels of gold and silver filled with delicious liquors, in which also had been mingled some *benjeh*. When he had fallen asleep, Ismael carried him through the gallery back to the dormitory, and, leaving him there, returned to his company. After a little time he went back, threw vinegar on his face, and then, bringing him out, ordered one of the Mamlooks to shake him. On awaking, and finding himself in the same place among the guests, he said . ' There is no god but God, and Mohammed is the Prophet of God ! ' The chief Ismael then drew near and caressed him, and he remained, as it were, immersed in intoxication, wholly devoted to the service of the chief, who then said unto him . ' O, such-a-one, know that what thou hast seen was not a dream, but one of the miracles of the imam Ali. Know that he has written thy name among those of his friends. If thou keep the secret thou art certain of thy felicity, but if thou speak of it thou wilt incur the resentment of the imam. If thou die thou art a martyr ; but beware of relating this to any person whatever. Thou hast entered by one of the gates to the friendship of the imam, and art become one of his family ; but if thou betray the secret, thou wilt become one of his enemies, and be driven from his house.' Thus this man became one of the servants of the chief Ismael. who in this manner surrounded himself with trusty men, until his reputation was established. This is what is related to the chief Ismael and his Devoted."

To these romantic tales of the Paradise of the Old Man of the Mountain we must add to another of an even more mystical character, furnished by the learned and venerable Sheik Agd-ur-Rahman (Servant of the Compassionate, *i.e.*, of God) Ben Ebubekr Al-Jeriri of Damascus, in the twenty-fourth chapter of his work entitled, *A Choice Book for Discovering the Secrets of the Art of Imposture.*

Asteroids : (*See* **Astrology.**)

Astolpho : A hero of Italian romance. He was the son of Otho, King of England. He was transformed into a myrtle by Alcina, a sorceress, but later regained his human form through Melissa. He took part in many adventures, and cured Orlando of his madness. *Astolpho* is the allegorical representation of a true man lost through sensuality.

Astral Body is in Theosophy that body which functions in the Astral World. Like the rest of man's five bodies, it is composed of matter, relatively, however, much finer than that which composes the ordinary physical body. It is the instrument of passions, emotions, and desires, and, since it interpenetrates and extends beyond the physical body, it is the medium through which these are conveyed to the latter. When it separates from the denser body— as it does during sleep, or by the influence of drugs, or as the result of accidents—it takes with it the capacity for feeling, and only with its return can pain or any other such phenomena be felt. During these periods of separation the *astral body* is an exact replica of the physical, and as it is extremely sensitive to thought, the apparitions of dead and dying—of which so much is heard in the new science of the Borderland—resemble even to the smallest details the physical bodies which they have lately left. The Astral World is, of course, easily attainable to clairvoyants of even moderate powers, and the appropriate body is therefore clearly visible. In accordance with theosophic teaching on the subject of thought, the latter is not the abstraction it is commonly considered to be, but built up of definite forms the shape of which depends on the quality of the thought, and it also causes definite vibrations, which are seen as colours. Hence, clairvoyants are able to tell the state of a man's development from the appearance of his *astral body*. A nebulous appearance betokens imperfect development, while an ovoid appearance betokens a more perfect development. As the colours are indicative of the kind of thought, the variety of these in the *astral body* indicates the possessor's character.

Inferior thoughts beget loud colours, so that rage, for instance, will be recognised by the red appearance of the *astral body*, and on the contrary, higher thoughts will be recognisable by the presence of delicate colours, religious thought for instance, causing a blue colour. This teaching holds true for the bodies higher than the *astral*, but, the coloration of the *astral body* is much more familiar to dwellers in the physical world than is the coloration of the higher bodies, with the feelings of which they are relatively unacquainted. There is a definite theory underlying the emotional and other functions of the *astral body*. The matter of which the latter is composed is not, of course, alive with an intelligent life, but it nevertheless possesses a kind of life sufficient to convey an understanding of its own existence and wants. The stage of evolution of this life is that of descent, the turning point not having yet, so far as it is concerned, been reached. He who possesses the body has, on the other hand, commenced to ascend, and there is, therefore, a continual opposition of forces between him and his *astral body*. Hence, his *astral body* accentuates in him such of grosser, retrograde thoughts as he may nourish since the direction of these thoughts coincides with its own direction. If, however, he resists the opposition of his *astral body*, the craving of the latter gradually becomes weaker and weaker till at last it disappears altogether. And the constitution of the *astral body* is thereby altered, gross thoughts demanding for their medium gross *astral* matter, pure thoughts demanding fine *astral* matter. During physical life the various kinds of matter in the *astral body* are intermingled, but at physical death the elementary life in the matter of the *astral* body seeks instinctively after self-preservation, and it therefore causes the matter to rearrange itself in a series of seven concentric sheaths, the densest being outside and the finest inside. Physical vision depends on the eyes, but *astral* vision depends on the various kinds of *astral* matter being in a condition of receptiveness to different undulations. To be aware of fine matter, fine matter in the *astral body* is necessary, and so with the other kinds. Hence, when the rearrangement takes place, vision only of the grossest kinds of matter is possible since only that kind is represented in the thick outer sheath of the *astral body*. Under these circumstances, the new denizen of the *astral* sphere sees only the worst of it, and also only the worst of his fellow denizens, even though they are not in so low a state as himself. This state is not, of course eternal, and in accordance with the evolutionary process, the gross sheath of *astral* matter wears slowly away, and the man remains clothed with the six less gross sheaths. These also, with the passage of time, wear away, being resolved into their compound elements, and at last when the final disintegration of the least gross sheath of all takes place, the individual leaves the Astral World and passes into the Mental. This rearrangement of the *astral body* is not, however, inevitable, and those who have learned and know, are able at physical death to prevent it. In such cases the change appears a very small one, and the so-called dead continue to live their lives and do their work much as they did in the physical body. (*See* **Astral World, Avichi Theosophy.**)

Astral World. (**Plane or Sphere**) : Kama World is, in Theosophy, the second lowest of the seven worlds, the world of emotions, desires, and passions. Into it man passes at physical death, and there he functions for periods which vary with the state of his development, the primitive savage spending a relatively short time in the *Astral World*, the civilised man spending relatively longer. The appropriate body is the *astral* (q.v.), which though composed of matter as is the physical body, is nevertheless of a texture vastly finer than the latter. Though it is in its aspect of the after-death abode that this world is of most importance and most interest, it may be said in passing, that even during physical life, man—not only clairvoyants who attain it easily, but also ordinary men—may and do temporarily inhabit it. This happens during sleep, or by reason of the action of anæsthetics or drugs, or accidents, and the interpenetrating astral body then leaves its denser physical neighbour, and taking with it the sense of pleasure and pain, lives for a short time in its own world. Here again the state of the savage differs from that of his more advanced fellows, for the former does not travel far from his immediate surroundings, while the latter may perform useful, helpful work for the benefit of humanity. Further, it may in passing be noted that disembodied mankind are not the only inhabitants of the *Astral World*, for very many of its inhabitants are of an altogether non-human nature— lower orders of the *devas* or angels, and nature-spirits or elementals, both good and bad, such including fairies which are just beyond the powers of human vision, and the demons present to the vision of delirium tremens. It will however be sufficient now to turn attention to the *Astral World* as the state immediately following physical death and containing both heaven and hell as these are popularly conceived.

There are seven divisions which correspond to the seven divisions of matter, the solid, liquid, gaseous, etheric, super-etheric, subatomic and atomic, and, as mentioned in the article on the Astral Body, this plays a most important part in the immediate destiny of man in it. If through ignorance, he has permitted the rearrangement of the matter of his astral body into sheaths, he is cognisant only of part of his surroundings at a time, and it is not till after experience, much of which may be extremely painful, that he is able to enjoy the bliss which the higher divisions of the *Astral World* contain. The lowest of these divisions, the seventh, is the environment of those of gross and unrestrained passions, since it and most of the matter of their astral bodies is of the same type, and it constitutes a very hell, and the only hell which exists. This is *Avichi*, the place of desires which cannot be satisfied because of the absence of the physical body, which was the means of their satisfaction. The tortures of these desires are the analogue of the torments of hell-fire in the older Christian orthodoxy. Unlike that orthodoxy, however, theosophy teaches that the state of torment is not eternal, but passes away in time when the desires through long gnawing without fulfilment, have died at last, and it is therefore more correct to look on *Avichi* as a purgatorial state. The ordinary man, however, does not experience this seventh division of the *Astral World*, but according to his character finds himself in one or other of the three next higher divisions. The sixth division is very little different from his physical existence, and he continues in his old surroundings among his old friends, who are, of course, unaware of his presence, and indeed, often does not realise that he is dead so far as the physical world is concerned. The fifth and fourth divisions are in most respects quite similar to this, but their inhabitants become less and less immersed in the activities and interests which have hitherto engrossed them, and each sheath of their astral bodies decays in turn as did the gross outer sheath of the sensualist's body. The three higher divisions are still more removed from the ordinary material world, and their inhabitants enjoy a state of bliss of which we can have no conception ; worries and cares of earth are altogether absent, the insistence of lower desires has worn out in the lower divisions, and it is now possible to live continually in an environment of the loftiest thoughts and aspirations. The third division is said to correspond to the spiritualistic " summerland," where the inhabitants live in a world of their own creation—of the creation of their thoughts.

Its cities and all their contents, scenery of life, are all formed by the influence of thought. The second division is what is properly looked on as heaven, and the inhabitants of different races, creeds, and beliefs, find it each according to his belief. Hence, instead of its being the place taught of by any particular religion, it is the region where each and every religion finds its own ideal. Christians, Mohammedans, Hindus, and so on, find it to be just as they conceived it would be. Here, and in the first and highest division, the inhabitants pursue noble aims freed from what of selfishness was mingled with these aims on earth. The literary man, his thoughts of fame ; the artist, the scholar, the preacher, all work without incentive of personal interest, and where their work is pursued long enough, and they are fitted for the change, they leave the *Astral World* and enter one vastly higher—the Mental. It was, however, mentioned that the rearrangement of the matter of the astral body at physical death, was the result of ignorance, and those who are sufficiently instructed do not permit this rearrangement to take. They are not, therefore, confined to any one division, and have not to progress from division to division, but are able to move through any part of the *Astral World*, labouring always in their various lines of action to assist the great evolutionary scheme. (*See* **Astral Body, Worlds, Planes or Spheres, Theosophy, Avichi, Summerland.**)

Astrology : The art of divining the fate or future of persons from the juxtaposition of the sun, moon and planets. *Judicial astrology* foretells the destinies of individuals and nations, while *natural astrology* predicts changes of weather and the operation of the stars upon natural things.

History.—In Egyptian tradition, we find its invention attributed to Hermes Trismegistus, or Thoth, by whom, under different names, is represented the various revelations of truth, both theological and natural ; for he is the Mercury of the Romans, the eloquent deliverer of the messages of the gods. The name of Ptolemy, the greatest of which *astrology* can boast, belongs also to Egypt, but to the comparatively recent period when Imperial Rome flourished. In Imperial Rome *astrology* was held in great repute, especially under the reign of Tiberius, who himself obtained that knowledge of the science from Thrasyllus, which enabled him to foretell the destiny of Galba, then consul. When Claudius was dying from the effects of Locusta s poison, Agrippina cautiously dissembled his progressive illness ; nor would she announce his decease till the very moment arrived, which the astrologers had pronounced fortunate for the accession of Nero. Augustus had discouraged the practice of *astrology* by banishing its professors from Rome, but the favour of his successors recalled them, and though occasional edicts, in subsequent reigns, restrained, and even punished all who divined by the stars ; and though Vitellius and Domitian revived the edict of Augustus, the practices of the astrologers were secretly encouraged, and their predictions extensively believed. Domitian himself, in spite of his hostility, was in fear of their denouncements. They prophesied the year, the hour, and the manner of his death, and agreed with his father in foretelling that he should perish not by poison, but by the dagger.

After the age of the Antonines and the work of Censorinus, we hear little of *astrology* for some generations. In the eighth century the venerable Bede and his distinguished scholar, Alcuin, are said to have pursued this mystic study. In that immediately following, the Arabians revived and encouraged it. Under the patronage of Almaimon, the Mirammolin, in the year 827, the *Megale Syntaxis* of Ptolemy was translated under the title of " Almagest," by Al. Hazen Ben Yusseph. Albumasar added to this work, and the astral science continued to receive new force from the labours of Alfraganus, Ebennozophim, Alfaragius, and Geber.

The conquest of Spain by the Moors carried this knowledge, with all their other treasures of learning into Spain, and before their cruel expulsion it was naturalized among the Christian savants. Among these the wise Alonzo (or Alphonso) of Castile, has immortalized himself by his scientific researches, and the Jewish and Christian doctors, who arranged the tables which pass under his name, were convened from all the accessible parts of civilized Europe. Five years were employed in their discussion, and it has been said that the enormous sum of 400,000 ducats was disbursed in the towers of the Alcazar of Galiana, in the adjustment and correction of Ptolemy's calculations. Nor was it only the physical motions of the stars which occupied this grave assembly. The two kabalistic volumes, yet existing in cipher, in the royal library of the kings of Spain, and which tradition assigns to the hand of Alonzo himself, betoken a more visionary study. and in spite of the denunciations against his orthodoxy, which were thundered in his ears on the authority of Tertullian, Basil and Bonaventure, the fearless monarch gave his sanction to such masters as practised truly the art of divination by the stars, and in one part of his code enrolled astrology among the seven liberal sciences.

In Germany many eminent men have been addicted to this study; and a long catalogue might be made of those who have considered other sciences with reference to astrology, and written on them as such. Faust has, of course, the credit of being an astrologer as well as a wizard, and we find that singular but splendid genius, Cornelius Agrippa, writing with as much zeal against astrology as on behalf of other occult sciences.

To the believers in astrology, who flourished in the sixteenth and seventeenth centuries, must be added the name of Albert von Wallenstein, Duke of Friedland. He was indeed an enthusiast in the cause, and many curious anecdotes are related of this devotion. That he had himself studied astrology, and under no mean instructors, is evidenced by his biography and correspondence.

Of the early progress of astrology in England, little is known. Bede and Alcuin we have already mentioned as addicted to its study. Roger Bacon could scarcely escape the contagion of the art. But it was the period of the Stuarts which must be considered as the acme of astrology among us. Then Lilly employed the doctrine of the magical circle, and the evocation of spirits from the Ars Notoria of Cornelius Agrippa, and used the form of prayer prescribed therein to the angel Salmonœus, and entertained among his familiar acquaintance the guardian spirits of England, Salmael and Malchidael. His ill success with the divining rod induced him to surrender the pursuit of rhabdomancy, in which he first engaged, though he still perserved in asserting that the operation demanded secrecy and intelligence in the agents, and, above all, a strong faith, and a competent knowledge of their work. The Dean of Westminster had given him permission to search for treasure in the cloisters of the abbey in the dead of the night. On the western side, the rods turned over each other with inconceivable rapidity, yet, on digging, nothing but a coffin could be discovered. He retired to the abbey, and then a storm arose which nearly destroyed the west end of the church, extinguished all the candles but one, and made the rods immovable. Lilly succeeded at length in charming away the demon, but no persuasion could induce him to make another experiment in that species of divination.

The successor of Lilly was Henry Coley, a tailor, who had been his amanuensis, and traded in prophecy with success almost equal to that of his master.

While astrology flourished in England it was in high repute with its kindred pursuits of magic, necromancy, and alchemy, at the court of France. Catherine de Medici herself was an adept in the art. At the revolution, which commenced a new era in this country, astrology declined, and notwithstanding the labours of Partridge, and those of Ebenezer Sibley, it has only in recent years recovered its importance.

Signs.—There are twelve signs of the Zodiac, divided in astrology into "Northern and "Commanding" (the first six), and "Southern' and "Obeying" (last six). They are as follow :—

Aries, the house of Mars, and exaltation of the sun, or the first sign of the zodiac, is a vernal, dry, fiery, masculine, cardinal, equinoctial, diurnal, movable, commanding, eastern, choleric, violent, and quadrupedian sign. These epithets will be presently explained. The native, that is, the person born under its influence, is tall of stature, of a strong but spare make, dry constitution, long face and neck, thick shoulders, piercing eyes, sandy or red hair, and brown complexion. In disposition he will be warm, hasty and passionate. The aspects of the planets may, however, materially alter these effects. This sign rules the head and face. Among diseases, it produces small-pox, and epilepsy, apoplexy, headache, hypochondriasis, baldness, ringworm, and all diseases of the head and face, paralysis, fevers, measles, and convulsions. It presides over the following countries: England, France, Germany, Syria, Switzerland, Poland and Denmark ; and over the cities of Naples, Capua, Padua, Florence, Verona, Ferrara, Brunswick, Marseilles, Cæsarea, and Utrecht. Its colours are red and white.

Now to explain this terminology, before examining another sign, there are said to be four triplicities among the signs, viz. : the earthly triplicity, including Taurus, Virgo, and Capricorn ; the airy, which includes Gemini, Libra and Aquarius ; the fiery, under which are reckoned Aries, Leo, and Sagittarius ; and the watery, which claims Cancer, Scorpio and Pisces. The signs are further divided into diurnal and nocturnal: Aries diurnal, Taurus nocturnal, and so on alternately, the diurnal signs being all masculine, and the nocturnals feminine. The terms tropical, equinoctial, vernal, etc., need no comment. Fixed, common, movable, refer to the weather. Signs which are named after quadrupeds are, of course, quadrupedal. Such as are called after human states of occupations as humane. A person born under a fiery masculine diurnal sign, is hot in temper, and bold in character. If it be a quadrupedal sign, he is somewhat like to the animal after which the sign is called. Thus in Taurus, the native is bold and furious ; in Leo, fierce and cruel. Cardinal signs are those occupying the four cardinal points. The first six from Aries are termed commanding, and the latter six, obeying signs. Cancer, Scorpio and Pisces are called fruitful or prolific ; and Gemini, Leo, and Virgo, barren. Sagittarius, because usually represented as a centaur, is said to be humane, and productive of humane character in the former fifteen degrees, but of a savage, brutal and intractable disposition in the latter.

We shall now proceed with the signs. Taurus is cold and dry, earthly, melancholy, feminine, fixed and nocturnal, southern, the night-house of Venus. When influential in a nativity, it usually produces a person with a broad forehead, thick lips, dark curling hair, of quality rather brutal, melancholy, and slow in anger, but when once enraged, violent, furious, and difficult to be appeased. The diseases under this sign are all such as attack the throat, scrofula, quinsey, imposthumes and wens. The sign rules the neck and throat. Places subject to it are stables, cowhouses, cellars and low rooms, and all places used for or by cattle. Of kingdoms, Russia, Ireland, Sweden, Persia and Parthia, and of cities, Leipsic, Parma, Mantua, Novogorod, and eleven others.

Gemini is masculine and diurnal, aerial, hot and moist. The native is tall, and straight of body, with long arms; the hands and feet well formed, the complexion rather dark, the hair brown, the eye hazel; strong and active in person, sound and acute in judgment; lively, playful, and generally skilful in business. Diseases under this sign are those to which the arms, hands and shoulders are subject, with aneurisms, frenzy and insanity. Places: hilly and high grounds, the tops of houses, wainscoted rooms, halls and theatres, barns, storehouses and stairs; kingdoms, Armenia, Brabant, Lombardy, Sardinia and Egypt; cities: London, Bruges, Cordova, Metz and seven others. It is the day-house of Mercury, and rules the colours red and white.

Cancer is the only house of the moon, and the first sign of the watery northern triplicity. It is a watery, cold, moist, phlegmatic, feminine, movable nocturnal, solstitial, and exceedingly fruitful sign, more so than any other. The native is fair and pale, short and small; the upper part of the body larger in proportion to the lower; a round face, light hair, and blue or grey eyes; phlegmatic, and heavy in disposition; weak in constitution, and of a small voice. Diseases: All disorders of the breast and stomach over which parts the sign rules; cancers, consumption, asthma, dropsy and surfeits. Kingdoms: Scotland, Holland, Zealand, Burgundy, Numidia and Carthage; places: the sea and all rivers, swamps, ponds, lakes, wells, ditches, and watery places. Cities: Constantinople, Tunis, York and New York, Genoa, Venice, Algiers, Amsterdam, Cadiz, and sixteen others. The colours ruled by this sign are green and russet.

Leo is a sign of a very different nature. It is the only house of the sun; fiery, hot, dry, masculine, choleric, commanding, eastern, and a very barren sign. When this sign ascends in a nativity, the individual will be of a tall and powerful frame, well-shaped, of an austere countenance, of light, yellowish hair, large piercing eyes, commanding aspect, and ruddy complexion. The character will be fierce and cruel, but yet open, generous and courteous. Such was Richard Cœur-de-Lion. But the latter part of the sign is weaker and more brutal. This sign is even more modified by planetary influences than any others. Among diseases it causes all affections of the heart, over which together with the back and the vertebræ of the neck, it rules; fevers, plague, jaundice and pleurisy. Of places, it governs woods, forests, deserts and hunting-grounds, fireplaces and furnaces; of kingdoms: Italy, Chaldæa, Turkey and Bohemia; of cities: Bath, Bristol, Taunton, Rome, Damascus, Prague, Philadelphia, and nineteen others. Its colours are red and green.

Virgo is an earthy, cold, dry, barren, feminine, southern, melancholy, commanding sign. It is the house and exaltation of Mercury. The native is handsome and well-shaped, slender, of middle stature, and of a clear, ruddy or brown complexion, dark hair and eyes, the face rather round, and the voice sweet and clear, but not strong; the character amiable and benevolent, witty and studious, but not persevering; and if not opposed by planetary aspects, apt to oratory. This sign rules the viscera, and is answerable for all diseases affecting them. Of places: cornfields and granaries, studies and libraries; of kingdoms: Greece, Crete, Mesopotamia and Assyria; of cities: Jerusalem, Paris, Corinth, and twelve others. Its colours are blue and black.

Libra is a sign aerial, sanguine, hot, moist, equinoctial cardinal, movable, masculine, western and diurnal, humane, and the day-house of Venus. The native is tall and well-made, very handsome, of a fine ruddy complexion in youth, but which changes to a deep red with advancing years. The hair long and flaxen, the eyes grey, the disposition courteous, and the character just and upright. Of kingdoms it governs Ethiopia, Austria, Portugal, and Savoy; and of cities, Antwerp, Frankfort, Vienna, Charlestown in America, and twenty-seven others. The colours which it rules are crimson and tawny; and of places, mountains, saw-pits and woods newly felled.

Scorpio, the night-house of Mars, is a cold, phlegmatic, feminine, nocturnal, fixed, northern, and watery sign. The native is of a strong, robust, corpulent body, of a middle stature, broad visage, dark but not clear complexion, dark grey eyes or light brown, black hair or very dark brown, short, thick legs and thick neck. Of places it governs swampy grounds and stagnant waters, places which abound in venomous creatures, orchards and ruinous houses, especially near water. Of kingdoms: Fez, Bavaria, Norway and Mauritania; of cities: Messina, and others; of colours: brown.

Sagittarius is a fiery, hot, dry, masculine, diurnal, eastern, common, bicorporeal, obeying sign, the day-house and joy of Jupiter. The native is well-formed and rather above the middle stature, with fine chestnut hair, but inclined to baldness, a visage somewhat long but ruddy and handsome; the body strong, stout and hardy. He is inclined to horsemanship and field-sports, careless of danger, generous and intrepid, but hasty and careless. This sign rules the hips, and is the cause of gout, rheumatism and disorders which affect the muscles. Accidents and disorders occasioned by intemperance come under the government of this sign. Of kingdoms: Spain, Hungary, Sclavonia and Arabia; of places: stables and parks; and of colours, green and red.

Capricornus is an earthy, cold, dry, feminine, nocturnal, movable, cardinal, solstitian, domestic, southern, quadrupedal sign; the house of Saturn, and the exaltation. The native is of slender stature, long thin countenance, small beard, dark hair and eyes, long neck, narrow chest and chin, tall usually, though not always; in disposition, cheerful and collected; talented and upright. Ruling the knees and hips, it governs all diseases which afflict them, and also all cutaneous diseases, such as leprosy, etc., and melancholy diseases such as hypochondriasis and hysteria. The kingdoms which it rules are India, Thrace, Mexico and Saxony; and the cities, Oxford, Bradenburg and nineteen others. The places over which it has power are workshops and fallow grounds, and its colours, black and brown.

Aquarius is an airy, hot, moist, rational, fixed, humane, diurnal, sanguine, masculine, western, obeying sign, the day-house of Saturn. The native is a well-made and robust person, rather above the middle stature, long face, but of a pleasing and delicate countenance, clear, bright complexion, with flaxen hair, often sandy; of a disposition fair open and honest. As this sign rules the legs and ankles, it causes all diseases which affect them: lameness, white swelling, cramp, and gout. Of places it denotes mines and quarries, aeroplane machines, roofs of houses, wells, and conduits. Of kingdoms: Tartary, Denmark and Westphalia; and of cities: Hamburg, Bremen, and fifteen more. Its colours are grey and sky-blue.

Lastly, Pisces is a watery, cold, moist, feminine, phlegmatic, nocturnal, common, bicorporeal, northern, idle, effeminate, sickly, and extremely fruitful sign, only less so than Cancer; the house of Jupiter, and the exaltation of Venus. The native is short and ill-shaped, fleshy, if not corpulent, with thick, round shoulders, light hair and eyes, the complexion pale, and the head and face large; of a weak and vacillating disposition, well-meaning, but devoid of energy. This sign rules the feet, and causes lameness and every kind of disorder occasioned by watery humours. Of places : all such as are under Cancer, save the sea and rivers ; of kingdoms : Lydia, Calabria, Pamphylia and Normandy ; of cities : Compostella, Alexandria, Rheims. Ratisbon, and eleven others ; and of colours, it rules white.

Planets. The influence and effects of the planets are still more important than those of the signs, and they are as follow : We commence with the most remote of the planets, Uranus. The days and hours are, as we have seen divided among the planets, but as none were left vacant, the appropriation of any to Uranus would, of course, throw out almost all the ancient calculations. If these then are to be preserved, the newly-discovered planet has no influence ; but if this be the case, by what analogy can any be assigned to the others ? However, when this question was likely to be debated, Uranus was rolling on in its far-off orbit, and occasioning no uneasiness whatever to astrologers or magicians. Leaving out all mention of the astronomical elements, we proceed to notice that Uranus is by nature extremely cold and dry, melancholy, and one of the infortunes. The native is of small stature, dark or pale complexion, rather light hair, of a highly nervous temperament, sedate aspect, but having something singular in his appearance ; light grey eyes, and delicate constitution. If the planet be well dignified, he is a searcher into science, particularly chemistry, and remarkably attached to the wonderful. He possesses an extraordinary magnanimity and loftiness of mind, with an uncontrollable and intense desire for pursuits and discoveries of an uncommon nature. If ill-dignified, then the native is weak, sickly, and short-lived, treacherous, and given to gross imposture, unfortunate in his undertakings, capricious in his tastes, and very eccentric in his conduct. No planet, save Saturn, is so actively and powerfully malevolent as this. His effects are truly malefic. They are, however of a totally unexpected, strange and unaccountable character. He rules over places dedicated to unlawful arts, laboratories, etc. The regions under his immediate governance are Lapland, Finland, and the Poles. Professions : necromancers and Gœtic magicians ; cities : Upsala and Mexico. The name of his angel has not been found out, but he is known to be very hostile to the female sex, and when his aspects interfere in the period of marriage, the result is anything but happiness.

Saturn is by nature cold and dry ; is a melancholy, earthy, masculine, solitary, diurnal, malevolent planet, and the great infortune. When he is lord of the ascendant, the native is of a middle stature, the complexion dark and swarthy, or pale ; small black eyes, broad shoulders, black hair, and ill-shaped about the lower extremities. When well dignified, the native is grave and wise, studious and severe, of an active and penetrating mind, reserved and patient, constant in attachment, but implacable in resentment, upright and inflexible ; but if the planet be ill-dignified at the time of birth, then the native will be sluggish, covetous, and distrustful ; false, stubborn, malicious, and ever discontented. This planet is said to be well dignified in the horoscope of the Duke of Wellington, and to have been ill-dignified, but singularly posited in that of Louis XI. of France. The diseases he signifies are quartan agues, and such as proceed from cold and melancholy ; all impediments in the sight, ear, and teeth ; rheumatism, consumption, disorders affecting the memory, the spleen, and the bones. Saturn, in general, signifies husbandmen, day-labourers, monks, Jesuits, sectarians, sextons, and such as have to do with the dead ; gardeners, dyers of black, and thirty-three other professions, which Lilly enumerates. He mentions also forty-eight plants,

including all anodynes and narcotic poisons, which are under the rule of this planet. Among animals, the cat, the ass, hare, mole, mouse, wolf, bear, and crocodile ; all venomous creatures. Among fishes, the eel, tortoise and shell-fish ; among the birds, the bat, and the owl ; among metals and minerals, lead, the loadstone, and all dross of metals ; over the sapphire, lapis lazuli, and all stones that are not polishable, and of a leaden or ashy colour.

" He causeth the air to be dark and cloudy, cold and hurtful, with thick and dense vapours. He delighteth in the eastern quarter, causing eastern winds ; and in gathering any plant belonging to him the ancients did observe to turn their faces to the east in his hour. Those under him do rarely live beyond fifty-seven years ; and if he be well placed, seldom less than thirty. But his nature is cold and dry, and these qualities are destructive to man. Black is the colour which he ruleth. Of countries under his influence are Bavaria, Saxony, and Styria ; Ravenna, Constance and Ingoldstadt among cities. His friends are Jupiter, Mars and Mercury ; his enemies, the Sun and Venus. We call Saturday his day, for then he begins to rule at sunrise, and rules the first hour and the eighth of that day. His angel is Cassel."

The next planet is Jupiter. He is a diurnal, masculine planet, temperately hot and moist, airy, and sanguine ; the greater fortune and lord of the airy triplicity. The native, if the planet be well dignified, will be of an erect carriage and tall stature ; a handsome ruddy complexion, high forehead, soft, thick brown hair ; a handsome shape and commanding aspect ; his voice will be strong, clear and manly, and his speech grave and sober. If the planet be ill dignified, still the native will be what is called a good-looking person, though of smaller stature, and less noble aspect. In the former case, the understanding and character will be of the highest possible description ; and in the latter case, though careless and improvident, immoral and irreligious, he will never entirely lose the good opinion of his friends. Yet he will be, as Sancho Panza expresses it : " Haughty to the humble, and humble to the haughty." The diseases it rules are apoplexy and inflammation of the lungs ; disorders affecting the left ear, cramps, and palpitations of the heart. Plants : the oak, spice, apples, and one hundred and seventy-two others ; gems : topaz, amethyst, hyacinth and bezoar ; minerals : tin, pewter and firestone ; animals : the ox, horse, elephant, stag, and all domestic animals ; weather : pleasant, healthful, and serene west-north and north-west winds ; birds : the eagle, peacock, pheasant, etc. Of fishes, he rules the whale and the dolphin ; of colours : blue, when well posited ; of professions : the clergy, the higher order of law students, and those who deal in woollen goods ; when weak, the dependents on the above, with quacks, common cheats, and drunkards. Places : all churches, palaces, courts, and places of pomp and solemnity. He rules the lungs and blood, and is friendly with all the planets, save Mars. Countries : Spain, Hungary and Babylon ; his angel is Zadkiel.

The next planet is Mars ; a masculine, nocturnal, hot, and dry planet ; of the fiery triplicity ; the author of strife, and the lesser infortune. The native is short, but strongly made, having large bones, ruddy complexion, red or sandy hair and eyebrows, quick, sharp eyes, round, bold face, and fearless aspect. If well dignified, courageous and invincible, unsusceptible of fear, careless of life, resolute and unsubmissive. If ill dignified, a trumpeter of his own fame, without decency or honesty ; fond of quarrels, prone to fightings, and given up to every species of fraud, violence and oppression. Nero was an example of this planet's influence, and the gallows is said to terminate most generally the career of those born in low life under its government. This plant rules the head, face, gall, left ear, and the smell. Disease: plague, fevers, and all complaints arising from excessive heat; all wounds by iron or steel, injuries by poison, and all evil effects from intemperate anger. Herbs and plants: mustard, radish, with all pungent and thorny plants; gems . the bloodstone, jasper, ruby and garnet; of minerals . iron, arsenic, antimony, sulphur and vermilion; animals . the mastiff wolf, tiger and all savage beasts; birds . the hawk, kite, raven, vulture, and generally birds of prey; weather: thunder and lightning, fiery meteors, and all strange phenomena; kingdoms: Lombardy and Bavaria; cities: Jerusalem and Rome. He signifies soldiers, surgeons, barbers and butchers. Places: smiths' shops, slaughterhouses, fields of battle, and brick-kilns. His friends are all the planets, save the Moon and Jupiter. His colour is red, and his angel is Samael.

We now come to the Sun, a masculine, hot, and dry planet, of favourable effects. The native is very like one born under Jupiter, but the hair is lighter, the complexion redder, the body fatter, and the eyes larger. When well dignified, the solar man is affable, courteous, splendid and sumptuous, proud, liberal, humane, and ambitious. When ill dignified, the native is arrogant, mean, loquacious, and sycophantic; much resembling the native under Jupiter, ill dignified, but still worse. Diseases: all those of the heart, mouth and throat; epilepsy, scrofula, tympanitis, and brain-fevers. Herbs and plants: laurel, vervain, St. John's wort, orange, hyacinth, and some hundreds beside; gems: carbuncle, the diamond, the ætites; minerals: gold; animals: the lion, the boar, the horse; birds: the lark, the swan, the nightingale, and all singing birds; fish: the star-fish and all shell-fish; countries: Italy, Bohemia, Chaldæa and Sicily; of cities: Rome; colour yellow; weather, that which is most seasonable; professions: kings, lords and all dignified persons, braziers, goldsmiths, and persons employed in mints; places: kings' courts, palaces, theatres, halls, and places of state. His friends are all the planets, save Saturn; and his angel is Michael.

The influence of the asteroids, Juno, Pallas, Ceres, and Vesta, have never been calculated, and they are said by modern astrologers to act beneficially, but feebly.

The Moon is a far more important planet; feminine, nocturnal, cold, moist, and phlegmatic. Her influence in itself is neither fortunate nor unfortunate. She is benevolent or otherwise, according to the aspects of other planets towards her; and under these circumstances she becomes more powerful than any of them. The native is short and stout, with fair, pale complexion, round face, grey eyes, short arms, thick hands and feet, very hairy, but with light hair; phlegmatic. If the Moon be affected by the Sun at the time of birth, the native will have a blemish on or near the eye. When the Moon is well dignified the native is of soft, engaging manners, imaginative, and a lover of the arts, but wandering, careless, timorous, and unstable, loving peace, and averse from activity. When ill dignified, then the native will be of an ill shape, indolent, worthless and disorderly. Diseases: palsy, epilepsy, scrofula and lunacy, together with all diseases of the eyes; herbs: lily, poppies, mushrooms, willow, and about two hundred others; minerals and gems: pearls, selenite, silver and soft stones; colour: white; animals: the dog, the cat, the otter, the mouse, and all amphibious creatures; birds: the goose, duck, bat and waterfowl in general; fish: the eel, the crab, and the lobster; weather: she increases the effect of other planets; countries: Denmark, Holland, Flanders, and North America; cities: Amsterdam, Venice, Bergen-op-Zoon, and Lubeck; places: fountains, baths, the sea, and in watery places; professions: queens and dignified women midwives, nurses, all who have to do with water, sailors. Her angel is Gabriel.

Venus is a feminine planet, temperately cold and moist, the author of mirth and sport. The native is handsome, well-formed, but not tall; clear complexion, bright hazel or black eyes, dark brown or chestnut hair, thick, soft, and shining; the voice soft and sweet, and the aspect very prepossessing. If well dignified, the native will be cheerful, friendly, musical, and fond of elegant accomplishments; prone to love, but frequently jealous. If ill dignified, the native is less handsome in person and in mind, altogether vicious, given up to every licentiousness; dishonest and atheistical. Herbs and plants: the fig-tree, myrrh, myrtle, pomegranate, and about two hundred and twenty more; animals: the goat, panther, hart, etc.; birds: the sparrow, the dove, the thrush, and the wren; gems: the emerald, chrysolite, beryl, chrysoprasus; countries: Spain, India and Persia; cities: Florence, Paris and Vienna; mineral: copper; colour: green; occupations: all such as minister to pomp and pleasure; weather: warm, and accompanied with showers. Her angel is Hanael.

Mercury is the last of the planets which we nave to consider. He is masculine, melancholy, cold, and dry. The native is tall, straight, and thin, with a narrow face and high forehead, long straight nose, eyes black or grey, thin lips and chin, scanty beard, with brown hair; the arms, hands and fingers, long and slender; this last is said to be a peculiar mark of a nativity under Mercury. If the planet be oriental at the time of birth, the native will be very likely to be of a stronger constitution, and with sandy hair. If occidental, sallow, lank, slender, and of a dry habit. When well dignified, he will be of an acute and penetrating mind, of a powerful imagination, and a retentive memory; eloquent, fond of learning, and successful in scientific investigation. If engaged in mercantile pursuits, enterprising and skilful. If ill dignified, then the native is a mean, unprincipled character, pretending to knowledge, but an imposter, and a slanderer, boastful, malicious, and addicted to theft. Diseases: all that affect the brain, head, and intellectual faculties; herbs and plants: the walnut, the valerian, the trefoil, and about one hundred more; animals: the dog, the ape, the weasel, and the fox; weather: rain, hailstones, thunder and lightning, particularly in the north; occupations: all literate and learned professions; when ill dignified, all pretenders, quacks, and mountebanks. Places: schools, colleges, markets, warehouses, exchanges, all places of commerce and learning; metal, quicksilver; gems: cornelian, sardonyx, opal, onyx, and chalcedony; his colour is purple. His friends are Jupiter, Venus, and Saturn; his enemies Mars, the Sun, and the Moon. His angel is Raphael.

The *Aspects* of the Planets are five, thus distinguished: 1. Conjunction, when two planets are in the same degree and minute of a sign, which may be of good or evil import, according to the nature of the planets, and their relation to each other as friendly or the contrary. 2. Sectile, when two planets are 60° distant from each other, it is called the aspect of imperfect love or friendship, and is generally a favourable omen. 3. Quartile, when two planets are 90° distant from each other, making the aspect of imperfect hatred, and inclining to enmity and misfortune. 4. Trine, when the distance is 120°, promising the most perfect unanimity and peace. 5. Opposition, when two planets are 180° apart, or exactly opposite each other, which is considered an aspect of perfect hatred, and implies every kind of misfortune.

The Planets are said to be in their *joys* when situated in the houses where they are most strong and powerful, thus:

Saturn in Aquarius, Jupiter in Sagittarius, Mars in Scorpio, the Sun in Leo, Venus in Taurus, Mercury in Virgo, and the Moon in Cancer. Cogent reasons are given why the planets should joy in these houses rather than others.

The *Dragon's Head* and *Dragon's Tail* are the points, called nodes, in which the ecliptic is intersected by the orbits of the planets, particularly by that of the moon. These points are, of course, shifting. The *Dragon's Head* is the point where the moon or other planet commences its northward latitude ; it is considered masculine and benevolent in its influence. The *Dragon's Tail* is the point where the planets' southward progress begins ; it is feminine and malevolent.

The *Part of Fortune* is the distance of the moon's place from the sun, added to the degrees of the ascendent.

The Twelve Planetary *Houses* are determined by drawing certain great circles through the intersection of the horizon and meridian, by which the whole globe or sphere is apportioned into twelve equal parts. In practice these lines are projected by a very simple method on a plane. The space in the centre of the figure thus described may be supposed to represent the situation of the earth, and is generally used to write down the exact time when the figure was erected, and for whose nativity, or for what question. Each division or house rules certain events in this order, reckoned from the east : 1, life or person ; 2, riches ; 3, brethren or kindred ; 4, parents ; 5, children ; 6, servants and sickness ; 7, marriage ; 8, death ; 9, religion ; 10, magistracy ; 11, friends ; 12, enemies. These categories are made to comprehend all that can possibly befall any individual, and the prognostication is drawn from the configuration of the planets in one or more of these " houses."

The *Horoscope* denotes the configuration of the planets in the twelve houses ascertained for the moment of nativity, or the hour of the question. The Ascendent (a term sometimes used instead of horoscope) is the planet rising in the east or first house, which marks the general character of the child then born. Hyleg is another term for the lord of life ; Anareta for the destroyer of life, which are considered the chief places in a horoscope.

The *Characters* used in *astrology*, to denote the twelve signs, the planets, etc., are as follows :

Signs of the Zodiac.

| Aries. | Taurus | Gemini | Cancer |
| the ram. | the bull. | the twins. | the crab. |

| Leo | Virgo | Libra | Scorpio |
| the lion. | the Virgin. | the balance. | the scorpion. |

| Sagittarius | Capricornus | Aquarius | Pisces |
| the archer. | the goat. | the water carrier. | the fishes |

Planetary Signs.

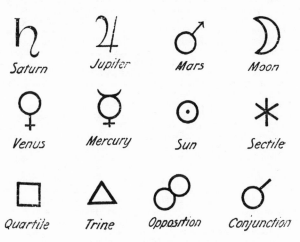

| Saturn | Jupiter | Mars | Moon |

| Venus | Mercury | Sun | Sectile |

| Quartile | Trine | Opposition | Conjunction |

These characters represent natural objects, but they have also a hieroglyphic or esoteric meaning that has been lost. The figure of Aries represents the head and horns of a ram ; that of Taurus, the head and horns of a bull ; that of Leo, the head and mane of a lion ; that of Gemini, two persons standing together, and so of the rest. The physical or astronomical reasons for the adoption of these figures have been explained with great learning by the Abbé Pluche, in his *Histoire du Ciel*, and Dupuis, in his *Abrégé de l'Origine de tous les Cultes*, has endeavoured to establish the principles of an astro-mythology, by tracing the progress of the moon through the twelve signs, in a series of adventures, which he compares with the wanderings of Isis. This kind of reasoning is suggestive, certainly, but it only establishes analogies, and proves nothing.

Nativities.—The cases in which astrological predictions were chiefly sought, were in Nativities ; that is in ascertaining the fate and fortunes of any individual from the positions of the stars at the time of his birth ; and in questions called *horary*, which comprehended almost every matter which might be the subject of astrological inquiry. The event of sickness, the success of any undertaking, the reception of any suit, were all objects of horary questions. A person was said to be born under that planet which ruled the hour of his birth. Thus two hours every day are under the control of Saturn. The first hour after sunrise on Saturday is one of them. A person therefore born on Saturday in the first hour after sunrise, has Saturn for the lord of his ascendant ; those born in the next hour, Jupiter ; and so on in order. Venus rules the first hour on Friday ; Mercury on Wednesday Jupiter on Thursday, the sun and moon on Sunday and Monday, and Mars on Tuesday. The next thing is to make a figure divided into twelve portions, which are called houses, as directed above. The twelve houses are equal to the twelve signs, and the planets, being always in the zodiac, will therefore all fall within these twelve divisions or houses. The line, which separates any house from the preceding, is called the cusp of the house. The first house is called the ascendant, and the east angle ; the fourth the imum cœli, or the north angle ; the seventh, the west angle ; and the tenth, the medium cœli, or the south angle. Having drawn this figure, tables and directions are given for the placing of the signs, and as one house is equal to one sign when one is given, the rest are given also. When the signs and planets are all placed in the houses, the next thing is to augur, from their relative position, what influence they will have on the life and fortunes of the native.

The House of Life implies all that affects, promotes, or endangers life. Saturn or Mars in this house denotes a short or unfortunate life, while Jupiter and Venus have, when free from evil aspects, an exactly contrary effect. The sign ascending will considerably modify the person and character of the native, so that to form an astrological judgment of this it will be necessary to combine the indications of the sign and the planet. In what are called horary questions, this house relates to all questions of life, health, and appearance, such as stature, complexion, shape, accidents and sickness. It shows the events of journeys and voyages, with respect to the life and health of those engaged in them. When the question is of a political nature it signifies the people in general, and being of the same nature as Aries, all that is said of that sign may be transferred to this house. The second house, which is of the same nature as the sign Taurus, is called the house of riches. It signifies the advancement in the world with respect to opulence of the querent ; and here the operations of the planets are, as in other cases, according to their own nature, Jupiter, Venus, Mercury, and the Sun being fortunate, if well aspected, only denoting different causes of wealth ; Saturn, Mars, the Moon, and Uranus, unfortunate. In horary questions, it signifies the money of the querent, or the success in a pecuniary point of view of any expedition of undertaking. It concerns loans, lawsuits, and everything by which riches may be gained or lost. In political questions it signifies the treasury, public loans, taxes, and subsidies ; the younger branches of the blood-royal, and the death of national enemies. The third house is the house of kindred, particularly of brothers, and was probably so designated on account of the third sign Gemini, of which nature it is said to be. It denotes kindred, and the planets in this house are full of signification. Saturn signifies coldness and distrust ; Mars, sudden, violent and hasty quarrels ; Herschel, all unaccountable estrangements ; Jupiter denotes steady friendships, Venus great love between brothers and sisters, and good fortune by means of the latter ; the Sun, warm attachment ; the Moon, indifference. In horary questions, this house signifies the health, fortune and happiness of the querent's parents, his own patrimony and inheritance, and the ultimate consequences, either good or bad, of any undertaking in which he may be engaged. In political cases it denotes the landed interest of a nation : the ancient and chartered rights of all classes, which have been handed down to them from their ancestors ; and all public advocates and defenders of these interests and rights.

The fifth house, which has the same government, and partakes of the same character as Leo, is called the House of Children. In nativities, therefore, it denotes the children of the native, and their success and also his own success by means of them. It also has some reference to women. The health and welfare of children, whether present or absent, are determinable by the planets in this house. It also denotes all questions relative to amusement, simply, as it would seem, on account of the fondness of youth for such pursuits. In political questions consequently, we find this house taken to signify the rising generation, theatres, exhibitions, public festivals, and all national amusements ; all increase in the population ; music and musical taste, sculpture, painting, and the advancement of the fine arts in general. The sixth house is that of servants, but it also denotes sickness and private enemies. It is usually considered an evil house and but few configurations of the planets which can take place in it are fortunate. It is of the nature, and shares the government of Virgo. When the lord of the ascendant is placed in this house, it denotes a low station, and if in addition to this he be ill dignified, the native will not rise above menial employments. In horary *astrology* it points out servants and cattle, dependents, and small shopkeepers ; uncles and aunts by the father's side ; tenants, stewards, shepherds and farmers. If, however, the question be political, then this house indicates the under-servants of the government ; the common seamen in the navy, private soldiers in the army, and the general health of the nation. This last refers chiefly to contagious and epidemic disorders.

The seventh house, which is of the same nature as Libra, and has the same government, is the House of Marriage. If Saturn be found here, he denotes unhappiness from constitutional causes ; Mars from difference of temper ; Herschel, as usual, from some strange and unaccountable dislike. The other planets are mostly causers of good, unless exception be made in the case of the Moon. In horary questions, this house denotes love, speculations in business, partners in trade, lawsuits, and litigation ; it is the House of Thieves, and sets forth thier conduct and character. In queries of a political nature, it signifies the event of any war, and the consequences of a treaty ; it personates the victorious nation, army, or navy, and indicates outlaws and fugitives, with the places in which they have taken their retreat.

The eighth house is the House of Death. It denotes wills, legacies, and all property depending upon the death of others ; the power, means, and influence of adversaries ; the opposing parties in lawsuits. It is of the nature of Scorpio, and has the same government. If Mars be unfortunately placed in this house, it portends a violent death to the native. Saturn is often productive of suicide, and Herschel of the mysterious disappearance of the unhappy individual, whose horoscope is so marked. Jupiter, on the contrary, and Venus, point out a late and quiet departure. In horary questions its significance has been already noticed, but it also denotes the portion or dowry of women, and seconds in duels. In political questions it has a signification of a very different character, viz., the privy council of a king or queen, their friends, and secrets of state. It does, however, bear some mark of its appropriation to death, by being made to denote the rate of mortality among the people. The ninth house is that of religion, science, and learning. It has the same government and nature as Sagittarius. Jupiter is the most fortunate planet in it, and if joined with Mercury, then the native is promised a character at once learned, estimable, and truly religious. The Sun and Venus are likewise good significators here, but the Moon denotes a changeable mind, and frequent alterations in religious principles. Mars is the worst planet in this house, and portends an indifference, or even an active hostility to religion. In horary questions the ninth house is appropriated to the church and the clergy ; all ecclesiastical matters, dissent, heresy, schism, dreams, visions, and religious delusions. It also denotes voyages and travels to distant lands, and in questions of a political nature, the religion of the nation, and all the higher and more solemn courts of justice, such as Chancery, etc.

The tenth house is one of the most important of all. It is the House of Honour, Rank, and Dignity ; of the nature and rule of Capricorn. In this house the planets are more powerful than in any other, save only the House of Life. They point out the employment, success, preferment, and authority of the native. Saturn is here the worst planet, but the Moon and Herschel are also mischievous, the latter by preventing the native from attaining that rank to which his services, learning, or merit entitle him, and doing this by a series of inexplicable disappointments. Jupiter and the Sun signify advancement by the favour of distinguished men, and Venus, of distinguished women. In horary questions, the tenth house signifies the mother of the querist ; and politically the sovereign. This is a house in which Mars is not unfortunate, if well placed ; denoting war-like achievements and consequent honours.

The eleventh house is the House of Friends : it is of the nature of Aquarius, and has the same rule. It denotes, of course, friends, well-wishers, favourites, and flatterers, but is said to be a house in which evil planets are increased in strength, and good planets diminished. The Sun is the best planet in it, and Mars the worst. In horary questions it has the same signification as in a nativity, and also denotes the expectations and wishes of the querist. It is said to be much influenced by the sign which is in it, and to signify legacies, if the sign be one of the earthy triplicity, and honour with princes, if it be one of the fiery triplicity. In political questions, the eleventh house signifies the allies of the public, with whom no particular treaty is at the same time binding ; and also the general council of the nation, and newly acquired rights.

Lastly, the twelfth house, which, of course, partakes the rule and character of Pisces, is the House of Enemies, and denotes sorrow, sickness, care, anxiety, and all kinds of suffering. Yet evil planets are weaker, according to some writers, and good planets stronger than in certain other houses. Very few configurations in this house are esteemed for the native, but its evil effects are, of course, greatly modified by the planetary influences. In horary questions it signifies imprisonment, treason, sedition, assassination, and suicide ; and in questions which are of a political character, it points out deceitful treaties, unsuccessful negotiations, treachery in the offices of state, captivity to princes, and general ill fortune. The criminal code, and the punishment of culprits, dungeons, and circumstances connected with prison discipline are also denoted by this house. Saturn is the worst, and Venus the best planet to be present in it.

Having taken notice of the signs, the planets, and the houses, it is next necessary for the astrologer to note also the aspects of the planets one towards another, which aspects decide whether the planet is of good or evil signification. These aspects are as follows—omitting the less important :

1. The Trine, marked △ when two planets are four signs, or 120° apart.

2. The Sectile, marked ✳ when two planets are two signs, or 60° apart.

3. The Quintile, (5-tile) when two planets are . . 72° apart.

These are all fortunate aspects, and are here placed according to their importance.

4. The Conjunction, ☌ when two stars or planets are of the same sign.

This is a fortunate aspect with the fortunate, and evil with evil planets.

5. The Opposition, ☍ when two planets are six signs or 180° apart.

6. The Quartile, ☐ when two planets are three signs or 90° apart.

7. The Semi-quartile ½☐ when the two planets are 45° apart.

These three last aspects are evil, and evil in the order in which they are here placed.

Horary questions are subjects of astrological calculations. They are so called, because the scheme of the heavens is erected for the hour in which the question is put. Thus, let a person be sick, and the question be of his recovery, the Houses will now signify as follows, says Blagrave :—

" 1. The patient's person
2. His estate
3. His kindred
4. His father or his grave
5. His children
6. His sickness and servants
7. His wife and his physician
8. His death
9. His religion
10. His mother and his physic
11. His friends
12. His enemies."

And according to the position of the planets the above particulars are to be judged of. If the question be of stolen goods, a distribution of the houses is again made according to similar rules. And here the colour denoted by the signs is pertinent ; for let Mercury signify the thief, then the sign in which that planet is found will denote the personal appearance and complexion of the thief. If the question be one concerning marriage, then it points out that of the future bride or bridegroom ; and so on.

For full information on astrology, reference is to be made to the works of Ptolemy, Firmicius Maternus, Censorinus, Alchabitius, Junctinus, Marcolini da Forli, Fabricius, Vossius, Cardan, Baptista Porta, Campanella, Chavigny, Guynaus, Kottero, Camerarius, Sir G. Wharton, William Lilly, Sir C. Haydon, Henry Coley, and Ebenezer Sibley. Later compendiums, however, have appeared, and we ought not to omit the *Dictionnaire Infernal*, of Collin de Plancy. and the works of Sepharial and Alan Leo.

For an interesting and most practical course of rhymed mnemonic lessons on astrology see *The Palace of the King*. by Isabella M. Pagan, the well-known Theosophist and writer on astrological subjects.

Athanor : This occult hill is surrounded by mist excepting the southern side, which is clear. It has a well, which is four paces in breadth, from which an azure vapour ascends, which is drawn up by the warm sun. The bottom of the well is covered with red arsenic. Near it is a basin filled with fire from which rises a livid flame odourless and smokeless, and never higher or lower than the edge of the basin. Also there are two black stone reservoirs, in one of which the wind is kept, and in the other the rain. In extreme drought the rain-cistern is opened and clouds escape, which water the whole country. The term is also employed to denote moral and philosophical alchemy.

Atlantis : a supposed sunken continent. which. according to some accounts, occupied most of the area of the present Atlantic Ocean. It is dealt with here because of late years several accounts purporting to come from certain spirit " controls" have been published which give a more or less detailed description of the history, life and manners of its inhabitants, and it is of interest to Theosophists. The question regarding the existence of such a continent is a very vexed one indeed. It appears to have originated at an early date, for Plato in his *Timæus* states that the Atlantians overran Europe and were only repulsed by the Greeks. It is stated that the Hindu priesthood believed. and still believe that it once existed ; and there are shadowy legends among the American native races which would seem to assist these beliefs. At the same time definite proof is conspicuous by its absence. Brasseur de Bourbourg held that *Atlantis* was an extension of America which stretched from Central America and Mexico, far into the Atlantic, the Canaries, Madeiras and Azores being the only remnants which were not submerged ; and many similar fantastic theories have been advanced. Donnelly undertook to prove the existence of such a continent by modern scientific methods, and located the *Atlantis* of Plato as an island opposite the entrance to the Mediterranean—a remnant of the lost continent. He thought that *Atlantis* was the region where men first arose from barbarism to civilisation, and that all the civilised peoples of Europe and America derived their culture thence: that it was indeed the antediluvian world of the Garden of Eden; that the Atlantians founded a colony in Egypt; and that the Phœnician alphabet was the Atlantian alphabet: that not only the Aryan but the Semitic people, and perhaps the "Turanian" races, emerged therefrom: that it perished in a terrible revolution of nature in which the whole island sank into the ocean with nearly all its inhabitants; and that only a few persons escaped to tell the story of the catastrophe, which has survived to our time in the flood and deluge legends of the Old and New worlds. Even some serious scientists have not disdained to examine the question, and it is claimed that ocean deposits show remains of what must have been at one time a land above the ocean. The theory that the Atlantians founded the civilisations of Central America and Mexico has been fully proven to be absurd, as that civilisation is distinctly of an aboriginal nature, and of comparatively late origin. (*See* Spence, *Myths of Mexico and Peru.*) The late Dr. Augustus le Plongeon and his wife spent many years in trying to prove that a certain Queen Móo of Yucatan, founded a colony in Egypt; but as they professed to be able to read hieroglyphs that no one else could decipher, and many of which were not hieroglyphs at all but ornamental designs, and as they placed side by side and compared with the Egyptian alphabet a "Mayan" alphabet, which certainly never originated anywhere but in their own ingenuity, we cannot have much faith in their conclusions. We do not learn from Dr. le Plongeon's works by what course of reasoning he came to discover that the name of his heroine was the rather uneuphonious one of Móo, but probably he arrived at it by the same process as that by which he discovered the "Mayan" alphabet. He further assumes that his story is taken up where he ends it by the *Manuscript Troano*, which is, however, chiefly calendric and not historical. Some years ago a French scientist left a large sum of money for research in connection with the sunken continent of *Atlantis*, and this has been fully taken advantage of by a certain author, who is pursuing his investigations in a practical manner.

The claims of certain spiritualists and occultists to restore the history of *Atlantis* are about as successful as those of the pseudo-scientists who have approached the question. They claim to have reconstructed almost the entire history of the island-continent by means of messages from spirit controls, which acquaint us minutely with the polity, life, religion and magical system of the Atlantians; but in the face of scientific knowledge and probability these accounts fail to convince, and are obviously of the nature of imaginative fiction. There is also a certain body of occult tradition concerning *Atlantis* which may either have originated from oriental sources, or else have come into being in the imaginations of later occultists; and this is to some extent crystallised in the works in question. It would be rash to say that such a continent as *Atlantis* never existed; but it would be equally foolish to say so dogmatically without a backing of much greater proof than we at present possess on the subject.

Atmadhyana : In the Rajah Yoga philosophy of S'rimat Sankaracharya, *Atmadhyana* is one of the stages necessary to acquire the knowledge of the unity of the soul with Brahman. It is the fourteenth stage and is the condition of highest joy arising from the belief, "I am Brahman."

Atman : translated "Soul," but better rendered "Self," and meaning in the Hindu religion the union of the soul with God. It is believed that the soul is neither body nor mind, nor even thought, but that these are merely conditions by which the soul is clouded so that it loses its sense of oneness with God. In the Upanishads it is said "The Self, smaller than small, greater than great, is hidden in the heart of the creature;" and "In the beginning there was Self."

Atmic or Nirvanic Plane : (*See* **Spiritual World**).

Attea Society : (*See* **Italy**).

Attic Mysteries : (*See* **Mysteries**).

Attwood, Mrs. : The author of a work entitled, *A Suggestive Inquiry with the Hermetic Mystery*, published anonymously at London, in 1850. Owing to the circumstance that it was supposed to have revealed certain alchemical secrets, it was shortly afterwards withdrawn from circulation.

Atziluth : One of the three worlds of the Kabala; the supreme circle; the perfect revelation. According to Eliphas Levi, it is represented in the *Apocalypse* by the head of the mighty angel with the face of a sun.

August Order of Light : An Oriental order introduced into this country in 1882 by Mr. Maurice Vidal Portman. Its object is the development of practical occultism, and it is continued at Bradford, Yorkshire, as "The Oriental Order of Light." It has a ritual of three degrees, Novice, Aspirans, Viator. It adopted Kabalistic forms, and is governed by a Grand Master of the Sacred Crown or *Kether* of the Kabala.

August Spirits, the Shelf of the : In the country of Japan, every house has a room set apart, called the spirit chamber, in which there is a shelf or shrine, with tablets bearing the names of the deceased members of the family, with the sole addition of the word *Mitama* (spirit). This is a species of ancestor worship, and is known as "home" worship.

Ankh : The Egyptian symbol of life, perhaps the life which remains to one after death. It is conjectured that it symbolises the union of the male and female principles, the origins of life, and that like the American cross, it typifies the four winds, the rain-bringers and fertilizers. It has been found manufactured in every description of material, and is sometimes encountered in combination with the dad or tat symbol (q.v.) It is usually carried in the right hand by divinities.

Aura : An emanation said to surround human beings, chiefly encircling the head, and supposed to proceed from the nervous system. It is described as a cloud of light suffused with various colours. This is seen clairvoyantly, being imperceptible to the physical sight.

Some authorities trace the existence of the *aura* in such scriptural instances as the bright light shining about Moses, which the children of Israel were unable to look upon, when he descended from the mountain bearing the stone tablets engraved with the Ten Commandments; in the exceedingly brilliant light which shone round about St. Paul's vision at the time of his conversion; and in the transfiguration of Jesus Christ, when his raiment shone so brightly that no fuller on earth could whiten it. Many of the mediæval saints were said to be surrounded with a cloud of light. Of St. John of the Cross it is told that when at the altar or kneeling in prayer, a certain brightness darted from his face; St. Philip Neri was constantly seen enveloped in light; St. Charles Borromeo was similarly illuminated. This is said to be due to the fact that when a person is engaged in lofty thought and spiritual aspiration, the auric colours become for the time being, more luminous and translucent, therefore more easily discernible. In Christian art, round the heads of saints and the sacred characters, is to be found portrayed the halo or nimbus which is supposed to represent the *aura*; sometimes the luminous cloud is shown around the whole of the body as well as the head, when it is called *aureola*. It is also thought that the colours of the body and clothing in mediæval paintings and stained glass are intended to represent the auric colours of the person portrayed. The crowns and distinctive head-dresses worn by the kings and priests of antiquity, are said to be symbolic of the *aura*. In many of the sacred books of the East, representations of the great teachers and holy men are given with the light extending round the whole of the body. Instances of this may be found in the temple caves of India and Ceylon, in the Japanese Buddhistic books, also in Egypt, Greece, Mexico and Peru. In occult literature the tradition of the *aura* is an old one, Paracelsus, in the 16th century, making mention of it in the following terms : " The vital force is not enclosed in man, but radiates round him like a luminous sphere, and it may be made to act at a distance. In these semi-natural rays the imagination of man may produce healthy or morbid effects. It may poison the essence of life and cause diseases, or it may purify it after it has been made impure, and restore the health." Again : " Our thoughts are simply magnetic emanations, which, in escaping from our brains, penetrate into kindred heads and carry thither, with a reflection of our life, the mirage of our secrets." A modern theosophical description is as follows : " The *aura* is a highly complicated and entangled manifestation, consisting of many influences operating within the same area. Some of the elements composing the *aura* are projected from the body, others from the astral principles, and others again from the more spiritual principles connected with the " Higher Self," or permanent Ego ; and the various *auras* are not lying one around the other, but are all blended together and occupy the same place. Guided by occult training. the clairvoyant faculty may make a complete analysis of the various elements in the *aura*, and can estimate the delicate tints of which it is composed—though all blended together—as if each were seen separately."

Classified more exactly, the divisions of the *aura* are stated to be : 1, the health *aura* ; 2, the vital *aura* ; 3, the " Karmic " *aura*, that of the animal soul in man ; 4, the *aura* of character ; 5, the *aura* of the spiritual nature.

The " health *aura* " is thus described : " It is almost colourless, but becomes perceptible by reason of possessing a curious system of radial striation, that is to say, it is composed of an enormous number of straight lines, radiating evenly in all directions from the body." The second, or " vital " *aura*, is said to be to a certain extent under the control of the will, when it circulates within the " linga charira " or astral body, of a " delicate rosy tint, which it loses, becoming bluish as it radiates outward." The third *aura* is " the field of manifestation, or the mirror in which every feeling, every desire is reflected." Of this *aura* the colours constantly change, as seen by the clairvoyant vision. " An outburst of anger will charge the whole *aura* with deep red flashes on a dark ground, while sudden terror will, in a moment, change everything to a ghastly grey." The fourth *aura* is that of the permanent character, and is said to contain the record of the past earth-life of the personality. The fifth *aura* is not often seen even by clairvoyants, but it is described by those who have seen it, only in the cases where the spiritual nature is the most powerful factor, as " outshining all the rest of the *auras* with startling brilliancy." The auric colours, it is declared, cannot be adequately described in terms of the ordinary colours discernible to the physical vision, being very much brighter, and of more varied hues and shades. The symbolic meaning of these is roughly of the following order : Rose, pure affection ; brilliant red, anger and force ; dirty red, passion and sensuality ; yellow, of the purest lemon

colour, the highest type of intellectual activity ; orange, intellect used for selfish ends, pride and ambition ; brown, avarice. Green is a colour of varied significance ; its root meaning is the placing of one's self in the position of another. In its lower aspects it represents deceit and jealousy ; higher up in the emotional gamut, it signifies adaptability, and at its very highest, when it tells on the colour of foliage, sympathy, the very essence of thinking for other people. In some shades green stands for the lower intellectual and critical faculties, merging into yellow. Blue indicates religious feeling and devotion, its various shades being said to correspond to different degrees of devotion, rising from fetishism to the loftiest religious idealism. Purple represents psychic faculty, spirituality, regality, spiritual power arising from knowledge, and occult pre-eminence.

Auspices, or College of Diviners : (*See* **Divination**).

Austatikco-Pauligaur : A class of Persian evil spirits. They are eight in number, and keep the eight sides of the world. Their names are as follows :—(1) Indiren, the king of these genii ; (2) Augne-Baugauven, the god of fire ; (3) Eemen king of death and hell ; (4) Nerudee, earth in the figure of a giant ; (5) Vaivoo, god of the air and winds ; (6) Varoonon, god of clouds and rain ; (7) Gooberen, god of riches ; (8) Essaunien. or Shivven.

Austral Virtue : (*See* **Fludd**).

Australia : *Native Magic.*—From birth to death, the native Australian or blackfellow is surrounded by magical influences. In many tribes the power to perform magic, " sympathetic " or otherwise, is possessed by only a few people ; but among the central tribes it is practised by both men and women—more often, however, by the former, who conserve the knowledge of certain forms of their own. There is also among them a distinct class of medicine-men, whose duty it is to discover whose magic has caused the death of anyone. Among the central tribes, unlike many others, magic is not made a means of profit or emolument. A heavy taboo rests on a great many things that the boy or young man would like to do, and this is for the behoof of the older men of the tribe, who attach to themselves the choicest morsels of food and so forth. Among girls and women the same law applies ; and the latter are sternly forbidden to go near the places where the men perform their magical ceremonies. To terrify them away from such spots, the natives have invented an instrument called a " bull-roarer "—a thin slip of wood swung round at the end of a string, which makes a screaming, whistling noise, which the women believe is the voice of the Great Spirit. The natives preserve long oval pieces of wood, which they call *churingas*. In these are supposed to remain the spirits of their ancestors, so that in reality they are of a fetish nature. These are kept concealed in the most secret manner.

Sympathetic Magic is of course rife amongst such a primitive people. Certain ceremonies are employed to control nature so as to ensure a plentiful supply of food and water, or to injure an enemy. One of the commonest forms of these is the use of the pointed stick or bone, which is used in one form or another by all Australian tribes. The former is a small piece of wood, varying in length from three to eighteen inches, resembling a skewer, and tapering to a point. At the handle end it is topped with a knob of resin, to which is attached a strand of human hair. Magical songs are sung over it, to endow it with occult potency. The man who wishes to use it goes into the bush singly, or with a friend, where he will be free from observation, and planting the stick in the ground, mutters over it what he desires to happen to his enemy. It is then left in the ground for a few days. The evil magic is supposed to proceed from the stick to the man, who often succumbs, unless a medicine-man, chances to discover the implement.

The Australian savage has a special dread of magic connected with places at a distance, and any magical apparatus purchased or obtained from far-away tribes is supposed to possess potency of much greater kind than if it had been made among themselves. Thus certain little stones traded by Northern tribes are supposed to contain a very powerful form of evil magic called *mauia*. These are wrapped up in many folds of bark and string, According to their traditions this type of magic was first introduced by a Batman, who dropped it to earth where it made a great explosion at a certain spot, whence it can still be procured. Sticks procured from a distance, with which the natives chastise their wives, are sufficient by their very sight to make the women obey their husbands. Much mystery surrounds what are known as "debil-debil" shoes, which consist of a pad of emu feathers, rounded at both ends, in order that no one should be able to trace in which direction the wearer is journeying. These are supposed to be worn by a being called *kurdaitcha*, to whom deaths are attributed. Like other savages, the Australian native believes that death is always due to evil magic. A man may become a *kurdaitcha* by submitting to a certain ceremony, in which the little toe of his foot is dislocated. Dressed up and painted grotesquely, he sets out accompanied by a medicine-man and wearing the *kurdaitcha* shoes, when he desires to slay an enemy. When he spears him, the medicine-man closes up the wound, and the victim returns to consciousness oblivious of the fact that he is full of evil magic ; but in a while he sickens and dies ; and then it is known that he has been attacked by a *kurdaitcha*. Many long and elaborate ceremonies are connected with the *churinga*, and these have been well described by Messrs. Spencer and Gillen, Howitt, Fison, and others.

Spiritualism in Australia has both a public and private representation. The latter is far more general than the former in every country except America, but although demonstrations of spirit power are more commonly known in Australia amongst individuals and families, than on the rostrum, or through the columns of the journals, they are less available for the purposes of historical record. It seems that many Australian colonists had heard of the Spiritualist movement before settling in the country, and on their arrival, pursuing the customary methods of unfoldment through the spirit circle, a deep interest was awakened long before public attention was called to the subject. In Sydney, Melbourne, Ballarat, Geelong, Brisbane, and numerous other towns and mining districts, communion with spirits was successfully practised in circles and families, up to about 1867. After that epoch it seems to have become the subject of various journalistic reports of the usual adverse, eulogistic, or non-committal character. At or about that period, a large number of influential persons became interested in the matter, and not a few whose names were a sufficient guarantee of their good faith, began to detail wonderful experiences in the columns of the public journals. The debate and denial, rejoinder and defence, called forth by these narratives, served as propaganda of the movement, and rendered each freshly recorded manifestation, the centre of an ever-widening circle of interest.

In Victoria a gentleman of considerable wealth and learning, writing under the *nom de plume* of "Schamlyn," entered into a warm controversy with the editor of the *Collingwood Advertiser*, in defence of Spiritualism. Another influential supporter, and for a time became a pillar of strength in its maintenance, was a gentleman connected with the editorial department of the *Melbourne Argus*, one of the leading journals of Victoria, and an organ well calculated to exert a powerful sway over the minds of its readers.

As the tides of public opinion moved on, doctors, lawyers, merchants, and men of eminence began to joins the ranks. Tidings of phenomena of the most astounding character poured in from distant towns and districts. Members of the press began to share the general infection, and though some would not, and others could not avow their convictions, their private prepossessions induced them to open their columns for debate and correspondence on the subject. To add to the stimulus thus imparted, many of the leading colonial journals indulged in tirades of abuse and misrepresentation, which only served to increase the contagion without in the least diminishing its force. At length the clergy began to arouse themselves and manifest their interest by furious abuse. Denunciation provoked retort ; discussion compelled investigation. In Sydney, many converts of rank and influence suddenly appeared. The late Hon. John Bowie Wilson, Land Minister, and a champion of temperance, became an open convert to Spiritualism, and by his personal influence no less than his public defence of the cause made converts unnumbered. Amongst the many others whose names have also been recorded in the ranks of Spiritualism in Sydney may be mentioned Mr. Henry Gale, Mrs. Wilson and Mrs. Gale, Mrs. Woolley and Mrs. Greville, besides a number of other ladies ; Mr. Greville, M.P., and several other members of the New South Wales Parliament and Cabinet ; Hon. J. Windeyer, Attorney-General of the Colony, subsequently one of the judges ; Mr. Alfred De Lissa, an eminent barrister ; Mr. Cyril Haviland, a literary man ; Mr. Macdonald ; Captain Barron ; Mr. Milner Stephen a barrister of eminence, his wife and family, and many others. Another who did more to advance the cause of Spiritualism, and crystallize its scattered fragments into concrete strength than any other individual in the ranks was Mr. Wm. Terry, the well-known and enterprising editor of the Melbourne *Harbinger of Light* Spiritual organ,

"About 1869" says Mr. H. Tuttle, "the necessity for a Spiritualistic journal was impressed deeply on the mind of Mr. Terry. He could not cast it off, but pondered over the enterprise. At this time, an exceedingly sensitive patient described a spirit holding a scroll on which was written "Harbinger of Light" and the motto, "Dawn approaches, error is passing away ; men arising shall hail the day." This influenced him, and in August 1870, he set to work to prepare the first number, which appeared on the 1st of September of that year.

"There was no organisation in Australian Spiritualism, and Mr. Terry saw the advantage and necessity of associative movement. He consulted a few friends, and in November, 1870, he organised the first Victorian Association of Spiritualists. A hall was rented, and Sunday services, consisting of essays and reading by members, enlivened by appropriate hymns, were held. In October, 1872, impressed with the desirability of forming a Lyceum, he called together a few willing workers, and held the first session on October 20th, 1872. It is, and has been from the first in a flourishing condition, numbering one hundred and fifty members, with a very handsome and complete outfit, and excellent library. He has remained an officer ever since, and conductor four sessions. He assisted in the establishment of the Spiritualist and Free-thought Association, which succeeded the original one, and was its first president. He has lectured occasionally to appreciative audiences, and his lectures have been widely circulated. His mediumship, which gave such fair promise, both in regard to writing and speaking, became controlled, especially for the relief of the sick. Without the assistance of advertising he has acquired a fine practice. With this he combines a trade in Reform and Spiritualistic publications, as extensive as the colony, and the publication of the

Harbinger of Light, a Spiritual journal that is an honour to the cause, and well sustains the grand philosophy of immortality. No man is doing more for the cause, or has done more efficient work."

A short but interesting summary of the rise and progress of Spiritualism in Australia is given in the American *Banner of Light*, 1880, in which Mr. Terry's good service is again alluded to, and placed in line with that of several other pioneers of the movement, of whom mention has not yet been made. It is as follows :—

" The *Harbinger of Light*, published at Melbourne, Australia, furnishes a review of the origin of its publication and the work it has accomplished during the ten years just closed. At its advent in 1870, considerable interest had been awakened in the subject of Spiritualism, by the lectures of Mr. Nayler, in Melbourne, and Mr. Leech, at Castlemaine. The leaders of the church became disturbed, and seeing their gods in danger, sought to stay the progress of what would eventually lessen their influence and possibly their income. But Mr. Nayler spoke and wrote with more vigour ; the addresses of Mr. Leech were published from week to week in pamphlet form, and widely distributed. At the same time, Mr. Charles Bright, who had published letters on Spiritualism in the *Argus*, over an assumed name, openly identified himself with the movement, and spoke publicly on the subject. Shortly after, eleven persons met and formed an association, which soon increased to eighty members. A hymn-book was compiled, and Sunday services began. As elsewhere, the press ridiculed, and the pulpit denounced Spiritualism as a delusion. A number of articles in the *Argus* brought some of the facts prominently before the public, and the growing interest was advanced by a public discussion between Messrs. Tyerman and Blair. In 1872, a Sunday school, on harmonial principles, was established, Mr. W. H. Terry, the proprietor of the *Harbinger*, being its first conductor. Almost simultaneously with this was the visit of Dr. J. M. Peebles, whose public lectures and work in the Lyceum served to consolidate the movement. A controversy in the *Age*, between Rev. Mr. Potter, Mr. Tyerman and Mr. Terry, brought the facts and teachings of Spiritualism into further notice.

" Soon came Dr. Peebles, Thomas Walker, Mrs. Britten and others, who widened the influence of the spiritualistic philosophy, and aided the *Harbinger* in its efforts to establish Spiritualism on a broad rational basis. Mr. W. H. Terry is deserving of all praise for his unselfish and faithful exertions in carrying the *Harbinger* through the years of as hard labour as ever befell any similar enterprise, and we bespeak for him, in his continued efforts to make known the evidences of a future existence, and the illuminating truths of Spiritualism, the hearty co-operation and sympathy of all friends of the cause."

Writing to the *Banner of Light* on the subject of Mr. Tyerman's accession to the Spiritual ranks, an esteemed American correspondent says :—

" The Rev. J. Tyerman, of the Church of England, resident in one of the country districts, boldly declared his full reception of Spiritualism as a great fact, and his change of religious faith consequent upon the teachings of spirits. Of course, he was welcomed with open arms by the whole body of Spiritualists in Melbourne, the only city where there was any considerable number enrolled in one association. He soon became the principal lecturer, though not the only one employed by the Association, and well has he wielded the sword of the new faith. He is decidedly of the pioneer stamp, a skilful debater, a fluent speaker, ready at any moment to engage with any one, either by word of mouth or as a writer. So widely, indeed, did he make his influence felt, and so individual was it, that a

new society grew up around him, called the Free-Thought and Spiritualist Propaganda Society, which remained in existence till Mr. Tyerman removed to Sydney, when it coalesced with the older association, under the combined name of Melbourne Spiritualist and Free-Thought Association."

Another valuable convert to the cause of Spiritualism, at a time when it most needed good service, was Mrs. Florence Williams, the daughter of the celebrated English novelist, G. P. R. James, and the inheritor of his talent, originality of thought, and high culture. This lady for a long time officiated at the first Spiritual meetings convened for Sabbath Day exercises, as an acceptable and eloquent lecturer, and her essays would have formed an admirable epitome of spiritual revelations at the time in which they were delivered.

The visits of several zealous propagandists have been alluded to in previous quotations, Amongst the first to break ground as a public exponent of Spiritualism, was the Rev. J. M. Peebles, formerly a minister of Battle Creek, Michigan. Mr. Peebles was well known in America as a fine writer and lecturer, and as such was justified in expecting courteous, if not eulogistic mention from the press of a foreign country, with whom his own was on terms of amicable intercourse. How widely different was the journalistic treatment he experienced may be gathered from his own remarks addressed to the *Banner of Light* some five years after his first visit, and describing in graphic terms the changed spirit which marked alike the progress of the movement and the alteration in the tone of public opinion. Mr. Peebles says :—

" Relative to Spiritualism and its divine principles, public sentiment has changed rapidly, and for the better, during the past five years. Upon my late public appearance in Melbourne, the Hon. John McIlwraith, ex-Mayor of the city, and Commissioner to our Centennial Exhibition, took the chair, introducing me to the audience. On my previous visit some of the Spiritualists seemed a little timid. They preferred being called investigators, remaining a good distance from the front. Then my travelling companion, Dr. Dunn, was misrepresented, and meanly vilified in the city journals ; while I was hissed in the market, caricatured in *Punch*, burlesqued in a theatre, and published in the daily press as an ' ignorant Yankee,' an ' American trickster,' a ' long-haired apostate,' and ' a most unblushing blasphemer.' But how changed ! Recently the secular press treated me fairly. Even the usually abusive *Telegraph* published Mr. Stevenson's article assuring the Rev. Mr. Green that I was willing to meet him at once in a public discussion. The *Melbourne Argus*, one of the best daily papers in the world, the *Australasian*, the *Herald*, and the *Age*, all dealt honourably by me, reporting my lectures, if briefly, with admirable impartiality. The press is a reflector ; and those audiences of 2,000 and 2,500 in the great Opera House on each Sunday for several successive months, were not without a most striking moral significance. It seemed to be the general opinion that Spiritualism had never before occupied so prominent yet so favourable a position in the eyes of the public. . . . ."

Efficient service was rendered to the cause of Spiritualism by Mr. Thomas Walker, a young Englishman, first introduced in the Colonies by the Rev. J. M. Peebles. Alleging himself to be a " trance speaker " under the control of certain spirits, whom he named, Mr. Walker lectured acceptably in Sydney, Melbourne, and other places in the Colonies on the Spiritual rostrum. In March, 1878, Mr. Walker maintained a public debate with a Mr. M. W. Green, a minister of a denomination termed " the Church of Christ." This gentleman had acquired some reputation in the Colonies as a preacher, and as one who had bitterly opposed, and taken every possible opportunity, to misrepresent Spiritualism. The debate, which was held in the Temperance Hall, Melbourne, attracted large audiences, and been extended for several nights beyond the period originally agreed upon.

The following extracts are taken from the *Melbourne Age*, one of the leading daily journals of the city. They are dated August 20th, 1878, and read thus :

" Spiritualism is just now very much to the front in Melbourne. The lectures of Mrs. Emma Hardinge-Britten, delivered to crowded audiences at the Opera House every Sunday evening, have naturally attracted a sort of wondering curiosity to the subject, and the interest has probably been intensified by the strenuous efforts that are being made in some of the orthodox pulpits to prove that the whole thing is an emanation from the devil. The announcement that the famous Dr. Slade had arrived to strengthen the ranks of the Spiritualists, has therefore been made at a very critical juncture, and I should not be surprised to find that the consequence will be to infuse a galvanic activity into the forces on both sides. Though I do not profess to be a Spiritualist, I own to having been infected with the fashionable itch for witnessing ' physical manifestations,' as they are called, and accordingly I have attended several circles with more or less gratification. But Dr. Slade is not an ordinary medium even among professionals. The literature of the Spiritualists is full of his extraordinary achievements, attested to all appearance by credible witnesses, who have not been ashamed to append their names to their statements. . . . I see that on one occasion, writing in six different languages was obtained on a single slate, and one day, accompanied by two learned professors, Dr. Slade had a sitting with the Grand Duke Constantine, who obtained writing on a new slate held by himself alone. From St. Petersburg, Dr. Slade went to Berlin, where he is said to have obtained some marvellous manifestations in the house of Professor Zöllner, and where he was visited by the court conjurer to the Emperor, Samuel Bellachini. . . . My object in visiting Dr. Slade can be understood when I was introduced to him with my friend, whom I shall call Omega, and who was bent on the same errand. Dr. Slade and Mr. Terry constituted the circle of four who sat around the table in the centre of the room almost as immediately as we entered it. There was nothing in the room to attract attention. No signs of confederacy, human or mechanical. The hour was eleven in the morning. The window was unshuttered, and the sun was shining brightly. The table at which we sat was a new one, made especially by Wallach Brothers, of Elizabeth Street, of polished cedar, having four slight legs, one flap, and no ledges of any kind underneath. As soon as we examined it Dr. Slade took his seat on one side, facing the window, and the rest of us occupied the other three seats. He was particularly anxious that we should see he had nothing about him. It has been said that he wrote on the slate by means of a crumb of pencil stuck in his finger-nails, but his nails were cut to the quick, while his legs and feet were ostentatiously placed away from the table in a side position, exposed to view the whole time. He first produced a slate of the ordinary school size, with a wet sponge, which I used to it. A chip of pencil about the size of a grain of wheat was placed upon it on the table ; we joined hands, and immediately taps were heard about the table, and in answer to a question—' Will you write ? '— from Dr. Slade, three raps were given, and he forthwith took up the slate with the pencil lying on it, and held half of it under the table by his finger and thumb, which clasped the corner of the half that was outside the table, and was therefore easily seen by all present. His left hand re-

mained near the centre of the table, resting on those of the two sitters on either side of him. Several convulsive jerks of his arm were now given, then a pause, and immediately the sound of writing was audible to every one, a scratching sound interrupted by the tap of the pencil, which indicated, as we afterwards found, that the t's were being crossed and the i's dotted. The slate was then exposed, and the words written were in answer to the question which had been put by Omega as to whether he had psychic power or not. I pass over the conversation that ensued on the subject, and go on to the next phenomenon. To satisfy myself that the ' trick ' was not done by means of sympathetic writing on the slate, I had ten minutes previously purchased a slate from a shop in Bourke Street, containing three leaves, and shutting up book fashion. This I produced, and Dr. Slade readily repeated his performance with it. It was necessary to break the pencil down to a mere crumb, in order to insert it between the leaves of the slate. This done, the phenomenon at once recurred with this rather perplexing difference, that the slate, instead of being put half under the table, forced itself by a series of jerks on to my neck, and reposed quietly under my ear, in the eyes of everyone present. The scratching then commenced ; I heard the t's crossed and the i's dotted by the moving pencil, and at the usual signal I opened the slate, and found an intelligible reply to the question put. . . . The next manifestation was the levitation of one of the sitters in his chair about a clear foot from the ground, and the levitation of the table about two feet. I ought to have mentioned that during the whole of the *séance* there was a good deal of by-play going on. Everyone felt the touch of hands more or less, and the sitters' chairs were twice wrenched from under them, or nearly so, but the psychic could not possibly have done it. . . . "

Says Mrs. Emma Hardinge Britten, in her *Nineteenth Century Miracles* :—" As personal details are more graphic than the cold narrations of passing events, we deem it expedient in this place to give our readers an inside view of Spiritualism in Australia, by republishing one of the many articles sent by the author to the American Spiritual journals during her sojourn in the Colonies. The following excerpt was written as the result of personal experience, and at a time when Spiritualism, in the usual inflated style of journalistic literature, was ' in the zenith of its triumphs.' It is addressed to the Editor of the *Banner of Light*, and reads as follows :—

" ' Spiritualism in these colonies finds little or no public representation outside of Melbourne or Sydney, nevertheless warm friends of the cause are scattered all over the land, and endeavours are being made to enlarge the numerous circles into public meetings, and the fugitive efforts of whole-hearted individuals into associations as powerful as that which exists in Melbourne. At present, the attempt to effect missionary work in any portions of Australia outside Sydney or Melbourne, becomes too great a burden to the luckless individual, who has not only to do the work, but to bear the entire cost of the undertaking, as I have had to do in my visits to various towns in Victoria. Expenses which are cheerfully divided amongst the many in the United States, become all too heavy for endurance when shouldered upon the isolated workers ; hence the paucity of public representation, and the impossibility of those who visit the Colonies, as I have done, effecting any important pioneer work beyond the two great centres I have named. Mr. Walker at Sydney, and I at Melbourne, have been favoured with the largest gatherings ever assembled at Colonial Sunday meetings.

" ' Having, by desire of my spirit guides, exchanged rostrums, he filling my place at Melbourne, and I his at Sydney, we find simultaneously at the same time, and on the same Sundays, the lessees of the two theatres we occupied raising their rent upon us one hundred and fifty per cent. The freethinkers and Spiritualists had occupied the theatre in Sydney four years at the rate of four pounds per Sunday. For my benefit the landlord raised the rent to ten pounds, whilst the same wonderful spirit of accordance caused the Melbourne manager to increase upon Mr. Walker from eight pounds to a demand of twenty. With our heavy expenses and small admission fees this was tantamount to driving us out altogether. Both of us have succeeded after much difficulty, and fighting Christian warriors with the Christian arms of subtlety and vigilance, in securing other places to lecture in ; and despite the fact that the press insult us, the pulpit curse us, and Christians generally devote us to as complete a prophecy of what they would wish to us to enjoy everlastingly as their piety can devise, we are each attracting our thousands every Sunday night, and making such unmistakable marks on public opinion as will not easily be effaced again. . . .

" ' Dr. Slade's advent in Melbourne since last September has been productive of an immense amount of good. How far his labours here will **prove** remunerative I am not prepared to say. Frankly speaking, I do not advise Spirit Mediums or speakers to visit these colonies on financial advancement intent. There is an abundant crop of Medium power existing, interest enough in the cause, and many of the kindest hearts and clearest brains in the world to be found here ; but the lack of organisation, to which I have before alluded, and the imperative necessity for the workers who come here to make their labours remunerative, paralyses all attempts at advancement, except in the sensation line. Still I feel confident that with united action throughout the scattered force of Spiritualistic thought in these Colonies, Spiritualism might and would supersede every other phase of religious thought in an incredibly short space of time. I must not omit to mention that the friends in every place I have visited have been more than kind, hospitable and appreciative. The public have defied both press and pulpit in their unstinted support of my lectures. The press have been equally servile, and the Christian world equally stirred, and equally active in desperate attempts to crush out the obvious proofs of immortality Spiritualism brings.

" ' In Melbourne, I had to fight my way to comply with an invitation to lecture for the benefit of the City Hospital. I fought and conquered ; and the hospital committee revenged itself for a crowded attendance at the Town Hall by taking my money without the grace of thanks, either in public or private, and the simply formal acknowledgment of my services by an official receipt. In Sydney, where I now am, I was equally privileged in lecturing for the benefit of the Temperance Alliance, and equally honoured, after an enthusiastic and successful meeting, by the daily press of the city in their utter silence concerning such an important meeting, and their careful record of all sorts of such trash as they disgrace their columns with. So mote it be. The wheel will turn some day !

During the years 1881 and '82 the Australian colonists were favoured with visits from three more well-known American Spiritualists. The first of these was Professor Denton, an able and eloquent lecturer on geology, and one who never failed to combine with his scientific addresses, one or more stirring lectures on Spiritualism. The second propagandist was Mrs. Ada Foye, one of the best test-writing, rapping, and seeing Mediums, who has ever appeared in the ranks of Spiritualism ; whilst the third was Mrs. E. L. Watson, a trance-speaker.

Professor Denton's lectures created a wide-spread interest amongst all classes of listeners.

It now becomes necessary to speak of one of the most

arbitrary acts of tyranny on the part of the Victorian Government towards Spiritualism which the records of the movement can show. This was the interdict promulgated by " the Chief Secretary " against the proprietor of the Melbourne Opera House, forbidding him to allow Spiritualists to take money at the door for admission to their services, and in effect, forbidding them to hold services there at all. A similar interdict was issued in the case of Mr. Proctor, the celebrated English lecturer on astronomy. The excuse for this tyrannical procedure in Mr. Proctor's case, might have been justified on the ground, that the Chief Secretary was entirely ignorant of the fact, that astronomy had anything to do with religion, or that it was not orthodox to talk about the celestial bodies on a Sunday, except in quotations from Genesis, or Revelations ; but in the case of " the Victorian Association of Spiritualists " it was quite another point. Spiritualism was their religion, and Spiritual lectures their Sabbath Day exercises. Messrs. Walker, Peebles, and Mrs. Britten, had occupied the Opera House for months together, and admission fees had been charged at each of their Sunday services, without let or hindrance. The result of many gatherings for the purpose of denouncing their policy may be judged by a perusal of the following paragraph published in the *Harbinger of Light* of March, 1882 :—

" On Friday last a letter was received from the Government by the Executive of the Victorian Association of Spiritualists, intimating that the former had no desire to suppress the lectures, but endorsed the permit of May 1879. The directors of the Opera House Company were interviewed, and on the understanding that no money be taken at the doors, consented to the opening of the House. The fact being announced in Saturday's papers drew a large audience to hear Mr. Walker's lecture on Sunday, ' Lord Macaulay on Roman Catholicism.' The services will be continued as heretofore. Seats in dress circle or stalls may be hired by month or quarter, at W. H. Terry's 84, Russel Street."

During Dr. Slade's visit to Sydney, a very able and energetic worker in Spiritualism became convinced of its truth, in the person of Mr. E. Cyril Haviland, the author of two excellent pamphlets and many articles, tracts, and good literary contributions on this subject. Mr. Haviland, Mr. Harold Stephen, and several other gentlemen of literary repute in Sydney, combined during the author's last visit to form a " Psychological Society," the members of which like the persons above named, represented some of the most accomplished writers and advanced thinkers of the city.

Mr. L. E. Harcus, an able and fluent writer, furnished a report of the origin and growth of this society for the *Banner of Light* of March 1880.

Austria : (For ancient magic among the Teutonic people of Austria, *See* **Teutons.** *See also* **Hungary.**)

In Austria, Spiritualism was first promulgated by M. Constantine Delby of Vienna. He was a warm adherent of Allan Kardec, and founded a society under legal auspices, besides starting a Spiritual journal. The society numbered but few members, in fact Spiritualism never obtained much foothold in Vienna. At Buda-Pesth it was quite otherwise. In a short time a considerable amount of interest was awakened, and many persons of note began to take part in the circles that were being formed there, amongst these were Mr. Anton Prohasker and Dr. Adolf Grunhut. At length a society was formed, legalised by the State, of which Baron Edmund Vay, was elected president. Mr. Lishner, of Pesth, built a handsome séance room which the society rented. At that time there were one hundred and ten members, many of them being Hebrews, though all Christians. Baron Vay was the honorary president, Dr. Grunhut, was the active president, and these and Mr. Prohasker were amongst the most devoted and faithful workers. The principles of the society, indeed the basis of it were taken from the *Geist Kraft Stoff* of Baroness Adelma Von Vay and the works of Allan Kardec —purely Christian Spiritism. It never encouraged paid Mediumship. All the officers were voluntary and honorary. It had no physical Medium, but good trance, writing and seeing mediums.

Autography : A term sometimes used to denote the spiritualistic phenomenon of " direct " writing (q.v.).

Auto-Hypnotization : (*See* **Hypnotism.**)

Ansuperomin : A sorcerer of the time of St. Jean de Lus, who, according to information supplied by Pierre Delamere, a councillor of Henry IV, was seen several times at the " sabbath," mounted on a demon in the shape of a goat, and playing on the flute for the witches' dance.

Automatic Writing and Speaking : Writing executed or speech uttered without the agent's volition, and sometimes without his knowledge. The term is used by psychical researchers and applied particularly to the trance phenomena of the séance-room. By spiritualists, writing or speaking produced under these conditions, are said to be performed " under control "—that is, under the controlling agency of the spirits of the dead—and are therefore not judged to be truly " automatic." The general consensus of opinion, however, ascribes such performances to the subconscious activity of the agent. Automatic writing and speaking necessarily imply some deviation from the normal in the subject, though such abnormality need not be pronounced, but may vary from a slight disturbance of the nerve-centres occasioned by excitement or fatigue to hystero-epilepsy or actual insanity. When the phenomena are produced during a state of trance or somnambulism the agent may be entirely unconscious of his actions. On the other hand the automatic writing may be executed while the agent is in a condition scarcely varying from the normal and quite capable of observing the phenomena in a critical spirit, though perhaps ignorant of a word in advance of what he is actually writing. Between these states of full consciousness or complete unconsciousness there are many intermediate stages. The secondary personality, as displayed in the writings or utterances, may gain only a partial ascendancy over the primary, as may happen in dreams or in the hypnotic trance. As a rule automatic speech and writings display nothing more than a revivifying of faded mental imagery, thoughts and conjectures and impressions which never came to birth in the upper consciousness. But at times there appears an extraordinary exaltation of memory, or even of the intellectual faculties. Cases are on record where lost articles have been recovered by means of automatic writing. Foreign languages which have been forgotten, or with which the subject has small acquaintance, are spoken or written fluently. Hélène Smith, the subject of Professor Flournoy, even went so far as to invent a new language, purporting to be that of the Martians, but in reality showing a marked resemblance to French—the mother-tongue of the medium. Automatic writing and speaking have been produced in considerable quantities, mainly in connection with spiritualistic circles, though it existed long before the advent of spiritualism in the speaking with " tongues " of the early ecstatics. These unintelligible outpourings are still to be met with, but are no longer a marked feature of automatic utterance. But, though the matter and style may on occasion transcend the capabilities of the agent in his normal state, the great body of automatic productions does not show an erudition or literary excellence beyond the scope of the natural resources of the automist. The style is involved, obscure, inflated, yet possessing a super-

ficial smoothness and a suggestion of flowing periods and musical cadences. The ideas are often shallow and incoherent, and all but lost in a multitude of words. The best known of automatic writings are the *Spirit Teachings* of the Rev. Stanton Moses, the works of A. J. Davis, J. Murray Spear, and Charles Linton, and, perhaps most important of all, the *Trance Utterances* of Mrs. Piper, these last offering no inconsiderable evidence for telepathy. A good deal of poetry has been produced automatically, notably by the Rev. T. L. Harris. Among those who are known to have produced automatic writings are Goethe, Victor Hugo, Victorien Sardou, and other eminent men of letters. (For the hypothesis of spirit control, *see article* **Spiritualism.**)

Avenar : An astrologer who promised to the Jews, on the testimony of the planets, that their Messiah should arrive without fail in 1444. or at the latest. in 1464. He gave. for his guarantors, Saturn, Jupiter, " the crab, and the fish." All the Jews kept their windows open to receive the messenger of God, who did not arrive.

Avenir : (**Journal**) (*See* **France**).

Avicenna : Named *Aben Sina* by Hebrew writers, but properly, *Ebor Sina*, or—to give his long array of names in full—*Al-Sheikh Al-Rayis Abu Ali Al-Hossein ben Abdallah ben Sina*, born at Kharmatain, near Bokhara, in the year of the Hegira 370, or A.D. 980. He was educated at Bokhara, and displayed such extraordinary precocity that when he had reached his tenth year, he had completely mastered the Koran, and acquired a knowledge of algebra, the Mussulman theology, and the *His ab ul-Hind*, or arithmetic of the Hindoos. Under Abdallah Al- Natheli he studied logic, Euclid, and the Almagest. and then, as a diversion, devoted himself to the study of medicine. He was only twenty-one years old when he composed his Kitab al-Majmu or, *The Book of the Sum Total*, whose mysteries he afterwards endeavoured to elucidate in a commentary in twenty volumes. His reputation for wisdom and erudition was so great that on the death of his father he was promoted by Sultan Magdal Douleth to the high office of Grand Vizier, which he held with advantage to the State until a political revolution accomplished the downfall of the Samanide dynasty. He then quitted Bokhara. and wandered from place to place, increasing his store of knowledge, but yielding himself to a life of the grossest sensuality. About 1012 he retired to Jorjan, where he began his great work on medicine. which is still held in some repute as one of the earliest systems of that art with any pretensions to philosophical completeness. It is arranged with singular clearness, and presents a very admirable resumé of the doctrines of the ancient Greek physicians. Avicenna subsequently lived at Rui, Kazwin, and Ispahan, where he became physician to the Persian sovereign, Alaeddaulah. He is said to have been dismissed from this post on account of his debauched living. He then retired to Hamadan, where, worn out with years of sensual indulgence, he died, at the age of 58, in 1038. His works on philosophy, mathematics, and medicine, are nearly one hundred in number, and include at least seven treatises on the Philosopher's Stone. His *Book of the Canon of Medicine* acquired an European celebrity, and has been several times translated into Latin. Contemporary with Avicenna were numerous votaries of the alchemistical science, and almost every professor of medicine was an astrologer The influence of the stars upon the conditions of the human body was generally accepted as a first principle in medicine ; and the possible transmutation of metals engaged the attention of every enquiring intellect. At the same time, the Arabians were almost the sole depositaries of human knowledge ; and. in the East glowed that steadily-shining light which, never utterly extinct, had withdrawn its splendour and its glory from the classic lands of the West. "They cultivated with success," says Gibbon, "the sublime science of astronomy, which elevates the mind of man to disdain his diminutive planet and monentary existence." The names of Mesua and Geber, of Rhazis and Avicenna, are ranked with the Grecian masters ; in the city of Bagdad, eight hundred and sixty physicians were licensed to exercise their lucrative profession ; in Spain, the life of the Catholic princes was entrusted to the skill of the Saracens, and the school of Salerno, their legitimate offspring, revived in Italy and Europe the precepts of the healing art.

Avichi : is the Theosophic hell. Though it is a place of torment, it differs in great degree from the ordinary conception of hell. Its torments are the torments of fleshly cravings, which for want of a physical body, cannot be satisfied. A man remains after death exactly the same entity as he was before it, and, if in life, he has been obsessed with strong desires or passions, such obsession still continues, though, in the astral plane in which he finds himself the satisfaction of these desires or passions is impossible. Of course, the manner of these torments is infinite, whether it be the confirmed sensualist who suffers them, or more ordinary men who, without being bound to the things of the flesh, have nevertheless allowed the affairs of the world to bulk too largely in their lives, and are now doomed to regret the small attention they have bestowed on higher matters. Avichi is a place of regrets for things done and things undone. Its torments are not, however, eternal, and with the passing of time—of which there is no measure in the astral plane—they are gradually discontinued, though at the cost of terrible suffering.

Avidya in Theosophy is the ignorance of mind which causes man before starting on the Path to expend vain effort and pursue vain courses. It is the antithesis of *Vidya*. (*See* Path, *and* Vidya, *and* Theosophy.)

Awyntyrs of Arthure at the Tern Wathelyn : an Arthurian poem of the fourteenth or fifteenth centuries. It is believed to be of Scottish origin, but its authorship is doubtful. Amongst other adventures, the poem relates one which King Arthur and his queen Guinevere, accompanied by their favourite knight Sir Gawane, had whilst hunting in the wilds of Cumberland. They were overtaken by darkness, while separated from the rest of the party, and the ghost of the queen's mother appears to them. The apparition tells of the torments to which it is being subjected, and entreats that prayers will be offered up for its release. This the queen and Sir Gawane promise, and on their return to Carlisle millions of masses are ordered to be sung on its behalf.

Axinomancy : Divination by means of a hatchet or a woodcutter's axe. It is by this form of divination that the diviners predicted the ruin of Jerusalem, as is seen from Psalm LXXIII. François de la Tour-Blanche, who remarked upon this, does not tell us how the diviners made use of the hatchet. We can only suppose that it was by one of the two methods employed in ancient times and still practised in certain northern countries. The first is as follows : When it is desired to find a treasure, a round agate must be procured, the head of the axe must be made red-hot in the fire, and so placed that its edge may stand perpendicularly in the air. The agate must be placed on the edge. If it remains there, there is no treasure, if it falls, it will roll quickly away. It must, however, be replaced three times, and if it rolls three times towards the same place, there the treasure will be found. If it rolls a different way each time, one must seek about for the treasure.

The second method of divination by the axe is for the purpose of detecting robbers. The hatchet is cast on the ground, head-downwards, with the handle rising perpendicularly in the air. Those present must dance round it in a ring, till the handle of the axe totters and it falls to the ground. The end of the handle indicates the direction in which the thieves must be sought. It is said by some that if this divination is to succeed, the head of the axe must be stuck in a round pot, but this, as Delancre says, is absurd. For how could an axe be fixed in a round pot, any more than the pot could be sewed or patched if the axe had broken it to pieces ?

Ayperor : A count of the infernal empire. (The same as Ipès.)

Azael : One of the angels who revolted against God. The rabbis say that he is chained on sharp stones, in an obscure part of the desert, awaiting the last judgment.

Azam, Dr. : (*See* **Hypnotism**).

Azazel : A demon of the second order, guardian of the goat. At the feast of expiation, which the Jews celebrate on the tenth day of the seventh month, two goats are led to the High Priest, who draws lots for them, the one for the Lord, the other for Azazel. The one on which the lot of the Lord fell was sacrificed, and his blood served for expiation. The High Priest then put his two hands on the head of the other, confessed his sins and those of the people, charged the animal with them, and allowed him to be led into the desert and set free. And the people, having left the care of their iniquities to the goat of Azazel —also known as the scape-goat—return home with clean consciences. According to Milton, Azazel is the principal standard-bearer of the infernal armies. It is also the name of the demon used by Mark the heretic for his magic spells.

Azer : An angel of the elemental fire. Azer is also the name of the father of Zoroaster.

Azoth : (*See* **Philosopher's Stone**).

Aztecs : (*See* **Mexico and Central America**).

B

Ba : The Egyptian conception of the soul, which in the form of a man-headed bird left the body after death and winged its flight to the gods. It returned at intervals to the mummy for the purpose of comforting it and reassuring it concerning immortality. Sometimes it grasps the *ankh* (q.v.) and the *nif* (q.v.) and is occasionally represented as flying down the tomb-shaft to the deceased, or perched on the breast of the mummy. It was sometimes carved on the lid of mummy cases. In the *Book of the Dead* a chapter promises abundance of food to the *Ba*, so that the conception does not appear to have been entirely spiritual.

Baalberith : According to Wierius, a demon of the second order ; master of the Infernal Alliance. He is said to be secretary and keeper of the archives of Hell.

Baalzephon : Captain of the guard and sentinels of Hell, according to Wierius.

Baaras : A marvellous plant known to the Arabs as the "Golden Plant," and which is supposed to grow on Mount Libanus, underneath the road which leads to Damascus. It is said to flower in the month of May, after the melting of the snow. At night it can be seen by torchlight, but through the day it is invisible. It was held to be of great assistance to alchemists in the transmutation of metals. It is alluded to by Josephus. (Lib. VIII., Chap. 25.)

Babau : A species of ogre with which the nurses in the central parts of France used to frighten their charges. He was supposed to devour naughty children in salad. The ending "au" suggests a Celtic origin. For example, "Y Mamau," the Welsh for "fairies."

Babiagora : Certain lakes of a gloomy nature, which lie between Hungary and Poland, which have figured in various stories of witchcraft. Pools, such as these, are often used for purposes of divination, as by gazing down into clear water the mind is disposed to contemplation, often of a melancholy character. This form of divination is termed " Hydromancy " (q.v.) and is similar to crystal-gazing.

Babylonia : The conservative element in the religion of Babylonia was one of its most marked and interesting features. All the deities retained, even after they reached their highest development, traces of their primitive demoniac characters, and magic was never divorced from religion. The most outstanding gods were Ea, Anu and Enlil, the elder Bel. These formed a triad at the dawn of history, and appear to have developed from an animistic group of world spirits. Although Ea became specialised as a god of the deep, Anu as a god of the sky, and Enlil as an earth god, each had also titles which emphasised that they had attributes overlapping those of the others. Thus Ea was Enki, earth lord, and as Aa was a lunar deity, and he had also solar attributes. In the legend of Etana and the Eagle, his heaven is stated to be in the sky. Anu and Enlil as deities of thunder, rain and fertility, linked closely with Ea, as Dagan, of the flooding and fertilising Euphrates. Each of these deities were accompanied by demon groups. The spirits of disease were the " beloved sons of Bel " ; the fates were the seven daughters of Anu ; the seven storm demons, including the dragon and serpent, were of Ea's brood. In one of the magical incantations translated by Mr. R. C. Thompson, occurs the following description of Ea's primitive monster form :

> The head is the head of a serpent,
> From his nostrils mucus trickles,
> The mouth is beslavered with water ;
> The ears are those of a basilisk,
> His horns are twisted into three curls,
> He wears a veil in his head-band,
> The body is a sun-fish full of stars,
> The base of his feet are claws,
> The sole of his foot has no heel ;
> His name is Sassu-wunnu,
> A sea monster, a form of Ea.

Ea was " the great magician of the gods " ; his sway over the forces of nature was secured by the performance of magical rites, and his services were obtained by mankind, who performed requisite ceremonies and repeated appropriate spells. Although he might be worshipped and propitiated in his temple at Eridu, he could also be conjured in reed huts. The latter indeed appear to have been the oldest holy places. In the Deluge myth, he makes a revelation in a dream to his human favourite, Pir-napishtim, the Babylonian Noah, of the approaching disaster planned by the gods, by addressing the reed hut in which he slept : " O, reed hut, hear ; O, wall, understand." The sleeper received the divine message from the reeds. The reeds were to the Babylonian what rowan branches were to northern Europeans : they protected them against demons. The dead were buried wrapped in reed mats.

When the official priesthood came into existence it included two classes of magicians, the " Ashipu," who were exorcists, and the " Mashmashu," the " purifiers." The Ashipu priests played a prominent part in ceremonies, which had for their object the magical control of nature : in times of storm, disaster, and eclipse they were especially active. They also took the part of " witch doctors." Victims of disease were supposed to be possessed of devouring demons :

> Loudly roaring above, gibbering below,
> They are the bitter venom of the gods. . .
> Knowing no care, they grind the land like corn :
> Knowing no mercy, they rage against mankind,
> They spill their blood like rain,
> Devouring their flesh and sucking their veins.
> (Thompson's translation.)

It was the business of the Ashipu priests to drive out the demon. Before he could do so he had to identify it. Having done so, he required next to bring it under his influence. This he accomplished by reciting its history and detailing its characteristics. The secret of the magician's power was his knowledge. To cure toothache, for instance, it was necessary to know the " Legend of the Worm," which, vampire-like, absorbed the blood of victims, but specialised in gums. The legend relates that the worm came into existence as follows : Anu created the heaven, the heavens created the earth, the earth created the rivers, and the rivers created the canals, then the canals created marshes, and the marshes created the " worm." In due time the worm appeared before Shamash, the sun god, and Ea, god of the deep, weeping and hungry. " What will you give me to eat and drink ? " it cried. The gods promised that it would get dried bones and scented wood. Apparently the worm realised that this was the " food of death," for it made answer : " What are dry bones to me ? Set me upon the gums that I may drink the blood of the teeth and take away the strength of the gums." When the worm heard this legend repeated, it came under the magician's power, and was dismissed to the marshes, while Ea was invoked to smite it. Different demons were exorcised by different processes. A fever patient might receive the following treatment :

Sprinkle this man with water,
Bring unto him a censer and a torch,
That the plague demon which resteth in the body of the man,
Like water may trickle away.

Another method was to fashion a figure of dough, wax, clay or pitch. This figure might be placed on a fire or mutilated, or placed in running water to be washed away. As the figure suffered, so did the demon it represented.

By the magic of the word of Ea.

A third method was to release a raven at the bedside of the sick man so that it would conjure the demon of fever to take flight likewise. Sacrifices were also offered, as substitutes for patients, to provide food for the spirit of the disease. A kid was slain and the priest muttered,

The kid is the substitute for mankind ;
He hath given the kid for his life,
He hath given the head of the kid for the head of the man.

A pig might be offered :

Give the pig in his stead
And give the flesh of it for his flesh,
The blood of it for his blood, etc.

The cures were numerous and varied. After the patient recovered the house was purified by the " mashmashu " priests. The ceremony entailed the sprinkling of sacred water, the burning of incense, and the repetition of magical charms. Houses were also protected against attack, by placing certain plants over the doorways and windows. An ass's halter seems to have been used, as horse-shoes have been in Europe, to repel witches and evil spirits.

The purification ceremonies suggest the existence of taboo. For a period a sick man was " unclean " and had to be isolated. To each temple was attached a " House of Light " in which fire ceremonies were performed, and a " House of Washing " where patients bathed in sacred water. Oil was also used as anointment to complete the release from uncleanness. Ioods were also tabooed at certain seasons. It was unlawful for a man to eat pork on the 30th of Ab (July-August) or the 27th of Tisri, and other dates. Fish, ox flesh, bread, etc. were similarly tabooed on specific dates. A man's luck depended greatly on his observance of these rules. But although he might observe all ceremonies, he might still meet with ill-fortune on unlucky days. On the festival day of Marduk (Merodach) a man must not change his clothes nor put on white garments, nor offer up sacrifices. Sure disaster would overcome a king if he drove out in a chariot, or a physician if he laid hands on the sick, or a priest who sat in judgment, and so on. On lucky days good fortune was the heritage of everyone. Good fortune meant good health in many cases, and it was sometimes assured by worshipping the dreaded spirit of disease called Ura. A legend related that this demon once made up his mind to destroy all mankind. His counsellor Ishun, however, prevailed upon him to change his mind, and he said, " Whoever will laud my name I will bless with plenty. No one will oppose the person who proclaims the glory of my valour. The worshipper who chants the hymn of praise to me will not be afflicted by disease, and he will find favour in the eyes of the King and his nobles."

Ghosts.—Among the spirits who were the enemies of mankind the ghosts of the dead were not the least virulent, and especially the ghosts of those who had not been properly buried. These homeless spirits (the grave was the home of the dead) wandered about the streets searching for food and drink, or haunted houses. Not infrequently they did real injury to mankind. Of horrible aspect, they appeared before children and frightened them to death. They waylaid travellers and mocked those who were in sorrow. The scritch-owl was a mother who had died in childbed and wailed her grief nightly in solitary places. Occasionally she appeared in monstrous form and slew wayfarers. Adam's " first wife Lilith " was a demon who had once been beautiful and was in the habit of deceiving lovers, and working ill against them. A hag, Labartu, haunted mountains and marshes and children had to be charmed against her attacks. She also had a human history. The belief that the spirits of the dead could be conjured from their graves to make revelations was also prevalent in *Babylonia*. In the Gilgamesh epic, the hero visits the tomb of his old friend and fellow-warrior Ea-Bani. The ghost rises like a " weird gust " and answers the various questions addressed to it with great sadness. Babylonian outlook on the future life was tinged by profound gloom and pessimism. It was the fate of even the ghosts of the most fortunate and ceremonially buried dead to exist in darkness and amidst dust. The ghost of Ea-Bani said to Gilgamesh :

" Were I to inform thee the law of the underworld
  which I have experienced,
Thou wouldest sit down and shed tears all day
  long."

Gilgamesh lamented :
" The sorrow of the underworld hath taken hold upon
  thee."

Priests who performed magical ceremonies had to be clothed in magical garments. They received inspiration from their clothing. Similarly the gods derived power from the skins of animals with which they were associated from the earliest time. Thus Ea was clad in the skin of the fish—probably the fish totem of the Ea tribe.

The dead were not admitted to the heavens of the gods. When a favoured human being, like Utnapishtim, the Babylonian Noah, joined the company of the gods, he had assigned to him an island Paradise where Gilgamesh visited him. There he dwelt with his wife. Gilgamesh

was not permitted to land, and held converse with his immortal ancestor, sitting in his boat. The deities secured immortality by eating the " food of life " and drinking the " water of life." DONALD MACKENZIE.

Bacchic Mysteries : (*See* **Greece**).

Bachelor : The name given to his satanic majesty, when he appeared in the guise of a great he-goat, for the purpose of love intercourse with the witches.

Bacis : A famous augur of Beotia. Many persons who ventured to predict the future adopted the name of *Bacis*.

Bacon, Roger, was born near Ilchester in Somerset, in 1214. In his boyhood he displayed remarkable precocity, and in due time, having entered the order of St. Francis, he studied mathematics and medicine in Oxford and Paris. Returning to England, he devoted attention to philosophy and also wrote Latin, Greek, and Hebrew Grammars. He was a pioneer of astronomy and was acquainted with the properties of lenses, so that he may have foreshadowed the telescope. In the region of the mechanical sciences, his prophecies are noteworthy since he not only speaks of boats which may be propelled without oars, but of cars which may move without horses, and even of machines to fly in the air. To him we are indebted for important discoveries in the science of pure chemistry. His name is for ever associated with the making of gunpowder, and if the honour cannot be wholly afforded him, his experiments with nitre were at least a far step towards the discovery. His study of alchemical subjects led him, as was natural, to a belief in the philosopher's stone by which gold might be purified to a degree impossible by any other means, and also to a belief in the elixir of life whereby on similar principles of purification, the human body might be fortified against death itself. Not only might man become practically immortal by such means but, by knowledge of the appropriate herbs, or by acquaintance with planetary influences, he might attain the same consummation. As was natural in an ignorant age, Bacon was looked on with considerable suspicion which ripened into persecution. The brethren of his order practically cast him out, and he was compelled to retire to Paris, and to submit himself to a régime of repression. A prolific penman, he was forbidden to write, and it was not till 1266 that Guy de Foulques, the papal legate in England—subsequently Pope Clement IV.—hearing of *Bacon*'s fame, invited him to break his enforced silence. *Bacon* hailed the opportunity and in spite of hardship and poverty, finished his *Opus Majus, Opus Minus* and *Opus Tertium*. These works seem to have found favour with Clement, for the writer was allowed to return to Oxford, there to continue his scientific studies and the composition of scientific works. He essayed a compendium of philosophy of which a part remains, but its subject-matter was displeasing to the ruling powers and *Bacon*'s misfortunes began afresh. His books were burned and again he was thrown into prison, where he remained for fourteen years, and during that period it is probable that he continued to write. About 1292 he was again at liberty, and within the next few years—probably in 1294—he died. *Bacon*'s works were numerous and, while many still remain in manuscript, about a dozen have been printed at various times. Many are obscure treatises on alchemy and deserve little attention, but the works he wrote by invitation of Clement are the most important. The *Opus Majus* is divided into six parts treating of the causes of error, the relation between philosophy and theology, the utility of grammar, mathematics, perspective and experimental science. The *Opus Minus*, of which only part has been preserved, was intended to be a summary of the former work. The *Opus Tertium* though written after the other two, is an introduction to them, and also in part supplementary to them. These works, large though they be, seem to have been only the forerunners of a vast work treating of the principles of all the sciences, which, however, was probably little more than begun. Much of *Bacon's* work and many of his beliefs must, of course, be greatly discounted, but judging the man in relation to his time, the place he takes is a high one. His devotion to the experimental sciences was the point wherein he differed from most from his contemporaries, and to this devotion is to be accounted the fame which he then possessed and still possess.

But no sketch of *Bacon's* life would be complete without some account of the legendary material which has gathered around his name, and by virtue of which he holds rank as a great magician in the popular imagination. When, in the sixteenth century, the study of magic was pursued with increased zeal, the name of *Friar Bacon* became more popular, and not only were the traditions worked up into a popular book, entitled *The History of Friar Bacon*, but one of the dramatists of the age, Robert Green, founded upon them a play, which was often acted, and of which there are several editions. The greater part of the history of *Friar Bacon*, as far as it related to that celebrated personage, is evidently the invention of the writer, who appears to have lived in the time of Queen Elizabeth ; he adopted some of the older traditions, and filled up his narrative with fables taken from the common story books of the age. We are here first made acquainted with two other legendary conjurers, Friars Bungay and Vandermast ; and the recital is enlivened with the pranks of Bacon's servant Miles.

According to this legendary history, *Roger Bacon* was the son of a wealthy farmer in the West of England, who had placed his son with the parish priest to gain a little scholarship. The boy soon showed an extraordinary ability for learning, which was encouraged by the priest, but which was extremely disagreeable to the father, who intended him for no other profession but that of the plough. Young *Bacon* fled from home, and took shelter in a monastery, where he followed his studies to his heart's content, and was eventually sent to complete them at Oxford. There he made himself a proficient in the occult sciences, and attained to the highest proficiency in magic. At length he had an opportunity of exhibiting his skill before the court, and the account of his exploits on this occasion may be given as a sample of the style of this quaint old history.

" The king being in Oxfordshire at a nobleman's house, was very desirous to see this famous friar, for he had heard many times of his wondrous things that he had done by his art, therefore he sent one for him to desire him to come to the court. *Friar Bacon* kindly thanked the king by the messenger, and said that he was at the king's service and would suddenly attend him, ' but, sir,' saith he to the gentleman, ' I pray you make haste or else I shall be two hours before you at the court.' ' For all your learning", answered the gentleman, ' I can hardly believe this, for scholars, old men, and travellers, may lie by authority.' ' To strengthen your belief ' said *Friar Bacon*, ' I could presently show you the last wench that you kissed withal, but I will not at this time.' ' One is as true as the other,' said the gentleman, ' and I would laugh to see either.' ' You shall see them both within these four hours,' quoth the friar, ' and therefore make what haste you can.' ' I will prevent that by my speed,' said the gentleman, and with that he rid his way ; but he rode out of his way, as it should seem, for he had but five miles to ride, and yet was he better than three hours a-riding them, so that *Friar Bacon* by his art was with the king before he came.

" The king kindly welcomed him, and said that he long time had desired to see him, for he had as yet not heard of his like. *Friar Bacon* answered him, that fame had belied him, and given him that report that his poor studies had never deserved, for he believed that art had many sons more excellent than himself was. The king commended him for his modesty, and told him that nothing could become a wise man less than boasting : but yet withal he requested him now to be no niggard of his knowledge, but to show his queen and him some of his skill ' I were worthy of neither art or knowledge,' quoth *Friar Bacon*, ' should I deny your majesty this small request ; I pray seat yourselves, and you shall see presently what my poor skill can perform.' The king, queen, and nobles sat them all down. They having done so, the friar waved his wand, and presently was heard such excellent music, that they were all amazed, for they all said they had never heard the like. ' This is,' said the friar, ' to delight the sense of hearing,—I will delight all your other senses ere you depart hence.' So waving his wand again, there was louder music heard, and presently five dancers entered, the first like a court laundress, the second like a footman, the third like a usurer, the fourth like a prodigal, the fifth like a fool. These did divers excellent changes, so that they gave content to all the beholders, and having done their dance they all vanished away in their order as they came in. Thus feasted two of their senses. Then waved he his wand again, and there was another kind of music heard, and whilst it was playing, there was suddenly before them a table, richly covered with all sorts of delicacies. Then desired he the king and queen to taste of some certain rare fruits that were on the table, which they and the nobles there present did, and were very highly pleased with the taste ; they being satisfied, all vanished away on the sudden. Then waved he his wand again, and suddenly there was such a smell, as if all the rich perfumes in the whole world had been then prepared in the best manner that art could set them out. Whilst he feasted thus their smelling, he waved his wand again, and there came divers nations in sundry habits, as Russians, Polanders, Indians, Armenians, all bringing sundry kinds of furs, such as their countries yielded, all which they presented to the king and queen. These furs were so soft to the touch that they highly pleased all those that handled them. Then, after some odd fantastic dances, after their country manner, they vanished away. Then asked *Friar Bacon* the king's majesty if that he desired any more of his skill. The king answered that he was fully satisfied for that time, and that he only now thought of something that he might bestow on him, that might partly satisfy the kindness he had received. *Friar Bacon* said that he desired nothing so much as his majesty's love, and if that he might be assured of that, he would think himself happy in it. ' For that,' said the king, ' be thou ever sure, in token of which receive this jewel,' and withal gave him a costly jewel from his neck. The friar did with great reverence thank his majesty, and said, ' As your majesty's vassal you shall ever find me ready to do you service ; your time of need shall find it both beneficial and delightful. But amongst all these gentlemen I see not the man that your grace did send for me by ; sure he hath lost his way, or else hath met with some sport that detains him so long ; I promised to be here before him, and all this noble assembly can witness I am as good as my word—I hear him coming. With that entered the gentleman, all bedirted, for he had rid through ditches, quagmires, plashes, and waters, that he was in a most pitiful case. He, seeing the friar there, looked full angrily, and bid a plague on all his devils. for they had led him out of his way, and almost drowned him. ' Be not angry, sir,' said *Friar Bacon*, ' here is an old friend of yours that hath more cause, for she hath tarried these three hours for you,'—with that he pulled up the hangings, and behind him stood a kitchen-maid with a basting-ladle in her hand—' now am I as good as my word with you, for I promised to help you to your sweetheart,—how do you like this ? ' ' So ill,' answered the gentleman, ' that I will be avenged of you.' ' Threaten not,' said *Friar Bacon*, ' lest I do you more shame, and do you take heed how you give scholars the lie again ; but because I know not how well you are stored with money at this time, I will bear your wench's charges home.' With that she vanished away."

This may be taken as a sort of exemplification of the class of exhibitions which were probably the result of a superior knowledge of natural science, and which were exaggerated by popular imagination. They had been made, to a certain degree, familiar by the performances of the skilful jugglers who came from the east, and who were scattered throughout Europe ; and we read not unfrequently of such magical feats in old writers. When the Emperor Charles IV. was married in the middle of the fourteenth century to the Bavarian Princess Sophia in the city of Prague, the father of the princess brought a waggon-load of magicians to assist in the festivities. Two of the chief proficients in the art, Zytho the great Bohemian sorcerer, and Gouin the Bavarian, were pitted against each other, and we are told that after a desperate trial of skill, Zytho, opening his jaws from ear to ear, ate up his rival without stopping till he came to his shoes, which he spit out, because, as he said, they had not been cleaned. After having performed this strange feat, he restored the unhappy sorcerer to life again. The idea of contests like this seems to have been taken from the scriptural narrative of the contention of the Egyptian magicians against Moses.

The greater number of *Bacon's* exploits are mere adaptations of mediæval stories, but they show, nevertheless, what was the popular notion of the magician's character. Such is the story of the gentleman who, reduced to poverty and involved in debt, sold himself to the evil one, on condition that he was to deliver himself up as soon as his debts were paid. As may be imagined without much difficulty, he was not in haste to satisfy his creditors, but at length the time came when he could put them off no longer, and then, in his despair, he would have committed violence on himself had not his hand been arrested by *Bacon*. The latter, when he had heard the gentleman's story, directed him to repair to the place appointed for his meeting with the evil one, to deny the devil's claim, and to refer for judgment to the first person who should pass " In the morning, after that he had blessed himself, he went to the wood, where he found the devil ready for him. So soon as he came near, the devil said : ' Now, deceiver, are you come ? Now shall thou see that I can and will prove that thou hast paid all thy debts, and therefore thy soul belongest to me.' ' Thou art a deceiver,' said the gentleman, ' and gavest me money to cheat me of my soul, for else why wilt thou be thine own judge ?—let me have some others to judge between us.' ' Content,' said the devil, ' take whom thou wilt.' ' Then I will have,' said the gentleman, ' the next man that cometh this way.' Hereto the devil agreed. No sooner were these words ended, but *Friar Bacon* came by, to whom this gentleman spoke, and requested that he would be judge in a weighty matter between them two. The friar said he was content, so both parties were agreed ; the devil told *Friar Bacon* how the case stood between them in this manner. ' Know, friar, that I seeing this prodigal like to starve for want of food, lent him money, not only to buy him victuals, but also to redeem his lands and pay his debts, conditionally that so soon as his debts were paid, that he should give himself freely to me ; to this, here is

his hand '—showing him the bond. ' Now, my time is expired, for all his debts are paid, which he cannot deny.' ' This case is plain, if it be so that his debts are paid.' ' His silence confirms it,' said the devil, ' therefore give him a just sentence.' ' I will,' said *Friar Bacon*, ' but first tell me,'—speaking to the gentleman—' didst thou never yet give the devil any of his money back, nor requite him in any ways ? ' ' Never had he anything of me as yet,' answered the gentleman. ' Then never let him have anything of thee, and thou art free. Deceiver of mankind,' said he, speaking to the devil, ' it was thy bargain never to meddle with him so long as he was indebted to any ; now how canst thou demand of him anything when he is indebted for all that he hath to thee ? When he payeth thee thy money, then take him as thy due ; till then thou hast nothing to do with him, and so I charge thee to be gone.' At this the devil vanished with great horror, but *Friar Bacon* comforted the gentleman, and sent him home with a quiet conscience, bidding him never to pay the devil's money back, as he valued his own safety."

Bacon now met with a companion, Friar Bungay, whose tastes and pursuits were congenial to his own, and with his assistance he undertook the exploit for which he was most famous. He had a fancy that he would defend England against its enemies, by walling it with brass, preparatory to which they made a head of that metal. Their intent was to make the head speak, for which purpose they raised a spirit in a wood, by whose directions they made a fumigation, to which the head was to be exposed during a month, and to be carefully watched, because if the two friars did not hear it before it had ceased speaking, their labour would be lost. Accordingly, the care of watching over the head while they slept was entrusted to *Bacon's* man Miles. The period of utterance unfortunately came while Miles was watching. The head suddenly uttered the two words, " Time is." Miles thought it was unnecessary to disturb his master for such a brief speech, and sat still. In half an hour, the head again broke silence with the words, " Time was." Still Miles waited until, in another half hour, the head said, " Time is past," and fell to the ground with a terrible noise. Thus, through the negligence of Miles, the labour of the two friars was thrown away.

The king soon required *Friar Bacon's* services, and the latter enabled him, by his perspective and burning-glasses, to take a town which he was besieging. In consequence of this success, the kings of England and France made peace, and a grand court was held, at which the German conjurer, Vandermast, was brought to try his skill against *Bacon*. Their performances were something in the style of *Bacon's* former exhibition before the king and queen. Vandermast, in revenge, sent a soldier to kill *Bacon*, but in vain. Next follow a series of adventures which consist of a few mediæval stories very clumsily put together among which are that known as the Friar and the Boy, that which appeared in Scottish verse, under the title of *The Friars of Berwick*, a tale taken from the Gesta Romanorum, and some others. A contention in magic between Vandermast and Bungay, ended in the deaths of both. The servant Miles next turned conjurer, having got hold of one of *Bacon's* books, and escaped with a dreadful fright, and a broken leg. Everything now seemed to go wrong. *Friar Bacon* " had a glass which was of that excellent nature that any man might behold anything that he desired to see within the compass of fifty miles round about him." In this glass he used to show people what their relations and friends were doing, or where they were. One day two young gentlemen of high birth came to look into the glass, and they beheld their fathers desperately fighting together, upon which they drew their swords and slew each other. Bacon was so shocked that he broke his glass, and hearing about the same time of the deaths of Vandermast and Bungay, he became melancholy, and at length he burnt his books of magic, distributed his wealth among poor scholars and others, and became an anchorite. Thus ended the life of *Friar Bacon,* according to " the famous history," which probably owed most of its incidents to the imagination of the writer.

Bacoti : A common name for the augurs and sorcerers of Tonquin. They are often consulted by the friends of deceased persons for the purpose of holding communication with them.

Backstrom, Dr. Sigismund : (*See* **Rosicrucians**).

Bad : A Jinn of Persia who is supposed to have command over the winds and tempests. He presides over the twenty-second day of the month.

Badger : To bury the foot of a badger underneath one's sleeping-place is believed by the Voodoo worshippers and certain Gypsy tribes to excite or awaken love.

Bael : A demon cited in the Grand Grimoire (q.v.), and head of the infernal powers. It is with him that Wierius commences his inventory of the famous *Pseudonomarchia Daemonum.* He alludes to *Bael* as the first monarch of hell, and says that his estates are situated on the eastern regions thereof. He has three heads, one, that of a crab, another that of a cat, and the third that of a man. Sixty-six legions obey him.

Bagoe : A pythoness, who is believed to have been the Erithryean sibyl. She is said to have been the first woman to have practised the diviner's art. She practised in Tuscany, and judged all events by the sound of thunder.

Bagommedes : a knight mentioned by Gautier in the *Conte du Graal.* It is said that he was fastened to a tree by Kay and left hanging head downwards, until released by Perceval. On *Bagommede's* return to the court he challenged Kay, but was prevented by Arthur from slaying him.

Bahaman : A jinn who, according to Persian tradition, appeased anger, and in consequence governed oxen, sheep, and all animals of a peaceful disposition.

Bahir : (" Brightness.") A mystical Hebrew treatise of the twelfth or thirteenth century, the work of a French rabbi, by name Isaac ben Abraham of Posquières, commonly called " Isaac the Blind." (*See* **Kabala**).

Baian : son of Simeon, King of the Bulgarians, and a mighty magician, who could transform himself into a wolf whenever he desired. He could also adopt other shapes and render himself invisible. He is alluded to by Ninauld in his *Lycanthropie* (page 100).

Balan : A monarch great and terrible among the infernal powers, according to Wierius. He has three heads, those of a bull, a man, and a ram. Joined to these is the tail of a serpent, the eyes of which burn with fire. He bestrides an enormous bear. He commands forty of the infernal legions, and rules over finesse, ruses and middle courses.

Balasius : To describe this stone in fewer words than Leonardus has used would be impossible. It is " of a purple or rosy colour, and by some is called the placidus or pleasant. Some think it is the carbuncle diminished in its colour and virtue ; just as the virtue of the female differs from that of the male. It is often found that the external part of one and the same stone appears a *balasius,* and the internal a carbuncle, from whence comes the saying that the *balasius* is the carbuncle's house. The virtue of the *balasius* is to overcome and repress vain thoughts and luxury ; to reconcile quarrels among friends ; and it befriends the human body with a good habit of health. Being bruised and drunk with water, it relieves infirmities in the eyes, and gives help in disorders of the liver ; and what

is still more surprising, if you touch the four corners of a house, garden or vineyard, with the *balasius,* it will preserve them from lightning, tempest, and worms."

Balcoin, Marie : a sorceress of the country of Labour, who attended the infernal Sabbath in the reign of Henry IV of France. In the indictment against her it was brought forward that she had eaten at the Sabbatic meeting the ear of a little child. For her numerous sorceries she was condemned to be burnt.

Balkan Peninsula : *See* **Slavs ; Greece, Modern ; Vampire, etc.**

Ballou, Adin : A Universalist minister who in 1842 formed the Hopedale Community (q.v.). He was one of those whose doctrines prepared the way for spiritualism in America, and who, after that movement had been inaugurated, became one of its most enthusiastic protagonists (*See* **America, U.S. of**).

Balor : a mighty King of the Formorians, usually styled " *Balor* of the Evil Eye," in Irish mythical tales. It was believed that he was able to destroy by means of an angry glance. When his eyelid became heavy with years, it is said that he had it raised by means of ropes and pulleys, so that he might continue to make use of his magical gift : but his grandson, Lugh, the Sun-god, crept near him one day when his eyelid had drooped momentarily, and slew him with a great stone which sank through his eye and brain.

Balsamo, Peter : (*See* **Cagliostro**).

Baltazo : One of the demons who possessed a young woman of Laon, Nicole Aubry, in the year 1566. He went to sup with her husband, under the pretext of freeing her from demon-possession, which he did not accomplish. It was observed that at supper he did not drink, which shows that demons are averse to water.

Baltus, Jean François : A learned Jesuit who died in 1743. In his *Reply to the History of the Oracles of Fontenelle,* published in Strasbourg in 1709, he affirmed that the oracles of the ancients were the work of demons, and that they were reduced to silence during the mission of Christ upon the earth.

Banshee : An Irish supernatural being of the wraith type. The name implies " female fairy." She is usually the possession of a specific family, to a member or members of whom she appears before the death of one of them. Mr. Thistleton Dyer, writing on the *Banshee* says :

" Unlike, also, many of the legendary beliefs of this kind, the popular accounts illustrative of it are related on the evidence of all sections of the community, many an enlightened and well-informed advocate being enthusiastic in his vindication of its reality. It would seem, however, that no family which is not of an ancient and noble stock is honoured with this visit of the *Banshee,* and hence its non-appearance has been regarded as an indication of disqualification in this respect on the part of the person about to die. ' If I am rightly informed,' writes Sir Walter Scott, ' the distinction of a *Banshee* is only allowed to families of the pure Milesian stock, and is never ascribed to any descendant of the proudest Norman or the boldest Saxon who followed the banner of Strongbow, much less to adventurers of later dates who have obtained settlements in the Green Isle.' Thus, an amusing story is contained in an Irish elegy to the effect that on the death of one of the Knights of Kerry, when the *Banshee* was heard to lament his decease at Dingle—a seaport town, the property of those knights—all the merchants of this place were thrown into a state of alarm lest the mournful and ominous wailing should be a forewarning of the death of one of them, but, as the poet humorously points out, there was no necessity for them to be anxious on this point. Although, through misfortune, a family may be brought down from high estate to the rank of peasant tenants, the *Banshee* never leaves nor forgets it till the last member has been gathered to his fathers in the churchyard. The Mac-Carthys, O'Flahertys, Magraths, O'Neils, O'Rileys, O'Sullivans, O'Reardons, have their *Banshees*, though many representatives of these names are in abject poverty.

"'The *Banshee*,' says Mr. McAnally, 'is really a disembodied soul, that of one who in life was strongly attached to the family, or who had good reason to hate all its members. Thus, in different instances, the *Banshee's* song may be inspired by different motives. When the *Banshee* loves those she calls, the song is a low, soft chant, giving notice, indeed, of the close proximity of the angel of death, but with a tenderness of tone that reassures the one destined to die and comforts the survivors ; rather a welcome than a warning, and having in its tones a thrill of exultation, as though the messenger spirit were bringing glad tidings to him summoned to join the waiting throng of his ancestors.' To a doomed member of the family of the O'Reardons the *Banshee* generally appears in the form of a beautiful woman, ' and sings a song so sweetly solemn as to reconcile him to his approaching fate.' But if, during his lifetime, the *Banshee* was an enemy of the family, the cry is the scream of a fiend, howling with demoniac delight over the coming death agony of another of his foes.

" Hence, in Ireland, the hateful '*Banshee* ' is a source of dread to many a family against which she has an enmity. ' It appears,' adds McAnally, ' that a noble family, whose name is still familiar in Mayo, is attended by a *Banshee* of this description—the spirit of a young girl, deceived, and afterwards murdered by a former head of the family. With her dying breath she cursed her murderer, and promised she would attend him and his forever. After many years the chieftain reformed his ways, and his youthful crime was almost forgotten even by himself, when one night, as he and his family were seated by the fire, the most terrible shrieks were suddenly heard outside the castle walls. All ran out, but saw nothing. During the night the screams continued as though the castle were besieged by demons, and the unhappy man recognised in the cry of the *Banshee* the voice of the young girl he had murdered. The next night he was assassinated by one of his followers, when again the wild unearthly screams were heard exulting over his fate. Since that night the ' hateful *Banshee* ' has, it is said, never failed to notify the family, with shrill cries of revengeful gladness, when the time of one of their number has arrived."

" Among some of the recorded instances of the *Banshee's* appearance may be mentioned one related by Miss Lefrau, the niece of Sheridan, in the Memoirs of her grandmother, Mrs. Frances Sheridan. From this account we gather that Miss Elizabeth Sheridan was a firm believer in the *Banshee*, and firmly maintained that the one attached to the Sheridan family was distinctly heard lamenting beneath the windows of the family residence before the news arrived from France of Mrs. Frances Sheridan's death at Blois. She added that a niece of Miss Sheridan made her very angry by observing that as Mrs. Frances Sheridan was by birth a Chamberlaine, a family of English extraction, she had no right to the guardianship of an Irish fairy, and that therefore the *Banshee* must have made a mistake. Then there is the well-known case related by Lady Fanshawe who tells us how, when on a visit in Ireland, she was a-wakened at midnight by a loud scream outside her window. On looking out she saw a young and rather handsome woman, with dishevelled hair, who vanished before her eyes with another shriek. On communicating the circumstance in the morning, her host replied, ' A near relation of mine died last night in the castle, and before such an event happens, the female spectre whom you have seen is always visible."

" This weird apparition is generally supposed to assume the form of a woman, sometimes young, but more often old. She is usually attired in a loose white drapery, and her long ragged locks hang over her thin shoulders. As night time approaches she occasionally becomes visible, and pours forth her mournful wail—a sound said to resemble the melancholy moaning of the wind. Oftentimes she is not seen but only heard, yet she is supposed to be always clearly discernible to the person upon whom she specially waits. Respecting the history of the *Banshee*, popular tradition in many instances accounts for its presence as the spirit of some mortal woman whose destinies have become linked by some accident with those of the family she follows. It is related how the *Banshee* of the family of the O'Briens of Thomond was originally a woman who had been seduced by one of the chiefs of that race— an act of indiscretion which ultimately brought about her death."

Bantu Tribes : (*See* **Africa**).

Baphomet : The goat-idol of the Templars (q.v.) and the deity of the sorcerers' Sabbath. The name is composed of three abbreviations : Tem. ohp. Ab, *Templi omnium hominum pacis abhas*, " the father of the temple of universal peace among men." Some authorities hold that the Baphomet was a monstrous head, others that it was a demon in the form of a goat. An account of a veritable Baphometic idol is as follows : " A pantheistic and magical figure of the Absolute. The torch placed between the two horns, represents the equilbrating intelligence of the triad. The goat's head, which is synthetic, and unites some characteristics of the dog, bull, and ass, represents the exclusive responsibility of matter and the expiation of bodily sins in the body. The hands are human, to exhibit the sanctity of labour ; they make the sign of esotericism above and below, to impress mystery on initiates, and they point at two lunar crescents, the upper being white and the lower black, to explain the correspondences of good and evil, mercy and justice. The lower part of the body is veiled, portraying the mysteries of universal generation, which is expressed solely by the symbol of the caduceus. The belly of the goat is scaled, and should be coloured green, the semicircle above should be blue ; the plumage, reaching to the breast, should be of various hues. The goat has female breasts, and thus its only human characteristics are those of maternity and toil, otherwise the signs of redemption. On its forehead, between the horns and beneath the torch, is the sign of the microcosm, or the pentagram with one beam in the ascendant, symbol of human intelligence, which, placed thus below the torch, makes the flame of the latter an image of divine revelation. This Pantheos should be seated on a cube, and its footstool should be a single ball, or a ball and a triangular stool."

Wright (*Narratives of Sorcery and Magic*), writing on the Baphomet says :—" Another charge in the accusation of the Templars seems to have been to a great degree proved by the depositions of witnesses ; the idol or head which they are said to have worshipped, but the real character or meaning of which we are totally unable to explain. Many Templars confessed to having seen this idol, but as they described it differently, we must suppose that it was not in all cases represented under the same form. Some said it was a frightful head, with long beard and sparkling eyes ; others said it was a man's skull ; some described it as having three faces ; some said it was of wood, and others of metal ; one witness described it as a painting (*tabula picta*) representing the image a man (*imago hominis*) and said that when it was shown to him, he was ordered to ' adore Christ, his creator.' According to some it was a gilt figure, either of wood or metal ; while others described it as painted black and white. According to another deposition, the idol had four feet, two before and two behind ; the one belonging to the order at Paris, was said to be a silver head, with two faces and a beard. The novices of the order were told always to regard this idol as their saviour. Deodatus Jaffet, a knight from the south of France, who had been received at Pedenat, deposed that the person who in his case performed the ceremonies of reception, showed him a head or idol, which appeared to have three faces, and said, ' You must adore this as your saviour, and the saviour of the order of the Temple ' and that he was made to worship the idol, saying, ' Blessed be he who shall save my soul.' Cettus Ragonis, a knight received at Rome in a chamber of the palace of the Lateran, gave a somewhat similar account. Many other witness s spoke of having seen these heads, which, however, were, perhaps, not shown to everybody, for the greatest number of those who spoke on this subject, said that they had heard speak of the head, but that they had never seen it themselves ; and many of them declared their disbelief in its existence. A friar minor deposed in England that an English Templar had assured him that in that country the order had four principal idols, one at London, in the Sacristy of the Temple, another at Bristelham, a third at Brueria (Bruern in Lincolnshire), and a fourth beyond the Humber.

" Some of the knights from the south added another circumstance in their confessions relating to this head. A templar of Florence, declared that, in the secret meetings of the chapters, one brother said to the others, showing them the idol, ' Adore this head. This head is your God and your Mahomet.' Another, Gauserand de Montpesant, said that the idol was made in the figure of Baffomet (*in figuram Baffometi*) ; and another, Raymond Rubei, described it as a wooden head, on which was painted the figure of *Baphomet*, and he adds, ' that he worshipped it by kissing its feet, and exclaiming *Xalla*,' which he describes as ' a word of the Saracens ' (*verbum Saracenorum*). This has been seized upon by some as a proof that the Templars had secretly embraced Mahometanism, as *Baffomet* or *Baphomet* is evidently a corruption of Mahomet ; but it must not be forgotten that the Christians of the West constantly used the word Mahomst in the mere signification of an idol, and that it was the desire of those who conducted the prosecution against the Templars to show their intimate intercourse with the Saracens. Others, especially Von Hammer, gave a Greek derivation of the word, and assumed it as a proof that gnosticism was the secret doctrine of the temple. . . . ''

Baptism : It was said that at the witches' Sabbath children and toads were baptised with certain horrible rites. This was called the *baptism* of the devil.

Baptism of the Line : A curious rite is performed on persons crossing the equator for the first time. The sailors who are to carry it out dress themselves in quaint costumes. The *Father of the Line* arrives in a cask, accompanied by a courier, a devil, a hair-dresser, and a miller. The unfortunate passenger has his hair curled, is liberally sprinkled with flour, and then has water showered upon him, if he is not ducked. The origin of this custom is not known, nor is it quite clear what part the devil plays in it. It is said, however, that it may be averted by tipping the sailors.

Baquet : A large circular tub which entered largely into the treatment which D'Eslon, the friend and follower of Mesmer, prescribed for his patients. Puységur tells us in his book *Du Magnétisme Animal*, that in the *baquet* were placed some bottles, arranged in a particular manner, and partly covered with water. It was fitted with a lid in which were several holes, through which passed iron rods, connecting the patients, who sat round the contrivance, with the interior of the tub. The operator was armed with a shorter iron rod. While the patients waited for the symptoms of the magnetic treatment, someone played upon a pianoforte, a device which is frequently adopted at séances. The symptoms included violent convulsions, cries, laughter, and vomiting. This state they called the *crisis*, and it was supposed to hasten the healing process. A commission appointed in 1784 by the French government through the *Faculté de Médecine* and the *Societé royale de Médecine*, reported that such practices were exceedingly dangerous, and in nowise proved the existence of the magnetic fluid. Dr. Bell a " professor of animal magnetism " set up a similar institution in England in 1785, using a large oak *baquet*.

Bar-Lgura : (Semitic demon) : Sits on the roofs of houses and leaps on the inhabitants. People so afflicted are called *d'baregara*.

Barqu : A demon in whose keeping was the secret of the Philosophers' stone.

Barguest, the : A goblin or phantom of a mischievous character, so named from his habit of sitting on bars or gates. It is said that he can make himself visible in the day time. Rich in the *Encyclopædia Metropolitana* relates a story of a lady, whom he knew, who had been brought up in the country. She had been passing through the fields one morning, when a girl, and saw, as she thought, someone sitting on a stile : however, as she drew near, it vanished.

Barnaud, Nicholas : A medical doctor of the sixteenth century who claimed to have discovered the Philosophers' Stone. He published a great number of short treatises on the subject of Alchemy, which are contained in the third volume of the *Theatrum Chimicum* of Zetzner, published at Strasburg, in 1659.

Baron Chaos : (*See* Busardiar).

Bartholomew : (*See* Dee).

Baru : Caste of priests. (*See* **Semites.**)

Basil : an astrologer. (*See* Italy).

Basilideans : A gnostic sect founded by Basilides of Alexandria, who claimed to have received his esoteric doctrines from Glaucus, a disciple of the Apostle Peter. The system had three grades—material, intellectual, and spiritual, and possessed two allegorical statues, male and female. The doctrine had many points of resemblance to that of the Ophites (q.v.), and ran on the lines of Jewish Kabalism.

Bassantin, James : a Scottish astrologer, the son of the Laird of Bassantin, in the Merse, was born in the reign of James IV. ; and, after studying mathematics at the University of Glasgow, he travelled for farther information on the Continent. He subsequently went to Paris, where for some years he taught mathematics in the University. He returned to Scotland in 1562. The prevailing belief of that age, particularly in France, was a belief in judicial astrology. In his way home through England, as we learn from Sir James Melville's Memoirs, he met with his brother, Sir Robert Melville, who was at that time engaged, on the part of the unfortunate Mary, in endeavouring to effect a meeting between her and Elizabeth ; when he predicted that all his efforts would be in vain ; " for, first, they will neuer meit togither, and next, there will nevir be bot dissembling and secret hattrent (hatred) for a whyle, and at length captivity and utter wrak for our Quen by England." Melville's answer was, that he could not credit such news, which he looked upon as " false, ungodly, and unlawful ; " on which *Bassantin* replied, " Sa far as Melanthon, wha was a godly thologue, has declared and written anent the naturall scyences, that are lawfull and daily red in dyvers Christian Universities ; in the quhilkis, as in all other artis, God gives to some less, to some mair and clearer knawledge than till othirs ; be the quhilk knawledge I have also that at length, that the kingdom of England sall of rycht fall to the crown of Scotland, and that ther are some born at this instant that sall bruik lands and heritages in England. Bot, alace, it will cost many their lyves, and many bluidy battailes will be fouchen first, and the Spaniatris will be helpers, and will take a part to themselves for their labours." The first part of *Bassantin's* prediction, which he might very well have hazarded from what he may have known of Elizabeth's character and disposition, and also from the fact that Mary was the next heir to the English throne, proved true. *Bassantin* was a zealous Protestant and a supporter of the Regent Moray. He died in 1568. His principal work is a Treatise or Discourse on Astronomy, written in French, which was translated into Latin by John Tornæsius (M. de Tournes), and published at Geneva in 1599. He wrote four other treatises. Although well versed for his time in what are called the exact sciences, *Bassantin*, or, as his name is sometimes spelt, *Bassantoun*, had received no part of a classical education. Vossius observes, that his *Astronomical Discourse* was written in very bad French, and that the author knew " neither Greek nor Latin, but only Scots." *Bassantin's* Planetary System was that of Ptolemy.

Bat : There is an Oriental belief that the bat is specially adapted to occult uses. In the Tyrol it is believed that the man who wears the left eye of a bat may become invisible, and in Hesse he who wears the heart of a bat bound to his arm with red thread will always be lucky at cards. (*See* **Chagrin**).

Bataille, Dr. : Author of *Le Diable au XIX. Siècle*. Under the pseudonym of Dr. Hecks he purports to have witnessed the secret rites and orgies of many diabolic societies, but a merely perfunctory examination of his work is sufficient to brand it as wholly an effort of the imagination.

Bathym, also called Marthim, a duke of the Infernal Regions. He has the appearance of a robust man, says Wierius, but his body ends in a serpent's tail. He bestrides a steed of livid colour. He is well versed in the virtues of herbs and precious stones. He is able to transport men from one place to another with wondrous speed. Thirty legions obey his behests.

Baton, the Devil's : There is preserved in the *marche d' Ancâne*, Tolentino, a *bâton* which it is said that the devil used.

Battle of Loquifer, The : a tale incorporated in the Charlemagne saga, supposed to have been written about the twelfth century. Its hero is Renouart, the giant brother-in-law of William of Orange, and the events take place on the sea. Renouart and his barons are on the shore at Porpaillart, when a Saracen fleet is seen. He is persuaded to enter one of the ships, which immediately set sail ; and he is told by Isembert, a hideous monster, that the Saracens mean to flay him alive. Renouart, armed only with a huge bar of wood, kills this creature, and makes the Saracens let him go, while they return to their own country. It is arranged that Renouart will fight one Loquifer, a fairy giant and leader of the Saracens ; and on the issue of this combat the war will depend. They meet on an island near Porpaillart. Loquifer is in possession of a magical balm, which heals all his wounds immediately, and is concealed in his club ; but Renouart, who is assisted by angels, at length succeeds in depriving Loquifer of his club, so that his strength departs. Renouart slays him, and the devil carries off his soul. The romance goes on to tell of a duel between William of Orange and Desrame, Renouart's father, in which the latter is slain. Renouart is comforted by fairies, who bear him to Avalon

where he has many adventures. He is finally wrecked, but is rescued by mermaids, and awakes to find himself on the sands at Porpaillart, from which spot he had been taken to Avalon.

Bauer, George : who Latinized his name (a boor or husbandman) into " Agricola," was born in the province of Misnia, in 1494. An able and industrious man, he acquired a considerable knowledge of the principles of medicine, which led him, as it led his contemporaries, to search for the *elixir vitæ* and the Philosopher's Stone. A treatise on these interesting subjects, which he published at Cologne in 1531, secured him the favour of Duke Maurice of Saxony, who appointed him the superintendent of his silver-mines at Chemnitz. In this post he obtained a practical acquaintance with the properties of metals which dissipated his wild notions of their possible transmutation into gold ; but if he abandoned one superstition he adopted another, and from the legends of the miners imbibed a belief in the existence of good and evil spirits in the bowels of the earth, and in the creation of explosive gases and fire-damp by the malicious agency of the latter. *Bauer* died in 1555.

Bave : Daughter of the wizard Calatin. She figures in the famous Irish legend *The Cattle Raid of Quelgny*. By taking the form of one of Niam's handmaids she succeeded in enticing her away from Cuchulin, and led her forth to wander in the woods.

Bayemon : The grimoire of Pope Honorius gives this name as that of a powerful demon whom it addresses as monarch of the western parts of the Infernal Regions. To him the following invocation is addressed : " O *King Bayemon*, most mighty, who reigneth towards the western parts, I call upon thee and invoke thy name in the name of the Divinity. I command thee in the name of the Most High to present thyself before this circle, thee and the other spirits who are thy subjects, in the name of Passiel and Rosus, for the purpose of replying to all that which I demand of thee. If thou dost not come I will torment thee with a sword of heavenly fire. I will augment thy pains and burn thee. Obey, O *King Bayemon*.

Bealings Bells : In February, 1834, a mysterious outbreak of bell-ringing was heard at the residence of Major Moor, F.R.S.,—Bealings, near Woodbridge, Suffolk. From the 2nd of February to the 27th of March the bells of the house rang at frequent intervals, and without any visible agency. The Major meanwhile took careful note of the condition of the atmosphere, state of the wires, and any physical cause which might affect the bells, but, as Mr. Podmore justly points out, he omitted to take precautions against trickery in his own household, and has not even left on record the names of its members, or any facts concerning them.

Beans : A forbidden article of diet. The consumption of beans was prohibited by Pythagoras and Plato to those who desire veracious dreams, as they tend to inflate ; and for the purpose of truthful dreaming, the animal nature must be made to lie quiet. Cicero, however, laughs at this discipline, asking if it be the stomach and not the mind with which one dreams ?

Bearded Demon : The demon who teaches the secret of the Philosophers' Stone. He is but little known. The *démon barbu* is not to be confused with Barbatos, a great and powerful demon who is a duke in Hades, though not a philosopher ; nor with Barbas, who is interested in mechanics. It is said that the *bearded demon* is so called on account of his remarkable beard.

Beaumont, John : Author of a *Treatise on Spirits, Apparitions*, etc., published in 1705. He is described as " a man of hypochondriacal disposition, with a considerable degree of reading, but with a strong bias to credulity." Labouring under this affection, he saw hundreds of imaginary men and women about him, though, as he adds, he never saw anything in the night-time, unless by fire or candlelight, or in the moonshine. " I had two spirits," he says, " who constantly attended me, night and day, for above three months together, who called each other by their names ; and several spirits would call at my chamber door, and ask whether such spirits lived there, and they would answer they did. As for the other spirits that attended me, I heard none of their names mentioned only I asked one spirit, which came for some nights together, and rung a little bell in my ear, what his name was, who answered *Ariel*. The two spirits that constantly attended myself appeared both in women's habit, they being of a brown complexion, about three feet in stature ; they had both black loose net-work gowns, tied with a black sash about the middle, and within the net-work appeared a gown of a golden colour, with somewhat of a light striking through it. Their heads were not dressed in top-knots, but they had white linen caps on, with lace on them about three fingers' breadth, and over it they had a black loose net-work hood."

" I would not," he says, " for the whole world, undergo what I have undergone, upon spirits coming twice to me ; their first coming was most dreadful to me, the thing being then altogether new, and consequently most surprising, though at the first coming they did not appear to me but only called to me at my chamber-windows, rung bells, sung to me, and played on music, etc.; but the last coming also carried terror enough ; for when they came, being only five in number, the two women before mentioned, and three men (though afterwards there came hundreds), they told me they would kill me if I told any person in the house of their being there, which put me in some consternation ; and I made a servant sit up with me four nights in my chamber, before a fire, it being in the Christmas holidays, telling no person of their being there. One of these spirits, in women's dress, lay down upon the bed by me every night ; and told me, if I slept, the spirits would kill me, which kept me waking for three nights. In the meantime, a near relation of mine went (though unknown to me) to a physician of my acquaintance, desiring him to prescribe me somewhat for sleeping, which he did, and a sleeping potion was brought me ; but I set it by, being very desirous and inclined to sleep without it. The fourth night I could hardly forbear sleeping ; but the spirit, lying on the bed by me, told me again, I should be killed if I slept ; whereupon I rose and sat by the fireside, and in a while returned to my bed ; and so I did a third time, but was still threatened as before ; whereupon I grew impatient, and asked the spirits what they would have ? Told them I had done the part of a Christian, in humbling myself to God, and feared them not ; and rose from my bed, took a cane, and knocked at the ceiling of my chamber, a near relation of mine then lying over me, who presently rose and came down to me about two o'clock in the morning, to whom I said, " You have seen me disturbed these four days past, and that I have not slept : the occasion of it was, that five spirits, which are now in the room with me, have threatened to kill me if I told any person of their being here, or if I slept ; but I am not able to forbear sleeping longer, and acquaint you with it, and now stand in defiance of them ; and thus I exerted myself about them and notwithstanding their continued threats I slept very well the next night, and continued to do so, though they continued with me above three months, day and night."

Beausoleil, Jean du Chatelot, Baron de : German mineralogist and alchemist, who lived during the first half of the seventeenth century. He travelled over most European countries looking for metals with the aid of a divining ring. In 1626 his instruments were seized under the pretext that

they were bewitched, and he himself prisoned in the Bastille, where he died in 1645. In 1617 he published a work entitled *Diorisinus, id est definitis verae philisophiæ de materia prima lapidis philosophalis. Beausoleil* was the greatest of French metallurgists of his time.

Bechard : A demon alluded to in the *Key of Solomon* as having power over the winds and the tempests. He makes hail, thunder and rain.

Bed : Graham's Magnetic : A magnetic contrivance made use of by one Graham, physician and magnetist of Edinburgh. His whole house, which he termed the Temple of Hygeia, was of great magnificence, but particularly did splendour prevail in the room wherein was set the *magnetic bed*. The *bed* itself rested on six transparent pillars ; the mattresses were soaked with oriental perfumes ; the bed-clothes were of satin, in tints of purple and sky-blue. A healing stream of magnetism, as well as fragrant and strengthening medicines, were introduced into the sleeping apartment through glass tubes and cylinders. To these attractions were added the soft strains of hidden flutes, harmonicons, and a large organ. Permission to use this celestial couch, so soothing to shattered nerves, was accorded only to those who sent a written application to its owner, inclosing £50 sterling.

Bees : It is maintained by certain demonologists that if a sorceress ate a queen-bee before being captured, she would be able to sustain her trial and tortures without making a confession. In some parts of Brittany it is claimed for these insects that they are very sensitive to the fortunes and misfortunes of their master, and will not thrive unless he is careful to tie a piece of black cloth to the hive when a death occurs in the family, and a piece of red cloth when there is any occasion of rejoicing. Solinus writes that there are no bees in Ireland, and even if a little Irish earth be taken to another country, and spread about the hives, the bees will be forced to abandon the place, so fatal to them is the earth of Ireland. The same story is found in the *Origines* of Isodore. " Must we seek," says Lebrun, " the source of this calumny of Irish earth ? No ; for it is sufficient to say that it is a fable, and that many bees are to be found in Ireland."

Belin, Albert : A Benedictine, born at Besançon in 1610. His principal works are a treaty on talismans and a dissertation upon astral figures, published at Paris in 1671, and again in 1709. He also wrote *Sympathetic Powder Justified*, an alchemical work, and *Adventures of an unknown philosopher in the search for and the manufacture of the Philosopher's Stone*. This latter work is divided into four books and speaks very clearly of the manner in which the stone is made. (Paris, 1664 and 1674).

Bell, Dr. : (*See* **Spiritualism**.)

Belle-Fleur, La : (*See* **Antichrist**.)

Bellenden, Sir Lewis : (*See* **Scotland**.)

Belli Paaro : A secret society of Liberia, Africa, the cult of which consists in a description of brotherhood with departed spirits. Dapper, an early author, says of this society : " They have also another custom which they call *Belli Paaro*, of which they say it is a death, a new birth and an incorporation in the community of spirits or soul with whom the common folk associate in the bush, and help to eat the offerings prepared for the spirits." This description is far from clear, but it is obvious enough that those who join the society desire to be regarded as spiritualised, or as having died and having been brought to life again ; and that their society is nothing more than a confraternity of all those who have passed through this training in common.

Belloc, Jeanne : A sorceress of the district of Labour, in France, who in the reign of Henry IV. was indicted for sorcery at the age of 84 years. In answer to Pierre Delancre who interrogated her, she stated that she commenced to repair to the sabbatic meetings of Satan in the winter of the year 1609, that she was there presented to the Devil who kissed her, a mark of approbation which he bestowed upon the greatest sorcerers only. She related that the Sabbath was a species of bal masqué, to which some came in their ordinary forms, whilst others joined the dance in the guise of dogs cats, donkeys, pigs and other animals.

Belocolus : A white stone with a black pupil, said to render its bearer invisible in a field of battle.

Belomancy : The method of divination by arrows, dates as far back as the age of the Chaldeans. It existed among the Greeks, and still later among the Arabians. The manner in which the latter practised it is described elsewhere, and they continued its use though forbidden by the Koran. Another method deserves mention. This was to throw a certain number of arrows into the air, and the direction in which the arrow inclined as it fell, pointed out the course to be taken by the inquirer. Divination by arrows is the same in principle as Rhabdomancy (q.v.).

Belphegor : The demon of discoveries and ingenious inventions. He appears always in the shape of a young woman. The Moabites, who called him *Baalphegor,* adored him on Mount Phegor. He it is who bestows riches.

Benedict IX. : At a time when the papacy was much abused —about the tenth and eleventh centuries—the papal crown was more than once offered for sale. Thus the office fell into the hands of a high and ambitious family who held it for a boy of twelve—*Benedict IX.* As he grew older the boy lost no opportunity of disgracing his position by his depraved mode of life. But, like his predecessors in the papal chair, he excelled in sorcery and various forms of magic. One of the most curious stories concerning him tells how he made the Roman matrons follow him over hill and dale, through forests and across rivers, by the charm of his magic, as though he were a sort of Pied Piper.

Benemmerinnen : Hebrew witches who haunt women in childbirth for the purpose of stealing new-born infants.

Benjees, The : A people of the East Indies, given over to the worship of the Devil ; and whose temples and pagodas are filled with horrible statues of him. The king of Calicut had a temple wholly filled with awful figures of the devil, and which was lighted only with the gleam of many lamps. In the centre was a copper throne, on which was seated a devil, made of the same metal, with a large tiara on his head, three huge horns and four others which come out of his forehead. On his tongue and in his hand were two figures—souls, which the Indians say, he s preparing to devour.

Bensozia : According to Don Martin in his *Religion de Gaulois,* " chief deviless " of a certain Sabbatic meeting held in France in the twelfth and thirteenth centuries. She was, he says, the Diana of the ancient Gauls, and was also called Nocticula, Herodias, and " The Moon." One finds in the manuscripts of the church at Couserans, that the ladies of the fourteenth century were said to go on horseback to the nocturnal revelries of Bensozia. All of them were forced to inscribe their names in a Sabbatic catalogue along with those of the sorcerers proper, and after this ceremony they believed themselves to be fairies. There was found at Montmorillon in Poitou, in the eighteenth century, a portion of an ancient temple, a bas-relief with the figure of a naked woman carved upon it, and it is not unlikely, thinks Collin de Plancy, that this figure was the original deity of the *Bensozia* cult.

Beowulf : an Anglo-Saxon saga of great interest. The events in this poem probably took place about the fifth century. *Beowulf,* himself, was most likely one of the Sons of Light or Men of the Sun, whose business it was to fight the powers of darkness until they themselves fell.

It is related in this legend how *Beowulf* fought the monster, Grendel, and succeeded in defeating him—the giant escaping only by leaving his arm in *Beowulf's* grip. But Grendel's mother, a mer-woman, came to revenge him and slew many people. *Beowulf,* hearing of this, took up the quarrel, and diving to the bottom of the sea, where her palace lay, killed her after a fierce fight. Later on *Beowulf* was made regent of Gothland, and afterwards king, and he reigned for about forty years. He was poisoned by the fangs of a dragon during a mighty struggle, and died from the effects. He was buried on a hill named Hronesnas, and was deeply mourned by his people.

Berande : A sorceress burnt at Maubec, in France, in 1577. She was confronted by a damsel whom she accused of sorcery, which the girl denied, whereat the beldame exclaimed, " Dost thou not remember how at the last dance at the Croix du Paté, thou didst carry a pot of poison ? " The damsel at this confessed, and was burnt along with her accuser.

Bereschith : Universal Genesis, one of the two parts into which the Kabala was divided by the rabbins.

Berigard of Pisa : Alchemist. (1578 ? — 1664). Owing to his residing for many years at Pisa, this alchemist is commonly known by the appellation given above ; but in reality he was not an Italian but a Frenchman, and his name was *Claude Guillermet de Bérigard,* or, as it is sometimes spelt, *Beauregard.* The date of his birth is uncertain, some authorities assigning it to 1578, and others placing it considerably later ; but they are agreed in saying that Moulins was his native town, and that, while a young man, he evinced a keen love for science in its various branches, and began to dabble in alchemy. He appears to have studied for a while at the Sorbonne, at Paris ; and, having acquired some fame there on account of his erudition, he was appointed professor of natural philosophy at the University of Pisa. This post he held until the year 1640, whereupon he was assigned an analogous position at Padua, and it was probably in the latter town that his death occurred in 1664. His most important contribution to scientific literature is *Dubitationes in Dialogum Ealilæi pro Terræ immobilitate,* a quarto published at Florence in 1632 ; but he was likewise author of *Circulus Pisanus,* issued at Udine in 1643, wherein he concerns himself chiefly with commenting on Aristotle's ideas on physics. *Bérigarde's* writings are virtually forgotten nowadays, but they are interesting as documents illustrating the progress of scientific knowledge throughout the seventeenth century.

Berkeley, Old Woman of : (*See* **England.**)

Bermechobus : The supposed writings of St. Methodius of Olympus (martyred 311 A.D.) or the saint of the same name who was Patriarch of Constantinople and who died in 846. The real name of the work is Bea-Methodius, a contraction for *Beatus Methodivo,* which was misprinted " Bermechobus." The work is of the nature of a prophetic Apocalypse, and foretells the history of the world. It was handed down by the Gnostics and was printed in the *Liber Mirabilis* (q.v.). There are no grounds, however, for the supposition that the work should be referred to either of the saints above mentioned. It recounts how Seth sought a new country in the east and came to the country of the initiates, and how the children of Cain instituted a system of black magic in India. The author identifies the Ishmaelites with those tribes who overthrew the Roman power, and tells of a powerful northern people whose reign will be over-turned by Anti-Christ. A universal kingdom will thereafter be founded, governed by a prince of French blood, after which a prolonged period of justice will supervene.

Bernheim : (*See* **Hypnotism.**)

Berthome du Lignon : called Champagnat, a sorcerer brought to trial at Montmorillon, in Poitou, in 1599. He confessed that his father had taken him to the Sabbath of the sorcerers in his youth, that he had promised the Devil his soul and his body, that His Satanic Majesty had shown him marks of his favour, and that he had even visited him in prison on the previous night. He further confessed having slain several persons and beasts with the magical powders given him by the Enemy of Mankind.

Bertrand, Alexandre—His Traité du Somnambulisme et du Magnetisme Animal en France : (*See* **Hypnotism ; Spiritualism.**)

Beryl : *Beryl*, said to preserve wedded love, and to be a good medium for magical vision.

Bezoar : (red). A precious stone supposed to be possessed of magical properties, and found in the bodies of certain animals. At one time these stones would fetch ten times their weight in gold, being used as a remedy against poison and contagion ; and for this purpose they were both taken internally, and worn round the neck. It is said that there are nine varieties of *bezoar*, differing greatly in composition ; but they may be generally divided into those which consist mainly of mineral and those which consist of organic matter. A strange origin was assigned to this stone by some of the early naturalists. It is said that the oriental stags when oppressed with years fed upon serpents, which renewed their youth. In order to counteract the poison which was absorbed into their system, they plunged into a running stream keeping their heads only above water. This caused a viscous fluid to be distilled from their eyes, which was indurated by the heat of the sun, and formed the *bezoar*.

Bhikshu : (*See* **India.**)

Biarbi : (*See* **Fascination.**)

Bible des Bohemians : (*See* **Tarot.**)

Bible of the Devil : This was without doubt a grimoire (q.v.) or some such work. But Delancre says that the Devil informed sorcerers that he possessed a bible consisting of sacred books, having a theology of its own, which was dilated upon by various professors. One great magician, continues Delancre, who was brought before the Parliament of Paris, avowed that there dwelt at Toledo sixty-three masters in the faculty of Magic who took for their text-book the Devil's Bible.

Bibliomancy : A method of discovering whether or not a person was innocent of sorcery, by weighing him against the great Bible in the Church. If the person weighed less than the Bible, he was innocent. (*See* **Witchcraft.**)

Biffant : A little-known demon, chief of a legion who entered the body of one Denise de la Caille (q.v.) and who was obliged to sign with his claws the *proces verbal* of exorcisms.

Bifrons : A demon of monstrous guise who, according to Wierius, often took the form of a man well versed in Astrology and planetary influences. He excels in geometry, is acquainted with the virtues of herbs, precious stones and plants, and it is said that he is able to transport corpses from one place to another. He it is also who lights the strange corpse-lights above the tombs of the dead. Twenty six of the infernal regions obey his behests.

Bigois or Bigotis : A sorcerer of Tuscany who, it is said, composed a learned work on the nature of prognostications, especially those connected with thunder and lightning. The book is said to be irretrievably lost. It is thought that *Bigois* is the same as Bagoe (q.v.), a sibly of Erithryea, but this is merely of the nature of surmise.

Binah : In the supreme triangle of the *Kabala* the three sides are reason, which they name *Kether ;* necessity, *Chochmah ;* and liberty, *Binah.*

Biragues, Flaminio de : Author of an infernal-facetious work entitled *l'Enfer de la mere Cardine*, which treats of the dreadful battle in Hell on the occasion of the marriage of Cerberus with Cardine (Paris, 1585 and 1597.) It is a satire on the demonography of the times. Didot reprinted the work in 1793. The author was a nephew of a Chancellor of France, Rene de Biragues.

Birds : It is a common belief among savage tribes that the souls of the dead are conveyed to the land of the hereafter by *birds*. Among some West African peoples, for instance, a *bird* is bound to the body of the deceased and then sacrificed, so that it may carry the man's soul to the after-world. The Bagos also offer up a *bird* on the corpse of a deceased person for the same reason. The South Sea Islanders, again, bury their dead in coffins shaped like the *bird* which is to bear away their spirits, while the natives of Borneo represent Tempon-Telon's Ship of the Dead (q.v.) as having the form of a *bird*. The Indian tribes of North-West America have rattles shaped like ravens, with a large face painted on the breast. The probable significance is that the raven is to carry the disembodied soul to the region of the sun.

Birog : A Druidess of Irish legendary origin. She it was who, by her magic, brought Kian and Ethlinn together.

Birraark : Australian necromancers. (*See* **Necromancy.**)

Biscar, Jeanette : A sorceress of the district of Labour in France, who was transported to the witches' Sabbath by the Devil in the form of a goat. As a reward she was suspended in mid-air head downwards.

Bisclaveret : The name of the were-wolf (q.v.) in Brittany. It is believed to be a human being, transformed by magic into a fearsome man-devouring beast, which roams about the woods, seeking whom it may slay.

Bitru : Otherwise called Sytry, a great Prince of Hell, according to the demonographer Wierius. He appeared in the form of a leopard with the wings of a griffin. But when he adopted a human appearance for the nonce it was invariably one of great beauty. It is he who awakes lust in the human heart. Seventy legions obey his commands.

Bitumen, in Magic : *Bitumen* was greatly used in magical practices. Images for the purpose of sympathetic magic were often made of this substance ; and it was used in the ceremonies for the cleansing of houses in which any uncleanness had appeared—being spread on the floor like clay.

Black Earth : (*See* **Philosopher's Stone.**)

Black Hen, Fast of The : In Hungary and the adjacent countries it is believed that whoever has been robbed and wishes to discover the thief must take a *black hen* and along with it fast strictly for nine Fridays. The thief will then either return the plunder or die. This is called " taking up a black fast " against anyone. A great deal of lore concerning *black hens* may be found in the works of Gubernatis and Friedrich.

Black Magic : Middle Ages. *Black Magic* as practised in mediæval times may be defined as the use of supernatural knowledge for the purposes of evil, the invocation of diabolic and infernal powers that they may become the slaves and emissaries of man's will ; in short, a perversion of legitimate mystic science. This art and its attendant practices can be traced from the time of the ancient Egyptians and Persians, from the Greeks and Hebrews to the period when it reached its apogee in the Middle Ages, thus forming an unbroken chain ; for in mediæval magic may be found the perpetuation of the popular rites of paganism—the ancient gods had become devils, their mysteries orgies, their worship sorcery.

Some historians have tried to trace the areas in Europe most affected by these devilish practices. Spain is said to have excelled all in infamy, to have plumbed the depths of the abyss. The south of France next became a hotbed of sorcery, whence it branched northwards to Paris and the countries and islands beyond, southward to Italy, finally extending into the Tyrol and Germany.

In *Black Magic* human perversity found the means of ministering to its most terrible demands and the possible attainment of its darkest imaginings. To gain limitless power over god, demon and man ; for personal aggrandisement and glorification ; to cheat, trick and mock ; to gratify base appetites ; to aid religious bigotry and jealousies ; to satisfy private and public enmities ; to further political intrigue ; to encompass disease, calamity and death—these were the ends and aims of *Black Magic* and its followers.

So widespread, so intense was the belief in the Powers of Evil that it may truly be said the Devil reigned supreme, if the strength and fervour of a universal fear be weighed against the weak and wavering manifestations of love and goodwill, peace and charity enjoined by religion in the worship of God.

Under the influence of this belief the world became to the mind and imagination of man a place of dread. At set of sun, at midnight, in twilight of dawn and eve, the legions of evil were abroad on their mission of terror. A running stream, a lake, or thick forest, held each its horde of malevolent spirits lying in wait for the lonely wayfarer, while the churchyard close to the House of God, the place of the gallows away from the habitation of man, the pestilential marsh, wilderness and mysterious cavern, the barren slopes and summits of mountains, were the dread meeting-places of the Devil and his myrmidons, the scenes of their infamous orgies, the temples of their blasphemous rites.

And the night was troubled by evil and ominous winds blowing from the Netherworld, heavy with the beating of the innumerable wings of the birds of ill-omen presaging woe ; the darkness was faintly lit by the flitting phosphorescent forms of sepulchral larvæ, waiting to batten on the souls and bodies of man ; of stryges infesting the tombs and desecrating the dead ; of incubi and succubi surrounding the homes of the living to bring dishonour and madness to sleeping man and woman and beget monstrous and myriad life ; of ravenous vampires in search of victims for their feast of blood. Moon and stars might illumine the darkness, but in their beams were spells and enchantments, in their rising and waning the inexorable workings of Fate, while against their light could be seen the dishevelled or naked forms of warlock and witch passing overhead to their diabolical Sabbaths. The familiar happenings and actions of life might be nothing but the machinations of sorcery— to eat and drink might be to swallow evil ; to look upon beauty in any form, the sesame to malign influence ; to laugh, but to echo infernal mockery and mirth.

In this fruitful soil of superstition and grotesque ignorance, *Black Magic* sowed and reaped its terrible harvest of evil, persecution, madness and death. Such a state of mind must, of necessity, have induced a weakness of will and imagination specially prone to the influence of hypnotic suggestion by a stronger will, and even more ready to fall an easy prey to self-hypnotism, which must have often been the result of such an atmosphere of foreboding and dread.

The simplest ailments or most revolting diseases, catalepsy and somnambulism, hysteria, and insanity, all these were traced to the power of *Black Magic*, caused through the conjurations of sorcery. It followed that curative medicine was also a branch of magic, not a rational science, the cures being nothing if not fantastic in the last degree —incantations and exorcisms, amulets and talismans of precious stones, metals or weird medicaments rendered powerful by spells ; philtres and enchanted drinks, the cure of epilepsy by buried peachblossoms, and though in

the use of herbs and chemicals was laid the foundation of the curative science of to-day, it was more for their enchanted and symbolic significance that they were prescribed by the magicians.

History shows us that the followers of the Black Art swarmed everywhere. In this fraternity as in others there were grades, from the pretenders, charlatans and diviners of the common people, to the various secret societies and orders of initiates, amongst whom were kings and queens, and popes, dignitaries of church and state, where the knowledge and ritual were carefully cherished and preserved in manuscripts, some of which are extant at the present day, ancient grimoires (q.v.), variously termed the Black, the Red, the Great Grimoire, each full of weird rites, formulæ and conjurations, evocations of evil malice and lust in the names of barbaric deities ; charms and bewitchments clothed in incomprehensible jargon, and ceremonial processes for the fulfilment of imprecations of misfortune, calamity, sin and death.

The deity who was worshipped, whose powers were invoked in the practice of *Black Magic*, was the Source and Creator of Evil, Satanas, Belial, the Devil, a direct descendant of the Egyptian Set, the Persian Ahriman, the Python of the Greeks, the Jewish Serpent, Baphomet of the Templars, the Goat-deity of the Witches' Sabbath. He was said to have the head and legs of a goat, and the breasts of a woman.

To his followers he was known by many names, among these being debased names of forgotten deities, also the Black One, the Black He-goat, the Black Raven, the Dog, the Wolf and Snake, the Dragon, the Hell-hound, Hellhand, and Hell-bolt. His transformations were unlimited, as is indicated by many of his names ; other favourite and familiar forms were a cat, a mouse, a toad, or a worm, or again, the human form, especially as a young and handsome man when on his amorous adventures. The signs by which he might be identified, though not invariably, were the cloven hoof, the goat's beard, cock's feathers, or ox's tail.

In all his grotesquery are embedded ancient mysteries and their symbols, the detritus of dead faiths and faded civilizations. The Greek Pan with the goat limbs masquerades as the Devil, also the goat as emblematic of fire and symbol of generation, and perhaps traces of the Jewish tradition where two goats were taken, one pure, the other impure, the first offered as sacrifice in expiation of sin, the other, the impure burdened with sins by imprecation and driven into the wilderness, in short, the scapegoat. In the Hebrew Kabala, Satan's name is that of Jehovah reversed. He is not a devil, but the negation of deity.

Beneath the Devil's sway were numberless hordes and legions of demons and spirits, ready and able to procure and work any and every evil or disaster the mind of man might conceive and desire. In one Grimoire it tells of nine orders of evil spirits, these being False Gods, Lying Spirits, Vessels of Iniquity, Revenge led by Asmodeus, Deluders by the Serpent, Turbulents by Merigum, Furies by Apollyon, Calumniators by Astaroth, and Tempters by Mammon. These demons again are named separately, the meaning of each name indicating the possessor's capacity, such as destroyer, devastator, tumult, ravage, and so forth.

Again each earthly vice and calamity was personified by a demon, Moloch, who devours infants ; Nisroch, god of hatred, despair, fatality ; Astarte, Lilith and Astaroth, deities of debauchery and abortion ; Adramelek, of murder, and Belial, of red anarchy.

According to the Grimoires, the rites and rules are multifarious, each demon demanding special invocation and procedure. The ends that may be obtained by these means are sufficiently indicated in the headings of the chapters : To take possession of all kinds of treasure ; to like in opulence ; to ruin possessions ; to demolish buildings and strongholds ; to cause armed men to appear ; to excite every description of hatred, discord, failure and vengeance ; to excite tempests ; to excite love in a virgin, in a married person ; to procure adulteries ; to cause enchanted music and lascivious dances to appear ; to learn all secrets from those of Venus to Mars ; to render oneself invisible ; to fly in the air and travel ; to operate under water for twenty-four hours ; to open every kind of lock without a key, without noise and thus gain entrance to prison, larder or charnel-house ; to innoculate the walls of houses with plague and disease ; to bind familiar spirits ; to cause a dead body to revive ; to transform one's self ; to transform men into animals or animals into men.

These rites fell under the classification of divination, bewitchments and necromancy. The first named was carried out by magical readings of fire, smoke, water or blood ; by letters of names, numbers, symbols, arrangements of dots ; by lines of hand or finger nails ; by birds and their flight or their entrails ; by dice or cards, rings or mirrors.

Bewitchments were carried out by means of nails, animals, toads or waxen figures and mostly to bring about suffering or death. In the first method nails were consecrated to evil by spells and invocations, then nailed crosswise above the imprint of the feet of the one who is destined for torment. The next was by selection of some animal supposed to resemble the intended victim and attaching to it some of his hair or garments. They gave it the name and then proceeded to torture it, in whole or part according to the end desired, by driving nails, red-hot pins and thorns into the body to the rhythm of muttered maledictions. For like purpose a fat toad was often selected, baptised, made to swallow a host, both consecrated and execrated, tied with hairs of the victim upon which the sorcerer had previously spat, and finally buried at the threshold of the bewitched one's door, whence it issued as nightmare and vampire for his undoing.

The last and most favoured method was by the use of waxen images. Into the wax was mixed baptismal oil and ash of consecrated hosts, and out of this was fashioned a figure resembling the one to be bewitched. It was then baptised, receiving the persons name in full ; received the Sacraments, and next subjected to curses, torture by knives or fire ; then finally stabbed to the heart. It was also possible to bewitch a person by insufflation, breathing upon them, and so causing a heaviness of their will and corresponding compliance to the sorcerer.

Necromancy (q.v.) was the raising of the dead by evocations and sacrilegious rites, for the customary purposes of evil. The scene of operation might be about pits filled with blood and resembling a shambles, in a darkened and suffocating room, in a churchyard or beneath swinging gibbets, and the number of ghosts so summoned and galvanized into life might be one of legion.

For whatever end, the procedure usually included profanation of Christian ritual, such as diabolical masses and administration of polluted sacrements to animals and reptiles ; bloody sacrifices of animals, often of children ; of orgiastic dances, generally of circular formation, such as that of the Witches' Sabbath in which undreamed-of evil and abominations, all distortions and monstrosities of reality and imagination took part, to end in a nightmare of obscene madness.

For paraphernalia and accessories the sorcerers scoured the world and the imagination and mind of man, bending all things, beautiful or horrible to their service. The different planets ruled over certain objects and states and invocations, for such were of great potency if delivered under their auspices. Mars favoured wars and strife, Venus love, Jupiter ambition and intrigue, Saturn malediction and death.

Vestments and symbols proper to the occasion must be donned. The electric furs of the panther, lynx and cat added their quota of influence to the ceremonial. Colours also must be observed and suitable ornaments. For operations of vengeance the robe must be the hue of leaping flame, or rust and blood, with belt and bracelets of steel, and crown of rue and wormwood. Blue, Green and Rose were the colours for amorous incantations ; whilst for the encompassing of death black must be worn, with belt of lead and wreath of cypress, amid loathsome incense of sulphur and assafœtida.

Precious stones and metals also added their influence to the spells. Geometrical figures, stars, pentagrams, columns, triangles, were used ; also herbs, such as belladonna and assafœtida ; flowers, honeysuckle, being the witches' ladder, the arum, deadly nightshade and black poppies ; distillations and philtres composed of the virus of loathsome diseases, venom of reptiles, secretions of animals, poisonous sap and fungi and fruits, such as the fatal manchineel, pulverised flint, impure ashes and human blood. Amulets and talismans were made of the skins of criminals, wrought from the skulls of hanged men, or ornaments rifled from corpses and thus of special virtue, or the pared nails of an executed thief.

To make themselves invisible the sorcerers used an unguent compounded from the incinerated bodies of new-born infants and mixed with the blood of night-birds. For personal preparation a fast of fifteen days was observed. When that was past, it was necessary to get drunk every five days, after sundown, on wine in which poppies and hemp had been steeped.

For the actual rites the light must be that of candles made from the fat of corpses and fashioned in the form of a cross ; the bowls to be of skulls, those of parricides being of greatest virtue ; the fires must be fed with cypress branches, with the wood of desecrated crucifixes and blood-stained gibbets ; the magic fork fashioned of hazel or almond, severed at one blow ; the ceremonial cloth to be woven by a prostitute, whilst round about the mystic circle must be traced with the embers of a polluted cross. Another potent instrument of magic was the mandragore to be unearthed from beneath gallows where corpses are suspended, by a dog tied to the plant. The dog is killed by a mortal blow after which its soul will pass into the fantastic root, attracting also that of the hanged man.

The history of the Middle Ages is shot through with the shadows cast by this terrible belief in *Black Magic*. Machinations and counter-machinations in which church and state, rich and poor, learned and ignorant were alike involved ; persecutions and prosecutions where the persecutor and judge often met the fate they dealt to the victim and condemned—a dreadful phantasmagoria and procession where we may find the haughty Templars, the blood-stained Gilles de Laval, the original of Bluebeard ; Catherine de Medici and Marshals of France ; popes, princes and priests. In literature also we find its trace, in weird legends and monstrous tales : in stories of spells and enchantments ; in the tale of Dr. Faustus and his pact with the Devil, his pleasures and their penalty when his soul must needs pass down to Hell in forfeit ; we may find its traces in lewd verses and songs. Art, too, yields her testimony to the infernal influence in pictures, sculptures and carvings, decorating palace and cathedral ; where we may find the Devil's likeness peeping out from carven screen and stall, and his demons made visible in the horde of gargoyles grinning and leering from niche and corner, and clustering beneath the eaves.   K. N.

(*See* **Evocation ; Familiars ; Grimoires ; Magic ; Necromancy, etc.**)

Black Mass : It is known from the confessions of witches sorcerers that the devil also has mass said at his Sabbath. Pierre Aupetit, an apostate priest of the village of Fossas, in Limousine, was burned for having celebrated the mysteries of the Devil's mass.   Instead of speaking the holy words of consecration the frequenters of the Sabbath said : " Beelzebub, Beelzebub, Beelzebub."   The devil in the shape of a butterfly, flew round those who were celebrating the mass, and who ate a black host, which they were obliged to chew before swallowing.

Black Pullet, The : A French magical publication supposedly printed in 1740, purporting to be a narrative of an officer who was employed in Egypt.   While in Egypt the narrator fell in with a magician to whom he rendered considerable service, and who when he expired left him the secret of manufacturing a *black pullet* which had much skill in gold-finding.   In it we find much plagiarism from the *Comte de Gabalis* (See Elementary Spirits,) and the whole work if interesting, is distinctly derivative.   It contains many illustrations of talismans and magical rings.   The receipt for bringing the *black pullet* into existences describes that a black hen should be set to hatch one of its own eggs, and that during the process a hood should be drawn over its eyes so that it cannot see.   It is also to be placed in a box lined with black material.   The chick thus hatched will have a particular instinct for detecting the places wherein gold is hidden.

Black Veil of the Ship of Theseus : (*See* **Philosopher's Stone.**)

Blackwell, Anna : The most prominent disciple of Allen Kardec in this country, and the ablest exponent of his views. *Miss Blackwell* herself had psychic experiences—she had seen visions, and spirit forms had appeared on her photographs.

Blake, William : (1757—1827) Poet, Mystic, Painter and Engraver, is one of the most curious and significant figures in the whole history of English literature, and a man who has likewise exerted a wide influence on the graphic arts. He was born in London on the 28th of November, 1757. It would seem that his parents and other relatives were humble folk, but little is known definitely about the family while their ancestry is a matter of discussion.   Mr. W. B. Yeats, who is an ardent devotee of *Blake*, and has edited his writings, would have it that the poet was of Irish descent but though it is true that the name *Blake* is common in Ireland to this day, especially in Galway, Mr. Yeat's contention is not supported by much trustworthy evidence, and it is contradicted by Mr. Martin J. Blake in his genealogical work, *Blake Family Records*.

William manifested æsthetic predilections at a very early age, and his father and mother did not discourage him herein, but offered to place him in the studio of a painter. The young man demurred however, pointing out that the apprenticeship was a costly one, and saying generously that his numerous brothers and sisters should be considered, and that it was not fair that the family's exchequer should be impoverished on his behalf.   Thereafter engraving was suggested to him as a profession, not just because it necessitated a less expensive training than painting, but also as being more likely than the latter to yield a speedy financial return ; and accepting this offer, *Blake* went at the age of fourteen to study under James Basire, an engraver whose plates are but little esteemed to-day, yet who enjoyed considerable reputation while alive, and was employed officially by the Society of Antiquaries.   Previous to this a more noted manipulator of the burin, William Ryland, a protégé of George III, had been suggested as one who would probably give a capital training to the boy : but the latter, on being taken to see Ryland, evinced a strong dislike for him, and refused stoutly to accept his teaching, declaring that the man looked as though born to be hanged.   And it is interesting to note that the future artist of the *Prophetic Books* was right, for only a few years later Ryland was convicted of forgery, and forfeited his life in consequence.

Blake worked under Basire for seven years, and during the greater part of his time the pupil was engaged mainly in doing drawings of Westminster Abbey, these being destined to illustrate a huge book then in progress, the *Sepulchral Monuments* of Richard Gough.   It is said that *Blake* was chosen by his master to go and do these drawings not so much because he showed particular aptitude for draughtmanship, as because he was eternally quarrelling with his fellow-apprentices : and one may well believe, indeed, that the young artist was convinced of his superiority to his *confrères*, and made enemies by failing to conceal this conviction.   Whilst at the Abbey, *Blake* asserted that he saw many visions.   In 1778, he entered the Royal Academy School, then recently founded : and here he continued his studies under George Moser, a chaser and enameller who engraved the first great seal of George III. Yet it was not to Moser that the budding visionary really looked for instruction, he was far more occupied with studying prints after the old masters, especially Michael Angelo and Raphael ; and one day Rosa found him engaged thus, reproved him kindly but firmly, and told him he would be acting more wisely if he took Charles le Brun as his exemplar.   He even hastened to show the pupil a volume of engravings after that painter, so redolent always of the worst tendencies of *le grand siécle* ; and, with this incident in mind, it may be assumed that *Blake* was deeply grateful when, a little later he had shaken off the futile shackles of the Royal Academy, and began to work on his own account.   He had to work hard, however, for meanwhile his affections had been engaged by a young woman, Catherine Boucher, and funds were of course necessary ere it was possible for the pair to marry.   But *Blake* slaved manfully with his burin, engraving illustrations for magazines and the like ; and in 1782 he had his reward, his marriage being solemnized in that year.   His wife's name indicates that she was of French origin, and it would be interesting to know if she was related to François Boucher. or to the fine engraver of the French Empire, Boucher-Desnoyers ; but waiving these speculations, it is pleasant to recall that the marriage proved a singularly happy one, *Blake's* spouse clinging to him lovingly throughout all his troubles and privations, and ever showing a keen appreciation of his genius.   As regards Catherine's appearance there still exists a small pencil-drawing by *Blake*, commonly supposed to be a portrait of his wife ; and it shows a slim, graceful woman, just the type of woman predominating in *Blake's* other pictures ; so it may be presumed that she frequently acted as his model, or—for *Blake* had no fondness for drawing from nature—that her appearance gradually crystallised itself in his brain, and thus transpired in the bulk of his works.

After his marriage *Blake* took lodgings in Green Street, Leicester Fields ; and feeling, no doubt, that engraving was but a poor staff for a married man to lean upon, he opened a print shop in Broad Street.   He made many friends at this period, the most favoured among them being Flaxman, the sculptor ; and the latter introduced him to Mr. Matthew, a clergyman of artistic tastes, who, manifesting keen interest in the few poems which *Blake* had already written, generously offered to defray the cost of printing them.   The writer gladly accepted the offer and the result was a tiny volume, *Poetical Sketches* by W. B. Thus encouraged, *Blake* gave up his printselling business, while simultaneously he went to live in Poland Street, and soon after this removal he published his *Songs of Innocence*, the letterpress enriched by designs from his own hand. Nor was this the only remarkable thing about the book, for the whole thing was printed by the author himself, and by a new method of his own invention—a method which can scarcely be detailed here owing to lack of space, but which the reader will find described adequately in Mr. Arthur Hind's monumental *History of Engraving and Etching*. *Blake* lived in Poland Street for five years, and during this time he achieved and issued *The Book of Thel*, *The Marriage of Heaven and Hell*, and the first book of *The French Revolution*. In 1792 he removed to Hercules Buildings, Lambeth; and while staying here he was forced by dire poverty to do much commercial work, notably a series of illustrations to Young's *Night Thoughts*, yet he found leisure for original drawing and writing also, and to this period of his life belong the *Gates of Paradise* and *Songs of Experience*. In a while he tired of London however, and so he went to Felpham, near Bognor, in Sussex, taking a cottage there hard by where Aubrey Beardsley was to live at a later date, and here he composed *Milton*, *Jerusalem*, and a large part of the *Prophetic Books*, while he made a new friend, William Hayley, who repeatedly aided him with handsome presents of money. The Sussex scenery, besides—afterwards to inspire Whistler and Conder—appealed keenly to the poet, and in one of his lyrics he exclaims :—

"Away to sweet Felpham, for Heaven is there," while to Flaxman he wrote :—

"Felpham is a sweet place for study, because it is more spiritual than London. Heaven opens here on all sides her golden gates; her windows are not obstructed by vapours, voices of celestial inhabitants are more distinctly heard, and their forms more distinctly seen, and my cottage is also a shadow of their houses."

Yet *Blake* tired of Sussex as he had tired of his former home, and in 1803 he returned to London, taking a house in South Bolton Street. Here again he endured much poverty, and was then forced into doing illustrations to Virgil, and also a series of designs for Blair's *Grave*; but later his financial horizon was brightened by help from John Linnell, the landscape painter, and shortly afterwards the artist did some of his finest things, for instance his *Spiritual Portraits*, and his drawings for *The Book of Job*, while after completing these he commenced illustrating the *Divine Comedy* of Dante. In 1821 he again changed his home, taking up his abode now in Fountain Court, Strand, and here he continued to work at the Dante drawings; but only seven of them were ever published, for *Blake's* health was beginning to fail, his energies were slackening, and he died in 1827.

Sixteen years before his death *Blake* held a public exhibition of his drawings, engravings, illustrations and the like; and the affair was treated with haughty disdain, the only paper which saw fit to print a criticism being *The Examiner*, edited by Leigh Hunt. It is customary for *Blake's* idolators of to-day to attempt to heap scorn on those who thus expressed callousness towards his work, and to vituperate more particularly the many people among his contemporaries who showed him frank antagonism, but is not all this noisy blaming of his bygone enemies and critics unnecessarily severe ? For it must be borne in mind that the artist came as a complete novelty, the mysticism permeating his pictures having virtually no parallel in English painting prior to his advent. And it should be remembered, too, that *Blake* as a technician has many grave limitations; and limitations which must have

been exasperating to people accustomed to the art of that amazing century which begot masters like Ramsay, Gainsborough and Romney, Watteau and Fragonard, De la Tour and Clodion, all of them producing works eminently graceful and pre-eminently decorative. Now comparing him to any of these men, *Blake's* modelling appears sadly timid and amateurish, as witness his drawing of himself, or his copy of Laurence's portrait of Cowper; while passing to his draughtsmanship, this is frequently inaccurate, and nowhere embodies the fluency and charming rhythm reflected by nearly all the artists aforesaid. His colour again is often thin and tawdry; while as to his composition, he is admirable only on very rare occasions, the incontestable truth being that, in the bulk of his pictures, the different parts have little or no relation to one another. This is true especially of those of his works which include a vast assembly of figures, yet even in various others of simpler cast this lack of anything like arrangement is equally paramount, and to choose an example, one need only look at " The Door of Death " in *America*. This is two pictures rather than one, and the spectator's gaze wanders from side to side, fretted and bewildered.

It were injustice to *Blake* himself, to omit noting these technical flaws in his workmanship, yet it were no less unjust, if not actually ridiculous, to write at any length contrasting him with the other masters of his century; for his outlook and intention were wholly different from theirs, and, lacking their charm and decorative value, he transcends these men withal in divers respects. He is a prince among mystics, his finest drawings are flushed with weirdness and mystery, and he reincarnates visions and phantasies as no one else has done in line and colour, not even Rosetti. For *Blake* contrived to remain a child throughout the whole of his life, and so, for him, dreams were an actuality, the things he saw in his trances were real and living, and he perpetuated all these things with just that obvious and definite symbolism which a child would naturally use. When he wants to express " Vain Desire " he draws a man trying to reach the stars with the aid of an enormous ladder; in the " Resurrection of the Dead " he delineates actual bodies soaring heavenwards, and when his topic is morning, he shows a nude form shining from the dusky mountain tops; while for *Blake* " The Door of Death " is an actual stone portal, and when illustrating the text in Job, " With dreams upon my bed Thou scarest me," he is not content to depict a sleeper with a frightened expression on his face, but draws all around the sleeper the imaginary horrors which tormented him— serpents, chains, and distorted human creatures. Now in the hands of most men all this sort of thing would yield nothing but the laughable, yet somehow *Blake's* drawings, even those which are weakest technically, invariably possess just that curious air of distinction which is the dominant characteristic of all truly great pictures. In fine, he expressed the outlook of a child with a sublime mastery never vouchsafed to children.

If *Blake* the draughtsman and illustrator was a fierce iconoclast, turning his back resolutely on the styles current in his time, most assuredly *Blake* the poet, enacted a kindred *role*, evincing a sublime contempt for the trammels of Augustanism, and thus making straight the way for Burns, for Wordsworth, and for the divine Shelley. Yet just as Burns was tinged slightly by the typical failings of the pastoral century, so also *Blake* would seem to have found it difficult originally to break his shackles : for occasionally one finds him employing expletives, and this suggests that at first he thought with Pope and his school that verse is futile unless precise; while some of his pictures of child life in *Songs of Innocence* are unduly pretty and idyllic, almost as idyllic as the scenes in Goldsmith's

Deserted Village. Unlike Lowry and Mr. Kenneth Grahame those exquisite adepts in the delineation of children, *Blake* shows only one side of childlife : for his children are nearly all out for a holiday, they are seldom vexed, or cross, or angry, and their eyes are hardly ever dim with tears. At least, however, they are prone to dream dreams and see visions : and it is significant that, in one poem, the writer describes a child unto whom are revealed things hidden from his father's eyes :—

> " Father, O father ! what do we here,
> In this land of unbelief and fear ?
> The land of dreams is better far
> Above the light of the morning star."

That verse and many others besides, charm at once by a fusion of complete naturalness with rare beauty : and the genius of *Blake* in his earlier poems is really this, that with the simple language of childhood, and out of the simple events of childlife, he makes a noble and enduring art—an art, charged as surely as his own drawings with an air of distinction.

Had *Blake* contented himself with writing his *Poetical Sketches*, his *Songs of Innocence* and the subsequent *Songs of Experience*, the charge of madness could not well have been levelled at him by his contemporaries. It was his later writings like *The Book of Thel* and the *Prophetic Books* which begot this imputation, for in these later poems the writer casts his mantle of simplicity to the winds, he sets himself to give literary form to visions, and he is so purely spiritual and ethereal, so far beyond the realm of normal human speech, that mysticism frequently devolves into crypticism. His rhythm, too, is often so subtle that it hardly seems rhythm at all ; yet even in his weirdest flights *Blake* is still the master, he still embodies that curious something which differentiates great art from the rank and file of æsthetic products. And if, as observed before, the colouring in many of his water-colour drawings is sadly thin and poor, the very reverse is true, and true abundantly of the poems written towards the close of his life. Glowing and gorgeous tones are omnipresent in these, they have the barbaric pomp of Gautier's finest prose, the glitter and opulence of Berlioz' or Wagner's orchestration, nay the richness and splendour of a sunset among towering mountains.

No account of *Blake* would be complete without some account of the literature which has grown up around his name, a literature whereof many items are more than worthy of the topic they celebrate. The earliest systematic biography of the master is that by Alexander Gilchrist, 1863, a book, the more valuable inasmuch as it contains many reproductions of *Blake's* drawings, notably the whole of the Job set : and since Gilchrist's day the artist's life has been rewritten by Alfred I. Story, 1893, and by Edwin J. Ellis, 1907, while his letters have been collected and annotated by Frederick Tatham, 1906. Much interesting and important matter concerning *Blake* is contained in *The Life and Letters of Samuel Palmer, by* A. W. Palmer, 1892 in *A Memoir of Edward Calvert* by Samuel Calvert, 1893, and in *The Life of John Linnell* by A. T. Story, 1892, while as regards critical studies of the master, perhaps the best is Swinburne's eloquent tribute, 1868, and further works of note are those of Richard Garnett, Mr. Arthur Symons and M. Basil de Selincourt. The student should also consult *Ideas of Good and Evil* by W. B. Yeats, 1903, and *The Rosetti Papers* by W. M. Rossetti, 1903, while he will find it advisable to look also at an edition of the *Job* illustrations containing an able introduction by Mr. Laurence Binyon, 1906. To speak finally of editions of *Blake's* own writings these are of course numerous, but the only one which is really complete is that edited by E. J. Ellis, 1906.　　　　　　　　　　　　　　　　W. G. B-M.

Blanchfleur : Granddaughter of the Duke of Ferrara and heroine of the romance *Florice and Blanchefleur*, which is probably of Spanish origin. She and Florice, son of the King of Murcia, loved each other from infancy, and she gave him a magical ring. He was banished for his love and *Blanchfleur* was eventually shipped to Alexandria to be sold as a slave. Florice, however, found her there, partly by aid of the mystic ring, and they were happily united.

Blavatsky, Helena Petrovna : was born at Ekaterinoslav Russia, on the 31st of July, 1831. She was the daughter of Colonel Peter Hahn, a member of a Mecklenburg family settled in Russia. She married, at the age of seventeen Nicephore Blavatsky, a Russian official in Caucasia, a man very much older than herself. Her married life was of short duration as she separated from her husband in a few months. The next year or so she occupied chiefly in travelling, Texas Mexico, Canada and India, were each in turn the scene of her wanderings, and she twice attempted to enter Tibet. on one occasion she managed to cross its frontier in disguise but lost her way, and after various adventures was found by a body of horsemen and escorted homewards. The period between 1848 and 1858, she described as the " veiled" time of her life, refusing to divulge anything that happened to her in these ten years, save stray allusions to a seven years' stay in Little and Great Tibet, or in a " Himalayan Retreat." In 1858 she returned to Russia, where she soon achieved distinction as a spiritualistic medium. Later on she went to the United States where she remained for six years, and became a naturalised citizen. She became prominent in spiritualistic circles in America about 1870. It was there that she founded her school of Theosophy. The idea occurred to her of combining her spiritualistic " control " with Buddhistic legends about Tibetan sages, and she professed to have direct " astral " communication with two Tibetan mahatmas.

With the aid of Col. Henry Olcott, she founded in New York, in 1875, the Theosophical Society with a threefold aim : (1) to form a universal brotherhood of man ; (2) to study and make known the ancient religions, philosophies and sciences ; (3) to investigate the laws of nature and develop the divine powers latent in man. In order to gain converts to Theosophy she was obliged to appear to perform miracles. This she did with a large measure of success, but her " methods " were on several occasions detected as fraudulent. Nevertheless' her commanding personality secured for her a large following, and when she died, in 1891, she was at the head of a large body of believers in her teaching, numbering about 100,000 persons. (*See* **Theosophy.**)

Blindfolding a Corpse : The Afritans of the Shari River in Central America were wont to blindfold a corpse before burying it, to prevent it from returning to haunt the survivors.

Blockula : (See **Scandinavia.**)

Bluebeard : (*See* **Gilles de Laval.**)

Bodhisattva : is the official in the theosophical hierarchy who has charge of the religion and education of the world. He is the founder of religions, instituting these either directly or through one of his messengers, and after a faith has been founded, he puts it in charge of a Master, though he still continues the direction of it.

Bodin, Jean · a jurisconsult and student of demonology, who died of the plague in 1596. An Angevin by birth, he studied law in youth and published his *Republique*, which La Harpe calls " the rerm of the spirit of law," but it is his *Demonomanie des Sorciers* by which he is known to occultists. In this work he defended sorcery, but propagated numerous errors. By his *Colloquium heptaplomeron de abdites rerum sublimium varcanus* he aroused very unfavourable opinions regarding his religious views. In it he discusses in the form of dialogue the theological opinions of Jews, Mussulmans, and deists to the disadvantage of the Christian faith, and although he died a Catholic he professed in his time the tenets of Protestantism, Judaism, sorcery, atheism and deism. The *Demonomanie* was published in Paris, in 1581, and again under the title of *Flèau des demons et des sorciers* at Wiort, in 1616. In its first and second books Bodin demonstrates that spirits have communication with mankind, and traces the various characteristics and forms which distinguish good spirits from evil. He unfolds the methods of diabolic prophecy and communication, and those of evocation of evil existences of pacts with the Devil, of journeys through the air to the sorcerers' Sabbath, of infernal ecstasies, of spells by which one may change himself into a werewolf, and of carnal communion with incubi and succubi. The third book speaks of the manner of preventing the work of sorcerers and obviating their charms and enchantments, and the fourth of the manner in which sorcerers may be known. He concludes his study by refuting the work of John Wier or Wierius (q.v.) who, he asserts, was in error in believing sorcerers to be fools and people of unsound mind, and states that the books of that author should be burned " for the honour of God."

Sir Walter Scott says : " *Bodin*, a lively Frenchman, explained the zeal of Wierius to protect the tribe of sorcerers from punishment, by stating that he himself was a conjurer and the scholar of Cornelius Agrippa, and might therefore well desire to save the lives of those accused of the same league with Satan. Hence they threw on their antagonists the offensive names of witch-patrons and witch-advocates, as if it were impossible for any to hold the opinion of Naudæus, Wierius, Scot, etc., without patronizing the devil and the witches against their brethren of mortality. Assailed by such heavy charges, the philosophers themselves lost patience, and retorted abuse in their turn, calling *Bodin*, Delrio, and others who used their arguments, witch-advocates, and the like, as the affirming and defending the existence of the crime seemed to increase the number of witches, and assuredly augmented the list of executions. But for a certain time the preponderance of the argument lay on the side of the Demonologists.

Boehme, Jakob : (1575-1624) : German Mystic. The name o this illustrious mystic and philosopher, who has excited so wide and lasting an influence, is sometimes spelt *Beem* or *Behm*, *Behmon* or *Behmont*, while commoner still is the form used at the head of this article ; but it is probable that *Jakob's* name was really *Böhme*, for that spelling savours far more of bygone Germany than any of the multifarious others do. Born in 1575, at Altsteidenberg, in Upper Lusatia, the philosopher came of humble peasant stock, and accordingly his education consisted in but a brief sojourn at the village school of Seidenberg, about a mile from his own home, while the greater part of his childhood was spent in tending his father's flocks on the grassy sides of a mountain, known as the Landskrone. This profession doubtless appealed to a boy of speculative and introspective temperament, but betimes it transpired that *Jakob* was not strong enough physically to make a good shepherd, and consequently he left home at the age of thirteen, going to seek his fortune at Görlitz, the nearest town of any size.

To this day Görlitz is famous for its shoemakers, while in *Boehme's* time it was a very centre and stronghold of the cobbling industry ; so it was to a cobbler that the boy went first in search of employment, and very soon he had found what he wanted. Unfortunately, the few authentic records of his career offer little information concerning his early years, but apparently he prospered tolerably well,

it being recorded that in 1599 he became a master-shoemaker, and that soon afterwards he was married to Katharina, daughter of Hans Kantzschmann, a butcher. The young couple took a house near the bridge in Neiss Voistadt —their dwelling is still pointed out to the tourist—and some years later *Boehme* sought to improve his business by adding gloves to his stock in trade, a departure which sent him periodically to Prague to acquire consignments of the goods in question.

It is likely that *Boehme* began to write soon after becoming a master-cobbler, if not even at an earlier period, but it was not till he was approaching forty that his gifts became known and appreciated. About the year 1612, he composed a philosophical treatise, *Aurora, oder die Morgenröte un Aufgang*, and, though this was not printed till much later, manuscript copies were passed from hand to hand, the result being that the writer soon found himself the centre of a local circle of thinkers and scholars, many of them people far above him in the social scale. These did not say that the cobbler should stick to his last, but realised that his intellect was an exceptionally keen one ; and *Boehme* would no doubt have proceeded to print and publish his work but for an unfortunate occurrence, just that occurrence which has always been liable to harass the man of bold and original mind. In short, a charge of heresy was brought against him by the Lutheran Church ; he was loudly denounced from the pulpit by Gregorius Richter, pastor primarius of Görlitz, and anon, the town council, fearing to contend with the omnipotent ecclesiastical authorities, took po session of the original manuscript of *Boehme's* work, and bade the unfortunate author desist from writing in the meantime. So far as can be ascertained, he obeyed instructions for a little while, perhaps fearing the persecution which would await him if he did otherwise, but by 1618 he was busy again, compiling polemical and expository treatises ; while in 1622, he wrote certain short pieces on repentance, resignation, and the like. These last were the only things from his pen which were published in book form during his lifetime, and with his consent, nor were they of a nature likely to excite clerical hostility ; but a little later *Boehme* circulated a less cautious theological work, *Der Weg zu Christa*, and this was the signal for a fresh outburst of hatred on the part of the church, Richter storming from his pulpit once again. The philosopher, however, contrived to go unscathed, and, during a brief sojourn at Dresden, he had the pleasure of listening to sundry orations made in his praise by some of his admirers, whose number was now greatly increased. But *Boehme* was not destined to survive this triumph long, for, struck down by fever at Dresden, he was carried with great difficulty to his home at Görlitz, and there he died in 1624, his wife being absent at the time

Boehme's literary output divides itself easily and naturally into three distinct sections, and indeed he himself observed this, and drew up a sort of specification wherein he virtually indicated his successive aims. At first he was concerned simply with the study of the deity, and to this period belongs his *Aurora ;* next he grew interested in the manifestation of the divine in the structure of the world and of man, a predilection which resulted in four great works, *Die Drei Principien Gottlichens Wes Wescus, Vom Dreifachen Leben der Menschen, Von der Menschwerdung Christi*, and *Von der Geburt and Bezlichnung Aller Wescu ;* while finally, he devoted himself to advanced theological speculations and researches, the main outcome being his *Von Christi Testamenten* and his *Von der Chadenwahl : Mysterium Magnum.* Other notable works from his hand, are his seven *Quellgeister*, and likewise his study of the three first properties of eternal nature, a treatise in which some of his ardent devotees have found Sir Adam

Newton's formulæ anticipated. and which certainly resembles Schelling's *Theogonische Natur.*

Alchemist or not himself, *Boehme's* writings demonstrate that he studied Paracelsas closely, while they also reflect the influence of Valentine Weigel, and of the earliest protestant mystic, Kaspar Schwenhfeld. Nor was it other than natural that the latter should appeal keenly to the philosopher of Görlitz, he too being essentially a stout Protestant, and having little or nothing in common with the mystics of other forms of Christianity. That is to say, he is seldom or never dogmatic, but always speculative, true Teuton that he was; while his writings disclose none of those religious ecstasies which fill the pages of Santa Theresa, and he never talks of holding converse with spirits or angels, or with bygone saints; he never refers to miracles worked on his behalf, practically the one exception being a passage where he tells how, when a shepherd boy on the Landskrone, he was vouchsafed an apparition of a pail of gold. At the same time, he seems to have felt a curious and constant intimacy with the invisible world, he appears to have had a strangely perspicacious vision of the *Urgrund,* as he calls it, which is, being literally translated, primitive cause; and it was probably his gift in these particular ways, and the typically German clearness with which he sets down his ideas and convictions, which chiefly begot his vast and wide influence over subsequent people inclined to mysticism. Throughout the latter half of the seventeenth century, his works were translated into a number of different languages, and found a place in the library of nearly every broadminded English theologian; while they proved a great and acknowledged source of inspiration to William Law, the author of *Christian Perfection* and *A Serious Call to a Devout Life.* Since then, various religious bodies, regarding *Boehme* as their high priest, have been founded in Great Britain and in Holland; while in America, too, the sect known as Philadelphians owe their dominant tenets to the mystic of Görlitz.   W. S. B-M.

Bogey : Perhaps derived from the Slavonic *bog,* god. Other forms of the name of this ancient sprite, spectre or goblin are bug-a-boo, boo (Yorkshire), boggart, bogle (Scotland), boggle, bo-guest, bar-guest, boll, boman, and bock. Bull-beggar is probably a form of bu and bogey allied to boll (Northern), an apparition.

Boguet Henri : Grand Justice of the district Saint Claude, in Burgundy, who died in 1619. He was the author of a work full of peurile and ferocious zeal against sorcerers. This book, published at the commencement of the seventeenth century, was latterly burnt because of the inhumanities which crowded its pages. It is entitled *Discours des sorciers,* with many instructions concerning how to judge sorcerers and their acts. It is, in short, a compilation of procedures, at the majority of which the author has himself presided, and which exhibit the most incredible absurdities and criminal credulity. In its pages we discover the proceedings against the unfortunate little Louise Maillat, who at the age of eight was possessed of eight demons, of Françoise Secretain, a sorceress, who had meetings with the said demons, and who had the Devil for her lover, and of the sorcerers Gros-Jacques and Willirmoz. Claude Gailiard and Roland Duvernois and many others figure in the dreadful role of the sanguinary author's dread judgments. *Boguet* details the horrible doings of the witches' Sabbath, how the sorcerers caused hail to fall of which they made a powder to be used as poison, how they used an unguent which carried them to the Sabbath, how a sorcerer was enabled to slay whom he would by means of a mere breath, and how, when arraigned before a judge they cannot shed tears. He further enlarges on the Devil's mark which was found on the skins of these

unfortunates, of how all sorcerers and magicians possess the power of changing their forms into those of wolves, and how, for these offences they were burnt at the stake without sacrament, so that they were destroyed body and soul. The work terminates with instructions to judges of cases of sorcery, and is often known as the *Code des Sorciers.*

Boh : A magical word greatly used to frighten children. "Boe," a Greek word is synonymous with the Latin "Clamor" signifying our English "cry;" and it is possible that the cry of the ox "boo' may have suggested this exclamation, as this sound would quite naturally be very terrifying to a young child. One also suspects some connection between this monosyllable and the "Bogle-boe" or "bwgwly" of Welsh people. According to Warton, it was the name of a fierce Gothic general, whose name like those of other great conquerors was remembered as a word of terror.

Bohmius, Jean : The author of a work entitled Pyschologie, a treatise on spirits, published at Amsterdam in 1632. Of its author nothing is known.

Bolomancy : (*See* **Belomancy.**)

Bonati : A Florentine astrologer who flourished in the thirteenth century. He lived in a most original manner, and perfected the art of prediction. When the army of Martin IV, beseiged Forli, a town of the Romagna, defended by the Count of Montferrat, *Bonati* announced to the Count that he would succeed in repulsing the enemy, but that he would be wounded in the fray. The event justified his prediction, and the Count who had taken with him the necessary materials to staunch his wound in case the prophecy came true, became a devout adherent of astrology. *Bonati* became a Franciscan towards the close of his life, and died in 1300. His works were published by Jacobus Cauterus under the title of Liber Astronomicus, at Augsberg, in 1491.

Boniface VIII., Pope, who gained an unenviable notoriety in Dante's *Inferno* has been regarded by many as an exponent of the black art, and so romantic are the alleged magical circumstances connected with him that they are worthy of repetition. *Boniface,* a noted jurisconsult, was born at Anagni, about 1228, and was elected Pope in 1294. He was a sturdy protagonist of papal sapremacy, and before he had been seated two years on the throne of St. Peter he quarrelled seriously with Phillippe le Bel, King of France, whom he excommunicated. This quarrel originated in the determination of the king to check in his own dominions the power and insolence of the church and the ambitious pretensions of the see of Rome. In 1303, Phillippe's ministers and agents, having collected pretended evidence in Italy, boldly accused *Boniface* of heresy and sorcery, and the king called a council at Paris to hear witnesses and pronounce judgment. The pope resisted, and refused to acknowledge a council not called by himself; but the insults and outrages to which he was exposed proved too much for him, and he died the same year, in the midst of these vindictive proceedings. His enemies spread abroad a report, that in his last moments he had confessed his league with the demon, and that his death was attended with "so much thunder and tempest, with dragons flying in the air and vomiting flames, and such lightning and other prodigies, that the people of Rome believed that the whole city was going to be swallowed up in the abyss." His successor, Benedict XI. undertook to defend his memory but he died in the first year of his pontificate (in 1304), it was said by poison, and the holy see remained vacant during eleven months. In the middle of June, 1305, a Frenchman, the archbishop of Bordeaux, was elected to the papal chair under the title of Clement V.

It was understood that Clement was raised to the papacy

in a great measure by the king's influence, who is said to have stipulated as one of the conditions, that he should allow of the proceedings against *Boniface*, which were to make his memory infamous. Preparations were again made to carry on the trial of *Boniface*, but the king's necessities compelled him to seek other boons of the supreme pontiff, in consideration of which he agreed to drop the prosecution, and at last, in 1312, *Boniface* was declared in the council of Vienne, innocent of all the offences with which he had been charged.

If we may place any faith at all in the witnesses who were adduced against him, *Boniface* was at bottom a freethinker, who concealed under the mitre the spirit of mockery which afterwards shone forth in his countryman Rabelais, and that in moments of relaxation, especially among those with whom he was familiar, he was in the habit of speaking in bold—even in cynical—language, of things which the church regarded as sacred. Persons were brought forward who deposed to having heard expressions from the lips of the pope, which, if not invented or exaggerated, savour of infidelity, and even of atheism. Other persons deposed that it was commonly reported in Italy, that *Boniface* had communication with demons, to whom he offered his worship, whom he bound to his service by necromancy, and by whose agency he acted. They said further, that he had been heard to hold conversation with spirits in the night ; that he had a certain "idol," in which a "diabolical spirit" was enclosed, whom he was in the habit of consulting ; while others said he had a demon enclosed in a ring which he wore on his finger. The witnesses in general spoke of these reports only as things which they had heard ; but one a friar, brother Bernard de Sorano, deposed, that when *Boniface* was a cardinal, and held the office of notary to Nicholas III., he lay with the papal army before the castle of Puriano, and he (brother Bernard) was sent to receive the surrender of the castle. He returned with the cardinal to Viterbo, where he was lodged in the palace Late one night, as he and the cardinal's chamberlain were looking out of the window of the room he occupied, they saw Benedict of Gaeta (which was *Boniface* s name before he was made pope) enter a garden adjoining the palace, alone, and in a mysterious manner. He made a circle on the ground with a sword, and placed himself in the middle, having with him a cock, and a fire in an earthen pot (*in quadam olla terrea*). Having seated himself in the middle of the circle, he killed the cock and threw its blood in the fire, from which smoke immediately issued, while Benedict read in a certain book to conjure demons. Presently brother Bernard heard a great noise (*rumorem magnum*) and was much terrified. Then he could distinguish the voice of some one saying, "Give us the share," upon which Benedict took the cock threw it out of the garden, and walked away without uttering a word. Though he met several persons on his way, he spoke to nobody, but proceeded immediately to a chamber near that of brother Bernard, and shut himself up. Bernard declared that, though he knew there was nobody in the room with the cardinal, he not only heard him talking all night, but he could distinctly perceive a strange voice answering him.

Bonnevault, Pierre : A sorcerer of Poitou in the seventeenth century, who was arrested as he was on his way to the Devil's Sabbath. He confessed that on the first occasion he had been present at that unholy meeting he had been taken thither by his parents and dedicated to the Devil, to whom he had promised to leave his bones after death, but that he had not bargained to leave his infernal majesty his immortal soul. He admitted that he called Satan master, that the Enemy of Man had assisted him in various magical acts, and that he, *Bonnevault*, had slain various

persons through Satanic agency. In the end he was condemned to death. His brother Jean, accused of sorcery at the same time, prayed to the Devil for assistance, and was raised some four or five feet from the ground and dashed back thereon, his skin turning at the same time to a blue-black hue. He confessed that he had met at the Sabbath a young man through whom he had promised one of his fingers to Satan after his death. He also told how he had been transported through the air to the Sabbath how he had received powders to slay certain people whom he named, and for these crimes he received the punishment of death.

Bonnevault, Maturin de : Father of the preceding also accused of sorcery, visited by experts who found upon his right shoulder a mark resembling a small rose, and when a long pin was thrust into this he displayed such signs of distress that it was judged that he must be a sorcerer, indeed, he confessed that he had espoused Berthomée de la Bedouche, who with her father and mother practised sorcery, and how he had gone to seek serpents and toads for the purposes of their sorceries. He said that the Sabbath was held four times yearly, at the feasts of Saint John the Baptist, Christmas, Mardi gras and Páques. He had slain seven persons by sorcery, and avowed that he had been a sorcerer since he was seven years of age. He met a like fate with his sons.

Book of Celestial Chivalry : Appeared in the middle of the sixteenth century. It is of Spanish origin ; and treats of supposititious knightly adventures, in a semi-romantic, semi-mystical vein.

Book of Sacred Magic : (*See* **Abraham the Jew.**)

Book of Secrets : (*See* **Kabala.**)

Book of the Dead : An arbitrary title given to an Egyptian funerary work called *pert em hru*, the proper translation of which is : "coming forth by day," or "manifested in the light." There are several versions or recensions of this work, namely those of Heliopolis, Thebes and Sais, these editions differing only inasmuch as they were edited by the colleges of priests founded at these centres. Many papyri of the work have been discovered, and passages from it have been inscribed upon the walls of tombs and pyramids, and on sarcophagi and mummy-wrappings. It is undoubtedly of extremely early date : how early it would indeed be difficult to say with any exactness, but in the course of centuries it was greatly added to and modified. In all about 200 chapters exist, but no papyrus has been found containing all these. The chapters are quite independent of one another, and were probably all composed at different times. The main subject of the whole is the beatification of the dead, who were supposed to recite the chapters in order that they might gain power and enjoy the privileges of the new life.

The work abounds in magical references, and it is its magical side alone which we can consider here. The whole trend of the *Book of the Dead* is thaumatmagic, as its purpose is to guard the dead against the dangers which they have to face in reaching the other world. As in most mythologies, the dead Egyptian had to encounter malignant spirits, and was threatened by many dangers before reaching his haven of rest. He had also to undergo judgment by Osiris, and to justify himself before being permitted to enter the realms of bliss. This he imagined he could in great part accomplish by the recitation of various magical formulæ, and spells, which would ward off the evil influences opposed to him. To this end every Egyptian of means had buried with him a papyrus of the *Book of the Dead*, in which was contained at least all the chapters necessary to his encounter with such formidable adversaries as he would meet at the gates of Amenti (q.v.), the Egyptian Hades, and which would assist him in making replies during his ceremony of justification. First amongst these spells were the " words of power " (See " Egypt "). The Egyptians believed that to discover the " secret " name of a god was to gain complete ascendancy over him. Sympathetic magic was in vogue in Egyptian burial practice, for we find in Egyptian tombs of the better sort, paintings of tables laden with viands of several descriptions, the inscriptions attached to which convey the idea of boundless liberality. Inscriptions like the following are extremely common—" To the *Ka* or soul of so-and-so, 5,000 loaves of bread, 500 geese, and 5.000 jugs of beer." Those dedications cost the generous donors little, as they merely had the objects named painted upon the wall of the tomb, imagining that their *kas* or astral counterparts would be eatable and drinkable by the deceased. This of course is merely an extension of the neolithic savage conception that articles buried with a man had their astral counterparts and would be of use to him in another world.

Pictorial representation played a considerable part in the magical ritual of the *Book of the Dead*. One of the pleasures of the dead was to sail over Heaven in the boat of Ra, and to secure this for the deceased one must paint certain pictures and mutter over them words of power. On this, Budge in his *Egyptian Magic* says : " On a piece of clean papyrus a boat is to be drawn with ink made of green *abut* mixed with *anti* water, and in it are to be figures of Isis, Thoth, Shu, and Khepera, and the deceased ; when this had been done the papyrus must be fastened to the breast of the deceased, care being taken that it does not actually touch his body. Then shall his spirit enter into the boat of Ra each day, and the god Thoth shall take heed to him, and he shall sail about with him into any place that he wisheth. Elsewhere it is ordered that the boat of Ra be painted ' in a pure place,' and in the bows is to be painted a figure of the deceased ; but Ra was supposed to travel in one boat (called Atet) until noon, and another (called Sektet) until sunset, and provision had to be made for the deceased in both boats. How was this to be done ? On one side of the picture of the boat a figure of the morning boat of Ra was to be drawn, and on the other a figure of the afternoon boat ; thus the one picture was capable of becoming two boats. And, provided the proper offerings were made for the deceased on the birthday of Osiris, his soul would live for ever, and he would not die a second time. According to the rubric to the chapter in which these directions are given, the text of it is as old, at least, as the time of Hesepti, the fifth king of the 1st. dynasty, who reigned about B.C. 4350, and the custom of painting the boat upon papyrus is probably contemporaneous. The two following rubrics from Chapters CXXXIII. and CXXXIV., respectively, will explain still further the importance of such pictures :—

" 1. ' This chapter shall be recited over a boat four cubits in length, and made of green porcelain (on which have been painted) the divine sovereign chiefs of the cities ; and a figure of heaven with its stars shall be made also, and this thou shalt have made ceremonially pure by means of natron and incense. And behold, thou shalt make an image of Ra in yellow colour upon a new plaque and set it at the bows of the boat. And behold, thou shalt make an image of the spirit which thou dost wish to make perfect (and place it) in this boat, and thou shalt make it to travel about in the boat (which shall be made in the form of the boat) of Ra ; and he shall see the form of the god Ra himself therein. Let not the eye of any man whatsoever look upon it, with the exception of thine own self, or thy father, or thy son, and guard (this) with great care. Then shall the spirit be perfect in the heart of Ra, and it shall give unto him power with the company of the gods ; and the gods shall look upon him as a divine being like

unto themselves ; and mankind and the dead shall fall down upon their faces and he shall be seen in the underworld in the form of the radiance of Ra.'

" 2. ' This chapter shall be recited over a hawk standing and having the white crown upon his head, (and over figures of) the gods Tem, Shu, Tefnut, Seb, Nut, Osiris, Isis, Suti, and Nephthys, painted in yellow colour upon a new plaque, which shall be placed in (a model of) the boat (of Ra), along with a figure of the spirit whom thou wouldst make perfect. These thou shalt anoint with cedar oil, and incense shall be offered up to them on the fire, and feathered fowl shall be roasted. It is an act of praise to Ra as he journeyeth, and it shall cause a man to have his being along with Ra day by day, whithersoever the god vayageth ; and it shall destroy the enemies of Ra in very truth regularly and continually.' "

It was understood that the words of power were not to be spoken until after death. They were " a great mystery " but " the eye of no man whatsoever must see it, for it is a thing of abomination for every man to know it. Hide it, therefore, the Book of the Lady of the Hidden Temple is its name." This would seem to refer to some spell uttered by Isis-Hathor which delivered the god Ra or Horus from trouble, or was of benefit to him, and it is concluded that it may be equally efficacious in the case of the deceased.

Many spells were included in the *Book of the Dead* for the purpose of preserving the mummy against mouldering, for assisting the owner of the papyrus to become as a god and to be able to transform himself into any shape he desired. Painted offerings were also provided for him in order that he might give gifts to the gods. Thus we see that the *Book of the Dead* was undoubtedly magical in its character, consisting as it did of a series of spells or words of power, which enabled the speaker to have perfect control over all the powers of Amenti. The only moment in which the dead man is not master of his fate is when his heart is weighed by Thoth before Osiris. If it does not conform to the standard required for justification, he is cast out ; but this excepted, an absolute knowledge of the *Book of the Dead* safeguarded the deceased in every way from the danger of damnation. So numerous are the spells and charms for the use of the deceased, that to merely enumerate them would be to take up a good deal of space. A number of the chapters consist of prayers and hymns to the gods, but the directions as to the magical uses of the book are equally numerous, and the conception of supplication is mingled with the idea of circumvention by sorcery in the most extraordinary manner.

Book of the Sum Total : (*See* **Avicenna and Jean de Menug.**)

Book of Thel : (*See* **Blake.**)

Boolya : (*See* **Magic.**)

Borack : Mahomet's mare which he has put in Paradise. She has a human face, and stretches at each step as far as the furthest sight can reach.

Boreal Virtue : (*See* **Fludd.**)

Borri, Josephe-François : An alchemistical imposter of the seventeenth century, born at Milan, in 1627. In youth his conduct was so wayward that at last he was compelled to seek refuge in a church in dread of the vengeance of those whom he had wronged. However, he speedily cloaked his delinquencies under the cloak of imposture and hypocrisy, and he pretended that God had chosen him to reform mankind and to re-establish His reign below. He also claimed to be the champion of the Papal power against all heretics and Protestants, and wore a wondrous sword which he alleged Saint Michael had presented him with. He said that he had beheld in heaven a luminous palm-branch which was reserved for him. He held that the Virgin was divine in nature, that she had conceived through inspiration, and that she was equal to her Son, with Whom she was present in the Eucharist, that the Holy Spirit was incarnate in her, that the second and third Persons of the Trinity were inferior to the Father. According to some writers *Borri* proclaimed himself as the Holy Spirit incarnate. He was arrested after the death of Innocent X by order of the Inquisition, and on 3rd of January, 1661, condemned to be burnt as a heretic. But he succeeded in escaping to Germany where he received much money from the Queen Christina to whom he claimed that he could manufacture the Philosophers' Stone. He afterwards fled to Copenhagen, whence he wished to sail to Turkey. But he was tracked to a small village hard by and arrested along with a conspirator. He was sent back to Rome, where he died in prison, August 10th, 1695. He is the author of a work entitled, The Key of the Cabinet of the Chevalier Borri (Geneva, 1681) which is chiefly concerned with elementary spirits, and it is this work which the Abbé de Villars has given in an abridged form as the *Comte de Gabalis* (q.v.).

Borroughs, George : (*See* **America, U.S. of.**)

Bors, Bohors or Boort : One of King Arthur's knights. He was associated with Sir Galahad and Lancelot in their search for the Holy Grail. He is the hero of many magical adventures, one of which we relate. During the quest for the Holy Grail, a damsel offers him her love, which he refuses ; and she, with twelve other damsels, thereupon threatens to throw herself from a tower. *Bors*, though of a kindly disposition, thinks they had better lose their souls than his. They fall from the tower, *Bors* crosses himself, and the whole vanishes, being a deceit of the devil. After the quest is ended *Bors* comes to Camelot ; he relates his adventures, which it is said were written down and kept in the Abbey of Salisbury.

Botanomancy : A method of divination by means of burning the branches of vervein and brier, upon which were carved the questions of the practitioner.

Bottle Imps : A class of German spirits, similar in many ways to Familiars. The following is the prescription of an old alchymist, given by the Bishop of Dromore in his *Relics of Ancient Poetry*, for the purpose of securing one of these fairies. First, take a broad square crystal or Venetian glass, about three inches in breadth and length. Lay it in the blood of a white hen on three Wednesdays or three Fridays. Then take it and wash it with holy water and fumigate it. Then take three hazel sticks a year old ; take the bark off them ; make them long enough to write on them the name of the fairy or spirit whom you may desire three times on each stick, which must be flat on one side. Bury them under some hill haunted by fairies on the Wednesday before you call her ; and on the Friday following dig them out, and call her at eight, or three, or ten o'clock, which are good times for this purpose. In order to do so successfully one must be pure, and face toward the East. When you get her, tie her to the glass.

Bourru : A monkish apparition spoken of in many tales as that of an imaginary phantom which appears to the Parisians, walking the streets in the darkest hours of the night, and glancing in at the windows of timid folk— passing and re-passing a number of times. Nurses are wont to frighten their small charges with the *Monk Bourru*. The origin of the spectre is unknown.

Boville (or Bovillus), Charles de : A Picard who died about 1553. He desired to establish in his work *De sensu* the opinion, anciently held, that the world is an animal,—an idea also imagined by Felix Nogaret. Others works by *Boville* are his *Lettres*, his *Life of Raymond Lully*, his *Traite des douze nombres*, and his *Trois Dialogues sur l'Immortalitè de l'Ame, le Rèsurrection, et la Fin du Monde*.

Bowls, Magical (*See* **Magic.**)

Boxhorn, Mark Querius : A celebrated Dutch critic, born at Bergen-op-Zoom, in 1612. His *Treatise on Dreams* (Leyden 1639) is of great rarity.

Braccesco, Jean : A canon and alchemist of Brescia, who flourished in the seventeenth century He gave much study to the hermetic philosophy, and commented upon the work of Geber. His most curious work is *The Tree of Life* a dissertation upon the uses of the Philosophers' Stone in medicine. (Rome. 1542.)

Bradlaugh, Charles : A prominent member of the Committee of the London Dialectical Society, appointed in 1869 to investigate the alleged phenomena of spiritualism. He and Dr. Edmunds were among those who served on sub-committee No, 5, which held séances with Home, at which the phenomena were not at all satisfactory. The two investigators named therefore signed a minority report, containing a careful and critical treatment of the evidence.

Bragadini, Mark Antony : An alchemist of Venice, beheaded in 1595, because he boasted that he had made some gold from a recipe which he had received from a demon. He was tried at Munich, by order of Duke William II. Two black dogs which accompanied him were also arrested, charged with being familiars, and duly tried. They were shot with an arquebuse in the public square.

Brahan Seer, The : Coinneach Odhar (Kenneth Ore). Although Coinneach Odhar is still spoken of and believed in as a seer throughout the Highlands, and especially in the county of Ross and Cromarty, his reputation is of comparatively recent growth. The first literary reference to him was made by Hugh Miller in his *Scenes and Legends of the North of Scotland* (1835). About half a century later a collection of the *Seer's* predictions was published by the late Mr. Alexander Mackenzie, Inverness, the author of several clan histories. Many of these alleged foretellings are of a trivial character. The most important prophecies attributed to Coinneach (Kenneth) are those which refer to the house of Seaforth Mackenzies. One, which is supposed to have been uttered in the middle of the seventeenth century, foretold that the last of the Seaforths would be deaf. It was uttered at Brahan Castle, the chief seat of the Seaforths, near Dingwall, after the seer had been condemned to death by burning, by Lady Seaforth for some offensive remark. He declared to her ladyship that he would go to heaven, but she would never reach it. As a sign of this he declared that when he was burned a raven and a dove would hasten towards his ashes. If the dove was the first to arrive it would be proved his hope was well founded. The same legend is attached to the memory of Michael Scott—a rather suggestive fact. According to tradition, Kenneth was burned on Chanonry Point, near Fortrose. No record survives of this event. The first authentic evidence regarding the alleged seer, was unearthed by Mr. William M. Mackenzie, editor of *Barbour's Bruce*, who found among the Scottish Parliamentary records of the sixteenth century an order, which was sent to the Ross-shire authorities, to prosecute several wizards, including Coinneach Odhar. This was many years before there was a Seaforth. It is quite probable that Kenneth was burned, but the legendary cause of the tale must have been a " filling in " of late tradition. Kenneth's memory apparently had attached to it many floating prohecies and sayings including those attributed to Thomas and Michael Scott. The sayings of " True Thomas " were hawked through the Highlands in Gaelic chap books, and so strongly did the bard appeal to the imaginations of the eighteenth century folks of Inverness, that they associate him with the Fairies and Fingalians (Fians) of the local fairy mound, Tom-na-hurich. A Gaelic saying runs, " When the horn is blown, True Thomas will come forth."

Thomas took the place of Fingal (Finn or Fionn) as chief of the " Seven Sleepers " in Tom-na-hurich, Inverness. At Cromarty, which was once destroyed by the sea, Thomas is alleged to have foretold that it would be thrice destroyed. Of course, the Rhymer was never in Cromarty and probably knew nothing about it. As he supplanted Fingal at Inverness, so at Cromarty he appears to have supplanted some other legendary individual. The only authentic historical fact which remains is that Coinneach Odhar was a notorious wizard, and of mature years, in the middle of the sixteenth century. Wizards were not necessarily seers. It is significant that no reference is made to Kenneth in the letters received by Pepys from Lord Reay, regarding second-sight in the seventeenth century, or in the account of Dr. Johnson's Highland tour, although the learned doctor investigated the problem sympathetically.

In the Scottish Highlands no higher compliment could be paid to the memory of any popular man than to attribute to him the gift of " second sight." Rev. John Morrison, minister of Petty, near Inverness, who was a bard, was one of the reputed seers of this order. Many of his " wonderful sayings " were collected long after his death. Rev. Dr. Kennedy, a Dingwall Free Church minister, and a man of strong personality and pronounced piety, is reputed to have had not only the " gift of prophecy " but also the " gift of healing." He was himself a believer in " second sight " and stated that his father was able to foretell events. In his *The Days of the Fathers in Ross-shire* (1861), he makes reference to several individuals who were similarly " gifted " with what he believed to be a God-given power. One of his seers was reputed to have foretold the " Disruption " of the Church of Scotland about sixteen years before the event took place. By this time the seers had acquired the piety of the people who believed in them. Even the notorious Kenneth, the *Brahan seer* a Pagan and a wizard, became glorified by doubtful tradition, like the notorious Michael Scott, one of his prototypes.

References to second sight in the Highlands are made in the following publications : Kirk's *Secret Commonwealth of Elves, Fauns and Fairies* ; Martin's *Western Isles of Scotland* ; *Deuterosophia (Second Knowledge) or a Brief Discourse concerning Second Sight* by Rev. John Frazer (Edinburgh, Ruddiman, Aned and Co, 1763), *Miscellanies* by John Aubrey, F.R.S (London, 1696). That there is sufficient evidence to justify the serious investigation of " Second sight " phenomena in the Scottish Highlands, no doubt can remain. But that is no reason why the " *Brahan Seer* " legends should be accepted as genuine, especially when it is found that Kenneth died before the Seaforth branch of the Mackenzies came into existence. Whoever foretold the fall of that house, it was certainly not the " notorious wizard " of the Scottish Parliamentary records. No doubt, Kenneth made himself notorious by tyrannizing over a superstitious people in the sixteenth century, and was remembered on that account. During his lifetime he must have been credited with many happenings supposed to have been caused by his spells. After his death he gathered an undeserved reputation for prophecy and piety by the snowball process—a not unfamiliar happening in the past of the Scottish Highlands, where Sir William Wallace, St. Patrick, St. Bean, and others were reputed to have been giants who flung glaciated boulders from hill-top to hill-top across wide glens and over lochs of respectable dimensions.

DONALD MACKENZIE.

Brahma Charin : (*See* India.)

Braid : (*See* Hypnotism.)

Breathings, The : One of the methods of *yoga* practice. There are three varieties of breathing amongst *yogis* : (1) by quite emptying the lungs. and holding them so as long as possible ; (2) by filling the lungs as full as may be ; and (3) by merely retaining whatever breath happens to be in them. It is thus possible to suppress thought, thereby saving up much vital force.

Bredis : French medium. (*See* France.)

Briah : In the *Kabala*, the third of the three stages of spirit progress, the three original ranks or classes. Men are called upon to proceed from the lower to the higher. In the *Apocalypse Briah* is represented as the feet of " the mighty angel with the face of the sun."

Briatic World : (*See* Kabala.)

Bricoriu surnamed " of the Poisoned Tongue": an Ulster chieftain mentioned in the myth of Cuchulain, a mediæval Irish romance. It is said that upon one occasion he asked certain warriors to a feast, and started the question of which of them was the greatest. Conall, Laery, and Cuchulain, were selected, and a demon called " The Terrible " was requested to decide the point. He suggested whoever could cut off his, The Terrible's, head to-day, and allow his own head to be cut off on the morrow, would be the most courageous, and therefore most deserve the title of champion. Cuchulain succeeded in beheading the devil, who immediately picked up his head and vanished. The next day he reappeared in his usual form in order to cut off Cuchulain's head. On his placing his head on the block, the demon told him to rise, and acknowledged that he was champion of Ireland.

Bridge of Souls : The superstition that the souls of the dead sought the other world by means of a bridge is pretty widely disseminated. The Rev. S. Baring Gould in his *Book of Folklore* says : " As peoples became more civilised and thought more deeply of the mystery of death, they conceived of a place where the souls lived on, and being puzzled to account for the rainbow, came to the conclusion that it was a bridge by means of which spirits mounted to their abode above the clouds. The Milky Way was called variously the Road of the Gods or the Road of Souls. Among the Norsemen, after Odin had constructed his heavenly palace, aided by the dwarfs, he reared the bridge Bifrost, which men call the rainbow, by which it could be reached. It is of three colours ; that in the middle is red, and is of fire, to consume any unworthy souls that would venture up the bridge. In connection with this idea of a bridge uniting heaven and earth, up which souls ascended, arose the custom of persons constructing bridges for the good souls of their kinsfolk. On runic grave-stones in Denmark and Sweden we find such inscriptions as these: ' Nageilfr had this bridge built for Anund, his good son.' ' The mother built the bridge for her only son.' ' Holdfast had the bridge constructed for Hame, his father, who lived in Viby.' ' Holdfast had the road made for Igul and for Ura, his dear wife.' At Sundbystein, in the Uplands, is an inscription showing that three brothers and sisters erected a bridge over a ford for their father.

The bridge as a means of passage for the soul from this earth to eternity must have been known also to the Ancients for in the cult of Demeter, the goddess of Death, at Eleusis, where her mysteries were gone through, in order to pass at once after death into Elysium, there was an order of Bridge priestesses ; and the goddess bore the name of the Lady of the Bridge. In Rome also the priest was a bridge-builder pontifex, as he undertook the charge of souls. In Austria and parts of Germany it is still supposed that children's souls are led up the rainbow to heaven. Both in England and among the Chinese it is regarded as a sin to point with the finger at the bow. With us no trace of the idea that it is a *Bridge of Souls* remains. Probably this was thought to be a heathen belief and was accordingly forbidden, for children in the North of England to this day when a rainbow appears, make a cross on the ground with a couple of twigs or straws, " to cross out the bow." The West Riding recipe for driving away a rainbow is : " Make a cross of two sticks and lay four pebbles on it, one at each end."

Brig of Dread, The : There is an old belief, alluded to by Sir Walter Scott, that the soul, on leaving the body, has to pass over the *Brig of Dread*, a bridge as narrow as a thread, crossing a great gulf. If the soul succeed in passing it he shall enter heaven, if he fall off he is lost.

Brimstone : Pliny says that houses were formerly hallowed against evil spirits by the use of *Brimstone*.

Brisin : An enchantress who figures in the *Morte d'Arthur*. She plays an important part in the annunciation of Galahad and the allurement of Lancelot.

British National Association of Spiritualists : A society formed in 1873, mainly through the instrumentality of Mr. Dawson Rogers, to promote the interests of spiritualism in Great Britain. It numbered among its original vice-presidents and members of council the most prominent spiritualists of the day—Benjamin Coleman, Mrs. Makdongall Gregory, Sir Charles Isham, Messrs. Jacken, Dawson Rogers, and Morell Theobald, Drs. Wyld, Stanhope Speer, and many others—while many eminent people of other lands joined the association as corresponding members. The *B.N.A.S.* in 1882 decided to change its name to " The Central Association of Spiritualists." Among its committees was one for systematic research into the phenomena of spiritualism, in which connection some interesting scientific experiments were made in 1878. Early in 1882 conferences were held at the Association's rooms, presided over by Professor Barrett, which resulted in the formation of the Society for Psychical Research. Many members of the latter society were recruited from the council of the B.N.A.S., such as the Rev. Stainton Moses, Dr. George Wyld, Messrs. Dawson Rogers, and Morell Theobald. The *B.N.A.S.* was at first associated with the *Spiritualist*, edited by W. H. Harrison, but in 1879 the reports of its proceedings were transferred to *Spiritual Notes*, a paper which, founded in the previous year, came to an end in 1881, as did also the *Spiritualist*. In the latter year Dawson Rogers founded *Light*, with which the society was henceforth associated. From the beginning of its career, the *B.N.A.S.* has held itself apart from religious and philosophical dogmatism, and has included among its members spiritualists of all sects and opinions.

British Spiritual Telegraph : Spiritualistic journal. (*See* Spiritualism.)

Britten, Mrs. Emma Hardinge : *Mrs. Emma Hardinge*, afterwards *Mrs. Hardinge Britten*, was a distinguished " inspirational " speaker, a native of London, but whose first championship of spiritualism was carried out in America. In 1865 she came to Britain with the intention of retiring from active service, but was persuaded by the spiritualists there to continue her labours. Her eloquent extempore lectures, delivered presumably under spirit control, dealt often with subjects chosen by the audience, and were of a lofty and erudite character. She was the author of a *History of Modern American Spiritualism*, and a careful, if biased resumé of spiritualism in all parts of the world, entitled *Nineteenth Century Miracles*.

Broceliande : A magic forest in Brittany, which figures in the Arthurian legend. It was in this place that Merlin was enchanted by Nimue or Viviana, Lady of the Lake, and imprisoned beneath a huge stone. The name *Broceliande* is often employed as symbolic of the dim unreality of legendary scenery.

Brohou, Jean : A physician of Coutarces, in the seventeenth century. He was the author of an *Almanack* or *Journal of Astrology*, with prognostications for the year 1572,

(Rouen, 1571), and a *Description d'une Merveilleuse et Prodiigeuse Comète*, with a treatise on comets, and the events they prognosticate (Paris, 1568).

Broichan, or Druid : (*See* Celts.)

Broom : In Roumania and Tuscany it is thought that a *broom* laid beneath the pillow will keep witches and evil spirits away.

Broomstick : Witches were wont to ride through the air on switches or *broomsticks*, on their nocturnal journey to the Sabbath. Does the broomstick magically take the place of a flying horse ?

Brotherhood of the Trowel : An esoteric society which sprang up at Florence towards the end of the fifteenth century, which was composed of eminent architects, sculptors and painters ; and continued in existence for over four hundred years. Their patron was St. Andrew, whose festival was commemorated annually by ceremonies allied to the old Mysteries.

Brothers of Purity : An association of Arab philosophers founded at Bosra in the tenth century. They had forms of initiation, and they wrote many works which were afterwards much studied by the Jews of Spain.

Brown, John Mason : on prophecy by American medicine man. (*See* Divination.)

Browne, Sir Thomas : A learned English medical man who died in 1682 at an advanced age. Besides his famous *Religio Medici* and *Urn Burial*, he was chiefly celebrated by the manner in which he combatted popular errors in a work entitled *Pseudodoxia Epadinium*, an essay on popular errors,—an examination of many circumstances in his time received as veritable facts, and which he proved to be false or doubtful. But frequently the learned author replaces one error by another, if on the whole his book is wonderfully accurate considering the date of its composition. The work is divided into seven books, the first of which deals with those errors which spring from man's love of the marvellous ; the second, errors arising from popular beliefs concerning plants and metals, the third, absurd beliefs connected with animals ; the fourth book treats of errors relative to man ; the fifth, errors recorded by pictures ; the sixth deals with cosmographical and historical errors ; and the seventh, with certain commonly accepted absurdities concerning the wonders of the world. For the publication of this work he was charged with atheism, which drew from him his famous *Religio Medici*.

Bruhesen, Peter Van : A Dutch doctor and astrologer who died at Bruges, in 1571. He published in that town in 1550 a *Grand and Perpetual Almanack* in which he scrupulously indicated by the tenets of judicial astrology the correct days for bathing, shaving, hair-cutting and so forth. The work caused offence to a certain magistrate of Bruges who plied the tonsorial trade, with the result that there appeared against *Bruhesen's* volume another *Grand and Perpetual Almanack*, with the flippant subtitle *a scourge for empirics and charlatans*. This squib was published by a rival medico, François Rapaert, but Peter Haschaerts, a surgeon, and a protagonist of astrological science, warmly defended *Bruhesen* in his *Astrological Buckler*.

Bruillant : One of the actors mentioned in the *Grand Saint Graal*. He it was who discovered the Grail Sword in Solomon's ship, and with it slew Lambor. For this use of the holy sword, however, the whole of Britain suffered, for no wheat grew, the fruit trees bare no fruit, and there was no fish in the sea. *Bruillant* himself was punished with death.

Buckingham, Duke of : (*See* England.)

Buddhic Plane : (*See* Intuitional World.)

Buer : According to Wierius, a demon of the second class. He has naturally the form of a star, and is gifted with a knowledge of philosophy and of the virtues of medicinal herbs. He gives domestic felicity and health to the sick. He has charge over fifteen legions.

Buguet : A French photographer who came to London in 1874 and there produced spirit photographs with considerable skill. Many persons claimed to recognise their friends in the spirit pictures, and even after *Buguet* had been arrested, and had confessed that he had resorted to trickery, there were yet a number of persons who refused to believe that he was a fraud, and thought that he had been bribed to confess trickery of which he was innocent. (*See* **Spirit Photography.**)

Bune : According to Wierius a most powerful demon, and one of the Grand Dukes of the Infernal Regions. His form is that of a man. He does not speak save by signs only, He removes corpses, haunts cemeteries, and marshals the demons around tombs and the places of the dead. He enriches and renders eloquent those who serve him. Thirty legions of the infernal army obey his call. The demons who own his sway called Bunis, are regarded by the Tartars as exceedingly evil. Their power is great and their number immense. But their sorcerers are ever in communication with these demons by means of whom they carry on their dark practices.

Burgot, Pierre : A werewolf, burned at Besançon in 1521 with Michel Verdun (q.v.).

Burial with Feet to the East : It was formerly the custom among Christians to bury their dead with the feet towards the east and head towards the west. Various reasons are given for this practice, some authorities stating that the corpse was placed thus in preparation for the reserrection, when the dead will rise with their faces towards the east. Others think this mode of burial is practised in imitation of the posture of prayer.

Burma : A country east of India and south of China, and a province of British India, inhabited by an indigenous stock of Indo-Chinese type which originally migrated from Western China, at different periods, and which is now represented by three principal divisions, the Talaings, the Shans, and the Bama, or Burmese proper, although groups of several other allied races are found in the more remote portions of the country. The civilised part of the community, which, roughly speaking, is perhaps one half of the population, recognizes a religion the constituents of which are animism (q.v.) and Indian Brahmanic demonolatry, modified to some extent by Buddhistic influences, and this cult is steadily making progress in the less enlightened and outlying tribes. We have here to do only with that portion of the popular belief which deals with the more directly occult and with superstition, and we shall refrain from any description of Burmese religion proper which presents similar features to those cults from which it takes its origin, and which are fully described elsewhere.

The Burmese believe the soul immaterial and independent of the body, to which it is only bound by special attraction. It can quit and return to the body at will, but can also be captured and kept from returning to it. After death the soul hovers near the corpse as an invisible butterfly, known as *leippya*. A witch or demon may capture the *leippya* while it wanders during the hours of sleep, when sickness is sure to result. Offerings are made to the magician or devil to induce him to release the soul. The Kachins of the Northern Hills of Burma believe that persons having the evil eye possess two souls, the secondary soul being the cause of the malign influence.

Belief in Spirits.—Belief in spirits, mostly malign, is very general in *Burma*, and takes a prominent place in the religious belief of the people. The spirits of rain, wind and the heavenly bodies are in that condition of evolution which usually results in their becoming full-fledged deities, with whom placation gives place to worship. But the spirits of the forest are true demons with well-marked animistic characteristics. Thus the *nat* or *seiktha* dwells in every tree or grove. His nature is usually malign, but occasionally we find him the tutelar or guardian of a village. In any case he possesses a shrine where he may be propitiated by gifts of food and drink. Several of these demoniac figures have almost achieved godhead, so widespread have their cults become, and Hmin Nat, Chiton, and Wannein Nat, may be instanced as fiends of power, the dread of which has spread across extensive districts. The *nats* are probably of Indian origin, and although now quite animistic in character may at one time have been members of the Hindu pantheon. Many spirit families such as the *Seikkaso, Akathaso,* and *Bommaso,* who inhabit various parts of the jungle trees, are of Indian origin. The fulfilment of every wish depends upon the *nats* or spirits, who are all powerful as far as man is concerned. They are innumerable. Every house has its complement, who swarm in its several rooms and take up their abode in its hearth, door-posts, verandahs, and corners. The *nats* also inhabit or inspire wild beasts, and all misfortune is supposed to emanate from them. The Burmans believe that the more materialistic dead haunt the living with a malign purpose. The people have a great dread of their newly deceased ancestors, whom they imagine to haunt the vicinity of their dwellings for the purpose of ambushing them. No dead body may be carried to a cemetery except by the shortest route, even should this necessitate the cutting a hole in the wall of the house. The spirits of those who have died a violent death haunt the scene of their fatality. Like the ancient Mexicans (*See* **Ciupipiltin**), the Burmans have a great dread of the ghosts of women who have died in childbed. The Kachins believe such women to turn into vampires (*swawmx*) who are accompanied by their children when these die with them. The spirits of children are often supposed to inhabit the bodies of cats and dogs. The Burmans are extremely circumspect as to how they speak and act towards the inhabitants of the spirit-world, as they believe that disrespect or mockery will at once bring down upon them misfortune or disease. An infinite number of guardian spirits is included in the Burman demonological system, and these are chiefly supposed to be Brahmanic importations. These dwell in the houses like the evil *nats*, and are the tutelars of village communities, and even of clans. They are duly propitiated, at which ceremonies rice, beer, and tea-salad are offered to them. Women are employed as exorcists in a case of driving out the evil *nats*, but at the festivals connected with the guardian *nats* they are not permitted to officiate.

Necromancy and Occult Medicine.—Necromancy is of general occurrence among the Burmese. The *weza* or wizards are of two kinds, good and evil, and these are again each subdivided into four classes, according to the materials which they employ, as, for example, magic squares, mercury or iron. The native doctors profess to cure the diseases caused by witchcraft, and often specialise in various ailments. Besides being necromantic, medicine is largely astrological. There is said to be in Lower Burma a town of wizards at Kale Thaungtot on the Chindwin River, and many journey thence to have the effects of bewitchment neutralised by its chief. Sympathetic magic is employed to render an enemy sick. Indian and native alchemy and cheiromancy are exceedingly rife. Noise is the universal method of exorcism, and in cases of illness the patient is often severely beaten, the idea being that the fiend which possesses him is the sufferer.

Mediums and Exorcists.—The *tumsa* or *natsaw* are magicians, diviners, or " wise " men and women who practise their arts in a private and not in a hierophantic capacity among the rural Burmans. The wise man physician who works in iron (*than weza*) is at the head of his profession, and sells amulets which guard the purchasers from injury. female mediums profess to be the spouses of certain *nats*, and can only retain their supernatural connection with a certain spirit so long as they are wed to him. With the exorcists training is voluntary and even perfunctory. But with the mediums it is severe and prolonged. Among the civilised Burmans. a much more exhaustive apprenticeship is demanded. Indeed a thorough and intricate knowledge of some departments of magical and astrological practice is necessary to recognition by the brotherhood, the entire art of which is medico-magical, consisting of the eorcism of evil spirits from human beings and animals. The methods employed are such as usually accompany exorcism among all semi-civilised peoples, that is, dancing, flagellation of the afflicted person, induction of ectasy, oblation to the fiend in possession, and noise.

Prophecy and Divination.—These are purely popular in *Burma*, and not hierophantic, and in some measure are controlled bv the use of the *Deitton*, an astrological book of Indian origin. The direction in which the blood of a sacrificed animal flows, the knots in. torn leaves, the length of a split bamboo pole, and the whiteness or otherwise of a hard-boiled egg, serve among others as methods of augury. But by far the most important mode of divination in use in Burma is that by means of the bones of fowls. It is indeed universal as deciding all the difficulties of Burmese existence. Those wing or thigh bones in which the holes exhibit regularity are chosen. Pieces of bamboo are inserted into these holes, and the resulting slant of the stick defines the augury. If the stick slants outwards it decides in favour of the measure under test. If it slants inwards, the omen is unfavourable. Other methods of divination are by the entrails of animals and by the contents of blown eggs.

Astrology.—Burmese astrology derives both from Indian and Chinese sources, and powerfully affects the entire people. Every Burman is fully aware from his private astrologer, of the trend of his horoscope regarding the near future, and while active and enterprising on his lucky days, nothing will induce him to undertake any form of work should the day be *pyatthadane* or ominous. The *Bedinsaya*, or astrologers proper, practise a fully developed Hindu astrology, but they are few in number, and are practically neglected for the rural soothsayers, who follow the Chinese system known as *Hpewan*, almost identical with the Taoist astrological tables of Chinese diviners. From this system are derived horoscopes, fortunes, happy marriages, and prognostications regarding business affairs. But in practice the system is often confounded with the Buddhist calendar and much confusion results. The Buddhist calendar is in popular use, whilst the *Hpewan* is purely astrological. Therefore the Burman who is ignorant of the latter must perforce consult an astrologer who is able to collate the two regarding his lucky and unlucky days. The chief horoscopic influences are day of birth, day of the week, which is represented by the symbol of a certain animal, and the position of the dragon's mouth to the terminal syllables of the day-names.

Magic.—Burmese magic consists in the making of charms the manufacture of occult medicine which will cause hallucination, second sight, the prophetic state, invisibility, or invulnerability. It is frequently " sympathetic." (*See* **Magic**) and overlaps into necromancy and astrology. It does not appear to be at all ceremonial, and is to a great extent unsophisticated, save where it has been influenced by Indian and Buddhist monks, who also draw on native sources to enlarge their own knowledge.

LITERATURE.—Temple, *The Thirty-seven Nats*, 1906 ; Scott and Hardiman, *Gazeteer of Upper Burma and the Shan States*, 1900-1901 ; *The Indian Antiquary*, Vols. XVII.-XXXVI. ; Fielding Hall, *The Soul of a people.*

Busardier : An alchemist of whom few particulars are on record. He lived at Prague with a noble Courtier. Falling sick and feeling the approach of death, he sent a letter to his friend Richtausen, at Vienna, asking him to come and stay with him during his last moments. Richtausen set out at once but on arriving at Prague found that *Busardier* was dead. On inquiring if the adept had left anything behind him the steward of the nobleman with whom he had lived stated that only some powder had been left which the nobleman desired to preserve. Richtausen by some means got possession of the powder and took his departure. On discovering this the nobleman threatened to hang his steward if he did not recover the powder. The steward surmising that no one but Richtausen could have taken the powder, armed himself and set out in pursuit. Overtaking him on the road he at the point of the pistol, made Richtausen hand over the powder. Richtausen however contrived to abstract a considerable quantity.

Richtausen knowing the value of the powder presented himself to the Emperor Ferdinand, himself an alchemist, and gave him a quantity of the powder. The Emperor assisted by his Mine Master, Count Russe, succeeded in converting three pounds of mercury into gold by means of one grain of the powder. The Emperor is said to have commemorated the event by having a medal struck bearing the effigy of Apollo with the caduceus of Mercury and an appropriate motto.

Richtausen was ennobled under the title of Baron Chaos.

Mr. A. E. Waite in his *Lives of the Alchemists* states that " Among many transformations performed by the same powder was one by the Elector of Mayence, in 1651. He made projections with all the precautions possible to a learned and skilful philosopher. The powder enclosed in gum tragacanth to retain it effectually, was put into the wax of a taper, which was lighted, the wax being then placed at the bottom of a crucet. These preparations were undertaken by the Elector himself. He poured four ounces of quicksilver on the wax, and put the whole into a fire covered with charcoal above, below and around. Then they began blowing to the utmost, and in about half an hour on removing the coals, they saw that the melted gold was over red, the proper colour being green. The baron said the matter was yet too high and it was necessary to put some silver into it. The Elector took some coins out of his pocket, put them into the melting pot, combined the liquefied silver with the matter in the crucet, and having poured out the whole when in perfect fusion into a lingot, he found after cooling, that it was very fine gold, but rather hard, which was attributed to the lingot. On again melting, it became exceedingly soft and the Master of the Mint declared to His Highness that it was more than twenty-four carats and that he had never seen so fine a quality of the precious metal."

Butter, Witches' : The devil gives to the witches of Sweden cats which are called carriers, because they are sent by their mistresses to steal in the neighbourhood. The greedy animals on such occasions cannot forbear to satisfy their own appetites. Sometimes they eat to repletion and are obliged to disgorge their stolen meal. Their vomit is always found in kitchen gardens, is of a yellow colour, and is called witches' butter.

Byron, Lord (*See* **Haunted Houses.**)

Byron, Sir John : (*See* **Haunted Houses.**)

C

Caacrinolaas : According to Wierius (q.v.) Grand President of Hell, also known as Caasimolar and Glasya. He is figured in the shape of a god with the wings of a griffon. He is supposed to inspire knowledge of the liberal arts, and to incite homicides. It is this fiend who can render man invisible. He commands thirty-six legions.

Cabiri, or more properly **Cabeiri :** A group of minor deities of Greek origin, of the nature and worship of whom very little is known. The name appears to be of Semitic origin, signifying the " great gods," and the *Cabiri* seem to have been connected in some manner with the sea, protecting sailors and vessels. The chief seats of their worship were Lemnos, Samothrace, Thessalia and Bœotia. They were originally only two in number —the elder identified with Dionysus, and the younger identified with Hermes, who was also known as Cadmilus. Their worship was at an early date amalgamated with that of Demeter and Ceres, with the result that two sets of *Cabiri* came into being— Dionysus and Demeter, and Cadmilus and Ceres. A Greek writer of the second century B.C. states that they were four in number—Axisros, Axiokersa, Axiokersos, and Casmilus, corresponding, he states to Demeter, Persephone, Hades and Hermes. The Romans identified the *Cabiri* with the Penates. In Lemnos a festival of these deities was held annually and lasted nine days, during which all domestic and other fires were extinguished, and sacred fire was brought from Delos. From this fact it has been judged that the *Cabiri* may have been volcanic demons ; but this view has latterly been abandoned. It was in Samothracia that the cult of the *Cabiri* attained its widest significance, and in this island as early as the fifth century B.C. their mysteries were held with great éclat, and attracted almost universal attention. Initiation into these was regarded as a safeguard against misfortune of all kinds, and persons of distinction exerted all their influence to become initiates. In 1888 interesting details as to the bacchanal cult of the *Cabiri* were obtained by the excavation of their temple near Thebes. Statues of a deity called Cabeiros were found, attended by a boy cup-bearer. His attributes appear to be bacchic.

The *Cabiri* are often mentioned as powerful magicians, and Herodotus and other writers speak of the *Cabiri* as sons of Vulcan. Cicero, however, regards them as the children of Proserpine ; and Jupiter is often named as their father. Strabo, on the other hand, regards them as the ministers of Hecate and Bochart recognises in them the three principal infernal deities, Pluto, Proserpine, and Mercury. It is more than likely that they were originally of Semitic or Egyptian origin—more probably the former ; but we find a temple of Memphis consecrated to them in Egypt. It is not unlikely, as Herodotus supposes, that the cult is Pelasgian in origin, as it is known that the Pelasgians occupied the island of Samothrace, and established there certain mysteries, which they afterwards carried to Athens. There are also traditions that the worship of the *Cabiri* originally came from the Troad, a Semitic centre. Kenrick in his *Egypt before Herodotus* brings forward the following conclusions concerning the *Cabiri* :—

" 1. The existence of the worship of the *Cabiri* at Memphis under a pigmy form, and its connection with the worship of Vulcan. The coins of Thessalonica also establish this connection ; those which bear the legend ' Kabeiros ' having a figure with a hammer in his hand, the pileus and apron of Vulcan, and sometimes an anvil near the feet.

" 2. The *Cabiri* belonged also to the Phœnician theology. The proofs are drawn from the statements of Herodotus. Also the coins of Cossyra, a Phœnician settlement, exhibit a dwarfish figure with the hammer and short apron, and sometimes a radiated head, apparently allusive to the element of fire, like the star of the Dioscuri.

" 3. The isle of Lemnos was another remarkable seat of the worship of the *Cabiri* and of Vulcan, as representing the element of fire. Mystic rites were celebrated here over which they presided, and the coins of the island exhibit the head of Vulcan, or a Cabirus, with the pileus, hammer and forceps. It was this connection with fire, metallurgy, and the most remarkable product of the art, weapons of war, which caused the *Cabiri* to be identified with the Cureks of Etolia, the Idæi Dactyli of Crete, the Corybantes of Phrygia, and the Telchines of Rhodes. They were the same probably in Phœnician origin, the same in mystical and orgiastic rites, but different in number, genealogy, and local circumstances, and by the mixture of other mythical traditions, according to the various countries in which their worship prevailed. The fable that one Cabirus had been killed by his brother or brothers was probably a moral mythus representing the result of the invention of armour, and analogous to the story of the mutual destruction of the men in brazen armour, who sprang from the dragon's teeth sown by Cadmus and Jason. It is remarkable that the name of the first fratricide signifies a ' lance,' and in Arabic a ' smith.'

" 4. The worship of the *Cabiri* prevailed also in Imbros, near the entrance of the Hellespont, which makes it probable that the great gods in the neighbouring island of Samothrace were of the same origin. The *Cabiri*, Curetes, and Corybantes appear to have represented air as well as fire. This island was inhabited by Pelasgi, who may have derived from the neighbouring country of Thrace and Phrygia, and with the old Pelasgic mysteries of Ceres. Hence the various explanations given of the Samothracan deities, and the number of them so differently stated, some making them two, some four, some eight, the latter agreeing with the number of early Egyptian gods mentioned by Herodotus. It is still probable that their original number was two, from their identification with the Dioscuri and Tyndaridæ, and from the number of the Patæci on Phœnician vessels. The addition of Vulcan as their father or brother made them three, and a fourth may have been their mother Cabira.

" 5. The Samothracian divinities continued to be held in high veneration in late times, but are commonly spoken of in connection with navigation, as the twin Dioscuri or Tyndaridæ ; on the other hand the Dioscuri are spoken of as the Curetes or Corybantes. The coins of Tripolis exhibit the spears and star of the Dioscuri, with the legend ' *Cabiri*.'

" 6. The Roman Penates have been identified with the Dioscuri, and Dionysius states that he had seen two figures of ancient workmanship, representing youths armed with spears, which, from an antique inscription on them, he knew to be meant for Penates. So, the 'Lares ' of Etruria and Rome.

" 7. The worship of the *Cabiri* furnishes the key to the wanderings of Æneas, the foundation of Rome, and the War of Troy itself, as well as the Argonautic expedition. Samothrace and the Troad were so closely connected in this worship, that it is difficult to judge in which of the two it originated, and the gods of Lavinium, the supposed colony from Troy, were Samothracian. Also the Palladium, a pigmy image, was connected at once with Æneas and the Troad, with Rome, Vesta, the Penates, and the religious belief and traditions of several towns in the south of Italy. Mr. Kenrick also recognises a mythical personage in Æneas, whose attributes were derived from those of the *Cabiri*, and continues with some interesting observations on the Homeric fables. He concludes that the essential part of the War of Troy originated in the desire to connect together and explain the traces of an ancient religion. It fine, he notes one other remarkable circumstance, that the countries in which the Samothracian and Cabiriac worship prevailed were peopled either by the Pelasgi, or by the Æolians, who of all the tribes comprehended under the general name Hellenes, approach the most nearly in antiquity and language to the Pelasgi ' We seem warranted, then (our author observes), in two conclusions ; first that the Pelasgian tribes in Italy, Greece and Asia were united in times reaching high above the commencement of history, by community of religious ideas and rites, as well as letters, arts, and language ; and, secondly, that large portions of what is called the heroic history of Greece, are nothing else than fictions devised to account for the traces of this affinity, when time and the ascendancy of other nations had destroyed the primitive connection, and rendered the cause of the similarity obscure. The original derivation of the Cabiriac system from Phœnicia and Egypt is a less certain, though still highly probable conclusion.

" 8. The name *Cabiri* has been very generally deduced the Phœnician 'mighty' and this etymology is in accordance with the fact that the gods of Samothrace were called ' Divi potes.' Mr. Kenrick believes, however, that the Phœnicians used some other name which the Greeks translated ' Kabeiros,' and that it denoted the two elements of fire and wind."

Pococke in his *India in Greece* will have it that the *Cabiri* are the 'Khyberi " or people of the " Khyber," or a Buddhist tribe—a totally unlikely origin for them.

In the *Generations* of Sanconiathon, the *Cabiri* are claimed for the Phœnicians, though we understand the whole mystically. The myth proceeds thus. Of the Wind and the Night were born two mortal men, Æon and Protogonus. The immediate descendants of these were, 'Genus' and 'Genea,' man and woman To Genus were born three mortal children, Phôs, Pur, and Phlox, who discovered fire, and these again begat " sons of vast bulk and height, whose names were given to the mountains in which they dwelt, Cassiul, Libanus, Antilibanus, and Brathu. The issue of these giant men by their own mothers were Meinrumus, Hypsuranius, and Usous. Hypsuranius inhabited Tyre ; and Usous becoming a huntsman, consecrated two pillars to fire and the wind, with the blood of the wild beasts that he captured. In times long subsequent to these, the race of Hypsuranius gave being to Agreus and Halieus, inventors, it is said, of the arts of hunting and fishing. From these descended two brothers, one of whom was Chrysor or Hephæstus ; in words, charms and divinations ; he also invented boats, and was the first that sailed. His brother first built walls with bricks, and their descendants in the second generation seem to have completed the invention of houses, by the addition of courts, porticos, and crypts. They are called Aletæ and Titans, and in their time began husbandry and hunting with dogs. From the Titans descended Amynus, a builder, and Magus, who taught men to construct villages and tend flocks ; and of these two were begotten Misor (perhaps Mizraim), whose name signifies Well-freed ; and Sydic, whose name denotes the Just ; these found the use of salt. We now come to the important point in this line of wonders. From Misor descended Taautus (Thoth, Athothis, or Hermes Trismegistus), who invented letters ; and from Sydic descended the Dioscuri, or *Cabiri*, or Corybantes, or Samothraces. These, according to Sanconiathon, first built a complete ship, and others descended from them who discovered medicine and charms. All this dates prior to Babylon and the gods of Paganism,

the elder of whom are next introduced in the ' Generations.' Finally, Sanconiathon settles Poseidon (Neptune) and the *Cabiri* at Berytus ; but not till circumsision, the sacrifice of human beings, and the portrayal of the gods had been introduced. In recording this event, the *Cabiri* are called husbandmen and fishermen, which leads to the presumption that the people who worshipped those ancient gods were at length called by their name.

But little is known regarding the methods of initiation:— " The candidate for initiation was crowned with a garland of olive, and wore a purple band round his loins. Thus attired, and prepared by secret ceremonies (probably mesmeric), he was seated on a throne brilliantly lighted, and the other initiates then danced round him in hieroglyphic measures. It may be imagined that solemnities of this nature would easily degenerate into orgies of the most immoral tendency, as the ancient faith and reverence for sacred things perished, and such was really the case. Still, the primitive institution was pure in form and beautiful in its mystic signification, which passed from one ritual to another, till its last glimmer expired in the freemasonry of a very recent period. The general idea represented was the passage through death to a higher life, and while the outward senses were held in the thrall of magnetism, it is probable that revelations, good or evil, were made to the high priests of these ceremonies."

It is extremely difficult to arrive at any scientific conclusion regarding the origin of the *Cabiri*, but, to summarise, they were probably of Semitic origin, arriving in Greece through Phœnician influence ; and that they approximated in character to the gods with whom the Greeks identified them is extremely likely. (*See* Strabo, L. 10 ; Varro, *De Lingua Latina*, L. 4 ; Herodotus, L. 3, c. 37 ; Eusebius, *Praep Evang* ; Pausanius, L. 9 ; Bryant, *Antient Mythology*, Vol. III.)

Cacodaemons : Deities of inferior rank, one of whom it was believed by many was attached to each mortal from his birth as a constant companion, and were capable of giving impulses, and acting as a sort of messenger between the gods and men. The *cacodaemons* were of a hostile nature, as opposed to the agathodaemons who were friendly. It is said that one of the cacodaemons who appeared to Cassius was a man of huge stature, and of a black hue. The belief in these daemons is probably traditional, and it is said that they are the rebellious angels who were expelled from heaven for their crimes. They tried, but in vain, to obtain a settlement in various parts of the universe ; and their final abode is believed to be all the space between the earth and the stars. There they abide, hated by all the elements, and finding their pleasure in revenge and injury. Their king was called Hades by the Greeks, Typhon by the Egyptians, and Ahrimanes by the Persians and Chaldæans.

Cacodemon : The name given by the ancients to an evil spirit. He changed his shape so frequently that no one could tell in what guise he most generally appeared to man. Each person was also supposed to have a good and bad genius, the evil being the *cacodemon*. The astrologers also called the twelfth house of the sun, which is regarded as evil, that of *cacodemon*.

Cactomite : A marvellous stone, said to possess occult properties, which was known to the ancients, and which was probably the cornelian. Any one wearing it was supposed to be assured of victory in battle.

Caer : The daughter of Ethal Anubal, Prince of the Danaans of Connaught, and mentioned in Irish myths. It was said that she lived year about in the form of a maiden and of a swan. She was beloved by Angus Og, who also found himself transformed into a swan ; and all who heard the rapturous song of the swan-lovers were plunged into a deep sleep, lasting for three days and nights.

Cætulum (*See* **Lithomancy.**)

Cagliostro : one of the greatest occult figures of all time. It was the fashion during the latter half of the XIXth century to regard *Cagliostro* as a charlatan and impostor, and this point of view was greatly aided by the savage attack perpetrated on his memory by Carlyle, who alluded to him as the " Prince of Quacks." Recent researches, however, and especially those made by Mr. W. R. H. Trowbridge in his *Cagliostro : the Splendour and Misery of a Master of Magic* (1910), go to show that if *Cagliostro* was not a man of unimpeachable honour, he was by no means the quack and scoundrel that so many have made him out to be. In the first place it will be well to give a brief outline of his life as known to us before Mr. Trowbridge's examination of the whole question placed *Cagliostro's* circumstances in a different light, and then to check the details of his career in view of what may be termed Mr. Trowbridge's discoveries.

We find that Carlyle possessed a strong prejudice in regard to *Cagliostro*, and that he made no allowance for the flagrant mendacity of the documentary evidence regarding the so-called magician ; and this leads up to the fact that although documents and books relating to *Cagliostro* abound, they possess little or no value. An account compiled from all these sources would present the following features :

Cagliostro's father whose name is alleged to have been Peter Balsamo, a person of humble origin, died young, and his mother, unable to support him, was glad to receive assistance for this purpose from one of her brothers ; but from infancy he showed himself averse to proper courses, and when placed in an religious seminary at Palermo, he more than once ran away from it, usually to be recaptured in undesirable company. Sent next to a Benedictine convent, where he was under the care of a Father Superior, who quickly discovered his natural aptitude, he became the assistant of an apothecary attached to the convent, from whom he learned the principles of chemistry and medicine ; but even then his desire was more to discover surprising and astonishing chemical combinations than to gain more useful knowledge. Tiring of the life at last, he succeeded in escaping from the convent, and betook himself to Palermo where he associated with rascals and vagabonds. He was constantly in the hands of the police, and his kind uncle who tried to assist him was rewarded by being robbed of a considerable sum. Engaged in every description of rascality, he was even said to have assisted in the assassination of a wealthy canon. At this time it is asserted that he was only fourteen years of age, but, later, becoming tired of lesser villainies he resolved upon a grand stroke, upon which to lay the foundations of his fortunes.

At Palermo resided an avaricious goldsmith named Marano, a stupid, superstitious man who believed devotedly in the efficacy of magic. He became attracted to *Cagliostro*, who at the age of seventeen posed as being deeply versed in occultism, and had been seen evoking spirits. Marano made his acquaintance and confided to him that he had spent a great deal of money upon quack alchemists ; but that he was convinced that in meeting him (*Cagliostro*) he had at last chanced upon a real master of magic. *Cagliostro* willingly ministered to the man's superstitions, and told him as a profound secret that in a field at no great distance from Palermo lay a buried treasure which, by the aid of magic ceremonies he could absolutely locate. But the operation necessitated some expensive preliminaries—at least 60 oz. of gold would be required in connection with it. To this very considerable sum Marano demurred, and *Cagliostro* cooly asserted that he would enjoy the vast treasure alone. But the credulity of Marano was too strong for his better sense, and at length he agreed to furnish the necessary funds.

At midnight they sought the field where it was supposed the treasure was hid. *Cagliostro* proceeded with his incantations and Marano, terrified at their dreadful nature, fell prostrate on his face, in which position he was unmercifully belaboured by a number of scoundrels whom *Cagliostro* had collected for that purpose. Palermo rang with the affair, but *Cagliostro* managed to escape to Messina, where he adopted the title of " Count."

It was in this town that he first met with the mysterious Althotas. He was walking one day in the vicinity of the harbour when he encountered a person of singular dress and countenance. This man, apparently about fifty years of age, was dressed as an oriental, with caftan and robes, and was accompanied by an Albanian greyhound. Attracted by his appearance *Cagliostro* saluted him, and after some conversation the stranger offered to tell the pseudo-count the story of his past, and to reveal what was actually passing in his mind at that moment. *Cagliostro* was interested and made arrangements for visiting the stranger, who pointed out to him the house in which he resided, requesting him to call a little before midnight, and to rap twice on the knocker, then three times more slowly, when he would be admitted. At the time appointed *Cagliostro* duly appeared and was conducted along a narrow passage lit by a single lamp in a niche of the wall. At the end of this was a spacious apartment illuminated by wax candles, and furnished with everything necessary for the practice of alchemy. Althotas expressed himself as a believer in the mutability of physical law rather than of magic, which he regarded as a science having fixed laws discoverable and reducible to reason. He proposed to depart for Egypt, and to carry *Cagliostro* thither with him—a proposal which the latter joyfully accepted. Althotas acquainted him with the fact that he possessed no funds, and upon *Cagliostro's* expressing some annoyance at this circumstance laughed at him, telling him that it was an easy matter for him to make sufficient gold to pay the expenses of their voyage. Authorities differ greatly regarding the personality of Althotas ; but we will leave this part of the *Cagliostro* mystery for the moment.

Embarking upon a Genoese ship they duly came to Alexandria where Althotas told his comrade that he was absolutely ignorant regarding his birth and parentage, and said that he was much older than he appeared to be, but that he was in possession of certain secrets for the preservation of strength and health. " Nothing " he said " astonishes me ; nothing grieves me, save the evils which I am powerless to prevent ; and I trust to reach in peace the term of my protracted existence." His early years had been passed near Tunis on the coast of Barbary, where he had been the slave of a wealthy Mussulman pirate. At twelve years of age he spoke Arabic fluently, studied botany, and read the Koran to his master, who died when Althotas was sixteen. Althotas now found himself free, and master of a very considerable sum which had been bequeathed him by his late owner.

Accompanied by *Cagliostro* he penetrated into Africa and the heart of Egypt, visiting the Pyramids, making the acquaintance of the priests of different temples, and receiving from them much hidden knowledge. (The slightest acquaintance with Egyptian history would have saved the author of this statement from making such an absurd anachronism). Following upon their Egyptian tour, however, they visited the principal kingdoms of Africa and Asia, and they are subsequently discovered at Rhodes pursuing alchemical operations. At Malta they assisted the Grand-master Pinto, who was infatuated with alchemical experiments, and from that moment Althotas completely disappears—the memoir of *Cagliostro* merely stating that during their residence in Malta he passed away.

Cagliostro on the death of his comrade repaired to Naples. He was in funds, for Pinto had well provided him before he left Malta. In Naples he met with a Sicilian prince, who conceived a strong predilection for his society, and invited him to his castle near Palermo. This was dangerous ground but *Cagliostro* was nothing if not courageous, and besides he was curious to revisit the haunts of his youth. He had not been long in Palermo when one day he travelled to Messina where he encountered by chance one of his confederates in the affair of Marano the goldsmith. This man warned him strongly not to enter the town of Palermo, and finally persuaded him to return to Naples to open a gambling-house for the plucking of wealthy foreigners. This scheme the pair carried out, but the Neapolitan authorities regarded them with such grave suspicion that they betook themselves to the Papal States. Here they parted company, and regarding this time the alleged memoir of *Cagliostro* is not very clear. It however leads us to believe that the so-called Count had no lack of dupes, and from this obscurity he emerges at Rome where we find him established as an empiric, retailing specifics for all the diseases that flesh is heir to. Money flowed in upon him, and he lived in considerable luxury.

It was at this time that he met the young and beautiful Lorenza Feliciani, to whom he proposed marriage; her father dazzled by *Cagliostro's* apparent wealth and importance consented, and the marriage took place with some ceremony. All biographers of *Cagliostro* agree in stating that Lorenza was a thoroughly good woman, honest, devoted and modest. The most dreadful accusations have been made concerning the manner in which *Cagliostro* treated his wife, and it has been alleged that he thoroughly ruined her character and corrupted her mind. But we shall discover later that this account has been coloured by the unscrupulous imagination of the Jesuitical writers of the Roman Inquisition. All biographers agree that *Cagliostro* hastened his wife's ruin, but it is difficult to know how they came by their data; and in any case they disagree substantially in their details. *Cagliostro's* residence now became the resort of card-sharpers and other undesirables, and it is said that he himself assumed the title and uniform of a Prussian colonel; but he and his confederates quarrelled and with his wife he was forced to quit Rome with a so-called Marquis D'Agriata. They took the road to Venice, and reached Bergamo, which through their rogueries they had speedily to leave. They then made the best of their way through Sardinia and Genoa, and indeed spent several years in wandering through Southern Europe. At last they arrived in Spain by way of Barcelona, where they tarried for six months, proceeding afterwards to Madrid and Lisbon. From Lisbon they sailed to England, where *Cagliostro* lived upon his wits, duping certain foreigners. An English life of *Cagliostro* gives an account of his adventures in London, and tells how he was robbed of a large sum in plate, jewels and money; how he hired apartments in Whitcomb Street, where he spent most of his time in studying chemistry and physics, giving away much money and comporting himself generously and decently on all sides.

In 1772 he returned to France with his wife and a certain Duplaisir. At this time it is said that Duplaisir eloped with Lorenza, and that *Cagliostro* obtaining an order for her arrest, she was imprisoned in a penitentiary, where she was detained for several months. On her release, it is alleged, an immediate reconciliation occurred between husband and wife. At this time *Cagliostro* had attracted much attention in Paris by his alchemical successes. It was the period of mystic enthusiasm in Europe, when princes, bishops, and the nobility generally were keen to probe the secrets of nature, and when alchemy and the allied sciences were the pursuits and hobbies of the great. But according to his Italian biographer *Cagliostro* went too far and raised such hopes in the breasts of his dupes that at last they entertained suspicions of his honesty, so that he was forced to flee to Brussels, whence he made his way to his native town of Palermo, where he was speedily arrested by the goldsmith Marano. A certain nobleman, however, interested himself on his behalf, and procured his release, and he embarked with his wife who had accompanied him, for Malta. From that island they soon retired to Naples, and from there to Marseilles and Barcelona. Their progress was marked by considerable state, and having cheated a certain alchemist of 100,000 crowns under the pretence of achieving some alchemical secret, they hurried to England.

It was during his second visit to London that the Count was initiated into Masonry, and conceived his great idea of employing that system for his own behoof. With this grand object in view he incessantly visited the various London Lodges, and ingratiated himself with their principals and officials. At this period he is said to have picked up in an obscure London bookstall a curious manuscript which is said to have belonged to a certain George Gaston, concerning whom nothing is known. This document dealt with the mysteries of Egyptian Masonry, and abounded in magical and mystical references. It was from this, it is alleged, that *Cagliostro* gathered his occult inspirations. He studied it closely and laid his plans carefully. After another and somewhat harassed tour through Holland, Italy and Germany, he paid a visit to the celebrated Count de St. Germain. In his usual eccentric manner, St. Germain arranged their meeting for the hour of two in the morning, at which time *Cagliostro* and his wife, robed in white garments, and cinctured by girdles of rose colour, presented themselves before the Count's temple of mystery. The drawbridge was lowered, and a man of exceptional height led them into a dimly lighted apartment where folded doors sprang suddenly open, and they beheld a temple illuminated by hundreds of wax lights. The Count of St. Germain sat upon the altar, and at his feet two acolytes swung golden censers. In the *Lives of the Alchemystical Philosophers* this interview is thus detailed. "The divinity bore upon his breast a diamond pentagram of almost intolerable radiance. A majestic statue, white and diaphanous, upheld on the steps of the altar a vase inscribed, 'Elixir of Immortality,' while a vast mirror was on the wall, and before it a living being, majestic as the statue, walked to and fro. Above the mirror were these singular words—'Store House of Wandering Souls.' The most solemn silence prevailed in this sacred retreat, but at length a voice, which seemed hardly a voice, pronounced these words—' Who are you? Whence come you? What would you?' Then the Count and Countess *Cagliostro* prostrated themselves, and the former answered after a long pause, ' I come to invoke the God of the faithful, the Son of Nature, the Sire of Truth. I come to demand of him one of the fourteen thousand seven hundred secrets which are treasured in his breast, I come to proclaim myself his slave, his apostle his martyr.'

" The divinity did not respond, but after a long silence, the same voice asked :—' What does the partner of thy long wanderings intend ?'

" ' To obey and to serve,' answered Lorenza.

" Simultaneously with her words, profound darkness succeeded the glare of light, uproar followed on tranquillity, terror on trust, and a sharp and menacing voice cried loudly :—' Woe to those who cannot stand the tests .'

" Husband and wife were immediately separated to undergo their respective trials, which they endured with exemplary fortitude, and which are detailed in the text of their memoirs. When the romantic mummery was over, the two postulants were led back into the temple with the promise of admission to the divine mysteries. There a man mysteriously draped in a long mantle cried out to them :—' Know ye that the arcanum of our great art is the government of mankind, and that the one means to rule them is never to tell them the truth. Do not foolishly regulate your actions according to the rules of common sense ; rather outrage reason and courageously maintain every unbelievable absurdity. Remember that reproduction is the palmary active power in nature, politics and society alike ; that it is a mania with mortals to be immortal, to know the future without understanding the present, and to be spiritual while all that surrounds them is material.'

" After this harangue the orator genuflected devoutly before the divinity of the temple and retired. At the same moment a man of gigantic stature led the countess to the feet of the immortal Count de St. Germain who thus spoke :—

" ' Elected from my tenderest youth to the things of greatness, I employed myself in ascertaining the nature of veritable glory. Politics appeared to me nothing but the science of deception, tactics the art of assassination, philosophy the ambitious imbecility of complete irrationality ; physics fine fancies about Nature and the continual mistakes of persons suddenly transplanted into a country which is utterly unknown to them ; theology the science of the misery which results from human pride ; history the melancholy spectacle of perpetual perfidy and blundering. Thence I concluded that the statesman was a skilful liar, the hero an illustrious idiot, the philosopher an eccentric creature, the physician a pitiable and blind man, the theologian an anatical pedagogue, and the historian a word-monger. Then did I hear of the divinity of this temple. I cast my cares upon him, with my incertitudes and aspirations. When he took possession of my soul he caused me to perceive all objects in a new light ; I began to read futurity. This universe so limited, so narrow, so desert, was now enlarged. I abode not only with those who are, but with those who were. He united me to the loveliest women of antiquity. I found it eminently delectable to know all without studying anything, to dispose of the treasures of the earth without the solicitations of monarchs, to rule the elements rather than men. Heaven made me liberal ; I have sufficient to satisfy my taste ; all that surrounds me is rich, loving, predestinated.

" When the service was finished the costume of ordinary life was resumed. A superb repast terminated the ceremony. During the course of the banquet the two guests were informed that the Elixir of Immortality was merely Tokay coloured green or red according to the necessities of the case. Several essential precepts were enjoined upon them, among others that they must detest, avoid, and calumniate men of understanding, but flatter, foster, and blind fools, that they must spread abroad with much mystery the intelligence that the Count de St. Germain was five hundred years old, and that they must make gold, but dupes before all."

There is no good authority for this singular interview, but if it really occurred it only probably served to confirm *Cagliostro* in the projects he had mapped out for himself.

Travelling into Courland, he and his wife succeeded in establishing several Masonic Lodges according to the rite of what he called Egyptian Freemasonry. Persons of high rank flocked around the couple, and it is even said that he plotted for the sovereignty of the Grand Duchy. Be this as it may, it is alleged that he collected a very large treasure of presents and money, and set out for St. Petersburg, where he established himself as a physician.

A large number of cures have been credited to *Cagliostro* throughout his career, and his methods have been the subject of considerable controversy. But there is little doubt that the basis of them was a species of mesmeric influence. It has been said that he trusted simply to the laying on of hands ; that he charged nothing for his services ; that most of his time was occupied in treating the poor, among whom he distributed vast amounts of money. The source of this wealth was said to have been derived from the Masonic Lodges, with whose assistance and countenance he had undertaken this work.

Returning to Germany he was received in most of the towns through which he passed as a benefactor of the human race. Some regarded his cures as miracles, others as sorceries, while he himself asserted that they were effected by celestial aid.

For three years *Cagliostro* remained at Strasburg, fêted and lauded by all. He formed a strong friendship with the famous Cardinal-archbishop, the Prince de Rohan who was fired by the idea of achieving alchemical successes. Rohan was extremely credulous, and leaned greatly to the marvellous. *Cagliostro* accomplished supposed transmutations under his eyes, and the Prince delighted with the seeming successes lavished immense sume upon the Count. He even believed that the elixir of life was known to *Cagliostro* and built a small house in which he was to undergo a physical regeneration. When he had sucked the Prince almost dry, *Cagliostro* repaired to Bordeaux, proceeding afterwards to Lyons, where he occupied himself with the foundation of headquarters for his Egyptian Masonic rite. He now betook himself to Paris, where he assumed the rôle of a master of practical magic, and where it is said he evoked phantoms which he caused to appear at the wish of the enquirer in a vase of clear water, or mirror. Mr. Waite thinks in this connection that fraud was an impossibility, and appears to lean to the theory that the visions evoked by *Cagliostro* were such as occur in crystal-gazing, and that no one was more astonished than the Count himself at the results he obtained. Paris rang with his name and he won the appellation of the " Divine *Cagliostro*." Introduced to the Court of Louis XVI. he succeeded in evoking apparitions in mirrors before many spectators—these including many deceased persons specially selected by those present. His residence was isolated and surrounded by gardens, and here he established a laboratory. His wife affected great privacy, and only appeared in a diaphanous costume at certain hours, before a very select company. This heightened the mystery surrounding them, and the élite of Parisian society vied with one another to be present at their magic suppers, at which the evocation of the illustrious dead was the principal amusement. It is even stated that deceased statesmen, authors and nobles took their seats at *Cagliostro's* supper-table.

But the grand object of *Cagliostro* appears to have been the spread of his Egyptian Masonic rite. The lodges which he founded were androgynal, that is they admitted both men and women ; the ladies being instructed by the Master's wife, who figured as the Grand Mistress of the Order —her husband adopting the title of Grand Copt. There is little doubt that a good deal of money was subscribed by the neophytes of the various lodges : the ladies who joined, each sacrificing on the altar of mysticism no less than 100 louis ; and *Cagliostro's* immense wealth, which has never been doubted by any authority on his life, in the strictest probability found its source in the numerous gifts which showered in upon him from the powerful and wealthy for the purpose of furthering his masonic schemes.

But although he lived in considerable magnificence, *Cagliostro* by no means led a life of abandoned luxury; for there is the best evidence that he gave away vast sums to the poor and needy, that he attended the sick hand and foot, and in short played the part of healer and reformer at one and the same time.

A great deal of mystery surrounded the doings of the Egyptian Masonry in its headquarters in the Faubourg Saint Honoré, and the séances for initiation took place at midnight. Figuier and the Marquis de Luchet have both given striking accounts of what occurred during the female initiations:

" On entering the first apartment," says Figuier, "the ladies were obliged to disrobe and assume a white garment, with a girdle of various colours. They were divided into six groups, distinguished by the tint of their cinctures. A large veil was also provided, and they were caused to enter a temple lighted from the roof, and furnished with thirty-six arm-chairs covered with black satin Lorenza clothed in white, was seated on a species of throne, supported by two tall figures, so habited that their sex could not be determined. The light was lowered by degrees till surrounding objects could scarcely be distinguished, when the Grand Mistress commanded the ladies to uncover their left legs as far as the thigh, and raising the right arm to rest it on a neighbouring pillar. Two young women then entered sword in hand, and with silk ropes bound all the ladies together by the arms and legs. Then after a period of impressive silence, Lorenza pronounced an oration, which is given at length, but on doubtful authority, by several biographers, and which preached fervidly the emancipation of womankind from the shameful bonds imposed on them by the lords of creation.

" These bonds were symbolised by the silken ropes from which the fair initiates were released at the end of the harangue, when they were conducted into separate apartments, each opening on the Garden, where they had the most unheard-of experiences. Some were pursued by men who unmercifully persecuted them with barbarous solicitations; others encountered less dreadful admirers, who sighed in the most languishing postures at their feet. More than one discovered the counterpart of her own love but the oath they had all taken necessitated the most inexorable inhumanity, and all faithfully fulfilled what was required of them. The new spirit infused into regenerated woman triumphed along the whole line of the six and thirty initiates, who with intact and immaculate symbols re-entered triumphant and palpitating, the twilight of the vaulted temple to receive the congratulations of the sovereign priestess.

" When they had breathed a little after their trials, the vaulted roof opened suddenly, and, on a vast sphere of gold, there descended a man, naked as the unfallen Adam, holding a serpent in his hand, and having a burning star upon his head.

" The Grand Mistress announced that this was the genius of Truth, the immortal, the divine *Cagliostro*, issued without procreation from the bosom of our father Abraham, and the depositary of all that hath been, is, or shall be known on the universal earth. He was there to initiate them into the secrets of which they had been fraudulently deprived. The Grand Copt thereupon commanded them to dispense with the profanity of clothing, for if they would receive truth they must be as naked as itself. The sovereign priestess setting the example unbound her girdle and permitted her drapery to fall to the ground, and the fair initiates following her example exposed themselves in all the nudity of their charms to the magnetic glances of the celestial genius, who then commenced his revelations.

" He informed his daughters that the much abused

magical art was the secret of doing good to humanity. It was initiation into the mysteries of Nature, and the power to make use of her occult forces. The visions which they had beheld in the Garden where so many had seen and recognised those who were dearest to their hearts, proved the reality of hermetic operations. They had shewn themselves worthy to know the truth; he undertook to instruct them by gradations therein. It was enough at the outset to inform them that the sublime end of that Egyptian Freemasonry which he had brought from the very heart of the Orient was the happiness of mankind. This happiness was illimitable in its nature, including material enjoyments as much as spiritual peace, and the pleasures of the understanding.

The Grand Copt at the end of this harangue once more seated himself upon the sphere of gold and was borne away through the roof; and the proceedings ended, rather absurdly in a ball. This sort of thing was of course as the breath of his nostrils to *Cagliostro*, who could not have existed without the atmosphere of theatrical mysticism, in which he perfectly revelled.

It was at this period that *Cagliostro* became implicated in the extraordinary affair of the Diamond Necklace. He had been on terms of great intimacy with the Cardinal de Rohan. A certain Countess de Lamotte had petitioned that prince for a pension on account of long aristocratic descent. De Rohan was greatly ambitious to become First Minister of the Throne, but Marie Antoinette, the Queen, disliked him and stood in the way of such an honour. Mme. Lamotte soon discovered this, and for purposes of her own told the Cardinal that the Queen favoured his ambitions, and either forged, or procured someone else to forge, letters to the Cardinal purporting to come from the Queen, some of which begged for money for a poor family in which her Majesty was interested. The letters continued of the begging description, and Rohan, who was himself heavily in debt, and had misappropriated the funds of various institutions, was driven into the hands of money-lenders. The wretched Countess de Lamotte met by chance a poor woman whose resemblance to the Queen was exceedingly marked. This person she trained to represent Marie Antoinette, and arranged nightly meetings between her and Rohan, in which the disguised woman made all sorts of promises to the Cardinal. Between them the adventuresses mulcted the unfortunate prelate in immense sums. Meanwhile a certain Bähmer, a jeweller, was very desirous of selling a wonderful diamond necklace in which, for over ten years he had locked up his whole fortune. Hearing that Mme. de Lamotte had great influence with the Queen, he approached her for the purpose of getting her to induce Marie Antoinette to purchase it. She at once corresponded with De Rohan on the matter, who came post haste to Paris, to be told by Mme. de Lamotte that the Queen wished him to be security for the purchase of the necklace, for which she had agreed to pay 1,600,000 livres, or £64,000, in four half-yearly instalments. He was naturally staggered at the suggestion but however, affixed his signature to the agreement, and Mme. de Lamotte became the possessor of the necklace. She speedily broke it up, picking the jewels from their setting with an ordinary penknife. Matters went smoothly enough until the date when the first instalment of 400,000 livres became due. De Rohan, never dreaming that the Queen would not meet it, could not lay his hands on such a sum, and Bähmer noting his anxiety mentioned the matter to one of the Queen's ladies-in-waiting, who retorted that he must be mad, as the Queen had never purchased the necklace at all. He went at once to Mme. de Lamotte who laughed at him, said he was being fooled, that it had nothing to do with her, and told him to go to the Cardinal. The terrified jeweller did not however take her advice, but went to the King.

The amazed Louis XVI. listened to the story quietly enough, and then turned to the Queen who was present, who at once broke forth in a tempest of indignation. As a matter of fact Bähmer had for years pestered her to buy the necklace, but the crowning indignity was that De Rohan, whom she cordially detested, should have been made the medium for such a scandalous disgrace in connection with her name, and she at once gave directions that the Cardinal should be arrested. The King acquiesced in this, and shortly afterwards the Countess de Lamotte, *Cagliostro* and his wife, and others, followed him to the Bastille.

The trial which followed was one of the most sensational and stirring in the annals of French history. The King was greatly blamed for allowing the affair to become public at all, and there is little doubt that such conduct as the evidence displayed as that of aristocrats assisted to hasten the French Revolution.

It was Mme. de Lamotte who charged *Cagliostro* with the robbery of the necklace, and she did not hesitate to invent for him a terrible past, designating him an empiric, alchemist, false prophet, and Jew. This is not the place to deal with the trial at length, and it will suffice to state that *Cagliostro* easily proved his complete innocence. But the Parisian public looked to *Cagliostro* to supply the comedy in this great drama, and assuredly they were not disappointed, for he provided them with what must be described as one of the most romantic and fanciful, if manifestly absurd, life stories in the history of autobiography. His account of himself which is worth quoting at length is as follows :—

" I cannot," he says, " speak positively as to the place of my nativity, nor to the parents who gave me birth. All my inquiries have ended only in giving me some great notions, it is true, but altogether vague and uncertain, concerning my family.

" I spent the years of my childhood in the city of Medina in Arabia. There I was brought up under the name of Acharat, which I preserved during my progress through Africa and Asia. I had my apartments in the palace of the Muphti Salahaym. It is needless to add that the Muphti is the chief of the Mahometan religion, and that his constant residence is at Medina.

" I recollect perfectly that I had then four persons attached to my service : a governor, between forty-five and sixty years of age, whose name was Althotas, and three servants, a white one who attended me as *valet de chambre* and two blacks, one of whom was constantly about me night and day.

" My governor always told me that I had been left an orphan when only about three months old, that my parents were Christians and nobly born ; but he left me absolutely in the dark about their names and the place of my nativity. Some words, however, which he let fall by chance have induced ms to suspect that I was born at Malta. Althotas, whose name I cannot speak without the tenderest emotion, treated me with great care and all the attention of a father. He thought to develope the talent I displayed for the sciences. I may truly say that he knew them all, from the most abstruse down to those of mere amusement. My greatest aptitude was for the study of botany and chemistry.

" By him I was taught to worship God, to love and assist my neighbours, and to respect everywhere religion and the laws. We both dressed like Mahometans and conformed outwardly to the worship of Islam ; but the true religion was imprinted in our hearts.

" The Muphti, who often visited me, always treated me

with great goodness and seemed to entertain the highest regard for my governor. The latter instructed me in most of the Eastern languages. He would often converse with me on the pyramids of Egypt, on those vast subterraneous caves dug out by the ancient Egyptians, to be the repository of human knowledge and to shelter the precious trust from the injuries of time.

" The desire of travelling and of beholding the wonders of which he spoke grew so strong upon me, that Medina and my youthful sports there lost all the allurements I had found in them before. At least, when I was in my twelfth year, Althotas informed me one day that we were going to commence our travels. A caravan was prepared and we set out, after having taken our leave of the Muphti who was pleased to express his concern at our departure in the most obliging manner.

" On our arrival at Mecca we alighted at the palace of the Cherif. Here Althotas provided me with sumptuous apparel and presented me to the Cherif, who honoured me with the most endearing caresses. At sight of this prince my senses experienced a sudden emotion, which it is not in the power of words to express, and my eyes dropped the most delicious tears I have ever shed in my life. His, I perceived, he could hardly contain.

" I remained in Mecca for the space of three years ; not a day passed without my being admitted to the sovereign's presence, and every hour increased his attachment and added to my gratitude. I sometimes surprised his gaze riveted upon me, and turned to heaven with every expression of pity and commiseration. Thoughtful, I would go from him a prey to an ever-fruitless curiosity. I dared not question Althotas, who always rebuked me with great severity, as if it had been a crime in me to wish for some information concerning my parents and the place where I was born. I attempted in vain to get the secret from the negro who slept in my apartment. If I chanced to talk of my parents he would turn a deaf ear to my questions. But one night when I was more pressing than usual, he told me that if ever I should leave Mecca I was threatened with the greatest misfortunes, and bid me, above all, *beware of the city of Trebizond*.

" My inclination, however, got the better of his forebodings—I was tired of the uniformity of life I led at the Cherif's court. One day when I was alone the prince entered my apartment ; he strained me to his bosom with more than usual tenderness, bid me never cease to adore the Almighty, and added, bedewing my cheeks with his tears : ' *Nature's unfortunate child, adieu !* '

" This was our last interview. The caravan waited only for me and I set off, leaving Mecca never to re-enter it more

" I directed my course first to Egypt, where I inspected these celebrated pyramids which to the eye of the superficial observer only appear an enormous mass of marble and granite. I also got acquainted with the priests of the various temples, who had the complacence to introduce me into such places as no ordinary traveller ever entered before. The next three years of my progress were spent in the principal kingdoms of Africa and Asia. Accompanied by Althotas, and the three attendants who continued in my service, I arrived in 1766 at the island of Rhodes, and there embarked on a French ship bound to Malta.

" Notwithstanding the general rule by which all vessels coming from the Levant are obliged to enter quarantine, I obtained on the second day leave to go ashore. Pinto, the Grand Master of the Knights of Malta, gave us apartments in his palace, and I perfectly recollect that mine were near the laboratory.

" The first thing the Grand Master was pleased to do was to request the Chevalier d'Aquino, of the princely house of Caramanica, to bear me company and do me the honours of the island. It was here that I first assumed; European dress and with it the name of Count *Cagliostro*, nor was it a small matter of surprise to me to see Althotas appear in a clerical dress with the insignia of the Order of Malta.

" I have every reason to believe that the Grand Master Pinto was acquainted with my real origin. He often spoke to me of the Cherif and mentioned the city of Trebizond, but never would consent to enter into further particulars on the subject. Meanwhile he treated me with the utmost distinction, and assured me of very rapid preferment if I would consent to take the cross. But my taste for travelling and the predominant desire of practising medicine, induced me to decline an offer that was as generous as it was honourable.

" It was in the island of Malta that I had the misfortune of losing my best friend and master, the wisest as well as the most learned of men, the venerable Althotas. Some minutes before he expired, pressing my hand, he said in a feeble voice, ' My son, keep for ever before your eyes the fear of God and the love of your fellow-creatures ; you will soon be convinced by experience of what you have been taught by me.'

" The spot where I had parted for ever from the friend who had been as a father to me, soon became odious. I begged leave of the Grand Master to quit the island in order to travel over Europe ; he consented reluctantly, and the Chevalier d'Aquino was so obliging as to accompany me. Our first trip was to Sicily, from thence we went to the different islands of the Greek Archipelago, and returning, arrived at Naples, the birthplace of my companion.

" The Chevalier, owing to his private affairs, being obliged to undertake a private journey, I proceeded alone to Rome, provided with a letter of credit on the banking house of Signor Bellone. In the capital of the Christian world I resolved upon keeping the strictest *incognito*. One morning, as I was shut up in my apartment, endeavouring to improve myself in the Italian language, my *valet de chambre* introduced to my presence the secretary of Cardinal Orsini, who requested me to wait on his Eminence. I repaired at once to his palace and was received with the most flattering civility. The Cardinal often invited me to his table and procured me the acquaintance of several cardinals and Roman princes, amongst others, Cardinals York and Ganganelli, who was afterwards Pope Clement XIV. Pope Rezzonico, who then filled the papal chair, having expressed a desire of seeing me, I had the honour of frequent interviews with his Holiness.

" I was then (1770) in my twenty-second year, when by chance I met a young lady of quality, Seraphina Feliciani, whose budding charms kindled in my bosom a flame which sixteen years of marriage have only served to strengthen. It is that unfortunate woman, whom neither her virtues, her innocence, nor her quality of stranger could save from the hardships of a captivity as cruel as it is unmerited."

Cagliostro is reticent regarding his life between the period last dealt with, and the date of his coming to Paris. But although proved innocent he had through his very innocence offended so many persons in high places that he was banished, amidst shouts of laughter from everyone in the court. Even the judges were convulsed, but on his return from the court-house the mob cheered him heartily. If he had accomplished nothing else he had at least won the hearts of the populace by his kindness and the many acts of faithful service he had lavished upon them, and it was partly to his popularity, and partly to the violent hatred of the Court, that he owed the reception accorded

to him. He was re-united to his wife, and shortly afterwards took his departure for London where he was received with considerable éclat. Here he addressed a letter to the people of France, which obtained wide circulation and predicted the French Revolution, the demolishment of the Bastille, and the downfall of the monarchy. Following upon this the *Courier de l'Europe* a French paper published in London, printed a so-called exposure of the real life of *Cagliostro* from beginning to end. From that moment, however, his descent was headlong ; his reputation had studying medicine, and living very quietly : but he made he could find no rest for the sole of his foot. At last he came to Rome, whither Lorenza, his wife accompanied him. At first he was well received there, and even entertained by several cardinals, privately the grand mistake of attempting to further his masonic ideas within the bounds of the Papal States. Masonry was of course anathema to the Roman Church, and upon his attempting to found a Lodge in the Eternal City itself, he was arrested on the 27th September, 1789, by order of the Holy Inquisition, and imprisoned in the Castle of Saint Angelo. His examination occupied his inquisitors for no less than eighteen months, and he was sentenced to death on the 7th April, 1791. He was, however, recommended to mercy, and the Pope commuted his sentence to perpetual imprisonment in the Castle of Saint Angelo. On one occasion he made a desperate attempt to escape : requesting the services of a confessor he attempted to strangle the Brother sent to him, but the burly priest, whose habit he had intended to disguise himself in proved too strong for him, and he was quickly overpowered. After this he was imprisoned in the solitary Castle of San Leo near Montefeltro, the situation of which stronghold is one of the most singular in Europe, where he died and was interred in 1795. The manner of his death is absolutely unknown, but an official commissioned by Napoleon to visit the Italian prisons gives some account of *Cagliostro's* quarters there.

" The galleries," he reports, " which have been cut out of the solid rock, were divided into cells, and old dried-up cisterns had been converted into dungeons for the worst criminals, and further surrounded by high walls, so that the only possible egress, if escape was attempted, would be by a staircase cut in the rock and guarded night and day by sentinels.

" It was in one of these cisterns that the celebrated *Cagliostro* was interred in 1791. In recommending the Pope to commute the sentence of death, which the Inquisition had passed upon him, into perpetual imprisonment, the Holy Tribunal took care that the commutation should be equivalent to the death penalty. His only communication with mankind was when his jailers raised the trap to let food down to him. Here he languished for three years without air, movement, or intercourse with his fellow-creatures. During the last months of his life his condition excited the pity of the governor, who had him removed from this dungeon to a cell on the level with the ground, where the curious, who obtain permission to visit the prison, may read on the walls various inscriptions and sentences traced there by the unhappy alchemist. The last bears the date of the 6th of March 1795."

The Countess Cagliostro was also sentenced by the Inquisition to imprisonment for life. She was confined in the Convent of St. Appolonia, a penitentiary for women in Rome, where it was rumoured that she died in 1794.

Cagliostro's manuscript volume entitled " Egyptian Freemasonry " fell with his other papers into the hands of the Inquisition, and was solemnly condemned by it as subversive to the interests of Christianity. It was publicly burned, but oddly enough the Inquisition set apart one of its brethren to write—" concoct " is the better word —some kind of Life of *Cagliostro* and in this are given several valuable particulars concerning his Masonic methods as follows :

" It may be unnecessary to enter into some details concerning Egyptian Masonry. We shall extract our facts from a book compiled by himself, and now in our possession, by which he owns he was always directed in the exercise of his functions, and from which those regulations and instructions were copied, wherewith he enriched many mother lodges. In this treatise, which is written in French, he promises to conduct his disciples to perfection by means of physical and moral regeneration, to confer perpetual youth and beauty on them, and restore them to that state of innocence which they were deprived of by means of original sin. He asserts that Egyptian Masonry was first propagated by Enoch and Elias, but that since that time it has lost much of its purity and splendour. Common masonry, according to him, has degenerated into mere buffoonery, and women have of late been entirely excluded from its mysteries ; but the time was now arrived when the Grand Copt was about to restore the glory of masonry, and allow its benefits to be participated by both sexes.

" The statutes of the order then follow in rotation, the division of the members into three distinct classes, the various signs by which they might discover each other, the officers who are to preside over and regulate the society, the stated times when the members are to assemble, the erection of a tribunal for deciding all differences that may arise between the several lodges or the particular members of each, and the various ceremonies which ought to take place at the admission of the candidates. In every part of this book the pious reader is disgusted with the sacrilege, the profanity, the superstition, and the idolatry with which it abounds—the invocations in the name of God, the prostrations, the adorations paid to the Grand Master, the fumigations, the incense, the exorcisms, the emblems of the Divine Triad, of the moon, of the sun, of the compass, of the square, and a thousand other scandalous particulars, with which the world is at present acquainted.

" The Grand Copt, or chief of the lodge, is compared to God the Father. He is invoked upon every occasion ; he regulates all the actions of the members and all the ceremonies of the lodge, and he is even supposed to have communication with angels and with the Divinity. In the exercise of many of the rites they are desired to repeat the *Veni* and the *Te Deum*—nay, to such an excess of impiety are they enjoined, that in reciting the psalm *Memento Domine David*, the name of the Grand Master is always to be substituted for that of the King of Israel.

" People of all religions are admitted into the society of Egyptian Masonry—the Jew, the Calvinist, the Lutheran are to be received into it as well as the Catholic—provided they believe in the existence of God and the immortality of the soul, and have been previously allowed to participate in the mysteries of the common masonry. When men are admitted, they receive a pair of garters from the Grand Copt, as is usual in all lodges, for their mistresses ; and when women are received into the society, they are presented by the Grand Mistress with a cockade, which they are desired to give to that man to whom they are most attached.

" We shall here recount the ceremonies made use of on admitting a female.

" The candidate having presented herself, the Grand Mistress (Madame Cagliostro generally presided in that capacity) breathed upon her face from the forehead to the chin, and then said, ' I breathe upon you on purpose to inspire you with virtues which we possess, so that they

may take root and flourish in your heart, I thus fortify your soul, I thus confirm you in the faith of your brethren and sisters, according to the engagements which you have contracted with them. We now admit you as a daughter of the Egyptian lodge. We order that you be acknowledged in that capacity by all the brethren and sisters of the Egyptian lodges, and that you enjoy with them the same prerogatives as with ourselves.'

" The Grand Master thus addresses the male candidate : ' In virtue of the power which I have received from the Grand Copt, the founder of our order, and by the particular grace of God, I hereby confer upon you the honour of being admitted into our lodge in the name of Helios, Mene, Tetragrammaton.'

" In a book said to be printed at Paris in 1789, it is asserted that the last words were suggested to *Cagliostro* as sacred and cabalistical expressions by a pretended conjuror, who said that he was assisted by a spirit, and that this spirit was no other than a cabalistical Jew, who by means of the magical art had murdered his own father before the incarnation of Jesus Christ.

" Common masons have been accustomed to regard St. John as their patron, and to celebrate the festival of that saint. *Cagliostro* also adopted him as his protector, and it is not a little remarkable that he was imprisoned at Rome on the very festival of his patron. The reason for his veneration of this great prophet was, if we are to believe himself, the great similarity between the Apocalypse and the rites of his institution.

" We must here observe that when any of his disciples were admitted into the highest class, the following execrable ceremony took place. A young boy or girl, in the state of virgin innocence and purity, was procured, who was called the pupil, and to whom power was given over the seven spirits that surround the throne of their divinity and preside over the seven planets. Their names according to *Cagliostro's* book are Anael, Michael, Raphael, Gabriel, Uriel, Zobiachel, and Anachiel. The pupil is then made use of as an intermediate agent between the spiritual and physical worlds, and being clothed in a long white robe, adorned with a red ribbon, and blue silk festoons, he is shut up in a little closet. From that place he gives responses to the Grand Master, and tells whether the spirits and Moses have agreed to receive the candidates into the highest class of Egyptian masons. . . .

" In his instructions to obtain the moral and physical regeneration which he had promised to his disciples, he is exceedingly careful to give a minute description of the operations to which they have to submit. Those who are desirous of experiencing the moral regeneration are to retire from the world for the space of forty days, and to distribute their time into certain proportions. Six hours are to be employed in reflection, three in prayer to the Deity, nine in the holy operations of Egyptian Masonry, while the remaining period is to be dedicated to repose. At the end of the thirty-three days a visible communication is to take place between the patient and the seven primitive spirits, and on the morning of the fortieth day his soul will be inspired with divine knowledge, and his body be as pure as that of a new-born infant.

" To procure a physical regeneration, the patient is to retire into the country in the month of May, and during forty days is to live according to the most strict and austere rules, eating very little, and then only laxative and sanative herbs, and making use of no other drink than distilled water, or rain that has fallen in the course of the month. On the seventeenth day, after having let blood certain white drops are to be taken, six at night and six in the morning, increasing them two a day in progression. In three days more a small quantity of blood is again to be let from the arm before sunrise, and the patient is to retire to bed till the operation is completed. A grain of the *panacea* is then to be taken ; this panacea is the same as that of which God created man when He first made him immortal. When this is swallowed the candidate loses his speech and his reflection for three entire days, and he is subject to frequent convulsions, struggles, and perspirations. Having recovered from this state, in which however, he experiences no pain whatever, on that day, he takes the third and last grain of the panacea, which causes him to fall into a profound and tranquil sleep ; it is then that he loses his hair, his skin, and his teeth. These again are all reproduced in a few hours, and having become a new man, on the morning of the fortieth day he leaves his room, enjoying a complete rejuvenescence, by which he is enabled to live 5557 years, or to such time as he, of his own accord, may be desirous of going to the world of spirits."

To revert to the question of the researches of Mr. Trowbridge, it will appear to any unbiassed reader of his work that he has proved that *Cagliostro* was not the same as Joseph Balsamo with whom his detractors have identified him. Balsamo was a Sicilian vagabond adventurer, and the statement that he and *Cagliostro* were one and the same person originally rests on the word of the editor of the *Courier de l' Europe*, a person of the lowest and most profligate habits, and upon an anonymous letter from Palermo to the Chief of the Paris police. Mr. Trowbridge sees in the circumstance that the names of the Countess *Cagliostro* and the wife of Balsamo were identical nothing but a mere coincidence, as the name Lorenza Feliciani is a very common one in Italy. He also proves that the testimony of the handwriting experts as to the remarkable similarity between the writing of Balsamo and *Cagliostro* is worthless, and states that nobody who had known Balsamo ever saw *Cagliostro*. He also points out that Balsamo, who had been in England in 1771, was " wanted " by the London police : how was it then that six years afterward they did not recognise him in Count *Cagliostro* who spent four months in a debtors' prison there, for no fault of his own ? The whole evidence against *Cagliostro's* character rests with the editor of the *Courier de l'Europe* and his Inquisition biographer, neither of whom can be credited for various good reasons. Again, it must be recollected that the narrative of the Inquisition biographer is supposed to be based upon the confessions of *Cagliostro* under torture in the Castle of St. Angelo. Neither was the damaging disclosure of the editor of the *Courier de l'Europe* at all topical, as he raked up matter which was at least fourteen years old, and of which he had no personal knowledge whatsoever. Mr. Trowbridge also proves that the *dossier* discovered in the French archives in 1783, which was supposed to embody the Countess Cagliostro's confessions regarding the career of her husband when she was imprisoned in the Salpetriére prison, is palpably a forgery, and he further disposes of the statements that *Cagliostro* lived on the immoral earnings of his wife.

It is distinctly no easy matter to get at the bed-rock truth regarding *Cagliostro* or to form any just estimate of his true character. That he was vain, naturally pompous, fond of theatrical mystery, and of the popular side of occultism, is most probable. Another circumstance which stands out in relation to his personality is that he was vastly desirous of gaining cheap popularity. He was probably a little mad. On the other hand he was beneficent, and felt it his mission in the then king-ridden state of Europe to found Egyptian Masonry for the protection of society in general, and the middle and lower classes in particular. A born adventurer, he was by no means a rogue, as his lack of shrewdness has been proved on many

occasions. There is small question either that the various Masonic lodges which he founded and which were patronised by persons of ample means, provided him with extensive funds, and it is a known fact that he was subsidised by several extremely wealthy men, who, themselves dissatisfied with the state of affairs in Europe, did not hesitate to place their riches at his disposal for the purpose of undermining the tyrannic powers which then wielded sway. There is reason to believe that he had in some way and at some period of his life acquired a certain working knowledge of practical occultism, and that he possessed certain elementary psychic powers of hypnotism and telepathy. His absurd account of his childhood is almost undoubtedly a plagiarism of that stated in the first manifesto to the public of the mysterious Rosicrucian Brotherhood, (q.v) as containing an account of the childhood of their Chief. But on the whole he is a mystery, and in all likelihood the clouds which surround his origin and earlier years will never be dispersed. It is probably better that this should be so, as although *Cagliostro* was by no means an exalted character, he was yet one of the most picturesque figures in the later history of Europe ; and assuredly not the least aid to his picturesqueness is the obscurity in which his origin is involved. Consult—*Cagliostro*. W. R. H. Trowbridge ; *Cagliostro and Company*. Franz Funck-Brentano ; Waite, *Lives of the Alchemysts*.

Cagnet Bombec of Jonquieres : A song detailing an operation in Alectromancy. (*See* **Alectromancy.**)

Cahagnet, Alphonse : A French cabinet-maker who became interested in somnambulic phenomena about the year 1845, and thenceforward recorded and analysed the trance utterances of various somnambules. His *Arcanes de la vie future devoilées*, published in January, 1848, contained much information concerning the various spheres, and the conditions under which discarnate siprits lived. This was followed in 1849 by a second volume, describing séances held with Adéle Maginot. Through this medium sitters could communicate with their deceased friends or with those who were far away, evidences of clairvoyance, diagnosis and cure of disease were given, and, in short, all the phenomen of American-French mediumship were anticipated. A third volume of *Arcanes* was published later. *Cahagnets'* work is notable in many ways. His own good faith was transparent, he took great pains to procure the written testimony of the sitters, and thus the trance utterances of his somnambules are among the best attested of their kind.

Cailleach, or Harvest Old Wife : In the Highlands of Scotland, there is to be found the belief that whoever is last with his harvesting will be saddled with the Harvest Old Wife to keep until the next year.

The first farmer to be done, made a doll of some blades of corn, which was called the " old wife," and sent it to his nearest neighbour. He, in turn, when finished, sent it on to another, and so on until the person last done had the " old woman " to keep. Needless to say this fear acted as a spur to the superstitious Highlanders. (*See* **Scotland.**)

Caiumarath, or Kaid-mords : According to the Persians, the first man. He lived a thousand years and reigned five hundred and sixty. He produced a tree, from the fruits of which were born the human race. The devil seduced and corrupted the first couple, who after their fall, dressed themselves in black garments and sadly awaited the resurrection, for they had introduced sin into the world.

Cala, Charles : A Calabrian who wrote on the occult in the seventeenth century. He published his *Memorie historiche dell'apparitione delle cruce prodigiose da Carlo Cala* at Naples in 1661.

Calatin Clan : A poisonous multiform monster of Irish legend. This creature was composed of a father and his twenty-seven sons, any one of whose weapons could, by the merest touch, kill a man within nine days. This monstrosity was sent against Cuchulain, who succeeded in catching its eight-and-twenty spears on his shield. The Clan, however managed to throw him down and ground his face in the gravel. Cuchulain was assisted by the son of an Ulster exile, who cut off the creature's heads while Cuchulain hacked it to pieces.;

Calen : Chilian sorcerers. (*See* **American Indians.**)

Calif, Robert. (*See* **America, U.S. of**)

Calmecacs : Training College of Aztec priests. (*See* **Mexico and Central America.**)

Calmet, Dom Augustin : A Benedictine of the congregation of Saint-Vannes, and one of the most diligent and active of his order, who died in 1757 at his abbey of Sesones. He was the author of a *Dictionnaire de la Bible* and of many well-known commentaries on the scriptures. But he is chiefly famous among occultists for his *Dissertation sur les apparitions des anges, des demons et des esprits, et sur les revenans et vampires de Hongrie, de Bohème, de Moravie et de Silésie.* (Paris 1746, and 1751—the latter being the best edition). It was translated into English in 1759, and is alluded to in the article " Vampire." The greatest faith in the supernatural (some might perhaps stigmatise it as credulity) marks the work. But he notices unfavourable theories equally with those which suit his hypotheses, and if he places too much credence in the classical authors, he is never dull. He became the butt of Voltaire, who wrote beneath his portrait in verse of questionable quality :

" Des oracles sacrés que Dieu daigna nous rendre
Son travail assidu perca l'obscurité
Il fit plus, il les crut avec simplicité
Et fut, par ses vertus, digne de les entendre."

Calundronius : A magic stone without form or colour which has the virtues of resisting malign spirits, destroying enchantments, giving to the owner an advantage over his enemies, and of dissipating despair.

Cambions : Offspring of the incubi and succubi (q.v.), according to Bodin and Delamare. Some are more kindly disposed to the human race than others. Luther says of them in his *Colloquies* that they show no sign of life before seven years of age. He says that he saw one which cried when he touched it. Maïole states, according to Boguet in his *Discours des Sorciers* (chap. XIV.), that a Galician mendicant was in the habit of exciting public pity by carrying about a *Campion.* One day, a horseman observing him to be much hampered by the seeming infant in crossing a river, took the supposed child before him on his horse. But he was so heavy that the animal sank under the weight. Some time afterwards the mendicant was taken and admitted that the child he habitually carried was a little demon whom he had trained so carefully that no one refused him alms whilst carrying it.

Cambodia : The *Cambodia* of to-day is bounded by French Cochin-China, Annam, Siam and the Gulf of Siam. Of its population of 1,500,000 inhabitants, the main part is composed of the Khmèr people, and Chinese, Annamese Malays and aboriginal elements are also represented.

Magic.—Magic is mixed up to a surprising degree with the daily life of this people. They consult sorcerers upon the most trivial matters, and are constantly at great pains to discover whether any small venture is likely to prove lucky or unlucky. There are two kinds of sorcerers (or sorceresses), the soothsayers (àp thmop) and the medicine-sorcerers (*kru*). Of these the latter enjoy the highest reputation as healers and exorcists, while the former are less respected, dealing, as they do in charms and philtres for the sake of gain, or in evil incantations and spells to indulge their spite and hatred. The outcast *kru*, however, can be ministers of destruction as well as of healing. One of the means used to take the life of an enemy is the old device favoured by witches. They make a wax figure of the victim, prick it at the spot where they wish to harm him, and thus bring disease and death upon him. Another plan is to take two skulls from which the tops have been removed, place them against each other, and convey them secretly under the bed of a healthy man where they have very evil results. Sometimes by means of spells they transform wood-shavings or grains of rice into a large beetle, or into worms, which enter the body of their victim and cause his illness, and, perhaps his death. If the man thus attacked happens to possess the friendship of a more powerful sorcerer, however, the latter may afford him his protection, and thus undo the mischief,. The more harmless occupations of the wizards consist in making philtres and amulets to insure the admiration of women, the favour of the king, and success at play.

Evil Spirits.—The evil spirits, to whom they ascribe the most malicious intent, are called *pray.* Of these the most fearsome variety is the " wicked dead" (*khmoc pray*), which includes the spirits of women who have died in childbed. From their hiding-place in the trees these spirits torment inoffensive passers-by with their hideous laughter, and shower down stones upon them. These practices are, of course, calculated either to kill or to drive the unfortunate recipients of their attentions insane. Among the trees there are also concealed mischievous demons who inflict terrible and incurable diseases upon mankind.

Those who have suffered a violent death are also greatly to be feared. From the nethermost regions they return, wan and terrible, to demand food from human beings, who dare not deny it to them. Their name *beisac* signifies " goblin," and they have the power to inflict all manner of evil on those who refuse their request. So the good Cambodian, to avert such happenings, puts his offering of rice or other food in the brushwood to appease the goblins. The *pray*, it may be said, require to have their offerings laid on the winnowing fan that enters so largely into Cambodian superstition.

Were-wolves, both male and female, strike terror into the hearts of the natives. By the use of certain magical rites and formulae, men can become endowed with supernatural powers, such as the ability to swallow dishes, and are thereupon changed to were-wolves. Women who have been rubbed with oil which a wizard has consecrated are said to lose their reason, and to flee away to the woods They retain their human shape for seven days. If during that time a man shall undergo the same process of being rubbed with consecrated oil, and shall follow the *toman* to the woods, and strike her on the head with a heavy bar— then, the Cambodians say, she shall recover her reason and may return home. If, on the other hand, no such drastic remedy is to be found, at the end of seven days the woman shall turn into a tigress. In order to cure men who have the powers of a were-wolf, one must strike them on the shoulder with a hook.

The Cambodians believe that ghosts issue from dead bodies during the process of decomposition. When this ceases the ghosts are no longer seen, and the remains are changed into owls and other nocturnal birds.

Most hideous of all the evil spirits in *Cambodia*, are the *srei ap* or ghouls, who, represented only by head and alimentary canal, prowl nightly in search of their gruesome orgies. They are known by their terrible and blood-shot eyes, and are much feared, since even their wish to harm can inflict injury. When anyone is denounced as a ghoul she is treated with great severity, either by the authorities, who may sentence her to banishment or death, or by the villagers, who sometimes take the law into their own hands and punish the supposed offender.

Astrology, etc.—The science of astrology is not without its votaries in *Cambodia*. Astrologers, or, as they are called, *horas*, are attached to the court, and their direct employment by the king gives them some standing in the country. At the beginning of each year they make a calendar, which contains, besides the usual astronomical information, weather and other predictions. They are consulted by the people on all sorts of subjects, and are believed to be able to avert the calamities they predict.

It is not surprising that in such a country, where good and evil powers are ascribed so lavishly, much attention should be paid to omens, and much time spent in rites to avert misfortune. The wind, the fog, the trees, are objects of fear and awe, and must be approached with circumspection lest they send disease and misfortune, or withhold some good. For instance, trees whose roots grow under a house bring ill-luck to it. The bamboo and cotton-plant are also dangerous when planted near a house, for should they grow higher than the house, they would wish, out of a perverted sense of gratitude, to provide a funeral cushion and matting for the occupants.

Animals receive their share of superstitious veneration. Tigers are regarded as malevolent creatures, whose whiskers are very poisonous. Elephants are looked upon as sacred, and particularly so white elephants. Monkeys they will on no account destroy. Should a butterfly enter the house, it is considered extremely unlucky, while a grasshopper, on the contrary, indicates coming good-fortune.

There are other superstitions relating to household objects, customs, etc., which do not differ greatly from those of other countries.

LITERATURE.—E. Aymonier, *Le Cambodge*, Paris, 1900-02. A. Leclerc, *Le Buddhisme Cambodge, Paris*, 1899 ; *Cambodge, Contes et Legendes*, Paris, 1894.

Camuz, Philippe : A Spanish writer of romances who lived in the sixteenth century. To him is attributed a life of Robert the Devil, *La Vida de Roberto el Diablo*, published at Seville in 1629.

Candelabrum : (*See* **Necromancy.**)

Candles Burning Blue : There is a superstition that candles and other lights burn blue at the apparition of spirits, probably because of the sulphurous atmosphere accompanying the spectres.

Candles, Magical : (*See* **Magic.**)

Capnomancy : Was the observation of smoke, which consisted in two principal methods. The more important was the smoke of the sacrifices, which augured well if it rose lightly from the altar, and ascended straight to the clouds ; but the contrary if it hung about. Another method was to throw a few jasmine or poppy seeds upon burning coals. There was yet a third practice by breathing the smoke of the sacrificial fire.

Caqueux or Cacoux : Formerly a caste of rope-makers dwelling in Brittany, who in some of the cantons of that country were treated as pariahs, perhaps because the ropes they manufactured were to the people the symbols of slavery and death by hanging. Be that as it may, they were interdicted from entering the churches, and were regarded as sorcerers. They did not hesitate to profit by this evil reputation, but dealt in talismans which were supposed to render their wearers invulnerable, and also acted as diviners. They were further credited with the ability to raise and sell winds and tempests like the sorcerers of Finland It is said that they were originally of Jewish origin, separated like lepers from other folk. Francois II, Duke of Brittany, enacted that they should

wear a mark composed of red cloth on a part of their dress where it could be readily seen. (*See* Cambry, Voyage dans le Finistére, t.3, p. 146).

Carbuncle : The ancients supposed this stone to give out a native light without reflection, and they ranked it fifth in order after diamonds, emeralds, opals, and pearls. It is among the gems ruled by the sun, and is both male and female—the former distinguished by the brightness which appears as if burning within it, while the latter throws it out. It takes no colour from any other gem applied to it, but imparts its own. The virtue of the *carbuncle* is to drive away poisonous air, repress luxury, and preserve the health of the body. It also reconciles differences among friends.

Cardan, Jerome : A so-called magician, who lived about the end of the fifteenth, or the beginning of the sixteenth, century. He was contemporary with Faustus and Paracelsus, to whom, as to the other necromancers of his age, he was entirely dissimilar. He has left in his *Memoirs* a frank and detailed analysis of a curiously complicated and abnormal intellectuality, sensitive, intense, and not altogether free from the taint of insanity. He declares himself subject to strange fits of abstraction and exaltation, the intensity of which became at length so intolerable that he was forced to inflict on himself severe bodily pain as a means of banishing them. He would, he tells us, talk habitually of those things which were most likely to be distasteful to the company ; he would argue on any side of a question, quite irrespective of whether he believed it right or wrong, and he had an extraordinary passion for gambling. He tells us of three peculiarities, in which we may trace the workings of a diseased imagination, and in the third, at least, that abnormal delicacy of perception which characterised him. The first was the faculty of projecting his spirit outside his body, to the accompaniment of strange physical sensations. The second was the ability to perceive sensibly anything he desired to perceive. As a child, he explains, he saw these images involuntarily and without the power of selection, but when he reached manhood he could control them to suit his choice. The third of his peculiar qualities was, that before every event of moment in his life, he had a dream which warned him of it. Indeed, he himself has written a commentary of considerable length on Synesius's treatise on dreams, in which he advances the theory that any virtuous person can acquire the faculty of interpreting dreams, that, in fact, anyone can draw up for himself a code of dream-interpretations by merely studying carefully his own dreams. We cannot put much faith in *Cardan's* wonderful dreams, however. His is not the type of mind to which we would go for an accurate statement concerning mental phenomena, but such significant dreams as he may have had, were probably, as has already been suggested, the result of his abnormal sub-conscious perceptiveness. In one instance at least, his prediction was not entirely successful. He foretold the date of his own death, and, at the age of seventy-five, was obliged to abstain from food in order to die at the time he had predicted.

Carpenter : (*See* **Spiritualism.**)

Carpocratians : A sect of Gnostics founded by Carpocrites of Alexandria. It taught that Christ derived the mysteries of his religion from the Temple of Isis in Egypt, where he had studied for six years, and that he taught them to his apostles, who transmitted them to Carpocrites. This body used theurgic incantations, and had grips, signs and words, symbols and degrees. It is believed to have endured for some centuries. (*See* **Gnostics.**)

Carrahdis : A class of native priests in New South Wales, Australia.

Carver, Jonathan, Narrative of : (*See* **Divination.**)

Cassaptu, Babylonian Witch. (*See* **Semites.**)

Castle of the Interior Man, The : The mystical name given to the seven stages of the soul's ascent towards the Divinity. These seven processes of psychic evolution are briefly as follows : (1) The state of prayer, being concentration on God ; (2) The state of mental prayer, in which one seeks to discover the mystic significance of all things ; (3) The obscure night, believed to be the most difficult, in which self must be utterly renounced ; (4) The prayer of quietism, complete surrender to the will of God ; (5) The state of union, in which the will of man and the will of God become identified ; (6) The state of ecstatic prayer, in which the soul is transported with joy, and love enters into it ; (7) The state of ravishment, which is the mystic marriage, the perfect union, and the entrance of God and Heaven into the interior man.

Catabolignes : Demons who bore men away, killed them, and broke and crushed them having this power over them. We are told that a certain Campester wrote a book wherein it is related how these demons treated their agents, the magicians and sorcerors.

Catalepsy : A condition involving the sudden suspension of sensation and volition, and the partial suspension of the vital functions. The body assumes a rigid and statuesque appearance, sometimes mistaken for death, and the patient remains unconscious throughout the attack. On occasion, the cataleptic state may be marked by symptoms of intense mental excitement, and by apparently volitional speech and action. Sometimes the symptoms are hardly distinguishable from those of hysteria. The period covered by the attack may vary from a few minutes to several days, though the latter only in exceptional cases ; it may, however, recur on trifling provocation in the absence of resistence from the will-power of the patient. The affection is caused by a pathological condition of the nervous system, generally produced by severe or prolonged mental emotion, and it must not be confused with the hypnotic trance. The belief that it may occur in a perfectly healthy person is, on the whole, fallacious. There is some reason to suppose that *catalepsy*, like ecstacy and mediumistic faculties, may at times prove contagious. Dr. Pététin, in his *Electricité Animale* (1808) makes mention of as many as eight cases met with in a restricted area, although *catalepsy* is in ordinary circumstances of rare occurrence. Pététin also mentions certain strange phenomena witnessed by him in connection with the state of spontaneous *catalepsy* (*see* **Stomach, Seeing with**), which would seem to show that persons in this condition are amenable to suggestion in a high degree. The true physical reasons for catalepsy are still practically unknown to science. But there seem to be good reasons for believing that it can be self-induced in certain cases. Many Eastern fakirs have been known to cast themselves into a cataleptic sleep lasting for months and cases have even been known where they permitted themselves to be buried, being exhumed when the grass had grown over their graves. (*See* Dendy, *Philosophy of Mystery*.)

Cathari : (*See* **Gnostics.**)

Catoptromancy, or Enoptromancy is a species of divination by the mirror, which Pausanius describes : " Before the Temple of Ceres at Patras, there was a fountain, separated from the temple by a wall, and there was an oracle, very truthful, not for all events, but for the sick only. The sick person let down a mirror, suspended by a thread, till its base touched the surface of the water, having first prayed to the goddess and offered incense. Then looking in the mirror, he saw the presage of death or recovery, according as the face appeared fresh and healthy, or of a ghastly aspect." Another method of using the mirror was to place it at the back of a boy's or girl's head, whose eyes were bandaged. In Thessaly, the response appeared in characters of blood on the face of the moon, probably represented in the mirror. The Thessalian sorceresses derived their art from the Persians, who always endeavoured to plant their religion and mystic rites in the countries they invaded.

Cats, Elfin : These are to be found in the Scottish Highlands, and are said to be of a wild breed, as large as dogs, black in colour, with a white spot on the breast, and to have arched backs and erect bristles. By some, these cats are said to be witches in disguise.

Cauldron Devils : An abyss at the summit of the Peak of Teneriffe. A stone cast into the gulf resounds as though a copper vessel were being struck by a huge hammer, and on this account its name has been bestowed on it by the Spaniards. The natives of the Island are persuaded that the infernal regions are there, where dwell for ever the souls of the wicked.

Causimomancy : Divination by fire. It is a happy presage when combustible objects cast into the fire do not burn.

Cazotte, Jacques (1720-1792) : A French romance writer, and the reputed author of the famous *Prophétie de Cazotte*, concerning the Revolution. His sympathies were not with the revolutionary party. His letters were seized, and he and his daughter Elizabeth thrown into prison. During the September massacres, Elizabeth saved his life by flinging herself between him and the cut-throats who sought to kill him. He escaped, but was re-arrested, condemned, and beheaded. He was the author of the celebrated occult romance *Le Diable Amoureux*.

Celestial Light : The sacred light of all the ages, which is " as the lightning which shineth from the west to the east." It is the halo which surrounds certain visions of a mystical character, but can only be seen by those who have lived ascetically, when respiration is feeble, and life has almost left the body.

Cellini, Benvenuto : This celebrated Italian artist and craftsman had several most interesting adventures with demons and professors of the black art. In his *Life* he writes as follows.

" It happened, through a variety of odd accidents, that I made acquaintance with a Sicilian priest, who was a man of genius, and well versed in the Latin and Greek authors. Happening one day to have some conversation with him, when the subject turned on the subject of necromancy, I, who had a great desire to know something of the matter, told him, that I had all my life felt a curiosity to be acquainted with the mysteries of this art. The priest made answer, ' That the man must be of a resolute and steady temper who enters upon that study.' I replied, ' That I had fortitude and resolution enough, if I could but find an opportunity.' The priest subjoined, ' If you think you have the heart to venture, I will give you all the satisfaction you can desire.' Thus we agreed to enter upon a plan of necromancy. The priest one evening prepared to satisfy me, and desired me to look out for a companion or two. I invited one Vincenzio Romoli, who was my intimate acquaintance : he brought with him a native of Pistoia, who cultivated the black art himself. We repaired to the Colloseo, and the priest, according to the custom of necromancers, began to draw circles upon the ground with the most impressive ceremonies imaginable : he likewise brought hither assafœtida, several precious perfumes and fire, with some compositions also which diffused noisome odours. As soon as he was in readiness, he made an opening to the circle, and having taken us by the hand, ordered the other necromancer, his partner, to throw the perfumes into the fire at the proper time, intrusting the care of the fire and the perfumes to the rest ; and then he began his incantations. This ceremony lasted above an hour and a half, when there appeared several legions of devils insomuch that the amphitheatre was quite filled with them. I was busy about the perfumes, when the priest, perceiving there was a considerable number of infernal spirits, turned to me and said, ' *Benvenuto*, ask them something.' I answered, ' Let them bring me into the company of my Sicilian mistress, Angelica.' That night we obtained no answer of any sort ; but I had received great satisfaction in having my curiosity so far indulged. The necromancer told me, it was requisite we should go a second time, assuring me, that I should be satisfied in whatever I asked ; but that I must bring with me a pure immaculate boy.

" I took with me a youth who was in my service, of about twelve years of age, together with the same Vincenzio Romoli, who had been my companion the first time and one Agnolino Gaddi, an intimate acquaintance, whom I likewise prevailed on to assist at the ceremony. When we came to the place appointed, the priest having made his preparations as before, with the same and even more striking ceremonies, placed us within the circle, which he had likewise drawn with a more wonderful art, and in a more solemn manner, than at our former meeting. Thus having committed the care of the perfume and the fire to my friend Vincenzio, who was assisted by Agnolino Gaddi, he put into my hand a pintacula or magical chart, and bid me turn it towards the places that he should direct me ; and under the pintacula I held the boy. The necromancer having begun to make his tremendous invocations, called by their names a multitude of demons, who were the leaders of the several legions, and questioned them by the power of the eternal uncreated God, who lives for ever, in the Hebrew language, as likewise in Latin and Greek ; insomuch that the amphitheatre was almost in an instant filled with demons more numerous than at the former conjuration. Vincenzio Romoli was busied in making a fire, with the assistance of Agnolino, and burning a great quantity of precious perfumes. I. by the direction of the necromancer, again desired to be in the company of my Angelica. The former thereupon turning to me, said, ' Know, they have declared, that in the space of a month you shall be in her company.'

" He then requested me to stand resolutely by him, because the legions were now above a thousand more in number than he had designed ; and, besides these were the most dangerous ; so that, after they had answered my question, it behoved him to be civil to them, and dismiss them quietly. At the same time the boy under the pintacula was in a terrible fright, saying, that there were in that place a million of fierce men, who threatened to destroy us ; and that, moreover, four armed giants of an enormous stature were endeavouring to break into our circle. During this time, whilst the necromancer, trembling with fear, endeavoured by mild and gentle methods to dismiss them in the best way he could, Vincenzio Romoli, who quivered like an aspen leaf, took care of the perfumes. Though I was as much terrified as any of them, I did my utmost to conceal the terror I felt ; so that I greatly contributed to inspire the rest with resolution ; but the truth is, I gave myself over for a dead man, seeing the horrid fright the necromancer was in. The boy placed his head between his knees, and said, ' In this posture I will die ; for we shall all surely perish.' I told him that all these demons were under us, and what he saw was smoke and shadow ; so I bid him hold up his head and take courage. No sooner did he look up, but he cried out, ' The whole amphitheatre is burning, and the fire is just falling upon us ;' so covering his eyes with his hands, he again exclaimed that destruction was inevitable, and he desired to see no more. The necromancer entreated me to have a good heart, and take care to to burn the proper perfumes ; upon which

I turned to Romoli, and bid him burn all the most precious perfumes he had. At the same time I cast my eye upon Agnolino Gaddi, who was terrified to such a degree that he could scarce distinguish objects, and seemed to be half-dead. Seeing him in this condition, I said, ' Agnolino, upon these occasions a man should not yield to fear, but should stir about and give his assistance ; so come directly and put on some more of these perfumes.' Poor Agnolino, upon attempting to move, was so violently terrified that the effects of his fear overpowered all the perfumes we were burning. The boy, hearing a crepitation, ventured once more to raise his head, when, seeing me laugh, he began to take courage, and said, ' That the devils were flying away with a vengeance.'

" In this condition we stayed till the bell rang for morning prayer. The boy again told us, that there remained but few devils, and these were at a great distance. When the magician had performed the rest of his ceremonies, he stripped off his gown and took up a wallet full of books which he had brought with him. We all went out of the circle together, keeping as close to each other as we possibly could, especially the boy, who had placed himself in the middle, holding the necromancer by the coat, and me by the cloak. As we were going to our houses in the quarter of Banchi, the boy told us that two of the demons whom we had seen at the amphitheatre, went on before us leaping and skipping, sometimes running upon the roofs of the houses, and sometimes upon the ground. The priest declared, that though he had often entered magic circles, nothing so extraordinary had ever happened to him. As we went along, he would fain persuade me to assist with him at consecrating a book, from which, he said, we should derive immense riches : we should then ask the demons to discover to us the various treasures with which the earth abounds, which would raise us to opulence and power ; but that those love-affairs were mere follies, from whence no good could be expected. I answered, ' That I would readily have accepted his proposal if I understood Latin : ' he redoubled his persuasions, assuring me, that the knowledge of the Latin language was by no means material. He added, that he could have Latin scholars enough, if he had thought it worth while to look out for them ; but that he could never have met with a partner of resolution and intrepidity equal to mine, and that I should by all means follow his advice. Whilst we were engaged in this conversation, we arrived at our respective homes, and all that night dreamt of nothing but devils."

Celonitis or Celontes : This wonderful stone is found in the tortoise, and its property is to resist fire. Its healing virtues are two-fold, similar to those of the Asinius. Carried under the tongue on the day of the new moon, and for the fifteen days following, during the lunar ascension, it inspires its fortunate possessor to foretell future events every day from sunrising to six o'clock ; and in the decrease during the intervening hours.

Celts : Magic among the Celtic peoples in ancient times was so closely identified with Druidism that its origin may be said to have been Druidic. That Druidism was of Celtic origin, however, is a question upon which much discussion has been lavished, some authorities, among them Rhys, believing it to have been of non-Celtic and even non-Aryan origin. This is to say that the earliest non-Aryan or so-called " Iberian " or Megalithic people of Britain introduced the immigrant *Celts* to the Druidic religion. An argument in favour of this theory is that the continental *Celts* sent their neophyte Druid priests to Britain to undergo a special training at the hands of the Druids there, and there is little doubt that this island was regarded as the headquarters of the cult. The people of Cisalpine Gaul, for instance, had no Druidic priesthood. (*See* Rice Holmes'

Cæsar's Conquest, pp. 532-536). Cæsar has told us that in Gaul Druidic seminaries were very numerous , and that in them severe study and discipline were entailed upon the neophytes, the principal business of whom was to commit to memory countless verses enshrining Druidic knowledge and tradition. That this instruction was astrological and magical we have the fullest proof, and it is with these aspects of the Celtic religion alone that we have to deal in this place.

The Druids were magi as they were hierophants in the same sense that the American-Indian medicine-man is both magus and priest. That is, they were medicine-men on a higher-scale, and possessed a larger share of transcendental knowledge than the shamans of more barbarous races. Thus they may be said to be a link between the shaman and the magus of mediæval times. Many of their practices were purely shamanistic, whilst others were more closely connected with mediæval magical rite. But they were not the only magicians among the *Celts*, for we find that magic power is frequently the possession of women and the poetic craft. The art magic of Druidism had many points of comparison with most magical systems, and may be said to have approximated more to that black magic which desires power for the sake of power alone, than to any more transcendental type. Thus it included the power to render oneself invisible, to change the bodily shape, to produce an enchanted sleep, to induce lunacy, and the utterance of spells and charms which caused death. Power over the elements was also claimed, as in the case of Broichan, a Caledonian Druid who opposed Saint Columbia, as we read in Adamnan's *Life* of that saint as follows :

" Broichan, speaking one day to the holy man, says : ' Tell me, Columba, at what time dost thou propose to sail forth ? ' " On the third day,' says the Saint, ' God willing and life remaining, we propose to begin our voyage.' ' Thou wilt not be able to do so,' says Broichan in reply, ' for I can bring the wind contrary for thee, and bring dark clouds upon thee.' The Saint says : ' The omnipotence of God rules over all things, in Whose Name all our movements, He Himself governing them, are directed.' What more need be said ? On the same day as he had purposed in his heart the Saint came to the long lake of the river Ness, a great crowd following. But the Druids then began to rejoice when they saw a great darkness coming over, and a contrary wind with a tempest. Nor should it be wondered at that these things can be done by the art of demons, God permitting it, so that even winds and waters are roused to fury.

" For it was thus that legions of devils once met the holy bishop Germanus in mid-ocean, what time he was sailing from the Gallican Gulf (the British Channel!) to Britain in the cause of man's salvation, and stirred up dangerous storms and spread darkness over the sky and obscured daylight. All which storms, however, were stilled at the prayer of St. Germanus, and, quicker than said, ceased, and the darkness was swept away.

" Our Columba, therefore, seeing the furious elements stirred up against him, calls upon Christ the Lord, and entering the boat while the sailors are hesitating, he with all the more confidence, orders the sail to be rigged against the wind. Which being done, the whole crowd looking on meanwhile, the boat is borne along against the contrary winds with amazing velocity. And after no great interval, the adverse winds veer round to the advantage of the voyage amid the astonishment of all. And thus, throughout that whole day, the blessed man's boat was driven along by gentle favouring breezes, and reached the desired haven. Let the reader, therefore, consider how great and saintly was that venerable man through whom Al-

mighty God manifested His glorious Name by such miraculous powers as have just been described in the presence of a heathen people.'

The art of rain-making, bringing down fire from the sky, and causing mists, snow-storms and floods was also claimed by the Druids. Many of the spells probably in use among the Druids survived until a comparatively late period, and are still in use in some remote Celtic localities—the names of Saints being substituted for those of Celtic deities, —as in Well-worship (q.v.) a possibly Druidic cultus, and certain ritual practices which are still carried out in the vicinity of megalithic structures. In pronouncing incantations, the usual method employed was to stand upon one leg, to point to the person or object on which the spell was to be laid with the fore-finger, at the same time closing an eye, as if to concentrate the force of the entire personality upon that which was to be placed under ban. A manuscript preserved in the Monastery of St. Gall and dating from the eighth or ninth century, has preserved magical formulæ for the preservation of butter and the healing of certain diseases in the name of the Irish god Diancecht. These and others bear a close resemblance to Babylonian and Etruscan spells, and this goes to strengthen the hypothesis often put forward with more or less ability that Druidism had an eastern origin. All magical rites were accompanied by spells. Druids often accompanied an army to assist by their magical art in confounding the enemy.

There is little doubt that the conception of a Druidic priesthood has descended down to our own time in a more or less debased condition in British Celtic areas. Thus the existence of guardians and keepers of wells said to possess magical properties, and the fact that certain familiar magical spells and formulæ are handed down from one gen ration to another, is a proof of the survival of Druidic tradition, however feeble. Females are generally the conservators of these mysteries, but that there were Druid priestesses is fairly certain.

There are also indications that to some extent Scottish witchcraft was a survival of Celtic religio-magical practice. (*See* **Witchcraft, Scottish** in article **Scotland.**)

Amulets were extensively worn by the *Celts*, the principal forms in use being phallic (against the evil eye), coral, the " serpent's egg "—some description of fossil. The person who passed a number of serpents together forming such an " egg " from their collected spume had to catch it in his cloak ere it fell to earth, and then make all speed over a running-stream where he was safe from the reptiles' vengeance. Totemic amulets were also common. (*See* **Scotland and Ireland.**)

LITERATURE—H. d'Arbois de Jubainville, *Les Druides et les dieux celtiques a forme d'animaux*, Paris, 1906 ; Gomme *Ethnology in Folklore*, London 1892 ; T. R. Holmes, *Cæsar's Conquest of Gaul*, London 1899, *Cæsar's Conquest of Britain*, 1907 ; S. Reinach, *Cultes, mythes et religions* Paris, 1905 ; J. Rhys, *Celtic Britain*, London 1882 ; *Celtic Heathendom*, London 1888 ; C. Squire, *Mythology of the ancient Britons*, London, 1905.

Central America : (*See* **Mexico and Central America.**)

Central Association of Spiritualists : (*See* **British National Association of Spiritualists.**)

Cepionidus : A stone of many colours, said to reflect the likeness of the beholder.

Ceraunius, or Cerraclus, is described as a pyramidal crystalline stone, tinged with saffron, and is said to fall from the clouds. It preserves from drowning, from injury by lightning, and gives pleasant dreams.

Ceraunoscopy : Divination practised by the ancients by the examination of the phenomena of the air.

Ceremonial Magic : Ceremonial magic is chiefly occupied

with the art of dealing with spirits. Its rites are supposedly religious, and the rituals which contain it partake largely of the nature of religious observances. It is not, as generally supposed, a reversed Christianity or Judaism, nor does it partake of the profanation of religious ritual. It is in effect an attempt to derive power from God for the successful control of evil spirits. In the Grimoires and Keys of Black Magic, the operator is constantly reminded that he must meditate continually on the undertaking in hand, and centre every hope in the infinite goodness of the Great Adonai. The god invoked in Black Magic is not Satan as is so often supposed, but the Jehovah of the Jews, and the Trinity of the Christians. The foundation of practical magic is almost certainly the belief in the power of divine words to compel the obedience of all spirits to those who could pronounce them. Such words and names were supposed to invoke or dismiss the denizens of the spirit world, and these with suitable prayers were used in all magical ceremonies. Again it was thought that it was easier to control evil spirits than to enlist the sympathies of angels.

He who would gain such power over demons is exhorted in the magical texts which exist to observe continence and abstinence, to disrobe as seldom and sleep as little as possible during the period of preparation, to meditate continually on his undertaking and centre all his hopes on the Great Adonai. The fast should be most austere, and human society must be avoided as much as possible. The concluding days of the fast should be additionally strict—sustenance being reduced to bread and water. Daily ablutions are necessary, and these must be made in water which has been previously exorcised according to the ritual : especially must this be observed immediately before the ceremony. Certain periods of the day and night are ruled by certain planets and these are to be found in the book known as the *Key of Solomon the King* (q.v). (*See also* **Astrology.**) The Book of Black Magic taught that the hours of Saturn, Mars and Venus are good for communion with spirits,—the hour of the first named planet for invoking souls in Hell ; and that of the second those who have been slain in battle. In fact these hours and seasons are ruled by the laws of astrology. In the preparation of the instruments employed, the ceremonies of purifying and consecrating, must be carefully observed. An aspergillum composed of mint, marjoram, and rosemary should be used for the first and should be contained in a pot of glazed earth. For fumigation a chafing dish should be used filled with freshly kindled coal and perfumed with aloe-wood or mace, benzoin or storax.

The experiment of holding converse with spirits should be made in the day and hour of Mercury : that is the 1st or 8th, or the 15th or 22nd (*See* **Necromancy**). The *Grand Grimoire* says that when the night of action has arrived, the operator shall take a rod, a goat-skin, a blood-stone, two crowns of vervain, and two candlesticks with candles ; also a new steel and two new flints, enough wood to make a fire, half a bottle of brandy, incense and camphor, and four nails from the coffin of a dead child. Either one or three persons must take part in the ceremony—on of whom only must address the spirit. The Kabbalistic circle is formed with strips of kid's skin fastened to the ground by the four nails. With the blood-stone a triangle is traced within the circle, beginning at the eastern point. The letters *a e a j* must be drawn in like manner, as also the Name of the Saviour between two crosses. The candles and vervain crowns are then set in the left and right sides of the triangle within the circle, and they with the brazier are set alight—the fire being fed with brandy and camphor. A prayer is then repeated. The operator must be careful

to have no alloyed metal about him except a gold or silver coin wrapped in paper, which must be cast to the spirit when he appears outside the circle. The spirit is then conjured three times. Should the spirit fail to appear, the two ends of the magic rod must be plunged into the flames of the brazier. This ritual is known as the Rite of Lucifuge, and is believed to invoke the demon Lucifuge Rofocale.

For further information concerning the ceremonial of magic, *See* **Necromancy** and the articles on the various rituals of magic, such as **Arbatel, Key of Solomon, Grimorium Verum**, etc. (*See* **Magic.**)

Ceroscopy : Divination by wax. The process was as follows. Fine wax was melted in a brass vessel until it became a liquid of uniform consistence. It was then poured slowly into another vessel filled with cold water, in such a way that the wax congealed in tiny discs upon the surface of the water. The magician then interpreted the figures thus presented as he saw fit.

Chagrin or **Cagrino :** An evil spirit believed in by the Continental Gypsies. It has the form of a hedgehog, is yellow in colour, and is a foot and a half in length and a span in breadth. "I am certain," says Wlislocki, "that this creature is none other than the equally demoniac being called Harginn, still believed in by the inhabitants of North-western India. Horses are the special prey of the *Chagrin*, who rides them into a state of exhaustion, as does the Guecubu (q.v.) of Chili. The next day they appear sick and weary, with tangled manes and bathed in sweat. When this is observed they are tethered to a stake which has been rubbed with garlic juice, then a red thread is laid on the ground in the form of a cross, or else some of the hair of the animal is mixed with salt, meal and the blood of a bat and cooked to bread, with which the hoof of the horse is smeared. The empty vessel which contained the mixture is put in the trunk of a high tree while these words are uttered :

" Tarry, pipkin, in this tree,
Till such time as full ye be."

Chain, Forming a : In spiritualism, a term denoting the joining of the hands of the sitters round a table, whereby the magnetic current is strengthened and reinforced. The Baron de Guldenstubbé gives the following directions for forming a chain. " In order to form a chain, the twelve persons each place their right hand on the table, and their left hand on that of their neighbour, thus making a circle round the table. Observe that the medium or mediums if there be more than one, are entirely isolated from those who form the chain."

Dr. Lapponi, in his *Hypnotism and Spiritism* (trans. London, 1906), gives an account of the usual procedure for the formation of a chain. " He (the medium) makes those present choose a table, which they may examine as much as they like, and may place in whatever part of the room they choose. He then invites some of the assistants to place their hands on the table in the following manner : The two thumbs of each person are to be touching each other, and each little finger is to be in communication with the little finger of the persons on either side. He himself completes the *chain* with his two hands. The hands of all altogether rest on the edge of the table. (*See* **Planetary Chains.**)

Chain-Period : (*See* **Planetary Chains.**)

Chakras : These are, according to theosophists, the sense organs of the etheral body (q.v.) and receive their name from their appearance which resembles vortices. Altogether there are ten *chakras*—visible only to clairvoyants—but of these it is advisable to use only seven. They are situated, not on the denser physical body, but opposite certain parts of it as follows : (1) the top of the head, (2) between the eyebrows, (3) the throat, (4) the heart, (5) the spleen—(where vitality is indrawn from the sun), (6) the solar plexus, (7) the base of the spine. The remaining three *chakras* are situated in the lower part of the pelvis and normally are not used, but are brought into play only in Black Magic. It is by means of the *chakras* that the trained occultist can become acquainted with the astral world. (*See* **Theosophy.**)

Chalcedony : A good specific against phantasy and the illusions of evil spirits. It also quickens the power of the body, and renders its possessor fortunate in law. To the latter effect it must be perforated and suspended by hairs from an ass. The black variety prevents hoarseness and clears the voice.

Chams : A race of Indo-Chinese origin, numbering about 130,000 souls, settled in Annam, Siam, Cochin-China, and Cambodia. They have some reputation among the surrounding population as sorcerers; this corruption probably arising from the mythic influence of a conquered race. Their magicians claim to be able to slay at a distance, or to bring ruin and disease by the aid of magical formulæ. Among the Cambodian *Chams*, sorcerers are cordially detested by the common people, as they are believed to be the source of all the evil which befalls them, and the majority of them usually end their days by secret assassination. They are nearly always of the female sex, and enter the sisterhood by means of a secret initiation held in the depths of the forest at the hour of midnight. Indeed the actual method of initiation is known to us. The woman who desires to become a sorceress procures the nest of a termite, and sacrifices thereon a cock (*See* **Cock**), cutting it in two from the head to the tail, and dancing in front of it in a condition of complete nudity, until by force of her incantations the two halves of the bird approach one another and it becomes once more alive and gives vent to a crow. Sorceresses are said to be known by the tendency of their complexion to alter its hue, and by their swollen and bloodshot eyes. They possess numerous rites for the propitiation of evil spirits, in which, in common with the neighbouring and surrounding populations, they implicitly believe. Thus in building a house numerous propitiatory rites must be observed, accompanied by invocation of the protecting deities. They believe in lucky and unlucky days, and are careful not to undertake anything of importance unless favoured by propitious omens. They possess many peculiar superstitions. Thus they will not disturb grain which has been stored during the day time, as they say it is then asleep, and wait until nightfall before supplying themselves from it. They also have many magical agricultural formulæ, such as the " instruction " to, and " passing " of, the standing rice-stems in the harvest field before they are cut and garnered, so that they may be worthy to be stored. The Brahmanic *Chams* believe that the souls of good men betake themselves to the sun, those of women to the moon, and those of the coolie class into clouds, but these are only places of temporary sojourn, until such time as all finally come to reside within the centre of the earth. The belief in metempsychosis is also highly popular. See E. Aymonier, *Les Tchames et leur Religions*, Paris, 1891; Aymonier Chaton, *Dictionnaire Cam-Française*, Paris, 1906; Cahaton, *Nouvelles recherches sur les chams*, Paris, 1901.

Changelings : The substitution of a little old mannikin of the elf race, for a young child. There are many tales representative of this belief in Scotland. The *changeling* grows up peevish and misshapen, always crying, and gives many proofs of its origin to those versed in such matters. There are many ways of getting rid of him, such as sticking a knife into him, making him sit on a gridiron with a fire below, dropping him into a river, etc.,—which one would

imagine would prove fairly successful The changeling sometimes gives himself away by unthinking reference to his age.

Chaomandy : (*See* **Ceraunoscopy.**)

Chaos : (See **Philosopher's Stone.**)

Charcot, Prof. J. M. : (See **Hypnotism**.)

Charlemagne ; or Charles the Great : The greatest of Frankish kings ; was the elder son of Pepin the Short, and succeeded his father in 768 A.D. He is included in this work chiefly because of his close connection with the supernatural so far as legend is concerned. Again and again in the pages of French romance, notably in these romances dealing with the adventures of William of Orange, do we find the Emperor visited by angels who are the direct messengers of the heavenly power. This of course is to symbolise his position as the head and front of Christendom in the world. He was its champion and upholder, surrounded as he was on all sides by the forces of paganism,—the Moors on his southern borders, and the Prussians and Saxons on his flank. *Charles* was regarded by the Christians of Europe as the direct representative of heaven, whose mission it was to Christianise Europe and to defend the true faith in every way. No less do we find him and his court connected with the realm of fäery. Notices of the encounters of the fairy folk by his paladins are not so numerous in the original French romances which deal with him and them ; but in the hands of Boiardo, Ariosto, and Pulci, they dwelt in an enchanted region where at any moment they might meet with all kinds of supernatural beings. But both in the older and later romances the powers of magic and enchantment are ever present. These are chiefly instanced in magical weapons such as the Sword Durandal of Roland which cannot be shivered ; the magical ointments of giants like Ferragus, which rubbed on their bodies make them invulnerable ; the wearing of armour which exercises a similar guardianship on the body of its possessor, and so forth. But we find heroes like Ogier, the Dane, penetrating into fairy land itself, and wedding its queen. This was the fate of a great many mediæval heroes, and Ogier finds in the enchanted realm King Arthur, and several other paladins. The analogous cases of Tom-a-Lincolne, Tannhäuser and Thomas the Rhymer, will readily occur to the reader. The magical and the marvellous is everywhere in use in the romances which deal with *Charlemagne*. Indeed in this respect they entirely put in the shade the later romances proper, as distinguished from the Chansons de Geste.

Charm (Carmen) : A magical formula, sung or recited to bring about a supposedly beneficial result, or to confer magical efficacy on an amulet. In popular usage the same word is employed to designate the incantation and the object which is charmed. For the material object (*See* **Amulet :**) for the recital (*See* **Spells.**)

Charnock, Thomas : Alchemist. (1524 ? — 1581). Comparatively little biographical matter concerning this English alchemist is forthcoming, but it is recorded that he was born somewhere in the Isle of Thanet, Kent ; while as to the date, this is revealed inasmuch as one of his manuscripts, dated 1574, is stated by the writer to have been penned in " the fifty yeare of my age." As a young man he travelled all over England in search of alchemistic knowledge, but eventually he fixed his residence at Oxford, and here he chanced to make the acquaintance of a noted scientist. The latter, greatly impressed with the youth's cleverness, straightway appointed him his confidant and assistant in general ; and, after working in this capacity for a number of years, *Charnock* found himself the sole legatee of his patron's paraphernalia, and likewise of the various secrets written in his note-books. Armed thus, he proceeded to devote himself more eagerly than ever to the quest of gold-production ; but in 1555, just as he imagined himself on the verge of triumph, his hopes were frustrated by a sudden explosion in his laboratory ; while in 1557, when he again thought that success was imminent, the press-gang arrived at his house and laid violent hands on him, being anxious for recruits wherewith to swell the English army then fighting the French. The alchemist was bitterly chagrined on being kidnapped in this wise, and, lest his secrets should be discovered by prying eyes, he set himself to destroy all his precious *impedimenta.*

> "With my worke made such a furious faire
> That the gold flew forth in the aire,"—

so he writes concerning this iconoclasm. and, subsequent to this event, he proceeded to France as a soldier, and took part in the disastrous campaign which culminated in the English being worsted at Calais by the Duc de Guise. How *Charnock* fared during the expedition is not known, and it is likely that he found small pleasure in the rough life ; but be that as it may, he returned to England safely, and in 1562 he was married to one Agnes Norton. Thereafter he settled at Stockland, in the county of Somerset, and here he continued to pursue scientific researches, apparently unmolested by further visitations from the military powers. Nor would it seem that the clergy molested him either, or looked askance on his alchemistic studies ; for on his death, which occurred in 1581, his mortal remains were duly interred at Otterhampton Church, Bridgwater.

That facetious antiquary and historian, Anthony Wood, in his *Athenæ Oxoniensis*, credits *Charnock* with a considerable amount of writing, and it is possible that several items enumerated are in reality from some other pen than the alchemist's. However, there are certain books which the latter undoubtedly wrote, notably *Ænigma ad Alchimiam*, issued in 1572 ; while no less interesting than this is the *Breviary of Natural Philosophy*, which is couched in verse, was published originally in 1557, and was subsequently reprinted in the *Theatrum Chemicum* of Elias Ashmole.

Chase, Warren : (*See* **Spiritualism.**)

Chazel, Comte de : (*See* **Rosicrucians.**)

Chela : (*See* **Adept.**)

Chelidonius : A stone taken out of a swallow ; good against melancholy and periodical disorders. To cure fever it must be put in a yellow linen cloth, and tied about the neck.

Chenevix, Richard : (*See* **Spiritualism.**)

Cherubim : Certain mystic appearances of the angelic type, often represented as figures wholly or partly human, and with wings proceeding from the shoulders. We find the first mention of these beings in connection with the expulsion of Adam and Eve from the Garden of Eden ; and they are frequently spoken of in later biblical history. Sometimes the cherubim have two or more faces, or are of composite animal form.

Chesed : Under this name the Jewish Kabalists signified the attribute of mercy.

Chesme : A cat-shaped well—or fountain—spirit or nymph of the Turks. She inveigles youths to death much in the same manner as the Lorelei.

Chevaliers de l' Enfer : These are demons more powerful than those of no rank, but less powerful than titled demons —counts, marquises, and dukes. They may be evoked from dawn to sunrise, and from sunset to dark.

Chilan Balam, Books of : (*See* **Mexico and Central America.**)

Children in Poltergeist Cases : (*See* **Poltergeist.**)

China : Although it can hardly be said that any system of magic worthy of the name ever originated in China, and though magical practice was uncommon, yet instances are not wanting of the employment of magical means in the Celestial Empire, and the belief in a supernatural world

peopled by gods, demons and other beings is very strong in the popular Chinese mind.

"Although the Chinese mind possessed under such a constitution but few elements in which magic could strike root and throw out its ramifications and influence, yet we find many traces giving evidence of the instinctive movement of the mind, as well as of magical influence ; though certainly not in the manner or abundance that we meet with it in India. The great variety of these appearances is, however, striking, as in no other country are they so seldom met with.

"As the King, as it were, microcosmically represents the human races in fortune or misfortune before the divinity so must his eye be constantly directed to those signs in which the will of the Most High is revealed ; ' He must observe dreams as much as the phenomena of nature, the eclipses and the positions of the stars ; and, when all else is wanting, he must consult the oracle of the tortoise, or the Plant Tsche, and direct his actions accordingly.' He is therefore, as it were, the universal oracle of the people, as the popular mind is relieved from every flight of imagination by a highly remarkable mental compulsion." . . .

"It is easy to understand from these circumstances wherefore we find so few of these phenomena of magic and the visionary and ecstatic state, in other parts of the East so frequent, and therefore they are scattered and uncertain. Accounts are, however, not wanting to show that the phenomena as well as theories of prophecy were known in more remote times. Under the Emperor Hoei Ti, about A.D. 304, a mystical sect arose in *China* calling themselves the teachers of the emptiness and nothingness of all things. They also exhibited the art of binding the power of the senses, and producing a condition which they believed perfection."

Demonism and Obsession. The Chinese are implicit believers in demons whom they imagine surround them on every hand. Says Peebles : " English officials, American missionaries, mandarins and many of the Chinese literati (Confucians, Taoists and Buddhist believers alike) declare that spritism in some form, and under some name, is the almost universal belief of *China*. It is generally denominated ' ancestral worship.' "

"There is no driving out of these Chinese," says Father Gonzalo, " the cursed belief that the spirits of their ancestors are ever about them, availing themselves of every opportunity to give advice and counsel."

"The medium consulted," remarks Dr. Doolittle, " takes in the hand a stick of lighted incense to dispel all defiling influences, then prayers of some kind are repeated, the body becomes spasmodic, the medium's eyes are shut, and the form sways about, assuming the walk and peculiar attitude of the spirit when in the body. Then the communication from the divinity begins, which may be of a faultfinding or a flattering character. . . . Sometimes these Chinese mediums profess to be possessed by some specified historical god of great healing power, and in this condition they prescribe for the sick. It is believed that the ghoul or spirit invoked actually casts himself into the medium, and dictates the medicine."

"Volumes might be written upon the gods, genii and familiar spirits supposed to be continually in communication with this people," writes Dr. John L. Nevius, in his works, *China and The Chinese.* " The Chinese have a large number of books upon this subject, among the most noted of which is the ' Liau-chai-chei,' a large work of sixteen volumes. . . . Tu Sein signifies a spirit in the body, and there are a class of familiar spirits supposed to dwell in the bodies of certain Chinese who became the mediums of communication with the unseen world. Individuals said to be possessed by these spirits are visited by multitudes, particularly those who have lost recently relatives by death, and wish to converse with them. . . . Remarkable disclosures and revelations are believed to be made by the involuntary movements of a bamboo pencil, and through a similar method some claim to see in the dark. Persons considering themselves endowed with superior intelligence are firm believers in those and other modes of consulting spirits."

The public teacher in Chen Sin Ling (W. J. Plumb says) : " In the district of Tu-ching, obsessions by evil spirits or demons are very common." He further writes that " there are very many cases also in Chang-lo." Again he says :

" When a man is thus afflicted, the spirit (*Kwei*) takes possession of his body without regard to his being strong or weak in health. It is not easy to resist the demon's power. Though without bodily ailments, possessed persons appear as if ill. When under the entrancing spell of the demon, they seem different from their ordinary selves.

" In most cases the spirit takes possession of a man's body contrary to his will, and he is helpless in the matter. The kwei has the power of driving out the man's spirit, as in sleep or dreams. When the subject awakes to consciousness, he has not the slightest knowledge of what has transpired.

" The actions of possessed persons vary exceedingly. They leap about and toss their arms, and then the demon tells them what particular spirit he is, often taking a false name, or deceitfully calling himself a god, or one of the genii come down to the abodes of mortals. Or, perhaps, it professes to be the spirit of a deceased husband or wife. There are also kwei of the quiet sort, who talk and laugh like other people, only that the voice is changed. Some have a voice like a bird. Some speak Mandarin—the language of *Northern China*—and some the local dialect ; but though the speech proceeds from the mouth of the man, what is said does not appear to come from him. The outward appearance and manner is also changed.

" In Fu-show there is a class of persons who collect in large numbers and make use of incense, pictures, candles and lamps to establish what are called ' incense tables.' Taoist priests are engaged to attend the ceremonies, and they also make use of ' mediums.' The Taoist writes a charm for the medium, who, taking the incense stick in his hand, stands like a graven image, thus signifying his willingness to have the demon come and take possession of him. Afterward, the charm is burned and the demon-spirit is worshipped and invoked, the priest, in the meanwhile going on with his chanting. After a while the medium begins to tremble, and then speaks and announces what spirit has descended, and asks what is wanted of him. Then, whoever has requests to make, takes incense sticks, makes prostrations, and asks a response respecting some disease, or for protection from some calamity. In winter the same performances are carried on to a great extent by gambling companies. If some of the responses hit the mark, a large number of people are attracted. They establish a shrine and offer sacrifices, and appoint days, calling upon people from every quarter to come and consult the spirit respecting diseases. . . .

" There is also a class of men who establish what they call a ' Hall of Revelations.' At the present time there are many engaged in this practice. They are, for the most part, literary men of great ability. The people in large numbers apply to them for responses. The mediums spoken of above are also numerous. All of the above practices are not spirits seeking to possess men ; but rather men seeking spirits to possess them, and allowing themselves to be voluntarily used as their instruments.

" As to the outward appearance of persons when possessed, of course, they are the same persons as to outward form as at ordinary times ; but the colour of the countenance may change. The demon may cause the subject to assume a threatening air, and a fierce, violent manner, The muscles often stand out on the face, the eyes are closed, or they protrude with a frightful stare. These demons sometimes prophesy.

" The words spoken certainly proceed from the mouths of the persons possessed ; but what is said does not appear to come from their minds or wills, but rather from some other personality, often accompanied by a change of voice. Of this there can be no doubt. When the subject returns to consciousness, he invariably declares himself ignorant of what he has said.

" The Chinese make use of various methods to cast out demons. They are so troubled and vexed by inflictions affecting bodily health, or it may be throwing stones, moving furniture, or the moving about and destruction of family utensils, that they are driven to call in the service of some respected scholar or Taoist priest, to offer sacrifices, or chant sacred books, and pray for protection and exemption from suffering. Some make use of sacrifices and offerings of paper clothes and money in order to induce the demon to go back to the gloomy region of Yan-chow. . . As to whether these methods have any effect, I do not know. As a rule, when demons are not very troublesome, the families afflicted by them generally think it best to hide their affliction, or to keep these wicked spirits quiet by sacrifices, and burning incense to them."

An article in the *London Daily News* gives lengthy extracts from an address upon the Chinese by Mrs. Montague Beaucham, who had spent many years in *China* in educational work. Speaking of their spiritism, she said, " The latest London craze in using the planchette has been one of the recognized means in *China* of conversing with evil spirits from time immemorial." She had lived in one of the particular provinces known as demon land, where the natives are bound up in the belief and worship of spirits. " There is a real power," she added, " in this necromancy. They do healings and tell fortunes." She personally knew of one instance that the spirits through the planchette had foretold a great flood. The boxer rising was prophesied by the planchette. These spirits disturbed family relations, caused fits of frothing at the mouth, and made some of their victims insane. In closing she declared that " Chinese spiritism was from hell," the obsession baffling the power of both Christian missionaries and native priests.

Dr. Nevius sent out a circular communication for the purpose of discovering the actual beliefs of the Chinese regarding demonism through which he obtained much valuable information. Wang Wu-Fang, an educated Chinese wrote :

" Cases of demon possession abound among all classes. They are found among persons of robust health, as well as those who are weak and sickly. In many unquestionable cases of obsession, the unwilling subjects have resisted, but have been obliged to submit themselves to the control of the demon. . . .

" In the majority of cases of possession, the beginning of the malady is a fit of grief, anger or mourning. These conditions seem to open the door to the demons. The outward manifestations are apt to be fierce and violent. It may be that the subject alternately talks and laughs ; he walks awhile and then sits, or he rolls on the ground, or leaps about ; or exhibits contortions of the body and twistings of the neck. . . . It was common among them to send for exorcists, who made use of written charms, or chanted verses, or punctured the body with needles These are among the Chinese methods of cure.

" Demons are of different kinds. There are those which clearly declare themselves ; and then those who work in secret. There are those which are cast out with difficulty, and others with ease.

" In cases of possession by familiar demons, what is said by the subject certainly does not proceed from his own will. When the demon has gone out and the subject recovers consciousness, he has no recollection whatever of what he has said or done. This is true almost invariably.

" The methods by which the Chinese cast out demons are enticing them to leave by burning charms and paper money, or by begging and exhorting them, or by frightening them with magic spells and incantations, or driving them away by pricking with needles, or pinching with the fingers, in which case they cry out and promise to go.

" I was formerly accustomed to drive out demons by means of needles. At that time cases of possession by evil spirits were very common in our villages, and my services were in very frequent demand. . . . "

The Rev. Timothy Richard, missionary, also writing in response to Dr. Nevius' circular, says :

" The Chinese orthodox definition of spirit is, ' the soul of the departed ;' some of the best of whom are raised to the rank of gods. . . . There is no disease to which the Chinese are ordinarily subject that may not be caused by demons. In this case the mind is untouched. It is only the body that suffers ; and the Chinese endeavour to get rid of the demon by vows and offerings to the gods. The subject in this case is an involuntary one. . . .

" Persons possessed range between fifteen and fifty years of age, quite irrespective of sex. This infliction comes on very suddenly, sometimes in the day, and sometimes in the night. The demoniac talks madly, smashes everything near him, acquires unusual strength, tears his clothes into rags, and rushes into the street, or to the mountains or kills himself unless prevented. After this violent possession, the demoniac calms down and submits to his fate, but under the most heart-rending protests. These mad spells which are experienced on the demon's entrance return at intervals, and increase in frequency, and generally also in intensity, so that death at last ensues from their violence.

" A Chefoo boy of fifteen was going on an errand. His path led through fields where men were working at their crops. When he came up to the men and had exchanged a word or two with them, he suddenly began to rave wildly ; his eyes rolled, then he made for a pond near by. Seeing this, the people ran up to him, stopped him from drowning himself and took him home to his parents. When he got home, he sprang up from the ground to such a height as manifested almost a superhuman strength. After a few days he calmed down and became unusually quiet and gentle ; but his own consciousness was lost. The demon spoke of its friends in Nan-Kin. After six months this demon departed. He has been in the service of several foreigners in Chefoo since. In this case no worship was offered to the demon.

" Now we proceed to those, who involuntarily possessed, yield to and worship the demon. The demon says he will cease tormenting the demoniac if he will worship him, and he will reward him by increasing his riches. But if not, he will punish his victim, make heavier his torments and rob him of his property. People find that their food is cursed. They cannot prepare any, but filth and dirt comes down from the air to render it uneatable. Their wells are likewise cursed ; their wardrobes are set on fire, and their money very mysteriously disappears. Hence arose the custom of cutting off the head of a string of cash that it might not run away. . . . When all efforts to rid themselves of the demon fail, they yield to it, and say

' Hold ! Cease thy tormenting and we will worship thee ! ' A picture is pasted upon the wall, sometimes of a woman, and sometimes of a man, and incense is burned, and prostrations are made to it twice a month. Being thus reverenced, money now comes in mysteriously, instead of going out. Even mill-stones are made to move at the demon's orders, and the family becomes rich at once. But it is said that no luck attends such families, and they will eventually be reduced to poverty. Officials believe these things. Palaces are known to have been built by them for these demons, who, however, are obliged to be satisfied with humbler shrines from the poor. . . .

" Somewhat similar to the above class is another small one which has power to enter the lower regions. These are the opposite of necromancers, for instead of calling up the dead and learning of them about the future destiny of the individual in whose behalf they are engaged, they lie in a trance for two days, when their spirits are said to have gone to the Prince of Darkness, to inquire how long the sick person shall be left among the living. . . .

" Let us now note the different methods adopted to cast out the evil spirits from the demoniacs. Doctors are called to do it. They use needles to puncture the tips of the fingers, the nose, the neck. They also use a certain pill, and apply it in the following manner : the thumbs of the two hands are tied tightly together, and the two big toes are tied together in the same manner. Then one pill is put on the two big toes at the root of the nail, and the other at the root of the thumb nails. At the same instant the two pills are set on fire, and they are kept until the flesh is burned. In the application of the pills, or in the piercing of the needle, the invariable cry is : ' I am going ; I am going immediately. I will never dare to come back again. Oh, have mercy on me this once. I'll never return ! '

" When the doctors fail, they call on people who practise spiritism. They themselves cannot drive the demon away, but they call another demon to do it. Both the Confucianists and Taoists practise this method. . . . Sometimes the spirits are very ungovernable. Tables are turned, chairs are rattled, and a general noise of smashing is heard, until the very mediums themselves tremble with fear. If the demon is of this dreadful character, they quickly write another charm with the name of the particular spirit whose quiet disposition is known to them. Lu-tsu is a favourite one of this kind. After the burning of the charm and incense, and when prostrations are made, a little frame is procured, to which a Chinese pencil is attached. Two men on each side hold it on a table spread with sand or millet. Sometimes a prescription is written, the pencil moving of its own accord. They buy the medicine prescribed and give it to the possessed. . . . Should they find that burning incense and offering sacrifices fails to liberate the poor victim, they may call in conjurors, such as the Taoists, who sit on mats and are carried by invisible power from place to place. They ascend to a height of twenty or fifty feet, and are carried to a distance of four or five *li* (about half a mile). Of this class are those who, in Manchuria call down fire from the sky in those funerals where the corpse is burned. . . .

" These exorcists may belong to any of the three religions in *China*. The dragon procession, on the fifteenth of the first month, is said by some to commemorate a Buddhist priest's victory over evil spirits. . . . They paste up charms on windows and doors, and on the body of the demoniac, and conjure the demon never to return. The evil spirit answers : ' I'll never return You need not take the trouble of pasting all these charms upon the doors and windows.'

" Exorcists are specially hated by the evil spirits. Sometimes they feel themselves beaten fearfully ; but no hand is seen. Bricks and stones may fall on them from the sky or housetops. On the road they may without any warning be plastered over from head to foot with mud or filth ; or may be seized when approaching a river, and held under the water and drowned."

In his *Social Life among the Chinese*, Dr. Doolittle says : " They have invented several ways by which they find out the pleasure of gods and spirits. One of the most common of their utensils is the *Ka-pue*, a piece of bamboo root, bean-shaped, and divided in the centre, to indicate the positive and the negative. The incense lighted, the Ka-pue properly manipulated before the symbol god, the pieces are tossed from the medium's hand, indicating the will of the spirit by the way they fall."

The following manifestation is mental rather than physical : " The professional takes in the hand a stick of lighted incense to expel all defiling influences ; prayers of some sort are repeated, the fingers interlaced, and the medium's eyes are shut, giving unmistakable evidence of being possessed by some supernatural or spiritual power. The body sways back and forward ; the incense falls, and the person begins to step about, assuming the walk and peculiar attitude of the spirit. This is considered as infallible proof that the divinity has entered the body of the medium. Sometimes the god, using the mouth of the medium, gives the supplicant a sound scolding for invoking his aid to obtain unlawful or unworthy ends.

" *Divination*," writes Sir John Burrows, " with many strange methods of summoning the dead to instruct the living and reveal the future, is of very ancient origin, as is proved by Chinese manuscripts antedating the revelations of the Jewish Scriptures."

An ancient Chinese book called *Poh-shi-ching-tsung*, consisting of six volumes on the " Source of True Divination," contains the following preface :

" The secret of augury consists in the study of the mysteries and in communications with gods and demons. The interpretations of the transformations are deep and mysterious. The theory of the science is most intricate, the practice of it most important. The sacred classic says : ' That which is true gives indications of the future.' To know the condition of the dead, and hold with them intelligent intercourse, as did the ancients, produces a most salutary influence upon the parties. . . . But when from intoxication or feasting, or licentious pleasures, they proceed to invoke the gods, what infatuation to suppose that their prayers will move them Often when no response is given, or the interpretation is not verified, they lay the blame at the door of the augur, forgetting that their failure is due to their want of sincerity. . . . It is the great fault of augurs, too, that, from a desire of gain, they use the art of divination as a trap to ensnare the people."

Peebles adds ; " Naturally undemonstrative and secretive, the higher classes of Chinese seek to conceal their full knowledge of spirit intercourse from foreigners, and from the inferior castes of their own countrymen, thinking them not sufficiently intelligent to rightly use it. The lower orders, superstitious and money-grasping, often prostitute their magic gifts to gain and fortune-telling. These clairvoyant fortune-tellers, surpassing wandering gypsies in ' hitting ' the past, infest the temples, streets and roadsides, promising to find lost property, discover precious metals and reveal the hidden future."

Ghosts.—The Chinese are strong in the belief that they are surrounded by the spirits of the dead. Indeed ancestor-worship constitutes a powerful feature in the national faith, but as it deals with religion it does not come within the scope of this article. Suffice it to say that the Celestial has ever before him the likelihood and desirability of communion with the dead. On the death of a person they make a hole in the roof to permit the soul to effect its escape from the house. When a child is at the point of death, its mother will go into the garden and call its name, hoping thereby to bring back its wandering spirit.

" With the Chinese the souls of suicides are specially obnoxious, and they consider that the very worst penalty that can befall a soul is the sight of its former surroundings. This, it is supposed that, in the case of the wicked man, ' they only see their homes as if they were near them ; they see their last wishes disregarded, everything upside down, their substance squandered, strangers possess the old estate ; in their misery the dead man's family curse him, his children become corrupt, land is gone, the wife sees her husband tortured, the husband sees his wife stricken down with mortal disease ; even friends forget, but some, perhaps, for the sake of bygone times, may stroke the coffin and let fall a tear, departing with a cold smile.' "

" In *China*, the ghosts which are animated by a sense of duty are frequently seen : at one time they seek to serve virtue in distress, and at another they aim to restore wrongfully held treasure. Indeed, as it has been observed, ' one of the most powerful as well as the most widely diffused of the people's ghost stories is that which treats of the persecuted child whose mother comes out of the grave to succour him.' "

" The Chinese have a dread of the wandering spirits of persons who have come to an unfortunate end. At Canton, 1817, the wife of an officer of Government had occasioned the death of two female domestic slaves, from some jealous suspicion it was supposed of her husband's conduct towards the girls ; and, in order to screen herself from the consequences, she suspended the bodies by the neck, with a view to its being construed into an act of suicide. But the conscience of the woman tormented her to such a degree that she became insane, and at times personated the victims of her cruelty, or, as the Chinese supposed, the spirits of the murdered girls possessed her, and utilised her mouth to declare her own guilt. In her ravings she tore her clothes and beat her own person with all the fury of madness ; after which she would recover her senses for a time, when it was supposed the demons quitted her, but only to return with greater frenzy, which took place a short time previous to her death. According to Mr. Dennys, the most common form of Chinese ghost story is that wherein the ghost seeks to bring to justice the murderer who shuffled off its mortal coil."

Poltergeists (q.v.) are not uncommon in *China*, and several cases of their occurrence have been recorded by the Jesuit missionaries of the eighteenth century in Cochin China. Mr Dennys in his *Folk Lore of China*, mentions a case in which a Chinaman was forced to take refuge in a temple by the usual phenomena—throwing about of crockery, &c., after the decease of a monkey.

Secret Societies. For an account of secret societies in *China*, *See* **Thion-ti-Hwir** and **Triad Society.**

It has sometimes been claimed that the systems of Confucius and Lao-Tze are magical or kabalistic, but such claims have been advanced by persons who did not appreciate their proper status as philosophic systems. (*See* **Y-Kin, Book of.**)

Symbolism. There are numerous mysteries of meaning in the strange symbols, characters, personages, birds, beasts, etc. which adorn all species of Chinese art objects. For example a rectangular Chinese vase is feminine, representing the creative or ultimate principle. A group of seemingly miscellaneous art objects, depicted perhaps upon a brush tray, are probably the *po-ku*, or ' hundred antiques,' emblematic of culture and implying a delicate compliment to the recipient of the tray. Birds and animals occur with frequency on Chinese porcelains, and, if one will observe closely, it is a somewhat select menagerie, in which certain types are emphasised by repetition. For instance, the dragon is so familiar as to be no longer remarked, and yet his significance is perhaps not fully understood by all. There are, in fact, three kinds of dragons, the *lung* of the sky, the *li* of the sea, and the *kiau* of the marshes. The *lung* is the favourite kind, however, and may be known when met by his having ' the head of a camel, the horns of a deer, the eyes of a rabbit, ears of a cow, neck of a snake, belly of a frog, scales of a carp, claws of a hawk, and palm of a tiger.' His special office is to guard and support the mansions of the gods, and he is naturally the peculiar symbol of the Emperor, or Son of Heaven.

A less familiar beast is the *chi-lin*, which resembles in part a rhinoceros, but has head, feet, and legs like a deer, and a tufted tail. In spite of his unprepossessing appearance he is of a benevolent disposition, and his image on a vase or other ornament is an emblem of good government and length of days. A strange bird, having the head of a pheasant, a long flexible neck and a plumed tail, may often be seen flying in the midst of scroll-like clouds, or walking in a grove of treepeonies. This is the *fenghuang*, the Chinese phœnix, emblem of immortality and appearing to mortals only as a presage of the auspicious reign of a virtuous Emperor. The tortoise (*kuei*), which bears upon its back the seagirt abode of the Eight Immortals, is a third supernatural creature associated with strength, longevity, and (because of the markings on its back) with a mystic plan of numerals which is a key to the philosophy of the unseen.

Colours have their significance, blue being the colour of the heavens, yellow of the earth and the Emperor, red of the sun, white of Jupiter or the Year Star, while each dynasty had its own particular hue, that of the Chou dynasty being described as ' blue of the sky after rain where it appears between the clouds.'

One could go on indefinitely ' reading ' the meaning of the seemingly fantastic creations of the Chinese artist-devotee, but enough has been said to show that the strange beings, the conventional arrangements, the apparently haphazard conjunction of objects in his decorative schemes are far from being matter of chance, but add to their decorative properties the intellectual charm of significance.

Chirothesy, Diepenbroek's Treatise on : (*See* **Healing by Touch**.)

Chips of Gallows : Chips from a gallows and places of execution are said to make efficacious amulets against ague.

Chiton : An evil spirit. (*See* **Burma**.)

Chochurah : The name under which the Jewish Kabalists designate Wisdom.

Chov-hani : The Gypsy name for a witch.

Chrisoletus : Is stone, which if bound round with gold and carried in the left hand drives away night-hags and preserves from melancholy, illusions and witches. Its virtue is the greater if a hole be made in it, and the hairs of an ass passed through.

Christian Circle, The : (*See* **Spain**.)

Chrysolite : A stone preventive of fever and madness, which also disposes to repentance. If set in gold, it is a preservative against nocturnal terrors.

Chrysoprase : A stone good for weakness of sight, and for rendering its possessor joyful and liberal : its colour is green and gold.

Churchyard : It is not difficult to understand how the churchyard has come to be regarded as the special haunt of ghosts. The popular imagination may well be excused for supposing that the spirits of the dead continue to hover over the spot where their bodies are laid. The ancient Greeks thought that the souls of the dead were especially powerful near their graves or sepulchres, because of some natural tie binding soul and body, even after death. The more gross and earthly a soul was, the less willing was it to leave the vicinity of its body, and in consequence, spectres encountered in a *churchyard* were more to be feared than those met with elsewhere. The apparitions witnessed at the tombs of saints, however, were to be regarded rather as good angels than the souls of the saints themselves.

Chymical Nuptials of Christian Rosenkreutz : (*See* **Rosicrucians**.)

Circe : (*See* **Greece**.)

Circles, Spiritualistic : A group of persons who meet at intervals for the purpose of holding séances for spirit communication. It is essential that at least one among them be a medium ; occasionally there are several mediums in one circle. But indeed all the members of a circle must be chosen with care, if the séances are to be productive of phenomena. The Baron de Guldenstubbé, in his *Practical Experimental Pneumatology, or the Reality of Spirits and the Marvellous Phenomenon of their Direct Writing*, published early in the history of the movement, gives directions for the forming of a circle after the American fashion.

" Setting aside the moral conditions," he says, " which are equally requisite it is known that American Circles are based on the distinction of positive and electric or negative magnetic currents.

" The circles consist of twelve persons, representing in equal proportions the positive and negative or sensitive elements. This distinction does not follow the sex of the members, though generally women are negative and sensitive, while men are positive and magnetic. The mental and physical constitution of each individual must be studied before forming the circles, for some delicate women have masculine qualities, while some strong men are, morally speaking, women. A table is placed in a clear and ventilated spot ; the medium is seated at one end and entirely isolated ; by his calm and contemplative quietude he serves as a conductor for the electricity and it may be noted that a good somnambulist is usually an excellent medium. The six electrical or negative dispositions, which are generally recognised by their emotional qualities and their sensibility, are placed at the right of the medium, the most sensitive of all being next to him. The same rule is followed with the positive personalities, who are at the left of the medium, with the most positive among them next to him. In order to form a chain, the twelve person each place their right hand on the table, and their left hand on that of the neighbour, thus making a circle round the table. Observe that the medium or mediums, if there be more than one, are entirely isolated from those who form the chain."

The formation of a circle is accomplished on similar lines at the present day. M. Camille Flammarion states that the alternation of the sexes is generally provided to " reinforce the fluids." That the séance may be as productive when the circle is composed of a few investigators, following no rules, but their own, has been abundantly proved in recent years. The one indispensable feature is the medium.

Clairaudience (" Clear Hearing") : The ability to hear sounds inaudible to the normal ear, such as " spirit " voices ; a faculty analogous to clairvoyance, (q.v.), but considerably less frequently met with. If *clairaudience* be ascribed to auditory, as clairvoyance to visual, hallucination, its comparative rareness is accounted for, since visual hallucination is the more common of the two. At the same time there are a goodly number of instances of the clairaudient faculty on record, some of them of a very picturesque nature. (*See* **Spirit Music**). Perhaps the best known case is that of Joan of Arc, but she was not the only martyr who heard the voices of saints and angels urging them to the performance of some special task. In spiritualistic circles the faculty is frequently claimed by mediums, but distinction must be made between the " inner voice," in which the latter are supposed to receive communications from the denizens of the other world, and an externalised voice comparable to an actual physical sound. Frequently some such physical sounds form the basis of an auditory hallucination, just as the points of light in a crystal are said to form *points de repère* round which the hallucination of the visualiser may shape itself.

Clairvoyance (*i.e.,* "clear vision") : A term denoting the supposed supernormal faculty of seeing persons and events which are distant in time or place, and of which no knowledge can reach the seer through the normal sense-channels. *Clairvoyance* may be roughly divided into three classes— retrocognition and premonition, or the perception of past and future events respectively, and the perception of contemporary events happening at a distance, or outside the range of the normal vision. *Clairvoyance* may include psychometry, second sight, and crystal-gazing, all of which see. For the early history of *clairvoyance, see* **Divination.** In prophecy, we have a form of *clairvoyance* extending back into antiquity, and second-sight also is an ancient form. It is notable that spiritualism in Great Britain was directly heralded, about the third decade of the nineteenth century, by an outbreak of *clairvoyance.* Among the clairvoyants of that period may be mentioned Alexis Didier (q.v.), whose phenomena suggested that telepathy at least entered into his feats, which included the reading of letters enclosed in sealed packets, the playing of *écarté* with bandaged eyes, and others of a like nature. *Clairvoyance* remains to the present day a prominent feature of the spiritualistic séance. Though there exists a quantity of evidence, collected by the members of the Society for Psychical Research and other scientific investigators, which would seem to support the theory of a supernormal vision, yet at the same time it must be acknowledged that many cases of *clairvoyance* lend themselves to a more mundane explanation. For instance, it has been shown that it is almost, if not quite, impossible so to bandage the eyes of the medium that he cannot make some use of his normal vision. The possibility of hyperæsthesia during trance must also be taken into account, nor must we overlook the hypothetical factor of telepathy, which may conceivably play a part in clairvoyant performances. A private enquiry agency might also be suggested as a possible source of some of the knowledge displayed by the professional clairvoyant. The crystal is, as has been indicated, a favourite mode of exercising the clairvoyant faculty, presumably because the hypnotic state is favourable to the development of the supernormal vision, though it might also be suggested that the condition thus induced favoured the rising into the upper consciousness of knowledge sub-consciously gleaned. The term *clairvoyance* is also used to cover the power to see discarnate spirits, and is thus applied to mediumship generally.

Clan Morna : In Irish romance one of the divisions of the Fianna, whose treasure bag containing magic weapons and precious jewels of the Danaan age was kept by Fia of that clan.

Clavel : Author of *Histoire Pittoresque de la Francmazonnerie.* He hints in it that when Freemasonry in Austria was suppressed by Charles VI., the Order of Mopses was established in its place.

Cledonism, or in full, **Cledonismantia,** is the good or evil presage of certain words uttered without premeditation when persons come together in any way. It also regulated the words to be used on particular occasions. Cicero says

the Pythagoreans were very attentive to these presages ; and according to Pausanius, it was a favourite method of divination at Smyrna, where the oracles of Apollo were thus interpreted.

Cleromancy was practised by throwing black and white beans, little bones or dice, and perhaps, stones ; anything, in short, suitable for lots. A method of practising *cleromancy* in the streets of Egypt is mentioned under the head of Sortilege, and the same thing was common in Rome. The Thriæan lots, named before, meant indifferently the same thing as *cleromancy* ; it was nothing more than dicing, only that the objects used bore particular marks or characters, and were consecrated to Mercury, who was regarded as the patron of this method of divination. For this reason an olive leaf, called " the lot of Mercury," was generally put in the urn in order to propitiate his favour.

Clidomancy should be exercised when the sun or moon is in Virgo. the name should be written upon a key the key should be tied to a Bible, and both should be hung upon the nail of the ring-finger of a virgin, who must thrice softly repeat certain words. According as the key and book turns or is stationary, the name is to be considered right or wrong. Some ancients added the seven Psalms with litanies and sacred prayers, and then more fearful effects were produced upon the guilty ; for not only the key and the book turned, but either the impression of the key was found upon him, or he lost an eye. Another method of practising with the Bible and key, is to place the street door key on the fiftieth-psalm, close the volume and fasten it very tightly with the garter of a female ; it is then suspended to a nail and will turn when the name of the thief is mentioned. By a third method, two persons suspend the Bible between them ; holding the ring of the key by their two forefingers.

Clothes, Phantom : (*See* **Phantom Dress.**)

Cloven Foot : There is an old belief, buttressed by countless tales of apparitions, that the Devil always appears with a *cloven foot*, as a sort of distinguishing mark. It has been suggested that the Evil One, having fallen lower than any man, is not permitted to take the perfect human form, but must have some sort of deformity, *i.e.*, the *cloven foot*.

Cock : The *cock* has always been connected with magical practice in the various parts of the world throughout the ages, and is to be considered in more than one light in this connection. He is the herald of the dawn, and many examples might be cited of assemblies of demons and sorcerers where his shrill cry, announcing dayspring, has put the infernal Sabbath to rout. It is said that for the purpose of averting such a contingency, sorcerers were wont to smear the head and breast of the *cock* with olive oil, or else to place around his neck a collar of vine-branches. In many cases the future was divined through the instrumentality of this bird. (*See* **Alectryomancy**). It was also believed that in the stomach of the *cock* was found a stone, called Lappilus Alectorius, from the Greek name of the bird, the virtue of which was to give strength and courage, and which is said to have inspired the gigantic might of Milo of Crotona.

Originally a native of India, the *cock* arrived in Europe in early times, via Persia, where we find him alluded to in the Zoroastrian books as the beadle of Sraosa, the sun, and affrighter of demons. Among the Arabs, it is said that he crows when he becomes aware of the presence of jinns. The Jews received their conception of the *cock* as a scarer of evil spirits from the Persians, as did the Armenians, who say that he greets with his clarion call the guardian angels, who descend to earth with the day, and that he gives the key-note to the angelic choirs of heaven to commence their daily round of song. In India, too, and among the Pagan Slavs, he was supposed to scare away demons from dwelling places, and was often the first living creature introduced into a newly-built house. The Jews, however, believe that it is possible for the *cock* to become the victim of demons, and they say that if he upsets a dish he should be killed. The *cock* is often used directly in magical practice. Thus, in Scotland, he is buried under the patients' bed in cases of epilepsy. The Germans believed that if a sorcerer throws a black *cock* into the air, thunder and lightning will follow, and among the Chams of Cambodia, a woman who wishes to become a sorceress sacrifices a live *cock* on a termite's nest, cutting the bird in two from the head to the tail, and placing it on an altar, in front of which she dances and sings, until the two halves of the bird come together again, and it comes to life and crows. His name was often pronounced by the Greeks as a cure for the diseases of animals, and it was said by the Romans that locked doors could be opened with his tail feathers. The bird was often pictured on amulets in early times, and figured as the symbol of Abraxas, the principal deity of a Gnostic sect.

The *cock* is often regarded as the guide of souls to the underworld, and in this respect was associated by the Greeks with Persephone and Hermes, and the Slavs of pagan times often sacrificed *cocks* to the dead, and to the household serpents in which they believed their ancestors to be reincarnated. Conversely, the *cock* was sometimes pictured as having an infernal connection, especially if his colour be black. Indeed he is often employed in black magic, perhaps the earliest instance of this being in the Atharia Veda. A black *cock* is offered up to propitiate the Devil in Hungary, and a black hen was used for the same purpose in Germany. The Greek syrens, the Shedim of the Talmud, and the Izpuzteque, whom the dead Aztec encounters on the road to Mictlan, the Place of the Dead, all have *cock's* feet. There is a widespread folk-belief that once in seven years the *cock* lays a little egg. In Germany it is necessary to throw this over the roof, or tempests will wreck the homestead, but should the egg be hatched, it will produce a cockatrice or basilisk. In Lithuania they put the *cock's* egg in a pot, and place it in the oven. From this egg is hatched a Kauks, a bird with a tail like that of a golden pheasant, which, if properly tended, will bring its owner great good luck. Gross mentions in a chronicle of Bâle, in Switzerland, that in the month of August, 1474, a *cock* of that town was accused and convicted of laying an egg, and was condemned to death. He was publicly burned along with his egg, at a place called Kablenberg, in sight of a great multitude of people.

The *cock* was also regarded as having a connection with light and with the sun, probably because of the redness of his comb, and the fiery sheen of his plumage, or perhaps because he heralds the day. It is the *cock* who daily wakens the heroes in the Scandinavian Asgard. (*See* **Alectromancy.**)

Cock Lane Ghost : The supposed cause of a mysterious outbreak of rappings, apparitions, and similar manifestations which broke out at a house in Cock Lane, Smithfield, London, in 1762. The disturbance was of the usual character of poltergeist hauntings, but for some reason or other it attracted wide-spread attention in London. Crowds flocked to the haunted spot, and claimed to have witnessed the manifestations. The ghost purported to be the spirit of a former resident in the Cock Lane house, a Mrs. Kent, and stated that she had been murdered by her husband. The tenant of the house at the time of the disturbance was a man named Parsons, and it was more than surmised that he had invented the ghost for the purpose of blackmailing the deceased's woman's husband. The disturbance was finally traced to Parson's daughter, a girl of eleven, and

Parsons himself was prosecuted and pilloried. (*See* Andrew Lang's *Cock Lane and Common Sense*, (1894).

Coffin Nails : In Devonshire it is said that a ring made from three nails or screws that have been used to fasten a coffin, and dug up in a churchyard, will act as a charm against convulsions and fits of every kind.

Coffin, Walter : (*See* **Psychological Society**).

Coleman, Benjamin : (*See* **British National Association of Spiritualists.**)

Coleridge, Samuel Taylor : English author and mystic (1772-1834). *Samuel Taylor Coleridge*, one of the greatest of English poets and critics, was born in the year 1772 at Ottery St. Mary, Devonshire, his father being John Coleridge, a clergyman and schoolmaster, who enjoyed considerable reputation as a theological scholar, and was author of a Latin grammar. Samuel's childhood was mostly spent at the native village, and from the first his parents observed that his was no ordinary temperament, for he showed a marked aversion to games, he even eschewed the company of other children, and instead gave his time chiefly to promiscuous reading. " At six years of age," he writes in one of his letters to his friend, Thomas Poole, " I remember to have read *Belisarius, Robinson Crusoe*, and *Philip Quarll*, and then I found the *Arabian Nights Entertainments*," while in this same letter he tells how the boys around him despised him for his eccentricity, the result being that he soon became a confirmed dreamer, finding in the kingdom of his mind a welcome haven of refuge from the scorn thus levelled at him.

By the time he was nine years old, *Coleridge* had shown a marked predilection for mysticism, in consequence whereof his father decided to make him a clergyman ; and in 1782 the boy left home to go to Christ's Hospital, London. Here he found among his fellow pupils at least one who shared his literary tastes, Charles Lamb, and a warm friendship quickly sprang up between the two ; while a little later *Coleridge* conceived an affection for a young girl called Mary Evans, but the progress of the love affair was soon arrested, the poet leaving London in 1790 to go to Cambridge. Beginning his university career as a sizar at Jesus College, he soon became known as a brilliant conversationalist, yet he made enemies by his extreme views on politics and religion, and in 1793, finding himself in various difficulties, he went back to London where he enlisted in the 15th Dragoons. Bought out soon afterwards by his relations, he returned to Cambridge, and in 1794, he published his drama, *The Fall of Robespierre*, while in the following year he was married to Sarah Fricker, and in 1796 he issued a volume of *Poems*. He now began to preach occasionally in Unitarian chapels, while in 1797 he met Wordsworth, with whom he speedily became intimate, and whom he joined in publishing *Lyrical Ballads*, this containing some of *Coleridge's* finest things, notably *The Ancient Mariner*. Nor was this the only masterpiece he wrote at this time, for scarcely was it finished, ere he composed two other poems of like worth, *Christabel* and *Kubla Khan* ; while in 1798 he was appointed Unitarian minister at Shrewsbury, and after holding this post for a little while, he went to travel in Germany, the requisite funds having been given him by Josiah and Thomas Wedgwood, both of whom were keen admirers of *Coleridge's* philosophical powers, and were of opinion that study on the continent would be of material service to him.

Among *Coleridge's* first acts on returning from Germany was to publish his translation of Schiller's *Wallenstein*, while simultaneously he took a cottage at Keswick, intending to live there quietly for many years. But peace and quiet are benefits usually sought in vain by poets, and *Coleridge* was no exception herein, for early in life he had begun to take occasional doses of laudanum, and now this practice developed into a habit which ruled his whole life. In 1804 he sought relief by going to Malta, while afterwards he visited Rome, and though, on returning to England, he was cheered by finding that a small annuity had been left him by the Wedgwoods, he was quite incapable of shaking off this deadly drug habit. As yet, however, it had not begun to vitiate his gifts altogether ; and, after staying for awhile with Wordsworth at Grasmere, he delivered a series of lectures on poetry at Bristol and subsequently in London. Especially in the Metropolis his genius was quickly recognised, and he was made a pensioner of the Society of Literature, this enabling him to take a small house at Highgate, and there he mainly spent his declining years, while it was in Highgate Cemetery that his remains were interred after his death in 1834.

Everything from *Coleridge's* hand is penetrated by a wealth of thought. Apart from his purely metaphysical works, of which the most notable are *Aids to Reflection* and *Confessions of an Enquiring Spirit*, his *Biographia Literaria* and other fine contributions to critical literature are all of a mystical temper ; for *Coleridge*—more, perhaps, than any other critics, not even excepting Goethe and Walter Pater—is never content with handling the surface of things, but always reflects a striving to understand and lay bare the mysterious point where artistic creation begins. For him, literature is a form of life, one of the most mysterious forms of life, and while he is supremely quick at noticing purely æsthetic merit, and equally quick at marking defect, it is really the philosophical element in his criticism which gives it its transcendant value and interest.

Coleridge's metaphysical predilections are not more salient in his prose than in his verse. In a singularly beautiful poem, *To the Evening Star*, he tells that he gazes thereon,

"Till I, myself, all spirit seem to grow."

And in most of his poems, indeed, he is " all spirit," while often he hypnotises the reader into feeling something of the author's spirituality. Here and there, no doubt, he attempts to express in words things too deep and mysterious to be resolved into that sadly limited mode of utterance, the result being a baffling and even exasperating obscurity ; but waiving altogether *Coleridge's* metaphysical poems, may it not be said justly that he introduced the occult into verse with a mastery wholly unsurpassed in English literature ? May it not be said that *The Ancient Mariner*, and more especially *Christabel*, are the most beautiful of all poems in which the supernatural plays an important part ?

Coley, Henry : (*See* **Astrology.**)

College of Teutonic Philosophers, R. C. (*See* **Michael Maer**).

Collegia : Roman craftsmen's society. (*See* **Freemasonry**).

Colloquy of the Ancients : A collection of Ossianic legends, made into one about the thirteenth or fourteenth centuries. It relates how the Fian heroes, Keelta and Oisin, each with eight warriors, met to talk over the glorious past for the last time. Then Oisin returns to the Fairy Mound of his mother, and Keelta meets with St. Patrick and his monks at Drumdreg. Keelta tells the saint many tales, interspersed with lyrics, with which he is delighted, and he eventually baptises Keelta and his warriors and grants them absolution.

Commentary on the Ancient War of the Knights : (*See* **Alchemy.**)

Community of Sensation : The term applied by the early mesmerists to a phenomenon of the hypnotic trance, wherein the somnambule seemed to *share the sensations* of the operator. Thus an hypnotic subject, insensible to pain and utterly indifferent to any stimulus applied to his own organism, would immediately respond to such stimuli applied to the hypnotist. If the latter had his nose tweaked or his hair pulled, the entranced subject, though in a separate apartment, would rub the corresponding part of his own person, with every sign of pain and indignation. The most common sensations shared in this wise were those of tasting and smelling, but apparent community of sight and even hearing were not unknown. In the days of Reichenbach such experiences were largely attributed to fraud, but they have since been proved to be genuine trance phenomena, probably arising from unconscious suggestion and hyperæsthesia, or, in the few cases where that hypothesis will not cover the ground, telepathic communication between operator and subject. *Community of sensation* is not, however, confined to the trance condition. Many instances of *community of sensation* arising spontaneously in the cases of persons in *rapport* with one another are to be found in the *Journal* and *Proceedings* of the Society for Psychical Research.

Compacts with the Devil : An anonymous writer has handed down to us the agreement entered into between Louis Gaufridi and the devil :

" I, Louis, a priest, renounce each and every one of the spiritual and corporal gifts which may accrue to me from God, from the Virgin, and from all the saints, and especially from my patron John the Baptist, and the apostles Peter and Paul and St. Francis. And to you, Lucifer, now before me, I give myself and all the good I may accomplish, except the returns from the sacrament in the cases where I may administer it ; all of which I sign and attest."

On his side Lucifer made the following agreement with Louis Gaufridi :

" I, Lucifer, bind myself to give you, Louis Gaufridi, priest, the faculty and power of bewitching by blowing with the mouth, all and any of the women and girls you may desire ; in proof of which I sign myself Lucifer."

Bodin gives the following : " Magdalen of the Cross, native of Cordova in Spain and abbess of a convent, finding that she was suspected by the nuns and fearing that she would be burnt if charged, desired to anticipate them, and obtain the pardon of the pope by confessing that from the age of twelve years, a bad spirit in the form of a black Moor had desired her chastity, and that she had given in, and this had gone on for thirty years or more, she usually sleeping with him. Through his means while in the church, she was raised up, and when the nuns took the Sacrament after the consecration, the host came even to her in the air, in the sight of the other nuns who regarded it as sacred and the priest also, who used to complain at that time of a host."

According to Don Calmet there is to be seen at Molsheim in the chapel of St. Ignatius in the church of the Jesuit fathers a well-known inscription giving the history of a young German nobleman named Michel Louis, of the family of Boubenhoren, who was sent when quite young to the court of the Duke of Lorraine to learn French and there lost all his money at cards. Reduced to despair he decided to give himself up to the devil if that spirit of evil could or would give him good money, for he was afraid that he would be able to supply him only with counterfeit. While thinking this over a young man his own age, well-built and well-clothed, suddenly appeared before him and asking him the cause of his distress, put out his hand full of money and invited him to prove its worth, telling him to look him up again on the morrow. Michel returned to his companions who were still playing, won back all he had lost and all that of his companions. Then he called on his devil who asked in return three drops of blood which he collected in an acorn shell, and offering a pen to Michel told him to write to his dictation. This consisted of unknown words, which were taken down on two different notes, one of which the devil retained, and the other was put into the arm of Michel in the same places from which the blood had been taken. The devil then said: "I undertake to serve you for seven years, after which you belong to me without reserve." The young man agreed, though with some dread, and the devil did not fail to appear to him, day and night in various forms, inspiring him to things varied, unknown and curious and always with a tendency of evil. The fatal period of seven years was drawing to a end, and the young man was then about twenty years of age. He went home to his father, where the devil to whom he had given himself inspired him to poison his father and mother, burn the castle and kill himself. He tried to carry out all these crimes, but God prevented their success—the gun with which he would have killed himself missed fire twice, and the poison failed to act on his parents. Getting more and more uneasy he confided the unhappy condition he was in to some of his father's servants and begged them to get help. At the same time the devil seized him, twisting his body around and stopping very short of breaking his bones. His mother, who followed the teachings of Svenfeld and had enlisted her son in them, finding no help in her cult against the demon who possessed or obsessed him, was forced to put him in the care of some monks. But he soon left them and escaped to Islade whence he was sent back to Mo'sheim by his brother, canon of Wissbourg, who put him again into the hands of the Fathers of the Society. It was then that the demon made the most violent efforts against him, appearing to him in the form of wild animals. One day among others the demon, in the form of a man, wild and covered with hair, threw on the ground a note or contract different from the true one which he had got from the young man, so as to try by this false show to get him out of the hands of those who were looking after him and to prevent his making a full confession. Finally the 20th October, 1603, was set aside for proof in the Chapel of St. Ignatius, and for the reproduction of the true contract containing the deal made with the demon. The young man made profession of the orthodox catholic faith, renounced the demon and received the holy Eucharist Then with terrible cries he said that he saw two goats of immense size standing with their fore feet in the air and each holding between its hoofs one of the contracts or compacts. But when the exorcism was begun and the name of St. Ignace was invoked the two goats disappeared and there issued from the arm or left hand of the young man practically without pain and leaving no scar, the contract, which fell at the feet of the exorcist. There still remained the contract which had been retained by the demon. The exorcisms were begun again, St. Ignatius was invoked and a mass was promised in his honour, when a stork appeared, large, deformed and ill-shapen, and dropped from its beak the second contract, which was found on the altar."

There is frequent mention among the ancients of certain demons who show themselves, especially towards midday, to those with whom they are on familiar terms. They visit such persons in the form of men or animals or allow themselves to be enclosed in a letter, account or phial or even in a ring, wide and hollow within. "Magicians are known," adds Leloyer, "who make use of them, and to my great regret I am forced to admit that the practice is only too common."

Housdorf in his *Théâtre des exemples du 8e commandement*," quoted by Goulart, says: "A doctor of medicine forgot himself so far as to form an alliance with the enemy of our salvation whom he called up and enclosed in a glass from which the seducer and familiar spirit answered him. The doctor was fortunate in the cure of ailments, and amassed great wealth in his practice, so much so that he left his children the sum of 78,000 francs. Shortly before his death, when his conscience began to prick him, he fell into such a frenzy that he never spoke but to invoke the devil or blaspheme the Holy Ghost and it was in this unfortunate condition that he passed away."

Goulart repeats, from Alexander of Alexandria, the story of a prisoner who had invoked the help of the devil and had visited the lower regions:

"The overlord of a small town in the principality of Sulmona and Kingdom of Naples, proved very miserly and arrogant in his rule, so much so that his subjects were too poor to live beside his harsh treatment of them. One of them, honest, but poor and despised, gave a sound beating for some reason to a hunting dog of this overlord, and the death of the dog angered the latter so much that he had the poor man seized and shut up in a dungeon. After some days the warders, who kept the gates carefully locked went to open them as usual to give him a crust of bread, but he was not to be found in his cell. Having looked for him everywhere, again and again, and finding no trace of him nor his method of escape, they at last reported this wonderful affair to their master, who at first ridiculed, and then threatened them, but realising at length the truth of it, he was no less astonished than they. Three days after this alarming incident, and with all the doors of the prison and dungeon closed as before, this same prisoner, unbeknown to anyone, was found shut up in his own dungeon. He was much distracted, and asked to be taken without delay before the overlord as he had a matter of much importance to communicate. When taken there he said that he had come back from the lower regions. His case was that, not being able to stand any longer the rigors of prison life, overcome with despair, fearing death and lacking any good advice, he had invoked the help of the devil that he might release him from his confinement. That soon after, the Evil One, in a terribly hideous form, had appeared in his dungeon where they made a bargain, after which he was dragged out, not without severe injury, and projected into subterranean passages, wonderfully hollowed out, like the bottom of the earth; there he had seen the dungeons of the wicked, their tortures and their miseries, dark and terrible. Kings, princes and high lords were plunged into abysses of darkness where, with indescribable torture, they were seared with a raging fire. That he had seen popes, cardinals and other prelates, beautifully dressed, and other kinds of persons in varying garb, suffering other anguish in gulfs of great depth, where the torture was incessant. Proceeding, he said he had recognised some acquaintances and especially a former great friend of his who, recognising him in return, enquired as to his condition. The prisoner told him that their land was in the hands of a cruel master, whereupon the other charged him to command this cruel master, on returning, to renounce his tyrannical ways, otherwise his place would be one of the neighbouring seats, which was shown to the prisoner. And (continued this shade) in order that the said overlord may have faith in your report recall to him the secret counsel and talks we had together when engaged in a certain war, the chiefs in which he named, and then he gave in detail the secret, their agreement, the words and promises given on each side. The prisoner gave them all distinctly one by one in their order, and the lord was much astonished at the message, wondering how things committed to himself and not revealed by him to anybody, could be so easily and so boldly unfolded to him by a poor subject of his who told them as if he had read them in a book. Further, the prisoner enquired of his friend in the lower regions, whether it could be true that all the magnificently dressed persons that he saw were conscious of their torments. The other answered that they were seared with an eternal fire, overwhelmed with torture and indescribable anguish, and that all this scarlet and golden raiment was nought but the colouring of the glowing fire. Wishing to test this he drew near to touch this scarlet effect and the other begged him to go, but the fierceness of the fire had scorched the whole of the palm of his hand, which he showed all roasted and cooked as in the embers of a great fire. The poor prisoner being released, to those who met him on his way home he appeared stupid. He neither saw nor heard anything, was always deep in thought, spoke little and replied very shortly to the questions put to him. His face, too, had become so hideous, his appearance so will and ill-favoured that his wife and children had difficulty in recognising him again, and when they did it was only to weep and cry at this change in him. He lived but a few days after his return and so great was his distraction that he had great difficulty in looking after his affairs."

Crespet describes the mark with which Satan brands his own :

"It may be assumed that it is no fallacy but very evident that Satan's mark on sorcerers is like leprosy, for the spot is insensitive to all punctures, and it is in the possession of such marks that one recognises them as true sorcerers for they feel the puncture no more than if they were leprous, nor does any blood appear, and never indeed, does any pain that may be inflicted cause them to move the part."

"They receive, with this badge, the power of injuring and of pleasing, and, secretly or openly, their children are made to participate in the oath and connection which the fathers have taken with the devil. Even the mothers with this in view, dedicate and consecrate their children to the demons, not only as soon as born but even when conceived, and so it happens that, through the ministrations of these demons, sorcerers have been seen with two pupils in each eye, while others had the picture of a horse in one eye and two pupils in the other, and such serve as marks and badges of contracts made with them, for these demons can engrave and render in effigy such or similar lines and features on the bodies of the very young embryo."

"These marks," says Jacques Fontaine, "are not engraved on the bodies of sorcerers by the demons for recognition purposes only, as the captains of companies of light-horse know those of their number by the colour of their coats, but to imitate the creator of all things, to show his power and the authority he has gained over those miserable beings who have allowed themselves to be caught by his cunning and trickery, and by the recognition of these marks of their master to keep them in his power. Further, to prevent them, as far as possible, from withdrawing from their promises and oaths of fidelity, because though breaking faith with him the marks still remain with them and serve, in an accusation, as a means of betraying them, with even the smallest amount of evidence that may be brought forward."

"Louis Gaufridy, a prisoner, who had just been condemned to be burnt . . . . was marked in more than thirty places over the body and on the loins especially there was a mark of lust so large and deep, considering the site, that a needle could be inserted for the width of three fingers across it without any feeling being shown by the puncture."

The same author shows that the marks on sorcerers are areas which have mortified· from the touch of the devil's finger.

"About 1591, Leonarde Chastenet, an old woman of eighty, was taken up as a sorceress while begging in Poitou. Brought before Mathurin Bonnevault, who deponed to having seen her at the meeting of witches, she confessed that she had been there with her husband, and that the devil, a very disgusting beast, was there in the form of a goat. She denied that she would have carried out any witchcraft, but nineteen witnesses testified to her having caused the death of five labourers and a number of animals.

"Finding her crimes discovered and herself condemned she confessed that she had made a compact with the devil, given him some of her hair, and promised to do all the harm she could. She added that at night in prison the devil had appeared to her, in the form of a cat, to which she expressed the wish to die, whereupon this devil presented her with two pieces of wax telling her to eat them and she would die, but she had been unwilling to do it. She had the pieces of wax with her, but on examination their composition could not be made out. She was then condemned and the pieces of wax burnt with her."

Compass Brothers :—Between the years 1400 and 1790, there existed at Lubeck a guild of this name, which met twice a year. Their badge was a compass and sector suspended from a crowned letter " C," over which was a radiated triangular plate. In 1485 they adopted chains composed of these emblems united by eagles' tails. They appear to have been a magical or Kabbalistic society.

Conan Mac Morna :—A figure in the Ossianic cycle of Irish legend, described as scoffing and deriding all that was high and noble. One day while hunting, he and others of the Fians, entered a magnificent palace which they found empty and began to feast. It soon became apparent, however, that the palace was enchanted, and the walls shrank to the size of a fox's hole. *Conan* seemed to be unaware of the danger and continued to eat ; but two of the Fians pulled him off his chair, to which some of his skin stuck. To soothe the pain a black sheep-skin was placed on his back, on to which it grew, and he wore it till he died.

Conary Mor :—A legendary High King of Ireland. It is said that his great-grandfather destroyed the Fairy Mound of Bri-Leith, and thus brought down ill-fate upon *Conary Mor*. When a child he left his three foster-brothers on the Plains of Liffey, and followed a flock of beautiful birds down to the shore. These were transformed into armed men, who told him that they belonged to his father and were his kin. His *geise* (or taboo) was made known to him. and later he was proclaimed King of Erin. His reign was good, happy and prosperous, until the Danaan folk lured him to the breaking of his *geise*. It is told how *Conary*, dying of thirst after battle, sent his warrior Mac Cecht to bring him water. Mac Cecht had much difficulty in obtaining this, and on his return found that *Conary* had been beheaded : the water, however, was raised to the mouth of the bodyless head—which, it is said, thanked Mac Cecht for his deed.

Conferentes :—Gods of the ancients, spoken of by Arnobe, whom Leloyes identifies with incubi.

Conjuretors :—Magicians who claim to have the power to evoke demons and tempests

Conte Del Graal :—One of the " Quest " versions of the legend of the Holy Grail (q.v.) compiled by various authors. It tells how Perceval was reared to the life of a forester by his mother ; but forsaking her he becomes a member of the Court of King Arthur. Thence he goes forth as a knight-errant, and his numerous adventures are recited. During these, he meets with certain mysteries, but returns to the court. The adventures of Gauvain, another of the knights are fully detailed. Perceval, himself, sets forth again, and wanders about for five years in a very godless state of mind. One Good Friday he meets with a band of pilgrims, who remonstrate with him for riding armed on a holy day ; and he turns aside to confess to a hermit who turns out to be his uncle. From him he learns that only the sinless can find the Grail, and that he has sinned in abandoning his mother, and thus causing her death. In a continuation of the legend by a different author, Perceval appears to continue his search, but apparently unsuccessfully; and finally, by yet another compiler we are told that Perceval after many adventures marries Blanchfleure. The nature and origin of the Grail are described in these continuations of the legend.

Control :—A spiritualistic term, denoting the spirit who *controls* the physical organisation of a medium.—(*See* **Spiritualism.**)

Convulsionaries of St. Medard : During the first half of the eighteenth century there occurred in the cemetery of St. Medard, Paris, an extraordinary outbreak of convulsions and religious extasy, whose victims were the Jansenists, at that time suffering much persecution at the hands of the government and the church. The outbreak commenced with a few isolated cases of miraculous healing. One, Mlle. Morsaron, a paralytic, having for her confessor an enthusiastic Jansenist, was recommended by him to seek the tomb of St. Francis de Paris, in the cemetery of St. Medard. When she had repaired thither a few times she recovered her health. The news spread abroad, and other cures followed. Violent convulsions became a feature of the crisis which preceded these cures. At length the healing by Deacon Paris of a more than usually obstinate case, by a crisis of more than ordinary severity, was the signal for a violent outburst of epidemic frenzy. People of both sexes and all ages repaired to the tomb of the holy deacon, where the most appalling scenes were witnessed. People from the provinces helped to swell the ranks, till there was not a vacant foot of ground in the neighbourhood of St. Medard. At length, on January 27th, 1732, the cemetery was closed by order of the king. On its closed gate a wit inscribed the lines :

> De par le roi défense à Dieu
> De faire miracle en ce lieu.

However the king's ordinance did not put an end to the epidemic, which spread from Paris to many other towns. Ten years after its commencement—in 1741—it seemed to have died away, but in 1759 it burst out in Paris with renewed vigour, accompanied by scenes still more awful. In the following year it disappeared once more, though isolated examples persisted so late as 1787.

Cook, Florence : An English medium, the first to present the phenomenon of materialisation in its complete form. In the production of the crowning physical manifestation, she was associated at the outset of her mediumistic career—at the beginning of the decade 1870-80—with the medium Herne, but ere long dispensed with his assistance. So that she might not be under the necessity of taking fees for her services, a wealthy Manchester spiritualist, Mr. Charles Blackburn, paid her a sum of money annually. She was thus practically a private medium, and for the most part, her séances were held in her own home. Her principal control was the now famous spirit Katie King. Mr.— now Sir William — Crookes, who investigated the phenomena produced in Miss Cook's presence, declared his conviction that Katie and the medium were two separate entities, and was satisfied of the supernormal nature of the former. Not all the sitters, however, were equally convinced. Many persons traced a resemblance in form and feature between medium and control, and it has been suggested that the apparent differences were achieved by a change in the mode of hair-dressing, by tip-toeing, and other mechanical means.

Coral (red) : It stops bleeding, preserves houses from thunder, and children from evil spirits, goblins, and sorceresses.

It also strengthens digestion, and if taken in powder as soon as the child is born, preserves it from epilepsy.

Corbenic : A magic castle of the Arthurian legend, in which it is said the Holy Grail was kept. It was guarded by two lions. Lancelot tries to enter it by his own strength, instead of leaning on his Creator, and as a result is struck dumb by a fiery wind. In this state he remains for fourteen days without food or drink.

Cordovero : A famous Kabalist of the sixteenth century.

Cornwall : (*See* **Sea Phantoms and Superstitions.**)

Corpse Candles : Mysterious lights supposed to presage death. They are also called *fetch-lights* and *dead men's candles.*

Coscinomancy is practised with a sieve, and a pair of tongs or shears, which are supported upon the thumb nails of two persons, who look one upon the other, or the nails of the middle finger may be used. Potter, in his *Greek Antiquities,* says : " It was generally used to discover thieves, or others suspected of any crime, in this manner : they tied a thread to the sieve by which it was upheld, or else placed a pair of shears, which they held up by two fingers, then prayed to the gods to direct and assist them ; after that they repeated the names of the persons under suspicion, and he, at whose name the sieve whirled round or moved, was thought guilty." In the *Athenian Oracle* it is called " the trick of the sieve and scissors, the coskiomancy of the ancients, as old as Theocritus," he having mentioned in his third idyll, a woman who was very skilful in it. Saunders, in his *Chiromancy,* and Agrippa, at the end of his works, gives certain mystic words to be pronounced before the sieve will turn. It was used to discover love secrets as well as unknown persons. According to Grose, a chapter in the Bible is to be read, and the appeal made to St. Peter or St. Paul.

Costume, Phantom : (*See* **Phantom Dress.**)

Counter Charms : Charms employed to counteract the effect of other charms. When magicians wish to disenchant animals they sprinkle salt in a porringer with some blood from one of the bewitched creatures, and repeat certain formulæ for nine days.

Counts of Hell : Demons of a superior order in the infernal hierarchy, who command numerous legions. They may be evoked at all hours of the day, provided the evocation takes place in a wild, unfrequented spot.

Courier de l'Europe : (*See* **Cagliostro**).

Cox, Sergeant : ((*See* **Psychological Society**).

Cramp-Rings, Hallowing : A ceremony which took place in England on Good Friday. It consisted of the repetition of certain psalms and prayers, during which the king rubbed the rings between his hands. It was said that rings thus consecrated on Good Friday by the kings of England, had the power of curing cramp ; and the rings, which were given away were much in request even by foreign ambassadors.

Critomancy : Divination by means of observing viands and cakes. The paste of cakes which are offered in sacrifice, is closely examined, and from the flour which is spread upon them, omens are drawn.

Crollius, Oswald : A disciple of the school of Paracelsus, and author of the *Book of Signatures*—the preface to which contains a good sketch of hermetic philosophy. The writer seeks to demonstrate that God and Nature have, so to speak, signed all their works, that every product of a given natural force is as the sum of that force, printed in indelible characters, so that he who is initiated in the occult writings can read as in an open book the sympathies and antipathies of things, the properties of substances, and all other secrets of creation. " The characters of different writings," says Eliphas Levi, " were borrowed primitively from these natural signatures existing in stars and flowers, in mountains and the smallest pebble ; the figures of crystals, the marks on minerals, were impressions of the thought which the Creator had in their creation. . . . . But we lack any grammar of this mysterious language of worlds, and a mathematical vocabulary of this primitive and absolute speech. King Solomon alone is credited with having accomplished the dual labour, but the books of Solomon are lost. The enterprise of *Crollius* was not the reconstitution of these, but an attempt to discover the fundamental principles obtaining in the universal language of the creative world. It was recognised in these principles that the original hieroglyphics, based on the prime elements of geometry, corresponded to the constitutive and essential laws of forms, determined by alternating or combined movements, which, in their turn, were determined by equilibratory attractions. Simples were distinguished from composites by their external figures ; and by the correspondence between figures and numbers it became possible to make a mathematical classification of all substances revealed by the lines of their services. At the root of these endeavours, which are reminiscences of Edenic science, there is a whole world of discoveries awaiting the sciences. Paracelsus had defined them, *Crollius* indicates them, another, who shall follow, will realise and provide the demonstration concerning them. What seemed the folly of yesterday will be the genius of to-morrow, and progress will hail the sublime seekers who first looked into this lost and recovered world, this Atlantis of human knowledge.''

Crosland, Mrs. Newton : An early spiritualistic medium. Under the name of Camilla Toulmin, she published, in 1857, *Light in the Valley*, a record of her experiences. There is a trend of Swedenborgian mysticism in her writings. (*See* **Spiritualism.**)

Cross-Correspondences : Correspondences found in the script of two or more automatic writers acting without collusion, and under such conditions that the possibility of communication by normal means is removed. Since the beginning of the present century efforts have been made by members of the Society for Psychical Research to prove, by the production of script containing *cross-correspondence*, the existence of discarnate intelligences, and their ability to operate through the physical organism of a medium. The first instances were of a spontaneous character, and occurred in the trance utterances of Mrs. Thompson and those of another medium, Miss Rawson. Thereafter the idea was conceived of deliberately cultivating them, and several ladies—Mrs. Verrall, Mrs. Holland, and others— who had been successful in producing automatic script, sent it to the Society for Psychical Research, where the writings were found to show more numerous correspondences than mere coincidence would warrant. It was arranged that experiments should be made under stricter test conditions. Frequently the script of Mrs. Verrall was of an allusive and enigmatical character, so that she herself was unable to interpret it until the key had been supplied by the writings of a second automatist. Sometimes three automatists succeeded in producing writings having a decided connection wth each other. Two obscure writings have been rendered intelligible by means of a third, perhaps in itself equally obscure. In at least one case correspondences occurred in the script of no less than six automatists, under somewhat curious circumstances. Mr. Piddington, a well known member of the Society for Psychical Research, had written a '' test '' letter, which he proposed should be opened after his death. The contents, which dealt emphatically with the number seven, he told to no one. On hearing, however, of the remarkable *cross-correspondences*—all dealing with the number seven— he opened his letter, four years after it was written, and

supplied the clue. In 1906, Mrs. Piper was brought to this country so that the correspondences might be studied to better advantage. The experiments were successful to a surprising degree, and seemed to place beyond a doubt the operation in all the writings of an intelligence other than the automatist's. Mr. Podmore, however, would refer the phenomena of *cross-correspondences*, at least in part, to the operation of a complex form of telepathy—a possible, but in view of the facts, not very probable, explanation.

Crow : The cawing of a *crow* is an omen of evil.

Crow's Head : (*See* **Philosopher's Stone.**)

Crystal : *Crystal* prevails against unpleasant dreams, dissolves enchantments, and is a medium for magical visions. Being bruised with honey, it fills the breasts with milk. Leonardus appears to have indulged a little spite against this beautiful mineral. '' The principal use of *crystal*,'' he says, '' is for making cups, rather than anything else that is good.''

Crystalomancy, or Crystal Gazing : A mode of divination practised from very early times with the aid of a crystal globe, a pool of water, a mirror, or indeed any transparent object. Divinations by means of water, ink, and such substances are also known by the name of hydromancy (*q.v.*). *Crystal gazing* may be a very simple or a very elaborate performance, according to the period in which it was practised, but in every case the object is to induce in the clairvoyant a form of hypnosis, so that he may see visions in the crystal. The '' crystal '' most in favour among modern crystal gazers is a spherical or oval globe, about four inches in diameter, and preferably a genuine crystal ; but as a crystal of this size and shape is necessarily expensive, a sphere of glass is frequently substituted, and with very good results. It must, however, be a perfect sphere of oval, free from speck or flaw, highly polished, and contained in a stand of polished ebony, ivory, or boxwood. Among the Hindus, a cup of treacle or a pool of ink is made to serve the same purpose. Precious stones were much used by crystallomancers in the past, the favourite stone being the beryl in pale sea green or reddish tints. By the ancients *crystallomancy* was practised with a view to the invocation of spirits, and very elaborate preparations and ceremonials were considered necessary. He who would practise invocations in this wise must, in the first instance, be a man of pure life and religious disposition. For the few days immediately preceding the inspection of the crystal, he must make frequent ablutions, and subject himself to strict religious discipline, with prayer and fasting. The crystal, as well as the stand on which it rests, must be inscribed with sacred characters, as must also the floor of the room in which the invocation is to take place. A quiet, retired spot is suggested for the purpose, where the magician may be free from all disturbance. Besides these matters of solitude and cleanliness, there is the question of the mental attitude to be considered, and this is no less important than the material preparations. A perfect faith is an essential condition of success. If the magician would be accompanied by one or two of his friends, they also must conform to the same rules and be guided by the same principles. The time of the invocation is chosen according to the position in the heavens of the various planets, all preparations having been made during the increase of the moon. All the instruments and accessories used in the performance—the sword, rod and compasses, the fire and the perfume to be burned thereon, as well as the crystal itself—are consecrated or '' charged '' prior to the actual ceremony.

During the process of invocation, the magician faces the east and summons from the crystal the spirit he desires. Magic circles have previously been inscribed on the floor, and it is desirable that the crystallomancer remain within these for some little time after the spirit has been dismissed. It was essential that no part of the ceremonial be omitted, otherwise the invocation would be a failure. Paracelsus, however, and others declared that all such elaborate ceremonies were unnecessary, and that the *magnes microcosmi*, the magnetic principle in man, was in itself sufficient to achieve the desired object. At a later period, though the ceremonial was not abolished, it became decidedly less imposing. If the person on whose behalf the divination was to be performed was not himself gifted with the clairvoyant faculty, he sought for a suitable medium, the best for the purpose being a young boy or girl, born in wedlock, and perfectly pure and innocent. Prayers and magical words were pronounced prior to the ceremony, and incense and perfumes were burned. Sometimes the child's forehead was anointed, and he himself provided with garments suitable to the impressive nature of the ceremony. Some writers mention a formula of prayers, known as the Call, which preceded the inspection of the crystal. Finally, the latter having been charged, it was handed over to the medium. The first indication of the clairvoyant vision was the appearance of a mist or cloud in the crystal. This gradually cleared away, and the vision made its appearance.

Modern *Crystal gazing* is carried on in much the same manner, though the preparations are simpler. The crystal is spherical and of the size of an orange ; when in use it may be held between the agent's finger and thumb, or, if the end be slightly flattened, placed on a table ; alternatively it may be held in the palm of the hand against a background of black cloth. The operation may be more readily carried out in a subdued light. A medium or clairvoyant person acts as the seer and if the divination be made for anyone else it is advisable that he be allowed to hold the crystal in his hand for a few minutes before it is passed into the hands of the clairvoyant. The object of crystal gazing is, as has been said, the induction of an hypnotic state giving rise to visionary hallucinations, the reflection of light in the crystal forming *points de repère* for such hallucinations. The value of elaborate ceremonials and impressive rituals thus lies in their potency to affect the mind and imagination of the seer. So far, the mystery of crystal vision is no mystery at all. But the remarkable frequency with which, according to reliable witnesses, visions seen in the crystal have tallied with events happening elsewhere at the same moment, or even with future events, is a fact for which science has not yet found an adequate explanation. It has been suggested that if telepathy operates with greater freedom during the hypnotic state, so it may be also with the self-induced hypnosis of crystal gazing. And this, though it cannot be said to cover the entire ground, is perhaps, on the whole, the best explanation yet offered. There are many well-attested cases wherein the crystal has been successfully used for the purpose of tracing criminals, or recovering lost or stolen property. The telepathic theory, however, will hardly apply to these instances wherein events have been witnessed in the crystal *before* their actual occurrence. Such mysteries as these must be left to the art of the psychical researcher to unravel.

Crucifixion, Gnostic Conception of : As soon as Christ was born according to the Gnostic speculative view of Christianity, Christos, united himself with Sophia (Holy Wisdom). descended through the seven planetary regions, assuming in each an analogous form to the region, and concealing his true nature from its genii, whilst he attracted into himself the spark of Divine Light they severally retained in their angelic essence. Thus Christos, having passed through the seven Angelic Regions before the "Throne," entered into the man Jesus, at the moment of his baptism in the Jordan. From that time forth, being supernaturally gifted, Jesus began to work miracles. Before that, he had been completely ignorant of his mission. When on the cross, Christos and Sophia left his body, and returned to their own sphere. Upon his death, the two took the man "Jesus," and abandoned his material body to the earth ; for the Gnostics held that the true Jesus did not (and could not) physically suffer on the cross, and die, and that Simon of Cyrene, who bore his cross, did in reality suffer in his room : "And they compelled one, Simon a Cyrenian, who passed by, coming out of the country, the father of Alexander and Rufus, to bear his cross " (St. Mark XV. 21). The Gnostics contended that a portion of the real history of the Crucifixion was never written.

At the resurrection Christos and Sophia gave the man Jesus another body, made up of ether (Rosicrucian Aetherœum). Thence-forward he consisted of the two first Rosicrucian principles only, soul and spirit ; which was the reason that the disciples did not recognise him after the resurrection. During his sojourn upon earth after he had risen, he received from Sophia, or Holy Wisdom, that perfect knowledge or illumination, that true "Gnosis," which he communicated to the small number of the Apostles who were capable of receiving the same.

Ciupipiltin : Vampires in ancient Mexico. (*See* **Mexico and Central America**.)

Cursed Bread : Used for purposes of divination, or ordeal by flour or bread. A piece of bread, about an ounce in weight, over which a spell had been cast, was administered to the suspected person. Should it cause sickness or choking the man was said to be guilty, but if he remained well he was regarded as innocent. Barley bread was often used for this form of divination, being more likely to cause choking. This method of trial was practised amongst the Anglo-Saxons.

Curses : (*See* **Spells.**)

Cyamal : The head-chief of the Egbo Assembly, a secret council of Old Calabar.

D

Dactylomancy: A term covering various forms of divination practised with the aid of rings. One method resembles the table-rapping of modern spiritualism. A round table is inscribed with the letters of the alphabet, and a ring suspended above it. The ring, it is said, will indicate certain letters, which go to make up the message required. It was used, according to Ammianus Marcellinus, to find Valen's successor, and the name Theodosius was correctly indicated. Solemn services of a religious character accompanied this mode of divination. Another form of *dactylomancy*, of which there is no detailed account, was practised with rings of gold, silver, copper, iron or lead, which were placed on the finger-nails in certain conjunctions of the planets. A wedding ring is, however, most in favour for purposes of this sort. Another way is to suspend the ring within a glass tumbler, or just outside of it so, that the ring on being swung may easily touch the glass. As with table-rapping, a code may then be arranged, the glass being struck once for an affirmative, twice for a negative answer, and so on. Suspended above a sovereign, the ring will indicate the person from whose head hair has been taken, or, if requested, any other member of the company.

Dactyls : A class of sorcerers and scientific physicians who had their origin in Phrygia. Their number is given differently by different authorities. Some say it equals the number of fingers on the hands—five male and five female. Pausanias says five, Perecydes fifty-two, twenty right and thirty-two left; while Orpheus the Argonaut mentions a large number. The *dactyls* were magicians, exorcists, conjurors, soothsayers. Plutarch says that they made their appearance in Italy as sorcerers; while their magical practices and mysteries threw the inhabitants of Samothrace into consternation. They were credited with the discovery of minerals and the notes of the musical scale; also with the discovery and use of the Ephesian mines They introduced fire into Crete, musical instruments into Greece. They were good runners and dancers, skilled in science and learning, and from them came the first wise men. They are said by some to have been the magnetic powers and spirits, whose head was Hercules.

Daemonologie : by King James VI. and I. : It is customary nowadays to sneer at the writings of this royal author, and as Horace Walpole remarks, his majesty really has more critics than readers; while it should be borne in mind that in his own day the king's books were greatly admired, winning the encomiums of Bacon, Izaak Walton, and numerous equally eminent men of letters. In general, however, it was *Basilicon Doron* which elicited their homage, and compared to this last the king's study of demonology is but a mediocre performance. Published in 1597, it is couched " in forme of ane dialogue," the speakers being Philomathes and Epistemon; and the former, being very incredulous as regards all kinds of magic, asks Epistemon to enlighten him. Thereupon many famous acts of witchcraft are adduced, but, when Philomathes requests to be told precisely why the black art should be considered iniquitous, his interlocutor fails conspicuously to give a satisfactory answer. He merely inveighs against the practice in question, and accordingly there is something distinctly trite in the subsequent pages, wherein Epistemon is represented as being converted to the other speaker's point of view, and declaring loudly that all sorcerers and the like " ought to be put to death according to the Law of God, the civill and imperiall Law, and municipall Law of all Christian Nations."

Daiver-Logum : The dwelling place of the daivers (q.v.) a species of Hindoo genii. Besides the daivers, who number three hundred and thirty millions, there dwell in the *Daiver-Logum* those heroes and prophets who are not yet fit for the paradise of Shiva or of Vishnu.

Daivers and Daivergoel : Hindoo genii inhabiting the Daiver-Logum, a world of their own. They are, it seems, related to the Persian divs, from which it is suggested that the word " devil " is derived. They possess material bodies as well as spiritual, and have many human attributes, both good and evil. Their king is called Daivuntren, or Indiren, his wife Inderannee, and his son Seedcra-hudderen. The latter records the actions of human beings, by which they must at last be judged. In Daivuntren's immense court of audience there is room not only for the *daivers* themselves, but for a multitude of attendants, or companions. These are the kuinarer, the musicians of Daiver-Logum; Dumbarim, Nardir, the drummers; Kimprusher, winged beings of great beauty, who wait on the *daivers*; Kundagaindoorer, similar beings, the messengers of Vishnu; Paunner, the jugglers; Viddiaser, the bards; Tsettee, those beings who attend them in their aerial flights; Kannanader, or Dordanks, the messengers who lead devotees of Shiva and Vishnu to paradise, and the wicked to hell. There is yet another class of *daivergoel*, or genii, which comprises the eight keepers of the eight sides of the world, known by their general name of Aushtatiken-Pauligaur. These are Indiren, or Daivuntren, their king; Augne-Bangauven, god of fire; Eemen, king of death and hell; Nerudee, the earth-element personified as a giant; Vaivoo,

god of the air and winds; Varooner, god of the clouds and rain; Gooberen, god of riches; and Essaunien, Shiva himself, in one of his 1,008 incarnations.

Dalan : A druid who figures in the medieval Irish legend of Conary Mor (q.v.).

Dalton, Thomas : The history of this alchemist is veiled in obscurity, but he appears to have lived about the middle of the fifteenth century; and, as he is mentioned in the *Ordinall of Alchimy* by Thomas Norton, it is likely that he was a pupil or at least a friend of the latter. *Dalton* was a churchman, resident at an abbey in Gloucester; and it is reported that, on one occasion, he was brought before the king, Edward IV., in whose presence he was charged with the surreptitious practice of magic, in those days a capital crime. His accuser was one Debois, to whom the unfortunate alchemist had at one time been chaplain, and this Debois affirmed upon oath that he had seen the accused create a thousand pounds of pure gold within the space of a single day. Thereupon *Dalton* reminded his accuser that he had sworn never to reveal this or any kindred facts. Debois acknowledged his perfidy herein, yet added that he was acting for the good of the commonwealth. The alchemist then addressed the king himself, telling him that he had been given the powder of projection by a certain Canon of Litchfield, and that since then he had been in so constant a state of trepidation that he had ultimately destroyed the precious article. Edward accordingly granted him his freedom, at the same time giving him money sufficient for his journey home; but on his way there he was seized by a certain Thomas Herbert, who had heard of the accusation brought against the churchman, and was naturally inquisitive. Herbert carried his victim to the castle of Gloucester, and, incarcerating him in a cell there, tried every means to make him disclose the secret at issue. All was in vain, however, and at length *Dalton* was condemned to death by his persecutor, and brought out to be beheaded in the courtyard of the castle. He placed his head on the block, and, crying out to God to receive his soul, he called upon the executioner to strike speedily; but now a strange scene was enacted, for hardly was the axe raised ere Herbert sprang forward to avert it, at the same time declaring that he dared not shed innocent blood. In short, the projected execution was no more than a dastardly ruse, the persecutor imagining that the alchemist would confess all when his life was at stake; and, as the plan had failed, *Dalton* was allowed to go free. So he returned to his abbey in Gloucestershire, and there he lived quietly and unmolested for the rest of his days.

Damear : A mystical city. (*See* **Rosicrucians.**)

Damian, John : Alchemist, Abbot of Tungland. (*See* **Scotland.**)

Danaans, The : The people of the goddess Dana, often mentioned in Irish medieval romance. They were one of the three Nemedian families who survived the Fomorian victory, and returned to Ireland at a later period. By some it was said that they came " out of heaven," and by others that they sprang from four cities, in which they learned science and craftsmanship, and from each of which they brought away a magical treasure. From Falias they brought the Stone of Destiny (Lia Fail) (q.v.); from Gorias an invincible sword; from Finias a magical spear; and from Murias the Cauldron of the Dagda. They were believed to have been wafted to Ireland on a magic cloud, carrying their treasures with them. After a victorious battle they took possession of the whole of Ireland, except Connacht which was given to the vanquished. The *Danaans* were the representatives of power and beauty, of science and poetry, to the writer of the myth; to the common people they were gods of earth. In their battles they were subject to death, but it was by magical powers that they conquered their mortal foes.

D'Ancre, Marechale : (*See* **France.**)

Dandis : (*See* **India.**)

Daphnomancy : Divination by means of the laurel. A branch is thrown in the fire, if it crackles in burning it is a happy sign, but if it burns without doing so, the prognostication is false.

Dark, The : A druid of Irish medieval legend, who turned Saba into a fawn because she did not return his love.

Darkness of the Sages : (*See* **Philosopher's Stone.**)

D'Ars, Cure : (*See* **France.**)

Davenport Brothers (Ian and William) : Two American mediums who gave séances for physical phenomena in America and Britain during the decade 1860-70. They seem to have attained to a considerable measure of fame, and to have won a great many people to the belief that their performances were genuine spirit manifestations. On their coming to England in 1864 they were accompanied by a chaplain, the Rev. J. B. Ferguson, who helped to inspire confidence in their good faith. The usual plan of their séances was as follows : The *Brothers Davenport* took their seats *vis-à-vis* in a small walnut cabinet " made very like a wardrobe or clothes-press." Any two gentlemen from among the audience were requested to bind them firmly to their benches, so as to preclude any possibility of their freeing their hands. Musical instruments were then placed in the cabinet, apparently out of reach of the medium, and the lights were lowered. Soon the musical instruments began to play within the cabinet, dim " spirit hands " were seen in front of it. At the conclusion of the séance, however, the mediums were found tied as securely as ever. They met with a check, however, on their provincial tour, for at Liverpool there were two men among the audience who possessed the secret of a special knot. The " Tom Fool's knot," as it was called, baffled the spirits, and the mediums were mobbed. Later in a séance given before a committee of the Anthropological Society, they shirked nearly all the conditions, and succeeded in accomplishing nothing which could not be done by a skilful conjurer. Tolmagne, Anderson, and other conjurers emulated their feats, and Maskelyne and Cooke so successfully that mediums had no resource but to class them as "fellow-adepts."

Davey, S. T. : A member of the Society for Psychical Research who in 1886 gave imitations of the slate-writing performances of Eglinton and Slade, with a view to exposing their fraudulent methods. By simple conjuring he succeeded in emulating all their feats. (*See* **Slate-writing, Spiritualism.**)

Davies, Lady : Eleanor Tuchet, daughter of George, Lord Audley, married Sir John Davies, an eminent lawyer in the time of James the First, and author of a poem of considerable merit on the Immortality of the Soul. This lady was a person of many talents ; but what she seems most to have valued herself upon, was her gift of prophecy ; and she accordingly printed a book of Strange and Wonderful Predictions. She professed to receive her prophecies from a spirit, who communicated to her audibly things about to come to pass, though the voice could be heard by no other person. Sir John Davies was nominated lord chief justice of the king's bench in 1626. Before he was inducted into the office, lady Eleanor, sitting with him on Sunday at dinner, suddenly burst into a passion of tears. Sir John asked her what made her weep. To which she replied " These are your funeral tears." Sir John turned off the prediction with a merry answer. But in a very few days he was seized with an apoplexy, of which he presently died. She also predicted the death of the duke of Buckingham in the same year. For this assumption of the gift of prophecy, she was cited before the high-commission-court and examined in 1634.

Davis, Andrew Jackson : Known as the " Poughkeepsie Seer " from his residence in Poughkeepsie, N.Y., was a prophet, clairvoyant, and mystic philosopher, who commenced his mission to the world about 1844, some time before the Rochester Rappings had inaugurated the movement known as " modern spiritualism." In 1847 he published a volume of trance discourses, *The Principles of Nature, Her Divine Revelations, and A Voice to Mankind*. In the same year he issued the first number of the *Univercœlum*, a periodical devoted to clairvoyance and trance phenomena generally, which continued till 1849. Not until 1850, however, did *Davis* and his followers identify themselves with the spiritualists. In his *Revelations* the Poughkeepsie Seer propounds his Harmonial Philosophy, afterwards to be elaborated in many volumes. His mission, revealed to him by Galen and Swedenborg, was the prophesying of a new dispensation, preceded by a social revolution. He was associated, throughout his career, with many prominent spiritualists.

Death-Coach : There is a widespread superstitious belief that death goes round in a coach picking up souls. The form of the belief varies, of course, with the locality. In some parts of England and Wales the death-coach passes silently at midnight, without sound of hoof or wheels. Both coach and horse are black, and a black hound runs in front. In some localities the horses and coachman are headless, which doubtless adds to the effectiveness of the apparition. The Breton peasant hears the approach at midnight of a cart with a creaking axle. It is the *Ankon* death— and when the cart stops before a dwelling some-one within must die.

Death-watch : The ticking of the *death-watch*—a small insect found in decaying wood— is thought by the superstitious to presage death.

Decem Viri : (*See* **Sibylline Books.**)

Dectera : A figure of Irish medieval romance. She was the daughter of Cathbad the Druid, and mother of Cuchulain (q.v.). She and fifty other maidens disappeared from the court of Conor mac Nessa. Three years later, while pursuing a flock of birds which were spoiling the crops, the king and courtiers came upon a magnificent palace inhabited by a youth of noble mien and a beautiful woman and fifty maidens. These were recognised as *Dectera* and her companions, and the youth as Lugh, the sun-god. Conor summoned *Dectera* to him, but she sent him instead her new-born son, Cuchulain.

Dee, John : Born in London 1527, this remarkable mathematician and astrologer is supposed to have been descended from a noble old Welsh House, the Dees of Nant y Groes in Radnorshire ; while he himself affirmed that among his direct ancestors was Roderick the Great, Prince of Wales. *Dee's* father appears to have been a gentleman server at the court of Henry VIII., and, being consequently in tolerably affluent circumstances, he was able to give his son a good education. So at the age of fifteen *John* proceeded to Cambridge, and after two years there he took his degree as Bachelor of Arts ; while a little later on his becoming intensely interested in astronomy and the like, he decided to leave England and go and study abroad. In 1547, accordingly, he went to the Low Countries, where he consorted with numerous scholars, and whence he eventually brought home the first astronomer's staff of brass, and also two globes constructed by Gerard Mercetor ; but *Dee* was not destined to remain in his native land for long, and in 1548 he lived for some time at Louvain, and in 1550 he spent several months in Paris, lecturing there on the principles of geometry. He was offered, indeed, a permanent post at the Sorbonne ; but he declined this, and in 1551 he returned to England, where, having been recommended to Edward VI., he was granted the rectory of Upton-upon-Severn, Worcestershire.

The astrologer was now in a delightful and enviable position, having a comfortable home and assured income, and being able to devote himself exclusively to the studies he loved. But hardly had he begun to enjoy these bene-fits ,ere an ugly cloud darkened his horizon, for, on the accession of Queen Mary in 1553, he was accused of try-ing to take the new sovereign's life by thaumaturgic means, and was imprisoned at Hampton Court. He gained his liberty soon afterwards, but he felt very conscious that many people looked on him askance on account of his scientific predilections ; and, in a preface which he wrote for an English translation of Euclid, he complains bitterly of being regarded as " a companion of the helhounds, a caller and a conjuror of wicked and damned spirits." How-ever, during the reign of Queen Elizabeth his fortunes began to improve again ; and after making another long tour abroad, going on this occasion so far afield as St. Helena, he took a house at Mortlake on the Thames, and while staying there he rapidly became famous for his inti-mate knowledge of astronomy. In 1572 on the advent of a new star, people flocked to hear *Dee* descant on the subject ; while five years later, on the appearance of a mysterious comet, the scholar was again vouchsafed ample opportunity of displaying his learning, Elizabeth herself being among those who came to ask him what this addition to the stellar bodies might portend.

The most romantic circumstances in *Dee's* life, however, are those which deal with his experiments in crystallomancy. Living in comparative solitude—practising astrology for bread, but studying alchemy for pleasure— brooding over Talmudic mysteries and Rosicrucian theories—immersed in constant contemplation of wonders which he longed to penetrate—and dazzled by visions of the elixir of life and the Philosopher's Stone, *Dee* soon attained to such a condition of mystic exaltation that his visions became to him as realities, and he persuaded himself that he was the favoured of the Invisible. In his *Diary* he records that he first saw in his crystal-globe—that is, saw spirits— on the 25th of May, 1581. In another year he had at-tained to a higher level, and one day, in November, 1582, while on his knees and fervently praying, he became aware of a sudden glory which filled the west window of his lab-oratory, and in whose midst shone the bright angel Uriel. It was impossible for *Dee* to speak. His tongue was frozen with awe. But Uriel smiled benignly upon him, gave him a convex piece of crystal, and told him that when he wished to communicate with the beings of another world he had but to examine it intently, and they would imme-diately appear and reveal the mysteries of the future. Then the angel vanished.

Dee, however, found from experience that it was needful to concentrate all one's faculties upon the crystal before the spirits would obey him. In other words, it was neces-sary to stimulate the imagination to the highest pitch, until the soul became a willing agent in its self-deception. Bring the will to bear upon the imagination, and it is possible to realize a spirit in every shadowy corner—to hear the song of the spirits in the low crooning of the evening wind— to read in the starry heavens the omens and por-tents of the future. One may become with marvellous ease the deceiver of one-self,—the dupe of one's own de-lusions,—and brood upon a particular subject until one passes the mysterious border between sanity and madness —passes from imagination into mania.

Dee could never remember what the spirits said in their frequent conversations with him. When the excitement was over, he forgot the fancies with which he had been beguiled. He resolved, therefore, to discover some fellow-

worker, or neophyte, who should converse with the spirits while he himself, in another part of the room, sat and re-corded the interesting dialogue. He found the assistant he sought in one Edward Kelly, who unhappily possessed just the requisite boldness and cunning for making a dupe of the amiable and credulous enthusiast.

Edward Kelly was a native of Lancashire, born, accord-ing to *Dee's* own statement, in 1555. We know nothing of his early years, but after having been convicted at Lan-caster of coining—for which offence he lost his ears—he removed to Worcester, and established himself as a druggist. Sensual, ambitious, and luxurious, he longed for wealth, and despairing of securing it by honest industry, began to grope after the Philosopher's Stone, and to employ what magical secrets he picked up in imposing upon the ignorant and profligate. *Dee* sought knowledge for the love of it ; Kelly as a means to gratify his earthly passions. He con-cealed the loss of his ears by a black skull-cap, and being gifted with a good figure and tolerably handsome counte-nance, looked the very incarnation of mysterious wisdom, Before his acquaintance with *Dee* began, he had obtained some repute as a necromancer and alchymist, who could make the dead utter the secrets of the future. One night he took a wealthy dupe with some of his servants, into the park of Walton le Dale, near Preston in Lancashire, and there alarmed him with the most terrific incantations. He then inquired of one of the servants whose corpse had been last buried in the neighbouring churchyard, and being told that a poor man had been interred there within a very few hours, exhumed the body, and pretended to draw from it oracular utterances.

Dee appears to have had a *skryer*, or seer before his in-troduction to Kelly, who was named Barnabas Saul. He records in his *Diary* on the 9th of October, 1581, that the unfortunate medium was strangely troubled by a " spiritual creature " about midnight. On the 2nd of December he willed his skryer to look into the " great crystalline globe " for the apparition of the holy angel Anael. Saul looked and saw. But his invention appears to have become ex-hausted by the following March, when he confessed that he neither saw nor heard any spiritual creature any more ; whereat the enthusiastic *Dee* grew strangely dissatisfied, and soon dismissed the unsatisfactory and unimaginative medium. Then came Edward Kelly (who appears to have been also called Talbot), and the conferences with the spirits rapidly increased in importance as well as curiosity.

A clever rogue was Kelly. Gifted with a fertile fancy and prolific invention, he never gazed into the " great crystalline globe " without making some wondrous discoveries, and by his pretended enthusiasm gained the entire confidence of the credulous *Dee*. The mathema-tician, despite his learning and his profound intellect, became the easy tool of the plastic, subtle Skryer. The latter would sometimes pretend that he doubted the inno-cent character of the work upon which he was engaged ; would affect a holy horror of the unholy ; and profess that the spirits of the crystal were not always " spirits of health," but—perish the thought !—" goblins damn'd ;" demons whose task it was to compass their destruction. The conferences held between Kelly and the spirits were meanwhile, carefully recorded by *Dr. Dee* ; and whoever has stomach for the perusal of a great deal of absurdity and not a little blasphemy, may consult the folio published in 1659 by the learned Méric Casaubon, and entitled " A True and Faithful Relation of what passed between *Dr. John Dee* and some Spirits ; tending, had it succeeded, to a General Alteration of most States and Kingdoms in the World."

Two such shining lights could not hide themselves under a bushel, and their reputation extended from Mortlake even to the Continent. *Dee* now declared himself possessed of the *elixir vitae*, which he had found he said, among the ruins of Glastonbury Abbey; so that the curious were drawn to his house by a double attraction. Gold flowed into his coffers in an exhaustless stream, but his experiments in the transmutation of metals absorbed a great portion of his substance.

At this time the court of England was visited by a Polish nobleman named Albert Laski, Count Palatine of Siradz, who was desirous to see the magnificence of the famous "Gloriana." Elizabeth received him with the flattering welcome she always accorded to distinguished strangers, and placed him in charge of the splendid Leicester. He visited all the England of the sixteenth century worth showing, and especially her two Universities, but was sorely disappointed at not finding the famous *Dr. Dee* at Oxford. "I would not have come hither," he said to the Earl, "had I wot that *Dee* was not here." Leicester undertook to introduce him to the learned philosopher on their return to London, and so soothed his discontent.

A few days afterwards the Pole and Leicester were waiting in the ante-chamber at Whitehall for an audience of the Queen, when *Dr. Dee* arrived. Leicester embraced the opportunity, and introduced him to Albert Laski. The interview between two genial spirits was interesting, and led to frequent visits from Laski to *Dee's* house at Mortlake. Kelly soon perceived what a Pactolus this Pole would prove, and as he was imbued with all the extravagant superstitions of the age relative to the elixir and the Philosopher's Stone, it was easy enough to play upon his imagination, and entangle him in the meshes of an inextricable deception. *Dee*, in want of money to prosecute his splendid chimeras, and influenced by Kelly's artful suggestions, lent himself in some measure to the fraud, and speedily the "great crystalling globe" began to reveal hints and predictions which inflamed the ardent fancy of the "noble Polonian." But Kelly imposed upon *Dee* as well as upon Laski. He appears to have formed some wild but magnificent projects for the reconstruction of Europe, to be effected through the agency of the Pole, and thenceforth the spirits could converse upon nothing but hazy politics.

On a careful perusal of *Dee's Diary*, it is impossible to come to any other conclusion than that he was imposed upon by Kelly, and accepted his revelations as the actual utterances of the spirits; and it seems probable that the clever, plastic, slippery Kelly not only knew something of the optical delusions then practised by the pretended necromancers, but possessed considerable ventriloquial powers, which largely assisted in his nefarious deceptions.

Kelly had undoubtedly conceived some extravagant notions of a vast European monarchy, in which Laski was to play the part of a *Roi fainéant* and he himself of a *Maire du Palais*. To this point all the spiritual revelations now tended, and they were managed, it must be owned, with consummate skill. Laski was proved, by the agency of Madinie, to be descended from the Anglo-Norman family of the Lacies. Then an angel named Murifre, who was clothed like a husbandman, pointed out Laski as destined to effect the regeneration of the world.

But it did not answer Kelly's purposes to bring matters too suddenly to a conclusion, and with the view of showing the extreme value of his services, he renewed his complaints upon the wickedness of dealing with spirits, and his fear of the perilous enterprises they might enjoin. He threatened, moreover, to abandon his task, a threat which completely perturbed the equanimity of *Dr. Dee*. Where indeed, could he hope to meet with another *skryer* of such infinite ability? Once when Kelly expressed his desire of riding from Mortlake to Islington on some pretended business, the doctor grew afraid that it was only an excuse to cover his absolute evasion. "Whereupon," says the doctor, "I asked him why he so hasted to ride thither, and I said if it were to ride to Mr. Harry Lee I would go thither, and to be acquainted with him, seeing now I had so good leisure, being eased of the book writing. Then he said that one told him the other day that the duke (Laski) did but flatter him, and told him other things both against the duke and me. I answered for the duke and myself, and also said that if the forty pounds annuity which Mr. Lee did offer him was the chief cause of his mind setting that way (contrary to many of his former promises to me), that then I would assure him of fifty pounds yearly, and would do my best, by following of my suit, to bring it to pass as soon as I possibly could; and thereupon did make him promise upon the Bible.

"Then Edward Kelly again upon the same Bible did swear unto me constant friendship, and never to forsake me; and moreover said that unless this had so fallen about he would have gone beyond the seas, taking ship at Newcastle within eight days next.

"And so we plight our faith each to the other, taking each other by the hand, upon these points of brotherly and friendly fidelity during life, which covenant I beseech God to turn to his honour, glory, and service, and the comfort of our brethren (his children) here on earth."

Kelly now returned to his crystal and his visions, and Laski was soon persuaded that he was destined by the spirits to achieve great victories over the Saracens, and win enduring glory. But for this purpose it was needful he should return to Poland, and to Poland the poor dupe went, taking with him the learned *Dr. Dee*, the invaluable Edward Kelly, and their wives and families. The spirits continued to respond to their inquiries even while at sea, and so they landed at the Brill on the 30th of July 1583, and traversed Holland and Friesland to the opulent free town of Lubeck. There they lived sumptuously for a few weeks, and with recruited strength set out for Poland. On Christmas Day they arrived at Stettin, where they remained till the middle of January 1584. They gained Lasco, the Pole's principal estate, early in February. Immediately the grand work commenced for the transmutation of iron into gold, boundless wealth being obviously needful for so grand an enterprise as the regeneration of Europe. Laski liberally supplied them with means, but the alchymists always failed on the very threshold of success. Day by day the prince's trees melted away in the deceptive crucible; he mortgaged his estates, he sold them, but the hungry furnace continued to cry for "More! more!" It soon became apparent to the philosopher's that Laski's fortune was nearly exhausted. Madinie, Uriel, and their comrades made the same discovery at the same time, and, moreover, began to doubt whether Laski, after all, was the great regenerator intended to revolutionize Europe. The whole party lived at Cracow from March 1584 until the end of July, and made daily appeals to the spirits in reference to the Polish prince. They grew more and more discouraging in their replies, and as Laski began slowly to awake to the conviction that he had been a monstrous dupe, in order to rid himself of the burthen, he proposed to furnish them with sufficient funds for a journey to Prague, and letters of introduction to the Emperor Rudolph. At this very moment the spirits discovered that it was necessary *Dee* should bear a divine message to the Emperor, and Laski's proposal was gladly accepted.

At Prague the two philosophers were well received by the Emperor. They found him very willing to believe in the existence of the famous stone, very courteous to *Dee* as a man of European celebrity, but very suspicious of the astute and plausible Kelly. They remained some months at Prague, living upon the funds which Laski had supplied, and cherishing hopes of being attached to the imperial service. At last the Papal Nuncio complained to the countenance afforded to heretical magicians, and the Emperor ordered them to quit his dominions within four-and-twenty hours. They precipitately complied, and by so doing escaped a prison or the stake, to which the Nuncio had received orders from Rome to consign them (May 1586).

They now proceeded to Erfurdt, and from thence to Cassel, but meeting with a cold reception, made their way once more to Cracow. Here they earned a scanty living by telling fortunes and casting nativities ; enduring the pangs of penury with an almost heroic composure, for they, the pretended possessors of the Philosopher's Stone, durst not reveal their indigence to the world, if they would not expose themselves to universal ridicule. After a while, they found a new dupe in Stephen, king of Poland, to whom Kelly's spirits predicted that the Emperor Rudolph would shortly be assassinated, and that the Germans would elect him to the Imperial throne. But he in his turn grew weary of the ceaseless demands for pecuniary supplies. Then arose a new disciple in the person of Count Rosenberg, a nobleman of large estates at Trebona, in Bohemia. At his castle they remained for upwards of two years, eagerly pursuing their alchemical studies, but never approaching any nearer to the desired result.

Dee's enthusiasm and credulity had degraded him into the tool and slave of Kelly ; but the latter was nevertheless very wroth at the superior respect which *Dee*, as really a man of surprising scholarship and considerable ability, enjoyed. Frequent quarrels broke out between them, aggravated by the criminal passion which Kelly had conceived for the doctor's young and handsome wife, and which he had determined to gratify. He matured at length an artful plan to obtain the fulfilment of his wishes. Knowing *Dee's* entire dependence upon him as a *skryer*, he suddenly announced his intention of resigning that honoured and honourable office, and only consented to remain on the doctor's urgent entreaties. That day (April 18, 1587) they consulted the spirits. Kelly professed to be shocked at the revelation they made, and refused to repeat it. *Dee's* curiosity was aroused, and he insisted upon hearing it, but was exceedingly discomposed when he found that the spirits enjoined the two philosophers to have their wives in common. Kelly expressed his own abhorrence of the doctrine, and when the spirits repeated it, with a mixture of socialistic extravagance to the effect that sin was only relative, and could not be sinful if ordered by God, protested they must be spirits of evil, not of good,— once more resigned his post as *skryer*,—and left the Castle.

Dee now attempted to convert his son Arthur into a medium, but the lad had neither the invention, the faith, nor the deceptive powers for such an office, and the philosopher, deprived of those conferences with the other world which he had so long enjoyed, began to lament the absence of his old confederate. At this juncture Kelly suddenly returned. Again he consulted the crystal, and again was ordered to practise the socialistic rule of all things in common. *Dee* was too delighted at his return to oppose any longer the will of the spirits. The two wives resisted the arrangement for some time, but finally yielded to what was represented to be the will of Heaven, and *Dee* notes in his *Diary* that " on Sunday the 3rd of May, *anno* 1587 (by the new account), I, *John Dee*, Edward Kelly, and our two wives covenanted with God, and subscribed the same for indissoluble and inviolable unities, charity, and friendship keeping, between us four, and all things between us to be common, as God by sundry means willed us to do."

The alchemists now resumed their pursuits with eagerness ; but discord soon crept into this happy family of four. The wives, never very well content with the socialistic theory, quarrelled violently ; the husbands began to be pinched for want of means ; and *Dee* turned his eyes towards England as a pleasanter asylum than the castle of Trebona was likely to prove for his old age. He obtained permission from Queen Elizabeth to return, and separated finally from Kelly. The latter, who had been knighted at Prague, took with him an elixir found at Glastonbury Abbey, and ventured to proceed to the Bohemian capital. He was immediately arrested by order of the Emperor, and flung into prison. Obtaining his release after some months ' imprisonment, he wandered over Germany, telling fortunes, and angling for dupes with the customary magical baits, but never getting a whit nearer that enjoyment of boundless resources which the possession of the Philosopher's Stone should have ensured him. Arrested a second time as a heretic and a sorcerer, and apprehending perpetual imprisonment, he endeavoured to escape, but fell from the dungeon-wall, and broke two of his ribs and both of his legs. He expired of the injuries he had received in February 1593.

Dr. Dee set out from Trebona with a splendid train, the expenses of his journey apparently being defrayed by the generous Bohemian noble. Three waggons carried his baggage ; three coaches conveyed himself, his family, and servants. A guard of twenty-four soldiers escorted him ; each carriage was drawn by four horses. In England he was well received by the Queen, as far as courteous phrases went, and settling himself at Mortlake, he resumed his chemical studies, and his pursuit of the Philosopher's Stone. But nothing prospered with the unfortunate enthusiast. He employed two *skryers*—at first a rogue, named Bartholomew, and afterwards a charlatan named Heckman—but neither could discover anything satisfactory in the " great crystalline globe." He grew poorer and poorer ; he sank into absolute indigence ; he wearied the Queen with ceaseless importunities ; and at length obtained a small appointment as Chancellor of St. Paul's Cathedral, which in 1595 he exchanged for the wardenship of Manchester College. He performed the duties of this position until age and a failing intellect compelled him. to resign it about 1602 or 1603.

He then retired to his old house at Mortlake, where he practised as a common fortune-teller, gaining little in return but the unenviable reputation of a wizard, " a conjuror, a caller, or invocator of devils." On the 5th of June 1604, he presented a petition to James the First, imploring his protection against such injurious calumnies, and declaring that none of all the great number of " the very strange and frivolous fables or histories reported and told of him (as to have been of his doing) were true."

Dee is an exceptionally interesting figure, and he must have been a man of rare intellectual activity. He made calculations to facilitate the adoption in England of the Gregorian calendar ; and he virtually anticipated the Historical Manuscripts Commission, addressing to the crown a petition wherein he wrote on the desirability of carefully preserving the old, unpublished records of England's past, many of which documents were at this period domiciled in the archives of monasteries. Moreover he was a voluminous writer on science, and, though lack of space makes it impossible to give a full list of his works here, it certainly behoves to mention the following : *Monas Hieroglyphica* 1564, *De Trigono* 1565, *Testamentum Johannis Dee Philosophi Summi ad Johannem Guryun Transmissum* 1568, *An Account of the Manner in which a certayn Copper-smith in the Land of Moores, and a certayn Moore transmuted Copper to Gold*, 1576.

Deitton : An astrological book of Indian origin in use in Burma, the same as the *Dittharana* (q. v.) (*See* **Burma.**)

De la Motte, Madame : (*See* **Cagliostro.**)

Deleuze, Billot : (*See* **France.**)

Deleuze, Jean Philippe François : French naturalist and adept in animal magnetism. He was born at Sisteron, in 1753, and died in 1835. It is by his advocacy of animal magnetism that he is principally remembered, and his works on this subject include : *Histoire Critique du Magnétisme,* (1813-1819) ; *Insruction Pratique sur le Magnétisme Animale,* (1819 and 1836) ; *Défense du Magnétisme,* (1819) ; *Mémoire sur la Faculté de Prevision,* (1836). He believed in *rapport* between patient and magnetiser, in diagnosis of disease by clairvoyants, and other supernormal phenomena. (*See* **Hypnotism.**)

Delirium : (*See* **Visions.**)

De Lisle : (circa. 1710). French Alchemist. A considerable amount of matter concerning this French alchemist is contained in Langlet de Fresnoy's invaluable book, *Histoire de la Philosophie Hermetique,* while Figuier writes at some length on the subject ; but neither of these writers furnishes *de Lisle's* Christian name, and neither gives the exact date of his birth. The place where the event occurred is likewise unknown, although it is commonly held that the alchemist was a Provençal ; while his position in the social hierarchy is likewise a matter of conjecture, the tradition that he sprang from humble peasant stock being practically vitiated by the *particule* in his name. True that this is usually spelt *Delisle,* but one may be fairly certain that that is a mere perversion, and that originally the two syllables were written separately.

De Lisle is known to have been active during the first decade of the eighteenth century, so it may be assumed that he was born towards the close of *le grand siècle* ; while it would seem that, at an early age, he entered the service of a scientist whose name is unrecorded, but who is supposed to have been a pupil of Lascaris. This nameless scientist, it appears, got into trouble of some sort, the likelihood being that he was persecuted on account of his hermetic predilections ; and accordingly he left Provence and set out for Switzerland, taking with him his young henchman, *de Lisle. En route* the latter murdered his patron and employer, thereafter appropriating all his alchemistic property, notably some precious transmuting powder ; and then, about the year 1708, he returned to his native France, where he soon attracted attention by changing masses of lead and iron into silver and gold. Noble and influential people now began to court his society and his scientific services, and betimes he found himself safely and comfortably housed in the castle of La Palud, where he received many visitors from day to day, demonstrating his skill before them. Anon, however, he grew weary of this life ; and, having contracted a *liaison* with a Madame Alnys, he commenced wandering with her from place to place, a son being eventually born to the pair. At this time Madame Alnys' husband was still living, but that did not prevent *de Lisle* from continuing to elicit patronage and favour from the rich and great, and in 1710, at the Chateau de St. Auban, he performed a curious experiment in the presence of one St. Maurice, then president of the royal mint. Going into the grounds of the *château* one evening, *de Lisle* showed St. Maurice a basket sunk in the ground, and bade him bring it into the *salle-à-manger* where it was duly opened, its contents transpiring to be merely some earth of a blackish hue. No very precious material ! thought St. Maurice, accustomed to handling ingots and nuggets ; but *de Lisle,* after distilling a yellow liquid from the earth, projected this on hot quicksilver, and speedily produced in fusion three ounces of gold, while subsequently he succeeded in concocting a tolerable quan-

tity of silver. Some of the gold was afterwards sent to Paris, where it was put through a refining process, and three medals were struck from it, one of which, bearing the inscription *Aurum Arte Factum,* was deposited in the cabinet of his most Christian majesty. Thereupon *de Lisle* was invited to come to Paris himself, and visit the court ; but he declined the offer, giving as his reason that the southern climate he chiefly lived in was necessary to the success of his experiments, the preparations he worked with being purely vegetable. The probability is that, having been signally triumphant in duping his *clientèle* so far, he felt the advisability of refraining from endeavours which might prove futile, and vitiate his reputation.

We hear nothing of *de Lisle* later than 1760, so presumably he died about that time ; but his son by Madame Alnys seems to have inherited some part of his father's predilections, together with a fair quota of his skill. Wandering for many years through Italy and Germany, he affected transmutations successfully before various petty nobles ; while at Vienna he succeeded in bringing himself under the notice of the Duc de Richelieu, who was acting then as French ambassador to the Viennese court, and Richelieu afterwards assured the Abbé Langlet that he not only saw the operation of gold-making performed, but did it himself by carrying out instructions given him by Alnys. The latter gradually acquired great wealth, but, falling under suspicion, he was imprisoned for a space at Marseilles, whence he ultimately escaped to Brussels. Here he continued, not altogether unsuccessfully, to engage in alchemy ; while here too he became acquainted with Percell, the brother of Langlet du Fresnoy, to whom he is supposed to have confided some valuable scientific secrets. Eventually, however, the mysterious death of one Grefier, known to have been working in Alnys' laboratory, made the Brussels authorities suspicious about the latter's character, so he left the town stealthily, never to be heard of again.

Demonius : A stone so called from the supposed demoniacal rainbow that appears in it.

Demonocracy : The government of demons ; the immediate influence of evil spirits ; the religion of certain peoples of America, Africa, and Asia, who worship devils.

Demonography : The history and description of demons and all that concerns them. Authors who write upon this subject—such as Wierus, Delancre, Leloyer—are sometimes called demonographers.

Demonology : That branch of magic which deals with malevolent spirits. In religious science it has come to indicate knowledge regarding supernatural beings who are not deities. But, it is in regard to its magical significance only that it falls to be dealt with here. The Greek term *Daimon,* originally indicated " genius " or " spirit," but in England it has come to mean a being actively malevolent. Ancient *Demonology* will be found dealt with in the articles Egypt, Semites, Genius and Devil-Worship, and savage *demonology* under the heads of the various countries and races where it had its origin. According to Michael Psellus, demons are divided into six great bodies. First, the demons of fire. Second, those of the air. Third, those of the earth. The fourth inhabit the waters and rivers, and cause tempests and floods ; the fifth are subterranean, who prepare earthquakes and excite volcanic eruptions. The sixth, are shadows, something of the nature of ghosts. St. Augustine comprehends all demons under the last category. This classification of Psellus is not unlike that system of the middle ages, which divided all spirits into those belonging to the four elements, fire, air, earth, and water, or salamanders, sylphs, undines, and gnomes.

The mediæval idea of demons was, of course, in a direct

line from the ancient Christian and Gnostic supposition. The Gnostics, of early Christian times, in imitation of a classification of the different orders of spirits by Plato, had attempted a similar arrangement with respect to an hierarchy of angels, the gradation of which stood as follows:—The first and highest order was named seraphim, the second cherubim, the third was the order of thrones, the fourth of dominions, the fifth of virtues, the sixth of powers, the seventh of principalities, the eighth of archangels, the ninth, and lowest, of angels. This classification was, in a pointed manner, censured by the apostles, yet still, strange to say, it almost outlived the pneumatologists of the middle ages. These schoolmen, in reference to the account that Lucifer rebelled against heaven, and that Michael, the archangel, warred against him, long agitated the momentous question: " What orders of angels fell on this occasion ? " At length, it became the prevailing opinion that Lucifer was of the order of Seraphim. It was also proved after infinite research, that Agares, Belial, and Barbatos, each of them deposed angels of great rank, had been of the order of virtues ; that Bileth, Focalor, and Phœnix, had been of the order of thrones ; that Goap had been of the order of powers, and that Purson had been both of the order of virtues and of thrones ; and Murmur, of thrones and of angels. The pretensions of many other noble devils were likewise canvassed, and, in equally satisfactory manner, determined. Afterwards, it became an object of enquiry to learn : " How many fallen angels had been engaged in the contest ? " This was a question of vital importance, which gave rise to the most laborious research, and to a variety of discordant opinions. It was next agitated : " Where the battle was fought— in the inferior heaven, in the highest region of the air, in the firmament, or in Paradise ? " " How long it lasted ?— whether during one second, or moment of time (*punctum temporis*), two, three, or four seconds ? " These are queries of very difficult solution, but the notion which ultimately prevailed was, that the engagement was concluded in exactly three seconds from the date of its commencement ; and that while Lucifer, with a number of his followers, fell into hell, the rest were left in the air to tempt man. A still newer question rose out of all these investigations : " Whether more angels fell with Lucifer, or remain in heaven with Michael ? " Learned clerks, however, were inclined to think that the rebel chief had been beaten by a superior force, and that, consequently, devils of darkness were fewer in number than angels of light.

These discussions which, during the number of successive centuries interested the whole of Christendom, too frequently exercised the talents of the most erudite persons in Europe. The last object of demonologists was to collect, in some degree of order, Lucifer's routed forces, and to reorganise them under a decided form of subordination or government. Hence, extensive districts were given to certain chiefs who fought under this general. There was Zimimar, " the lordly monarch of the north," as Shakespeare styles him, who had his distinct province of devils ; there was Gorson, the King of the South ; Amaymon, the King of the East ; and Goap, the Prince of the West. These sovereigns had many noble spirits subordinate to them, whose various ranks were settled with all the preciseness of heraldic distinction ; there were Devil Dukes, Devil Marquises, Devil Counts, Devil Earls, Devil Knights, Devil Presidents, and Devil Prelates. The armed force under Lucifer seems to have comprised nearly twenty-four hundred legions, of which each demon of rank commanded a certain number. Thus, Beleth, whom Scott has described as " a great king and terrible, riding on a pale horse, before whom go trumpets and all melodious music," commanded eighty-five legions ; Agares, the first

duke under the power of the East, commanded thirty-one legions ; Leraie, a great marquis, thirty legions ; Morax, a great earl and a president, thirty-six legions ; Furcas, a knight, twenty legions ; and, after the same manner, the forces of the other devil chieftains were enumerated.

Such were the notions once entertained regarding the history, nature, and ranks of devils. Our next object will be to show that, with respect to their strange and hideous forms the apparitions connected with the popular belief on this subject, were derived from the descriptive writings of such demonologists, as either maintained that demons possessed a decided corporeal form, and were mortal, or that, like Milton's spirits, they could assume any sex, and take any shape they chose.

When, in the middle ages, conjuration was regularly practised in Europe, devils of rank were supposed to appear under decided forms, by which they were as well recognised as the head of any ancient family would be by his crest and armorial bearings. Along with their names and characters were registered such shapes as they were accustomed to adopt. A devil would appear, either like an angel seated in a fiery chariot, or riding on an infernal dragon, and carrying in his right hand a viper ; or assuming a lion's head, a goose's feet, and a hare's tail ; or putting on a raven's head, and mounted on a strong wolf. Other forms made use of by demons were those of a fierce warrior, or of an old man riding upon a crocodile with a hawk in his hand. A human figure would arise having the wings of a griffin ; or sporting three heads, two of them being like those of a toad and of a cat ; or defended with huge teeth and horns, and armed with a sword ; or displaying a dog's teeth and a large raven's head ; or mounted upon a pale horse, and exhibiting a serpent's tail ; or gloriously crowned, and riding upon a dromedary ; or presenting the face of a lion ; or bestriding a bear, and grasping a viper. There are also such shapes as those of an archer, or of a Zenophilus. A demoniacal king would ride upon a pale horse ; or would assume a leopard's face and griffin's wings ; or put on the three heads of a bull, of a man, and a ram, with a serpent's tail, and the feet of a goose ; and, in this attire, bestride a dragon, and bear in his hand a lance and a flag ; or, instead of being thus employed, goad the flanks of a furious bear, and carry in his fist a hawk. Other forms were those of a goodly knight ; or of one who bore lance, ensigns, and even a sceptre ; or of a soldier, either riding on a black horse, and surrounded by a flame of fire, or wearing on his head a duke's crown, and mounted on a crocodile or assuming a lion's face, and, with fiery eyes, spurring on a gigantic charger ; or, with the same frightful aspect, appearing in all the pomp of family distinction, on a pale horse ; or clad from head to foot in crimson raiment, wearing on his bold front a crown, and sallying along on a red steed. Some infernal duke would appear in his proper character, quietly seated on a griffin ; another spirit of a similar rank would display the three heads of a serpent, a man, and a cat ; he would also bestride a viper, and carry in his hand a firebrand. Another of the same type would appear like a duchess, encircled with a fiery zone, and mounted on a camel ; a fourth, would wear the aspect of a boy, and amuse himself on the back of a two-headed dragon. A few spirits, however, would be content with the simple garbs of a horse, a leopard, a lion, an unicorn, a night raven, a stork, a peacock, or a dromedary, the latter animal speaking fluently the Egyptian language. Others would assume the more complex forms of a lion or of a dog, with a griffin's wings attached to each of their shoulders, or of a bull equally well gifted ; or of the same animal, distinguished by the singular feature of a man's face ; or of a crow clothed with human flesh ; or of a hart with a fiery tail. To certain other noble devils were assigned such shapes as those of a dragon with three heads, one of these being human ; of a wolf with a serpent's tail, breathing forth flames of fire ; of a she-wolf exhibiting the same caudal appendage together with griffin's wings, and ejecting from her mouth hideous matter. A lion would appear, either with the head of a branded thief, or astride upon a black horse, and playing with a viper, or adorned with the tail of a snake, and grasping in his paws two hissing serpents.

These were the varied shapes assumed by devils of rank. " It would, therefore," says Hibbert, " betray too much of the aristocratical spirit to omit noticing the forms which the lower orders of such beings displayed. In an ancient Latin poem, describing the lamentable vision of a devoted hermit, and supposed to have been written by St. Bernard in the year 1238, those spirits, who had no more important business upon earth than to carry away condemned souls, were described as blacker than pitch ; as having teeth like lions, nails on their fingers like those of a wild-boar, on their fore-head horns, through the extremities of which poison was emitted, having wide ears flowing with corruption, and discharging serpents from their nostrils. The devout writer of these verses has even accompanied them from drawings, in which the addition of the cloven feet is not omitted. But this appendage, as Sir Thomas Brown has learnedly proved, is a mistake, which has arisen from the devil frequently appearing to the Jews in the shape of a rough and hairy goat, this animal being the emblem of sin-offering."

It is worthy of further remark, that the form of the demons described by St. Bernard differs little from that which is no less carefully pourtrayed by Reginald Scot, three hundred and fifty years later, and, perhaps, by the demonologists of the present day. " In our childhood," says he, " our mother's maids have so terrified us with an ouglie divell having horns on his head, fier in his mouth, and a tail on his breech, eies like a bason, fangs like a dog, clawes like a beare, a skin like a niger, and a voice like a roaring lion—whereby we start and are afraid when we hear one cry bough."

Wit the view of illustrating other accounts of apparitions, we must advert to the doctrines of *demonology* which were once taught. Although the leading tenets of this occult science may be traced to the Jews and early Christians, yet they were matured by our early communication with the Moors of Spain, who were the chief philosophers of the dark ages, and between whom and the natives of France and Italy much communication subsisted. Toledo, Seville, and Salamanca, became the great schools of magic. At the latter city, prelections on the black art were, from a consistent regard to the solemnity of the subject, delivered within the walls of a vast and gloomy cavern. The schoolmen taught that all knowledge and power might be obtained from the assistance of the fallen angels. They were skilled in the abstract sciences, in the knowledge of precious stones, in alchemy, in the various languages of mankind and of the lower animals, in the *belles lettres*, in moral philosophy, pneumatology, divinity, magic, history, and prophecy. They could control the winds, the waters, and the influence of the stars ; they could raise earthquakes, induce diseases, or cure them, accomplish all vaster mechanical undertakings, and release souls out of purgatory. They could influence the passions of the mind, procure the reconcilation of friends or foes, engender mutual discords, induce mania and melancholy, or direct the force and objects of the sexual affections. According to Wierus, demons are divided into a great many classes, and into regular kingdoms and principalities, nobles and commoners. Satan is by no means the great sovereign of this monarchy, but his place is taken by Beelzebub. Satan is

alluded to by Wierus as a dethroned monarch, and Chief of the Opposition ; Moloch, Chief of the Army ; and Pluto, Prince of Fire ; and Leonard, Grand Master of the Sphere. The masters of these infernal courts are, Adramelech, Grand Chancellor ; Astaroth, Grand Treasurer ; and Nergal, Chief of the Secret Police ; and Baal, Chief of the Satanic Army. According to this authority, each state in Europe has also its infernal ambassadors. Belphegor is thus accredited to France, Mammon to England, Belial to Turkey, Rimmon to Russia, Thamuz to Spain, Hutjin to Italy, and Martinet to Switzerland. Berbiguier, writing in 1821, has given a sketch of the Infernal Court. He says : " This court has representatives on earth. These mandatories are innumerable. I give nomenclature and degree of power of each : Moreau, magician and sorcerer of Paris, represents Beelzebub ; Pinel, a doctor of Salpêtrière, represents Satan ; Bouge, represents Pluto ; Nicholas, a doctor of Avigum, represents Moloch ; and so on. " Altogether," says Wierus, " there are in the infernal regions 6666 legions, each composed of the same number of devils."

Demonology and Witchcraft by Sir Walter Scott : This work occupies a curious and pathetic place in Sir Walter Scott's vast literary output. Four years subsequent to his financial *débâcle*, in 1826, the author sustained a mild apoplectic shock, and it was shortly after this that John Murray, who was then issuing a series known as " The Family Library," asked Sir Walter to contribute thereto a volume on *demonology*. Consent was given readily, but, as an entry in Scott's journal makes manifest, he did not care greatly for the work, and really engaged in it just because he was still in the throes of writing off his debts, and had to accept every commission which was offered him. In short, the book was begun from a purely commercial motive, and was composed when the writer's mental faculties were perforce sluggish, the natural result being that it is infinitely inferior to his other writings. But despite its inferiority herein, Sir Walter's volume has its interest for students of occultism. The writer is lame enough in what might be called the speculative parts of his book—those pages, for instance, in which he tries laboriously to account for the prevalence in the middle-ages of belief in witchcraft and the like—but his wonderful and well-stored memory stood him in good stead when writing those passages concerned purely with facts, and thus there is considerable value in his account of *demonology* in France and in Sweden, and in all that he says about Joan of Arc. Moreover, his intimate knowledge of early Scottish literature gives a singular importance to all those of his chapters which are concerned with his native land, while it is interesting to find that here and there, he offers something of a sidelight on his own immortal novels, as for example, when he treats of those spectres which he had dealt with previously in *Woodstock*.

Demonomancy : Divination by means of demons. This divination takes place by the oracles they make, or by the answers they give to those who evoke them.

Demonomania : The mania of those who believe all that is told concerning demons and sorcerers, such as Bodin, Delancre, Leloyer, and others. Bodin's work is entitled *Demonomania of the Sorcerers*, but in this case it signifies devilry.

De Morgan, Mrs. : The author of a mystico-spiritual work entitled *From Matter to Spirit*, published in 1863. *Mrs. de Morgan*, whose interest in spiritualism was awakened at the séances of Mrs. Hayden, was the wife of Professor de Morgan, who himself offered emphatic testimony to the genuineness of Mrs. Hayden's mediumship.

Deoca, or The Woman of the South : A Princess of Munster, who is mentioned in Irish medieval legend. It is said that she was betrothed to Lairgnan, and asked of him as a marriage gift the children of Lir, who had been magically changed by their stepmother into four wonderful singing swans. The hermit who looked after them refused to give them to Lairgnan, who then seized them. When brought into the presence of *Deoca* they were transformed into their human form—withered, white-haired, miserable beings. The hermit baptised them before they died, and sorrowed for them so much that he himself was laid in their grave.

Dermot of the Love-spot : The typical lover of Irish legend, and the hero of the myth of *Dermot* and Grania. It was in this wise that he got the love-spot. One night he and three companions entered a hut for a night's shelter, in which dwelt an old man, a young girl (Youth), a wether (the World) and a cat (Death). During the night the girl put the love-spot on Dermot's forehead, and henceforth, it is said, no woman could see him without loving him. He came to be loved by Grania, the betrothed of Finn, who forced him to run away with her. They were pursued all over Ireland, but after sixteen years of outlawry, *Dermot* was allowed to return to his patrimony. He was killed by the Boar of Ben, Bulben, (q.v.) an enchanted animal, who had been his step-brother. His body was borne away on a gilded bier by the People of Dana, and was given a soul by Angus Og, the Irish God of Love, that he might return each day and talk with him. *Dermot* was of the type of solar hero ; and the bier on which his body was borne away is, of course, the sunset.

Dervishes : A sect of Mohammedan priests. In some cases they exercise a semi-esoteric doctrine. Their various " paths " or systems are of great antiquity, and probably are derived from the ancient rites of Persia and Egypt, bearing also a strong resemblance to Magism. Taking the *Bektash* as typical of all, we find that in the fifteenth century *Bektash* of Bokhara received his mantle from Ahmed Yesevee, who claimed descent from the father-in-law of Mohammed. He established a " path," consisting nominally of seven degrees, only four of which, however, are essential. These aim at the establishment of an affinity between the aspirant and the Sheik, from whom he is led through the spirit of the founder, and that of the Prophet to Allah. The initiatory ceremony provides a severe test. The aspirant is tried for a year with false secrets, and his time of probation having expired, a lamb is slain, from the carcass of which a cord is made for his neck and a girdle of initiation for his loins. Two armed attendants then lead him into a square chamber, where he is presented to the Sheik as " a slave who desires to know truth." He is then placed before a stone altar, on which are twelve escallops. The Sheik, who is attended by eleven others, grips the hand of the aspirant in a peculiar way, and administers the oath of the Order, in which the neophyte promises to be poor, chaste and obedient. He is then informed that the penalty of betraying the Order is death. He then says : " Mohammed is my guide, Ali is my director," and is asked by the Sheik, " Do you accept me as your guide ? " The reply being made in the affirmative, the Sheik says : " Then I accept you as my son." He is then invested with a girdle on which are three knots, and receives an alabaster stone as a token. The sign of recognition is the same as that in the first degree of masonry. Amongst their important symbols are the double triangles and two triangles joined at the apex. One of their maxims is that " the man must die that the saint must be born." As a jewel they make use of a small marble cube with red spots, to typify the blood of the martyred Ali. These dervish sects are by no means popular with the orthodox Mussulmans, as they devote themselves entirely to the well-being of their order rather than to Mohammedanism.

A notable exercise indulged in by several Dervish sects, is that of gyration in circles for extended periods of time, or prolonged dancing. The object of this is obscure, some authorities contending that it is engaged in to bring about a condition of ecstasy, whilst others see in it a planetary or astronomic significance.

D'Eslon : (*See* **Hypnotism.**)

Desmond, Gerald, sixteenth earl of *Desmond*, who was killed in 1583, had some repute as a magician, and was known as the " Great Earl." Many curious stories are current concerning him. He dwelt in his castle on a small island in Lough Gur, and there, in time, he brought his young bride, to whom he was so passionately attached that he could deny her nothing. Seeking him one day in the chamber where he worked his magic spells, she demanded to know the secret of the Black Cat. In vain he told her of the terrible things she must witness ; she would not be dissuaded. So he warned her solemnly that if she uttered a word the castle would sink to the bottom of Lough Gur, and set to work. Terrible indeed were the sights she beheld, but she stood firm and uttered neither word nor cry, until her husband lay down on the floor and stretched till he reached almost from end to end of the room. Then she uttered a wild shriek, and the castle sank instantly to the bottom of Lough Gur, where it still remains. Once in every seven years *Desmond*, mounted on a white horse, rises from the water and rides round the Lough. His horse is shod with silver shoes, and when these wear out the spell will be broken, *Desmond* will return, and his vast estates shall once more be restored to him.

D'Espagnet, Jean : A Hermetic philosopher who left two treatises *Enchiridion Physicæ Restitutæ* and *Arcanum Philosophiæ Hermeticæ* which have also been claimed as the works of one calling himself the " Chevalier Imperial." " The Secret of Hermetic Philosophy " embraces the practical side of the *Magnum Opus* and the " Enchiridion " treats of the physical possibility of transmutation. *D'Espagnet* also wrote the preface to the *Tableau de l' Inconstance des Démons* by Pierre Delancre. The " Arcanum " is better known as the " Canons of Espagnet " and has been claimed as a treatise on mystical Alchemy. The Author states, however, that " the science of producing Nature's grand Secret is a perfect knowledge of nature universally and of Art, concerning the realm of Metals ; the practice whereof is conversant in finding the principles of Metals by analysis."

The authorities cited by Espagnet are those who like Trévisan are known to have devoted their lives to practical Alchemy. Nevertheless, it may be granted that while much of the matter treats of a physical object it may be extended to the psychic side of Hermetic Art.

" Deuce Take You " : A vulgar saying which had its origin in antiquity. The *deuce* is practically synonymous with the devil, the word being derived from *Dusins*, the ancient name given by the Gauls to a sort of demon or devil.

Devas : In Theosophy, constitute one of the ranks or orders of spirits who compose the hierarchy which rules the universe under the Deity. Their numbers are vast and their functions are not all known to mankind, though generally these functions may be said to be connected with the evolution of systems and of life. Of *Devas* there are three kinds—Bodiless Devas, Form Devas and Passion Devas. Bodiless Devas belong to the higher mental world, their bodies are composed of mental Elemental Essence, and they belong to the first Elemental kingdom. Form Devas belong to the lower mental world, and while their bodies are composed also of mental Elemental Essence, they belong to the second Elemental kingdom. Passion Devas belong to the astral world and their bodies are composed of astral Elemental Essence. Devas are creatures superlatively great and superlatively glorious, of vast knowledge and power, calm yet irresistible, and in appearance altogether magnificent.

Devil : A name derived from the Greek *Diabolos*, "slanderer." The name for the supreme spirit of evil, the enemy of God and man. In primitive religious systems there is no conception of evil, and the gods are neither good nor bad, as we conceive these terms, but may possess " good " and " bad " attributes at one and the same time. Thus we have very few traces of beings which are absolutely evil in the older religions, and it may be broadly stated that the conception of Satan as we have it to-day is almost purely Hebrew and Christian. In Egypt and Babylon, figures like Apepi and Tiawath, although clearly in the line of evolution of a Satanic personality, are by no means rulers of the infernal regions. Again the Hades of the Greeks is merely a ruler of the shades of the dead, and not an enemy of Olympus or mankind. It is strange that in Mexico, Mictlantecutli, lord of hell, is a much more directly Satanic figure than any European or Asiatic ruler of the realms of the dead. But in some mythologies, there are frequent allusions to monsters who may quite easily have coloured our conception of Satan. Such is the Hindu serpent Ahi, and the Hebrew Leviathan, the principle of Chaos. In the Teutonic mythology we have the menacing shape of Loki, originally a god of fire, but afterwards the personification of evil. The conception of Satan, too, appears to have some deeply-rooted connection with the ancient serpent-worship, which seems to have penetrated most oriental countries. Thus we find the Tempter in the Old Testament in the guise of a serpent. The serpent or dragon is being generally regarded as the personification of night who swallows the sun and envelopes the world in darkness.

The Hebrew conception of Satan it is thought, arose in the post-exilic period, and exhibits traces of Babylonian or Assyrian influence. It is not likely that before the captivity any specific doctrine respecting evil spirits was held by the Hebrews. Writing on this subject, Mr. F. T. Hall in his book *The Pedigree of the Devil* says :—

" The term ' Satan ' and ' Satans ' which occur in the Old Testament, are certainly not applicable to the modern conception of Satan as a spirit of evil ; although it is not difficult to detect in the Old Hebrew mind a fruitful soil, in which the idea, afterwards evolved, would readily take root. The original idea of a ' Satan ' is that of an ' adversary,' or agent of ' opposition.' The angel which is said to have withstood Balaam is in the same breath spoken of as ' The angel of the Lord,' and a ' Satan.' When the Philistines under Achish their king were about to commence hostilities against the Israelites under Saul and David and his men were about to march with the Philistines ; the latter objected, lest, in the day of battle, David should become a ' Satan ' to them, by deserting to the enemy. When David, in later life, was returning to Jerusalem, after Absalom's rebellion and death ; and his lately disaffected subjects were, in turn, making their submission ; amongst them came the truculent Shimei : Abishai, David's nephew, one of the fierce sons of Zeruiah, advised that Shimei should be put to death : this grated upon David's feelings, at a time when he was filled with exuberant joy at his own restoration ; and he rebuked Abishai as a ' Satan.' Again Satan is said to have provoked David to number Israel, and at the same time, that ' the Lord moved David to number Israel ; ' a course strenuously opposed by Joab, another of the sons of Zeruiah. Solomon in his message to Hiram, king of Tyre, congratulated himself on having no ' Satans ' and that this peaceful immunity from discord enabled him to build the Temple, which had been

forbidden to his warlike father, David. This immunity was not, however, lasting ; for Hadad, the Edomite, and Regon, of Zobah, became ' Satans ' to Solomon, after his profuse luxury had opened the way for curruption and disaffection. In all these cases, the idea is simply identical with the plain meaning of the word : a Satan is an opponent, an adversary. In the elaborate curse embodied in the 109th Psalm, the writer speaks of his enemies as his ' Satans' and prays that the object of his anathema may have ' Satan ' standing at his right hand. The Psalmist himself, in the sequel, fairly assumes the office of his enemy's ' Satan,' by enumerating his crimes and failings, and exposing them in their worst light. In the 71st Psalm, enemies (v. 10) are identified with ' Satans ' or adversaries (v. 13).

" The only other places in the Old Testament where the word occurs, are in the Book of Job, and the prophecy of Zechariah. In the Book of Job, Satan appears with a distinct personality, and is associated with the sons of God, and in attendance with them before the throne of Jehovah. He is the cynical critic of Job's actions, and in that character he accuses him of insincerity and instability ; and receives permission from Jehovah to test the justice of this accusation, by afflicting Job in everything he holds dear. We have here the spy, the informer, the public prosecutor, the executioner ; all embodied in Satan, the adversary : these attributes are not amiable ones, but the writer does not suggest the absolute antagonism between Jehovah and Satan, which is a fundamental dogma of modern Christianity.

" In the prophecy of Zechariah, Satan again, with an apparent personality, is represented as standing at the right hand of Joshua, the high-priest, to resist him : he seems to be claiming strict justice against one open to accusation ; for Joshua is clothed in filthy garments—the type of sin and pollution. Jehovah relents, and mercy triumphs over justice : the filthy garments are taken away, and fair raiment substituted. Even here, the character of Satan, although hard, is not devoid of virtue, for it evinces a sense of justice."

The Babylonians, among whom the Hebrews dwelt during the Captivity, believed in the existence of vast multitudes of spirits, both good and bad, but there is nothing to show that the Hebrews took over from them any extensive pantheon, either good or evil. Indeed the Hebrew and Babylonian religions possessed many things in common, and there was no necessity that the captive Jews should borrow an animism which they probably already possessed. At the same time it is likely that they adopted the idea of an evil agency from their captors, and as the genius of their religion was averse to polytheism, the probabilities are that they welded the numerous evil forces of Babylonian into one central figure. Again, it must have occurred to them that if the world contained an evil principle, it could not possibly emanate from God, whom they regarded as all-good, and it was probably with the intention of separating all evil from God that the personality of Satan (having regard to the amount of evil in the universe) was invested with such importance.

In later Judaism we find the conception of Satan strongly coloured by Persian dualism, and it has been supposed that Asmodeus of the Book of Tobit is the same as Aeshara Daewa of the Ancient Persians. Both " Satan " and " Satans " were mentioned in the Book of Enoch, and in Ecclesiasticus he was identified with the serpent of Genesis, and in the " Book of the Secrets of Enoch " his revolt against God and expulsion from Heaven are described. In the Jewish Targinn, Samael, highest of the angels, merges with Satan into a single personality.

The Satan of the New Testament is merely a reproduction of these later Jewish forms. In Matthew he is alluded to as the " Prince of Demons," and in Ephesians is spoken of as ruling over a world of evil beings who dwell in the lower heavens. Thus he is prince of the powers of the air. In Revelation the war in Heaven between God and Satan is described, and his imprisonment is foreshadowed after the overthrow of the Beast and the Kings of the earth, when he will be chained in the bottomless pit for one thousand years. After another period of freedom he is finally cast into the lake of brimstone for ever. According to the orthodox Christian belief of the present day, Satan has been endowed with great powers for the purpose of tempting man to prove his fortitude. In the middle ages, the belief in Satan and Satanic agencies was overwhelming, and was inherited by Protestantism from Roman Catholicism. This is not the place to enter into a discussion as to the likelihood of the existence of an evil being, but the great consensus of theological opinion is in favour of such a theory.

Devil Worship : (1). The worship of Satan or Lucifer. (2). The worship by semi-civilised or barbarous people; of deities having a demoniac form.

The Worship of Satan or diabolism is spasmodic and occasionally epidemic. It dates from the early days of dualism (q.v.) and perhaps originated in the Persian dual system when the opposing deities Ormuzd and Ahriman symbolised the good and bad principles respectively. Instances of pure Satanism are comparatively rare, and it must not be confounded with the Sabbatic orgies of witchcraft which partake more of the nature of (2), or with the evocation of the Evil One, for the purpose of making a pact with him. Modern groups practising Satanism are small and obscure, and, unorganised as they are, details concerning them are conspicuous by their absence.

Plentiful details, however, are forthcoming concerning the cultus of Lucifer, but much discrimination is required in dealing with these, the bulk of the literature on the subject being manifestly imaginative and wilfully misleading. The members of the church of Lucifer are of two groups, those who regard the deity they adore as the evil principle, thus approximating to the standpoint of the Satanists, and those who look upon him as the true god in opposition to Adonai or Jehovah, whom they regard as an evil deity who has with fiendish ingenuity miscreated the world of man to the detriment of humanity.

Modern diabolic literature is written from the point of view of the Roman Catholic Church, and much may be said for the theory that it was composed to subserve the necessities of that institution. But this cannot be wholly true, as it is a substantial fact that hosts are frequently abstracted from Catholic churches for the purpose of Satanic rite which requires the destruction of the consecrated wafer as a ritual act. In 1894 a hundred consecrated hosts were stolen from Nôtre Dame by an old woman under circumstances that clearly proved that the vessels which contained them were not the objects of the theft, and an extraordinary number of such larcencies occurred in all parts of France about the end of last century, no less than thirteen churches in the diocese of Orleans being thus despoiled. In the diocese of Lyons measures were taken to transform the tabernacles into strong-boxes, and in eleven of the dioceses similar acts were recorded. In Italy, Rome, Liguria and Solerus suffered, and even in the Island of Mauritius an outrage of peculiar atrocity occurred in 1895. It has been asserted by many writers such as Archbishop Meurin and Dr. Bataille that Freemasonry is merely a mask for Satanism, that is, that in recent years an organisation of which the ordinary mason is ignorant has grown up which has diabolism for its special object. This it is asserted is recruited from the higher branches of masonry and initiates women. Needless to say, the

change is indignantly denied by masons, but it must be remembered that the persons who bring it are Catholics, who have a direct interest in humiliating the fraternity. Bataille and Margiotta have it that the order of the Palladium or Sovereign Council of Wisdom, was constituted in France in 1737, and this, they infer, is one and the same as the legendary Palladium of the Templars, better known by the name of Baphomet (q.v.) In 1801 one Isaac Long, a Jew, carried the "original image" of Baphomet to Charleston in the United States, and it is alleged that the lodge he founded then became the chief in the Ancient and Accepted Scotch Rite. He was succeeded in due course by Albert Pike, who, it is alleged, extended the Scotch Rite, and shared the Anti-Catholic Masonic chieftainship with the Italian patriot Mazzini. This new directory was established, it is asserted, as the new Reformed Palladium Rite or the Reformed Palladium. Assisted by Gallatin Mackey, one Longfellow, Holbrook and a Swiss, Phileas Walder by name, Pike erected the new rite into an occult fraternity with world-wide powers, and practised the occult arts so well that we are asked to believe that the head lodge at Charleston was in constant communication with Lucifer ! Dr. Bataille in a wholly ludicrous work *Le Diable au XIX Siècle*, states among other things that in 1881 his hero " Dr. Hacks " in whom his own personality is but thinly disguised, visited Charleston in March 1881, where he met Albert Pike, Gallatin Mackey and other Satanists. Mackey showed him his *Arcula Mystica* in appearance like a liqueur stand, but in reality a diabolical telephone, worked like the Urim and Thummim. Miss Diana Vaughan, once a Palladist, Grand Mistress of the Temple, and Grand Inspectress of the Palladium, was converted to Roman Catholicism, and in *Memoirs of an ex-Palladist*, (1895) she has given an exhaustive account of her dealings with the Satanists of Charleston. She claims to be descended from the alchemist Thomas Vaughan, and recounts her adventures with Lucifer. These are so wholly absurd that we must request freedom from the necessity of recounting them. There is little doubt that Miss Vaughan was either the victim of hallucination or else the instrument of the Roman Catholic Church in its attempts to brand Masonry as a vehicle of Satanism. The publications of Margiotta and Gabriel Pages are equally puerile, and we may conclude that, if Satanism and the worship of Lucifer exists, that the rites of their churches are carried on in such a secret manner, that few, even mystics of experience, can be aware of them.

When applied to the ceremonies of barbarous races, devil-worship is a misnomer, as the " devils " adored by them are deities in their eyes, and only partake of the diabolic nature in the view of missionaries and others. But inasmuch as the gods possess a demoniac form they may be classed as diabolic. Among these may be enumerated many South American and African tribes. The Uapès of Brazil worship Jurupari, a fiend-like deity, to whom they consecrate their young men. His cult is invested with the utmost secrecy. The myth of his birth states that he was born of a virgin who conceived after drinking a draught of *chahiri*, or native beer. She possessed no sexual parts, and could not give birth to the god until bitten by a fish whilst bathing. When arrived at man's estate Jurupari invited the men of the tribe to a drinking-bout, but the women refused to provide the liquor, and thus gained his illwill. He devoured the children of the tribe because they had eaten of the *uacu* tree which was sacred to him. The men, enraged at the loss of their offspring, fell upon him, and cast him into a fire, from the ashes of which grew the *paxiuba* tree, which the Uapès say is the bones of Jurupari. Whilst it was night the men cut down the tree and fashioned it into sacred instruments which must never be seen by the women, on account of the dislike Jurupari conceived for them. Should a woman chance to see the sacred symbols pertaining to the worship of Jurupari, she is at once poisoned. On hearing the " Jurupari music " of the priests on the occasion of one of his festivals the women of the tribe wildly rush into concealment, nor dare to emerge from it until all chance of danger is past. In all probability this custom proceeds from the ancient usage common to most American tribes that the rites of initiation of the men of the tribe must not be witnessed by the women thereof, probably on account of some more or less obscure totemic reason or sex-jealousy analagous to the exclusion of women from the rites of freemasonry, to which, strange to say, the worship of Jurupari bears a strong resemblance.

This is a good example of the " *devil worship* " of savage races. The Chinese also placate devils (*see* **China**) as do the people of Burma and Cambodia (*q.v.*) but in no sense can their oblations to evil spirits be classed as " worship," any more than the gods of classic times may be regarded as devils, simply because they were so labelled by early Christianity. (*See* **Gnostics, Obeah, Ju-ju, Devil, Demonology,** etc.)

LITERATURE :—Huysman, *La Bas* ; Bataille, *Le Diable au XIX siècle* ; Rosen, *Satan et Cie* ; Meurin, *La synagogue du Satan* ; Papus, *Le Diable et L'Occultisme* ; Waite, *Devil-Worship in France* ; Julie Bois, *Petites Religions de Paris : Satanisme et la Magie* ; Spence, article " *Brazil* " in *Encyclopædia of Religion and Ethics.*

Devil's Bridge : A bridge thrown across the Afon Mynach, near Aberystwyth. The story goes that an old woman who had lost her cow saw it on the opposite side of the chasm to that on which she stood, but knew not how to reach it. At that juncture the Evil One appeared to her in the shape of a monk, and promised to throw a bridge across, if she would give him the first living thing that would pass over it. The old lady agreed, the bridge was completed, and the crafty fiend begged that she would try it. But the old woman had observed his cloven hoof, and knee bent backwards, so she took a crust from her pocket and flung it across the ravine, bidding her little dog go fetch it. The Evil One was outwitted, as he generally is in such tales.

Devil's Chain : There is a tradition in Switzerland that St. Bernard has the devil chained in some mountains in the neighbourhood of the Abbey of Clairvanx. From this comes the custom, observed by the farmers of the country, of striking three blows with the hammer on the anvil every Monday morning before setting to work. By this means the devil's chain is strengthened, so that he may not escape.

Devil's Girdle, The : Witches in mediaeval times were often accused of wearing the *Devil's Girdle*, probably as a mark of allegiance to the Evil One. Magical girdles were commonly worn, and a modern writer suggests that the magnetic belts advertised at the present day had their origin in this practice.

Devil's Pillar : There are preserved at Prague three stones of a pillar which the devil brought from Rome to crush a priest, with whom he had made a compact, and to kill him while he said mass. But St. Peter, says the legend, threw the devil and his pillar into the sea three times in succession, which diversion gave the priest time for repentance. The devil was so chagrined that he broke the pillar and saved himself.

Devil's Sonata : (*See* **Visions.**)

Devils, Afraid of Bells : It was an old superstition that evil spirits were afraid of bells and fled from the sound of them.

Devon, Witchcraft in : The belief in witchcraft is not yet dead in Devonshire, as was shown in a curious case heard in Crediton County Court not many years ago, when a young woman alleged that she was given a potion in a grocer's shop, and that as a result, either of the draught or of the incantation delivered while she was in the shop, she was getting thinner every day. Only those who have lived long in Devon can realise the widespread belief that still exists in remote corners of the county of the power of " the evil eye," and of the credence given to all kinds of weird superstitions. " Witches " are believed to be able to exercise a malign influence even after death unless they are buried with their toes downwards. Not very long ago, a woman suspected of being a witch, was buried in this way within twenty miles of Tiverton. In no part of the country is witchcraft more believed in than in the Culm Valley. There is a local saying that there are enough witches in the valley to roll a hogshead of cider up the Beacon Hill, at Culmstock, and old people living in the locality are not ashamed to say that they believe in witchcraft. The witches are of two kinds—" black " and " white." The former profess to have the power to condemn those on whom they are asked to cast a spell, to all kinds of misfortunes ; the latter impose on credulous clients by making them believe that they can remove evil spells and bring good fortune—for a consideration, of course. For obvious reasons visits to " witches " are generally kept dark, but every now and again particulars leak out. In the Culmstock district, not so very long ago, a young girl went with her mother to a witch, in order to get a spell cast over an errant swain, who was suspected of bestowing his affections on another young lady. The witch professed to be able to bring the young man back to his first love, or to condemn him to all kinds of torture, but her price was prohibitive, and so the young man was left to marry whom he would. Farmers are the witches' most profitable clients, and it is a noteworthy fact that they generally contrive to visit the " wise woman " when they are away from home, " at market." A few years ago, farmers used to go to Exeter for many miles round to consult a witch whenever they had any misfortune, and it is commonly reported that they can get the same sort of advice in the city at the present day. At many farmhouses Bibles are kept in the dairies to prevent witches from retarding the butter-making operations. " I'm 'witched," or " I must have been 'witched," are expressions heard in Devon every day in the week. Generally speaking, it is animals that are supposed to sustain the most harm from being " overlooked." The loss of cattle that have died has been put down to the power of evil spirits, and according to many superstitious people, witches have a peculiar power over pigs. A man who believed his pigs had been bewitched was told, not so long ago, to take the heart of a pig, stick it full of pins and needles, and roast it at the fire. He did this believing this would check the mortality among his swine.

Diadochus : According to Marbodaeus, this gem resembles the beryl in its properties, and was most valuable in divination. It serves for the invocation of spirits, and oracular responses could be discovered in it. Albertus Magnus writes it Diacodos, and it is possibly to this stone that Braithwaite alludes in his *English Gentleman* : " For as the precious stone Diacletes, though it have many rare and excellent sovereignties in it, yet loseth them all if put in a dead man's mouth." Marbodaeus mentions this in his verses as a property of the *diadochus.* The words of Leonardus are too curious to omit : " It disturbs devils beyond all other stones, for, if it be thrown in water, with the words of its charm sung, it shows various images of devils, and gives answer to those that question it. Being held in the mouth, a man may call any devil out of hell, and receive satisfaction to such questions as he may ask." He names it Diacodas or Diacodus.

Diagrams, Magical : (*See* **Magic**.)

Diakka: A term used by Andrew Jackson Davis to signify wicked, ignorant, or undeveloped spirits. It is believed that at death no sudden or violent change takes place in the character and disposition of an individual. Those who are mischievous, unprincipled, sensual, during their lives remain so, for a time at least, after they die. Hudson Tuttle says, " As the spirit enters the spirit world just as it leaves this, there must be an innumerable host of low, undeveloped, uneducated, or in other words, evil spirits." There is, indeed, a special sphere or plane for these *diakka*, where they are put on probation. It is they who are responsible for the fraud and trickery often witnessed at seánces ; they not only deceive the sitters, but the medium as well. The way to avoid their influence is to live a pure, refined, and religious life, for these evil spirits are naturally attracted to those whose minds most resemble their own.

Diamond : This gem possesses the most marvellous virtues. It gives victory to him who carries it bound on his left arm whatever the number of his enemies. Panics, pestilences, enchantments—all fly before it ; hence, it is good for sleep-walkers and for the insane. It deprives the lodestone of its virtue, and one variety, the Arabian *diamond*, is said to attract iron more powerfully than the magnet itself. The ancients believed that neither fire nor blows would overcome its hardness, unless macerated with fresh goat's blood ; and Cyprian, Austin, Isidore, and others of the fathers, adopting this notion, have used it to illustrate the method by which the blood of the Cross softens the heart of man. If bound to a magnet, the *diamond*, according to the belief of the ancients, will deprive it of its virtue.

Diancecht : A Danaan magician of Irish medieval legend. He it was who restored to Nuada of the Silver Hand (q.v.) his lost limb and thus his throne.

Diaphane : The Kabalistic term for the imagination.

Dickenson, Edmund : *Dr. Edmund Dickenson*, physician to King Charles the Second, a professed seeker of the hermetic knowledge, produced a book entitled, *De Quinta Essentia. Philosophorum* ; which was printed at Oxford in 1686, and a second time in 1705. A third edition of it was printed in Germany in 1721. In correspondence with a French adept, the latter explains the reasons why the Brothers of the Rosy Cross concealed themselves. As to the universal medicine, Elixir Vitae, or potable form of the preternatural menstruum, he positively asserts that it is in the hands of the " Illuminated," but that, by the time they discover it, they have ceased to desire its uses, being far above them : and as to life for centuries, being wishful for other things, they decline availing themselves of it. He adds that the adepts are obliged to conceal themselves for the sake of safety, because they would be abandoned in the consolations of the intercourse of this world (if they were not, indeed, exposed to worse risks), supposing that their gifts were proven to the conviction of the bystanders as more than human, when they would become simply abhorrent. Thus, there are excellent reasons for the its conduct ; they proceed with the utmost caution, and instead of making a display of their powers, as vain-glory is the least distinguishing characteristic of these great men, they studiously evade the idea that they have any extraordinary or separate knowledge. They live simply as mere spectators in the world, and they desire to make no disciples, converts nor confidants. They submit to the obligations of life, and to relationships—enjoying the fellowship of none, admiring none, following none, but themselves. They obey all codes, are excellent citizens, and only preserve silence in regard to their own private beliefs, giving the world the benefit of their acquirements up to a certain point ; seeking only sympathy at some angles of their multiform character, but shutting out curiosity where they do not desire its inquisitive eyes.

Didot Perceval : So-called because the only MS. of this legend discovered belonged to A. F. Didot, the famous collector. This version of the Grail Legend lays great stress on the illness of the Fisher King. It tells how the Table Round was constructed, and relates the adventures of Sir Perceval, which are much the same as those told in the *Conte del Graal* and include the Good Friday incident. It is said that he, with his brother-in-law, Brons, were instructed in the mystic expressions which Christ whispered to Joseph of Arimathea when on the cross.

Diepenbroeks, Treatise on : (*See* **Healing by Touch.**)

Dilston : (*See* **Haunted Houses.**)

Dionysiac Mysteries : (*See* **Mysteries.**)

Direct Writing : A term used in spiritualism for spirit writing which is produced *directly*, and not by the hand of a medium, or through a mechanical contrivance such as a psychograph or planchette.. The best known form of *direct writing* is that made popular by the mediums Slade and Eglinton—slate-writing (q.v.) But the spirits are not dependent solely on prepared materials, but can produce *direct* writing anywhere, and under any circumstances. Thus during a poltergeist disturbance at Stratford, Conn., in 1850-51, *direct writing* was found on turnips which sprang apparently from nowhere. An unfinished letter left for a few moments would be found completed in a different hand, though during the interval it might have been inaccessible to any normal agency. *Direct writing* may also be produced at spiritualistic séances, either by means of slate-writing, or by putting scraps of paper and pencil into a sealed drawer or a closed box. A sound as of writing will shortly be heard, and on the paper being withdrawn it will be found to contain some sort of message from the spirit world. Experiments on these lines were carried out by a noted spiritualist, Baron de Guldenstubbé, in 1856. Paper and pencil he locked in a small box, the key of which he carried about with him. At the end of thirteen days he found some writing on the paper ; and on that same day the experiment was repeatedly performed, each time with success. Another method he adopted was to visit galleries, churches, and other public places, and to leave writing materials on the pedestals of statues, on tombs, and so on. In this way he obtained writing in English, French, German, Latin, Greek, and other languages purporting to come from Plato, Cicero, St. Paul, Juvenal, Spencer, and Mary Stuart. The Baron was accompanied on these expeditions by the Comte d'Ourches and others of his friends, while on one occasion a medium is mentioned as being present. It is probable, indeed, that a medium was essential to these spirit performances ; for, though the medium's physical organism is not used as an agent, the writings generally take place in the vicinity of one gifted with supernormal faculties. Not only is legible hand-writing produced in this way ; sometimes mysterious hieroglyphs are inscribed, which can only be deciphered by those who possess mediumistic powers.

Dithorba : Brother of Red Hugh and Kimbay of Irish medieval legend. He was killed by his niece Macha, and his five sons expelled from Ulster. They resolved to wrest the sovereignty of Ireland from Macha, but she discovers them in the forest, overpowers them by her mesmeric influence, and carries them to her palace on her back. They build the famous Irish city of Emain Macha under her supervision.

Divination : The method of obtaining knowledge of the unknown or the future by means of omens. Astrology (q.v.), and oracular utterances (*See* **Oracles**), may be regarded as branches of *divination*. The derivation of the word supposes a direct message from the gods to the diviner or augur. It is practised in all grades of barbarism and civilisation. The methods of *divination* are many and various, and strangely enough in their variety are confined to no one portion of the globe. Crystal-gazing has been relegated to a separate article. Shell-hearing and similar methods are allied to crystal-gazing and may be classed with it, as that method of *divination* which arises from the personal consciousness of the augur. Of the same class are *divination* by dreams, automatic writing, and so forth. What might be called *divination* by "luck" is represented by the use of cards, the casting of lots, the use of knuckle-bones as in Africa and elsewhere, cocoanuts as in Polynesia. Haruspication, or the inspection of entrails, *divination* by foot-print in ashes, by the flight of birds, by meeting with ominous animals, represents the third class of augury.

The art of *divination* is usually practised among savages by the shaman caste; among less barbarous people by the augur, as in Rome and ancient Mexico; and even amongst civilised people by persons who pretend to *divination*, such as the spiritualistic medium or the witch. The art is undoubtedly of great antiquity. It was employed in ancient Egypt side by side with astrology, and *divination* by dream was constantly resorted to,—a class of priests being kept apart, whose office it was to interpret dreams and visions. We find instances of dreams recorded in the Egyptian texts : as for example those of Thothmes IV. king of Egypt in 1450 B.C., and Nut-Amen, king of the Eastern Soudan and Egypt about 670 B.C. The Egyptian magician usually set himself to procure dreams for his clients by such devices as the drawing of magical pictures and the reciting of magical words ; and some of these are still extant, such as that in the British Museum papyrus No.122. We find, however, that in Egypt augury was usually effected by astrological methods.

In ancient China the principal method of *divination* was by means of the oracles ; but we find such forms as the examination of the marks on the shell of a tortoise, which reminds us of the examination of the back of a peccary by the Maya of Central America. We find a Chinese monarch consulting the fates in this manner in 1146 B.C. and finding them unfavourable ; but as in Egypt, most soothsaying was accomplished by means of astrology. Omens, however, were by no means ignored, and were given great prominence, as many tales in the ancient books testify.

In ancient Rome a distinct caste or college of priests called Augurs was set apart to interpret the signs of approval or disapproval sent by the gods in reference to any coming event. This college probably consisted originally of but three members, of whom the king himself was one ; and it was not until the time of Cæsar that the members were increased to sixteen. The college remained in existence as late as the fourth century, and its members held office for life. The tenets of the Roman augurs were, that for signs of the gods one must look towards the sky and glean knowledge of the behests of the divine beings from such omens as the lightning-flash, and the flight of birds. On a windless night, the augur took up his position on a hill which afforded an extensive view. Marking out a space for himself, he pitched a tent within it, and seating himself therein with covered head requested the gods for a sign, and waited for an answer. He faced southwards, thus having the east, or lucky quarter, on his left, and the west, or unfavourable portion of the sky, on his right. He carefully observed every sign which came within the purview of his vision : such as lightning, the appearance of birds, and so forth. The song or utterance of birds was also carefully hearkened to ; and these were divided into birds of good omen and evil omen : while others referred to definite persons and events. The reading of omens

was also effected by the feeding of birds and observing the manner in which they ate. The course of animals and the sounds uttered by them were also closely watched, and all unusual phenomena were regarded as omens or warnings. Sortilege or the casting of lots was often resorted to by the caste of augurs. The election of magistrates was nearly always referred to the Auspices or College of Diviners, as were the setting out of an army for war, and the passing of laws.

In the East generally, *divination* appears to have been effected by crystal-gazing, dreams and similar methods of self-hallucination, or self-hypnotism. *Divination* flourished in Chaldea and Assyria among the Babylonians and Ethiopians, and appears to have been very much the same as in Egypt. In the Jewish *Talmud* we notice that witches are said to divine by means of bread-crumbs. Among the Arabs, the future is often foretold by means of the shapes seen in sand. The Burmese and Siamese pierce an egg at each end, and having blown the contents on the ground, trace within them the outline of things to be. (*See* **Burma.**) *Divination* by astrology too is very common in oriental countries, and prophetic utterance is likewise in great favour.

It is remarkable that among the native races of America the same arts of *divination* as are known to the peoples of the Old World were and are in vogue. These arts, as a rule, are the preserve of the medicine-man and priestly class. In ancient Mexico there was a college of augurs corresponding in purpose to the Auspices of ancient Rome, the members of which occupied themselves with observing the flight and listening to the songs of birds, from which they drew their conclusions. In Mexico, the *Calmecac* or college of priests had a department where divination was taught in all its branches, but there were many *ex officio* prophets and augurs, and the reader is referred to the article on **Mexico** for an account of the astrological methods of casting nativities, and so forth. Oracles were common, and in this connection an amusing Peruvian story may be recalled. A certain *huaca* or oracle was reported to be of evil influence ; orders were given to destroy it ; and upon its being broken up a parrot found means to escape from within it,—thus giving us a pretty shrewd idea of the means employed by the priesthood to effect oracular utterance. In Peru, still other classes of diviners predicted by means of the leaves of tobacco, or the grains or juice of coca, the shapes of grains of maize, taken at random, the forms assumed by the smoke rising from burning victims, the viscera of animals, the course taken by spiders, and the direction in which fruits might fall. The professors of these several methods were distinguished by different ranks and titles, and their training was a long and arduous one. The American tribes as a whole were very keen observers of bird life. Strangely enough the bird and serpent are combined in their symbolism, and indeed in the names of several of their principal deities. The bird appeared to the American savage as a spirit, in all probability under the spell of some potent enchanter—a spell which might be broken by some great sorcerer or medicine man alone. As among the ancient Romans, the birds of America were divided into those of good and evil omen ; and indeed certain Brazilian tribes appear to think that the souls of departed Indians enter into the bodies of birds. The shamans of certain tribes of Paraguay act as go-betweens between the members of their tribes and such birds as they imagine enshrine the souls of their departed relatives. This usage would appear to combine the acts of augury and necromancy.

The priesthood of Peru practised oracular methods by "making idols speak," and this they probably accomplished by ventriloquial arts. The *piagés* or priests of the Uapès of Brazil have a contrivance known to them as the *paxiuba*, which consists of a tree-stem about the height of a man, on which the branches and leaves have been left. Holes are bored in the trunk beneath the foliage, and by speaking through these the leaves are made to tremble, and the sound so caused is interpreted as a message from Jurupari one of their principal deities. But all over the American continent from the Eskimos to the Patagonians, the methods of oracular *divination* are practically identical. The shaman or medicine-man raises a tent or hut which he enters carefully closing the aperture after him. He then proceeds to make his incantations, and in a little while the entire lodge trembles and rocks, the poles bend to breaking point, as if a dozen strong men were straining at them, and the most violent noise comes from within, seemingly now emanating from the depths of the earth, now from the air above, and now from the vicinity of the hut itself. The reason for this disturbance has never been properly accounted for ; and medicine-men who have been converted to Christianity have assured scientific workers amongst Indian tribes that they have not the least idea of what occurred during the time they occupied these enchanted lodges, for the simple reason that they were plunged in a deep sleep. After the supernatural sounds have to some extent faded away, the medicine-man proceeds to question the spirit he has evoked,—the answers of whom for sheer ambiguity are equal to those of the Pythonesses of ancient Greece. There is little doubt that the shamans who practise this method of oracular utterance are the victims of hallucination, and many cases are on record in which they have excited themselves into a condition of permanent lunacy.

America is the touchstone of the science of anthropology, and since we have adopted it as the continent from which to draw the majority of our illustrations, it will be as well if we conclude the article on American lines for the sake of comparison. We find then that *divination* by hypnosis is well-known in the western continent. Jonathan Carver, who travelled among the Sioux about the latter end of the eighteenth century, mentions it as in use amongst them. The " Ghost Dance " religion of the Indians of Nevada had for one of its tenets the belief in hypnotic communion with the dead. *Divination* by means of dreams and visions is extremely common in both sub-continents of the western hemisphere, as is exemplified by the derivation of the word " priest " in the native languages : by the Algonquians they are called " dreamers of the gods," by the Maya " listeners," and so forth. The ability to see visions was usually quickened by the use of drugs or the swallowing or inhalation of cerebral intoxicants, such as tobacco, *maguey*, coca, the snake-plant, and so forth. Indeed many Indian tribes, such as the Creeks, possessed numerous plants which they cultivated for this purpose. A large number of instances are on record in which Indian medicine-men are said to have divined the future in a most striking manner, and perhaps the following will serve to illustrate this :

In his autobiography, Black Hawk, a celebrated Sac chief, relates that his grandfather had a strong belief that in four years' time ' he should see a white man, who would be to him as a father.' Supernaturally directed, as he said, he travelled eastward to a certain spot, and there, as he had been informed in dreams, met with a Frenchman who concluded an alliance on behalf of his country with the Sac nation. Coincidence is certainly possible here, but it can hardly exist in the circumstances of Jonathan Carver. While he was dwelling with the Killistenœs, they were threatened with a famine, and on the arrival of certain traders, who brought them food in exchange for skins and other goods, their very existence depended. The diviners of the tribe were consequently consulted by

the chief, and announced that the next day, at high noon exactly, a canoe would make its appearance with news of the anxiously looked-for expedition. The entire population came down to the beach in order to witness its arrival, accompanied by the incredulous trader, and, to his intense surprise, at the very moment forecasted by the shamans, a canoe rounded a distant headland, and, paddling speedily shorewards, brought the patient Killistenœs news of the expedition they expected.

John Mason Brown has put on record an equally singular instance of the prophetic gift on the part of an American medicine-man. (*See Atlantic Monthly*, July, 1866.) He was engaged several years previously in searching for a band of Indians in the neighbourhood of the Mackenzie and Coppermine rivers ; but the difficulties of the search induced the majority of his band to return, until out of ten men who originally set out only three remained. They had all but concluded to abandon their search when they stumbled upon a party of braves of the very tribe of which they were in search. These men had been sent out by their medicine-men to find three whites, of whose horses, accoutrements, and general appearance the shaman had given them an exhaustive account ere they set out, and this the warriors related to Brown before they saw his companions. Brown very naturally inquired closely of the medicine-man how he had been able to foretell their coming. But the latter, who appeared to be ' a frank and simple-minded man,' could only explain that ' he saw them coming, and heard them talk on their journey.'

Crystal-gazing is in common use amongst many Indian tribes. The Aztecs of Mexico were wont to gaze into small polished pieces of sandstone, and a case is on record where a Cherokee Indian kept a divining crystal wrapped up in buckskin in a cave, occasionally " feeding " it by rubbing over it the blood of a deer. At a village in Guatemala, Stephens saw a remarkable stone which had been placed on the altar of the church there, but which had previously been used as a divining-stone by the Indians of the district. *Divination* by arrow was also commonly resorted to.

According to Fuentes, the chronicler of Guatemala the reigning king of Kiche, Kicah Tanub, when informed by the ambassador of Montezuma II. that a race of irresistible white men had conquered Mexico and were proceeding to Guatemala, sent for four diviners, whom he commanded to tell him what would be the result of this invasion. They asked for time to discover the future fate of his kingdom, and taking their bows discharged some arrows against a rock. They returned to inform their master that, as no impression had been made upon the rock by the arrowheads, they must prognosticate the worst and predicted the ultimate triumph of the white man— a circumstance which shows that the class to which they belonged stood in no fear of royalty. Kicah Tanub, dissatisfied, sent for the ' priests,' obviously a different class from the diviners, and requested their opinions. From the ominous circumstance of an ancient stone—which had been brought from afar by their forefathers—having been broken, they also augured the fall of the Kiche empire.

Many objects such as small clay birds, boats or boat-shaped vessels, etc., have been discovered in sepulchral mounds in North America, and it is conjectured that these may have been used for purposes of *divination*. As any object might become a fetish, it is probable that any object might become a means of augury. The method employed appears to have been so to treat the object that the probable chances for or against the happening of a certain event would be discovered—much, indeed, as some persons will toss coins to " find out " whether an expected event will come to pass or not. Portents, too, were implicitly believed in by the American races, and this branch of augury was, we find, one of the accomplishments of Nezahualpilli, king of Tezcuco, near Mexico, whom Montezuma consulted concerning the terrible prodigies which startled his people prior to the advance of the Spaniards upon his kingdom, and which were supposed to predict the return of Quetzacloatl, the legendary culture-hero of Anahuac, to his own again. These included earthquakes, tempests, floods, the appearances of comets and strange lights, whilst mysterious voices were heard in the air—such prodigies, indeed, as tradition usually insists upon as the precursors of the downfall of a mighty empire.

The various methods of *divination* have each been accorded a separate article : thus the reader is referred to **Axinomancy, Belomancy, Capnomancy,** and so forth ; and in the articles dealing with the various countries a goodly number of instances of divinatory practice will be discovered.

Divine Name, The : In Jewish mysticism great stress is laid upon the importance of the *Divine Name*. It consists of forty-two letters ; not, as Moses Maimonides points out, comprised in one word, but in a phrase of several words, which conveyed an exact notion of the essence of God. With the priestly decadence in the last days of the Temple, a name of twelve letters was substituted for the *Divine Name*, and as time went on even this secondary name was not divulged to every priest, but only to a few. The longer name was sometimes said to contain forty-five or seventy-two letters. The ten Sefiroth are also supposed, in a mystical sense, to be the names of the Deity. The *Divine Name Jahveh* is greater than " I am that I am," since the latter signifies God as He was before the creation, the Absolute, the Unknowable, the Hidden One ; but the former denotes the Supreme Manifestation, the immanence of God in the Cosmos.

Divine World : Formerly known as the Adi Plane—is in the theosophic scheme of things, the first or highest world, (in Theosophy) the world first formed by the divine impulse in the creative process. It is unattainable by man in his present state. (*See* **Theosophy** and **Solar System**.)

Divining Rod : A forked rod, or branch of tree, which in the hands of certain people is said to indicate, by means of spasmodic movements of varying intensity, the presence of water and minerals underground. Traces of the rod used for purposes of divination are to be found in the records of Ancient Egypt. Cicero and Tacitus both wrote of the rod " virgula divina." This ancient *divining rod* was a form of rhabdomancy (q.v.) or divination by means of little pieces of stick. In Germany it was known as the " wishing-rod " and was used just as fortune-tellers use cards, coffee or tea-grounds at the present day. Agricola's *De Re Metallica* published at Basle, at the beginning of the sixteenth century, makes reference to another rod which he calls the virgula furcata," the forked, rod to distinguish it from the " virgula divina." This rod, he said, was used by miners to discover mineral lodes ; rhabdomancy having nothing to do with this use of the *divining rod*. Melancthon mentions this use of the rod and ascribed the behaviour of the " instrument " in the discovery of metallic ores to the law of sympathy, according to the belief then obtaining that metals, trees and other natural objects had certain subtle relationships with each other ; and believers in this theory pointed to the fact that trees which grew above mineral lodes droop as though attracted downwards ; the modern scientific explanation of this natural phenomenon being that it is due to the poverty of the soil. In Sebastian Minister's *Cosmography*, also of the sixteenth century, may be found engravings of these " mineral diviners " at work. The priests of that time persecuted them as demons in disguise ; they were also included in the witchcraft persecutions, suffering tortures and burning

to death. Among miners on the Continent the use of the " virgula furcata " became universal, especially in the Harz Mountains and throughout Saxony. In Germany it was called the Schlag-Ruthe, " striking-rod " from the fact of its appearing to strike when held over mineral ores.

Robert Boyle, the " father of chemistry " is the first to make mention of the *divining rod* in England. In an essay of his published in 1663 may be found the following " A forked hazel twig is held by its horns, one in each hand, the holder walking with it over places where mineral lodes may be suspected, and it is said that the fork by dipping down will discover the place where the ore is to be found. Many eminent authors, amongst others our distinguished countryman Gabriel Plat, ascribe much to this detecting wand, and others, far from credulous or ignorant, have as eye-witnesses spoken of its value. When visiting the lead-mines of Somersetshire I saw its use, and one gentleman who employed it declared that it moved without his will, and I saw it bend so strongly as to break in his hand. It will only succeed in some men's hands, and those who have seen it may much more readily believe than those who have not." Some authorities on the subject state that it was first brought into England in the time of Queen Elizabeth. In the State papers of that reign may be found recorded the fact that commissioners were sent to Germany to study the best methods of mining and brought back with them German miners from the Harz Mountains ; and that these " foreigners " introduced the *divining rod* into England seems highly probable. It was first used for water finding, however, in Southern France, and not until a century later was it used in England for this purpose. It became the " dowsing rod " in England and Somersetshire might be called the home of the " dowser." Locke the philosopher, a Somersetshire man referred in 1691 to the " dowsing rod " and De Quincey, also belonging to the county, tells of singular cases of " jousers " as he calls them. Down to the present day this means of finding water is used, farmers and owners of large estates sending for a " dowser " when they wish to find a spring of water. These men are not geologists, who might have a scientific knowledge of the locality, they are often merely labourers. The rods are mostly cut from the hazel, but all kinds of nut and fruit trees have been used, white and black thorn and privet also being favourites. Pieces of watch-spring and copper-wire are also used ; and in some cases the forked rod is dispensed with, the peculiar sensation felt in the arms, hands and body being sufficient to indicate the water. These dowsers wander over the ground with the ends of the fork grasped in the palms of the hands and the rod downwards and when this moves, turning suddenly in his hand, upwards, it is said for water, downwards for minerals, at that spot will be found the desired object, absolute correctness frequently being achieved. In later years attempts have been made to scientifically investigate the question and amongst amateur " dowsers " we find the names of Lord Farrer and the late Mr. Andrew Lang. As to the theory for these movements the electrical or magnetic theory was exploded by Father Kircher in 1654 who balanced the rod on a frictionless support like a delicate pair of scales and found that in this position nothing would induce it to move over hidden water or metal. It must be held by some human being before the movements take place. Chevreul, the French savant, in 1854 put forward the theory of involuntary muscular action. A modern scientist gives his opinion that very possibly it is due to a faculty in the " dowser " akin to that possessed by a medium : " some transcendental perceptive power unconsciously possessed by certain persons, a faculty analogous to what is called clairvoyance. Not exactly to be described as ' clear-seeing ' but rather, a dim, obscure impression not reaching the brain through the organ of vision, seldom ever rising to the level of a conscious impression, but one able to start the nervous reflex action which caused the muscles to twitch and the rod or other ' autoscope' to move. Doubtless, changes of blood pressure and pulse rate also occur in the dowser ; and if this be so, quite possibly modern instrumental appliances for recording these will ultimately supersede the primitive forked twig." He goes on to say that : "The ' dowser' in fact, 'feels for' and subconsciously discerns the hidden object, whether it be water, hidden treasure or even a malefactor concealing himself from justice, who was pursued and discovered by the agency of the famous dowser Jacques Aymar, using his supernormal powers in 1692." See Sir W. F. Barrett F.R.S. *Lecture on The Dowsing Rod.* A. E. Waite, *The Occult Sciences.*

Divs : The *div* of ancient Persia, pronounced *deo, deu,* or *dive,* is supposed to be the same as the European devil of the middle ages. In the romances of Persia they are represented as male and female, but the male *divs* are considered the more dangerous, and it is from their character, personified in a supposed chief, that the devil is painted with his well-known attributes. The male *divs,* according to the legends of Persia, were entrusted with the government of the world for seven thousand years anterior to the creation of Adam, and they were succeeded by the female *divs* or peris, who under their chief, Gian ben Gian, ruled other two thousand years. The dominion of the peris was terminated by Eblis (the devil of the Koran) who had been created from the elements of fire, and whose abode was previously with the angels. Eblis or Haris, as he is also called, became the leader of the rebellious angels when they were commanded to do homage to the first created man, and being joined by the whole race of genii, the male and female *divs,* whom he had formerly subjugated, he was like them deprived of grace. Eblis and his immediate followers were condemned to suffer for a long period in the infernal regions, but the remainder were allowed to wander over the earth, a constant source of misery to themselves and to the human race, whose obedience is put to the test by their devices, and secured by the example of their degradation and sufferings. They are supposed to assume various forms, especially that of the serpent, and in the drawings annexed to the Persian romances they are represented much as our own devils, ogres, and giants, in the tales of the middle ages. The writers of the later ages, both Arabian and Persian, have localised the abode of these evil genii in the mountain Kaf ; their capital is Aherman-abad, the abode of Aherman their chief, who is identified with the Ahremanes of the Manicheans, that remarkable sect being said to have borrowed their doctrines from Zoroaster. The distinction of sex is a remarkable characteristic of the *divs,* and its evil results in a system of diabolic superstition may be read in the stories of the Ephialtae and Hyphialtae, or nightmare.

Evidently the same in origin as the Persian *divs,* are the daivers of the Hindoos, who inhabit a world which is called, after them, Daiver-Logum. We may borrow a brief account of them from Kindersley's *Specimens of Hindoo Literature.* "The daivers," he says, " perpetually recur in their romances, and other literary works, and are represented as possessing not only material bodies, but as being subject to human frailties. Those saints and heroes who may not as yet be considered worthy of the paradises of Shivven or of Veeshnoo, are represented as inhabiting the Daiver-Logum (or Sorgum). These daivers are in number no less than three hundred and thirty millions. The principal are—I. ' Daivuntren ' or ' Indiren' their king ; to whom report is made of all that happens among them. His court of audience is so capacious as to

contain not only the numerous daivers, but also the prophets, attendants, etc. They are represented in the mythological romances of the Hindoos, as having been engaged in bloody wars, and with various success against the giants (Assoores). The family of Daivuntren consists of his wife ' Inderaunee,' and his son ' Seedera-budderen ' (born from a cow), who records the actions of men, by which they are finally to be judged. II. The attendants or companions of these daivers are—1. The 'Kinnarer,' who sing and play on musical instruments. 2. ' Dumbarim Nardir,' who also perform on a species of drum. 3. ' Kimprusher,' who wait on the daivers and are represented with the wings and fair countenances of angels. 4. ' Kunda-gaindoorer,' similar winged beings who execute the mandates of Veeshnoo. 5. ' Paunner ' a species of jugglers, who amuse the daivers with snake dancing, etc. 6. ' Viddiaser,' their bards, who are acquainted with all arts and sciences, and entertain them with their histories and discourses. 7. ' Tsettee,' who attend them in their aerial journeys. 8. ' Kanuanader,' or ' Dovdanks,' messengers, who conduct the votaries of Veeshnoo and Shivven to their respective paradises, and the wicked to hell (Narekah), of which ' Eemen ' is sovereign. III. The third class of daivergoel, daivers, or genii, are the eight keepers of the eight sides of the world, literally signified by their general name of ' Aushtatikcu-Pauligaur ; they are—1. ' Indiren,' who is no other than Daivuntren, named above. 2. ' Augne-Baugauven,' the god of fire. 3. 'Eemen' king of death and the infernal regions. 4. ' Nerudee,' the element of earth represented under the figure of a giant. 5. ' Vaivoo,' god of air and winds. 6. ' Varoonen,' god of clouds and rain. 7. ' Gooberen,' god of riches. 8. 'Essaunien,' or Shivven himself, in one of his 1,008 appearances on earth." To these principal daivers, Kindersley adds without sufficient reason the ' Reeshees ' of the Hindoos, and their tutelary god of virtue, "Derma-Daive."

For the true oriental doctrine of these evil genii the *Zend-Avesta* may be consulted, which associates the idea of evil more especially with the peris or female *divs,* contrary to the later romances of Islamism. This anomaly reappears in our own fairy tales, the same characters, which at times, are invested with the most malignant attributes, being often described under forms of sylph-like grace and beauty.

Djemscheed, The Cup of : A divination cup, which has been the subject of many of the poems and myths of ancient Persia. It was believed to have been found while digging the foundations of Persepolis, filled with the elixir of immortality. In this magical cup was mirrored the whole world, and everything, good and evil, was revealed therein. The Persians had great faith in these revelations ; and attributed the prosperity of their empire to the possession of this famous cup.

Doctrine of Correspondence : (*See* **Swedenborg.**)

Donn : Son of Midir the Proud ; an Irish hero of medieval legend. In the *Colloquy of the Ancients* we are told how Finn and Kelta and five other champions were out hunting one day, and followed a beautiful faun until it vanished under ground. Seeking shelter in a noble mansion, they were entertained by *Donn mac Midir* and his brother ; and their aid was asked against the rest of the Danaan folk. It seems that thrice in the year they had to fight their fairy foes, and all their followers had been killed excepting the eight-and-twenty warriors themselves. The faun which they had followed had been an enchanted maiden sent to entice them. After a year of successful fighting, the Danaans were obliged to make peace.

Double Triangle : (*See* **Magic.**)

D'Ourches, Comte : French magnetist and necromancer, associated about 1850 with Baron de Guldenstubbé in the attempt—successful only after six months of endeavour—to establish in France spiritualistic circles such as were being formed at the time in America. After a time they were successful in obtaining such manifestations as raps, the vibration of piano-chords, and direct writing.

Dovantes : (*See* **Daivers and Daivergoel.**)

Dowie, The Prophet : (*See* **America, U.S. of.**)

Dowsers : (*See* **Divining Rod.**)

Dowsing, George : (*See* **England.**)

Draconites : otherwise dentrites, draconius, or obsianus, is described by Albertus Magnus as a shining black stone of pyramidal figure. It is not very easy to obtain, as it must be taken out of the head of a dragon, cut off while the beast is still panting. It subdues all sorts of poison, and endows its possessor with invincible courage. The kings of the East esteemed it a great treasure.

Dragon : A purely fabulous monster of enormous size, common to almost all countries. Descriptions of its appearance vary ; but it appears to have been of a reptilian nature, often of a red or green colour, sometimes with several heads which vomited forth fire and vapours, and a large and clumsy tail. It was of enormous strength ; but the ancients believed that it could be charmed by music, and the *dragon* which guarded the golden fleece was soothed by the voice of Medea. In India at the time of Alexander the Great, a *dragon* was worshipped as a god ; and in occult history it is the manifestation of hell. The *dragon*, however, is best known in legendary history as the terrible monster, whose duty it was to provide the hero with opportunities of valour, and in this capacity it has figured in many a tale. The legend of St. George and the Dragon is familiar to everyone, and also the *dragon* that was slain by Sir Lancelot, one of the knights of King Arthur's Round Table. In Revelation the *dragon*, a representation of the Evil One, is overcome by the Archangel Michael. On one side of the coin given to those who were cured of possession, about the time of Henry VII., there was portrayed an angel standing with both feet on a *dragon*. The idea of the dragon is perhaps evolved from the conception of the earth, as a living being, a notion which would gain currency from Earthquake and related phenomena.

Dragon's Head : (*See* **Astrology.**)

Dragon's Tail : (*See* **Astrology.**)

Dreams : The occult significance of *dreams* was a matter of speculation among the wise at an early period in the history of civilisation. In the articles upon Babylonia and Egypt we have to some extent outlined the methods by which the wise men of those countries divined the future from visions seen in sleep, and to these we must refer the reader, as well as to the articles dealing with other countries, savage and civilised, where we will discover a good deal of data relating to *dreams* and dream-lore. In this place we can only indicate some of the more outstanding theories of antiquity regarding the nature and causes of *dreams* and the manner in which the ancient diviners generally interpreted them.

Dreams were regarded as of two kinds—false and true, in either case emanating from a supernatural intelligence, evil or good. By the ancients sleep was regarded as a second life, in which the soul was freed from the body and therefore much more active than during the waking state. The acts it observed and the scenes through which it passed were thought to have a bearing on the future life of the dreamer, but it is possible that the dream-life was regarded as supernatural and "inverted," and that the events which the bodiless spirit beheld were the opposites of those which would later occur on the earth-plane. The idea thus originated that "*dreams* go by contraries," as both popular belief and the many treatises upon the sub-

ject of nightly visions assure us is the case.

However the belief in the divinatory character of *dreams* arose, there is every proof that their causes and nature exercised some of the greatest minds of antiquity. Aristotle believed them to arise solely from natural causes. Posidonius the Stoic was of the opinion that they were of three kinds, the first automatic, and coming from the clear sight of the soul, the second from spirits and the third from God. Cratippus, Democritus, and Pythagoras held doctrines almost identical or differing only in detail, Later, Macrobius divided *dreams* into five kinds : the dream, the vision, the ocular dream, the insomnium and the phantasm. The first is a figurative and mysterious representation which requires an interpretation ; the second was an exact representation of a future event in sleep ; the third was a dream representing some priest or divinity, who declared to the sleeper things to come ; the fourth was an ordinary *dream* not deserving of attention, and the fifth was a disturbed half-awake *dream*, a species of nightmare. Other writers divide *dreams* into accidental *dreams* and those which were induced for the purposes of divination. We are told by Herodotus that in the temple of Bel in Babylon a priestess lay on a bed ready to dream visions of the second class, and that the beds of such soothsayers were often made of the skin of a ram is well known. The ancient Hebrews obtained such *dreams* by sleeping among tombs, and this especial gateway to the supernatural world seems to have been, and still is known to the majority of nations, barbarous and the reverse, as intimately as hypnotic and other methods of reaching its planes and hearing its pronouncements. Sleep was, of course, often induced by drugs, whether the soma of the Hindoos, the peyollotl of the ancient Mexicans, the haschish of the Arabs, or the opium of the Malays or Chinese, and these narcotics which have the property of inducing speedy sleep and of heightening the inward vision were and are greatly prized by professional dreamers all over the world, especially as they rendered dreaming almost immediately possible.

With the nature of ecstatic vision we have dealt under the heading of Hypnotism and now that we have outlined the older theories regarding the cause and nature of *dreams* (for with the modern and purely physiological theories on the subject we have no concern in this place), we may pass on to consider the methods by which *dreams* were read or divined. As has been remarked, this was generally undertaken by a special class of diviners, who in ancient Greece were known as Oneiocritikoi, or interpreters of dreams. The first treatise on the subject is that of Artemidorus, who lived in the time of Antoninus Pius. He differentiates between the *dreams* of Kings and those of commoners, as he believes that the visions of royalty must have reference to the commonwealth and not to the individual. Dreams which represent something as happening to the individual who *dreams* them, show that they have a personal significance, whereas if the *dream* relates to another it will concern him alone. He details the numerous species of *dreams* throughout five books, and then adduces numerous examples. Neither for rule nor illustration have we any space here, and indeed, the literature, popular and otherwise, which treats of oneiromancy is so extensive and so readily accessible that no necessity arises for so doing. Suffice it to say that the rules of Artemidorus are far from clear, and according to them, any dream might signify any event, and any interpretation of the same might be considered justifiable. The method of testing *dreams* according to Amyraldus is his *Discours sur les Songes divins* (Saumur, 1625) is whether the instructions and advice that they contain make for good or ill—a test it is impossible to apply until after the result is known. But Amyraldus surmounts this difficulty by proposing to test *dreams* by the evidence they show of divine knowledge—by asking oneself in short, whether the *dream* it was desired to examine gave any evidence of such things as God alone could know. It would seem from an examination of such *dreams* as were submitted to the diviners of antiquity that the symbolism they exhibited was of a character so profound that it could only be unriddled by an interpreter who received divine aid, such as was afforded in the case of Moses or Daniel. It is plain, however, that the most far-fetched interpretations were given to many of the most epoch-making *dreams* of antiquity, and indeed, the oneio-critical system is one of the weakest spots in the armour of occult science, and was the first of its departments to fall into disrepute and become the prey of the charlatan. There are not wanting serious students of the occult who doubt entirely the occult significance of *dreams*, and it must be granted that no good reason exists for classing them generally with the vision, or a condition of second sight or ecstasy. *See* H. Hutchinson, *Dreams and their Meanings*, London, 1901 ; J. C. Colquohoun, *Magic, Witchcraft and Animal Magnetism*, London, 1851 ; H. Christmas, *The Cradle of the Twin Giants*, London, 1849, and many other popular and more advanced handbooks on the subject.

Dreams of Animals : It was believed by many that animals dreamed. Pliny says : " Evident it is, that horses, dogs, kine, oxen, sheepe and goats, doe dreame. Whereupon it is credibly also thought that all creatures that bring forth their young quicke and living, doe the same. As for those that lay egges, it is not so certian that they dreame; but resolved it is that they doe sleepe."

Dress, Phantom : The question of the apparel worn by apparitions has of late years aroused considerable controversy. Says Mr. Podmore : " The apparition commonly consists simply of a figure, clothed as the percipient was accustomed to see the agent clothed ; whereas to be true to life the phantasm would as a rule have to appear in bed. In cases where the vision gives no information as to the agent's clothing and surroundings generally—and, as already said, such cases form the great majority of the well attested narratives—we may suppose that what is transmitted is not any part of the superficial content of the agent's consciousness, but an impression from the underlying massive and permanent elements which represent his personal identity. The percipient's imagination is clearly competent to clothe such an impression with appropriate imagery, must indeed so clothe it if it is to rise into consciousness at all." " The ghosts, it will have been observed, always appear clothed. Have clothes also ethereal counterparts ? Such was and is the belief of many early races of mankind, who leave clothes, food, and weapons in the graves of the dead, or burn them on the funeral pile, that their friends may have all they require in the spirit world. But are we prepared to accept this view ? And again, these ghosts commonly appear, not in the clothes which they were wearing at death—for most deaths take place in bed—but in some others, as will be seen from an examination of the stories already cited. Are we to suppose the ethereal body going to its wardrobe to clothe its nakedness withal ? or that, as in the case of Ensign Cavalcante's appearance to Frau Reiken, the ghost will actually take off the ethereal clothes it wore at death and replace them with others ? It is scarcely necessary to pursue the subject. The difficulties and contradictions involved in adapting it to explain the clothes must prove fatal to the ghost theory."

Mr. Thistleton Dyer says on the subject :

" It is the familiar dress worn in lifetime that is, in most cases, one of the distinguishing features of the ghost, and when Sir George Villiers wanted to give a warning to his son, the Duke of Buckingham, his spirit appeared to one of the Duke's servants ' in the very clothes he used to wear.' Mrs. Crowe, in her *Night Side of Nature* gave an account of an apparition which appeared at a house in Sarratt, Hertfordshire. It was that of a well-dressed gentleman, in a blue coat and bright gilt buttons, but without a head. It seems that this was reported to be the ghost of a poor man of that neighbourhood who had been murdered, and whose head had been cut off. He could, therefore, only be recognised by his ' blue coat and bright gilt buttons.' Indeed, many ghosts have been nicknamed from the kinds of dress in which they have been in the habit of appearing. Thus the ghost at Allanbank was known as ' Pearlin Jean,' from a species of lace made of thread which she wore ; and the ' White Lady ' at Ashley Hall—like other ghosts who have borne the same name—from the white drapery in which she presented herself. Some lady ghosts have been styled ' Silky,' from the rustling of their silken costume, in the wearing of which they have maintained the phantom grandeur of their earthly life. There was the ' Silky ' at Black Heddon who used to appear in silken attire, oftentimes ' rattling in her silks '; and the spirit of Denton Hall—also termed ' Silky '—walks about in a white silk dress of antique fashion. This last ' Silky ' was thought to be the ghost of a lady who was mistress to the profligate Duke of Argyll in the reign of William III., and died suddenly, not without suspicion of murder, at Chirton, near Shields—one of his residences. The ' Banshee of Loch Nigdal,' too, was arrayed in a silk dress, green in colour. These traditions date from a period when silk was not in common use, and therefore attracted notice in country places. Some years ago a ghost appeared at Hampton Court, habited in a black satin dress with white kid gloves. The White ' Lady of Skipsea ' makes her midnight serenades clothed in long, white drapery. Lady Bothwell, who haunted the mansion of Woodhouselee, always appeared in white ; and the apparition of the mansion of Houndwood, in Berwickshire—bearing the name of ' Chappie '—is clad in silk attire.

" One of the ghosts seen at the celebrated Willington Mill was that of a female in greyish garments. Sometimes she was said to be wrapped in a mantle, with her head depressed and her hands crossed on her lap. Walton Abbey had its headless lady who used to haunt a certain wainscotted chamber, dressed in blood-stained garments, with her infant in her arms ; and, in short, most of the ghosts that have tenanted our country houses have been noted for their distinctive dress.

" Daniel Defoe, in his *Essay on the History and Reality of Apparitions*, has given many minute details as to the dress of a ghost. He tells a laughable and highly amusing story of some robbers who broke into a mansion in the country, and, while ransacking one of the rooms, they saw, in a chair, ' a grave, ancient man, with a long full-bottomed wig, and a rich, brocaded gown,' etc. One of the robbers threatened to tear off his ' rich brocaded gown,' another hit at him with a firelock, and was alarmed at seeing it pass through the air ; and then the old man ' changed into the most horrible monster that ever was seen, with eyes like two fiery daggers red hot.' The same apparition encountered them in different rooms, and at last the servants, who were at the top of the house, throwing some ' hand grenades ' down the chimneys of these rooms, the thieves were dispersed. Without adding further stories of this kind, which may be taken for what they are worth, it is a generally received belief in ghost lore that spirits are accustomed to appear in the dresses which they wore in their lifetime—a notion credited from the days of Pliny the Younger to the present day.

" But the fact of ghosts appearing in earthly raiment has excited the ridicule of many philosophers, who, even admitting the possibility of a spiritual manifestation, deny that there can be the ghost of a suit of clothes. George Cruikshank, too, who was no believer in ghosts, sums up the matter thus : ' As it is clearly impossible for spirits to wear dresses made of the materials of earth, we should like to know if there are spiritual outfitting shops for the clothing of ghosts who pay visits on earth.' Whatever the objections may be to the appearance of ghosts in human attire, they have not hitherto overthrown the belief in their being seen thus clothed, and Byron, describing the ' Black Friar ' who haunted the cloisters and other parts of Newstead Abbey, tells us that he was always

arrayed

In cowl, and beads, and dusky garb.

Indeed, as Dr. Tylor remarks, ' It is an habitual feature of the ghost stories of the civilised, as of the savage world, that the ghost comes dressed, and even dressed in well-known clothing worn in life.' And he adds that the doctrine of object-souls is held by the Algonguin tribes, the islanders of the Fijian group, and the Karens of Burmah —it being supposed that not only men and beasts have souls, but inorganic things. Thus, Mariner, describing the Fijian belief, writes : ' If a stone or any other supstance is broken, immortality is equally its reward ; nay, artificial bodies have equal good luck with men, and hogs, and yams. If an axe or a chisel is worn out or broken up, away flies its soul for the service of the gods. The Fijians can further show you a sort of natural well, or deep hole in the ground, at one of their islands, across the bottom of which runs a stream of water, in which you may clearly see the souls of men and women, beasts and plants, stocks and stones, canoes and horses, and of all the broken utensils of this frail world, swimming, or rather tumbling along, one over the other, pell-mell, into the regions of immortality.' As it has been observed, animistic conceptions of this kind are no more irrational than the popular idea prevalent in civilised communities as to spirits appearing in all kinds of garments."

Druidic Language : (*See* **Shelta Thari.**)

Druids : (*See* **Celts.**)

Drum, Magic : (*See* **Lapland.**)

Drummer of Tedworth : A poltergeist who haunted the house of Mr. John Mompesson, of Tedworth, Wilts, about the year 1661 and onwards. In March of that year Mompesson had had a vagrant drummer brought before a justice of the peace, whereby his drum was confiscated. The instrument was taken to the house of Mompesson, during the latter's absence, and immediately a violent poltergeist disturbance broke out. Apparitions were seen by members of the household, pieces of furniture were seen to move of themselves, small objects were flung about by invisible hands, the younger children were levitated as they lay in their beds, and there was a continual sound of drumming every night. The drummer, understood to be the cause of the trouble, was transported, when peace once more reigned in the afflicted household ; but ere long he managed to return, when the disturbances broke out with renewed vigour. There is no first-hand account of this poltergeist, save that of Joseph Glanvil— *Sadducismus Triumphatus,* 1668—and though Glanvil is our authority for the whole story, that part of it which he himself declares to have witnessed is certainly not the most marvellous, but describes scratchings and pantings heard in the vicinity of the childrens' beds.

Du Potet : One of the original founders of spiritualism in France, and one of the first experimentalists in table-turning, either in that country or elsewhere. (*See* France).

Du-Sith (Black Elf.) : A little man, believed to be of fairy origin, who killed Sir Lachlan Mor M'Clean at the battle of Trai-Gruinard, in Islay, Scotland, in the year 1598. The story runs that this little man offered his services to Sir James Macdonald, the opponent of Sir Lachlan ; and that the latter's death was caused by an arrow which struck him on the head, and was afterwards found to be an Elf-bolt. In reply to a question of Macdonald's the little man replied : '' I am called *Du-sith,* and you were better to have me with you than against you.''

Duad : (*See* **God.**)

Dual Personality : In every form of cerebral dissociation there is a disturbance of consciousness. Sometimes, and especially in the trance, there occurs what is known as '' split consciousness,'' and the split may be so pronounced that the subject seems to have two or more distinct personalities. The secondary personality may differ from the primary in many ways, and possess entirely distinct intellectual and moral characteristics. The entranced subject may allude to his normal consciousness in the third person, may criticise its opinions and attitude, or even express direct antagonism towards it. The secondary personality sometimes alternates with the primary in such a way as to suggest that two spirits are struggling to possess the same physical organisation. Another peculiarity of this state is that whereas the normal consciousness generally knows nothing of the others, the secondary personalities have full knowledge of each other and of the normal conciousness. *Dual personality* is not confined to the trance state, but may arise spontaneously. R. L. Stevenson makes effective use of it in his *Strange Case of Dr. Jekyll and Mr. Hyde.*

Duguid, David : A Glasgow painting medium who achieved considerable success in his line. He was a cabinet-maker, who in 1866 found himself possessed of mediumistic faculties. At first an ordinary rapping medium, he speedily developed the power of painting in trance, even in the dark. A still higher stage of mediumship was reached when direct drawings were produced in his presence. These drawings, generally copies of Dutch masters, purporting to be done by the original artists, are said not to have been without some merit, apart from the fact that they were done in complete darkness. The two principal controls were Ruysdael and Steen. In 1869 control of the medium's organism was taken by Hafed, prince of Persia at the beginning of the Christian era, and Archmagus. Hafed related his many adventures through *Duguid's* mediumship in a series of sittings extending over some years. A Persian of princely birth, he had borne arms in his country's defence. After extensive travels, he was admitted to the magi, and ultimately became Archmagus. He was of those who bore rich gifts to Bethlehem at the birth of Christ. Finally he met his death in the arena at Rome. *Hafed, Prince of Persia,* was afterwards published in book form. (*See* **Spiritualism**).

Duk-duk, The : Members of a secret society of New Pomerania, who are also called Spirits.

Dumbarin-Nardar : One of the classes of attendants or companions of the Hindoo daivers, whose special duty it is to play upon a kind of drum.

Dupuis, Charles François : 1742-1809. *Charles François Dupuis* was born at Trie le-Chateau, and educated by his father and afterwards at the College d'Harcourt. At the age of twenty-four he was made professor of rhetoric at Lisieux ; but his inclination led him into the field of mathematics. In his work, *Origine de tous les Cultus* he attempts to explain not only all the mysteries of antiquity, but also the origin of all religious beliefs. In his *Memoire* *explicatif du Zodiaque chronologique et mythologique* (1806) he maintains a common origin for the astronomical and religious opinions of the Greeks, Egyptians, Chinese, Persians, and Arabians.

Durandal : A magical sword belonging to Roland of legendary fame.

Duum Vira : (*See* **Sibylline Books.**)

E

Ea : (*See* **Babylonia.**)

Earth laid upon a Corpse : It is related in Pennant's *Tour* that it was the custom in the Highlands of Scotland to lay on the breast of the deceased a wooden platter containing a little earth and a little salt—the former to symbolize the corruptibility of the body, the latter the incorruptibility of the soul.

Ebennozophim : (*See* **Astrology.**)

Eber Don : Chief of the Milesian invaders of Ireland. Many of their ships were lost in a storm which the Danaans (q.v.) raised by magic.

Eblis, or **Haris** as he is also called : the " Satan " of the Mohammedans. It is said that he was an inmate of Azazil, the heaven nearest God ; and when the angels were commanded to bow down to the first man, *Eblis* was the chief of those who rebelled. They were cast out of Azazil, and *Eblis* and his followers were sentenced to suffer in hell for a long time. It is supposed that he was composed of the elements of fire ; and that he succeeded the peris in the government of the world.

Ech-Uisque : A Gaelic word meaning water-horse. The *Ech-uisque* was a goblin of Highland folk-lore, understood to be a favourite form assumed by the Kelpie, in order to lure souls to his master the Devil. In the disguise of a fine steed, beautifully accoutred, the Kelpie grazed innocently by the wayside. The weary traveller, passing by, and believing this splendid animal to have strayed from his master, was tempted to make use of him to help him on his way ; and the deceitful Kelpie, remaining quiet as a lamb until the traveller was fairly mounted, would then with a fiendish yell of triumph plunge headlong into an adjacent pool. It was believed that the soul of the unfortunate man, who had had no time to prepare for death, would thus be safely secured to the Evil One ; while the Kelpie received the body in payment for his trouble.

Echo D'Outre Tombe (Journal) : (*See* **France.**)

Eckartshausen, K. Von : Author of *The Cloud on the Sanctuary* (1800). *Eckartshausen*, by birth and education an intensely religious man, at first wrote several little books of devotion that had great vogue in France and Germany. He later turned his attention to larger works of a more profound character, such as that mentioned above. According to *Eckartshausen* the requisite faculty of true communion with the church is the inward conception of things spiritual and with this sense present, is possible the beginning of Regeneration understood as the process of gradually eliminating original sin. His work on the Interior Church is in two parts : first, elucidation of his doctrine ; second, a series of dogmas or assertions derived therefrom.

Ectenic Force : A supposed physical force emanating from the person of the medium, and directed by his will, by means of which objects may be moved without contact in apparent defiance of natural laws. The existence of such a force was first postulated by Count Agenor de Gasparin, to explain the phenomena of table-turning and rapping, and the name *Ectenic Force* was bestowed upon the supposed agency by de Gasparin's colleague, M. Thury. The experiments of Thury and de Gasparin are declared to offer some of the most convincing evidence that spiritualism can produce, and have influenced more than one eminent student of psychic research. If it be true that tables were moved without contact, then such a theory is indeed necessary, but the evidence for this type of phenomena is not abundant.

Eddy, Mrs. Mary Baker : (*See* **New Thought.**)

Eden, Garden of : (*See* **Paradise.**)

Eel : The *eel* is credited with the possession of many marvellous virtues. If he is left to die out of the water, his body steeped in strong vinegar and the blood of a vulture, and the whole placed under a dunghill, the composition will raise from the dead anything brought to it, and will give it life as before. It is also said that he who eats the still warm heart of an *eel* will be seized with the spirit of prophecy, and will predict things to come. The Egyptians worshipped the *eel*, which their priests alone had the right to eat. Magic *eels* were made in the eighteenth century of flour and the juice of mutton. There may be added a little anecdote told by William of Malmesbury. A dean of the church of Elgin, in the county of Moray in Scotland, having refused to cede his church to some pious monks, was changed, with all his canons, into *eels*, which the brother cook made into a stew.

Egbo, The : or **Esik,** is a secret society of Calabar, near the Niger delta. The name means " tiger," and the society is divided into eleven grades, of which the first three are not open to slaves. Members, as a rule, buy themselves into the higher grades in their turn, and the money thus obtained is shared amongst the *Nyampa* who form the inner circle. The king is president of the society under the title of *Cyamba*. Each grade has its special festival day, on which their *Idem* or spirit-master exercises complete control. Whenever an *Egbo* day is announced, slaves, women, and children take flight in all directions, as the ambassador of the Idem, armed with a heavy whip, goes through the village and lashes everyone whom he may encounter. The Idem is usually a hermit who lives in the distant bush-land, and when he appears it is in a fantastic guise of mats and branches, which covers him from head to foot, and with a black mask on his face. The principals of the order themselves are linked together by a garb of leaves so gathered up that they seem to move in a connected mass.

" The Order of *Free Egbos*, (says Froebenius) is said to have originated at the fairs which were held at a great palm-oil market in the interior, midway between Calabar and the Kamerun. As the place became the scene of much disorder, while the European trade made it necessary for the maintenance of public credit that all engagements should be strictly carried out, this institution was formed as a sort of Hanseatic Union under the most influential traders, for the mutual safeguarding of their interests. Later it acquired the political character of a *Vehmgericht* or secret tribunal, by bringing within its sphere of action the whole police of the Calabars and the Kamerun. The kings always sought to secure for themselves the Grandmastership of the Order, since otherwise their authority would sink to a mere shadow. European skippers have frequently found it to their advantage to be enrolled in the lower grades, in order thereby the more easily to recover their debts. A member of the *Egbo* has the right to claim as his own property the slave of his debtor, wherever he may find him, merely by fastening a yellow strip to his dress or loincloth. Even in the interior of the continent the standing of an *Egbo* is still respected and feared, and affords one a certain immunity from molestation, such as is absolutely needed for the extensive commercial speculations in Africa.

"In the Kamerun, as a preliminary to their acceptance into the *Free Egbos*, the young men are sent for a protracted period to the Mokokos, a bush tribe in the interior ; with these they live naked in the fields, and only now and then dart out, clad in green leaves, to have a bath in the river. All women, and especially slaves, are prohibited, under heavy penalties, from approaching the forest where they reside. In the Kamerun, it is customary to pay particular honour to a visitor, above all if he be a European, by introducing the *Egbo* goat, which the people are otherwise seldom allowed to set eyes upon.

"Holman reports that the whole of the Old Calabar district is subject to the rule of the so-called *Egbo* laws. These are promulgated at a secret Council, the *Egbo* Assembly, which is held in the 'Palaver-house' erected for this special purpose. In virtue of his sovereign rights, the head-chief presides, under the title of *Cyamab*, over this assembly. Amongst the members of the *Egbo* there are different ranks, which must be acquired in their due order, one after the other. Holman quotes Englishmen who state that Europeans have bought themselves into the *Egbo*, and even into the Yampai, in order to be thus better able to get in their money. He gives the following as the names and prices of the different grades of *Egbo* :

1	Abungo	..	..	..	125 bars
2	Aboko	..	..	..	75 bars
3	Makairo	..	..	..	400 copper bars
4	Bakimboko	..	..	..	100 bars
5	Yampaiç	..	..	..	850 copper bars

"To these must be added rum, clothes, membo, etc. The Yampai is the only grade whose members are allowed to sit in Council. The sums paid for the various titles of the *Egbo* are distributed exclusively amongst the Yampai, who, however, are not limited to a single share, since every Yampai can multiply his title as often as he can purchase shares, and these give him a claim to the receipt of the corresponding quotas from the profits of the whole institution."

Egg, Orphean : The cosmic doctrine of the Greek sage Orpheus. He says : "God, the uncreated and incomprehensible Being, created all things ; the ether proceeded from him ; from this the unshapely chaos and the dark night arose, which at first covered all things. The unshapen mass was formed into the shape of an egg, from which all things have proceeded." The whole universe has the form of an egg, and everything in it strives to attain the same form. The Orphean theory has something in common with the doctrines of the magnetic philosophers.

Eglamour of Artoys, Sir : A magical English legend of French origin. The poem tells of the winning of Christabell by *Eglamour*. Christabell's father will agree to the union if *Eglamour* will fulfil three tasks. He must conquer the giant, Sir Maroke ; bring from a distant land the head of an enormous boar, and kill a powerful dragon which has been devastating the country round Rome. In these adventures he is successful, but is kept in Rome by illness. Meantime, Christabell has given birth to a son, and is banished by her angry father. Her son is stolen from her by a griffin, and taken to Israel, where he is adopted by the king and named Degrabell. Many years afterwards, *Sir Eglamour* and Degramour meet in a tournament for the hand of Christabell. The former is successful, and eventually their identities are revealed. *Eglamour* and Christabell are married, and return to their native country with their son.

Eglinton, William : A well known English medium, who in 1876 succeeded Slade as the principal exponent of slate-writing (q.v.) That *Eglinton's* performances in this direction were very skilfully carried out there is abundant evidence, for several practised conjurers, as well as many other investigators, were entirely at a loss to explain the *modus operandi*. Yet on one occasion, at least, *Eglinton* was seen—by Professor Lewis Cargill—to write the " spirit " messages himself. This was in 1886, when his slate-writing was attracting attention. Some ten years earlier, when he was giving materialisation séances, there were discovered in his portmanteau a false beard and some muslin draperies, which were found to correspond with fragments cut from the hair and garments of the materialised spirit. Nor were these the only occasions on which he made use of fraudulent means of producing mediumistic phenomena. It may be objected that *Eglinton* was " controlled " to procure draperies and fake hair, but it necessarily casts a dark shadow on his mediumship.

Egypt : To the peoples of antiquity as well as to those of the modern world, *Egypt* appeared as the very mother of magic. The reason for this widespread belief is not far to seek. In *Egypt* the peoples of the ancient world found a magical system much more highly developed than anything within their native knowledge, and again the cult of the dead with which Egyptian religion was so deeply imbued, appeared to the stranger to savour strongly of magical practice. It must be borne in mind that, if the matter of the magical papyri be omitted, the notices which we possess of Egyptian magic are almost wholly foreign, so that it is wiser for a proper understanding of Egyptian occultism to derive our facts concerning it from the original native sources as far as is possible. Like all other systems, the magic of the Egyptians was of two kinds, that which was supposed to benefit either the living or the dead, and that which has been known throughout the ages as " black " magic or necromancy.

The contents of the Westcar Papyrus show that as early as the fourth dynasty, the working of magic was a recognised art in *Egypt*, but in reality we must place the beginnings of Egyptian magical practice in neolithic times. Throughout the centuries magical practice varied considerably, but the principal means for its working remained the same. That is to say, the Egyptians relied for magical effect upon amulets, magical figures, pictures, and formulæ, magical names and ceremonies, and the general apparatus of the occult sciences.

The objects for which magic was exercised were numerous. It exorcised storms, protected against wild beasts, poison, disease, wounds, and the ghosts of the dead. One of the most potent methods of guarding against misfortune of any kind was the use of *Amulets*. It must not be assumed that all ornaments or objects discovered on the mummy are of magical potency. These are frequently the possession of the *Ka* or double (q.v.), necessary to its comfort in a future existence. The small crowns, sceptres, and emblems of Osiris, usually executed in *faience*, are placed beside the dead person in order that he may wear them when he becomes one with Osiris, and therefore a king. The scarab, fashioned in the likeness of a scarabæus beetle, symbolised resurrection. The *dad* symbolised the human skeleton, and, therefore, perhaps, the dead and dismembered Osiris. It has an influence on the restoration of the deceased. The *uza*, or eye, signifies the health necessary to the dead man's soul. The so-called " palettes " at one time supposed to have been employed for the mixing of paint, are now known to have been amulets inscribed with words of power placed on the breasts of the dead in neolithic times. The amulet of the *menat* was worn, or held, with the sistrum by gods, kings, and priests, and was supposed to bring joy and health to the wearer. It represented the vigour of the two sexes.

Spells.—The simplest type of spell in use in *Egypt*, was

that in which the exorcist threatens the evil principle, or assures it that he can injure it. Generally, however, the magician requests the assistance of the gods, or he may pretend to that which he desires to exorcise that he is a god. Invocations, when written, were usually accompanied by a note to the effect that the formula had once been employed successfully by a god—perhaps by a deified priest. An incomprehensible and mysterious jargon was employed, which was supposed to conceal the name of a certain deity who was thus compelled to do the will of the sorcerer. These gods were almost always those of foreign nations, and the invocations themselves appear to be attempts at various foreign idioms, employed, perhaps, as sounding more mysterious than the native speech. Great stress was laid upon the proper pronunciation of these names, and failure in all cases was held to lie at the door of mis-pronunciation. The *Book of the Dead* (q.v.) contains many such " words of power," and these were intended to assist the journey of the dead in the underworld of Amenti. It was believed that all supernatural beings, good and evil, possessed hidden names, which if a man knew, he could compel them to do his will. The name, indeed, was as much part of a man as his body or soul. The traveller through Amenti must tell not only the divine gods their names, but must prove that he knew the names of a number of the supposedly inanimate objects in the dreary Egyptian Hades, if he desired to make any progress. (*See* **Gnostics** and **Names Magical.**)

Magical Books.—Many magical books existed in *Egypt* which contained spells and other formulæ for exorcism and necromantic practice. Thus Medical Papyri in the Leipsic collection contain formulæ spoken whilst preparing drugs ; the Ebers Papyrus contains such spells ; the Harris Magical Papyrus, dating from the New Kingdom, and edited by Chabas, contains spells against crocodiles. The priestly caste, who compiled those necromantic works, was known as *Kerheb*, or " scribes of the divine writings," and even the sons of Pharaohs did not disdain to enter their ranks.

The Ritual of Egyptian Magic. In many instances the ritual of Egyptian magic possesses strong similarities to the ceremonial of other systems and countries. Wax figures were employed in lieu of the bodies of persons to be bewitched or harmed and models of all kinds were utilised in order that the physical force directed against them might react upon the persons or animals it was desired to injure. But the principal rite in which ceremonial magic was employed was the very elaborate one of mummification. As each bandage was laid in its exact position certain words of power were uttered which were supposed to be efficacious in the preservation of the part swathed. After evisceration, the priest uttered an invocation to the deceased, and then took a vase of liquid containing ten perfumes, with which he smeared the body twice from head to foot, taking especial care to anoint the head thoroughly. The internal organs were then placed on the body, and the backbone immersed in holy oil, supposed to be an emanation from the gods Shu and Seb. Certain precious stones were then laid on the mummy, each of which had its magical significance. Thus crystal lightened his face, and cornelian strengthened his steps. A priest who personified the jackal-headed god, Anubis, then advanced, performed certain symbolical ceremonies on the head of the mummy, and laid certain bandages upon it. After a further anointing with oil the deceased was declared to have " received his head." The mummy's left hand was filled with thirty-six substances used in embalming, symbolic of the thirty-six forms of the god Osiris. The body was then rubbed with holy oil, the toes wrapped in linen, and after an appropriate address the ceremony was completed.

Dreams. The art of procuring dreams and their interpretation was much practised in *Egypt*. As instances of dreams recorded in Egyptian texts may be quoted those of Thothmes IV. (B.C. 1450) and Nut-Amen, King of Egypt (B.C. 670). The Egyptian magician procured dreams for his clients by drawing magical pictures and the recitation of magical words. The following formulæ for producing a dream is taken from British Museum Papyrus, No. 122, lines 64 ff. and 359 ff.

" To obtain a vision from the god Bes : Make a drawing of Besa, as shewn below, on your left hand, and envelope your hand in a strip of black cloth that has been consecrated to Isis and lie down to sleep without speaking a word, even in answer to a question. Wind the remainder of the cloth round your neck. The ink with which you write must be composed of the blood of a cow, the blood of a white dove, fresh frankincense, myrrh, black writing ink, cinnabar, mulberry juice, rain-water, and the juice of wormwood and vetch. With this write your petition before the setting sun, saying, ' Send the truthful seer out of the holy shrine, I beseech thee, Lampsuer, Sumarta, Baribas, Dardalam, Iorlex : O Lord send the sacred deity Anuth, Anuth, Salbana, Chambré, Breith, now, now, quickly, quickly. Come in this very night.' "

" To procure dreams : Take a clean linen bag and write upon it the names given below. Fold it up and make it into a lamp-wick, and set it alight, pouring pure oil over it. The word to be written is this : ' Armiuth, Lailamchouch, Arsenophrephren, Phtha, Archentechtha.' Then in the evening, when you are going to bed, which you must do without touching food (*or*, pure from all defilement), do thus : Approach the lamp and repeat seven times the formula given below : then extinguish it and lie down to sleep. The formula is this : ' Sachmu . . . . epaema Ligotereench : the Aeon, the Thunderer, Thou that hast swallowed the snake and dost exhaust the moon, and dost raise up the orb of the sun in his season, Chthetho is the name ; I require, O lords of the gods, Seth, Chreps, give me the information that I desire.' "

Medical Magic. Magic played a great part in Egyptian medicine. On this point Weidemann says : " The Egyptians were not great physicians : their methods were purely empirical and their remedies of very doubtful value, but the riskiness of their practice arose chiefly from their utter inability to diagnose because of their ignorance of anatomy. That the popular respect for the human body was great we may gather from the fact that the Paraskhistai who opened the body for embalmment were persecuted and stoned as having committed a sinful although necessary deed. The prescribed operations in preparing a body for embalmment were never departed from, and taught but little anatomy, so that until Greek times the Egyptians had only the most imperfect and inaccurate ideas of the human organism. They understood nothing about most internal diseases, and especially nothing about diseases of the brain, never suspecting them to be the result of organic changes, but assuming them to be caused by demons who had entered into the sick. Under these circumstances medicines might be used to cause the disappearance of the symptoms, but the cure was the expulsion of the demon. Hence the Egyptian physician must also practise magic.

" According to late accounts, his functions were comparatively simple, for the human body had been divided into thirty-six parts, each presided over by a certain demon, and it sufficed to invoke the demon of the part affected in order to bring about its cure—a view of matters fundamentally Egyptian. In the Book of the Dead we find that different divinities were responsible for the well-being of the bodies of the blessed ; thus Nu had charge of the hair, Râ of the face, Hathor of the eyes, Apuat of the ears, Anubis of the lips, while Thoth was guardian of all parts of the body together. This doctrine was subsequently applied to the living body, with the difference that for the great gods named in the Book of the Dead there were substituted as gods of healing the presiding deities of the thirty-six decani, the thirty-six divisions of the Egyptian zodiac, as we learn from the names given to them by Celsus and preserved by Origen. In earlier times it was not so easy to be determined which god was to be invoked, for the selection depended not only on the part affected but also on the illness and symptoms and remedies to be used, etc.

"Several Egyptian medical papyri which have come down to us contain formulas to be spoken against the demons of disease as well as prescriptions for the remedies to be used in specified cases of illness. In papyri of older date these conjurations are comparatively rare, but the further the art of medicine advanced, or rather receded, the more numerous they became."

"It was not always enough to speak the formulas once ; even their repeated recitation might not be successful, and in that case recourse must be had to other expedients : secret passes were made, various rites were performed, the formulas were written upon papyrus, which the sick person had to swallow, etc., etc. But amulets were in general found to be most efficacious, and the personal intervention of a god called up, if necessary, by prayers or sorcery."

Magical Figures. As has been said the Egyptians believed that it was possible to transmit to the figure of any person or animal the soul of the being which it represented. In the Westcar Papyrus we read how a soldier who had fallen in love with a governor's wife was swallowed by a crocodile when bathing, the saurian being a magical replica of a waxen one made by the lady's husband. In the official account of a conspiracy against Rameses III. (ca B.C. 1200) the conspirators obtained access to a magical papyrus in the royal library and employed its instructions against the king with disastrous effects to themselves. These, too, made waxen figures of gods and of the king for the purpose of slaying the latter.

Astrology : The Egyptians were fatalists, and believed that a man's destiny was decided before he was born. The people therefore had recourse to astrologers. Says Budge : " In magical papyri we are often told not to perform certain magical ceremonies on such and such days, the idea being that on these days hostile powers will make them to be powerless, and that gods mightier than those to which the petitioner would appeal will be in the ascendant. There have come down to us fortunately, papyri containing copies of the Egyptian calendar, in which each third of every day for three hundred and sixty days of the year is marked lucky or unlucky, and we know from other papyri *why* certain days were lucky or unlucky, and why others were only partly so." " From the life of Alexander the Great by Pseudo-Callisthenes we learn that the Egyptians were skilled in the art of casting nativities, and that knowing the exact moment of the birth of a man they proceeded to construct his horoscope. Nectanebus employed for the purpose a tablet made of gold and silver and acacia wood, to which were fitted three belts. Upon the outer belt was Zeus with the thirty-six *decani* surrounding him ; upon the second the twelve signs of the Zodiac were represented ; and upon the third the sun and moon. He set the tablet upon a tripod, and then emptied out of a small box upon it models of the seven stars that were in the belts, and put into the middle belt eight precious stones ; these he arranged in the places wherein he supposed the planets which they represented would be at the time of the birth

of Olympias, and then told her fortune from them. But the use of the horoscope is much older than the time of Alexander the Great, for to a Greek horoscope in the British Museum is attached ' an introductory letter from some master of the art of astrology to his pupil, named Hermon, urging him to be very exact and careful in his application of the laws which the ancient Egyptians, with their laborious devotion to the art, had discovered and handed down to posterity.' Thus we have good reason for assigning the birthplace of the horoscope to Egypt. In connection with the horoscope must be mentioned the " sphere " or " table " of Democritus as a means of making predictions as to life and death. In a magical papyrus we are told to ' ascertain in what month the sick man took to his bed, and the name he received at his birth. Calculate the course of the moon, and see how many periods of thirty days have elapsed ; then note in the table the number of days left over, and if the number comes in the upper part of the table, he will live, but if in the lower part he will die.' "

Ghosts. The conception that the *ka* or double of man wandered about after death, greatly assisted the Egyptian belief in ghosts.

"According to them a man consisted of a physical body, a shadow, a double, a soul, a heart, a spirit called the *khu*, a power, a name, and a spiritual body. When the body died the shadow departed from it, and could only be brought back to it by the performance of a mystical ceremony ; the double lived in the tomb with the body, and was there visited by the soul whose habitation was in heaven. The soul was, from one aspect, a material thing, and like the *ka*, or double, was believed to partake of the funeral offerings which were brought to the tomb ; one of the chief objects of sepulchral offerings of meat and drink was to keep the double in the tomb and to do away with the necessity of its wandering about outside the tomb in search of food. It is clear from many texts that, unless the double was supplied with sufficient food, it would wander forth from the tomb and eat any kind of offal and drink any kind of dirty water which it might find in its path. But besides the shadow, and the double, and the soul, the spirit of the deceased, which usually had its abode in heaven, was sometimes to be found in the tomb. There is, however, good reason for stating that the immortal part of man which lived in the tomb and had its special abode in the statue of the deceased was the ' double.' This is proved by the fact that a special part of the tomb was reserved for the *ka*, or double, which was called the ' house of the *ka*,' and that a priest, called the ' priest of the *ka*,' was specially appointed to minister therein."

Esoteric Knowledge of the Priesthood. The esoteric knowledge of the Egyptian priesthood is now believed to have been of the description with which the Indian medicine man is credited plus a philosophy akin to that of ancient India. Says Davenport Adams :

"To impose upon the common people, the priesthood professed to lead lives of peculiar sanctity. They despised the outer senses, as sources of evil and temptation. They kept themselves apart from the *profanium vulgus*, ' and,' says Iamblicus, ' occupied themselves only with the knowledge of God, of themselves, and of wisdom ; they desired no vain honours in their sacred practice, and never yielded to the influence of the imagination.' Therefore they formed a world within a world, fenced round by a singular awe and wonder, apparently abstracted from the things of earth, and devoted to the constant contemplation of divine mysteries. They admitted few strangers into their order, and wrapt up their doctrines in a hieroglyphical language, which was only intelligible to the initiated. To these various precautions was added the solemnity of a terrible oath, whose breach was invariably punished with death."

"The Egyptian priests preserved the remaining relics of the former wisdom of nature. These were not imparted as the sciences are, in our age, but to all appearances they were neither learned nor taught; but as a reflection of the old revelations of nature, the perception must arise like an inspiration in the scholar's mind. From this cause appear to have arisen those numerous preparations and purifications the severity of which deterred many from initiation into the Egyptian priesthood; in fact, not infrequently resulted in the scholar's death. Long fasting, and the greatest abstinence, appear to have been particularly necessary: besides this, the body was rendered insensible through great exertions, and even through voluntarily inflicted pain, and therefore open to the influence of the mind. The imagination was excited by representations of the mysteries; and the inner sense was more impressed by the whole than—as is the case with us—instructed by an explanation of simple facts. In this manner the dead body of science was not given over to the initiated, and left to chance whether it would become animated or not, but the living soul of wisdom was breathed into them.

"From this fact, that the contents of the mysteries were rather revealed than taught—were received more from inward inspiration and mental intoxication, than outwardly through endless teaching, it was necessary to conceal them from the mass of the people.

So says Schubert, dealing with the same subject: "The way to every innovation was closed, and outward knowledge and science could certainly not rise to a high degree of external perfection; but that rude sensuality, inclination for change and variety, was suppressed as the chief source of all bodily and spiritual vices, is clear, as well as that here, as in India, an ascetic and contemplative life was recommended.

"They imparted their secret and divine sciences to no one who did not belong to their caste, and it was long impossible for foreigners to learn anything; it was only in later times that a few strangers were permitted to enter the initiation after many severe preparations and trials. Besides this, their functions were hereditary, and the son followed the footsteps of his father."

"Concerning that which passed within the temples, and of the manner in which the sick were treated, we have but fragmentary accounts; for to the uninitiated the entrance was forbidden, and the initiated kept their vows. Even the Greeks, who were admitted to the temples, have been silent concerning the secrets, and have only here and there betrayed portions. Jablonski says, ' that but few chosen priests were admitted into the sanctum, and that admission was scarcely ever permitted to strangers even under the severest regulations.'"

Dealing with the subject of hypnotism in *Egypt*, Montfauçon says: "Magnetism was daily practised in the temples of Isis, of Osiris, and Serapis. In these temples the priests treated the sick and cured them, either by magnetic manipulation, or by other means producing somnambulism." Presenting a painting of a mesmeric scene, he says: "Before a bed or table, on which lie the sick, stands a person in a brown garment, and with open eyes, and the dog's head of Anubis. His countenance is turned towards the sick person; his left hand is placed on the breast, and the right is raised over the head of his patient, quite in the position of a magnetiser.

Egyptian Masonry : (*See* **Cagliostro**.)

El Buen Sentido : (*See* **Spain**.)

El Criterio : (*See* **Spain**.)

El Havarevna : (*See* **Rosicrucians**.)

Elbegast : A dwarf mentioned in the medieval semi-traditional saga-cycle *Dietrich of Bern*. He is friendly towards Dietrich and helps him in his search for the giant Grimm.

Elder : As an Amulet. Blockwick recommends as a charm against erysipelas an " *elder* on which the sun never shined." " If the piece betwixt the two knots be hung about the patient's neck, it is much commended. Some cut it in little pieces, and sew it in a knot, in a piece of a man's shirt, which seems superstitious."

Elder Tree : The *elder* had wonderful influence as a protection against evil. Wherever it grew, witches were powerless. In this country, gardens were protected by having *elder trees* planted at the entrance, and sometimes hedges of this plant were trained round the garden. There are very few old gardens in country places in which are not still seen remains of the protecting *elder tree.* " In my boyhood " says Napier, " I remember that my brothers, sisters, and myself were warned against breaking a twig or branch from the *elder* hedge which surrounded my grandfather's garden. We were told at the time as a reason for this prohibition, that it was poisonous; but we discovered afterwards that there was another reason, viz., that it was unlucky to break off even a small twig from a bourtree bush." In some parts of the Continent this superstition feeling is so strong that, before pruning it, the gardener says: " *Elder, elder, may I cut thy branches ?* " If no response be heard, it is considered that assent has been given and then, after spitting three times, the pruner begins his cutting. According to Montanus, *elder* wood formed a portion of the fuel used in the burning of human bodies as a protection against evil influences; and, the drivers of hearses had their whip handles made of *elder* wood for a similar reason. In some parts of Scotland, people would not put a piece of *elder* wood into the fire, and Napier says " Pieces of this wood lying about unused when the neighbourhood was in great straits for firewood; but none would use it, and when asked why ? the answer was : " We don't know, but folks say it is not lucky to burn the bourtree." It was believed that children laid in a cradle made wholly or in part of elderwood, would not sleep well, and were in danger of falling out of the cradle. *Elder* berries gathered on St. John's Eve, would prevent the possessor suffering from witchcraft, and often bestowed upon him magical powers. If the *elder* were planted in the form of a cross upon a new-made grave, and if it bloomed, it was a sure sign that the soul of the dead person was happy.

Eleazar : A Jewish magician who had much success as an exorcist. His method was to fasten to the nose of the possessed a ring in which was set a root used by Solomon, and very efficacious.

Eleazar of Garniza : A Hebrew author who has left many works, of which several have been printed. Among his books was a *Treatise on the Soul*, and a *Kabalistic Commentary on the Pentateuch.*

Electric Girls : Girls in whose presence certain phenomena occurred, similar in nature to the time-honoured phenomena of the poltergeist (q.v.), but ascribed to the action of some new physical force, probably electricity. The best known of these *electric girls* was perhaps Angelique Cottin, a Normandy peasant girl, whose phenomena were first observed about 1846. Finally she was taken to Paris and placed under the observation of Dr. Tanchon and others, who testified to the actuality of the phenomena. These included the movement of objects without contact, or at a mere touch from Angelique's petticoats, the agitation in her presence of the magnetic needle, and the blowing of a cold wind. She was also able to distinguish between the poles of a magnet at a touch. A commission appointed by the Academy of Sciences, however, could observe nothing but the violent movements of her chair, which were probably caused by muscular force. Other *electric girls* practised about the same time, and even after the beginning of the spiritualistic movement in America they were occasionally heard of. They are worthy of note as a link between the poltergeist and the spiritualistic medium.

Electrobiology : A mode of producing hypnotism by looking steadily at metallic discs. The process was discovered about the middle of last century, and its fame spread by numerous lecturers in England and America.

Electrum : Amber is the subject of some curious legends under this name, but there is also a metallic *electrum*, known to the French in modern times as Orbas. A cup of this metal, according to Pliny, has the property of discovering poison, by exhibiting certain semi-circles like rainbows in the liquor, which it also keeps sparkling and hissing as if on the fire. A black species of *electrum* or amber is the proper *gargates* of Pliny, and the jet of the present day. The occult virtues of *electrum* are of the tell-tale character.

Elementary Spirits : The unseen intelligences who inhabit the four elements, of the finest essence of which they are composed. The creatures of the air are called sylphs ; of the earth gnomes ; of fire salamanders ; and of water, nymphs or undines. The best authority on the subject is the Abbé de Villars, who published early in the eighteenth century a short treatise entitled *Comte de Gabalis*, from which a good deal of what follows is drawn. According to this work the creatures of the elements were before the Fall subject to Adam in all things, and we are led to understand that by means of certain performances this ancient communication may be restored, and that man may once more have at his beck and call the *elementary spirits*. The Abbé gives a brief sketch of the nature of these peoples. The air, he says, is filled with a great number of beings of human form, somewhat fierce in appearance, but really of a docile nature. They are much interested in the sciences, and are subtle, officious towards the sages, hostile towards the foolish and the ignorant. Their wives and daughters are of a masculine type of beauty, such as is depicted in the Amazons. The seas and rivers are inhabited as well as the air, beings dwelling therein whom the sages designated undines, or nymphs. The female population much exceeds the male, the women being exceedingly beautiful, so that among the daughters of men there is none to equal them. The earth is filled almost to the centre with gnomes, people of small stature, the guardians of subterranean treasure, minerals and precious stones. They are ingenious, friendly towards men, and easy to command. They provide the children of the sages with all the money they require, asking no other reward for their services than the glory of performing them. The gnomides, their wives, are small of stature but very good-looking, and they dress very curiously. As for the salamanders, the inhabitants of the region of fire, they serve the philosophers, but are not over-anxious for their company, while their daughters and wives are rarely seen. Their women are very beautiful, beyond all the other elementals, since they dwell in a purer element. Their habits, mode of life, manners and laws are admirable, and the attractions of their minds are greater even than that of their persons. The Supreme Being they know and religiously adore, but have no hope of eternal enjoyment of Him, since their souls are mortal. True it is that, being composed of the purest parts of the elements wherein they dwell, and having no contrary qualities, they can live for several centuries ; yet are they much troubled because of their mortal nature. It was, however, revealed to the philosophers that an *elementary spirit* could attain to immortality by being united in marriage with a human being. The children born of such unions are more noble and heroic than the children of human men and women, and some

of the greatest figures of antiquity—Zoroaster, Alexander, Hercules, Merlin, to mention a few—are declared to have been the children of *elementary spirits*.

The salamanders, the Comte de Gabalis goes on to say, are composed of the most subtle particles of the sphere of fire, conglobated and organised by the action of the Universal Fire, so called because it is the principle of all the motions of nature. The sylphs are composed of the purest atoms of the air ; the nymphs, of the most delicate particles of water ; and the gnomes, of the finest essence of earth. Adam was in complete accord with these creatures because, being composed of that which was purest in the four elements, he contained in himself the perfections of these four peoples, and was their natural king. But since by reason of his sin he had been cast into the excrements of the elements, there no longer existed the harmony between him, so impure and gross, and these fine and ethereal substances. The Abbé then gives a recipe whereby the resultant state of things may be remedied and the ancient correspondence restored. To attain this end we must purify and exalt the element of fire which is within us. All that is necessary is to concentrate the fire of the world by means of concave mirrors, in a globe of glass. There will then be formed within the globe a solary powder, which, having purified itself from the admixture of other elements, becomes in a very short time a sovereign means of exalting the fire which is in us, and makes us, so to speak, of an igneous nature. Thenceforward these creatures of the fire become our inferiors, and, delighted at the restoration of mutual harmony between themselves and the human race, they will show towards man all the good-will they have for their own kind. Sylphs, gnomes, and nymphs are more familiar with man than are the salamanders, on account of their shorter term of life, and it is therefore easier to get into touch with them. To accomplish the restoration of our empire over the sylphs, gnomes, or nymphs, we must close a glass full of air, earth, or water, and expose it to the sun for a month, at the end of which period its various elements must be separated according to science. This process is most easy in the case of water and earth. "Thus," says the Comte, "without characters, without ceremonies, without barbarous words, it is possible to rule absolutely over these peoples." Other authorities prescribe other means of obtaining dominion over the spirits of the elements. Eliphas Levi, for instance, states that anyone desirous of subjugating the elementals must first perform the four trials of antique initiation ; but as the original trials are no longer known similar ones must be substituted. Thus he who would control the sylphs must walk fearlessly on the edge of a precipice, he who would win the service of the salamanders must take his stand in a burning building, and so on, the point of the ordeals being that the man should show himself unafraid of the elements whose inhabitants he desires to rule. In mediæval times the evocation and exorcism of *elementary spirits* was much practised, the crystal being a favourite means of evoking them. The exorcism of earth is performed by means of breathing, sprinkling of water, and burning of incense, and the repetition of a formula of prayer to the gnomes. Air is exorcised by breathing towards the four cardinal points, and by the recital of prayers to the air-spirits (sylphs). The casting of salt, incense, sulphur, camphor, and white resin into a fire is declared efficacious in the exorcism of that element. In the case of water, breathing and laying on of hands, repetition of formulæ, mixing of salt and ashes of incense, and other ceremonials are to be observed. In every instance a special consecration of the four elements is a primary and essential part of the proceedings.

As has been said, it is possible for a human being to

confer immortality on an *elementary spirit* by the ceremony of marriage. But this does not always occur ; sometimes the reverse is the case, and the elementals share their mortality with their human mate. In literature, at all events, countless stories relate how men have risked and lost their immortality by marrying a sylph or an undine. According to the Comte de Gabalis, however, it would seem to be a matter of choice whether a man confers his immortality on his ethereal partner, or whether he partakes of her mortal nature ; for it is therein suggested that those who have not been predestined to eternal happiness would do well to marry with an elemental, and spare themselves an eternity of woe.

Not every authority has painted so attractive a picture of the creatures of the elements as has the Abbé de Villars. By some it is believed that there are numberless degrees among these beings, the highest resembling the lowest angels, while the lowest may often be mistaken for demons, which, of course, they are not. Not only do multitudinous variations of form and disposition characterise the elementals of our own planet ; the other planets and the stars are the abode of countless hosts of *elementary spirits*, differing from those of our own world perhaps more than the latter differ from one another. All the forms of beasts, insects, and reptiles may be taken by the lower elementals, as well as strange combinations of the shapes of different animals. The inhabitants of each element have their peculiar virtues and vices which serve to distinguish them. The sylphs are capricious and inconstant, but agile and active ; the undines, jealous and cold, but observant ; the salamanders, hot and hasty, but energetic and strong ; and the gnomes, greedy of gold and treasures, but nevertheless hard-working, good-tempered and patient. One who would seek dominion over any of these must practise their virtues ; but carefully avoid their faults, thus conquering them, as it were, on their own ground. Each species can only dwell in its own proper element. Thus a sylph may not invade the sphere of a salamander, or *vice versa*, while both would be decidedly out of their element in the regions of the nymphs or the gnomes. Four rulers have been set over the four species—Gob, ruler of the gnomes ; Paralda, of the sylphs ; Djin, of the salamanders ; and Necksa, of the nymphs. To the dwellers in each element is assigned a point of the compass, where lies their special kingdom. To the gnomes is given the north ; to the salamanders, the south ; to the sylphs, the east ; and to the undines, the west. The gnomes influence those of a melancholic disposition, because they dwell in the gloom of subterranean caverns. The salamanders have an effect on those of sanguine temperament, because their home is in the fire. The influence of the undines is upon the phlegmatic, and of the sylphs upon those of a bilious temperament. Though as a rule they are invisible to human eyes, they may on occasion become visible to those who invoke them, to the sages and philosophers, or even to the multitude. In the reign of king Pepin, Zedekias suggested to the sylphs that they should appear to men, whereupon the air was seen to be full of them, sometimes ranged in battle, or in an aerial navy. It was said by the people that they were sorcerers—an opinion to which Charlemagne and Louis the Debonnair subscribed, the latter at least imposing heavy penalties on the supposed sorcerers. So that they might behold their admirable institutions, certain men were raised up in the air, and while descending were seen by their fellowmen on earth. The latter regarded them as stragglers of the aerial army of sorcerers, and thought that they had come to poison the fruits and fountains. These unfortunate persons were thereupon put to death, along with many others suspected of connection with the sorcerers.

To return to the consideration of the nature of these spirits, we find them collated in the *Comte de Gabalis* with the oracles of antiquity, and even with the classic pantheons of Greece and Rome. Pan, for example, was the first and oldest of the nymphs, and the news of his death, communicated by the people of the air to the inhabitants of the waters, was proclaimed by them in a voice that was heard sounding over all the rivers of Italy—" The great Pan is dead ! " Mr. A. E. Waite considers that the " angels" evoked in mediæval magic, as well as the " devils " of the Sabbath, were higher or lower elementals. Others may see in the brownies and domestic spirits of folk-lore some resemblance to the subjugated *elementary spirit*. Even the familiar poltergeist, where he does not clearly establish his identity as the spirit of a deceased person, may be regarded with propriety as an elemental. The Theosophists use the word " elemental " in a different sense, to denote the " astral remains " (*See* **Shell**) of one who has lived an evil life on earth, and who is loath to leave the scene of his pleasures. With some occultists, again, " elemental " really signifies a sub-human being, probably identical with an *elementary spirit*, but of a mental and moral status considerably lower than that of a human being.

M. J.

Eleusis, Mysteries of : (*See* **Mysteries.**)

Elf Arrows : The superstitious name given to triangular flints, *Belemnites*, which are found in many countries, but notably in Scotland. It was believed that these stones were arrows shot by the elves, which prove fatal to cattle, —the cure being to touch them with the arrow with which they have been hit, and give them to drink of water in which the arrow has been dipped. It is even on record that an Irish bishop was thus shot at by an evil spirit ; and it is said that they are manufactured by the Devil with the help of attendant imps who roughhew them, while the Archfiend finishes the work. Cases are on record where they have been known to be made and used by the witches of Scotland within historic times. Similar superstitions regarding these remnants of the stone age prevail in Italy, Africa, and Turkey.

Elf-Fire : The *Ignis fatuus*, or " foolish fire." This is the name given to fire obtained by rubbing two pieces of wood together, and which is used in superstitious ways. Amongst the Russian peasantry it is believed that these wandering lights are the souls of still-born children, who do not desire to lure people from the path, but who get no rest until they find their bodies.

Elixir of Life : No doubt exists that the mediæval alchemists and mystics believed that they were perfectly justified in their search for the *Elixir of Life*, the universal medicine, and the renewal of youth. This, with the quest for gold, became the grand aim of alchemy, and although this search may have had a psychical and mystical side, it most certainly had a physical one. But there does not seem to have been any standard method of accomplishing the manufacture of the *elixir*. Thus in *Petit Albert* one is instructed to take 8lbs. of sugar of mercury as the foundation of such a mixture ; while Bernard Trévisan believes that the precipitation of the philosopher's stone into mercurial water results in the manufacture of the *elixir*. This he states, will when elaborated to the Red, transmute copper and other metals into pure gold, and if elaborated to the White, will produce unalloyed silver.

But the application of the *elixir* to the prolongation of life was undoubtedly the chief reason for its continued search. The retired alchemist in his later years, wearied with his quest for gold, craved the boon of youth and desired renewed health and strength to assist him to carry out his great purpose. As an illustration of the alchemical conception of the *elixir of life*, we quote the following from a work dealing with the secret of rejuvenescence, originally supposed to have been written by Arnold de Villanova, and published by Longueville-Harcourt at Paris in 1716 :—

" To renew youth is to enter once more into that felicitous season which imparts to the human frame the pleasures and strength of the morning. Here it is to no purpose that we should speak of that problem so much discussed by the Wise, whether the art can be carried to such a pitch of excellence that old age should itself be made young. We know that Paracelsus has vaunted the metamorphic resources of his Mercury of Life which not merely rejuvenates men but converts metals into gold ; He who promised unto others the years of the sybils, or at least the 300 winters of Nestor, himself perished at the age of thirty-seven. Let us turn rather to Nature, so admirable in her achievements, and deem her not capable alone of destroying what she has produced at the moment she has begotten them. Is it possible that she will refuse unto man, for whom all was created, what she accords to the stags, the eagles, and the serpents, who do annually cast aside the mournful concomitants of senility, and do assume the most brilliant, the most gracious amenities of the most joyous youth ? Art, it is true, has not as yet arrived at that apex of perfection wherefrom it can renew our youth ; but that which was unachieved in the past may be accomplished in the future, a prodigy which may be more confidently expected from the fact that in isolated cases it has actually already taken place, as the facts of history make evident. By observing and following the manner in which nature performs such wonders, we may assuredly hope to execute this desirable transformation, and the first condition is an amiable temperament, such as that which was possessed by Moses, of whom it is written that for one hundred and twenty years his sight never failed him.

" The stag, eagle, and sparrow-hawk renew their youth. Aldrovandus has written on the rejuvenescence of the eagle. Among the birds of the air, we are told by Pliny that the raven and the phœnix live, each of them six hundred years. No one denies that the stag is renewed by feeding on vipers and serpents, while the apes of Caucasus, whose diet is pepper, prove a sovereign remedy for the lion, who grows young by devouring their flesh. Those who have written of the elephant maintain that his normal life is extended through three centuries, while the horse, which alone in creation participates in the natures of man, of the lion, of the ox, the sheep, the mule, the stag, the wolf, the fox, the serpent, and the hare, from each deriving three of its qualities, has occasionally survived with undiminished vigour the lapse of a hundred years. The serpent, who is instrumental in the rejuvenescence of the stag, himself renews his youth at the shedding of his scales, from all which considerations, it follows that it is not beyond belief that a like prodigy may be found in the superior order of the same productions whence man has been himself derived, for man is assuredly not in a worse condition than the beasts whom he rules."

Trithemius (q.v.) on his death-bed dictated a receipt which he said would preserve mind, health and memory with perfect sight and hearing, for those who made use of it. It consists of among other things, calomel, gentian, cinnamon, aniseed, nard, coral, tartar, mace, and five grammes of it were to be taken night and morning in wine or brodium during the whole of the first month ; during the second month, in the morning only ; during the third month thrice in the week, and so continuing through life. This is a more understandable receipt than that of Eugenius Philalethes, who says : " Ten parts of cœlestiall

slime ; separate the male from the female, and each afterwards from its own earth, physically, mark you, and with no violence. Conjoin after separation in due, harmonic vitall proportion ; and straightway, the Soul descending from the pyroplastic sphere, shall restore, by a mirific embrace, its dead and deserted body. Proceed according to the Volcanico magica theory, till they are exalted into the Fifth Metaphysical Rota. This is that world-renowned medicine, whereof so many have scribbled, which, notwithstanding, so few have known."

In his *History of Magic* Eliphas Levi gives Cagliostro's great secret of rejuvenescence in the following terms :

" Let us now turn to the secret of physical regeneration to attain which——according to the occult prescription of the Grand Copht—a retreat of forty days, after the manner of a jubilee, must be made once in every fifty years, beginning during the full moon of May in the company of one faithful person only. It must be also a fast of forty days, drinking May-dew—collected from sprouting corn with a cloth of pure white linen—and eating new and tender herbs. The repast should begin with a large glass of dew and end with a biscuit or crust of bread. There should be slight bleeding on the seventeenth day. Balm of Azoth should then be taken morning and evening, beginning with a dose of six drops and increasing by two drops daily till the end of the thirty-second day. At the dawn which follows thereafter renew the slight bleeding ; then take to your bed and remain in it till the end of the fortieth day.

" On the first awakening after the bleeding, take the first grain of Universal Medicine. A swoon of three hours will be followed by convulsions, sweats and much purging, necessitating a change both of bed and linen. At this stage a broth of lean beef must be taken, seasoned with rice, sage, valerian, vervain and balm. On the day following take the second grain of Universal Medicine, which is Astral Mercury combined with Sulphur of Gold. On the next day have a warm bath. On the thirty-sixth day drink a glass of Egyptian wine, and on the thirty-seventh take the third and last grain of Universal Medicine. A profound sleep will follow, during which the hair, teeth, nails and skin will be renewed. The prescription for the thirty-eighth day is another warm bath, steeping aromatic herbs in the water, of the same kind as those specified for the broth. On the thirty-ninth day drink ten drops of Elixir of Acharat in two spoonsful of red wine. The work will be finished on the fortieth day, and the aged man will be renewed in youth.

" By means of this jubilary regimen, Cagliostro claimed to have lived for many centuries. It will be seen that it is a variation of the famous Bath of Immortality in use among the Menandrian Gnostics."

Aristeus is stated to have left to his disciples a secret which rendered all metals diaphanous, and man immortal. The process would appear to consist in a mystic treatment of the atmosphere, which is to be congealed and distilled until it develops the divine sparkle, and subsequently becomes liquified. It is then subjected to heat and undergoes several other processes, when the elixir emerges.

There is surprisingly little literature upon the subject of the *Elixir of Life*. But a more prolonged notice on the subject will be found under the article " Philosopher's stone " (q.v.).

Ellide : The dragon-shaped ship of Frithjof, the hero of an Icelandic legend. It was said to be golden-headed, with open jaws, its under part scaled with blue and gold, its tail twisted and of silver, its sails red-bordered and black. When its wings were outspread, it could skim the calmest seas. This ship had been given to one of Frithjof's forefathers as a reward for kindness by Aegir, the sea-god.

Elliot : (*See* **Spiritualism.**)

Elliotism : (*See* **Hypnotism.**)

Eloge de l'Enfer : A critical, historical, and moral work, an edition of which was published at The Hague in 1759. It is very satirical, very heavy, and somewhat lacking in wit.

Elongation : The phenomenon of *elongation* is a fairly common one at spiritualistic séances. It may be described as a stretching out of the medium's body, till his height is increased by from three inches to nearly a foot. The feat is ascribed to spirit agencies. There are accounts by witnesses of standing in the social and scientific world of *elongations* of Herne, Home, Morse, and other well-known mediums. These manifestations usually made their appearance only when the light was low, but there were several exceptions. In describing an *elongation* of Home, Lord Lindsay says : " Home looked as if he was pulled up by the neck, the muscles seemed in a state of tension. He stood firmly upright in the middle of the room, and before the *elongation* commenced I placed my foot on his instep." The same witness also declares that the increase in Home's height on this occasion was eleven inches. Most accounts describe a violent swaying motion on the part of the medium as preceding the *elongation*, which some critics have regarded as a convenient mode of covering the use of mechanism, which might be concealed in the medium's boots.

Elymas, the Sorcerer : A magician of Paphos, in Cyprus, who openly defied the apostle Paul before the Roman governor. The latter, who did not know whether to credit Paul or *Elymas*, summoned them both before him, when the apostle suffered the indignity referred to. " Oh, full of all subtlety and mischief," said Paul, in righteous anger, " child of the devil, enemy of all righteousness, wilt thou not cease to pervert the right ways of the Lord ? And, now, behold, the hand of the Lord is upon thee, and thou shalt be blind, not seeing the sun for a season." It is not related in what manner *Elymas* exercised his talents, or what were the characteristics of his sorceries, but we are told that the sentence of Paul immediately took effect, and " there fell on him a mist and a darkness ; and he went about, seeking some to lead him by the hand."

Emanations : Variously defined as subtle fluid, astral influence, psychic force, physical effluence, magnetism, radiations and vibrations. They are said to proceed from and surround all bodies and objects in nature, and when brought into contact through this medium, influencing and re-acting on each other, the result being either interpenetration or repulsion. The attractive properties of the magnet were known to the ancients, some authorities claiming that it was used in their religious rites and mysteries, in Egypt, Greece and Rome. They adduced as evidence the iron rings and wings used in the Samothracian mysteries, the iron wings worn by the priests of Jupiter to increase their magical power, and in the various symbols ascribed to the pagan gods. It is said too that meteoric stones, because of their supposed radiation of force, were also made use of in the religious rites, either being worshipped, or employed for purposes of divination and soothsaying. Small ones were worn by the priests and Pliny tells of the temple of Arsinoe which was vaulted with magnetic stone in order to receive a hovering statue of its patron. Cedrenus gives an account of an ancient image in the Serapium at Alexandria being suspended by magnetic force.

The most ancient writing extant in which this theory of *emanations* may be traced is ascribed to Timæus of Locris in which he ascribes the creation of the universe to the divine *emanations* of God, an imparting of His being to unformed matter. By this union a world-soul was created which vitalises and regulates all things. Claudian in his *Idyl of the Magnet* uses it as a symbol of the informative spirit of things, the laws of nature, creative and existent.

The mysticism of the seventeenth and eighteenth centuries mainly depends on these ideas of radiations emanating from all things but especially the stars, magnets and human beings, of a force which would act on all things and was controlled by the indwelling spirit. The writings of Paracelsus abound with instances of the theory. He asserts that every substance in itself contains something of the nature of the loadstone ; that the astral light, which is one of the finer media of nature, finer than the luminiferous ether, exists throughout planetary space especially around the brain and spinal cords of human beings ; (*See* article **Aura**) that we are all but organised magnets having each our poles which attract and repel ; that our thoughts are magnetic *emanations* escaping from our brains. His theory of the universe was that it emanated from a great first Being and there was a reciprocity in all things. In man too there exists an astral quality, emanating from the stars, which, whether physical or not, when compared with the physical body may be considered a spirit. This life stands in connexion with the stars from which it sprang and draws to it their power like a magnet. He calls this Sidereal life the magnes microcosmi and makes use of it to explain the manifestations of nature—it glows in the flower, glides in the stream, moves in the ocean and shines in the sky. Van Helmont speaks of an ethereal spirit, pure and living, which pervades all things. Robert Fludd explained sympathy and antipathy by the action of the emanatory spheres surrounding man—in sympathy the *emanations* proceeding from the centre, in antipathy the opposite movement taking place. He maintained that these sensitive *emanations* are to be found also amongst animals and plants, drawing an argument from the fact that if dead and inert substances, such as the earth and magnet seem to be, should have their *emanations* and their poles, their living forms must needs have them likewise. In the writings of Maxwell, a Scotch physician, is to be found the statement : " There is a linking together of spirits, an incessant outpouring of the rays of our body into another." Athanasius Kircher elaborated the theory deriving all natural phenomena from the action of magnetic radiation ; the arts and sciences being also *emanations*. Wirdig, Bartholin and many more pursued and developed their philosophical investigations along these lines.

Descartes asserted that all space is filled with a fluid matter which he held to be elementary, the foundation and fountain of all life, enclosing all globes and keeping them in motion. In Newton's doctrine of attraction, which he called the Divine Sensorium, the idea of emanation and magnetism is found. The following quotation is from his *Fundamental Principles of Natural Philosophy* : " Here the question is of a very subtle spirit which penetrates through all, even the hardest bodies and which is concealed in their substance. Through the strength and activity of this spirit, bodies attract each other and adhere together when brought into contact. Through it electrical bodies operate at the remotest distances as well as near at hand, attracting and repelling ; through this spirit the light also flows and is refracted and reflected and warms bodies." Mesmer enunciated the following propositions : " Between the heavenly bodies, the earth and human beings, there exists a mutual or interchangeable influence. The medium of this influence is an universally distributed fluid which suffers no vacuum, is of a rarity with which nothing can compare and has the property of receiving and transmitting all impressions of movement. Animal bodies experience the mutual effect of this agent, because it penetrates the nerves and affects them directly. In the human body particularly are observed properties analagous to those of the magnet. It is shown by experiment that a matter flows out so fine that it penetrates all bodies without apparently losing any of its activity. This may be communicated to other bodies, animate or inanimate, such as mirrors ; it is communicated, propagated, augmented by sound. Its virtues may be accumulated, concentrated and transported." On this theory he based his famous " Animal Magnetism " (q.v.) and its practice for the cure of disease, in fact all human ailments. Baron von Reichenbach, a man of scientific attainments, a chemist and metallurgist of some repute, conducted a series of experiments to investigate this theory. He procured the aid of a large number of sensitives, clairvoyants and mediums. These persons he placed in dark rooms, and then submitted to their spiritual sight magnets, shells, crystals, minerals, animals, human hands and a great variety of animate and inanimate objects, known only to himself but detected by the sensitives through the luminous *emanations* given forth by each substance. These *emanations* or flames differed in colour, size and intensity according to the nature of the object examined. The sensations experienced seemed mainly of two kinds—temperature and perceptions of light and colour. The poles of the magnet emitted flames, reddish yellow from the south pole, bluish green from the north ; a similar polarity was observed in the luminous *emanations* from crystals. The human fingers radiated light. Elementary substances each had their distinctive light and colour, the metals giving the most vivid impressions. Iron, copper, bismuth, mercury and others gave off a red glow, each differing from the others ; the flames emitted by lead, cobalt and palladium were blue ; those of silver, gold, cadmium, diamond were white. The clairvoyants also perceived the luminous matter over the bodies of the sick in hospitals ; and a column of misty vapour hovering over a newly made grave. This radiance emitted by the various substances, was capable of illuminating other objects. It could be concentrated by a lens, reflected by a mirror but produced no effect on a thermometer and was liable to be absorbed by the glass of the percipient's spectacles. A large number of the sensitives fully corroborated each other's statements and observations, two artists amongst them sketching their clairvoyant visions. These experiments of the Baron's were conducted for years with the most persevering attention and he arrived at the conclusion that from every object in the human, animal, vegetable and mineral kingdom there emanated a force which could be detected under favourable conditions as flames or luminous radiations. Some observers defined these as the universal life of things. Reichenbach in his writings and descriptions of the experiments called them the " Od Force " or " Odyle." Modern Spiritualism claims that all physical phenomena such as materialisations, (q.v.) levitation, (q.v.) apports, (q.v.) table-rapping etc. are produced by the spirits' manipulations of the medium's more physical *emanations* in such a way as to give them power to manifest materially and control matter. The finer phases of mediumship are traced to a similar use of the psychic aura or force emitted from the medium's personality. Theosophy has elaborated the theory of *emanations* into grandiose conceptions of astral light, influences, auras, etc. In Paris, in 1901, a peculiar phenomenon produced through the agency of a young Roumanian gentleman was investigated by Dr. Rozier. Broussay could occasion a gaseous bubbling of water when this was enclosed in a bottle and over this ebullition he had more or less control. In Dr. Rozier's presence this was carried out by the following process. A white glass bottle was taken, a quarter filled with water, and the neck of this was firmly closed up by Broussay's hand. It was then turned upside down and held tightly so that no moisture could possibly escape. On watching the water thus brought into touch with the hand minute air bubbles formed rapidly and rose in threadlike lines to the surface. After lapse of a minute or two the appearance intensified and the bubbles rose in greater number until the effect resembled soda water in effervesence. When the experiment was at its height the bubbles seemed to fly from every part of the hand which was exposed to the water and gathered round the neck of the bottle while a crackling sound was audible. Light had no effect on the experiment and the temperature of M. Broussay was normal, 37deg. to 38deg. at most. This experiment is similar to a favourite performance given by Indian jugglers, who will boil an egg in from five to ten minutes at most without fire to heat the water. An explanation of this phenomenon is given as being due to the electric vibrations passing along the surface of the skin and raising the temperature of the water above boiling point—the definition of electricity in this case being that as it is neither matter nor energy, though energy may be expended in moving or creating it, it is quite probably generated by the brain cells, a manifestation of cerebral force and will vibrations. Later investigations in the subject of *emanations* were set in motion by certain results detected in connection with a study of the famous " X " rays, when it was found that a new species of radiations was emitted by the focus tube, which traversed aluminium, black paper, wood, etc. These new rays were plane-polarized from the moment of their emission ; were susceptible of rotatory and elliptic polarization and could be refracted, reflected and diffused. The wave-lengths of the " N " rays are much smaller than those of light and they also appear to be without heat. They can be obtained from various sources other than the Röntgen tube, and certain bodies seem to have the property of retaining or storing the rays for a considerable time. The human body is said to emit them unceasingly. Though non-luminous in themselves the rays will, if allowed to fall upon a phosphorescent body, increase its glow. A small spark or flame is similarly influenced. In photography the existence of the " N " rays is well demonstrated, those pictures taken without the rays being very faint while those obtained while the " N " rays were in action were much stronger. Pebbles exposed to sunlight spontaneously emit " N " rays and bodies such as Rupert's drops, hardened steel, hammered brass, etc, are permanent sources of the rays. These rays were named after the initial letter of the town of Nancy where the researches were made that led to their discovery by Professor Blondlot. Further experiments proved that all matter possesses the power of radiation and those potentialities can be seen and registered by a fluorescent screen just as those of the animal and human organism. Whenever muscular and nerve energies are manifesting rays are emitted, and it was found that they would pass through certain substances whereas others would intercept and store them. For example, they passed through an oak board three or four centimetres thick, black paper, aluminium, etc, but water stopped them or even a cigarette paper if wet. Fresh water intercepted them but if the liquid were salt the rays passed through. Dr. Baraduc for many years pursued his studies in the emission of human fluidic forces and used the biomètre for registering vibrations emitted from human bodies. This instrument consists of a needle suspended by a fine thread and covered with a glass shade. When the hand approaches this shade, without touching it the needle is deflected. As the result of long observation he formed the opinion that the variations in the movements of the needle were caused by various conditions, physical, mental and moral in the persons who approached it and that by these means he was able to estimate those conditions. Dr. Baraduc also experimented in photography on these lines. He took photographs of the *emanations* given off from the hands of persons in varied, mental, moral and physical states. In these the lines of radiation varied considerably. In one, described by him as a psychic hand, the luminosity seemed to radiate from the lower base of the palm ; another, where all the lines were confused, was a photograph taken from the hand of a man in mental distress. Dr. Baraduc also photographed some stones which were said to have been used in the initiation rites of pre-Christian religions and the stream of rays emanating from these stones was distinctly visible on the plates ; also some holy water at Lourdes just after a miraculous cure had been effected, and there again the influence was strong. He photographed with similar result the sacred wafer during the moment of elevation in a Roman Catholic Church. He also photographed both his son and his wife, the one four minutes after death and the other twenty-four hours after death, and in each instance there was seen stretching from the lifeless body a great stream of force which extended right up to the ceiling of the room and then turned down again. In the one case the face of the son could be recognised by anyone who had known him and could be seen close to the body. In the other case the profile of Dr. Baraduc's wife was to be seen halfway up the room. (*See article* **Thought Photography**.)

Emerald : A good preservative against decay, promotes childbirth, arrests dysentery, and heals the bites of venomous animals. It is the most grateful of all jewels to the eyes, and reflects images like a looking-glass. Nero is said to have had one of immense size, in which he beheld the combats of the gladiators.

Emerald Table, The : A symbolic work on the hermetic art by Hermes Trismegistus.

Emerick, Catherine : (*See* **Germany**.)

Enchantments : (*See* **Spells**.)

Enchiridion of Pope Leo, The : Is a collection of charms, cast in the form of prayers, which have nothing in common with those of the Church. It is concerned chiefly with worldly, rather than spiritual advantages. It was perhaps printed at Rome in 1523, and again in 1606. Its magical virtue rests on a supposed letter from Charlemagne to Pope Leo, in which he states that since receiving the *Enchiridion* he has never ceased to be fortunate. The charms it contains are supposed to be effectual against all the dangers to which human flesh is heir—poison, fire, wild beasts and tempests. When a copy of the book has been secured, it must be placed in a small bag of leather, carried on the person, and one page at least read daily. The reading must be done upon the knees with the face turned to the east, and works of piety must be performed in honour of the celestial spirits, whose influence it is desired to attract. The first chapter of the Gospel according to St. John is declared to be the most potent in the book. As for the symbols, they are mostly of oriental origin. It also includes the mysterious prayers of Pope Leo, and certain conjurations of a semi-magical character, including the seven mysterious orisons, which are merely clumsy imitations of the Roman ritual.

Enchiridion Physicae Restitutae : (*See* **D'Espagnet**.)

Endless Cord, Tying Knots in : About the years 1877-88 Professor Zöllner of Leipsic investigated the phenomena of the medium Slade, and particularly anything which might prove a fourth dimension of space, in which hypothesis Professor Zöllner was at that time greatly interested. The tying in an endless cord of such knots as could ordinarily only be made if the ends of the cord were free provided such a test. In December, 1877, Zöllner visited Slade with two pieces of hempen cord, the free ends of each

being sealed to a piece of cardboard. To ensure the cord always being in sight Zöllner hung it round his neck, and kept Slade's hands continually in view. Under these circumstances four knots were produced, apparently on the original sealed cord.

England : (For the pre-Saxon inhabitants of *England, See* **Celts**.) The Anglo-Saxon system of magic was of course Teutonic. Their pretenders to witchcraft were called *wicca, scin-laeca, galdor-craeftig, wiglaer,* and *morthwyrtha. Wiglaer* is a combination from *wig,* an idol or a temple, and *laer,* learning. He was the wizard, as *wicca* was the witch. Scinlaeca was a species of phantom or apparition, and was also used as a name of the person who had the power of producing such things : it is, literally, " a shining dead body." *Galdor-craeftig* implies one skilled in incantations ; and *morth-wyrtha* is, literally, " a worshipper of the dead."

Another general appellation for such personages was *dry,* a magician.

The laws visited these practices with penal severity. The best account that can be given of them will be found in the passages proscribing them.

" If any *wicca,* or *wiglaer,* or false swearer, or *morthwyrtha,* or any foul, contaminated, manifest *horcwenan* (whore, quean or strumpet), be any where in the land, man shall drive them out." " We teach that every priest shall extinguish all heathendom, and forbid *wilweorthunga* (fountain-worship), and *licwiglunga* (incantations of the dead), and *hwata* (omens), and *galdra* (magic), and man-worship, and the abominations that men exercise in various sorts of witchcraft, and in *frithspottum,* and with elms and other trees, and with stones, and with many phantoms."

From subsequent regulations, we find that these practices were made the instruments of the most fatal mischief ; for penitentiary penalties are enjoined if any one should destroy another by *wicce craefte* ; or if any should " drive sickness on a man" ; or if death should follow from the attempt.

They seem to have used philtres ; for it is also made punishable if any should use witchcraft for another's love, or should give him to eat or to drink with magic. They were also forbid to *wiglian* (or to divine) by the moon. Canute renewed the prohibitions. He enjoined them not to worship the sun or the moon, fire or floods, wells or stones, or any sort of tree ; not to love *wiccecraeft,* or frame death-spells, either by lot or by torch ; nor to effect any thing by phantoms. From the *Poenitentiale* of Theodore we also learn, that the power of letting loose tempests was also pretended to.

Another name for magical arts among the Anglo-Saxons was *unlybban wyrce,* " destructive of life." The penitence is prescribed for a woman who kills a man by *unlybban.* One instance of philtre using is detailed to us. A woman resolving on the death of her step-son, or to alienate from him his father's affection, sought a witch, who knew how to change minds by arts and enchantments. Addressing such a one with promises and rewards, she enquired how the mind of the father might be turned from the child, and be fixed on herself. The magical medicament was immediately made, and mixed with the husband's meat and drink. The catastrophe of the whole was the murder of the child and the discovery of the crime by the assistant, to revenge the step-mother's ill-treatment.

The charms used by the Anglo-Saxons were innumerable. They trusted in their magical incantations for the cure of disease, for the success of their tillage, for the discovery of lost property, and for the prevention of casualties. Specimens of their charms for these purposes still remain to us. Bede tells us, that " many, in times of disease (neglecting the sacraments) went to the erring medicaments of idolatry, as if to restrain God's chastisements by incantations, phylacteries, or any other secret of the demoniacal arts.''

Their prognostications, from the sun, from thunder, and from dreams, were so numerous, as to display and to perpetuate superstition. Every day of every month was catalogued as a propitious or unpropitious season for certain transactions. We have Anglo-Saxon treatises which contain rules for discovering the future and disposition of a child, from the day of its nativity. One day was useful for all things ; another, though good to tame animals was baleful to sow seeds. One day was favourable to the commencement of business ; another to let blood ; and others wore a forbidding aspect to these and other things. On this day one must buy, on a second sell, on a third hunt, on a fourth do nothing. If a child was born on such a day, it would live ; if on another, its life would be sickly ; if on another, he would perish early. In a word, the most alarming fears, and the most extravagant hopes, were perpetually raised by these foolish superstitions, which tended to keep the mind in the dreary bondage of ignorance and absurdity, which prevented the growth of knowledge, by the incessant war of prejudice, and the slavish effects of the most imbecile apprehensions.

The same anticipations of futurity were made by noticing on what day of the week or month it first thundered, or the new moon appeared, or the new-year's day occurred. Dreams likewise had regular interpretations and applications ; and thus life, instead of being governed by counsels of wisdom, was directed by those solemn lessons of gross superstition, which the most ignorant peasant of our days would be ashamed to avow.

Although witchcraft was of early origin in *England*, we do not find many notices of it in the literature of the country, nor does it seem to have been systematically punished until past Reformation times. That is not to say, that no prosecution ever took place against witchcraft in Plantagenet and early Tudor times, but that in all probability the vogue of sorcery was so widespread, and so powerful was supposed to be the protection of a Church that nothing like a crusade was directed against it. Again it was regarded as a political offence to employ sorcery against the ruling powers, and as such it was punished severely enough, as is witnessed by the execution of the Duchess of Gloucester in Henry VI.'s reign, and the Duke of Buckingham in 1521. In Henry VI.'s time Lord Hungerford was beheaded for consulting certain soothsayers concerning the duration of the King's life.

L. S.

According to Sir William Blackstone, '' To deny the possibility, nay, the actual existence of witchcraft and sorcery is at once flatly to contradict the revealed Word of God in various passages of the Old and New Testaments, and the thing itself is a truth to which every nation in the world hath in its turn borne testimony.''

At very early periods the Church fulminated against those who practised it. In 696 a Canon of Council held at Berkhampstead condemned to corporal punishment those who made sacrifices to evil spirits, and at subsequent dates Statutes against Witchcraft were enacted by the Parliaments of Henry VIII., Elizabeth and James I. Mr. Inderwick says, '' For centuries in this country strange as it may now appear, a denial of the existence of such demoniacal agency was deemed equal to a confession of Atheism and to a disbelief in the Holy Scriptures themselves. But not only did Lord Chancellors, Lord Keepers, benches of Bishops and Parliament attest the truth and the existence of witchcraft, but Addison writing as late as 1711, in the pages of the *Spectator*, after describing himself as hardly pressed by the arguments on both sides of

this question expresses his own belief that there is and has been, witchcraft in the land.''

It is in the twelfth Century that a first distinct glimpse is obtained of the bond between the *Evil One* and his victim. The tale of the old woman of Berkeley which Southey's Ballad has familiarised, is related by William of Malmesbury on the authority of a professed eye-witness. When the devil informed the witch of the near expiry of her contract, she summoned the neighbouring monks and her children, and after confessing her criminal compact displayed great anxiety lest Satan should secure her body as well as her soul. She gave directions to be sewn in a stag's hide and placed in a stone coffin, shut in with lead and iron, to be loaded with heavy stones and the whole fastened down with three iron chains. In order to baffle the power of the demons, she further directed fifty psalms to be sung by night, and fifty masses to be sung by day, and that at the end of three nights, if her body was still secure, she said that it might be buried with safety. All these precautions however, proved of no avail. The monks bravely resisted the efforts of the fiends on the first and second nights, but on the third night in the middle of a terrific uproar an immense demon burst into the monastery and in a voice of thunder commanded the dead witch to rise. She replied that she was bound with chains, which however the demon snapped like thread, the coffin lid fell aside, and on the witch arising the demon bore her off on a huge black horse and galloped into the darkness, while her shrieks resounded through the air. The first trial for witchcraft in England occurred during the tenth year of the reign of King John, when according to the *Abbreviato-Placitorum*, the wife of Ado the merchant, accused one Gideon of the crime. He proved his innocence however, by the ordeal of the red-hot iron. A trial was reported with more detail in the year 1324. Certain citizens of Coventry had suffered at the hands of the prior whose extortions were approved of and supported by two of Edward II.'s favourites. By way of revenge they plotted the death of the prior, the favourites, and the King.

In order to carry this into effect they consulted John of Nottingham, a famous Magician of the time, and his servant Robert Marshall of Leicester. Marshall however, betrayed the plot and stated that together with his master they fashioned images of wax to represent the King, his two favourites, the prior, his caterer and steward, and one Richard de Lowe—the latter being brought in merely as an experimental lay-figure in which to test the effect of the charm. At an old ruined house near Coventry, on the Friday following Holy Cross Day, John gave his man a sharp pointed leaden branch and commanded him to plunge it into the forehead of the figure representing Richard de Lowe. This being done John dispatched his servant to Lowe's house to find out the result of the experiment. Lowe it seems had lost his senses and went about screaming '' Harrow.'' On the Sunday before Ascension John withdrew the branch from the image's forehead, and thrust it into the heart, where it remained till the following Wednesday when the unfortunate victim died. Such was the evidence of Marshall, but the judges gave it little belief, and after several adjournments the trial was abandoned.

The first enactment against witchcraft in *England* was by the Parliament of 1541. In 1551 further enactments were levelled at it, but it was not until 1562 that Parliament defined witchcraft as a Capital Crime. Thenceforth followed the regular persecution of Witches. Many burnings occurred during the latter years of Elizabeth's reign.

At the village of Worboise, (q.v.) in the County of Huntingdon in 1589 dwelt two country gentlemen, Robert

Throgmorton and Sir Samuel Cromwell. Mr. Throgmorton's family consisted of his wife and five daughters of whom the eldest Joan, a girl of fifteen was possessed with a mind and imagination well stocked with ghost-and witch-lore. On one occasion she had to pass the cottage of a labouring family of the name of Samuel. This family consisted of a man, his wife, and their grown-up daughter. Mother Samuel was sitting at the door wearing a black cap, and busily engaged in knitting. Joan declared that she was a witch, ran home and fell into strange convulsive fits, stating that Mother Samuel had bewitched her. In due course the other daughters respectively were attacked with similar fits, and attributed the blame to Mother Samuel. The parents now began to suspect that their children were really bewitched and reported the matter to Lady Cromwell, who, as an intimate friend of the family took the matter up and along with Sir Samuel ordered that the alleged witch should be put to ordeal. Meanwhile the children let loose their imagination and invented all sorts of weird and grotesque tales about the old woman. Eventually Throgmorton had the poor old woman dragged to his grounds where she was subjected to torture, pins being thrust into her body to see if blood could be drawn. Lady Cromwell tore out a handful of the old crone's hair which she gave to Mrs. Throgmorton requesting her to burn it as an antidote against witchcraft. Suffering under these injuries the old woman invoked a curse against her torturers which was afterwards remembered, though she was allowed her liberty. She thereafter suffered much persecution at the hands of the two families, all ills and misfortunes occurring amongst their cattle and stock being laid to her charge. Eventually Lady Cromwell was seized with an illness that caused her death, and upon old Mother Samuel was laid the responsibility. Repeated efforts were made to persuade her to confess and amend what she had done. At last, tormented beyond endurance, she let herself be persuaded to pronounce an exorcism against the spirits and confessed that her husband and daughter were also associates with her and had sold themselves to the devil. On the strength of this confession the whole family were imprisoned in Huntingdon Gaol. At the following Session the three Samuels were put upon trial indicted with various offences and " bewitching unto death " the Lady Cromwell. In the agony of torture the old woman confessed all that was required, but her husband and daughter strongly asserted their innocence. All were sentenced to be hanged and burned. The executions were carried out in April 1595.

It is related that in 1594 the Earl of Derby attributed the cause of his death to witchery, though he had no idea of the person who had bewitched him.

The Accession of James I. himself a great expert in witchcraft and the author of the famous treatise on demonology (q.v.) gave a great impetus to the persecution of witches in *England*. " Poor old women and girls of tender age were walked, sworn, shaved, and tortured, the gallows creaked and the fires blazed."

In 1606 there were tried at King's Lynn the wife of one Henry Smith a grocer, for cursing a sailor who had struck a boy, and for cursing her neighbours because they were more prosperous in their trades than she was.

After hearing the most absurd evidence she was convicted and sentenced to death. Upon the scaffold she confessed to various acts of witchcraft.

In 1633 arose the famous case of the Lancashire Witches (q.v.). On the assertion of a boy called Robinson, that he had been carried off and witnessed a witches' Sabbath at the Hoare Stones, some eighteen women were brought to trial at Lancaster Assizes.

As the result of the severe legislation against witchcraft,

there arose a class of self-constituted impugners or witch-finders who to their personal advantage were the means of the sacrifice of many innocent lives.

The most famous of these witch-finders was Matthew Hopkins of Manningtree, in Essex. He assumed the title of " Witch-finder General," and with an assistant, and a woman whose duty was to examine female suspects for devil's marks, he travelled about the Counties of Essex, Sussex, Huntingdon, and Norfolk. In one year this murderer—for want of a better name—caused the death of sixty people. His general test was that of swimming. The hands and feet of accused were tied together crosswise. She was wrapped in a sheet and thrown into a pond. If she sank as frequently happened, she was deemed innocent, but at the cost of her life, if she floated she was pronounced guilty and forthwith executed. Another test was to repeat the Lord's Prayer without a single falter or stumble, a thing accredited impossible of a witch. On one occasion she was weighed against the Church Bible, obtaining her freedom if she outweighed it. It is alleged but without certainty, that on his impostures being found out an angry crowd subjected him to his own test by swimming, but whether he was drowned or executed authorities fail to agree.

In his *Witch, Warlock and Magician* Mr. Adams says, " I think there can be little doubt that many evil-disposed persons availed themselves to the prevalent belief in witchcraft as a cover for their depredations on the property of their neighbours, diverting suspicion from themselves to the poor witches, who through accidental circumstances had acquired notoriety as the devil's accomplices. It would also seem probable that not a few of the reputed witches similarly turned to account their bad reputation."

It was not till the close of the seventeenth Century that convictions began to be discouraged by the Courts. But an old superstition dies hard, and in the early part of the eighteenth Century witchcraft was generally believed in, in England, even among the educated classes.

Probably the revolution of opinion was effected between the Restoration and the Revolution. According to Dr. Parr, the last execution of witches in *England* took place at Northampton where two were hung in 1705, and at the same place five others suffered a like fate in 1712. Hutchison commenting on this in his *Historical Essay* says, " This is the more shameful as I shall hereafter prove from the literature of that time, a disbelief in the existence of witches had become almost universal among educated men, though the old superstition was still defended in the Judgment Seat, and in the pulpit." Wesley who had more influence than all the Bishops put together says, " It is true likewise that the English in general, and, indeed, most of the men of learning in Europe, have given up all accounts of witches and apparitions as mere old wives' fables. I am sorry for it. The giving up of witchcraft, is in effect giving up the Bible. But I cannot give up to all the Deists in Great Britain the existence of witchcraft, till I give up the credit of all history sacred and profane."

Every year however, diminished the old belief, and in 1736, a generation before Wesley stated the above opinions, the laws against witchcraft were repeated, but as illustrative of the long lived prevalence of the superstition in 1759 Susannah Hannaker of Wengrove, in Wiltshire, was put to the ordeal of weighing, but she fortunately outweighed the Bible. Cases of ducking supposed witches occurred in 1760 at Leicester, in 1785 at Northampton, and in 1829 at Monmouth, while as recently as 1863 a Frenchman died as the result of an illness caused by his having been ducked as a Wizard, at Castle Hedingham in Essex, and on September 17th, 1875, an old woman named Ann Turner, a reputed witch, was killed by a feeble-minded man at Long Compton in Warwickshire.

A. J. B. G.

See Wright. *Narrative of Sorcery and Magic* ; and Mackay. *Extraordinary Popular Delusions.*

Magic. Magic in *England* in early times is of course one with witchcraft, and it is only when we discern the stupendous figure of Roger Bacon (q.v.) that we find any thing like separation between the two. Of course, the popular traditions concerning Bacon are merely legendary, but they assist to crystallise for us the idea of an English magician of medieval times. The Elizabethan History of Friar Bacon was probably the first which placed these traditions on record. Here we have no concern with the Bacon of science, for the Bacon of magic is a magician who cheated the Devil, who made a brazen head that spoke, and who engaged in all manner of black magic.

In *England* the popular belief in magic was strengthened by the extraordinary effects of natural processes then known only to a small number of individuals who concealed their knowledge with the most profound secrecy. In *England*, as we approach the age of the Reformation, we find that the study of magic and alchemy have become extremely common among the Romish clergy. The rapid rise to power of men like Wolsey and Cromwell led people to think that they had gained their high positions through diabolical assistance. The number of Magicians in the reign of Henry VIII. was exceedingly great, as is witnessed by documents in the Record Office. At the height of Wolsey's greatness, a magician who is described as " one Wood, gent." was dragged before the Privy-council, charged with some misdemeanour which was connected with the intrigues of the day. In a paper addressed to the lords of the council, Wood states that William Nevill had sent for him to his house at Oxford, it being the first communication he had ever had with that " person." After he had been at Weke a short time, Neville took him by the arm and led him privately into the garden, and, to use the quaint language of the original, " ther demawndyd of me many questyons, amowng all other askyd (if it) were not possible to have a rynge made that should brynge man in favor with hys prynce, saying my lord cardinale had suche a rynge that whatsomevere he askyd of the kynges grace that he hadd yt, ' and master Cromwell, when he and I were servauntys in my lord cardynales housse, dyd hawnt to the company of one that was seyne in your faculté, and shortly after no man so grett with my lord cardynale as master Cromwell was.' " Neville added, that he had spoken " with all those who have any name in this realm, ': who had assured him that in the same way he might become " great with his prince," and he ended by asking of the reputed magician what books he had studied on the subject. The latter continued, " and I, at the harté desire of hym showyd that I had rede many bokes, and specyally the boke of Salamon, and how his rynges be made and what mettell, and what vertues they had after the canon of Salamon." He added, that he had also studied the magical work of Hermes. William Neville then requested him to undertake the making of a ring, which he says that he declined, and so went away for that time. But Neville sent for him again, and entered into further communication with him on the old subject, telling him that he had with him another conjurer, named Wade, who could show him more than he should ; and, among other things, had showed him that " he should be a great lord," This was an effective attempt to move Wood's jealousy ; and it appears that Neville now prevailed upon him to make " moldes," probably images, " to the entent that he showld wed mastres Elezebeth Gare," on whom he seemed to have set his love. Perhaps

she was a rich heiress. Wood then enters into excuses for himself, declaring that, although at the desire of " some of his friends," he had " called to a stone for things stolen," he had not undertaken to find treasures, and he concluded with the naive boast, " but to make the phylosofer's stone, I will chebard (i.e, jeopard) my lyffe to do hyt, yf hyt plesse the kynges good grace to command me do hyt." This was the pride of science above the low practitioner's. He even offered to remain in prison until he had performed his boast, and only asked " twelve months upon silver, and twelve and a half upon gold."

The search for treasures, which the conjurer Wood so earnestly disclaims, was, however, one of the most usual occupations of our magicians of this period. The frequent discoveries of Roman or Saxon, or medieval deposits, in the course of accidental digging—then probably more common than at present—was enough to whet the appetite of the needy or the miserly, and the belief that the sepulchral barrow, or the long deserted ruin, or even the wild and haunted glen, concealed treasures of gold and silver of great amount has been carried down to our own days in a variety of local legends. Hidden treasures were under the particular charge of some of the spirits who obeyed the magician's call, and we still trace his operations in many a barrow that has been disturbed, and ruined floor that has been broken up. That these searches were not always successful will be evident from the following narrative :—

In the reign of Henry VIII. a priest named William Stapleton was placed under arrest as a conjurer, and as having been mixed up in some court intrigues, and at the request of Cardinal Wolsey he wrote an account of his adventures, still preserved in the Roll's House records (for it is certainly addressed to Wolsey, and not, as has been supposed, to Cromwell). Stapleton says that he had been a monk of the mitred abbey of St. Benet in the Holm, in Norfolk, where he was resident in the nineteenth year of Henry VIII. i.e. in 1527 or 1528, at which time he borrowed of one Dennys, of Hofton, who had procured them of the vicar of Watton, a book called *Thesaurus Spirituum*, and after that another, called *Secreta Secretorum*, a little ring, a plate, a circle, and also a sword for the art of digging, in studying of which he spent six months. Now it appears that Stapleton had small taste for early rising, and after having been frequently punished for being absent from matins and negligent of his duty in church he obtained a licence of six months from the abbot to go into the world, and try and raise money to buy a dispensation from an order which seemed so little agreeable to his taste. The first person he consulted with was his friend Dennys, who recommended him to try his skill in finding treasure, and introduced him to two " knowing men," who had " placards " or licences from the king to search for treasure trove, which were not unfrequently bought from the crown at this period. These men lent him other books and instruments belonging to the " art of digging," and they went together to a place named Sidestrand in Norfolk, to search and mark out the ground where they thought treasure should lie. It happened, however, that the lady Tyrry, to whom the estate belonged, received intelligence of their movements, and after sending for them and subjecting them to a close examination, ordered them to leave her grounds.

After this rebuff, the treasure-seekers went to Norwich, where they became acquainted with another conjurer named Godfrey, who had a " shower " of spirit, " which spirit," Stapleton says, " I had after myself," and they went together to Felmingham, and there Godfrey's boy did " scry " unto the spirit, but after opening the ground they found nothing there. There are Roman barrows at Felmingham, which, when examined recently, appeared to have been opened at a former period in search of treasure. The disappointed conjurers returned to Norwich, and there met with a stranger, who brought them to a house in which it was supposed that treasure lay concealed, and Stapleton again applied himself to his incantations, and called the spirit of the treasure to appear, but he turned a deaf ear to their charms, " for I suppose of a truth," is the pithy observation of the operator, " that there was none."

Disappointed and disgusted, Stapleton now gave up the pursuit. In Norfolk, however, he soon met with some of his old treasure-seeking acquaintances, who urged him to go to work again, which he refused to do unless his books were better. They told him of a man of the name of Leech, who had a book, to which the parson of Lesingham had bound a spirit called " Andrea Malchus ;" and to this man he went. Leech let him have all his instruments, and told him further that the parson of Lesingham and Sir John of Leiston (another ecclesiastic) with others, had called up of late by the means of the book in question three spirits, Andrea Malchus (before mentioned), Oberion and Inchubus. " When these spirits," he said, " were all raised, Oberion would in nowise speak. And then the parson of Lesingham did demand of Andrea Malchus, and so did Sir John of Leiston also, why Oberion would not speak to them. And Andrea Malchus made answer, " For because he was bound unto the lord cardinal." And that also they did entreat the said parson of Lesingham, and the said Sir John of Leiston, that they might depart as at that time ; and whensoever it might please them to call them up again, they would gladly do them any service they could."

When Stapleton had made this important acquisition, he repaired again to Norwich, where he had not long been, when he was found by a messenger from the personage whom he calls the lord Leonard Marquees, who lived at " Calkett Hall," and who wanted a person expert in the art of digging. He met lord Leonard at Walsingham, who promised him that if he would take pains in exercising the said art he would sue out a dispensation for him to be a secular priest, and to make him his chaplain. The lord Leonard proceeded rather shrewdly to make trial of the searcher's talents ; for he directed one of his servants to hide a sum of money in the garden, and Stapleton " hewed " for it, and one, Jackson " scryed," but he was unable to find the money. Yet, without being daunted at this slip Stapleton went directly with two other priests, Sir John Shepe and Sir Robert Porter, to a place beside Creke Abbey, where treasure was supposed to be, and Sir John Shepe called the spirit of the treasure, and I shewed to him, but all came to no purpose."

Stapleton now went to hide his disappointment in London, and remained there some weeks, till the lord Leonard, who had sued out his dispensation as he promised, sent for him to pass the winter with him in Leicestershire, and towards spring he returned to Norfolk. And there he was informed that there was " much money " hidden in the neighbourhood of Calkett Hall, and especially in the Bell Hill (probably an ancient tumulus or barrow), and after some delay, he obtained his instruments, and went to work with the parish priest of Gorleston, but " of truth we could bring nothing to effect." On this he again repaired to London, carrying his instruments with him, and on his arrival he was thrown into prison at the suit of the lord Leonard, who accused him of leaving his service without permission, and all his instruments were seized. These he never recovered, but he was soon liberated from prison, and obtained temporary employment in the church.

But his conjuring propensities seem still to have lingered about him, and we find this ex-monk and hermit, and now secular priest, soon afterwards engaged in an intrigue which led him eventually into a much more serious danger. It appears by Stapleton's statements, that one Wright, a servant of the Duke of Norfolk, came to him, and " at a certain season shewed me that the duke's grace, his master was soore vexed with a spyrytt by the enchantment of your grace " (he is addressing Wolsey). Stapleton says, that he refused to interfere, but that Wright went to the duke and told him that he, Stapleton, knew of his being enchanted by Cardinal Wolsey, and that he could help him ; upon which the duke sent for Stapleton, and had an interview with him. It had previously been arranged by Wright and Stapleton (who says that he had been urged into the plot by the persuasion of Wright, and by the hope of gain and prospect of obtaining the duke's favour) that he should say he knew that the duke was persecuted by a spirit, and that he had " forged " an image of wax in his similitude, which he had enchanted, in order to relieve him. The Duke of Norfolk appears at first to have placed implicit belief in all that Stapleton told him ; he inquired of him if he had certain knowledge that the Lord Cardinal had a spirit at his command, to which he replied in the negative. He then questioned him as to his having heard anyone assert that the cardinal had a spirit ; on which Stapleton told him of the raising of Oberion by the parson of Lesingham and Sir John of Leiston, and how Oberion refused to speak, because he was the lord cardinal's spirit. The duke, however, soon after this, became either suspicious or fearful, and he eventually sent Stapleton to the cardinal himself, who appears to have committed him to prison, and at whose order he drew up the account here abridged.

The foregoing is the history of a man who, after having been a victim to his implicit belief in the efficiency of magical operations was himself driven at last to have recourse to intentional deception. The number of such treasure-hunters appears to have been far greater among his contemporaries, of almost all the classes of society, than we should at first glance be led to suppose. A few years before the date of these events, in the 12th year of Henry VIII., or A.D. 1521, the king had granted to Robert, Lord Curzon, the monopoly of treasure-seeking in the counties of Norfolk and Suffolk, and Lord Curzon immediately delegated to a man, named William Smith, of Clopton, and a servant or retainer of his own, named Amylyon, not only the right of search thus given to him, but the power to arrest and proceed against any other person they found seeking treasures within the two counties. It appears that Smith and Amylyon had in some cases used this delegated authority for purposes of extortion ; and in the summer of the same year, Smith was brought up before the court of the city of Norwich, at the suit of William Goodred, of Great Melton, the minutes of the proceedings against him still remaining on the records. We here again find priests concerned in these singular operations.

It appears that the treasure-diggers, who had received their " placard " of Lord Curzon in March, went to Norwich about Easter, and paid a visit to the schoolmaster, named George Dowsing, dwelling in the parish of St. Faith, who, they had heard, was " seen in astronymye." They shewed him their license for treasure-seeking, which authorised him to press into their service any persons they might find who had skill in the science ; so that it would appear that they were not capable of raising spirits themselves without the assistance of " scholars." The schoolmaster entered willingly into their project, and they went, about two or three o'clock in the morning, with one or two other persons who were admitted into their confidence, and dug in ground beside " Butter Hilles," within the walls of the city, but " found nothing there." These " hilles," also, were probably tumuli. They next proceeded to a place called " Seynt William in the Wood by Norwich," where they excavated two days (or rather two nights), but with no better success.

They now held a meeting at the house of one Saunders, in the market of Norwich, and called to their assistance two ecclesiastics, one named Sir William, the other Sir Robert Cromer, the former being the parish priest of St. Gregory's. At this meeting, George Dowsing raised " a spirit or two," in a glass ; but one of the priests, Sir Robert Cromer, " began and raised a spirit first." This spirit, according to the depositions, was seen by two or three persons. Amylyon deposed that " he was at Saunders's where Sir Robert Cromer held up a stone, but he could not perceive anything in it ; but that George Dowsing caused to rise in a glass a little thing of the length of an inch or thereabout, but whether it was a spirit or a shadow he cannot tell, but the said George said it was a spirit." However, spirit or no spirit, they seem to have had as little success as ever in discovering the treasure.

Unable after so many attempts, to find the treasure themselves, they seem now to have resolved on laying a general contribution on everybody who followed the same equivocal calling. They went first and accused a person of the name of Wikman, of Morley Swanton, in the county of Norfolk, of " digging of hilles," and, by threatening to take him before Lord Curzon, they obtained from him ten shillings. Under the same pretext, they took from a lime-burner of Norwich, named White, a " christal-stone," and twelvepence in money in order that he " should not be put to further trouble." They took both books (probably conjuring books) and money from John Wellys, of Hunworth, near Holt Market, whom, similarly, they accused of " digging of hilles." And of another person, labouring under the same charge, they took " a christal stone and certain money."

With the era of Dr. Dee (q.v.) Edward Kelly, (q.v.) their school, a much more definite system of magico-astrology was evolved on English soil. Although Dee was credulous and Kelly was a rogue of the first water, there is little doubt that the former possessed psychic gifts of no mean character. His most celebrated followers were William Lilly (q.v) and Elias Ashmole (q.v) not to speak of Simon Forman (q.v.) and Evans (q.v.). Lilly gathered about him quite a band of magicians, Ramsey, Scott, Hodges, and others, not to speak of his " skryers " Sarah Skelhorm and Ellen Evans. But these may be said to be the last of the practical magicians of *England.* Their methods were those of divination by crystal-gazing and evocation of spirits, combined with practical astrology.

Spiritualism. For the beginnings of spiritualism in *England* we must go back to the middle of the seventeenth century when Maxwell and Robert Fludd (q.v.) flourished and wrote concerning the secrets of mysticism and magnetism. Fludd was a Paracelsian pure and simple and regarded man as the microcosm of the universe in miniature. He was an ardent defender of the Rosicrucians, concerning whom he wrote two spirited works, as well as his great *Tractatus Apologeticus* and many other alchemical and philosophical treatises. The part of the *Tractatus* which deals with natural magic is one of the most authoritative ever penned on the subject, and divides the subject most minutely into its several parts. Thomas Vaughan (q.v.) is likewise a figure of intense interest about this period. He was a supreme adept of spiritual alchemy and his many works written under the Pseudonym of Eugenius Philalethes show him to have possessed an exalted mind. It is to men of this type, magi, perhaps, but

none the less spiritualists, that the whole superstructure of English spiritualism is indebted.

(See further **Spiritualism in England** under article **Spiritualism.)**

Enguerraud de Marigny : *(See* **France.)**

Ennemoser, Joseph (1787-1854) : A doctor and philosopher of Germany, who devoted himself largely to the study of magnetism. He was made a professor at Bonn in 1819, and at Munich in 1841. Among his works may be mentioned his *Histoire du magnétisme* (1844) ; *le Magnétisme dans ses rapports avec la nature et la religion* (1842) ; and *Introduction à la pratique du mesmerisme* (1852) ; *History of Magic (English trans. by Howitt)*, 1854.

Enoch : Seventh master of the world after Adam, and author of the *Kabala* and *Book of the Tarot.* He is identical with the Thoth of the Egyptians, the Cadmus of the Phœnicians, and the Palamedes of the Greeks. According to tradition he did not die, but was carried up to heaven, whence he will return at the end of time.

Enoch, Book of : An Apochryphal book of the Old Testament, written in Hebrew about a century before Christ. The original version was lost about the end of the fourth century, and only fragments remained, but Bruce the traveller brought back a copy from Abyssinia, in 1773 in Ethiopia, probably made from the version known to the early Greek fathers. In this work the spiritual world is minutely described, as is the region of Sheol (q.v.) the place of the wicked. The book also deals with the history of the fallen angels, their relations with the human species and the foundations of magic. The book says : " that there were angels who consented to fall from heaven that they might have intercourse with the daughters of earth. For in those days the sons of men having multiplied, there were born to them daughters of great beauty. And when the angels, or sons of heaven, beheld them, they were filled with desire ; wherefore they said to one another : Come let us choose wives from among the race of man, and let us beget children'. Their leader Samyasa, answered thereupon and said : ' Perchance you will be wanting in the courage needed to fulfil this resolution, and then I alone shall be answerable for your fall.' But they swore that they would in no wise repent and that they would achieve their whole design. Now there were two hundred who descended on Mount Armon, and it was from this time that the mountain received its designation, which signifies Mount of the Oath. Hereinafter follow the names of those angelic leaders who descended with this object : Samyasa, chief among all, Urakabarameel, Azibeel, Tamiel, Ramuel, Danel, Azkeel, Sarakuyal, Asael, Armers, Batraal, Anane, Zavebe, Sameveel, Ertrael, Turel, Jomiael, Arizial. They took wives with whom they had intercourse, to whom also they taught Magic, the art of enchantment and the diverse properties of roots and trees. Amazarac gave instruction in all secrets of sorcerers ; Barkaial was the master of those who study the stars ; Akibeel manifested signs ; and Azaradel taught the motions of the moon." In this account we see a description of the profanation of mysteries. The fallen angels exposed their occult and heaven-born wisdom to earthly women, whereby it was profaned, and brute force taking advantage of the profanation of divine law, reigned supreme. Only a deluge could wipe out the stain of the enormity, and pave the way for a restitution of the balance between the human and the divine, which had been disturbed by these unlawful revelations. A translation of the *Book of Enoch* was published by Archbishop Lawrence in 1821, the Etheopic text in 1838, and there is a good edition by Dillman (1851). Philippi and Ewald have also written special works on the subject.

Epworth, Poltergeist, The : In December, 1716, a disturbance of a poltergestic character broke out in the Parsonage of Epworth, the home of John Wesley. The evidence consists in contemporary letters written to Samuel Wesley by his mother and two of his sisters ; letters written nine years after the events to John Wesley by his mother and four of his sisters, and a copy of an account by Samuel Wesley the elder. The disturbances, consisting of rappings, loud and varied noises, were heard by every member of the household. Mrs. Wesley says in a letter, " Just as we (Mr. and Mrs. Wesley) came to the bottom of the broad stairs, having hold of each other, on my side there seemed as if somebody had emptied a bag of money at my feet, and on his as if all the bottles under the stairs (which were many) had been dashed in a thousand pieces." The disturbances lasted for about two months, though occasional manifestations were heard after that period. Hetty, one of the five daughters of the Wesley household, is the only one who has not left a record of her experiences, although it would seem that the poltergeist was most active in her neighbourhood.

Equilibrium : Magical harmony depends upon equilibrium. In occult operations if the will of the operator be always at the same tension and directed along the same line, moral impotence will ensue. (*See* **Levi—Ceremonial Magic.**)

Eric of the Windy Hat : According Hector of Boêce, the king of Sweden, *Eric* or Henry, surnamed the *Windy Hat*, could change the wind merely by turning his hat or cap on his head, to show the demon with whom he was in league which way he wished the wind to blow. The demon obeyed the signal so promptly that the king's hat might have served the people for a weather-cock.

Eromanty : One of six kinds of divination practised among the Persians by means of air. They enveloped their heads in a napkin and exposed to the air a vase filled with water, over which they mutter in a low voice the objects of their desires. If the surface of the air shows bubbles it is regarded as a happy prognostication.

Esdaile : (*See* **Hypnotism.**)

Eskimos : The religion of the *Eskimos* is still to a great extent in the magical stage. Their shamans or medicine-men, whom they call *Angekok* partake more of the character of magicians than that of priests and they invariably consult them before starting on a hunting expedition, or when prostrated by illness. The nature of the ceremonies employed on those occasions may be inferred from the account of Captain Lyon, who on one occasion employed an angekok named Toolemak, to summon a Tomga or familiar spirit in the cabin of a ship.

All light having been carefully excluded from the scene of operations, the sorcerer began by vehemently chanting to his wife, who, in her turn, responded with the *Amna-aya*, the favourite song of the *Eskimo*. This lasted throughout the ceremony. Afterwards, Toolemak began to turn himself round very rapidly, vociferating for Tomga, in a loud powerful voice and with great impatience, at the same time blowing and snorting like a walrus. His noise, agitation, and impatience increased every moment, and at length he seated himself on the deck, varying his tones, and making a rustling with his clothes.

Suddenly the voice seemed smothered, and was so managed as to give the idea that it was retreating beneath the deck, each moment becoming more distant, and ultimately sounding as if it were many feet below the cabin, when it ceased entirely. In answer to Captain Lyon's queries, the sorcerer's wife seriously declared that he had dived and would send up Tomga.

And, in about half a minute, a distant blowing was heard approaching very slowly, and a voice differing from that which had first been audible was mixed with the blowing, until eventually both sounds became distinct, and the old beldame said that Tomga had come to answer the stranger's questions. Captain Lyon thereupon put several queries to the sagacious spirit, receiving what was understood to be an affirmative or a favourable answer by two loud slaps on the deck.

A very hollow yet powerful voice, certainly differing greatly from that of Toolemak, then chanted for some time, and a singular medley of hisses, groans, and shouts, and gobblings like a turkey's followed in swift succession. The old woman sang with increased energy, and as Captain Lyon conjectured that the exhibition was intended to astonish " the Kabloona," he said repeatedly that he was greatly terrified. As he expected, this admission added fuel to the flame, until the form immortal, exhausted by its own might, asked leave to retire. The voice gradually died away out of hearing, as at first, and a very indistinct hissing succeeded. In its advance it sounded like the tone produced by the wind upon the bass cord of an Æolian harp ; this was soon changed to a rapid hiss, like that of a rocket, and Toolemak with a yell, announced the spirit's return.

At the first distant sibilation Captain Lyon held his breath, and twice exhausted himself ; but the *Eskimo* conjurer did not once respire, and even his returning and powerful yell was uttered without previous pause or inspiration of air.

When light was admitted, the wizard, as might be expected, was in a state of profuse perspiration, and greatly exhausted by his exertions, which had continued for at least half an hour. Captain Lyon then observed a couple of bunches, each consisting of two strips of white deerskin and a long piece of sinew, attached to the back of his coat. These he had not seen before, and he was gravely told that they had been sewn on by Tomga while he was below.

The angekoks profess to visit the dwelling-place of the spirits they invoke and give circumstantial descriptions of these habitations. They have a firm belief in their own powers.

Dr. Kane considers it a fact of psychological interest, as it shows that civilised or savage wonder-workers form a single family, that the angekoks have a firm belief in their own powers. " I have known," he says, " several of them personally, and can speak with confidence on this point. I could not detect them in any resort to jugglery or natural magic ; their deceptions are simply vocal, a change of voice, and perhaps a limited profession of ventriloquism, made more imposing by the darkness." They have, however, like the members of the learned professions everywhere else, a certain language or jargon of their own, in which they communicate with each other.

" While the angekoks are the dispensers of good, the *issintok*, or evil men, are the workers of injurious spells, enchantments, and metamorphoses. Like the witches of both Englands, the Old and the New, these malignant creatures are rarely submitted to trial until they have suffered punishment—the old " Jeddart justice "—*castigat auditque*. Two of them, in 1818, suffered the penalty of their crime on the same day, one at Kannonak, the other at Upernavik. The latter was laudably killed in accordance with the " old custom " . . . . custom being everywhere the apology for any act revolting to moral sense. He was first harpooned, then disembowelled ; a flap let down from his forehead to cover his eyes and prevent his seeing again—he had, it appears, the repute of an evil eye ; —and then small portions of his heart were eaten, to ensure that he should not come back to earth unchanged."

Esoteric Languages : Artificial languages invented by certain castes for the better preservation of secrets, or for the purpose of impressing the vulgar with the mysteries and superior nature of those who employed the tongues in question. " They conversed with one another in eager undertones in a language I did not understand." This is one of the stock phrases of the mystery novel of the nineteenth century, and has probably given rise to a great deal of misconception as to the true character and multiplicity of esoteric tongues. As a matter of fact, these are particularly rare. It is stated by several ancient au-thors that the Egyptian priests possessed a secret language of their own ; but what its nature was we are unable to state, as no fragments of it are now extant,—probably because it was not reduced to writing. At the same time many Egyptian magical formulæ are in existence (*See* **Egypt**) which teem with words and expressions of secret meaning ; but examination of these shows that they are merely foreign, usually Syrian, words slightly changed. We know, for example, that the secret dialects of the medicine-men among the North-American Indians are chiefly composed either of archaic expressions or the idioms of other tribes. But there are examples of the de-liberate manufacture of a secret tongue, such as the *Shelta Thari* (q.v) or language of the ancient caste of bronze-workers, still spoken by the tinkler classes of Great Britain, and the secret language of the *Ndembo* caste (q.v.) of the Lower Congo. It is probable that the Jewish priesthood cast a veil of secrecy over the sacred names of the Deity, and the higher ranks of their heavenly hierarchy, by sub-stituting other names for them, such as " Adonai" for " Jahveh." This of course arose from the Egyptian con-ception that the name of the god must be concealed from the vulgar, as to know it was to possess magical power over the deity. The spells and incantations of mediæval magic are full of oriental names and idioms, but much jargon also found its way into these. It was considered in the middle ages that the primitive language of the world was lost to man, and it was thought that this might only be recovered through magical agency, or the reversion to a state of complete innocence. Others believed it to be Hebrew ; and it is on record that James IV. of Scotland isolated two infants on the island of Inchkeith, in the Firth of Forth along with a dumb woman who cared for them ; and that in course of time they " spak gude Ebrew." A similar tradition acquaints us with the circumstance that a certain Egyptian king isolated two children in a like manner, who on coming to the period of speech met the first persons they beheld after their time of solitude with the word *beccos*, the Greek for bread. But these instances, it is unnecessary to say, are purely legendary. In many savage tribes, secret jargons or dialects are in use among the priesthood or the initiated of secret societies ; and in several brotherhoods of modern origin, symbolic words are constantly in use for the purpose of veiling veritable meaning. The Rosicrucians (q.v.) are said to have con-stituted and employed an arcane tongue.

Esplanadian : A mediæval Spanish legend. It tells how Ama-dis of Gaul and his wife Oriana of the Firm Island had the wicked enchanter Archelous in their keeping, but set him free in answer to his wife's entreaties. Certain calamities happen which are attributed to Archelous, and Amadis' son *Esplandian* is carried off by the enchantress Urganda. The legend goes on to relate *Esplandian's* adventures, how he is given a magic sword, and kills a dragon. With this sword he succeeds in killing Archelous himself, and his nephew, and he then sets free a kinsman. His next oppo-nent is Matroed, son of Arcobone, whom he also vanquishes ; and finally the stronghold of Archelous is utterly destroyed, and the land freed from the pagan influence of Matroed.

Esquiros, Alphonse : (*See* **France.**)

Essence, Elemental : (*See* **Evolution of Life.**)

Essence, Monadic : (*See* **Evolution of Life.**)

Essenes, The : A mystical Jewish sect, the tenets of which are only partly known. They first appeared in history about 150 years B.C. They were very exclusive and pos-sessed an organisation peculiar to themselves. They ex-ercised strict asceticism, and great benevolence. They had fixed rules for initiation, and a succession of strictly separate grades. Their system of thought deviated greatly from the normal development of Judaism, and was more in sympathy with Greek philosophy and oriental ideas. The tendency of the society was practical, and they re-garded speculation on the universe as too lofty for the human intellect. So far as can be judged there was nothing occult in their beliefs.

Etain : The second wife of Midir the Proud, of Irish fame. Fuamnach, Midir's first wife, became jealous of her beauty and turned her into a butterfly, and she was blown out of the palace by a magic storm. For seven years she was tossed hither and thither through Ireland, but then was blown into the fairy palace of Angus on the Boyne. He could not release her from the spell, but during the day she fed on honey-laden flowers, and by night in her natural form gave Angus her love. Fuamnach discovered her hiding-place, and sent a dreadful tempest which blew *Etain* into the drinking-cup of Etar, wife of an Ulster chief. Etar swallowed her, but she was born her daughter, and as such married Eochy, High King of Ireland.

Ether sometimes spoken of as *koilon* is in theosophic as in scientific teaching, all pervading, filling all space and inter-penetrating all matter. Despite this, it is of very great density, 10,000 times more dense than water and with a pressure of 750 tons per square inch. It is capable of being known only by clairvoyants of the most highly developed powers. This *ether* is filled with an infinitude of small bubbles pretty much like the air-bubbles in treacle or some such viscid substance, and these were formed at some vastly remote period by the infusion of the breath of the Logos into the *ether*, or, as Madame Blavatsky phrased it, they are the holes which Fohat, the Logos, dug in space. Of these bubbles—not of the *ether*—matter is built up in its degree of density varying with the number of bubbles com-bined together to form each degree. (*See* **Solar System**, **Theosophy.**)

Etheric Double is, in Theosophy, the invisible part of the ordinary, visible, physical body which it interpenetrates and beyond which it extends for a little, forming with other finer bodies the " aura " (q.v.) The term *etheric* is used because it is composed of that tenuous matter by the vi-brations of which the sensation of light is conveyed to the eye. This matter, it must however be noted is not the omnipresent ether of space, but is composed of physical matter known as etheric, super-etheric, sub-atomic, and atomic. The term *double* is used because it is an exact replica of the denser physical body. The sense organs of the *etheric double* are the *chaksams* (q.v.) and it is through these *chaksams* (q.v.) that the physical body is supplied with the vitality necessary for its existence and its well-being during life. The *etheric double* thus plays the part of a conductor, and it also plays the part of a bridge between the physical and astral bodies, for without it man could have no communication with the astral world and hence neither thoughts nor feelings. Anæsthetics for instance drive out the greater part of the *double*, and the subject is then impervious to pain. During sleep it does not leave the physical body, and, indeed, in dreams the etheric part of the brain is extremely active, especially when, as is often the case, the dreams are caused by attendant physical circumstances, such as noise. Shortly after death, the *etheric double* finally quits the physical body though it does not move far away from that body, but is composed of the four subdivisions of physical matter above alluded to. With the decay of the latter, the *double* also decays and thus to a clairvoyant, a burying ground presents a most unpleasant sight. (*See also* **Vitality, Etheric Vision, Theosophy, Shell.**)

Etheric Vision is in Theosophy, the power of sight peculiar to the Etheric Double (q.v.). It is of considerably greater power than physical vision, and by its aid many of the phenomena of the physical world may be examined as may also many creatures of a non-human nature which are ordinarily just outside the range of physical vision. It responds readily to stimuli of various kinds and becomes active under their influence.

Ethlinn : Daughter of Balor, King of the Fomorians of Irish magical legend. She was Balor's only child, and as he had been informed by a druid that he would be killed by his grandson, he had *Ethlinn* imprisoned in a tower and guarded by twelve women, who were forbidden to tell her that such beings as men existed. Balor stole a magic cow from Kian, who in revenge obtained access to *Ethlinn* disguised as a woman. They had three children whom Balor ordered to be drowned, but one of them fell from the napkin in which they were being taken to their doom, and was carried off by the Druidess Birog to its father Kian. This child became Lugh, the great sun-god, who eventually fulfilled the prophecy and killed his grandfather, Balor.

Etteilla : An eighteenth century student of the Tarot. By profession he was a barber, his true name being Alliette ; but on entering upon his occult labours he read it backwards, after the Hebrew fashion—*Eteilla*. He had but little education, and was ill acquainted with the philosophy of the initiates. Nevertheless he possessed a profound intuition, and, if we believe Eliphas Levi, came very near to unveiling the secrets of the Tarot. Of his writings Levi says that they are " obscure, wearisome, and in style barbarous." He claimed to have revised the *Book of Thot*, but in reality he spoilt it, regarding as blunders certain cards whose meaning he had failed to grasp. It is commonly admitted that he failed in his attempt to elucidate the Tarot, and ended by transposing the keys, thus destroying the correspondence between the numbers and the signs. It has also been said of him that he had degraded the science of the Tarot into the cartomancy, or fortune-telling by cards, of the vulgar.

Evergreens : The custom of decorating houses at Christmastide with *evergreen* plants—holly, ivy, box, laurel, mistletoe —is sometimes said to have originated when Christianity was introduced into this country, to typify the first British church, built of *evergreen boughs*. More probably it extends back into antiquity. In Druidic times people decorated their houses with *evergreen* plants so that the sylvan spirits might repair thither to shelter from the severity of winter, till their leafy bowers should be renewed.

Everitt, Mrs. : An English medium who gave private séances so early as 1855. To these sessions were admitted her private friends, and enquirers introduced by them. When a prayer had been said and the lights turned out the spirits manifested themselves by raps, table-tiltings, lights and spirit voices. Mr. Morell Theobald, a prominent spiritualist, was neighbour and friend to Mr. and *Mrs. Everitt*, and was first attracted to the subject through their instrumentality.

Evocations : (*See* **Necromancy**).

Evolution of Life, according to theosophists, began when the Logos, in his second aspect, sent forth the second life wave. This life wave descends from above through the various worlds causing an increasing heterogeneity and thereafter ascends, causing a return to its original homogeneity. Our present state of knowledge of life in these worlds extends no farther than the mental world. In the higher division of that world it has ensouled the relatively fine matter appropriate thereto—if that matter is atomic it is known as " monadic essence " if non-atomic, as " elemental essence," and this is known as the first elemental kingdom. What we may call the inhabitants of this kingdom are the higher order of angels. The life wave having functioned sufficiently long in the higher mental world, now presses down to the lower level of that world, where it appears as the second elemental kingdom, the inhabitants of which are some of the lower orders of angels, the Form Devas. Again pressing down, the life wave manifests itself in the astral world, forming the third elemental kingdom, the inhabitants of which are the lowest orders of angels, the Passion Devas. It now enters the physical world and, in the fourth elemental kingdom, ensouls the etheric part of minerals with the elementary type of life which these possess. The middle of this kingdom represents the farthest descent of the life wave, and thereafter its course is reversed and it commences to ascend. The next kingdom into which it passes is the fifth elemental kingdom, the vegetable world, whence it passes to the sixth elemental kingdom, the animal world, and lastly to the seventh elemental kingdom, man. During its stay in each kingdom, the life wave progresses gradually from elementary to highly specialised types and when it has attained these latter, it passes to the next kingdom. This, of course, of necessity means that successive currents of this great second life wave have come forth from the Logos, since, if it were otherwise, there would be only one kingdom in existence at a time. In each kingdom, also, the souls of the bodies which inhabit it differ from those of the other kingdoms. Thus, in the seventh kingdom, that of man, each individual has a soul. In the animal kingdom on the contrary, one soul is distributed among different bodies, the number of which varies with the state of evolution. To one soul may be allotted countless bodies of a low type of development, but, as the development increases, the soul comes to have fewer bodies allotted to it until in the kingdom of man there is but one.

Exorcism : To exorcise, according to the received definitions, says Smedley, is to bind upon oath, to charge upon oath, and thus, by the use of certain words, and performance of certain ceremonies, to subject the devil and other evil spirits to command and exact obedience. Minshew calls an " exorcist " a " conjuror ;" and it is so used by Shakespeare ; and *exorcism*, " conjuration." It is in the general sense of casting out evil spirits, however, that the word is now understood.

The trade of *exorcism* has probably existed at all times In Greece, Epicurus and Æschines, were sons of women who lived by this art, and each was bitterly reproached, the one by the Stoics, theother by Demosthenes, for having assisted his parent in her dishonourable practices.

We read in the Acts of the Apostles (XIX. 13) of the failure and disgrace of " certain of the vagabond Jews, exorcists," who, like the Apostles, " took upon them to call over them that had evil spirits the Name of the Lord Jesus." " God," says Josephus, " enabled Solomon to learn that skill which expels demons, which is a science useful and sanative to men. He composed such incantations also, by which distempers are alleviated, and he left behind him the manner of using *exorcisms*, by which they drive away demons, so that they never return. And this method of cure is of great force unto this day ; for I have seen a certain man of my own country, whose name was Eleazar, releasing people that were demoniacal, in the presence of Vespasian and his sons, and his captains, and the whole multitude of his soldiers. The manner of the cure was this. He put a ring that had a root of one of those sorts mentioned by Solomon to the nostrils of the demoniac, after which he drew out the demon through his nostrils; and when the man fell down immediately, he adjured him to return unto him no more, making still mention of Solomon, and reciting the incantation which he composed. And when Eleazar would persuade and demonstrate to the spectators that he had such a power, he set, a little way off, a cup or basin full of water, and commanded the demon as he went out of the man to overturn it, and thereby to let the spectators know that he had left the man." Some pretended fragments of these conjuring books of Solomon are noticed in the *Codex Pseudepigraphus* of Fabricus; and Josephus himself has described one of the antidemoniacal roots, in a measure reminiscent of the perils attendant on gathering the "mandrake." Another fragment of antiquity bearing on this subject is the *exorcism* practised by Tobit, upon which it is by no means easy to pronounce judgment. Grotius, in a note on that history, states that the Hebrews attributed all diseases arising from natural causes to the influence of demons; and this opinion it is well known, has been pushed much farther than Grotius intended, by Hugh Farmer and others of his school. These facts are derived in great measure from Bekker's most ingenious, though forgotten volumes *Le Monde Enchanté*, to which the reader may be referred for almost all that can be written on the necessity of *exorcism*.

Bekker relates an instance of *exorcism* practised by the modern Jews, to avert the evil influence of the demon Lilis, whom the Rabbis esteem to be the wife of Satan. During the hundred and thirty years, says Rabbi Elias, in his *Thisbi* which elapsed before Adam was married to Eve, he was visited by certain she devils, of whom the four principal were Lilis, Naome, Ogére, and Machalas; these, from their commerce with him, produced a fruitful progeny of spirits. Lilis still continues to visit the chambers of women recently delivered, and endeavours to kill their babes, if boys on the eighth day, if girls, on the twenty-first, after their birth. In order to chase her away, the attendants describes circles on the walls of the chamber, with charcoal, and within each they write, "Adam, Eve, Lilis, avaunt!" On the door also of the chamber they write the names of the three angels who preside over medicine, Senoi, Sansenoi, and Sanmangelof,—a secret which it appears was taught them, somewhat unwittingly, by Lilis herself.

A particular ecclesiastical order of exorcists does not appear to have existed in the Christian church till the close of the third century; and Mosheim attributes its introduction to the prevalent fancies of the Gnostics. In the Xth. Canon of the Council of Antioch, held A.D. 341 exorcists are expressly mentioned in conjunction with subdeacons and readers, and their ordination is described by the IVth. Council of Carthage, 7. It consisted, without any imposition of hands, in the delivery, by the Bishop of a book containing forms of *exorcism*, and directions that they should exercise the office upon "Energumens," whether baptized or only catechumens. The fire of *exorcism*, as St. Augustine terms it, always preceded baptism. Catechumens were exorcised for twenty days previous to the administration of this sacrament. It should be expressly remarked, however, that in the case of such catechumens as were not at the same time energumens, these *exorcisms* were not directed against any supposed demoniacal possession. They were, as Cyril describes them, no more than prayers collected and composed out of the words of Holy Writ, to beseech God to break the dominion and power of Satan in new converts, and to deliver them from his slavery by expelling the spirit of wickedness and error.

Thus in the Greek Church, as Rycaut mentions, before baptism, the priest blows three times upon the child to dispossess the devil of his seat; and this may be understood as symbolical of the power of sin over the unbaptized, not as an assertion of their real or absolute possession.

The exorcists form one of the minor orders of the Romish Church. At their ordination the bishop addresses them as to their duties, and concludes with these words:—Take now the power of laying hands upon the energumens, and by the imposition of your hands, by the grace of the Holy Spirit, and the words of *exorcism*, the unclean spirits are driven from obsessed bodies. One of the completest manuals for a Romish exorcist which ever was compiled, is a volume of nearly 1300 pages, entitled, *Thesaurus Exorcismorum et Conjurationum terribilium, potentissimorum, efficacissimorumque, cum Practica probatissima, quibus, Spiritus maligni, Dæmones, malecifiaque omnia de corporibus humanis tanquam Flagellis Fustigusque fugantur, expelluntur. Doctrinis refertissimus atque uberrimus; ad maximam Exorcistarum commodi-Tatem in lucem editus et recusus, Coloniæ,* 1608. It contains the following Tracts: F. Valerii Polydori Patavini, Ordinis Minor, etc. "Practica Exorcistarum," two parts; F. Hieronymi Mengi Vitellianensis, "Flagellum Dæmonum;" Ejusdem "Fustis Dæmonium;" F. Zachariæ Vicecomitis, "Complementum Artis Exorcistiæ;" Petri Antonii Stampæ, "Fuga Satanæ."

From the first of these treatises, it appears that the energumens were subjected to a very severe corporal as well as spiritual discipline. They were first exercised in Præxorcizationes" which consist of confessions, postulations, protestations, concitations, and interrogations. The *exorcisms* themselves are nine in number: 1. "ex Sanctis nominibus Dei," which are thus enumerated, "Schemhamphoras, Eloha, Ab, Bar, Ruachaccocies Jehovah, Tetragrammaton, Heheje, Haja hove vejhege, El Sabaoth, Agla, Adonai, Cados, Sciadai, Alpha and Omega, Agios and Yschiros, O Theos and Athanatos; 2. ex omnium Sanctorum ordine; 3. ex præcipuis animadversione dignis Sanctorum Angelorum; 4. ex actibus vitæ gloriosæ Virg. Mariæ; 5. ex gestis, Domini Nostri Jesu Christi; 6. ex institutis venerabilium Sacramentorum; 7. ex præcipuis S. Ecclesiæ Dogmatibus; 8. Apocalypsis (Apocalypsews) Beati Joannis Apostoli." All these are accompanied with appropriate psalms, lessons, litanies, prayers, and adjurations. Then follow eight "Postexorcizationes." The three first are to be used according as the demon is more or less obstinately bent on retaining possession. If he is very sturdy, a picture of him is to be drawn, "effigie horribili ac turpi," with his name inscribed under it, and to be thrown into the flames, after having been signed with the cross, sprinkled with holy water and fumigated. The fourth and fifth are forms of thanksgiving and benediction after liberation. The sixth refers to "Incubi" and "Succubi." The seventh is for a haunted house, in which the service varies during every day of the week. The eighth is to drive away demoniacal storms and tempests—for which purpose are to be thrown into a huge fire large quantities of Sabinæ, Hupericonis, Palmæ Christi, Arthemesize, Verbenæ, Aristolochiæ rotundæ, Rutæ, Aster, Attici, Sulphuris et Assæ fetidæ. The second part of the treatise "Dispersio Dæmonum" contains many recipes for charms and amulets against possession. Besides these, there are directions for the diet and medicine of the possessed, as bread provided "contra Diaboli nequitiam et maleficiorum turbinem." Mutton "pro obsessi nutrimento atque Maleficii et Dæmonis detrimento." Wine "pro maleficiatis nutriendis et maleficiis Diabolicisque quibuscunque infestationibus destruendis." Holy water for the same purpose, whenever wine is forbidden. A draught " ad omne maleficium indifferenter solvendum et Diabolum conterendum." Four separate lavements and a night draught for the delirious ; two emetics " pro materialibus instrumentis maleficialibus emittendis." And finally, there is a conserve " virtuosius corroborativa ventriculi a maleficialium instrumentorum materialium vomitione fessi."

In the " Flagellum Dæmonum " are contained numerous cautions to the exorcist himself, not to be deceived by the arts of the demon, particularly when he is employed with possessed women. If the devil refuses to tell his name, the demoniac is to be fumigated. If it be necessary to break off the *exorcism* before the evil spirits be wholly expelled, they are to be adjured to quit the head, heart, and stomach of the energumen, and to abscond themselves in the lower parts of his body, " puta in ungues mortuos pedum."

In the " Fustis Dæmonum " the exorcist is directed, whenever the evil spirit persists in staying, to load him with vituperative addresses. After this railing latinity, redoubled precaution is necessary, and if the demons still refuse to tell their names, the knowledge of which is always great gain, the worst names that can be thought of are to be attributed to them, and fumigations resorted to. The seventh *exorcism* in this treatise is " mirabilis efficaciæ pro his qui in matrimonis a Dæmonibus vel maleficis diabolica arte impediuntur seu maleficiantur." Among other things, they are to be largely anointed with holy oil ; and if all adjurations fail, they are to be strenuously exhorted to patience. In the last form, dumbness is attacked, and a very effectual remedy against this infirmity is a draught of holy water with three drops of holy wax, swallowed on an empty stomach.

Father Vicecomes, in his *Complementum Artis Exorcisticæ*, explains the several signs of possession or bewitchment ; also, in how many separate ways the evil spirit notifies his departure, sometimes by putting out the light, now and then by issuing like a flame, or a very cold blast, through the mouth, nose, or ears. He then writes many prescriptions for emetics, perfumes, and fumigations, calculated to promote these results. The writer concludes with a catalogue of the names of some of the devils of commonest occurrence, which is of very narrow dimensions : Astaroth, Baal, Cozbi, Dagon, Aseroth, Baalimm, Chamo, Beelphegor, Astarte, Bethage, Phogor, Moloch, Asmodæus, Bele, Nergel, Melchon, Asima, Bel, Nexroth, Tartach, Acharon, Belial, Neabaz, Merodach, Adonides, Beæmot, Jerobaal, Socothbenoth, Beelzebub, Leviathan, Lucifer, Satan, Mahomet.

The *Fuga Satanæ* of Stampa is very brief, and does not contain any matter which deserves to be added to the much fuller instructions given by Mengs and Vicecomes. Several of the forms used by Mengs are translated and satirized, in the coarse ridicule which characterized those times, in a little tract entitled *A Whip for the Devil, or the Roman Conjuror*, 1683. A century and a half before this, Erasmus had directed his more polished and delicate wit to the same object ; and his pleasant dialogue *Exorcismus seu Spectrum* is an agreeable and assuredly an unexaggerated picture of these practices.

Those who desire to peruse a treatise on practical *exorcism* should consult the *Histoire admirable de la possession et conversion d'une Penitente, seduite par un Magicien, la faisant Sorcière et Princesse des Sorciers, au païs de Provence, conduite à la Scte. Baume, pour y estre exorcizée, l'an MDCX. au mois de Novembre, soubs l'authorité de R.P.F. Sebastien Michælis, Prieur de Convente Royale de la Scte. Magdalene' a S. Maximin et dudict lieu de la Scte. Baume*, Paris, 1613. The possessed in this case, Magdalaine de Palha, was

exorcised during four months ; she was under the power of five princes of the devils, Beelzebub, Leviathan, Baalberith, Asmodeus and Astaroth, " avec plusieurs autres inférieurs." Beelzebub abode in her forehead, Leviathan in the middle of her head, Astaroth in the hinder part of it ; " la partie de la tête ou ils estoient faisoit, contre nature, un perpetual mouvement et battement ; estans sortis la partie ne bougeoit point."

A second sister of the same convent, Loyse, was also possessed by three devils of the highest degree, Verin, Gresil, and Soneillon ; and of these, Verin, through the proceedings of the exorcists, appears to have turned king's evidence, as it were ; for, in spite of the remonstrances and rage of Beelzebub, " qui commença a rugir et a jetter des cris comme feroit un taureau échauffé," he gave important information and instruction to his enemies, and appeared grievously to repent that he was a devil. The daily Acts and Examinations, from the 27th of November to the following 23rd of April, are specially recorded by the exorcist himself, and all the conversations of the devils are noted down verbatim. The whole business ended in a tragedy, and Louis Gaufridi, a priest of Marseilles, who was accused of witchcraft on the occasion was burned alive at Aix.

Michaelis is eminently distinguished in his line. We find him three years afterwards engaged in exorcising three nuns in the convent of St. Brigette, at Lisle. Whether the two unhappy women, Marie de Sains and her accomplice, Simone Dourlet, who were supposed to have been the causes of this possession, were put to death or not, does not appear. The proceedings may be found in a *Histoire véritable et mémorable de ce qui c'est passé sous l'Exorcisme de trois filles possedées au païs de Flandre*, Paris 1623 ; and they are in some respects an appendix to those against Louis Gaufridi, whose imputed enormities are again related in a second volume of this work.

This transaction appears to have been the work of superstition alone ; but one of far deeper dye, and of almost unparalleled atrocity, occurred at Loudun (q.v.) in 1634, when Grandier (q.v.), curé and canon of that town, was mercilessly brought to the stake partly by the jealousy of some monks, partly to gratify the personal vengeance of Richelieu, who had been persuaded that this ecclesiast had lampooned him, an offence which he never forgave. Some Ursline nuns were tortured to feign themselves possessed, and Grandier was the person accused of having tenanted them with devils. Tranquille, one of the exorcists, published a *Véritable relation des juste procédures observées au fait de la possession des Ursulines de Loudun, et au procés de Grandier*, Paris 1634 ; and by a singular fatality, this reverend personage himself died within four years of the iniquitous execution of his victim, in a state of reputed possession, probably distracted by the self-accusations of remorse.

The last acknowledgment of *exorcism* in the Anglican Church, during the progress of the Reformation, occurs in the first Liturgy of Edward VI. in which is given the following form at baptism : " Then let the priest, looking upon the children, say, ' I command thee, unclean spirit, in the name of the Father, of the Son, and of the Holy Ghost, that thou come out and depart from these infants, whom our Lord Jesus Christ has vouchsafed to call to His holy baptism, to be made members of His Body and of His Holy congregation. Therefore, thou cursed spirit, remember thy sentence, remember thy judgment, remember the day to be at hand wherein thou shalt burn in fire everlasting prepared for thee and thy angels. And presume not hereafter to exercise any tyranny towards these infants whom Christ hath bought with His precious blood, and by this His holy baptism calleth to be of His flock.' " On the remonstrance of Bucer, in his censure of the liturgy, that that *exorcism* was not originally used to any but demoniacs, and that it was uncharitable to imagine that all were demoniacs who came to baptism, it was thought prudent by our reformers to omit it altogether, in their review of the liturgy in the 5th and 6th of Edward VI.

The LXXIId canon thus expresses itself on *exorcism*, " No minister shall, without the license of the bishop of the diocese, first obtained and had under his hand and seal, —attempt upon any pretence whatever, either of obsession or possession, by fasting or prayer, to cast out any devil or devils : under pain of the imputation of imposture or cosenage, and deposition from the ministry."

Extispicy, or **Extispicium** so named from *exta* and *spicere*, to view, consider, was applied to the inspection of entrails chiefly. The officers were Extispices or Aruspices, and one of the instruments they used was called by the same name as the craft, an *extispicium*. The Erturians were the first and also the most learned, who practised *extispicy*, and Romulus is said to have chosen his first Aruspices from among them. The art was also practised throughout Greece, where it had a consecrated priesthood confined to two families. The Roman Aruspices had four distinct duties, to examine the victims before they were opened, to examine the entrails, to observe the flame as the sacrifice was burnt, and also to examine the meat and drink-offering which accompanied it. It was a fatal sign when the heart was wanting, and this is said to have been the case with two oxen that were immolated on the day when Cæsar was killed. If the priest let the entrails fall, or there was more bloodiness than usual, or if they were livid in colour, it was understood to be a portent of instant disaster. Itruvius has attempted to account for the origin of *extispicy* by the custom of examining the viscera of animals, before settling an encampment, to ascertain if the neighbourhood was healthy, an explanation to which little value can be attached.

Eye-biters : In the time of Queen Elizabeth there came among the cattle of Ireland a disease whereby they grew blind. The witches to whose malevolence this evil was attributed were called *eye-biters*, and many of them were executed.

F

Fabre, Pierre Charles : (French Alchemist — Fl. 1630.) Hardly any biographical details concerning this French alchemist are forthcoming. Mr. Waite, in his *Lives of the Alchemystical Philosophers*, declares that *Fabre* was a native of Montpellier ; but we do not find any evidence to support this statement, and it is possible that he has confounded *Fabre* the alchemist with a painter of the same name, who was born at Montpellier, and after whom the Musée Fabre at that town is called. Pierre Jean Fabre appears to have been a doctor of medicine, and to have been renowned in his own day as a scholar of chemistry, a subject on which he compiled several treatises ; while, though it is not recorded that he ever won any marked successes in the field of alchemy, he certainly wrote numerous things dealing wholly or partly with that topic. Of these the most important are *Alchimista Christianus* and *Hercules Pischymicus*, both published at Toulouse, the first in 1632, the second two years afterwards ; and in the latter he maintains that the mythological " labours of Hercules " are allegories, embodying the arcana of hermetic philosophy. The philosopher's stone, he declares complacently, may be found in all compounded circumstances, and is formed of salt, mercury and sulphur.

Fagail : The " parting gift " of the fairies, of Gaelic origin. This may be of a pleasant or unpleasant nature—it may be death, or the conversion of a man who worked badly, was ugly, and of rude speech, into the best workman, the best looking man, and the best speaker in the place.—Campbell's *Superstitions of the Scottish Highlands.*

Fairies : A species of supernatural beings, and one of the most beautiful and important of mythological conceptions. The belief in *fairies* is very ancient and widespread, and the same ideas concerning them are to be found among rude and uncultivated races as in the poesy of more civilised peoples. Of British *fairies* there are several distinct kinds, and these differ considerably in their characteristics. In Ireland, where the belief is strongest, the *fairies* are called " good people," and are of a benevolent but capricious and mischievous disposition. The pixies of England are very similar. The industrious domestic spirit known as Puck, or Robin Goodfellow, is of the fairy kind ; so also are the brownies of Scotland. It is supposed that the hard work of the latter has given them the swarthiness from which they take their name, the other being called *fairies* from their fairness.

Scottish fairy mythology resembles that of Ireland, though of a more sombre cast. In Highland Scotland *fairies* are called *daoine sithe* or " men of peace," and it is believed that every year the devil carries off a tenth part of them. They steal human children, and leave in their places fairy changelings, fretful, wizened, unchildish things. Flint arrow-heads are believed, both in Ireland and Scotland, to be fairy weapons, and the water in which they are dipped is a cure for many ills. Fairy music may often be heard in certain spots, and like the *fairies* themselves it is of exquisite beauty. As in the myth of Persephone, mortals who eat or drink in fairyland are doomed to remain there for ever. If a fairy marry with a human being, there is generally some condition imposed on the latter which, being broken, leads to his undoing. Many fairy legends are found all over Europe, varying a little with the locality but identical in their essential points. The conception of *fairies* is probably animistic. (*See* **Animism.**)

Fairfax, Edward : An English poet of the sixteenth century, author of a work on *Demonology*, wherein he treats somewhat credulously of sorcery.

Falconet, Noel : A physician who died in 1734. Among his works was one entitled *Letters and Remarks on the so-called Potable Gold.*

Familiars : Spirits attendant upon a magician, sorcerer, or witch. The idea probably arose out of that of fetishism (q.v.) especially as many *familiars* were supposed to reside in rings, lockets, or other trinkets worn by the wizard or sorcerer. From Delrio we learn that these spirits were called by the Greeks " Paredrii," as being ever assiduously at hand ; and by the Latins, beside " Familiares," " Martinelli," or " Magistelli," for which names he does not assign any reason. The black dog of Cornelius Agrippa is among the best known *familiars* of modern times. His story rests on the authority of Paulus Jovius, (" Elogia " ci.) and it has been copied by Thevet, among others, in his *Hist. des Hommes plus Illustres et Sçavans*, XVIII. Jovius relates that Agrippa was always accompanied by the devil in the shape of a black dog, and that, perceiving the approach of death, he took a collar ornamented with nails, disposed in magical inscriptions from the neck of the animal, and dismissed him with these memorable words, " Abi perdita Bestia quæ me totum perdidisti." (Away, accursed beast, through whose agency I must now sink into perdition.) The dog thus addressed, it is said, ran hastily to the banks of the Saone, into which he plunged headlong, and was never afterwards seen. Le Loyer says :—" With regard to the demons whom they imprisoned in rings and charms, the magicians of the school of Salamanca and Toledo, and their master Picatrix, together with those in Italy who made traffic of this kind of ware, knew better than to say whether or not they had appeared to those who had been in possession or bought them. And truly I cannot speak without horror of those who pretend to such vulgar familiarity with them, even to speaking of the nature of each particular demon shut up in a ring ; whether he be a Mercurial, Jovial, Saturnine, Martial, or Aphrodisiac spirit ; in what form he is wont to appear when required ; how many times in the night he awakes his possessor ; whether benign or cruel in disposition ; whether he can be transferred to another ; and if, once possessed, he can alter the natural temperament, so as to render men of Saturnine complexion Jovial, or the Jovials Saturnine, and so on. There is no end of the stories which might be collected under this head, to which if I gave faith, as some of the learned of our time have done, it would be filling my paper to little purpose. I will not speak therefore of the crystal ring mentioned by Joalium of Cambray, in which a young child could see all that they demanded of him, and which eventually was broken by the possessor, as the occasion by which the devil too much tormented him. Still less will I stay my pen to tell of the sorcerer of Courtray, whose ring had a demon enclosed in it, to whom it behoved him to speak every five days. In fine, the briefest allusion must suffice to what they relate of a gentleman of Poitou, who had playfully taken from the bosom of a young lady a certain charm in which a devil was shut up. " Having thrown it into the fire," the story goes, " he was incessantly tormented with visions of the devil till the latter granted him another charm, similar to the one he had destroyed, for the purpose of returning to the lady and renewing her interest in him." Heywood writes, if not much more fully on the subject than Le Loyer does, and evidently attaches a far greater degree of credibility to the narratives which he brings forward. " Grillandus is of opinion, that everie Magition and Witch, after they have done their homage to the devell, have a familiar spirit given to attend them, whom they call ' Magistellus,' ' Magister,' ' Martinettus ' or ' Martinellus ' " and these are sometimes visible to men in the shape of a dog, a rat, an aethiope, etc. So it is reported of one Magdalena Crucia, that she had one of these paredrii to attend her like a blackemore. Glycas tells us, that Simon Magus had a great black dog tyed in a chaine, who, if any man came to speak with him whom he had no desire to see was ready to devoure him. His shadow likewise he caused still to go before him ; making the people beleeve that it was the soule of a dead man who still attended him.

" These kindes of familiar spirits are such as they include or keepe in rings hallowed, in viols, boxes, and caskets ; not that spirits, having no bodies, can be imprisoned there against their wills, but that they seem to be confined of their own free-will and voluntarie action.

" Johannes Leo writeth, that such are frequent in Africke, shut in caves, and bear the figure of birds called Aves Hariolatrices, by which the Magitions raise great summes of money, by predicting by them of things future. For being demanded of any difficulty, they bring an answer written in a small scroll of paper, and deliver it to the magition in their bills. Martinus Anthonius Delrius, of the Society of Jesus, a man of profound learning and judgment, writeth, that in Burdegell there was an advocate who in a viol kept one of these Paradrii inclosed. Hee dying, his heires knowing thereof, were neither willing to keepe it, nor durst they breake it ; and demanding counsell, they were persuaded

to go to the Jesuit's Colledge, and to be directed by them. The fathers commanded it to be brought before them and broken ; but the executors humbly besought them that it might not be done in their presence, being fearfull least some great disaster might succeed thereof. At which they smiling, flung it against the wall, at the breaking thereof there was nothing seen or heard, save a small noise, as if the two elements of water and fire had nearly met together, and as soone parted.

" Philostratus tells us, that Apollonius Tyaneus was never without such rings ; and Alexander Neapolitanius affirmeth, that he received them of Jarcha, the great prince of the Gymnosophists, which he took of him as a rich present, for by them he could be acquainted with any deep secret whatsoever. Such a ring had Johannes Jodocus Rosa, a citizen of Cortacensia, who every fifth day had conference with the spirit enclosed using it as a counsellor and director in all his affairs and interprises whatsoever. By it he was not onely acquainted with all newes as well forrein as domesticke, but learned the cure and remedy for all griefs and diseases ; insomuch that he had the reputation of a learned and excellent physition. At length, being accused of sortilege or enchantment, at Arnham, in Guelderland, he was proscribed, and in the year 1548 the chancellor caused his ring, in the public market, to be layd upon an anvil, and with an iron hammer beaten to pieces.

" Mengius reporteth from the relation of a deare friend of his (a man of approved fame and honestie) this historie. In a certain town under the jurisdiction of the Venetians, one of their præstigious artists (whom some call Pythonickes), having one of these rings, in which he had two familiar spirits exorcised and bound, came to a predicant or preaching friar, a man of sincere life and conversation ; and confessed unto him that hee was possessed of such an enchanted ring, with such spirits charmed, with whom he had conference at his pleasure. But since he considered with himselfe, that it was a thing dangerous to his soule, and abhominable both to God and man, he desired to be cleanly acquit of it, and to that purpose he came to receive of him some godly counsell. But by no persuasion would the religious man be induced to have any speech at all with these evil spirits (to which motion the other had before earnestly solicited him), but admonished him to cause the magicke ring to be broken, and that to be done with all speed possible. At which words the *familiars* were heard (as it were) to mourne and lament in the ring, and to desire that no such violence might be offered unto them ; but rather than so, that it would please him to accept the ring, and keepe it, promising to do him all service and vassallage ; of which, if he pleased to accept, they would in a short time make him to be the most famous and admired predicant in all Italy. But he perceiving the devils cunning, under this colour of courtesie, made absolute refusall of their offer ; and withall conjured them to know the reason why they would so willingly submit themselves to his patronage ? After many evasive lies and deceptious answers, they plainly confessed unto him, that they had of purpose persuaded the magition to heare him preach ; that by that sermon, his conscience being pricked and galled, he might be weary of the ring, and being refused of the one, be accepted of the other ; by which they hoped in short time so to have puft him up with pride and heresie, to have percipitated his soule into certaine and never ending destruction. At which the churchman being zealously inraged, with a great hammer broke the ring almost to dust, and in the name of God sent them thence to their own habitation of darkness, or whither it pleased the highest powers to dispose them.

" Of this kinde doubtlesse was the ring of Ggyes (of whom Herodotus doth make mention), by vertue of which he had power to walke invisible ; who, by the murder of his sovereign Candaules, married his queene, and so became King of Lydia. Such, likewise, had the Phocensian tyrant, who, as Clemens Stromaeus speaketh, by a sound which came of itselfe, was warned of all times, seasonable and unseasonable, in which to manage his affairs ; who, notwithstanding, could not be forewarned of his pretended death, but his *familiar* left him in the end, suffering him to be slain, by the conspirators. Such a ring, likewise, had one Hieronimus, Chancellor of Mediolanum, which afterwards proved to be his untimely ruine." (*Hierarchie of the Blessed Angels, vii.; The Principats, p. 475, etc.*)

Sometimes the *familiar* annexed himself voluntarily to a master, without any exercise of magic skill or invocation on his part, nor could such a spirit be disposed of without exorcism, as we learn from the following story cited by Delrio (vi., c. ii., s. 3., q. 3.) :—" A certain man (pater familias—head of a family), lived at Trapani, in Sicily, in whose house it is said, in the year 1585, mysterious voices had been heard for a period of some months. This *familiar* was a dæmon, who, in various ways, endeavoured to annoy man. He had cast huge stones, though as yet he had broken no mortal head ; and he had even thrown the domestic vessels about, but without fracturing any of them. When a young man in the house played and sung, the demon, hearing all, accompanied the sound of the lute with lascivious songs, and this distinctly. He vaunted himself to be a dæmon ; and when the master of the house, together with his wife, went away on business to a certain town, the dæmon volunteered his company. When he returned, however, soaked through with rain, the spirit went forward in advance, crying aloud as he came, and warning the servants to make up a good fire," etc. In spite of these essential services, the paterfamilias called in the aid of a priest and expelled the *familiar*, though not without some difficulty.

A learned German physician has given an instance in which the devil of his own accord enclosed himself in a ring as a *familiar*, thereby proving how dangerous it is to trifle with him.

Paracelsus was believed to carry about with him a *familiar* in the hilt of his sword. Naudé assures us, that he never laid this weapon aside even when he went to bed, that he often got up in the night and struck it violently against the floor, and that frequently when overnight he was without a penny, he would show a purseful of gold in the morning. (*Apologie pour les Grands Hommes soupçonnez de Magie, xiv., p. 281.*) After this, we are not a little disconcerted with the ignoble explanation which he gives of this reputed demon, namely, that although the alchemists maintain that it was no other than the philosopher's stone, he (Naudé) thinks it more rational to believe, if indeed there was anything at all in it, that it was two or three doses of laudanum, which Paracelsus never went without, and with which he effected many strange cures.

The feats of Kelly, " Speculator " to Dr. Dee, may be read in the life of the last-named writer. Of Dr. Dee himself and the spirits Ash, Il, Po, Va, and many others, who used to appear to him, by Kelly's ministry, in a beryl, much may be found in Merie Casaubon's *Relation of what passed for many years between Dr. John Dee and some spirits.* This narrative comprises the transactions of four-and-twenty years, from 1583 to 1607. *Familiars* partook of that jealousy which is always a characteristic of spiritual beings, from the time of Psyche's Cupid downwards, in their intercourse with mortals. This feeling is strongly exemplified in a narrative given by Froissart, and translated by Lord Berners, which relates :—" How a spyrite, called Orthone, serued the lorde of Corasse a long time, and brought euer tidynges from all parts of the worlde."

Fanny : (*See* **Poltergeists**)

Fantasmagoriana : The title of a collection of popular stories, dealing mainly with apparitions and spectres, which was published in Paris in 1812. The contents were for the most part translated from the German.

Faraday : (*See* **Spiritualism.**)

Fascination : From Latin *fascinare*, to enchant. The word in its general acceptation signifies charm, enchant, to bewitch, by the eyes, the looks ; generally, to charm or enchant ; to hold or keep in thraldom by charms, by powers of pleasing.

A belief in *Fascination* (strictly so called) appears to have been very generally prevalent in most ages and countries. For its existence in Greece and Rome we may quote the wish of Theocritus that an old woman might be with him to avert this ill by spitting, or the complaint of Menalcas, in Virgil, that some evil eye has fascinated his lambs. The Romans, indeed, with their usual passion for increasing the host of heaven, deified this power of ill, and enrolled a god " fascinus " among their objects of worship. Although he was a " numen," the celebration of his rites was intrusted by a singular incongruity, to the care of the vestal virgins ; and his phallic attribute was suspended round the necks of children and from the triumphal chariots. Lucretius, writing *Of Natural Witchcraft for Love, etc.*, says : " But as there is *fascination* and witchcraft by malicious and angry eyes unto displeasure, so are there witching aspects tending contrariwise to love, or, at the least, to the procuring of good will and liking. For if the *fascination* or witchcraft be brought to pass or provoked by the desire, by the wishing or coveting any beautiful shape or favour, the venom is strained through the eyes, though it be from afar, and the imagination of a beautiful form resteth in the heart of the lover, and kindleth the fire where it is afflicted. And because the most delicate, sweet and tender blood of the beloved doth there wander, his countenance is there represented, shining in his own blood, and cannot there be quiet, and is so haled from thence, that the blood of him that is wounded, reboundeth, and slippeth into the wounder."

Varius, Prior of the Benedictine Convent of Sta. Sophia in Benevento, published a Treatise, *De Fascino*, in 1589. He first points to whole nations which have been reported to possess the power of *fascination*. Thus the idolatrous " Biarbi " and " Hamaxobii," on the authority of Olaus Magnus, are represented to be " most deeply versed in the art of fascinating men, so that by witchcraft of the eyes, or words, or of aught else (a very useful latitude of expression) they so compel men that they are no longer free, nor of sane understanding, and often are reduced to extreme emaciation, and perish by a wasting disease." He then proceeds to similar marvels concerning animals. Wolves, if they see a man first, deprive him of all power of speech ; a fact yet earlier from Theocritus. The shadow of the hyæna produces the same effect upon a dog ; and this sagacious wild beast is so well acquainted with its own virtue, that whenever it finds dog or man sleeping, its first care is to stretch its length by the side of the slumberer, and thus ascertain his comparative magnitude with its own. If itself be larger of the two, then it is able to afflict its prey with madness, and it fearlessly begins to nibble his hands or paws (whichever they may be) to prevent resistance ; if it be smaller, it quietly runs away. It may be as well to know, (though not immediately bearing on *fascination*), that an attack from a hyæna, if it approaches on the right hand, is peculiarly dangerous ; if from the left, it may be beaten off without much trouble. Lastly, tortoises lay their eggs and afterwards hatch them, as is very credibly affirmed, by virtue of their eyes alone.

The tenth chapter of the *First Book of Vairus* inquires : " An aliqui se fascinare possint ? " a question which is decided in the affirmative, by the example of the Basilisk of Narcissus, and of one less known, though equally unfortunate, Eutelis. In the twelfth chapter he affirms, that the more wicked any person is, the better is he adapted to exercise evil *fascination*. From this book we may extract two useful cautions : " Let no servant ever hire himself to a squinting master, and let jewellers be cautious to whose hands, or rather eyes, they intrust their choicest wares." A friend of Vairus told him, that he had seen a person who was gifted with an eye of such fascinating power, that once while he was looking attentively on a precious stone of fine water, exquisite cutting, and admirable polish, in the hands of a lapidary, the jewel of its own accord split into two parts.

In his Second Book, after disputing against " natural " *fascination*, which he treats as visionary, Vairus determines that all *fascination* is an evil power, attained by tacit or open compact with the devil.

A second writer on this matter is John Lazarus Gutierrez, a Spanish physician, who may be believed to be equally well qualified for the consideration of mystery. His *Opusculum de Fascino* appeared in 1653. On his own experience he does not state much, but in his *Dubium* (III.) he cites Mendoza for an account of a servant of a Tyrolese nobleman, who could bring down a falcon from her very highest flight by steadily looking at her. From Antonius Carthaginensis, also, he produces two other wonders. The first, of a man in Guadalazara, who was in the habit of breaking mirrors into minute fragments solely by looking at them ; the second, of another in Ocana, who used to kill his own children, as well as those of other folks, by the contagion of his eyes ; nay, still more, occasionally, in like manner, to be the cause of death to many valuable horses.

From Cardan, Gutierrez extracts the following symptoms by which a physician may determine that his patient is fascinated :—Loss of colour, heavy and melancholy eyes, either overflowing with tears or unnaturally dry, frequent sighs, and lowness of spirits, watchfulness, bad dreams, falling away of flesh. Also, if a coral or jacinth worn by him loses its colour, or if a ring, made of the hoof of an ass, put on his finger, grows too big for him after a few days' wearing. According to the same writer, the Persians used to determine the sort of *fascination* under which the patient laboured, by binding a clean linen cloth round his head, letting it dry there, and remarking whether any and what spots arose on it.

But the most curious fact which we learn from Gutierrez is that the Spanish children in his time wore amulets against *fascination*, somewhat resembling those in use among the Romans. The son of Gutierrez himself wore one of these ; it was a cross of jet, (" agavache ") and it was believed that it would split if regarded by evil eyes, thus transferring their venom from the child upon itself. In point of fact, the amulet worn by young Gutierrez did so split one day, while a person was steadfastly looking at him ; and, in justice to the learned physician, we must add, that he attributes the occurrence to some accidental cause, and expresses his conviction that the same thing would have happened under any other circumstances. Throughout his volume, indeed, all his reasoning is brought forward to explode the superstition.

A third similar work is that of John Christian Fromman, a physician of Saxe-Coburg, who published his *Tractatus de Fascinatione* in 1675.

We have already learned from Vairus, that all those who are immoderately praised, especially behind their backs, persons of fair complexion, and of handsome face or figure, particularly children, are most exposed to *fascination*, and this notion probably arose from such children attracting from strangers more attention than others less indebted to nature. It was an impression of his own personal beauty which induced Polyphemus to put in practice the spitting charm which Cotattaris had taught him. So we read in Theocritus, Frommann adds, that children in unwashed baby linen are easily subject to *fascination*, and so also is any fair one who employs two lady's maids to dress her hair ; moreover, that all those who lie in bed very late in the morning, especially if they wear nightcaps, all who break their fast on cheese or peas, and all children who, having been once weaned, are brought back to the breast, will, even against their inclination, be gifted with the power of fascinating both men and beasts.

In order to ascertain whether a child be fascinated, three oak apples may be dropped into a basin of water under its cradle, the person who drops them observing the strictest silence ; if they swim the child is free, if they sink it is affected ; or a slice of bread may be cut with a knife marked with three crosses, and both the bread and the knife left on the child's pillow for a night ; if marks of rust appear in the morning the child is fascinated. If on licking the child's forehead with your tongue a salt taste is perceived, this also is an infallible proof of *fascination*.

The following remedies against *fascination* rest upon the authorities either of Vairus or Frommann, or both of them ; several of them may be traced to Pliny :—An invocation of Nemesis ; the root of the " Satyrios Orchis ;" the skin of a hyæna's forehead ; the kernel of the fruit of a palm tree ; " Alyssum " (madwort) hung up anywhere in the house ; the stone " Catochites ;" spitting on the right'shoe before it be put on ; hyssop ; lilies ; fumigations ; sprinklings ; necklaces of jacinth, sapphire, or carbuncle ; washings in river water, provided silence be kept ; licking a child's forehead, first upward, next across, and lastly up again, and then spitting behind its back ; sweeping its face with the bough of a pine tree ; laying it on the ground, covered up in a linen cloth, and then sprinkling it in the form of a cross, with three handfuls of earth, dug where the eaves drop, and brought thence at three separate times within an hour ; laying turf from a boy's grave under a boy's pillow, from a girl's under a girl's ; silently placing near a child the clothes in which it was baptized ; if, as is sometimes the case, a child appears to derive no benefit from washing, taking three scrapings from the plaster of each of the four walls of its bedroom, and sprinkling them on its linen ; three " lavements " of three spoonfuls of milk ; giving in a drink the ashes of a rope in which a man has been hanged ; drawing water silently, and throwing a lighted candle into it in the name of the Holy Trinity, then washing the patient's legs in this water, and throwing the remainder behind its back in the form of a cross ; hanging up the key of the house over the child's cradle ; laying on it crumbs of bread, a lock with the bolt shut, a looking-glass, or some coral washed in the font in which it was baptized ; hanging round its neck fennel seeds, or bread and cheese.

Vairus states, that huntsmen, as a protection against *fascination*, were used to split an oak plant, and pass themselves and their dogs between it. As amulets against love *fascination*, he recommends sprinkling with the dust in which a mule has rolled itself ; a bone which may be found in the right side of a toad ; or the liver of a chameleon. Vida has given a highly elaborate description of one who possessed this destructive power in his eye, after enjoining especial caution respecting those who are permitted to look at the silkworms. Some instances of yet more modern belief in *fascination* than those to which we have referred above, may be found collected in Brand's *Popular Antiquities*. It appears even in our own days to be prevalent among the inhabitants of the western islands of Scotland, who use nuts, called Molluca beans, as amulets against it. Dallaway, in his *Account of Constantinople* remarks, that " Nothing can exceed the superstition of the Turks respecting the evil eye of an enemy or infidel. Passages from the Koran are painted on the outside of the houses, globes of glass are suspended from the ceiling, and a part of the superfluous caparison of their horses is designed to attract attention and divert a sinister influence."

Delrio has a very short notice of *fascination* ; he divides it into " Poetica seu Vulgaris," that resulting from obscure physical causes, which he treats as fabulous ; " Philosophica," which he considers to be contagion ; and " Magica," to which he heartily assents.

Fat of the Sorcerers : It was said at one time that the devil made use of human fat for his sorceries. The witches anointed themselves with this fat in order to go to the Sabbath by way of the chimney.

Fatimites : (*See* **Arabs**.)

Faust : A magician of the sixteenth century, famous in legend and literature. There is sound proof that such a person existed. Trithemius (q.v.) mentions him in a letter written in 1507, in which he speaks of him in terms of contempt, as a fool and a mountebank who pretended that he could restore the writings of the ancients were they wiped out of human memory, and blasphemed concerning the miracles of Christ. Mudt, a canon of the German Church also alludes to him in a letter as a charlatan. Johann Gast, a Protestant pastor of Basel, appears to have known Faust, and considers a horse and dog belonging to him to have been familiar spirits. Wier (q.v.), the great protector of witches, mentions *Faust* in a work of his, as a drunkard who had studied magic at Cracow. He also mentions that in the end Satan strangled him after his house had been shaken by a terrific din. From other evidence it is pretty clear that *Faust* was a wandering magician or necromancer, whose picturesque character won him wide publicity or notoriety. By the end of the century in which he flourished he had become the model of the mediæval magician, and his name was for ever linked with those of Virgil, Bacon, Pope Silvester and others.

The origins of the *Faust* legend are of very great antiquity. The essentials underlying the story are the pact with Satan, and the supposed vicious character of purely human learning. The idea of the pact with Satan belongs to both Jewish and Christian magico-religious belief, but is probably more truly Kabalistic than anything else, and can scarcely be traced further back ; unless it resides in the savage idea that a sacrificed person takes the place of the deity, to which he is immolated during the period of life remaining to him before his execution, and afterwards becomes one with the god. The wickedness of believing in the all-sufficiency of human knowledge is a favourite theme with the early Lutherans, whose beliefs strongly coloured the *Faust* legend ; but vivid hues and wondrously carven outlines were also afforded its edifice by the thought of the age in which it finally took shape ; and in the ancient *Faust-* books we find tortuous passages of thought and quaintnesses of conception which recall to our minds the artistry of the Renaissance.

The *Faust-book* soon spread over Europe ; but to England is due the honour of the first dramatic representation of the story by Christopher Marlowe, who in the *Tragicall History of Dr. Faustus* produced a wondrous, if unequal drama,—the outstanding passages of which contained most of his best work. Lessing wrote a *Faust* play during the German revival of the eighteenth century, but it remained to Goethe to crown the legend with the creation of the greatest psychological drama the world has ever seen. The manner in which Goethe differed from his predecessors in his treatment of the story lies in the circumstance that he gives a different character to the pact between *Faust* and Mephistopheles, whose nature again is totally at variance with the devils of the old *Faust-books*. From Lessing Goethe received the idea of *Faust's* final salvation. It may be said that though in some respects Goethe adopted the letter of the old legend he did not adopt its spirit. Probably the story of *Faust* has given to thousands their only idea of mediæval magic, and this idea has lost nothing in the hands of Goethe, who has cast about the subject a much greater halo of mystery than it perhaps really contains. (*See* **Goethe**.)

Fay, Annie Eva : A medium. (*See* **Spiritualism**.)

Feliciani, Lorenza : (*See* **Cagliostro**.)

Fendeurs : A supposed French Rosicrucian Society, concerning which very little is known. It flourished in the middle of the seventeenth century ; and its members claimed that it was of Scottish origin.

Feortini : (*See* **Visions**.)

Ferarius : This alchemist is supposed to have been an Italian priest of the thirteenth century, but nothing is known concerning his career. Various chymical writings ascribed to him are embodied in that curious collection, the *Theatrum Chimicum*, prominent among them being *De Lapide Philosophorum* and *Thesaurus Philosophiæ* ; and in the former the author observes, rather tritely, that in alchemy the first thing to be ascertained is what is really signified by the myrionimous *argentum vivum sapientium*. But he does not volunteer any information in this particular, and his works in general are obscure, and of but little interest.

Ferdinand D. Schertz : (*See* **Magia Posthuma**.)

Fern : The common *Fern*, it was believed, was in flower at midnight on St. John's Eve, and whoever got possession of the flower would be protected from all evil influences, and would obtain a revelation of hidden treasure. *Fern* seed was supposed to render one invisible.

Ferrier, Susan : (*See* **Fiction, Occult English**.)

Fetch : According to Irish belief, the apparition of a living person ; the Irish form of the wraith (q.v.) It resembles in every particular the individual whose death it is supposed to foretell, but it is generally of a shadowy or ghostly appearance. The *fetch* may be seen by more than one person at the same time and, like the wraith of England and Scotland, may appear to the person it represents. There is a belief, too, that if the *fetch* be seen in the morning, it indicates long life for the original : but if it be seen at night, his speedy demise may be expected. The *Fetch* enters largely into the folk-tales of Ireland ; and it is hardly surprising that so many tales have been woven around it, for there is something gruesome in the idea of being haunted by one's own " double " which has frequently been turned to account by more sophisticated writers than the inventors of folk-tales.

Patrick Kennedy, in his *Legendary Fiction of the Irish Celt*, speaking of the Irish *fetch*, gives the following tale of *The Doctor's Fetch*, based, it is stated, on the most authentic sources : " In one of our Irish cities, and in a room where the mild moonbeams were resting on the carpet and on a table near the window, Mrs. B., wife of a doctor in good practice and general esteem, looking towards the window from her pillow, was startled by the appearance of her husband standing near the table just mentioned, and seeming to look with attention on the book which was lying open on it. Now, the living and breathing man was by her side apparently asleep, and, greatly as she was surprised and affected, she had sufficient command of herself to remain without moving, lest she should expose him to the terror which she herself at the moment experienced.

After gazing on the apparition for a few seconds, she bent her eyes upon her husband to ascertain if his looks were turned in the direction of the window, but his eyes were closed. She turned round again, although now dreading the sight of what she believed to be her husband's *fetch*, but it was no longer there. She remained sleepless throughout the remainder of the night, but still bravely refrained from disturbing her partner.

" Next morning, Mr. B., seeing signs of disquiet on his wife's countenance while at breakfast, made some affectionate inquiries, but she concealed her trouble, and at his ordinary hour he sallied forth to make his calls. Meeting Dr. C, in the street, and falling into conversation with him, he asked his opinion on the subject of *fetches*. ' I think,' was the answer, ' and so I am sure do you, that they are mere illusions produced by a disturbed stomach acting upon the excited brain of a highly imaginative or superstitious person.' ' Then,' said Mr. B., ' I am highly imaginative or superstitious, for I distinctly saw my own outward man last night standing at the table in the bedroom, and clearly distinguishable in the moonlight. I am afraid my wife saw it too, but I have been afraid to speak to her on the subject.'

" About the same hour on the ensuing night the poor lady was again roused, but by a more painful circumstance. She felt her husband moving convulsively, and immediately afterwards he cried to her in low, interrupted accents, ' Elleo, my dear, I am suffocating ; send for Dr. C.' She sprang up, huddled on some clothes, and ran to his house. He came with all speed, but his efforts for his friend were useless. He had burst a large blood-vessel in the lungs, and was soon beyond human aid. In her lamentations the bereaved wife frequently cried out, ' Oh ! the *fetch*, the *fetch !* ' and at a later period told the doctor of the appearance the night before her husband's death.

Fetishism : The term *fetishism* is employed in more than one sense. Thus it may mean in some cases pure idolatry or the worship of inanimate objects. Again in older works of travel, it is even used to signify African religion. But taken in its general and more modern sense, it signifies any inanimate object which appears to the savage as the residence of a spirit. Thus a carved doll, a necklace of teeth, a flint stone into which a shaman or medicine-man has succeeded in coaxing a spirit to reside, is regarded by the savage as a fetish. But larger objects are occasionally adopted as fetishes, and in the adoption of these in contradistinction to the smaller fetishes we can trace the evolution of the idol. As a general rule the fetish is an object peculiar in shape or material, for such is considered by the shaman as being more likely to attract a wandering spirit than any more ordinary substance. Thus we find as fetishes peculiarly shaped stones, tufts of human hair and bones, parts of animals and birds, and so forth. Fossils are not uncommonly employed as fetishes, possibly because of their freakish formation.

The origin of *fetishism* is undoubtedly animistic (*See* **Animism**). The savage intelligence regards everything that surrounds it as possessing the property of life—water, the earth, trees, stones and so forth. But this is modified by the idea that many of these objects are under the power of some spell or potent enchantment. Thus the rocks and trees are the living tombs of imprisoned spirits, resembling the dryads of folk-lore ; so that it is not at all strange to the savage mind to perceive an imprisoned intelligence more or less powerful, in any object, no matter how uncommon its form. In fact, according to the savage mind, spirit was dependent to a great extent upon material body. The wandering spirit, according to the barbarian, could not fare much better, materially speaking, than a wandering savage : it would suffer the rigours of hunger and cold,

and would be only too agreeable to be at rest for a while where it would be treated with every deference and properly attended to. For this purpose a shaman will either manufacture or search for a fitting residence for this spirit, and he will proceed by various rites to attempt to coax some wandering intelligence to take up its home therein.

There is of course a point at which the fetish commences to develop into a god. This happens when fetishes survive the test of experience and achieve a more than personal or tribal popularity. Thus amongst the Zuñi Indians a fetish called " The Knife-feathered Monster " has practically become the tribal god of war, and a pony and sheep fetish are at present in course of evolving as deities in the pantheon of this people. Amongst the Zuñi there appears to have been the conception that their fetishes were totemistic. *Fetishism* and totemism are not incompatible with one another, but often flourish side by side ; but the basic difference between a fetish and a totem is that the fetish spirit is the bond slave of the person who owns its abode, whereas the totem is his patron spirit, personal or tribal. Nevertheless the fetish partakes more of the nature of those spirits which are subservient to man, as for example the Arabian Jinn, than of those which subsequently develop into gods. They are more of the race of faery, of the little folk who dwelt in the crevices of rocks and trees, the smaller swarm of the supernatural, than of the strain of Olympus. A capital example of a fetish, which will be familiar to all, is that which occurs in the story of Aladdin and his lamp. Here we have the subservient nature-spirit—the original conception of which must have been that it dwelt in the lamp or the ring, and was only freed therefrom on the summons of its temporary master to perform some special piece of work. But a fetish is not necessarily a piece of personal property : it may belong collectively to an entire community or family, and it is usually an heirloom.

The savage naturally attaches great importance to those fetishes which assist him in the chase. Thus the Zuñi Indians, who possess perhaps the most complete fetishistic system of any barbarous people, have a special temple-house set apart for their tribal fetishes of the hunt, which they call the Prey-gods. On setting out for the hunt, the Zuñi Indian will visit the fetish-house, and sprinkle a little maize meal on a platter placed before that fetish which he wishes to employ in his expedition. In this office he is usually assisted by a medicine-man set aside for the purpose, whose special duty it is to see that the fetishes are properly placated and returned when their services are no more required. Let us suppose that he selects the fetish of the mountain-lion. This is a stone object, shaped in the likeness of that animal. Once in the open country, the hunter places the mouth of the fetish to his own and suspires deeply, imagining that by so doing he is breathing in the hunting instinct of the mountain-lion. He then forcibly emits his breath. The Indian idea is that beasts of prey are able by the emission of breath to render the game helpless over a wide area, and this the hunter believes he has successfully and magically imitated. When he meets with his game, after slaying it, his first act is to excise the liver, which he smears upon the lips of the fetish, which is then duly returned to the fetish-house. Most of the objects belonging to a medicine-man or shaman are believed to be fetishes,—that is, they possess a certain quality of life that other, and more ordinary, objects do not have.

The word fetish is derived from the Portuguese *feitiço* which implies " something made," and was applied by early voyagers in West Africa to the wooden figures, stones and so forth, regarded as the residence of spirits. *Fetishism* in Africa appears to be generally confined to the coasts, but in America it is prevalent more or less over the whole hemisphere. That it was once prevalent in Europe is practically certain from the nature of many objects found in prehistoric and early historic graves, and in certain parts of Asia, it is by no means extinct. The material conception of *fetishism* survives in the charm, amulet or mascot, which is regarded as a luck-bringer, although the spiritual significance connected with it has quite vanished. (*See* **Charms and Amulets, Familiar**).

Fey : To possess second sight. (*See* **Teutons.**)

Fiction, English Occult : English literature, as it is known to-day, really begins with the Elizabethan age ; for the writers prior to that time, excellent as many of them are, elicit comparatively little interest nowadays save among experts. And, by the time of Elizabeth's advent, the old " miracle plays " had gone out of fashion ; yet tales about the miraculous doings of mythical heroes continued to find favour, and many new things of this kind were written.

A few of the Restoration dramatists dealt in magic and the like, but throughout the Georgian age people were mostly too prosaic, too matter-of-fact, to care for things of that sort, and they were eschewed by the majority of prominent writers of the day. However, after the great artistic movement commonly styled the Renaissance of Wonder, the old interest in the occult began to revive apace, and, ere the nineteenth century was very far advanced, a literature suitable to this budding taste was being purveyed on a voluminous scale. Among the first to enter the lists, *soi disant*, was William Godwin, with his novel of *St. Truyne the Rosicrucian* ; while Godwin's daughter, Mary, chiefly remembered nowadays as the second wife of Shelley, merits notice as a mystical writer by virtue of her story of *Frankenstein*. A little before the advent of this authoress, numerous occult tales had been written by Matthew Lewis, notably *Tales of Terror* and the drama of *Castle Spectre*, staged successfully at Drury Lane in 1798 ; while not long after Lewis a further novelist came to swell the muster-roll, Bulwer Lytton, whose taste for the mystic is seen especially in *Zanoni*, *A Strange Story*, and *Haunters and the Haunted*. His essays of this kind, nevertheless, were never very satisfactory in the real literary sense ; and as Leslie Stephen once discovered, they too often smacked of the theatrical. But Sir Walter Scott, on the other hand, writing just before Lytton's time, not only showed a keen fondness for occult matter, but frequently utilised it to genuine artistic purpose. In *The Monastery* a mysterious sylph rises from a fountain ; astrology is introduced into *Guy Mannering*, *The Fortunes of Nigel*, and *Quentin Durward ;* while a splendid ghost story is told in *Redgauntlet*, and ghosts figure also in *Woodstock*. In *The Bride of Lammermoor*, besides, the author deals incidentally with that firm belief in prophecy which was long a prominent part of Scottish life ; while in *Waverley*, again, he depicts a Highland chief as awestruck and unmanned by the sight of a peculiar omen. Highland superstitions, indeed, appealed with particular potency to Sir Walter's romantic temper ; while he was not the only writer of his time who dealt ably with this branch of the occult, another being Susan Ferrier in her novels of *Destiny* and *The Chief's Daughter*. Nor should we fail ere leaving this period, to mention Ann Radcliffe, for in almost all her novels the supernatural figures prominently.

While the last-named trio were at work thus in Britain, some good stories in which magic occurs were being written in America by Washington Irving ; and, not very long after his day, a second American arose to treat brilliantly of weirdness and wizardry, Edgar Allan Poe. Then, reverting to England, ghosts appear in a few of Dickens' novels, and Charles Reade manifests here and there a love of the occult ; while coming to slightly later times, a writer

who manifested this predilection abundantly is Robert Louis Stevenson. His *Dr. Jekyll and Mr. Hyde* is among the best of all modern novels in which the supernatural plays a salient rôle, and many of his short stories pertain also to the category of occult, for example, the tale of the magic bottle in *Island Nights Entertainments ;* while, about the date these were being composed, Oscar Wilde was writing what is one of the most beautiful things dealing with invisible powers, *The Picture of Dorian Gray*. Much inferior to this masterpiece, yet possessing considerable excellence, are George du Maurier's *Peter Ibbetson*, *Trilby* and *The Martian*, in each of which the supernatural is prominent ; while a further work which should certainly be cited is Lafcadio Hearn's *Dead Love*, a tiny tale of magic which the author thought lightly of, but which future generations are almost sure to prize on account of its lovely wording, at some places worthy of Théophile Gautier himself, who was Hearn's acknowledged master.

These recent authors do not by any means conclude the list, for a wealth of occult *fiction* has been written since their day. Among its most remarkable items is *The Ghost Ship* of Richard Middleton, a singularly promising storyteller and poet who died by his own hand lately at the early age of twenty-nine ; while many contemporary novelists have introduced magic into their books, for instance, Mr. Rider Haggard in *She*, the late Mr. Bram Stoker in *Dracula*, and Mr. F. A. Anstey in *Vice Versa* and *The Brass Bottle*. In fact, were one to cite all the living wont to trade in the occult, an article of formidable size would be the result, and accordingly the attempt must be eschewed ; but at least it is essential to mention Mr. Theodore Watts-Dunton's *Aylwin*, this reflecting really fine treatment of mystic matter, and being couched throughout in a style of exceptional beauty. Mr. Arthur Symons is another great writer of to-day who loves the borderland between dreams and realities, as witness many pages in his *Spiritual Adventures ;* while the invisible world has always appealed powerfully to Mr. W. B. Yeats, and is employed to good purpose here and there in his stories of the Irish peasantry. It is less the ghost than the fairy which he delights in, true Celt that he is ; and his predilection herein sets one dreaming of fairy-tales in general, and summons a curious medley of names. William Morris wrote a host of beautiful fairy-stories, some of them concerned with the promulgation of socialistic ideas, but others innocent of anything of that sort ; while the voluminous works of Ruskin include what can only be defined as a fairy tale, *The King of the Golden River*. Numerous contemporary writers have likewise done good work in this field—Lord Dunsany, Mr. J. M. Barrie, and more especially Mr. Laurence Housman—while a remarkable fairy play has been written lately by Mr. Graham Robertson, and has been staged with surprising triumph. Then, reverting for a moment to defunct authors, fairies occur in that charming volume by H. D. Lowry, *Make Believe*, and in Richard Middleton's book, *The Day Before Yesterday ;* while no account of this particular domain of literature would be complete without mention of the work of Lewis Carrol, and also of Jean Ingelow's lovely story, *Mopsa the Fairy*. This last is possibly the best of all fairy stories, and one which has been most widely and wisely cherished ; and it stands out very clearly in the memory of nearly every man of imaginative temperament, reminding him of his own childhood.

Figuier, Guillaume Louis : A French writer and chemist, born at Montpellier in 1819. His uncle, Pierre Figuier, was professor of chemistry at the School of Pharmacy, Montpellier, and Louis, having taken his degree of doctor of medicine, and studied chemistry at the laboratory of Balard in Paris, was made professor of chemistry at the School of Pharmacy, Montpellier. He later—1853 —

exchanged this post for a similar one in the School of Pharmacy of Paris. Thereafter many honorary degrees in science and medicine were conferred upon him by various faculties. In 1857 he finally left off teaching and devoted himself to the popularising of science, mainly physiology and medical chemistry. He published from time to time many notable works, and was not more distinguished for his prodigious output than for its literary quality. Of those works having a bearing on occult matters the principal are : *le Lendemain de la mort ou La Vie future selon la science* (1872) dealing with the transmigration of souls ; *l' Alchimie et les Alchimistes* (1854) ; *Histoire du merveilleux dans les temps modernes* (1859-60); *les Bonheurs d' outre tombe* (1892.) He tried to popularize science by introducing on the stage plays whose heroes were savants and inventors. His attempt however, met with but a cold reception. In 1889 he published a volume of dramas and comedies, *la Science au Thèâtre*. He died at Paris in 1894.

Fingitas : The tradition concerning this stone is remarkable. It is described as quite transparent and hard like marble. It is related that a certain king built a temple of it which needed no windows, the light being admitted into it as if it had been all open to the day.

Finias : One of the four great cities whence the Irish mythical Danaans were said to have sprung.

Finn Mac Cummal : In Irish romance, Captain of the Fianna and the centre of the Ossianic tales. His father Cumhal, chief of the clan Basena, was slain at Castle Knock by the rival clan Morna, but his mother succeeded in saving him from the enemy. He was brought up in hiding and given the name of *Finn* from the clearness of his skin. He learned science and poetry from the druid Finegas who dwelt on the river Boyne. The druid had been unable to catch the salmon of knowledge until *Finn* became his pupil, and when he did succeed in catching it, he told *Finn* to watch it while it was cooking but not to partake of it. *Finn*, however, burned his fingers as he turned the spit and put one of them in his mouth. Seeing this, Finegas bade him eat the salmon and he became filled with the wisdom of all ages. Afterwards he took service with King Cormac to whom he revealed his name and lineage. Cormac promised him the leadership of the Fianna if he succeeded in killing the fire-blowing demon that came yearly to set Tara in flames. *Finn* slew the demon and bore his head back to Tara. The Fianna were therefore ordered to swear allegiance to *Finn* as their captain, which, led by Goll mac Morna, their former captain, they all did. Under *Finn*, the Fianna rose to great eminence, an eminence which at length became tyrannical and from which they were thrown at the battle of Bowra. *Finn's* end is shrouded in mystery. According to popular tradition he and his great companions lie sleeping in an enchanted cave whence they shall arise in the hour of their country's need, like Arthur, Barbarossa and Charlemagne.

Fioravanti, Leonardi : An Italian alchemist doctor and surgeon of the sixteenth century. He was a voluminous writer whose best known work is a *Summary of the Arcana of Medicine, Surgery and Alchemy*, published in Venice in 1571. It embraces an application of the principles and methods of Hermes to the Science of Medicine. The author's account of the *petra philosophorum* shews its designation to be purely arbitrary. It is a mixture of mercury, nitre and other ingredients intended as a stomachic and has no connection with the transmuting *lapis* of the alchemists.

Fire : Many nations have adored this element. In Persia a chimneyless enclosure was made, and into it *fire* was introduced. Essences and perfumes were cast into the *fire* by the great persons of the nation. When a Persian king was at the point of death all the *fires* in the principal towns of the kingdom were extinguished, and were not rekindled until the crowning of his successor. Certain Tartars never accost foreigners who have not purified themselves by passing between two fires ; they are also careful to drink with their faces turned to the south, in honour of the element of *fire*. In some parts of Siberia it is believed that *fire* is inhabited by a being who dispenses good and evil ; they offer him perpetual sacrifices. According to the kabalists, this was the element of the Salamanders. (See also **Fire Ordeal**.)

Fire, Magical : (*See* **Magic.**)

Fire-Mist, Children of the : (*See* **Lords of the Flame.**)

Fire-ordeal : The *fire-ordeal* is of great antiquity, and probably arose from the conception of the purifying influence of fire. Among the Hindoos, from the earliest times until comparatively recently, those who were suspected of wrongdoing were required to prove their guilt or innocence by walking over red-hot iron. If they escaped unharmed their innocence was placed beyond a doubt. The priestesses of a Cappodocian goddess, Diana Parasya, walked barefooted on red-hot coals, attributing their invulnerability to the powers of the divinity. In Europe trial by fire was of two kinds—traversing the flames, or undergoing the ordeal of hot iron. The latter form comprised the carrying in the hand of red-hot irons, the walking over iron bars or glowing ploughshares, and the thrusting of the hand into a red-hot gauntlet. An early instance of the former mode in European history is that of Pierre Barthelémy, who in 1097 declared to the Crusaders that heaven had revealed to him the place where was concealed the spear that had pierced the Saviour's body. To prove his assertion he offered to undergo the ordeal by fire, and was duly required to walk a path about a foot in width and some fourteen feet in length, on either side of which were piled blazing olive-branches. The judgment of the fire was unfavourable, and twelve days later the rash adventurer expired in agony. Books also were sometimes submitted to the trial by fire. This method was adopted to decide the claims of the Roman and Mozaratian liturgies, the former emerging victorious from the flames. Among savage people the *fire-ordeal* is also to be met with, and especially in New Zealand, India, Fiji, and Japan. It may be suspected that the issue of these ordeals was not always left on the knees of the gods. There is no doubt that the ancient Egyptians were acquainted with substances which rendered the body partly immune. Albertus Magnus gives a recipe for this purpose. It is made up of powdered lime, made into a paste with the white of an egg, the juice of the radish, the juice of the marsh mallow, and the seeds of the fleabane. A first coat of this mixture is applied to the body and allowed to dry, when a second coat is applied. If the feet are constantly oiled, or moistened with sulphuric acid, they may be rendered impervious. Possibly the ancients were not unaware of the fire-resisting properties of asbestos. The *fire-ordeal* has remained to this day as one of the phenomena of spiritualism. D. D. Home frequently handled live coals, and laid them on a handkerchief without damaging the material in the least. On one occasion he enclosed a glowing coal in his hands and blew upon it until it became white hot. A well known instance is that related by Mrs. S. C. Hall, when Home placed a burning coal on the head of Mr. Hall, whose white hair was then drawn over the still glowing coal. In an account given by Mrs. Homewood and Lord Lindsay of a séance with the same medium we are told that Home took a chimney from a lighted lamp and thrust it into the fire, making it so hot that a match applied to it ignited instantly, and then thrust it into his mouth, touching it with his tongue, without any apparent ill effects. Another account states that Home placed his face right in the fire among the burning coals " moving it about as though bathing it in water." Other mediums, both in England and America, emulated this feat with some measure of success. It has been suggested that the state of trance generally accompanying such exploits, and corresponding to the ecstasy of the shaman performing a similar feat, may produce anæsthesia, or insensibility to the pain of burning. But how it comes that the skin is not scorched, nor the material of the handherchief marked by the burning coal, it is not easy to say.

Flamel, Nicholas, was born at Pontoise, of a poor but respectable family, about the beginning of the fourteenth century. He received a good education, of which his natural abilities enabled him to make the best use. Repairing to Paris, he obtained employment as a public scrivener,—sitting at the corner of the Rue de Marivaux, copying or inditing letters and other documents. The occupation brought with it little profit, and *Flamel* tried in succession poetry and painting with an equally unsatisfactory result. His quick wits suggested that as he could make no money by teaching mankind, it might be more profitable to cheat them, and he took up the pursuit of Astrology, casting horoscopes and telling fortunes. He was right in his conjectures, and soon throve so vigorously that he was enabled to take unto himself a wife named Petronella. But those who begin to study the magic art for profit or amusement generally finish by addicting themselves to it with a blindly passionate love. *Nicholas* devoted himself both day and night to his fascinating but deceptive pursuits ; and soon acquired a thorough knowledge of all that previous adepts had written upon the *elixir vitæ*, the universal Alkahest, and the Philosopher's Stone. In 1297 he lighted upon a manual of the art which would have been invaluable if it had been intelligible. He bought it for two florins. It contained three times seven leaves written with a steel instrument upon the bark of trees. The caligraphy was as admirable as the Latin was cryptical. Each seventh leaf was free from writing, but emblazoned with a picture ; the first, representing a serpent swallowing rods ; the second, a serpent crucified on a cross ; and the third, the arid expanse of a treeless desert, in whose depths a fountain bubbled, with serpents trailing their slimy folds from side to side. The author of this mysterious book purported to be " Abraham, the patriarch, Jew, prince, philosopher, Levite, priest, and astrologer," (q.v.) who added to his other claims upon the wonder of mankind a knowledge of Latin. He had included within these precious pages a complete exposition of the art of transmuting metals ; describing every process, explaining the different vessels, and pointing out the proper seasons for making experiments. In fact, the book would have been perfect, but for one deficiency ; it was addressed not so much to the tyro as to an adept, and took it for granted that its student was already in possession of the Philosopher's Stone. This was a terrible obstacle to the inquiring *Flamel*. The more he studied the book the less he understood it. He studied the letterpress, and he studied the illustrations ; he invited the wise men of France to come and study them, but no light was thrown upon the darkness. For thrice seven years he pored over these perplexing pages, until at length his wife suggested that a Jewish Rabbi might be able to interpret them. As the chiefs of the Jews were principally located in Spain, to Spain went *Flamel*, and there he remained for two years. From one of the Hebrew sages he obtained some hints which afforded a key to the patriarchal mysteries, and returning to Paris he recommenced his studies with a new vigour. They were rewarded with success. On the 13th of February, 1382, o.s., *Flamel* made a projection on Mercury, and produced some virgin silver. On the 25th of the following April he converted some Mer-

cury into gold, and found himself the fortunate possessor of an inexhaustible treasure. But his good fortune did not end here. *Flamel*, continuing his researches discovered the elixir of life, which enabled him to prolong his life— and accumulate gold—to the venerable age of 116. He further administered the life-giving potion to his wife, who reached nearly as great a longevity as himself, dying in the year preceding his own death, A.D. 1414. As they had no children, they spent their wealth upon churches and hospitals, and several of the religious and charitable institutions of France still attest their well-directed benevolence. There is no doubt that *Flamel* practised alchemy, and one of his works on the fascinating science—a poem entitled *The Philosophic Summary*—was printed as late as 1735. In Salmon's valuable and very curious *Bibliotheque des Philosophes Chimiques* are preserved some specimens of the drawings in Abraham's treatise on metallurgy and of his own handwriting. But *Flamel* was neither an enthusiast nor a dupe. His alchemical studies were but the disguises of his usurious practices. To account for the immense wealth he acquired by money-lending to the young French nobles, and by transacting business between the Jews of France and those of Spain, he invented the fiction of his discovery of the Philosopher's Stone. He nevertheless obtained great repute as a magician, and his followers believed that he was still alive though retired from the world, and would live for six centuries.

Flammarion, Camille : (*See* **Spiritualism.**)

Fletcher, Anna : (*See* **Germany.**)

Flight of Birds in Augury : (*See* **Divination.**)

Flournoy Prof. : (*See* **Automatic Writing and Speaking.**)

Fludd, or Flud, Robert : This Rosicrucian and alchemist was born in 1574 at Milgate House, in the parish of Bearsted, Kent, his father being one Sir Thomas Fludd, a knight who enjoyed the patronage of Queen Elizabeth, and served her for several years as " Treasurer of War in the Low Countries." At the age of seventeen Robert entered St. John's College, Oxford, and five years later he took his degree as Bachelor of Arts ; while shortly afterwards, on his deciding to take up medical science, he left England and went to prosecute his studies on the Continent. Going first to Spain, he travelled thence to Italy, and subsequently stayed for some time in Germany, where he is said to have supported himself by acting as pedagogue in various noble households ; but soon he was home again, and in 1605 his *alma mater* of Oxford conferred on him the degrees of Bachelor of Medicine and Doctor of Medicine, while five years later he became a Fellow of the College of Physicians. Having thus equipped himself thoroughly for the medical profession, Fludd went to London and took a house in Fenchurch Street, a quiet place in those days, though now a noisy centre of commerce ; and here he soon gained an extensive practice, his success being due not merely to his genuine skill, but to his having an attractive and even magnetic personality. But busy though he was in this way, he found leisure to write at length on medicine ; while anon he became an important and influential member of the Fraternity of the Rosy Cross, and at the same time he commenced alchemical experiments. He preached the great efficacy of the magnet, of sympathetic cures, of the weapon-salve ; he declared his belief in the Philosopher's Stone, the universal alkahest or solvent, the *elixir vitæ* ; he maintained that all things were animated by two principles—condensation, the Boreal, or northern virtue ; and rarefaction, the Austral, or southern virtue. He asserted that the human body was controlled by a number of demons, that each disease had its peculiar demon, each demon his particular place in the frame of humanity, and that to conquer a disease—say in the right leg—you must call in the aid of the demon who ruled the left, always proceeding by this rule of contraries. As soon as the doctrines of the Rosy Cross Brotherhood were promulgated *Fludd* embraced them with all the eagerness of which his dreamy intellect was capable ; and several German writers having made an attack upon them, he published a defence in 1616, under the title of *Apologia Compendiaria Fraternitatem de Rosea-Cruce Suspicionis et Infamiæ Maculis Aspersam Abluens*, which procured him a wide-spread reputation as one of the apostles of the new fraternity. He met with the usual fate of prophets, and was lustily belaboured by a host of enemies—by Mersenne, Gassendi, and Kepler. *Fludd* was by no means discomfited, and retorted upon his opponents in an elaborate treatise, *Summum Bonum, quod est Magiæ, Cabalæ, Alchimiæ, Fratrum Roseæ-Crucis Verorum, et adversus Mersenium Calumniatorem*. He made at a later period and aventurous attempt to identify the doctrines of the Rosicrucians with what he was pleased to call the Philosophy of Moses (*Philosophia Mosaica, in quâ sapientia et scientia Creationis explicantur*), published at Ghent, 1638, and wrote numerous treatises on alchemy and medical science. He founded an English school of Rosicrucians. *Fludd* is one of the high priests of the Magnetic Philosophy, and learnedly expounds the laws of ostral medicine, the doctrines of sympathies, and the fine powers and marvellous effects of the magnet. When two men approach each other—such was his theory—their magnetism is either active or passive ; that is, positive or negative. If the emanations which they send out are broken or thrown back, there arises antipathy, or *Magnetismus negativus* : but when the emanations pass through each other, the positive magnetism is produced, for the magnetic rays proceed from the centre to the circumference. Man, like the earth, has his poles, or two main streams of magnetic influence. Like a little world, he is endowed with a magnetic virtue which, however, is subjected to the same laws as, on a larger scale, the magnetic power of the universe. How these principles may be developed in the cure or prevention of disease, the reader must learn from the mystic pages of Robertus à Fluctibus himself.

Fludd died in 1637 at a house in Coleman Street, to which he had removed a few years before ; but ere his demise he had won a fairly wide reputation by his chymical ability, and had also issued a considerable number of books, prominent among them being *Tractatus Apologeticus integritatem Societatis de Rusae Cruce defendans*, Leyden 1617, *Veritatis Proscenium*, Frankfort 1621, *Medicina Catholica*, Frankfort 1629, *Monochordum Mundi Syhiphoniacum*, Frankfort, 1622.

Flute, Charm of the : The flute is often mentioned in history as being used for the purpose of charming animals, and the serpent seems to have been peculiarly delighted with its music. It is said that adders will swell at the sound of the flute, raising themselves up, twisting about and keeping proper time. A Spanish writer says that in India he had often seen the Gentiles leading about enchanted serpents, making them dance to the sound of a flute, putting them round their necks, and touching them without harm ; and to this day a musical instrument of this nature is used by the snake-charmers of that country. In opposition to this, Hippocrates mentions a man, Nicanor, who fainted whenever he heard the sound of a flute.

Flying Dutchman, The : Sailors in Holland long believed that a certain Dutch skipper, van Straaten by name, was condemned as a penalty for his sins to sail for year after year through the seas beating around the Cape of Storms, this being the old name for the Cape of Good Hope ; and crews returning to the Zudyer Zee after voyaging in the region aforesaid, use to declared that they had seen van Straaten's mysterious craft, and had fled from it in terror. This legend is probably a very old one, albeit the exact date at which it became current is indeterminate ; and it should be added that the story is found in the folklore of various countries besides Holland, notably Germany. Several German versions call the ill-starred seaman von Falkenberg, and maintain that it was not near South Africa, but in the North Sea that his spectral barque commonly hovered ; while some of them contend further that the devil was wont to pay periodic visits to the captain on board his ship, and that frequently the two were seen playing dice on deck, the stakes at issue being von Falkenberg's soul. The tale soon found its way from folk-lore into actual literature, among the greatest of those writers utilising it being Heinrich Heine, and in his rendering the sailor has a chance of salvation. That is to say, the fates allow him to put foot on *terra firma* once every seven years ; and if, during his brief period of respite, he contrives to win the affection of an unsullied maiden, liberation from perennial sea-wandering will be granted him as reward. Heine's form o the story appealed keenly to Wagner, who was always prone to regard woman devoutly as before all else a regenerating force ; and accordingly the great composer wrote a music-drama on the subject of *The Flying Dutchman*, or as he calls it in German, *Der Fliegende Holländer*, in which the scene is mostly laid in the North Sea, while the sailor himself is called van Derdecken, and the maiden to whom he makes advances is Senta. This opera was first staged at Dresden in 1843, and, though it can hardly be said that it won speedy appreciation, at least it did not elicit quite the scorn meted out originally to the majority of Wagner's works. Marryat has also a novel on the subject.

Fohat is in Theosophy, the power of the Logos. (*See* **Theosophy, Logos.**)

Fong-Chur : A mysterious operation practised in China, in the disposition of buildings, and particularly of tombs. If someone should chance to build in a position contrary to his neighbours, so that the corner of his house faced the side of a house belonging to someone else, the latter believes that the worst of misfortune will befall him. Long-standing feuds may result from the unfortunate action. The remedy consists in placing in a chamber a dragon or other monster in terra-cotta, facing the corner of the fatal edifice. The terrible gaze of the monster will repulse the evil influence. Incense is burned before the dragon, and he is treated with much respect.

Fong Onhang : Fabulous birds to which the Chinese attribute almost the same qualities as are attributed to the phœnix. The women adorn themselves with the image of this bird, in gold, silver, or brass, according to their means.

Forgities : A gem said to assuage anger.

Fontaine, John : This Flemish alchemist and poet appears to have lived at Valenciennes towards the close of the thirteenth century. Two books are ascribed to him, *La Fontaine des Amoureux de Science* and *La Fontaine Perilleuse*, both of which are written in French and were published at Paris, the first-named in 1561 and the second eleven years later. His claims to the authorship of the latter work have frequently been disputed, but the former is almost certainly his, and a curious production it is. At the outset the author professes himself an adept in hermetic philosophy, and thereafter he proceeds, in poetry of an allegorical style which recalls *The Romaunt of the Rose*, to describe the different processes to be gone through ere achieving a transmutation. There is little in this metrical treatise which indicates that the writer was an alchemist of any great ability, but he certainly possessed a distinct gift for making pleasant if hardly powerful verses.

Fontenettes, Charles. : Author of a *Dissertation sur une fille de Grenoble, qui depuis quatre ans ne boit ni ne mange*, 1737. This prodigy was commonly attributed to the devil, but

Fontenettes explained that it was due to a less sinister cause.

Fork, Magical : (*See* Magic.)

Formicarium : (*See* Germany.)

Fortune-telling : *Fortune-telling* in Britain, was formerly included under the crime of Witchcraft, and was made punishable by death under the Statute of 1563 C. 73. This Act was repealed by 9 George II. C. 5, which ordained that no prosecution should thereafter be made on charge of Witchcraft, also by the said Act all persons professing to occult skill or undertaking to tell fortunes might be sentenced to imprisonment for one year, and to stand pillory and find surety for their future good behaviour.

Punishment by pillory is now abolished. By Act 5 George IV. c. 83 fortune-tellers were included along with other vagrants under the general category of rogues and vagabonds, and were liable to imprisonment for three months. This Act was made applicable to Scotland by 34 and 35 Vict. C. 24.

No prosecution occurred under it until the case of *Smith* (23 R (I.C.) 77). The old Act extended to Scotland as aforesaid enacted that " every person pretending or professing to tell fortunes or using any subtle craft, means, or device, by palmistry or otherwise to deceive, and impose on any of His Majesty's Subjects " shall be deemed a vagabond and rogue within the meaning of the Act and shall be punishable as therein provided. In the case above referred to the complainer, a woman named Jone Lee or Smith, was charged in the Police Court at Glasgow, with a contravention of the above enactment in respect that at a time and place specified, did pretend to tell the fortunes of " a person named " who was thereby induced to pay the accused the sum of sixpence. The accused was convicted of the contravention " as libelled " and brought a suspension. The Court *quashed* the conviction, holding that the complaint was irrelevant in that it did not set forth that the accused had pretended to tell fortunes with intent to deceive and impose on any one. Lord Young, one of the judges, in the course of his opinion says " It has never been imagined, so far as I have ever heard, or thought, that writing, publishing, or selling books on the lines of the hand, or even on astrology—the position of the stars at birth and the rules upon which astrologers proceed in telling fortunes therefrom. I say that I have never heard of publishing, or selling such books is an offence, or that reading such books, and telling fortunes therefrom is an offence. Roguery and knavery might be committed that way, but it would be a special case. I am not in any way suggesting that a spae wife or anyone else may not through that means commit knavery and deception, and so be liable to punishment."

It would thus appear that *fortune-telling* is of itself no offence, unless it is accompanied by fraud, impositions, or intent to deceive. While it might be an offence for the palmist or fortune-teller knowingly to accept payment from a half witted or obviously apparent ignorant person, it can hardly be pretended that the ordinary person who consults a professional fortune teller or chrystal gazer and tenders payment in return for their skill at delineations of character or forecasting of the future, feels that he has been imposed upon should the delineations be at fault, or the forecast turn out inaccurate.   A.J.B.G.

Fountain Spirits of Behmen : According to Jacob Behmen, there were in nature seven active principles, the " *Fountain Spirits*, or " Mothers of Existence." These were—the astringent quality ; the sweet quality ; the bitter quality ; the quality of fire ; the quality of love ; the quality of sound ; and the quality of essential substance. The reciprocal action of these antipathetic qualities resulted in Supreme Unity. Each is at once the parent and the child of all the rest, for they generate and are generated by each other. They are typified by the seven golden candlesticks of the Apocalypse.

Fourth Dimension of Space : There are three known dimensions in space typified in the three geometric figures—a line, having length, a surface, length and breadth, a cube, length, breadth and thickness. It has been conjectured that a *fourth dimension* may exist in addition to length, breadth, and thickness. Spiritualists have claimed to find proof of a *fourth dimension* in certain of the physical phenomena of the séance-room such as the tying of knots in endless cords, and the passage of matter through matter.

Fowler, Miss Lottie : (*See* Spiritualism.)

Fox Family : (*See* Spiritualism.)

Fox, Sisters : Two American girls who in 1847 practically commenced the practice of spirit-rapping in Arcadia, New York. An account of their doings is given in the article (**Spiritualism**). They latterly became professional mediums ; but were to a great extent discredited.

Fragarach (The Answerer) : In Irish legend a sword that could pierce any mail. It was one of the magical gifts brought by Lugh from the Land of the Living.

France : Magical practice in pre-Roman *France* was vested in the druidic cast, and was practically identical with that of the same body in Britain, from which, indeed, it drew its inspiration. It is not likely that Roman magic gained any footing in Gaul, but we have little evidence to show whether this was or was not the case. In the early Frankish period of the Merovingian dynasty, we find the baleful personality of Fredegonda, wife of Hilperic, king of Soissons, " a woman whose glance was witchcraft." She destroyed many people on the pretext of sorcery, but there is no doubt that she herself experimented in black magic, and protected many practitioners of the art. Thus she saved a sorceress who had been arrested by Ageric, bishop of Verdun, by hiding her in the palace. (*See* Fredegonda.) The practice of magic was not punished under the rule of the early French kings, except in those in high places, with whom it was regarded as a political offence, as in the case of the military leader Mummol, who was tortured by command of Hilperic for sorcery. One of the Salic laws attributed to Pharamond by Sigebert states that ; " If any one shall testify that another has acted as *hèrèburge* or *strioporte*—titles applied to those who carry the copper vessel to the spot where the vampires perform their enchantments—and if he fail to convict him, he shall be condemned hereby to a forfeit of 7,500 *deniers*, being 180½ *sous*. . . . If a vampire shall devour a man and be found guilty, she shall forfeit 8,000 *deniers*, being 200 *sous*."

The Church legislated also against sorcerers and vampires, and the Council of Agde, in Languedoc, held in A.D. 506, pronounced excommunication against them. The first Council of Orleans, convened in 541, condemned divination and augury, and that of Narbonne, in 589, besides excommunicating all sorcerers, ordained that they should be sold as slaves for the benefit of the poor. Those who had dealings with the Devil were also condemned to be whipped by the same Council. Some extraordinary phenomena are alleged to have occurred in *France* during the reign of Pepin le Bref. The air seemed to be alive with human shapes, mirages filled the heavens, and sorcerers were seen among the clouds, scattering unwholesome powders and poisons with open hands ; crops failed, cattle died, and many human beings perished. It is perhaps possible that such visions were stimulated by the teachings of the famous Kabalist, Zedekias, who presided over a school of occult science, where he refrained indeed from unveiling the hidden secrets of his art, and contented himself by spreading the theory of elemental spirits, who, he stated, had before the fall of man been subservient to him.

It was thought that the visions alluded to above signified the descent of sylphs and salamanders in search of their former masters. Says Eliphas Levi :

" Voyages to the land of sylphs were talked of on all sides as we talk at the present day of animated tables and fluidic manifestations. The folly took possession even of strong minds, and it was time for an intervention on the part of the Church, which does not relish the supernatural being hawked in the public streets, seeing that such disclosures, by imperilling the respect due to authority and to the hierarchic chain of instruction, cannot be attributed to the spirit of order and light. The cloud-phantoms were therefore arraigned and accused of being hell-born illusions, while the people—anxious to get something into their hands—began a crusade against sorcerers. The public folly turned into a paroxysm of mania ; strangers in country places were accused of descending from heaven and were killed without mercy ; imbeciles confessed that they had been abducted by sylphs or demons ; others who had boasted like this previously either would not or could not unsay it ; they were burned or drowned, and, according to Garinet, the number who perished throughout the kingdom almost exceeds belief. It is the common catastrophe of dramas in which the first parts are played by ignorance or fear.

" Such visionary epidemics recurred in the reigns following, and all the power of Charlemagne was put in action to calm the public agitation. An edict, afterwards renewed by Louis the Pious, forbade sylphs to manifest under the heaviest penalties. It will be understood that in the absence of the aerial beings the judgments fell upon those who had made a boast of having seen them, and hence they ceased to be seen. The ships in air sailed back to the port of oblivion, and no one claimed any longer to have journeyed through the blue distance. Other popular frenzies replaced the previous mania, while the romantic splendours of the great reign of Charlemagne furnished the makers of legends with new prodigies to believe and new marvels to relate."

Around the figure of Charlemagne (q.v.) clusters such an immense amount of the matter of faëry that it is reserved for treatment in a special article, and it will suffice to state here that it almost partakes of the nature of true myth. It is stated that the *Enchiridion* (q.v.) (which may well be stigmatised as an early text-book of occult absurdity having no claim to figure in the true genealogy of occult literature) was presented to Charlemagne by Pope Leo III.

Eliphas Levi presents a picturesque condition of affairs in the *France* of Charlemagne in the following passage :

" We know that superstitions die hard and that degenerated Druidism had struck its roots deeply in the savage lands of the North. The recurring insurrections of Saxons testified to a fanaticism which was (a) always turbulent, and (b) incapable of repression by moral force alone. All defeated forms of worship—Roman paganism, Germanic idolatry, Jewish rancour conspired against victorious Christianity. Nocturnal assemblies took place ; thereat the conspirators cemented their alliance with the blood of human victims ; and a pantheistic idol of monstrous form, with the horns of a goat, presided over festivals which might be called *agapæ* of hatred. In a word, the Sabbath was still celebrated in every forest and wild if yet unreclaimed provinces. The adepts who attended them were masked and otherwise unrecognisable ; the assemblies extinguished their lights and broke up before daybreak, the guilty were to be found everywhere, and they could be brought to book nowhere. It came about therefore that Charlemagne determined to fight them with their own weapons.

" In those days, moreover, feudal tyrants were in league with sectarians against lawful authority ; female sorcerers were attached to castles as courtesans ; bandits who frequented the Sabbaths divided with nobles the blood-stained loot of rapine ; feudal courts were at the command of the highest bidder ; and the public burdens weighed with all their force only on the weak and poor. The evil was at its height in Westphalia, and faithful agents were despatched thither by Charlemagne entrusted with a secret mission. Whatsoever energy remained among the oppressed, whosoever still loved justice, whether among the people or among the nobility, were drawn by these emissaries together, bound by pledges and vigilance in common. To the initiates thus incorporated they made known the full powers which they carried from the emperor himself, and they proceeded to institute the Tribunal of Free Judges.

A great deal of this, of course, is only what might be expected from the French magus. It is not likely that the Sabbath was yet celebrated in such an extreme manner as in later times, nor was the Vehmgericht founded by Charlemagne, or indeed, founded at all, for four and a half centuries after his day.

From the reign of Robert the Pious to that of St. Louis, there is not much to relate that can strike the imagination of the student of occult history. In the time of the latter monarch flourished the famous Rabbi Jachiel, the celebrated Kabalist. There is some reason to believe that he had glimmerings of the uses of electricity, for on the approach of night a radiant star appeared in his lodging, the light being so brilliant that no eye could gaze thereon without being dazzled, while it darted rainbow colours. It appeared to be inexhaustible, and was never replenished with oil or other combustible substance. When the Rabbi was annoyed by intruders at his door he struck a nail fixed in his cabinet, producing simultaneously a blue spark on the head of the nail and the door-knocker, to which, if the intruder clung, he received a severe shock. Albertus Magnus (q.v.) lived at the same period.

The next circumstance of interest which falls to be noted is the prosecutions of the Templars (q.v.) who were brought to trial by Philip the Fair. Other prosecutions for sorcery were those of Joan of Arc, Gilles de Laval (q.v.), lord of Raiz, the prototype of Bluebeard, a renowned sorcerer, who with two assistants, Prelati and Sillé, practised diabolical rites at his castle of Machecoul, celebrating the black mass in the most revolting manner. He had been in the habit of slaughtering children to assist him in his search for the philosopher's stone. We now near the period of those astounding prosecutions for sorcery which are fully noted under the article " Witchcraft " and elsewhere. As early as the thirteenth century the charge of sorcery had been made as one of the means of branding with infamy the heretical Waldenses (q.v.), who were accused of selling themselves to the Devil, and of holding sabbatical orgies where they did homage to the enemy of mankind. About the middle of the fifteenth century *France* became the theatre of wholesale oppression against suspected sorcerers, but one finds leading up to this a series of events which prove that the outburst in question was by no means a novelty in that country. In 1315 Enguerraud de Marigny, who had conducted the execution of the Templars a minister of Philip the Fair, was hanged along with an adventurer named Paviot, for attempting to compass the deaths of the Counts of Valois and St. Paul. In 1334 the Countess of Artois and her son were thrown into prison on a suspicion of sorcery. In 1393, in the reign of Charles VI., it was considered that his sister-in-law, the Duchess of Orleans, who was a viscomte and the daughter of the Duke of Milan, had rendered the King mad by sorcery. The ministers of the court resolved to pit a magician against her, and one Arnaud Guillaume (q.v.) was brought from Guienne as a suitable adversary to the noble lady. He possessed a book to which he gave the strange title of *Smagorad*, the original of which, he said, was given by God to Adam, to console him for the loss of his son Abel, and he asserted that the possessor of this volume could hold the stars in subjection, and command the four elements. He assured the King's advisers that Charles was suffering from the malignity of a sorcerer, but in the meantime the young monarch recovered, and the possessor of the patriarchal volume fell back into his original obscurity. Five years later the King had another attack, and two Augustine friars were sent from Guienne for the purpose of effecting a cure. But their conduct was so outrageous that they were executed. A third attack in 1403 was combated by two sorcerers of Dijon, Poinson and Briquet. For this purpose they established themselves in a thick wood not far from the gates of Dijon, where they made a magic circle of iron of immense weight, which was supported by iron columns of the height of a middle-sized man, and to which twelve chains of iron were attached. So great was the popular anxiety for the King's recovery, that the two sorcerers succeeded in persuading twelve of the principal persons of the town to enter the circle, and allow themselves to be fastened by the chains. The sorcerers then proceeded with their incantations, but they were altogether without result. The bailiff of Dijon, who was one of the twelve, and had averred his incredulity from the first, caused the sorcerers to be arrested, and they were burnt for their pretences.

The Duke of Orleans appears to have fallen under the same suspicion of sorcery as his Italian consort. After his murder by order of the Duke of Burgundy—the commencement of those troubles which led to the desolation of *France*—the latter drew up various heads of accusation against his victim as justifications of the crime, and one of these was, that the Duke of Orleans had attempted to compass his death by means of sorcery. According to this statement, he had received a magician—another apostate friar— into his castle of Mountjoie, where he was employed in these sinister designs. He performed his magical ceremonies before sunrise on a neighbouring mountain, where two demons, named Herman and Astramon, appeared to him ; and these became his active instruments in the prosecution of his design.

About the year 1400 the belief in the nightly meetings of the witches' Sabbath had become almost universal. It would indeed be difficult to attempt to trace the origin of this practice, which does not seem altogether referable to the survival of pagan belief. (*See* **Witchcraft.**) The wholesale nature of the prosecutions against sorcerers and witches prove that there must have been an extraordinary number of them in the country. In Paris alone, in the time of Charles IX, there were no less than thirty thousand sorcerers, and it is computed that *France* contained more than three times that number in the reign of Henry III., not a town or village being exempt from their presence. They belonged to all classes, and generally met the same fate, regardless of rank, age or sex. Children of the tenderest years and nonagenarians were alike committed to the flames, and the terror of being publicly accused as a sorcerer hung like a black cloud over the life of every successful man, as the charge was one which envy readily seized upon for the destruction of its object. No elaborate or perfect creed regarding witchcraft had at this epoch been evolved in England, but in *France* and other continental countries it had been assuming a form systematic and complete. There were probably two reasons for this, the decrees of ecclesiastical councils and the numerous treatises of scholars who professed to illustrate their various

theories regarding sorcery by alleged statements from the mouths of its innumerable victims. Indeed the writings of these men served to standardise the sorcery creed of all continental countries. During the earlier part of the sixteenth century, trials for witchcraft in *France* are of rare occurrence, and there are no cases of great importance recorded till after the year 1560. In 1561 a number of persons were brought to trial at Vernon, accused of having held their Sabbath as witches in an old ruined castle in the shape of cats ; and witnesses deposed to having seen the assembly, and to having suffered from the attacks of the pseudo-feline conspirators. But the court threw out the charge, as worthy only of ridicule. In 1564, three men and a woman were executed at Poitiers, after having been made to confess to various acts of sorcery ; among other things, they said that they had regularly attended the witches' Sabbath, which was held three times a year, and that the demon who presided at it ended by burning himself to make powder for the use of his agents in mischief. In 1571, a mere conjurer, who played tricks upon cards, was thrown into prison in Paris, forced to confess that he was an attendant on the Sabbath, and then executed. In 1573, a man was burnt at Dôle, on the charge of having changed himself into a wolf, and in that form devoured several children. Several witches, who all confessed to having been at the Sabbaths, were in the same year condemned to be burnt in different parts of *France*. In 1578, another man was tried and condemned in Paris for changing himself into a wolf ; and a man was condemned at Orleans for the same supposed crime in 1583. As *France* was often infested by these rapacious animals, it is not difficult to conceive how popular credulity was led to connect their ravages with the crime of witchcraft. The belief in what were in England called *wer-wolves* (men-wolves), and in *France loups-garous*, was a very ancient superstition throughout Europe. It is asserted by a serious and intelligent writer of the time that, in 1588, a gentleman, looking out of the window of his château in a village two leagues from Apchon, in the mountains of Auvergne, saw one of his acquaintances going a-hunting, and begged he would bring him home some game. The hunter, while occupied in the chase, was attacked by a fierce she-wolf, and after having fired at it without effect, struck it with his hunting-knife, and cut off the paw of his right fore-leg, on which it immediately took to flight. The hunter took up the paw, threw it into his bag with the rest of his game, and soon afterwards returned to his friend's château, and told him of his adventure, at the same time putting his hand into the bag to bring forth the wolf's paw in confirmation of his story. What was his surprise at drawing out a lady's hand, with a gold ring on one finger ! His friend's astonishment was still greater when he recognised the ring as one which he had given to his own wife ; and, descending hastily into the kitchen, he found the lady warming herself by the fire, with her right arm wrapped in her apron. This he at once seized, and found to his horror that the hand was cut off. The lady confessed that it was she who, in the form of a wolf, had attacked the hunter ; she was, in due course of time, brought to her trial and condemned, and was immediately afterwards burnt at Rioms.

In 1578, a witch was burnt at Compiègne ; she confessed that she had given herself to the devil, who appeared to her as a great black man, on horseback, booted and spurred. Another avowed witch was burnt the same year, who also stated that the evil one came to her in the shape of a black man. In 1582 and 1583, several witches were burnt, all frequenters of the Sabbaths. Several local councils at this date passed severe laws against witchcraft, and from that time to the end of the century, the number of miserable persons put to death in *France* under the accusation was very great. In the course only of fifteen years, from 1580 to 1595, and only in one province, that of Lorraine, the president Remigius burnt nine hundred witches, and as many more fled out of the country to save their lives; and about the close of the century, one of the French judges tells us that the crime of witchcraft had become so common that there were not jails enough to hold the prisoners, or judges to hear their causes. A trial which he had witnessed in 1568, induced Jean Bodin, a learned physician, to compose his book *De la Demonomanie des Sorciers*, which was ever afterwards the text-book on this subject.

Among the English witches, the evil one generally came in person to seduce his victims, but in *France* and other countries, this seems to have been unnecessary, as each person, when once initiated, became seized with an uncontrollable desire of making converts, whom he or she carried to the Sabbath to be duly enrolled. Bodin says, that one witch was enough to corrupt five hundred honest persons. The infection quickly ran through a family, and was generally carried down from generation to generation, which explained satisfactorily, according to the learned commentator on demonology just mentioned, the extent to which the evil had spread itself in his days. The novice, at his or her reception, after having performed the preliminaries, and in general received a new and burlesque rite of baptism, was marked with the sign of the demon in some part of the body least exposed to observation, and performed the first criminal act of compliance which was afterwards to be so frequently repeated, the evil one presenting himself on these occasions in the form of either sex, the reverse to that of the victim.

Towards the end of the sixteenth century, the witchcraft infatuation had risen to its greatest height in *France*, and not only the lower classes, but persons of the highest rank in society were liable to suspicions of dealing in sorcery. We need only mention that such charges were publicly made against King Henry III. and Queen Catherine de Medicis, and that, early in the following century, they became the ground of state trials which had a fatal conclusion.

In 1610, during the reign of Louis XIII., occurred the *cause célèbre* of the marechale d'Ancre. Among the servants attached to the train of Marie de Medici was a certain Eleanora Dori, who married one, Concini, a prodigal spendthrift. Marie de Medici, as guardian to her son, was virtually ruler of *France*, and considerable power was exercised by these favourites of hers. The result was that the peers of France leagued themselves together against the upstarts, but with little result at first, as Concini was created Marechal of *France*, with the title of Marquis d'Ancre. His wife, who was very superstitious, fell sick, and attributed her ill-health to the effects of sorcery. The upshot was that d'Ancre was assassinated by the nobles during a hunting expedition. The mob dragged the corpse of d'Ancre from its grave and hanged it on the Pont Neuf. His wretched widow was accused of sorcery, and of having bewitched the Queen Mother. The exorcists who had assisted her to free herself from illness had advised the sacrifice of a cock, and this was now represented as a sacrifice to the infernal powers. Added to this, the astrological nativities of the royal family were found in her possession, as were, it is said, a quantity of magical books, and a great number of magical characters. After being tortured without result she was beheaded and burnt, and strangely enough the anger of the Parisian mob turned to general commiseration. Many other interesting cases occurred in *France* in the seventeenth century, among others that of the Ursulines at Aix (q.v.), for the enchantment of whom Louis Gaufridi was burnt, the Nuns of Louviais, and the nuns of Assonne. The case of the Ursulines of Loudon

(q.v.), is fully dealt with elsewhere. (*See* **Urban Grandier).**

The eighteenth century in *France* was fairly prolific in occult history. At a time when Europe was credulous about nothing but magic, *France* did not escape the prevailing craze. Perhaps the most striking personality of this age in the occult connection was the Comte de Saint Germain (q.v.), who was credited with possessing the secrets of alchemy and magic. His family connections were unknown, and his conversation suggested that he had lived for many centuries. Another mysterious adept was an alchemist calling himself Lascaris (q.v.) who literally sowed his path through Europe with gold. Then followed Cagliostro (q.v.), who attained a fame unrivalled in the history of French occultism. He founded many masonic lodges throughout the country, and assisted in many ways to bring about the French Revolution. A school of initiates was founded by Martines de Pasqually, which appears in some measure to have incorporated the teachings of the later European adepts. One of the most important figures at this time is Louis Claude de Saint-Martin, known as " Le Philosophe Inconnu " who came under the influence of Pasqually (q.v.), and later, under that of the writings of Boehme, whose works he translated. Cazotte (q.v.) was the first of these names who were associated with both magic and the Revolution, which, indeed, owed much in its inception to those mysterious brotherhoods of *France* and Germany, who during the eighteenth century sowed the seeds of equality and Illuminism throughout Europe. Another was Loiséaut (q.v.), who formed a mystical society, which met in great secrecy, awaiting a vision of John the Baptist, who came to them to foretell the Revolution. The spiritual director of this circle was a monk named Dom Gerle (q.v.) one of the first mesmerists in Paris, who is said to have foretold the dreadful fame of Robespierre by means of Catherine Théot, his medium. He was expelled by the members of the circle, acting on the advice of one of their number, Sister Françoise André, who cherished a notion to preserve the crown for the future reign of Louis XVII., and thus gave rise to that multitude of stories connected with the so-called " Saviours " of the youthful " Capet." This sect, or a portion of it, became notorious under the leadership of Vintras (q.v.), when its meetings degenerated into the most dreadful debauchery. The appearance of Mlle. Lenormand as a prophetess at the end of the eighteenth century may be said to close the occult history of that age. With the beginning of the nineteenth century we find the craze for magnetism rampant. In his works *The Reform of Philosophy* and *Yes or No*, Wronski pretended to have discovered the first theorems of the Kabala, and later beguiled rich persons of weak intellect into paying him large sums in return for knowledge of the Absolute. The Saviours of Louis XVII. were formally condemned in 1853 by the Pope as practitioners of black magic, but they in turn condemned the Pope, and their leader, Vintras, constituted himself Sovereign Pontiff, but he was arrested on the charge of roguery and after five years' imprisonment, found an asylum in England.

The Baron du Potet did much to advance the science of Mesmer and by this time was being seriously followed by Cahagnet and others (*See* **Mesmerism).** In the middle of the nineteenth century all sorts of absurdities swayed occult Paris. The tale of Alphonse Esquiros (q.v.) entitled *The Magician* founded a school of magic phantasy, which was assiduously nursed by Henri Delaage (q.v.), who was said to have the gift of ubiquity, and who made a collection of processes from the old magicians for acquiring physical beauty.

Spiritualism. The Comte d'Ourches was the first to introduce into *France* automatic writing and table-writing.

Baron Guldenstubbé, in his *Practical Experimental Pneumatology; or, the Reality of Spirits and the Marvellous Phenomena of their Direct Writing*, gives an account of his discovery as follows :

" It was in the course of the year 1850, or about three years prior to the epidemic of table-rapping, that the author sought to introduce into *France* the circles of American spiritualism, the mysterious Rochester knockings and the purely automatic writings of mediums. Unfortunately he met with many obstacles raised by other mesmerists. Those who were committed to the hypothesis of a magnetic fluid, and even those who styled themselves Spiritual Mesmerists, but who were really inferior inducers of somnambulism, treated the mysterious knockings of American spiritualism as visionary follies. It was therefore only after more than six months that the author was able to form his first circle on the American plan, and then thanks to the zealous concurrence of M. Rousaan, a former member of the *Sociètè des Magnètiseurs Spiritualistes*, a simple man who was full of enthusiasm for the holy cause of spiritualism. We were joined by a number of other persons, amongst whom was the Abbé Châtel, founder of the Eglise Française, who, despite his rationalistic tendencies, ended by admitting the reality of objective and supernatural revelation, as an indispensable condition of spiritualism and all practical religions. Setting aside the moral conditions which are equally requisite, it is known that American circles are based on the distinction of positive and electric or negative magnetic currents.

" The circles consist of twelve persons, representing in equal proportions the positive and negative or sensitive elements. This distinction does not follow the sex of the members, though generally women are negative and sensitive, while men are positive and magnetic. The mental and physical constitution of each individual must be studied before forming the circles, for some delicate women have masculine qualities, while some strong men are, morally speaking, women. A table is placed in a clear and ventilated spot ; the medium is seated at one end and entirely isolated ; by his calm and contemplative quietude he serves as a conductor for the electricity, and it may be noted that a good somnambulist is usually an excellent medium. The six electrical or negative dispositions, which are generally recognised by their emotional qualities and their sensibility, are placed at the right of the medium, the most sensitive of all being next him. The same rule is followed with the positive personalities, who are at the left of the medium, with the most positive next to him. In order to form a chain, the twelve persons each place their right hand on the table. Observe that the medium or mediums, if there be more than one, are entirely isolated from those who form the chain.

" After a number of séances, certain remarkable phenomena have been obtained, such as simultaneous shocks, felt by all present at the moment of mental evocation on the part of the most intelligent persons. It is the same with mysterious knockings and other strange sounds ; many people, including those least sensitive, have had simultaneous visions, though remaining in the ordinary waking state. Sensitive persons have acquired that most wonderful gift of mediumship, namely, automatic writing, as the result of an invisible attraction which uses the non-intelligent instrument of a human arm to express its ideas. For the rest, non-sensitive persons experience the mysterious influence of an external wind, but the effect is not strong enough to put their limbs in motion. All these phenomena, obtained according to the mode of American spiritualism, have the defect of being more or less indirect, because it is impossible in these experiments to dispense with the mediation of a human being or medium. It is

the same with the table-turning which invaded Europe in the middle of the year 1853.

" The author has had many table experiences with his honourable friend, the Comte d'Ourches, one of the most instructed persons in Magic and the Occult Sciences. We attained by degrees the point when tables moved, apart from any contact whatever, while the Comte d'Ourches has caused them to rise, also without contact. The author has made tables rush across a room with great rapidity, and not only without contact but without the magnetic aid of a circle of sitters. The vibrations of piano-chords under similar circumstances took place on January 20, 1856, in the presence of the Comte de Szapary and Comte d'Ourches. Now all such phenomena are proof positive of certain occult forces, but they do not demonstrate adequately the real and substantial existence of unseen intelligences, independent of our will and imagination, though the limits of these have been vastly extended in respect of their possibilities. Hence the reproach made against American spiritualists, because their communications with the world of spirits are so insignificant in character, being confined to mysterious knockings and other sound vibrations. As a fact, there is no direct phenomenon at once intelligent and material, independent of our will and imagination, to compare with the direct writing of spirits, who have neither been invoked or evoked, and it is this only which offers irrefutable proof as to the reality of the supernatural world.

" The author, being always in search of such proof, at once intelligent and palpable, concerning the substantial reality of the supernatural world, in order to demonstrate by certain facts the immortality of the soul, has never wearied of addressing fervent prayers to the Eternal, that He might vouchsafe to indicate an infallible means for strengthening that faith in immortality which is the eternal basis of religion. The Eternal, Whose mercy is infinite, has abundantly answered this feeble prayer. On August 1st, 1856, the idea came to the author of trying whether spirits could write directly, that is, apart from the presence of a medium. Remembering the marvellous direct writing of the Decalogue, communicated to Moses, and that other writing, equally direct and mysterious, at the feast of Belshazzar, recorded by Daniel ; having further heard about those modern mysteries of Stratford in America, where certain strange and illegible characters were found upon strips of paper, apparently apart from mediumship, the author sought to establish the actuality of such important phenomena, if indeed within the limits of possibility.

" He therefore placed a sheet of blank letter paper and a sharply pointed pencil in a box, which he then locked, and carried the key about him, imparting his design to no one. Twelve days he waited in vain, but what was his astonishment on August 13th, 1856, when he found certain mysterious characters traced on the paper. He repeated the experiment ten times on that day, placing a new sheet of paper each time in the box, with the same result invariably. On the following day he made twenty experiments but left the box open, without losing sight of it. He witnessed the formation of characters and words in the Esthonian language with no motion of the pencil. The latter being obviously useless he decided to dispense with it and placed blank paper sometimes on a table of his own, sometimes on the pedestals of old statues, on sarcophagi, on urns, etc., in the Louvre, at St. Denis, at the Church of St. Etienne du Mont, etc., Similar experiments were made in different cemeteries of Paris, but the author has no liking for cemetries, while most saints prefer the localities where they have lived on earth to those in which their mortal remains are laid to rest."

We are now launched upon the sea of modern spiritualism in *France*, which occupied the entire activities of occultists in that country for several decades, and which it will be better to trace from the period of its importation into the country.

Very soon after public attention had been drawn to the subject of magnetism in *France* by Mesmer and d'Eslon, several men distinguished for learning and scientific attainments, followed up their experiments with great success. Amongst these was the Baron Dupotet, whose deep interest in the subject of magnetism induced him to publish a periodical which, under the title of *Journal de Magnètisme*—still forms a complete treasury of well collated facts, and curious experiments·in occult force. From this work we learn that the Baron's investigations commenced in the year 1836, since which period up to 1848, he chronicled the production of the following remarkable phases of phenomena, the occurrence of which is testified to by numerous scientific and eminent witnesses. Through the Baron's magnetized subjects was evolved, clairvoyance, trance-speaking, and healing ; *stigmata* or raised letters and figures on the subject's body ; elevation of somnambulists into the air ; insensibility to fire, injury or touch. In the presence of the magnetized objects also, heavy bodies were moved without human contact, and objects were brought from distant places through walls and closed doors. Sometimes the " Lucides " described scenes in the spirit world, found lost property, prophesied and spoke in foreign languages.

In 1840, Baron Dupotet writes that he had " rediscovered in magnetism the magic of antiquity." " Let the *savants*," he says, " reject the doctrine of spiritual appearances ; the enquirer of to-day is compelled to believe it ; from an examination of undeniable facts." . . . " If the knowledge of ancient magic is lost, all the facts remain on which to reconstruct it."

But of all the revealers to whom French Spiritualism is indebted for indubitable proof of super-mundane intercourse, none stands more prominent in truthfulness and worth, than M. Cahagnet, the well-known author of "*The Celestial Telegraph*," a work translated into English in 1848.

M. Cahagnet was an unlearned mechanic, a man of the people and though a sensible and interesting writer, was neither well read, nor highly educated. He affirms that he was a " materialist " when first his attention was attracted to the subject of animal magnetism, but being of a thoughtful nature, he determined to devote all the leisure he could spare to a thorough examination of its possibilities. When he found that he possessed the power to induce the magnetic sleep in others, he proceeded on the plan then generally adopted by mesmerists, namely, to try how far he could succeed in biologizing his subjects, that is to say, to substitute his own senses, mind, and will, for those of the sleeper.

In the course of these experiments M. Cahagnet discovered that he could effect remarkable cures of disease, and being naturally of a benevolent disposition, he determined to bend all his energies in this desirable direction. He soon found, however, that he was destined to realize the aphorism, " he builded wiser than he knew." A new and most perplexing obstacle arose to confound his philosophy and scatter his theories to the winds ; this was the fact, that some of his subjects, instead of representing what simply he willed, or manifesting—in accordance with his views of biology—merely the influence of his mind, began to transcend both will and mind, and wander off in space, to regions they persisted in calling the " land of spirits," and to describe people, whom they emphatically affirmed to be the souls of those whom the world called dead.

For a long time M. Cahagnet strove vehemently to combat what he termed these " wild hallucinations," but when he found them constantly recurring, and vast numbers of those who had come to witness the experiments in magnetism recognising in the descriptions given by the somnambulists the spirits of those whom they had known on earth, and mourned as dead, conviction became inevitable, and the magnetizer, like his visitors, was compelled to admit a new and wonderful phase of lucidity, and one which carried the vision of the clairvoyant from earth to heaven, ·and pierced the veil which separated the mortal from the realms of immortality. It was after a long series of carefully conducted experiments of the above description, that M. Cahagnet was finally persuaded to give the results of his wonderful séances to the world, under the name and style of *The Celestial Telegraph*, or, *Secrets of the Life to Come.*

The author of *Art Magic* says : " The narrow conservatism of the age, and the pitiful jealousy of the Medical Faculty, rendered it difficult and harassing to conduct magnetic experiments openly in Europe within several years of Mesmer's decease. Still such experiments were not wanting, and to show their results, we give a few excerpts from the correspondence between the famous French Magnetists, MM. Deleuze and Billot, from the years 1829 to 1840. By these letters, published in 1836, it appears that M. Billot commenced his experiments in magnetizing as early as 1789, and that during forty years, he had an opportunity of witnessing facts· in clairvoyance, ecstasy, and somnambulism, which at the time of their publication transcended the belief of the general mass of readers. On many occasions in the presence of entranced subjects, spirits recognised as having once lived on earth in mortal form—would come *in bodily presence* before the eyes of an assembled multitude and at request bring flowers, fruits, and objects, removed by distance from the scene of the experiments.

" M. Deleuze frankly admits that his experience was more limited to those phases of somnambulism in which his subjects submitted to amputations and severe surgical operations without experiencing the slightest pain. . . . In a letter dated 1831 M. Billot writing to Deleuze says :—

" ' I repeat, I have seen and known all that is permitted to man. I have seen the stigmata arise on magnetized subjects ; I have dispelled obsessions of evil spirits with a single word. I have seen spirits bring those material objects I told you of, and when requested, make them so light that they would float, and, again, a small *boiteau de bonbons* was rendered so heavy that I failed to move it an inch until the power was removed.

" ' To those who enjoyed the unspeakable privilege of listening to the " somnambules " of Billot, Deleuze, and Cahagnet, another and yet more striking feature of unanimous revelation was poured forth. Spirits of those who had passed away from earth strong in the faith of Roman Catholicism—often priests and dignitaries of that conservative Church, addressing prejudiced believers in their former doctrine, asserted that there was no creed in Heaven —no sectarian worship, or ecclesiastical dogmatism there prevailing.

" ' They taught that God was a grand Spiritual Sun—life on earth a probation—the spheres, different degrees of comprehensive happiness or states of retributive suffering—each appropriate to the good or evil deeds done on earth. They described the ascending changes open to every soul in proportion to his own efforts to improve.

" ' They all insisted that man was his own judge, incurred a penalty or reward for which there was no substitution. They taught nothing of Christ, absolutely denied the idea of vicarious atonement—and represented man as his own Saviour or destroyer.

" ' They spoke of arts, sciences, and continued activities, as if the life beyond was but an extension of the present on a greatly improved scale. Descriptions of the radiant beauty, supernal happiness, and ecstatic sublimity manifested by the blest spirits who had risen to the spheres of Paradise, Heaven, and the glory of angelic companionships melts the heart, and fills the soul with irresistible yearning, to lay down life's weary burdens and be at rest with them.' "

Having shown that Spiritualism arose in *France* as in Germany from the awakening of psychic powers evolved by magnetism, and traced the footprints of the great temple builders who have laid the foundation stones of the spiritual edifice in the human system and steadily worked upwards from matter to force, and from thence to spirit in every gradation of sphere, life and progress, we recall the pithy words of the Baron de Potet, who, in addressing the would-be leaders of public opinion in his essay on the " Philosophical Teaching of Magnetism," says :

" You *savants* of our country ; you have not shown yourselves better informed than the Siamese.

" For these sixty years it has been shouted in your ears : *The Magnetizers march to the discovery of a moral world* ; all the phenomena they produce indisputably proves its existence.

" You have declared that they were impostors, imbeciles, and the most illustrious amongst you have only pronounced a verdict which will attest to future ages your ignorance or your insincerity.

" Before the soul is disengaged from matter, it can, and does, converse with pure spirits. Already it can gaze prophetically on its own future destiny, by regarding the condition of those who have gone before—but a step— yet one which the eye of spirit alone can measure, and if men are spirits already, who can stay the eagle glance of the soul into the land of its own inheritance ? "

In following up the history of Spiritualism in *France*, although we find it has gained an immense foothold, and exerted a wide-spread influence upon the popular mind, it is nevertheless evident, that one of the chief obstacles to its general acceptance has been its lack of internal unity, and the antagonistic sentiments which have prevailed amongst its acknowledged leaders.

Two of those who have figured most prominently in the grand drama of French Spiritualism, and in all probability exerted more influence upon public opinion than any other members of its *dramatis personæ*, were MM. Allan Kardec and Pierart, the respective editors of the two leading Spiritual journals, entitled *La Revue Spirite* and *La Revue Spiritualiste*. These may also be regarded as the representatives of the two opposing factions known as Spiritualists and Spiritists, the former teaching that the soul of man undergoes but one mortal birth, and continues its progress through eternity in spiritual states, the latter affirming the doctrine of Re-incarnation, and alleging that the one spirit in man can and does undergo many incarnations in different mortal forms.

M. Kardec and his followers represented the " Spiritists " or Re-incarnationists—M. Pierart leading the ranks of the opposing faction most commonly called Spiritualists.

In respect to the question of testimony, it must be remembered that M. Kardec derived his communications chiefly from those writing and trance mediums who might have proved the most susceptible to his influence, and is said to have persistently banished from his circles, not only Mr. Home, M. Bredif, and other physical mediums, but all those who did not endorse his favourite dogma through their communications.

Says the author of *Nineteenth Century Miracles* : It

must not be supposed that the schism which divided the two leaders of French Spiritualism was confined to the immediate sphere of action in which they moved. Scattered sympathisers with the writings of Allan Kardec, may be found all over the Continent of Europe, and in small numbers in America also. Few people who read works put forward with authoritative pretentions have the faculty of thoroughly digesting what they read, hence, when M. Kardec's books were translated into the English language, and it became the publisher's interest to aid in their circulation, they found more readers than thinkers, and their plausible style attracted more admiration than sincere conviction. In *France*, no doubt M. Kardec's personal influence, and strong phychological power, admirably fitted him for a propagandist, and when we remember how readily any doctrines eloquently advocated will command adherents, especially among restless and excitable natures, we need be at no loss to discover why M. Kardec's writings have become so popular and his opinions so generally accepted by his readers. Little or no spiritual literature was disseminated in the French language when Allan Kardec's works were first published. He possessed that indomitable energy and psychological influence in which his much harassed rival Pierart was wanting. Thus in a measure, the field of Continental spiritual propagandism was his own, nor did he fail to make use of his great opportunities.

"The successes achieved by Kardec's journal, *La Revue Spirite*, communicated a wave of influence also, which propagated journals of a similar character all over the country. Thus in 1864, there were no less than ten spiritualistic periodicals published in *France*, under fhe following titles : *La Revue Spirite*, *La Revue Spiritualiste*, and *L'Avenir*, Paris ; four *Spiritist* journals published in Bordeaux, which, in 1865, became merged into *L' Union Spirite Bordelaise* ; *La Medium Evangelique*, Toulouse ; *L'Echo d'outre Tombe*, Marseilles ; and *La Vérité*, Lyons. The editors of these journals are said to have been all followers of Allan Kardec, with the exception of M. Pierart, editor of *La Revue Spiritualiste*."

It must be remarked that the doctrines of the Re-incarnationists, although defended with great ability by their propagandists, who included many of the most capable minds of France, were not suffered to pass without severe castigation on the part of their English neighbours ; and it becomes necessary to note how the French spiritual schism was received on the other side of the Channel. In the *London Spiritual Magazine* of 1865, the editor, in commenting on the ominous silence of the *Spirite* journals concerning Dr. Maldigny's opera of Swedenborg says :—

" It is worthy of note that the journals of the Kardec school, so far as we have seen them, do not take the least notice of this opera. The *Avenir* of Paris, which appears weekly, but greatly wants facts, has not a word to say about it. . . . . It is greatly to be regretted that the main object of the Kardecian journals seems to be, not the demonstration of the constantly recurring facts of Spiritualism, but the deification of Kardec's doctrine of Re-incarnation.

" To this doctrine—which has nothing to do with Spiritualism, even if it had a leg of reason or fact to stand on— all the strength, and almost all the space of these journals is devoted.

" These are the things which give the enemies of Spiritualism a real handle against it, and bring it into contempt with sober minds. Re-incarnation is a doctrine which cuts up by the roots all individual identity in the future existence. It desolates utterly that dearest yearning of the human heart for reunion with its loved ones in a permanent world. If some are to go back into fresh physical bodies, and bear new names, and new natures, if they are to become respectively Tom Styles, Ned Snooks, and a score of other people, who shall ever hope to meet again with his friends, wife, children, brothers and sisters ? When he enters the spirit-world and enquires for them, he will have to learn that they are already gone back to earth, and are somebody else, the sons and daughters of other people, and will have to become over and over the kindred of a dozen other families in succession ! Surely, no such most cheerless crochet could bewitch the intellects of any people, except under the most especial bedevilment of the most sarcastic and mischievous of devils."

In the January number for 1866, a still stronger article on this subject appears from the pen of Wm. Howitt, who writes the following fearless words of protest against the doctrine of Re-incarnation :

" In the *Avenir* of November 2nd, M. Pezzani thinks he has silenced M. Pierart, by asserting that without Re-incarnation all is chaos and injustice in God's creation : ' In this world there are rich and poor, oppressed and oppressors, and without Re-incarnation, God's justice could not be vindicated.' That is to say, in M. Pezzani's conception, God has not room in the infinite future to punish and redress every wrong, without sending back souls again and again into the flesh. M. Pezzani's idea, and that of his brother Re-incarnationists is, that the best way to get from Paris to London is to travel any number of times from Paris to Calais and back again. We English, that the only way is to go on to London at once. . . . As to M. Pezzani's notions of God's injustice without Re-incarnation, if souls were re-incarnated a score of times, injustice between man and man, riches and poverty, oppression and wrong, all the enigmas of social inequality would remain just then as now.

" In noticing these movements in the Spiritist camp in *France*, we should be doing a great injustice if we did not refer to the zealous, eloquent, and unremitting exertions of M. Pierart in the *Revue Spiritualists*, to expose and resist the errors of the *Spirite* to which we have alluded. The doctrine of Re-incarnation, M. Pierart has persistently resisted and denounced as at once false, unfounded on any evidence, and most pernicious to the character of Spiritualism."

Allan Kardec died on March 31st, 1869.

Notwithstanding the fact that the experimental method of receiving communications through physical mediumship was not in favour with M. Allan Kardec and his followers, there is an abundant amount of phenomena of all kinds recorded in M. Pierart's excellent journal, *La Revue Spiritualiste*, also in many other European journals devoted to the subject. From this we are about to select such facts of a representative character as will give a general view of French Spiritualism in the nineteenth century.

The celebrated "Curé D'Ars," the founder of the D'Ars "Providence," and many other noble works of charity, Jean Baptiste Vianney, was born in the vicinity of Lyons, in 1786, in a humble sphere of life. His natural capacity was by no means remarkable, and at school he was only remembered as a somewhat dull scholar. Circumstances having opened up the way for his becoming a priest, although he had only Latin enough to say mass, and no learning beyond the routine of his profession, yet his amiable nature and unaffected piety won him friends wherever he went. After some changes of fortune and the rejection of two good offers of rich positions, which in his extreme humility he did not deem himself fit for, he accepted the pastoral charge of the little agricultural village of D'Ars, now in the arrondisement of Trevoux.

Very soon his reputation for beneficence drew round him a much larger circle of poor dependents than he could provide for, and then it was that he commenced his extra-ordinary life of faith, supplicating in fervent prayer for whatever means were necessary to carry out his divine mission of blessing to his unfortunate fellow creatures. In this way the sphere of his benevolence, and the wonderful results of the means he employed to maintain it, reached proportions that could scarcely be credited.

But now a still more wonderful thing was to happen in the enchanted region of D'Ars. Persons afflicted with disease began to experience sudden cures whilst praying before the altar, or making confessions to the Curé. The fame of this new miracle soon spread abroad, until the Abbé Monnin declares that upwards of 20,000 persons annually came from Germany, Italy, Belgium, and all parts of *France*, and even from England, and that in less than six years this number increased to an average of 80,000. Diseases of every kind that had been pronounced incurable, were dissipated at once. The indefatibagle Curé gave himself up to the work, heart and soul. His church stood open day and night, and the immense crowds that surrounded it, were obliged to wait for hours and sometimes days, to reach the good healer. No one was allowed to take precedence of the rest, except in cases of extreme poverty or extreme suffering. Princes, nobles, and great ladies, often drove up as near as they could to the church in grand carriages, and manifested the utmost astonishment when informed that notwithstanding their rank, they could not be admitted except in turn. The Curé only permitted himself to take four hours sleep, namely from eleven to three, and when he came to the confessional again, the church and all the approaches to it were crowded with those who had waited all night to secure their places. Omnibuses were established to convey patients from Lyons to D'Ars, and the Saône was covered with boats full of anxious pilgrims.

There can be no doubt that the first well marked impulse which experimental spiritualism received through the invocatory processes of the circle, in *France*, as in many other countries of Europe, was due to the visits of Mr. D. D. Home, the celebrated non-professional physical medium, and subsequently to the large influx of professional mediums, who found in *France* an excellent field for the demonstration of their peculiar gifts.

Of Mr. Home's séances it would be superfluous to write, he himself having related them in two volumes published at different periods of his career, and his many admiring friends having sufficiently described the marvels of which they were witnesses in numerous magazines and newspaper articles.

Mr. Home's manifestations were given in *France* almost exclusively to personages of rank, or those distinguished by literary fame. He was a guest of royalty, the nobility, and persons of the highest position. During his residence in Paris, under the Imperial *régime*, he was a frequent and ever-welcome visitor at the court of the late Emperor Louis Napoleon. A record of the manifestations produced through his mediumship was kept by command of the Empress, and frequently read to her favoured friends. Amongst these memoranda is one which went the round of the papers at the time of its occurrence, hence there can be no impropriety in alluding to it now. It stated that on one occasion a séance was held at the Tuileries, when none were present save the Emperor, the Empress, the Duchess de Montebello, and Mr. D. D. Home.

On the table were placed pen, ink, and paper, and presently a spirit hand was seen, which dipped the pen in the ink and deliberately wrote the name of the first Napoleon, in a perfect facsimile of that monarch's handwriting. The Emperor asked if he might be permitted to kiss this wonderful hand, when it instantly rose to his lips, subsequently passing to those of the Empress, and Mr. Home.

The Emperor carefully preserved this precious autograph, and inscribed with it a memorandum to the effect that the hand was warm, soft, and resembled exactly that of his great predecessor and uncle.

As an evidence of the wide popularity to which the subject of Spiritualism had attained in 1869, M. Pierart quotes in one of his numbers of that year, an article from the *Siécle*, a leading paper, but one which has hitherto contained many notices inimical to Spiritualism. The writer, M. Eugène Bonnemère, says :

" Although somnambulism has been a hundred times annihilated by the Academy of Medicine, it is more alive than ever in Paris ; in the midst of all the lights of the age, it continues, right or wrong, to excite the multitude. Protean in its forms, infinite in its manifestations, if you put it out of the door, it knocks at the window ; if that be not opened, it knocks on the ceiling, on the walls ; it raps on the table at which you innocently seat yourselves to dine or for a game of whist. If you close your ears to its sounds, it grows excited, strikes the table, whirls it about in a giddy maze, lifts up its feet, and proceeds to talk through mediumship, as the dumb talk with their fingers.

" You have all known the rage for table-turning. At one time we ceased to ask after each other's health, but asked how your table was. ' Thank you, mine turns beautifully ; and how goes yours on ? ' Everything turned ; hats and the heads in them. One was led almost to believe that a circle of passengers being formed round the main-mast of a ship of great tonnage, and a magnetic chain thus established, they might make the vessel spin round till it disappeared in the depth of the ocean, as a gimlet disappears in a deal board. The Church interfered ; it caused its thunders to roar, declaring that it was Satan himself who thus raised the devil in the tables, and having formally forbade the world to turn, it now forbade the faithful to turn tables, hats, brains, or ships of huge size. But Satan held his own. The sovereign of the nether world passed into a new one, and that is the reason that America sends us mediums, beginning so gloriously with the famous Home, and ending with the Brothers Davenport. One remembers with what a frenzy everyone precipitated himself in pursuit of mediums. Everyone wished to have one of his own ; and when you introduced a young man into society, you did not say, ' He is a good waltzer,' but, ' He is a medium.' Official science has killed and buried this Somnambulism a score of times ; but it must have done it very badly, for there it is as alive as ever, only christened afresh with a new name."

Amongst the many distinguished adherents of Spiritualism in the department of French literature, none have more bravely asserted and defended their belief than Camille Flammarion, the celebrated astronomer ; Victor Hugo, Alexandre Dumas, and Victorien Sardou, the renowned writer of French comedy. M. Sardou was himself a medium of singularly happy endowments. He executed a number of curious drawings, purporting to represent scenes in the spirit world, amongst which was an exquisite and complex work of art entitled, " The House of Mozart."

Francis I., Duke of Brittany : (*See* **Summons by the Dying.**)

Frank, Christian : A visionary, who died in 1590 ; he frequently changed his religion, which fact gained for him the surname of Weathercock. He believed the religion of Japan to be the best, because he had read that its ministers were ecstatics.

Frank, Sebastian : A visionary of the sixteenth century, of whose life little is known. In 1531, he published a treatise on *l'Arbu de la science du bien et du mal, dont Adam a mangé la mort, et dont encore aujourd'hui tous les hommes la mangent.*

According to him, the sin of Adam is but an allegory, and the tree only the person, will, knowledge, and life of Adam. *Frank* died in 1545.

" Frankenstein," by Mrs. Shelley. (*See* **Fiction, Occult English.**)

Fraud : A very large part is played by *fraud* in spiritualistic practices, both in the physical and psychical, or automatic, phenomena, but especially in the former. The frequency with which mediums have been convicted of *fraud* has, indeed, induced many people to abandon the study of psychical research, judging the whole bulk of the phenomena to be fraudulently produced. Yet the question of *fraud* is itself an interesting and complicated one, not unworthy of the attention of the student, for we find in connection with spiritualism not only simple deception practised with a view to gaining pecuniary advantages, but also many instances of systematic and apparently deliberate trickery where there is no evident reward to be obtained, and even cases where the medium is, so far as can be judged, entirely innocent and ignorant of the *fraud* he obviously practises. And it may be added that after all precautions have been taken which science and commonsense can suggest, there remains a portion of the phenomena which still continues to be inexplicable, and which justifies the interest now so widely shown in psychic science.

In considering the important factor of *fraud*, we must distinguish between conscious and unconscious *fraud*, though, as will be shown hereafter, it is at times possible for the one to shade imperceptibly into the other. Conscious *fraud* most often appears in connection with the physical phenomena. Almost at the outset of the spiritualistic movement, *i.e.*, in 1851, three doctors, professors of the University of Buffalo, N.Y., demonstrated that the rappings which attended the Sisters Fox were produced by the manipulation of the knee and toe joints, a fact which was shortly afterwards corroborated by Mrs. Cluver, a relative of the Fox family. Since that time many mediums have at one time or another been convicted of *fraud*, and every phase of physical mediumship been discredited. Slate-writing, spirit photography, materialisation, have all in turn been exposed, though the latter, at least, seems able to survive any number of exposures. Time and again, sitters have beheld the form and features of the medium in the materialised spirit ; shadowy figures in filmy draperies, have been shown to be mannikins wrapped in muslin, and false beards and white draperies have been found about the person of the medium. Apports have been smuggled into the séance-room—jewels, flowers, perfumes, *objets d'art*—in order to be showered upon the sitters by generously-disposed " spirits." Threads and human hairs have been used to move furniture and other objects. Sometimes more elaborate and complicated machinery is provided, but more often the medium depends upon sleight of hand and skilful suggestion to accomplish his ends. Conjurers have frequently been admitted to séances, and have failed to discover the *modus operandi* of the various feats, but this fact, though a great deal has been made of it by spiritualists, cannot be taken to have any significance, since conjurers are often quite mystified by each other's performances.

Another phase of *fraud* is that illustrated by many instances of *soi-disant* clairvoyance, where the medium acquires her information by muscle-reading, or by judicious enquiry previous to the séance. *Fraud* of this kind may be either conscious or unconscious.

Under the heading of unconscious *fraud* must be classed a large group of automatic phenomena. In many of the more pronounced cases af automatism, the normal consciousness of the agent is not responsible for his acts, while, on the other hand, there is a slighter degree of automatism, where the agent may be partly conscious of, and responsible for, his productions. This latter state, if it be frequently induced, and if the will power of the automatist be somewhat relaxed, may pass into the more profound stage ; so that *fraud* which is at first conscious and voluntary may in time become unconscious and spontaneous. And thus it is extremely difficult to know just when an accusation of *fraud* may with justice be brought against a medium. There is evidence that many trance mediums reproduce in their discourses information subconsciously acquired at some more or less remote period ; the trance utterances of Mrs. Piper, Mrs. Thomson, and others, reveal this peculiarity. It is true that extensive and apparently fraudulent arrangements are sometimes made before a séance, but may it not be possible that, previous to a " physical " or " psychical " séance, such preparations may be made automatically in a state approximating to the mediumistic trance ? If the hypnotic subject is not responsible—or is only partly so—for the fulfilment of a post-hypnotic promise, would it not be within reason to suppose that the medium, in gaining information concerning possible sitters, in secreting apports about the person, is the victim of a similar dissociation of consciousness? There are facts not a few which would support such a conclusion.

Spiritualists themselves are, from time to time, called upon to face exposures of undoubted *fraud*, and on these occasions various apologies of a more or less ingenious nature, are offered for the erring medium. Sometimes it is said that the medium is controlled by mischievous spirits (*diakka*), who make use of his physical organism to perform tricks and deceptions. Again, it is stated that the medium feels an irresistible impulse to perform the action which he knows is in the mind of the control. Thus Eusapia Palladino would extend her hand involuntarily in the direction in which movement of furniture was to take place, though without actual contact—that is, perceiving that the spirits desired to move the object, she herself was impelled to attempt a physical (and fraudulent) forestalling of the action. Certain of the investigators who examined the phenomena in connection with the latter medium have also declared that their production costs Eusapia a great deal of pain and fatigue, and that she therefore seizes readily upon an opportunity of producing them easily and without trouble. Such an opportunity, they held, only presented itself when their rigorous precautions were relaxed. The same has also been stated in connection with other mediums. In the case of a materialisation séance, when the spirit form is grasped and found to be the medium herself, these apologists offer an explanation, as follows : A certain amount of the medium's physical energy is imparted to the spirit. If the latter be roughly handled, spirit and medium will unite for their joint benefit, either within or without the cabinet—if the medium possesses most energy, she will draw the spirit to her, if the most of the energy is with the materialised spirit, it is the medium who will instantly be attracted to the spirit. That it is the latter alternative which invariably takes place is a fact which has no significance for good spiritualists. Or they may insist, as did Sergeant Cox, on one occasion, that the medium is controlled to impersonate a spirit. But whatever be the reason for *fraud*, it is clear that not the most ingenuous medium is to be trusted for a moment, though his character in normal life be blameless, and no object in committing *fraud* be apparent ; and that investigators must rely only on the strictest vigilance and the most up-to-date scientific methods and apparatus.

Fredegonda : (*See* **France.**)

Freemasonry—History and Origin : Though it would not be exactly correct to say that the history of *Freemasonry* was lost in the mists of antiquity, it is competent to remark

that althuogh to a certain degree traceable, its records are of a scanty nature, and so crossed by the trails of other mystical brotherhoods, that disentanglement is an extremely difficult process. The ancient legend of its foundation at the time of the building of the Temple at Jerusalem is manifestly traditional. If one might hazard an opinion, it would seem that at a very early epoch in the history of civilization, a caste of builders in stone arose, who jealously guarded the secret of their craft. In all probability this caste was prehistoric. It is not unreasonable to assume this when we possess plenty of proof that an ancient caste of bronze-workers flourished in every country in Europe and Asia ; and if this be admitted, and it cannot well be refuted in the light of recent researches,—(*see Journal of the Gypsy Lore Society* for 1913)—there is nothing absurd or impossible in the contention that a similar school of workers in stone should have arisen at a like early period. We know that it is probable that the old caste of bronze-workers had an esoteric language of their own, which has come down to us as the Shelta Thari (q.v.) spoken generally by the tinkler people of Great Britain and Ireland. If such a caste can elaborate a secret language and cling jealously to the " mysteries " of metal-working, there is no reason to doubt the existence of a similar caste of masons. We tender this theory for what it is worth, as it is unsupported by any great authority on the subject. Where such a caste of operative masons arose is altogether a separate question, and cannot be dealt with here ; but it must obviously have been in a country where working in stone was one of the principal arts. It is also almost certain that this early brotherhood must have been hierophantic. Its principal work to begin with would undoubtedly consist in the raising of temples and similar structures, and as such it would come into very close contact with the priesthood, if indeed it was not wholly directed by it. In early civilization but two classes of dwelling receive the attention of the architect,—the temple and the palace. For example, among the ruins of Egypt and Babylon, remains of the private house are rare, but the temple and the royal residence are everywhere conspicuous, and we know that among the ruins of Central America temples and palaces alone remain—the huts of the surrounding dwellers having long ago disappeared. The temple is the nucleus of the early city. Around the worship of the gods crystallises commerce, agriculture, and all the affairs of life. All roads lead to the temple. Striding for a moment over the gap of years between early Babylon and Egypt and mediæval Britain, we find the priesthood in close touch with the masons. A mediæval cathedral took more than one generation to erect, and in that time many masons came and went around the fane. The lodge was invariably founded hard by the rising cathedral or abbey, and apprentices and others were entered as opportunity offered : indeed a man might serve his apprenticeship and labour all through his life upon the one building, without ever seeing any work elsewhere. The evidence as to whether the master-masons were also architects is very conflicting, and it has been held that the priests were the architects of the British cathedrals,—the master-masons and operatives merely carrying out their designs. There is good evidence however that this is not wholly true. Authorities are at one in declaring that of all arts architecture is by far the most intricate. It is undoubtedly the one which requires a long and specific training. Questions of stress and strain of the most difficult description arise, and it seems incredible that anyone with the most superficial knowledge of the subject should believe that ecclesiastics, who had not undergone any special training should be qualified to compose plans of the most perfect and intricate description for the most noble and remarkable edifices ever raised in this country.

We know that professional architects existed at a very early period ; and why the priesthood should be credited with their work, it is difficult to understand ; but instances are on record where the priests of a certain locality have taken to themselves the credit of planning the cathedral of the diocese. Be this as it may, the " mystery " of building was sufficiently deep to require extensive knowledge and experience and to a great extent this justifies the jealousy with which the early masons regarded its secrets. Again, this jealousy with which it was kept from the vulgar gaze may have been racial in its origin, and may have arisen from such considerations as the following : " Let no stranger understand this craft of ours. Why should we make it free to the heathen and the foreigner ? " This also smacks of priestcraft, but if masonry originated hierophantically, it certainly did not continue a preserve of any religion, and is nowadays probably the chiefest abomination of the Roman Catholic hierarchy, which has not hesitated to publish and disseminate the grossest libels regarding it. It is to Britain that we must look for evidence as to the evolutionary line of masonry. Before the founding of the Grand Lodge, we find that York and the North of England in general was regarded as the most ancient seat of the fraternity in this island. Indeed without stretching probabilities too far, the line of evolution so far as York is concerned is quite remarkable. We know for example that in the early days of that city a temple of Serapis existed there, which was afterwards a monastery of the Begging Friars, and the mysteries of this god existed beside the Roman Collegia or Craftsmen's Society. It is also considered that the crypt of York Minster affords evidence of the progress of masonry from Roman to Saxon times. It is stated that it has a mosaic pavement of blue and white tiles laid in the form employed in the first degree of masonry, and is said to show the sites of three seats used by the master and his wardens during the construction of the building. It is also an undoubted fact that the craft occasionally met in this crypt during last century. There is thus reason to believe even though the evidence be of a scanty nature (but the foregoing does not embrace all of it) that the early masons of Britain were probably influenced by Romano-Egyptian mystical societies, and that their own craft societies drew some of their practices and constitutions from these alien schools. Masonic tradition goes to show that even in the beginning of the fourteenth century masonry in Britain was then regarded as a thing of great antiquity. Lodge records for the most part only date back to the sixteenth century in the oldest instances, but ancient manuscripts are extant which undoubtedly relate to masonry. Thus the old charges embodied in the Regius MS. which was unearthed in 1839 by Mr, Halliwell Phillips are dated at 1390, and contain a curious legend of the craft, which tells how the necessity of finding work of some description drove men to consult Euclid, who recommended masonry as a craft to them. It goes on to tell how masonry was founded in Egypt, and how it entered England in the time of Athelstan. The necessity for keeping close counsel as regards the secrets of the craft is insisted upon in rude verse. The Cooke MS. dates from the first part of the fifteenth century, and likewise contains versions of the old charges. Egypt is also regarded here as the mother-land of masonry, and Athelstan is the medium for the introduction of the craft into the island of Britain. But that this manuscript was used among masons at a later date was proved by the discovery of a more modern version dated about 1687, in 1890, and known as the William Watson MS. In all about seventy of these old charges and pseudo-histories have been discovered since 1860. They have all much in common and are of English origin.

A great deal has been written to attempt to prove that British freemasonry borrowed extensively from continental secret societies, such as the Steinmetzin of Germany, the Rosicrucians (q.v.) and similar fellowships. The truth probably lies however in the circumstance that the coming and going of students of occultism throughout Europe was so constant, and so frequent were their communications that practically all those societies were in touch with one another. Again many persons belonged to several of them at once, and imported the rules and constitution of one body into another. No student of occultism can fail to be struck with the close resemblance of the constitutions of nearly all the mystical fellowships of the middle ages, and the resemblance of the verbiage employed by their founders and protagonists. It must also be insisted that the speculative or mystic part of masonry was in the middle ages merely a tradition with the brotherhood, whatever it may have been in earlier times, and whatever close connection the craft may have had with hierophantic or mystic philosophy. The speculative element, we repeat, was merely traditional and symbolical as at present, and not practical ; but this tradition was to serve to keep alight the flame of speculative mysticism which was to be aroused again at the end of the mediæval period. When political freedom awoke in Europe, the necessity for the existence of secret societies vanished, but the persons who delighted in their formation and management still remained. The *raison d'être* of these fellowships had disappeared, but the love of mysticism, not to say the mysterious, was perhaps stronger than ever. What then occurred ? Simply this : that all those persons who found the occupation of floating and managing real secret societies gone, cast about for anything in the shape of a mystical fellowship that they could find. They soon discovered the craft of masonry which although operative possessed mystical traditions. The attraction was mutual, and astrologers, alchemists and others soon crowded the lodges, to such purpose that at the lodge held in 1646 in London, there was not an operative mason present, and at that held in 1682, the speculative branch was overwhelming in its numbers. Harking back a little, it is noteworthy that the freemasons in mediæval times formed a fellowship or guild closely resembling in its constitution that of similar trade guilds both in Britain and the continent ; such as the Weavers, Tailors, Fishmongers, and so forth. But although these guilds preserved their " mysteries," where they possessed them, with considerable jealousy, they do not appear to have embedded in their constitutions the same ancient practices and ritual which go to show so strongly that masonry is undoubtedly an institution of great antiquity.

It has also been suggested that freemasonry was introduced into Europe by the Knights Templar. It would be difficult to discover a similar institution which in the opinion of some authorities had not been founded by that order ; and it is difficult to believe that the haughty chivalry of Norman times would have claimed any connection whatsoever with an operative craft. There are, however, many connections between alchemy and masonry. For example in the *Ordinall of Alchymy* compiled by Thomas Norton, (q.v.), the freemasons are alluded to as workers in it. In 1630, we find Fludd (q.v.) using language which smacks strongly of freemasonry. His society was divided into degrees, and the Masons' Company of London had a copy of the masonic charges presented by him. Vaughan also appears to have been a freemason, and many masons of the middle of the seventeenth century, such as Robert Moray and Elias Ashmole, were diligent students of occult science. and Sir Christopher Wren was a student of hermetic art.

It has often been put forward that Scotland was the original home of freemasonry in these islands, but although the craft was undoubtedly ancient in that country, there does not appear to be any adequate proof that it was older than in England. Some of the Scottish lodges, such as No. 1 Edinburgh, Kilwinning, and Aberdeen, possess very ancient records, and it is probable that this has led to the assumption that the brotherhood was of greater antiquity in North Britain than in England. But the circumstance that the craft was probably introduced into England in Roman times, where it has in all likelihood flourished ever since, tends to dispose of such a theory. The history of modern freemasonry begins with the formation of the Grand Lodge of England, which was inaugurated on St. John the Baptist's Day 1717 by several old lodges. This represented the first central governing body of the fraternity, and before this time each lodge had been self-governing. Many lodges speedily came under its ægis, and Ireland formed a Grand lodge of her own in 1725 but Scotland did not follow till 1736, and even then many lodges held aloof from the central body, only 33 out of 100 falling into line. From one or other of these three governing bodies all the regular lodges throughout the world have arisen, so that modern masonry may truthfully be said to be of entirely British origin. This is not the place to enter into an elaborate discussion of the history and affairs of modern masonry, and we are chiefly exercised regarding its mystical position and tendencies. Regarding these we must be brief. As regards the lower ranks of the craft, it consists almost entirely in these islands at least of persons who have in great measure treated it as a mere friendly society, and it is only in the higher ranks that any real idea of the true significance of the mystical tenets preserved and taught is retained. The ordinary mason, who preserves a cryptic and mysterious silence when the affairs of his craft are alluded to, merely serves as a laughing-stock to the modern well-equipped mystic. Certain signs and handgrips are in use amongst masons, and the possession of these, and of a ritual the significance of which he rarely comprehends, the average brother fondly imagines, renders him somewhat superior to the layman. It is extremely doubtful if among even the higher ranks of masonry, the deepest significance of the tradition of the craft is thoroughly realised, and if the absurd works which every now and then emanate from eminent masons regarding the history of their craft be accepted as criteria of their higher knowledge, it must indeed be of slight proportions. Regarding the grand secret, or secrets, of masonry, the layman may rest comfortably assured that if he has failed to join the brotherhood, he has missed no fact of supreme importance by so doing. There is no " secret " at all. The original secrets in connection with the craft were those of operative masons, who were jealous of their position as workmen, and who rightly enough did not believe in giving away business secrets to all and sundry ; but the so-called " secrets " of modern speculative masonry are merely such as have brought alchemy, astrology, and the kindred sciences into unthinking disrepute among those who do not recognise their significance in the history of human thought. This is not to say that masonry as a whole consists of mere claptrap. The trend of its entire constitution is nowadays frankly mystical, but it is a mysticism which is only half understood by the lower ranks of the craft, and which is imperfectly recognised by its higher officers. Its tenets are unquestionably mystic and lofty, but masonic transcendentalism has scarcely kept in line with the more modern forms of mysticism. From time to time new degrees have been formed which have in some measure rectified this, but the number of masons qualified to understand the nature of the vast and mighty truths conveyed in these, is naturally extremely small, and it is as a friendly society that the brotherhood effects its greatest good.

As has been said, continental masonry is undoubtedly the offspring of British systems. This is not to say that in France and Germany there were no masonic lodges in existence before the formation of the English Grand Lodge ; but all modern lodges in these countries undoubtedly date from the inception of the English central body. French masonry possessed and possesses many rites which differ entirely from those accepted by the British craft. We find the beginnings of modern French masonry in the labours of Martinez Pasqually (q.v.), St. Martin (q.v.), and perhaps to a great extent in those of Cagliostro (q.v.) who toiled greatly to found his Egyptian rite in France. It is noticeable, however, that he had become a member of a London lodge before attempting this. In *France*, masonry has always had more or less a political complexion, and nowadays the extreme enmity existing between it and the Roman Catholic church in that country favours the inclusion in its ranks of persons possessing ideals by no means in consonance with the very upright standard of British masonry. In Germany, it has been said that the Steinmetzin approximated very strongly in mediæval times to the British masons, if they were not originally one and the same ; but the later lodges in Germany all date from that founded in 1733.

The entrance of masons into the various degrees involves an elaborate system of symbolic ritual, of which the essence is uniform throughout all lodges. The members are classified in numerous degrees, of which the first three are entered apprentice, fellow-craft, and master-mason. Each lodge possesses its own byelaws, subject to the Book of Constitution of the Grand Lodge.

Wild stories have been circulated, chiefly by the Roman Catholic enemies of masonry, regarding the practice of diabolic occultism in the higher ranks of the craft. To begin with, it is extremely unlikely that more than three or four persons connected with it possess the requisite knowledge to thus offend against the Christian proprieties, and the childish asseverations of French writers on the subject may be dismissed with a smile. The " occultism " and " transcendentalism " of the majority of zealous brethren are usually of the mildest character possible, and are in some measure related to the mysterious attitude of the average mason, when dark hints as to lodge doings are whispered of among his admiring relatives.

French Commission on Magnetism : (*See* **Spiritualism, Hypnotism.**)

Friar Rush (German Rausch) : A house-spirit supposed to have been sent from the infernal regions to keep the monks and friars of the seventeenth century in the same state of wickedness that they then existed in. He gained admittance to monastic houses as a scullion ; is probably representative of the spirit of inebriety. A German myth.

Friends of God : A mystical society founded in Germany in the fourteenth century, for the purpose of ministering to the poor by preaching and sacrament. Its members included men and women of every rank and station ; not only monks and nuns, but knights, farmers, artizans, merchants. Their law was : " That universal love, commanded by Christ, and not to be gainsaid by his vicar." Their prophecies and warnings roused the ire of certain of the clergy, and they were charged with sectarianism.

Fritzlar, Martin Von : German alchemist. (Circa, 1750.) The dates of the birth and death of this alchemist have never been ascertained, but he is known to have lived in the first half of the eighteenth century, while he appears to have been a Hessian, resident chiefly at the village of Fritzlar. While a young man, he studied pharmacy, intending to make it his profession ; but he soon grew interested in the quest of gold-making, and, when the celebrated alchemist, Lascaris, came to Germany, Martin hastened to his presence with a view to gleaning his secrets. Along with several other young men, the Hessian was allowed to witness numerous experiments, and while he watched them, it seemed to him that the great secret lay open before him ; but afterwards, when he made attempts on his own account, he found that Lascaris had duped him shamefully, and had even taken advantage of his ignorance. Thereupon, in contradistinction to the majority of thwarted alchemists, he renounced the futile search altogether, vowed fealty to his original calling, and devoted the rest of his life thereto.

Fumigation in Exorcism : One of the most important rites during the exorcism of an evil spirit, appears to have been the *fumigation* of the victim ; and for this, various prescriptions are given throughout occult history. If it is found difficult to dislodge the demon, a picture of him is sometimes drawn, which is to be thrown into the fire after having " been signed with the cross, sprinkled with holy water, and *fumigated*." At other times, if the evil spirit refuses to give his name, the exorcist will *fumigate* the possessed one.

Futhorc : (*See* **Teutons**).

G

Galactides or Galaricides : Perhaps a species of emerald. It is greatly valued by magicians, its property being to make magical writings heard, and ghosts appear, to return answers. It promotes love and friendship.

Galeotti, Martius : Italian Astrologer. (1442-1494). Born in 1442, this Italian astrologer and theologian, appears to have been a native of Narni, in Umbria ; but it would seem that he left Italy while a young man, and settled for a while at Boulogne. Here, he gave grave offence to the Church of Rome by promulgating the doctrine that good works are not the road to salvation, and that this is only to be obtained by faith in Christ ; and, finding the priests around him growing daily more and more hostile, *Galeotti* saw fit to leave France for Hungary, where he became secretary to the king, Matthias Covirnus, and also tutor to the latter's son, Prince John. His secretarial and tutorial duties, however, did not occupy the whole of his time ; and, besides making himself an expert astrologer, he wrote a book called, *De jocose Dictis et Factis Regis Matthiæ Covirni.* Some of the tenets contained therein were the means of his incurring fresh ill-will from the clergy ; and eventually, their rancour became so great, indeed, that the writer was seized and taken to Venice, where he was imprisoned for a while. He was released anon, chiefly owing to the influence of the Pope, Sixtus IV, whose tutor he is said to have been at an earlier and indeterminate date ; and, thereupon, *Galeotti* returned to France, where he came under the notice of the king, Louis XI, who appointed him his state-astrologer. Thenceforth, for many years, the Italian acted in this onerous capacity, sometimes living within the precincts of the royal castle of Plessis-les-Tours, sometimes at the town of Lyons ; and once, in 1478, while staying at the latter place, and being informed that Louis was approaching, he rode out to meet him, fell from his horse, and died shortly afterwards as a result of injuries sustained in the fall.

An especial interest attaches to *Galeotti* in that he appears in Sir Walter Scott's inimitable story of mediæval France, *Quentin Durward.* Early in the tale, soon after Quentin has entered the Scots Guard of Louis XI., the latter and his new guardsman are depicted as visiting the astrologer, the King being anxious for a prophecy regarding Quentin's immediate future. The scene is a very memorable and graphic one, among the best in the whole book ; and it is historically valuable, moreover, containing, as it does, what is probably a fairly accurate description of the kind of study used generally by an astrologer in the middle ages. *Galeotti* is represented, " curiously examining a specimen, just issued from the Frankfort Press, of the newly invented art of printing " ; and the King questions him about this novel process, whereupon the seer speaks of the vast changes it is destined to bring about throughout the whole world. Now, it was by no means thoughtlessly or carelessly, that Sir Walter introduced this passage, for, though the novelist himself does not refer to the matter in his notes, and though Andrew Lang says nothing thereon in those annotations which he furnished for the " Border Waverley," it is a fact that Louis was keenly interested in printing ; and, soon after the craft first made its appearance, the King commissioned the director of his mint, one Nicholas Janson or Jenson, to give up his present post in favour of studying typography, with a view to its being carried on in France.

Galigai, Leonora : Wife of the Maréchal d'Ancre Concino Concini, who was killed by the populace, in 1617. She was believed to be a sorceress, and was said to have bewitched the Queen. In her possession were found three volumes full of magic characters, besides charms and amulets. At her trial, it was established that the Maréchal and his wife had consulted magicians, astrologers, and sorcerers, and had made use of waxen images, and that they had brought sorcerers from Nancy to sacrifice cocks, besides working many other sorceries and deeds of darkness. It is said that on her own confession, she was condemned, and was beheaded and burnt in 1617. But when President Courtin asked her by what charm she had bewitched the Queen, she replied, proudly : " My spell was the power of a strong mind over a weak one."

Galitzin, Prince : (*See* **St. Martin**).

Garatronicus : A red-coloured stone, which Achilles is believed to have carried with him in battle. It renders its possessor invincible.

Garden of Pomegranates : A tract reflecting the later spirit of Kabalism (q.v.).

Gardner, Dr. : (*See* **Spirit-Photography**).

Gargates : A black species of electrum or amber, now called jet. To electrum are attributed many occult virtues of a tell-tale character, and according to Pliny, a cup of this substance had the property of discovering poison, by showing certain half-circles, like rainbows, in the liquor, which also sparkles and hisses as if on fire.

Garinet, Jules : Author of a *History of Magic in France*, Paris, 1818. In this curious work will be found a description of the Sabbath, a dissertation on demons, a discourse on the superstitions connected with magic among the ancients and the moderns.

Garlic : A species of onion, cultivated throughout Europe, to which is attributed certain occult properties. It is believed by the Greeks and the Turks that the use of this vegetable, or even the mention of its name, is a sure charm against the " evil eye," and against vampires (q.v.). New-built houses and the sterns of boats belonging to Greece and Turkey, have long bunches of *garlic* hanging from them as a preventive against the fatal envy of any ill-disposed person.

Garnet : Preserves the health and promotes joy, but in the case of lovers, discord.

Garnier, Gilles : A werwolf, condemned at Dôle, under Louis XIII., for having devoured a number of children. He was burned alive, and his body, after being reduced to ashes, was scattered to the winds.

Gassner : (*See* **Hypnotism**).

Gastromancy, or Divination from the Belly, is now generally explained by ventriloquism, the voice in both cases sounding low and hollow, as if issuing from the ground. Salverte enforces this opinion, and adds : " The name of *Engastrimythes*, given by the Greeks to the Pythiæ (priestesses of Apollo) indicates that they made use of this artifice.'' The explanation is only partial, and the text of Isaiah : '' Thy voice shall die as one that hath a familiar spirit,'' is inapplicable in such an argument. Those who are experienced in clairvoyance are aware that the voice is often reduced very low, in consequence of a change in the respiration. This was the case with some of the ancient Pythonesses, though instances may have occurred when ventriloquism was resorted to, as by the wizards of Greenland in our own time.

Another method of practising the ancient *gastromancy* connects it with crystal-seeing, as vessels of glass, round, and full of clear water, were used, which were placed before several lighted candles. In this case, a young boy or girl was generally the seer, and the demon was summoned in a low voice by the magician. Replies were then obtained from the magical appearances seen in the illuminated glass vessels.

Gaudillon, Pierre : A sorcerer, who was burned in 1610, for going about at night in the form of a hare.

Gaufridi, Louis : A French ecclesiastic, burned as a sorcerer at Aix, in 1611. He was a curé at Marseilles, where his attractive person and manners gained for him a footing in high society, but for all his priestly garb, he led an evil life. A girl whom he had seduced was sent by her parents to a convent of Ursulines, and here *Gaufridi* followed her, making the credulous nuns believe that a legion of demons possessed the convent. At the instance of the exorcist, who relieved the '' possessed '' nuns *Gaufridi* was tried at Aix, and condemned to be burned alive.

Gauher-Abad : Meaning the Abode of Jewels. This was the name given to one of the capitals of the peris of Persian romance. These were beings of an angelic or well-disposed nature, who inhabited the earth, along with the divs or evil-disposed, before the creation of man. After this event, the peris became inhabitants of the ærial regions, and had three capitals : Shad-u-kam (pleasure and desire), Gauherabad, and Amber-abad (city of Ambergris).

Gauthier, Jean : An alchemist. Charles IX. of France, deceived by his promises, had him provided with a hundred and twenty thousand pounds, with which to make gold, and the adept set to work. But after he had worked for a week, he ran away with the King's money. He was pursued, captured, and hanged.

Gauthier of Bruges : It is related that a Franciscan monk, made a bishop by Pope Nicholas III., and deposed by Clement V., appealed to God against his deposition, and asked that he should be buried with his act of appeal in his hand. Some time after his death, Pope Clement V., visited Poitiers, and, finding himself one day in a Franciscan monastery, asked to see the remains of him whom he had deposed. He caused the tomb to be opened, and was horrified to see *Gauthier of Bruges* presenting his act of appeal, with a withered hand.

Gbalo : An order of priests among the Ga people of the Gold Coast, west of Togoland.

Geber, otherwise Abou Moussah Djafar al Sofi, was a native of Haman, in Mesopotamia, or, according to other accounts, a Spanish Moor, born at Savile, somewhere about the end of the eighth century, though all dates concerning him are extremely doubtful. Practically nothing is known of his life. He undertook wide experiments in metallurgy and chemistry, with the object of discovering the constituent elements of metals, in the course of which he stumbled upon nitric acid and red oxide of mercury. It is, indeed, upon actual discoveries that his reputation is based, and not upon the many spurious treatises which have been attributed to him, and which embrace the entire gamut of the sciences. His alleged extant works, which are in Latin, cannot but be regarded with suspicion, especially as several mediæval writers adopted his name. It is believed, however, that

the library at Leyden, and the Imperial Library at Paris, contain Arabic manuscripts, which might be referred to his authorship. His *Sum of Perfection,* and his *Investigation into the Perfection of Metals* are his most important works, a complete edition of which was published at Dantzic, in 1682, and again in the *Bibliotheca Chemica Curiosa, of* Mangetus, published at Cologne, in 1702. The *Sum of Perfection* professes to draw its inspiration from alchemical authors, who lived previous to *Geber,* but as alchemy was then not very far advanced, the derivation is an unlikely one. We are told in its pages that success in the great art is only to be achieved by rigid adherence to natural law. A spirit of great strength and a dry water are spoken of as the elements of the natural principle. The philosophical furnace and its arrangement is dealt with in detail, as is the philosopher's vessel, a vase of glass with several intricate details difficult of comprehension. There is no dubiety, however, regarding the absolutely physical basis of metallurgy, upon which the work is composed, and it contains no hint of allegory or the achievement of success through supernatural agency.

Gehenna (otherwise Hell) : The word is derived from the Hebrew *ge* and *Hinnom,* the Valley of Hinnom—originally a valley in Palestine where the Jews passed their children through the fire to Moloch, the god of the Ammonites. *Gehenna* is popularly regarded as a place of torment to which the wicked are consigned when they leave this earth : it is pictured as a bottomless pit, lit only by the fire which is never quenched. In Dante and Milton, we have diverse descriptions of Hell—the one of unutterable anguish, horror and despair ; the other more sublimely imaginative, and pierced with rays of faith and love. The locality of Hell, and the duration of its torments, have for centuries been the subject of much questioning. By some, it is believed, that there is a purgatorial region—a kind of upper *Gehenna,* '' in which the souls of just men are cleansed by a temporary punishment '' before they are admitted to Heaven. It was believed that during this period the soul could revisit the places and persons whom it had loved. By the Persians, *Gehenna* was understood as the place inhabited by the divs, or rebellious angels, and to which they had been confined when they refused to bow down before the first man. *Gehenna* is used in the New Testament for Hell, and is practically synonymous with the Greek '' Hades.''

Gematria : along with *temurah,* was the science of the dual interpretation of the Kabalistic alphabet, which composed the notary art, which is fundamentally the complete science of the *tarot* (q.v.) signs and their complex and varied application to the definition of all secrets.

Genealum Dierum : (*See* **Avicenna.**)

Genius : Is generally used as the name of a superior class of ærial beings, holding an intermediate rank between mortals and immortals. That, at least, appears to be the signification of '' Daemon,'' the corresponding term in Greek. It is probable, that the whole system of Demonology was invented by the Platonic philosophers, and engrafted by degrees on the popular mythology. The Platonists professed, however, to derive their doctrines from the '' theology of the ancients,'' so that this system may have come originally from the East, where it formed a part of the tenets of Zoroaster. This sage ascribed all the operations of nature to the agency of celestial beings, the ministers of one supreme first cause, to whose most visible and brilliant image, Fire, homage was paid as his representative. Some Roman writers speak of '' the *Genius* '' as '' the God of Nature,'' or '' Nature '' itself, but their notions seem to have been modified by, if not formed from, etymological considerations, more likely to mislead than to afford a certain clue to the real meaning of the term. At a later period, they supposed almost every created thing, animate or inanimate, to be protected by its guardian *genius*, a sort of demi-god, who presided over its birth, and was its constant companion till its death. Thus, Censorinus, who lived about the middle of the third century, wrote as follows : " The *genius* is a god supposed to be attendant on everyone from the time of his birth. . . . Many think the *genius* to be the same as the lars of the ancients. . . . We may well believe that its power over us is great, yea, absolute. . . . Some ascribe two *genii* at least to those who live in the houses of married persons." Euclid, the Socratic philosopher, gives two to every one, a point on which Lucilius, in his " Satires," insists we cannot be informed. To the *genius*, therefore, so powerful through the whole course of one's life, they offered yearly sacrifices. As the birth of every mortal was a peculiar object of his guardian *genius's* solicitude, the marriage-bed was called the genial bed, " lectus genialis " ; the same invisible patron was supposed also to be the author of joy and hilarity, whence a joyous was called a genial life, " genialis vita." There is a curious passage relating to the functions of the Greek demons in the *Symposium* of Plato, in which he says : (*Speech of Socrates*) " from it (*i.e.*, the agency of *genii*) proceed all the arts of divination, and all the science of priests, with respect to sacrifices, initiations, incantations, and everything, in short, which relates to oracles and enchantments. The deity holds no direct intercourse with man ; but, by this means, all the converse and communications between the gods and men, whether asleep or awake, take place ; and he who is wise in these things is a man peculiarly guided by his *genius*." We here see the origin of the connection between demonology and magic ; an association perpetually occurring in the romances of the East, if the Jinns of the Mussulmans can be identified with the *genii* of the Platonists. (*See also* **Jinn.**)

Germany : For early German magic, see **Teutons.**

Magic as formulated and believed in by the Germans in the Middle Ages, bears, along with traces of its unmistakable derivation from the ancient Teutonic religion, the impress of the influence wrought by the natural characteristics of the country upon the mind of its inhabitants Deep forests, gloomy mountains, limitless morasses, caverned rocks, mysterious springs, all these helped to shape the weird and terrible imagination which may be traced in Teutonic mythology, and later in the darker and more repulsive aspects of magic and witchcraft, which first arose in *Germany*, and then obtained ready credence.

As the clash and strife of Teuton and Roman, of Christian and Heathen have left indelible records in folk-lore and history, so we may find them as surely in the magical belief of the Middle Ages. The earlier monkish legends are replete with accounts of magic and sorcery, indicating plainly the process by which the ancient deities had become evil and degraded upon the introduction of the newer religion. Miracles are recounted, where these evil ones are robbed of all power at the name of Christ, or before some blessed relic, then chained and prisoned beneath mountain, river and sea in eternal darkness, whilst it was told how misfortune and death were the unvarying rewards for those who still might follow the outcast gods.

Again, the sites and periods of the great religious festivals of the Teutons are perpetuated in those said to be the place and time of the Witches' Sabbath and other mysterious meetings and conclaves. Mountains especially retained this character—as the Venusberg, the Horselberg, and Blocksberg, now become the Devil's realm and abode of the damned. Chapels and cathedrals were full of relics, whose chief virtue was to exorcise the spirits of evil, while the bells must be blessed, as ordained by the Council of Cologne, in order that " demons might be affrighted by their sound, calling Christians to prayers ; and when they

fled, the persons of the faithful would be secure ; that the destruction of lightnings and whirlwinds would be averted, and the spirits of the storm defeated."

Storms were always held to be the work of the Devil, or the conjuration of his followers. In their fury might be heard the trampling of his infernal train above the tossing forests or holy spires, and here is seen the transformation Odin and his hosts had undergone. Another instance of this is found when the Valkyries, the Choosers of the Slain, riding to places of battle, have become the mediæval witches riding astride broom-sticks, on their missions of evil. Castles of flames, where the Devil holds wild revel ; conclaves of corpses revivified by evil knowledge ; unearthly growths, vitalized by hanged men's souls, springing to life beneath gallows and gibbets ; little men of the hills, malicious spirits, with their caps of mist and cloaks of invisibility ; in these may be seen the meeting of the Heathen and Christian stories, and the origins of that terrible belief in magic, and its train of terror and death, which is one of the darkest mysteries of the Middle Ages.

Witchcraft was at first derided as a delusion by men of sense and education, and belief in it was actually forbidden by some of the earlier councils. It was in the fifteenth and sixteenth centuries that it attained prominence, helped greatly thereto by the fact that magic, sorcery and witchcraft had now become a crime in the eyes of the Church —a crime punishable by confiscation and death. It may be truly said that the Holy Fathers and Inquisitors first systematised and formulated Black Magic. Under such authority, belief in it flourished, filling the people with either an abject fear or unholy curiosity.

The motives for laying the charge of sorcery and witchcraft at a person's door were, of course, many besides that of care for the soul ; for personal feuds, political enmities, religious differences and treasury needs found in this an unfailing and sure means of achieving their infamous ends. However this might be, the charges were hurled at high and low, and death thereby reaped a plentiful harvest.

The famous Council of Constance began the years of terror with its proscription of the doctrines of Wyclif and the burning of John Huss and Jerome of Prague. At this time, too, a work was published by one of the Inquisitors, called the *Formicarium*, a comprehensive list of the sins against religion and in the fifth volume an exhaustive account was given of that of sorcery. The list of crimes accomplished by witches is detailed, such as second sight, ability to read secrets and foretell events ; power to cause diseases, death by lightning and destructive storms ; to transform themselves into beasts and birds ; to bring about illicit love, barrenness of living beings and crops ; their enmity against children and practice of devouring them.

Papal bulls appeared for the appointment of Inquisitors, who must not be interfered with by the civil authorities, and the Emperor and reigning princes took such under their protection. The persecutions rose to a ferocity unparalleled in other countries, till the following century, and hundreds were burned in the space of a few years. Two Inquisitors of this time, Jacob Sprenger, and Henricus Institor, compiled the famous *Malleus Maleficarum*, a complete system of witchcraft, also a perfect method of proving the innocent capable and guilty of any and every crime. Yet it was meant partly as an apology—a pointing out of the necessity for the extermination of such a horde of evil-doers. At this time, too, appeared the bull of Pope Innocent VIII., another comprehensive method and process for trials and tortures.

These persecutions were intermittent throughout the fifteenth and sixteenth centuries, breaking out again with renewed vigour in the seventeenth century. It was stimulated in this by the increasing strife between Catholics and Protestants and the condition of the country, devastated by wars, plague and famine, was an ever-ready and fruitful source of charges that might be brought against sorcery. Two cities, Bamberg and Würzburg attained an unenviable fame for sanguinary trials and number of victims.

In the first-named city, Prince-Bishop George II., and his suffragan, Frederic Forner, prosecuted the holy inquisition with such energy that between the years 1625 and 1630 nine hundred trials took place, six hundred people being burned. Confessions of whatever the holy fathers wished, were wrung from the victims under extreme and merciless torture. Rich and poor, learned and ignorant, were gathered into the toils, the number often being so great that names were never taken and written down, the prisoners being cited as No. 1, 2, 3, and so on.

At Würzburg, Lutheranism was gaining ground, and here again the charge of sorcery was brought against its followers. The bishop, Philip Adolph, who came to the see in 1623, did not dare to openly prosecute them, so took this means of punishing those unfaithful to the Church. In Hauber's *Bibliotheca Magica* may be found a list of twenty-nine burnings, covering a short period prior to 1629. Each burning consisted of several victims, the numbers ranging from two up to ten or more. It is a strange procession we see here, winding their way to death through the flames and bitter smoke, a procession pathetic and terrible. Old men and women, little girls and boys and infants, all emissaries of the Evil One ; noble ladies and washerwomen ; vicars, canons, singers and minstrels ; Bannach, a senator, " the fattest citizen in Würzburg " ; a very rich man, a keeper of the pot-house, the bishop's own nephew and page, " the most beautiful girl in Würzburg," a huckster, a blind girl, living beings beside the decapitated dead—the procession is endless as the conditions were various.

Strangely, it was at Würzburg, in 1749, that the last trial for witchcraft took place, that of Maria Renata, of the Convent of Unterzell. She was condemned on all the old charges, of consorting with the Devil, bewitchments and other infernal practices, and burned there in the month of June, the last victim of cruel superstition.

Towards the end of the seventeenth century, disbelief in the truth of witchcraft and criticism of the wholesale burnings began to be heard, though earlier than this, some had dared to lift their voices against the injustice and ignorance of it all. Cornelius Saos, a priest in Mainz, had, before 1593, stated his doubt of the whole proceedings, but suffered for his temerity. Johannes Wier, physician to the Duke of Cleves, Thomas Erast, another physician, Adam Tanner, a Bavarian Jesuit, and last, but not least, Frederick Spree, also a Jesuit, who, more than all helped to end the reign of terror and superstition.

Alchemy, the forerunner of modern chemistry, belonged in those days to the realm of magic, and was therefore Satanic in its derivation, and its followers liable to the charge of sorcery and the penalty of death. In this fraternity we find emperors and princes, often devoted to the study themselves, or taking into their service well-known practisers of the art, as when Joachim I. had Johannes Trithemius as teacher of astrology and " defender of magic," and the Emperor Rudolph employing Michael Maier as his physician.

Germany supplies a long roll of names famous for their discoveries made in the name of magic, men who by their search for knowledge and truth laid themselves open to much terrible suspicion. Here we find Paracelsus,—that inexplicable figure who in his search for the Elixir of Life discovered laudanum, perhaps in some magical distillation of black poppies at midnight hour ; the great Cornelius Agrippa ; Basil Valentine, prior and chemist ; Henry

Kühñrath, physician and philosopher, and a train of students, all tirelessly searching for the elusive mysteries of life, the innermost secrets of nature.

These men were awesome figures to the ignorant mind. Popular imagination was ever busy weaving strange tales about their doings, such as infernal dealings and pacts with the Devil. Such knowledge as the alchemists gained could only be acquired by infernal means, and the soul of the magician was often the price promised and inexorably demanded by the Evil One. These myths and imaginings centred themselves about one magician especially, and in the Faust legend we may find embalmed the general attitude and belief of the Middle Ages towards learning and any attempt to extend the realm of knowledge.

The Alchemists were also mystics as their writings abundantly testify, but most notable of all in this department of occultism was Jacob Böhme, the son of peasants, the inspired shoemaker.

During the Thirty Years' War many wild preachers, seers and fanatics appeared, exhorting and prophesying. No doubt the condition of the country contributed towards producing these states of hallucination and hysteria, and in contrast to the terror, misfortune and sorrow on all sides we have accounts of ecstatics absorbed in supernatural visions. Anna Fleischer of Freiburg was such an one, as was Christiana Poniatowitzsch, who journeying throughout Bohemia and *Germany* related her visions and prophesied.

At the end of the seventeenth century the old tenets of magic were undergoing a gradual change. Alchemy began to separate itself from them, and became merged in the science of chemistry. The residue of the magical beliefs formed their protagonists in members of all kinds of secret societies, many of which were founded on those of the Middle Ages. Freemasonry—whose beginnings are attributed by some to a certain guild of masons banded together for the building of Strasburg Cathedral, but by other authorities to Rosicrucianism—formed the basis and pattern for many other secret societies.

In the eighteenth century these flourished exceedingly. Occultism became rampant. We hear of Frederick William working with Steinert in a house specially built for evocations ; of Schroepfer, proprietor of a café with his magic punch and circles for raising the spirits of the dead ; of Lavater with two spirits at his command ; of the Mopses, a society whose rites of initiation were those of the Templars and Witches' Sabbath in a mild and civilized form ; and of Carl Sand, the mystical fanatic who killed Kotzebue.

The Illuminati, whose teachings, spreading to France, did so much towards bringing about the many violent changes there, were banded together as a society by Adam Weishaupt and fostered by Baron von Knigge, a student of occultism. The object of this society is said to have originally been that of circumventing the Jesuits, but in its development it absorbed mysticism and supernaturalism, finally becoming political and revolutionary as it applied its philosophies to civil and religious life. Though it was disbanded and broken up in 1784 its influence was incalculable and widespread in its effects for long afterwards.

Many other names occur, coming under the category of mysticism : Jüng Stilling, seer, prophet and healer ; Anton Mesmer, the discoverer and apostle of animal magnetism ; the Marquis de Puységur, magnetist and spiritualist ; Madame von Krudener, preacher of peace and clemency to monarchs and princes ; Zschokke the mystical seer, and Dr. Justinus Kerner, believer in magnetism and historian of those two famous cases of possession and mediumship, the " Maid of Orlach " and the " Seeress of Prevorst."

Early in the nineteenth century occurred the remarkable cures said to be affected by Prince Hohenlohe, a dignitary of the Church. He was led to believe in the power of healing through the influence of a peasant named Martin Michel. Most of these cures took place at Würzburg, the scenes of former sanguinary witch-burnings, and it is said that upwards of four hundred people, deaf, dumb, blind and paralytic were cured by the power of fervent prayer.

About this time also occurred the famous case of " stigmata " in the person of the ecstatic, Katherine Emerick, the nun of Dülmen. The remarkable features were the appearance of a bloody cross encircling the head ; marks of wounds in hands, feet and side, and crosses on the breast, with frequent bleedings therefrom. This persisted for many years and the case is mentioned by several notable men of the time.

In nineteenth century Occultism we find, as in the earlier periods, stories of hauntings and doings of mischievous sprites existing beside learned disquisitions by educated men ; as that on the " fourth dimension in space " by Zöllner in his *Transcendental Physics*, and another on the luminous emanations from material objects in Baron von Reichenbach's treatise on the *Od or Odylic Force* ; thus betraying an unmistakeable likeness to its precursor, the magic of the Middle Ages.

Spiritualism. The movement of modern spiritualism, which left such a deep impress on America, France and England, affected *Germany* in a much less degree. But it would be indeed surprising if the country which gave so great attention to magnetism, wherein somnambules and clairvoyants were so plentiful, the country of seers and mystics, did not interest itself in the wide-spread phenomena of spiritualism. And investigators there were in *Germany*, though we have no record of any in the period immediately following the Rochester Rappings. Fichte declared for the facts of spiritualism ; Hartmann, also, the author of the *Philosophy of the Unconscious*, desired to give the phenomena a definite place in philosophy. Carl du Prel, in his *Philosophy of Mysticism*, points to spiritualistic manifestations as evidence of a subconscious region in the human mind. Du Prel also founded a monthly magazine, *The Sphinx*, devoted to the interests of spiritualism, and Aksakoff, the well-known Russian spiritualist, published the results of his researches in *Germany*, and in the German language, because he was not permitted to publish them in Russian. Another philosophic exponent of the spiritualistic doctrine was Baron Hellenbach, who founded on its tenets a distinct hypothesis of his own— namely, that no change of world, or " sphere," occurs at birth or death, but merely a change in the mode of perception. So much for the philosophical attitude towards the phenomena. The popular view-point was doubtless more influenced by the performances of the mediums who from time to time found their way to *Germany*. The most important of these was Henry Slade, who sought refuge in that country from his English persecutors. His remarkable manifestations in *Germany*, under the observation of Zöllner the astronomer, left nothing to be desired from a spiritualistic point of view.

Gerson, Jean Charlier de : The learned and pious chancellor of the University of Paris, who died in 1429. He was the author of the *Examination of Spirits*, which contained rules for distinguishing true revelations from false ; and of *Astrology Reformed*, which had a great success.

Gert, Berthomine de : A sorceress of the town of Préchac in Gascogny, who confessed about the year 1608 that when a sorceress returning from the Sabbath was killed on the way, the devil was in the habit of taking her shape and making her reappear and die in her own dwelling so as to preserve her good reputation. But if he who had killed her had a wax candle about him, and made with it the sign of the cross on the body of the witch, the devil could not

with all his strength remove her, and so was forced to leave her there.

Gervais : Archbishop of Rheims, died in 1067. His death was revealed to a Norman knight, returning from a pilgrimage to Rome, by a hermit whom he met on the way, and who told him that on the previous night he had been disturbed by a vision of demons making a great noise. They had, they said, been carrying the body of *Gervais* from Rheims, but because of his good deeds he had been taken from them. On his return to Rheims the knight found that *Gervais* was dead, and that the time of his death corresponded exactly with the time of the hermit's vision.

Ghor-Boud-Des, The : The people of " Ghor-bund-land." Mr. Pococke in his *India in Greece* maintains that these people are the same as the " Corybantes," or ministers of the gods, otherwise known as the Cabiri.

Ghost Seers : Sir William Hamiliton has observed, " however astonishing, it is now proved, beyond all rational doubt, that in certain abnormal states of the nervous organism, perceptions are possible through other than the ordinary channels of the senses." But, without entering into this metaphysical question, folk-lore holds that persons born at a particular time of the day have the power of seeing ghosts. " Thus it is said in Lancashire," says Mr. Thiselton Dyer, " that children born during twilight are supposed to have this peculiarity, and to know who of their acquaintance will next die. Some say that this property belongs also to those who happen to be born exactly at twelve o'clock at night, or, as the peasantry say in Somersetshire, " a child born in chime-hours will have the power to see spirits." The same belief prevails in Yorkshire, where it is commonly supposed that children born during the hour after midnight have the privilege through life of seeing the spirits of the departed. Mr. Henderson says that " a Yorkshire lady informed him she was very near being thus distinguished, but the clock had not struck twelve when she was born. When a child she mentioned this circumstance to an old servant, adding that ' Mamma was sure her birthday was the 23rd, not the 24th, for she had inquired at the time.' ' Ay, Ay,' said the old woman, turning to the child's nurse, ' mistress would be very anxious about that, for bairns born after mid-night see more things than other folk.' "

This superstition prevails on the Continent, and, in Denmark, Sunday children have prerogatives far from enviable. Thorpe, tells how " in Fyer there was a woman who was born on a Sunday, and, like other Sunday children had the faculty of seeing much that was hidden from others. But, because of this property, she could not pass by a church at night without seeing a hearse or a spectre. The gift became a perfect burden to her ; she therefore sought the advice of a man skilled in such matters, who directed her, whenever she saw a spectre to say, " Go to Heaven ! but when she met a hearse, " Hang on ! " Happening sometime after to meet a hearse, she, through lapse of memory cried out, " Go to Heaven ! " and straightway the hearse rose in the air and vanished. Afterwards, meeting a spectre she said to it, " Hang on ! " when the spectre clung round her neck, hung on her back, and drove her down into the earth before it. For three days her shrieks were heard before the spectre would put an end to her wretched life."

It is a popular article of faith in Scotland that those who are born on Christmas Day or Good Friday have the power of seeing spirits, and even of commanding them, a superstition to which Sir Walter Scott alludes in his *Marmion* (stanza 22). The Spaniards imputed the haggard and downcast looks of their Philip II. to the disagreeable visions to which this privilege subjected him.

Among uncultured tribes it is supposed that spirits are visible to some persons and not to others. The " natives " of the Antilles believed that the dead appeared on the road when one went alone, but not when they went together ; among the Finns the ghosts of the dead were to be seen by the Shamans, and not by men generally, unless in dreams. It is, too, a popular theory with savage races that the soul appears in dreams to visit the sleeper, and hence it has been customary for rude tribes to drink various intoxicating substances, under the impression that when thrown into the state of ecstasy they would have pleasing visions. On this account certain tribes on the Amazon use certain narcotic plants, producing an intoxication lasting twenty-four hours. During this period they are said to be subject to extraordinary visions, in the course of which they acquire information on any subject they may specially require. For a similar reason the inhabitants of North Brazil, when anxious to discover some guilty person, were in the habit of administering narcotic drinks to seers, in whose dreams the criminal made his appearance. The Californian Indians would give children certain intoxicants in order to gain from the ensuing vision information about their enemies. And the Darien Indians used the seeds of the *Datura sanguines* to produce in children prophetic delirium, during which they revealed the whereabouts of hidden treasures.

Gilles de Laval : Lord of Raiz, and Marshal of France, the " Blue Beard " of our nursery legends, and a famous sorcerer, was born about the year 1420, of one of the most famous families of Brittany. His father died when he was in his twentieth year, and the impetuous lad found himself possessed of unlimited power and wealth. By birth, he was connected with the Roceys, the Craons, and the Montmorencys. Through his father's decease he became the lord of fifteen princely domains, yielding a revenue of three hundred thousand livres. He was handsome, lithe, well-limbed, but distinguished by the appendage of a beard of bluish black. His address was fascinating, his erudition extensive, his courage unimpeachable. Everything seemed to promise a splendid and illustrious career, instead of that dark and miserable history which has associated the name of Blue Beard with so many traditions of horror and legends of atrocious crimes.

At the outset he did nothing to justify an evil augury. He served with zeal and gallantry in the wars of Charles VI. against the English, and had fought under Joan of Arc in the ever memorable Siege of Orléans. His exploits procured him from a grateful king the reward of the high dignity of Marshal of France. From this point his career tended downwards. He retired to his Castle of Champtocé and indulged in the display of the most luxurious state. Two hundred horsemen accompanied him on his travels, and his train, when he went hunting, exceeded in magnificence that of the King himself. His retainers wore the most sumptuous dresses ; his horses were caparisoned with the richest trappings ; his castle gates were thrown open day and night to all comers, for whom an ox was daily roasted whole, and sheep, and pigs, and poultry, wine, mead, and hippocras provided in sufficient quantities for five hundred persons. He carried the same love of pomp into his devotion. His principal chaplain, whom he called a bishop, a dean, a chanter, two arch-deacons, four vicars, a schoolmaster, twelve assistant chaplains, and eight choristers, composed his ecclesiastical establishment. Each of these had his horse and his servant ; all were dressed in robes of scarlet and furs, and had costly appointments. Sacred vessels, crucifixes, all of gold and silver, were transported with them wherever their lord went, together with many organs, each carried by six men. He was exceedingly desirous that all the priests of his chapel should be entitled to wear the mitre, and he sent many embassies to Rome to obtain this privilege, but without success. He maintained a choir of twenty-five young children of both

sexes, and these he caused to be instructed in singing by the best masters of the day. He had also his comedians, his morris-dancers, and his jugglers, and every hour was crowned with some sensual gratification or voluptuous pleasure.

In 1443, this magnificent young seigneur wedded Catherine, the heiress of the noble House of Thouars, an event which afforded him fresh occasions of displaying his insane passion for luxurious pomp. He gave the most splendid banquets ; he figured in the most chivalric tournaments. His guests, who came from all parts to share in the revels of Champtocé, knew not which to admire the most, his skill in all knightly exercises, or his profound erudition. " He had espoused a young woman of high birth," says Eliphas Levi, " and kept her practically shut up in his castle at Machecoul, which had a tower with the entrance walled up." A report was spread by the Marshal that it was in a ruinous state, and no one sought to penetrate therein. This, notwithstanding, Madame de Raiz, who was frequently alone during the dark hours, saw red lights moving to and fro in this tower ; but she did not venture to question her husband, whose bizarre and sombre character filled her with extreme terror.

The legal state maintained by the Lord of Retz was ordered on so extensive a scale that it even exhausted his apparently inexhaustible revenues, and to procure the funds for his pleasures and his extravagance, he was compelled to sell several of his baronies. Then the Marshal attempted to dispose of his seignory of Ingrande. But his heirs-at-law, indisposed to see their valuable inheritance gradually pared away into nothing, solicited the interference of the King, and a royal edict prohibited him from selling his paternal estates. In this predicament, most men would have curtailed their profusion, and endeavoured to economize their income, but *Gilles de Retz* was unable to live in diminished splendour. The luxuries that surrounded him were all that for him made life. To have shorn him of his magnificence would have been to strike a death-blow at his heart. Money, therefore, became the principal object of his desires, and to obtain money it seemed to his excited imagination only necessary that he should turn alchemist.

He sent accordingly into Italy, Spain, and Germany, and invited the adepts in the great science to repair from every land to the splendours of Champtocé. Amongst those who obtained the summonses, and continued attached to him during the remainder of his career, were Prélati, an alchemist of Padua, and a physician of Poitou, whose name is not given. At their instigation he built a stately laboratory, and joined by other adepts, eagerly began the search for the Philosophers' Stone. For a twelve month the furnaces blazed away right merrily, and a thousand chemical combinations disposed of the Marshal's gold and silver. Meanwhile, the alchemists feasted on the most luxurious viands, and quaffed the rarest wines ; and so admirable were their quarters that, as far as they were concerned, they would have prosecuted the quest of the elixir vitæ, or the Philosophers' Stone, until death cut short their labours.

The impetuosity of the Lord of Retz could not abide such lingering processes. He wanted wealth, and he wanted it immediately. If the grand secret could not be discovered by any quicker method, he would have none of it, nor, indeed, as his resources were fast melting away, would it avail him much if the search occupied several years. At this junction the Poitousan physician and the Paduan alchemist whispered to him of quicker and bolder methods of attaining the desired alkehest, if he had the courage to adopt them. *Gilles de Retz* immediately dismissed the inferior adepts, and put himself in the hands of the two abler and subtler masters. These persuaded him that the Evil One could at once reveal to them the secret, and offered to summons him *ex tenebris*, for the Marshal to conclude with him whatever arrangement he thought best. As long as he saved his soul, the Lord of Retz professed himself willing to do anything the devil might command.

In this frame of mind he went to the physician at midnight to a solitary recess in the neighbouring wood, where the physician drew the magic circle and made the customary conjurations. *Gilles* listened to the invocation with wonder, and expectant that every moment the Spirit of Darkness would burst upon the startled silence. After a lapse of thirty minutes, the physician manifested signs of the greatest alarm; his hair seemed to stand on end, his eyes glared with unutterable horror; he talked wildly, his knees shook, a deadly pallor overspread his countenance, and he sank to the ground. *Gilles* was a man of dauntless bravery, and gazed upon the strange scene unmoved. After awhile the physician pretended to recover consciousness. He arose, and turning to his master, inquired if he had not remarked the wrathful countenance of the devil. *De Retz* replied that he had seen no devil. Whereupon the physician declared he had appeared in the fashion of a wild leopard, and had growled at him horribly. "You," he said to his lord, "would have been the same, and heard the same, but for your want of faith. You could not determine to give yourself up wholly to his service, and therefore he thrust a mist before your eyes." *De Retz* acknowledged that his resolution had somewhat faltered, but that now his choice was made, if indeed the Evil One could be coerced into speaking, and revealing the secret of the universal alkahest. The physician said that there grew certain herbs in Spain and Africa which possessed the necessary power, and offered to go in search of them himself if the Lord of Laval would supply the funds. As no one else would be able to detect the herbs so miraculously gifted, *De Retz* thanked the physician for his voluntary self-denial, and loaded him with all the gold he could spare. The physician then took leave of his credulous patron, who never saw him again.

De Retz, as soon as the physician had quitted Champtocé, was once more seized with the fever of unrest. His days and nights were consumed in ceaseless visions of gold; gold, without which he must abandon his gilded pomp and unholy pleasures; gold, without which he could not hope to brave his enemies or procure exemption from the just punishment of his crimes. He now turned for help to the alchemist Prélati, who agreed to undertake the enterprise it *De Retz* furnished him with the charms and talismans necessary in so troublesome a work. He was to sign with his blood a contract that he would obey the devil in all things, and to offer up a sacrifice of the hands, eyes, blood, heart and lungs of a young child. The madman having willingly consented to these terms, Prélati went out alone on the following night, and after an absence of three hours, returned to his impatient lord. His tale was a monstrously extravagant one, but *De Retz* swallowed it greedily. The devil had appeared in the shape of a comely young man of twenty, who desired to be called Barron, and had pointed out to him a store of ingots of pure gold, buried under an oak in the neighbouring wood, which was to become the property of the Lord of Laval if he fulfilled the conditions of his contract. But this bright prospect was over-clouded by the devil's injunction that the gold was not to be searched for until a period of seven times seven weeks had elapsed, or it would turn to slates and dust. *De Retz* was by no means willing to wait so many months for the realisation of his wishes, and desired Prélati to intimate to the devil that he should decline any further correspondence with him if matters could not be expedited. Prélati persuaded

him to wait for seven times seven days, and then, the two repaired with pick-axe and shovel to dig up the treasure. After some hard work they lighted upon a load of slates inscribed with hieroglyphical characters. Prélati broke out into a fit of rage, and culminated the Evil One as a liar, a knave, a rogue—*De Retz* heartily joining in his fierce denunciations. He persuaded his master, however, to give the devil a further trial, and led him on from day to day with dark oracular hints and pretended demoniac intimations, until he had obtained nearly all the valuables remaining to his unhappy dupe. He was then preparing to escape with his plunder, when a catastrophe occurred, which involved him in his lord's ruin.

On Easter Day, in the year 1440, having communicated solemnly in his chapel, and bade farewell to the lady of Machecoul, telling her that he was departing to the Holy Land, the poor creature was even then afraid to question, so much did she tremble at his presence; she was also several months in her pregnancy. The Marshal permitted her sister to come on a visit as a companion during his absence. Madame de Raiz took advantage of this indulgence, after which *Gilles de Laval* mounted his horse, and departed. To her sister, Madame de Raiz communicated her fears and anxieties. What went on in the castle? Why was her lord so gloomy? What signified his repeated absences? What became of the children who disappeared day by day? What were those nocturnal lights in the walled-up tower? These and the other problems excited the curiosity of both women to the utmost degree. What, all the same, could be done? The Marshal had forbidden them expressly even to approach the tower, and before leaving he had expressed this injunction. It must assuredly have a secret entrance, for which Madame de Raiz and her sister Anne proceeded to search through the lower rooms of the castle, corner by corner, stone after stone. At last, in the chapel, behind the altar, they came upon a copper button, hidden in a mass of sculpture. It yielded under pressure, a stone slid back, and the two curiosity-seekers, now all in a tremble, distinguished the lowermost steps of a staircase, which led them to the condemned tower.

At the top of the first flight there was a kind of chapel, with a cross upside down and black candles; on the altar stood a hideous figure, no doubt representing the demon. On the second floor, they came upon furnaces, retorts, alembics, charcoal—in a word, all the apparatus of alchemy. The third flight led to a dark chamber where the heavy and fetid atmosphere compelled the young women to retreat. Madame de Raiz came into collision with a vase, which fell over, and she was conscious that her robe and feet were soaked by some thick and unknown liquid. On returning to the light at the head of the stairs, she found that she was bathed in blood.

Sister Anne would have fled from the place, but in Madame de Raiz curiosity was even stronger than disgust or fear. She descended the stairs, took a lamp from the infernal chapel and returned to the third floor, where a frightful spectacle awaited her. Copper vessels filled with blood were ranged the whole length of the walls, bearing labels with a date on each, and in the middle of the room there was a black marble table, on which lay the body of a child, murdered quite recently. It was one of those basins which had fallen, and black blood had spread far and wide over the grimy and worm-eaten wooden floor. The two women were now half-dead with terror. Madame de Raiz endeavoured at all costs to efface the evidence of her indiscretion. She went in search of a sponge and water, to wash the boards, but she only extended the stain, and that which at first seemed black, became all scarlet in hue. Suddenly a loud commotion echoed through the castle, mixed with the cries of people calling to Madame de Raiz.

She distinguished the awe-stricken words: "Here is Monseigneur come back." The two women made for the staircase, but at the same moment they were aware of the trampling of steps and the sound of other voices in the devil's chapel. Sister Anne fled upwards to the battlement of the tower; Madame de Raiz went down trembling, and found herself face to face with her husband, in the act of ascending, accompanied by the apostate priest and Prélati.

Gilles de Laval seized his wife by the arm, and without speaking, dragged her into the infernal chapel. It was then that Prélati observed to the Marshal: "It is needs must, as you see, and the victim has come of her own accord. . . ." "Be it so," answered his master. "Begin the Black Mass. . . ." The apostate priest went to the altar, while *Gilles de Laval* opened a little cupboard fixed therein, and drew out a large knife, after which he sat down close to his spouse, who was now almost in a swoon, and lying in a heap on a bench against the wall. The sacrilegious ceremonies began. It must be explained that the Marshal, so far from taking the road to Jerusalem, had proceeded only to Nantes, where Prélati lived; he attacked this miserable wretch with the uttermost fury, and threatened to slay him if he did not furnish the means of extracting from the devil that which he had been demanding for so long a time. With the object of obtaining delay, Prélati declared that terrible conditions were required by the infernal master, first among which would be the sacrifice of the Marshal's unborn child, after tearing it forcibly from the mother's womb. *Gilles de Laval* made no reply, but returned at once to Machecoul, the Florentine sorcerer and his accomplice, the priest, being in his train. With the rest we are acquainted.

Meanwhile, Sister Anne, left to her own devices on the roof of the tower, and not daring to come down, had removed her veil, to make signs of distress at chance. They were answered by two cavaliers, accompanied by a posse of armed men, who were riding towards the castle; they proved to be her two brothers, who, on learning the spurious departure of the Marshal for Palestine, had come to visit and console Madame de Raiz. Soon after they arrived with a clatter in the court of the castle, whereupon *Gilles de Laval* suspended the hideous ceremony, and said to his wife: "Madame, I forgive you, and the matter is at an end between us if you do now as I tell you. Return to your apartment, change your garments, and join me in the guest-room, whither I am going to receive your brothers. But if you say one word, or cause them the slightest suspicion, I will bring you hither on their departure; we shall proceed with the Black Mass at the point where it is now broken off, and at the consecration you will die. Mark where I place this knife."

He rose up and led his wife to the door of her chamber, and subsequently received her relations and their suite, saying that this lady was preparing herself to come and salute her brothers. Madame de Raiz appeared almost immediately, pale as a spectre. *Gilles de Laval* never took eyes off her, seeking to control her by his glance. When her brother suggested that she was ill, she answered that it was the fatigue of pregnancy, but added in an undertone: "Save me, he seeks to kill me." At the same moment, Sister Anne rushed into the hall, crying: "Take us away; save us, my brothers, this man is an assassin," and she pointed to *Gilles de Laval*. While the Marshal summoned his people, the escort of the two visitors surrounded the women with drawn swords, and the Marshal's people disarmed instead of obeying him. Madame de Raiz, with her sister and brothers, gained the drawbridge, and left the castle.

Terrible rumours were now bruited through all the country-side. It was noticed that many young girls and boys had disappeared. Some had been traced to the Castle of Champtocé, and not beyond. The public voice accused him of murder, and of crimes even worse than murder—of lust in its foulest and most disgusting shapes. It was true that no one dared openly accuse a baron so powerful as the Lord of Retz. It was true that whenever the circumstances of the disappearance of so many children were alluded to in his presence, he always manifested the greatest astonishment. But the suspicions of the people once aroused are not easily allayed; and the Castle of Champtocé and its lord soon acquired a fearful reputation, and were surrounded with an appalling mystery.

The continued disappearance of young boys and girls had caused so bitter a feeling in the neighbourhood that the Church had felt constrained to intervene, and on the earnest representations of the Bishop of Nantes, the Duke of Brittany ordered *De Retz* and his accomplice to be arrested. Their trial took place before a commission composed of the Bishop of Nantes, Chancellor of Brittany, the Vicar of the Inquisition, and Pierre l'Hôpital, the President of the Provincial Parliament. *De Retz* was accused of sorcery, sodomy, and murder. At first he displayed the most consummate coolness, denounced his judges as worthless and impure, and declared that rather than plead before such shameless knaves he would be hung like a dog, without trial. But the overwhelming evidence brought against him—the terrible revelations made by Prélati and his servants of his abandoned lust, of his sacrifices of young children for the supposed gratification of the devil, and the ferocious pleasure with which he gloated over the throbbing limbs and glazing eyes of those who were equally the victims of his sensuality and his cruelty—this horrible tale, as it unfolded day by day the black record of his enormities, shook even his imperturbable courage, and he confessed everything. The blood-stained chronicle showed that nearly one hundred children had fallen victims to this madman and his insane greed of the Philosophers' Stone. Both *De Retz* and Prélati were doomed to be burned alive, but in consideration of his rank the punishment of the Marshal was somewhat mitigated. He was strangled before he was given over to the flames. On the scaffold, he exclaimed to Prélati, with a hideous assumption of religious confidence: "Farewell, friend Francis. In this world we shall never meet again, but let us rest our hopes in God—we shall see each other in Paradise." The sentence was executed at Nantes, on the 23rd of February, 1440. "Notwithstanding his many and atrocious cruelties," says the old chronicler, Monstrelet, "he made a very devout end, full of penitence, most humbly imploring his Creator to have mercy on his manifold sins and wickedness. When his body was partly burned, some ladies and damsels of his family requested his remains of the Duke of Brittany, that they might be interred in holy ground, which was granted. The greater part of the nobles of Brittany, more especially those of his kindred, were in the utmost grief and confusion at his shameful death."

The Castle of Champtocé still stands in its beautiful valley, and many a romantic legend flowers about its gray old walls. "The hideous, half-burnt body of the monster himself," says Trollope, "circled in flames, pale, indeed, and faint in colour, but more lasting than those the hangman kindled around his mortal form in the meadow under the walls of Nantes—is seen on bright moonlight nights, standing now on one topmost point of craggy wall, now on another, and is heard mingling his moan with the sough of the night-wind. Pale, bloodless forms, too, of youthful growth and mien, the restless, unsepulchred ghosts of the unfortunates who perished in these dungeons unassoiled, may at similar times be seen flitting backwards and forwards in numerous groups across the space enclosed by the ruined walls, with more than mortal speed, or glancing hurriedly from window to window of the fabric, as still seeking to escape from its hateful confinement."

Girard, Jean-Baptiste : A Jesuit born at Pôle in 1680, much persecuted by the Jansenists. They accused him of having seduced a girl named Catherine Cadière, who showed symptoms of possession, and had to be sent to a convent of Ursulines at Brest. His enemies found it impossible to implicate him in the affair, and the parliament of Aix, before which he was tried, were forced to acquit him.

Gladen, The Root of : Regarded as a remedy for a disease called the " Elf cake," which causes a hardness of the side. The following is the prescription given in *A Thousand Notable Things* for the making up of the medicine :—" Take a root of gladen, and make powder thereof, and give the diseased party half a spoonful thereof, to drink in white wine, and let him eat thereof so much in his pottage at one time, and it will help him within awhile."

Glamis Castle : (*See* **Haunted Houses.**)

Glamour : (*See* **Gypsies.**)

Glamourie : The state of mind in which witches beheld apparitions and visions of many kinds. Of the same nature as phantasy.

Glanvil, Joseph : (1636—1680) An English philosopher who wrote several works dealing with occult affairs, was born at Plymouth, and became a Church of England clergyman with charges at Frome Selwood and Streat and Walton. In 1666 he was appointed to the Abbey Church, Bath, made a prebendary of Worcester Cathedral, and was chaplain in ordinary to Charles II. from 1672. In his *scepsis Scientifica* (1665) his *Sorcerers and Sorcery* (1666) and his *Sadducismus Triumphatus* (printed 1681) he undertook the defence of the belief in the supernatural, and supplied many illustrations in support of his theory.

Glas Ghairm : A rhyme or spell of Scottish origin, by the use of which one could keep a dog from barking, and open a lock, and supposed to be of special value to young men in their courtship days. About twenty years ago a well-known character in Skye, named Archibald the Light-headed, was believed to know this incantation ; but he repeated it so quickly that no one could understand what he said. This poor man was insane ; but the fear which dogs had of him was ascribed to his knowledge of the *Glas Ghairm*. It was believed that this rhyme had some reference to the safety of the Children of Israel on the night before the Exodus : " against any of the children of Israel shall not a dog move his tongue, against man or beast."

Glauber, Johann Rudolph : German mediciner and alchemist, born at Carlstadt, in 1603. No authentic records concerning his life appear to exist, although he was a profuse writer and left many treatises on medicine and alchemy. He discovered and prepared many medicines of great value to pharmacy, some of which are in common use, for example the familiar preparation known as Glauber's Salts. He was a firm believer in the Philosophers' Stone and elixir vitæ. Concerning the former, he states : " Let the benevolent reader take with him my final judgment concerning the great Stone of the Wise ; let every man believe what he will and is able to comprehend. Such a work is purely the gift of God, and cannot be learned by the most acute power of human mind, if it be not assisted by the benign help of a Divine Inspiration. And of this I assure myself that in the last times, God will raise up some to whom He will open the Cabinet of Nature's Secrets, that they shall be able to do wonderful things in the world to His Glory, the which, I indeed, heartily wish to posterity that they may enjoy and use to the praise and honour of God."

Some of *Glauber's* principal works are, *Philosophical*

Furnaces, Commentary on Paracelsus, Heaven ot the Philosophers, or Book of Vexation, Miraculum Mundi, The Prosperity of Germany, Book of Fires.

Gloriana : (*See* **Dee.**)

Glosopetra, or Gulosus : This stone is said to fall from Heaven in the wane of the moon. It is shaped like the human tongue, and was used by magicians to excite the lunar motions.

Gloucester, Eleanor Cobham, Duchess of : Wife of Humphrey of Gloucester, uncle of Henry VI., and Lord Protector of England during the King's minority. Though Humphrey was very popular in England, he was not without enemies, and one of the most bitter of these was Henry Beaufort, Cardinal of Winchester, great-uncle to the King. He it was who brought a charge of witchcraft against the *Duchess of Gloucester*, hoping thus to destroy her husband's power as the actual head of the realm and heir to the throne in the event of the King's death. It was supposed that the *Duchess* had first resorted to witchcraft in order to gain the affections of Humphrey, whose second wife she was. Then, when she had married him, and the death of the Duke of Bedford had removed the last barrier but one between her and a crown, she set about the secret removal of that barrier, which was, of course, the unfortunate King. To assist her in her evil designs, she sought the advice of Margery Jourdain (the Witch of Eye), Roger Bolingbroke, Thomas Southwel, and John Hume, or Hun, a priest. All five were accused of summoning evil spirits, and plotting to destroy the King. They were also suspected of making a waxen image, which was slowly melted before a fire, in the expectation that as the image was consumed, the life of the King would also waste away. For the supposed practice of this common device of witches, they were put upon trial. The priest, Hun, turned informer, and Bolingbroke, having abjured his evil works, was called upon to give evidence. Margery Jourdain was burned as a witch, and the *Duchess of Gloucester* was sentenced to walk through the streets of London on three separate occasions bearing a lighted taper in her hand, and attended by the Lord Mayor, sheriffs, and others. Afterwards, she was banished to the Isle of Man.

Gnosticism : Under the designation " Gnostics," several widely-differing sects were included, the term, derived from the Greek, meaning, " to know " in opposition to mere theory, and sharing this significance with the words, " wizard," " witch," which also indicate in their original meaning : " those who know."

Simultaneously with Christianity, these sects assumed a definite form, the eastern provinces of the Roman Empire being their sphere of operations at first. Their doctrines were an admixture of Indian, Egyptian, Babylonian, and Christian creeds, astrology and magic, with much of the Jewish *Kabbala* also. From Alexandria, that centre of mystic learning, much of their distinctive beliefs and ritual were derived, while it seems certain that to a certain extent they became affiliated with Mithraism (q.v.), to whose sheltering kindness Occidental Christianity also owed much. Most of the sects had a priesthood of the mysteries, and. these initiated priests practised magic arts astrology, incantations, exorcisms, the fashioning of charms talismans and amulets, of which many are extant at the present day. It is said that the Grecian mysteries, the Eleusinian and Cabiric, for instance, were celebrated by the Gnostic sects down to a late date. They were looked upon as heretics and sorcerers by the Church, and were the victims of relentless persecution. In Persia also they were put to death, but some embraced Islamism, and transmitted their doctrines to the Dervish sects (q.v.). Manicheism, a later sect was founded by Manes, who belonged to the Order of the Magi, and was famous for his skill in astrology, medicines and magic. This sect was anathema to the Church, and its later variants, Paulicians, Cathari, Albigensis, Lollards, and later still the Carbonari, never failed to arouse the persecuting fervour of the Church.

Apollonius of Tyana (q.v.), a Pagan, was supposed to have some connection with the Gnostics. The first Gnostic of eminence was Simon Magus (q.v.) contemporary with the Christian apostles. The Simonians are said to have interpreted the Creation in Genesis as symbolic of the gestation of the fœtus, the temptation of Eve and the Garden of Eden having a like character. The Carpocratians, one of the Gnostic sects, derived their mysteries and rites from Isis worship. They used Theurgic incantations, symbols and signs. The Ophites also adopted Egyptian rites, and, as their name indicates, these included much of serpent symbolism, an actual serpent being the central object of their mysteries. Marcos, disciple of Valentinus, and founder of the Marcian sect, celebrated Mass with two chalices, pouring wine from the larger into a smaller, and on pronouncing a magical formula, the vessel was filled with a liquor like blood, which swelled up seething. Other sects practised divination and prophecy by means of female somnambules. Some of the sects became degraded in doctrine and ritual, this often being of an orgiastic character.

The Gnostic talismans were mostly engraved on gems, the colour and traditional qualities of the jewel being part of its magical efficacy. They used spells and charms and mystic formulæ, said to " loose fetters, to cause blindness in one's enemies, to procure dreams, to gain favour, to encompass any desire whatsoever." In a Greek Gnostic Papyrus is to be found the following spell of Agathocles, for producing dreams : " Take a cat, black all over, and which has been killed ; prepare a writing tablet, and write the following with a solution of myrrh, and the dream which thou desirest to be sent, and put in the mouth of the cat. The text to be transcribed runs : ' Keimi, Keimi, I am the Great One, in whose mouth rests Mommom, Thoth, Nauumbre, Karikha, Kenyro, Paarmiathon, the sacred Ian icê ieu aêoi, who is above the heaven, Amekheumen, Neunana, Seunana, Ablanathanalba,' (here follow further names, then,) ' Put thyself in connection with N.N. in this matter (as to the substance of the dream named,) but if it is necessary then bring for me N.N. hither by thy power ; lord of the whole world, fiery god, put thyself in connexion with N.N.' Again, there follows a list of meaningless names, the formula ending : ' Hear me, for I shall speak the great name, Thoth ! whom each god honours, and each demon fears, by whose command every messenger performs his mission. Thy name answers to the name (vowels) a, e, ê, i, o, u, ô, iauoeêaô oueê ôia. I named thy glorious name, the name for all needs. Put thyself in connection with N.N., Hidden One, God, with respect to this name, which Apollobex also used." The repetition of apparently meaningless syllables was always held to be of great efficacy in magical rites, either as holding the secret name of the powers invoked, or of actual power in themselves. In Atanasi's *Magic Papyrus*, Spell VII., directs you to lay the link of a chain upon a leaden plate, and having traced its outline, to write thereon, round the circumference, the common Gnostic legend in Greek characters (reading both ways) continuously. Within the circle was written the nature of the thing which it was desired to prevent. The operation was called " The Ring of Hermes." The link was then to be folded up on the leaden plate, and thrown into the grave of one dead before his time, or else into a disused well. After the formula above given, was to follow in Greek : " Prevent thou such and such a person from doing such and such a thing "—a proof that the long string of epithets all referred to the same power. These

instances might be multiplied, although much of the more valuable parts of the Gnostic doctrines were destroyed by every persecutor who arose, and this was easily done, for the sacred and mystic teachings, the prayers and spells were inscribed on perishable parchments. That much of the evil was imputed to them by the Church because of their more philosophic habit of thought in opposition to faith and dogma, is beyond doubt.

Goat : The devil is frequently represented under the shape of a *goat*, and as such presided over the witches' Sabbath. The *goat* is also the " emblem of sinful men at the day of judgment." (*See* **Baphomet ; Witchcraft.**)

Goblin : A spirit formerly supposed to lurk in houses. They were generally of a mischievous and grotesque type. Hobgoblins, according to Junius, were so called because they were wont to hop on one leg.

God : According to the ancient magical conception of *God* in the scheme of the universe, evil is the inevitable contrast and complement of good. *God* permits the existence of the shadow in order that it may intensify the purity of the light. Indeed he has created both and they are inseparable the one being necessary to and incomprehensible without the other.

The very idea of goodness loses its meaning if considered apart from that of evil—Gabriel is a foil to Satan and Satan to Gabriel. The dual nature of the spiritual world penetrates into every department of life material and spiritual. It is typified in light and darkness, cold and heat, truth and error, in brief, the names of any two opposing forces will serve to illustrate the great primary law of nature— viz. the continual conflict between the positive or good and the negative or evil.

For a scriptural illustration of this point, let the story of Cain and Abel be taken. The moral superiority of his brother is at first irksome to Cain, finally intolerable. He murders Abel, thus bringing on his own head the wrath of *God* and the self-punishment of the murderer. For in killing Abel he has done himself no good, but harm. He has not done away with Abel's superiority, but has added to himself a burden of guilt that can be expiated only by much suffering.

Suffering is shewn in the Scriptures to be the only means by which evil is overcome by good. Cain re-appears in the story of the prodigal son, who after privation and suffering is restored to his father who forgives him fully and freely.

The possibility of sin and error is therefore entirely consistent with and even inseparable from life, and the great sinner a more vital being than the colourless character, because having greater capacity for evil he has also greater capacity for good, and in proportion to his faults so will his virtues be when he turns to *God*. " There is more joy in heaven over one sinner that repenteth than over ninety and nine just persons," because more force of character, more power for good or evil is displayed by the sinner than by the feebly correct. And that power is the most precious thing in life.

This great dual law, right and wrong, two antagonistic forces, call them what we will, is designated by the term duad. It is the secret of life and the revelation of that secret means death. This secret is embodied in the myth of the Tree of Knowledge in Genesis. At death the discord will be resolved, but not till then.

From the duad is derived the triad on which is based the doctrine of the Trinity. Two forces producing equilibrium, the secret of nature, are designated by the duad, and these Three, call them life, good, evil, constitute one law. By adding the conception of unity to that of the triad we arrive at the tetrad, the perfect number of four, the source of all numerical combinations. According to theology there are three persons in *God*, and these three form one Deity. Three and one make four because unity is required to explain the Three. Hence, in almost all languages, the name of *God* consists of four letters. Again, two affirmations make two negations either possible or necessary. According to the Kabalists the name of the Evil one consisted of the same four letters spelled backward, signifying that evil is merely the reflection or shadow of good—"The last reflection or imperfect mirage of light in shadow."

All which exists in light or darkness, good or evil, exists through the tetrad. The triad or trinity, then, is explained by the duad and resolved by the tetrad.

Godfrey : A priest of Provence, who had seduced several women. One of them, a nun, to save herself, asserted that *Godfrey* had bewitched her.

Arrested and imprisoned, he was tortured until he confessed that he was a magician, and that he had, by means of his breathing and other enchantments, corrupted this woman and several others. He was even induced, in his extreme agony, to speak of his presence at the Witches' Sabbath, and to give a long description of it. After these confessions had been cruelly extorted from the anguish of failing nature, the Parliament of Aix condemned him, on the 30th of April, 1611, to be burnt alive, as guilty of magic, sorcery, impiety, and abominable lust—a sentence which was carried into execution without delay.

This horrible affair gave rise to an adventure which has been related by the Abbé de Papon.

"The process," said he, "contained many depositions upon the power of the demons. Several witnesses protested that after being anointed with a magic oil, *Godfrey* transported himself to the Sabbath, and afterwards returned to his chamber down the shaft of the chimney. One day, when these depositions had been read to the Parliament, and the imagination of the judges excited by a long recital of supernatural events, there was heard in the chimney an extraordinary noise, which suddenly terminated with the apparition of a tall black man. The judges thought it was the devil come to the rescue of his disciple, and fled away swiftly, with the exception of a councillor Thorton, their reporter, who, finding himself entangled in his desk, could not follow them. Terrified by what he saw, with trembling body and staring eyes, and repeatedly making the sign of the cross, he in his turn affrighted the pretended demon, who was at a loss to understand the magistrate's perturbation. Recovering from the embarrassment he made himself known, and proved to be a chimney sweeper who, after having swept the chimney of the Messieurs des Comptes, whose chimneys joined those of the Tournelle, had by mistake descended into the chamber of the Parliament."

Goethe, Johann Wolfgang : German Author, (1749-1832) : *Johann Wolfgang Goethe*, probably the most celebrated of all German writers, was born at Frankfurt-on-the-Main in 1749, his father being a lawyer of some eminence. At an early age the boy showed a persistent fondness for drawing, and assimilated the rudiments of learning with surprising ease ; while in 1759, on a French nobleman of æsthetic tastes coming to stay with the Goethes, a warm friendship between him and the future author sprang up, and proved the means of accelerating the latter's intellectual development. Shortly after this a French theatre was founded at Frankfurt, and here young Goethe became conversant with Racine ; while simultaneously he made some early attempts at original writing, and began to learn Italian, Latin and Greek, English and even Hebrew. Very soon, however, a little cloud came to darken his horizon— just the cloud which has dimmed the blue skies for so

many youths—for at the age of fifteen he became desperately enamoured of a young girl, and as his parents disapproved of the match the pair were separated straightway. At first *Goethe* declared himself broken-hearted, and being intensely virile, as all men of might are, he sought consolation in loose-living. But a broken heart seldom proves a fatal malady, and the disappointed lover's restoration to mental health was facilitated betimes by his removal from his native town to Leipsic, where he entered the university, intending to become a lawyer.

At Leipsic *Goethe* showed slender affection for the actual curriculum, and instead he continued in essay writing and drawing, while he even took lessons in etching. He also found time for another love-affair, but this was cut short in 1768 by his undergoing a serious illness ; and, on his recovering therefrom, he decided to leave his present *alma mater* in favour of that of Strasburg. Arrived there, he became intimate with Jung Stilling, while his taste for letters was strengthened, Homer and Ossian being the masters for whom he chiefly avowed affection ; while, though he continued to show himself callous as regards law, he succeeded in becoming an advocate in 1771, whereupon he returned to Frankfort.

Goethe had already written a quantity of verse and prose, and now, in his native town, he began to do critiques for some of the newspapers there, while simultaneously he commenced writing *Goetz von Berlichingen* and *Werther*. These were followed shortly by *Prometheus*, and in 1774 the author started working at *Faust*, while the following year witnessed the production of some of his best love poems, these being addressed to Lilli Schönemann, daughter of a Frankfurt banker. Nothing more than poetry, however, was destined to result from this new devotion ; and scarcely had it come and gone ere *Goethe's* whole life was changed, for meanwhile his writings had become famous, and now the young Duke Carl August of Weimar, anxious for a trusty henchman, invited the rising author to come to his court. The invitation was accepted, *Goethe* became a member of the privy-council, while subsequently he was raised to the rank of Geheimrath and then ennobled.

Goethe's life at Weimar was a very busy one. Trusted implicitly by the Duke, he directed public roads and buildings, he attended to military and academic affairs, and he founded a court theatre. But though having all these outlets for his energy he continued to write voluminously, among the most important works he produced during his first years at the Duke's court being *Iphigenia* and *Wilhelm Meister* ; while in 1787 he made a lengthy stay in Italy, visiting Naples, Pompei, Rome and Milan. Returning to Weimar, he began writing *Egmont* ; while in 1795 he made the acquaintance of Schiller, with whom he speedily became very intimate, and along with whom he worked on the *Horen*, a journal designed to elevate the literary tastes of the masses. About this period, too, *Goethe* wrote his play of *Hermann und Dorothea*, and likewise did sundry translations from Voltaire, Diderot and Benvenuto Cellini ; while the year 1806 is a significant one in his history, marked as it is alike by his marriage and by the entry of Napoleon into Weimar. The conquering general and the German poet each found much in the other to admire, and the latter was decorated with the cross of the Legion of Honour ; nor did his literary activities show any signs of flagging as yet, for in 1811 he wrote *Dichtung und Wahrheit*, in 1821 *Wilhelm Meister's Wanderjahre*, and a little later he commenced working at a second part of *Faust*. During the time he was engaged thus he had two famous visitors, Beethoven coming from Vienna and Thackeray from London ; and, though the composer imagined himself coldly received, the novelist on the contrary spoke with enthusiasm of the welcome accorded him. But *Goethe* was now well-stricken in years, his health was beginning to fail, and he died early in 1832.

Few great writers, not even Disraeli or Sir Walter Scott, had fuller lives than *Goethe*. His love-affairs, besides those cited above, were countless, and his early taste for the graphic arts continued to the end of his days, resulting in his making a vast collection of treasures; while his interest in mysticism, by virtue of which he is included in this volume, manifested itself in divers forms besides the writing of *Faust*. For, something of a nympholept as he was, Goethe's mind was essentially an aspirational and speculative one, and during his childhood at Frankfurt he used to do symbolical drawings of the soul's aspirations to the deity, while subsequently he became immersed in the study of the Christian religion. Anon he grew sceptical on this subject, his ideas being altered not only by his own ruminations but by his readings in various iconoclastic philosophers, especially Rousseau; and it would seem that latterly his intellect was less engaged by Christianity than by those other and probably more ancient Eastern faiths, his leanings in this direction being demonstrated by sundry works from his pen, notably his *West-östliche Divan*. One of his note-books, moreover, shows that while a young man at Strassburg he made a close study of Giordano Bruno and other early scientists; while as a boy he was a keen student of alchemy, reading deeply in Welling and van Helmont, Basil Valentine and Paracelsus, and even fitting up a laboratory where he spent long hours in arduous experiments. No doubt it was while engaged in this way that he first conceived the idea of writing a drama on the subject of Dr. Faustus, but be that as it may, his alchemistic and other scientific researches certainly stood him in good stead when ultimately composing this work. The story's main outlines are so well known already—not only by reason of Calderon's and Marlowe's versions, but by the operas of Gounod, Schumann and Berlioz—that it were superfluous if not impertinent to offer anything of the nature of a paraphrase or synopsis here; but it should be said, in drawing to a conclusion, that after all it is mainly on account of *Faust* that *Goethe* takes rank as a mystic, and a great mystic, for his rendering of the immortal theme is acknowledged as among the finest things in the whole of mystical literature.

Goetia : (*See* **Key of Solomon the King.**)

Golden Key : Under this title have been published many volumes purporting to reveal an infallible method of attaining success in a lottery. *La Clef d'or*, or *La Véritabie trésor de la fortune*, reprinted from time to time at Lille, is based on the doctrine of sympathetic numbers, which the author claims to have discovered. Each number drawn, he declares, has five sympathetic numbers which directly follow it. Thus the number 4 has for its sympathetic numbers 30, 40, 50, 20, and 76. Knowing this, of course, it is an easy matter to win fortune at a lottery.

Gormogons : A Jacobite Masonic Society, perhaps related to the Lodges of Harodim (q.v.) They employed pseudonyms like the latter, and had an ambassador at Rome. Their history is sketched in a pamphlet dated 1724, entitled " Two Letters to a Friend," and in the work of Prichard (1730). The Duke of Wharton and the Chevalier Ramsay who were well-known Jacobites, were members of the Order. They had a cipher and secret reception of their own, and used a jargon in which the names of places and individuals were hidden and transposed. A plate of Hogarth's is extant in which the Order is lampooned under the title of " The Mystery of Masonry brought to light by ye *Gormogons*."

Graal, The Lost Book of the : The origin of the *Graal* legend, which is of course speculative. Seven ancient books are cited as being the possible cradle of the story, but none of them quite meet the case. In the Huth Merlin, a " Book of the Sanctuary " is referred to, but this is a book of records, not containing any special spiritual allusion.

If, and it is very doubtful if, such a book ever existed, it was most probably a. Mass book, extant about 1100. Its contents would relate to a Mass following the Last Supper, in which Christ gave Himself, the Priest serving. The mystery is threefold. (1) of Origin, which is part of the mystery of the Incarnation. (2) of Manifestation, which would have taken place had the world been worthy. (3) of Removal : this world being unworthy, the *Graal* was said to be removed, yet not hidden, for it is always discernible by anyone worthy, or qualified to see it. As has been said, it is not probable that such a Mass-book ever existed.

Grail, Holy : A portion of the Arthurian cycle of romance, of late origin embodying a number of tales dealing with the search for a certain vessel of great sanctity, called the " grail " or " graal." Versions of the story are numerous— the most celebrated of them being the Conte del Graal, the Grand St. Graal, Sir Percyvalle, Quete del St. Graal, and Guyot; but there are many others. These overlap in many respects, but the standard form of the story may perhaps be found in the Grand St. Graal—one of the latest versions, which dates from the thirteenth century. It tells how Joseph of Arimathea employed a dish used at the last supper to catch the blood of the Redeemer which flowed from his body before his burial. The wanderings of Joseph are then described. He leads a band to Britain, where he is cast into prison, but is delivered by Evelach or Mordrains, who is instructed by Christ to assist him. This Mordrains builds a monastery where the *Grail* is housed. Brons, Joseph's brother-in-law, has a son Alain, who is appointed guardian of the *Grail*; and this Alain having caught a great fish, with which he feeds the entire household, is called the Rich Fisher, which title becomes that of the *Grail* keepers in perpetuity. Alain placed the *Grail* in the castle of Corbenic, and thence in due time come various knights of King Arthur's court in quest of the holy vessel, but only the purest of the pure can approach its vicinity; and in due time Percival attains to sight of the marvel.

It is probable that the *Grail* idea was originated by early mediæval legends of the quest for talismans which conferred great boons upon the finder : as for example, the Shoes of Swiftness, the Cloak of Invisibility, the Ring of Gyges, and so forth; and that these stories were interpreted in the light and spirit of mediæval Christianity and mysticism. They may be divided into two classes : those which are connected with the quest for certain talismans, of which the *Grail* is only one, and which deal with the personality of the hero who achieved the quest; and secondly those which deal with the nature and history of the talismans.

A great deal of controversy has raged around the probable Eastern origin of the *Grail* Legend, and much erudition has been employed to show that Guyot, a Provençal poet who flourished in the middle of the twelfth century, found at Toledo in Spain an Arabian book by an astrologer, Flegitanis, which contained the *Grail* story. But the name " Flegitanis " can by no means be an Arabian proper name; and it might perhaps be the Persian *felekedâneh*, a Persian combined word which signifies " astrology," and in this case it would be the title of an astrological work. Professor Bergmann and others believed that the Holy Legend originated in the mind of Guyot himself; but this conclusion was strongly combated by the late Alfred Nutt. There is, however, good reason to believe that the story may have been brought from the East by the Knights Templar.

The *Grail* Legend has often been held by certain writers

to buttress the theory that the Church of England or the Catholic Church has existed since the foundation of the world. From early Christian times the genealogy of these churches is traced back through the patriarchs to numerous apocryphal persons; but we are not informed as to whether it possessed hierophants in neolithic and paleolithic times, or how it originated. This mischievous and absurd theory, which in reality would identify Christianity with the grossest forms of paganism, is luckily confined to a small band of pseudo-mystics, comprising for the most part persons of small erudition and less liberality of outlook. The *Grail* Legend was readily embraced by those persons, who saw in it a link between Palestine and England and a plea for the special and separate foundation of the Anglican Church by direct emissaries from the Holy Land. Glastonbury was fixed as the headquarters of the *Grail* immigrants, and the finding of a glass dish in the vicinity of the cathedral there not many years ago was held to be confirmation of the story by many of the faithful. The exact date of this vessel cannot successfully be gauged, but there is not the least reason to suppose that it is more than a few hundred years old. (*See* **Tradition.**)

Grail Sword : Associated with the Holy *Grail* in Arthurian Legend. Its history begins with King David who bequeathed it to Solomon who was bidden to re-cast the pommel. In Solomon's time it was placed in a ship built and luxuriously furnished by Solomon's wife. Subsequently discovered by the Knights of the Quest, it was assumed and worn by Galahad.

Gram : A magic sword thrust into a tree by Odin and pulled out by Sigmund. It bestowed upon its possessor exceptional powers and performed many miracles.

Grand Copt: (*See* **Cagliostro.**)

Grand Grimoire, The : A work pretended to be edited by a suppositious person, Antonia del Rabina, who, it is alleged, prepared his edition from a copy transcribed from the genuine writings of King Solomon. The work is divided into two parts : the first containing the evocation of Lucifuge Rocofale (*See* " **Ceremonial Magic** " in article " **Magic** ") ; the second being concerned with the rite of making pacts with demons. The work is regarded as one of the most atrocious of its type ; but there is little reason for such heavy condemnation, as its childish and absurd. character must be patent to everyone. Eliphas Levi says that it pretends to confer the Powder of Protection, that great mystery of the sages, but that in reality it confers the Powder of Consecration—whatever that may imply. The first portion of the Grand Grimoire in a process for the evocation of evil spirits to assist the operator to discover hidden treasure. The second part, that which deals with facts, suggests the surrender of the magician body and soul to the demon, and it is in this that the diabolical excellencies of the work consist. But the pact, as it stands, is grossly unfair to the devil, for the working of it is such, that the magician can very readily slip through his fingers.

Grand Lodge : Foundation of. (*See* **Freemasonry.**)

Grandier, Urbain : *Urbain Grandier*, a canon of the French church, and a popular preacher of the town of Loudun in the district of Poiriers, was in the year 1634 brought to trial upon the accusation of magic. The first cause of his being thus called in question was the envy of his rival preachers, whose fame was eclipsed by his superior talents. The second cause was a libel falsely imputed to him upon cardinal Richelieu. *Grandier*, besides his eloquence, was distinguished for his courage and resolution, for the gracefulness of his figure, and the extraordinary attention he paid to the neatness of his dress and the decoration of his person, which last circumstance brought upon him the imputation of being so much devoted to the service of the

fair. About this time certain nuns of the convent of Ursulines at Loudun (q.v.) were attacked with a disease which manifested itself by very extraordinary symptoms, suggesting to many the idea that they were possessed with devils. A rumour was immediately spread that *Grandier*, urged by some offence he had conceived against these nuns, was the author, by the skill he had in the arts of sorcery, of these possessions. It unfortunately happened that the same capuchin friar who assured cardinal Richelieu that *Grandier* was the writer of the libel against him, also communicated to him the story of the possessed nuns, and the suspicion which had fallen on the priest on their account. The cardinal, seized with avidity on this occasion of private vengeance, wrote to the counsellor of state at Loudun, to cause a strict investigation to be made into the charges, and in such terms as plainly implied that what he aimed at was the destruction of *Grandier*. The trial took place in the month of August, 1634 ; and, according to the authorised copy of the trial, *Grandier* was convicted upon the evidence of Astaroth, a devil of the order of Seraphims, and chief of the possessing devils, of Easas, of Celsus, of Acaos, of Cedon, of Asmodeus of the order of thrones, of Alex, of Zabulon, of Naphthalim, of Cham, of Uriel, and of Achas of the order of principalities, and sentenced to be burned alive. In other words, he was convicted upon the evidence of twelve nuns, who, being asked who they were, gave in these names, and professed to be devils that, compelled by the order of the court, delivered a constrained testimony. The sentence was accordingly executed, and *Grandier* met his fate with heroic constancy. At his death an enormous drone fly was seen buzzing about his head, and a monk, who was present at the execution, attested that, whereas the devils are accustomed to present themselves in the article of death to tempt men to deny God their Saviour, this was Beelzebub (which in Hebrew signifies the God of flies), come to carry away to hell the soul of the victim.

Graterakes, Valentine : An Irish mesmerist born in the county of Waterford in 1628. In 1662, he dreamed that he had received the gift of healing by laying on of hands. He ignored the dream, but as it occurred again on several occasions, he made an experiment upon his wife which was quite successful. He practised the laying on of hands for practically all diseases, and in 1666 went to London where he was summoned to court. Whilst there he healed many persons, but the insults of the courtiers proved too much for him and he was forced to withdraw to a house near London, where he continued his cures. In his *Critical History of Animal Magnetism* Pechlin says, " Amongst the most astonishing cures which history records, are those of an Irish gentleman in London, Oxford, and other cities of England and Ireland. He himself published in London in 1666 a full account of them. ' *Val. Graterakes*, Esq., of Waterford, in the kingdom of Ireland, famous for curing several diseases and distempers by the stroak of his hand only : London, 1660.' "

Pechlin believes that no doubt whatever can be entertained of the reality of his cures, as they are related in his own work ; and they are, therefore worthy of being translated into all languages. Pechlin caused a number of letters and testimonials to be printed, which place the veracity and the character of *Graterakes* in the clearest light. In the first place, Joh. Glanville, the author of *Scepsis Scientifica*, in which he treated all learning and human science as open to doubt, and who was also a chaplain to Charles II., says in a letter that *Graterakes* was a simple, amiable, and pious man, a stranger to all deceit. The same testimony was given to him by George Rust, Bishop of Dromore in Ireland. The bishop says that he was three weeks at his house, where he had an opportunity of observing his sound morals, and the great number of his cures of the sick. Through the simple laying on of hands he drove the pains to the extremities of the limbs. Many times the effect was very rapid and as if by magic. If the pains did not immediately give way, he repeated his rubbings, and always drove them from the nobler parts to the less noble, and finally into the limbs.

The Bishop relates still further :—" I can as eye-witness assert that *Graterakes* cured dizziness, very bad diseases of the eyes and ears, old ulcers, goitre, epilepsy, glandular swellings, scirrhous indurations, and cancerous swellings. I have seen swellings disperse in five days which were many years old, but I do not believe by super-natural means ; nor did his practice exhibit anything sacred. The cure was sometimes very protracted, and the diseases only gave way through repeated exertions ; some altogether resisted his endeavours."

It appeared to the bishop that something healing, something balsamic flowed from him. *Graterakes* himself was persuaded that his power was an especial gift of God. He healed even epidemic complaints by his touch, and on that account he believed it his duty to devote himself to the cure of diseases.

To the bishop's may be added the testimonies of two physicians, Faireklow and Astel, who very assiduously inquired into the reality of his cures.

" I was struck," says Faireklow, " with his gentleness and kindness to the unhappy, and by the effects which he produced by his hand."

Astel says,—" I saw *Graterakes* in a moment remove most violent pains merely by his hand. I saw him drive a pain from the shoulder to the feet. If the pains in the head or the intestines remained fixed, the endeavour to remove them was frequently followed by the most dreadful crises, which even seemed to bring the patient's life into danger ; but by degrees they disappeared into the limbs, and then altogether. I saw a scrofulous child of twelve years with such swellings that it could not move, and he dissipated merely with his hand the greatest part of them. One of the largest, however, he opened, and so healed it with his spittle." Finally Astel says that he saw a number of other cures, and repeats the testimonies of Rust and Faireklow on the character of *Graterakes*.

The celebrated Robert Boyle, President of the Royal Society of London, says :—" Many physicians, noblemen, clergymen, etc., testify to the truth of *Graterakes'* cures, which he published in London. The chief diseases which he cured were blindness, deafness, paralysis, dropsy, ulcers, swellings, and all kinds of fevers." Finally, it is said that ' he laid his hand on the part affected, and so moved the disease downwards."

Graterakes was undoubtedly one of the most celebrated of the early mesmerists, and there is no question that the science owed considerable popularity to his cures. There was nothing of the charlatan about him, and he appears as an unaffected and simple person, whose whole desire was to make the best of the gift which he had received.

Great White Brotherhood : (*See* **Adept.**)

Greatrakes : (*See* **Healing by Touch.**)

Greece : That magic in its widest sense was native to the imagination and genius of the Greeks is apparent in their theogony and mythology, essentially magical in conception and meaning, in their literature, sculpture and history. The natural features of the country appealed powerfully to the quality of their imagination. Mountains and valleys, mysterious caves and fissures, vapours and springs of volcanic origin ; groves,—these according to their character, were dedicated to the gods. Parnassus was the abode of the sun-god, Apollo ; the lovely vale of Aphaca that of Adonis ; the oak-groves of Dodona favoured of Zeus, the gloomy caves with their roar of subterranean waters the Oracle of Trophonius. Innumerable instances of magical wonder-working are found in the stories of their deities and heroes. The power of transformation is shown in a multitude of cases, amongst them those of Bacchus who, by waving a spear, could change the oars of a ship into serpents, the masts into heavy-clustered vines, tigers, lynxes and panthers to appear amidst the waves, and the terrified sailors leaping overboard to take the shape of dolphins ; in those wrought by Circe who by her magic wand and enchanted philtre turned her lovers into swine. The serpent-staff of Hermes gave, by its touch, life or death, sleep or waking ; Medusa's head turned its beholders into stone ; Hermes gave Perseus wings that he might fly and Pluto a helmet which conferred invisibility. Prome-theus moulds a man of clay and to give it life steals celestial fire from heaven ; Odysseus to peer into the future descends to Hades in search of Tiresias the Soothsayer ; Achilles is made invulnerable by the waters of the Styx.

Dedicated by immemorial belief there were places where the visible spirits of the dead might be evoked, Heraclea, Acheron, piaces where men in curiosity, in longing or remorse strove to call back for a fleeting moment those who had passed beyond mortal ken. In the month of March, when the spring blossoms broke through the earth and snowed the trees with white, the Festival of the Flowers was held at Athens, also the Commemoration of the Dead, when their spirits were thought to rise from their graves and wander about the familiar streets, striving to enter the dwellings of man and temples of the gods but shut out therefrom by the magic of branches of whitethorn, or by knotted ropes and pitch.

Oracles : Of great antiquity and eminently of Greek charac-ter and meaning were *the Oracles*. For centuries they ministered to that longing deeply implanted in human nature the longing to know the future, and to invoke divine foresight and aid in the direction of human affairs, from those of a private citizen to the multitudinous needs of a great state. Divination and prophecy were therefore the great features of the oracles. This was inspired by various means, by intoxicating fumes natural or artificial, by the drinking of mineral springs, by signs and tokens, by dreams. The most famous Oracles were those at Delphi, Dodona, Epi-daurus, and that of Trophonius, but others of renown were scattered over the country. Perhaps one of the earliest was that of *Aesculapius* son of Apollo, and called the Healer, the Dream-sender because his healing was given through the medium of dreams that came upon the applicant while sleeping in the temple-courts, the famous temple-sleep. This temple, situated at Epidaurus, was surrounded by sacred groves and whole companies of sick persons lingered there in search of lost health and enlightenment through divine dreams. Famous beyond all was that of Apollo, the *Delphian oracle* on the Southern Slopes of Parnassus where kings and princes, heroes and slaves of all countries journeyed to ask the questions as to the future and what it might hold for them. The temple was built above a volcanic chasm, amid a wildness of nature which suggested the presence of the unseen powers. Here the priestess, the Pythia, so named after the serpent Pytho whom Apollo slew, was seated on a tripod placed above the gaseous vapours rising from the chasm. Intoxicated to a state of frenzy, her mouth foaming, wild torrents of words fell from her lips, and these were shaped into coherence and meaning by the attendant priests and given to the waiting questioner standing before the altar crowned with laurel, the symbol of sleep and dreams and sacred to Apollo. Priests and priestesses were also crowned with these leaves, and they were burned as incense ; before the Pythias chamber hung a falling screen of laurel branches while at the festival of the Septerion every ninth year a bower of laurel was erected in the forecourt of the temple. One writer has left strange details such as the rule that the sacred fire within the temple must only be fed with fir-wood ; and, though a woman was chosen as the medium of the prophetic utterance yet no woman might question the oracle. The *Oracle of the Pelasgic Zeus at Dodona*, the oldest of all, answered by signs rather than inspired speech, the rustling of the leaves in the sacred groves, by means of lots and the falling of water, by the wind-moved clanging of brazen-bowls, two hollow columns standing side by side. The three priestesses, Peliades, meaning doves, were given titles signifying the Diviner of the future ; the friend of man, Virtue : the virgin-ruler of man, Chastity. For two thousand years this oracle existed, from the time when it was consulted by those heroes of the ancient myths, struggling in the toils of Fate, Hercules, Achilles, Ulysses and Aeneas, down to the latest vestiges of Greek national-ity. The *Oracle of Trophonius* was also of great renown. Here there were numerous caverns filled with misty vapours and troubled by the noise of hidden waters far beneath. In this mysterious gloom the supplicants slept sometimes for nights and days, coming forth in a somnambulic state from which they were aroused and questioned by the attendant priests. Frightful visions were generally re-counted, accompanied by a terrible melancholy, so that it passed into a proverb regarding a sorrowful man " He has been in the cave of Trophonius." Thus it may be seen that magic in the sense of secret revelations, miraculous cures and prophetic gifts, of abnormal powers, had always existed for the Greeks, the oracles were a purely natural human way of communing with their gods upon earth. But magic in the lower sense of sorcery was unknown till Asiatic and Egyptian influences were introduced. The native conception of Fate as inexorable and inescapable for gods, kings and slaves alike was inimical to the spontaneous growth of a form of magic which had for its primary aim a certain command of the destinies of man. Good and evil and the perpetual strife between these two principles, the belief in demonology, these were foreign to the Greek mind, they were imported. It is said that to the Pytha-gorean school may be traced the first mention of good and evil demons and not till after the Persian War was there a word in the Greek language for magic. As these foreign beliefs were thus gradually introduced and assimilated they were ascribed to the native deities, gradually becoming incorporated with the ancient histories and rites.

After the invasion by the Persians, *Thessaly*, where their stay was of lengthy duration, became famous for its sorcer-esses and their practices which embraced a wide than-maturgical field, from calling down the moon to brewing magical herbs for love or death, so much so that Apuleius in his romance, *The Golden Ass*, says, that when in Thessaly he was in the place " where, by common report of the world, sorcery and enchantments were most frequent. I viewed the situation of the place in which I was, nor was there anything I saw that I believed to be the same thing which it appeared to be. Insomuch that the very stones in the street I thought were men bewitched and turned into that figure, and the birds I heard chirping, the trees with-out the walls, and the running waters, were changed from human creatures into the appearances they were. I persuaded myself that the statues and buildings could move ; that the oxen and other brute beasts could speak and tell strange tidings ; that I should hear and see oracles from heaven conveyed in the beams of the Sun."

Sorceresses.—Homer tells the tale of Circe the enchant-ress, with her magic philtres and magic songs but makes no mention of Medea, the arch-sorceress of later times. Round her name the later beliefs clustered, to her were attributed all the evil arts, she became the witch par excellence, her infamy increasing from age to age. The same may be said of Hecate, the moon-goddess, at first sharer with Zeus of the heavenly powers, but later become an ominous shape of gloom, ruler and lover of the night and darkness, of the world of phantoms and ghouls. Like the Furies she wielded the whip and cord ; she was followed by hell hounds, by writhing serpents, by lamiæ, strygæ and empusæ, figures of terror and loathing. She presided over the dark mysteries of birth and death ; she was worshipped at night in the flare of torches. She was the three-headed Hecate of the cross-roads where little round cakes or a lizard mask set about with candles were offered to her in propitiation, that none of the phantom mob might cross the threshold of man. *Love-magic and death-magic*, the usual forms of sorcery became common in Greece as else-where. Love philtres and charms were eagerly sought, the most innocent being bitten apples and enchanted garlands. Means of protection against the evil eye became a necessity for tales of bewitchment were spread abroad, and of mis-fortune and death being brought upon the innocent and unwary by means of a waxen figure moulded in their image and tortured by the sorceress. In tombs and secret places leaden tablets were buried inscribed with the names of foes and victims, pierced through with a nail in order to bring disaster and death upon them. At this time it became law that none who practised sorcery might participate in the Eleusinian Mysteries, and at Athens, a Samian Sorceress, Theoris, was cast to the flames.

Orphic Magic.—The introduction of Egyptian influences were due generally to the agency of Orpheus and Pythagoras, who, while in Egypt, had been initiated into the mysteries. The story of Orpheus shows him as pre-eminently the wonder-worker, but one of beneficence and beauty. To men of his time everything was enchantment and prodigy. By the irresistible power of his music he constrained the rocks, trees and animals to follow him, at his behest storms arose or abated. He was the necromancer, who by his golden music overcame the powers of darkness, and descend-ing to the world of shades, found his beloved Eurydice, and but for the fatal and disobedient look into her face ere they gained the upper air would have brought her back to the living world. Jealous women tore him limb from limb, and his head floating down the waters of the Hebrus was cast on the rocky shores of Lesbos where, still retaining the power of speech, it uttered oracles, the guidance of which people from all parts sought, even those of Babylon. He was said to have instructed the Greeks in medicine and magic, and for long afterwards remedies, magical formulæ, incantations and charms were engraved upon Orphean tablets and the power of healing was ascribed to the Orphean Hymns. Pythagoras, Philosopher and geometrician, to the populace a magician, indefatigable in the pursuit of know-ledge, wielded an immense influence on the thought of his time. After his return from Egypt he founded a school where to those who had previously undergone severe and drastic discipline he communicated his wide and varied knowledge. He was also credited with miraculous powers such as being visible at the same hour in places far apart as Italy and Sicily ; of taming a bear by whispering in its ear ; of calling an eagle from its flight to alight on his wrist.

Mysteries.—Among the greatest features of religious life were the mysteries held at periodic intervals in connection with the different deities, such as the *Samothracian*, the *Bacchic* and most famous of all, the *Eleusinian*. Their origin is to be traced mostly to a pre-historic nature-worship and vegetation-magic. All these mysteries had three trials or baptisms by water, fire and air, and three specially sacred emblems, the phallus, egg and serpent, generative emblems.

sacred in all secret rites. The Samothracian centred round four mysterious deities, Axieros the mother, her children Axiocersos, male, Axiocersa, female, from whom sprang Casindos the originator of the universe. The festival probably symbolized the creation of the world, also the harvest and its growth. Connected with this was the worship of Cybele, goddess of the earth, of the cities and fields. Her priests, the Corybantes, dwelt in a cave where they held their ceremonies, including a wild and orgiastic weapon-dance, accompanied by the incessant shaking of heads and clanging of swords upon shields. The cult of *Bacchus* was said by some to have been carried into *Greece* from Egypt by Melampus. He is the god of the vine and vegetation, and his mysteries typified the growth of the vine and the vintage ; the winter sleep of all plant life and its renewal in spring. Women were his chief attendants, the Bacchantes,who, clashing cymbals and uttering wild cries in invocation of their god, became possessed by ungovernable fury and homicidal mania. Greatest of all in their relation to Hellenic life were the *Eleusinian Mysteries*. These were the paramount interest and function of the state religion exerting the widest, strongest influence on people of all classes. The rites were secret and their details are practically unknown, but they undoubtedly symbolised the myth of Demeter, corn-goddess, and were held in spring and September. Prior to initiation a long period of purification and preparation was enforced during which the higher meaning of the myth was inculcated, the original meaning having become exalted by the genius of the Greeks into an intimate allegory of the soul of man, its birth, life and death, its descent into Hades and subsequent release therefrom. After this there came the central point of the mysteries, the viewing of certain holy and secret symbols ; next, a crowning with garlands, signifying the happiness which arises from friendship with the divine. The festival also embodied a scenic representation of the Story of Demeter ; the rape of Persephone, the sorrow of the mother, her complaints before Zeus, the final reconciliation. Women played a great part in this, the reason being that as they themselves " produce," so by sympathetic magic their influence was conveyed to the corn, as when crying aloud for rain they looked upward to the skies, then down to the earth with cries of " Conceive ! " These priestesses were crowned with poppies and corn, symbolical attributes of the deity they implored. (*See* article **Mysteries.**)

Divination.—Besides the priests and priestesses attached to the different temples there was an order of men called interpreters whose business it was to read futurity by various means such as the flight of birds and entrails of victims. These men often accompanied the armies in order to predict the success or failure of operations during warfare and thus avert the possibility of mistakes in the campaign: they fomented or repressed revolutions in state and government by their predictions. The most celebrated interpreters were those of Elis, where in two or three families this peculiar gift or knowledge was handed down from father to son for generations. But there were others who were authorised by the state—men who traded on the credulity of the rich and poor, women of the lowest dregs of humanity, who professed to read the future in natural and unnatural phenomena, in eclipses, in thunder, in dreams, in unexpected sight of certain animals, in convulsive movement of eyelids, tingling of the ears, in sneezing, in a few words casually dropped by a passer-by. In the *literature* and *philosophies* of *Greece* magic in all its forms is found as theme for imagination, discussion and belief. In the hands of the tragic poets, sorceresses such as Circe and Medea become figures of terror and death, embodiments of evil. Pythagoras left no writings but on his theories were founded those of Empedocles and Plato.

In the verses of Empedocles he teaches the theory of re-incarnation, he himself remembering previous existences wherein he was a boy, a girl, a plant, fish and bird. He also claimed to teach the secrets of miraculous medicine, of the re-animation of old age, of bringing rain, storm, or sunshine, of recalling the dead. Aristides the Greek orator gives exhaustive accounts of the many dreams he experienced during sleep in the temples and the cures prescribed therein. Socrates tells of his attendant spirit or genius who warned him, and others through his agency, of impending danger, also foretelling futurity.

Xenophon, treating of divination by dreams, maintains that in sleep the human soul reveals her divine nature, and being freed from trammels of the body gazes into futurity. Plato, while inveighing against sorcery, took the popular superstitions relating to magic, demons and spirits and by his genius purified and raised them, using them as a basis for a spiritual and magical theory of things, unsurpassed for intellectual beauty. On his teaching was founded the school of Neo-Platonists who were among the most fervid defenders of magic. Aristotle states that prediction is a purely natural quality of the imagination, while Plutarch in his writings, wherein much may be found on magic and dreams, gives an exhaustive account or the somnambulic states of the oracular priestess, Pythia, attributing them to possession by the divinity.   K.N.

Greece Modern : Although superstition is rife in the Hellenic archipelago it partakes more of the nature of Slavonic tradition than that of the ancient inhabitants of the country, and is more or less petty and ill-defined. But the most notable circumstance in modern Greek superstition is that which relates to Vampirism. The Vampire is called *Broucolack* by the modern Hellenes, and appears to date from mediæval times. Says Calmet, " It is asserted by the modern Greeks, in defence of their schism, and as a proof that the gift of miracles, and the episcopal power of the keys, subsists in their church more visibly and evidently than in the church of Rome, that, with them, the bodies of excommunicated persons never rot, but swell up to an uncommon size, and are stretched like drums, nor ever corrupt or fall to dust, till they have received absolution from some bishop or priest. And they produce many instances of carcasses which have been in their graves uncorrupted, and which have afterwards putrefied as soon as the excommunication was taken off."

"They do not, however, deny that a body's not corrupting is sometimes a proof of sanctity, but in this case they expect it to send forth an agreeable smell, to be white or ruddy, and not black, stinking, and swelled like a drum, as the bodies of excommunicated persons generally are. We are told, that in the time of Manuel, or Maximus, patriarch of Constantinople, the Turkish emperor having the mind to know the truth of the Greek notion concerning the incorruption of excommunicated bodies, the patriarch ordered the grave of a woman, who had lived in a criminal commerce with an archbishop of Constantinople, to be opened. Her body being found entire, black and much swelled, the Turks put it into a chest, under the emperor's seal, and the patriarch having repeated a prayer, and given absolution to the deceased, the chest was opened three days after and the body was found reduced to ashes. It is also a notion which prevails among the Greeks, that the bodies of these excommunicated persons frequently appear to the living, both day and night, and speak to them, call upon them, and disturb them several other ways.

"Leo Allatius is very particular upon this head, and says, that in the isle of Chio, the inhabitants never answer the first time they are called, for fear of its being a spectre ; but if they are called twice, they are sure it is not a Broucolack (this is the name they give these spirits). If any one appears at the first call, the spectre disappears, but the person certainly dies.

"They have no way to get rid of these evil genii, but to dig up the body of the person that has appeared, and burn it after having repeated over it certain prayers. By this means the body being reduced to ashes, appears no more. And they look upon it as a clear case, that either these mischievous and spiteful carcasses come out of their graves of their own accord, and occasion the death of the persons that see or speak to them ; or that the devil himself makes use of these bodies to frighten and destroy mankind. They have hitherto discovered no remedy which more infallibly rids them of these plagues, than to burn or mangle the bodies which were made use of for these cursed purposes. Sometimes the end is answered by tearing out the heart and letting the bodies rot above ground before they burn them again, or by cutting off the head, or driving a large nail through the temples.

Sir Paul Rycaut, in his *History of the Present State of the Greek Church*, observes, that the opinion that, excommunicated bodies are preserved from putrefaction, prevails, generally, not only among the Greeks, but also among the Turks, and he gives us a fact which he had from a Caloyer of Candia, who confirmed it to him upon oath. The caloyer's name was Sophronius, a man well known and respected in Smyrna.

There died in the island of Milo, a man, who was excommunicated for a fault which he had committed in the Morea, and he was buried in a private place, without any ceremonies, and in unconsecrated ground. His relations and friends expressed great dissatisfaction at his being treated in this manner, and very soon after the inhabitants of the island were tormented every night by frightful apparitions, which they attributed to this unhappy man. Upon opening the grave his body was found entire, and his veins swelled with blood, and a consultation being held upon the subject, the caloyers dismembering his body, cutting it in pieces, and boiling it in wine, which, it seems, is the usual manner of proceeding there in those cases.

However, the friends of the deceased prevailed upon them, by dint of entreaty, to delay the execution, and in the meantime sent to Constantinople to get absolution for him from the patriarch. Till the messenger could return the body was laid in the church, and prayers and masses were said daily for the repose of his soul. One day while Sophronius, the caloyer above mentioned, was performing the service, there was heard on a sudden a great noise in the coffin, and upon examination the body was found reduced to ashes, as if it had been dead seven years. Particular notice was taken of the time when the noise was heard, and it was found to be the very morning when the absolution was signed by the patriarch. Sir Paul Rycaut, who has recorded this event, was neither a Greek nor Roman Catholic, but a staunch Protestant of the Church of England.

He observes upon this occasion, that the notion among the Greeks is, that an evil spirit enters into the excommunicated carcass and preserves it from corruption by performing the usual functions of the human soul in a living body. They fancy, moreover, that these corpses eat by night, and actually digest and are nourished by their food ; that several have been found of a fresh, ruddy colour, with their veins ready to burst with blood, full forty days after their death, and that upon being opened there has issued from them as large a quantity of warm fresh blood as would come from a young person of the most sanguine constitution. And this opinion prevails so universally, that every one is furnished with a story to this purpose. Father Theophilus Raynard, author of a particular treatise upon this subject, asserts that this coming again of deceased

persons is an undoubted truth, and supported by unquestionable facts. But to pretend that these spectres are always excommunicated persons, and that the schismatical Church of *Greece* has a privilege of preserving from putrefaction the bodies of those that die under her sentence, is what cannot be maintained, since it is certain that excommunicated bodies rot as well as others, and that several who have died in the communion of the church, Greek as well as Roman, have continued uncorrupted. There have even been instances of this nature among the heathens, and frequently among other animals, whose carcasses have been found unputrefied in the ground, and among the ruins of old buildings. Whoever will examine more accurately into this matter, may consult father Goard's *Rituel des Grecs*, p. 687, 688. Matthew Paris's *History of England*, t. ii. p. 687. Adam of Bremen, c. ixxv. Albert of Stade, under the year 1050 ; and M. Ducange, *Glossar. Latinit.* at the word " Imblocatus."

M. De Tournefort has given, in his travels, an account of the digging up an imaginary Broucolack in the island of Mycone, where he was on the 1st of January, 1701. His words are as follow :—" We were present at a very different scene in the same island, upon occasion of one of those dead corpses, which they suppose to come to life again after their burial. The man, whose story I am going to relate, was a peasant in Mycone, naturally ill-natured and quarrelsome (a circumstance of consequence in such cases) ; he was murdered in the fields, nobody knew how, or by whom.

" Two days after his being buried in a chapel in the town it was noised about that he was seen in the night walking about in a great hurry ; that he came into houses and tumbled about their goods, griped people behind, and played a thousand little monkey tricks. At first it was only laughed at, but it soon grew to be a very serious affair when the better sort of people joined in the complaint. The Papas themselves gave credit to it, and no doubt had their reasons for so doing. Masses, to be sure, we said, but the peasant was incorrigible, and continued his old trade. After several meetings of the chief people of the town, and of the priests and monks, it was concluded to be necessary, in obedience to some old ceremonial, to wait till nine days after the burial.

" On the tenth day, a mass was said in the chapel where the body lay, in order to drive out the devil, which was imagined to have taken possession of it. When the mass was over the body was taken up, and preparations were made for pulling out its heart. The butcher of the town, an old clumsy fellow, began with opening the belly instead of the breast. He groped a long while among the entrails without finding what he looked for, till at last somebody said he should cut up the diaphragm, and then the heart was pulled out, to the admiration of the spectators. In the meantime the carcass stunk so abominably that they were obliged to burn frankincense ; but the smoke mixing with the fumes of the corpse, increased the stink and began to heat the poor people's brains. Their imagination, already affected with the spectacle before them, grew full of whimsies, and they took it into their heads that a thick smoke came from the body ; nor durst we say that it was only the smoke of the incense.

" In the chapel and the square before it they were incessantly bawling out Broucolack, which is the name they give to these pretended redivivi. From hence the bellowing was communicated to the streets and seemed to be invented on purpose to split the roof of the chapel. Several there present averred that the blood of the offender was red, and the butcher swore that the body was still warm, whence they concluded that the deceased was guilty of a heavy crime for not being thoroughly dead, or rather for suffering himself to be re-animated by the devil, which is the notion they have of a Broucolack. They then roared out that word in a stupendous manner. Just at this time there came in a flock of people, who loudly protested that they plainly saw the body was not grown stiff when it was carried from the fields to the church to be buried, and that consequently it was a true Broucolack, which word continued to be the burden of the song.

" I question not but they would have sworn it did not stink if we had not been there so thoroughly were their heads turned upon this occasion, and so strongly were they infatuated with the notion of these spectres. As for us, we got as close to the body as we could, that we might observe what passed more exactly, and were almost poisoned with the stink. When they asked us what we thought of the corpse we told them we believed it to be completely dead, and having a mind to cure, or, at least, not to exasperate their prejudices, we presented to them that it was no wonder the butcher should feel some warmth, by groping in the entrails, which were then putrefying, that it was no extraordinary thing for it to emit fumes since the same will happen upon turning up a dunghill, and that as for the pretended redness of the blood, it was still visible by the butcher's hands, that it was a mere stinking nasty smear.

" After all our reasoning they resolved upon going to the sea-shore, and there burning the dead man's heart. But, notwithstanding this execution, he did not grow more peaceable, but made more noise than ever. He was accused of beating people in the night, breaking down doors, and even roofs of houses, shattering windows, tearing clothes, and emptying casks and bottles. It was a ghost of a very thrifty constitution; nor do I believe that he spared any house but the consul's, where we lodged. In the meantime nothing could be more deplorable than the condition of this island. Not a head in it but was turned; the wisest among them were seized like the rest. In short, it was a real disorder of the brain, as dangerous as lunacy or madness. Whole families quitted their houses, and brought their beds from the remotest parts of the town into the great square, there to spend the night. Every one complained of some fresh insult, and nothing could be heard but groans at the approach of night. The most sensible people among them thought proper to retire into the country.

" When the prepossesion was so general, we thought it our best way to hold our tongues. Had we opposed it we should have been treated not only as fools, but as infidels. Indeed, how was it possible to bring a whole nation to its senses ? Those who believed in their hearts that we doubted the truth of the fact, came and reproached us with our incredulity, and endeavoured to prove that there were such things as Broucolacks, by quotations out of the *Buckler of Faith*, written by father Richard, a Jesuit missionary. Their argument was this : He was a Latin, and therefore you ought to believe him, nor should we have got anything by denying the consequence. We were entertained every morning with a recital of the new pranks of this night-bird, who was even charged with being guilty of the most abominable sins.

" Some of the citizens, who were most zealous for the public good, took it into their heads that there had been a defect in the most essential part of the ceremony. They were of opinion that mass ought not to have been said, till after the heart had been pulled out. With this precaution they insisted that the devil must needs have been worsted, and would not have ventured to come again ; whereas, by mass being said first, he had time enough given him to make off, and return to his post when the danger was over.

" After all these wise reflections, they were as much perplexed as at first setting out. They meet night and morning, debate, and make processions for three days and three nights. The Papas are obliged to fast, and run from house to house with sprinklers on their hands. Holy water is plentifully scattered about, even to the washing of the doors, and filling the mouth of the poor Broucolack.

" We repeated it so often to the magistrates, that we should not fail in Christendom to appoint a watch by night upon such an occasion, in order to observe what passed in the town, that at last they apprehended some vagabonds who had certainly a hand in these disorders ; but either they were not the principal agents, or they were dismissed too soon. For two days after, to make themselves amends for the fast they had kept in prison, they begun to empty the wine casks of such as had been silly enough to leave their houses in the night, so that nothing was left but to have recourse again to prayers.

" One day, as they were repeating a certain form, after having stuck a number of naked swords in the grave where the carcass lay (which they dug up three or four times a day to gratify the whim of whoever came by), an Albanian, who happened to be at Mycone, took upon him to pronounce with an air of great wisdom, that it was ridiculous to make use of the swords of Christians in such a case as this. " Are you so blind," says he, " as not to see that the hilt of these swords, being made in the form of a cross, hinders the devil from coming out of the carcass ? I am surprised that you do not take the Turkish sabres." But the expedient of this wise personage had no effect : the Broucolack was still unruly ; the whole island continued in a strange consternation, and they were utterly at a loss what saint to invoke, when all of a sudden, as if they had given one another the word, they begun to bawl all over the city that they had waited too long, that the Broucolack should be burned to ashes, and then they defied the devil to harbour there any longer, and that it was better to have recourse to this extremity, than to have the island totally deserted. For, in fact, several whole families had begun to pack up in order to retire to Syra or Tinos.

" The magistrates, therefore, gave orders to carry the Broucolack to the point of St. George's Island, where they got ready a great pile, with pitch and tar, for fear the wood should not burn fast enough of itself. The remnant of this miserable carcass was thrown into it and soon consumed. It was the 1st of January, 1701, and we saw the flame as we returned from Delos. It might properly be called a rejoicing bonfire, as no more complaints were heard of the Broucolack. They only said that the devil had at last met with his match, and some ballads were made to turn him into ridicule.

" It is a notion which prevails all over the Archipelago that the devil re-animates no carcasses but those of the Greek communion. The inhabitants of Santorini are terribly afraid of these bug-bears : those of Mycone, after their whims were dissipated, were equally afraid of a prosecution from the Turks, and from the bishop of Tinos. Not a single Papas would venture to be at St. George's when the body was burnt, for fear the bishop should insist upon a fee for their taking up and burning a body without his leave. As for the Turks, they did not fail, at their next visit, to make the Myconians pay heavily for their treatment of this poor devil, who became in every respect an object of abomination and horror to all the country."

Greeley, Horace : (*See* **Spiritualism.**)

Green Lion : (*See* **Philosopher's Stone.**)

Gregory, Mrs. Makdougail : (*See* **British National Association of Spiritualists.**)

Gregory the Seventh : A pope of the eleventh century, against whom a charge of necromancy was brought. He is chiefly notable for his bitter and prolonged struggle with

Henry IV., Emperor of Germany. A quarrel arose between them regarding the gift by Henry of ecclesiastical dignities, to account for which he was summoned before Gregory. He refused to appear, was excommunicated, and, in return, had the pope kidnapped by brigands. *Gregory*, however, was rescued by the people of Rome, and on his release commanded the Germans to elect a new emperor, Rudolph, duke of Suabia. Henry, attended by a very small retinue, thereupon repaired to Canossa, where *Gregory* at that time resided, to arrange for terms of peace. He was there treated with such severity and studied neglect that his desire to come to terms with the pope left him, and on his return he elected an anti-pope, Clement III. In the struggle which ensued Henry defeated Rudolph in battle and *Gregory* was sentenced as a sorcerer. He died in exile at Salerno.

As a magician he is not very conspicuous, for his fame rests chiefly on a prophecy he made publicly that Rudolph would be victorious, and that " before St. Peter's day," on the fulfilment of which saying he staked his papal crown. The unfortunate Rudolph, entirely trusting to *Gregory's* oracular utterance, renewed the battle six times and finally perished without having obtained the promised victory. Other stories credit *Gregory* with the power of making lightning with a motion of his hand, and causing thunder to dart from his sleeve. It is related by Benno that on one occasion he left his magical book behind him at his villa. Entrusting two of his servants with the task of returning for it, he warned them not to look into it on pain of the most awful punishment. However, curiosity overcame the fears of one of them, and, opening the book he pronounced some words. Immediately a band of imps appeared and asked what was their command. The terrified servants begged that the demons would cast down so much of the city wall as lay in their way, and thus they escaped the penalty of their disobedience.

Of a lofty and severe cast of mind, Gregory's motive was not so much fraud as profound enthusiasm and strength of purpose, which sustained him through the struggle with Henry to the end of his life.

Grihestha : (*See* **India**.)

Grimoire : A text-book of Black Magic. The three best known grimoires are the *Grimorium Verum*, the *Grand Grimoire*, and the *Grimoire of Pope Honorius*. Black magic (q.v.) is of course an ignorant and superstitious perversion of the true science, and the grimoires well illustrate this—their most noticeable feature being their utter futility. The grimoires, in fact, cannot be taken seriously, and the diabolic practices contained in their pages are more absurd than fearsome. Before entering upon them, the rites of the church are practised as a preliminary and fasting is observed. The great object of the *grimoires* is to invoke the infernal powers, and at the same time to trick them. The fiends are treated as imbeciles. In the *grimoire*, the magician is instructed how, when selling them his soul, he may deceive them by a play upon words. One of the chief desires of the sorcerer of the middle ages was to discover hidden treasure by means of Satanic agency, and having found it to devote himself to good deeds and the distribution of his wealth among the poor.

Abstinence from every species of impurity is strongly insisted upon for the space of an entire quarter of the moon, and the sorcerer most solemnly promises the grand Adonai (q.v.), the Master of all Spirits, that he shall not eat more than two meals per diem, and that these shall be prefaced by prayer. The operator must change his apparel as seldom as possible, and sleep only on occasion, meditating continually on his undertaking, and centring all his hopes in the infinite goodness of Adonai, who is

undoubtedly the supreme deity, and not as might be thought a master-fiend. But the *grimoires* teem with mystifications, and it is frequently difficult to discern their real meaning. In the three grimoires alluded to, the infernal hierarchy is described at length—(*See* **Demonology**) ; but the principal contents of these works are evocations and spells for the gaining over of the diabolical powers to the purposes of the sorcerer. That they were employed by veritable professors of the art of black magic is rather unlikely, as the real black magician had very much higher aims than the mere unearthing of buried treasure, and it is most probable that they were for the most part in use among amateurs of the art, who dabbled in it merely in the hope of enriching themselves.

Grimoire of Honorius, The : A magical work published at Rome in 1629, and not, as is generally thought, connected in any way with Kabbalistic magic. The work is indeed permeated with Christian ideas. It is extremely unlikely that it is the work of the Roman Bishop known as Honorius. The work has been called " a malicious and somewhat clever imposture," since it pretends to convey the sanction of the Papal Chair to the operators of necromancy. It deals with the evocation of the rebellious angels.

Grimorium Verum, The : This magical text-book was first published in 1517, and purported to be translated from the Hebrew. It is based to some extent upon the Key of Solomon (q.v.), and is quite honest in its statement that it proposes to invoke " devils," which it refers to the four elements, so that these would appear to be of the type of elementary spirits (q.v.). A part of the account it gives regarding the hierarchy of spirits is taken from the Lemegeton (q.v.). The work is divided into three portions : the first describing the characters and seals of the demons, with the forms of their evocation and dismissal ; the second gives a dscription of the supernatural secrets which can be learned by the power of the demons ; and the third is the key of the work and its proper application. But these divisions only outline what it purports to place before the reader, as the whole work is a mass of confusion. The plates which supply the characters do not apply to the text. The book really consists of two parts—*the Grimorium Verum* itself, and a second portion, which consists of magical secrets. The first supplies directions for the preparation of the magician based on those of the Clavicle of Solomon. Instructions for the manufacture of magical instruments, and the composition of a parchment on which the characters and seals are to be inscribed, as well as the processes of evocation and dismissal. The second part contains the " admirable secrets" of the pretended Albertus Magnus, the " Petit Albert" and so forth. The work is only partially diabolical in character, and some of its processes might claim to be classed as White Magic.

Grossetete, Robert : Bishop of Lincoln from 1235, and generally known as Robert of Lincoln. Among his many accomplishments he is said to have numbered some proficiency in the art of magic. Born of poor parents, he was early compelled to earn his own living, and even at times to beg for bread. He was at length " discovered " by the Mayor of Lincoln, who was attracted by his appearance and the shrewdness of his remarks, and had him sent to school, where his remarkable capacity for study so helped his advancement that he was enabled to complete his education at Oxford, Cambridge, and Paris. The illustrious Roger Bacon characterised him and his friend, Friar Adam de Marisco, as the most learned men of their time. He was well skilled in the sciences of mathematics and astronomy, and a master of Greek and Hebrew. As a member of the clergy he distinguished himself chiefly by his vigorous denunciation of the abuses in the court of Rome, and particularly of the pope, Innocent IV., whose rule added but little lustre to the church. *Grossetête* did not hesitate to point out the misdeeds of the ecclesiastical dignitaries, many of whom had never even visited their various sees. And he openly pronounced Innocent to be the Antichrist.

His essays in necromancy include (Gower tells us) the making of a brazen head, which would answer questions and foretell the future. However, this would appear to be no unique accomplishment, as both Pope Silvester II., and Roger Bacon are credited with it.

Gruagach : That is "long-haired one," from the Gaelic *gruag,* a wig : a fairy being with protective duties, to be met with in Scottish legends, and which apparently may be of either sex. The *Gruagach* appears to have been particularly associated with cattle, and milk was laid aside for him every evening — otherwise no milk would be got at next milking. Usually this being was of a beneficent nature, although occasionally it showed mischievous traits by loosing the cattle in the byres so that the herds had to get up, sometimes several times during a night, to tie them up : this apparently caused the *Gruagach* much delight. There are many tales in different parts of Scotland about the *Gruagach,* from which one gathers that this fairy commonly had long hair and was well dressed, of whichever sex it might happen to be. (*See* **Scotland**).

Gualdi : Dr. Campbel, in his well-known work *Hermippus Redivivus or the Sage's Triumph over old age and the grave* relates that this person was probably a Rosicrucian who lived for several hundreds of years. The particulars concerning him are as follows, but they cannot be verified, and are regarded by Godwin as apocryphal :—
He sojourned at Venice for several months, and was known by the name of the "Sober Signior" among the common people, on account of the regularity of his life, the composed simplicity of his manners and the quietness of his costume : for he always wore dark clothes, and these of a plain, unpretending style. Three things were remarked of him during his stay at Venice. The first was, that he had a small collection of fine pictures, which he readily showed to everybody that desired it : the next, that he was perfectly versed in all arts and sciences, and spoke always with such minute particularity as astonished—nay, silenced—all who heard him, because he seemed to have been present at the things which he related, making the most unexpected corrections in small facts sometimes. And it was, in the third place, observed that he never wrote or received any letter, never desired any credit, but always paid for everything in ready money, and made no use of bankers, bills of exchange, or letters of credit. However, he always seemed to have enough, and he lived respectably, though with no attempt at splendour or show.

Signor *Gualdi* met, shortly after his arrival at Venice, one day, at the coffee-house which he was in the habit of frequenting, a Venetian nobleman of sociable manners, who was very fond of art, and this pair used to engage in sundry discussions, and they had many conversations concerning the various objects and pursuits which were interesting to both of them. Acquaintance ripened into friendly esteem, and the nobleman invited Signor *Gualdi* to his private house, whereat—for he was a widower— Signor *Gualdi* first met the nobleman's daughter, a very beautiful young maiden of eighteen, of much intelligence, and of great accomplishments. The nobleman's daughter was just introduced at her father's house from a convent, or pension, where she had been educated by the nuns. This young lady, in short, from constantly being in his society, and listening to his narratives, gradually fell in love with the mysterious stranger, much for the reasons of Desdemona ; though Signor *Gualdi* was no swarthy Moor, but only

a well-educated gentleman—a thinker rather than a doer. At times, indeed, his countenance seemed to grow splendid in expression, and he boasted certainly wondrous discourse, and a strange and weird fascination would grow up about him, as it were, when he became more than usually pleased and animated. Altogether, when you were set thinking about him, he seemed a puzzling person, and of rare gifts, though when mixing with the crowd you would scarcely distinguish him from the crowd ; nor would you observe him unless there was something akin to him in you excited by his talk.

The Venetian nobleman was now on a footing of sufficient intimacy with Signor *Gualdi* to say to him one evening, at his own house, that he understood that he had a fine collection of pictures, and that, if agreeable, he would pay him a visit one day for the purpose of viewing them. The nobleman's daughter, who was present, and who was pensively looking down upon the table thinking deeply of something that the Signor had just said, raised her eyes eagerly at this expression of wish by her father, and, as accorded with her feelings, she appeared, though she spoke not, to be desirous to make one of the party to see the pictures. It was natural that she should secretly rejoice at this opportunity of becoming more intimately acquainted with the domestic life of one whom she had grown to regard with feelings of powerful interest. She felt that the mere fact of being his guest, and under the roof which was his, would seem to bring her nearer to him, and, as common with lovers, it seemed that their being thus together would, in feeling at least, appear to identify both. Signor *Gualdi* was very polite, and readily invited the nobleman to his house, and also extended the invitation to the young lady, should she feel disposed to accompany her father, since he divined from the expression of her face that she was wishful to that effect. The day for the visit was then named, and the Signor took his departure with the expression of friendship on all sides which usually ended their meetings.

It followed from this arrangement, that on the day appointed, the father and daughter went to Signor *Gualdi's* house. They were received by the Signor with warm kindness, and were shown over his rooms with every mark of friendliness and distinction. The nobleman viewed Signor *Gualdi's* pictures with great attention, and when he had completed his tour, he expressed his satisfaction by telling the Signor that he had never seen a finer collection, considering the number of pictures. They were now in Signor *Gualdi's* own chamber—the last of his set of rooms,— and they were just on the point of turning to go out, and *Gualdi* was removing the tapestry from before the door to widen the egress, when the nobleman, who had paused to allow him thus to clear the way, by chance cast his eyes upwards over the door, where there hung a picture evidently of the stranger himself. The Venetian looked upon it with doubt, and after a while his face fell ; but it was soon cleared, as if with relief. The gaze of the daughter was also riveted upon the picture, which was very like *Gualdi* but she regarded it with a blush. The Venetian looked from the picture to *Gualdi,* and back again from *Gualdi* to the picture. It was some time before he spoke.

" That picture was intended for you, sir," said he at last, hesitating, to Signor *Gualdi.* A slight cold change passed over the eyes of the stranger ; but he only made reply by a low bow. " You look a moderately young man, —to be candid with you, sir, I should say about forty-five, or thereabouts—and yet I know, by certain means of which I will not now further speak, that this picture is by the hand of Titian who has been dead nearly a couple of hundred years. How is this possible ? " he added, with a polite, grave smile. " It is not easy," said Signor *Gualdi* quietly, " to know all things that are possible, for very frequent mistakes are made concerning such ; but there is certainly nothing strange in my being like a picture painted by Titian." The nobleman easily perceived by his manner, and by a momentary cloud upon his brow, that the stranger felt offence. The daughter clung to her father's arm, secretly afraid that this little unexpected demur might pass into coolness, and end with a consummation of estrangement, which she feared excessively ; she dreaded the rupture of their intimacy with the stranger ; and, contradictory as it may seem, she wanted to withdraw, even without the point she dreaded being cleared up into renewed pleasant confidence. However, this little temporary misunderstanding was soon put to an end by Signor *Gualdi* himself, who, in a moment or two, resumed his ordinary manner, and he saw the father and daughter down-stairs, and forth to the entrance of his house, with his usual composed politeness—though the nobleman could not help some feeling of restraint, and his daughter experienced a considerable amount of mortification ; and she could not look at Signor *Gualdi*,—or, rather, when she did, she looked too much.

This little occurence remained in the mind of the nobleman. His daughter felt lonely and dissatisfied afterwards, eager for the restoration of the same friendly feeling with Signor *Gualdi*, and revolving in her mind numberless schemes to achieve it. The Venetian betook himself in the evening to the usual coffee-house, and he could not forbear speaking of the incident among the group of people collected there. Their curiosity was roused, and one or two resolved to satisfy themselves by looking at the picture attentively the next morning. But to obtain an opportunity to see the picture on this next morning, it was necessary to see the Signor *Gualdi* somewhere, and to have his invitation to his lodgings for the purpose. The only likely place to meet with him was at the coffee-house ; and thither the gentlemen went at the usual time, hoping, as it was the Signor's habit to present himself, that he would do so. But he did not come—nor had he been heard of from the time of the visit of the nobleman the day before to the Signor's house—which absence, for a first time almost that he had been in Venice, surprised everybody. But as they did not meet with him at the coffee-house—as they thought was sure—one of the persons who had the oftenest conversed with the Signor, and therefore was the freer in his acquaintance, undertook to go to his lodgings and inquire after him, which he did ; but he was answered by the owner of the house, who came to the street-door to respond to the questioner, that the Signor had gone, having quitted Venice that morning early, and that he had locked up his pictures with certan orders, and had taken the key of his rooms with him.

This affair made a great noise at the time in Venice, and an account of it found its way into most of the newspapers of the year in which it occurred. In these newspapers, and elsewhere, an outline of the foregoing particulars may be seen. The account of the Signor *Gualdi* will also be met with in *Les Mémoires historiques* for the year 1687.

Guecubu : Among the Araucanians, a people of Chili, the *Guecubu* are evil spirits, who do all in their power to thawrt and annoy the Great spirit, Togin, and his ministers.

Guillaume de Carpentras : An astrologer who made for King René of Sicily, and for the Duke of Milan, astrological spheres, from which horoscopes were drawn. He made for Charles VIII. of France one which cost twelve hundred crowns. This sphere contained many utilities, and was so contrived that all the movements of the planets, at any hour of the day and night, were to be found there.

Guillaume de Paris : He is said by the demonologists to have made speaking statues, like those made by Roger Bacon—

a thing which could only be done by diabolical agency.

Guinefort : A strange story has been left on record by Father Etienne Bourbon, a Dominican, who died in 1262. He relates that while he was preaching in the diocese of Lyons, many women came to him confessing that they had taken their children to *St. Guinefort*. Curious to know what sort of saint it might be whose cult called for confession, Father Bourbon enquired into the matter, and found that *Guinefort* was a dog ! It was, in fact, that dog which had given rise to the well-known fable of the dog and the serpent, wherein a dog is killed under the unjust suspicion that it has slain a child, which in reality it has saved from the attack of a serpent. This dog-martyr it was to whose " shrine " the women brought their children.

A similar story is told of a dog named Ganelon, whose tomb was in Auvergne, in the neighbourhood of a fountain. The adventure took place during the reign of Louis le Debonnaire. Two or three centuries later it was found that the waters of the fountain possessed medicinal virtues, but cures were attributed to the unknown occupant of the tomb—that is, until a certain bishop found among the archives of the Château the anecdote of Ganelon.

Guldenstubbe, Baron de : A famous mystic, who was one of the first in France to recognise the importance of spiritualistic phenomena. With the Comte d'Ourches, he held many experiments in table-turning, automatic writing, and so forth, and published a work entitled *Practical Experimental Pneumatology or The Reality of Spirits and the Marvellous Phenomenon of their Direct Writing.* (*See article* **France** *and* **Circles.**)

Guppy, Mrs. : Née Miss Nichol, a celebrated English medium who began to exercise her powers about 1866. At that time she lived with Mrs. Sim, a sister of Dr. Alfred Russel Wallace, who was a frequent witness of her phenomena. Thereafter her mediumistic powers developed apace and the circle of her sitters grew as the manifestations became more ambitious. Raps were heard and apports of fruit and flowers conveyed to the séance-room. A. R. Wallace states that on one occasion " the room and the table shook violently," and Miss Nichol herself was several times levitated—(*See* **Levitation**). Soon after the formal commencement of her mediumship she married Mr. Samuel Guppy. In January, 1872 she gave a materialisation séance, the first serious attempt of the kind in this country, She and her husband were also instrumental in introducing spirit-photography (q.v.) into England. On the death of Mr. Guppy she was married a second time to Mr. W. Volckman.

Guppy, Samuel : (*See* **Spiritualism.**)

Gurney, Edmund : A distinguished psychologist and student of psychic science. He was born at Horsham in 1847, and educated at Blackheath and Trinity College, Cambridge, where he obtained a fellowship. He devoted himself thereafter to the study of medicine and passed the second M.B. Cambridge examination in 1880. . Thus equipped, he turned to the investigation of psychical research, seeking, in common with most psychical researchers, to find evidence for the survival of consciousness and personality after death. He chose for exploration the region of unconscious or subconscious activity—what Mr. Myers, himself a worker in the same field, has designated the " subliminal consciousness." From 1874 to 1878 *Gurney* and Myers worked with professional mediums, getting but poor results, but on the founding of the Society for Psychical Research experiments of a more scientific nature were made. These resulted in two volumes of *Phantasms of the Living,* by Messrs. Myers, Podmore, and *Gurney*, which went some way towards establishing telepathy on a sound basis. To the same end were directed Mr. *Gurney's* careful hypnotic experiments between 1885 and 1888, and his contributions to the *Proceedings* of the S.P.R. He was, indeed, an ideal student of psychic research, acute, patient, exact, logical, and entirely disinterested. Besides his psychological works he wrote *The Power of Sound* (1880), an essay on music, and a collection of essays entitled Tertium Quid (1887). He died in June, 1888, from an overdose of narcotic medicine.

Gustenhover : A goldsmith who resided at Strasburg in 1603. In a period of much danger he gave shelter to one M. Hirschborgen who is described as good and religious. In return for the hospitality of his host he gave him some powder of projection and departed on his journey.

Gustenhover indiscreetly made transmutation before many people, which in due course reached the ears of Rudolph II. himself, an amateur alchemist. He forthwith ordered the Strasburg magistrates to send the goldsmith to him. He was accordingly arrested and guarded with the greatest vigilance. On learning that he was to be sent to the Emperor at Prague he disclosed the whole business and requesting the magistrates to meet together asked them to procure a crucet and charcoal, and without his coming near them to melt some lead. On the metal being molten he then gave them a small quantity of a reddish powder on which being thrown into the crucet produced a considerable amount of pure gold.

On being brought into the presence of the Emperor he confessed that he had not himself prepared the magical powder and was wholly ignorant of the nature of its composition. This the Emperor refused to believe in spite of the repeated protestations of the goldsmith. The powder being at length exhausted, *Gustenhover* was set to the now impossible task of making more gold. He sought refuge from the fury of the Emperor by an alchemical blasphemy accursed by all sons of the doctrine. Convinced that the alchemist was concealing his secret, the Emperor had him imprisoned for the rest of his life.

It is believed that Hirschborgen who presented *Gustenhover* with the powder was no other than Alexander Sethon (q.v.), who at that period was travelling Germany in various disguises.

Guyon, Madame (1648—1717) : Jeanne Marie Bouvières de la Mothe, a celebrated mystic and quietest who suffered much persecution at the hands of the Church of Rome. She was born at Montargis on April 13th, 1648, and early showed a passion for martyrdom and religious exercises. As she grew older vanity took the place of devotion, for she was both witty and beautiful. At the age of sixteen she was forced into a marriage with the wealthy M. Guyon, more than twenty years her senior, in whose household she was exposed to insult and cruelty. Broken in spirit she turned once more to religion, and consulted a Franciscan, who advised her to seek God in her heart rather than in outward observances. From that time she became a mystic, aiming at the suppression of all human hopes and fears, and desires, and the attainment of a completely disinterested love of God. She embraced every form of suffering, physical and mental, and even eschewed spiritual joys. In 1680 M. Guyon died, and his widow was released from bondage. Henceforth she embraced the doctrine of quietism. In losing the gifts," she said, "she had found the Giver, and had reached an ideal state of resignation and self-suppression." She went to Paris, expounded her theories with earnestness and charm, and gathered an illustrious circle about her. Here also she made friends with Fénélon. But the persecutions of the Church increased She herself requested that a commission be appointed to examine her doctrine and writings. Three commissioners were chosen, among them Bossuet, the champion of the Church, her erstwhile friend and now her bitter enemy.

Her writings were condemned, and she herself incarcerated at Vincennes. For four years she lay in the dungeons of the Bastile, while Bossuet used every means to calumniate her name and doctrine. In 1702, her health broken, she was released and sent to Blois where she died in 1707. Her last years were blessed with peace and resignation, and such a submission to trials as she had ever shown.

Gwion Bach : In Welsh romance and myth, son of Gwreang. Set by Ceridwin to stir the magic cauldron of science and inspiration intended to be drunk by her son, *Gwion* tasted the liquid and became gifted with supernatural sight. He fled, pursued by Ceridwin, and the pair were changed successively into a hare and a greyhound, a fish and an otter, a bird and a hawk, a grain of wheat and a black hen, which ultimately swallowed the wheat. (Compare the metamorphoses of Ceridwen and *Gwion Bach* with that of the Queen of Beauty and the Djinn in the *Arabian Nights*, Tale of the Second Calendar). Later *Gwion* was placed in a bag and flung into the sea by Ceridwin. He was drawn out by Elphin, son of Cwyddus, and was now called Taliesin (Radiant Brow).

Gypsies : The name Gypsy, an abbreviation of " Egyptian," has been used for centuries by English-speaking people to denote a member of a certain caste of turbulent wanderers who travelled Europe during the Middle Ages, and whose descendants, in a much-decayed condition, are still found in most European countries. Many other names, such as " Saracen " and " Zigeuner," or " Cigan," have been applied to these people, but " Egyptian " is the most; widespread in time and place. It does not relate to Egypt, but to the country of " Little Egypt " or " Lesser Egypt," whose identity has never been clearly established. Two Transylvanian references of the years 1417 and 1418 indicate that Palestine is the country in question, but there is some reason to believe that " Little Egypt" included other regions in the Levant. *Gypsies* speak of themselves as Romané, and of their language as Romani-tchib (*tchib*=: tongue). Physically, they are black-haired and brown-skinned, their appearance, like their language, suggesting affinities with Hindustan. But, although possessing marked racial characteristics, for the most part, they must also be regarded as a caste or organization. In recent centuries, if not in earlier times, many of their over-lords were not of Gypsy blood, but belonged to the nobility and *petite noblesse* of Europe, and were formally appointed by the kings and governments of their respective countries to rule over all the *Gypsies* resident within those countries. The title of baron, count, or regent of the *Gypsies* was no proof that the official so designated was of Gypsy race. This fact must always be borne in mind in any consideration of the Gypsy system.

The rulers thus appointed, being empowered by Christian princes, and under Papal approval, were necessarily Christian. Moreover, their vassals were at least Christian by profession. Although their behaviour was often wildly inconsistent with such a profession, it was in the character of Christian pilgrims that they asked and obtained hospitality from the cities and towns of Mediæval Europe. On the other hand, they seem to have practised rites which could not be described as Christian. This twofold character is illustrated in connection with the services which they still hold in the crypt of the church of Les Saintes Maries de la Mer, in the Île de la Camargue, Bouches-du-Rhône. In this church the Festival of the Holy Marys is annually celebrated on 25th May, and to it the *Gypsies* come in great numbers. The crypt is specially reserved for them, because it contains the shrine of Saint Sara of Egypt, whom they regard as their patron saint. Throughout the night of 24th—25th May they keep watch over her shrine, and on the 25th they take their departure. Among the Gypsy votive offerings presented in the crypt, some are believed to date back to about the year 1450. All this would appear to indicate that the *Gypsies* were Christians. Another statement, however, tends to qualify such a conclusion. This is the assertion that the shrine of Saint Sara rests upon an ancient altar dedicated to Mithra ; that the *Gypsies* of that neighbourhood who are known as " Calagues," are descended from the Iberians formerly inhabiting the Camargue ; and that their cult is really the Mithraic worship of fire and water, upon which the veneration of Saint Sara is super-imposed.

Confirmation of this view may be obtained from the worship of fire still existing among the *Gypsies* of Southern Hungary. The ceremonies observed at child-birth, in order to avert evil during the period between birth and baptism, may be taken as evidence. Prior to the birth of the child, the *Gypsies* light a fire before the mother's tent, and this fire is not suffered to go out until the rite of baptism has been performed. The women who light and feed the fire croon, as they do so, the following chant :—

> Burn ye, burn ye fast, O Fire !
> And guard the babe from wrathful ire
> Of earthy Gnome and Water-Sprite,
> Whom with thy dark smoke banish quite !
> Kindly Fairies, hither fare,
> And let the babe good fortune share,
> Let luck attend him ever here,
> Throughout his life be luck aye near !
> Twigs and branches now in store,⎫
> And still of branches many more,⎬ *bis*.
> Give we to thy flame, O Fire !⎭
> Burn ye, burn ye, fast and high,
> Hear the little baby cry !

It will be noted that the spirits of the Earth and Water are here regarded as malevolent, and only to be overcome by the superior aid of fire. Nevertheless, those women who are believed to have learned their occult lore from the unseen powers of Earth and Water are held to be the greatest magicians of the tribe. Moreover, the water-being is not invariably regarded as inimical, but is sometimes directly propitiated. As when a mother, to charm away convulsive crying in her child, goes through the prescribed ceremonial in all its details, of which the last is this appeal, as she casts a red thread into the stream :—" Take this thread, O Water-Spirit, and take with it the crying of my child ! If it gets well, I will bring thee apples and eggs !" The water-spirit appears again in a friendly character when a man, in order to recover a stolen horse, takes his infant to a stream, and, bending over the water, asks the invisible genius to indicate, by means of the baby's hand, the direction in which the horse has been taken. In these two instances we have a clear survival of the worship of water and the watery powers. It may be questioned whether these rites ought to be ascribed to Mithraism in its later stages, or whether they own an earlier origin.

One definite statement with regard to Gypsy lore is afforded by Joseph Glanvil, in a passage which inspired Matthew Arnold's poem of " The Scholar-Gypsy." " There was lately a lad in the University of Oxford," says Glanvil (*Vanity of Dogmatising*, 1661), " who was, by his poverty, forced to leave his studies there, and at last to join himself to a company of vagabond *Gypsies*." Glanvil goes on to say that " after he had been a pretty while exercised in the trade," this scholar-gypsy chanced to meet two of his former fellow-students, to whom he stated :—" that the people he went with were not such impostors as they were taken for, but that they had a traditional kind of learning among them, and could do wonders by the powers of imagination, their fancy binding that of others ; that himself had learned much of their art, and when he had

compassed the whole secret, he intended," he said, " to leave their company, and give the world an account of what he had learned."

Here we have clear indications of the possession of a body of esoteric learning, which included the knowledge and exercise of hypnotism. Even among modern *Gypsies* this power is exercised. De Rochas states that the Catalan *Gypsies* are mesmerists and clairvoyants, and the present writer has experienced an attempt on the part of a South Hungarian Gypsy to exert this influence. The same power, under the name of *glamour*, was formerly an attribute of the Scottish *Gypsies*. Glamour is defined by Sir Walter Scott as " the power of imposing on the eyesight of the spectators, so that the appearance of an object shall be totally different from the reality." And, in explanation of a reference to " the *Gypsies' glamour'd gang*," in one of his ballads, he remarks : " Besides the prophetic powers ascribed to the *Gypsies* in most European countries, the Scottish peasants believe them possessed of the power of throwing upon bystanders a spell to fascinate their eyes and cause them to see the thing that is not. Thus in the old ballad of ' Johnnie Faa,' the elopement of the Countess of Cassillis with a Gypsy leader is imputed to fascination—

> ' Sae soon as they saw her weel-faur'd face,
> They cast the *glamour* o'er her.' "

Scott also relates an incident of a Gypsy who " exercised his glamour over a number of people at Haddington, to whom he exhibited a common dung-hill cock, trailing, what appeared to the spectators, a massy oaken trunk. An old man passed with a cart of clover, he stopped and picked out a four-leaved blade ; the eyes of the spectators were opened, and the oaken trunk appeared to be a bulrush." The quatrefoil, owing to its cruciform shape, acted as a powerful antidote to witchcraft. Moreover, in the face of this sign of the Cross, the Gypsy was bound to desist from the exercise of what was an unlawful art. As to the possibility of hypnotizing a crowd, or making them " to see the thing that is not," that feat is achieved to-day by African witch-doctors. What is required is a dominant will on the one hand and a sufficiently plastic imagination on the other

Scott introduces these statements among his notes on the ballad of " Christie's Will," in relation to the verse—

> " He thought the warlocks o' the rosy cross,
> Had fang'd him in their nets sae fast ;
> Or that the *Gypsies*' glamour'd gang
> Had lair'd his learning at the last."

This association of Rosicrucians with *Gypsies* is not inapt, for hypnotism appears to have been considered a Rosicrucian art. Scott has other suggestive references in this place. " Saxo Grammaticus mentions a particular sect of Mathematicians, as he is pleased to call them, who, ' per summam ludificandorum oculorum peritiam, proprios alienosque vultus, varus rerum imaginibus, adumbraie callebant ; illicibusque formis veros obscurare conspectus." Merlin, the son of Ambrose, was particularly skilled in this art, and displays it often in the old metrical romance of Arthour and Merlin. The jongleurs were also great professors of this mystery, which has in some degree descended, with their name, on the modern jugglers." *

It will be seen that various societies are credited with the possession, in an eminent degree, of the art of hypnotism, during the Middle Ages. Presumably, it was inherited from one common source. How much the *Gypsies* were associated with this power may be inferred from a Scottish Act of Parliament of the year 1579, which was directed against " the idle people calling themselves Egyptians, or any other that fancy themselves to have knowledge of

*See also Scott's note 2M appended to *The Lay of the Last Minstrel*.

prophecy, *charming*, or other abused sciences." For the term "charming," like "glamour" and other kindred words (*e.g.* "enchantment," "bewitched," "spellbound") bore reference to the mesmeric influence.

The statement made by Glanvil's scholar-gypsy would lead one to believe that the *Gypsies* inhabiting England in the seventeenth century possessed other branches of learning. They have always been famed for their alleged prophetic power, exercised through the medium of astrology and chiromancy or palmistry, and also by the interpretation of dreams ; this last-named phase being distinctly specified in Scotland in 1611.† It does not appear that any modern *Gypsies* profess a knowledge of astrology. Nevertheless, it is interesting to note that Groome ‡ was shown by a Welsh Gypsy-man the form of the written charm employed by his mother in her fortune-telling, and that form is unquestionably a survival of the horoscope. Both mother and son were obviously unaware of that fact, and made no profession of astrology ; but they had inherited the scheme of the horoscope from ancestors who were astrologers.

The practice of chiromancy is still a Gypsy art, as it has been for ages. A curious belief was current in mediæval times to the effect that the three Kings or Magi who came to Bethlehem were *Gypsies*, and in more than one religious play they are represented as telling the fortunes of the Holy Family by means of palmistry. This circumstance has evoked the following suggestive remarks from C. G. Leland.||

"As for the connection of the Three Kings with *Gypsies*, it is plain enough. *Gypsies* were from the East ; Rome and the world abounded in wandering Chaldean magipriests, and the researches which I am making have led me to a firm conclusion that the *Gypsy* lore of Hungary and South Slavonia has a very original character as being, firstly, though derived from India, not *Aryan*, but Shamanic, that is, of an Altaic, or Tartar, or 'Turanian' stock. . . . . Secondly, this was the old Chaldean-Accadian 'wisdom' or sorcery. Thirdly—and this deserves serious examination—it was also the old Etruscan religion whose magic formulas were transmitted to the Romans. . . . .

"The Venetian witchcraft, as set forth by Bernoni, is evidently of Sclavic-Greek origin. That of the Romagna is Etruscan, agreeing very strangely and closely with the Chaldean magic of Lenormant, and marvellously like the *Gypsies'*. It does not, when carefully sifted, seem to be like that of the Aryans. . . . . nor is it Semitic. To what degree some idea of all this, and of *Gypsy* connection with it, penetrated among the people and filtered down, even into the Middle Ages, no one can say. But it is very probable that through the centuries there came together some report of the common origin of *Gypsy* and 'Eastern ' or Chaldean lore, for, since it *was* the same, there is no reason why a knowledge of the truth should not have been disseminated in a time of a traditions and earnest study in occultism."

These surmises on the part of a keen and accomplished student of every phase of magic, written and unwritten, are deserving of the fullest consideration. By following the line indicated by Leland it may be possible to reach an identification of the "traditional kind of learning" possessed by the *Gypsies* in the seventeenth century.

DAVID MACRITCHIE.

Gyromancy : Was performed by going round continually in a circle, the circumference of which was marked by letters. The presage was drawn from the words formed by the letters on which the inquirers stumbled when they became too giddy to stand. The object of this circumcursation was simply to exclude the interference of the will, and reduce the selection of letters to mere chance. In some species of enchantment, however, the act of turning round was to produce a prophetic delirium. The religious dances, and the rotation of certain fanatics on one foot, with their arms stretched out, are of this nature. These cases really indicate a magical secret, of which, however, the deluded victims rarely possessed any knowledge. In the phenomenon known as St. Vitus's Dance, and the movements of the convulsionaries, manifestations of spiritual intelligence were quite common. The tendancy of the spiritual force is to act spirally, rhythmically, whether in the use of language or of the bodily members.

H

Habondia : Queen of the fairies, witches, harpies, furies; and ghosts of the wicked. This definition is according to the statement of Pierre Delancre, in his work on the *Inconstancy of Demons*.

Hackley, Frederick : (*See* **Rosicrucians.**)

Hackworld House : (*See* **Haunted Houses.**)

Hafed, Prince of Persia : (*See* **Duguid, David.**)

Hag of the Dribble, or "Gwrach y Rhibyn" : One of the Welsh banshees, whose pleasure it is to carry stones across the mountains in her apron, then loosing the string, she lets the stones shower down, thus making a "dribble." It is believed that at twilight this hag flaps her raven wing against the window of those who are doomed to die, and howls "A a a ui ui Anni."

Haggadah : The general name for the narrative or fabular portion of the Rabbinical literature.

Hajoth Hakados : One of the spheres of angels, by whose agency Jehovah's providence is spread. The Jews believe that these angels inhabit one of the hierarchies named "Jehovah," and that the simple essence of the divinity flows through the *Hajoth Hakados* to the angel "Metratton" and to the ministering spirit "Reschith Hajalalim."

† *Register of the Privy Council*, Vol. IX., p. 256.
‡ *In Gypsy Tents*, p. 376.
|| *Journal of the Gypsy Lore Society*, April, 1889, pp. 246-7.

Hallucination : A false perception of sensory vividness arising without the stimulus of a corresponding sense-impression. In this it differs from illusion, which is merely the misinterpretation of an actual sense-perception. Visual and auditory *hallucinations* are the most common, and especially the former ; but *hallucination* of the other senses may also be experienced, though it is not so readily distinguishable. Human figures and voices most frequently form the subject of a *hallucination*, but in certain types other classes of objects may be seen—as, for instance, the rats and insects of *delirium tremens*. Though *hallucination* is often associated with various mental and physical diseases, it may, nevertheless, occur spontaneously while the agent shows no departure from full vigour of body and mind, and may be induced—*i.e.*, in hypnotism—in about 90 per cent. of all subjects. The essential difference between sane and insane *Hallucinations* is that in the former case the agent can, by reflection, recognise the subjective nature of the impression, even when it has every appearance of objectivity ; whereas in the latter case the patient cannot be made to understand that the vision is not real.

Until comparatively recently **Hallucinatory** percepts were regarded merely as intensified memory-images, but as the most intense of ordinary representations do not possess that sensory vividness which is yet a feature of the smallest sensation received from the external world, it follows that other conditions must be present besides the excitement of the brain-elements which is the correlate of representation. It is true that the seat of excitement is the same both in actual sense-perceptions and in memory images but in the former case the stimulus is peripherally originated in the sensory nerve, whereas in the latter it takes its rise in the brain itself. Now if any neural system becomes highly excited—a state which may be brought about by emotion, ill-health, drugs, or a number of causes—it may serve to divert from their proper paths any set of impulses arising from the sense organs, and as any impulse ascending through the sensory nerves produces an effect of sensory vividness—normally, a true perception—the impulses thus diverted give to the memory images an appearance of actuality, not distinguishable from that produced by a corresponding sense-impression. In hypnosis a state of cerebral dissociation is induced, whereby any one neural system may be abnormally excited, and *hallucination* thus very readily engendered. Drugs which excite the brain also induce *hallucinations*.

The question or whether there is any relation between the *hallucination* and the person it represents is, and has long been, a vexed one. Countless well-authenticated stories of apparitions coinciding with a death or some other crisis are on record, and would seem to establish some causal connection between them. In former times apparitions were considered to be the " doubles " or " ethereal bodies " of the originals, and modern spiritualists believe that they are the spirits of the dead—or, mayhap, of the living, temporarily forsaking the physical organism. But the main theory among those who believe in such a causal connection between agent and *hallucination*—and in view of the statistics collected by Professor Sidgwick and others (*See* " **Psychic Research** "), it is difficult not to believe—is that of telepathy, or thought-transference. That the cerebral machinery for the transmission of thought should be specially stimulated in moments of intense excitement, or at the approach of dissolution, is not to be wondered at ; and thus it is sought to account for the appearance of hallucinatory images coinciding with death or other crises. Moreover, the dress and appearance of the apparition does not necessarily correspond with the actual dress and appearance of its original. Thus a man at the point of death, in bed and wasted by disease, may appear to a friend as if in his ordinary health, and wearing his ordinary garb. Nevertheless there are notable instances where some remarkable detail of dress is reproduced in the apparition. It seems clear, however, that it is the agent's general personality which is, as a rule, conveyed to the percipient, and not, except in special cases, the actual matter of his surface-consciousness.

A similar explanation has been offered for the hallucinatory images which many people can induce by gazing in a crystal, or even in a pool of water, or a drop of ink, and which are often declared to give information, and reproduce scenes and people of whom the agent has no knowledge. It is suggested that those images which do not arise in the subliminal consciousness of the agent may have been telepathically received by him from other minds. (*See* " **Crystal-gazing.**")

Collective Hallucination is a term applied to *hallucinations* which are shared by a number of people. There is no evidence, however, of the operation of any other agency than suggestion (q.v.) or at the most, telepathy.

Ham : A Norwegian storm-fiend in the shape of an eagle with black wings, sent by Helgi to engulf Frithjof as he sailed for the island of Yarl Angantyr in the Saga of Grettir.

Hamaxobii : (*See* **Fascination.**)

Hambaruan : Among the Dayaks of Borneo the *hambaruan*, or soul of a living man, may leave the body at will, and go where it chooses ; it is, however, liable to capture by evil spirits. If this should happen, the man falls ill, and, if his soul is not speedily liberated, dies.

Hammurabi, Law of, against witchcraft: (*See* **Semites.**)

Hamon : A sacred stone like gold, shaped as a ram's horn. If its possessor is in the posture of contemplation, it gives the mind a representation of all divine things.

Hand of Glory : The hand of a dead man, in which a lighted candle has been placed. It was formerly believed in Ireland and Mexico to be an instrument of magic. If the candle and its gruesome candlestick be taken into a house the sleeping inmates will be prevented from waking, and the candle itself will remain invisible. To be truly efficacious, however, both hand and candle must be prepared in a special manner.

Hands of Spirits : There are instances in occult history where the hand only of a spirit has become visible to the human eye. During the reign of James I. a vision of this kind came to a certain clerk who was engaged in writing a will which was to disinherit a son. It took the form of a fine white hand, which appeared between the candle and the parchment, casting a shadow on the latter. It came three times, till the clerk, becoming alarmed, threw down his pen and refused to finish the work. In the Book of Daniel it is related : " In the same hour came forth fingers of a man's hand, and wrote over against the candlestick upon the plaster of the wall of the king's palace : and the king (Belshazzar) saw the part of the hand that wrote." There are also many instances of writing being done without human hands, and a Mr. Wolf, of Ohio, states that he has shaken hands with spirits, as " substantially " as one man shakes hands with another. After a certain vision, it is recorded that Daniel was touched by a hand, which set him upon his knees and upon the palms of his hands.

Hanon-Tramp : The name given by the Germans to a certain kind of nightmare (q.v.). This particular nightmare takes the form of a demon, which suffocates people during sleep. It is believed by the French peasantry that this is " the destruction that wasteth at noon-day," as it is supposed that people are most exposed to its attacks at that time. Its method of suffocation is to press on the breast and thus impede the action of the lungs.

Hansen, Mr., of Copenhagen : (*See* **Telepathy.**)

Hantu Penyardin : A Malay Vampire. (*See* **Vampire.**)

Hantu Pusaka, a Malay Demon : (*See* **Malays.**)

Hare, Dr. : (*See* **Spiritualism.**)

Harodim : A degree of Freemasonry very popular in the North of England, and especially in the County of Durham, and probably founded in Gateshead in 1681. It was brought under the Grand Lodge in 1735. They were the custodians of the Ritual of All Masonry, or the Old York Ritual. There were nine lodges in all. A London version of this society was the Harodim-Rosy-Cross, of Jacobite origin, probably carried to London by the Earl of Derwentwater. This latter may have been a Scotch rite in very early times.

Harris, Thomas Lake, 1823—1906 : An American spiritualist born in Buckinghamshire, who, with his parents, emigrated to the United States when he was of a tender age. He adopted the profession of a preacher of the Universalist Church, but afterwards became a Swedenborgian. He attached himself to Davis (q.v.), but after the latter's exposure he deserted him and established himself as a preacher at New York, where he gathered round him a considerable congregation. When about twenty-seven years of age, he began to pose as the possessor of prophetic power, and produced a number of poems, which are not without a certain merit of their own. These he was able to improvise with such rapidity as to lead many to the belief that he was indeed divinely inspired. Somewhere about the year 1859 he visited London, where in certain circles his verse was admired. On returning to America, he founded a small community near New York, of which he became the head. Its members were of a heterogeneous description, composing American ladies of means, Japanese, clergymen, and the author, Laurence Oliphant, with his wife and mother. This community *Harris* called the Brotherhood of the New Life, and a little later on it was decided to change its site to the shores of Lake Erie. The principal industry of the community was wine-making, and for this *Harris* was called to account by the temperance party, but he summarily dismissed their objections by stating that the wine he made was the direct vehicle of the Divine Breath. His theology was a curious one: he believed that the Creator was androgyne, and he favoured married celibacy. The mode of breathing professed by him appears to have been imitated from that in vogue among certain Buddhist castes, but it was to be the mark of the faithful. In 1881 the Oliphants seceded from his rule, and charged him with fraud. They took legal proceedings against him, and succeeded in recovering considerable sums in this manner. Oliphant believed to the last that *Harris* possessed psychical powers, but there is no doubt at all that he was extremely avaricious and licentious as his books of verse, issued to a select circle, prove. In 1891 he proclaimed that he had renewed his youth, and that he had discovered what amounted to the elixir of life. On his death in 1906 his disciples would not believe that he had passed away, but thought he was only sleeping. He died in March, and it was not util June that his demise was publicly acknowledged by his followers. His whole philosophy was directed towards the breaking down of the established order of the relations of the sexes. His sect had a jargon of its own, and its language was often inflated and absurd. But with all his failings, and they were many, *Harris* was a man of considerable gifts, among which may be noted some poetic fervour and fluency and force of character.

Haruspication : (*See* **Divination.**)

Hasidim (" Pious Ones ") : Devotees of a mystical phase of Judaism. They are first heard of in the pre-Maccabean age. In the first centuries of the Christian era we again hear of the *Hasidim*, sometimes supposed to be the descendants of the earlier sect. The later *Hasidim* were saints and workers of miracles, gifted with esoteric wisdom and the prophetic faculty. Early in the eighteenth century there arose yet another sect of the same name, having for its aim the revival of spirituality in the Jewish religion. Representatives of this mystic body are still to be found in Hungary, Poland, and Russia.

Hasona : (*See* **Magic.**)

Hassan Sabah : (*See* **Assassins.**)

Hastraun : A small mystical sect of Judaism, whose members were to be found in some parts of Palestine and Babylon. They practised some sort of communism, and were known also as " fearers of sin."

Hatha Yoga : The earliest and therefore most simple form of the *Yoga* practice. An English translation of the *Hatha Yoga Pradipika* of Swatmaram Swami was published in 1893. This book consists of four chapters : the first containing advice as to surroundings, conduct, postures, etc. ; the second dealing with breathing practice, preparation, purification ; the third gives ten *Mudras* which confer miraculous powers ; and the fourth is a sort of supplement, and deals with the results of *Yoga* practice. The fruits of *Yoga* are detailed, and are of a very omniscient character.

Hauffe, Frederica : Better known as the " Seeress of Provost," a somnambule who came under the observation of

Dr. Justinus Kerner, a well-known poet and physician, early in the nineteenth century. A natural trance and convulsive patient, she came to Kerner to be magnetised, but he endeavoured at first to treat her by medicinal means. Finding these unavailing, however, he resorted to magnetism. Henceforward the Seeress passed the greater part of her life in trance, displaying all the usual somnambulic phenomena. (*See* **Magnetism** under article **Hypnotism.**) She saw and conversed with apparitions, developed remarkable clairvoyant faculties, and dealt also in mysticism, describing intricate symbolical circle-systems. She was also the author of a " primitive " language, constructed with some ingenuity, which purported to be that tongue, spoken by the patriarchs of old, wherein the words conveyed in some mystic manner the properties of the things they designated. Dr. Kerner and others were sometimes able to see *Frau Hauffe's* ghostly interlocutors, as dim grey pillars of cloud. Physical phenomena of a poltergeistic character were also of common occurrence in her presence.

Haunted Houses : Not long ago a number of the daily papers contained, throughout several consecutive weeks, an advertisement offering for sale " an ancient Gothic Mansion, known as Beckington Castle, ten miles from Bath and two from Frome " ; and the writer of this advertisement after expatiating on the noble scenery around Beckington, and the rare architectural beauty of the house itself, proceeded to say that the place was the more desirable because it was reported to be haunted ! No doubt there are people who long for a house containing a *bona fide* ghost, and it is sometimes said that the rich tradesman, anxious to turn himself into a squire, invariably looks out for a haunted manor, while some waggish writers have declared, indeed, that nowadays ghosts are to be bought at Whitely's, and that the demand for them among American millionaires is stupendous. And, if the purchaser of Beckington Castle had to pay an additionally high price because the place rejoiced in a veritable ghost, in reality anything of this sort usually makes a house almost unsaleable. At Lossiemouth, for example, on the east coast of Scotland, a fine old mansion stood untenanted for years, and was eventually sold for a merely nominal sum ; and the reason was, simply, that according to popular tradition the building was paraded nightly by a female figure draped in white, her throat bearing an ugly scar, and her hands tied behind her back with chains. Nor is it merely concerning old Manors in the country that stories of this nature are current, and, even in many densely-populated towns there exist to this day houses reputed to be haunted, which are quite unsaleable.

It would seem that royal palaces, closely watched and guarded as they are nowadays, and invariably have been, are not altogether destitute of such inhabitants. For a legend contends that Windsor Castle is frequently visited by the ghost of Sir George Villiers, and it is said, moreover, that once, in the reign of Charles I., this ghost appeared to one of the king's gentlemen-in-waiting, and informed him that the Duke of Buckingham would shortly fall by the hand of an assassin—a prophecy which was duly fulfilled soon after, as all readers of *Les Trois Mousquetaires* will doubtless remember, the incident figuring in that immortal story. Then at Hackwood House, near Basingstoke, there is a room in which no one dares to sleep, all dreading " the grey woman " supposed to appear there nightly ; while Wyecoller Hall, near Colne, boasts a spectre horseman who visits the place once a year, and rides at full speed through the garden. Very different is the legend attached to Dilston, in Tyneside, where a bygone Lady Windermere is said to appear from time to time, and indulge in loud lamentations for her unfortunate husband, who was executed for his share in the Jacobite rising of 1715 ; while at Salmesbury Hall, Blackburn, there is a ghost of yet another kind, the people of the neighbourhood affirming that periodically they see a weird lady and her knight promenading the grounds of the Hall, indulging the while in silken dalliance. It need hardly be said, perhaps, that ghosts of this particular nature are remarkably common, and bulk largely in the spiritual lore of nearly every county ; but the more gruesome apparitions predominate withal, and among these is the ghost of Amy Robsart, which still haunts the manor of Cumnor, in Oxfordshire. For it must be borne in mind that Amy was a real woman, and not a mere creation of Sir Walter Scott's brain. She was married in 1550 to the Earl of Leicester, and her tragic death is commonly laid to his charge ; but a tradition exists to the effect that Queen Elizabeth was really the responsible person, and recalling an authentic portrait of Amy, which bespeaks her a woman of charm and of no ordinary beauty, it is easy to believe that the ill-favoured queen hated her and took strong measures to get her out of the way.

Numerous rectories rejoice in the ghost of a clergyman, erstwhile murdered by his infuriated parishioners ; and there are several *haunted* monasteries and convents, while at Holy Trinity Church at York a phantom nun appears occasionally on winter evenings, and walks about muttering paternosters. The story concerning her is that, on one occasion, during a period of civil-war, a band of soldiers were minded to sack the edifice in question, and on approaching it with this intention they were confronted by an abbess, who bade them beware of the divine wrath they would surely incur if they committed an act of sacrilege. They laughed at her piety, and, never thinking she would offer any resistance, they tried to march *en masse* into the building, but, hardly had they commenced the assault, ere their opponent snatched a sword from one of them, and stood bravely on the defensive. A fierce battle ensued, the abbess proving herself a veritable amazon, and slaying a host of her foes ; yet she lost her life ultimately, and her ghost it is which still frequents the church she sought to defend.

There are few parts of England so rich in romance as Sherwood Forest, once the scene of Robin Hood's exploits ; and there is at least one place in this region which claims a number of ghosts, Newstead Abbey, the seat of Lord Byron's ancestors. A part of the garden there is popularly known as " the devil's wood," a name which points to the place having been infested once by minions of the foul fiend, while one of the rooms in the house is *haunted* by a certain " Sir John Byron, the little, of the grey beard," who presumably ended his days in some uncanny fashion. His portrait hangs over the hall in the dining-room, and a young lady, staying at Newstead about the middle of last century, contended stoutly that once she had entered this room to find the portrait gone, and its subject seated by the fireside reading a black-letter folio ! The poet Byron himself cherished very fondly all the ghostly traditions which clung round his home, and it is recorded that, on his learning that there were stone coffins underneath the house, he straightway had one of them dug up and then opened. He used some of its gruesome contents to " decorate " his own library, while he had the coffin itself placed in the great hall, through which thereafter the servants were afraid to pass by night. He also utilised the supernatural lore of Newstead in one of his poems, and from this we learn that a spectre friar was wont to parade the mansion whenever some important event was wont to befall its owners :—

" When an heir is born he is heard to mourn,
And when ought is to befall
That ancient line, in the pale moonshine

He walks from hall to hall.
His form you may trace, but not his face,
'Tis shadowed by his cowl ;
But his eyes may be seen from the folds between,
And they seem of a parted soul.
Say nought to him as he walks the hall,
And he'll say nought to you :
He sweeps along in his dusky pall,
As o'er the grass the dew.
Then, gramercy ! for the black friar ;
Heaven sain him, fair or foul,
And whatsoe'er may be his prayer,
Let ours be for his soul."

Passing from England to Ireland we find many *haunted houses* ; for instance, Dunseverick in Antrim, where dwells still the soul of a bygone chief, so wicked in his lifetime that even hell's gates are closed to him. And passing from Ireland to Scotland we find numerous *haunted* buildings too, notably Holyrood Palace and the castles of Hermitage and Glamis. It is the ghost of the murdered Rizzio which frequents Holyrood, yet it should be added that the vision is seldom seen nowadays ; and mayhap the fates, aware that the Italian minstrel was shamefully treated, have at length accorded his soul a resting-place more cosy than the dismal Edinburgh Palace. But the ghost of Hermitage, on the contrary, is still considerably addicted to exercise, and in truth his story marks him as having been a man of rare activity and ambition. Lord Soulis was his name, and, possibly after hearing of Faustus' exploits, he vowed that he too would exorcise the devil, who generously made his appearance betimes. " Vast power will be yours on earth," said the evil one to Soulis " if you will but barter your soul therefor " ; so his lordship signed the requisite compact with his life's blood, and thenceforth his days were given over to the enjoyment of every conceivable pleasure. Anon, however, he felt that his end was near, and calling some of his vassals around him he told them of the awful fate awaiting him after death. Thunderstruck they were, but soon after Soulis was gone it occurred to them that, could they but destroy his mortal remains completely, they might save his soul from the clutches of Beelzebub. So having sheathed the corpse in lead they flung it into a burning fiery furnace, and manifestly this cremation saved his lordship from the nether regions, for had he gone there his soul would not have been active still at Hermitage.

The ghost-story associated with Glamis Castle, the family seat of the Earl of Strathmore, is quite different from the rank and file of supernatural tales, and bears a more naked semblance of veracity than pertains to any of these. It is a matter of common knowledge that there is a secret chamber at Glamis, a chamber which enshrines a mystery known only to a few members of the Strathmore family, and three or four generations ago a lady, staying as a visitor at Glamis, vowed she would solve the riddle. Her first difficulty was to locate the actual room, but one afternoon, when all the rest of the household were going out, she feigned a headache and thus contrived to be left completely alone. Her next move was to go from room to room, putting a handkerchief in the window of each, and having done this she went outside and walked round the castle to see whether any room had evaded her search. Very soon she observed a window which had no handkerchief in it, so she hastened indoors again, thinking that her quest was about to be rewarded. But try as she might she could not find the missing room ; and while she was searching the other guests returned to the house, along with them being the then Lord Strathmore. He was fiercely incensed on learning what had been going forward, and that night shrieks were heard in a long corridor in the castle. The guests ran out of their rooms to find out what was wrong, and in the dim light they perceived a curious creature with an inhuman head, wrestling with an aged man-servant who eventually contrived to carry the monster away. There the story ends, but as remarked before it bears a semblance of truth, the probability being that some scion of the Glamis castle family was mad or hideously deformed, and was accordingly incarcerated in a room to which access was difficult and secret. And no doubt endless other ghost-stories rest on some basis of this sort, for, while the diverting practice of showing freaks in public is a comparatively new one, freaks themselves are among the world's most ancient institutions, perhaps almost as ancient as spectres and visions. It is impossible in this place to allude to the host of less famous haunted residences, an allusion to which their owners might take strong exception.   W.B.G.M.

Hayden, Mrs. : The first spiritualistic medium to visit England. *Mrs. Hayden* was the wife of W. B. Hayden, editor of the *Star Spangled Banner.* Her séance phenomena consisted mainly of raps, by means of which communication with the spirits was established. Her supernormal faculties were testified to by Professor de Morgan in a letter dated July, 1853, and by Robert Chambers in *Chambers' Journal,* May, 1853.

Hayti : (*See* **West Indian Islands.)**

Hazel Tree : The Hazel was dedicated to the god Thor, and, in the Roman Catholic Church, was esteemed a plant of great virtue for the cure of fevers. When used as a divining rod, the rod, if it were cut on St. John's Day or Good Friday, would be certain to be a successful instrument of divination. A hazel rod was a badge of authority, and it was probably this notion which caused it to be made use of by schoolmasters. Among the Romans, a *hazel* rod was also a symbol of authority.

Head of Baphomet : An interesting discovery was made public in 1818 dealing with the history of secret societies. There was found, among the antiquities of the imperial museum of Vienna some of those idols named *heads of Baphomet,* which the Templars adored. These heads represent the divinity of the gnostics, named *Mété* or Wisdom. For a long time there was preserved at Marseilles one of these gilded heads, seized in a retreat of the Templar when the latter were pursued by the law. (*See* **Baphomet.)**

Healing by Touch : In England and Scotland, and in France also, the idea that a touch of the royal hand was a sure remedy for scrofula was long prevalent, and consequently this complaint acquired betimes the now familiar name of " king's evil." In France, so far as can be ascertained, this interesting practice dates from the reign of Louis IX., and in England from that of Edward III., who is recorded to have performed a considerable number of cures. He was wont to wash the affected part of the sufferer, but gradually the use of actual ablutions was discontinued, and most subsequent kings contented themselves with mere touching, while at the same time prayers were offered up on behalf of the patient. Anon the religious ceremony used on such occasions grew more elaborate, while, during the reign of Henry VII., a special " king's evil " petition was drawn up by a body of divines for insertion in the Service Book, and there it prevailed for a surprisingly long time thereafter, being found in some editions printed as late as the beginning of the eighteenth century.

The idea that kings ruled by divine right emanated mainly from Scotland, and so it is natural to assume that the early inhabitants of that land regarded their sovereigns as capable of miracles. There is little or no evidence, nevertheless, that the Stuarts, prior to the Union of the Crowns, practised touching for king's evil; but scarcely was Charles I. on the British throne ere he began to demonstrate his powers herein, and scrofulous persons flocked from far and near accordingly. Indeed, they came in such numbers, that early in the fifth year of his reign, Charles found it essential to specify certain times for their reception at court, and the proclamation which he issued on the subject may be read in the *Historical Collections* of John Rushworth, sometime secretary to Oliver Cromwell. Here it is stated that, in the future, those who wish to benefit from the king's thaumaturgic gift will be welcomed at Michaelmas or Easter, but it is clear that his Majesty saw fit to make exceptions to this rule, for, during his visit to Edinburgh in 1633, he ministered to numerous unfortunates in the month of June. It was at Holyrood that he received them, the palace being transformed *pro tempore* into a veritable Lourdes, and Sir James Balfour, the Historian, who was knighted at this time, and created Lyon King-at-Arms, affirms in an unpublished manuscript, still extant in the Advocates Library, Edinburgh, that Charles successfully " heallit 100 persons of the cruelles or kingis eivell, yong and olde."

Reverting to the proclamation cited above, therein the king speaks at length of the many cures wrought by his " royal predecessors." Now this, of course, may allude purely to the Plantagenets or Tudors, but it is equally possible that these references indicate touching for scrofula on the part of the early Stuarts, and be that as it may, Charles I. was not the only member of that dynasty who essayed the act. John Evelyn, in his *Diary,* writes repeatedly of Charles the Second's activities in this relation, while Samuel Pepys refers to the same thing, and in one passage he says the sight failed to interest him in the least, for he had seen it often before. Clearly, then, quite a host of the Merry Monarch's subjects were " heallit " by the royal *touch,* nor did the practice end with the ousting of the Stuarts in 1689. The Chevalier de St. George essayed it on several occasions, and his son Prince Charles, when in Scotland in 1745, made at least one attempt, though whether with success or not is unrecorded.

In the infancy of the world, and during a time when these laws of nature were but partially known and understood by man, it was most natural that these inexplicable powers should be directly ascribed to a divine influence. Healing of the sick was supposed to proceed alone from God, or through the priest' and saints His servants. Faith was therefore necessary to the cure, and the magical powers were therefore transferred by words, prayers, and ceremonies, and the science was transmitted among the mysteries. *Healing by touch,* by laying on of hands, and by the breath, belonged to this secret influence ; also the use of talismans and amulets, which were composed of organic as well as inorganic substances,—minerals, stones, and plants ; the wearing of rings, of images of saints, and other symbolical objects ; lastly, *healing* the sick by words and prayers.

As regards the semblance which this science bears to magnetism, it is certain that not only were the ancients acquainted with an artificial method of treating disease but also with somnambulism itself. Among others, Agrippa von Nettesheim speaks of this plainly when he says, in his *Occulta philosophia,* p. 451 :—" There is a science, known but to very few, of illuminating and instructing the mind, so that at one step it is raised from the darkness of ignorance to the light of wisdom. This is produced principally by a species of artificial sleep, in which a man forgets the present, and, as it were, perceives the future through the divine inspiration. Unbelieving wicked persons can also be deprived of this power by secret means."

The *healing* of the sick by the *touch* and the laying on of hands is to be found among primitive peoples, the Indians, the Egyptians, and especially among the Jews. In Egypt sculptures have been found where one hand of the operator is placed on the stomach and the other on the back. Even the Chinese, according to the accounts of the early missionaries (Athan. Kircher, *China Illustrata*), healed sickness by the laying on of hands. In the Old Testament we find numerous examples, of which we shall extract a few.

When Moses found his end approaching, he prayed for a worthy successor, and we find the following passage (Numbers, xxvii., 18, 20) :—" And the Lord said unto Moses, Take thee Joshua, the son of Nun, a man in whom is the spirit, and lay thine hand upon him." .... " And thou shalt put some of thine honour upon him, that all the congregation of the children of Israel may be obedient."

Another instance is to be found in the *healing* the seemingly dead child by Elisha, who stretched himself three times upon the child, and called upon the Lord. The manner in which Elisha raised the dead son of the Shunamite woman is still more remarkable. He caused Gehazi to proceed before him to lay his staff upon the face of the child. As this was of no avail, Elisha went up into the room, and laid himself upon the child, etc., and his hands upon the child's hands, so that the child's body became warm again. After that the child opened his eyes. Elisha's powers even survived his death. " And Elisha died, and they buried him ; and the bands of the Moabites invaded the land in the coming of the year. And it came to pass, as they were burying a man, that, behold, they spied a band of men ; and they cast the man into the sepulchre of Elisha ; and when the man was let down, and touched the bones of Elisha, he revived and stood upon his feet." (2 Kings, xiii., 20, 21). Naaman the leper, when he stood before Elisha's house with his horses and chariots, and had been told to wash seven times in the Jordan, said, " Behold I thought, he will surely come out to me, and stand, and call upon the name of the Lord his God, and strike his hand over the place, and recover the leper." (2 Kings, v. 4).

The New Testament is particularly rich in examples of the efficacy of laying on of the hands. " Neglect not the gift that is in thee, which was given thee by prophecy, with the laying on of the hands of the presbytery." (1 Timothy, iv., 14), is the principal maxim of the Apostles, for the practical use of their powers for the good of their brethren in Christ. In St. Mark we find (xvi., 18) :—" They shall lay hands on the sick and they shall recover." St. Paul was remarkable for his powers : " And it came to pass that the father of Publius lay sick of a fever and of a bloody flux ; to whom Paul entered in, and prayed and laid his hands on him and healed him." (Acts, xxviii., 8). " And Ananias went his way, and entered into the house, and putting his hands on him, said, Brother Saul, the Lord, even Jesus that appeared unto thee in the way as thou camest, hath sent me that thou mayest receive thy sight and be filled with the Holy Ghost. And immediately there fell from his eyes as it had been scales, and he received sight." (Acts, ix., 17, 18). In St. Mark we find :— " And they brought young children to him, that he might *touch* them ; and his disciples rebuked those who brought them. But Jesus said, ' Suffer the little children to come unto me, for of such is the kingdom of heaven.' And he took them up in his arms, put his hands upon them, and blessed them." " And they bring unto him one that was deaf and had an impediment in his speech, and they besought him to put his hand upon him. And he took him aside from the multitude, and put his fingers into his ears, and he spit and touched his tongue ; and, looking up to heaven, he sighed, and said unto him, ' Ephphatha,'— that is, Be opened. And straightway his ears were opened,

and the string of his tongue was loosed, and he spake plain." (Mark, vii., 33).

Other passages may be met with in Matth. ix., 18 ; Mark v., 23 ; vi., 5 ; viii., 22 ; x., 13 ; xvi., 18 ; Luke v., 13 ; xviii., 15 ; John ix., 17 ; Acts ix., 17, etc., etc. In the histories of the saints, innumerable examples are recorded, and the command, " In my name shall they cast out devils ; they shall speak with new tongues ; they shall take up serpents ; and if they drink any deadly thing it shall not hurt them ; they shall lay their hands on the sick and they shall recover," applies to all true followers of Christ. Those, however, who are wanting in the power of the spirit and in faith cannot perform these acts like the saints, on whom they cast doubts because they cannot imitate them.

The saints accomplished everything through faith in Christ, and therefore were able to perform such miracles. We shall make mention of a few of the most remarkable accounts. St. Patrick, the Irish apostle, healed the blind by laying on his hands. St. Bernard is said to have restored eleven blind persons to sight, and eighteen lame persons to the use of their limbs, in one day at Constance. At Cologne he healed twelve lame, caused three dumb persons to speak, ten who were deaf to hear ; and, when he himself was ill, St. Lawrence and St. Benedict appeared to him, and cured him by touching the affected part. Even his plates and dishes are said to have cured sickness after his death. The miracles of SS. Margaret, Katherine, Elizabeth, Hildegarde, and especially the miraculous cures of the two holy martyrs Cosmas and Damianus, belong to this class. Among others, they freed the Emperor Justinian from an incurable sickness. St. Odilia embraced a leper, who was shunned by all men, in her arms, warmed him, and restored him to health.

Remarkable above all others are those cases where persons who were at the point of death have recovered by holy baptism or extreme unction. The Emperor Constantine is one of the most singular examples. Pyrrhus, king of Epirus, had the power of assuaging colic and affections of the spleen by laying the patients on their backs and passing his great toe over them. (Plutarch. Vita Pyrrhi : " Digitum maximum pedis divinitatem habuisse adeo quod igne non potuit comburi.") The Emperor Vespasian cured nervous affections, lameness, and blindness, solely by the laying on of his hands (Suelin, Vita Vespas). According to Coelius Spartianus, Hadrian cured those afflicted with dropsy by touching them with the points of his fingers, and recovered himself from a violent fever by similar treatment. King Olaf healed Egill on the spot by merely laying his hands upon him and singing proverbs (*Edda*, p, 216). The kings of England and France cured diseases of the throat by *touch*. It is said that the pious Edward the Confessor, and in France that Philip the First, were the first who possessed this power. The formula used on such occasions was, " Le roi te touche, allez at guerissez ; " so that the word was connected with the act of touching. In England the disease was therefore called " King's Evil." In France this power was retained until the time of the Revolution, and it is said that at the coronation the exact manner of touching, and the formula—" Le roi te touche, dieu te guerisse "—were imparted to the monarch. In the reign of Louis XIII. the Duke d'Epernon is said to have exclaimed, when Richelieu was made generalissimo against the Spaniards, " What ! has the king nothing left but the power of healing wens ? "

Among German princes this curative power was ascribed to the Counts of Hapsburg, and also that they were able to cure stammering by a kiss. Pliny says, " There are men whose whole bodies possess medicinal properties,—as the Marsi, the Psyli, and others, who cure the bite of serpents merely by the touch." This he remarks especially of the Island of Cyprus ; and later travellers confirm these cures by the touch. In later times, the Salmadores and Ensalmadores of Spain became very celebrated, who healed almost all diseases by prayer, laying on of hands, and by breathing. In Ireland, Valentine Greatrakes (q.v.) cured at first " king's evil " by touch. In the seventeenth century, the gardener Levret and the notorious Streeper performed cures in London by stroking with the hand. In similar manner cures were performed by Michael Medina, and the Child of Salamanca ; also Marcellus Empiricus (Sprengel, Gesch. der Med. Part 2, p. 179). Richter, an innkeeper at Royen, in Silicia, cured, in the years 1817-18, many thousands of sick persons in the open fields, by touching them with his hands. Under the Popes, laying on of hands was called Chirothesy. Diepenbroek wrote two treatises on it, and, according to Lampe, four-and-thirty Chirothetists were declared to be holy. Mesmer (q.v.) and his assistants also employed manipulations largely.

Hearn, Lafcadio : (*See* **Fiction, Occult English.**)

Heart : It is said in Ecclesiates that the *heart* of the wise is at the right side, the *heart* of the foolish at the left. But this saying must be placed in the same category as that of Jonas, who said of some of the Ninevites that they did not know their right hand from their lelt—that is, they could not distinguish good from evil.

Heat and Light : Spiritualistic Journal. (*See* **Spiritualism.**)

Heavenly Man, The : According to the *Zohar*, the first of the Sephiroth, or divine emanations. Before the creation God was without form, above and beyond all attributes. But when He had created the *Heavenly Man* He used him as a Chariot in which to descend. And desiring to make Himself known by His attributes, " He let Himself be styled as the God of pardon, the God of Justice, the God Omnipotent, the God of Hosts and He who is (Jahveh)." The *Heavenly Man* is to be distinguished from the " earthly man." The creation of the earthly man was, indeed, the work of the *Heavenly Man*—that is, of the first emanation from God, the Supreme Manifestation, the Divine activity.

Hecate : Originally a Greek goddess of uncertain parentage. She appears to have been one of the Titans who ruled the heaven, earth and sea ; and could bestow gifts on mortals at pleasure. Later she was confounded with other goddesses until she became at length a mystic goddess having all the magic powers of nature at command. Magicians and witches besought her aid, and sacrifices were offered to her where three ways met of dogs, honey and female black lambs. Festivals were celebrated to her annually at Ægina. In appearance she was frightful, and serpents hung hissing around her shoulders.

Heckman : (*See* **Dee.**)

Hekalot : According to the *Zohar*, the seven halls of the world of *Yetsirah*, the divine halls into which the seekers for the Chariot (Merkabah) strive to enter. Here dwell the angels, presided over by *Metatron* ; likewise the souls of men not specially noted for their piety. (The souls of the pious dwell in the world of *Beriah*).

Hela, or " Death " : One of the offspring of Loki and the giantess Angurbodi. The gods becoming alarmed of her and the other monsters which were coming to life in Jotunheim, it was deemed advisable by All-father that they should be brought before him. Hela was cast into Niflheim, to which are sent all those who die of sickness or old age. She governs this world, which is composed of nine regions, into which she distributes those who come to her ; and in which she inhabits a strongly-protected abode. Niflheim is said to be " a dark abode far from the sun " ; its gates open to the " cutting north " : " its walls are formed of wreathed snakes and their venom is ever falling like rain " ; and it is surrounded by dark and poisonous streams. " Nidhog, the great dragon, who dwells beneath the central root of Ygdrassil, torments and gnaws the dead." It is said that one-half of Hela's body is livid, and the other half flesh-coloured. Hunger is her table ; Starvation, her knife ; Delay, her man ; Slowness, her maid ; Precipice, her threshold ; Care, her bed ; and Burning Anguish forms the hangings of her apartments.

Heliotrope : Said to render its possessor invisible if it be rubbed over with the juice of the herb of the same name ; stops bleeding, and averts danger from poison.

Hell : The derivation of this word is probably from the root *helan* to cover, designating a subterranean or hidden place. In Ward's *Mythology* we find it in the form of *Hel* as a " place of the dead " alone, by no means a place of punishment. The conception of such has a more or less clear train of evolution behind it. The Christian idea of a place of punishment was directly coloured by the Jewish conception of *Sheol*, which in turn took shape from Babylonian sources. When exactly the idea began to form itself as a place of punishment is not clear, as among the ancient Semites, Egyptians and Greeks, we find the under-world regarded as a place of the dead alone. Thus in Egypt we find Amenti distinctly a place of the dead, in which the tasks of life are for the most part duplicated. This is the case also among barbarian people, who merely regard the land of the dead as an extension of human existence, in which man led a more or less shadowy life. The savage does not believe in punishment after death, and conceives that any breach of moral rule is summarily dealt with in this life. It is only when a higher moral code emerges from totemic or similar rule that the idea of a place of punishment is invented by priest-craft. This is, however, not always the case : in Greece, Rome and Scandinavia, we find that Hades was merely looked upon as a place of the dead, where, like shadowy ghosts, mankind flit to and fro, gibbering and squeaking as phantoms are supposed to do. According to the Greeks, Hades was only some twelve feet under the surface of the ground, so that Orpheus would have had no very long journey from the subterranean spheres to reach earth once more. *Hell* is generally regarded as a sovereignty, a place definitely ruled in an ordinary manner by a monarch set there for the purpose by the celestial powers. Thus the Greek Hades ruled the Sad Sphere of the Dead ; Osiris was lord and governor of the Egyptian Amenti ; in Central America, we find twin rulers in the Kiche Hades, Xibalba, whose names are given as Hun-came and Vukub-came. These latter are actively malignant, unlike the Mictlan of the Mexican, whose empire was for the generality of the people. These could only exist there for the space of four years, after which they finally became entirely extinct. The Mexicans represent Mictlan as a huge monster with open mouth ready to devour his victims, and this we find paralelled in the Babylonian Tiawith. We thus see that at a certain stage in all mythologies, the conception of a place of the dead was confounded with the idea of a place of punishment. The Greeks generally bewailed the sad end of humanity which was condemned for ever to dwell in semi-darkness after death. The possibility of the existence of a place of reward never seemed to appeal to them. To the vivid Greek mind life was all in all, and it was left to the finer and altogether more upright Semitic conscience to evolve in the near East the conception of a place of punishment. Thus Sheol, from being regarded as a place of the dead became the home of fire, into which the wicked and unjust were thrust for their sins. This was certainly foreshadowed by Babylonian and Egyptian ideals, for we find the Egyptian unable to pass the test of justification simply rejected ; from the idea of rejection would soon spring the idea of active punishment. The Semitic conception of *Hell* was probably re-inforced on the introduction of Christianity into Europe, and coloured by the conception of the places of the dead belonging to the other mythologies of Europe. Thus the Scandinavian idea, which was also that of our Saxon forefathers, undoubtedly coloured the English conception of the place of punishment.

" 'Hela,' or ' Death,' in the prose *Edia*, is one of the offspring of Loki and the giantess Angurbodi ; their other two being the wolf Fenrir and the Midgard serpent. The gods were not long ignorant that these monsters continued to be bred up in Jötunheim, and having had recourse to divination, became aware of all the evils they would have to suffer from them ; their being sprung from such a mother was a bad presage, and from such a sire one still worse. Ali-father therefore deemed it advisable to send one of the gods to bring them to him. When they came he threw the serpent into that deep ocean by which the earth is engirdled. But the monster has grown to such an enormous size that, holding his tail in his mouth he encircles the whole earth. ' Hela ' he cast into Niflheim, and gave her power over nine worlds (regions), into which she distributes those who are sent to her, that is to say, all who die through sickness or old age. Here she possesses a habitation protected by exceedingly high walls and stronglybarred gates. Her hall is called Elvidner ; Hunger is her table ; Starvation, her knife ; Delay, her man ; Slowness, her maid ; Precipice, her threshold ; Care, her bed ; and Burning Anguish forms the hangings of her apartments. The one-half of her body is livid, the other half the colour of human flesh.' A description of Niflheim itself, the abode of Loki and his evil progeny, in given in the *Voluspa*. It is ' a dark abode far from the sun ' ; its gates are open to ' the cutting north ' ; ' its walls are formed of wreathed snakes, and their venom is ever falling like rain.' It is surrounded by the dark and poisonous streams ' Elivagar.' Nidhog, the great dragon, who dwells beneath the central root of Ygdrassil, torments and gnaws the dead."

The probabilities are that the ideas concerning the Celtic other-world had little to do in forming the British conception of Hell. The Brythonic "Annwyl" was certainly a subterranean locality, but it was by no means a place of punishment, being merely a microcosm of the world above, where folk hunted, ate and drank, as in early Britain. Nor was the Irish other-world much different and after crossing the waters of oblivion the possessed person found himself in a sphere in many ways resembling the earth-life.

In southern Europe again the idea of *Hell* appears to have been strongly coloured by both classical and Jewish conceptions. Our best picture of the mediæval conception of the place of punishment is undoubtedly the Inferno of Dante, who in most things followed the teaching of contemporary schoolmen in describing it. Acknowledging Virgil as his master, he follows him in many descriptions of Tartarus ; but we find the Semitic idea cropping up every here and there, as in the beginning of one of the cantos, where, what looks suspiciously like a Hebrew incantation, is set down. The *dramatis personæ* are classical ; thus we have Pluto and many of the breed of Tartarus. In later mediæval times the ingenuity of the monkish mind came to the rescue and conceptions which in some instances appear to be perfectly original sprang up. Thus, *Hell* obtained an annexe, Purgatory. Its inhabitants took on a form which may distinctively be alluded to as European, in contradistinction to the more satyr-like shape of the earlier hierarchy of Hades. We find grizzly forms of bird-like shape, with exaggerated beaks and claws, and the animal forms and faces of later mediæval gargoyles give us a capital idea of what the denizens of Hades seemed like in the eyes of the superstition of the sixteenth and seventeenth

centuries. It was only a modified version of these ideas which came down to our grandfathers, and one may suspect that such superstitions were not altogether disbelieved by our fathers. This is not the place to embark upon a theological discussion as to whether the *Hell* of the Christians exists, or does not exist ; but it may be interesting to remark that a great controversy has raged ever since the time of Origen as to the question whether or not the punishments of *Hell* are eternal. Those who denied that this was so were called Universalists, and believed in the final redemption of all. Enough has been said to show that most Eastern mythological systems possess a Hades which does not differ in any fundamental respect from that of most barbarian races, except that it is perhaps rather more specialised and involved. Many later writers, such as Swedenborg, Boehme, Blake and others (not to forget Milton), have given us vivid pictures of the hierarchy and general condition of *Hell*. For the most part these are based on the patristic writings. In the Middle Ages endless controversy took place as to the nature and offices of the various inhabitants of the place of punishment (*See* **Demonology**), and the descriptions of later visionaries are practically mere repetitions of the conclusions then arrived at.

The locality of *Hell* has also been a question of endless speculation ; some believed it to be resident in the sun, giving as their reason for this the fact the Greek name of that luminary *Helios* ; but such childish etymologies appear to have been in disfavour with most writers on the subject, and the grand popular idea that *Hell* is subterranean has had no real rival.

Hellawes : A sorceress, Lady of the Castle Nigramous. She attempted to win the love of Lancelot, but being unable to do so, she perished.

Hellenbach, Baron : (*See* **Germany**.)

Helmont, John Baptista van, must be ranked as one of the pioneers of science by reason of his experimental researches, his acute judgment, his penetrating attitude of mind leading him to say " Names do not trouble me, I contemplate the thing in itself as near as I can," and his untiring search for the truth, not for personal aggrandizement or power, but in the service of progress and for the good of mankind. He was born of a noble family in the year 1557 at Bois-le-Duc in Brabant. Studying at Louvain, he early attained distinction in the science of mathematics, lecturing on physics at the age of seventeen. Before he was twenty-two he had read Hippocrates and the Greek and Arabian authors and become eminent in the doctrines of Aristotle and Galen and the practice of medicine according to Vopiscus and Plempius. In the year 1599 he took his degree of doctor of medicine. After this some years were spent in the practice of physic, but meeting a follower of Paracelsus he became interested in his theories of chemical medicine to such a degree that he retired to the castle of Vilvord, near Brussels, to spend the rest of his life in the study of experimental chemistry on which he wrote various treatises, becoming famous throughout Europe for his scientific knowledge. He revolutionized medicine as known in his day, turning aside from the theories of Galen and the Arabs, and created an epoch in the history of physiology, being the first to recognize the functions of the stomach and its relation to the other organs of the body. His many and varied experiments led him to deal with aerial fluids, to which he gave the name of gas—carbonic acid gas being his discovery —and it is said that without him the chemistry of steel in all probability would have been unknown to science.

The writings of *van Helmont* contain many truths, foreshadowings of ideas and principles now accepted as indispensable commonplaces, though these almost of necessity are hidden under much of the incomprehensible beliefs and illusions prevalent in his time. Alchemy, with its visions of the Elixir of Life and the Philosopher's Stone represented to him another field for experiment and research and though he never pretended to the art of making the transmuting powder, he testified his belief in the transmutation of metals, having seen the experiment performed many times. Among other things he became a firm believer in Mineral and Human Magnetism, anticipating Mesmer in almost the very terms of the later exponent of the theory and basing his argument on the well-known facts of the sympathy or antagonism spontaneously arising between individuals and the influence exerted by a firm will over a weak imagination. To the last he declined to leave his retirement, though his fame brought him flattering invitations and offers from the Emperor and Elector Palatine. Almost unknown to his neighbours he yet attended any stricken by illness without accepting any fees for his services. He lived to the age of sixty-seven, dying at his castle of Vilvord in 1624.

Helvetius, John Frederick : A physician of the Hague who in 1667 published a work concerning a strange adventure of his life in which he claimed to have taken part in a veritable act of metallic transmutation by alchemical processes. The book was translated into English and published at London 1670 under the title *Of a Transmutation*. As it is one of the few exact descriptions of such an experiment, it has been thought well to append the passage recounting it in full, as follows :—

"On the 27th December, 1666, in the afternoon, a stranger, in a plain, rustic dress, came to my house at the Hague. His manner of address was honest, grave authoritative ; his stature was low, with a long face and hair black, his chin smooth. He seemed like a native of the north of Scotland, and I guessed he was about forty-four years old. After saluting me he requested me most respectfully to pardon his rude intrusion, but that his love of the pyrotechnic art made him visit me. Having read some of my small treatises, particularly that against the sympathetic powder of Sir Kenelm Digby and observed therein my doubt of the Hermetic mystery, it caused him to request this interview. He asked me if I still thought there was no medicine in Nature which could cure all diseases, unless the principal parts, as the lungs, liver, etc. were perished, or the time of death were come. To which I replied I never met with an adept, or saw such a medicine, though I read of much of it and often wished for it. Then I asked if he was a physician. He said he was a founder of brass, yet from his youth learned many rare things in chemistry, particularly of a friend—the manner to extract out of metals many medicinal arcana by the use of fire. After discoursing of experiments in metals, he asked me, would I know the philosophers' stone if I saw it ? I answered, I would not, though I read much of it in Paracelsus, Helmont, Basil, and others, yet I dare not say I could know the philosophers' matter. In the interim he drew from his breast pocket a neat ivory box, and out of it took three ponderous lumps of the stone, each about the size of a small walnut. They were transparent and of a pale brimstone colour, whereto some scales of the crucible adhered when this most noble substance was melted. The value of it I since calculated was twenty tons weight of gold. When I had greedily examined and handled the stone almost a quarter of an hour, and heard from the owner many rare secrets of its admirable effects in human and metallic bodies, also its other wonderful properties, I returned him this treasure of treasures, truly with a most sorrowful mind, like those who conquer themselves, yet, as was just, very thankfully and humbly. I further desired to know why the colour was yellow, and not red, ruby colour, or purple, as the philosophers write. He answered

that was nothing, for the matter was mature and ripe enough. Then I humbly requested him to bestow a little piece of the medicine on me, in perpetual memory of him, though but of the size of a coriander or hemp seed. He presently answered, " Oh no, this is not lawful, though thou wouldst give me as many ducats in gold as would fill this room, not for the value of the metal, but for some particular consequences. Nay, if it were possible," said he, " that fire could be burnt by fire, I would rather at this instant cast all this substance into the fiercest flames." He then demanded if I had a more private chamber, as this was seen from the public street. I presently conducted him into the best furnished room backward, not doubting but he would bestow part thereof or some great treasure on me. He entered without wiping his shoes, although they were full of snow and dirt. He asked me for a little piece of gold, and, pulling off his cloak, opened his vest, under which he had five pieces of gold. They were hanging to a green silk ribbon, and were of the size of breakfast plates. This gold so far excelled mine that there was no comparison for flexibility and colour. The inscriptions engraven upon them he granted me to write out ; they were pious thanksgivings to God, dated 20th August, 1666, with the characters of the Sun, Mercury, the Moon, and the signs of Leo and Libra.

" I was in great admiration, and desired to know where and how he obtained them. He answered, " A foreigner, who dwelt some days in my house, said he was a lover of this science, and came to reveal it to me. He taught me various arts—first, of ordinary stones and chrystals, to make rubies, chrysolites, sapphires, etc., much more valuable than those of the mine ; and how in a quarter of an hour to make oxide of iron, one dose of which would infallibly cure the pestilential dysentery, or bloody flux ; also how to make a metallic liquor to cure all kinds of dropsies, most certainly and in four days ; as also a limpid, clear water, sweeter than honey, by which in two hours of itself, in hot sand, it would extract the tincture of garnets, corals, glasses, and such like." He said more, which I *Helvetius*, did not observe, my mind being occupied to understand how a noble juice could be drawn out of minerals to transmute metals. He told me his said master caused him to bring a glass of rain-water, and to put some silver leaf into it, which was dissolved therein within a quarter of an hour, like ice when heated. " Presently he drank to me the half, and I pledged him the other half, which had not so much taste as sweet milk, but whereby, methought, I became very light-headed. I thereupon asked if this were a philosophical drink, and wherefore we drank this potion ; but he replied, I ought not to be so curious." By the said master's directions, a piece of a leaden pipe being melted, he took a little sulphureous powder out of his pocket, put a little of it on the point of a knife into the melted lead, and after a great blast of the bellows, in a short time he poured it on the red stones of the kitchen chimney. It proved most excellent pure gold, which the stranger said brought him into such trembling amazement that he could hardly speak ; but his master encouraged him saying, " Cut for thyself the sixteenth part of this as a memorial and give the rest away among the poor," which the stranger did, distributing this alms, as he affirmed if my memory fail not, at the Church of Sparenda. " At last," said he, " the generous foreigner taught me thoroughly this divine art."

" As soon as his relation was finished, I asked my visitor to show me the effect of transmutation and so confirm my faith ; but he declined it for that time in such a discreet manner that I was satisfied, he promising to come again in three weeks, to show me some curious arts in the fire, provided it were then lawful without prohibition. At the three weeks end he came, and invited me abroad for an hour or too. In our walk we discoursed of Nature's secrets, but he was very silent on the subject of the great elixir gravely asserted that it was only to magnify the sweet fame and mercy of the most glorious God ; that few men endeavoured to serve Him, and this he expressed as a pastor or minister of a church ; but I recalled his attention, entreating him to show me the metallic mystery, desiring also that he would eat, drink, and lodge at my house, which I pressed, but he was of so fixed a determination that all my endeavours were frustrated. I could not forbear to tell him that I had a laboratory ready for an experiment, and that a promised favour was a kind of debt. " Yes, true," said he, " but I promised to teach thee at my return, with this proviso, if it were not forbidden."

" When I perceived that all this was in vain, I earnestly requested a small crumb of his powder, sufficient to transmute a few grains of lead to gold, and at last, out of his philosophical commiseration, he gave me as much as a turnip seed in size, saying, " Receive this small parcel of the greatest treasure of the world, which truly few kings or princes have ever seen or known." " But," I said, " this perhaps will not transmute four grains of lead," whereupon he bid me deliver it back to him, which, in hopes of a greater parcel, I did, but he, cutting half off with his nail, flung it into the fire, and gave me the rest wrapped neatly up in blue paper, saying, " It is yet sufficient for thee." I answered him, indeed with a most dejected countenance, " Sir, what means this ? The other being too little, you give me now less." He told me to put into the crucible half an ounce of lead, for there ought to be no more lead put in than the medicine can transmute. I gave him great thanks for my diminished treasure, concentrated truly in the superlative degree, and put it charily up into my little box, saying I meant to try it the next day, nor would I reveal it to any. ' Not so, not so,' said he,' ' for we ought to divulge all things to the children of art which may tend alone to the honour of God, that so they may live in the theosophical truth.' I now made a confession to him, that while the mass of his medicine was in my hands, I endeavoured to scrape away a little of it with my nail, and could not forbear ; but scratched off so very little, that, it being picked from my nail, wrapped in a paper, and projected on melted lead, I found no transmutation, but almost the whole mass sublimed, while the remainder was a glassy earth. At this unexpected account he immediately said, " You are more dexterous to commit theft than to apply the medicine, for if you had only wrapped up the stolen prey in yellow wax, to preserve it from the fumes of the lead, it would have sunk to the bottom, and transmuted it to gold ; but having cast it into the fumes, the violence of the vapour, partly by its sympathetic alliance, carried the medicine quite away.' I brought him the crucible, and he perceived a most beautiful saffron-like tincture sticking to the sides. He promised to come next morning at nine o'clock, to show me that this tincture would transmute the lead into gold. Having taken his leave, I impatiently awaited his return, but the next day he came not, nor ever since. He sent an excuse at half-past nine that morning, and promised to come at three in the afternoon, but I never heard of him since. I soon began to doubt the whole matter. Late that night my wife, who was a most curious student and inquirer after the art, came soliciting me to make an experiment of that little grain of the stone, to be assured of the truth. ' Unless this be done,' said she, ' I shall have no rest or sleep this night.' She being so earnest, I commanded a fire to be made, saying to myself, ' I fear, I fear indeed, this man hath deluded me.' My wife wrapped the said matter in wax, and I cut half an ounce of lead, and put it into a

crucible in the fire. Being melted, my wife put in the medicine, made into a small pill with the wax, which presently made a hissing noise, and in a quarter of an hour the mass of lead was totally transmuted into the best and finest gold, which amaxed us exceedingly. We could not sufficiently gaze upon this admirable and miraculous work of nature, for the melted lead, after projection, showed on the fire the rarest and most beautiful colours imaginable, settling in green, and when poured forth into an ingot, it had the lively fresh colour of blood. When cold it shined as the purest and most splendid gold. Truly all those who were standing about me were exceedingly startled, and I ran with this aurified lead, being yet hot, to the goldsmith, who wondered at the fineness, and after a short trial by the test, said it was the most excellent gold in the world.

" The next day a rumour of this prodigy went about the Hague and spread abroad, so that many illustrious and learned persons gave me their friendly visits for its sake. Amongst the rest, the general Assay-master, examiner of coins of this province of Holland, Mr. Porelius, who with others earnestly besought me to pass some part of the gold through all their customary trials, which I did, to gratify my own curiosity. We went to Mr. Brectel, a silversmith, who first mixed four parts of silver with one part of the gold, then he filled it, put *aquafortis* to it, dissolved the silver, and let the gold precipitate to the bottom ; the solution being poured off and the calx of gold washed with water, then reduced and melted, it appeared excellent gold, and instead of a loss in weight, we found the gold was increased, and had transmuted a scruple of the silver into gold by its abounding tincture.

" Doubting whether the silver was now sufficiently separated from the gold, we mingled it with seven parts of antimony, which we melted and poured out into a cone, and blew off the regulus on a test, where we missed eight grains of our gold ; but after we blew away the red of the antimony, or superfluous *scoria*, we found nine grains of gold for our eight grains missing, yet it was pale and silverlike but recovered its full colour afterwards, so that in the best proof of fire we lost nothing at all of this gold, but gained, as aforesaid. These tests I repeated four times and found it still alike, and the silver remaining out of the *acquafortis* was of the very best flexible silver that could be, so that in the total the said medicine or elixir had transmuted six drams and two scruples of the lead and silver into most pure gold."

Henry III. of France : (*See* **France.**)

Hereburge, Frankish title for a witch : (*See* **France.**)

Hermes Trismegistus (' the thrice greatest Hermes ") : The name given by the Greeks to the Egyptian god Thoth or Tehuti, the god of wisdom, learning and literature. Thoth is alluded to in later Egyptian writings as " twice very great " and even as " five times very great " in some demotic or popular scripts. (ca. third century B.C.) To him was attributed as " scribe of the gods " the authorship of all sacred books which were thus called " Hermetic " by the Greeks. These, according to Clemens Alexandrinus were forty-two in number and were sub-divided into six portions, of which the first dealt with priestly education, the second with temple ritual and the third with geographical matter. The fourth division treated of astrology, the fifth of hymns in honour of the gods and a text-qook for the guidance of Kings, while the sixth was medical. It is unlikely that these books were all the work of one individual, and it is more probable that they represent the accumulated wisdom of Egypt, attributed in the course of ages to the great god of wisdom.

As " scribe of the gods " Thoth was also the author of all strictly sacred writing. Hence by a convenient fiction the name of *Hermes* was placed at the head of an extensive cycle of mystic literature, produced in post-Christian times. Most of this Hermetic or Trismegistic literature has perished, but all that remains of it has been gathered and translated into English. It includes the " Poimandres,"· the " Perfect Sermon," or the " Asclepius," excerpts by Stobacus, and fragments from the Church Fathers and from the philosophers, Zosimus and Fulgentius. Hitherto these writings have been neglected by theologians, who have dismissed them as the offspring of third century Neo-Platonism. According to the generally accepted view, they were eclectic compilations, combining Neo-Platonic philosophy, Philonic Judaism and Kabalistic theosophy in an attempt to supply a philosophic substitute for, Christianity. The many Christian elements to be found in these mystic scriptures were ascribed to plagiarism. By an examination of early mystery writings and traditions it has been proved with some degree of certainty that the main source of the Trismegistic Tractates is the wisdom of Egypt, and that they " go back in an unbroken tradition of type and form and context to the earliest Ptolemaic times."

The " Poimandres," on which all later *Trismegistic* literature is based, must, at least in its original form, be placed not later than the first century. The charge of plagiarism from Christian writings, therefore, falls to the ground. If it can be proved that the " Poimandres " belongs to the first century, we have in it a valuable document in determining the environment and development of Christian origins.

Mr. G. R. S. Mead, author of " Thrice Greatest Hermes " says in a illuminating passage :—

" The more one studies the best of these mystical sermons, casting aside all prejudices, and trying to feel and think with the writers, the more one is conscious of approaching the threshold of what may well be believed to have been the true adytum of the best in the mystery traditions of antiquity. Innumerable are the hints of the greatnesses and immensities lying beyond that threshold—among other precious things the vision of the key to Egypt's wisdom, the interpretation of apocalypsis by the light of the sun-clear epopteia of the intelligible cosmos."

Hermetic Magic : (*See* **Hermes Trismegistus.**)

Hermetic Society : (*See* **Alchemy.**)

Hermitage Castle : (*See* **Haunted Houses.**)

Herne, J. : A medium who was associated with Charles Williams (q.v.) during a part of the latter's career and who afterwards practised on his own account. Materialisation was a special feature of his séances. And Miss Florence Cook held her first materialisation séance in conjunction with *Herne.* He was one of the mediums present on the occasion of Mrs. Guppy's famous transit, and was himself on one occasion transported in like manner.

Heyd : A Norwegian sea-witch or storm-fiend in the shape of a white bear, alluded to in the saga of Grettir. With the other storm-fiend Ham, she was sent by Helgi to engulf Frithjof as he sailed for the island of Yarl Angantyr.

Heydon, John : English Astrologer (fl.—1667). In his useful if not invaluable Lives of the Alchemystical Philosophers, Waite speaks with great scorn of the English Astrologer, *John Heydon,* describing him as no better than a charlatan, and for that reason furnishing no facts whatsoever concerning his career.

The astrologer appears to have been born in 1629, his father being Francis Heydon, owner of a small estate called Sidmouth, in Devonshire. It was not in that romantic shire, however, that the astrologer first saw the light of day, but at a house in London boasting the pleasant name of Green Arbour ; and after some years spent here *Heydon* went to Worcestershire, when his education was attended to by various clergymen. Being a clever boy, his

parents naturally desired to send him to the University, but this was soon rendered virtually impossible by the outbreak of the great civil war, and thereupon *Heydon* took arms on behalf of the king, and fought in several battles. He is said to have been successful as a soldier, and to have won to the captaincy of a troop of horse under Prince Rupert, but on the ultimate triumph of the Roundhead party, the young man found it advisable to leave England, and for some years he sojourned in various countries on the Continent, notably Spain and Turkey. Indeed, if his contemporaneous biographers are to be trusted, he penetrated so far afield as Zante, the island in the Levant whose praise has been sung so beautifully by Edgar Allan Poe ; but by 1652 *Heydon* was back in his native England, and in 1655 we find him studying law and established in the Temple, a place almost sacred by virtue of its many literary associations. Nor was law his only study, for soon he was deep in that craft of astrology wherewith his name was destined to become associated, and on one occasion, having prophesied that Cromwell would shortly die by hanging, he was straightway imprisoned accordingly. So, at least, says Thomas Carte in his life of the great Marquis of Ormonde, that storehouse of information concerning England in Stuart and Cromwellian days.

Those who take an interest in the history of medicine will doubtless recall Nicholas Culpeper, who, after fighting for the Parliament in the Civil war, devoted a wealth of energy to compiling elaborate treatises on astrology and pharmacopœia, arts which went hand in hand in the seventeenth century. And it was the widow of this Culpeper whom *Heydon* took to wife, the year of their marriage being 1656, while it would seem that a daughter was born of their union, for among the astrologers' writings is a volume entitled *Advice to a Daughter* (1658). Whether *Heydon* continued living in the Temple after his marriage is not recorded, nor do we hear that he even attended greatly to legal business, and it is likely, on the contrary that astrology occupied all his time, while it appears that that imprisonment already mentioned was not the only one he suffered. He became intimate with many of the great scientists of the Restoration, but quarrelled with a number of them too ; while, though he always maintained that he was not actually affiliated with the Rosicrucians, it is a fact that he explained their theories publicly. Little is known about his later years, while the date of his death is unknown, and, before turning to the subject of his writings, it only behoves to state that his portrait was engraved by Thomas Cross.

Mr. Waite declares that *Heydon's* writings are sorry *pastiches,* and it cannot be questioned that the bulk of his work is derivative, Sir Thomas Browne being one whom he apes particularly. Nevertheless *Heydon* must be credited with considerable assiduity, and his Rosicrucian books alone are numerous, the best of them being probably *The New Method of Rosie-Crucian Physick* (1658), *The Rosie-Crucian Infallible Axiomater* (1660), *The Wise Man's Crown,* or *The Glory of the Rosie-Cross* (1664), and *The Rosie-Cross Uncovered* (1662). In addition to them he was author of *Theomagia or The Temple of Wisdom* (1664), and *The Prophetic Trumpeter, sounding an Allarum to England* (1655), the latter being dedicated to Henry Cromwell, while according to Wood's *Athenæ Oxonicsis, Heydon* was likewise the compiler of *A Rosiecrucian Theological Dictionary.* Yet another book from his pen was *Idea of the Law,* and at the end of this we find advertisements of several works of his, probably pamphlets, none of which is known to exist nowadays, but whose titles are worth recording here. One is called *The Familiar Spirit,* another *The Way to Converse with Angels,* while the others are *A New Method of Astrology, Of Scandalous Nativities,* and

Cabballa, or the Art by which Moses and Elijah did so many Miracles. It is quite possible, of course, that these pamphlets were advertised while yet in course of preparation, and that the author was prevented from bringing them to a finish, but their titles are significant, showing how far *Heydon* waded into the sea of mysticism, and suggesting that he was really more erudite therein than Mr. Waite imagines.

Hharis : (*See* **Eblis.**)

Hidden Interpretation : (*See* **Kabala**).

Hieroglyphs : *Hieroglyphs* were, and are, frequently made use of by the spirits in the so-called " direct " writing, *i.e.*, writing produced without a medium or any physical agent. Direct writing, though frequently produced at sèances, is perhaps most common in poltergeistic outbreaks, when the poltergeist is wont to distribute messages through the house. Thus in the disturbance in the house of Dr. Phelps, Stratford, in 1850–51, *hieroglyphs* were found on the walls and ceilings, while turnips covered with them were seen to grow from the pattern of the carpet. On this occasion the matter was investigated by Andrew Jackson Davis, who recognised the *hieroglyphs* as spiritual symbols, which he was inspired to interpret as friendly messages from high spiritual powers.

Hilarion : (*See* **Michael Maer.**)

Hippomancy : A method of divination practised by the ancient Celts, who kept certain white horses in consecrated groves. These were made to walk immediately after the sacred car, and auguries were drawn from their movements. The ancient Germans kept similar steeds in their temples. If on leaving these on the outbreak of hostilities they crossed the threshold with the left forefoot first, the presage was regarded as an evil one, and the war was abandoned.

Hirschborgen : (*See* **Gustenhover.**)

History of Human Follies : (*See* **Adelung, Jean Christophe**).

Hmana Zena : (Common Woman), Dalmatian name for a witch : (*See* **Slavs.**)

Hmin Nat : An evil spirit. (*See* **Burma.**)

Hobgoblin, Robin Goodfellow, or **Puck :** An English domestic fairy or brownie of nocturnal habits. He is of a happy disposition, and is believed to be one of the courtiers, probably the jester, at the court of Oberon. Reginald Scot, in his *Discovery of Witchcraft* says :—" Your grandames' maids were wont to set a bowl of milk for him for his pains in grinding of malt and mustard, and sweeping the house at midnight. This white bread, and bread and milk, was his standard fee." He is perhaps best known in Britain by his appellation of Puck, and his qualities and attributes are represented under this name in Shakespeare's " Midsummer's Night's Dream." By some he is believed to be the demon who leads men astray during the night. Sometimes he is clothed in a suit of leather close to his body, and sometimes he wore green. He is usually represented as full of tricks and mischief.

Hocus Focus : Words of magical import, which by some are believed to be derived from " Ochus Bochus." a magician and demon of the north. It is perhaps more probable, however, that as others say they are a corruption of the Latin words " hoc est corpus," and are an imitation of the act of transubstantiation practised by the priests of the Church of Rome.

Hod : The name assigned in the *Kabbala* to the number eight and meaning " Eternity "—that is, Eternity of the conquests achieved by mind over matter, active over passive, life over death.

Hodgson, Dr. : (*See* **Spiritualism.**)

Holland : For early matter see **Teutons**).

　Spiritualism.—Since the introduction of spiritualism into *Holland* , in 1857–8, no small part of its history has been enacted in that country, notwithstanding that the phlegmatic and by no means impressionable temperament of the Dutchman would seem to make but an indifferent medium of him. The first Dutch spiritualist of whom we have record is one J. N. T. Marthese, who, after studying psychic phenomena in foreign countries, finally returned to his native Holland, bringing with him the American medium Home. The latter held *séances* at the Hague, before several learned societies, and by command of Queen Sophia, a *séance* was given in her presence. The medium himself, in an account of the performance, tells us that the royal lady was obliged to sit out seven *séances*, on consecutive evenings, before any results were obtained. These results, however, were apparently satisfactory, for the Queen was thereafter a staunch supporter of the movement. During Home's visit, spiritualism gained a considerable hold on the people of *Holland*, and the practice of giving small private *séances* became fairly wide-spread. Spirit voices were heard at these gatherings, the touch of spirit hands was felt, and musical instruments were played upon by invisible performers. Particularly were these *séances* appreciated which were held at the house of Mr. T. D. Van Herwerden, in the Hague, and which were attended by many enthusiastic students of spiritualistic phenomena. His medium was, as a rule, a Japanese boy of his household, about fourteen years old, and very ignorant. The manifestations ranged from spirit rapping and table turning in the earlier *séances* to form materialisation in those of a later date. One of the principal spirits purported to be a monk, Paurellus, who had been assassinated some three hundred years previously in that city. Afterwards Mr. Van Herwerden was induced by his friends to publish his diary, under the title of *Experiences and Communications on a still Mysterious Territory.* For a time, as has been said, spiritualistic *séances* were only conducted in family circles, and were of a quite private nature. But as the attention of the intellectuals became more and more directed to the new science, societies were formed to promote research, and to throw light upon that which was obscure and perplexing. The first of these was the society called the " Oromase," or Ormuzd, which was founded by Major J. Revius, a friend of Marthese, in 1859, and which included among its numbers many people of high repute. They met at the Hague, and the records of their transactions were carefully preserved. Major Revius was president and continued to act in that capacity till 1871, the year of his death. The society's secretary, A. J. Rita, was also a prominent worker in " the cause." The " Oromase " library contained a fine collection of works on spiritualism, mesmerism, and kindred subjects, and included American, French, German and English books. Another society, the " Veritas," was founded in Amsterdam in 1869. The studies of this latter association were conducted in a somewhat less searching and scientific spirit than those of the " Oromase." Its mediums specialized in trance utterances and written communications from the spirits, and its members inclined to a belief in re-incarnation, which was at variance with the opinions of the older society. Rotterdam had, for a time, a society with similar objects known as the " Research after Truth," but it soon came to an end, though its members continued to devote themselves privately to the investigation of spirit phenomena. Other equally short-lived societies were formed in Haarlem and other towns. In all of these, however, there was a dearth of mediums able to produce form materializations, and to supply the want a number of foreign mediums hastened to Holland. Hitherto the comparatively private nature of the *séances*, and the high standing of those who took part in them, had prevented the periodicals from making any but the most cautious comments on the *séances*. But the advent of professional mediums on the scene swept away the barrier and let loose a flood of journalistic ridicule and criticism. This in turn provoked the supporters of spiritualism to retort, and soon a lively battle was in progress between the spiritualists and the sceptics. The consequence was, that " the cause " was boomed as much by the articles which derided it as by those which were in favour of it. Such mediums as Mrs. Margaret Fox Kane, the Davenport brothers, Rita, Home, Miss Cook, and Henry Slade, came over to *Holland*. Writers arose who were prepared to devote their abilities to the defence of spiritualism. Such an one was Madame Elise van Calcar, who not only wrote a novel expounding spiritualistic principles, but also conducted a monthly journal " On the Boundaries of Two Worlds," and held a sort of spiritualistic salon, where enthusiasts could meet and discuss their favourite subject. Dr. H. de Grood, Dr. J. Van Velzen, Dr. Van der Loef, Herr Schimmel, are among the other prominent Dutch authors who wielded their pens in defence of the same opinions. The writings of Professors Varley, Crookes, and Wallace were translated into the Dutch language, and lecturers helped to spread the belief in communication with the Other World. A mesmerist, Signor Donata, carried on the practice of " Animal Magnetism " in *Holland*, and endeavoured to identify the magnetic force emanating from the operator with the substance of which disembodied spirits are composed. Many exposures were made of unscrupulous mediums, and these, naturally, cast discredit upon the entire movement. But on the whole the mediums, professional or otherwise, were well received. Such phases of psychic phenomena as haunted houses and poltergeists are also very common, but are so similar to these manifestations in other countries that they require no separate treatment.

Holly : This name is probably a corruption of the word " holy " as this plant has been used from time immemorial as a protection against evil influence. It was hung round, or planted near houses, as a protection against lightning. Its common use at Christmas is apparently the survival of an ancient Roman custom, occurring during the festival to Saturn, to which god the holly was dedicated. While the Romans were holding this feast, which occurred about the time of the winter solstice, they decked the outsides of their houses with *holly* ; at the same time the Christians were quietly celebrating the birth of Christ, and to avoid detection, they outwardly followed the custom of their heathen neighbours, and decked their houses with *holly* also. In this way the *holly* came to be connected with our Christmas customs. This plant was also regarded as a symbol of the resurrection. The use of mistletoe along with *holly* is probably due to the notion that in winter the fairies took shelter under its leaves, and that they protected all who sheltered the plant. The origin of kissing under the mistletoe is considered to have come from our Saxon ancestors, who regarded this plant as dedicated to Freya, the goddess of love.

Holy Trinity Church, York : (*See* **Haunted Houses**).

Home, Daniel Dunglas (1833–1886) : One of the best known of spiritualistic mediums, was born near Edinburgh in 1833. At the age of nine he was taken by his aunt to America, where in 1850 he became a convert to the new doctrine of spiritualism and himself developed mediumistic powers. The next five years saw him occupied in giving séances in New York and elsewhere. In 1855 some of his friends subscribed a sum of money to send him to Europe. In England his séances were attended by many notable people, and on the Continent also he was admitted into the highest society. Until 1859 he had subsisted on the bounty of his wealthy friends—for at no time did he take actual fees for his services—but in that year he married a Russian lady of noble birth, young, charming, and possessed of means. But on her death in 1862 his financial circumstances were altered again. Four years later he was adopted by a wealthy widow, Mrs. Lyon, who made him large money gifts. In a few months, however, she tired of her adopted son and sued him in the law courts for the recovery of her " gifts." The charge of fraud was not proved, and many distinguished persons filed affidavits testifying to the actuality of *Home's* mediumistic powers, but the court was not satisfied that he had not influenced Mrs. Lyon, and judgment was given in her favour. During all this time he had largely exercised his faculties as a medium, and in 1870–72 he held a series of sittings with Sir William Crookes In 1871 he married again, and for the second time his wife was a Russian lady of means. From 1872 onwards he lived mostly on the Continent, where he died in 1886, after a long and painful illness. *Home's* mediumship presents many remarkable features. His séances were productive of both trance and physical phenomena, the latter including raps and table-tilting, levitation and elongation, materialisation, the fire-ordeal, and practically every form of manifestation. Unlike other mediums, he was never detected in fraud, though his mediumship was spread over so many years, and his phenomena are among the best-attested in the records of spiritualism. But a more important factor in *Home's* success was his wonderful personality. Though of lowly birth, he early acquired an ease and charm of manner which fitted him for the good society wherein he was destined to move. Artless and spontaneous and very affectionate, of pleasing manners and generous disposition, he won the hearts of all with whom he came in contact, and inspired in his sitters an emotional confidence which seems frequently to have over-ruled their judgment. Sir W. Crookes said of him that he was " one of the most lovable of men," whose " perfect genuineness and uprightness were beyond suspicion." Whether a medium should ever be " beyond suspicion " to a scientific investigator is, of course, open to question, but the instance shows abundantly that even scientists are not immune from the influence of *personal magnetism*.

Homunculas : An artificial man supposed to have been made by the alchemists, and especially by Paracelsus. To manufacture one, he states that the needful spagyric substances should be taken and shut up in a glass phial, and afterwards be placed to digest in horse-dung for the space of forty days. At the end of this time, there will be something which will begin to move and live in the bottle. This something is a man, but a man who has no body and is transparent. Nevertheless, he exists, and nothing remains but to bring him up—which is not more difficult to do than to make him. You may accomplish it by daily feeding him—during forty weeks, and without extricating him from his dung-hill—with the arcanum of human blood. At the end of this time you shall have a veritable living child, having every member as well-proportioned as any infant born of a woman. He will only be much smaller than an ordinary child, and his physical education will require more care and attention.

Hopedale Community : A socialistic and religious *community* founded in 1842 near Milford in Massachusetts, by the Rev. Adin Ballon. In 1850 various spirit manifestations made their appearance in the *Community*, while on the death of its founder in 1852, communications of a spiritualistic cast, purporting to come from him, were received through the hand of a living member of the *Community*. The little band at *Hopedale* did a good deal to help the advance of Spiritualism.

Hopkins, Matthew : Called the witchfinder; flourished in 1640. Of him Godwin says, "Nothing can place the credulity of the English nation on the subject of witchcraft in a more striking point of view, than the history of *Matthew Hopkins*, who, in a pamphlet published in 1647 in his own vindication, assumes to himself the surname of the Witch-finder. He fell by accident, in his native country of Suffolk, into contact with one or two reputed witches, and, being a man of an observing turn and an ingenious invention, struck out for himself a trade, which brought him such moderate returns as sufficed to maintain him, and at the same time gratified his ambition by making him a terror to many, and the object of admiration and gratitude to more, who felt themselves indebted to him for ridding them of secret and intestine enemies, against whom, as long as they proceeded in ways that left no footsteps behind, they felt they had no possibility of guarding themselves."

After two or three successful experiments, *Hopkins* engaged in a regular tour of the countries of Norfolk, Suffolk, Essex and Huntingdonshire. He united to him two confederates, a man named John Stern, and a woman whose name has not been handed down to us. They visited every town in their route that invited them, and secured to them the moderate remuneration of twenty shillings and their expenses, leaving what was more than this to the spontaneous gratitude of those who should deem themselves indebted to the exertions of *Hopkins* and his party. By this expedient they secured to themselves a favourable reception and a set of credulous persons who would listen to their dictates as so many oracles. Being three of them, they were enabled to play the game into one another's hands, and were sufficiently strong to overawe all timid and irresolute opposition. In every town to which they came, they inquired for reputed witches, and having taken them into custody, were secure for the most part of a certain number of zealous abettors, and took care that they should have a clear stage for their experiments. They overawed their helpless victims with a certain air of authority, as if they had received a commission from heaven for the discovery of misdeeds. They assailed the poor creatures with a multitude of questions constructed in the most artful manner. They stripped them naked, in search for the devil's marks in different parts of their bodies, which they ascertained by running pins to the head into those parts, that, if they were genuine marks, would prove themselves such by their insensibility. They swam their victims in rivers and ponds, it being an undoubted fact, that, if the persons accused were true witches the water, which was the symbol of admission into the Christian Church, would not receive them into its bosom. If the persons examined continued obstinate, they seated them in constrained and uneasy attitudes, occasionally binding them with cords, and compelling them to remain so without food or sleep for twenty-four hours. They walked them up and down the room, two taking them under each arm, till they dropped down with fatigue. They carefully swept the room in which the experiment was made, that they might keep away spiders and flies, which were supposed to be devils or their imps in that disguise.

The most plentiful inquisition of *Hopkins* and his confederates was in the years 1644, 1645, and 1646. At length there were so many persons committed to prison upon suspicion of witchcraft, that the government was compelled to take in hand the affair. The rural magistrates before whom *Hopkins* and his confederates brought their victims, were obliged, willingly or unwillingly, to commit them for trial. A commission was granted to the earl of Warwick and others to hold a session of jail-delivery against them for Essex at Chelmsford. Lord Warwick was at this time the most popular nobleman in England. He was appointed by the parliament lord high admiral during the civil war. He was much courted by the independent clergy, was shrewd, penetrating and active, and exhibited

a singular mixture of pious demeanour with a vein of facetiousness and jocularity. With him was sent Dr. Calamy, the most eminent divine of the period of the Commonwealth, to see (says Baxter) that no fraud was committed, or wrong done to the parties accused. It may well be doubted, however, whether the presence of this clergyman did not operate unfavourably to the persons suspected. He preached before the judges. It may readily be believed, considering the temper of the times, that he insisted much upon the horrible nature of the sin of witchcraft, which could expect no pardon, either in the world or the world to come.

He sat on the bench with the judges, and participated in their deliberations. In the result of this inquisition sixteen persons were hanged at Yarmouth in Norfolk, fifteen at Chelmsford, and sixty at various places in the county of Suffolk. Whitlocke in his Memorials of English Affairs, under the date of 1649, speaks of many witches being apprehended about Newcastle, upon the information of a person whom he calls the Witch-finder, who, as his experiments were nearly the same, though he is not named, we may reasonably suppose to be *Hopkins* ; and in the following year about Boston in Lincolnshire. In 1652 and 1653 the same author speaks of women in Scotland, who were put to incredible torture to extort from them a confession of what their adversaries imputed to them.

The fate of Hopkins was such as might be expected in similar cases. The multitude are at first impressed with horror at the monstrous charges that are advanced. They are seized, as by contagion, with terror at the mischiefs which seem to impend over them, and from which no innocence and no precaution appear to afford them sufficient protection. They hasten, as with an unanimous effort, to avenge themselves upon these malignant enemies, whom God and man alike combine to expel from society. But, after a time, they begin to reflect, and to apprehend that they have acted with too much precipitation, that they have been led on with uncertain appearances. They see one victim led to the gallows after another, without stint or limitation. They see one dying with the most solemn asseverations of innocence, and another confessing apparently she knows not what, what is put into her mouth by her relentless persecutors. They see these victims old, crazy and impotent, harassed beyond endurance by the ingenious cruelties that are practised against them. They were first urged on by implacable hostility and fury, to be satisfied with nothing but blood. But humanity and remorse also have their turn. Dissatisfied with themselves, they are glad to point their resentment against another. The man that at first they hailed as a public benefactor, they presently come to regard with jealous eyes, and begin to consider as a cunning imposter, dealing in cool blood with the lives of his fellow-creatures for a paltry gain, and, still more horrible, for the lure of a perishable and short-lived fame. The multitude, we are told, after a few seasons, rose upon *Hopkins* and resolved to subject him to one of his own criterions. They dragged him to a pond and threw him into the water for a witch. It seems he floated on the surface, as a witch ought to do. They then pursued him with hootings and revilings, and drove him for ever into that obscurity and ignominy which he had amply merited.

Horbehutet : The Egyptian winged disk. He was a solar deity who accompanied the sun-god, Ra, on his daily journey across Egypt for the purpose of warding off evil from him. His symbol was placed over the gates and doors of temples to protect them from malign influences.

Horoscope : (*See* **Astrology**).

Horse Shoes : Horse shoes were nailed on the thresholds in the Middle Ages to keep out witches.

Horse-Whispering : A secret method by which certain persons are able to acquire power over refractory horses. As is well known to students of gypsy lore, that interesting people appear to be in possession of some secret by which they are enabled to render vicious horses entirely tame; and opinions are divided as to whether this secret consists in the application of a certain odour or balm to the horse's muzzle, or whispering into its ear a spell or incantation. It is said, indeed, that the gypsy horse-charmer applies aniseed to the nose of the animal. But besides being practised by gypsies, *horse-whispering* is in vogue amongst many other peoples. Camden in his *Recital of Irish Superstitions* says :—" It is by no means allowable to praise a horse or any other animal unless you say ' God save him.' If any mischance befalls a horse in three days after, they find out the person who commended him, that he may whisper the Lord's Prayer in his right ear." It was said by Con Sullivan, a famous Irish horse-whisperer of the eighteenth century, that it is out of the power of the professors of the art to explain the source of their influence, —the same thing being affirmed by those who practise it in South America, where a couple of men will tame half a dozen wild horses in three days. The same art is widely practised in Hungary and Bohemia, and it was from a Bohemian gypsy that a family in the county of Cork claimed to hold a secret by which the wildest or most vicious horse could be tamed. For generations this secret was regularly transmitted as a parting legacy at the time of death from the father to the eldest son.

Throughout the North of Scotland there are disseminated members of a secret society for the breaking in of refractory horses, which is believed to be called the Horseman's Society, and which purports to be able to trace its origin away back into the dark ages Those only are admitted who gain their livelihood by the care and management of horses, and the more affluent and better educated are jealously excluded. Many farmers entertain a prejudice against the members of the society, but they are forced to admit that they are always very capable in the management of their teams, and can perform services which would otherwise require the calling in of a veterinary surgeon. They are usually skilled in the knowledge of herbs and simples, and a great deal of the marvellous is imputed to them. In fact it is stated that they hold their meetings at night and in the clear moonlight, going through various equestrian performances with horses borrowed for the occasion from their masters' stables. There is further said to be an inner circle in the society, where the black art and all the spells and charms of witchcraft are the objects of study, and the members of which can smite the horses and cattle with mysterious sickness, and even cast a glamour over human beings. Indeed a local writer goes so far as to say that the inner circle of the Horsemen employ hypnotic influence both on men and animals, as it is said certain North-American Indians, and some of the jungle tribes of Hindustan, do.

The famous Con Sullivan has already been alluded to, and his achievements were really wonderful. On one occasion his services were requisitioned by Colonel Westenra afterwards Earl of Rosmore, who possessed a racehorse called " Rainbow," of the most savage description, which would attack any jockey courageous enough to mount him by seizing him by the leg with his teeth, and dragging him from the saddle. A friend of the Colonel's told him that he knew a person who could cure Rainbow, and a wager of £1,000 was laid on the matter. Con Sullivan, who was known throughout the countryside as " The Whisperer " was sent for, and after being shut up alone with the animal for a quarter of an hour, he gave the signal for the admission of those who had been waiting on the result. When they entered, they found the horse extended on his back, playing like a kitten with Sullivan, who was quietly sitting by him ; but both horse and operator appeared exhausted, and the latter had to be revived with brandy. The horse was perfectly tame and gentle from that day. Another savage steed named " King Pippin " took an entire night to cure, but in the morning he was seen following Sullivan like a dog, lying down at the word of command, and permitting any person to put his hand into his mouth. Shortly afterwards he won a race at the Curragh. Sullivan is described by one who knew him well as an ignorant rustic of the lower class, but there can be no question as to his extraordinary powers.

The statement of Sullivan is probably correct, that the successful whisperer is not acquainted with the secret of his own power. " The reason," says Rich, " is obvious. A force proceeding immediately from the will or the instinctive life would be impaired by reflection in the understanding and broken up or at least diminished by one half. The violent trembling of the animal under this operation is like the creaking and shivering of the tables before they begin to ' tip,' and indicates a moral or nervous force acting physically, by projection perhaps from the spirit of the operator. None of these cases are, after all, more wonderful than the movement of our own limbs and bodies by mental force, for how does it move them with such ease ? And may not the same power that places its strong but invisible little fingers on every point of our muscular frames, stretch its myriad arms a little further into the sphere around us, and operate by the same laws, and with as much ease, on the stalwart frame of a horse, or even a clothes-horse ? "

House of Light : (*See* Babylonia.)

House of Washing : (*See* Babylonia.)

House of Wisdom : The *tarik* or " path " of the *House of Wisdom* was founded by Moslem mystics at Cairo in the ninth century, and had seven initiatory degrees. The original founder appears to have been one Abdallah, a Persian, who, believing in the Gnostic doctrine of the Aeons or Sephiroths, applied the system to the successors of Mohammed, stating that Ismael was the founder of his *tarik* and one of his descendants as the seventh Imaum. He established an active system of propaganda and sent missionaries far and wide. He was succeeded in his office as chief of the society by his son and grandson. After the institution had been in existence for some time it was transferred to Cairo, and assemblies were held twice a week, when all the members appeared clothed in white. They were gradually advanced through the seven degrees of which the *tarik* consisted, and over which a *Dai-al-doat* or " Missionary of missionaries " presided. A later chief, Hakem-bi-emir-Illah, increased the degrees to nine, and in 1004 erected a stately home for the society, which he elaborately furnished with mathematical instruments. As the institution did not meet with the approval of the authorities, it was destroyed in 1123 by the then Grand Vizier, but meetings continued elsewhere. The officers of the society were :—*Sheik, Dai-el-keber,* or Deputy, *Dai,* or Master, *Refik,* or Fellow, *Fedavie,* or Agent, *Lassik,* or Aspirant, *Muemini,* or Believer. The teaching was to the effect that there had been seven holy Imaums, that God had sent seven Lawgivers, who had each seven helpers, who in turn had each twelve apostles. (*See* **Assassins.**)

Houses, Twelve Planetary : (*See* **Astrology.**)

Howitt, William : A well-known English writer on spiritualism who became interested in the movement at an early stage. Besides his numerous contributions to the *Spiritual Magazine* and other periodicals, he wrote a *History of the Supernatural*, in two volumes, and translated Ennemoser's *History of Magic.* He did much to separate spiritualism from the socialistic and humanitarian doctrines with which it was confused in America.

Howling of Dogs : The howling of dogs at night presages death to those who are ill.

Huaca : Peruvian Oracle. (*See* **Divination.**)

Hudson : Photographer. (*See* **Spirit Photography.**)

Huet, Pierre-Daniel : A celebrated bishop of Avrenches, who died in 1721. One finds in his *Reminiscences* many interesting passages relating to the vampires by the Greek Archipelago. "Many strange things," he says "are told of the broucolagnes, or vampires of the Archipelago. It is said in that country that if one leads a wicked life, and dies in sin, he will appear again after death as he was wont in his lifetime, and that such a person will cause great affright among the living." *Huet* believed that the bodies of such people were abandoned to the power of the devil, who retained the soul within them for the vexation of mankind. Father Richard, a Jesuit, employed on a mission in these islands, provided *Huet* with details of many cases of vampirism. In the Island of St. Erini, the Thera of the ancients occurred one of the greatest chapters in the history of vampirism. He says that these people were tormented by vampires, that they were constantly disinterring corpses for the purpose of burning them *Huet* states that this evidence is worthy of credence as emanating from a witness of unimpeachable honesty, who has had ocular demonstrations of what he writes about. He further says that the inhabitants of these islands after the death of a person, cut off his feet, hands, nose, and ears, and they call this act *acroteriazein*. They hang all these round the elbow of the dead. It is noteworthy that the bishop appears to think that the modern Greeks may have inherited the practice of burning bodies from their fathers in classical times, and that they imagine that unless the corpse is given to the flames, all cannot be well with the soul of the deceased.

Human Nature : Spiritualistic Journal. (*See* **Spiritualism**).

Hun-Came : (*See* **Hell.**)

Hungerford, Lord : (*See* **England.**)

Huns : The ancient historians credited the Huns with a monstrous origin. They were often called *children of the devil*, because it was said that they were born of a union between demons and hideous witches, the latter cast out of their own county by Philimer, king of the Goths, and his army. The old writers state that the Huns were of horrible deformity, and could not be mistaken for anything but the children of demons. Besoldus, following Servin, claims that their name of *Huns* comes from a Celtic or barbaric word signifying *great magicians*. Many stories are told of their magic prowess, and of their raising spectres to assist them in battle.

Hydromancy : Divination by water, is said by Natalis Comes to have been the invention of Nereus, and according to Delrio, a most respectable authority in these matters, it is a method of divination than which *nulla fæcundior imposturis*. Iamblichus, he says, mentions one kind of *hydromancy* tó which the Emperor Andronicus Comnenus had recourse ; not in person, for regard for his character (a character richly demanding such caution !) forbade this humiliation. This worthy applied to Sethos, a diviner, who from his youth upward had been addicted to magic, and on that account had been deprived of sight by the Emperor Manuel. The question proposed by *hydromancy* was, who was to be the successor of Andronicus, a doubt which grievously perplexed the superstitious tyrant, and left him in hesitation as to the fittest victim whom his suspicious vengeance might first sacrifice. The evil spirit when summoned, showed upon the water the letters S.I., and upon being asked at what time the person so designated should succeed, he replied, before the Feast of the exalta-

tion of the Cross. His prediction was verified, for, within the time named, Isaac Angelus had thrown Andronicus to be torn in pieces by the infuriated populace of Constantinople. It should be remembered here that the devil spells, as he repeats the Lord's Prayer, not in the natural order, but backwards. S.I., when inverted, would fairly enough represent Isaac, according to all laws of magic.

The same story is related with great spirit by Nicetas. The arts with which the tempter cheats the ear of his votary are vividly displayed, and there is one very picturesque touch, when the fiend is asked respecting time, which we are surprised should have escaped Delrio, who evidently borrows from this source, though he refers to Iamblichus. The annalist has already remarked that he neither knows, nor indeed wishes to know, the method of practising hydromancy, but Delrio, on the contrary, describes several kinds. In one a ring was suspended by a thread in a vessel of water, and this being shaken, a judgment was formed according to the strokes of the ring against the sides of the vessel. In a second, three pebbles were thrown into standing water, and observations were drawn from the circles which they formed. A third depended upon the agitations of the sea, whence the learned Jesuit deduces a custom prevalent among the Oriental Christians of annually baptizing that element ; at the same time taking especial care to show that the betrothment of the Adriatic by the Doge of Venice has a widely different origin. A fourth divination was taken from the colour of water, and certain figures appearing in it, which Varro says afforded numerous prognostics of the event of the Mithridatic War. But this branch was of sufficient importance to deserve a separate name, and we read accordingly of divination by fountains, these being the waters most frequently consulted. Among the most celebrated fountains for this purpose were those of Palicorus in Sicily, which invariably destroyed the criminal who ventured to adjure them falsely in testimony of his innocence. A full account of their usage and virtue is given by Macrobius. Pausanias has described a fountain near Epidaurus, dedicated to Ino, into which on her festival, certain loaves were wont to be thrown. It was a favourable omen to the applicant if these offerings were retained ; on the other hand, most unlucky if they were washed up again. So, also, Tiberius cast golden dice into the fountain of Apomus, near Padua, where they long remained as a proof of the imperial monster's good fortune in making the highest throw. Several other instances of divining springs may be found collected by the diligence of Boissard ; and to a belief in them Delrio thinks a custom of the ancient Germans is referable, who threw their new-born children into the Rhine, with a conviction that if they were spurious they would sink, if legitimate they would swim. In a fifth method, certain mysterious words were pronounced over a cup full of water, and observations were made upon its spontaneous ebullition. In a sixth, a drop of oil was let fall on water in a glass vessel, and this furnished as it were a mirror upon which many wonderful objects became visible. This, says Delrio, is the *Modus Fessanus*. Clemens Alexandrinus is cited for a seventh kind, in which the women of Germany watched the sources, whirls, and courses of rivers, with a view to prophetic interpretation ;. the same fact is mentioned by Vives in his *Commentary upon St. Augustine*. In modern Italy, continues the learned Jesuit, diviners are still to be found who write the names of any three persons suspected of theft upon a like number of little balls, which they throw into the water and some go to so profane an extent as to abuse even holy water for this most unsanctified purpose. Boissard, as cited above, has explained more fully than Delrio two of these methods of *hydromancy*, that by the ring suspended in a vessel of water, and the method by its spontaneous ebullition. A very similar account is given by Wierus.

In a fragment of Varro's book, *de Cultu Deorum*, the practice of *hydromancy* is attributed to Numa. Upon this statement St. Augustine has commented in the passage to which we have already referred, and he mentions that the practice of *hydromancy* was attributed by Varro to the Persians, and afterwards to the philosopher Pythagoras. Strabo in like manner has ascribed the practice to the Persians.

Hydromancy is, in principle, the same thing as divination by the crystal or mirror, and in ancient times a natural basin of rock kept constantly full by a running stream, was a favourite medium. The double meaning of the word " reflection " ought here to be considered, and how gazing down into clear water, the mind is disposed to self-retirement and to contemplation, deeply tinctured with melancholy. Rocky pools and glomy lakes figure in all stories of witchcraft—witness the Craic-pol-nain in the Highland woods of Laynchork ; the Devil's Glen in the county of Wicklow, Ireland ; the Swedish Blokula ; the witch mountains of Italy ; and the Bibiagora, between Hungary and Poland. Similar resorts in the glens of Germany were marked, as Tacitus mentions, by salt springs ; for this again there was an additional good reason, which would carry us far from the present subject to explain.

It was really only another form of divination by the gloomy water pool that attracted so much public attention at that time, when Mr. Lane, in his work on *Modern Egypt* testified to its success as practised in Egypt and Hindostan. That gentleman having resolved to witness the performance of this species of sorcery, the magician commenced his operations by writing forms of invocation to his familiar spirits on six slips of paper, a chafing dish with some live charcoal in it was procured, and a boy summoned who had not yet reached the age of puberty. Mr. Lane inquired who were the persons that could see in the fluid mirror, and was told that they were a boy not arrived at puberty, a virgin, a black female slave, and a pregnant woman. To prevent any collusion between the sorcerer and the boy, Mr. Lane sent his servant to take the first boy he met. When all was prepared, the sorcerer threw some incense and one of the strips of paper into the chafing-dish ; he then took hold of the boy's right hand, and drew a square with some mystical marks on the palm ; in the centre of the square he poured a little ink, which formed the magic mirror, and desired the boy to look steadily into it without raising his head. In this mirror the boy declared that he saw, successively, a man sweeping, seven men with flags, an army pitching its tents, and the various officers of state attending on the Sultan. The rest must be told by Mr. Lane himself.

" The sorcerer now addressed himself to me, and asked me if I wished the boy to see any person who was absent or dead. I named Lord Nelson, of whom the boy had evidently never heard, for it was with much difficulty that he pronounced the name after several trials. The magician desired the boy to say to the Sultan, ' My master salutes thee and desires thee to bring Lord Nelson ; bring him before my eyes that I may see him speedily.' The boy then said so, and almost immediately added, ' A messenger has gone and brought back a man dressed in a black (or rather, dark blue) suit of European clothes ; the man has lost his left arm.' He then paused for a moment or two, and looking more intently and more closely into the ink, said ' No, he has not lost his left arm, but it is placed on his breast.' This correction made his description more striking than it had been without it ; since Lord Nelson generally had his empty sleeve attached to the breast of his coat ; but it was the right arm that he had lost. With

out saying that I suspected the boy had made a mistake, I asked the magician whether the objects appeared in the ink as if actually before the eyes, or as if in a glass, which makes the right appear left. He answered that they appeared as in a mirror. This rendered the boy's description faultless. Though completely puzzled, I was somewhat disappointed with his performances, for they fell short of what he had accomplished in many instances in presence of certain of my friends and countrymen. On one of these occasions an Englishman present ridiculed the performance, and said that nothing would satisfy him but a correct description of the appearance of his own father, of whom he was sure no one of the company had any knowledge. The boy, accordingly, having called by name for the person alluded to, described a man in a Frank dress, with his hand placed on his head, wearing spectacles, and with one foot on the ground and the other raised behind him, as if he were stepping down from a seat. The description was exactly true in every respect ; the peculiar position of the hand was occasioned by an almost constant headache, and that of the foot or leg by a stiff knee, caused by a fall from a horse in hunting. On another occasion Shakespeare was described with the most minute exactness, both as to person and dress, and I might add several other cases in which the same magician has excited astonishment in the sober minds of several Englishmen of my acquaintance." So far Mr. Lane, whose account may be compared with that given by Mr. Kinglake, the author of *Eöthen*.

It may be worth adding, that in another case of *hydromancy* known to Elihu Rich, the boy could see better without the medium than with it—though he could also see reflected images in a vessel of water. This fact may be admitted to prove that such images are reflected to the eye of the seer from his own mind and brain ; how the brain becomes thus enchanted, or the eye disposed for vision, is another question ; certainly it is no proof that the recollected image in the mind of the inquirer is transferred to the seer, as proofs can be shown to the contrary.

Hyena : A many-coloured stone, taken from the eye of the animal so called. Put under the tongue, it enables its possessor to foretell future events. It cures the gout and quartan ague.

Hyle : The name given by the Gnostics to one of the three degrees in the progress of spirits.

Hyperæsthesia : An actual or apparent exaltation of the perceptive faculties, characteristic of the hypnotic state. The smallest suggestion, whether given by word, look, gesture, or even breathing or unconscious movement, is instantly seized upon and interpreted by the entranced subject, who for this reason is often termed " sensitive." The phenomenon of *hyperæsthesia*, observed but wrongly interpreted by the early magnetists and mesmerists, was largely responsible for the so-called clairvoyance, thought-reading, community of sensation, and other kindred phenomena. The realisation of suggestion and *hyperæsthesia* was the great achievement of Bertrand and Braid, which brought hypnotism into the domain of scientific fact. The significance of *hyperæsthesia* in connection with every form of psychic phenomena can hardly be over estimated. Nor is it met with only in the trance state. It enters into the normal existence to an extent that is but imperfectly understood. Dreams, for instance, frequently reproduce impressions which have been recorded in some obscure stratum of consciousness, while much that we call intuition is made up of inferences subconsciously drawn from indications too subtle to reach the normal consciousness. *Hyperæsthesia* has been defined above as " an actual or *apparent* exaltation of the perceptive faculties." The reason for this is that modern scientists declare that it is not known whether the senses are actually sharpened or not. Most probably the *hyperæsthetic* perception is merely a normal perception which by reason of the state of cerebral dissociation operates in a free field. Very slight sense-impressions may be recorded in the brain during normal consciousness, but such is the inhibiting effect of the excitement occasioned by other similar impressions, that they do not reach full consciousness.

Hypnosis : (*See* **Hypnotism**).

Hypnotism : A peculiar state of cerebral dissociation distinguished by certain marked symptoms, the most prominent and invariable of which is a highly-increased suggestibility in the subject. The hypnotic state may be induced in a very large percentage of normal individuals, or may occur spontaneously. It is recognised as having an affinity with normal sleep, and likewise with a variety of abnormal conditions, among which may be mentioned somnambulism, ecstasy, and the trances of Hindu fakirs and savage medicine-men. In fact, in one or other of their forms, hypnosis and its kindred have been known in practically all countries and all times.

Hypnotism is no longer classed with the occult sciences. It has gained, though only within comparatively recent years, a definite scientific status, and no mean place in legitimate medicine. Nevertheless its history is inextricably interwoven with occultism, and even to-day much hypnotic phenomena is classed as " spiritualistic " ; so that the consideration of *hypnotism* in this place is very necessary to a proper understanding of much of the occult science of our own and former times.

The Early Magnetists.—So far back as the 16th century hypnotic phenomena were observed and studied by men of science, who attributed them to *magnetism*, an effluence radiating from every object in the universe, in a greater or less degree, and through which all objects might exercise a mutual influence one on another. From this doctrine was constructed the " sympathetic " system of medicine, by means of which the magnetic effluence of the planets, the actual magnet, or of the physician, was brought to bear upon the patient. Paracelsus is generally supposed to be the originator of the sympathetic system, as he was its most powerful exponent. Of the magnet he says :—

" The magnet has long lain before all eyes, and no one has ever thought whether it was of any further use, or whether it possessed any other property, than that of attracting iron. The sordid doctors throw it in my face that I will not follow the ancients ; but in what should I follow them ? All that they have said of the magnet amounts to nothing. Lay that which I have said of it in the balance, and judge. Had I blindly followed others, and had I not myself made experiments, I should in like manner know nothing more than what every peasant sees—that it attracts iron. But a wise man must enquire for himself, and it is thus that I have discovered that the magnet, besides this obvious and to every man visible power, that of attracting iron, possesses another and concealed power." —That of healing the sick.

And there is no doubt that cures were actually effected by Paracelsus with the aid of the magnet, especially in cases of epilepsy and nervous affections. Yet the word "magnet" is most frequently used by Paracelsus and his followers in a figurative sense, to denote the *magnes microcosmi*, man himself, who was supposed to be a reproduction in miniature of the earth, having, like it, his poles and magnetic properties From the stars and planets, he taught, came a very subtle effluence which affected man's mind or intellect, while earthly substances radiated a grosser emanation which affected his body. The human mummy especially was a " magnet " well suited for remedial purposes, since it draws to itself the diseases and poisonous properties of other substances. The most

effective mummy was that of a criminal who had been hanged, and it was applied in the following manner. " If a person suffer from disease, " says Paracelsus, " either local or general, experiment with the following remedy. Take a magnet impregnated with mummy, and combined with rich earth. In this earth sow some seeds that have a likeness to, or homogeneity with, the disease ; then let this earth, well sifted and mixed with mummy, be laid in an earthen vessel, and let the seeds committed to it be watered daily with a lotion in which the diseased limb or body has been washed. Thus will the disease be transplanted from the human body to the seeds which are in the earth. Having done this, transplant the seeds from the earthen vessel to the ground, and wait till they begin to flourish into herbs. As they increase, the disease will diminish, and when they have reached their mature growth, will altogether disappear." The quaint but not altogether illogical idea of " weapon-salve "—anointing the weapon instead of the wound—was also used by Paracelsus, his theory being that part of the vital spirits clung to the weapon and exercised an ill effect on the vital spirits in the wound, which would not heal until the ointment had first been applied to the weapon ; this also was an outcome of the magnetic theory.

Towards the end of the 16th century Paracelsus was worthily succeeded by J. B. van Helmont, a scientist of distinction and an energetic protagonist of magnetism. " Material nature," he writes, " draws her forms through constant magnetism from above, and implores for them the favour of heaven ; and as heaven, in like manner, draws something invisible from below, there is established a free and mutual intercourse, and the whole is contained in an individual." Van Helmont believed also in the power of the will to direct the subtle fluid. There was, he held, in all created things. a magic or celestial power through which they were allied to heaven. This power or strength is greatest in the soul of man, resides in a less degree in his body, and to some extent is present in the lower animals, plants, and inorganic matter. It is by reason of his superior endowment in this respect that man is enabled to rule the other creatures, and to make use of inanimate objects for his own purposes. The power is strongest when one is asleep, for then the body is quiescent, and the soul most active and dominant ; and for this reason dreams and prophetic visions are more common in sleep. " The spirit," he says, " is everywhere diffused, and the spirit is the medium of magnetism ; not the spirits of heaven and of hell, but the spirit of man, which is concealed in him as the fire is concealed in the flint. The human will makes itself master of a portion of its spirit of life, which becomes a connecting property between the corporeal and the incorporeal, and diffuses itself like the light." To this ethereal spirit he ascribes the visions seen by " the inner man " in ecstasy, and also those of the " outer man " and the lower animals. In proof of the mutual influence of living creatures he asserts that men may kill animals merely by staring hard at them for a quarter of an hour. That Van Helmont was not ignorant of the power of imagination is evident from many of his writings. A common needle, he declares, may by means of certain manipulations, and the will-power and imaginations of the operator, be made to possess magnetic properties. Herbs may become very powerful through the imagination of him who gathers them. And again :— " I have hitherto avoided revealing the great secret, that the strength lies concealed in man, merely through the suggestion and power of the imagination to work outwardly, and to impress this strength on others, which then continues of itself, and operates on the remotest objects. Through this secret alone will all receive its true illumination—

all that has hitherto been brought together laboriously of the ideal being out of the spirit—all that has been said of the magnetism of all things—of the strength of the human soul—of the magic of man, and of his dominion over the physical world." Van Helmont also gave special importance to the stomach as the chief seat of the soul, and recounts an experience of his own in which, on touching some aconite with his tongue, he finds all his senses transferred to his stomach. In after years this was to be a favourite accomplishment of somnambules and cataleptic subjects. (*See* **Stomach, Seeing with.**)

A distinguished English magnetist was Robert Fludd, who wrote in the first part of the 17th century. Fludd was an exponent of the microcosmic theory, and a believer in the magnetic effluence from man. Not only were these emanations able to cure bodily diseases, but they also affected the moral sentiments ; for if radiations from two individuals were, on meeting, flung back or distorted, negative magnetism, or antipathy resulted, whereas if the radiations from each person passed freely into those from the other, the result was positive magnetism, or sympathy. Examples of positive and negative magnetism were also to be found among the lower animals and among plants. Another magnetist of distinction was the Scottish physician, Maxwell, who is said to have anticipated much of Mesmer's doctrine. He declares that those who are familiar with the operation of the universal spirit can, through its agency cure all diseases, at no matter what distance. He also suggests that the practice of magnetism, though very valuable in the hand of a well-disposed physician, is not without its dangers, and is liable to many abuses.

While the theoretical branch of magnetism was thus receiving attention at the hands of the alchemical philosophers, the practical side was by no means neglected. There were in the seventeenth and eighteenth centuries a number of " divine healers," whose magic cures were without doubt the result of hypnotic suggestion. Of these perhaps the best known and most successful were Valentine Greatrakes, an Irishman, and a Swabian priest named Gassner. Greatrakes was born in 1628, and on reaching manhood served for some time in the Irish army, thereafter settling down on his estate in Waterford. In 1662 he had a dream in which it was revealed to him that he possessed the gift of curing king's evil. The dream was repeated several times ere he paid heed to it, but at length he made the experiment, his own wife being the first to be healed by him. Many who came to him from the surrounding country were cured when he laid his hands upon them. Later the impression came upon him strongly that he could cure other diseases besides king's evil. News of his wonderful powers spread far and wide, and patients came in hundreds to seek his aid. Despite the fact that the Bishop of the Diocese forbade the exercise of these apparently magical powers, Greatrakes continued to heal the afflicted people who sought him. In 1666 he proceeded to London, and though not invariably successful, he seems to have performed there a surprising number of cures, which were testified to by Robert Boyle, Sir William Smith, Andrew Marvell, and many other eminent people. He himself describes them in a work entitled " Val. Greatrakes, Esq., of Waterford, in the kingdom of Ireland, famous for curing several diseases and distempers by the stroak of his hand only : London, 1660." His method of healing was to stroke the affected part with his hand, thus driving the disease into the limbs and so finally out of the body. Sometimes the treatment acted as though by magic, but if immediate relief was not obtained the rubbing was continued, and but few cases were dismissed as incurable. Even epidemic diseases he healed by a touch. It is said that during the treatment the patient's fingers and toes

remained insensible to external stimuli, and frequently he himself showed every symptom of such a magnetic crisis as was afterwards to become a special feature of mesmeric treatment. Personally Greatrakes was a simple and pious gentleman, persuaded that his marvellous powers were a divinely-bestowed gift, and most anxious to make the best use of them. The other healer mentioned, Gassner, belongs to a somewhat later period—about the middle of the eighteenth century. Gassner was a priest of Bludenz in Vorarlberg, where his many cures gained for him a wide celebrity. All diseases, according to him, were caused by evil spirits possessing the patient, and his mode of healing thus consisted of exorcising the demons. He too was a man of kindly disposition and piety, and made a large use of the Scriptures in his healing operations. The ceremony of exorcism was a rather impressive one. Herr Gassner sat at a table, the patient and spectators in front of him, A blue red-flowered cloak hung from his shoulders ; the rest of his clothing, we are told, was " clean, simple, and modest." On his left was a window, on his right, the crucifix. His fine personality, deep learning, and noble character inspired the faith of the patient and his friends and doubtless played no small part in his curative feats. Sometimes he made use of magnetic manipulations, stroking or rubbing the affected part, and driving the disease, after the manner of Greatrakes, into the limbs of the patient. The formula of exorcism he generally pronounced in Latin, with which language the demons showed a perfect familiarity. Not only could he control sickness by these means, but the passions also were amenable to his treatment. " Now anger is apparent, now patience, now joy, now sorrow, now hate, now love, now confusion, now reason,—each carried to the highest pitch. Now this one is blind, now he sees, and again is deprived of sight, etc." These curious results suggest the phreno-magnetism of later years, where equally sudden changes of mood were produced by touching with the finger-tips those parts of the subject's head which phrenology associated with the various emotions to be called forth.

Hitherto it will be seen that the rational and supernatural explanations of magnetism had run parallel with one another, the former most in favour with the philosophers, the latter with the populace. It was reserved for Emanuel Swedenborg (q.v.) (1688–1772), the Swedish philosopher and spiritualist, to unite the doctrine of magnetism with that of spiritualism—*i.e.*, the belief in the action in the external world of the discarnate spirits of deceased human beings. That Swedenborg accepted some of the theories of the older magnetists is evident from his mystical writings, from which the following passage has been extracted.

" In order to comprehend the origin and progress of this influence (*i.e.*, God's influence over man), we must first know that that which proceeds from the Lord is the divine sphere which surrounds us, and fills the spiritual and natural world. All that proceeds from an object, and surrounds and clothes it, is called its sphere.

" As all that is spiritual knows neither time nor space, it therefore follows that the general sphere or the divine one has extended itself from the first moment of creation to the last. This divine emanation, which passed over from the spiritual to the natural, penetrates actively and rapidly through the whole created world, to the last grade of it, where it is yet to be found, and produces and maintains all that is animal, vegetable, and mineral. Man is continually surrounded by a sphere of his favourite propensities ; these unite themselves to the natural sphere of his body, so that together they form one. The natural sphere surrounds every body of nature, and all the objects of the three kingdoms. Thus it allies itself to the spiritual world. This is the foundation of sympathy and antipathy, of union and separation, according to which there are amongst spirits presence and absence.

" The angel said to me that the sphere surrounded man more lightly on the back than on the breast, where it was thicker and stronger. This sphere of influence peculiar to man operates also in general and in particular around him by means of the will, the understanding, and the practice.

" The sphere proceeding from God, which surrounds man and constitutes his strength, while it thereby operates on his neighbour and on the whole creation, is a sphere of peace, and innocence ; for the Lord is peace and innocence. Then only is man consequently able to make his influence effectual on his fellow man, when peace and innocence rule in his heart, and he himself is in union with heaven. This spiritual union is connected with the natural by a benevolent man through the touch and the laying on of hands, by which the influence of the inner man is quickened, prepared, and imparted. The body communicates with others which are about it through the body, and the spiritual influence diffuses itself chiefly through the hands, because these are the most outward or *ultimum* of man ; and through him, as in the whole of nature, the first is contained in the last, as the cause in the effect. The whole soul and the whole body are contained in the hands as a medium of influence."

Mesmerism or Animal Magnetism.—In the latter half of the eighteenth century a new era was inaugurated in connection with the doctrine of a magnetic fluid. The fresh impetus which the science of magnetism received at that period was due in a very large measure to the works of Franz Antoine Mesmer (q.v.), a physician from whose name the word " mesmerism " was taken. He was born at Wiel, near Lake Constance, in 1733, and studied medicine at the University of Vienna, taking his doctor's degree in 1766. In the same year he published his first work, *De Planetarum Influxu* (" De l'influence des Planettes sur le corps humain "). Though he claimed to have thereby discovered the existence of a universal fluid, to which he gave the name of *magnétisme animal*, there is no doubt that his doctrine was in many respects identical with that of the older magnetists mentioned above. The idea of the universal fluid was suggested to him in the first place by his observation of the stars, which led him to believe the celestial bodies exercised a mutual influence on each other and on the earth. This he identified with magnetism, and it was but a step—and a step which had already been taken by the early magnetists—to extend this influence to the human body and all other objects, and to apply it to the science of medicine. In 1776 Mesmer met with Gassner, the Swabian priest whose miraculous cures have already been considered ; and, setting aside the supernatural explanation offered by the healer himself, Mesmer declared that the cures and severe crises which followed on his manipulations were attributable to nothing but magnetism. Nevertheless this encounter gave a new trend to his ideas. Hitherto he himself had employed the magnet in order to cure the sick, but seeing that Gassner dispensed with that aid, he was led to consider whether the power might not reside in a still greater degree in the human body. Mesmer's first cure was performed on an epileptic patient, by means of magnets, but the honour of it was disputed by a Jesuit named Hell, who had supplied the magnetic plates, and who claimed to have discovered the principles on which the physician worked. Thereafter for a few years Mesmer practised in various European cities, and strove to obtain recognition for his theories, but without success. In 1778 however, he went to Paris, and there attained an immediate and triumphant success in the fashionable world, though the learned bodies still refused to have angthing to say to

him. Aristocratic patients flocked in hundreds to Mesmer's consulting-rooms, which were hung with mirrors, it being one of the physicians' theories that mirrors augmented the magnetic fluid. He himself wore, it is said, a shirt of leather, lined with silk, to prevent the escape of the fluid, while magnets were hung about his person to increase his natural supply of magnetism. The patients were seated round a *baguet* or magnetic tub, of which the following description is given by Seifert, one of Mesmer's biographers.

" This receptacle was a large pan, tub, or pool of water, filled with various magnetic substances, such as water, sand, stone, glass bottles (filled with magnetic water), etc. It was a focus within which the magnetism was concentrated, and out of which proceeded a number of conductors. These being bent pointed iron wands, one end was retained in the *baguet*, whilst the other was connected with the patient and applied to the seat of the disease. This arrangement might be made use of by any number of persons seated round the *baguet*, and thus a fountain, or any receptacle in a garden, as in a room, would answer for the purpose desired." For the establishment of a school of *Animal Magnetism* Mesmer was offered 20,000 livres by the French government, with an annual sum of 10,000 livres for its upkeep ; but this he refused. Later, however, the sum of 340,000 livres was subscribed by prospective pupils, and handed over to him. One of Mesmer's earliest and most distiguished disciples was M. D'Eslon, a prominent physician, who laid the doctrines of animal magnatism before the Faculty of Medicine in 1780. Consideration of Mesmer's theories was, however, indignantly refused, and D'Eslon warned to rid himself of such dangerous doctrine. Another disciple of Mesmer who attained to distinction in magnetic practise was the Marquis de Puységur, who was the first to observe and describe the state of induced somnambulism now as well known as the hypnotic trance. It has been suggested, and seems not improbable, that Mesmer himself knew something of the induced trance, but believing it to be a state full of danger, steadfastly set his face against it. However that may be, Puységur's ideas on the subject began to supersede those of Mesmer, and he gathered about him a distinguished body of adherents, among whom was numbered the celebrated Lavater. Indeed, his recognition of the fact that the symptoms attending the " magnetic sleep " were resultant from it, was a step of no small importance in the history of mesmerism. In 1784 a commission was appointed by the French government to enquire into the magnetic phenomena. For some reason or another its members chose to investigate the experiments of D'Eslon, rather than those of Mesmer himself. The commissioners, including among their number Benjamin Franklin, Lavoisier, and Bailly, observed the peculiar crises attending the treatment, and the *rapport* between patient and physician, but decided that imagination could produce all the effects, and that there was no evidence whatever for a magnetic fluid. The report, edited by M. Bailly, gives the following description of the crisis.

" The sick persons, arranged in great numbers, and in several rows around the *baquet* (bath), received the magnetism by means of the iron rods, which conveyed it to them from the *baquet* by the cords wound round their bodies, by the thumb which connected them with their neighbours, and by the sounds of a pianoforte, or an agreeable voice, diffusing magnetism in the air.

" The patients were also directly magnetised by means of the finger and wand of the magnetiser, moved slowly before their faces, above or behind their heads, or on the diseased parts.

" The magnetiser acts also by fixing his eyes on the subjects ; by the application of his hands on the region of the solar plexus ; an application which sometimes continues for hours.

" Meanwhile the patients present a very varied picture.

" Some are calm, tranquil, and experience no effect. Others cough and spit, feel pains, heat, or perspiration. Others, again, are convulsed.

" As soon as one begins to be convulsed, it is remarkable that others are immediately affected.

" The commissioners have observed some of these convulsions last more than three hours. They are often accompanied with expectorations of a violent character, often streaked with blood. The convulsions are marked with involuntary motions of the throat, limbs, and sometimes the whole body ; by dimness of the eyes, shrieks, sobs, laughter, and the wildest hysteria. These states are often followed by languor and depression. The smallest noise appears to aggravate the symptoms, and often to occasion shudderings and terrible cries. It was noticeable that a sudden change in the air or time of the music had a great influence on the patients, and soothed or accelerated the convulsions, stimulating them to ecstasy, or moving them to floods of tears.

" Nothing is more astonishing than the spectacle of these convulsions.

" One who has not seen them can form no idea of them. The spectator is as much astonished at the profound repose of one portion of the patients as at the agitation of the rest.

" Some of the patients may be seen rushing towards each other with open arms, and manifesting every symptom of attachment and affection.

" All are under the power of the magnetizer ; it matters not what state of drowsiness they may be in, the sound of his voice, a look, a motion of his hands, spasmodically affects them."

Though Mesmer, Puységur, and their followers continued to practise magnetic treatment, the report of the royal commission had the effect of quenching public interest in the subject, though from time to time a spasmodic interest in it was shown by scientists. M. de Jussieu, at about the time the commission presented its report, suggested that it would have done well to enquire into the reality of the alleged cures, and to endeavour to find a satisfactory explanation for the phenomena they had witnessed ; while to remedy the deficiency he himself formulated a theory of " animal heat," an organic emanation which might be directed by the human will. Like Mesmer and the others, he believed in action at a distance.

Mesmeric practitioners formed themselves into " Societies of Harmony," until the political situation in France rendered their existence impossible. Early in the nineteenth century Pététin and Delenze published works on magnetism. But a new era was inaugurated with the publication in 1823 of Alexandre Bertrand's *Traité du Somnambulisme*, followed three years later by a treatise *Du Magnétisme Animal en France*. Bertrand was a young physician of Paris, and to him belongs the honour of having discovered the important part played by suggestion in the phenomena of the induced trance. He had observed the connection between the magnetic sleep, epidemic ecstasy, and spontaneous sleep-walking, and declared that all the cures and strange symptoms which had formerly been attributed to " animal magnetism," " animal electricity," and the like, resulted from the suggestions of the operator acting on the imagination of a patient whose suggestibility was greatly increased. It is probable that had he lived longer—he died in 1831, at the age of thirty-six—Bertrand would have gained a definite scientific standing for the facts of the induced trance ; but as it was the practitioners of animal magnetism still held to the

theory of a fluid or force radiating from magnetizer to subject, while those who were unable to accept such a doctrine, ignored the matter altogether, or treated it as vulgar fraud and charlatanry. Nevertheless Bertrand's works and experiments revived the flagging interest of the public to such an extent that in 1831 a second French commission was appointed by the Royal Academy of Medicine. The report of this commission was not forthcoming till more than five years had elapsed, but when it was finally published it contained a definite testimony to the genuineness of the magnetic phenomena, and especially of the somnambulic state ; and declared that the commission was satisfied of the therapeutic value of " animal magnetism." The report was certainly not of great scientific worth. The name of Bertrand is not even mentioned therein, nor his theory considered ; on the other hand, a good deal of space is given to the more supernatural phenomena. clairvoyance, action at a distance, and the prediction by somnambulic patients of crises in their maladies. This is the more excusable, however, since these ideas were almost universally associated with somnambulism. Community of sensation (q.v.) was held to be a feature of the trance state, as was also the transference of the senses to the stomach—(*See* **Stomach, seeing with**), while thought-transference was suggested by some of these earlier investigators, notably by Deleuze, who suggested that thoughts were conveyed from the brain of the operator to that of the subject through the medium of the subtle magnetic fluid. Meanwhile the spiritualistic theory was becoming more and more frequently advanced to explain the " magnetic " phenomena, including both the legitimate trance phenomena and the multitude of supernormal phenomena which was supposed to follow the somnambulic state. This will doubtless account in part for the extraordinary animosity which the medical profession showed towards animal magnetism as a therapeutic agency. Its anæsthetic properties they ridiculed as fraud or imagination, notwithstanding that serious operations, even of the amputation of limbs, could be performed while the patient was in the magnetic sleep. Thus Dr. John Elliotson was forced to resign his professorship at the University College Hospital ; Dr. James Esdaile, a surgeon who practised at a government hospital at Calcutta, had to contend with much ignorance and stupid conservatism in his professional brethren ; and similar contemptuous treatment was dealt out to other medical men, against whom nothing could be urged but their defence of mesmerism. In 1841 James Braid, a Manchester surgeon, arrived independently at the conclusions which Bertrand had reached some eighteen years earlier. Once more the theory of abnormal suggestibility was offered to explain the various phenomena of the so-called " magnetic " sleep ; and once more it was utterly ignored, alike by the world of science and by the public. Braid's explanation was essentially that which is offered now. He placed the new science—hypnotism, he called it, on a level with other natural sciences, above the mass of mediæval magic and superstition in which he had found it. Yet even Braid does not seem to have entirely separated the chaff from the grain, for we find him countenancing the practice of phreno-magnetism (q.v.), a combination of mesmerism and phrenology wherein the entranced patient. whose head is touched by the operator's fingers, exhibits every sign of the emotion or quality associated with the phrenological organ touched. Braid asserts that a subject, entirely ignorant of the position of the phrenological organs, passed rapidly and accurately from one emotion to another, according to the portion of the scalp in contact with the hypnotist's fingers. His physiological explanation is a somewhat inadequate one, and we can only suppose that he was not fully appreciative of his own theory of suggestion. In 1843 two periodicals dealing with magnetism appeared—the *Zoist*, edited by Dr. Elliotson and a colleague, and the *Phreno-Magnet*, edited by Spencer T. Hall. The first, adopting a scientific tone, treated the subject mainly from a therapeutic point of view, while the latter was of a more popular character. Many of the adherents of both papers, and notably Elliotson himself, afterwards became spiritualists. In 1845 an additional impetus was given to animal magnetism by the publication in that year of Baron von Reichenbach's researches. Reichenbach claimed to have discovered a new force, which he called *odyle*, *od*, or *odylic force*, and which could be seen in the form of flames by "sensitives." In the human being these emanations might be seen to radiate from the finger-tips, while they were also visible in animals and inanimate things. Different colours issued from the different poles of the magnet. Reichenbach experimented by putting his sensitives in a dark room with various objects—crystals, precious stones, magnets, minerals, plants, animals—when they could unerringly distinguish each object by the colour and size of the flame visible to their clairvoyant eye. These emanations were so invariable and so permanent that an artist might paint them, and this, indeed, was frequently done. Feelings of temperature, of heat or cold, were also experienced in connection with the odylic force. Baron von Reichenbach's experiments were spread over a number of years, and were made with every appearance of scientific care and precision, so that their effect on the mesmerists of the time was very considerable. But notwithstanding the mass of dubious phenomena which was associated with hypnotism at that time, there is no doubt but that the induced trance, with its therapeutic and anæsthetic value, would soon have come into its own had not two circumstances occurred to thrust it into the background. The first was the application of chloroform and ether to the purposes for which *hypnotism* had hitherto been used, a substitution which pleased the medical faculty greatly, and relieved its members from the necessity of studying *hypnotism*. The second circumstance was the introduction of the movement known as modern spiritualism, which so emphasised the occult side of the trance phenomena as to obscure for nearly half a century the true significance of induced somnambulism.

Modern Views of Hypnotism.—But if the great body of medical and public opinion ignored the facts of *hypnotism* during the period following Braid's discovery, the subject did not fail to receive some attention from the more scientific portion of Europe, and from time to time investigators took upon themselves the task of enquiring into the phenomena. This was especially the case in France, where the science of mesmerism or *hypnotism* was most firmly entrenched, and where it met with least opposition. In 1858 Dr. Azam, of Bordeaux, investigated *hypnotism* from Braid's point of view, aided by a number of members of the Faculty of Paris. An account of his researches was published in 1860, but cast no new light on the matter. Later the same set of facts were examined by Mesnet, Duval, and others. In 1875 Professor Richet also studied the science of artificial somnambulism. It is, however, from Bernheim and the Nancy school that the generally accepted modern view of *hypnotism* is taken. Bernheim was himself a disciple of Liébeault, who, working on independent lines, had reached the conclusions of Bertrand and Braid and once more formulated the doctrine of suggestion. Bernheim's work *De la Suggestion*, published in 1884, embodied the theories of Liébeault and the result of Bernheim's own researches therein. According to this view, then, *hypnotism* is a purely psychological process, and is induced by mental influences. The "passes" of Mesmer and the magnetic philosophers, the elaborate preparations of the

baquet, the strokings of Valentine Greatrakes, and all the multitudinous ceremonies with which the animal magnetists were wont to produce the artificial sleep, were only of service in inducing a state of expectation in the patient, or in providing a soothing and monotonous, or violent, sensory stimulus. And so also with the modern methods of inducing *hypnosis*; the fixation of the eyes, the contact of the operators hand, the sound of his voice, are only effective through the medium of the subject's mentality. Other investigators who played a large part in popularising *hypnotism* were Professor J. M. Charcot, of the Salpêtrière, Paris, a distinguished pathologist, and R. Heidenhain, professor of physiology at Breslau. The former taught that the hypnotic condition was essentially a morbid one, and allied to hysteria; a theory which, becoming widely circulated, exercised a somewhat detrimental effect on the practice of hypnotism for therapeutic purposes, till it was at length proved erroneous. Even now a prejudice lingers, particularly in this country, against the use of the induced hypnotic trance in medicine. Heidenhain, again, laid stress on the physical operations to induce somnambulism, believing that thereby a peculiar state of the nervous system was brought about, wherein the control of the higher nerve centres was temporarily removed, so that the suggestion of the operator was free to express itself automatically through the physical organism of the patient. The physiological theory also is somewhat misleading; nevertheless its exponents have done good work in bringing the undoubted facts of hypnosis into prominence. Besides these theories there is another which is to be met with chiefly in its native France—the old doctrine of a magnetic fluid. But it is rapidly dying out. Among the symptoms which may safely, and without reference to the supernatural, be regarded as attendant on *hypnotism* are the *rapport* between patient and operator, implicit obedience on the part of the former to the smallest suggestion, whether given verbally or by look, gesture, or any unconscious action, anæsthesia, positive and negative hallucinations, the fulfilment of post-hypnotic promises, control of organic processes and of muscles not ordinarily under voluntary control. Other phenomena which have been allied from time to time with magnetism, mesmerism, or *hypnotism*, and for which there is not the same scientific basis, are clairvoyance, telekinesia, transference of the senses from the ordinary sense-organs to some other parts of the body, usually the finger tips or the pit of the stomach, community of sensation, and the ability to commune with the dead. The majority of these, like the remarkable phenomena of phreno-magnetism, can be directly traced to the effect of suggestion on the imagination of the patient. Ignorant as were the protagonists of mesmerism with regard to the great suggestibility of the magnetised subject, it is hardly surprising that they saw new and supernormal faculties and agencies at work during the trance state. To the same ignorance of the possibilities of suggestion and hyperæsthesia may be referred the common belief that the hypnotizer can influence his subject by the power of his will alone, and secure obedience to commands which are only mentally expressed. At the same time it must be borne in mind that if the growing belief in telepathy be accepted, there is a possibility that the operation of thought transference may be more freely carried out during hypnosis, and it is notable, in this respect, that the most fruitful of the telepathic experiments conducted by psychical researchers and others have been made with hypnotized percipients. (*See* **Telepathy**.)

Among numerous explanations of the physiological conditions accompanying the hypnotic state there is one, the theory of cerebral dissociation, which is now generally accepted of science, and which may be briefly outlined as follows. The brain is composed of innumerable groups of nerve cells, all more or less closely connected with each other by means of nervous links or paths of variable resistance. Excitement of any of these groups, whether by means of impressions received through the sense organs or by the communicated activity of other groups, will, if sufficiently intense, occasion the rise into consciousness of an idea. In the normal waking state the resistance of the nervous association-paths is fairly low, so that the activity is easily communicated from one neural group to another. Thus the main idea which reaches the upper stratum of consciousness is attended by a stream of other, subconscious ideas, which has the effect of checking the primary idea and preventing its complete dominance. Now the abnormal dominance of one particular system of ideas—that suggested by the operator—together with the complete suppression of all rival systems, is the principal fact to be explained in hypnosis. To some extent the physiological process conditioning hypnosis suggests an analogy with normal sleep. When one composes himself to sleep there is a lowering of cerebral excitement and a proportionate increase in the resistance of the neural links ; and this is precisely what happens during hypnosis, the essential passivity of the subject raising the resistance of the association-paths. But in normal sleep, unless some exciting cause be present, all the neural dispositions are at rest, whereas in the latter case such a complete suspension of cerebral activities is not permitted, since the operator, by means of voice, gestures, and manipulations of the patient's limbs, keeps alive that set of impressions relating to himself. One neural disposition is thus isolated, so that any idea suggested by the operator is free to work itself out in action, without being submitted to the checks of the sub-activity of other ideas. The alienation is less or more complete according as the degree of *hypnotism* is light or heavy, but a comparatively slight raising of resistance in the neural links suffices to secure the dominance of ideas suggested by the hypnotizer. Hyperæsthesia, than which perhaps no phenomenon is more frequently mentioned in connection with the hypnotic state, really belongs to the doubtful class, since it has not yet been decided whether or no an actual sharpening or refining of the senses takes place. Alternatively it may be suggested that the accurate perception of very faint sense-impressions, which seems to furnish evidence for hyperæsthesia, merely recalls the fact that the excitement conveyed through the sensory nerve operates with extraordinary force, being freed from the restriction of sub-excitement in adjacent neural groups and systems. In accepting this view-point we concede that in normal life very feeble sensory stimuli must act on nerve and brain just as they do in hypnosis, save that in the former case they are so stifled amid a multitude of similar impressions that they fail to reach consciousness. In any case the occasional abnormal sensitiveness of the subject to very slight sensory stimuli is a fact of hypnotism as well authenticated as anæsthesia itself, and the term " hyperæsthesia," if not entirely justified, may for want of a better be practically applied to the observed phenomenon. The hypnotic state is not necessarily induced by a second person. " Spontaneous " hypnotism and " autohypnotisation " are well known to science. Certain Indian fakirs and the shamans of uncivilised races can produce in themselves a state closely approximating to hypnosis, by a prolonged fixation of the eyes, and by other means. The mediumistic trance is also, as will be shown hereafter, a case in point.

Hypnotism and Spiritualism.—Spiritualism is a legacy directly bequeathed by the magnetic philosophers of mediæval times, and through them, from the still older astrologers and magi. It has been shown that at a very early date phenomena of a distinctly hypnotic character were ascribed to the workings of spiritual agencies, whether angelic or demoniac, by a certain percentage of the observers Thus Greatrakes and Gassner believed themselves to have been gifted with a divine power to heal diseases. Cases of ecstasy, catalepsy and other trance states were given a spiritual significance—*i.e.*, demons, angels, elementals, and so on, were supposed to speak through the lips of the possessed. Witchcraft, in which the force of hypnotic suggestion seems to have operated in a very large degree, was thought to result from the witches' traffic with the Prince of Darkness and his legions. Even in some cases the souls of deceased men and women were identified with these intelligences, though not generally until the time of Swedenborg. Though the movement known as " modern spiritualism " is usually dated from 1848, the year of the " Rochester Rappings," the real growth of spiritualism was much more gradual, and its roots were hidden in animal magnetism. Emanuel Swendenborg, whose affinities with the magnetists have already been referred to, exercised a remarkable influence on the spiritualistic thought of America and Europe, and was in a sense the founder of that faith. Automatic phenomena were even then a feature of the magnetic trance, and clairvoyance, community of sensation, and telepathy were believed in generally, and regarded by many as evidences of spiritual communication. In Germany Professor Jung-Stilling, Dr. C. Römer, Dr. Werner, and the poet and physician Justinus Kerner, were among those who held opinions on these lines, the latter pursuing his investigations with a somnambule who became famous as the " Seerers of Prevorst "—Frau Frederica Hauffe. Frau Hauffe could see and converse with the spirits of the deceased, and gave evidence of prophetic vision and clairvoyance. Physical phenomena were witnessed in her presence, knockings, rattling of chains, movement of objects without contact, and, in short, such manifestations as were characteristic of the poltergeist family. She was, moreover, the originator of a " primeval " language, which she declared was that spoken by the patriarchs. Thus Frau Hauffe, though only a somnambule, or magnetic patient, possessed all the qualities of a successful spiritualistic medium. In England also there were many circumstances of a supernatural character associated with mesmerism. Dr. Elliotson, who, as has been indicated, was one of the best-known of English magnetists, became in time converted to a spiritualistic theory, as offering an explanation of the clairvoyance and similar phenomena which he thought to have observed in his patients. France, the headquarters of the rationalist school of magnetism, had, indeed, a good deal less to show of spiritualistic opinion. Nonetheless even in that country the latter doctrine made its appearance at intervals prior to 1848. J. P. F. Deleuze, a good scientist and an earnest protagonist of magnetism, who published his *Histoire Critique du Magnétisme Animal* in 1813, was said to have embraced the doctrines of spiritualism before he died. Dr. G. P. Billot was another believer in spirit communication, and one who succeeded in obtaining physical phenomena in the presence of his somnambules. It is, however, in the person of Alphonse Cahagnet, a man of humble origin who began to study induced somnambulism about the year 1845, and who thereafter experimented with somnambules, that we encounter the first French spiritualist of distinction. So good was the evidence for spirit communication furnished by Cahagnet and his subjects that it remains among the best which the annals of the movement can produce. In America, Laroy Sunderland, Andrew Jackson Davis, and others who became pillars of spiritualism in that country were first attracted to it through the study of magnetism. Everywhere we find hypnotism and spiritualism identified with each other until in 1848 a definite split occurs, and the two go their separate ways. Even yet, however, the separation is not quite complete. In the first place, the mediumistic trance is obviously a variant of spontaneous or self-induced hypnotism, while in the second, many of the most striking phenomena of the séance-room have been matched time and again in the records of animal magnetism. For instance, the diagnosis of disease and prescription of remedies dictated by the control to the " healing medium " have their prototype in the cures of Valentine Greatrakes, or of Mesmer and his disciples. Automatic phenomena—speaking in " tongues " and so forth—early formed a characteristic feature of the induced trance and kindred states. While even the physical phenomena, movement without contact, apports, rappings, were witnessed in connection with magnetism long before the movement known as modern spiritualism was so much as thought of. In many instances, though not in all, we can trace the operation of hypnotic suggestion in the automatic phenomena, just as we can perceive the result of fraud in much of the physical manifestations. The question whether, after the factors of hypnotism and fraud have been removed, a section of the phenomena remains inexplicable say by the hypothesis of communication with the spirit-world is one which has been in the past, and is to-day, answered in the affirmative by many men of the highest distinction in their various walks of life, and one which we would do well to treat with due circumspection. This, however, is reserved for consideration elsewhere, the scope of the present article being to show how largely spiritualism has borrowed from the fact of hypnotism. (*See* **Suggestion.**)

In M. Larelig's biography of the celebrated painter, Wiertz, and also in the introductory and biographical note affixed to the *Catalogue Raisonné du Musée Wiertz*, by Dr. S. Watteau, 1865, is to be found a detailed description of an extremely curious hypnotic experiment in which Wiertz was the hypnotic subject and a friend, a doctor, the hypnotiser. Wiertz had long been haunted by a desire to know whether thought persisted in a head severed from the trunk. His wish was the reason of the following experiment being undertaken, this being facilitated through his friendship with the prison doctor in Brussels, and another outside practitioner. The latter had been for many years a hypnotic operator, and had more than once put Wiertz into the hypnotic state, regarding him as an excellent subject. About this time a trial for murder in the Place Saint-Géry had been causing a great sensation in Belgium and the painter had been following the proceedings closely. The trial ended in the condemnation of the accused. A plan was arranged and Wiertz, with the consent of the prison doctor, obtained permission to hide with his friend, Dr. D., under the guillotine, close to where the head of the condemned would roll into the basket. In order to carry out the scheme he had determined upon more efficiently, the painter desired his hypnotiser to put him through a regular course of hypnotic suggestion, and when in the sleep state to command him to identify himself with various people and tell him to read their thoughts and penetrate into their psychical and mental states. The following is a resumé given in *Le Progrès Spirite* :—" On the day of execution, ten minutes before the arrival of the condemned man, Wiertz, accompanied by his friend the physician with two witnesses, ensconced themselves underneath the guillotine, where they were entirely hidden from sight. The painter was then put to sleep, and told to identify himself with the criminal. He was to follow his thoughts and feel any sensations, which he was to express aloud. He was also ' suggested ' to take special note of mental conditions during decapitation, so that when the head fell in the basket he could penetrate the brain and give an account of its last thoughts. Wiertz became entranced almost immediately, and the four friends soon understood by the sounds overhead that the executioner was conducting the condemned to the scaffold, and in another minute the guillotine would have done its work. The hypnotized Wiertz manifested extreme distress and begged to be demagnetised, as his sense of oppression was insupportable. It was too late, however—the knife fell. ' What do you feel ? What do you see ? ' asks the doctor. Wiertz writhes convulsively and replies, ' Lightning ! A thunderbolt falls ! It thinks ; it sees ! ' ' Who thinks and sees ? ' ' The head. It suffers horribly. It thinks and feels but does not understand what has happened. It seeks its body and feels that the body must join it. It still waits for the supreme blow for death, but death does not come.' As Wiertz spoke the witnesses saw the head which had fallen into the basket and lay looking at them horribly ; its arteries still palpitating. It was only after some moments of suffering that apparently the guillotined head at last became aware that is was separated from its body. Wiertz became calmer and seemed exhausted, while the doctor resumed his questions. The painter answered :—' I fly through space like a top spinning through fire. But am I dead ? Is all over ? If only they would let me join my body again ! Have pity ! give it back to me and I can live again. I remember all. There are the judges in red robes. I hear the sentence. Oh ! my wretched wife and children. I am abandoned. If only you would put my body to me, I should be with you once more. You refuse ? All the same I love you, my poor babies. Miserable wretch that I am I have covered you with blood. When will this finish !—or is not a murderer condemned to eternal punishment ? ' As Wiertz spoke these words the witnesses thought they detected the eyes of the decapitated head open wide with a look of unmistakable suffering and of beseeching. The painter continued his lamentations. ' No, such suffering cannot endure for ever ; God is merciful. All that belongs to earth is fading away. I see in the distance a little light glittering like a diamond. I feel a calm stealing over me. What a good sleep I shall have ! What joy ! ' These were the last words the painter spoke. He was still entranced, but no longer replied to the questions put by the doctor. They then approached the head and Dr. D. touched the forehead, the temples, and teeth and found they were cold. The head was dead."

In the Wiertz Gallery in Brussels are to be found three pictures of a guillotined head, presumably the outcome of this gruesome experiment.

Hypocephalus : A disk of bronze or painted linen found under the heads of Græco-Roman mummies in Egypt. It is inscribed with magical formulæ and divine figures, and its object was probably to secure warmth for the corpse. There is frequently depicted upon such amulets a scene showing cynocephalus apes adoring the solar disk seated in his boat.

Iacchus : (*See* **Mysteries.**)

Iao, or I-ha-ho : A mystic name said by Clement of Alexandria to have been worn on their persons by the initiates of the Mysteries of Serapis. It is said to embody the symbols of the two generative principles.

Ichthyomancy : Divination by the inspection of the entrails of fish.

Ideas of Good and Evil : (*See* **Yeats.**)

Ifrits : Hideous spectres probably of Arabian origin, now genii of Persian and Indian mythology. They assume diverse forms, and frequent ruins, woods and wild desolate places, for the purpose of preying upon men and other living things. They are sometimes confounded with the Jinns or Divs of Persia.

Ignis Fatuus : A wavering luminous appearance frequently observed in meadows and marshy places, round which many popular superstions cluster. Its folk-names, Will o' the Wisp and Jack o' Lantern, suggest a country fellow bearing a lantern or straw torch (wisp). Formerly these lights were supposed to haunt desolate bogs and moorlands for the purpose of misleading travellers and drawing them to their death. Another superstition says that they are the spirits of those who have been drowned in the bogs, and yet another, that they are the souls of unbaptized infants. Science refers these ignes fatui to gaseous exhalations from the moist ground, or, more rarely, to night-flying insects.

Illuminati : The term used first of all in the 15th century by enthusiasts in the occult arts signifying those who claimed to possess " light " directly communicated from a higher source, or due to a larger measure of human wisdom. We first find the name in Spain about the end of the 15th century. Its origin is probably a late Gnostic one hailing from Italy, and we find all sorts of people, many of them charlatans, claiming to belong to the brotherhood. In Spain, such persons as laid claim to the title had to face the rigour of the Inquisition, and this is perhaps the reason that we find numbers of them in France in the early seventeenth century, as refugees.

Here and there small bodies of those called *Illuminati*, sometimes known as Rosicrucians rose into publicity for a short period. But it is with Weishaupt, Professor of Law at Ingolstadt, that the movement first became identified with republicanism. It soon secured a strong hold all through Germany, but its founder's object was merely to convert his followers into blind instruments of his supreme will. He modelled his organisation on that of the Jesuits, adopted their system of espionage, and their maxim that the end justified the means. He induced mysticism into the workings of the brotherhood, so that an air of mystery might prevade all its doings, adopted many of the classes and grades of Freemasonry, and held out hopes of the communication of deep occult secrets in the higher ranks.

Only a few of the members knew him personally, and thus although the society had many branches in all parts of Germany, to these people alone was he visible, and he began to be regarded by those who had not seen him almost as a god. He took care to enlist in his ranks as many young men of wealth and position as possible, and within four or five years the power of Illuminism became extraordinary in its proportions, its members even had a hand in the affairs of the state, and not a few of the German princes found it to their interest to having dealings with the fraternity. Weishaupt's idea was to blend philanthropy and mysticism. He was only 28 when he founded the sect in 1776, but he did not make much progress until a certain baron Von Knigge joined him in 1780. A gifted person of strong imagination he had been admitted master of most of the secret societies of his day, among them Freemasonry. He was also an expert occultist and the

supernatural had strong attractions for him. These two, rapidly spread the gospel of the Revolution throughout Germany. But they grew fearful that, if the authorities discovered the existence of such a society as theirs they would take steps to suppress it. With this in view they conceived the idea of grafting it on to Freemasonry, which they considered would protect it, and offer it means of spreading more widely and rapidly.

The Freemasons were not long in discovering the true nature of those who had just joined their organisation. A chief council was held with the view of thoroughly examining into the nature of the beliefs held by them and a conference of masons was held in 1782 at which Knigge and Weishaupt attended and endeavoured to capture the whole organisation of Freemasonry, but a misunderstanding grew up between the leaders of illuminism. Knigge withdrew from the society, and two years later those who had reached its highest grade and had discovered that mysticism was not its true object, denounced it to the Bavarian Government as a political society of a dangerous character. Weishaupt fled, but the damage had been done, for the fire kindled by *Illuminism* was soon to burst forth in the French Revolution.

The title *Illuminati* was later given to the French Martinists (q.v.)

Imhetep : An Egyptian deity, son of Ptah and Nut, to whom great powers of exorcism were attributed. He was often appealed to in cases of demoniac possession.

Imperator : Control of Rev. W. S. Moses. (*See* **Moses, William Stainton.**)

Impersonation : Mediums who are controlled by the spirit of a deceased person frequently *impersonate* that person, imitate his voice and gestures, his physical peculiarities and manners, and exhibit the symptoms of any disease from which he may have suffered. (*See* **Trance Personalities.**)

Incense, Magical : (*See* **Magic.**)

Incommunicable Axiom, The : It was believed that all magical science was embodied in knowledge of this secret. The *Axiom* is to be found enclosed in the four letters of the Tetragram arranged in a certain way ; in the words " Azoth " and " Inri " written kabalistically ; and in the monogram of Christ embroidered in the labarum. He who succeeded in elucidating it became humanly omnipotent from the magical standpoint.

Incubus : A spirit which has intercourse with mortal women. The concept may have arisen from the idea of the commerce of gods with women, rife in pagan times. For, modern and mediæval instances, we can do little more than refer to the pages in which they may be found, and the very names of the writers will sufficiently avouch their credibility. The history of Hector Boethius has three or four notable examples, which obtain confirmation from the pen of Cardan. One of these we may venture to transcribe in the quaint dress which Holinshed had given it. " In the year 1480 it chanced as a Scottish ship departed out of the Forth towards Flanders, there arose a wonderful great tempest of wind and weather, so outragious, that the maister of the ship, with other the mariners, woondered not a little what the matter ment, to see such weather at that time of the yeare, for it was about the middest of summer. At length, when the furious pirrie and rage of winds still increased, in such wise that all those within the ship looked for present death, there was a woman underneath the hatches called unto them above, and willed them to throw her into the sea, that all the residue, by God's grace, might yet be saved ; and thereupon told them how she had been haunted a long time with a spirit dailie comming unto hir in man's likenesse. In the ship there chanced also to be priest, who by the maister's appointment going down to this woman, and finding her like a most wretched and desperate person, lamenting hir great misfortune and miserable estate, used such wholesome admonition and comfortable advertisements, willing her to repent and hope for mercy at the hands of God, that, at length, she seeming right penitent for her grievous offences committed, and fetching sundrie sighs even from the bottome of her heart, being witnesse, as should appeare, of the same, there issued forth of the pumpe of the ship, a foule and evil-favoured blacke cloud with a mighty terrible noise, flame, smoke, and stinke, which presently fell into the sea. And suddenlie thereupon the tempest ceassed, and the ship passing in great quiet the residue of her journey, arrived in saftie at the place whither she was bound." ('Chronicles,' vol. v., 146, Ed. 1808). In another case related by the same author, the *Incubus* did not depart so quietly. In the chamber of a young gentlewoman, of excellent beauty, and daughter of a nobleman in the country of Mar, was found at an unseasonable hour, "a foule monstrous thing, verie horrible to behold," for the love of which "Deformed" nevertheless, the lady had refused sundry wealthy marriages. A priest who was in the company began to repeat St. John's Gospel, and ere he had proceeded far "suddenlie the wicked spirit, making a verie sore and terrible roaring noise, flue his waies, taking the roofe of the chamber awaie with him, the hangings and coverings of the bed being also burnt therewith."

Erastus, in his Tract "de Lamiis," Sprangerus, who assures us that himself and his four colleagues punished many old women of Ratisbon with death for this commerce, Zanchius ("de Operibus Dei," xvi., 4.) ; Dandidas ("in Aristotelis de Anima," ii., 29, 30) ; Reussus (v., 6) ; Godelman (ii., 5) ; Valesius ("de Sacra Phil.," 40) ; and Delrio, "passim," among others, will satiate the keenest curiosity on these points. From Bodinus, we learn that Joan Hervilleria, at twelve years of age, was solemnly betrothed to Beelzebub, by her mother, who was afterwards burnt alive for compassing this clandestine marriage. The bridegroom was very respectably attired, and the marriage formulary was simple. The mother pronounced the following words to the bridegroom : " Ecce filiam meam quam spospondi tibi," and then turning to the bride, " Ecce amicum tuum qui beabit te." It appears, however, that Joan was not satisfied with her spiritual husband alone, but became a bigamist, by inter-marrying with real flesh and blood. Besides this lady, we read of Margaret Bremont, who, in company with her mother, Joan Robert, Joan Guillemin, Mary, wife of Simon Agnus, and Wilhelma, spouse of one Grassus, were in the habit of attending diabolic assignations. These unhappy wretches were burnt alive by Adrian Ferreus, General Vicar of the Inquisition. Magdalena Crucia of Cordova, an abbess, was more fortunate. In 1545 she became suspected by her nuns of magic, an accusation very convenient when a superior was at all troublesome. She encountered them with great wisdom by anticipating their charge ; and going beforehand to the Pope, Paul III., she confessed a thirty years' intimate acquaintance with the devil, and obtained his pardon. (*See* **England**.)

India : *Mystical Systems.*—It would be beyond the scope of such a work as this to undertake to provide any account of the several religious systems of India, and we must confine ourselves to a description of the mysticism and demonology which cluster round these systems, and an outline of the magic and sorcery of the native peoples of the empire.

Hinduism.—It may be said that the mysticism of the Hindus was a reaction against the detailed and practical ceremonial of the *Vedas*. If its trend were summarised it might justly be said that it partakes strongly of disinterestedness ; is a pantheistic identifying of subject and object, worshipper and worship ; aims at ultimate absorp-

tion in the Infinite ; inculcates absolute passivity, the most minute self-examination, the cessation of the physical powers ; and believes in the spiritual guidance of the mystical adept. For the Indian theosophists there is only one Absolute Being, the One Reality. True, the pantheistic doctrine of *Ekam advitiyam* " the One without Second " posits a countless pantheon of gods, great and small, and a rich demonology ; but it has to be understood that these are merely illusions of the soul and not realities. Upon the soul's coming to fuller knowledge, its illusions are totally dispelled, but to the ordinary man the impersonality of absolute being is useless. He requires a symbolic deity to bridge the gulf betwixt the impersonal Absolute and his very material self, hence the numerous gods of Hinduism which are regarded by the initiated merely as manifestations of the Supreme Spirit. Even the rudest forms of idolatry in this way possess higher meaning. As Sir Alfred Lyall says : " It (Brahminism) treats all the worships as outward visible signs of the same spiritual truth, and is ready to show how each particular image or rite is the symbol of some aspect of universal divinity. The Hindus, like the pagans of antiquity adore natural objects and forces,—a mountain, a river, or an animal. The Brahmin holds all nature to be the vesture or cloak of indwelling divine energy which inspires everything that produces all or passes man's understanding."

The life ascetic has from the remotest times been regarded in *India* as the truest preparation for communion with the deity. Asceticism is extremely prevalent especially in connection with the cult of Siva, who is in great measure regarded as the prototype of this class. The Yogis or Jogis (disciples of the Yogi philosophy), practise mental abstraction, and are popularly supposed to attain to superhuman powers. The usual results of their ascetic practices are madness or mental vacancy, and their socalled supernatural powers are mostly prophetic, or in too many cases pure jugglery and conjuring. The Parama-Hamsas, that is " supreme swans " claim to be identical with the world-soul, and have no occupation except meditation on Brahma. They are said to be equally indifferent to pleasure or pain, insensible to heat or cold, and incapable of satiety or want. The Sannyasis are those who renounce terrestrial affairs : they are of the character of monks, and are as a general rule extremely dirty. The Dandis or staff-bearers are worshippers of Siva in his form of Bhairava the Terrible. Mr. J. C. Owen in his *Mystics, Ascetics and Sects of India* says of these Sadhus or holy men :— " Sadhuism whether perpetuating the peculiar idea of the efficacy of asceticism for the acquisition of far-reaching powers over natural phenomena or bearing its testimony to the belief of the indispensableness of detachment from the world as a preparation for the ineffable joy of ecstatic communion with the Divine Being, has undoubtedly tended to keep before men's eyes as the highest ideal, a life of purity and restraint and contempt of the world of human affairs. It has also necessarily maintained amongst the laity a sense of the rights and claims of the poor upon the charity of the more opulent members of the community. Further, Sadhuism by the multiplicity of the independent sects which have arisen in India has engendered and favoured a spirit of tolerance which cannot escape the notice of the most superficial observer."

One of the most esoteric branches of Hinduism is the Sakta cult. The Saktas are worshippers of the Sakti or female principle as a creative and reproductive agency. Each of the principal gods possesses his own Sakti, through which his creative acts are performed, so that the Sakta worshippers are drawn from all sects. But it is principally in connection with the cult of Siva that Sakta worship is practised. Its principal seat is the north-eastern part of

India—Bengal, Behar and Assam. It is divided into two distinct groups. The original self-existent gods were supposed to divide themselves into male and female energies, the male half occupying the right-hand and the female the left-hand side. From this conception we have the two groups of " right-hand " observers and " left-hand " observers. In the *Tantras* or mystical writings, Siva unfolds in the nature of a colloquy in answer to questions asked by his spouse Parvati, the mysteries of Sakta occultism. The right-hand worshippers are by far the most numerous. Strict secrecy is enjoined in the performance of the rites, and only one minor caste, the Kanlas, carry on the mystic and degraded rites of the *Tantras*.

Brahmanism.—Brahmanism is a system originated by the Brahmans, the sacerdotal caste of the Hindus, at a comparatively early date. It is the mystical religion of India *par excellence*, and represents the more archaic beliefs of its peoples. It states that the numberless individual existences of animate nature are but so many manifestations of the one eternal spirit towards which they tend as their final goal of supreme bliss. The object of man is to prevent himself sinking lower in the scale, and by degrees to raise himself in it, or if possible to attain the ultimate goal immediately from such state of existence as he happens to be in. The code of Manu concludes " He who in his own soul perceives the supreme soul in all beings and acquires equanimity towards them all attains the highest state of bliss." Mortification of animal instincts, absolute purity and perfection of spirit, were the moral ideals of the Brahman class. But it was necessary to pass through a succession of four orders or states of existence ere any hope of union with the deity could be held out. These were : that of *brahmacharin*, or student of religious matters ; *grihastha*, or householder ; *vanavasin*, or hermit ; and *sannyasin* or *bhikshu*, fakir or religious mendicant. Practically every man of the higher castes practised at least the first two of these stages, while the priestly class took the entire course. Later, however, this was by no means the rule, as the scope of study was intensely exacting, often lasting as long as forty-eight years, and the neophyte had to support himself by begging from door to door. He was usually attached to the house of some religious teacher ; and after several years of his tuition was usually married, as it was considered absolutely essential that he should leave a son behind him to offer food to his spirit and to those of his ancestors. He was then said to have become a " Householder " and was required to keep up perpetually the fire brought into his house upon his marriage day. Upon his growing older, the time for him arrived to enter the third stage of life, and he " cut himself off from all family ties except that (if she wished) his wife might accompany him, and went into retirement in a lonely place, carrying with him his sacred fire, and the instruments necessary to his daily sacrifices." Scantily clothed, and with hair and nails uncut, it is set down that the anchorite must live entirely on food growing wild in the forest—roots, herbs, wild grain, and so forth. The acceptance of gifts was not permitted him unless absolutely necessary, and his time was spent in reading the metaphysical portions of the *Veda*, in making offerings, and in practising austerities with the object of producing entire indifference to worldly desires. In this way he fits himself for the final and most exalted order, that of religious mendicant or *bhikshu*. This consists solely of meditation. He takes up his abode at the foot of a tree in entire solitude, and only once a day at the end of their labours may he go near the dwellings of men to beg a little food. In this way he waits for death, neither desiring extinction nor existence, until at length it reaches him, and he is absorbed in the eternal Brahma.

The purest doctrines of Brahmanism are to be found in the Vedanta philosophic system, which recognises the *Veda*, or collection of ancient Sanskrit hymns, as the revealed source of religious belief through the visions of the ancient *Rishis* or seers. It has been already mentioned that the Hindu regarded the entire gamut of animated nature as being traversed by the one soul, which journeyed up and down the scale as its actions in its previous existence were good or evil. To the Hindu the vital element in all animate beings appears essentially similar, and this led directly to the Brahmanical theory of transmigration, which has taken such a powerful hold upon the Hindu mind.

Demonology.—A large and intricate demonology has clustered around Hindu mythology. The gods are at constant war with demons. Thus Durga slays Chanda and Asura, and also despatches Durga, a fiend of similar name to herself. Vishnu also slays more than one demon, but Durga appears to have been a great enemy of the demon race. The Asuras, probably a very ancient and aboriginal pantheon of deities, later became demons in the popular imagination, and the Rakshasas were cloud-demons. They are described as cannibals, could take any form, and were constantly menacing the gods. They haunt cemeteries, disturb sacrifices, animate the dead, harry and afflict mankind in all sorts of ways. In fact they are almost an absolute parallel with the vampires of Slavonic countries; and this greatly assists the conclusions of Asikoff that the Slavonic vampires were originally cloud-spirits. We find the gods constantly harassed by demons ; and on the whole we may be justified in concluding that just as the Tuatha-de-danaan harassed the later deities of Ireland, so did these aboriginal gods lead an existence of constant warfare with the divine beings of the pantheon of the immigrant Aryans.

Popular Witchcraft and Sorcery.—The popular witchcraft and sorcery of *India* greatly resembles that of Europe. The Dravidian or aboriginal races of *India* have always been strong believers in witchcraft, and it is possible that here we have an example of the mythic influence of a conquered people. They are, however, extremely reticent regarding any knowledge they possess of it. It is practically confined to them, and this might lead to the hasty supposition that the Aryan races of *India* possess no witchcraft of their own. But this is strongly unlikely, and the truth probably lies quite in the other direction ; however, the extraordinarily high demands made upon the popular religious sense by Brahmanism probably crushed the superstitions of the lower cultus of a very early period, and confined the practice of minor sorcery to the lower castes, who were of course of Dravidian or aboriginal blood. We find witchcraft most prevalent among the more isolated and least advanced races, like the Kols, Bhils, and Santals. The nomadic peoples are also strong believers in sorcery, one of the most dreaded forms of which is the *Jigar Khor*, or liver-eater, of whom Abul Fazl says :— " One of this class can steal away the liver of another by looks and incantations. Other accounts say that by looking at a person he deprives him of his senses, and then steals from him something resembling the seed of a pomegranate, which he hides in the calf of his leg ; after being swelled by the fire, he distributes it among his fellows to be eaten, which ceremony concludes the life of the fascinated person. A *Jigar Khor* is able to communicate his art to another by teaching him incantations, and by making him eat a bit of the liver cake. These *Jigar Khors* are mostly women. It is said they can bring intelligence from a long distance in a short space of time, and if they are thrown into a river with a stone tied to them, they nevertheless will not sink. In order to deprive any one of this wicked power, they brand his temples and every joint of his body, cram his eyes with salt, suspend him for forty days in a subterranean chamber, and repeat over him certain incantations." The witch does not, however, devour the man's liver for two and a half days, and even if she has eaten it, and is put under the hands of an exorciser, she can be forced to substitute a liver of some animal in the body of the man whom she victimised. We also hear tales of witches taking out the entrails of people, sucking them, and then replacing them. All this undoubtedly illustrates, as in ancient France and Germany, and probably also in the Slavonic countries, the original combination of witch and vampire ; how, in fact, the two were one and the same. In *India* the arch-witch *Ralaratri*, or " black night " has the joined eyebrows of the Salvonic werewolf or vampire, large cheeks, widely-parted lips, projecting teeth, and is a veritable vampire. But she also possesses the powers of ordinary witchcraft,—second-sight, the making of philtres, the control of tempests, the evil eye, and so forth. Witches also take animal forms, especially those of tigers ; and stories of trials are related at which natives gave evidence that they had tracked certain tigers to their lairs, which upon entering they had found tenanted by a a notorious witch or wizard. For such witch-tigers the usual remedy is to knock out their teeth to prevent their doing any more mischief. Strangely enough the Indian witch, like her European prototype, is very often accompanied by a cat. The cat, say the jungle people, is aunt to the tiger, and taught him everthing but how to climb a tree. Zalim Sinh, the famous regent of Kota, believed that cats were associated with witches, and imagining himself enchanted ordered that every cat should be expelled from his province.

As in Europe, witches are known by certain marks. They are believed to learn the secrets of their craft by eating offal of all kinds. The popular belief concerning them is that they are often very handsome and neat, and invariably apply a clear line of red lead to the parting of their hair. They are popularly accused of exhuming dead children, and bringing them to life to serve occult purposes of their own. They cannot die so long as they are witches, and until, as in Italy, they can pass on their knowledge of witchcraft to someone else. They recite charms backwards, repeating two letters and a half from a verse in the *Koran*. If a certain charm is repeated " forwards," the person employing it will become invisible to his neighbour, but if he repeats it backwards, he will assume whatever shape he chooses. A witch can acquire power over her victim by getting possession of a lock of hair, the paring of nails, or some other part of his body, such as a tooth. For this reason natives of *India* are extremely careful about the disposal of such, burying them in the earth in a place covered with grass, or in the neighbourhood of water, which witches universally dislike. Some people even fling the cuttings of their hair into running water. Like the witches of Europe too, they are in the practice of making images of persons out of wax, dough, or similar substances, and torturing them, with the idea that the pain will be felt by the person whom they desire to injure. In *India* the witches' familiar is known as *Bir* or the " hero," who aids her to inflict injury upon human beings. The power of the witch is greatest on the 14th, 15th and 29th of each month, and in particular on the Feast of Lamps, and the Festival of Durga.

Witches are often severely punished amongst the isolated hill-folk and a diabolical ingenuity is shown in torturing them. To nullify their evil influence, they are beaten with rods of the castor-oil plant and usually die in the process. They are often forced to drink filthy water used by curriers in the process of their work, or their noses are cut off, or

they are put to death. As has been said, their teeth are often knocked out, their heads shaved and offal is thrown at them. In the case of women their heads are shaved and their hair is attached to a tree in some public place. They are also branded ; have a ploughshare tied to their legs ; and made to drink the water of a tannery. During the Mutiny, when British authority was relaxed, the most atrocious horrors were inflicted upon witches and sorcerers by the Dravidian people. Pounded *chilli* peppers were placed in their eyes to see if they would bring tears, and the wretched beings were suspended from a tree head downwards, being swung violently from side to side. They were then forced to drink the blood of a goat, and to exorcise the evil spirits that they had caused to enter the bodies of certain sick persons. The mutilations and cruelties practised on them are such as will not bear repetition, but one of the favourite ways of counteracting the spells of a witch is to draw blood from her, and the local priest will often prick the tongue of the witch with a needle, and place the resulting blood on some rice and compel her to eat it.

In Bombay, the aboriginal Tharus are supposed to possess special powers of witchcraft, so that the " Land of Tharus " is a synonym for witch-land. In Gorakhpur, witches are also very numerous, and the half-gypsy *Banjaras*, or grain-carriers, are notorious believers in witchcraft. In his interesting *Popular Religion and Folk-lore of Northern India*, Mr. W. Crooke, who has had exceptional opportunities for the study of the native character, and who has done much to clear up the dark places of Indian popular mythology, says regarding the various types of Indian witches :—

" At the present day the half-deified witch most dreaded in the Eastern Districts of the North-western Provinces is Lona, or Nona, a *Chamarin* or woman of the currier caste. Her legend is in this wise. The great physician Dhanwantara, who corresponds to Luqman Hakim of the Muhammadans, was once on his way to cure King Parikshit, and was deceived and bitten by the snake king Takshaka. He therefore desired his sons to roast him and eat his flesh, and thus succeed to his magical powers. The snake king dissuaded them from eating the unholy meal, and they let the cauldron containing it float down the Ganges. A currier woman, named Lona, found it and ate the contents, and thus succeeded to the mystic powers of Dhanwantara. She became skilful in cures, particularly of snake-bite. Finally she was discovered to be a witch by the extraordinary rapidity with which she could plant out rice seedlings. One day the people watched her, and saw that when she believed herself unobserved she stripped herself naked, and taking the bundle of the plants in her hands threw them into the air, reciting certain spells. When the seedlings forthwith arranged themselves in their proper places, the spectators called out in astonishment, and finding herself discovered, Nona rushed along over the country, and the channel which she made in her course is the Loni river to this day. So a saint in Broach formed a new course for a river by dragging his clothes behind him. . . . . .

" Another terrible witch, whose legend is told at Mathura, is Putana, the daughter of Bali, king of the lower world. She found the infant Krishna asleep, and began to suckle him with her devil's milk. The first drop would have poisoned a mortal child, but Krishna drew her breast with such strength that he drained her life-blood, and the fiend, terrifying the whole land of Braj with her cries of agony, fell lifeless on the ground. European witches suck the blood of children ; here the divine Krishna turns the tables on the witch.

" The Palwar Rajputs of Oudh have a witch ancestress.

Soon after the birth of her son she was engaged in baking cakes. Her infant began to cry, and she was obliged to perform a double duty. At this juncture her husband arrived just in time to see his demon wife assume gigantic and supernatural proportions, so as to allow both the baking and nursing to go on at the same time. But finding her secret discovered, the witch disappeared, leaving her son as a legacy to her astonished husband. Here, though the story is incomplete, we have almost certainly, as in the case of Nona Chamarin, one of the Melusina type of legend, where the supernatural wife leaves her husband and children, because he violated some taboo, by which he is forbidden to see her in a state of nudity, or the like.

" The history of witchcraft in *India*, as in Europe, is one of the saddest pages in the annals of the people. Nowadays, the power of British law has almost entirely suppressed the horrible outrages which, under the native administration were habitually practised. But particularly in the more remote and uncivilized parts of the country this superstition still exists in the minds of the people and occasional indications of it, which appear in our criminal records, are quite sufficient to show that any relaxation of the activity of our magistrates and police would undoubtedly lead to its revival in some of its more shocking forms."

The aborigines of *India* live in great fear of ghosts and invisible spirits, and a considerable portion of their time is given up to averting the evil influences of these. Protectives of every description litter their houses, and the approaches to them, and they wear numerous amulets for the purpose of averting evil influences. Regarding these, Mr. Crooks says :—

" Some of the Indian ghosts, like the *Ifrit* of the Arabian Nights, can grow to the length of ten *yojanas* or eighty miles. In one of the Bengal tales a ghost is identified because she can stretch out her hands several yards for a vessel. Some ghosts possess the very dangerous power of entering human corpses, like the Vetala, and swelling to an enormous size. The Kharwars of Mirzapur have a wild legend, which tells how long ago an unmarried girl of the tribe died, and was being cremated. While the relations were collecting wood for the pyre, a ghost entered the corpse, but the friends managed to expel him. Since then great care is taken not to leave the bodies of women unwatched. So, in the Panjab, when a great person is cremated the bones and ashes are carefully watched till the fourth day, to prevent a magician interfering with them. If he has a chance, he can restore the deceased to life, and ever after retain him under his influence. This is the origin of the custom in Great Britain of waking the dead, a practice which ' most probably originated from a silly superstition as to the danger of a corpse being carried off by some of the agents of the invisible world, or exposed to the ominous liberties of brute animals.' But in *India* it is considered the best course, if the corpse cannot be immediately disposed of, to measure it carefully, and then no malignant *Bhut* can occupy it.

" Most of the ghosts whom we have been as yet considering are malignant. There are, however, others which are friendly. Such are the German Elves, the Robin Goodfellow, Puck, Brownie and the Cauld Lad of Hilton of England, the Glashan of the Isle of Man, the Phouka or Leprehaun of Ireland. Such, in one of his many forms, is the *Brahmadaitya*, or ghost of a Brahman who has died unmarried. In Bengal he is believed to be more neat and less mischievous than other ghosts ; the Bhuts carry him in a palanquin, he wears wooden sandals, and lives in a Banyan tree.

Infernal Court.—Wierus and others, learned in the lore of the *infernal* regions, have discovered therein princes and high dignitaries, ministers, ambassadors, and officers of state, whose names would fill much space to little purpose Satan is no longer the soverign of Hades, but is, so to speak, leader of the opposition. The true leader is Beelzebub.

Initiation : The process of entry into a secret society or similar organisation. The idea of *initiation* was certainly inherited by the Egyptians and Asssyrians from older neoblithic peoples, who possessed secret organisations or " mysteries " analogous to those of the Medwiwin of the North American Indians or those of the Australian Blackfellows. We read of *initiation* into the various grades of the Egyptian priesthood and the " mysteries " of Eleusis and Bacchus. (*See* **Mysteries.**) These processes probably consisted of tests of courage and fidelity (as do the savage *initiations*) and included such acts as sustaining a severe buffeting, the drinking of blood, real and imaginary, and so forth. In the *Popol Vuh*, the saga of the Kiche Indians of Guatemala we have a picture of the *initiation* tests of two hero-gods on entrance to the native Hades. Indeed, most of the mysteries typified the descent of man into Hell, and his return to earth, based on the corn-mother legend of the resurrection of the wheat plant.

Initiation into the higher branches of mysticism, magic and theosophy has been largely written upon The process in regard to these is of course entirely symbolical, and is to be taken as implying a preparation for the higher life and the regeneration of the soul.

Institor, Henricus : (*See* **Malleus Maleficarum.**)

Instruments, Magical : (*See* **Magic.**)

Insufflation, says Eliphas Levi, " is one of the most important practices of occult medicine, because it is a perfect sign of the transmission of life. To inspire, as a fact, means to breath upon some person or thing, and we know already, by the one doctrine of Hermes, that the virtue of things has created words, and that there is an exact proportion between ideas and speech, which is the first form and verbal realisation of ideas. The breath attracts or repels, according, as it is warm or cold. The warm breathing corresponds to positive electricity, and the cold breathing to negative electricity. Electrical and nervous animals fear the cold breathing, and the experiment may be made upon a cat, whose familiarities are important. By fixedly regarding a lion or tiger and blowing in their face, they would be so stupefied as to be forced to retreat before us. Warm and prolonged *insufflation* restores the circulation of the blood, cures rheumatic and gouty pains, re-establishes the balance of the humours, and dispels lassitude. When the operator is sympathetic and good, it acts as a universal sedative. Cold *insufflation* soothes pains occasioned by congestions and fluidic accumulations. The two breathings must, therefore, be used alternately, observing the polarity of the human organism, and acting in a contrary manner upon the poles, which must be treated successfully to an opposite magnetism. Thus, to cure an inflamed eye, the one which is not affected must be subjected to a warm and gentle *insufflation*, cold *insufflation* being practised upon the suffering member at the same distance and in the same proportion. Magnetic passes have a similar effect to *insufflations*, and are a real breathing by transpiration and radiation of the interior air, which is phosphorescent with vital light ; slow passes constitute a warm breathing which fortifies and raises the spirits ; swift passes are a cold breathing of dispersive nature, neutralising tendencies to congestion. The warm *insufflation* should be performed transversely, or from below upward , the cold *insufflation* is more effective when directed downward from above."

Intuitional World : Formerly known as the Buddhic Plane, is in the theosophic scheme the fourth world, and from it come intuitions. (*See* **Theosophy, Solar System, and Intuition**).

Invocation : (*See* **Necromancy.**)

Ireland : For information regarding ancient *Ireland See* "**Celts.**" Although nominally Christianised, there is little doubt that the early mediæval Irish retained many relics of their former condition of paganism, especially those which possessed a magical tendency. This is made clear by the writings of Giraldus Cambrensis, the first account we have of Irish manners and customs after the invasion of the country by the Anglo-Normans. His description, for example, of the Purgatory of St. Patrick in Lough Derg, Co. Donegal, proves that the demonology of the Catholic Church had already fused with the animism of Irish native heathnesse. He says :—

"There is a lake in Ulster containing an island divided into two parts. In one of these stands a church of especial sanctity, and it is most agreeable and delightful, as well as beyond measure glorious for the visitations of angels and the multitude of the saints who visibly frequent it. The other part, being covered with rugged crags, is reported to be the resort of devils only, and to be almost always the theatre on which crowds of evil spirits visibly perform their rites. This part of the island contains nine pits, and should any one perchance venture to spend the night in one of them (which has been done, we know, at times, by some rash men), he is immediately seized by the malignant spirits, who so severely torture him during the whole night, inflicting on him. such unutterable sufferings by fire and water, and other torments of various kinds, that when morning comes scarcely any spark of life is found left in his wretched body. It is said that any one who has once submitted to these torments as a penance imposed upon him, will not afterwards undergo the pains of hell, unless he commit some sin of a deeper dye.

"This place is called by the natives the Purgatory of St. Patrick. For he, having to argue with a heathen race concerning the torments of hell, reserved for the reprobate, and the real nature and eternal duration of the future life, in order to impress on the rude minds of the unbelievers a mysterious faith in doctrines so new, so strange, so opposed to their prejudices, procured by the efficacy of his prayers an exemplification of both states even on earth, as a salutary lesson to the stubborn minds of the people."

The ancient Irish believed in the possibility of the transformation of human beings into animals, and Giraldus in another narrative of facts purporting to have come under his personal notice proves that this belief had lost none of its significance with the Irish of the latter half of the twelfth century. The case is also interesting as being one of the first recorded examples of lycanthropy (q.v.) in the British Isles, and that must be our excuse for quoting it at some length.

"About three years before the arrival of Earl John in *Ireland*, it chanced that a priest, who was journeying from Ulster towards Meath, was benighted in a certain wood on the borders of Meath. While, in company with only a young lad, he was watching by a fire which he had kindled under the branches of a spreading tree, lo ! a wolf came up to them, and immediately addressed them to this effect : ' Rest secure, and be not afraid, for there is no reason you should fear, where no fear is ! ' The travellers being struck with astonishment and alarm, the wolf added some orthodox words referring to God. The priest then implored him, and adjured him by Almighty God and faith in the Trinity, not to hurt them, but to inform them what creature it was in the shape of a beast uttered human words. The wolf, after giving catholic replies to all

questions, added at last : ' There are two of us, a man and a woman, natives of Ossory, who, through the curse of Natalis, saint and abbot, are compelled every seven years to put off the human form, and depart from the dwellings of men. Quitting entirely the human form, we assume that of wolves. At the end of the seven years, if they chance to survive, two others being substituted in their places, they return to their country and their former shape. And now, she who is my partner in this visitation lies dangerously sick not far from hence, and, as she is at the point of death, I beseech you, inspired by divine charity, to give her the consolations of your priestly office.'

"At this wood the priest followed the wolf trembling, as he led the way to a tree at no great distance, in the hollow of which he beheld a she-wolf, who under that shape was pouring forth human sighs and groans. On seeing the priest, having saluted him with human courtesy, she gave thanks to God, who in this extremity had vouchsafed to visit her with such consolation. She then received from the priest all the rites of the church duly performed, as far as the last communion. This also she importunately demanded, earnestly supplicating him to complete his good offices by giving her the viaticum. The priest stoutly asserting that he was not provided with it, the he-wolf, who had withdrawn to a short distance, came back and pointed out a small missal-book, containing some consecrated wafers, which the priest carried on his journey, suspended from his neck, under his garment, after the fashion of the country. He then intreated him not to deny them the gift of God, and the aid destined for them by Divine Providence ; and, to remove all doubt, using his claw for a hand, he tore off the skin of the she-wolf, from the head down to the navel, folding it back. Thus she immediately presented the form of an old woman. The priest, seeing this, and compelled by his fear more than his reason, gave the communion ; the recipient having earnestly implored it, and devoutly partaking of it. Immediately afterwards the he-wolf rolled back the skin and fitted it to its original form.

"These rites having been duly, rather than rightly performed, the he-wolf gave them his company during the whole night at their little fire, behaving more like a man than a beast. When morning came, he led them out of the wood, and, leaving the priest to pursue his journey pointed out to him the direct road for a long distance. At his departure, he also gave him many thanks for the benefit he had conferred, promising him still greater returns of gratitude, if the Lord should call him back from his present exile, two parts of which he had already completed."

"It chanced, about two years afterwards, that I was passing through Meath, at the time when the bishop of that land had convoked a synod, having also invited the assistance of the neighbouring bishops and abbots, in order to have their joint counsels on what was to be done in the affair which had come to his knowledge by the priest's confession. The bishop, hearing that I was passing through those parts, sent me a message by two of his clerks, requesting me, if possible, to be personally present when a matter of so much importance was under consideration ; but if I could not attend he begged me at least to signify my opinion in writing. The clerks detailed to me all the circumstances, which indeed I had heard before from other persons ; and, as I was prevented by urgent business from being present at the synod, I made up for my absence by giving them the benefit of my advice in a letter. The bishop and synod, yielding to it, ordered the priest to appear before the pope with letters from them, setting forth what had occurred, with the priest's concession, to which instrument the bishops and abbots who were present at the synod affixed their seals."

" In our own time we have seen persons who, by magical arts, turned any substance about them into fat pigs, as they appeared (but they were always red), and sold them in the markets. However, they disappeared as soon as they crossed any water, returning to their real nature ; and with whatever care they were kept, their assumed form did not last beyond three days. It has also been a frequent complaint, from old times as well as in the present, that certain hags in Wales, as well as in Ireland and Scotland changed themselves into the shape of hares, that, sucking teats under this counterfeit form, they might stealthily rob other people's milk."

In Anglo-Norman times sorcery was widely practised but notices are scarce. It is only by fugitive passages in the works of English writers who constantly animadvert against the superstitious nature and practices of the Irish that we glean any information concerning the occult history of the country. The great *cause célèbre* of the Lady Alice Kyteler (q.v.) shook the entire Anglo-Norman colony during several successive years in the first half of the fourteenth century. The party of the Bishop of Ossory the relentless opponent of the Lady Alice, boasted that by her prosecution they had rid *Ireland* of a nest of sorcerers, but there is reason to believe that *Ireland* could have furnished numerous similar instances of black magic had the actors in them been of similar rank to the ill-fated lady—that is of sufficient importance in the eyes of chroniclers.

In this connection a work on *Irish Witchcraft and Demonology* by Mr. St. John D. Seymour (1913), is of striking and pregnant interest. We do not gather from it that Mr. Seymour had any previous general knowledge of the subject he handles before writing this book, and he appears to take it for granted that witchcraft in *Ireland* is purely an alien system, imported into the island by the Anglo-Normans and Scottish immigrants to the north. This undoubtedly is the case so far as the districts of the Pale and of Ulster are concerned, but surely it cannot be applied to the Celtic districts of *Ireland*. Regarding these Mr. Seymour is silent, but it will occur to most readers that the analogy of Celtic Scotland, which abounded in witches and witch-customs, is powerful evidence that a system similar to that in vogue in the Highlands obtained in the aboriginal districts of *Ireland*. Early Irish works contain numerous references to sorcery, and practices are chronicled in them which bear a close resemblance to those of the shamans and medicine-men of savage tribes all over the world. Animal transformation, one of the most common feats of the witch, is alluded to again and again in the ancient Irish cycles, and there are few heroes in Hibernian legend who have not a fair stock of working magic at their finger-ends. Wonder-working druids, too, abound. Mr. Seymour will have it that " In Celtic *Ireland* dealings with the unseen were not regarded with such abhorrence, and indeed had the sanction of custom and antiquity." He also states that " the Celtic element had its own superstitious beliefs, but these never developed in this direction " (the direction of Witchcraft). This is very difficult to believe. The lack of records of such a system is no criterion that it never existed, and we have not the least hesitation in saying that a thorough examination of the subject would prove that a veritable system of witchcraft obtained in Celtic *Ireland* as elsewhere, although it may not have been of " Celtic " origin.

Be that as it may, Mr. Seymour's book is most interesting as dealing with those Anglo-Norman and Scottish portions of *Ireland* where the belief in witchcraft followed the lines of those in vogue in the mother-countries of the immigrant populations. He sketches the *cause célèbre* of the Kyteler case (q.v.), touches on the circumstances connected with the Earl of Desmond and notes the case of the Irish prophetess who insisted upon warning the ill-fated James I. of Scotland on the night of his assassination at Perth. It is not stated by the ancient chronicler, quoted by Mr. Seymour, from what part of *Ireland* the witch in question emanated—for a witch she undoubtedly was as she possessed a familiar spirit, Huthart, whom she alleged had made her cognisant of the coming catastrophe. Mr. Seymour does not seem to be aware of the history of this spirit. He is the Teutonic *Hudekin* (q.v.) or *Hildekin*, the wearer of the hood, sometimes also alluded to as *Heckdekin*, well known throughout Germany and Flanders as a species of house-spirit or brownie. Trithemius alludes to him as a " spirit known to the Saxons who attached himself to the Bishop of Hildesheim " and we find him cropping up here and there in occult history. From this circumstance it might with justice be inferred that the witch in question came from some part of *Ireland* which had been settled by Teutonic immigrants, and more probably from Ulster, but the data is insufficient to permit us to conclude this definitely.

From the most scanty materials, Mr. Seymour has compiled a book of outstanding interest. He passes in review the witchcraft trials of the XVI. century, the burning of Adam Dubh, of the Leinster trial of O'Toole and College Green in 1327 for heresy, and the passing of the statute against witchcraft in *Ireland* in 1586. The prevalence of witchcraft in *Ireland* during the sixteenth century is proved by him to have been very great indeed, but a number of the authorities he cites, as to the existence of sorcerers in the Green Isle, almost certainly refer to the more Celtic portions of it ; for example Rich and Stanihurst. He has an excellent note upon the enchantments of the Earl of Desmond who demonstrated to his young and beautiful wife the possibilities of animal transformation by changing himself into a bird, a hag, a vulture, and a gigantic serpent. Human relations with the Devil are dwelt upon at length by Mr. Seymour in a racy chapter, and we are told how he was cheated by a doctor of divinity and raised on occasion by certain sorcerers. Florence Newton, the witch of Youghal claims an entire chapter to herself, and worthily, for her case is one of the most absorbing in the history of witchcraft. At any rate, whatever her occult powers, she splendidly succeeded in setting a whole community by the ears. Ghostly doings and apparitions, fairy possession, and dealings with the 'wee folk' are also included in the volume ; and Mr. Seymour has not confined himself to *Ireland*, but has followed one of his countrywomen to America, where he shows how she gave congenial employment to the fanatic Cotton Mather (q.v.). Witchcraft notices of the seventeenth century in Antrim and Island Magee comprise the eighth chapter ; and the ninth and last bring down the affairs of sorcery in *Ireland* from the year 1807 to the present day. The last notice is that of a trial for murder in 1911, when a wretched woman was tried for killing another—an old-age pensioner—in a fit of insanity. A witness deposed that he met the accused on the road on the morning of the crime holding a statue or figure in her hand, and repeating three times " I have the old witch killed. I got power from the Blessed Virgin to kill her." It appears that the witch quoted in question threatened to plague the murderess with rats and mice ; a single rodent had evidently penetrated to her abode, and was followed by the bright vision of a lady who told the accused that she was in danger, and further informed her that if she received the old pensioner's pension-book without taking off her clothes and cleaning them and putting out her bed and cleaning up the house, she would " receive dirt for ever and rats and mice." This is not an isolated case, and shows how hard such superstitions die in the more remote portions of civilised countries.

We have reviewed Mr. Seymour's book at some length because it represents practically all that exists on the subject in question. But it would be interesting to see him further his researches by an examination into such of the native Irish records as exist. Such a course would most probably result in the rescue of a considerable amount of detail which would enable him to complete the occult history of his country.

Iron : Its occult virtues are thus described by Pliny, according to Holland :—" As touching the use of Yron and steele in Physicke, it serveth otherwise than for to launce, cut, and dismember withal ; for take the knife or dagger, an make an ymaginerie circle two or three times round with the point thereof upon a young child or an elder bodie, and then goe round withall about the partie as often, it is a singular preservative against all poysons, sorceries, or enchantments. Also to take any yron naile out of the coffin or sepulchre wherein man or woman lieth buried, and to sticke the same fast to the lintle or side post of a dore, leading either to the house or bed-chamber where any dooth lie who is haunted with Spirits in the night, he or she shall be delivered and secured from such phanasticall illusions. Moreover, it is said, that if one be lightly pricked with the point of sword or dagger, which hath been the death of a man, it is an excellent remedy against the pains of sides or breast, which come with sudden prickes or stitches."

In certain parts of Scotland and the North of Ireland, there is a belief in the potency of iron for warding off the attacks of fairies. An iron poker, laid across a cradle, will, it is believed, keep the fairies away while the child is baptised. The Rev. John G. Campbell in his *Superstitions of the Scottish Highlands* relates how when a child, he and another boy were believed to be protected from a fairy which had been seen at a certain spot by the possession, the one of a knife, and the other of a nail. This was at Appin in Argyllshire.

Irving's Church, Speaking with Tongues in : In 1831 an outbreak of speaking with tongues occurred in the congregation of Edward Irving, in London. For several years Irving had waited for such a visitation, and had instituted special early-morning services for the purpose of hastening it. At length, in July, 1831, the " visitation " came, first one and then another of the congregation speaking with " tongues " and with prophetic uutterance. *Irving* himself was not at first entirely disposed to accept the utterances as of divine origin. But the undoubted good faith and irreproachable doctrine of his flock reassured him. Robert Baxter, who was absent at the commencement of the outbreak, but who was himself influenced to prophesy at a later date, has left an account of his experiences. The phenomena did not greatly differ from that of similar outbreaks. The inspired speakers were often attended by physical symptoms, such as convulsions, and they spoke in loud, somewhat unnatural tones. Baxter declares that he spoke sentences in Latin, French, and unknown languages. At length, however, evil spirits began to appear in the company, some of the congregation admitting that they had been possessed by false spirits. The outbreak seen afterwards died out.

Isaac of Holland : Very little is known about the life of this alchemist, but he is commonly supposed to have lived and worked early in the fifteenth century, the principal reason for assigning his career to that period being that in his writings he refers to Geber, Dastin, Morien and Arnold de Villanova, but not to more modern authorities ; while again, he appears to have been acquainted with various chymical processes discovered towards the close of the

fourteenth century, and hence it may reasonably be deduced that he did not live anterior to that time. According to tradition *Isaac* worked along with his son, whose name is not recorded, and the pair are usually regarded as having been the first men to exploit chymistry in the Netherlands. They are said to have been particularly skilful in the manufacture of enamels and artificial gems, and it is noteworthy that no less distinguished an alchemist than Paracelsus attached value to the Dutchmen's researches while these are also mentioned with honour by the seventeenth century English scientist, Robert Boyle.

Isaac compiled two scientific treatises, the one entitled *De Triplici Ordine Elixiris et Lapidis Theoria*, and the other *Opera Mineralia Joannis Isaaci Hollandi, sive de Lapide Philosophico*, and both were published at the beginning of the seventeenth century The more important of the two is the last-named, wherein the author sets forth his ideas on the exalting of base metals into *Sol* and *Luna*, and shows by the aid of illustrations exactly what kind of vessels should be used for this purpose.

Isagoge : (*See* **Arbatel**.)

Isham, Sir Charles : (*See* **British National Association of Spiritualists**.)

Ismaelites : (*See* **Assassins**.)

Isomery : (*See* **Alchemy**.)

Issintok, Eskimo Sorcerers : (*See* **Eskimos**.)

Italy : (For Ancient *Italy see* **Rome**.) Magic and sorcery in mediæval *Italy* seem strangely enough to have centred round many great personalities of the church, and even several popes have been included by the historians of occult science in the ranks of Italian sorcerers and alchemists. There appears to have been some sort of tradition. the origin of which is by no means clear, that the popes had been given over to the practice of magic ever since the tenth century, and it was alleged that Silvester II. confessed to this charge on his death-bed. Levi states that Honorius III., who preached the Crusades, was an abominable necromancer, and author of a *grimoire* or book by which spirits were evoked, the use of which is reserved exclusively to the priesthood. Platina, quoting from Martinus Polonus, states that Silvester, who was a proficient mathematician and versed in the *Kabala* on one occasion evoked Satan himself and obtained his assistance to gain the pontifical crown. Furthermore he stipulated as the price of selling his soul to the Devil that he should not die except at Jerusalem, to which place he inwardly determined he would never betake himself. He duly became Pope, but on one occasion whilst celebrating mass in a certain church at Rome, he felt extremely ill, and suddenly remembered that he was officiating in a chapel dedicated to the Holy Cross of Jerusalem. He had a bed set up in the chapel, to which he summoned the cardinals, and confessed that he had held communication with the powers of evil. He further arranged that when dead his body should be placed upon a car of green wood, and should be drawn by two horses, one black and the other white ; that they should be started on their course, but neither led nor driven, and that where they halted there his remains should be entombed. The conveyance stopped in front of the Lateran, and at this juncture most terrible noises proceeded from it, which led the bystanders to suppose that the soul of Silvester had been seized upon by Satan in virtue of their agreement. There is no doubt whatsoever that most of these legends concerning papal necromancers are absolute inventions and can be traced through Platina and Polonus to Galfridus and Gervaise, the necromancer, whom Naudé has rightly termed " the greatest forger of fables, and the most notorious liar that ever took pen in hand ! " On a par with such stories is that of Pope Joan, who for several years sat on the papal throne although a woman, and who was supposed to be one of the blackest sorceresses of all time. To her many magic books are attributed. Levi has an interesting passage in his *Hisory of Magic*, in which he states that certain engravings in a Life of this female pope, purporting to represent her, are nothing else than ancient tarots representing Isis crowned with a tiara. "It is well-known," he says, "that the hieroglyphic figure on the second tarot card is still called 'The Female Pope,' being a woman wearing a tiara, on which are the points of the crescent moon, or the horns of Isis." It is much more possible that the author of the *grimoire* in question was Honorius II., the anti-pope, or perhaps another Honorius who is described as the son of Euclid and master of the Thebans. But all Italian necromancers and magicians were by no means churchmen—indeed mediæval *Italy* was hardly a place for the magically inclined, so stringent were the laws of the church against the Black Art. Astrology, however, flourished to some extent, and its practitioners do not appear to have been unduly persecuted. A Florentine astrologer, named Basil, who flourished at the beginning of the fifteenth century, obtained some repute for successful predictions; and is said to have foretold to Cosmo de Medici that he would attain exalted dignity, as the same planets had been in ascendency at the hour of his birth, as in that of the Emperor Charles V. Many remarkable predictions were made by Antiochus Tibertus of Romagna, who was for some time councillor to Pandolpho de Maletesta, Prince of Rimini. He foretold to his friend, Guido de Bogni, the celebrated soldier, that he was unjustly suspected by his best friend, and would forfeit his life through suspicion. Of himself he predicted that he would die on the scaffold, and of the Prince of Rimini, his patron, that he would die a beggar in the hospital for the poor at Bologna. It is stated that the prophecies came true in every detail.

Although the notices of sorcery in mediæval times are few and far between in Italian history, there is reason to suspect that although magic was not outwardly practised, it lurked hidden in by-paths and out-of-the-way places. We have an excellent portrait of the mediæval Italian magician in those popular myths regarding Virgil the Enchanter. The fame of Virgil the Poet had waxed so great in ancient *Italy*, that in due course of time his name was synonymous with fame itself. From that it is a short step to the attribution of supernatural power, and Virgil the Roman poet became in the popular mind the mediæval Enchanter. His myth is symptomatic of magic in mediæval *Italy* as a whole, and it may therefore be given here at some length.

When the popular myth of Virgil the Enchanter first grew into repute is uncertain, but probably the earliest faint conception arose about the beginning of the tenth century, and each succeeding generation embroidered upon it some fantastic impossibility. Soon, in the South of *Italy*—for the necromancer's fame was of southern origin—there floated dim, mysterious legends of the enchantments which he had wrought. Thus he fashioned a brazen fly, and planted it on the gate of fair Parthenope to free the city from the inroads of the insects of Beelzebub. On a Neapolitan hill he built a statue of brass, and placed in its mouth a trumpet; and lo! when the north wind blew there came from that trumpet so terrible a roar that it drove back into the sea the noxious blasts of Vulcan's forges, which, even to this day, seethe and hiss near the city of Puossola. At one of the gates of Naples he raised two statues of stone, and gifted them respectively with the power of blighting or blessing the strangers who, on entering the city, passed by one or the other of them. He constructed three public baths for the removal of every disease which afflicts the human frame, but the physicians, in a wholesome dread of losing their patients and their fees,

caused them to be destroyed. Other wonders he wrought, which in time assumed a connected form, and were woven into a life of the enchanter, first printed in French about 1490-1520. A still fuller history appeared in English, the well-known "Life of Virgilius," about 1508, printed by Hans Doesborcke at Antwerp. It sets forth with tolerable clearness the popular type of the mediæval magician, and will be our guide in the following biographical sketch.

"Virgil was the son of a wealthy senator of Rome, wealthy and powerful enough to carry on war with the Roman Emperor. As his birth was heralded by extraordinary portents, it is no marvel that even in childhood he showed himself endowed with extraordinary mental powers, and his father having the sagacity to discern in him an embryo necromancer, sent him, while still very young, to study at the University of Toledo, where the "art of magick" was taught with extraordinary success.

"There he studied diligently, for he was of great understanding, and speedily acquired a profound insight into the great Shemaia of the Chaldean lore. But this insight was due, not so much to nocturnal vigils over abstruse books, as to the help he received from a very valuable familiar. And this was the curious fashion in which he was introduced to the said familiar :—

"'Upon a tyme the scholers at Tolenten hadde lycence to goo to playe and sporte them in the fyldes after the usuance of the olde tyme; and there was also Virgilius therby also walkynge among the hylles all about. It fortuned he spyed a great hole in the syde of a great hyll, wherein he went to depe that he culde not see no more lyght, and than he went a lytell ferther therein, and then he sawe soon lyght agayne, and than wente he fourth streyghte. And within a lyteh wyle after he harde a voice that called, 'Virgilius, Virgilius,' and he loked aboute, and he colde nat see nobodye. Than Virgilius spake, and asked, 'Who calleth me?' Than harde he the voyce agayne, but he sawe nobodye. Than sayd he, 'Virgilius, see ye not that lytell bourde lyinge byside you there, marked with that worde?' Than answered Virgilius, 'I see that borde well enough.' The voyce said, 'Doo away that bourde, and lette me out theratte.'

"'Than answered Virgilius to the voyce that was under the lytell bourde, and sayd, 'Who art thou that talkest me so?' Than answered the devyll, 'I am a devyll conjured out of the body of a certeyne man, and banysshed here tyll the daye of jugement, without that I be delyvered by the handes of men. Thus, Virgilius, I pray thee delyver me out of this payn, and I shall show unto thee many bokes of nygromancy, and how thou shalt cum by it lytly, and shalte knowe the practyse therein, that no man in the science of nygromancy shall (sur)pass thee; and, moreover, I shall showe and informe thee so that thou shalt have all thy desyre, whereby methinke it is a great gyfte for so lytell a donyge, for ye may also thus all your poor frendys helpen, and make ryghte your ennemyes unmighty.'

"Thorough that great promise was Virgilius tempted. He badde the fynd showe the bokes to hym, that he myght have and occupy them at his wyll. And so the fynd showed hym, and then Virgilius pulled open a bourde, and there was a lytell hole, and thereat wrange the devyll out lyke a yeel, and cam and stode before Virgilius lyke a bigge man.

"'Thereof Virgilius was astonied, and merveyled greately thereof, that so great a man myght com out at so lytell a hole!

"'Then sayd Virgilius, 'Shulde ye well passe into the hole that ye cam out of?!' 'Yes, I shall well,' sayd the devyll. 'I holde the beste pledge that I have, ye shall not do it.' 'Well,' sayd the devyll, 'thereto I consente.'

And then the devyll wrange hymself into the lytell hole agen, and as he was therein, Virgilius kyvered the hole agen with the bourde close, and so was the devyll begyled, and myght not there come out agen, but there abydeth shutte styll therein. Than called the devyll dredefully (drearily) to Virgilius, and sayd, ' What have ye done ? ' Virgilius answered, ' Abyde there styll to your day apoynted.' And fro thensforth abydeth he there.' "

Virgil's father died soon after this event, and his estates being seized by his former colleagues, his widow sunk into extreme poverty. Virgil accordingly gathered together the wealth he had amassed by the exercise of his magical skill, and set out for Rome, to replace his mother in a position proper to her rank. At Toledo, however, he was a famous student; at Rome he was a despised scholar, and when he besought the Emperor to execute justice and restore to him his estate, that potentate—ignorant of the magician's power—simply replied, ' Methinketh that the land is well divided to them that have it, for they may help you in their need ; what needeth you for to care for the disheriting of one school-master Bid him take heed, and look to his schools, for he hath no right to any land here about the city of Rome.'

Four years passed, and only such replies as this were vouchsafed to Virgil's frequent appeals for justice. Growing at length a-weary of the delay, he resolved to exercise his wondrous powers in his own behalf. When the harvest-time came, he accordingly shrouded the whole of his rightful inheritance with a vapour so dense that the new proprietors were unable to approach it, and under its cover his men gathered in the entire crop with perfect security. This done, the mist disappeared. Then a great indignation possessed the souls of his enemies, and they assembled their swordsmen, and marched against him to take off his head. Such was their power that the Emperor for fear fled out of Rome, ' for they were twelve senators that had all the world under them ; and if Virgilius had had right, he had been one of the twelve, but they had disinherited him and his mother.' When they drew near, Virgil once more baffled their designs by encircling his patrimony with a rampart of cloud and shadow.

The Emperor, with surprising inconsistency, now coalesced with the senators against Virgil—whose magical powers he probably feared far more than the rude force of the senatorial magnates—and made war against him. But who can prevail against the arts of necromancy ? Emperor and senators were beaten, and from that moment Virgil, with marvellous generosity, became the faithful friend and powerful supporter of his sovereign. . . . . . "

It may not generally be known that Virgil, besides being the saviour of Rome, was the founder of Naples. This feat had its origin, like so many other great actions, in the power of love.

Virgil's imagination had been fired by the reports that reached him of the surpassing loveliness of the Sultan's daughter. Now the Sultan lived at Babylon (that is, at Cairo—the Babylon of the mediæval romancers), and the distance might have daunted a less ardent lover and less potent magician. But Virgil's necromantic skill was equal to a bridge in the air—where other glowing spirits have often raised fair castles !—and passing over it, he found his way into the Sultan's palace,—into the Princess's chamber,—and speedily overcoming her natural modesty, bore her back with him to his Italian bower of pleasaunce. There having enjoyed their fill of love and pleasure, he restored her to her bed in her father's palace. Meanwhile, her absence had been noted, but she was soon discovered on her return, and the Sultan repairing to her chamber, interrogated her respecting her disappearance. He found that she knew not who it was that had carried her off, nor whither she had been carried.

When Virgil restored the lady on the following night, she took back with her, by her father's instructions, some of the fruit plucked from the enchanter's garden ; and from its quality the Sultan guessed that she had been carried to a southern land " on the side of France." These nocturnal journeys being several times repeated, and the Sultan's curiosity growing ungovernable, he persuaded his daughter to give her lover a sleeping-draught. The deceived magician was then captured in the Babylonian palace, and flung into prison, and it was decreed that both he and his mistress should be punished for their love by death at the stake.

Necromancers, however, are not so easily outwitted. As soon as Virgil was apprized of the fate intended for him, he made, by force of his spells, the Sultan and all his lords believe that the great river of Babylon—the might Nilus—was overflowing in the midst of them, and that they swam and lay and sprang like geese ; and so they took up Virgilius and the Princess, tore them from their prison, and placed them upon the aerial bridge. And when they were thus out of danger, he delivered the Sultan from the river, and all the lords ; and lo, when they recovered their humanity, they beheld the enchanter bearing the beautiful Princess across the Mediterranean ; and they marvelled much, and felt that they could not hope to prevail against his supernatural power.

And in this manner did Virgilius convey the Sultan's daughter over the sea to Rome. And he was highly enamoured of her beauty. " Then he thought in his mind how he might marry her "—apparently forgetting that he was already married—" and thought in his mind to found in the midst of the sea a fair town with great lands belonging to it ; and so he did by his cunning, and called it Naples : and the foundation of it was of eggs. And in that town of Naples he made a tower with four corner s and on the top he set an apple upon an iron yard, and no man could pull away that apple without he brake it ; and through that iron set he a bottle, and on that bottle set he an egg ; and he hanged the apple by the stalk upon a chain, and so hangeth it still. And when the egg stirreth, so should the town of Naples quake ; and when the egg brake, then should the town sink. When he had made an end, he let call it Naples."

After accomplishing so much for his Babylonian beauty, Virgil did not marry her, but endowing her with the town of Naples and its lands, gave her in marriage to a certain grandee of Spain. Having thus disposed of her and her children, the enchanter returned to Rome, collected all his treasures, and removed them to the city he had founded, where he resided for some years, and established a school which speedily became of illustrious renown. Here he lost his wife, by whom he had had no issue ; built baths and bridges, and wrought the most extraordinary miracles. So passed an uncounted number of years, and Virgil at length abandoned Naples for ever, and retired to Rome.

" Outside the walls of the Imperial City he built a goodly town, that had but one gate, and was so fenced round with water as to bar any one from approaching it. And the entry of its one gate was made " with twenty-four iron flails, and on each side was there twelve men smiting with the flails, never ceasing, the one after the other ; and no man might come in without the flails stood still, but he was slain. And these flails were made with such a gin (contrivance) that Virgilius stopped them when he list to enter in thereat, but no man else could find the way. And in this castle put Virgilius part of his treasure privily ; and, when this was done, he imagined in his mind by what means he might make himself young again, because he thought to live longer many years, to do many wonders and marvellous things. And upon a time went Virgilius to the Emperor, and asked him of licence (of absence) by the space of three weeks. But the Emperor in no wise would grant it unto him for he would have Virgilius at all times by him."

Spiritualism.—We have perhaps our first indication of the rise and spread of spiritualism in *Italy* in the modern acceptance of the term in an article published in the *Civitta Catholica* the well-known Roman organ, entitled " Modern Necromancy." The conclusions of the article were :—

" 1st. Some of the phenomena may be attributed to imposture, hallucinations, and exaggerations in the reports of those who describe it, but there is a foundation of reality in the general sum of the reports which cannot have originated in pure invention or be wholly discredited without ignoring the value of universal testimony.

" 2nd. The bulk of the theories offered in explanation of the proven facts, only cover a certain percentage of those facts, but utterly fail to account for the balance.

" 3rd. Allowing for all that can be filtered away on mere human hypotheses, there are still a large class of phenomena appealing to every sense which cannot be accounted for by any known natural laws, and which seem to manifest the action of intelligent beings."

D. D. Home last visited the principal cities of *Italy* in 1852, and had been so active in his propaganda that numerous circles were formed after his departure. Violent journalistic controversies arose out of the foundation of these societies, with the result that public interest was so aroused that it could only be satisfied with the publication of a paper issued from Geneva, and edited by Dr Pietro Suth and Signor B. E. Manieri entitled *Il amore del Vero*. In the journal accounts of the spiritual movements in the various countries of Europe, and America, were published although the Church and press levelled the anathemas against the journal. In the spring of 1863 a society was proved at Palermo entitled Il Societa Spiritual di Palermo, which had for president Signor J. V. Paleolozo, and for members men of the stamp of Paolo Morelle, professor of Latin and Philosophy.

It was about the autumn of 1864 that lectures were first given on Spiritualistic subjects in Italy. They were started in Leghorn and Messina, and though of a very mixed character, and often partaking largely of the lecturer's peculiar idiosyncrasies on religious subjects, they served to draw attention to the upheaval of thought going on in all directions, in connection with the revelations from the Spirit world. It could not be expected that a movement so startling and unprecedented as that which opened up a direct communication between the natural and the Spirit worlds could gain ground in public acceptance without waking up all the latent elements of enthusiasm, fanaticism, and bigotry, which prevailed in the Italian as in every other community.

In the year 1870, there had been over a hundred different societies formed, with varying success, in different parts of *Italy*. Two of the most prominent flourishing at that date were conducted in Naples, and according to the French journal, the *Revue Spirite* represented the two opposing schools which have prevailed in Continental Spiritualism, namely, the " Reincarnationists " whom we have elsewhere classified as " Spiritists " and the " Immortalists," or those known in America and England merely as " Spiritualists." (*See* **France**.)

About 1868, an immense impulse was communicated to the cause of Spiritualism—at least in the higher strata of Italian Society—by the visit of Mr. and Mrs. Guppy to Naples, at which place they took up their residence for two or three years. Mrs. Guppy—née Miss Nichol—of London,

was renowned throughout Europe for her marvellous powers as a " Physical force Medium " and as Mr. Guppy's wealth and social standing enabled him to place his gifted wife's services at the command of the distinguished visitors who crowded his salons, it soon became a matter of notoriety that the highest magnates of the land, including King Victor Emmanuel and many of his nearest friends and counsellors, had yielded conviction to the truth of the astounding phenomena exhibited through Mrs. Guppy's Mediumship.

It was about the year 1863, that Spiritualism began to enjoy the advantage of fair and honourable representation in the columns of a new paper entitled, the *Annali dello Spiritismo*, or " Annals of Spiritualism." This excellent journal was commenced at Turin, and published by Signor Niceforo Filalete, with all the liberality, energy, and talent worthy alike of the subject and its editor.

From the columns of the *Annali* we learn that a Venetian Society of Spiritualists, named " Atea " elected General Giuseppe Garibaldi their honorary president, and received the following reply by telepraph from the distinguished hero, the liberator of *Italy*: " I gratefully accept the presidency of the Society Atea. Caprera, 23rd September."

The same issue of the *Annali* contains a verbatim report of a " grand discourse, given at Florence, by a distinguished literary gentleman, Signor Sebastiano Fenzi, in which the listeners were considerably astonished by a rehearsal of the many illustrious names of those who openly avowed their faith in Spiritualism.

The years 1863-4 appear to have been rich in Spiritualistic efforts. Besides a large number of minor associations, the existence of which was recorded from time to time the early numbers of the *Annali* and *Revue Spirite*, a society which continued for a long time to exert a marked influence in promoting the study of occult forces and phenomena, was formed about this time in Florence, under the title of The Magnetic Society of Florence. The members of this association were without exception persons remarkable for literary and scientific attainments, or those of high influential position in society.

About this time Mr. Seymour Kirkup, a name familiar to the early initiators of Spiritualism, resided in Florence, and communicated many records of spiritual phenomena to the *London Spiritual Magazine*. Nearly ten years after the establishment of the Magnetic Society of Florence, Baron Guitern de Bozzi, an eminent occultist, founded the Pneumatological Psychological Academy of Florence, but upon his demise it was discontinued.

Modern Sorcery.—In his *Aradia, or the Gospel of the Witches of Italy*, the late Charles Godfrey Leland gives a valuable account of the life and practice of the modern Italian *strega* or witch. He says : " In most cases she comes of a family in which her calling or art has been practised for many generations. I have no doubt that there are instances in which the ancestry remounts to mediæval, Roman, or it may be Etruscan times. The result has naturally been the accumulation in such families of much tradition. But in Northern *Italy*, as its literature indicates, though there has been some slight gathering of fairy tales and popular superstitions by scholars, there has never existed the least interest as regarded the strange lore of the witches, nor any suspicion that it embraced an incredible quantity of old Roman minor myths and legends, such as Ovid has recorded, but of which much escaped him and all other Latin writers. . . . . . Even yet there are old people in the Romagna of the North who know the Etruscan names of the Twelve Gods, and invocations to Bacchus, Jupiter, and Venus, Mercury, and the Lares or ancestral spirits, and in the cities are women who prepare strange amulets, over which they mutter spells, all known in the old Roman time and who can astonish even the learned by their legends of Latin gods, mingled with lore which may be found in Cato or Theocritus. With one of these I became intimately acquainted in 1886, and have ever since employed her specially to collect among her sisters of the hidden spell in many places all the traditions of the olden times known to them. It is true that I have drawn from other sources but this woman by long practice has perfectly learned what few understand, or just what I want, and how to extract it from those of her kind.

"Among other strange relics, she succeeded, after many years, in obtaining the following 'Gospel,' which I have in her handwriting A full account of its nature with many details will be found in an Appendix. I do not know definitely whether my informant derived a part of these traditions from written sources or oral narration, but believe it was chiefly the latter. . . . . .

"For brief explanation I may say that witchcraft is known to its votaries as *la vecchia religione*, or the old religion, of which Diana is the Goddess, her daughter *Aradia* (or Herodias) the female Messiah, and that this little work sets forth how the latter was born, came down to earth, established witches and witchcraft, and then returned to heaven. With it are given the ceremonies and invocations or incantations to be addressed to Diana and Aradia, the exorcism of Cain, and the spells of the holy-stone, rue, and verbena, constituting, as the text declares, the regular church-service, so to speak, which is to be chanted or pronounced at the witch-meetings. There are also included the very curious incantations or benedictions of the honey, meal, and salt, or cakes of the witch-supper, which is curiously classical, and evidently a relic of the Roman Mysteries."

Briefly the ritual of the Italian witches is as follows : At the Sabbath they take meal and salt, honey and water, and say a conjuration over these, one to the meal, one to the salt, one to Cain, one to Diana, the moon-goddess.

They then sit down naked to supper, men and women, and after the feast is over they dance, sing and make love in the darkness, quite in the manner of the mediæval Sabbath of the sorcerers. Many charms are given connected with stones, especially if these have holes in them and are found by accident. A lemon stuck full of pins we are told is a good omen. Love-spells fill a large space in the little work, which for the rest recounts several myths of Diana and Endymion in corrupted form. (*See also* **Leland's Etruscan-Roman Remains.**)

Iubdan : In Ultonian romance, the King of the Wee Folk. One day he boasted of the might of his strong man Glower, who could hew down a thistle at one blow. His bard Eisirt retorted that beyond the sea, there existed a race of giants, any one of whom could annihilate a whole battalion of the Wee Folk. Challenged to prove his words, Eisirt brought Creda, King Fergus' dwarf and bard. He then dared *Iubdan* to go to Fergus' palace and taste the king's porridge. *Iubdan* and Bebo, his queen, arrived at the palace at midnight, but in trying to get at the porridge so as to taste and be away before daybreak, *Iubdan* fell in. He was found in the pot next morning by the scullions, and he and Bebo were taken before Fergus, who after a while released them in exchange for a pair of water shoes, wearing which a man could go over or under water as freely as on land.

Ivunches : Chilian familiars. (*See* **American Indians.**)

Iynx : A Chaldean symbol of universal being, the name of which signifies "power of transmission." It was reproduced as a living sphere or winged globe. The first example was perhaps put forth by mind on the plane of reality, to be followed by three others called paternal and ineffable, and latterly by hosts of Iynxs of a subordinate character, described as "free intelligences." The *Iynx* is described by Eliphas Levi as "corresponding to the Hebrew Yod or to that unique letter from which all other letters were formed."

J

Jacinth, or Hyacinth : A stone which preserves from plague and from lightning, strengthens the heart, and brings wealth, honour, prudence, and wisdom. It is recommended by Albertus Magnus as a soporific, on account of its coldness, and is ordered by Psellus in cases of coughs, ruptures, and melancholy, to be drunk in vinegar. Marbodæus describes the wonderful properties of three species of the *jacinth* ; Pliny and Leonardus are also particular in their account of it.

Jacob's Ladder : According to the kabalistic view, *Jacob's Ladder*, which was disclosed to him in a vision, is a meta-phorical representation of the powers of alchemy, operating through visible nature. The "Ladder" was a "Rainbow," or prismatic staircase, set up between heaven and earth. Jacob's Dream implied a history of the whole hermetic creation. There are only two original colours, red and blue, representing "spirit" and "matter," for orange is red mixing with the yellow light of the sun, yellow is the radiance of the sun itself, green is blue and yellow, indigo is blue tinctured with red, and violet is produced by the mingling of red and blue. The sun is alchemic gold, and the moon is alchemic silver. In the operation of these two potent spirits, or mystic rulers of the world, it is supposed astrologically that all mundane things were produced.

Jadian, or Were-tiger : (*See* **Malays.**)

Jakin and Boas : The names of the two symbolical pillars of Solomon's Kabalistic temple, and which were believed

to explain all mysteries. The one was black and the other white, and they represented the powers of good and evil. It is said that they symbolise the need of "two" in the world : Human equilibrium requires two feet ; the worlds gravitate by means of two forces ; generation needs two sexes.

James IV. of Scotland : It was almost inevitable that the romantic nature of *James IV. of Scotland* should have encouraged the study of alchemy and the occult sciences in the manner he did. Dunbar in his *Remonstrance*, speaks of the patronage which he bestowed upon alchemists and charlatans, and in the Treasurer's accounts there are numerous payments for the "Quinta Essentia," including wages to the persons employed, utensils of various kinds and so forth. In a letter to one Master James Inglis, *James* says :—

"*James*, etc. . . . . . to dear Master James Inglis greeting. We graciously accept your kindness, by which in a letter brought to us you signify that you have beside you certain books learned in the philosophy of the true Alchemy, and that although most worthy men have sought them from you, you have nevertheless with difficulty kept them for our use, because you had heard of our enthusiasm for the art. We give you thanks ; . . . and we have sent our familiar, Master James Merchenistoun, to you, that he may see to the transfer hither of those books which you wish us to have ; whom receive in good faith in our name. Farewell. From our Palace at Edinburgh."

From the Treasurer's Accounts.

27 Sept.—Item, for a pan in Stirling for the quinta
    essencia, and " potingary " there.   vi. *s.*
29 Sept.—For aqua vitae for the quinta essencia. . .
18 Oct.—Gallons aqua vitae for quinta essencia. iii. *l.*
    iiij. *s.*
10 Nov.—For four cauldrons to quinta essencia   xlv. *s.*
24 Dec.—V cakes glass for quinta essentia.   xxv. *s.*
31 Dec.—Paid to William Foular apothecary (*potingair*
    for potingary to the King and Queen, dis-
    tillation of waters, aqua vitae, and potingary
    books in English, from the 17 day of Decem-
    ber, 1506.

(*See* Scotland.)

James VI. : (*See* Daemonologie.)

Japan : All that the word " magic " defines is to be found
amongst the Japanese, in their religious beliefs and rites
in their conception of Nature and in the national customs.
To them all forms and objects animate or inanimate possess,
equally with man, a soul with good or evil tendencies, and
these entities, either of their own volition or by evocation,
come into close touch with man either to his advantage or
detriment. Their folklore and traditions are wrought of
the marvellous and the Japanese thought of to-day is still
permeated with a belief in the supernatural.

The predominant feature of the Japanese religion,
Shintoism, is the worship of ancestors, allied to that of
Nature. There are twelve recognised sects of Shintoism—
all with ancestor-worship as their cardinal principle. The
belief of the Japanese is that the disembodied spirits
acquire the powers of deities and possess supernatural
attributes. They become potential for good or evil and
they exercise their potentialities in the same mundane
sphere upon which their interests and affections centred
during life. They thus become guardian divinities, and
as such the object of ceremonies in their honour is to show
gratitude for their services whilst upon earth and to solicit
a continuance of these services beyond the grave. On
this point Lafcadio Hearn wrote :—" An intimate sense of
relation between the visible and invisible worlds is the
special religious characteristic of Japan among all civilised
countries. To Japanese thought the dead are not less
real than the living. They take part in the daily life of the
people,—sharing the humblest sorrows and the humblest
joys. They attend the family repasts, watch over the
well-being of the household, assist and rejoice in the prosperity of their descendants. They are present at the
public pageants, at all the sacred festivals of Shinto, at
the military games, and at all the entertainments especially
provided for them. And they are universally thought of
as finding pleasure in the offerings made to them or the
honours conferred upon them." Every morning, before
the family shrine, to be found in all Japanese homes,
flowers are set and food-emblems placed as offerings of
pious affection, while ancient prayers are repeated, for on
the shrine, beside the symbols of the Sun-goddess and the
tutelary god of the family are put the memorial tablets
containing names, ages and dates of death of members of
the household. There are stories of the souls of ancestors
taking material form and remaining visible through centuries. In the month of July three days are set apart for
the celebration of the *Festival of the Dead.* At this time
it is thought that the disembodied souls return from the
dismal region of the Shades to gaze for a while upon the
beauty of their country and to visit their people. On the
first morning new mats are placed upon all altars and on
every household shrine, while in all the homes tiny meals
are prepared in readiness for the ghostly guests. The
streets at night are brilliant with many torches ; in front
of every house gaily-coloured lanterns are lit in welcome.

Those who have recently lost some relative go to the
cemeteries to pray and burn incense and leave offerings of
water and flowers set in bamboo vases. On the third day
the souls of those who are undergoing penance are fed, also
those who have no friends among the living to care for
them. The evening of this day is the time of the ghosts'
departure, and for this thousands of little boats are fashioned
and laden with food-offerings and tender messages of farewell. When the night falls, tiny lanterns are lit and hung
at the miniature prows and the ghosts are supposed to step
aboard. Then the craft are set free upon river, lake and
sea, the water gleaming with glow of thousands of lights.
On this day no sailor dreams of putting out to sea—for
this one night it belongs to the dead. It is believed that if
a ship fails to come to port before the sailing of the ghost-
fleet the dead arise from the deep and the sailors can hear
their mournful whispering, while the white breakers are
their hands clutching the shores, vainly trying to return.

In the Shinto pantheon there are deities representing
well nigh everything in heaven and earth ; from the mountain of Fiyiyama to the household kitchen, from Wisdom to
Scarecrows, from Caligraphy to Poverty, Laughter to
Small pox. When babes are a week old they are taken to
the temple and placed under the protection of some god
chosen by the parents, but in later years he may choose his
patron god for himself beside the tutelary one.

In remote parts of *Japan* may still be found traces of an
older form of Shinto in which phallic symbols had their
place as representing life-giving power and therefore used
as a magical exorcism of evil influences, especially that of
disease. In this connection appears a dwarf-god who is
said to have first taught mankind the art of magic and
medicine In Shinto there are no idols, their place being
taken by *shintia*, god-bodies, concrete objects in which
the divine spirit is supposed to dwell, such as the mirror,
jewel and sword of the Sun-goddess, worshipped at the
famous Ise shrine. Pilgrims from all parts of *Japan* make
their way to this shrine, acquiring merit and purification
thereby. These pilgrims receive from the priests objects
of talismanic properties called *harai*, these also serving as
evidence of having been at the holy place. In former days
they were recognised as passports. The term *harai* signifies
to " drive out," to " sweep away," and has reference to
the purification of the individual from his sins. These
objects are in the form of small envelopes or paper boxes
each containing shavings of the wands used by the Ise
priests at the half-yearly festivals held to purify the nation
in general from the consequences of the sins of the preceding
six months. The list includes witchcraft, also wounding
and homicide, these latter being regarded more as uncleanness than as a moral stigma. On the pilgrims return home
the *harai* are placed upon the " god's-shelf."

On fête-days are still practised the ancient *ordeals.*
These are three in number, the *Kugadachi*, in which priests,
wrought to ecstatic frenzy by participation in a rhythmic
dance, pour upon their bodies boiling water without
receiving harm from the process ; the *Hiwatari* consisting
of walking barefoot over a bed of live coals, priests and
people alike participating, and *Tsurugi-watari*, the climbing
of a ladder of sword-blades. These are regarded as tests
of purity of character, this being thought to confer an
immunity from hurt in these ordeals. The attendant
rites consist of exorcism of evil spirits by the waving of
wands and magical finger-knots, and invocation of the
gods who are then believed to be actually present.

Possession by Divinities.—In connection with some of the
Shinto sects occult rites are practised to bring about possession of a selected person by the actual spirits of the gods.
Priests and laymen alike develop and practice this art,
undergoing a period of purification by means of various

austerities. Prophecy, divination and the cure of disease are the objects of these rites. The ceremony may take place in a temple or ordinary house where the " gods' shelf " makes the shrine. In the rites *gohei*, the Shinto symbols of consecration are used, the pendant form for purification and exorcism of evil influences, and an upright *gohei* affixed to a wand signifying the *shintai*, or god-body, is the central object. The medium, called *nak aza* takes his seat in the midst. Next him in importance is the functionary, the *maeza* who presides over the ceremony. It is he who builds the magical pyre in a brass bowl and burns in the flames strips of paper inscribed with characters, effigies of disease and trouble. There is a clapping of hands to call the attention of the gods and chants are intoned, accompanied by the shaking of metal-ringed crosiers and the tinkle of pilgrim bells. After the fire is burnt out, the bowl is removed and sheets of paper placed in symbolic form, upon which is then put the upright *gohei* wand. There is further chanting, the medium closes his eyes and clasps his hands into which the *maeza* now thrusts the wand. All then await the advent of the god which is indicated by the violent shaking of the wand and convulsive throes on the part of the medium, who is now considered to have become the god. The *maeza* reverently prostrates himself before the entranced *nakaza*, and asks the name of the god who has deigned to come. This done and answered, he next offers his petitions, to which the god replies. The ceremony is concluded by a prayer and the medium is awakened by beating upon his back and the massaging of his limbs out of their cataleptic contraction. These possession-rites are also conducted by the pilgrims who ascend the mountain of Ontaké.

Buddhism, which shares with Shinto the devotions of *Japan*, enjoins meditation as a means of attaining to supernatural knowledge and occult power. It is said that to those who in truth and constancy put in force the doctrines of Buddha the following ten powers will be granted. (1). They know the thoughts of others. (2). Their sight, piercing as that of the celestials, beholds without mist all that happens in the earth. (3). They know the past and present. (4). They perceive the uninterrupted succession of the ages of the world. (5). Their hearing is so fine that they perceive and can interpret all the harmonies of the three worlds and the ten divisions of the universe. (6). They are not subject to bodily conditions and can assume any appearance at will. (7). They distinguish the shadowing of lucky or unlucky words, whether they are near or far away. (8). They possess the knowledge of all forms, and knowing that form is void, they can assume every sort of form ; and knowing that vacancy is form, they can annihilate and render nought all forms. (9). They possess a knowledge of all laws. (10). They possess the perfect science of contemplation. It is said that methods are thus known by which it is possible to so radically change the psychological condition of the individual that he is enabled to recognise the character of the opposition between subjective and objective. These two extremes are reconciled in a higher condition of consciousness, a higher form of life, a more profound and complete activity which concerns the inmost depths of the self. To the " Zen " monasteries, belonging to a Buddhist sect of that name, anyone who is so inclined may retire for temporary meditation and for the development of these special faculties, which are mainly produced by entering upon a calm mental state, not exactly passive, but in which the attention is not devoted to any one thing, but is evenly distributed in all directions, producing a sort of void and " waiting." The spirit thus obtains entire repose and a satisfaction of the thirst for the ideal. This mystical retirement is sought by statesmen and generals, by scientific professional and business-men, and it is said that the force which accumulates within them by practising the " Zen " methods is of effective service to them in practical life.

Many of the customs of the Japanese have a magical significance. At the Festival of the New Year extending over three days it is considered of the first importance to insure good luck and happiness for the coming year by means of many traditional observances. Houses are thoroughly cleansed materially and spiritually, this last is getting rid of the evil spirits by throwing out beans and peas from the open slides of the houses. The gateways are decorated with straw ropes made to represent the lucky, Chinese numbers of three, five and seven. Mirror cakes, associated with the sun-goddess are eaten, also lobsters, longevity being symbolised by their bent and ancient, appearance, the pine-tree branches used for decoration at this time also signifying long life.

Divination is performed by various methods : by divining rods, by the reading of lines and cracks in the shoulder-blade of a deer, and by the classical form taken from the Confucian " *Yih-king* " or *Book of Changes*, this involving the use of eight trigrams and sixty-four diagrams. One method of " raising spirits " used by the Japanese, especially by girls who have lost their lovers by death, is to put into a paper lantern a hundred rushlights and repeat an incantation of a hundred lines. One of these rushlights is taken out at the end of each line and the would-be ghost-seer then goes out in the dark with one light still burning and blows it out when the ghost ought to appear.

Charms are everywhere, fashioned of all substances and in all forms, such as strips of paper bearing magical inscriptions to avert evil, fragments of temples, carven rice-grains representing the gods of Luck, *sutras* to frighten the demons, copies of Buddha's footprint, and paper tickets bearing the name of a god are often affixed outside the doors of houses to combat the god of Poverty.

Nature and her manifestations are the result of indwelling soul-life and the Japanese mind, imbued with this belief has peopled nature with multiform shapes. There are dragons with lairs in ocean and river which yet can fly abroad in the air while from their panting breath come the clouds of rain and tempests of lightning. In the mountains and forests are bird-like gnomes who often beset way-faring men and women and steal away their wits. There are also mountain men, huge hairy monkeys, who help the wood-cutters in return for food, and mountain-women, ogres with bodies grown over with long white hair, who flit like evil moths in search of human flesh. Then legend tells of the *Senrim*, hermits of the mountains, who knew all the secrets of magic, wizards who were attended by wise toads and flying tortoises, who could conjure magical animals out of gourds, who could project their souls into space. To animals were also ascribed supernatural powers. The fox is believed to possess such gifts to an almost limitless extent, for he has miraculous vision and hearing, he can read the inmost thoughts of man, he can transform himself and assume any shape at will. He loves to delude mankind and work destruction thereby to this end often taking the form of a beautiful and seductive woman whose embrace means madness and death. To the agency of this animal is attributed demoniacal possession, this occurring mostly among ignorant and superstitious women of the lower classes. The cat is not regarded with any kindly feeling by the Japanese, this being ascribed to the fact that this animal, together with the serpent, were the only creatures who did not weep at Buddha's death. This animal has also the power of bewitchment and possesses vampire proclivities. Among sailors, however, the cat is held in estimation, for it is thought to possess the power of warding off the evil spirits which haunt the sea. The images of animals are thought to be also endowed with life. There are tales of bronze horses and deer, of huge carven dragons and stone tortoises wandering abroad at night, terrorising the people and only laid to rest by summary decapitation. Butterflies are thought to be the wandering souls of the living who may be dreaming or sunk in reverie ; white butterflies are the souls of the dead. Fireflies keep afar evil spirits, and an ointment compounded of their delicate bodies defies any poison.

Trees occupy a foremost place in the tradition and legends of *Japan*. The people regard them with great affection, and there are stories of men who, seeing a tree they loved withering and dying, committed *hara-kiri* before it praying the gods that their life so given might pass into the tree and give it renewed vigour. The willow is one of the most eerie of trees, the willow-spirit often becoming a beautiful maiden and wedding a human lover. The pine tree brings good fortune, especially in the matter of happy marriages. It is also a token of longevity. Tree spirits can sometimes be inimical to man and it is recorded of one that to stay its disturbing wanderings it was necessary to cut it down, when from the stump flowed a stream of blood.

The element of *Fire* figures largely in the Japanese world of marvels. It is worshipped in connection with the rites of the Sun-goddess and even the kitchen-furnace becomes the object of a sort of cult. There is the lamp of Buddha, while messages from Hades come to this world in the shape of fire-wheels, Phantom-fires flicker about and flames burn in the cemeteries ; there are demon-lights, fox-flames and dragon-torches. From the eyes and mouths of certain birds, such as the blue heron, fire darts forth in white flames. Globes of fire, enshrining human faces and forms, sometimes hang like fruit in the branches of the trees. The *dolls* of Japanese children are believed to be endowed with life, deriving a soul from the love expended upon them by their human possessors. Some of these dolls were credited with supernatural powers, they could confer maternity upon a childless woman, and they could bring misfortune upon any who ill-treated them. When old and faded, these dolls are dedicated to Kojin the many-armed, who dwells in the *enokie* tree, and there are reverently laid upon his shrine, bodies which once held a tiny soul. (*See* Lafcadio Hearn's *Kokoro*, Percival Lowell's *Occult Japan*, F. Hadland Davis' *Myths and Legends of Japan*.) K.N.

Jasper : Prevents fever and dropsy, strengthens the brain, and promots eloquence ; it is a preservative against defluxions, the nightmare, and epilepsy, and is often met with in the east as a counter-charm. Marbodæus mentions seventeen species of this stone, but that " like the emerald " is most noted for its magical virtues.

Jean : A magician, votary of Apollonius of Tyana. He went from town to town, wearing an iron collar, and making his living by the performance of deeds of charletanry. At Lyons he attained some measure of fame by his miraculous cures, and was admitted to the presence of the sovereign, to whom he presented a magnificent enchanted sword. In battle this weapon became surrounded by nine score drawn knives. *Jean* also gave this prince a shield containing a magic mirror which would divulge the greatest secrets The arms vanished, or were stolen.

Jean, or Iwan Easilowitz : Grand Duke of Muscory in the fourteenth century. When at the point of death he fell into terrible swoons, during which his soul made toilsome journeys. In the first he was tormented for having kept innocent prisoners in his dungeons, in the second, he was tortured still more for having ground the people under heavy tasks ; during the third voyage he died, but his body disappeared mysteriously before he could be buried, and it was thought that the devil had taken him.

Jean d'Arras : A French writer of the fourteenth century, who compiled a chronicle of *Melusine* from popular stories which he collected.

Jean de Meung : *Jean de Meung* owes his celebrity to his poetical genius rather than his alchemical powers ; to his *Roman de la Rose*, rather than to his rhyming treatise upon the hermetic philosophy. He was born about 1280, and flourished through the reigns of Louis X., Philip the Long, Charles IV., and Philip de Valois. He appears to have possessed a light and railing wit, and a keen appreciation of a jest ; and it may well be doubted whether he was altogether sincere in his praises of alchemy. Having composed a quatrain on woman, which stigmatized her in the strongest terms, the ladies of Charles VI.'s court resolved to revenge their affronted honour, and surrounding him in the royal antechanber, desired the courtiers present to strip him preparatory to their inflicting a sound flagellation. *Jean* solicited to be heard before he was condemned and punished ; and having obtained an interval of grace, set forth, with fluent eloquence, that he was certainly the author of the calumnious verses, but that they were not intended to vilipend all womankind. He referred only to the vicious and debased, and not to such models of purity as he saw around him. Nevertheless, if any lady present felt that the verses really applied to her, he was her very humble servant, and would submit to a well-deserved chastisement. Like most of the mediæval poets, *Jean de Meung* was a bitter enemy of the priesthood, and he contrived with great ingenuity a posthumous satire upon their inordinate greed. He bequeathed in his will, as a gift to the Cordeliers, a chest of immense weight. As his fame as an alchemist was wide-spread, the brotherhood accepted the legacy in the belief that the chest contained the golden results of his quest of the Philosopher's Stone. But when they opened it, their dismayed eyes rested only on a pile of *slates*, covered with the most unintelligible hieroglyphics and cabalistic characters. The perpetrator of this practical joke was hardly, we think, a very sincere believer in the wonders of alchemy. (*See* **Devon, Witchcraft in.**)

Jeanne, D'Arc : *Jeanne d'Arc* was born in the village of Domrémy, near Vaucouleurs, on the border of Champagne and Lorraine, on Jan. 6th, 1412. She was taught to spin and sew, but not to read or write, these accomplishments being unusual and unnecessary to people in her station of life. Her parents were devout, and she was brought up piously. Her nature was gentle, modest, and religious ; but with no physical weakness or morbidity ; on the contrary, she was exceptionally strong, as her later history shows.

At or about the age of thirteen, *Jeanne* began to experience what psychology now calls " auditory hallucinations." In other words, she heard " voices "—usually accompanied by a bright light—when no visible person was present. This, of course, is a common symptom of impending mental disorder ; but no insanity developed in *Jeanne d'Arc*. Startled she naturally was at first, but continuation led to familiarity and trust. The voices gave good counsel of a very commonplace kind, as, for instance, that she " must be a good girl and go often to church." Soon, however, she began to have visions ; saw St. Michael, St. Catharine, and St. Margaret ; was given instructions as to her mission ; eventually made her way to the Dauphin, put herself at the head of 6,000 men, and advanced to the relief of Orleans, which was surrounded by the victorious English. After a fortnight of hard fighting, the siege was raised, and the enemy driven off. The tide of war had turned, and in three months the Dauphin was crowned king at Rheims as Charles the Seventh.

At this point, *Jeanne* felt that her mission was accomplished. But her wish to return to her family was over-ruled by king and archbishop, and she took part in the further fighting against the allied English and Burgundian forces, showing great bravery and tactical skill. But in November, 1430, in a desperate sally from Compiégne—which was besieged by the Duke of Burgundy—she fell into the enemy's hands, was sold to the English, and thrown into a dungeon at their headquarters in Rouen.

After a year's imprisonment she was brought to trial before the Bishop of Beauvais, in an ecclesiastical court. The charges were heresy and sorcery. Learned doctors of the Church, subtle lawyers, did their best to entangle the simple girl in their dialectical toils; but she showed a remarkable power of keeping to her affirmations and of avoiding heretical statements. "God has always been my Lord in all that I have done," she said. But the trial was only pretence, for her fate was already decided. She was condemned to the stake. To the end, she solemnly affirmed the reality of her "voices," and the truth of her depositions. Her last word, as the smoke and flame rolled round her, was "Jesus." Said an English soldier, awestruck by the manner of her passing: "We are lost; we have burned a Saint." The idea was corroborated in popular opinion by events which followed, for speedy death—as if by Heaven's anger—overtook her judges and accusers. Inspired by her example and claims, and helped by dissension and weakening on the side of the enemy, the French took heart once more; and the English were all-but swept out of the country.

Jeanne's family was rewarded by ennoblement, under the name of De Lys. Twenty-five years after her death, the Pope acceded to a petition that the *procès* by which she was condemned should be re-examined. The result was that the judgment was reversed, and her innocence established and proclaimed.

The life of the Maid supplies a problem which orthodox science cannot solve. She was a simple peasant girl, with no ambitious hankering after a career. She rebelled pathetically against her mission. "I had far rather rest and spin by my mother's side, for this is no work of my choosing, but I must go and do it, for my Lord wills it." She cannot be dismissed on the "simple idiot" theory of Voltaire, for her genius in war and her aptitude in repartee undoubtedly prove exceptional mental powers, unschooled though she was in what we call education. We cannot call her a mere hysteric, for her health and strength were superb. It is on record that a man of science said to an Abbé :—"Come to the Salpétrière Hospital, and I will show you twenty Jeannes d'Arc." To which the Abbé responded : "Has one of them given us back Alsace and Lorraine ?" The retort was certainly neat. Still, though the Salpétrière hysterics have not won back Alsace and Lorraine, it is nevertheless true that many great movements have sprung from fraud or hallucination. May it not have been so with *Jeanne*? She delivered France, and her importance in history is great; but may not her mission and her doings have been the outcome of merely subjective hallucinations, induced by the brooding of her specially religious and patriotic mind on the woes of her country? The army, being ignorant and superstitious, would readily believe in the supernatural nature of her mission, and great energy and valour would result—for a man fights well when he feels that Providence is on his side.

This is the most usual kind of theory in explanation of the facts. But it is not fully satisfactory. How came it—one may ask—that this untutored peasant girl could persuade not only the rude soldiery, but also the Dauphin and the Court, of her Divine appointment? How came she to be given the command of an army? Surely a post of such responsibility and power would not be given to an ignorant girl of eighteen, on the mere strength of her own claim to inspiration. It seems, at least, very improbable.

Now it so happens (though the materialistic school of historians conveniently ignore or belittle it) that there is strong evidence in support of the idea that *Jeanne* gave the Dauphin some proof of the possession of supernormal faculties. In fact, the evidence is so strong that Mr. Andrew Lang called it "unimpeachable"—and Mr. Lang did not usually err on the side of credulity in these matters. Among other curious things, *Jeanne* seems to have repeated to Charles the words of a prayer which he had made *mentally ;* and she also made some kind of clairvoyant discovery of a sword hidden behind the altar of Fierbois church. Schiller's magnificent dramatic poem—"Die Jungfrau von Orleans"—though unhistorical in some details, is substantially accurate on these points concerning clairvoyance and mind-reading.

The best books on the Maid are those of Mr. Anatole France (two vols.), and Mr. Andrew Lang, giving respectively the sceptical and the believing side as to the explanation of her experiences. There is also a very useful little book by Miss C. M. Antony, with preface by Father R. H. Benson.

Jelaleddin, Rumi : A Sufi poet of the thirteenth century, A.D. He teaches the Sufi doctrine that the chief end of man is so to emancipate himself from human thoughts and wishes, human needs and the outward impressions of the senses, that he may become a mere mirror for the Deity. So refined an essence does his mind become that it is as nearly as possible nothing; yet while in this state it can, by a union with the Divine Essence, mysteriously become the All. In his teachings he declares that names and words must not be taken for the things they represent:—

"Names thou mayst know ; go, seek the truth they name
Search not the brook, but heaven, for the moon."

Jennings, Hargrave : (*See* **Rosicrucians.**)

Jesodoth : The angel through which Elohim, the source of knowledge, understanding and wisdom, was imparted to the earth. This belief is of Jewish origin.

Jet : Its virtues are thus described by Pliny, according to the version of Holland : "In burning, the perfume thereof chaseth away serpents, and bringeth women again that lie in a traunce by the suffocation or rising of the mother ; the said smoke discovereth the falling sicknesse and bewraieth whether a young damsel be a maiden or no ; the same being boiled in wine helpeth the toothache, and tempered with wax cureth the swelling glandules named the king's evil. They say that the magicians use this jeat stone much in their sorceries, which they practice by the means of red hot axes, which they call axinomancia, for they affirm that being cast thereupon it will burne and consume, if that ewe desire and wish shall happen accordingly." *Jet* is known in Prussia as black amber.

Jets : (*See* **Siberia.**)

Jettatura : The Italian name for the power of the "evil eye." In order to guard against it magicians say that horns must be worn on the body.

Jinn : Singular Jinnee, plural Jineeyeh, Arabian spirits, perhaps animistic, but more probably strictly mythological like the Persian divs (q.v.). The *jinn* were created out of fire, and occupied the earth for several thousand years before Adam ; they were perverse, and would not reform, although prophets were sent to reclaim them ; they were eventually driven from the earth, and took refuge in the outlying islands of the sea. One of the number named Azazeel (afterwards called Iblees) had been carried off as a prisoner by the angels ; he grew up amongst them, and became their chief, but having refused, when commanded, to prostrate himself before Adam, he was degraded to the condition of a sheytân, and becomes the father of the sheytâns, or devils. The *jinn* are not immortal, but destined ultimately to die : they eat and drink and propagate their species ; they live in communities, and are ruled over by princes : they can make themselves visible or invisible, and assume the forms of various animals, such as serpents, cats and dogs. There are good *jinn* and bad *jinns*. They frequent baths, wells, latrines, ovens, ruined houses, rivers, cross roads and market places. Finally, like the demons of the Rabbins, they ascend to heaven and learn the future by eavesdropping. But with all their power and knowledge, they are liable to be reduced to obedience by means of talismans or magic arts, and become obsequious servants until the spell is broken.

It is far from clear or certain, that the *jinn* of the east were borrowed from the mythology or philosophy of the west, and the practice of translating the Arabic word *jinn* by the Latin term " genius " arose more from an apparent resemblance in the names, than from any identity in the nature and functions of those imaginary beings. This similarity of name, however, must have been purely accidental, for the Arabs knew little or nothing of the Latin language, and not a single term derived immediately from it ; dæmon, therefore, and not genius was the word which they would have used if they had borrowed this part of their creed from the west. *Jinn* appears, moreover, to be a genuine Arabic word, derived from a root signifying " to veil " or " conceal " ; it, therefore, means properly, " that which is veiled and cannot be seen." " In one sense,' says Fruzàbàdi, author of the *Câmus*, " the word *Jinn* signifies any spiritual being concealed from all our senses, and, for that reason, the converse of a material being. Taken in this extensive sense, the word *Jinn* comprehends devils as well as angels, but there are some properties common to both angels and *Jinn* ; some peculiar to each. Every angel is a *Jinn*, but every *Jinn* is not an angel. In another sense, this term is applied peculiarly to a particular kind of spiritual beings ; for such beings are of three kinds ; the good, which are angels ; the bad, devils ; and the intermediate, comprehending both good and bad, who form the class of *Jinn*." Thus the Arabs acknowledge good and bad genii, in that respect agreeing with the Greeks, but differing from the Persians. The genii, so long familiarized to European readers by the Arabian Nights, were not the same beings, mentioned by the Arabian lexicographer, but the Divs and Dévatàs of Indian romance, dressed up in a foreign attire, to please the taste of readers in Persia and Arabia.

The principal differences, therefore, between the genii of the west and the *jinn* of the east, seem to have been these ; the genii were deities of an inferior rank, the constant companions and guardians of men, capable of giving useful or prophetic impulses, acting as a species of mediators and messengers between the gods and men. Some were supposed to be friendly, others hostile, and many believed one of each kind to be attached, from his birth, to every mortal. The former was called Agathodæmon, the latter Cacodæmon ; and one of the latter who appeared to Cassius is represented as a man of vast stature and of a black hue, whence, no doubt, that colour has been given, in latter times, to the devil. The good genius prompted men to good, the evil to bad actions. That of each individual was as a shadow of himself. Often he was represented as a serpent ; his age also varied ; he was generally crowned with a chaplet of plane leaves. In coins of Trajan and Hadrian the genius places a *patera* with his right hand on an altar, and holds a sort of scourge in his left. His sacrifices were wholly bloodless, consisting of wine and flowers, and the person who performed the oblation was the first to taste the cup. They were adored with prostrations, particularly on the birthday, which was placed under their especial care.

The Roman men swore by their Genius, the women by their Juno. The genius of the reigning Prince was an oath of extraordinary solemnity. There were local as well as individual genii, concerning whom many particulars may be found in " Vossius," *de Idol.*

The *Jinn*, on the contrary, who seem to be the lineal descendants of the Dévatés and Rakshasas of the Hindu mythology, were never worshipped by the Arabs, nor considered as anything more than the agents of the Deity. Since the establishment of Mohammedanism, indeed, they have been described as invisible spirits, and their feats and deformities which figure in romance are as little believed by Asiatics, as the tales of " Arthur's Round Table " are by ourselves. Their existence as superhuman beings is maintained by the Mussulman doctors, but that has little connection with their character and functions as delineated by poets.

Jinnistan : An imaginary country which, according to a popular belief among the Persians, was the residence of the *jinn* who had submitted to Solomon.

Johannites : A mystic sect who follow the tenets of the late Father John of Cronstadt, where they publish an organ, and pursue their propaganda by means of itinerant pamphlet-sellers. They are said to abduct Jewish children, and because of this rumour they have on more than one occasion come under police supervision. They have several times unsuccessfully fixed the date of the Last Judgment. They declared in Father John's life-time that all the powers of heaven had descended into Cronstadt, and were personified in the entourage of Father John. They exhorted all believers to make confession to Father John, who alone could rescue sinners from the depths of hell. The orthodox clergy would not know the Lord, but Father John would gather together in Cronstadt 144,000 of the blessed, and then " leave the earth." Another affirmation of theirs is that all children who are new-born are " little devils," who must be " stamped out " immediately after birth. The Johannites urged the people to sell all their possessions and send the proceeds to Father John, or entrust them to the keeping of the pamphlet-sellers. Evidence is forthcoming tending to show that Father John was unaware of the abuse of his name, and on one occasion, in reply to a telegram from Bishop Nikander, of Perm, he strongly repudiated any connection with certain Johannite propagandists in the Perm Government.

John King : A spirit. (*See* **Spiritualism**.)

John of Nottingham : English Magician. (*See* **England**.)

John XXII., Pope : Jacques Duèse, subsequently *Pope John XXII.*, was born at Cahors in France towards the close of the 12th century. The exact date of his advent is indeterminate, but it is reported that his parents were in affluent circumstances, and it has even been suggested that they belonged to the *noblesse*. Jacques was educated first at a Dominican priory in his native village, and afterwards at Montpellier ; while subsequently he proceeded to Paris, where he studied both law and medicine. Leaving the Sorbonne, he was still at a loss to know what profession to follow ; but, chancing to become intimate with one Bishop Louis, a son of Charles II., King of Naples, the young man decided to enter the church, being doubtless prompted to this step by the conviction that his new friend's influence would help him forward in the clerical career. Nor was the future pontiff disappointed herein, for in the year 1300, at the instance of the Neapolitan sovereign, he was elevated to the episcopal see of Fréjus, while in 1308 he was appointed Chancellor of Naples. He soon showed himself a man of no mean ability in ecclesiastical affairs, and in 1310 Pope Clement V. saw fit to summon him to Avignon, being anxious to consult him anent certain points ; while in 1312 Jacques was made Bishop of Porto, and four years later he was elected to the pontifical crown and sceptre.

Thenceforth he lived always at Avignon, but his life was by no means a quiet or untroubled one. Early in his reign the throne of Germany became vacant, Louis of Bavaria and Frederick of Austria both contended for it, and Jacques gave great offence by supporting the claims of the latter; while at a later date he raised a storm by preaching a somewhat heterodox sermon, its purport being that the souls of those who have died in a state of grace go straight into Abraham's bosom, and do not enjoy the beatific vision of the Lord till after the Resurrection and the last judgment. This doctrine was hotly opposed by many clerics, notably Thomas of England, who had the courage to preach against it openly at Avignon; and so great was the disfavour which John incurred, in fact, that for several years after his death in 1334 he was widely regarded as Anti-Christ.

Jacques has frequently been credited with avarice, and it is true that he made stupendous efforts to raise money, imposing numerous taxes unheard of before his *régime*. Indeed, he manifested considerable ingenuity in this relation, and so the tradition that he dabbled in hermetic philosophy is probably founded on hard fact. It must be conceded, on the one hand, that in the course of his reign he issued a stringent bull against alchemists; but then, this was directed rather against the charlatans of the craft than against those who were seeking the philosopher's stone with real earnestness, and with the aid of scientific knowledge. It is more than likely, moreover, that *Jacques* sent forth this mandate largely with a view to blinding those who had charged him with essaying the practice at issue himself; and, be that as it may, it is certain that he

believed in magic and was interested in science. His credulity as regards the former is demonstrated by his bringing a charge of sorcery against Géraud, Bishop of Cahors; while his scientific predilections are evinced by the fact that he kept up a laboratory in the palace at Avignon, and was wont to spend much time therein. Doubtless some of this time was given to physiological and pathological studies, for various works of a medical nature are ascribed to *Jacques*, in particular a collection of prescriptions, a treatise on diseases of the eye, and another on the formation of the fœtus. But it may well be supposed that the avaricious prelate's activities in his laboratory were also bestowed in some measure on alchemistic researches, and the theory is buttressed by his having been a friend of Arnold de Villanova; while more important still, among the writings attributed to *Jacques* is *L'Art Transmutatoire*, published at Lyons in 1557. Besides, the pontiff left behind him on his death a vast sum of money and a mass of priceless jewels, and it was commonly asserted, among the alchemists of the day, that these and also two hundred huge ingots had all been manufactured by the deceased. The story of the unbounded wealth he had amassed in this way gradually blossomed and bore fruit, and one of *Jacques'* mediæval biographers credits him with having concocted a quantity of gold equivalent to £660,000 sterling.

Judah Ha-Levi (1085-1140): Celebrated Hebrew theologian and mystic. He seems to have had some conception of elementary spirits, for of the angels he says that "some are created for the time being, out of the subtle elements of matter."

Jung-Stilling : (*See* **Spiritualism.**)

K

Ka : The Egyptian conception of one of the seven parts of man; a spiritual double or astral body. Not only did mankind possess a *Ka*, but animals and inanimate objects as well. Every mortal received a *Ka* at birth. When he died his *Ka* left him, but was supposed to hover near the body and occasionally to reanimate it. For this purpose statues were placed near the mummy in which the *Ka* might find a temporary shelter. The *Ka* was provided with food by the friends of the deceased who left provisions in the tomb for its use. (*See* **Egypt and Vampire.**)

Kabala, The : A Hebrew and Jewish system of theosophy. The word signifies "doctrines received from tradition." In ancient Hebrew literature the name was used to denote the entire body of religious writings, the Pentateuch excepted. It is only in the early middle ages that the system of theosophy known as Kabalism was designated by that name. We will first consider the *Kabala* as a literary production before proceeding to examine it in the light of a hand-book of Hebrew occultism. The main sources which went to the making of the *Kabala* are the *Sepher Yesirah* or Book of Creation, which is a combination of mediæval mysticism and science. The date of origin of this work has been matter of great argument, but it is perhaps safest to say that it seems to be earlier than the ninth century A.D. The *Bahir* or brilliant is first quoted by Nahmanides, and is usually attributed to his teacher, Ezra. It owes much to the *Sepher Yesirah*, and to a great extent foreshadows the *Zohar*, which is a commentary on the *Pentateuch*, including eleven dissertations on that book,— the most important of which are the *Book of Secrets*, the *Secret of Secrets*, the *Mysteries of the Pentateuch*, and the *Hidden Interpretation*. It pretends to the authorship of Simon ben Yohai in the second century, and it is alleged that he drew his sources from traditional dialogues between God and Adam in Paradise. It is further stated that it was

discovered in a cavern in Galilee where it had been hidden for one thousand years. It has been proved almost beyond doubt, however, that it was written in the thirteenth century, and the capture of Jerusalem by the Crusaders is alluded to. It is also believed that Moses de Leon, who died in 35, and who circulated and sold the *Zohar*, was himself its author. At the same time there is no doubt that it enshrines a large number of very ancient and important Hebrew traditions. The matter contained in the *Kabala* deals with the nature of God, the *sephiroth* or divine emanations, of angels and of man. God, known in the *Kabala* as En Soph, fills and contains the universe. As he is boundless, mind cannot conceive him, so in a certain mystical sense he is non-existent. The doctrine of the *sephiroth* is undoubtedly the most important to be met with in the pages of the *Kabala*. To justify his existence the Deity had to become active and creative, and this he achieved through the medium of the ten sephiroth or intelligences which emanated from him like rays proceeding from a luminary. The first *sephiroth* or emanation was the wish to become manifest, and this contained nine other intelligences or sephiroth, which again emanate one from the other—the second from the first, the third from the second, and so forth. These are known as the Crown, Wisdom, Intelligence, Love, Justice, Beauty, Firmness, Splendour, Foundation and Kingdom. From the junction of pairs of *sephiroth*, other emanations were formed : thus from Wisdom and Intelligence proceeded Love or Mercy and from Mercy and Justice, Beauty. The *sephiroth* are also symbolical of primordial man and the heavenly man, of which earthly man is the shadow. They form three triads which respectively represent intellectual, moral, and physical qualities : the first, Wisdom, Intelligence and Crown ; the second Love, Justice and Beauty ; the third Firmness, Splendour and Foundation. The whole is circled or bound by Kingdom, the ninth *sephiroth*. Each of these triads symbolises a portion of the human frame : the first the head ; the second the arms ; the third the legs. It must be understood that though those *sephiroth* are emanations from God they remain a portion, and simply represent different aspects of the One Being.

Kabalistic cosmology posits four different worlds, each of which forms a sephiric system of a decade of emanations, which were verified in the following manner : the world of emanations or the heavenly man, a direct emanation from the *En Soph*. From it is produced the world of creation, or the *Briatic* world of pure nature, but yet not so spiritual as the first. The angel Metatron inhabits it and constitutes the world of pure spirit. He governs the visible world and guides the revolutions of the planets. From this is formed the world of formation or the *Yetziratic* world, still less refined, which is the abode of angels. Finally from these emanates the world of action or matter, the dwelling of evil spirits, which contains ten hells, each becoming lower until the depths of diabolical degradation is reached. The prince of this region is Samael, the evil spirit, the serpent of Genesis, otherwise " the Beast." But the universe was incomplete without the creation of man ; the heavenly Adam, that is the tenth *sephiroth*, created the earthly Adam, each member of whose body corresponds to a part of the visible universe. The human form, we are told, is shaped after the four letters which constitute the Jewish tetragrammation, *Jhava*, thus, the letters J h a v a . The souls of the whole human race pre-exist in the world of emanations, and are all destined to inhabit human bodies. Like the *sephiroth* from which it emanates, every soul has ten potentces, consisting of a trinity of triads—spirit, soul, cruder soul or *neptesh*. Each soul, before its entrance into the world consists of male and female united into one being, but when it descends to this earth, the two parts are separated and animate different bodies. The destiny of the soul upon earth is to develop the perfect germs implanted in it, which must ultimately return to *En Soph*. If it does not succeed in acquiring the experience for which it has been sent to earth, it must re-inhabit the body three times till it becomes duly purified. When all the souls in the world of the *sephiroth* shall have passed through this period of probation and returned to the bosom of En Soph, the jubilee will commence ; even Satan will be restored to his angelic nature, and existence will be a Sabbath without end. The *Kabala* states that these esoteric doctrines are contained in the Hebrew scriptures, but cannot be perceived by the uninitiated ; they are, however, plainly revealed to persons of spiritual mind.

Next considering the *Kabala* as occult literature, we find it stated that the philosophical doctrines developed in its pages are found to have been perpetuated by the secret method of oral tradition from the first ages of humanity. " The *Kabala*," says Dr. Ginsburg, when explaining the story of its birth, " was first taught by God Himself to a select company of angels, who formed a theosophic school in Paradise. After the Fall the angels most graciously communicated this heavenly doctrine to the disobedient child of earth, to furnish the protoplasts with the means of returning to their pristine nobility and felicity. From Adam it passed over to Noah, and then to Abraham, the friend of God, who emigrated with it to Egypt, where the patriarch allowed a portion of this mysterious doctrine to ooze out. It was in this way that the Egyptians obtained some knowledge of it, and the other Eastern nations could introduce it into their philosophical systems. Moses, who was learned in all the wisdom of Egypt, was first initiated into the *Kabala* in the land of his birth, but became most proficient in it during his wanderings in the wilderness, when he not only devoted to it the leisure hours of the

whole forty years, but received lessons in it from one of the angels. By the aid of this mysterious science the law-giver was enabled to solve the difficulties which arose during his management of the Israelites, in spite of the pilgrimages, wars, and frequent miseries of the nation. He covertly laid down the principles of this secret doctrine in the first four books of the Pentateuch, but withheld them from Deuteronomy. Moses also initiated the seventy Elders into the secrets of this doctrine, and they again transmitted them from hand to hand. Of all who formed the unbroken line of tradition, David and Solomon were the most deeply initiated into the *Kabala*. No one, how-ever, dared to write it down till Schimeon ben Jochai, who lived at the time of the destruction of the second. After his death, his son, Rabbi Eleazar, and his secretary, Rabbi Abba, as well as his disciples, collated Rabbi Simon Ben Jochai's treatises, and out of these composed the celebrated work called Z H R, *Zohar*, Splendour, which is the grand storehouse of Kabalism."

The history of Kabalistic origins, however, is as has been shown almost wholly fabulous, and no evidence worthy of the name can be adduced in its support. The mysticism of the *Mishna* and the *Talmud* must be carefully distinguished from that of the Kabalistic writings, as they are un-doubtedly of very considerable antiquity. But the *Kabala* has certain claims upon the modern student of mysticism. Its philosophical value is not depreciated by its modern origin, and it is regarded by many as an absolute guide to knowledge in all the most profound problems of existence. Its thesis is extensive and profound, but examination unfortunately proves it to be merely a series of dogmatic hypotheses, a body of positive doctrine based on a central assumption which is incapable of proof. This tradition, says Eliphas Levi, wholly reposes on the single dogma of magic, that the Visible is for us a proportional measure of the Invisible. In fact it proceeds by analogy from the known to the unknown. At the same time, it is a most interesting effort of the human mind.

Mediæval magic was deeply indebted to Kabalistic combinations of the divine names for the terms of its rituals, and from it it derived the belief in a resident virtue in sacred names and numbers. Certain definite rules are employed to discover the sublime source of power resident in the Jewish scriptures. Thus the words of several verses in the scriptures which are regarded as containing an occult sense, are placed over each other, and the letters are formed into new words by reading them vertically ; or the words of the text are arranged in squares in such a manner as to be read vertically or otherwise. Words are joined together and re-divided, and the initial and final letters of certain words are formed into separate words. Again, every letter of the word is reduced to its numerical value, and the word is explained by another of the same quantity. Every letter of a word too is taken to be an initial of an abbreviation of it. The twenty-two letters of the alphabet are divided into two halves, one half is placed above the other, and the two letters which thus become associated are interchanged. This *a* becomes *l*, *b*, *m*, and so on. This cipher alphabet is called *albm* from the first interchanged pairs. The commutation of the twenty-two letters is effected by the last letter of the alphabet taking the place of the first, the last but one the place of the second and so forth. This cipher is called *atbah*. These permutations and combinations are much older than the *Kabala*, and obtained amongst Jewish occultists from time immemorial.

Lastly, it should be pointed out that the *Kabala* has been condemned nowhere more strongly than among the Jews themselves. Jewish orthodoxy has always been suspicious of it, and as Mr. A. E. Waite has well said :

" The best lesson we can learn from it is the necessity of scrupulously separating the experimental knowledge of the mystics from their bizarre fields of speculation."

Kabotermannekens : According to the Flemish peasants, little spirits which play tricks on the women of the country, particularly on those who work in the dairy.

Kaf : According to the Musulmans, a great mountain that stretches to the horizon on every side. The earth is in the middle of this mountain, they say, like a finger in the middle of a ring. Its foundation is the stone *Sakhrat*, the least fragment of which is capable of working untold marvels. This stone it is which causes earthquakes. It is made of a single emerald. The mountain, which is frequently spoken of in Eastern tales, is said to be the habitation of genii. To reach it one must pass through dark wildernesses, and it is essential that the traveller be guided by a supernatural being.

Kai : The seneschal of King Arthur, known in the French romances as Messire Queux, or Maitre Queux or Kuex. He is prominent in the *Morte d'Arthur*. In the tale of Kilhwuh and Olwen in the Mabinogion, he is identified with a personage whose " breath lasted nine nights and days under water " and who " could exist nine nights and nine days without sleep." A wound from his sword could not be cured ; he could make himself as tall as the highest tree, and so great was the heat of his nature that, during rain, whatever he carried remained dry. Originally a deity, a rain-and-thunder god, he had apparently degenerated, through a series of mythological processes, into a mere hero.

Kale Thaungto : A town of wizards in Lower Burma. (*See* **Burma.**)

Kalid : (*See* **Morien.**)

Kapila : believed by the Hindus to be the god Vishnu, son of Brahman, in the fifth of his twenty-four incarnations. He wrote a series of philosophical propositions known as the *Sutras*, in which he states it is by philosophical study alone that one may attain union with the deity.

Kardec, Allen : The *nom de guerre* of Denizard Rivail, the French spiritualist whose doctrines were largely accepted on the Continent and especially in France. The chief tenet in spiritism was the doctrine of re-incarnation. Rivail, before his conversion to spiritualism, had occupied himself a great deal with animal magnetism. In 1856 he was introduced into a spiritualistic circle by Victorien Sardou. His *Livre des Esprits* and the works with which he followed it were based largely on communications received through mediums. They had a wide circulation, and the doctrines of spiritism became much more popular, in France at least, than those of the rival spiritualism, which did not include re-incarnation among its tenets. The names *Allan* and *Kardec* which M. Rivail assumed were names he had borne in two former incarnations, revealed to him by mediumistic communications. He was the editor of *La Revue Spirite*, and the founder and president of the Parisian Society for Spiritualistic Studies, at which M. Camille Flammarion, then nineteen years of age, made his first acquaintance with psychic science in 1861. *Allan Kardec* died in 1869, his doctrines having by that time become firmly established. In Britain, however, they made but little headway, his only disciple of note in this country being Miss Anna Blackwell. (*See* **France** and **Spiritualism.**)

Karma is a doctrine common to Brahmanism, Buddhism and Theosophy though theosophists have not adopted it wholly as it is taught in the two religions mentioned. The word *karma* itself means " action," but it may be useful to remember that generally the doctrine teaches that everything done is done for eternity, that, in short, " thou shalt reap as thou didst sow." Action is not homogeneous but on the contrary, contains three elements, the thought which conceives it, the will which finds the means of accomplish-

ment, and the union of thought and will which brings the action to pass. It is plain, therefore, that thought is very potent for good or evil, for as the thought is, so will the action be. The miser, thinking of avarice, is avaricious, the libertine, thinking of vice, is vicious, and on the contrary, those of virtuous thoughts show virtue in their actions. Arising naturally from such teaching is the attention devoted to thought-power. Taking the analogy of the physical body which may be developed by regimen and training, based on natural scientific laws, theosophists teach that character may, in exactly the same way, be scientifically built up. Physical weakness can be eradicated and an opposite state of affairs brought about by special exercise of the weak part, and by a similar method, weakness of character may be converted into strength Every vice is considered to evidence the lack of a corresponding virtue, avarice for instance showing the absence of generosity. Instead, however, of allowing matters to rest at this, under the plea—arising from ignorance—that the man was naturally avaricious, theosophists, on the lines of scientific knowledge, teach that constant thought directed to generosity will in time change the man's nature in this respect. This result cannot, of course, be brought about in a day, and the length of time necessary depends on at least two factors, the strength of thought and the strength of the vice, for the latter may be the sum of the indulgence of many ages and hence correspondingly difficult to eradicate The doctrine of *karma* must, however, be considered not in its relation to one life only, but in the light of the theosophic teaching of re-incarnation (q.v.). Re-incarnation is carried on under the law of *karma* as well as of evolution. The new-born man bears within him the seeds of what he formerly was. His character is the same as it was. It is as he made it in past existences and accordingly as he made it, so does it continue unless he himself change it as he had the power to do. Each succeeding existence finds that character more definite in one direction or another and if it be evil, the effort to change it becomes increasingly difficult, indeed a complete change may not be possible until many existences of effort have passed. In such cases as these, the promptings of evil may be too strong to be resisted, yet the man who has an intelligent knowledge of the workings of *Karma*, though he must eventually yield, does so only after the most desperate struggle of which his nature is capable, and thus, instead of yielding weakly and increasing the power of the evil, he has helped to destroy its potency. Only in the most rare cases can he free himself with one effort. (*See also* **Theosophy** and **Evolution.**)

Katean Secret Society : A secret society of the Moluccas. Anyone who wished to become a member was introduced into the *Katean* house through an aperture in the form of a crocodile's jaws or a cassowary's beak. Having remained there for a few days he was secretly removed to a remote spot. At the end of two months he was permitted to return to his relatives—hitherto unaware of his whereabouts—a member of the *Katean Society*.

Kathari : An heretical sect who excited the wrath of the clergy in mediæval times. (*See* **Waldenses.**)

Katie King : A spirit. (*See* **Materialisation** and **Spiritualism.**)

Katika Lima : Malay system of Astrology. (*See* **Malays.**)

Katika Tujo : Malay system of Astrology. (*See* **Malays.**)

Kauks, hatched from cock's egg : (*See* **Cock.**)

Keingala : The weatherwise mare of Asmund in the saga of Grettir the Strong. Her master believed in her weather prophecies, and, in setting his second son, Grettir, to look after the horses, told him to be guided by *Keingala*, who would always return to the stable before a storm. As she persisted in remaining on the cold hillside, grazing on the scanty grass till the lad was nearly frozen with cold, Grettir determined to make her return home regardless of the weather. One morning before turning out the horses he tore off a long strip of her skin from wither to flank. This had the effect of making the mare soon seek her stable ; and the same thing occurring the next day, no storm impending, Asmund himself let out the horses, when he discovered what had been done.

Kelly, Edward : (*See* **Dee.**)

Kelpie, The : A water spirit which, in Scotland, is believed to haunt streams and torrents. Kelpies appear to be of a mischievous nature, and were often accused of stopping the water-wheels of mills, and of swelling streams. The *Kelpie* is occasionally used as a name of terror to frighten unruly children ; and it was believed that he also devoured women.

Kephalonomancy : A method of divination which is practised by making divers signs on the baked head of an ass. It was familiar to the Germans and the Lombards substituted for it the head of a goat. The ancients placed lighted carbon on an ass's head, and pronounced the names of those who were suspected of any crime. If a crackling coincided with the utterance of a name, the latter was taken as being that of the guilty person.

Kephu : a Karen Vampire. (*See* **Vampire.**)

Kepler, John—1571–1630 : A great mathematician and astrologer. He was born at Weil in Würtemburg and educated at a monastic school at Maulbrunn and afterwards at the university of Tübingen, where he studied philosophy, mathematics, theology and astronomy. In 1593 he became professor of mathematics and morals at Gratz in Styria, where he also continued his astrological studies. He had an unhappy home life, and was somewhat persecuted for his doctrines. In 1626 were printed the famous Rodolphine tables, which he had prepared along with Tycho de Brahe, the astronomer. He died at Ratisbon. The laws of the courses of the planets, deduced by Kepler from observations made by Tycho, and known as *The Three Laws of Kepler*, became the foundation of Newton's discoveries, as well as the whole modern theory of the planets. His services in the cause of astronomy have placed him high amongst the distinguished men of science, and in 1808 a monument was erected to his memory at Ratisbon. His most important work is his *Astronomia nova, seu Physica Coelestis tradita Commentariis de Motibus Stellae Martis* (1609) which is still regarded as a classic by astronomers.

Kerheb : Egyptian Scribes. (*See* **Egypt.**)

Kerner, Dr. : (*See* **Spiritualism.**)

Kether : The Kabbalistic name for the number one, and meaning " Reason "—the Crown, the equilibrating power. Also a Hebrew occult name for one of the three essentials of God—Reason.

Kevan of the Curling Locks : The lover of Cleena who went off to hunt in the woods, leaving her to be abducted by the fairies.

Key of Solomon the King : A magical treatise of mediæval origin, of which a number of manuscripts are extant. It is supposed to be the work of King Solomon (q.v.), but is manifestly of comparatively modern origin, and was probably written in the fourteenth or fifteenth century. It is permeated with late Jewish ideas, and its chief intention appears to be the finding of treasure, and the making of such experiments as have for their object the interference with the free will of others. The power of the Divine Name is much in evidence, and the entire work is an absurd combination of pomposity and nonsense.

The *Lemegeton*, or Leeser Key of Solomon, is much more noteworthy. Its earliest examples date from the seventeenth century, and it invokes the hierarchies of the abyss by legions and millions. It is divided into four parts, which control the offices of all spirits at the will of the operator. The first part, *Gœtia*, contains forms of conjuration for seventy-two demons with an account of their powers and offices. The second part, *Theurgia Gœtia*, deals with the spirits of the cardinal points, who are of mixed nature. The third book is called the *Pauline Art*—the significance of which name is unaccountable. It deals with the angels of the hours of the day and night, and of the signs of the Zodiac. The fourth part is entitled *Almadel*, which enumerates four other choirs of spirits. The usual homilies regarding purity of life are insisted upon, as is the circumstance that none of the conjurations shall be applied to the injury of another.

Khaib : The Egyptian name for the shadow, which at death was supposed to quit the body to continue a separate existence of its own. It was represented under the form of a sunshade.

Khu : The Egyptian name for one of the immortal parts of man, probably the spirit. The word means " clear " or " luminous " and is symbolised by a flame of fire.

Khwaja Ka Mulay : (*See* **Siberia.**)

Kian : In Irish legend, Father of Lugh. His magical cow with her wonderful supply of milk having been stolen by Balor, he revenged himself by making Balor's daughter, Ethlinn, the mother of three sons. Of these two were drowned by Balor, and the third Lugh, escaping by falling into a bay, was wafted back to his father, *Kian*. Some years later, while fighting in Ulster, *Kian* fell in with the three sons of Turenn whose house was at enmity with him. To escape their notice, he turned himself into a pig, but they recognised him and he was wounded by one of them. He begged to be restored to his human shape before dying. This being granted, he rejoiced in having outwitted his enemies, as they would now have to pay the blood-fine for a man instead of a pig. The brothers, determined that there should be no blood-stained weapon to publish the deed, stoned *Kian* and buried his body.

King Robert of Sicily : (English romance of the fourteenth century, author unknown). It has never been printed. It tells how *King Robert of Sicily* was beguiled by pride into sneering at a priest who read mass. To punish him, an angel was sent down by God, and he, assuming *Robert's* shape, transformed the *King* into the likeness of his own fool : he is sent out to lie with the dogs. He was at length allowed to resume his proper shape after a long and ignominious penance. See poem on the subject by Longfellow.

Kinocetus : A stone said to be good in casting out devils. .

Kirk, Robert : (*See* **Scotland.**)

Kischuph : In the *Kabala*, the higher magical influence. It is divided into two branches, an elementary and a spiritual, and includes exorcism. Sometimes *Kischuph* exhibits a striking resemblance to the witchcraft of mediæval times. Sorcerers were said to change themselves into animals, and go long distances in a very short time. They may also induce pain and disease and death in men and animals. Still further allied to witches are the " women who make a contract with the Schedim, and meet them at certain times, dance with them, and visit these spirits who appear to them in the shape of goats. In many countries such women are killed." This form of *Kischuph* is true sorcery ; the other form, material *Kischuph*, is rather evil sympathy, consisting of disturbing influences on the natural elements produced by exciting false " rapports " in various substances.

Kiss, Bewitched by means of a : Florence Newton, a notorious witch of the Middle Ages, was on several occasions accused of having bewitched people by means of a *kiss*. The first was a servant-maid who had refused alms to her. About a week later the witch kissed her violently, from which time she suffered from fits and was transported from place to place, now being carried mysteriously to the top of the house, now being placed between two feather beds, and so on. The witch also caused the death of one David Jones, who stood sentinel over her in prison, by kissing his hand, and by the same means brought about the death of the children of three Youghal aldermen.

Klinnrath, Henry : A German alchemist and hierophant of the physical side of the *Magnum Opus*. He was certainly aware of the greater issues of Hermetic theorems and may be regarded as a follower of Paracelsus. He was born in Saxony about the year 1560. At the age of 28 he graduated in medicine at the University of Basle. He practised in Hamburg and thereafter in Dresden where he died in poverty and obscurity in 1601, at the age of forty-five. The most remarkable of his works, some of which are still in Manuscript, is the *Anphitheatrum Sapientiæ Æternæ solius veræ, Christiano Kabbalisticum divino magicum, &c.* It is an unfinished work and appeared after his decease with a preface and conclusion by Erasmus Wohlfahrt. It is a purely mystical and magical treatise. The seven steps leading to the goal of universal knowledge are described in a commentary on the Wisdom of Solomon. The work has been described as being the voice of ancient chaos, and its curious folding plates are particularly suggestive.

Klinschor, or Klingsor : Lord of the Magic Castle wherein are kept Arthur's mother and other queens. He is nephew to Virgilius of Naples and is overcome by Gawain. He is alluded to in the *Parsival* of Wolfram von Eschenbach.

Knigge : (*See* **Illuminati.**)

Knox, John : (*See* **Scotland.**)

Koilon is the name applied to the ether by Mrs. Besant and Mr. C. W. Leadbeater in their book on Occult Chemistry. (*See* **Ether, Theosophy.**)

Kommasso : Evil spirits inhabiting trees. (*See* **Burma.**)

Koons' Spirit Room : A log séance-room erected in Dover, Athens County, Ohio, by a farmer, Jonathan Koons, in 1852. *Koons*, an early convert to spiritualism, had been told that he and his eight children would develop mediumistic powers, and the *spirit-room* was intended to be used for manifestations produced by their mediumship. The room was furnished with the appliances incidental to the spiritualistic séance—table for rappings, tambourines, and other musical instruments ; phosphorus, by means of which the spirits might show themselves. The phenomena witnessed by the sitters, including Charles Partridge, editor of the *Spiritual Telegraph*, were of a varied nature, but in the main identical with the other manifestations of the same period. The spirits who visited *Koon's* log building claimed to be a band—one hundred and sixty-five in number—of men who had lived before the time of Adam, and from whom were descended the well-known spirit personalities, John and Katie King.

Kosh : The wicked forest fiend of the Bangala of the Southern Congo.

Koshei : (*See* **Slavs.**)

Kostchtchie, or " Deathless " : A Russian goblin of the bogle-boe species. This horrid monster is described as having a death's head and fleshless skeleton, " through which is seen the black blood flowing and the yellow heart beating." He is armed with an iron club, with which he knocks down all who come in his path. In spite of his ugliness, he is said to be a great admirer of young girls and women. He is avaricious, hates old and young alike, and particularly those who are fortunate. His dwelling is said to be amongst the mountains of the Koskels and the Caucasus, where his treasure is concealed.

Kostka, Jean : The pseudonym of Jules Doinel. A late Gnostic and initiate of the 33rd degree, who, converted to the Christian standpoint, revealed his diabolic adventures in the pages of *La Verité* under the title of " Lucifer Unmasked." He tells of diabolic happenings in the private chapel of a lady, " Madame X." who figures frequently in his pages, and who is thought to be the late Countess of Caithness, of visions of Jansen, and the classical deities. It is certain from the evidence that *M. Kostka* never came into personal contact with a Satanic or Luciferian cultus, and that his diabolic experiences were merely those of the amateur Satanist.

Kramat : (*See* **Magic.**)

Krata Repoa, or Initiation into the ancient Mysteries of the Priests of Egypt, written by C. F. Koppen and J. W. B. Von Hymmen, and published at Berlin in 1782. The term *Krata Repoa*, said to be of Egyptian origin, possesses no affinity to that language so far as the present writer is aware. The work is divided into seven grades. That of Postophoris (a word used by Apuleius to signify a priest of Isis) corresponds to the apprentice or keeper of the sacred threshold. Secondly comes the degree of Neokaros, in which are to be found many ordeals and temptations. The third degree is the State of Death—of degree of judgment and of the passage of the Soul. The candidate was restored to light in the following degree, the Battle of the Shadows. In the fifth grade a drama of Vengeance was enacted, and the sixth is that of the astronomer before the gate of the gods. In the final grade the whole scheme of initiation was expounded. It has been thought that these degrees corresponded to the actual procedure of a secret society, and it may be that in some measure they did, as one of their authors was a prominent member of The African Builders (q.v.), but although there would seem to be elements of real tradition in the work, most of it is probably mere invention.

Krstaca : Dalmatian name for a witch. (*See* **Slavs.**)

Kund : (*See* **Scandinavia.**)

Kyphi : Among the Egyptians, an aromatic substance, with soothing and healing properties, prepared from sixteen materials according to the prescription of the sacred books.

L

Labadie, Jean : A fanatic of the seventeenth century, born in 1610 at Bourg, on the Dordogne. He declared himself a second John the Baptist, sent to announce the second coming of the Messiah. He even went so far as to claim some measure of divinity for himself. But to his ambition as a votary he joined a taste for more worldly pleasures, which he indulged under the mask of religion. He died in 1674. Among his works (which were condemned) was *Le Veritable Exorcisme, au l'unique moyen de chasser le diable du monde chrétien.*

Labartu : (*See* **Babylonia,** also **Semites.**)

Laburum is a kabbalistic sign, embodied in the Great Magical Monogram which is the seventh and most important pantacle of the Enchiridion.

Lacteus : A stone applied to rheumatic eyes.

Lady-bird : A rustic mode of divination was that practised with the *lady-bird* or lady-fly. The *lady-bird* was captured by a maid and bidden to fly " north, south, or east, or west " in the direction in which her lover lived. Whichever way the insect flew, there dwelt her future husband.

Lady of Lawers : One of the Breadalbane family, of Scottish origin, and married to Campbell of Lawers. This gentlewoman was believed to be gifted with prophetic powers, and her prophecies are said to be written in a book shaped like a barrel and kept in the charter room of Taymouth Castle : it is named " The Red Book of Balloch." These forecasts all have reference to the house and lands of Breadalbane ; we give the following as an example :—" When the red cairn on Ben Lawers fell the church would split. In the same year that the cairn, built by the sappers and miners on Ben Lawers, fell, the Disruption in the Church of Scotland took place."

Lam : A magical word in Hindu yoga practice.

Lamb : *Dr. Lamb* was a noted sorcerer in the time of Charles the First. The famous Richard Baxter, in his *Certainty of the World of Spirits*, printed in 1691, has recorded an appropriate instance of the miraculous performance of this man. Meeting two of his acquaintance in the street, and they having intimated a desire to witness some examples of his skill, he invited them home with him. He then conducted them into an inner room, where presently, to their no small surprise, they saw a tree spring up in the middle of the apartment. They had scarcely ceased wondering at this phenomenon, when in a moment there appeared three diminutive men, with little axes in their hands for the purpose of cutting down this tree. The tree was felled ; and the doctor dismissed his guests, fully satisfied of the solidity of his pretensions. That very night, however, a tremendous hurricane arose, causing the house of one of the guests to rock from side to side, with every appearance that the building would come down, and bury him and his wife in the ruins. The wife in great terror asked " Were you not at *Dr. Lamb's* to-day ? " The husband confessed it was true. " And did you not bring something away from his house ? " The husband owned that, when the little men felled the tree, he had picked up some of the chips, and put them in his pocket. Nothing now remained to be done but to produce the chips, and get rid of them as fast as they could. This ceremony performed, the whirlwind immediately ceased, and the remainder of the night passed quietly.

Dr. Lamb at length became so odious by his reputation for these infernal practices, that the populace rose upon him in 1640, and tore him to pieces in the streets. Nor did the effects of his ill-fame terminate here. Thirteen years after, a woman, who had been his servant maid, was apprehended on a charge of witchcraft, was tried, and in expiation of her crime was executed at Tyburn.

Lamps, Magic : There dwelt at Paris in the time of St. Louis, a famous Jewish Rabbi called Jachiel, a great manufacturer of prodigies, who was regarded by the Jews as one of their saints, and by the Parisians as a sorcerer. During the night when everyone was asleep, he was wont to work by the light of a magic lamp which cast through his chamber a glow like that of day itself. He never replenished this lamp with oil, nor otherwise attended to it, and folks began to hint that he had acquired it through diabolic agencies. If anyone chanced to knock at his door during the night they noticed that the lamp threw out sparks of light of various colours, but if they continued to rap the lamp failed and the Rabbi turning from his work touched a large nail in the middle of his table which connected magically with the knocker on the street-door, giving to the person who rapped upon it something of the nature of an electric shock. (*See* **France.**)

Lamps of this description were supposed to be known to the Rosicrucians, and it is said that in opening the tomb of a daughter of Cicero several *lamps* were found burning upon it. It is of course possible that the light from these was luminous or phosphorescent and not living flame.

The magic *lamp* of Aladdin will occur to everyone in this connection ; and romance abounds in such vehicles of light.

Lancashire Witches : A story with many pathetic and pitiable features, and one which is eloquent of the ignorance and credulity of the age, is that of the *Lancashire Witches*. Not very far from Manchester lies Pendelbury Forest, a gloomy though romantic and picturesque spot. At the time when it was inhabited by the witches—that is to say, about the beginning of the 17th century—it was held in such terror by law-abiding folks that they scarcely dared to approach it. They imagined it to be the haunt of witches and demons, the scene of all sorts of frightful orgies and diabolical rites. So that when Roger Nowel, a country magistrate, hit upon the plan of routing the witches out of their den, and thus ridding the district of their malevolent influence, he fancied he would be doing a public-spirited and laudable action. He promptly began by seizing Elizabeth Demdike and Ann Chattox, two women of eighty years of age, one of them blind, and the other threatened with blindness, both of them living in squalor and abject poverty. Demdike's daughter, Elizabeth Device, and her grandchildren, James and Alison Device, were included in the accusation, and Ann Redferne, daughter of Chattox was apprehended with her mother. Others were seized in quick succession—Jane Bulcock and her son John, Alice Nutter, Catherine Hewitt, and Isabel Roby. All of them were induced—by what means it were better not to enquire too closely—to make a more or less detailed confession of their communication with the Devil. When this had been extorted from them, they were sent to prison in Lancaster Castle, some fifty miles away, there to await trial for their misdeeds.

They had not lain in prison very long when the authorities were informed that about twenty *witches* had assembled on Good Friday, at Malkin's Tower, the home of Elizabeth Device, in order to compass the death of one Covel, to blow up the castle in which their companions were confined, and rescue the prisoners, and also to kill a man called Lister, which last purpose they accomplished by means of diabolical agency. In the summer assizes of 1612 the prisoners were tried for witchcraft, and were all found guilty. The woman Demdike had died in prison, and thus escaped a more ignominious death at the gallows. The principal witnesses who appeared against Elizabeth Device were her grandchildren, James and Jennet Device. Directly the latter entered the witness-box her grandmother set up a terrible yelling punctuated by bitter execrations. The child, who was only nine years of age, begged that the prisoner might be removed as she could not otherwise proceed with her evidence. Her request was granted, and she and her brother swore that the Devil had visited their grandmother in the shape of a black dog, and asked what were her wishes. She had intimated that she desired the death of one John Robinson, whereupon the fiend told her to make a clay image of Robinson and gradually crumble it to pieces, saying that as she did so the man's life would decay and finally perish. On such evidence ten persons were hanged, including the aged Ann Chattox.

It is shocking to reflect that, at a period when literature and learning were at their height, such cruelty could be tolerated, not only by the vulgar and uneducated, but by the learned judges who pronounced the sentence. The women were old and ignorant and probably weak-minded. No doubt they began in time to invest themselves with those powers, which their neighbours credited to them, and to believe themselves fit objects for the awe and terror of the people. It is even possible that they may have seen some sort of visions, or hallucinations, which they persuaded themselves were evil spirits attending on them Thus their own cunning and ignorance may have hastened their downfall.

Twenty-two years later a similar outrage, on the same spot, was narrowly avoided, by the shrewdness of the judge who tried the case. A certain misguided man, by name Edmund Robinson, thought to profit by the general belief in witchcraft. To this end he taught his young son, a boy of eleven to say that one day he encountered in the fields two dogs, with which he tried to catch a hare. But the animals would not obey his bidding, and at length he tied them to a post and whipped them, when they immediately turned into a *witch* and her imp. This monstrous story gained such credence that when Robinson declared that his son possessed a sort of second-sight, which enabled him to distinguish a *witch* at a glance, no one thought of denying his statement. Accordingly, he took the boy to the neighbouring churches, set him on a bench, and bade him point out the *witches*. No less than seventeen persons were thus accused and might have been hanged had not the judge's suspicions been aroused by the story, for the jury did not hesitate to convict them. However, the doubts of the worthy judge gained a respite for the prisoners, some of whom were sent to London for examination by the King's physician and by the king himself. The boy's story was investigated and found to be merely a tissue of lies, as, indeed, the child himself confessed it to be. (*See* Whitaker, *The History of Whalley*, p. 215.)

Lapis Exilis : A name applied to the Graal itself. It is this stone which causes the phoenix to renew her youth. *Lapis Exilis*, according to Wolfram von Eschenbach, was synonymous with the Holy Grail.

Lapis Judaicus : Also identified with the Graal and the Talismanic stone of inexhaustible feeding power. It is sometimes called Theolithos, and seems but another name for the Lapis Exilis (q.v.) It has been confounded with the Phoenix stone. Another legend clings to it : it is said to have fallen from the crown of Lucifer, as he was banished from heaven, and remains in the keeping of the angels of the air.

Lapland : The Laplanders have a reputation for magical practice which is almost proverbial throughout Europe, and certainly so among the peoples of the Scandinavian Peninsula. Indeed the Finns still credit them with extraordinary power in sorcery and divination. Many Scandinavian scions of nobility were in ancient times sent to *Lapland* to obtain a magical reputation, and Eric the son of Harold Haarfager found Gunhild, daughter of Asur Tote, sojourning among the Lapps in A.D. 922 for that purpose. English literature abounds with reference to *Lapland* witches. But Sorcery in *Lapland* was a preserve of the male shamans or magicians. Like the Celtic witches the Lapps were addicted to the selling of wind or tempests in knotted ropes.

Scheffer in his *Lapponia* (1674) writing of Lapp magic says :—" The melancholic constitution of the Laplanders, renders them subject to frightful apparitions and dreams, which they look upon as infallible presages made to them by the Genius of what is to befall them. Thus they are frequently seen lying upon the ground asleep, some singing with a full voice, others howling and making a hideous noise not unlike wolves.

" Their superstitions may be imputed partly to their living in solitudes, forests, and among the wild beasts partly to their solitary way of dwelling separately from the society of others, except who belong to their own families sometimes several leagues distance. Hereafter it may be added, that their daily exercise is hunting, it being observed that this kind of life is apt to draw people into various superstitions, and at last to a correspondence with spirits. For those who lead a solitary life being frequently destitute of human aid, have ofttimes recourse to forbidden means, in hopes to find that aid and help among the spirits, which they cannot find among men ; and what encourages them in it is impunity, these things being committed by them, without as much as the fear of any witnesses ; which moved Mr. Rheen to allege, among sundry reasons which he gives for the continuance of the impious superstitions of the Laplanders, this for one : because they live among inaccessible mountains, and at a great distance from the conversation of other men. Another reason is the good opinion they constantly entertain of their ancestors, whom they cannot imagine to have been so stupid as not to understand what God they ought to worship, wherefore they judge they should be wanting in their reverence due to them, if, by receding from their institutions, they should reprove them of impiety and ignorance.

" The parents are the masters, who instruct their own sons in the magical art. ' Those,' says Tornaeus, ' who have attained to this magical art by instructions receive it either from their parents, or from somebody else, and that by degrees which they put in practice as often as an opportunity offers. Thus they accomplish themselves in this art, especially if their genius leads them to it. For they don't look upon every one as a fit scholar ; nay, some are accounted quite incapable of it, notwithstanding they have been sufficiently instructed, as I have been informed by very credible people.' And Joh. Tornaeus confirms it by these words : " As the Laplanders are naturally of different inclinations, so are they not equally capable of attaining to this art.' And in another passage, they bequeath the demons as part of their inheritance, which is the reason that one family excels the other in this magical art. From whence it is evident, that certain whole families have their own demons, not only differing from the familiar spirits of others, but also quite contrary and opposite to them. Besides this, not only whole families, but also particular persons, have sometimes one, sometimes more spirits belonging to them, to secure them against the designs of other demons, or else to hurt others. Olaus Petri Niurenius speaks to this effect, when he says—' They are attended by a certain number of spirits, some by three, others by two, or at least by one. The last is intended for their security, the other to hurt others. The first commands all the rest. Some of those they acquire with a great deal of pains and prayers, some without much trouble, being their attendants from their infancy.' Joh. Tornaeus gives us a very large account of it. ' There are some,' says he, ' who naturally are magicians ; an abominable thing indeed. For those who the devil knows will prove very serviceable to him in this art, he seizes on in their very infancy with certain distemper, when they are haunted with apparitions and visions, by which they are, in proportion of their age, instructed in the rudiments of this art. Those who are a second time taken with this distemper, have more apparitions coming before them than in the first, by which they receive much more insight into it than before. But if they are seized a third time with this disease, which then proves very dangerous, and often not without the hazard of their lives, then it is they see all the apparitions the devil is able to contrive, to accomplish them in the magical art. Those are arrived to such a degree of perfection, that without the help of the drum (see infra), they can foretell things to come a great while before ; and are so strongly possessed by the devil, that they foresee things even against their will. Thus, not long ago, a certain Laplander, who is still alive, did voluntarily deliver his drum to me, which I had often desired of him before ; notwithstanding all this, he told me in a very melancholy posture, that though he had put away his drum, nor intended to have any other hereafter, yet he could foresee everything without it, as he had done before. As an instance of it, he told me truly all the particular accidents that had happened to me in my journey into *Lapland*, making at the same time heavy complaints, that he did not know what use to make of his eyes, those things being presented to his sight much against his will.'

" Lundius observes, that some of the Laplanders are seized upon by a demon, when they are arrived to a middle age, in the following manner :—Whilst they are busie in the woods, the spirit appears to them, where they discourse concerning the conditions, upon which the demon offers them his assistance, which done, he teaches them a certain song, which they are obliged to keep in constant remembrance. They must return the next day to the same place, where the same spirit appears to them again, and repeats the former song, in case he takes a fancy to the person ; if not, he does not appear at all. These spirits make their appearances under different shapes, some like fishes, some like birds, others like a serpent or dragon, others in the shape of a pigmee, about a yard high ; being attended by three, four, or five other pigmees of the same bigness, sometimes by more, but never exceeding nine. No sooner are they seized by the Genius, but they appear in the most surprising posture, like madmen, before bereaved of the use of reason. This continues for six months ; during which time they don't suffer any of their kindred to come near them, not so much as their own wives and children. They spend most of this time in the woods and other solitary places, being very melancholy and thoughtful scarce taking any food, which makes them extremely weak. It you ask their children, where and how their parents sustain themselves, they will tell you, that they receive their sustenance from their Genii. The same author gives us a remarkable instance of this kind in a young Laplander called Olaus, being then a scholar in the school of Liksala, of about eighteen years of age. This young fellow fell mad on a sudden, making most dreadful postures and outcries, that he was in hell, and his spirit tormented beyond what could be expressed. If he took a book in hand, so soon as he met with the name of Jesus, he threw the book upon the ground in great fury, which after some time being passed over, they used to ask him whether he had seen any vision during this ecstacy ? He answered that abundance of things had appeared to him, and that a mad dog being tied to his foot, followed him wherever he stirred. In his lucid intervals he would tell them, that the first beginning of it happened to him one day, as he was going out of the door of his dwelling, when a great flame passed before his eyes and touching his ears, a certain person appeared to him all naked. The next day he was seized with a most terrible headache, so that he made most lamentable outcries, and broke everything that came under his hands. This unfortunate person's face was as black as coal, and he used to say, that the devil most commonly appeared to him in the habit of a minister, in a long cloak ; during his fits he would say that he was surrounded by nine or ten fellows of a low stature, who did use him very barbarously, though at the same time the standers-by did not perceive the least thing like it. He would often climb to the top of the highest fir trees, with as much swiftness as a squirrel, and leap down again to the ground, without receiving the least hurt. He always loved solitude, flying the conversation of other men. He would run as swift as a horse, it being impossible for anybody to overtake him. He used to talk amongst the woods to himself no otherwise than if several persons had been in his company.

" I am apt to believe, that those spirts were not altogether unknown to the ancients, and that they are the same which were called by Tertullian *Paredri*, and are mentioned by Monsieur Valois, in his *Ecclesiastical History of Eusebius*.

" Whenever a Laplander has occasion for his familiar spirit, he calls to him, and makes him come by only singing the song he taught him at their first interview ; by which means he has him at his service as often as he pleases. And because they know them obsequious and serviceable, they call them *Sveie*, which signifies as much in their tongue, as the companions of their labour, or their helpmates. Lundius has made another observation, very well worth taking notice of, viz. :—That those spirits or demons never appear to the women, or enter into their service, of which I don't pretend to allege the true cause, unless one might say, that perhaps they do it out of pride, or a natural aversion they have to the female sex, subject to so many infirmities."

For the purposes of augury or divination the Lapps employed a magic drum, which, indeed, was in use among several Arctic peoples. Writing in 1827, De Capell Brooke states that the ceremonies connected with this instrument had almost quite disappeared at that date. The encroachments of Lutheranism had been long threatening the existence of the native shamanism. In 1671 the Lapp drum was formally banned by Swedish law, and several magicians were apprehended and their instruments burnt. But before that date the religion which the drum represented was in full vigour. The Lapps called their drum *Kannus* (Regnard, 1681), also *Kaunus, Kabdas, Kabdes Gabdas*, and *Keure* (Von Duben, 1873.) its Scandinavian designations being *troll-trumma*, or *Rune-bomme*, " magic or runic drum," otherwise *Spa-trumma*, " fortune-telling drum." J. A. Friis has shown that the *sampo* of the Finnish *Kalevala* is the same instrument. According to Von Düben, the best pictures and explanations of the drum are to be found in Friis's *Lappisk Mythologi* (Christiania, 1871), pp. 30–47, but there are good descriptions in Von Düben's own work (*On Lapland och Lapparne*, Stockholm, 1873), as also in the books of Scheffer, Leem, Jessen, and others. The appearance of the Lapp drum is thus described by Regnard in 1681 :—This instrument is made of a single piece of wood, hollowed in its thickest part in an oval form, the under part of which is convex, in which they make two apertures long enough to suffer the fingers to pass through, for the purpose of holding it more firmly. The upper part is covered with the skin of the reindeer, on which they paint in red a number of figures, and from whence several brass rings are seen hanging, and some pieces of the bone of the reindeer." A wooden hammer, or, as among the Samoyeds (1614), a hare's foot was used as a drum-stick in the course of the incantation. An *arpa* or divining-rod was placed on a definite spot showing from its position after sounding the drum what magic inference might be drawn. By means of the drum, the priest could be placed *en rapport* with the spirit world, and was thus enabled to divine the future ; to ascertain synchronous events occurring at remote distances ; to forecast the measure of success attending the day's hunting ; to heal the sick ; or to inflict people with disease and cause death. Although obsolete in *Lapland* these rites are still performed among the Samoyeds and other races of Arctic Asia and America. It is interesting to note how exactly the procedure among the Vaigatz Samoyeds in 1556 (*Pinkerton's Voyages*, London, 1808, 1, 63) tallies with that of the Sakhalin Ainos in 1883 (J. M. Dixon in Trans, Asiatic Soc. of Japan, Yokohama, 1883, 47). The same practices can be traced eastward through Arctic America, and the drum is used in the same fashion by the Eskimo shaman priests in Greenland (Henry Rink's *Tales*, etc., 1875, 60–61.) The shape of the drum varies a little according to locality. The form of the Eskimo drum is that of a tambourine.

" Their most valuable instrument of enchantment," says Tornaeus, " is this sorcerer's kettle-drum, which they call Kannas or Quobdas. They cut it in one entire piece out of a thick tree stem, the fibres of which run upwards in the same direction as the course of the sun. The drum is covered with the skin of an animal ; and in the bottom holes are cut by which it may be held. Upon the skins are many figures painted, often Christ and the Apostles, with the heathen gods, Thor, Noorjunkar, and others jumbled together ; the picture of the sun, shapes of animals, lands and waters, cities and roads, in short, all kinds of drawings according to their various uses. Upon the drum there is placed an indicator, which they call *Arpa*, which consists of a bundle of metallic rings. The drumstick is, generally, a reindeer's horn. This drum they preserve with the most vigilant care, and guard it especially from the touch of a woman. When they will make known what is taking place at a distance,—as to how the chase shall succeed, how business will answer, what result a sickness will have, what is necessary for the cure of it, and the like, they kneel down, and the sorcerer beats the drum ; at first with light strokes, but as he proceeds, with ever louder stronger ones, round the index, either till this has moved in a direction or to a figure which he regards as the answer which he has sought, or till he himself falls into ecstasy, when he generally lays the kettle-drum on his head. Then he sings with a loud voice a song which they call *Jogke*, and the men and women who stand round sing songs, which they call *Daura*, in which the name of the place whence they desire information frequently occurs. The sorcerer lies in the ecstatic state for some time—frequently for many hours, apparently dead, with rigid features ; sometimes with perspiration bursting out upon him. In the meantime the bystanders continue their incantations, which have for their object that the sleeper shall not lose any part of his vision from memory ; at the same time they guard him carefully that nothing living may touch him—not even a fly. When he again awakes to consciousness, he relates his vision, answers the questions put to him, and gives unmistakable evidence of having seen distant and unknown things. The inquiry of the oracle does not always take place so solemnly and completely. In everyday matters as regards the chase, etc., the Lapp consults his drum without falling into the somnambulic crisis. On the other hand, a more highly developed state of prophet vision may take place without this instrument, as has already been stated. Claudi relates, that at Bergen, in Norway, the clerk of a German merchant demanded of a Norwegian Finn-Laplander what his master was doing in Germany. The Finn promised to give him the intelligence. He began then to cry out like a drunken man, and to run round in a circle, till he fell, as one dead, to the earth. After a while he woke again, and gave the answer, which time showed to be correct. Finally, that many, while wholly awake, free from convulsions and a state of unconsciousness, are able to become clairvoyant, is placed beyond all doubt by the account of Tornaeus.

" The use which they make of their power of clairvoyance, and their magic arts, is, for the most part, good and innocent ; that of curing sick men and animals ; inquiring into far-off and future things, which in the confined sphere of their existence is important to them. There are instances however, in which the magic art is turned to the injury of others."

In addition to the works quoted, see Jessen's *Norske Finners og Lappers Hedenske Religion* (1765) ; Sioborg's *Tympanum Schamanico-lapponicum* (1808) ; Petitot's *Les Grands Esquimaux* (1887), and Abercromby's *Pre- and Proto-historic Finns* (1898.)

Larvae : (*See* **Magic.**)

Lascaris : (Alchemist of the Eighteenth Century.) It is impossible to determine the date at which this mysterious personage was born, or to say, exactly, whence he came and where he chiefly lived. He is commonly supposed to have been active about the beginning of the eighteenth century, while Germany is held to have been the principal scene of his activities ; but everything recorded concerning him reads like a romance, and suggests the middle ages rather than the day before yesterday. Sometimes he assured people that he was of Oriental origin, sometimes he maintained that his native land was the Ionian Isles, and that he was a scion of the Greek royal house of *Lascaris* ; while on other occasions he declared that he was an

archimandrite of a convent in the Island of Mytilene, and that his object in coming to Europe was to solicit alms for the ransom of Christian prisoners in the East. Such was his tale when, about 1700, he commenced wandering in Germany, and, while sojourning at Berlin, he happened to fall ill and sent for medical aid. This appeared shortly in the shape of a young apothecary, Johann Friedrich Bötticher by name, who chanced to be deeply interested in alchemy, so a friendship sprang up between physician and patient and ere *Lascaris* left the Prussian capital he gave Bötticher a packet of transmuting powder, at the same time instructing him how to use it successfully, yet refraining from telling him how to manufacture the powder itself. Nothing daunted, Bötticher set to work speedily, concocted considerable quantities of gold and silver, grew rich, and was raised to the peerage ; while simultaneously he began to find his society, and more especially his services as a scientist, courted by kings and nobles. Meanwhile, however, his supply of the precious powder had run short, and being unable to make more he found his reputation waning apace ; while worse still, he had spent his newly-acquired wealth speedily, and now he found himself reduced to penury. Ultimately he was incarcerated, but during his period of durance vile he set himself to the manufacture of porcelain, and by the sale of this he eventually restored his fallen fortunes.

We presume naturally that it was gratitude to his physician which inspired the crafty alchemist to give Bötticher the powder, but why did *Lascaris* make an analogous present at a later date ? The recipient on this occasion being one Schmolz de Dierbach, a lieutenant-colonel in the Polish Army. He, like the German apothecary, succeeded in making a quantity of gold, and, though we hear no more about him after this transmutation, we learn that a certain Baron de Creux was likewise favoured by *Lascaris*, the Baron's experiments proving just as successful as those of the others aforesaid. Nor were these the only people on whom our alchemist bestowed his indulgence, for one Domenico Manuel, the son of a Neapolitan mason, was likewise given a packet of transmutatory powder, and, armed thus, he wandered through Spain, Belgium, and Austria, performing operations before princes and noblemen, and reaping wealth accordingly. Pride was the inevitable result of this, and though there is no reason to suppose that any patent of nobility was ever conferred on Domenico, we find him styling himself now Comte Gautano, now Comte di Ruggiero ; while in one town he maintained that he was a Prussian major-general, and elsewhere he declared that he was field-marshal of the Bavarian forces. Going to Berlin in the course of his perambulations, he offered to make gold in the presence of the king ; but alas ! his operation proved utterly futile, and he was hanged as a charlatan in consequence. This was in 1709, and in the same year, according to tradition, *Lascaris* himself performed some successful transmutations before a German politician named Liebknech, a citizen of Wurtembourg. Nothing further is heard of the mysterious Greek alchemist, however, so it may be assumed that he died soon after these events. His was a curious career indeed : his generosity having scarcely a parallel in the whole history of hermetic philosophy.

Latent Impressions : (*See* **Telepathy.**)

Launay, Jean : A celebrated doctor of the Sorbonne, born in 1603 at Valderic, in the diocese of Contanas. He has left a pedantic dissertation *On the Vision of St. Simon Stock*, which he could not understand, being something of a Jansenist. It was published in Paris, in 1653 and 1663.

Laurel : A tree which Apuleius classes among the plants which preserve men from the influence of evil spirits. It was also believed to give protection from lightning.

Laurin or Der Kleine Rosengarten : A Tyrolese romance of the late thirteenth century. Laurin, a dwarf, possesses a magic rose-garden into which no one may enter without the loss of a hand or a foot. Dietrich and his follower Witege, enter it, and the latter rides through the rose bushes. Laurin, the dwarf, appears, on horseback and dismounts Witege. He is challenged by Dietrich and, assuming his cloak of invisibility, wounds him. Dietrich now persuades him to a wrestling match and wrenches off the dwarf's belt which gives him super-human strength. Thus he overthrows *Laurin*. *Laurin* then invites Dietrich and his followers to his mountain home, prepares them a banquet, makes them tipsy, and throws them all into a dungeon. They are released by Künhild, a mortal woman, who restores their weapons. They take *Laurin* prisoner and carry him to Bern where he becomes a Christian convert and receives Künhild in marriage.

Law, William : English Mystic and Theologian (1686–1761.) *William Law* was born at Kingscliffe, Northamptonshire, in the year 1686. His father followed the humble calling of a grocer, but it is manifest that he was in tolerably affluent circumstances nevertheless, and ambitious besides, for in 1705 *William* was sent to Cambridge University. Entering Emmanuel College, he became a fellow thereof in 1711, but on the accession of George I. he felt himself unable to subscribe the oath of allegiance, the inevitable consequence being that he forfeited his fellowship. In 1727 he went to Putney, having acquired there the post of tutor to the father of Edmund Gibbon, the historian of the Roman Empire in decline, and he acted in this capacity for ten years, winning universal esteem the while for his piety and his theological erudition. In 1737, on the death of his employer, *Law* retired to his native village of Kingscliffe, and it would seem that thenceforth he chiefly supported by the purses of some of his devotees, notably Miss Hester Gibbon, sister of his guardian pupil, and a widow named Mrs. Hutcheson. These two ladies had a united income of fully £3000 a year, so *Law* must have been comfortable indeed, yet wealth and luxury did not tend to corrupt his piety, and it is recorded that he was wont to get up every morning at five, and spend several hours before breakfast in prayer and meditations. At a considerably earlier stage in his career he had begun publishing theses on mysticism, and on religion in general ; and now, being blessed with abundance of leisure, and having acquired fresh inspiration from reading the works of Jacob Boehme, he produced year after year a considerable mass of writing. Thus his life passed away placidly, and he died in 1761.

Law's works amount in all to some twenty volumes. His *début* as a writer was made in 1717, with an examination of certain tenets lately promulgated from the pulpit by the Bishop of Bangor ; and this was followed soon afterwards by a number of analogous writings, while in 1726 he employed his pen to attack the theatre, bringing out a book entitled *The Absolute Unlawfulness of the Stage Entertainment fully Demonstrated*. In the same year he issued *A Practical Treatise upon Christian Perfection*, and this was followed shortly by *A Serious Call to a Devout and Holy Life, adapted to the State and Condition of all Orders of Christians*. This last is the best-known of his works, but others which it behoves to cite are *The Grounds and Reason of Christian Regeneration* (1739), *The Spirit of Prayer* (1749), *The Way to Divine Knowledge* (1752), *The Spirit of Love* (1752), and *Of Justification by Faith and Works* (1760). Most of the foregoing, but especially the *Serious Call*, have been reprinted again and again ; while in 1762 a collected edition of *Law's* works was published, and in 1893 there appeared a sort of anthology, made up of extracts from the writer, chosen by Dr. Alexander Whyte. In his preface the editor speaks of *Law's* " golden books," while he adds that

" In sheer intellectual strength *Law* is fully abreast of the very foremost of his illustrious contemporaries, while in that fertilising touch which is the true test of genius, *Law* stands simply alone." Numerous other encomiums no less enthusiastic than this have been offered to the mystic, and it is noteworthy that he has engaged the interest of many great writers. Sir Leslie Stephen, for example, deals with him in his *History of English Thought in the Eighteenth Century*, and again in his pleasant *Studies of a Biographer* ; while the mystic figures also in the brilliant pages of W. E. H. Lecky, and in Gibbon's *Autobiography* he is hailed as " a worthy and pious man, who believed all that he professed, and practised all that he enjoined."

Laya Yoga : That practice of the yogi by which he listens to sounds which can be heard within his own body when the ears are closed. These sounds are termed " The Nada," and are of all kinds, from the roar of the ocean to the humming of bees.

Lazare, Denys : A prince of Serbia who lived in the year of the Hegira, 788. He was author of a work entitled *Dreams*, published in 1686. He himself claimed to have had nocturnal visions.

Le Normand, Marie : Known as " The Sybil of the Faubourg Saint Germain," was born at Alençon in 1772 and died at Paris in 1843. She was one of the most famous occultists and diviners of her day ; but it might justly be said that her art was much more the product of sound judgment than of any supernatural gift. She predicted their futures to Marat, Robespierre, and St. Just, but we hear no more of her under the Directory. When Josephine Beauharnais came into prominence as the intended wife of Napoleon, Mlle. Le Normand was received at all those houses and salons where the future empress had any influence. Josephine was extremely credulous, and used to read her own fortunes to herself on the cards ; but when she found that *Mlle. Le Normand* was an adept at this art, she often had her in attendance to assist her in it. Even Napoleon himself who was not without his own superstitions, had his horoscope read by her. She soon set up her own salon in Paris where she read people's fortunes by means of the cards. It is not stated whether these cards were of the nature of Tarot cards, but it is more than likely that they were ; but we know that she occasionally divined the fortunes of others through playing the games of piquet, sept, and other card games. She did not hide her methods from others, but the Parisian society of her day appears to have thought that her power of divination lay not in the cards she manipulated but in her personality. It has been stated by Migne that she did use the Tarot, but as he calls them " German cards," one cannot attach much importance to his statement. After the fall of the Emperor she was the rage amongst the Russian, German and English officers in Paris, and even the Emperor Alexander and other potentates consulted her. Shortly after this she went to Brussels, where she read the fortune of the Prince of Orange, but as she tried to cheat the customs she soon found herself the occupant of a Belgian prison. By the year 1830 she had become quite forgotten, and when the newspapers announced her death on June 25th, 1843, the majority of people failed to remember her name. There is very little doubt that she was a harmless charlatan, though several contemporary historians appear to consider that she possessed mischievous tendencies ; but the air of omniscience and mystery with which she surrounded herself was so absurd that by the majority of people she was looked upon, probably with justice, as a mere impostor.

Leannan Sith : Gaelic words meaning " fairy sweetheart " who may be of either sex. Mortals are advised to have nothing to do with such beings, as no good ever comes of the connection ; so long as the fairy lover is pleased with his or her mortal, all goes well, but when offended, life may be the forfeit.

Lebrun, Charles : A celebrated painter, born at Paris in 1619, died in 1690. He wrote a *Traité sur la physionomie humaine comparée avec celle des aminaux.*

Lebrun, Pierre : An orator, born at Brignolles in 1661, died in 1729. He has left two works, namely, *Lettres qui découvrent l'illusion des philosophes sur la baquette, et qui détruisent leurs systèmes* (1693), and *Histoire critique des pratiques superstitieuses qui ont séduit les peuples et embarrassé les savants* (1702).

Ledivi : (*See* **Assassins.**)

Leg Cake : The name given in the Highlands of Scotland to a cake given to a herd when he came with the news that a mare had foaled, or to a dairy-maid when she brought word that a cow had calved.

Legions of Demons : (*See* **Demonology.**)

Lehman, Mr., of Copenhagen : (*See* **Telepathy.**)

Leicester, Earl of : (*See* **Dee.**)

Leippya, or soul. (*See* **Burma.**)

Lemegeton : (*See* **Key of Solomon.**)

Leo, Pope : (*See* **Enchiridion.**)

Lescoriere, Marie : A witch of the sixteenth century, arrested at the age of ninety years. On being examined she declared that she was no longer a witch ; that she prayed daily ; and that she had not visited the Sabbath for forty years. Questioned on the subject of the Sabbath, she confessed that she had seen the devil, and that he had visited her in the shape of a dog or a cat. On one occasion, she said, she had killed a neighbour by praying to the devil.

Leshy : (*See* **Slavs.**)

Lesser Key of Solomon : (*See* **Key of Solomon.**)

Levi, Eliphas : Alphonse Louis Constant, better known by his pen-name of *Eliphas Levi*, was a French occultist of the nineteenth century, who has been called " the last of the magi." He was born about 1810, the son of a shoemaker, and through the good offices of the parish priest was educated for the church at St. Sulpice. In due course he became a deacon, taking a vow of celibacy. Shortly after this he was expelled from St. Sulpice for teaching doctrines contrary to those of the Church. How he lived during the ensuing years is not known, but about 1839 under the influence of a political and socialistic prophet named Ganneau, he wrote a pamphlet entitled *The Gospel of Liberty,* for which he received six months imprisonment. In Paris, notwithstanding his vow of celibacy, he married a beautiful girl of sixteen, who afterwards had the marriage annulled. It was probably not until Madame Constant had left him that he studied the occult sciences. At all events his writings previous to this show little trace of occult influence. In 1855 he published his *Doctrine of Transcendental Magic,* followed in 1856 by the *Ritual of Transcendental Magic ;* in 1860 was issued his *History of Magic ;* in 1861 *The Key of the Grand Mysteries ; Fables and Symbols* in 1864 ; *Le Sorcier de Mendon* and *La Science des Esprits* in 1865. Most of his works have been translated by Mr. A. E. Waite. He died in 1875.

Levi's knowledge of the occult sciences was much more imaginative than circumstantial, and in perusing his works the reader requires to be on his guard against the adoption of hasty generalisations and hypotheses.

Leviathan : (*See* **Devil.**)

Levitation : A term in use among spiritualists to denote the raising in the air of the human body or other objects without visible means, and presumably through the agency of disembodied spirits. Thus the *levitation* of tables and other more or less weighty objects is a common feat among " physical " mediums, whether or not a supernatural explanation be required. The witches of olden times, too, were popularly supposed to make use of some occult mode

of locomotion in their nocturnal travels, being transported through the air by the arts of their master, the Devil. And the poltergeist was also thought to suspend in the air, without visible means of support, the agent through whom he manifested himself. As a spiritualistic phenomenon *levitation* of the human body became known at an early stage of the movement, being recorded in connection with the medium Gordon so early as 1851. But the most important of levitated mediums was D. D. Horne, and many accounts of his feats in this direction are given by witnesses who were themselves convinced of their genuineness. It may be noted, however, that *levitations* usually occurred in a darkened séance-room, when the only indication of any untoward happening was furnished by the medium's own exclamations, by the fact that his voice seemed to come from high in the air, and sometimes by his boots scraping the back of a chair or the hand of one of the sitters. The Rev. Stainton Moses, who also was levitated on several occasions, seems to have held his séances in darkness also, or at most by the light of the fire. Mrs. Guppy (née Nicholls) was before her marriage several times levitated, notwithstanding the fact that she was extremely stout, and a curious story concerning a later *levitation* is told in a letter in the *Echo* of June 8th, 1871, for whose (anonymous) author's trustworthiness the editor vouches. About that time the writer attended a circle with Messrs. Herne and Williams as mediums, the spirits present being the famous John and Katie King. One of the sitters jokingly expressed a wish that Mrs. Guppy (then in her home some three miles distant) might be brought to the séance-room, and to this Katie King was heard to assent. While the company were laughing at the absurdity of the idea, there was a loud bump, followed by shrieks and exclamations. A match was struck, and there in the centre of the table stood Mrs. Guppy, an account-book in one hand, a pen in the other, and apparently in a state of trance. Less than three minutes elapsed between the expression of the wish and the appearance of Mrs. Guppy. The writer adds : " The possibility of her being concealed in the room is as absurd as the idea of her acting in collusion with the media."

Pseudo-historical instances of *levitation* may be found in abundance, especially among the early saints. St. Dunstan, archbishop of Canterbury, was observed to rise from the ground shortly before his death in 988. St. Bernard Ptolomei, St. Philip Benitas, St. Albert of Sicily, and St. Dominic, founder of the Dominican order, were all seen to be levitated while engaged in their devotions. An ecstatic nun " rose from the ground with so much impetuosity, that five or six of the sisters could hardly hold her down." It is related by his biographers that Savonarola, shortly before he perished at the stake, remained suspended at a considerable height above the floor of his dungeon, absorbed in prayer. And such instances might easily be multiplied.

Leviticon : A gospel adopted by the French Templars, and alleged by them to have been discovered in the Temple at Paris, along with other objects. It was supposed to have been composed in the fifteenth century by a Greek monk, Nicephorus, who sought to combine Moslem tenets with Christianity.

Lewis, Matthew Gregory : Commonly known as " Monk " Lewis, English Author (1775-1818). Matthew Gregory Lewis was born in London in 1775. His father was Matthew Lewis, deputy secretary of war, and proprietor of several valuable estates in Jamaica ; while his mother was Anna Maria Sewell, a lady of cultured tastes, devoted to music and various other arts. The future author showed precocity while yet a child, and on reaching boyhood he was sent to Westminster School, but while he was there an ugly cloud rose to dim his horizon, his parents quarrelling and agreeing to separate. *Matthew* contrived to remain friendly with both his father and mother, and in 1771 he visited Paris, while about the same time he made his first literary efforts, and in 1792 he went to Weimar in Germany where he made the acquaintance of Goethe, and also learnt German thoroughly. Two years later he was appointed attaché to the British Embassy at the Hague, and while staying there he wrote his mystical story, *Ambrosio, or the Monk*, which earned him his now familiar *sobriquet* of " Monk Lewis ; " while in 1796 he entered Parliament as member for Hindon, in Wiltshire, and during the next few years he necessarily resided chiefly in London, or near it, becoming friendly the while with most of the notable people of the day. Meantime his interest in the occult had been developing apace, and in 1798 there was staged at Drury Lane a play of his, *Castle Spectre*, in which ghosts and the like play a prominent part, and which won great popularity among people interested in things of that nature ; while in 1788 he issued his *Tales of Terror*, and in 1801 a volume entitled *Tales of Wonder*, this being virtually an anthology of popular occult verses, some of which were supplied by Sir Walter Scott.

In 1812 *Lewis's* father died, and the author accordingly found himself a very rich man. His conscience was troubled, nevertheless, by the fact that his wealth was derived from slave labour, and so, in 1815, he sailed to Jamaica, intent on making arrangements for the generous treatment of the negroes on his estates. Returning to England in 1816, he went soon afterwards to Geneva, where he met Byron and Shelley, while in 1818 he paid a last visit to the West Indies, and died at sea while returning home.

Libellus Merlini : (Little Book of Merlin.) A Latin tract on the subject of the prophecies of Merlin written by Geoffrey of Monmouth about 1135. Geoffrey prefaces his account of the prophecies with one concerning the deeds of a supernatural youth named Ambrosius whom he deliberately confounded with Merlin. Vortigern, King of the Britons, asks Ambrose Merlin the meaning of a vision in which appear two dragons red and white in combat. Merlin replies that the Red Dragon signifies the British race which would be conquered by the Saxon, represented by the White Dragon. A long prophetic rhapsody follows, relating chiefly to the Saxon wars, and with this the work, as given in the Seventh Book of Geoffrey's Historia Regum Britanniae, concludes. It was, however, known in Iceland before 1218 in a form independent of the Historia. (H. C. Leach, *Modern Philology*, viii., pp. 607 et seq.) This tract must not be confounded with the *Vita Merlini* (1145 or 1148) generally attributed to Geoffrey.

Licking, a Charm : The following was believed to be a remedy for enchantment : to lick the child's forehead first upward, then across, and lastly up again ; and then to spit behind its back.

It is said that if on licking a child's forehead with the tongue a salt taste is perceived, this is an infallible proof of fascination.

Life Waves according to Theosophists, are three in number. It is necessary to remember that the Deity, the Logos (q.v.) has three aspects corresponding to the Christian Trinity. These aspects are first that of Will ; second, that of Wisdom ; and third, that of Activity, and each has its definite scope in the creation of a universe. When the Logos sets about the great work of creation he sends the first *life wave* through his aspect of Activity into the multitude of bubbles in the ether, and thereby forms the various kinds of matter. The universe having been thus far prepared, he through his aspect of Wisdom sends the second *life wave*, which bringing with it *life* as we usually understand that term and penetrating matter from above,

gradually descends to the grosser forms and again ascends to the finer forms. In its descent, this *life wave* makes for an ever-increasing heterogeneity, but in its ascent the process is reversed and it makes for an ever-increasing homogeneity. The work of creation is now far enough advanced to permit of the creation of man, for matter has now been infused with the capacity of form and provided with *life*, and the Logos, therefore, through his aspect of Will, bears forth the Divine Spark, the Monad, and, along with the form and the *life*, ensouls man. (*See* **Theosophy, Logos, Ether, Evolution, Solar System, Monad.**)

Light : Spiritualistic Journal. (*See* **Spiritualism.**)

Lignite is a beautiful stone like glass ; being hung about a child it preserves it from witchcraft, and if bound on the forehead it stops the bleeding of the nose, restores the loss of senses, and helps to foretell future events.

Likho : (*See* **Slavs.**)

Lilith : According to Wierus and other demonologists, *Lilith* was the prince or princess who presided over the demons known as succubi. The demons under *Lilith* bore the same name as their chief, and sought to destroy newborn infants. For this reason the Jews wrote on the four corners of a birth-chamber a formula to drive *Lilith* away. (*See* **Babylonia.**)

Limachie : This little curiosity, resembling a chip of a man's nail, is to be squeezed out of the head of a slug, which must be done the instant it is seen. It is a good amulet to preserve from fever.

Linton Charles : (*See* **Automatic Writing and Speaking.**)

Lippares or Liparia : He who has this stone " needs no other invention to catch wild beasts." On the other hand, no animal can be attacked by dogs or huntsman if it look upon it.

Liquor Alkahest : (*See* **Philalethes.**)

Litanies of the Sabbath : On Wednesdays and Saturdays, if the accounts speak truly, it was the custom to sing at the witches' Sabbath the following *Litanies* :—

Lucifer, Beelzebub, Leviathan, have pity on us.

Baal, prince of the seraphim ; Baalberith, prince of the cherubim ; Astaroth, prince of the thrones ; Rosier, prince of denominations ; Carreau, prince of the powers ; Belial, prince of the vertues ; Perrier, prince of the principalities ; Oliver, prince of the arch angels ; Junier, prince of the angels ; Sarcueil, Fume-bouche, Pierre-le-Feu, Carniveau, Terrier, Contellier, Candelier, Behemoth, Oilette, Belphegor, Sabathan, Garandier, Dolers, Pierre-Fort, Axaphat, Prisier, Kakos, Lucesme, pray for us.

It must be remarked that Satan is evoked in these *litanies* only in company with a crowd of others.

Lithomancy : A species of divination performed by stones, but in what manner it is difficult to ascertain. Gale, in a " note upon Iamblichus," confesses that he does not clearly understand the nature of it ; whether it refers to certain motions observable in idols, or to an insight into futurity obtained by demons (familiars) enclosed in particular stones. That these supernatural beings might be so commanded is clear from a passage of Nicephorus. The Rabbis have attributed Lev. XXVI., 1 to *Lithomancy* ; but the prohibition of stones there given is most probably directed against idolatry in general. Bulenger has a short chapter on *Lithomancy*. He shows from Tzetzes, that Helenus ascertained the fall of Troy by the employment of a magnet, and that if a magnet be washed in spring water, and interrogated, a voice like that of a sucking child will reply.

The pseudo-Orpheus has related at length this legend of Helenus. " To him," he says, " Apollo gave the true and vocal sideritis, which others call the animated ophites, a stone possessing fatal qualities, rough, hard, black, and heavy, graven everywhere with veins like wrinkles. For one and twenty days Helenus abstained from the nuptial couch, from the bath, and from animal food. Then, washing this intelligent stone in a living fountain, he cherished it as a babe in soft clothing ; and having propitiated it as a god, he at length gave it breath by his hymn of mighty virtue. Having lighted lamps in his own purified house, he fondled the divine stone in his hands, bearing it about as a mother bears her infant ; and you, if ye wish to hear the voice of the gods, in like manner provoke a similar miracle, for when ye have sedulously wiped and dandled the stone in your arms, on a sudden it will utter the cry of a new-born child seeking milk from the breast of its nurse. Beware, however, of fear, for if you drop the stone upon the ground, you will rouse the anger of the immortals. Ask boldly of things future, and it will reply. Place it near your eyes when it has been washed, look steadily at it, and you will perceive it divinely breathing. Thus it was that Helenus, confiding in this fearful stone, learned that his country would be overthrown by the Atridæ."

Photius, in his abstract of the life of Isodorus by Damascius, a credulous physician of the age of Justinian, speaks of an oracular stone, the bætulum, to which *Lithomancy* was attributed. A physician named Eusebius used to carry one of these wonder-working stones about with him. One night, it seems, actuated by an unaccountable impulse, he wandered out from the city Emesa to the summit of a mountain dignified by a temple of Minerva. There, as he sat down fatigued by his walk, he saw a globe of fire falling from the sky and a lion standing by it. The lion disappeared, the fire was extinguished, and Eusebius ran and picked up a bætulum. He asked it to what god it appertained, and it readily answered, to Gennæus, a deity worshipped by the Heliopolitæ, under the form of a lion in the temple of Jupiter. During this night, Eusebius said he travelled not less than 210 stadia, more than 26 miles. He never became perfectly master of the bætulum, but was obliged very humbly to solicit its responses. It was of a handsome, globular shape, white, a palm in diameter, though sometimes it appeared more, sometimes less ; occasionally, also, it was of purple colour. Characters were to be read on it, impressed in the colour called tingaribinus. Its answer seemed as if proceeding from a shrill pipe, and Eusebius himself interpreted the sounds. Damascius believed its animating spirit to be divine ; Isodorus, on the other hand, thought it demoniacal, that is, not belonging to evil or material demons, not yet to those which are quite pure and immaterial. It was with one of these stones, according to Hesychius, that Rhea fed Saturnus, when he fancied that he was devouring Jupiter, its name being derived from the skin in which it was wrapped, and such the commentator supposed to have been the *Lapides divi*, or *vivi*, which the insane monster Heliogabalus wished to carry off from the temple of Diana, built by Orestes at Laodicea. Bochart traces the name and the reverence paid to the bætylia, to the stone which Jacob anointed at Bethel. Many of these bætylia, Photius assures us from Damascius, were to be found on Mount Libanus.

Little, Robert Wentworth : (*See* **Rosicrucians.**)

Little World : The name given to a secret society which conspired in England, in the eighteenth century, to re-establish the Stuart dynasty. Many stories are told of this society—as, for instance, that the devil presided over their assemblies in person. The members were Freemasons.

Loathly Damsel, The : Kundrie or Kundry. The Grail Messenger. One would imagine that the holder of such an office would be saint-like, but Christian describes her as " a damsel more hideous than could be pictured outside hell." Wolfram refers to her in his work as " Kundrie la

Sorciére." Kundry in Wagner's music-drama " Parsifal " represents sin.

Lodestone : A precious stone believed to possess magical properties of diverse kinds. If one is ill, one must hold it in one's hands and shake it well. It cures wounds, snake-bites, weak eyes, headaches and restores hearing. The possessor of the *lodestone* may walk through reptiles in safety, even when they are accompanied by " black death." Orpheus says that " with this stone you can hear the voices of the gods and learn many wonderful things ; " that it has the property of unfolding the future ; and if held close to the eyes it will inspire with a divine spirit.

Lodge, Sir Oliver : (*See* **Spiritualism.**)

Logos : Fohat—is the term very commonly used in theosophy to designate the Deity. Along with the great religions, theosophy has as the beginning of its scheme a Deity who, in Himself, is altogether beyond human knowledge or conception, whether in the ordinary or the clairvoyant states. But when the Deity manifests Himself to man through his works of creation. He is known as the *Logos*. Essentially He is infinite but when He encloses a " ring-pass-not " within which to build a kosmos, He has set limits to Himself, and what we can know of Him is contained in these limits. To us He appears in a triple aspect— the Christian Trinity—but this is, of course, merely an appearance, and in reality He is a unity. This triple aspect shews Him as Will, Wisdom and Activity, and from each of these came forth one of the creative life waves which formed the universe. From the third came the wave which created matter, from the second, the wave which aggregated diffuse matter into form, and from the first, the wave which brought with it the Monad, that scintillation of Himself which took posession of formed matter, to start thereby the evolutionary process.

Loiseant : (*See* **France.**)

Loki : (*See* **Devil.**)

Lombroso, Professor Cesare : A celebrated Italian anthropologist. A few years before his death he took up the study of spiritualism and experimented extensively with the well-known medium Eusapia Palladino, in company with Messieurs Richet, Maxwell, Flammarion, and Professor Schiaparelli. He embodied the results of his investigations in several well-known works, and concluded that although man was probably not immortal, his " shell " or shadow, a mere conglomeration of thought forces, remained on earth behind him for some considerable time after his demise. (*See* " **After Death—What ?** " 1909.)

London Dialectical Society : In 1869 an important enquiry into the phenomena of spiritualism was undertaken by the *London Dialectical Society*. A committee of more than thirty members—including Alfred Russel Wallace, Sergeant Cox, Charles Bradlaugh, H. G. Atkinson, and Dr. James Edmunds—was formed, and resolved itself into six sub-committees. During the eighteen months over which their labours extended, the committee received a large quantity of evidence from believers in the phenomena, but very little from those antagonistic to the spirit hypothesis. In " The Dialectical Society's Report on Spiritualism," published by the Society, particulars are given both of the members' own experiences and of testimonies from witnesses whose character and position made their evidence valuable. Practically every form of manifestation, both physical and automatic, is covered in the report, which concluded thus :

" In presenting their report, your Committee, taking into consideration the high character and great intelligence of many of the witnesses to the more extraordinary facts, the extent to which their testimony is supported by the reports of the sub-committees, and the absence of any proof of imposture or delusion as regards a large portion of the phenomena ; and further, having regard to the exceptional character of the phenomena, and the large number of persons of every grade of society and over the whole civilised world who are more or less influenced by a belief in their supernatural origin, and to the fact that no philosophical explanation of them has yet been arrived at, deem it incumbent upon them to state their conviction that the subject is worthy of more serious attention and careful investigation than it has hitherto received."

The *Dialectical Society's* investigations are noteworthy as the first organised attempt to elucidate the problem of spiritualistic phenomena.

Lopez, Senor Manoel : (*See* **Spain.**)

Lopoukine, Chevalier : A Russian theologian to whom is attributed a tract, said to be translated from the Russian and entitled *Characteristics of the Interior Church* (1801). His teaching is similar to that of Eckhartshausen whose work has elsewhere been briefly described—it is a kind of Christian transcendentalism and in its tenour, resembles the higher literature of the Graal.

Lords of the Flame or Children of the Fire Mist, are, according to theosophists, adepts sent from the planet Venus to aid terrestrial evolution. It is necessary to explain that, in the evolution of the Solar System (q.v.) Venus is considerably in advance of the Earth, but by the efforts of these adepts directed towards intellectual development—the inhabitants of the earth are now really farther advanced than in ordinary course they would be. These adepts are not permanently inhabitants of the Earth, and, while a few yet remain, most of them have returned whence they came, the time of crisis at which they assisted having now passed. (*See* **Theosophy, Evolution, Chains.**)

Lost Word of Kabbalism : *Lost Word* in Masonry. A *word* relating to some mystic plan, which though it is held to have disappeared, will at some time be restored, and will then make the whole system plain. It is not really *lost*, only withheld for a season. In the same way the Graal was not *lost*, but withdrawn to its own place and the search for it occupied the noblest figures in chivalry. It represents the Key to the enigma of Creation ; in terms of Christianity, the Kingdom of Heaven.

Loudun, Nuns of : In the year 1633, the convent of Ursulines established at *Loudun* in France was the scene of an outbreak of diabolical possession. The numerous *nuns* who inhabited the convent showed signs of diabolic possession, spoke with tongues, and behaved in the most extraordinary and hysterical manner. The affair grew in volume until practically all the *nuns* belonging to the institution were in the same condition of temporary insanity. The Mother Superior of the convent, Jeanne de Belfiel, appears to have been of hysterical temperament, and she was not long in infecting the other inmates of the institution. She, with a sister named Claire and five other *nuns*, were the first to be obsessed by the so-called evil spirits. The outbreak spread to the neighbouring town and so scandalous did the whole affair become that Richelieu appointed a commission to examine into it. The devils were subjected to the process of exorcism, which, however, proved to be fruitless in this instance, and the attacks of the *nuns* continued. But on a more imposing ceremony being held, they took themselves off, but only for a little while, returning again with greater violence than ever. Suspicion, or rather injustice, fixed upon the person of Urbain Grandier (q.v.), confessor of the convent, as the head and source of the whole affair. He was arrested and accused of giving over the *nuns* to the possession of the Devil by means of the practice of sorcery. The truth is that the neighbouring clergy were madly jealous of Grandier because he had obtained two benefices in their diocese, of which he was not a native, and they had made up their minds to compass his destruction at the first possible moment. Despite his protests of innocence,

the unfortunate priest was haled before a council of judges of the neighbouring presidencies, who found upon his body the various marks which were the undoubted signs of a sorcerer, and it is said that the inquest brought to light the fact that Grandier had none too good a reputation. We must be very careful, however, to refrain from believing the worst about him, as the sources regarding this are undoubtedly tainted by religious prejudice. It is said that on his papers being seized much matter subversive of religious practice was found amongst them. They failed, however, to find that pact with Satan for which they had looked, although afterwards several versions of it were published by more or less credulous persons and sold as broadsheets. The unfortunate man was condemned to be burnt at the stake—a sentence which was duly carried out. After his death, however, the possession of the hysterical sisters did not cease ; the demons became more obstreperous than ever and flippantly answered to their names of Asmodeus, Leviathan, and Behemoth, and so forth. A very holy Brother called Surin was delegated to put an end to the affair. Frail and unhealthy, he possessed, however, an indomitable spirit, and after much wrestling in prayer succeeded in finally exorcising the demons. The whole affair is set forth in the *Historie des Diables de Loudun*, published in 1839, which gave a detailed account of one of the most extraordinary obsessions of modern times.

Loutherburg : (*See* **Spiritualism.**)

Loyer, Pierre Le : Sieur de la Brosse, royal councillor and demonographer, was born at Huillé in Anjou in 1550. He was the author of a work entitled *Discours et histoires des spectres, visions et apparitions des esprits, anges, demons et âmes se montrant aux hommes*. The work is divided into eight books dealing with the marvellous visions and prodigies of all the centuries, and the most celebrated authors sacred as well as profane, who have dealt with occult subjects, the cause of apparitions, the nature of good and evil spirits, of demons, of ecstasy, of the essence, nature and origin of souls, of magicians and sorcerers, of the manner of their communication, of evil spirits, and of impostors It was published at Paris in 1605 in one quarto volume. The first book deals with spectres, apparitions and spirits ; the second with the physics of *Loyer's* time, the illusions to which the senses are prone, wonders, the elixirs and metamorphases of sorceries and of philtres ; ·the third book establishes the degrees, grades and honours of spirits, gives a resumé of the history of Philinnion and of Polycrites, and recounts diverse adventures with spectres and demons ; the fourth book gives many examples of spectral appearances, of the speech of persons possessed of demons, of the countries and dwelling-places of these spectres and demons, of marvellous portents, and so forth ; the fifth treats of the science of the soul, of its origin, nature, its state after death, and of haunting ghosts ; the sixth division is entirely taken up with the apparition of souls, and shows how the happy do not return to earth, but only those whose souls are burning in purgatory ; in the seventh book the case of the Witch of Endor, and the evocation of the soul of Samuel, are dealt with, as is evocation in general and the methods practised by wizards and sorcerers in this science ; the last book gives some account of exorcism, fumigations, prayers, and other methods of casting out devils, and the usual means employed by exorcists to destroy these. The work as a whole is exceedingly curious if disputatious and a little dull in parts, and throws considerable light upon the occult science of the times.

Lubin : The fish whose gall was used by Tobias to restore his father's sight. It is said to be very powerful against ophthalmia, and its heart is potent in driving away demons.

Lucifer : Literally light-bringer, a name applied to the conception of the devil, who has often been likened to a fallen star or angel. The Miltonic conception of *Lucifer* as a force potent for good or evil, one who might have done good greatly, intensely proud and powerful exceedingly, is one which is inconsistent with enlightenment. He represents simply the absence of good ; a negative not a positive entity.

He presides over the east, according to the ideas of the old magicians. He was invoked on Mondays, in a circle in the centre of which was his name. As the price of his complaisance in appearing to the magician he asked only a mouse. Lucifer commands Europeans and Asiatics. He appears in the shape of a beautiful child. When he is angry his face is flushed, but there is nothing monstrous about him. He is, according to some students of demonology, the grand justiciary of Hades. He is the first to be invoked in the litanies of the Sabbath. (*See* **Devil-worship.**)

Lugh : In Irish romance, son of Kian, and father of Cuchulain. He was brought up by his uncle Goban, the Smith, and by Duach, King of Fairyland. It was prophesied of *Lugh* that he should eventually overcome his father's old enemy Balor, his own grandfather. So instead of killing the three murderers of his father, Kian, he put them on oath to obtain certain wonders, including the magical spear of the King of "Persia" and the pig-skin of the King of Greece, which, if laid on a patient, would heal him of his wound or cure him of his sickness. Thus equipped, *Lugh* entered the Battle of Moytura, against the Fomorians, and by hurling a stone which pierced through the eye to the brain of Balor, fulfilled the druidic prophecy. *Lugh* was the Irish Sun-god ; his final conquest of the Fomorians and their leader symbolises the victory of light and intellect over darkness. Balor was god of darkness, and brute force as embodied in the Fomorians. By his title of Ildanach, or "All Craftsman," *Lugh* is comparable to the Greek Apollo. He was widely worshipped by Continental Celts.

Lully, Raymond : The life of this alchemist was a curious and eventful one, and all its diverse chapters bespeak him a man of titanic physical and mental energy, quite incapable of doing anything in dilettante fashion, but instead throwing himself heart and soul into every quest which chanced to appeal to him. *Raymond's* father was a Spanish knight, who, having won the approval of John I., King of Arragon, was granted an estate in Majorca ; and it was in that island of the Balearic group that the future alchemist was born, probably in the year 1229, but the date is uncertain. Thanks to the royal favour which his father enjoyed, *Raymond* was appointed Seneschal of the Isles while he was still a mere youth ; but hardly had he acquired this position ere, much to the chagrin of his parents, he began to show a strong predilection for debauchery. He paid amorous addresses to women of all sorts, while at length, becoming enamoured of a married lady named Eleonora de Castello, he began to follow her wherever she went, making no attempt to conceal his illicit passion. On one occasion, indeed, he actually sought the lady while she was attending mass. And, so loud was the outcry against this bold, if not sacrilegious act, that Eleonora found it essential to write in peremptory style to her *cavaliere servente*, bidding him desist from his present course. The letter failed to cool the youth's ardour, but anon, when it transpired that the lady was smitten with the deadly complaint of cancer, her admirer's frame of mind began to alter speedily. Sobered by the frustration of his hopes, he vowed that henceforth he would live differently, consecrating his days to the service of God.

So *Raymond* espoused holy orders, but, as was natural in the case of a man of such active and impetuous temperament, he felt small inclination for monastic life. His aim was to carry the Gospel far afield, converting the children of Mahomet, and with this in view he began to study

Arabic ; while having mastered that tongue he proceeded to Rome, eager to enlist the Pope's sympathy in his project. *Raymond* failed in the latter particular, yet, nothing daunted he embarked on his own account at Genoa about the year 1291, and having reached Tunis he commenced his crusade. His ardour resulted in his being fiercely persecuted and ultimately banished ; so perforce he returned for a while to Europe, visiting Paris, Naples and Pisa, and exhorting all good Christians to aid his beloved enterprise. But in 1308 he ventured to go back to Africa, and at Algiers he made a host of converts, yet was once more forced to fly for his life before the angry Mussulmans. He repaired to Tunis, thinking to escape thence to Italy, but his former activities in the town were remembered, and consequently he was seized and thrown into prison. Here he languished for a long time, never failing to seize every opportunity which presented itself of preaching the gospel, but at last some Genoese merchants contrived to procure his release, and so he sailed back to Italy. Proceeding to Rome, he made further and strenuous efforts towards obtaining the Pope's support of a well-equipped foreign mission ; but *Raymond's* importunity herein proved abortive, and, after resting for a brief space at his native Majorca, the heroic zealot took his life in his hands, and returned to Tunis. Here he even proclaimed his presence publicly, but scarcely had he begun preaching when he reaped the inevitable harvest, and after being savagely attacked he was left lying on the sea-shore, his assailants imagining him dead. He was still breathing, however, when some Genoese found him, and carrying him to a ship they set sail for Majorca. But the missionary did not rally, and he died while in sight of his home, the date being 1315.

Raymond's proselytising ardour had made his name familiar throughout Europe, and, while many people regarded him as a heretic because he had undertaken a mission without the pope's sanction, there were others who admired him so much that they sought to make him a saint. But he was never canonized, and the reason, perhaps, lay in the well-known fact that he had engaged in alchemy. He is reported to have made a large sum of gold for the English king, and, while there is really no proof that he ever visited Britain, the remaining part of the story holds a certain significance. For it is said that *Lully* made the money on the strict understanding that it should be utilised for equipping a large and powerful band of missionaries, and the likelihood is that he thought to employ his chymical skill on behalf of his beloved object, and approached some European Sovereign with this in view, thus giving rise to the tradition about his dealings with the English monarch. Be that as it may, *Raymond's* voluminous writings certainly include a number of alchemistic works, notably *Alchimia Magic Naturalis*, *De Aquis Super Accurtationes*, *De Secretis Medicina Magna* and *De Conservatione Vitæ*; and it is interesting to find that several of these won considerable popularity and were repeatedly reprinted, while so late as 1673 two volumes of *Opera Alchima* purporting to be from *Raymond's* pen were issued at London. Five years before this a biography by Vernon had been published at Paris, while at a later date a German historian of chemistry, Gmelin, referred to Lully as a scientist of exceptional skill, and mentioned him as the first man to distil rosemary oil.

Luminous Bodies : Dead *bodies* are frequently supposed to glow in the dark with a sort of phosphorescent light. Possibly the belief arose from the idea that the soul was like a fire dwelling in the body.

Luther, Martin : The Rosicrucian. (*See* **Rosicrucians.**)

Lutin, The : *The Lutin* of Normandy in many respects resembled Robin Goodfellow. Like him he had many names, and like him had the power of assuming many forms ;

but the *Lutin's* pranks were usually of a more serious nature than those of the tricky spirit of Merrie England. Many a man laid his ruin at the *Lutin's* door, although it must be confessed that in these cases neighbours were uncharitable enough to say, that the *Lutin* had less to do with it than habits of Want-of-Thrift and Self-Indulgence. Thus, on market days, when a farmer lingered late over his ale, whether in driving a close bargain or in enjoying the society of a boon companion, he declared the *Lutin* was sure to play him some spiteful trick on his way home : his horse would stumble—he would be thrown—he would lose his purse—or else his way. If the farmer persisted in these habits, more serious would become the *Lutin's* tricks ; the sheep-pens would be unfastened, the cow-house and stable doors left open, and the flocks and cattle be found moving among the standing corn and unmown hay ; while every servant on the farm would swear to his own innocence, and unhesitatingly lay the blame on the *Lutin.* Similar tricks were played on the fishermen by the Nain Rouge—another name for the *Lutin.* He opened the meshes of the nets and set the fish free ; he removed the floats and let the nets sink to the bottom, or the sinkers, and let the nets float away on the retiring tide. True, if closely questioned, the fishermen would confess that on these occasions the night was dark and stormy, the bothy warm, and the grog plentiful, and that instead of drawing their nets at the proper time, they had delayed it till morning. Again, he would appear like a black nag, ready bridled and saddled, quietly feeding by the way-side; but woe to the luckless wight who mounted him !—unless, indeed, he did so for some charitable or holy purpose, in which case he was borne with the speed of the wind to his destination. In this form the *Lutin* played his wildest pranks and was called Le Cheval Bayard.

Lux : (*See* **Spain.**)

Lycanthropy : The transformation of a human being into an animal. The term is derived from the Greek words, *lukos* a wolf, and *anthropos* a man, but it is employed regarding a transformation into any animal shape. It is chiefly in these countries where wolves are numerous that we find such tales concerning them. (*See* **Wer-wolf.**) But in India, and some parts of Asia, the tiger takes the place of the wolf ; in Russia and elsewhere the bear, and in Africa the leopard.

It is usually savage animals regarding which these beliefs are prevalent, but even harmless ones also figure in them. There is considerable confusion as to whether such transformations were voluntary, or involuntary, temporary or permanent. The man as transformed into the animal may be the very individual himself, or, on the other hand may be only his double, that is his spirit may enter the animal and his body remain unchanged. Magicians and witches were credited with the power of transforming themselves into wolves and other animal shapes, and it was asserted that if the animal were wounded that the marks of the wound would be discovered upon the wizard's body.

The belief is current amongst many savage tribes that every individual possesses an animal form which he enters at death, or at will. This is effected either by magic or natural agency.

As has been said, the wolf is a common form of animal transformation in Europe. In ancient Greece the belief was associated with the dog, which took the place of the wolf. Other similar beliefs are found in India and Java and in the former country we find the wer-wolf in a sort of vampire form.

Guyon relates the history of an enchanter who used to change himself into different beasts.

" Certain people," said he, " persuaded Ferdinand, first Emperor of that name, to command the presence of a Polish enchanter and magician in the town of Nuremberg to learn the result of a difference he had with the Turks, concerning the kingdom of Hungary ; and not only did the magician make use of divination, but performed various other marvels, so that the king did not wish to see him, but the courtiers introduced him into his chamber. There he did many wonderful things, among others, he transformed himself into a horse, anointing himself with some grease, then he took the shape of an ox, and thirdly that of a lion, all in less than an hour. The emperor was so terrified by these transformations that he commanded that the magician should be immediately dismisssed, and declined to hear the future from the lips of such a rascal."

" It need no longer be doubted," adds the same writer, " that Lucius Apuleius Plato was a sorcerer, and that he was transformed into an ass, forasmuch as he was charged with it before the proconsul of Africa, in the time of the Emperor Antonine I., in the year 150 A.D., as Apollonius of Tyana, long before, in the year 60, was charged before Domitian with the same crime. And more than three years after, the rumour persisted to the time of St. Augustine, who was an African, who has written and confirmed it ; as also in his time the father of one Prestantius was transformed into a horse, as the said Prestantius declared. Augustine's father having died, in a short time the son had wasted the greater part of his inheritance in the pursuit of the magic arts, and in order to flee poverty he sought to marry a rich widow named Pudentille, for such a long time that at length she consented. Soon after her only son and heir, the child of her former marriage, died. These things came about in a manner which led people to think that he had by means of magic entrapped Pudentille, who had been wooed in vain by several illustrious people, in order to obtain the wealth of her son. It was also said that the profound knowledge he possessed—for he was able to solve difficult questions which left other men bewildered— was obtained from a demon or familiar spirit he possessed. Further, certain people said they had seen him do many marvellous things, such as making himself invisible, transforming himself into a horse or into a bird, piercing his body with a sword without wounding himself, and similar performances. He was at last accused by one Sicilius Œmilianus, the censor, before Claudius Maximus, proconsul of Africa, who was said to be a Christian ; but nothing was found against him.

Now, that he had been transformed into an ass, St. Augustine regards as indubitable, he having read it in certain true and trustworthy authors, and being besides of the same country ; and this transformation happened to him in Thessaly before he was versed in magic, through the spell of a sorceress, who sold him, and who recovered him to his former shape after he had served in the capacity of an ass for some years, having the same powers and habits of eating and braying as other asses, but with a mind still sane and reasonable as he himself attested. And at last to show forth his case, and to lend probability to the rumour, he wrote a book entitled *The Golden Ass,* a mélange of fables and dialogues, to expose the vices of the men of his time, which he had heard of, or seen, during his transformation, with many of the labours and troubles he had suffered while in the shape of an ass.

" However that may be, St. Augustine in the book of the *City of God,* book XVIII., chapters XVII. and XVIII., relates that in his time there were in the Alps certain sorceresses who gave a particular kind of cheese to the passers by, who, on partaking of it, were immediately changed into asses or other beasts of burden, and were made to carry heavy weights to certain places. When their task was over, they were permitted to regain their human shape."

" The bishop of Tyre, historian, writes that in his time, probably about 1220, some Englishmen were sent by their king to the aid of the Christians who were fighting in the Holy Land, and that on their arrival in a haven of the island of Cyprus a sorceress transformed a young English soldier into an ass. He, wishing to return to his companions in the ship, was chased away with blows from a stick, whereupon he returned to the sorceress who made use of him, until someone noticed that the ass kneeled in a church and did various other things which only a reasoning being could do. The sorceress who followed him was taken on suspicion before the authorities, was obliged to give him his human form three years after his transformation, and was forthwith executed."

" We read," says Loys Guyon, " that Ammonius, a peripatetic philosopher, about the time of Lucius Septimius Severus, in the year 196 A.D., had present at his lessons an ass whom he taught. I should think that this ass had been at one time a man, and that he quite understood what Ammonius taught, for these transformed persons retain their reason unimpaired, as St. Augustine and other writers have assured us."

" Fulgose writes, book VIII., chapter II., that in the time of Pope Leon, who lived about the year 930, there were in Germany two sorceresses who used thus to change their guests into beasts, and on one occasion she changed a young mountebank into an ass, who, preserving his human understanding, gave a great deal of amusement to the passers-by. A neighbour of the sorceresses bought the ass at a good price, but was warned by them that he must not take the beast to a river, or he would lose it. Now the ass escaped one day and running to a near-by lake plunged into the water, when he returned to his own shape. Apuleirs says that he regained his human form by eating roses.

" There are still to be seen in Egypt asses which are led into the market-place to perform various feats of agility and tricks, understanding all the commands they receive, and executing them : such as to point out the most beautiful woman of the company, and many other things that one would hardly believe ; and Belon, a physician, relates in his observations that he has seen them, and others also, who have been there, and who have affirmed the same to me."

" One day there was brought to St. Macarius, the Egyptian," says Calmet, " an honest woman who had been transformed into a mare by the wicked art of a magician. Her husband and all who beheld her believed that she had really been changed into a mare. This woman remained for three days without taking any food, whether suitable for a horse or for a human being. She was brought to the priests of the place, who could suggest no remedy. So they led her to the cell of St. Macarius, to whom God had revealed that she was about to come. His disciples wished to send her away, thinking her a mare, and they warned the saint of her approach, and the reason for her journey. He said to them : ' It is you who are the animals, who think you see that which is not ; this woman is not changed, but your eyes are bewitched." As he spoke he scattered holy water on the head of the woman, and all those present saw her in her true shape. He had something given her to eat and sent her away safe and sound with her husband."

Lytton, Bulwer : Author (1803–1873). According to his baptismal certificate, the full name of this once famous author was *Edward George Earle Lytton Bulwer-Lytton*, and in signing some of his early writings he used all these names with occasional variations in their order, an act which was regarded by many people as springing from pride and pompousness, and which elicited the withering satire of Thackeray in *Punch*. *Lytton* was born at London in 1803, and his father was a Norfolk squire, Bulwer of Heydon

Hall ; while his mother was Elizabeth Barbara Lytton, a lady who claimed kinship with Cadwaladr Vendigaid, the semi-mythical hero who led the Strathclyde Welsh against the Angles in the seventh century. As a child the future novelist was delicate, but he learnt to read at a surprisingly early age, and began to write verses before he was ten years old. Going first to a small private school at Fulham, he soon passed on to another one at Rottingdean ; and here he continued to manifest literary tastes, Byron and Scott being his chief idols at this time. So clever was the boy thought, indeed, that his relations decided it would be a mistake to send him to a public school ; and accordingly he was placed with a tutor at Ealing, under whose care he progressed rapidly with his studies. Thereafter he proceeded to Cambridge, where he took his degree easily, and won many academic laurels, while on leaving the University he travelled for a while in Scotland and in France, and then bought a commission in the army. He sold it soon afterwards, however, while in 1827 he was married, and now he began to devote himself seriously to writing, his first publications of note being the novels of *Falkland*, *Pelham* and *Eugene Aram*. These won an instant success, and placed considerable wealth in the author's hands, the result being that in 1831 he entered parliament as liberal member for St. Ives, Huntingdonshire ; and during the next ten years he was an active politician yet found time to produce a host of stories, for instance *The Last Days of Pompei* and *Ernest Maltravers*, *Zanoni* and *The Last of the Barons*. These were followed shortly by *The Caxtons*, and simultaneously *Lytton* achieved some fame as a dramatist, perhaps his best play being *The Lady of Lyons* ; while in 1851 he was instrumental in founding a scheme for pensioning authors, in 1862 he increased his reputation greatly by his novel entitled *A Strange Story*, and four years later his services to literature and politics were rewarded by a peerage. He now began to work at yet another story, *Kenelm Chillingly*, but his health was beginning to fail, and he died in 1873 at Torquay.

The works cited above constitute but a fragment of *Lytton's* voluminous achievement. Besides further novels too numerous to mention, he issued several volumes of verses notably *Ismael* and *The New Union*, while he did translations from German, Spanish and Italian, he produced a history of Athens, he contributed to endless periodicals, and was at one time editor of *The New Monthly Magazine*. But albeit so busy throughout the whole of his career, and while winning vast fame and opulence, *Lytton's* life was not really a happy one, various causes conducing to make it otherwise. Long before meeting his wife he fell in love with a young girl who died prematurely, and this loss seems to have left an indelible scar on his heart, while his marriage was anything but a successful one, the pair being divorced comparatively soon after their union. Now as a mere child *Lytton* had evinced a predilection for mysticism, while he had surprised his mother once by asking her whether she was "not sometimes overcome by the sense of her own identity" (almost exactly the same question was put to his nurse in boyhood by another mystic, William Bell Scott) ; *Lytton* sedulously developed his leaning towards the occult, and it is everywhere manifest in his literary output. It transpires, for example, in his poem *The Tale of a Dreamer*, and again in *Kenelm Chillingly*, while in *A Strange Story* he tries to give a scientific colouring to old-fashioned magic ; but neither this essay nor those others are really to be called triumphant in the artistic sense, and, as Sir Leslie Stephen shrewdly observes, *Lytton's* "attempts at the mysterious too often remind us of spirit-rapping rather than excite the thrill of supernatural awe." In a word *Lytton's* outlook on life was theatrical and his mysticism was not a little stagey.

M

Maat Kheru : According to Maspus, the Egyptian name of the true intonation with which the dead must recite those magic incantations which would give them power in Amenti, the Egyptian Hades,

Macionica : Slavonic name for a witch. (*See* **Slavs.**)

Mackay, Gallatin : A disciple of Albert Pike (q.v.) and one of the leaders of Masonry in Charleston, U.S.A. who was charged by Miss Diana Vaughan, Dr. Bataille and others with the practice of Satanism and sorcery—charges entirely without foundation. (*See* Waite, *Devil-Worship in France*.)

Mackenzie, Kenneth : (*See* **Rosicrucians.**)

Macrocosm, The : The whole universe (Greek *Macros*, long, Kosmos the world (f. "Microcosm"). A six-pointed star, formed of two triangles, and the sacred symbol of Solomon's seal. It represents the infinite and the absolute—that is, the most simple and complete abridgment of the science of all things. Paracelsus states that every magical figure and kabalistic sign of the pantacles which compel spirits may be reduced to two—the *Macrocosm* and the Microcosm (q.v.) It is the emblem of the world.

Macroprosopus, The : One of the four magical elements in the Kabala ; and probably representing one of the four simple elements,—air, water, earth, or fire. *Macroprosopus* means " creator of the great world."

Madre Natura : An old and powerful secret society, of Italy, who worshipped and idealised nature, and which seems to have been founded by members of the ancient Italian priesthood. It had a tradition that one of the Popes as Cardinal de Medici became a member of the fraternity, and for this there is good documentary evidence. It accepted the allegorical interpretation which the Neo-Platonists had placed upon the Pagan creeds during the first ages of Christianity.

Magi : Priests of ancient Persia, and the cultivators of the wisdom of Zoroaster. They were institutied by Cyrus when he founded the new Persian empire, and are supposed to have been of the Median race. Schlegel says (*Philosophy of History*), " they were not so much a hereditary sacerdotal caste as an order or association, divided into various and successive ranks and grades, such as existed in the mysteries —the grade of apprenticeship—that of mastership—that of perfect mastership." In short, they were a theosophical college ; and either its professors were indifferently " magi," or magicians, and " wise men " or they were distinguished into two classes by those names. Their name pronounced " Mogh " by the modern Persians, and " Magh " by the ancients signified " Wise," and such is the interpretation of it given by the Greek and Roman writers. Stobæus expressly calls the science of the *magi*, the service of the gods, so Plato. According to Ennemoser, " Magiusiah, Madschusie, signified the office and knowledge of the priest, who was called " Mag, Magius, Magiusi," and after-wards *magi* and " Magician." Brucker maintains that the primitive meaning of the word is " fire worshipper," " worship of the light," an erroneous opinion. In the modern Persian the word is " Mog," and " Mogbed " signifies high priest. The high priest of the Parsees at Surat, even at the present day, is called, " Mobed." Others derive the word from " Megh," " Meh-ab " signifying something which is great and noble, and Zoroaster's disciples were called " Meghestom." Salverte states that these Mobeds are still named in the Pehivi dialect " Magoi." They were divided into three classes :—Those who abstained from all animal food ; those who never ate of the flesh of any tame animals ; and those who made no scruple to eat any kind of meat. A belief in the transmi-gration of the soul was the foundation of this abstinence. They professed the science of divination, and for that purpose met together and consulted in their temples. They professed to make truth the great object of their study ; for that alone, they said, can make man like God " whose body resembles light, as his soul or spirit resembles truth." They condemned all images, and those who said that the gods are male and female ; they had neither temples nor altars, but worshipped the sky, as a represen-tative of the Deity, on the tops of mountains ; they also sacrificed to the sun, moon, earth, fire, water, and winds, says Herodotus, meaning, no doubt that they adored the heavenly bodies and the elements. This was probably before the time of Zoroaster, when the religion of Persia seems to have resembled that of ancient India. Their hymns in praise of the Most High exceeded, according to Dio Chrysostom, the sublimity of anything in Homer or Hesiod. They exposed their dead bodies to wild beasts. It is a question " whether the old Persian doctrine and wisdom or tradition of light did not undergo material alterations in the hands of its Median restorer, Zoroaster ; or whether this doctrine was preserved in all its purity by the order of the magi." He then remarks that on them devolved the important trust of the monarch's education, which must necessarily have given them great weight and influence in the state. They were in high credit at the " Persian gates "—for that was the Oriental name given to the capital of the empire, and the abode of the prince—and they took the most active part in all the factions that encompassed che throne, or that were formed in the vicinity of the court. In Greece, and even in Egypt, the sacerdotal fraternities and associations of initiated, formed by the mysteries, had in general but an indirect, though not unimportant influence on affairs of state ; but in the Persian monarchy they acquired a complete political ascendency. Religion, philosophy, and the sciences were all in their hands, they were the universal physicians who healed the sick in body and in spirit, and, in strict con-sistency with that character, ministered to the state, which is only the man again in a larger sense. The three grades of the *magi* alluded to are called by Herber the " disciples," the " professed," and the " masters." They were originally from Bactria, where they governed a little state by laws of their own choice, and by their incorporation in the Persian empire, they greatly promoted the consolidation of the conquests of Cyrus. Their fall dates from the reign of Darius Hystaspes, about 500 B.C., by whom they were fiercely persecuted ; this produced an emigration which extended to Cappadocia on the one hand, and to India on the other, but they were still of so much consideration at a later period, as to provoke the jealousy of Alexander the Great. (*See* **Persia.**)

Magia Posthuma : A short treatise on Vampirism published at Olmutz in 1706, and written by Ferdinand de Schertz. Reviewing it Calmet (q.v.) says in his *Dissertation on Vampires* : " The author relates a story of a woman that died in a certain village, after having received all the sacra-ments, and was buried with the usual ceremonies, in the Churchyard. About four days after her death, the inhabi-tants of the village were affrighted with an uncommon noise and outcry, and saw a spectre, sometimes in the shape of a dog, and sometimes in that of a man, which appeared to great multitudes of people, and put them to excessive pain by squeezing their throats, and pressing their breasts, almost to suffocation. There were several whose bodies he bruised all over, and reduced them to the utmost weak-ness, so that they grew pale, lean, and disfigured. His fury was sometimes so great as not to spare the very beasts, for cows were frequently found beat to the earth, half dead ; at other times with their tails tied to one another, and their hideous lowings sufficiently expressed the pain they felt. Horses were often found almost wearied to death, foaming with sweat, and out of breath, as if they had been running a long and tiresome race; and these calamities continued for several months.''

The author of the treatise examines into the subject in the capacity of a lawyer, and discusses both the matter of fact and the points of law arising from it. He is clearly of opinion that if the suspected person was really the author of these noises, disturbances, and acts of cruelty, the law will justify the burning of the body, as is practised in the case of other spectres which come again and molest the living. He relates also several stories of apparitions of this sort, and particularises the mischiefs done by them. One, among others, is of a herdsman of the village of Blow near the town of Kadam in Bohemia, who appeared for a considerable time together, and called upon several persons, who all died within eight days. At last, the inhabitants of Blow dug up the herdsman's body, and fixed it in the ground, with a stake driven through it. The man, even in this condition, laughed at the people that were employed about him, and told them they were very obliging to furnish him with a stick to defend himself from the dogs. The same night he extricated himself from the stake, frightened several persons by appearing to them, and occasioned the death of many more than he had hitherto done. He was then delivered into the hands of the hangman, who put him into a cart, in order to burn him without the town. As they went along, the carcass shrieked in the most hideous manner, and threw about its arms and legs, as if it had been alive, and upon being again run through with a stake, it gave a loud cry, and a great quantity of fresh, florid blood issued from the wound. At last the body was burnt to ashes, and this execution put a final stop to the spectre's appearing and infesting the village.

The same method has been practised in other places, where these apparitions have been seen, and upon taking them out of the ground, their bodies have seemed fresh and florid, their limbs pliant and flexible, without any worms or putrefaction, but not without a great stench. The author quotes several other writers, who attest what he relates concerning these spectres, which, he says, still appear in the mountains of Silesia and Moravia. They are seen, it seems, both by day and night, and the things which formerly belonged to them are observed to stir and change their place, without any person's being seen to touch them. And the only remedy in these cases, is to cut off the head, and burn the body of the persons that are supposed to appear.

Magic : Short for " magic art," from Greek *magein* the science and religion of the priests of Zoroaster ; or, according to Skeat, from Greek *megas*, great, thus signifying the " great " science.

History.—The earliest traces of magical practice are found in the European caves of the middle Palæolithic Age. These belong to the last interglacial period of the Pleistocene period, which has been named the Aurignacian, after the cave-dwellers of Aurignac, whose skeletons, artifacts and drawings link them with the Bushmen of South Africa. In the cave of Gargas, near Bagnères de Luchon, occur, in addition to spirited and realistic drawings of animals, numerous imprints of human hands in various stages of mutilation. Some hands had been first smeared with a sticky substance and then pressed on the rock ; others had been held in position to be dusted round with red ochre, or black pigment. Most of the imprinted hands have mutilated fingers ; in some cases the first and second joints of one or more fingers are wanting ; in others the stumps only of all fingers remain. A close study of the hand imprints makes it evident that they are not to be regarded as those of

lepers. There can be little doubt that the joints were removed for a specific purpose, and on this point there is general agreement among anthropologists. A clue to the mystery is obtained by the magical custom among the Bushmen of similarly removing finger joints. Mr. G. W. Stow in his *The Native Races of South Africa* makes reference to this strange form of sacrifice. He once came into contact with a number of Bushmen who " had all lost the first joint of the little finger " which had been removed with a " stone knife " with purpose to ensure a safe journey to the spirit world. Another writer tells of an old Bushman woman whose little fingers of both hands had been mutilated, three joints in all having been removed. She explained that each joint had been sacrificed as a daughter died to express her sorrow. No doubt, however, there was a deeper meaning in the custom than she cared to confess. F. Boas in his *Report on the N.W. Tribes of Canada* gives evidence of the custom among these peoples. When frequent deaths resulted from disease, the Canadian Indians were wont to sacrifice the joints of their little fingers so as, they explained, " to cut off the deaths." Among the Indian Madigas (Telugu Pariahs) the evil eye is averted by sacrificers who dip their hands in the blood of goats or sheep and impress them on either side of a house door. This custom is not unknown even to Brahmans. Impressions of hands are also occasionally seen on the walls of Indian Mohammedan mosques. As among the N.W. Canadian tribes, the hand ceremony is most frequently practised in India when epidemics make a heavy toll of lives. The Bushmen also remove finger joints when stricken with sickness. In Australia, where during initiation ceremonies the young men have teeth knocked out and bodies scarred, the women of some tribes mutilate the little fingers of daughters with purpose to influence their future careers. Apparently the finger chopping customs of Palæolithic times had a magical significance. On some of the paintings in the Aurignacian caves appear symbols which suggest the slaying with spears and cutting up of animals. Enigmatical signs are another feature. Of special interest are the figures of animal-headed demons, some with hands upraised in the Egyptian attitude of adoration, and others apparently dancing like the animal-headed dancing gods of the Bushmen. In the Marsonlas Palæolithic cave there are semi-human faces of angry demons with staring eyes and monstrous noses. In the Spanish Cave at Cogul several figures of women wearing half-length skirts and shoulder shawls, are represented dancing round a nude male. So closely do these females resemble such as usually appear in Bushmen paintings that they might well, but for their location, be credited to this interesting people. Religious dances among the Bushman tribes are associated with marriage, birth and burial ceremonies ; they are also performed to exorcise demons in cases of sickness. " Dances are to us what prayers are to you," an elderly Bushman once informed a European. Whether the cave drawings and wood, bone and ivory carvings of the Magdalenian, or late Palæolithic period at the close of the last ice epoch, are of magical significance is a problem on which there is no general agreement. It is significant to find, however, that several carved ornaments bearing animal figures or enigmatical signs are perforated as if worn as charms. On a piece of horn found at Lorthet, Hautes Pyrénées, are beautiful incised drawings of reindeer and salmon, above which appear mystical symbols. An ape-like demon carved on bone was found at Mas d'Azil : on a reindeer horn from Laugerie Basse a prostrate man with a tail is creeping up on all fours towards a grazing bison. These are some of the instances which lend colour to the view that late Palæolithic art had its origin in magical beliefs and practices—that hunters carved on the handles of weapons and implements, or scratched on cave walls, the images of the animals they desired to capture—sometimes with the secured co-operation of demons, and sometimes with the aid of magical spells.

Coming to historic times we know that the ancient Egyptians (*See* **Egypt**) possessed a highly-developed magical system, as did the Babylonians (*See* **Semites**), and other pristine civilisations. Indeed from these the mediæval European system of *magic* was finally evolved. Greece and Rome (both of which see) also possessed distinct national systems, which in some measure were branches of their religions; and thus like the Egyptian and Babylonian were preserves of the priesthood.

Magic in early Europe was, of course, merely an appendage of the various religious systems which obtained throughout that continent; and it was these systems which later generated into witchcraft (q.v.) But upon the foundation of Christianity, the church soon began to regard the practice of *magic* as foreign to the spirit of its religion. Thus the Thirty-sixth Canon of the Œcumenical Council held at Laodicea in 364 A.D. forbids clerks and priests to become magicians, enchanters, mathematicians or astrologers. It orders, moreover, that the Church shall expel from its bosom those who employ ligatures or phylacteries, because it says phylacteries are the prisons of the soul. The Fourth Canon of the Council of Oxia, A.D. 525, prohibited the consultation of sorcerers, augurs, diviners, and divinations made with wood or bread; and the Sixtieth Canon of the Council of Constantinople A.D. 692, excommunicated for a period of six years diviners, and those who had recourse to them. The prohibition was repeated by the Council of Rome in 721. The Forty-second Canon of the Council of Tours in 613 is to the effect that the priests shall teach to the people the inefficacy of magical practices to restore the health of men or animals, and later Councils practically endorsed the church's earlier views.

It does not appear, however, that what may be called "mediæval magic" took final and definite shape until about the twelfth century. Modelled upon the systems in vogue among the Byzantines and Moors of Spain, which were evolved from the Alexandrian system (*See* **Neoplatonism**), what might be called the "oriental" type of *magic* gained footing in Europe, and quite superseded the earlier and semi-barbarian systems in use among the various countries of that continent, most of which, as has been said, were the relics of older pagan practice and ritual. To these relics clung the witch and the wizard and the professors of lesser magic; whereas among the disciples of the imported system we find the magician—black and white,—the necromancer and the sorcerer. The manner in which the theosophy and the magic of the East was imported was probably two-fold; first, there is good evidence that it was imported into Europe by persons returning from the Crusades; and secondly, we know that in matters of wisdom, Byzantium fell heir to Alexandria, and that from Constantinople *magic* was disseminated throughout Europe, along with other sciences. It is not necessary to deal in the course of this article with the history of witchcraft and lesser sorcery, as that has already been done in the article "witchcraft" (q.v.); and we will confine ourselves strictly to the history of the higher branches of *magic*. But it is competent to remark that Europe had largely obtained its pneumotology from the orient through Christianity, from Jewish and early Semitic sources; and it is an open question how far eastern demonology coloured that of the Catholic Church.

Mediæval *magic* of the higher type has practically no landmarks save a series of great names. Its tenets experienced but little alteration during six centuries. From the eighth to the thirteenth century, there does not appear to have been much persecution of the professors of *magic*, but after that period the opinions of the church underwent a radical change, and the life of the magus was fraught with considerable danger. However, it is pretty clear that he was not victimised in the same manner as his lesser brethren, the sorcerers and wizards; but we find Paracelsus consistently baited by the medical profession of his day, Agrippa constantly persecuted, and even mystics like Bœhme imprisoned and ill-used. It is difficult at this distance to estimate the enormous vogue that *magic* experienced, whether for good or evil during the middle ages. Although severely punished, if discovered or if its professors became sufficiently notorious to court persecution, the power it seems to have conferred upon them was eagerly sought by scores of people—the majority of whom were quite unfitted for its practice, and clumsily betrayed themselves into the hands of the authorities. In the article entitled "Black Magic," we have outlined the history of that lesser *magic* known as sorcery or "black magic," and there have shown what persecutions overtook those who practised it.

As has already been mentioned, the history of higher *magic* in Europe is a matter of great names, and these are somewhat few. They do not include alchemists, who are strictly speaking not magicians, as their application of arcane laws was particular and not universal; but this is not to say that some alchemists were not also magicians. The two great names which stand out in the history of European *magic* are those of Paracelsus and Agrippa, who formulated the science of mediæval *magic* in its entirety. They were also the greatest practical magicians of the middle ages, as apart from pure mystics, alchemists and others, and their thaumaturgic and necromantic experiences were probably never surpassed. With these mediæval magic comes to a close and the further history of the science in Europe will be found outlined in the division of this article entitled "Modern Magic."

Scientific Theories regarding the Nature of Magic.— General agreement as to the proper definition of *magic* is wanting, as it depends upon the view taken of religious belief. According to Frazer, *magic* and religion are one and the same thing, or are so closely allied as to be almost identical. This may be true of peoples in a savage or barbarian condition of society, but can scarcely apply to *magic* and religion as fully fledged, as for example in mediæval times, however fundamental may be their original unity. The objective theory of *magic* would regard it as entirely distinct from religion, possessed of certain well-marked attributes, and traceable to mental processes differing from those from which the religious idea springs. Here and there the two have become fused by the super-imposition of religious upon magical practice. The objective idea of *magic*, in short, rests on the belief that it is based on magical laws which are supposed to operate with the regularity of those of natural science. The subjective view, on the other hand, is that many practices seemingly magical are in reality religious, and that no rite can be called magical which is not so designated by its celebrant or agent. It has been said that religion consists of an appeal to the gods, whereas *magic* is the attempt to force their compliance. Messrs. Hubert and Mauss believe that *magic* is essentially traditional. Holding as they do that the primitive mind is markedly unoriginal, they have satisfied themselves that *magic* is therefore an art which does not exhibit any frequent changes amongst primitive folk, and is fixed by its laws. Religion, they say, is official and organised, *magic* prohibited and secret. Magical power appears to them to be determined by the contiguity, similarity and contrast of the object of the act, and the object to be effected. Mr. Frazer believes all *magic* to be based on the law of sympathy—that is the assumption that things act on one another at a distance because of their being secretly linked together by invisible bonds. He divides sympathetic *magic* into homeopathic *magic* and contagious *magic*. The first is imitative or mimetic, and may be practised by itself ; but the latter usually necessitates the application of the imitative principle. Well-known instances of mimetic magic are the forming of wax figures in the likeness of an enemy, which are destroyed in the hope that he will perish. Contagious magic may be instanced by the savage anointing the weapon which caused a wound instead of the wound itself, in the belief that the blood on the weapon continues to feel with the blood on the body. Mr. L. Marillier divides *magic* into three classes : the *magic* of the word or act ; the *magic* of the human being independent of rite or formula ; and the *magic* which demands a human being of special powers and the use of ritual. Mr. A. Lehmann believes *magic* to be a practice of superstition, and founds it in illusion. The fault of all these theories is that they strive after too great an exactness, and that they do not allow sufficiently for the feeling of wonder and awe which is native to the human mind. Indeed they designate this " strained attention." We may grant that the attention of savages to a magical rite is " strained," so strained is it in some cases that it terrifies them into insanity ; and it would seem therefore as if the limits of " attention " were overpassed, and as if it shaded into something very much deeper. Moreover it is just possible that in future it may be granted that so-called sympathetic magic does not partake of the nature of magic at all, but has greater affinities (owing to its strictly natural and non-supernatural character) with pseudo-science.

Magic is recognised by many savage peoples as a force rather than an art,—a thing which impinges upon the thought of man from outside. It would appear that many barbarian tribes believe in what would seem to be a great reservoir of magical power, the exact nature of which they are not prepared to specify. Thus amongst certain American-Indian tribes we find a force called *Orenda* or spirit-force. Amongst the ancient Peruvians, everything sacred was *huaca* and possessed of magical power. In Melanesia, we find a force spoken of called *mana*, transmissible and contagious, which may be seen in the form of flames or even heard. The Malays use the word *kramat* to signify the same thing ; and the Malagasy the term *hasma*. Some of the tribes round Lake Tanganyika believe in such a force, which they call *ngai*, and Australian tribes have many similar terms, such as *churinga* and *boolya*. To hark back to America, we find in Mexico the strange creed named *nagualism*, which partakes of the same conception—everything *nagual* is magical or possesses an inherent spiritual force of its own.

Theories of the Origin of Magic.—Many theories have been advanced regarding the origin of *magic*—some authorities believing that it commenced with the idea of personal superiority ; others through animistic beliefs (*See* **Animism**); and still others through such ideas as that physical pains, for which the savage could not account, were supposed to be inflicted by invisible weapons. This last theory is, of course, in itself, merely animistic. It does not seem, however, that writers on the subject have given sufficient attention to the great influence exerted on the mind of man by odd or peculiar occurrences. We do not for a moment desire to advance the hypothesis that *magic* entirely originated from such a source, but we believe that it was a powerful factor in the growth of magical belief. To which, too, *animism* and *taboo* contributed their quota. The cult of the dead too and their worship would soon become fused with magical practice, and a complete demonology would thus speedily arise.

The Dynamics of Magic.—Magical practice is governed by well-marked laws limited in number. It possesses many classes of practitioner ; as, for example, the diviner or augur, whose duties are entirely different from those of the witch-doctor. Chief among these laws, as has been already hinted, is that of sympathy, which, as has been said, must inevitably be sub-divided into the laws of similarity, contiguity and antipathy. The law of similarity and homeopathy is again divisible into two sections : (1)—the assumption that like produces like—an illustration of which is the destruction of a model in the form of an enemy ; and (2)—the idea that like cures like—for instance, that the stone called the bloodstone can staunch the flow of bleeding. The law dealing with antipathy rests on the assumption that the application of a certain object or drug expels its contrary. There remains contiguity, which is based on the concept that whatever has once formed part of an object continues to form part of it. Thus if a magician can obtain a portion of a person's hair, he can work woe upon him through the invisible bonds which are supposed to extend between him and the hair in the sorcerer's possession. It is well-known that if the animal familiar of a witch be wounded, that the wound will react in a sympathetic manner on the witch herself. This is called " repercussion."

Another widespread belief is that if the magician procures the name of a person that he can gain magical dominion over him. This, of course, arose from the idea that the name of an individual was identical with himself. The doctrine of the Incommunicable Name, the hidden name of the god or magician, is well instanced by many legends in Egyptian history,—the deity usually taking extraordinary care to keep his name secret, in order that no one might gain power over him. The spell or incantation is connected with this concept, and with these, in a lesser degree, may be associated magical gesture, which is usually introduced for the purpose of accentuating the spoken word. Gesture is often symbolic or sympathetic ; it is sometimes the reversal of a religious rite, such as marching against the sun, which is known as walking " widdershins." The method of pronouncing rites is, too, one of great importance. Archaic or foreign expressions are usually found in spells ancient and modern ; and the tone in which the incantation is spoken, no less than its exactness, is also important. To secure exactness rhythm was often employed, which had the effect of aiding memory.

The Magician.—In early society, the magician, which term includes the shaman, medicine-man, piagé, witch-doctor, *et cetera*, may hold his position by hereditary right ; by an accident of birth, as being the seventh son of a seventh son ; to revelation from the gods ; or through mere mastery of ritual. In savage life we find the shaman a good deal of a medium, for instead of summoning the powers of the air at his bidding as did the magicians of mediæval days, he seems to find it necessary to throw himself into a state of trance and seek them in their own sphere. The magician is also often regarded as possessed by an animal or supernatural being. The duties of the priest and magician are often combined in primitive society, but it cannot be too strongly asserted that where a religion has been superseded, the priests of the old cult are, for those who have taken their places, nothing but magicians. We do not hear much of beneficent *magic* among savage peoples, and it is only in Europe that White Magic may be said to have gained any hold.

Mediæval Definition of Magic.—The definitions of *magic* vouchsafed by the great magicians of mediæval and modern times naturally differ greatly from those of anthropologists.

For example Eliphas Levi says in his *History of Magic* : " *Magic* combines in a single science that which is most certain in philosophy with that which is eternal and infallible in religion. It reconciles perfectly and incontestably those two terms so opposed on the first view—faith and reason, science and belief, authority and liberty. It furnishes the human mind with an instrument of philosophical and religious certainty, as exact as mathematics, and even accounting for the infallibility of mathematics themselves. . . . . . There is an incontestable truth, and there is an infallible method of knowing that truth ; while those who attain this knowledge and adopt it as a rule of life, can endow their life with a sovereign power, which can make them masters of all inferior things, of wandering spirits, or in other words, arbiters and kings of the world.'' Paracelsus says regarding *magic* : " The magical is a great hidden wisdom, and reason is a great open folly. No armour shields against *magic* for it strikes at the inward spirit of life. Of this we may rest assured, that through full and powerful imagination only can we bring the spirit of any man into an image. No conjuration, no rites are needful ; circle-making and the scattering of incense are mere humbug and jugglery. The human spirit is so great a thing that no man can express it ; eternal and unchangeable as God Himself is the mind of man ; and could we rightly comprehend the mind of man, nothing would be impossible to us upon the earth. Through faith the imagination is invigorated and completed, for it really happens that every doubt mars its perfection. Faith must strengthen imagination, for faith establishes the will. Because man did not perfectly believe and imagine, the result is that arts are uncertain when they might be wholly certain.'' Agrippa also regarded *magic* as the true road to communion with God—thus linking it with mysticism.

Modern Magic : With the death of Agrippa in 1535 the old school of magicians may be said to have ended. But that is not to say that the traditions of magic were not handed on to others who were equally capable of preserving them. We must carefully discriminate at this juncture between those practitioners of magic whose minds were illuminated by a high mystical ideal, and persons of doubtful occult position, like the Comte de Saint-Germain and others. At the beginning of the seventeenth century we find many great alchemists in practice, who were also devoted to the researches of transcendental magic, which they carefully and successfully concealed under the veil of hermetic experiment. These were Michael Meyer, Campe, Robert Flood, Cosmopolite, D'Espagnet, Samuel Norton, Baron de Beausoleil, and Van Helmont ; another illustrious name is also that of Philalethes. The eighteenth century was rich in occult personalities, as for example the alchemist Lascaris (q.v.) Martines de Pasqually, and Louis de Saint-Martin (q.v.) who founded the Martinist school, which still exists under the grandmastership of Papus. After this magic merges for the moment into mesmerism, and many of the secret magical societies which abounded in Europe about this period practised animal magnetism as well as astrology, Kabalism and ceremonial magic. Indeed mesmerism powerfully influenced mystic life in the time of its chief protagonist, and the mesmerists of the first era are in direct line with the Martinist and the mystical magicians of the late eighteenth century. Indeed mysticism and magnetism are one and the same thing, in the persons of some of these occultists (*See* **Secret Tradition**) the most celebrated of which were Cazotte, Ganneau, Comte, Wronski, Du Potet, Hennequin, Comte d'Ourches, and Baron de Guldenstubbé, and last of the initiates known to us, Eliphas Levi (all of which see).

That Black Magic and sorcery are still practised is a well-known fact, which requires no amplification in this

place (*See* **Devil Worship**) : but what of that higher magic which has, at least in modern times, attracted so many gifted minds ? We cannot say that the true line of magical adepts ended with Levi, as at no time in the world's history are these known to the vulgar ; but we may be certain that the great art is practised in secret as sedulously as ever in the past, and that men of temperament as exalted as in the case of the magacians of older days still privately pursue that art, which, like its sister religion, is none the less celestial because it has been evolved from lowly origins in the mind of man, whose spirit with the march of time reflects ever more strongly the light of heaven, as the sea at first dimly reddened by the dawn, at length mirrors the whole splendour of day.
(*See also* **Abraham the Jew, Black Magic, Ceremonial Magic, Egypt, Magic Darts, Magical Diagrams, Magical Instruments, Magical Numbers, Magical Union of Cologne, Magical Vestments, Mediæval Magic.**)

Magic Darts : The Laplanders, who passed at one time for great magicians, were said to launch lead darts, about a finger-length, against their absent enemies, believing that with the *magic darts* they were sending grevious pains and maladies. (*See* **Magic.**)

Magic Squares : (*See* **Abraham the Jew.**)

Magical Diagrams : These were geometrical designs, representing the mysteries of deity and creation, therefore supposed to be of special virtue in rites of evocation and conjuration.

The chief of these were the Triangle, the Double Triangle, forming a six-pointed star and known as the Sign or Seal of Solomon ; the Tetragram a four-pointed star formed by the interlacement of two pillars ; and the Pentagram, a five-pointed star.

These signs were traced on paper or parchment, or engraved on metals and glass and consecrated to their various uses by special rites.

The Triangle was based on the idea of trinity as found in all things, in deity, time and creation. The triangle was generally traced on the ground with the magic sword or rod, as in circles of evocation where the triangle was drawn within it and according to the position of the magician at its point or base so the spirits were conjured from heaven or hell.

The Double Triangle, the Sign of Solomon, symbolic of the Macrocosm, was formed by the interlacement of two triangles, thus its points constituted the perfect number six. The magicians wore it, bound on their brows and breasts during the ceremonies and it was engraved on the silver reservoir of the magic lamp.

The Tetragram was symbolic of the four elements and used in the conjuration of the elementary spirits—sylphs of the air, undines of the water, the fire salamanders and gnomes of the earth. In alchemy it represented the magical elements, salt, sulphur, mercury and azoth ; in mystic philosophy the ideas Spirit, Matter, Motion and Rest ; in hieroglyphs the man, eagle, lion and bull.

The Pentagram, the sign of the Microcosm, was held to be the most powerful means of conjuration in any rite. It may represent evil as well as good, for while with one point in the ascendant it was the sign of Christ, with two points in the ascendant it was the sign of Satan. By the use of the pentagram in these positions the powers of light or darkness were evoked. The pentagram was said to be the star which led the Magi to the manger where the infant Christ was laid.

The preparation and consecration of this sign for use in *magical* rites is prescribed with great detail. It might be composed of seven metals, the ideal form for its expression ; or traced in pure gold upon white marble, never before used for any purpose. It might also be drawn with vermilion upon lambskin without a blemish prepared under the auspices of the Sun. The sign was next consecrated with the four elements ; breathed on five times ; dried by the smoke of five perfumes, incense, myrrh, aloes, sulphur and camphor. The names of five genii were breathed above it, and then the sign was placed successively at the north, south, east and west and centre of the astronomical cross pronouncing the letters of the sacred tetragram and various Kabalistic names.

It was believed to be of great efficacy in terrifying phantoms if engraved upon glass, and the magicians traced it on their doorsteps to prevent evil spirits from entering and the good from departing.

This symbol has been used by all secret and occult societies, by the Rosicrucians, the Illuminati, down to the Freemasons of to-day. Modern Occultists translate the meaning of the pentagram as symbolic of the human soul and its relation to God.

The symbol is placed with one point in the ascendant. That point represents the Great Spirit, God. A line drawn from there to the left-hand angle at base is the descent of spirit into matter in its lowest form, whence it ascends to right-hand angle typifying matter in its highest form, the brain of man. From here a line is drawn across the figure to left angle representing man's development in intellect, and progress in material civilization, the point of danger, from which all nations have fallen into moral corruption, signified by the descent of the line to right angle at base. But the soul of man being derived from God cannot remain at this point, but must struggle upward, as is symbolised by the line reaching again to the apex, God, whence it issued.

Magical Instruments and Accessories : In *magical* rites these were considered of the utmost importance. Indispensable to the efficacy of the ceremonies were the altar, the chalice, the tripod, the censer ; the lamp, rod, sword, and magic fork or trident ; the sacred fire and consecrated oils ; the incense and the candles.

The altar might be of wood or stone, but if of the latter, then of stone that has never been worked or hewn or even touched by the hammer.

The chalice might be of different metals, symbolic of the object of the rites. Where the purpose was evil, a black chalice was used as in the profane masses of sorcerers and witches. In some talismans the chalice is engraved as a symbol of the moon.

The tripod and its triangular stand was also made in symbolic metals.

The censer might be of bronze, but preferably of silver.

In the construction of the lamp, gold, silver, brass and iron must be used, iron for the pedestal, brass for the mirror, silver for the reservoir and at the apex a golden triangle. Various symbols were traced upon it, including an androgynous figure about the pedestal, a serpent devouring its own tail, and the Sign of Solomon.

The rod must be specially fashioned of certain woods and then consecrated to its magical uses. A perfectly straight branch of almond or hazel was to be chosen. This was cut before the tree blossomed, and cut with a golden sickle in the early dawn. Throughout its length must be run a long needle of magnetized iron ; at one end there should be affixed a triangular prism, to the other, one of black resin, and rings of copper and zinc bound about it. At the new moon it must be consecrated by a magician who already possesses a consecrated rod.

The secret of the construction and consecration of *magical* rods was jealously guarded by all magicians and the rod itself was displayed as little as possible, being usually concealed in the flowing sleeve of the magician's robe.

The sword must be wrought of unalloyed steel, with copper handle in the form of a crucifix. Mystical signs were engraved on guard and blade and its consecration took place on a Sunday in full rays of the sun, when the sword was thrust into a sacred fire of cypress and laurel, then moistened with the blood of a snake, polished, and next, together with branches of vervain, swathed in silk. The sword was generally used in the service of Black Magic.

The magic fork or trident used in necromancy was also fashioned of hazel or almond, cut from the tree at one blow with an unused knife, from whose blade must be fashioned the three prongs. Witches and sorceresses are usually depicted using the trident in their infernal rites.

The fire was lit with charcoal on which were cast branches of trees, symbolic of the end desired. In Black Magic these generally consisted of cypress, alderwood, broken crucifixes and desecrated hosts.

The oil for anointing was compounded of myrrh, cinnamon, galingale and purest oil of Olive. Unguents were used by sorcerers and witches, who smeared their brows, breasts and wrists with a mixture composed of human fat and blood of corpses, combined with aconite, belladonna and poisonous fungi, thinking thereby to make themselves invisible.

Incense might be of any odoriferous woods and herbs, such as cedar, rose, citron, aloes, cinnamon, sandal, reduced to a fine powder, together with incense and storax. In Black Magic, alum, sulphur and assafœtida were used as incense.

The candles, belonging solely to practices of Black Magic were moulded from human fat and set in candlesticks of ebony carved in the form of a crescent.

Bowls also were used in these ceremonies, fashioned of different metals, their shape symbolic of the heavens. In necromantic rites skulls of criminals were used, generally to hold the blood of some victim or sacrifice.

Magical Numbers : Certain *numbers* and their combinations were held to be of *magical* power, by virtue of their representation of divine and creative mysteries.

The doctrines of Pythagoras furnished the basis for much of this belief. According to his theory *numbers* contained the elements of all things, of the natural and spiritual worlds and of the sciences. The real numerals of the universe are the primaries one to ten and in their combination the reason of all else may be found. To the Pythagoreans One represented unity, therefore God ; Two was duality, the Devil ; Four was sacred and holy, the number on which they swore their most solemn oaths ; Five was their symbol of marriage. They also attributed certain *numbers* to the gods, planets and elements ; one represented the Sun, two the Moon ; while five was fire, six the earth, eight the air, and twelve water.

Cornelius Agrippa in his work *Occult Philosophy* published in 1533, discourses upon *numbers* as those characters by whose proportion all things were formed. He enumerates the virtues of numerals as displayed in nature, instancing the herb cinquefoil, which by the power of the number five exorcises devils, allays fever and forms an antidote to poisons. Also the virtue of seven as in the power of the seventh son to cure king's evil.

One was the origin and common measure of all things. It is indivisible ; not to be multiplied. In the universe there is one God ; one supreme intelligence in the intellectual world, man ; in the sidereal world, one Sun ; one potent instrument and agency in the elementary world, the philosopher's stone ; one chief member in the human world, the heart ; and one sovereign prince in the nether world, Lucifer.

Two was the number of marriage, charity and social communion. It was also regarded sometimes as an unclean number ; beasts of the field went into the Ark by twos.

Three had a mysterious value as shown in Time's trinity —Past, Present and Future ; in that of Space—length, breadth and thickness ; in the three heavenly virtues—faith, hope and charity ; in the three worlds of man—brain, the intellectual ; heart, the celestial ; and body, elemental.

Four signifies solidity and foundation. There are four seasons, four elements, four cardinal points, four evangelists.

Five, as it divides ten, the sum of all *numbers*, is also the number of justice. There are five senses ; the Stigmata, the wounds of Christ were five ; the name of the Deity the Pentagram is composed of five letters ; it also is a protection against beasts of prey.

Six is the sign of creation, because the world was completed in six days. It is the perfect number, because it alone by addition of its half, its third and its sixth reforms itself. It also represents servitude by reason of the Divine injunction " Six days shalt thou labour."

Seven is a miraculous number, consisting of one, unity, and six, sign of perfection. It represents life because it contains body, consisting of four elements, spirit, flesh, bone and humour ; and soul, made up of three elements, passion, desire and reason. The seventh day was that on which God rested from his work of creation.

Eight represents justice and fulness. Divided, its halves are equal ; twice divided, it is still even. In the Beatitude eight is the number of those mentioned—peace-makers, they who strive after righteousness, the meek, the persecuted, the pure, the merciful, the poor in spirit, and they that mourn.

Nine is the number of the muses and of the moving spheres.

Ten is completeness because one cannot count beyond it except by combinations formed with other *numbers*. In the ancient mysteries ten days of initiation were prescribed. In ten is found evident signs of a Divine principle.

Eleven is the number of the commandments, while Twelve is the number of signs in the Zodiac, of the apostles, of the tribes of Israel, of the gates of Jerusalem.

This theory of *numbers* Agrippa applied to the casting of horoscopes. Divination by *numbers* was one of the favourite methods employed in the Middle Ages.

In *magical* rites, *numbers* played a great part. The instruments, vestments and ornaments must be duplicated. The power of the number three is found in the magic triangle : in the three prongs of the trident and fork ; and in the three-fold repetition of names in conjurations. Seven was also of great influence, the seven days of the week each representing the period most suitable for certain evocations and these corresponded to the seven magical works ; 1.—works of light and riches ; 2.—works of divination and mystery ; 3.—works of skill, science and eloquence ; 4.—works of wrath and chastisement ; 5.—works of love ; 6.—works of ambition and intrigue ; 7.—works of malediction and death.

Magical Papyri : (*See* Egypt.)

Magical Union of Cologne : A society stated in a MS. of the Rosicrucians at *Cologne* to have been founded in that city in the year 1115. In the *Rosenkreutzer in seiner blosse* of Weise it is stated that the initiates wore a triangle as symbolising power, wisdom and love. The more exalted orders among them were called Magos, and these held the greater mysteries of the fraternity.

Magical Vestments and Appurtenances : These were prescribed needful adjuncts to magical rites, whose colour, name, form and substance, symbolic of certain powers and elements, added, it was supposed, greater efficacy to the evocations.

Abraham the Jew, a magician of the Middle Ages, prescribed a tunic of white linen, with upper robe of

scarlet and girdle of white silk. A crown or fillet of silk and gold was to be worn on the head and the perfumes cast on the fire might be incense, aloes, storax, cedar, citron or rose.

According to other authorities on the subject it was advisable to vary colour of robe and employ certain jewels and other accessories according to the symbolism of the end desired. A magician of the nineteenth century, Eliphas Levi, gives a detailed description of ritual, from which the following is taken.

If the rites were those of White Magic and performed on a Sunday, then the vestment should be of purple, the tiara, bracelets and ring of gold, the latter set with a chrysolith or ruby. Laurel, heliotrope and sunflowers are the symbolic flowers, while other details include a carpet of lion-skins and fans of sparrow-hawk feathers. The appropriate perfumes are incense, saffron, cinnamon and red sandal.

If, however, the ceremonial took place on a Monday, the Day of the Moon, then the robe must be of white embroidered with silver and the tiara of yellow silk emblazoned with silver characters ; while the wreaths were to be woven of moonwort and yellow ranunculi. The jewels appropriate to the occasion were pearls, crystals and selenite ; the perfumes, camphor, amber, aloes, white sandal and seed of cucumber.

In evocations concerning transcendent knowledge, green was the colour chosen for the vestment, or it might be green shot with various colours. The chief ornament was a necklace of pearls and hollow glass beads enclosing mercury. Agate was the symbolic jewel ; narcissus, lily, herb mercury, fumitory, and marjoram the flowers ; whilst the perfumes must be benzoin, mace and storax.

For operations connected with religious and political matters, the magician must don a robe of scarlet and bind on his brow a brass tablet inscribed with various characters. His ring must be studded with an emerald or sapphire, and he must burn for incense, balm, ambergris, grain of paradise and saffron. For garlands and wreaths, oak, poplar, fig and pomegranate leaves should be entwined.

If the ceremonial dealt with amatory affairs, the vestment must be of sky-blue, the ornaments of copper, and the crown of violets. The magic ring must be set with a turquoise, while the tiara and clasps were wrought of lapis-lazuli and beryl. Roses, myrtle and olive were the symbolic flowers, and fans must be made of swan-feathers.

If vengeance was desired on anyone, then robes must be worn whose colour was that of blood, flame or rust, belted with steel, with bracelets and ring of the same metal. The tiara must be bound with gold and the wreaths woven of absinthe and rue.

To bring misfortune and death on a person, the vestment must be black and the neck encircled with lead. The ring must be set with an onyx and the garlands twined of cypress, ash and hellebore ; whilst the perfumes to be used were sulphur, scammony, alum and assafœtida.

For purposes of Black Magic, a seamless and sleeveless robe of black was donned, while on the head was worn a leaden cap inscribed with the signs of the Moon, Venus and Saturn. The wreaths were of vervain and cypress ; and the perfumes burned were aloes, camphor and storax.

Maginot, Adele : One of the mediums whose trance utterances have been recorded by the French spiritualist Alphonse Cahagnet, who published his *Arcanes de la vie future dévoilés* in 1848. Her *séances*, of which Cahagnet strove to obtain a written account from as many as possible of those present, are among the most valuable evidence which spiritualism can produce. Her descriptions of absent or deceased friends of the sitters were singularly accurate, though her supposed conversations with their spirits would appear to be fictitious. At the least her *séances* are excellent examples of telepathic communication.

Magnet : (*See* **Hypnotism.**)

Magnetism : (*See* **Spiritualism, Hypnotism.**)

Magnetismus Negativus : (*See* **Fludd.**)

Magnus Microcoism : (*See* **Crystallomancy.**)

Magpie : The chattering of a *Magpie* was formerly considered a sure omen of evil.

Mahan, Rev. Asa : (*See* **Spiritualism.**)

Mahatma : (*See* **Adept.**)

Maier, Michael : A German alchemist born at Rindsburg in Holstein about the year 1858. He was one of the principal figures in the Rosicrucian Controversy in Germany and the greatest adept of his time. He diligently pursued the study of medicine in his youth and settling at Rostock practised with such success that the Emperor Rudolph appointed him as his physician, ennobling him later for his services. Some adepts eventually succeeded in luring him from the practical work he followed so long into the mazy and tortuous paths of alchemy. In order to confer with those whom he suspected were possessed of the transcendent mysteries he travelled all over Germany. The *Biographie Universelle* states that in pursuit of these " ruinous absurdities " he sacrificed his health, fortune and time. On a visit to England he became acquainted with Robert Fludd the Kentish Mystic.

In the controversy which convulsed Germany on the appearance of his Rosicrucian Manifestoes, he took a vigorous and enthusiastic share and wrote several works in defence of the mysterious society. He is alleged to have travelled in order to seek for members of the " College of Teutonic Philosophers R.C.," and failing to find them formed a brotherhood of his own, based on the form of the *Fama Fraternibus*. There is no adequate authority for this statement, but it is believed that he eventually, towards the end of his life, was initiated into the genuine order. A posthumous pamphlet of *Maier's* called *Ulysses* was published by one of his personal friends in 1624. There was added to the same volume the substance of two pamphlets already published in German but which in view of their importance were now translated into Latin for the benefit of the European literati. The first pamphlet was entitled *Colloquium Rhodostauroticum trium personarium per Famem et Confessionem quodamodo revelatam de Fraternitate Rosæ Crucis.* The second was an *Echo Colloquii* by Hilarion on behalf of the Rosicrucian Fraternity. From these pamphlets it appears that *Maier* was admitted as a member of the mystical order. He became the most profuse writer on alchemy of his time. He died in the year 1622. Most of his works, many of which are adorned with curious plates, are obscure with the exception of his Rosicrucian Apologies. (*See* **Rosicrucians.**)

Maimonides, Moses (1135–1204) **:** A great Spanish-Hebrew philosopher and theologian, the author of the *Guide of the Perplexed*. His theories are Aristotelian and rational, but there remained in his view-point a touch of mysticism.

Malachite : Used to preserve the cradle of an infant from spells.

Malays : Magic among the *Malays* is for the most part of that type known as " sympathetic " (*See* **Magic**), that is, it possesses more of the nature of pseudo-science than that of wonder. Says Clifford :—

" The accredited intermediary between men and spirits is the *Pawang*; the *Pawang* is a functionary of great and traditional importance in a *Malay* village, though in places near towns the office is falling into abeyance. In the inland districts, however, the *Pawang* is still a power, and is regarded as part of the constituted order of Society, without whom no village community would be complete. It must be clearly understood that he had nothing whatever to do with the official Muhammadan religion of the mosque; the village has its regular staff of elders—the *Imam*, *Khatio*, and *Bilal*—for the mosque service. But the *Pawang* is quite outside this system and belongs to a different and much older order of ideas; he may be regarded as the legitimate representative of the primitive ' medicine-man,' or ' village-sorcerer,' and his very existence in these days is an anomaly, though it does not strike *Malays* as such. . . . .

" The *Pawang* is a person of very real significance. In all agricultural operations, such as sowing, reaping, irrigation works, and the clearing of jungle for planting, in fishing at sea, in prospecting for minerals, and in cases of sickness, his assistance is invoked. He is entitled by custom to certain small fees; thus, after a good harvest he is allowed in some villages five *gantangs* of padi, one *gantang* of rice (*beras*), and two *chupaks* of *emping* (a preparation of rice and cocoa-nut made into a sort of sweetmeat) from each householder."

The Pawang regulates taboos, and employs a familiar spirit known as *hantu pusaka*—a hereditary demon. He also acts as a medium and divines through trance. To become a magician " You must meet the ghost of a murdered man. Take the midrib of a leaf of the ' ivory ' cocoa-nut palm (*pelepah niyor gading*), which is to be laid on the grave, and two midribs, which are intended to represent canoe-paddles, and carry them with the help of a companion to the grave of the murdered man at the time of the full moon (the 15th day of the lunar month) when it falls upon a Tuesday. Then take a cent's worth of incense, with glowing embers in a censer, and carry them to the head-post of the grave of the deceased. Fumigate the grave, going three times round it, and call upon the murdered man by name :—

' Hearken, So-and-so,
And assist me ;
I am taking (this boat) to the saints of God,
And I desire to ask for a little magic.'

Here take the first midrib, fumigate it, and lay it upon the head of the grave, repeating ' *Kur Allah* ' (' Cluck, Cluck, God ! ') seven times. You and your companion must now take up a sitting posture, one at the head and the other at the foot of the grave, facing the grave post, and use the canoe-paddles which you have brought. In a little while the surrounding scenery will change and take upon itself the appearance of the sea, and finally an aged man will appear, to whom you must address the same request as before."

Malay magic may be sub-divided into preparatory rites, sacrificial, lustration, divination and possession. Sacrifice takes the form of a simple gift, or act of homage to the spirit or deity. Lustration is magico-religious and purificatory, principally taking place after child-birth. It may be performed by fire or water. Divination consists for the most part of the reading of dreams, and is, as elsewhere, drawn from the acts of men or nature. Omens are strongly believed in.

" When a star is seen in apparent proximity to the moon, old people say there will be a wedding shortly . . . .

" The entrance into a house of an animal which does not generally seek to share the abode of man is regarded by the *Malays* as ominous of misfortune. If a wild bird flies into a house it must be carefully caught and smeared with oil, and must then be released in the open air, a formula being recited in which it is bidden to fly away with all the ill-luck and misfortunes (*sial jambalang*) of the occupier. An iguana, a tortoise, and a snake, are perhaps the most dreaded of these unnatural visitors. They are sprinkled with ashes, if possible to counteract their evil influence.

" A swarm of bees settling near a house is an unlucky omen, and prognosticates misfortune."

So, too, omens are taken either from the flight or cries of certain birds, such as the night-owl, the crow, some kinds of wild doves, and the bird called the " Rice's Husband " (*laki padi*.)

Astrology.—Divination by astrology is, however, the most common method of forecasting the future. The native practitioners possess long tables of lucky and unlucky periods and reasons. These are mostly translations from Indian and Arabic sources. The oldest known of these systems of propitious and unpropitious seasons is known as *Katika Lima*, or the Five Times. Under it the day is divided into five parts, and five days form a cycle. To each division is given a name as follows : Maswara, Kala, S'ri, Brahma, Bisnu (Vishnu) names of Hindu deities, the last name in the series for the first day being the first in that of the second day, and so on until the five days are exhausted. Each of these has a colour, and according to the colour first seen or noticed on such and such a day will it be fortunate to ask a boon of a certain god. Another version of this system, known as the " Five Moments " is similar in origin, but possesses a Mohammedan nomenclature. Another scheme *Katika Tujoh* is based on the seven heavenly bodies, divides each day into seven parts, each of which is distinguished by the Arabic name for the sun, moon, and principal planets. The astrology proper of the *Malays* is purely Arabic in origin, but a system of Hindu invocation is in vogue by which the lunar month is divided into parts called *Rejang*, which resembles the *Nacshatras* or lunar houses of the Hindus. Each division has its symbol, usually an animal. Each day is propitious for something, and the whole system has been committed to verse for mnemonic purposes.

Demonology.—The demoniac form common to Malaysia is that of the Jinn, with some leaven of the older Hindu spirit. They are one hundred and ninety in number. They are sometimes sub-divided into " faithful " and " infidel," and further into the Jinns of the royal musical instruments, of the state, and of the royal weapons. The Afrit is also known. Angels also abound, and are purely of Arabic origin. Besides these the principal supernatural beings are as follows :—the *Polong*, or familiar ; the *Hantu Pemburu*, or spectre Huntsman ; the *Jadi-jadian*, or wertiger ; the *Hantu*, or ghost of the murdered ; the *Jemalang*, or earth-spirit.

Minor Sorcery.—The rites of minor sorcery and witchcraft, as well as those of the shaman, are widely practised among the *Malays*, and are practically identical in character with those in use among other peoples in a similar state of culture.

See :—W. W. Skeat, *Malay Magic* ; Swettenham, *Malay Sketches* ; Clifford, *In Court and Kampong* ; *Studies in Brown Humanity.*

Malchidael : (*See* **Astrology.**)

Mallebranche : A marker of the game of tennis, living in the Rue Sainte-Geneviéve, Paris, who in 1618 was visited by an apparition of his wife, who had died five years before She came to advise him to repent and live a better life, and to pray for her also. Both *Mallebranche* and his wife (for he had married a second time) heard the voice, but the apparition did not become visible. In 1618 a *brochure* was published at Paris, entitled : *Histoire nouvelle et remarquable de l'esprit d'une femme qui c'est apparue au Faubourg Saint-Marcel aprés qu'elle a demeué cinq ans entiers ensevelie ; elle a parlé a son mari, lui a commandé de faire prier pour elle, ayant commencé de parler le mardi 11 Decembre, 1618.*

Malleus Maleficarum : A large volume published in Germany at the end of the fifteenth century, written by two inquisi-

tors under the papal bull against witchcraft of 1484,— Jacob Sprenger and Henricus Institor. Says Wright concerning it : " In this celebrated work, the doctrine of witchcraft was first reduced to a regular system, and it was the model and groundwork of all that was written on the subject long after the date which saw its first appearance. Its writers enter largely into the much-disputed question of the nature of demons ; set forth the causes which lead them to seduce men in this manner ; and show why women are most prone to listen to their proposals, by reasons which prove that the inquisitors had but a mean estimate of the softer sex. The inquisitors show the most extraordinary skill in explaining all the difficulties which seemed to beset the subject ; they even prove to their entire satisfaction that persons who have become witches may easily change themselves into beasts, particularly into wolves and cats ; and after the exhibition of such a mass of learning, few would venture any longer to entertain a doubt. They investigate not only the methods employed to effect various kinds of mischief, but also the countercharms and exorcisms that may be used against them. They likewise tell, from their own experience, the dangers to which the inquisitors were exposed, and exult in the fact that they were a class of men against whom sorcery had no power. These writers actually tell us, that the demon had tried to frighten them by day and by night in the forms of apes, dogs, goats, etc. ; and that they frequently found large pins stuck in their night-caps, which they doubted not came there by witchcraft. When we hear these inquisitors asserting that the crime of which the witches were accused, deserved a more extreme punishment than all the vilest actions of which humanity is capable, we can understand in some degree the complacency with which they relate how, by their means, forty persons had been burnt in one place, and fifty in another, and a still greater number in a third. From the time of the publication of the *Malleus Maleficarum*, the continental press during two or three generations teemed with publications on the all-absorbing subject of sorcery.

" One of the points on which opinion had differed most was, whether the sorcerers were carried bodily through the air to the place of meeting, or whether it was an imaginary journey, suggested to their minds by the agency of the evil one. The authors of the *Malleus* decide at once in favour of the bodily transmission. One of them was personally acquainted with a priest of the diocese of Frisingen, who declared that he had in his younger days been carried through the air by a demon to a place at a very great distance from the spot whence he had been taken. Another priest, his friend, declared that he had seen him carried away, and that he appeared to him to be borne up on a kind of cloud. At Baldshut, on the Rhine, in the diocese of Constance, a witch confessed, that offended at not having been invited to the wedding of an acquaintance, she had caused herself to be carried thorugh the air in open daylight to the top of a neighbouring mountain, and there, having made a hole with her hands and filled it with water, she had, by stirring the water with certain incantations caused a heavy storm to burst forth on the heads of the wedding-party ; and there were witnesses at the trial who swore they had seen her carried through the air. The inquisitors, however, confess that the witches were sometimes carried away, as they term it, in the spirit ; and they give the instance of one woman who was watched by her husband ; she appeared as if asleep, and was insensible, but he perceived a kind of cloudy vapour arise out of her mouth, and vanish from the room in which she lay—this after a time returned, and she then awoke, and gave an account of her adventures, as though she had been carried bodily to the assembly. . . . . .

" The witches of the *Malleus Maleficarum* appear to have been more injurious to horses and cattle than to mankind. A witch at Ravenspurg confessed that she had killed twenty-three horses by sorcery. We are led to wonder most at the ease with which people are brought to bear witness to things utterly beyond the limits of belief. A man of the name of Stauff in the territory of Berne, declared that when pursued by the agents of justice, he escaped by taking the form of a mouse ; and persons were found to testify that they had seen him perform this transmutation.

" The latter part of the work of the two inquisitors gives minute directions for the mode in which the prisoners are to be treated, the means to be used to force them to a confession, the degree of evidence required for conviction of those who would not confess, and the whole process of the trials. These show sufficiently that the unfortunate wretch who was once brought before the inquisitors of the holy see on the suspicion of sorcery, however slight might be the grounds of the charge, had very small chance of escaping out of their claws.

" The *Malleus* contains no distinct allusion to the proceedings at the Sabbath. The witches of this period differ little from those who had fallen into the hands of the earlier inquisitors at the Council of Constance. We see plainly how, in most countries, the mysteriously indefinite crime of sorcery had first been seized on to ruin the cause of great political offenders, until the fictitious importance thus given to it brought forward into a prominent position, which they would, perhaps, never otherwise have held, the miserable class who were supposed to be more especially engaged in it. It was the judicial prosecutions and the sanguinary executions which followed, that stamped the character of reality on charges of which it required two or three centuries to convince mankind of the emptiness and vanity. One of the chief instruments in fixing the belief in sorcery, and in giving it that terrible hold on society which it exhibited in the following century, was the compilation of Jacob Sprenger and his fellow inquisitor. In this book sorcery was reduced to a system but it was not yet perfect ; and we must look forward, some half a century before we find it clothed with all the horrors which cast so much terror into every class of society."

Malphas : Grand president of the infernal regions, where he appears under the shape of a crow. When he appears in human form he has a very raucous voice. He builds impregnable citadels and towers, overthrows the ramparts of his enemies, finds good workmen, gives familiar spirits, receives sacrifices, and deceives the sacrificers. Forty legions are under his command.

Mamaloi : An obeah priestess. (*See* **West Indian Islands.**)

Mana : (*See* **Magic.**)

Mananan : Son of the Irish sea-god Lir, magician and owner of strange possessions. His magical boat " Ocean-sweeper " steered by the wishes of its occupant ; his horse Aonban, able to travel on sea or land ; and his sword Fragarach, a match for any mail ; were brought by Lugh from " The Land of the Living " (Fairyland). As lord of the sea he was the Irish Charon, and his colour-changing cloak would flap gaily as he marched with heavy tread round the camp of the hostile force invading Erin. He is comparable with the Cymric Manawiddan and resembles the Hellenic Proteus.

Mandragoras : Familiar demons who appear in the figures of little men without beards. Delrio states that one day a *mandragora*, entering at the request of a sorcerer, who was being tried before a court for wizardry, was caught by the arms by the judge, who did not believe in the existence of the spirit, to convince himself of its existence, and

thrown into the fire, where of course it would escape unharmed. *Mandragoras* are thought to be little dolls or figures given to sorcerers by the Devil for the purpose of being consulted by them in time of need ; and it would seem as if this conception had sprung directly from that of the fetish, which is nothing else than a dwelling-place made by a shaman or medicine-man for the reception of any wandering spirit who chooses to take up his abode therein. The author of the work entitled *Petit Albert* says that on one occasion, whilst travelling in Flanders and passing through the town of Lille, he was invited by one of his friends to accompany him to the house of an old woman who posed as being a great prophetess. This aged person conducted the two friends into a dark cabinet lit only by a single lamp, where they could see upon a table covered with a cloth a kind of little statue or *mandragora*, seated upon a tripod and having the left hand extended and holding a hank of silk very delicately fashioned, from which was suspended a small piece of iron highly polished. Placing under this a crystal glass so that the piece of iron was suspended inside the goblet, the old woman commanded the figure to strike the iron against the glass in such a manner as she wished, saying at the same time to the figure : " I command you, *Mandragora*, in the name of those to whom you are bound to give obedience, to know if the gentleman present will be happy in the journey which he is about to make. If so, strike three times with the iron upon the goblet." The iron struck three times as demanded without the old woman having touched any of the apparatus, much to the surprise of the two spectators. The sorceress put several other questions to the *Mandragora*, who struck the glass once or thrice as seemed good to him. But, as the author shows, the whole was an artifice of the old woman, for the piece of iron suspended in the goblet was extremely light and when the old woman wished it to strike against the glass, she held in one of her hands a ring set with a large piece of magnetic stone, the virtue of which drew the iron towards the glass.

The ancients attributed great virtues to the plant called *mandragoras* or mandrake, which was supposed to be somewhat in the shape of a man, and when plucked from the earth to emit a species of human cry. It was also worn to ward off various diseases. (*See* **Exorcism.**)

Manen : The priest of the Katean Secret Society of the Moluccas.

Manicheism : (*See* **Gnosticism.**)

Manieri, B. E. : (*See* **Italy.**)

Manu is a grade in the theosophical hierarchy below the Planetary Logoi or Rulers of the Seven Chains. The charge given to *Manus* is that of forming the different races of humanity and guiding its evolution. Each race has its own *Manu* who represents the racial type.

Manuscript Troano : (*See* **Atlantis.**)

Maranos : A Jewish secret fraternity which arose in Spain in the fourteenth and fifteenth centuries during the persecution of the Hebrew race in that country. Its members met in the greatest secrecy at inns, disguised, and used grips, signs and passwords. (*See Freemasons' Magazine*, 1860, III., p. 416.)

Marcellus Empiricus : A Gallic-Roman writer born at Bordeaux in the fourth century. He was *magister officiorum* under Theodosius (379–395.) He wrote a work called *De medicamentis conspiricis physicis ac rationalibus*, a collection of medical recipes, for the most part absurd and worthless, and having more in common with popular superstition than with medical science.

Marcians : (*See* **Gnostics.**)

Margaritomancy : Divination by pearls. A pearl was covered with a vase, and placed near the fire, and the names of suspected persons pronounced. When the name of the guilty one was uttered the pearl was supposed to bound upwards and pierce the bottom of the vase.

Margiotta, Domenico : Author of *Adriano Lemmi*, and *Palladism*, in which books he violently impeaches the Grand Master Lemmi of the crimes of Satanism and sorcery. These statements have been amply proved to be without foundation.

Marie Antoinette : (*See* **Cagliostro.**)

Marigny, Enguerrand de : A minister of Louis X., king of France. His wife and her sister were accused of having recourse to enchantments to harm the king, his brother Charles, and other barons, with the intention of freeing *Enguessand*, who was imprisoned. The ladies were arrested. Jacques Dulot, a magician, who was believed to have helped in these sorceries, was also committed to prison, where he took his own life, after his wife had been burnt. Dulot's suicide was considered a conclusive proof of *Marigny's* guilt, and the ex-minister was tried, condemned, and hanged on a gibbet which he himself had had erected during his term of office. The tide of popular opinion turned at the sight of his misfortune, and the judges dared not condemn his wife and sister-in-law. The king himself repented of having abandoned *Marigny* to his enemies, and in his will left a sum of money to his family.

Marriage of Heaven and Hell : (*See* **Blake.**)

Marrow of Alchemy : (*See* **Philalethes.**)

Marshall, Mrs. : An English medium who gave open séances from 1858 onwards. Unlike many of the early mediums she practised professionally, and was for some time the only professional medium of note in this country. The phenomena witnessed included communication by means of rapping, playing on musical instruments, touchings by invisible hands, and all the more familiar forms. A writer in *All the Year Round*, July 28th, 1860, characterised *Mrs. Marshall's* performance as a " dull and barefaced imposition," but Robert Bell, the celebrated dramatist, writing in the *Cornhill Magazine* was satisfied that the phenomena were genuine spirit manifestations. (*See* **Spiritualism.**)

Marsi, The : According to Pliny, these people were from the earliest times skilled in magical practices and sorceries. They were able to charm poisonous serpents by means of songs.

Marthese, J. N. T. : (*See* **Holland.**)

Martian Language : A *language* purporting to be that of the inhabitants of the planet Mars, written and spoken by the medium known as Hélène Smith. Hélène, the medium studied by a celebrated investigator, M. Flournoy, professor of psychology at Geneva, had in 1892 joined a spiritualistic circle, where she developed marvellous mediumistic powers. In 1896, after Professor Flournoy had begun his investigations, she was spirited during a trance to the planet Mars, and thereafter described to the circle the manners and customs and appearance of the *Martians*. She learned their *language*, which she wrote and spoke with ease and consistency. Unlike most of the " unknown tongues " automatically produced the *Martian language* was intelligible, its words were used consistently, and on the whole it had every appearance of a genuine *language*. That it was in any way connected with Mars is out of the question. The descriptions of that planet and its inhabitants are quite impossible. And the *language* itself bears a remarkable resemblance to French, the native tongue of the medium. The grammar and construction of both languages are the same, and even the vowel-sounds are identical, so that the source of the *Martian language* is not far to seek.

Martin, Saint (exorcist) : (*circa* 316–400). Most of the pristine luminaries of the Christian Church are credited with working miracles, and indeed the great majority of them maintained that, would the rude populace be won

for Christ, the one sure way was to show them extraordinary marvels. Even Columba, most engaging of saints, was not averse to practising deception with a view to making converts; and it has often been suggested, not without considerable reason, that some of these early thaumaturgists brought science to their aid. Perhaps *St. Martin* was among those who essayed this practice, and certainly the muster-roll of his miracles is formidable, for he is traditionally credited with considerably over two hundred.

Martin was born about the year 316 at Sabaria, in Pannonia. His parents were heathen, yet he very soon came into contact with Christians, and their teaching impressed him greatly. As a young man he entered the army, and it was soon after this step that, while stationed with his regiment at Amiens, he performed his famous act of charity, dividing his cloak with a beggar who was shivering with cold. The night after this generous act he was vouchsafed a vision, Christ appearing to him and giving him his blessing ; and thereupon *Martin* espoused the Christian faith formally, he was baptised and renounced soldiering once and for all. Going to Poitiers, he then made the acquaintance of Hilary, who wished to make him a deacon, but at his own request ordained him to the humbler office of an exorcist ; and a little later, during a visit to his home, *Martin* experienced the joy of winning his mother from heathendom to the new faith. However, his open zeal in opposing the Arians raised persecution against him, and for a considerable space he found it advisable to live at the island of Gallinaria, near Genoa, in which quiet retreat he had ample leisure for scientific researches and theological studies ; but by the year 365 he was back with Hilary at Poitiers, when he founded the Monasterium Locociagense. Then, in 371, the people of Tours chose him as their bishop, and for some time subsequently he showed great activity in trying to extirpate idolatry in his diocese, and in extending the monastic system. Nevertheless, he was anything but a fierce proseletyser, and at Trèves, in 385, he entreated that the lives of the Priscillianist heretics should be spared, while he ever afterwards refused to have anything to do with those bishops who had sanctioned their execution. Meanwhile, being anxious for another period of quiet study, *Martin* had established the monastery of Marmontier les Tours, on the banks of the Loire ; and here much of his remaining life was spent, yet it was at Candes that his death occurred about the year 400.

Martin left no writings behind him, the *Confessio* with which he is sometimes credited being undoubtedly spurious. His life was written by his ardent disciple, Sulpicius Severus, and a curious document it is, filled with accounts of the miracles and marvels worked by the quondam bishop. Thanks to his triumphs herein, *Martin* was duly sanctified by the church, and he is commemorated on the 11th of November ; but the feast of Martinmas, which occurs on that date, and which of course derives its name from him, is, nevertheless, a survival of an old pagan festival ; and it inherited certain usages thereof, this accounting for the fact that *Martin* is regarded as the patron saint of deep potations. Certain of his miracles, and other incidents in his life, were figured by numerous painters of note, perhaps the finest picture of him being one by the Flemish master, Hugo van der Goes, which is now in the Municipal Museum at Glasgow ; while it behoves to add that the term Martinet, signifying a severe and punctilious person, is not derived from the saint's name, but from one Jean Martinet, a French soldier who, during the reign of Louis XIV., won fame by his ardour in promoting discipline in his regiment.

Martini : (*See* **Alchemy.**)

Martinists : (*See* **St. Martin.**)

Mascots : (*See* **Amulets.**)

Mashmashu : (*See* **Babylonia.**)

Masleh : The angel whom the Jews believed ruled the Zodiac. According to one of their rabbinical legends, Masleh was the medium through which the power and influence of the Messiah was transmitted to the sphere of the Zodiac.

Massey, C. C. : (*See* **Psychological Society.**)

Master : (*See* **Adept.**)

Mastiphal : The name given to the prince of demons in an apocryphal book entitled *Little Genesis*, which is quoted by Cedrenus.

Materialisation : A term denoting the formation by a spirit of a temporary physical organisation, visible and palpable, by means of which it can come into touch with material objects. *Materialisation* is the most important of the physical phenomena of spiritualism, and in its earlier stages was confined to the materialising of heads and hands, or vague luminous figures. In common with much of the physical phenomena, it had its origin in America, where it was known at a comparatively early period in the history of the movement. So early as 1860 séances were held with the Fox sisters by Robert Dale Owen and others, at which veiled and luminous figures were witnessed. One sitter, Mr. Livermore, saw and recognised the spirit of his dead wife many times during a series of séances with Kate Fox, extending over some six years. In this case, however, there were no other sitters, and the séances were held in the dark, the whole atmosphere being peculiarly favourable to fraud. In 1871 another American medium, Mrs. Andrews, held sittings at which materialised forms were seen, and in the following year Mrs. Guppy and another medium attempted the production of a similar phenomenon in England, but without marked success. The mediums, Herne and Williams, succeeded a few months later in materialising shadowy forms and faces in a dark séance-room. It was, however, Miss Florence Cook, to whose phenomena Sir William Crookes has so abundantly testified, who was to give the most remarkable demonstration of this form of spirit manifestation. Miss Cook was, at the commencement of her spiritualistic career, a young girl of sixteen or seventeen years, described by a contemporary writer as " a pretty, Jewish-like little girl." She was at that time a private medium, though at the outset she held some *materialisation* séances with Herne. From her childhood, it was said, she had been attended by a spirit-girl, who stated that her name on earth had been Annie Morgan, but that her name in the spirit-world was Katie King. Under the latter name Miss Cook's control was destined to become very famous in spiritualistic circles. Usually the medium was put in a sort of cupboard, or cabinet, tied to her chair, and the cords sealed. A short interval would ensue, during which the sitters sang spiritualistic hymns, and at length there would emerge from the cabinet a form clad in flowing white draperies, and not to be distinguished from an ordinary human being. On one occasion a séance was held at Mr. Cook's house, at which several distinguished spiritualists were present. Among the invited guests was Mr. W. Volckman, who thought to test for himself the good faith of the medium and the genuineness of " Katie." After some forty minutes close observance of the materialised spirit Mr. Volckman concluded that Miss Cook and Katie were one and the same, and just as the white-robed figure was about to return to the cabinet he rushed forward and seized her. His indignant fellow-sitters released the " spirit," the light was extinguished, and in the confusion that followed the spirit disappeared. Miss Cook was found a few minutes later bound as when she was placed in the cabinet, the cords unbroken, the seal intact. She wore a black dress, and there was no trace of white draperies in the cabinet. Sir William Crookes, whose investigations into the phenomena

of this medium extended over a period of some years, had better opportunity of examining Katie's pretensions than Mr. Volckman had, and he had left it on record that the spirit form was taller than the medium, had a larger face and longer fingers ; and whereas Florence Cook had black hair and a dark complexion, Katie's complexion was fair, and her hair a light auburn. Moreover Sir William, enjoying as he did the complete confidence of Katie, had on more than one occasion the privilege of seeing her and Miss Cook at the same time. But Miss Cook was not the only medium who was controlled by Katie King, who, with her father, John King, became in time a most popular spirit with *materialisation* mediums. From that time onwards *materialisation* was extensively practised both by private and professional mediums, among the number being Mrs. Showers and her daughter, Rita, Miss Lottie Fowler, William Eglinton and D. D. Home ; while in recent years *materialisations* are stated to have occurred in the presence of Eusapia Palladino. Many sitters claimed to see in these draped figures and veiled faces the form and features of deceased relatives and friends, though frequently there was but the smallest ground for such a claim—parents recognised their daughter by her hair, a man recognised his mother by the sort of cap she wore, and so on. There is no doubt that fraud entered, and still enters, very largely into *materialisation* séances. Lay figures, muslin draperies, false hair, and similar properties have been found in the possession of mediums ; accomplices have been smuggled into the séance-room ; lights are frequently turned low or extinguished altogether. Add to this the fact that other spirits besides " Katie " have on being grasped resolved themselves into the person of the medium, and it will be seen that scepticism is not altogether unjustified. Then, as already mentioned, the rash and premature recognition of deceased friends in draped forms whose resemblance to the medium is patent to the less-interested observer, has also done much to ruin the case for genuine spirit *materialisation*. Yet that there is a case we must believe on the assertion of some of the most distinguished of modern investigators, men fully alive to the possibilities of fraud, trained to habits of correct observation. M. Flammarion felt constrained to attribute the *materialisations* he had witnessed in the presence of Eusapia Palladino to fluidic emanations from the medium's person, while judging the recognition accorded to them the result of illusion. Others state that the physical organisation formed by the spirit is composed of fine particles of matter drawn from the material world. By way of explaining the numerous exposures that have been made from time to time various theories of a more or less ingenious character have been advanced by spiritualists. In a case of obvious fraud they declare that the spirits have controlled the medium to secrete wigs and draperies in the cabinet. If a spirit on being held by a sitter proves to be the medium herself an explanation is also forthcoming. The medium, it is said, imparts to the spirit a certain portion of her vital energy, so that the spirit may " manifest." When the latter is ruthlessly grasped these two portions of the medium's vital spirits tend to re-unite, so that either the medium will draw the spirit into the cabinet, or the spirit will draw the medium out. The reason that the union generally takes place without the cabinet is that the medium has imparted to the control more of her energy than she had retained.

Mather, Cotton, and **Increase :** Father and son, two eminent divines of Boston, notorious for their crusade against persons suspected of witchcraft. (*See* **America, U.S. of.**)

Matikon : A mystical work printed at Frankfort in 1784, whose theories resemble the doctrines of the Brahmins. The following is an example of its teachings. Before the

Fall, Adam was a pure spirit, a celestial being, surrounded by a mystic covering which rendered him incapable of being affected by any poison of nature, or by the power of the elements. The physical body, therefore, is but a coarse husk in which, having lost his primitive invulnerability, man shelters from the elements. In his condition of perfect glory and perfect happiness Adam was a natural king, ruling all things visible and invisible, and showing forth the power of the Almighty. He also bore " a fiery, two-edged, all-piercing lance,"—a living word, which united all powers within itself, and by means of which he could perform all things.

Maurier, George Du : (See **Fiction, Occult English.**)

Maxwell, Dr. Scotch Physician : (See **Hypnotism.**)

Mayas : (See **Mexico** and **Central America.**)

Mayavi-rupa is the invisible part of the physical body. Its appearance is exactly similar to that of the physical body. (See **Seven Principles, Rupa, Theosophy.**)

Mbwiri : (See **Africa.**)

Medea : An enchantress, daughter of the king of Colchis, who fell in love with Jason when he came to that country, and enabled him to slay the sleepless dragon that guarded the golden fleece. She fled from Colchis with Jason who made her his wife, and from whom she exacted a pledge never to love another woman. Her young brother, having been found on board the ship they sailed in, she tore him in pieces and flung him into the sea. She accompanied Jason to Greece, where she was looked on as a barbarian, but having conciliated King Peleus who was now a very old man, she induced him to try to regain youth by bathing in a magic cauldron of which she was to prepare the contents. So great was his faith in her powers, that the old man unhesitatingly plunged into her cauldron and was boiled alive. Her reason for this frightful act of cruelty was to hasten the succession to the throne of Jason, who in due course would have succeeded Peleus ; but now the Greeks would have none of either him or *Medea*, and he was forced to leave Iolcos. Growing tired of the formidable enchantress to whom he had bound himself, Jason sought to contract an alliance with Glauce, a young princess. Dissembling her real intentions, *Medea* feigned friendship with the bride-elect and sent her as a wedding present a garment, which as soon as Glauce put it on, caused her to die in the greatest agony. She—*Medea*—parted from Jason ; having murdered her two children by him, she fled from Corinth in her car drawn by dragons, to Athens, where she married Argeus, by whom she had a son, Medus. But the discovery of an attempt on the life of Theseus, forced her to leave Athens. Accompanied by her son, she returned to Colchis, and restored her father to the throne, of which he had been deprived by his own brother Perses. A great amount of literature has been written around *Medea* : Euripides, Ennius, Aeschylus, and later, Thomas Corneille having made her the theme of tragedies. (See **Greece.**)

Medici, Catherine de : (See **France.**)

Medicine, Occult : " The whole power of the occult physician," says Eliphas Levi, " is in the conscience of his will, while his whole art consists in exciting the faith of his patient. ' If you have faith,' says the Master, ' all things are possible to him who believes.' The confidence must be dominated by expression, tone, gesture ; confidence must be inspired by a fatherly manner, and cheerfulness stimulated by seasonable and sprightly conversations. Rabelais, who was a greater magician than he seemed, made pantagruelism his special panacea. He compelled his patients to laugh, and all the remedies he subsequently gave them succeeded better in consequence ; he established a magnetic sympathy between himself and them, by means of which he communicated to them his own confidence

and good humour ; he flattered them in his prefaces, termed them his precious, most illustrious patients, and dedicated his books to them. So are we convinced that Gargantua and Pantagruel cured more black humours, more tendencies to madness, more atrabilious whims, at that epoch of religious animosities and civil wars, than the whole Faculty of medicine could boast. *Occult medicine* is essentially sympathetic. Reciprocal affection, or at least real good will, must exist between doctor and patient. Syrups and juleps have very little inherent virtue ; they are what they become through the mutual opinion of operator and subject ; hence homœopathic medicines dispenses with them and no serious inconvenience follows. Oil and wine, combined with salt or camphor, are sufficient for the healing of all afflictions, and for all external frictions or soothing applications, oil and wine, are the chief medicaments of the Gospel tradition. They formed the balm of the Good Samaritan, and in the Apocalypse, when describing the last plagues, the prophet prays the avenging powers to spare these substances, that is, to leave a hope and a remedy for so many wounds. What we term extreme unction was the pure and simple practice of the Master's traditional medicine, both for the early Christians and in the mind of the apostle Saint James, who has included the precept in his epistle to the faithful of the whole world. ' Is any man sick among you,' he writes, ' let him call in the priests of the church, and let them pray over him, anointing him with oil in the name of the Lord.' This divine therapeutic science was lost gradually, and Extreme Unction came to be regarded as a religious formality necessary as a preparation for death. At the same time, the thaumaturgic virtue of consecrated oil could not be altogether effaced from remembrance by the traditional doctrine, and it is perpetuated in the passage of the catechism which refers to Extreme Unction. Faith and charity were the most signal healing powers among the early Christians. The source of most diseases is in moral disorders ; we must begin by healing the soul, and then the cure of the body will follow quickly."

Mediæval Magic : In the belief of the mediæval professors of the science of *magic*, it conferred upon the adept power over angels, demons, elementary spirits and the souls of the dead, the possession of esoteric wisdom, and actual knowledge of the discovery and use of the latent forces and undeveloped energies resident in man. This was supposed to be accomplished by a combination of will and aspiration, which by sheer force germinate a new intellectual faculty of psychological perception, enabling the adept to view the wonders of a new world and communicate with its inhabitants. To accomplish this the ordinary faculties were almost invariably heightened by artificial means. The grandeur of the magical ritual overwhelmed the neophyte, and wondrously quickened his senses. Ceremonial *magic* was a marvellous spur to the latent faculties of man's psychic nature, just as were the rich concomitants of religious mysticism. In the *mediæval* mind, as in other periods of man's history, it was thought that *magic* could be employed both for good and evil purposes,—its branches being designated " white," and " black," as it is used for benevolent or wicked ends. The term " red " *magic* is also occasionally employed, as indicating a more exalted type of the art, but the designation is fanciful. White *magic*, to a great extent, concerned itself with the evocation of angelic forces and of the spirits of the elements. The angelology of the Catholic Church was undoubtedly derived from the ancient faith of Israel, which in turn was indebted to Egypt and Babylon ; and the Alexandrian system of successive emanations from the one and eternal substance, evolved a complex hierarchy of angels, all of whom appear to have been at the bidding of him who was in possession of the Incommunicable Name,—a concept borrowed purely from that of the Name of Power so greatly made use of in Egyptian *magic* (*See* **Egypt.**) The letters which composed this name were thought to possess a great measure of occult significance, and a power which in turn appears to have been reflected upon the entire Hebrew alphabet (*See* **Kabala**), which was thus endowed with mystical meaning, each of the letters representing a vital and creative number. Just as a language is formed from the letters of its alphabet, so from the secret powers which resided in the Hebrew alphabet, were evolved magical variations. From the letter " aleph " to that of " jod " the angelical world was symbolised. From " caf " to " tsed " were represented the several orders of angels who inhabited the various spheres, each of which was under the direction of a particular intelligence. From " tsed " to " thau " is in secret correspondence with the elemental world ; so that there were intelligences in correspondence with each of the Hebrew letters,—" aleph " with the Haioth-ha-kodesch of the seraphim, the first and supreme angelical rank ; " beth " the second letter with the ophanim or angels of the second order ; " gimel " with the aralim or angels of the third order, and so on to the tenth letter " jod," which completes the enumeration of the angelical spheres. The rest of the Hebrew alphabet, however, corresponds to individual principalities and powers—all of whom hold an important place in the mystical universe. Thus " caf " the eleventh letter is in correspondence with Mettatron who belongs to the first heaven of the astronomic world. Final " caf," the next letter, corresponds to the intelligences of the secret order whose supreme chief is Raziel ; and " lamed " the twelfth letter corresponds to those of the third sphere, that of Saturn, whose lord is Schebtaiel ; and so on : these intelligences under their queen, with the sixteenth letter " ain " and " pe " the seventeenth of the Hebrew alphabet, refer to the first of the mystical elements —that of Fire, which is ruled over by the seraphim. Final " pe " corresponds to the air where dwell the sylphs, who are presided over by Ariel. " Tsade " refers to water where dwell the nymphs under their queen Tharsis ; and " koph " corresponds to earth, the sphere of the gnomes, ruled over by the cherubim. The twentieth letter " resh " applies to the animal kingdom, including man. " Shin " corresponds to the vegetable world. " Tau " the last symbol of the Hebrew alphabet refers to the world of minerals. There are besides these many other species of angels and powers, as will be seen from reference to the articles on " Angels " and " Kabala." More exalted intelligences were conjured by rites to be found in the ancient book known as the *Key of Solomon*, and perhaps the most satisfactory collection of formulæ for the invocation of the higher angels is that included in the anonymous *Theosophia Pneumatica*, published at Frankfort in 1686, which bears a strong family resemblance to the *Treatise on Magic* by Arbatel. The names in this work do not tally with those which have been already given, but as it is admitted by occult students that the names of all unseen beings are really unknown to humanity, this does not seem of such importance as it might at first sight. It would seem that such spiritual knowledge as the *mediæval magus* was capable of attaining was insufficient to raise him above the intellectual limitations of his time, so that the work in question possesses all the faults of its age and type. But that is not to say that it is possessed of no practical value ; and it may be taken as well-illustrating the white *magic* of *mediæval* times. It classifies the names of the angels under the title of Olympic or Celestial Spirits, who abide in the firmament and constellations : they administer inferior destinies and accomplish and teach whatever is portended by the several stars in which they

are insphered. They are powerless to act without a special command from the Almighty. The stewards of Heaven are seven in number—Arathron, Bethor, Phaleg, Och, Hagith, Ophiel, and Phul. Each of them has a numerous host at his command, and the regions in which they dwell are 196 in all. Arathron appears on Saturday at the first hour, and answers for his territory and its inhabitants ; as do the others, each at his own day and hour : and each presides for a period of 490 years. The functions of Bethor began in the fiftieth year before the birth of Christ 430. Phagle reigned till A.D. 920 ; Och till the year 1410 ; Hagith governed until A.D. 1900. The others follow in succession. These intelligences are the stewards of all the elements, energising the firmament and, with their armies, depending from each other in a regular hierarchy. The names of the minor Olympian spirits are interpreted in divers ways, but those alone are powerful which they themselves give, which are adapted to the end for which they have been summoned. Generically, they are called Astra, and their power is seldom prolonged beyond one hundred and forty years. The heavens and their inhabitants come voluntarily to man and often serve against even the will of man, but how much more if we implore their ministry. That evil and troublesome spirits also approach men is accomplished by the cunning of the devil, at times by conjuration or attraction, and frequently as a penalty for sins ; therefore, shall he who would abide in familiarity with celestial intelligences take pains to avoid every serious sin ; he shall diligently pray for the protection of God to vanquish the impediments and schemes of Diabolus, and God will ordain that the devil himself shall work to the direct profit of the Theosophist. Subject to Divine Providence, some spirits have power over pestilence and famine, some are destroyers of cities, like those of Sodom and Gomorrah, some are rulers over kingdoms, some guardians of provinces, some of a single person. The spirits are the ministers of the word of God, of the Church and its members, or they serve creatures in material things, sometimes to the salvation of soul and body, or, again, to the ruin of both. But nothing, good or bad, is done without knowledge, order, and administration.

It is unnecessary to follow the angelical host farther here, as we have outlined it elsewhere. Many preparations, however, are described by the author of the *Theosophia Pneumatica* for the successful evocation of these exalted beings. The magus must ponder during his period of initiation on the method of attaining the true knowledge of God, both by night and day. He must know the laws of the cosmos, and the practical secrets which may be gleaned from the study of the visible and invisible creatures of God. He must further know himself, and be able to distinguish between his mortal and immortal parts, and the several spheres to which they belong. Both in his mortal and immortal natures, he shall strive to love God, to adore and to fear him in spirit and in truth. He must sedulously attempt to find out whether he is fitted for the practice of *magic*, and if so to what branch he should turn his talents, experimenting in all to discover in which he is most naturally gifted. He must hold inviolate such secrets as are communicated to him by spirits, and he must accustom himself to their evocation. He must keep himself, however, from the least suspicion of diabolical *magic*, which has to do with Satan, and which is the perversion of the theurgic power concealed in the word of God. When he has fulfilled these conditions, and before he proceeds to the practice of his art, he should devote a prefatory period to deep contemplation on the high business which he has voluntarily taken in hand, and must present himself before God with a pure heart, undefiled mouth and innocent hands. He must bathe frequently and wear clean garments, confess his sins and abstain from wine for the space of three days. On the eve of operation, he must dine sparely at noon, and sup on bread and water, and on the day he has chosen for the invocation he must seek a retired and uncontaminated spot, entirely free from observation. After offering up prayer, he compels the spirit which he has chosen to appear : that is, he has passed into a condition, when it is impossible that the spirit should remain invisible to him. On the arrival of the angel, the desire of the magus is briefly communicated to him, and his answer is written down. More than three questions should not be asked, and the angel is then dismissed into his special sphere. Besides having converse with angels, the magus had also power over the spirits of the elements. The reader is referred to the special article upon these, and we shall confine ourselves in this place to describing the manner of their evocation. To obtain power over the salamanders for example, the *Comte de Gabalis* gives the following receipt : " If you would recover empire over the salamanders, purify and exalt the natural fire that is within you. Nothing is required for this purpose but the concentration of the Fire of the World by means of concave mirrors in a globe of glass. In that globe is formed the ' solary ' powder, which being of itself purified from the mixture of other elements, and being prepared according to Art becomes in a very short time a sovereign process for the exaltation of the fire that is within you, and transmutes you into an igneous nature." There is very little matter extant to show in what manner the evocation of Elementary spirits was undertaken, and no ritual has survived which will acquaint us with the method of communicating with them. In older writers it is difficult to distinguish between angels and elementary spirits, and it is probable that the lesser angels of the older magicians were the sylphs of Paracelsus, and the more modern professors of the art. The lower hierarchies of the elementary spirits were also frequently invoked by the black magician. Eliphas Levi provides a method for the interrogation and government of elementary spirits ; but he does not acquaint us with its source, and it is merely fragmentary. " It is necessary," he says, " in order to dominate these intelligences, to undergo the four trials of ancient initiation, and as these are unknown, their room must be supplied by similar tests. To approach the salamanders, therefore, one must expose himself in a burning house. To draw near the sylphs he must cross a precipice on a plank, or ascend a lofty mountain in a storm ; and he who would win to the abode of the undines must plunge into a cascade or whirlpool. Thus power being acquired through courage and indomitable energy this fire, earth and water must be consecrated and exorcised."

The air is exorcised by the sufflation of the four cardinal points, the recitation of the prayer of the sylphs, and by the following formula :—The Spirit of God moved upon the water, and breathed into the nostrils of man the breath of life. Be Michael my leader, and be Sabtabiel my servant, in the name and by the virtue of light. Be the power of the word in my breath, and I will govern the spirits of this creature of Air, and by the will of my soul, I will restrain the steeds of the sun,, and by the thought of my mind, and by the apple of my right eye. I exorcise thee O creature of Air, by the Petagrammaton, and in the name Tetragrammaton, wherein are steadfast will and well-directed faith. Amen. Sela. So be it.

Water is exorcised by the laying on of hands, by breathing and by speech, and by mixing sacred salt with a little of the ash which is left in an incense pan. The aspergillus is made of branches of vervain, periwinkle, sage, mint, ash, and basil, tied by a thread taken from a virgin's distaff,

with a handle of hazelwood which has never borne fruit, and on which the characters of the seven spirits must be graven with the magic awl. The salt and ashes of the incense must be separately consecrated. The prayer of the undines should follow.

Fire is exorcised by casting salt, incense, white resin, camphor and sulphur therein, and by thrice pronouncing the three names of the genii of fire—Michael, Samael, and Anael, and then by reciting the prayer of the salamanders.

The Earth is exorcised by the sprinkling of water, by breathing, and by fire, and the prayer of the gnomes. Their signs are—the hieroglyphs of the Bull for the Gnomes who are commanded with the magic sword ; of the Lion for the Salamanders, who are commanded with the forked rod, or *magic* trident ; of the Eagle for the Slyphs, who are ruled by the holy pentacles ; and, finally, of Aquarius for the Undines, who are evoked by the cup of libations. Their respective sovereigns are Gob for the Gnomes, Djin for the Salamanders, Paralda for the Sylphs, and Necksa for the Undines. These names, it will be noticed, are borrowed from folklore.

The " laying " of an elementary spirit is accomplished by its adjuration by air, water, fire, and earth, by breathing, sprinkling, the burning of perfumes, by tracing on the ground the Star of Solomon and the sacred Pentagram, which should be drawn either with ash of consecrated fire or with a reed soaked in various colours, mixed with pure loadstone. The Conjuration of the Four should then be repeated, the magus holding the pentacle of Solomon in his hand and taking up by turns the sword, rod and cup,—this operation being preceded and terminated by the Kabalistic sign of the cross. In order to subjugate an elementary spirit, the magus must be himself free of their besetting sins ; thus a changeful person cannot rule the sylphs, nor a fickle one the undines, an angry man the salamanders, or a covetous one the gnomes. We have given elsewhere (*See* **Necromancy**) the formula for the evocation of spirits, so there is no necessity to repeat it in this place. The white magician did not concern himself as a rule with such matters as the raising of demons, animal transformations and the like, his whole desire being the exaltation of his spiritual nature ; and the questions put by him to the spirits he evoked were all directed to that end. (*See* **Magic**.)

Medina, Michael : (*See* **Healing by Touch**.)

Medium : A person supposed to be qualified in some special manner to form a link between the dead and the living. Through him the spirits of the departed may communicate with their friends still on earth, either by making use of the material organism of the *medium* himself (" automatic phenomena ") or by producing in the physical world certain manifestations which cannot be explained by known physical laws. The essential qualification of a *medium* is an abnormal sensitiveness, which enables him to be readily " controlled " by disembodied spirits. For this reason *mediums* are also known as *sensitives*. There is some doubt as to whether mediumship is an inherent faculty, or whether it may be acquired ; and among some spiritualists at least, the belief is held that all men are *mediums*, though in varying degrees, and consequently that all are in communication with the spirits, from whom proceeds what we call " inspiration." Those who are ordinarily designated " mediums " are but gifted with the common faculty in a higher degree than their fellows.

Mediumship, like all the central doctrines of spiritualism, dates back to very early times. Demoniacal possession affords an excellent instance ; so also does witchcraft, while the *somnambule* of the mesmerists was identical with the modern *medium*. In its usual application, however, the term *medium* is used only of those sensitives who belong to the modern spiritualistic movement, which had its origin in America in 1848 (*See* **Spiritualism.**) In this sense, then, Mrs. Fox and her daughters, the heroines of the Rochester Rappings, were the earliest *mediums*. The phenomena of their séances consisted mainly of knockings, by means of which messages were conveyed from the spirits to the sitters. Other *mediums* rapidly sprang up, first in America, and later in Britain and the Continent. Their mediumship was of two kinds, " physical " and automatic. These phases were to be found either separately or combined in one person, as in the case of the Rev. Stainton Moses (q.v.) Indeed, it was practically impossible to find a trance speaker who did not at one time or another practise the physical manifestations, until the time of Mrs. Piper, whose phenomena were purely subjective. The early rappings speedily developed into more elaborate manifestations. For a few years an epidemic of table-turning (q.v.) caused wide-spread excitement, and the motions of the table became a favourite means of communicating with the spirits. The playing of musical instruments without visible agency was a form of manifestation which received the attention of *mediums* from an early date, as was also the bringing into the séance-room of " apports " of fruit, flowers, perfume, and all manner of portable property. Darkness was found to facilitate the spirit-manifestations, and as there are certain physical processes, such as those in photography, to which darkness is essential, no logical objection could be offered to the dimness of the séance-room. The members of the circle were generally seated round a table, holding each other's hands, and they were often enjoined to sing or talk pending the materialisation of a spirit. All this, though offering grounds of suspicion to the incredulous, was plausibly explained by the spiritualists. As time went on, and the demand for physical manifestations increased, these became more daring and more varied. The moving of objects without contact, the levitation of heavy furniture, and of the persons of *medium* or sitters, the elongation of the human body, the fire-ordeal, were all practised by the *medium* Home. At the séances of the Davenport Brothers musical instruments were played and moved about the room, and objects moved without being touched, while the *mediums* were bound hand and foot in a small cabinet. The slate-writing of " Dr." Slade and William Eglinton had a considerable vogue. The tying of knots in endless cords, the passage of solids through solids, were commonplaces of the mediumistic circle. The crowning achievement, however, was the materialisation of the spirit-form. Quite early in the history of spiritualism hands were materialised, then faces, and finally the complete form of the " control." Thereafter the materialised spirits allowed themselves to be touched, and even condescended, on occasion, to hold conversations with the sitters. Further proof of the actuality of the spirit " control " was offered by spirit photography (q.v.).

To those for whom spiritualism was a religion, however, much the most important part of the mediumistic performances is the trance-utterances and the like which come under the heading of " automatic," or psychological phenomena. These dealt largely with the conditions of life on the other side of the grave, and in style they tended to be verbose and incoherent. The spirit-drawings, also, were lacking in depths and distinction. Clairvoyance and crystal vision are included in the psychological phenomena, and so also are the pseudo-prophetic utterances of *mediums*, and the speaking in unknown tongues. According to the spiritualistic hypothesis already referred to, that " all men are *mediums*," it would be necessary to class inspiration, not only the inspiration of genius, but all good or evil impulses—as spiritual phenomena, and that in turn suggests that the every-day life of the normal individual is to some extent directed by spirit " controls." And therein lies the responsibility of mediumship, for if he would be controlled by pure spirits from the higher spheres, it behoves the *medium* to live a well-conducted and principled life. Misuse of the divine gift of mediumship carries with it its own punishment, for the *medium* becomes the sport of base human spirits and elementals (q.v.), his will is sapped, and his whole being degraded. Likewise he must be wary of giving up his personality to the first spirit who comes his way, for the low and earth-bound spirits have least difficulty in communicating with the living, having still more affinity with the things of the earth than with those of the spirit.

Of the physical *mediums* perhaps the most successful was Daniel Dunglas Home (1833–1886), who claimed to be of Scottish birth. He went to America, however, at an early age, and it was there that his mediumistic powers were first developed, though not until he came to Britain in 1855 did he rise to fame. It is worthy of note that Home was never detected in fraud—as the bulk of physical *mediums* have been at one time or another—though his performances were similar in kind to those of other *mediums*. This may be due in part to the fact that he did not act as a professional *medium*, and his sitters, being either his guests or his hosts, were doubtless restrained by courtesy from a too close enquiry into his methods. Again, all who came into contact with him were impressed by his simple manners, and frank and affectionate disposition, so that he possessed the most valuable asset of a *medium*—the ability to inspire confidence in his sitters. *Mediums* of a different stamp, though widely popular in their day, were the brothers Davenport. Their performance consisted of allowing themselves to be securely bound in a cabinet by the sitters, and while thus handicapped producing the usual mediumistic phenomena. The Davenports were shown to be mere conjurers, however, and when Maskelyne and Cook successfully imitated their feats the exposure was complete. Slate-writing, which proved one of the most widely-accepted forms of psychic phenomena, had as its principal exponents Henry Slade and William Eglinton. The best argument which can be advanced against their feats is to be found in the pseudo-séances of Mr. S. J. Davey, given in the interests of the Society for Psychical Research. Mr. Davey's slate-writing exhibitions were so like to those of the professional *mediums* that the spiritualists refused to believe that he was conjuring, and hailed him as a renegade *medium* ! Automatic drawing was principally represented by David Duguid, a Glasgow *medium* who attained considerable success in that line. Prominent trance speakers and writers were Duguid, J. J. Morse, Mrs. Hardinge Britten, and Mrs. Cora L. V. Tappan-Richmond. One of the best-known and most respected of private *mediums* was the Rev. Stainton Moses (1839–92), a clergyman and schoolmaster, whose normal life, at least, was beyond reproach. He produced both automatic and physical manifestations, the former including the writing of a work *Spirit Teachings*, dictated from time to time by his spirit " controls," while the latter comprised levitations, lights, " apports," and so on. His position, character, and education gave to his support of spiritualism a stability of considerable value.

It is to later *mediums*, however, that we must look for proof worthy of scientific consideration, and of these the most important are Eusapia Palladino and Mrs. Piper. Eusapia Palladino, an Italian *medium*, was born in 1854, and for a good many years had acted as *medium* for scientific investigators. In 1892 séances were held at Milan, at which were present Professors Schiaparelli, Brofferio, Lobmroso, Richet, and others. In 1894 Professor Richet conducted some experiments with Eusapia at his house in the Ile Roubaud, to which he invited Professor Lodge, Mr.

Myers, and Dr. Ochorowiez. The phenomena occurring in Eusapia's presence were the ordinary manifestations of the mediumistic séance, but their interest lay in the fact that all the distinguished investigators professed themselves satisfied that the *medium*, with her hands, head, and feet controlled by the sitters, could not of herself produce the phenomena. Credible witnesses asserted that Eusapia possessed the ability to project false or psychic limbs from her person. Professor Lodge and Mr. Myers were disposed to look for a new force (ectenic force) emanating from the *medium*. In 1895, however, some séances with Eusapia were held at Mr. Myers' house at Cambridge, where it became apparent that she habitually freed a hand or a foot—in short, habitually resorted to fraud. Yet even these exposures were not conclusive for in 1898, after a further series of experiments, Mr. Myers and Professors Lodge and Richet once more declared their belief in the genuineness of this *medium's* phenomena.

Mrs. Piper, the Boston *medium* whose trance utterances and writings contain the best evidence forthcoming in recent years for the truth of spiritualism, first fell into a spontaneous trance in 1884, and in the following year was observed by Professor James of Harvard. Thereafter her case was carefully studied by the Society for Psychical Research. Her first important " control " was a French physician, Dr. Phinuit, who was probably a fiction, but in 1892 she was controlled by George Pelham, a young author who had died in February of that year. So complete was her impersonation of Pelham that more than thirty of his friends claimed to recognise him, and so well did he establish his identity by the mention of many private matters, known only to himself and a few of his friends, that the hypothesis of spirit-control was almost inevitable. In 1896 George Pelham gave place to " Imperator," " Rector," and other spirits, who had formerly controlled Stainton Moses. From that time, and especially after 1900, the interest of the sittings declined, and they offered less material for the investigator. Another automatic *medium*, Hélène Smith, came under the observation of Professor Flournoy. Hélène's trance utterances were spoken in the " Martian language," a variant of the " unknown tongue " of the early ecstatics, and she claimed to be a re-incarnation of Marie Antoinette and a Hindu princess.

Of the various theories advanced to explain the mediumistic manifestations the most important is the spiritualistic explanation, which claims that the phenomena are produced by the spirits of the dead acting on the sensitive organism of the *medium*. The evidence for such a theory, though some investigators of the highest distinction have found it satisfactory, is nevertheless generally acknowledged to be inconclusive. Conscious fraud, though it is no longer considered to cover the whole ground, yet plays a definite part in the phenomena of both " physical " and trance *mediums*, for it has been shown that the latter frequently collect, through private enquiry agents, information anent possible sitters which is later retailed by the " controls." The spiritualist's explanation of these lapses into fraud is that they are instigated by the spirits themselves. And it does not seem impossible that a genuine *medium* might have resort to fraud during a temporary failure of his psychic powers. Automatism covers a still wider field. That automatic utterances, writing, drawing, etc., may be quite involuntary, and without the sphere of the *medium's* normal consciousness, is no longer to be doubted. The psychological phenomena may be met with in small children, and in private *mediums* whose good faith is beyond question, and the state is recognised as being allied to hypnotism and hysteria. Besides automatism and fraud there are some other factors to be considered ere the possibility of transcendental faculties be touched upon.

On the part of the sitter as well as of the *medium* some deception may be practised. It has been said that the ability to inspire confidence in his sitters is essential to a successful *medium*, and if at the same time the sitters be predisposed to believe in the supernatural nature of the manifestations, it is easy to imagine a lessening of the attention and observation so necessary to the investigator. The impossibility of continued observation for even a short period is a fact that can only be proved by experiment. Memory defects and proneness to exaggeration are also accountable for many of the marvels of the séance-room, and possible hallucination must be considered. When the *medium* is in a trance, with its accompanying hyperæsthesia, unconscious suggestion on the part of the sitters might offer a rational explanation of so-called " clairvoyance." But when all these factors are removed the root problems of mediumship still remain. In the case of Mrs. Piper for instance, the least that can be said for her trance utterances is that they were telepathic ; that she gathered information from the minds of her sitters, or through them from other living minds. To not a few, however, they presented definite proof of spirit communication. To meet such instances Mr. Myers formulated his doctrine of transcendental faculties, crediting the *medium* with clairvoyance and pre-vision. But no really conclusive test has ever been complied with. Psychical researchers have left sealed letters, whose contents are known only to themselves, instructing that after their deaths the letters be submitted to a *medium*, but in no case have the contents been correctly revealed. Again, in the case of Eusapia Palladino, Mr. Myers, Sir Oliver Lodge, and others have inclined to the belief in a force emanating from the *medium* herself by which the physical manifestations are produced. Here, also, the evidence cannot be considered conclusive. Skilled and scientific investigators have from time to time been deceived by what has actually proved to be sleight of hand, and, in fact, the only trustworthy evidence possible would be that of automatic records.

At the same time the testimony of such distinguished gentlemen as Professor Richet, Sir O. Lodge, and others makes it evident that judgment must not be hastily pronounced on the *medium*, but rather that an earnest endeavour be made to solve the problems in that connection.

Healing Mediums.—The diagnosis and cure of disease have been extensively practised by spiritualistic *mediums*, following in the path of the older somnambules and magnetic subjects. These latter were wont not only to trace the progress of their own diseases, but also to diagnose and to prescribe a mode of treatment. At the outset it was not prescribed for the diseases of those with whom they were in *rapport* ; and likewise the *medium*, having established *rapport* between his control and the patient, was influenced to prescribe a mode of treatment. At the outset it was not considered proper for the *healing medium* to accept any remuneration for his services, but later healers usually demanded a fee. It is true that' *healing mediums*, like Christian Scientists, mesmerists, magnetists, and others, have effected a considerable proportion of *bona fide* cures, but whether by spirit influence or suggestion is a point on which there is too much diversity of opinion for it to be discussed here. It is claimed for many *mediums* that they have cured diseases of long standing, which were pronounced incurable—heart disease, consumption, cancers, paralysis, and many more. Some also have been credited with the power to heal instantaneously, as did the Curé d'Ars and other miraculous healers. The marvellous potency of the waters at Lourdes is considered by spiritualists to be the gift of discarnate beings, having been in the first instance revealed to a child by her spirit guide, in the form of a white angel.

Medium and Daybreak : Spiritualistic Journal. (*See* **Spiritualism.**)

Medium Evangelique, La (Journal) : (*See* **France.**)

Melusina : The most famous of the fays of France. Being condemned to turn into a serpent from the waist downwards every Saturday, she made her husband, Count Raymond of Lusignan, promise never to come near her on a Saturday. This prohibition finally exciting his curiosity and suspicion, he hid himself and witnessed his wife's transformation. Melusina was now compelled to quit her mortal husband and destined to wander about as a spectre till the day of doom. It is said also that the count immured her in the dungeon of his castle.

Mental World : Formerly known as the Manas Plane—is in the theosophic scheme of things, the third lowest of the seven worlds. It is the world of thought into which man passes on the death of the astral body, and it is composed of the seven divisions of matter in common with the other worlds. It is observed that the *mental world* is the world of thought, but it is necessary to realise that it is the world of good thoughts only, for the base have all been purged away during the soul's stay in the astral world. According as these thoughts are, is the power to perceive the *mental world*. Perfected man would be free of the whole of it, but the ordinary man has in his past imperfect experience, gathered only a comparatively small amount of thought and he is, therefore, unable to perceive more than a comparatively small part of his surroundings. It follows from this that though his bliss is inconceivably great, his sphere of action is very limited,—this limitation, however, becoming less and less with his abode there after each fresh incarnation. In the Heaven world-division into which he awakes after dying in the astral world, he finds vast, unthought-of means of pursuing what has seemed to him good, art, science, philosophy and so forth. Here, all these come to a glorious fruition of which we can have no conception, and at last the time arrives when he casts aside his mental body and awakens in his casual body to the still greater bliss of the higher division of the *mental world*. At this stage he has done with the bodies which form his mortal personality, and which form his home in successive incarnations, and he is now truly himself, a spirit, immortal and unchangeable except for increasing development and evolution. Into his casual body is worked all that he has experienced in his physical, astral and mental bodies, and when he still finds that experience insufficient for his needs, he descends again into grosser matter in order that he may learn yet more and more.

Mephis or **Memphitis :** A stone which, when bruised to powder and drunk in water, causes insensibility to torture.

Mercury : Or quicksilver. A metal which has been known of for many centuries, and which has played an important part in the history of alchemy. In its refined state it forms a coherent, very mobile liquid. The early alchemists believed that nature formed all metals of *mercury*, and that it is a living and feminine principle. It went through many processes, and the metal evolved was pure or impure according to the locality of its production.

Mercury of Life : (*See* **Elixir of Life.**)

Merlin : An enchanter of Britain who dwelt at the court of King Arthur. His origin is obscure, but early legends concerning him agree that he was the offspring of Satan. He was probably an early Celtic god, who in process of time came to be regarded as a great sorcerer. There appears to have been more than one *Merlin*, and we must discriminate between the Merlin of Arthurian romance and Merlin Caledonius ; but it is probable that originally the two conceptions sprang from the one idea.

Mesmer, Franz Antoine : An Austrian doctor, born at Weil about the year 1733. In 1766 he took a degree in medicine at Vienna, the subject of his inaugural thesis being *De planetarum Influxu* (De l'influence des Planettes sur le corps humain). The influence of the planets he identified with magnetism. On seeing the remarkable cures of Gassner he supposed that the magnetic force must also reside in the human body, and thereupon dispensed with magnets. In 1778 he went to Paris where he was very favourably received—by the public, that is, for the medical authorities there, as elsewhere, refused to countenance him. His method was to seat his patients round a large circular vat or *baquet*, in which various substances were mixed. Each patient held one end of an iron rod, the other end of which was in the baquet. In due time the crisis ensued. Violent convulsions, cries, laughter, and various physical symptoms followed, these being in turn superseded by lethargy. Many claimed to have been healed by this method. In 1784 the government appointed a commission of members of the *Faculté de Médecine*, the *Societé Royale de Médecine*, and the Academy of Sciences, the commissioners from the latter body including Franklin, Bailly, and Lavoisier. The report of the Committee stated, in effect, that there was no such thing as animal magnetism, and referred the facts of the crisis to the imagination of the patient. It had the effect of quenching to a considerable extent the public interest in mesmerism, as animal magnetism was called, for the time at least, though it was afterwards to be revived. *Mesmer* died in 1815.

Mesmerism : (*See* **Hypnotism.**)

Mesna : (*See* **Alchemy.**)

Metals in Animal Magnetism : It is recorded by the magnetists that the various *metals* exercised a characteristic influence on their patients. Physical sensations of heat and cold numbness, drowsiness, and so on were experienced by the somnambules on contact with *metals*, or even when *metals* were secretly introduced into the room. Dr. Elliotson, especially, gave much prominence to the alleged power of *metal* to transmit the magnetic fluid. Gold, silver, platinum, and nickel were good conductors, though the magnetism conveyed by the latter was of a highly dangerous character. Copper, tin, pewter, and zinc were bad conductors. Elliotson found that a magnetised sovereign would throw into the trance his sensitives the sisters Okey, and that though iron would neutralise the magnetic roperties of the sovereign, no other metal would do so. When Baron von Reichenbach propounded his theory of odylic force his sensitives saw a luminous emanation proceed from metals—silver and gold shone white ; lead, blue ; nickle, red, and so on. All these phenomena may be referred to suggestion.

Metempsychosis, or Transmigration : The passing of the soul at death into another body than the one it has vacated. The belief in *metempsychosis* was very wide-spread in ancient times, and still survives in Braminism and Buddhism, as well as in European folk-tales and superstitions. The Brahmins and Buddhists believe that the soul may enter another human body, or that of one of the lower animals, or even a plant or tree, according to its deserts in the previous incarnation. Thus it is doomed to successive incarnations, till by the suppression of all desires and emotions it loses itself in the Supreme Being. Very similar was the idea of Pythagoras and the Greeks, who believed that all material existence was a punishment for sins committed in a former incarnation. Indeed it is probable that Pythagoras derived his theory from the Brahminical doctrine. The ancient Egyptians would also seem to have believed in metempsychosis. Among certain savage tribes of Africa and America *transmigration* is generally subscribed to at the present day. These savages imagine the discarnate spirit very much out of its element till it has found another body to dwell in, which it does as speedily as possible. Totemism may perhaps facilitate a belief in the passing of the soul into the body of an animal. In Europe also in early times the belief in *metempsychosis* flourished, and several popular folk-tales, such as that known in Scotland as *The Milk-white Doo*, of which variants are found in many lands, contain references to the souls of the dead entering into beasts, birds, or fishes. In some places it is thought that witches are at death transformed into hares, and for this reason the people of these localities refuse to eat a hare. The Jewish Kabalists also believed in the doctrine of *metempsychosis*, and traces of it are to be found in the writings of Swedenborg.

Metratton : According to Jewish rabbinical legend, *Metratton*, the angel, is one of the agents by whom God the Father works. He receives the pure and simple essence of the divinity and bestows the gift of life upon all. He dwells in one of the angelic hierarchies.

Mexico and Central America : Occult science among the ancient Mexicans may be said to have been in that stage between the savage simplicities of medicine-men and the more sophisticated magical practices of the mediæval sorcerer. The sources which inform us regarding it are unfortunately of a most scanty description and are chiefly gleaned from the works of the early missionaries to the country, and from the legends and myths of the people themselves. Writing upon the sorcerers of *Mexico*, Sahagun, an early Spanish priest, states that the *naualli* or magician among the Mexicans is one who enchants men and sucks the blood of infants during the night. This would seem as if the writer had confounded the sorcerer with the vampire,—a mistake occasionally made by continental writers on magic. He proceeds to say that among the Mexicans this class is ignorant of nothing which appertains to sorcery, and possesses great craft and natural address ; that they hire themselves out to people to work evil upon their enemies, and to cause madness and maladies. " The necromancer," he says, " is a person who has made pact with a demon, and who is capable of transforming himself into various animal shapes. Such people appear to be tired of life and await death with complaisance. The astrologer practises among the people as a diviner, and has a thorough knowledge of the various signs of the calendar, from which he is able to prognosticate the fortunes of those who employ him. This he accomplishes by weighing the power of one planet against that of another, and thus discovering the resultant applies it to the case in point. These men were called into consultation at births and deaths, as well as upon public occasions, and would dispute with much nicety on their art." The astrological system of the Mexicans was like that of their calendar of the most involved description possible, and no mere summary of it could convey anything but a hazy notion of the system, for which the reader is referred to the author's *Civilisation of Ancient Mexico*, Sahagun's *Historia*, and Bulletin 28 of the United States *Bureau of Ethnology*. In connection with the astrological science of the Aztecs, however, it is worthy of note that the seventh calendric sign, was that under which necromancers, sorcerers and evil-doers were usually born. Says Sahagun : " These work their enchantments in obscurity for four nights running, when they choose a certain evil sign. They then betake themselves in the night to the houses where they desire to work their evil deeds and sorceries. . . . . . . For the rest these sorcerers never know contentment, for all their days they live evilly and know no peace."

The myths of the Mexicans give us a good working idea of the status of the enchanter or sorcerer in Aztec society. For example we find that the Toltec god, Quetzalcoatl, who in early times was regarded as a description of culture-hero, was bewitched by the god of the incoming and rival race, Tezcatlipoca, who disguised himself as a physician and prescribed for an illness of his enemy's an enchanted draught, which made him long for the country of his origin—that is, the home of the rains. From this we may judge that potions or philtres were in vogue amongst Mexican sorcerers. In their efforts to rid themselves of the entire Toltec race, the traditional aborigines of *Mexico*, Tezcatlipoca is pictured as performing upon a magical drum in such a manner as to cause frenzy amongst the Toltecs, who leaped by thousands into a deep ravine hard by their city ; and similar instances of the kind are occasionally to be met with. Wonderful stories are told of the feats of the Huaxteca, a people of Maya race, dwelling on the Gulf of Mexico. Sahagun relates that they could produce from space a spring with fishes, burn and restore a hut, and dismember and resurrect themselves. The Ocuiltec of the Toluca Valley also possessed a widespread reputation as enchanters and magicians.

Divination and Augury.—As has been said, divination was practised among the Aztecs by means of astrology ; but there were other and less-intricate methods in use. There was in existence a College of Augurs corresponding in purpose to the Auspices of Ancient Rome, the members of which occupied themselves with observing the flight and listening to the songs of birds, from which they drew their conclusions, and pretended to interpret the speech of all winged creatures. The *Calmecac*, or training college of the priests, had a department where divination was taught in all its branches. A typical example of augury from birds may be found in the account of the manner in which the Mexicans fixed upon the spot for the foundation of their city. Halting after years of wandering in the vicinity of the Lake of Tezcuco, they observed a great eagle with wings outspread perched on the stump of a cactus, and holding in its talons a live serpent. Their augurs interpreted this as a good omen as it had been previously announced by an oracle, and upon the spot where the bird had alighted, they drove the first piles upon which they afterwards built the city of *Mexico*,—the legend of the foundation of which is still commemorated in the arms of modern *Mexico*. Dreams and visions played a great part in Mexican divination, and a special caste of augurs called *Teopixqui*, or *Teotecuhtli* (masters or guardians of divine things) were set apart for the purpose of interpreting dreams and of divining through dreams and visions, which was regarded as the chief route between man and the supernatural. The senses were even quickened and sharpened by the use of drugs and the ecstatic condition was induced by want of sleep, and pertinacious fixing of the mind upon one subject, the swallowing or inhalation of cerebral intoxicants such as tobacco, the maguey, coca, the snake-plant or *ololiuhqui*, and similar substances. As among some tribes of the American-Indians, it was probably believed that visions came to the prophet or seer pictorially, or that acts were performed before him as in a play. They also held that the soul travelled through space and was able to visit those places of which it desired to have knowledge. It is also possible that they hypnotised themselves by gazing at certain small highly-polished pieces of sandstone, or that they employed these for the same purpose as crystal-gazers employ the globe. The goddess Tozi was the patron of those who used grains of maize or red beans in divination.

Charms and Amulets.—The amulet was regarded in *Mexico* as a personal fetish. The Tepitoton, or diminutive household deities of the Mexicans were also fetishistic. It is probable that most of the Mexican amulets were modelled on the various ornaments of the gods. Thus the traveller's staff carved in the shape of a serpent like that of Quetzalcoatl was undoubtedly of this nature, and was even occasionally sacrificed to. The frog was a favourite model for an amulet. As elsewhere, the thunderbolts thrown by the gods were supposed to be flint stones, and were cherished as amulets of much virtue, and as symbols of the fecundating rains.

Vampirism.—As has been seen, Sahagun confounds the Mexican necromancer with the vampire, and it is interesting to note that this folk-belief must have originated in America independently of any European connection. But we find another instance of what would seem something like vampirism in *Mexico*. This is found in connection with the *ciupipiltin* or ghosts of women who have died in childbirth. These haunt the cross-roads, crying and wailing for the little ones they have left behind them. But as in many other countries, notably in Burma, they are malevolent—their evil tendencies probably being caused by jealousy of the happiness of the living. Lest they should enter their houses and injure their children, the Mexicans at certain times of the year stopped up every possible hole and crevice. The appearance of these ghosts (Sahagun describes them as " goddesses ") at cross-roads is highly significant, for we know that the burial of criminals at such junctions was merely a survival of a similar disposal of the corpse of the vampire, whose head was cut off and laid at his side, and who was entombed at cross-roads for the purpose of confusing him as to his whereabouts.

Nagualism.—Both in Mexico and Central America a religio-magical system called Nagualism obtained, the purpose of which was to bring occult influence against the whites for their destruction. The rites of this strange cult usually took place in caverns and other deserted localities, and were naturally derived to a large extent from those of the suppressed native religion. Each native worshipper possessed a magical or animal spirit-guide, with which he was endowed early in life. This system certainly flourished as lately as half a century ago, and there is good reason to believe that it is not yet extinct.

Central America.—Notices upon magic and sorcery amongst the Maya, Kiche, and other Central American peoples are even rarer than those which relate to *Mexico*, and we have to fall back almost solely upon the native legends to glean anything concerning the subject at all. The great storehouse of Central American legend is the *Popol Vuh*, for an account of which the reader is referred to the author's *Popol Vuh*, London, 1909. We find in this interesting native mythi-history, that some of the elder gods are regarded as magicians, and the hero-twins, Xblanque and Hun-ahpu, whom they sent to earth to rid it of the Titan Vukub-cakix, are undoubtedly possessed of magical powers. As boys we find them equipped with magic tools, which enable them to get through an enormous amount of work in a single day, and when they descend into Xibalba, the Kiche Hades, for the purpose of avenging their father and uncle, they take full advantage of their magical propensities in combating the natives of that drear abode. Xibalba itself possesses sorcerers, for we find two within its borders, Xulu and Pacaw, who assist the hero-gods in many of their necromantic practices.

As regards divination, we find that the Maya possessed a caste of augurs, called *Cocomes* or the Listeners ; and prophecy appears to have been periodically practised by their priests. In the so-called books of *Chilan Balam* which are native compilations of events occurring in Central *America* previous to the Spanish Conquest, we find certain prophecies regarding, amongst other things, the coming of the Spaniards. These appear to have been given forth by a priest who bore the title, not the name, of " Chilan Balam," whose offices were those of divination and astrology but these pronouncements seem to have been coloured

at a later date by Christian thought, and hardly to be of a genuine aboriginal character. There are certain astrological receips in the books, all of which are simply borrowed from European almanacs of the century between 1550 and 1650. Amulets were in great vogue amongst the Maya, and they had the same fear of the last five days of the year as had the Mexicans, who regarded them as *nemontemi* or unlucky, and did no work of any description upon them. These days the Maya called *uyayayab*, and they considered that a demon entered their towns and villages at the beginning of this period. To avert this, they carried an image of him through the village in the hopes that he might afterwards avoid it.

Mezazoth, The : A schedule which, when fastened on the doorpost, possessed talismanic qualities. It is said in the *Talmud* that whoever has the *mezazoth* fixed on his door, and is provided with certain personal charms, is protected from sin.

Michael : An archangel ; in the Hebrew, " He who is equal to God." In Revelation it is said : " there was war in heaven. Michael and his angels fought against the dragon " : and from this it is deduced that Michael was the leader of the celestial hierarchy,—as against Lucifer, the head of the disobedient angels. Michael is mentioned by name four other times in the Scriptures ; in Daniel as the champion of the Jewish Church against Persia ; in Jude as the archangel who fought with Satan for Moses' body ; by Gabriel he is called the prince of the Jewish Church ; and in the prophecy of Enoch, " Michael . . . . . who commands the nations." His design according to Randle Holme is a banner hanging on a cross ; and he is represented as victory with a dart in one hand and a cross on his forehead. Bishop Horsley and others considered Michael as only another name for the Son of God. In one of the Jewish rabbinical legends he is the ruler of Mercury, to which sphere he " imparts benignity, motion and intelligence, with elegance and consonance of speech."

Michael Medina : (*See* **Healing by Touch.**)

Microcosm, The : Or the Pentagram, a little world (Greek *Micros*, small ; *Kosmos*, a world)—a five-pointed star, which represents Man and the summation of the occult forces. It was believed by Paracelsus that this sign had a marvellous magical power over spirits ; and that all magic figures and kabalistic signs could be reduced to two—*The Microcosm*, and the Macrocosm (q.v.).

Microprosopus, The : One of the four magical elements in the Kabala ; and probably representing one of the four simple elements—air, water, earth, or fire. The word means " creator of the little world."

Mictlan, the Mexican Hades : (*See* **Hell.**)

Mid-day Demons : The ancients frequently made mention of certain demons who became visible especially towards mid-day to those with whom they had a pact. They appeared in the form of men or of beasts, and let themselves be enclosed in a character, a figure, a vial, or in the interior of a hollow ring.

Midiwiwin, The : A secret society or exclusive association of the Ojibway Indians of North America. The myth of the foundation of this society is as follows : Michabo, the Creator, looking down to earth saw that the forefathers of the Ojibway were very helpless. . . . Espying a black object floating on the surface of a lake he drew near to it and saw that it was an otter—now one of the sacred animals of the *Midiwiwin*. He instructed it in the mysteries of that caste, and provided it with a sacred rattle, a sacred drum, and tobacco. He built a *Midiwigan*, or Sacred House of Midi, to which he took the otter and confided to it the mysteries of the *Midiwiwin*. In short, the society is one of these " medicine " or magical associations so common among the North-American Indians (q.v.). When

a candidate is admitted to a grade and is prepared to pass
on to the next, he gives three feasts, and sings three prayers
to the Bear Spirit in order to be permitted to enter that
grade. His progress through the various grades is assisted
by several snake-spirits ; and at a later stage by
the power of certain prayers or invocations,—a larger
snake appears and raises its body, thus forming an arch
under which the candidate takes his way to the higher
grade. When the Indian belongs to the second grade he is
supposed to receive supernatural power, to be able to see
into the future, to hear what comes afar off, to touch
friends and foes however far away they may be, and so on.
In higher grades he can assume the form of any animal.
The third grade confers enhanced power, and it is thought
that its members can perform extraordinary exploits, and
have power over the entire invisible world. The fourth
is still more exalted.

When an Indian is ready to undergo initiation, he
erects a wigwam in which he takes steam-baths for four
days, one on each day. On the evening of the day before
initiation he visits his teachers in order to obtain from
them instructions for the following day. Next morning
the priests approach with the candidate at their head, enter
the *Midiwigan*, and the proceedings commence. The
publications of the Bureau of American Ethnology contain several good accounts of the ritual of this society.

Militia Crucifera Evangelica : (*See* **Rosicrucians.**)

Mimetic Magic : (*See* **Magic.**)

Mines, Haunted : The belief that *mines* are *haunted* is an
ancient and universal one, probably arising from the many
weird sounds and echoes which are heard in them, and the
perpetual gloom. Sometimes the haunting spectres are
gigantic creatures with frightful fiery eyes. Such was the
German " Bergmönch, a terrible figure in the garb of a
monk, who could, however, appear in ordinary human
shape to those towards whom he was well-disposed."
Frequently weird knockings are heard in the *mines*. In
Germany these are attributed to the Kobolds, small black
beings of a malicious disposition. White hares or rabbits
are also seen at times. The continual danger attending the
life underground is productive of many supernatural
" warnings," which generally take the form of mysterious
voices. In the Midland Counties of England the " Seven
Whistlers " are well known and their warnings solemnly
attended to. A light blue flame settling on a full coal-tub
was called " Bluecap," and his work was to move the coal-
tub towards the trolley-way. Bluecap did not give his
services for nothing. Every fortnight his wages were left
in a corner of the *mine*, and duly appropriated. A more
mischievous elf was " Cutty Soames," who would cut the
traces, or soams, yoking an assistant putter to the tub.
Basilisks, whose terrible eyes would strike the miner dead,
were another source of dread to the worker underground.
These, as well as the other mysterious foes who dealt fatal
blows, may be traced to the dreaded, but by no means
ghostly, fire-damp. *Mines* of the precious metals are still
more jealously guarded by the supernatural beings. Gnomes
the creatures of the earth-element, are the special guardians
of subterranean treasure, and they are not over-anxious
that their province be disturbed. *Mines* containing
precious stones are equally well looked after. The Indians
of Peru declare that evil spirits haunt the emerald *mines*,
while a *mine* in the neighbourhood of Los Esmeraldos was
said to be guarded by a frightful dragon. It has also been
stated that the poisonous fumes and gases which ofttimes
destroy the lives of miners are baleful influences radiated
by evil spirits.

Mirabilis Liber : The greater part of this book is attributed
to Saint Césaire. It is a collection of predictions concerning
the saints and the sibyls. It is surprising to find in the

edition of 1522 a prophecy of the French Revolution. The
expulsion and abolition of the nobility, the violent death
of the king and queen, the persecution of the clergy, the
suppression of convents, are all mentioned therein, followed
by a further prophecy that the eagle coming from distant
lands would re-establish order in France.

Miraculum Mundi : (*See* **Glauber.**)

Mirendola, Giacomo Picus da : Italian Astrologer and
Kabalist (1463-1494). This astrologer's family played a
prominent part in a number of the civil wars which convulsed mediæval Italy, while they owned extensive lands
in the neighbourhood of Modena, the most valuable of their
possessions being a castle bearing their own name of
Mirandola ; and it was here, in the year 1463, that *Giacomo*
was born. He appears to have been something of an
Admirable Crichton, never showing any fondness for playing
children's games, but devoting himself to study from the
very outset ; and, according to tradition, before he was
out of his teens he had mastered jurisprudence and
mathematics, he had waded far into the seas of philosophy
and theology, and had even dabbled in those occult sciences
wherewith his name was destined to be associated afterwards. A boy of this kind naturally felt small inclination
to remain at home, and so it is not surprising to find that
Giacomo soon left his brothers to look after the family
estates, and proceeded to various universities in Italy and
France. While in the latter country his interest in astrology
and the like deepened apace, thanks partly to his making a
close study of the works of Raymond Lully ; and in 1486
Giacomo went to Rome, where he delivered a series of
lectures on various branches of science. While thus
engaged his erudition won high praise from some of his
hearers, but certain members of the clergy suspected him
of heresy, reported his doings to the Inquisition, and even
sought to have him excommunicated. The pope, however
was of course rather averse to quarrelling with a member
of so powerful a family as the Mirandolas, and accordingly
he waived violent measures, instead appointing a body
of Churchmen to argue with the scientist. A lengthy
altercation ensued, and throughout it the jury displayed
the most consummate ignorance, it being recorded, indeeds
that some of them imagined that " Kabal " was a man,
who had written against Christianity, and that the Kabalists were the disciples of this hypothetic person. *Giacomo*
must have been deeply chagrined by this stupidity on the
part of his opponents, he must have felt that to argue with
such people was utterly vain ; yet he published a defence of
the ideas and theories promulgated in his lectures, and in
1493 the pope, Alexander VI., brought the affair to a conclusion by granting the offender absolution. Thereupon
Mirandole went to live at Florence, and here he stayed
until his demise in 1494, occasionally essaying alchemy,
but chiefly busy with further kabalistic studies.

Apart from the *Apologia Pici Mirandoli* cited above,
Giacomo was author of several books of a theological
nature, the most important of these being his *Conclusiones
Philosophicæ, cabalisticæ et theologicæ*, published in 1486,
and his *Disputationes adversus Astrologiam Divinaticum*,
issued in 1495. His works appear to have been keenly
admired by such of his contemporaries as were not averse
to speculative thought, and it is interesting to find that a
collected edition of his writings was printed at Boulogne in
1496, and another at Venice two years later.

Mishna, The : A compilation of Hebrew oral traditions,
written about the end of the second century by a certain
Rabbi of Galilee. Its doctrines are said by the Jews to be
of great antiquity and they believe it to be the oral law
delivered by God to Moses, at the same time as he received
the written law. It forms the framework of the *Talmud*.
(*See* **Kabala.**)

Misraim, Rite of : (*See* **Cagliostro.**)

Mithraic Mysteries : (*See* **Mysteries.**)

Mitla, Subterranean Chambers of : (*See* **Subterranean Crypts.**)

Modern Times, The Socialist Community of : A community founded on Long Island, in 1851, which numbered among its members a good many spiritualists.

Moghrebi. Arab sorcerer : (*See* **Semites.**)

Mohanes : Shamans or medicine-men of the Indians of the Peruvian Andes. Joseph Skinner writing of them in his *State of Peru*, London 1805, says : " These admit an evil being, the inhabitant of the centre of the earth, whom they consider as the author of their misfortunes, and at the mention of whose name they tremble. The most shrewd among them take advantage of this belief, to obtain respect ; and represent themselves as his delegates. Under the denomination of *Mohanes*, or *Agoreros*, they are consulted even on the most trivial occasions. They preside over the intrigues of love, the health of the community, and the taking of the field. Whatever repeatedly occurs to defeat their prognostics, falls on themselves ; and they are wont to pay their deceptions very dearly. They chew a species of vegetable called *puripiri*, and throw it into the air, accompanying this act by certain recitals and incantations, to injure some, to benefit others, to procure rain, and the inundation of the rivers, or, on the other hand, to occasion settled weather, and a plentiful store of agricultural productions. Any such result having been casually verified on a single occasion, suffices to confirm the Indians in their faith, although they may have been cheated a thousand times. Fully persuaded that they cannot resist the influence of the *puripiri*, as soon as they know that they have been solicited by its means, they fix their eyes on the impassioned object, and discover a thousand amiable traits, either real or fanciful, which indifference had before concealed from their view.

" But the principal power, efficacy, and, it may be said misfortune, of the *Mohanes*, consist in the cure of the sick. Every malady is ascribed to their enchantments, and means are instantly taken to ascertain by whom the mischief may have been wrought. For this purpose the nearest relative takes a quantity of the juice of *floripondium*, and suddenly falls, intoxicated by the violence of the plant. He is placed in a fit posture to prevent suffocation, and on his coming to himself, at the end of three days, the *Mohan* who has the greatest resemblance to the sorcerer he saw in his visions, is to undertake the cure, or if, in the interim, the sick man has perished, it is customary to subject him to the same fate. When not any sorcerer occurs in the visions, the first *Mohan* they encounter has the misfortune to represent his image."

Methods of Medicine Men.—It cannot be denied, that the *Mohanes* have, by practice and tradition, acquired a profound knowledge of many plants and poisons, with which they effect surprising cures on the one hand, and do much mischief on the other ; but the mania of ascribing the whole to a preternatural virtue, occasions them to blend with their practice a thousand charms and superstitions. The most customary method of cure is to place two hammocks close to each other, either in the dwelling, or in the open air : in one of them the patient lies extended, and in the other the *Mohan*, or Agorero. The latter, in contact with the sick man, begins by rocking himself, and then proceeds by a strain *in falsetto*, to call on the birds, quadrupeds, and fishes, to give health to the patient. From time to time he rises on his seat, and makes a thousand extravagant gestures over the sick man, to whom he applies his powders and herbs, or sucks the wounded or diseased parts. If the malady augments, the Agorero, having been joined by many of the people, chants a short hymn, addressed to the soul of the patient, with this burden : " Thou must not go, thou must not go." In repeating this he is joined by the people, until at length a terrible clamour is raised, and augmented in proportion as the sick man becomes still fainter and fainter, to the end that it may reach his ears.

Molucca Beans as Amulets : (*See* **Fascination.**)

Monaciello, The : The *Monaciello* or Little Monk seems to have lived exclusively in that portion of Southern Italy called Naples. The precise place where he dwelt does not appear to be accurately known, but it is supposed to have been in the remains of Abbeys and Monasteries. When the *Monaciello* appeared to mortals, it was always at the dead of night ; and then only to those who were in sorest need, who themselves had done all that mortal could do to prevent or alleviate the distress that had befallen them, and after all humain aid had failed. Then it was that the Monk appeared, and mutely beckoning them to follow, he led them to where treasure was concealed—stipulating no conditions for its expenditure, demanding no promise of repayment, exacting no duty or service in return. Men have vainly asked, was it actual treasure he gave, or did it merely appear so to the external senses, to be changed into leaves or stones when the day and the occasion of its requirement had passed ? And if actual treasure, how did it come in the place of its concealment, and by whom was it there deposited ?

In Germany, the wood-spirit Rubezahl performed similar acts of beneficence and kindness to poor and deserving persons and the money he gave proved to be, or passed for the current coin of the realm ; while in Ireland, the O'Donoghue, who dwelt beneath the waters of an inland lake, and rode over its surface on a steed white as the foam of its waves, distributed treasures that proved genuine to the good, but spurious to the undeserving.

Monad is a theosophical term which literally means a unit (Greek Monas). The *Monad* is frequently described as a " Divine Spark," and this impression is particularly apt, for it is a part of the Logos, the Divine Fire. The Logos has three aspects, Will, Wisdom and Activity, and, since the *Monad* is part of the Logos, it also has these three aspects It abides continually in its appropriate world, the monadic, but, that the divine evolutionary purposes may be carried out, its ray is borne downwards through the various spheres of matter when the outpouring of the third life wave takes place. It first passes into the Spiritual Sphere by clothing itself with an atom of spiritual matter and thus manifests itself in an atomic body, as a spirit possessing three aspects. When it passes into the next sphere, the Intuitional, it leaves its aspect of Will behind and in the Intuitional Sphere, appears in an Intuitional body as a spirit possessing the aspects of Wisdom and Activity. On passing in turn, from this sphere to the next the higher mental, it leaves the aspect of Wisdom behind, and appears in a casual body as a spirit possessing the aspect of activity. To put this somewhat abstruse doctrine in another form, the *Monad* has, at this stage, manifested itself in three spheres. In the spiritual it has transfused spirit with Will, in the Intuitional it has transfused spirit with Wisdom, and in the higher Mental it has transfused spirit with Activity or Intellect, and it is now a human ego, corresponding approximately to the common term " soul," an ego which, despite all changes, remains the same until eventually the evolutionary purpose is fulfilled and it is received back again into the Logos. From the higher mental sphere the *Monad* descends to the lower mental sphere and appears in a mental body as possessing mind, then betakes itself to the astral sphere and appears in the astral body as possessing emotions, and finally to the hhysical sphere and appears in a physical body as possessing vitality. These three lower bodies, the mental, the astral, and the physical, constitute the human personality which dies at death and is renewed when the *Monad*, in fulfilment of the process of reincarnation, again manifests itself in these bodies. (*See* **Theosophy, Evolution, Sphere, Life Waves, Monadic Sphere, Logos.**)

Monen : A Kabalistic term covering that branch of magic which deals with the reading of the future by the computation of time and observance of the heavenly bodies. It thus includes astrology.

Money : *Money* which comes from the devil is of poor quality, and such wealth, like the fairy-money, generally turns to earth, or to lead, toads, or anything else worthless or repulsive. " A youth," says Gregory of Tours, " received a piece of folded paper from a stranger, who told him that he could get from it as much *money* as he wished, so long as he did not unfold it. The youth drew many gold pieces from the papers, but at length curiosity overcame him, he unfolded it and discovered within the claws of a cat and a bear, the feet of a toad and other repulsive fragments, while at the same moment his wealth disappeared." In popular superstition it is supposed that if a person hear the cuckoo for the first time with *money* in his pocket, he shall have some all the year, while if he greet the new moon for the first time in the same fortunate condition, he shall not lack *money* throughout the month.

Mongols : (*See* **Siberia.**)

Monk : A medium. (*See* **Spiritualism.**)

Moo : Queen of Yucatan. (*See* **Atlantis.**)

Moors : (*See* **Arabs.**)

Mopses, The : A secret association imported into Germany, which celebrated the rites of the gnostic Sabbath. It replaced the Kabalistic " goat " by the Hermetic " dog " as an object of worship. The candidate for the order was brought into the circle of adepts with the eyes bandaged in the midst of a great uproar, and after saluting the idol was initiated. The sign of recognition was a grimace. The whole doctrine of the society was that of black magic. The *Mopses* recruited only among Catholics, and for the oath at reception they substituted a solemn engagement on honour to reveal no secrets of the order,—the practices of which much resembled the Sabbath of mediæval sorcerers.

Morelle, Paolo : (*See* **Italy.**)

Morgan, Professor De : (*See* **Spiritualism.**)

Morgan le Fay : Sister of Arthur and wife of King Urien of Gore. Arthur gave into her keeping the scabbard of his sword Excalibur, but she gave it to Sir Accolon whom she loved and had a forged scabbard made. Arthur, however, recovered the real sheath, but was again deceived by her. She figures as a Queen of the Land of Faerie and as such appears in French and Italian romance. It was she who, on one occasion, threw Excalibur into a lake. She usually presents her favourites with a ring and retains them by her side as does Venus in Tannhaüser. Her myth is a parallel of that of Eos and Tithonus and is probably derived from a sun and dawn myth.

Morien : It is commonly supposed that *Morien*, or Morienus as he is sometimes styled, was born at Rome in the twelfth century, and it is also reported that, like Raymond Lully and several other early chymists, he combined evangelical ardour with his scientific tastes. While still a mere boy, and resident in his native city, *Morien* became acquainted with the writings of Adfar, the Arabian philosopher, and gradually the youth's acquaintance with these developed into tense admiration, the result being that he became filled with the desire to make the personal acquaintance of the author in question. Accordingly he bade adieu to Rome and set out for Alexandria, this being the home of Adfar ; and, on reaching his destination, he had not to wait long ere gaining his desired end. The learned Arabian

accorded him a hearty welcome, and a little while afterwards the two were living together on very friendly terms, the elder man daily imparting knowledge to the younger, who showed himself a remarkably apt pupil. For some years this state of affairs continued, but at length Adfar died, and thereupon *Morien* left Alexandria and went to Palestine, found a retreat in the vicinity of Jerusalem, and began to lead a hermit's life there.

Meanwhile the erudition of the deceased Arabian acquired a wide celebrity, and some of his manuscripts chanced to fall into the hands of Kalid, Soldan of Egypt. He was a person of active and enquiring mind, and observing that, on the cover of the manuscripts, it was stated that the secret of the philosopher's stone was written within, he naturally grew doubly inquisitive. He found, however, that he himself could not elucidate the precious documents ; and therefore he summoned *illuminati* from far and near to his court at Cairo, and offered a large reward to the man who should discover the mystery at issue. An endless number of people presented themselves in consequence, but the majority of them were mere charlatans, and thus the Soldan was duped mercilessly.

Betimes news of these doings reached the ears of *Morien*. It incensed him to think that his old preceptor's wisdom and writings were being made a laughing-stock, so he decided that he must go to Cairo himself, and not only see justice done to Adfar's memory, but also seize what might prove a favourable opportunity of converting Kalid to Christianity. The Soldan was inclined to be cynical when the hermit arrived, nor would he listen to the latter's attacks on the Mahommedan faith ; yet he saw fit to grant *Morien* a house wherein to conduct researches, and here the alchemist worked for a long time, ultimately perfecting the elixir. He did not, withal, make any attempt to gain the proferred reward ; and instead he took his leave without the Soldan's cognizance, simply leaving the precious fluid in a vase on which he inscribed the suggestive words : " He who possess all has no need of others."

But Kalid was at a loss to know how to proceed further, and for a long time he made great efforts to find *Morien* and bring him again to his court. Years went by, and all search for the vanished alchemist proved vain ; but once, when the Soldan was hunting in the neighbourhood of Jerusalem, one of his servants chanced to hear of a hermit who was wont to create gold. Convinced that this must be none other than *Morien*, Kalid straightway sought him out ; so once more the two met, and again the alchemist made strenuous efforts to win the other from Mahommedanism. Many discussions took place between the pair, both speaking on behalf of their respective religions, yet Kalid showed no inclination to desert the faith of his fathers. And therefore *Morien* relinquished the quest in despair, but it is said that, on parting with the Soldan, he duly instructed him in the mysteries of the transcendent science.

Nothing is known about *Morien's* subsequent history, and the likelihood is that the rest of his days were spent quietly at his hermitage. He is credited with sundry alchemistic writings, said to have been translated from Arabic, but it need hardly be said that the ascription rests on the slenderest evidence. One of these works is entitled *Liber de Distinctione Mercurii Aquarum*, and it is interesting to recall that a manuscript copy thereof belonged to Robert Boyle, one of the founders of the Royal Society ; while another is entitled *Liber de Compositione Alchemiæ*, and this is printed in the first volume of *Bibliotheca Chemica Curiosa*. Yet better known than either of these, and more likely to be really from *Morien's* pen, is a third treatise styled *De Re Metallica, Metallorum Transumtatione, et occulta summague Antiquorum Medicine Libellus*, which was repeatedly published, the first edition appearing at Paris in 1559.

Morrell, Theobald : (*See* **Spiritualism.**)

Morse, J. J. : A well-known English trance or inspirational medium who began to practice about 1870. Early in his career the phenomenon of " elongation " was witnessed in connection with him, but these physical manifestations soon ceased, and he developed trance-speaking faculties of a high order, and delivered numerous eloquent discourses to spiritualists throughout the country.

Morzine, Devils of : (*See* **Switzerland.**)

Moses, Rev. William Stainton : One of the best known mediums connected with modern spiritualism, and probably, after Home, one of the most successful. He was born in 1839, at Donington, in Lincolnshire, the son of a school-master, and was educated at Bedford Grammar School and Exeter College, Oxford. He made good progress at the University, but before his final examination his health broke down, and he was forced to go abroad. On his return he graduated Master of Arts, and in 1863 was ordained. From that time until 1870 he was a curate, first in the Isle of Man and afterwards in Dorsetshire. Again his health gave way, and he was obliged to abandon parish work, and seek a change of occupation. In 1870 he became tutor to the son of Dr. and Mrs. Stanhope Speer, with whom he resided, and who were henceforth among his staunchest supporters. A year or two later he was appointed English master in University College School, but increasing ill-health compelled him to retire in 1899. Towards the close of his life *Mr. Moses* suffered greatly from depression and kindred nervous disorders. His life as a clergyman and as a schoolmaster was beyond reproach, and his duties were discharged in a way that won respect alike for his intelligence and efficiency.

His attention was first directed to spiritualism by the reading of R. Dale Owen's book on *The Debatable Land,* in 1872. He attended numerous *séances,* held by such mediums as Home, and soon afterwards he himself developed powerful mediumistic tendencies, and gave *séances* to the Speers and a few select friends. The best accounts of his sittings are those written by Dr. and Mrs. Speers who kept separate records of the performances, and there are occasional accounts by others who were admitted to the circle. The phenomena were at first confined to raps and levitations of furniture, but gradually the manifestations became more varied and more pronounced. Toilet articles in *Mr. Moses'* room moved about of themselves and formed a cross on his bed, " apports " of perfume, pincushions, pearls, and other articles were brought by the spirits, and the medium himself would float about the room. Towards the end of the year " spirit lights " began to make their appearance, and seem to have created a profound impression on the sitters, though to judge from the descriptions they give, it would seem that Mr. Podmore's explanation of " bottles of phosphorus " is not far from the truth. Musical instruments also were heard playing in the air, besides raps, thuds, and other noises.

Perhaps his most important manifestations, however, were the automatic writings published under the title of *Spirit Teachings.* These purported to come from several spirits, " Imperator," " Rector," and others, and were mostly of a theological caste. Though of a high ethical tendency, they evinced a departure from Christianity, and suggested the religion of spiritualism as the only rational human creed. Unlike many automatic writings *Mr. Moses'* productions were not written in extravagantly high-flown language, nor were they altogether meaningless. But it must be remembered that he was a man of education and not likely to fall into such errors.

Other work done by him in connection with Spiritualism

was his assistance in the founding of the British National Association of Spiritualism, and to serve on the Councils of the Psychological Society, and the Society for Psychical Research. He severed his connection with the latter body, however, because of the position they took up with regard to certain professional mediums. He was also president of the London Spiritual Alliance from 1884 onwards. Among his most popular works, besides *Spirit Teachings,* were *Psychography,* *Spirit Identity,* and *The Higher Aspects of Spiritualism.*

Why did *Stainton Moses* become a medium ? There are few questions more puzzling than this to the student of spiritual psychology. That professional mediums, and those private mediums who have anything to gain by their performances, should carry on deception from year to year, is comprehensible. But that a clergyman, who had hitherto led an uneventful and exemplary life, should deliberately and systematically practise a series of puerile tricks for the purpose of mystifying his friends, is certainly not so. We are forced to admit, then, either that his observers were victims to hallucination and self-deception, or that the phenomena he produced were genuine manifestations from the spirit-world.

Moss-Woman The : The Moss or Wood Folk, dwelt in the forests of Southern Germany. Their stature was small and their form strange and uncouth, bearing a strong resemblance to certain trees with which they flourished and decayed. They were a simple, timid, and inoffensive race, and had little intercourse with mankind ; approaching only at rare intervals the lonely cabin of the wood-man or forester, to borrow some article of domestic use, or to beg a little of the food which the good wife was preparing for the family meal. They would also for similar purposes appear to labourers in the fields which lay on the outskirts of the forests. A loan or gift to the Moss-people was always repaid manifold. But the most highly-prized and eagerly-coveted of all mortal gifts was a draught from the maternal breast to their own little ones ; for this they held to be a sovereign remedy for all the ills to which their natures were subject. Yet was it only in the extremity of danger that they could so overcome their natural diffidence and timidity as to ask this boon—for they knew that mortal mothers turned from such nurslings with disgust and fear. It would appear that the Moss or Wood folk also lived in some parts of Scandinavia. Thus are we told that in the churchyard of Store Hedding, in Zealand, there are the remains of an oak wood which were trees by day and warriors by night.

Mountain Cove Community, The : A spiritualistic *community* founded in *Mountain Cove,* Fayette Co., Virginia, in the autumn of 1851, under the leadership of the Rev. James Scott and the Rev. T. L. Harris. Both mediums had settled in Auburn in the previous year, and had obtained a considerable following. While Harris was absent in New York the command to form a *community* at *Mountain Cove* was given through the mediumship of Scott, and about a hundred persons accompanied him to Virginia. The members were obliged to deliver up all their possessions, again at the command of the spirits. Dissensions arose and pecuniary difficulties were experienced, and only the advent of T. L. Harris in the summer of 1852 saved the *community* from dissolution. However, the dissensions and difficulties remained, and early in 1853 the *community* finally broke up.

Muscle-reading : The concentration of thought on any particular object produces a tendency to muscular activity. Thus if a name be thought of the muscles of the larynx may range themselves as if for the pronunciation of that name. This is known as " subconscious whispering." Or there may be an unconscious movement towards the object in the mind. It is the interpretation of these involuntary movements by a second person, or percipient, that frequently passes for genuine telepathy. The thought-reading exhibited on the public platform, when it is not the result of fraud, may be in reality *muscle-reading*. The act of reading these slight muscular indications of the thoughts may be unconscious or instinctive—indeed, must be so, since they are much too fine to be perceived by the grosser consciousness.

Myers, Frederic William Henry (1843–1901) : Poet, essayist, and student of psychic science, was born at Keswick, Cumberland, and educated at Cheltenham and Cambridge. In 1865 he became classical lecturer there, but in 1872 abandoned this post for that of school inspector. . He published several volumes of poems and essays, some of the former of considerable beauty, though it is chiefly as an essayist that he is known. He has done excellent work in the region of psychic science, being one of the original group who founded the Society for Psychical Research in 1882, and remaining to the end of his life one of its most useful members. Though he did not belong to the sceptical school of which Mr. F. Podmore is the chief representative, *Mr. Myers'* view-point was decidedly not that of the average spiritualist. The evidence for the survival of the soul after death he found not in the somewhat puerile " spirit " manifestations, but in the *subliminal Consciousness*, that wide region that lies beneath the threshold of man's ordinary consciousness, wherein *Mr. Myers* believed to discern traces of unused faculties, clairvoyance, retro-cognition, precognition, telekinesia, and so on. All the phenomena of trance, hypnotism, automatism, and spiritualism he grouped together as phenomena of the subliminal consciousness. The results of his researches were embodied in a posthumous work entitled *Human Personality and its Survival of Bodily Death* (1903). He also wrote the introduction to Gurney's *Phantasms of the Living*. He died at Rome in 1901 and was buried at Keswick.

Myomancy was a method of divination by rats or mice and is supposed to be alluded to in Isaiah lxvi., 17. Their peculiar cries, or some marked devastation committed by them, was taken for a prognostic of evil. Ælian relates that Fabius Maximus resigned the dictatorship in consequence of a warning from these creatures ; and Cassius Flaminius, according to Varro, retired from the command of the cavalry for no greater reason. From Herodotus we learn that the army of Sennacherib, when he invaded Egypt was infested by mice in the night, and their quivers and bows gnawed in pieces ; in the morning, therefore, being without arms, they fled in confusion, and many of them were slain. Such a foreboding of evil could not very well be questioned, or its consequences averted, by the commander, but very different was the case when one of Cato's soldiers told him in affright that the rats had gnawed one of his shoes. Cato replied that the prodigy would have been much greater if the shoe had gnawed a rat ! Horapollo in his curious work on the Hieroglyphics of Egypt, describes the rat as a symbol of destruction, and, what is more to our purpose, the Hebrew name of this animal is from a root which signifies to separate, divide, or judge ; and it has been remarked by one of the commentators on Horapollo that the mouse has a finely discriminating taste. An Egyptian MS. in the " Bibliothèque Royale " at Paris, contains the representation of a soul going to judgment, in which one of the figures is depicted with the head of a rat and the well-known wig. It is understood that the Lybian rats and the mouse of Scripture are the same as the Arabian *jerboa*, which is characterised by a long tail, bushy at the end, and short fore-legs. The mice and emerods of gold, I. Sam. v., 6, 7, were essentially charms having a precise symbolic meaning.

Mysteries : From the Greek work *muein*, to shut the mouth, and *mustes* an initiate : a term for what is secret or concealed. Although certain *mysteries* were undoubtedly part of the initiatory ceremony of the priests of ancient Egypt, we are ignorant of their exact trend, and the term is usually used in connection with certain semi-religious ceremonies held by various cults in ancient Greece. The *mysteries* were indeed secret cults, to which only certain initiated people were admitted after a period of preliminary preparation. After this initial period of purification came the mystic communication or exhortation, then the revelation to the neophyte of certain holy things, the crowning with the garlands, and lastly the communion with the deity. But the *mysteries* appear to have circled round the semi-dramatic representation or mystery-play of the life of a deity.

It has often been advanced as a likely theory to account for the prevalence of these mystic cults in Greece, that they are of pre-Hellenic origin, and that the Pelasgic aboriginal people of the country strove to conceal their religions from the the eyes of their conquerors. But against this has to be weighed the evidence that for the most part the higher offices of these cults were in the hands of aristocrats, who, it may be reasonably inferred, had but little to do with the inferior strata of the population which represented the Pelasgic peoples. Again, the divinities worshipped in the *mysteries* possess for the most part Greek names, and many of them are certainly gods evolved upon Hellenic soil at a comparatively late period. We find a number of them associated with the realm of the dead. The earth-god or goddess is in most countries often allied with the powers of darkness. It is from the underworld that grain arises, and therefore we are not surprised to find that Demeter, Ge, and Aglauros, are identified with the underworld. But there were also the mysteries of Artemis, of Hecate, and the Cherites,—some of which may be regarded as forms of the great earth-mother.

The worships of Dionysus, Trophonious, and Zagreus were also of a mysterious nature. The Eleusinian and Orphic *mysteries* are undoubtedly those of most importance to the occult student ; and from the results of archæology, such as vase-painting and so forth, we have been able to glean some general idea of the trend of these. That is not to say that the heart of the mystery is revealed to us by any such illustrations, but these supplemented by what the Christian fathers were able to glean regarding these mystic cults, enable us to push our investigations in the proper quarters. Important as such matter is, however, it is extremely slight in character.

Eleusis.—The *mysteries* of Eleusis had for their primal adoration Demeter, Kore or Persephone,—the mother and the daughter—whose myth is too well-known to require repetition here. Pluto, the third figure in the drama is so unimportant as to be relegated to the background. Other " nameless " divinities appear to have been associated with these, under the name of " the gods " and " the goddesses " ; but the theory that those are supposed to descend from an aboriginal period, when gods were nameless, is too absurd for discussion. The nameless god is of no value to anyone, not even a savage, and a mere nodding acquaintance with mythological science is surely sufficient to show that such nameless gods are merely those whose higher names are hidden and unspoken. In Egypt, for example, the concept of the Concealed Name was extremely common. The " name of power " of a god, if discovered, bestowed on the discoverer sway over that deity, and we must therefore dismiss the idea of the nameless divinities of Eleusis as not in accordance with mythological fact. A more probable view is that which would make these gods later titles of the married pair

Pluto and Kore; but this, in view of the facts just stated, is also unlikely. Dionysus is also a figure of some importance in the Eleusinian mystery, and it has been thought that Orphic influence brought about his presence in the cult; but traces of Orphic doctrine have not been discovered in what is known of the *mysteries*. A more baffling personality in the great ritual drama is that of Iacchus, who appears to be none other than Dionysus under another name. But Dionysus or Iacchus does not appear to be a primary figure of the mystery.

We find in early Greek legends allusions to the sacred character of the Eleusinian *mysteries*. From the fifth century their organisation was in the hands of the Athenian city,—the royal ruler of which undertook the general management, along with a committee of supervision. The rites took place at the city of Eleusis, and were celebrated by a hereditary priesthood, the Eumolpedie. They alone, or rather their high priest, could penetrate into the innermost holy of holies; but there were also priestesses and female attendants on the goddesses.

The celebration of the *mysteries*, so far as can be gleaned, was somewhat as follows: In the month of September, the Eleusinian Holy Things were taken from the sacred city to Athens, and placed in the Eleusinion. These probably consisted to some extent of small statues of the goddesses. Three days afterwards the catechumens assembled to hearken to the exhortation of one of the priests, in which those who were for any reason unworthy of initiation were solemnly warned to depart. All must be Greeks or Romans above a certain age, and women and even slaves were admitted; but foreigners and criminals might not partake. The candidates were questioned as to their purification, and especially as regards the food which they had eaten during that period. After this assembly, they betook themselves to the sea-shore and bathed in the sea, being sprinkled afterwards with the blood of pigs. A sacrifice was offered up, and several days afterwards the great Eleusinian procession commenced its journey along the sacred way, its central figure being a statue of Iacchus. Many shrines were visited on the way to Eleusis, where, upon their arrival, they celebrated a midnight orgy.

It is difficult to come at what occurred in the inner circle; but there appear to have been two grades in the celebration, and we know that a year elapsed before a person who had achieved one grade became fit for election to the higher. Regarding the actual ritual in the hall of mystery, a great deal of controversy has taken place, but it is certain that a dramatic representation was the central point of interest, the chief characters in which were probably Demeter and Kore, and that the myth of the lost daughter and the sorrowing mother was enacted before a highly-impressed audience. It has been stated that the birth of Iacchus was announced during the ceremony; but this has not been handed down to us on good authority. Of scenic display, there was probably little or none, as excavation has proved that there was not room for it, and we find nothing regarding scenery in the accounts presented in many inscriptions; but the apparel of the actors was probably most magnificent, and was heightened by the Rembrandtesque effect of gloom and torchlight.

But certain sacred symbols were also displayed before the eyes of the elect. These appear to have been small idols of the goddesses, of great antiquity and sanctity. We know that the original symbols of deity are jealously guarded by many savage priesthoods. For example, the Uapes of Brazil keep careful watch over the symbols of Jurupari, their god, and these are shown only to the initiated—any woman who casts eyes on them being instantly poisoned. It is also stated by Hippolytus that the ancients were shown a cut corn stalk, the symbol of Demeter and

Kore. This, however, can hardly be trusted any more than the theory that the Eleusinians worshipped the actual corn as a clan totem. Corn as a totem is not unknown elsewhere, as for example in Peru, where the *cconopa* or godlings of the maize fields were probably originally totemic; and we know that amongst savage people totemism often carries in its train the concept of the full-fledged mystery. But if the Eleusinian corn was a totem, it was certainly the only corn totem known to Greece, and corn totems are rare. The totem has usually initiated with the hunting condition of man: when he arrives at the agricultural stage we generally find that a fresh pantheon has slowly evolved, in which full-fledged gods took the place of the old totemic deities. The corn appears to him as a living thing. It is growth, and within it resides a spirit. Therefore the deity which is evolved from this concept is more likely to be of animistic than of totemistic origin.

The neophyte was then made one with the deity, by partaking of holy food or drink. It will be recalled that when Persephone reached the dark shores of Hades she partook of the food of the dead—thus rendering it impossible for her to return. Once the human soul eats or drinks in Hades, it may not return to earth. This belief is universal, and it is highly probable that it was symbolised in the Eleusinian *mysteries*. There was nothing, however, particularly secret about this sacrament, as it is painted on many vases which have been brought to light. A great deal of the ritual undoubtedly partook of the character of agricultural magic,—a description of sympathetic sorcery. Among barbarians the medicine-man sprinkles water over the soil to incite the rain-spirit to do likewise. It is not long ago since, in the Isle of Mull, a long carved stone in a certain churchyard was filled with water, until the depressions upon it overflowed, to symbolise a well-watered country. All sorts of imitative rites took place on similar occasions—most of which will be familiar to students of folklore. It has been thought that the token of the growing corn may have served as an emblem of man's resurrection, and the fact that most persons approach the Eleusinian *mysteries* for the purpose of ensuring themselves a happy immortality would go far to prove this. M. Foucart has ingeniously put forward the theory that the object of the Eleusinian *mysteries* was much the same as that of the Egyptian *Book of the Dead*,—to provide the initiates with elaborate rules for avoiding the dangers of the underworld, and to instruct them in the necessary magical formulæ. But it does not appear than any such purpose was attained in the *mysteries*; and we know of no magic formulæ recited in connection with them. Friendship with the Holy Mother and Daughter was to the Eleusinian votary the chief assurance of immortality.

A great many offshoots of the Eleusinian cult were established in several parts of Greece.

Dionysiac.—The most important cult next to the Eleusinian was the Orphic, which probably arose in Phrygia, and which came to be associated with the name of Dionysus, originally a god of vegetation, who was of course also a divinity of the nether world. In this case, it was also desired to enter into communion with him, that immortality might be assured. His celebrations were marked by orgies of a bacchic description, in which it was thought that the neophyte partook for the nonce of the character and the power of the deity himself. The rites of the cult of Dionysus were on a much lower grade than those of Eleusis, and partook more of the barbarian element, and the devouring of an animal victim was supposed to symbolise the incarnation, death and resurrection of the divinity. Later the Dionysiac *mysteries* became purified, but always retained something of their earlier hysteric character. The cult possessed a fairly wide propaganda, and does not appear to have been regarded by the sages of its time with great friendliness. The golden tablets relating to the Orphic mystery found in tombs in Greece, Crete and Italy, contain fragments of a sacred hymn. As early as the third century B.C. it was buried with the dead as an amulet to protect him from the dangers of the underworld, and the fragments bear upon them incantations of a magical character.

Attis and Sybele.—These *mysteries* arrived at a later period on Hellenic soil. Passionate and violent in the extreme, they yet gained considerable sway in a more degenerate age, and communion with the deity was usually attained by bathing in blood in the *taurobolium* or by the letting of blood.

These Phrygian *mysteries* were full of the conception of the re-birth of the god Attis, who was also of an agrarian character ; and in brief it may be said of these mystic cults as a whole that they were primarily barbarian agricultural rites to some extent intellectualised.

Mithraic Mysteries.—The Mithraic cult was of Persian origin, Mithra, a personification of Light being worshipped in that country some five hundred years before the Christian era. Carried into Asia Minor by small colonies of magi, it was largely influenced by the religions with which it was brought into contact. Chaldean Astrology contributed much of the occult traditions surrounding the creed of the Sun-god, while to a certain extent it became hellenized when the Magi strove to bring the more barbaric portion of their dogma and its usages into harmony with the Hellenic ideal. To the art of Greece also it owed that ideal representation of Mithra Tauroctonous which formed the central object in the temples of the cult. The wide geographical area it traversed and the immense influence thus exercised was, however, due to the Romans. The rites originally reached Rome, Plutarch tells us, through the agency of Cilician priates conquered and taken there by Pompey. Another source, doubtless, was through the large number of Asiatic slaves employed in Roman households. Again the Roman soldiery must have carried the Mithraic cult to Rome as they certainly were the means of its diffusion, as far north as the mountains of Scotland, and southwards to the borders of the Sahara Desert.

Mithraism may be said to have been the only living religion which Christianity found to combat. It was strong enough to exert a formative influence on certain Christian doctrines, such as those relative to the end of the world and the powers of hell. Mithra was essentially the divinity of beneficence. He was the genius of celestial light, endowing the earth with all its benefits. As in his character of the Sun he puts darkness to flight so by a natural transition he came to represent ethically truth and integrity, the sun of goodness which conquers the night of evil. To him was ascribed the character of Mediator betwixt God and man ; his creed promised a resurrection to a future life of happiness and felicity. Briefly the story of Mithra is this : His life he owed to no mortal mother. In the gloom of a cavern Mithra sprang to being from the heart of a rock, seen by none but humble shepherds. He grew in strength and courage, excelling all, and used his powers to rid the world of evil. Of all his deeds of prowess, however, that one became the central motive of his cult wherein, by slaying a bull, itself possessed of divine potentialities, he dowered the earth with fruitfulness and miraculous crops. From the spinal cord of the bull sprang the wheat of man's daily bread, from its blood the vine, source of the sacred drink of the *Mysteries*, and from its seed all the different species of useful animals. After this beneficent deed Mithra ruled in the heavens, yet still keeping watch and ward over mankind, granting the petitions asked in his name. Those who followed him, who were initiated into his *mysteries* passed under his divine

protection, especially after death when he would rescue their souls from the powers of darkness which fain would seize upon the dead. And yet again Mithra would come, when the earth was failing in her life-sustaining powers, and again he would slay a divine bull and give to all abundant life and happiness.

The *mysteries* and rites inspired the votaries with awe while giving to their hearts hope of a future life, transcending that which they had known. The temples, mithræums as they were called, were either built underground or were caves and grottoes in the depths of dark forests, symbolising the birthplace of their god. Among his worshippers were slaves and soldiery, high officials and dignitaries, all mingling fraternally in a religion which called them Brethren. The rites were of magical significance. In order to bring their lives into closer communion with the divinity of Mithra, the neophytes must pass through seven degrees of initiation successively assuming the names of Raven, Occult, Soldier, Lion, Persian, Runner of the Sun and Father. Each of these grades carried with them symbolic garments and masks, donned by the celebrants. The masks represented birds and animals and would seem to indicate the existence of belief in the doctrine of metempsychosis ; or perhaps they were a remnant of totemic belief. An almost ascetic habit of life was demanded, including prolonged fasting and purification. The oath of silence regarding the rites was taken, and before entering the higher grades a ceremony called the Sacrament was held where consecrated bread and wine were partaken of. Dramatic trials of strength, faith and endurance were gone through by all, a stoical attitude and unflinching moral courage being demanded as sign of fitness in the participant. The drinking of the sacred wine, and the baptism of blood, were supposed to bring to the initiate not only material benefit but wisdom ; they gave power to combat evil, the power to attain to an immortality such as that of their god. An order of priests were connected with this cult, who faithfully carried on the occult tradition and usages, such as that of initiation, the rites of which were arduous ; the tending of a perpetual fire on the altars ; prayers to the Sun at dawn, noon and evening. There were sacrifices and libations, musical rites including long psalmodies and mystic chants. The days of the week were each sacred to a Planet, the day of the Sun being held especially holy. There were seasonal festivals, the birth of the Sun being solemnized on the 25th of December, and the equinoxes were days of rejoicing, while the initiations were held preferably in the spring, in March or April. It is believed that in the earliest days of the cult some of the rites were of a savage and barbaric character, especially the sacrificial element, but these, as indicated, were changed and ennobled as the beneficence of Mithra took precedence of his warlike prowess. The Mithraic brotherhoods took temporal interests as well as spiritual ones under their care, were in fact highly organised communities, including trustees, councils, senates, attorneys and patrons, people of high status and wealth. The fact of belonging to such a body gave to the initiate, be he of noble birth or but a slave, a sense of brotherhood and comradeship which was doubtless a powerful reason of the ascendancy which the Mithraic cult gained over the Roman army, whose members, dispersed to the ends of the earth in lonely solitudes amid wild and barbaric races, would find in this feeling of fraternity, this sharing in the worship and ritual of the Sun-god, an infinite comfort and solace.

Mysteries of the Pentateuch : (*See* **Kabala.**)

Mystic City of God : (*See* **Agreda, Marie of.**)

Mysticism : The attempt of man to attain to the ultimate reality of things and enjoy communion with the Highest. *Mysticism* maintains the possibility of intercourse with God, not by means of revelation, or the ordinary religious channels, but by dint of introspection, culminating in the feeling that the individual partakes of the divine nature. *Mysticism* has been identified with pantheism by some authorities; but it differs from pantheism in that its motive is religious. But *mysticism* is greatly more speculative than ordinary religion and instead of commencing its flights of thought from the human side, starts from the divine nature rather than from man. The name *mysticism* cannot be applied to any particular system. Whereas religion teaches submission of the will and the ethical harmonies of life, *mysticism* strains after the realisation of a union with God Himself. The mystic desires to be as close to God as possible, if not indeed part of the Divine Essence Itself; whereas the ordinary devotee of most religious systems merely desires to walk in God's way and obey His will.

Mysticism may be said to have originated in the East, where it probably evolved from kindred philosophic concepts. The unreality of things is taught by most Asiatic religions, especially by Brahminism and Buddhism, and the sense of the worth of human personality in these is small (*See* **India**). The Sufis of Persia may be said to be a link between the more austere Indian mystics and those of Europe. We find Sufism first arising in the ninth century among the Persian Mahommedans, probably as a protest against the severe monotheism of their religion; but in all likelihood more ancient springs contribute to its revival. In the Persia of Hafiz and Saadi, pantheism abounded, and their magnificent poetry is read by Mahommedans as having a deep mystical significance, although for the most part it deals with love and intoxication. In all probability more is read into these poems than exists beneath the surface, but at the same time it is certain that many of them exhibit the fervour of souls searching for communion with the highest. The rise of Alexandrian Neoplatonism (q.v.) was the signal for the introduction of *mysticism* to a waiting Europe, and as this stage of *mysticism* has been fully reviewed in a special article on the subject, there is no necessity to follow it here. It may be mentioned, however, that Neoplatonism made a definite mark upon early Christianity, and we find it mirrored in many of the patristic writings of the sixteenth century. It was Erigena who in the ninth century transmitted to Europe the so-called writings of Dionysius the Areopagite thus giving rise to both the scholasticism and *mysticism* of the middle ages. Erigena based his own system upon that of Dionysius. This was the so-called "negative theology" which places God above all categories and designates Hmi as Nothing, or The Incomprehensible Essence from which the world of primordial causes is eternally created. This creation is the Word or Son of God, in Whom all substantial things exist; but God is the beginning and end of everything. On this system Christian *mysticism* may be said to have been founded with little variation. With Erigena reason and authority were identical, and in this he agrees with all speculative mystics; whereas scholasticism is characterised by the acceptance by reason of a given matter which is pre-supposed even when it cannot be understood. It seemed to Erigena that in the scholastic system religious truth was external to the mind, while the opposite view was fundamental to *mysticism*. That is not to say that *mysticism* according to Erigena is a mere subordination of reason to faith. *Mysticism* indeed places every confidence in human reason, and it is essential that it should have the unity of the human mind with the divine as its main tenet; but it accepts nothing from without, and it posits the higher faculty of reason over the realisation of absolute truth.

Mediæval mysticism may be said to have originated from a reaction of practical religion against dialectics in which the true spirit of Christianity was then enshrined. Thus St. Bernard opposed the dry scholasticism of Abelard. His *mysticism* was profoundly practical, and deals chiefly with the means by which man may attain the knowledge of God. This is to be accomplished through contemplation and withdrawal from the world. Thus asceticism is the soul of mediæval mysticism; but he mistakenly averred regarding self-love that it is proper to love ourselves for God's sake, or because God loved us; thus merging self-love in love for God. We must, so to speak, love ourselves in God, in Whom we ultimately lose ourselves. Thus St. Bernard is almost Buddhistic, and indeed his *mysticism* is of the universal type. Perhaps Hugh of St. Victor, a contemporary of St. Bernard's, did more to develop the tenets of *mysticism*; and his monastery of Augustinians near Paris became, under his influence, a great centre of *mysticism*. One of his apologists, Richard of St. Victor, declares that the objects of mystic contemplation are partly above reason, and partly, as regards intuition, contrary to reason. The protagonists of this theory, all of whom issued from the same monastery, were known as the Victorines, who put up a stout fight against the dialecticians and schoolmen. Bonaventura, who died in 1274, was a disciple of this school, and believer in the faculty of mystic intuition. In the twelfth and thirteenth centuries, the worldliness of the church aroused much opposition amongst laymen, and its cold formalism created a reaction towards a more spiritual régime. Many sects arose such as the Waldenses, the Kathari, and the Beguines, all of which strove to infuse into their teachings a warmer enthusiasm than that which burned in the heart of the church of their time. In Germany, *mysticism* made great strides, and Machthild of Magdeburg, and Elizabeth of Thuringia, were, if not the originators of *mysticism* in Germany, perhaps the earliest supporters of it. Joachim of Flores and Amalric of Bena wrote strongly in favour of the reformed church, and their writings are drenched with mystical terms, derived for the most part from Erigena. Joachim mapped out the duration of the world into three ages, that of the Father, that of the Son, and that of the Spirit,—the first of which was to commence with the year 1260, and to be inaugurated by the general adoption of the life monastic and contemplative. A sect called The New Spirit, or The Free Spirit, became widespread through northern France, Switzerland and Germany; and these did much to infuse the spirit of *mysticism* throughout the German land.

It is with Eckhart, who died in 1327, that we get the juncture of *mysticism* with scholastic theology. Of his doctrine it has been said: "The ground of your being lies in God. Reduce yourself to that simplicity, that root, and you are in God. There is no longer any distinction between your spirit and the divine,—you have escaped personality and finite limitation. Your particular, creature self, as a something separate and dependent on God, is gone. So also, obviously, your creaturely will. Henceforth, therefore, what seems an inclination of yours is in fact the divine good pleasure. You are free from law. You are above means. The very will to do the will of God is resolved into that will itself. This is the Apathy, the Negation, the Poverty, he commends. With Eckhart personally this self-reduction and deification is connected with a rigorous asceticism and exemplary moral excellence Yet it is easy to see that it may be a merely intellectual process, consisting in a man's thinking that he is thinking himself away from his personality. He declares the appearance of the Son necessary to enable us to realize our sonship; and yet his language implies that this realization is the perpetual incarnation of that Son—does, as it were, constitute him. Christians are accordingly not less the sons of God by grace than is Christ by nature. Believe yourself divine, and the Son is brought forth in you. The Saviour and the saved are dissolved together in the blank absolute substance.''

With the advent of the black death, a great spirit of remorse swept over Europe in the fourteenth century, and a vast revival of piety took place. This resulted in the foundation in Germany of a society of Friends of God, whose chief object was to strengthen each other in intercourse with the Creator. Perhaps the most distinguished of these were Tauler, and Nicolas of Basle, and the society numbered many inmates of the cloister, as well as wealthy men of commerce and others. Ruysbroeck (q.v.) the great Dutch mystic, was connected with them ; but his *mysticism* is perhaps more intensely practical than that of any other visionary. It is the machinery by which the union with God is to be effected which most attracts him. In Ruysbroeck's life-time a mystical society arose in Holland called the Brethren of the Common Lot, who founded an establishment at which Groot dispensed the principles of *mysticism* to Radewyn and Thomas à Kempis.

The attitude of *mysticism* at the period of the Reformation is peculiar. We find a mystical propaganda pretending to be sent forth by a body of Rosicrucians denouncing Roman Catholicism in the fiercest terms, and we also observe the spirit of *mysticism* strongly within those bodies which resisted the coldness and formalism of the Roman Church. On the other hand, however, we find the principles of Luther strongly opposed by some of the most notable mystics of his time. But the Reformation past, *mysticism* went on its way, divided, it is true, so far as the outward

theological principles of its votaries were concerned, but strongly united in its general principles.

It is with Nicholas of Kusa, who died in 1464, that *mysticism* triumphs over scholasticism. Nicolas is the protagonist of super-knowledge, or that higher igno.:ance which is the knowledge of the intellect in contra-distincton to the mere knowledge of the understanding. His doctrines coloured those of Giordano Bruno and his theosophy certainly preceded that of Paracelsus. The next great name we meet with in *mysticism* is that of Boehme (q.v.), who once and for all systematised German philosophy. The Roman Church produced many mystics of note in the sixteenth and seventeenth centuries, notably Francis of Sales, Mme. Guyon and Molinos,—the last two of which were the protagonists of Quietism, which set forth the theory that there should be no pleasure in the practice of *mysticism*, and that God did not exist for the enjoyment of man. Perhaps the greatest students of Boehme were William Law (q.v.), 1686 to 1761, and Saint Martin (q.v.), 1743 to 1803.

But all *mysticism* is not necessarily identified with sect, although undoubtedly its strongholds in this country to-day are to be found in certain circles of the Church of England. There are still with us mystics who, professing no definite theological tenets, are yet mystics in virtue of their desire for unity with, or proximity to the Deity, by what they call " magical " methods. These are obscure, and are probably the result of personal experiences, which it is not given to everyone to comprehend ; but which,. nevertheless, may be very real indeed. For a good summary of such *mysticism* the reader is referred to Mr. A. E. Waite's *Azoth or the Star in the East* ; *See* also Evelyn Underhill's *Mysticism* and *The Mystic Way*.

N

" N " Rays : (*See* **Emanations.**)

Nagualism : (*See* **Mexico.**)

Names, Magical : (*See* **Egypt.**)

Napellus : A plant with narcotic properties, with which Van Helmont experimented. He says that, having on one occasion roughly prepared the root, he tasted it with his tongue, and in a very short time found that the centre of thought and intellect was situated in the pit of his stomach. An unusual clarity and distinctness of thought rendered the experience a pleasant one, and he sought on future occasions to repeat it by the same means, but without success. After about two hours he felt a slight dizziness and thereupon thought in the normal fashion with his brain. But throughout the strange experience he was conscious that his soul still remained in the brain as a governing power.

Napper, Dr., of Sandford in Buckinghamshire, who, according to Lilly " outwent Forman in physic and holiness of life, cured the falling-sickness perfectly by constellated rings, and some diseases by amulets." He was probably of the stock of the Scottish Napiers though his family had been settled in England since Henry the Eighth's time.

Nastrond : The Scandinavian and Icelandic Hell, said to be of an icy temperature. It lies in the lowest depths of Niflheim ; it is a " dark abode far from the sun ; " its gates face " the cutting north ; " " its walls are formed of wreathed snakes, and their venom is ever falling like rain." It is surrounded by dark and poisonous streams, and Nidhog, the great dragon, who dwells beneath the central root of Ygdrassil, torments and gnaws the dead. Here it is that Loki is chained to a splintered rock, where the venom of the snake Skada falls on him unceasingly ; and it is believed that his shuddering is the cause of earthquakes.

Nat : An evil spirit. (*See* **Burma.**)

Nativities : (*See* **Astrology.**)

Natsaw : Burmese wizards. (*See* **Burma.**)

Nature Spirits or Elementals, according to theosophy, have bodies composed of the finer kinds of matter. There are countless hosts of them, divided into seven classes, which allowing for two unmanifested, belong to the ether, air, fire, water, and earth,—the last four being called by the Kabalists, sylphs, salamanders, undines, and gnomes respectively ; and at the head of each class is a deva or inferior god. *Nature spirits* work in unsuspected ways, sometimes lending their aid to human beings in the form of certain faculties, and those in the astral world are engaged in the creation of form out of the matter which the outpouring of the Logos has quickened, hence it is they who form minerals, flowers, and so on. These *nature spirits* of the astral worlds of course have bodies of astral matter, and they frequently from mischievous or other impulses, change the appearance of these bodies. They are just without the powers of ordinary vision, and many people of more acute vision can see them, while the action of drugs also may make them visible.

Navarez, Senor : (*See* **Spain.**)

Naylor, James : An English impostor of the seventeenth century, born in the diocese of York. He served for a time in the army, then joined the Quakers where his discourses gained for him a reputation for sanctity. Trading on the good opinion of the people, he resolved to set himself up for a sort of deity, and entered Bristol in 1656, mounted on a horse led by a man and a woman, while others ran behind chanting " Holy, holy, holy, is the god of Sabaoth." He was duly punished by having his tongue pierced with a hot iron, and his forehead marked with the letter " B " (blasphemer). This done, he was forced to ride into Bristol in disgrace, his face turned towards the horse's tail.

Ndembo, The : Or *Kita* is a secret society which has wide-spread ramifications on the lower Congo, and especially in the districts lying to the south of that river. Initiation is made through the ganga, or chief, who instructs the neophyte at a given signal suddenly to lie down as if dead. A shroud is spread over him, and he is carried off to an enclosure outside the village called *vela*, and is pronounced to have died a *Ndembo*. Perhaps twenty, thirty, or even fifty candidates " die " at the one time. It is then assumed that persons " dying " in this manner decay until only a single bone remains, and this the ganga takes charge of. The process varies from three months to as many years, and the ganga is supposed by art magic to bring every one of the dead back to life within that period. On a festival day of the *Ndembo*, the members march through the village in a grand procession amidst universal joy, carrying with them the persons who are supposed to have died. The neophytes who are supposed to have perished, comport themselves as if in reality they had come from another world. They take new names, pretend that everything in the terrestrial sphere is new to them, turn a deaf ear to their parents and relatives, and even affect not to know how to eat. They further desire to have everything they set eyes on, and if it is not granted to them immediately, they may fall upon the unhappy owner and beat and even kill him without any consequence to themselves ; as it is assumed that they are mere children in the affairs of the terrestrial sphere, and therefore know no better.

Those who have gone through this rite are called *Nganga*, or the " knowing ones," while the neophytes are designated *Vanga*. During their occupation of the *vela* they learn an esoteric language, which they constantly employ. Perhaps the best picture of their cult has been given by Bastian, who says :—

" The Great Nkissi (who here replaces the fetish) lives in the interior of the woodlands where nobody can see him. When he dies the Nganga carefully collect his bones in order to bring them back to life, and nourish them that they may again put on flesh and blood. But it is not well to speak about it. In the Ambamba country everybody must have died once, and when the Nganga (replacing the fetish-priest) shakes his calabash against a village, those men and youths whose hour is come fall into a state of lifeless torpor, from which they generally rise up in three days. But the man whom the Nkissi loves he carries off to the bush and often buries him for a series of years. When he again awakens to life, he begins to eat and drink as before, but his mind is gone, and the Nganga must himself educate him and instruct him in every movement, like the smallest child. At first that can only be done with the rod, but the senses gradually return, so that you can speak with him, and when his education is finished the Nganga takes him back to his parents. These would seldom recognise him but for the positive assurance of the Nganga, who at the same time reminds them of earlier occurrences. Whoever has not yet undergone the experience in Ambamba is universally despised, and is not allowed to join in the dances."

Necromancy : Or divination by means of the spirits of the dead, from the Greek words *nekros*, dead ; and *manteia*, divination. It is through its Italian form nigromancia that it came to be known as the "Black Art." With the Greeks it originally signified the descent into Hades in order to consult the dead rather than summoning the dead into the mortal sphere again. The art is of almost universal usage. Considerable difference of opinion exists among modern adepts as to the exact methods to be properly pursued in the necromantic art, and it must be borne in mind that *necromancy*, which in the Middle Ages was called sorcery, shades into modern spiritualistic practice. There is no doubt however, that *necromancy* is the touch-stone of occultism,

for if, after careful preparation the adept can carry through to a successful issue, the raising of the soul from the other world, he has proved the value of his art. It would be fruitless in this place to enter into a psychological discussion as to whether this feat is possible of accomplishment or not, and we will confine ourselves to the material which has been placed at our disposal by the sages of the past, who have left full details as to how the process should be approached.

In the case of a compact existing between the conjuror and the devil, no ceremony is necessary, as the familiar is ever at hand to do the behests of his masters. This, however, is never the case with the true sorcerer, who preserves his independence, and trusts to his profound knowledge of the art and his powers of command ; his object therefore is to " constrain" some spirit to appear before him, and to guard himself from the danger of provoking such beings. The magician, it must be understood always has an assistant, and every article named is prepared according to rules well known in the black art. In the first place they are to fix upon a spot proper for such a purpose ; which must be either in a subterraneous vault, hung round with black, and lighted by a magical torch ; or else in the centre of some thick wood or desert, or upon some extensive unfrequented plain, where several roads meet, or amidst the ruins of ancient castles, abbeys, monasteries, etc., or amongst the rocks on the sea shore, in some private detached churchyard, or any other solemn, melancholy place between the hours of twelve and one in the night, either when the moon shines very bright, or else when the elements are disturbed with storms of thunder, lightning, wind, and rain ; for, in these places, times, and seasons, it is contended that spirits can with less difficulty manifest themselves to mortal eyes, and continue visible with the least pain, in this elemental external world.

When the proper time and place is fixed on, a magic circle is to be formed, within which, the master and his associate are carefully to retire. The dimensions of the circle are as follow :—A piece of ground is usually chosen, nine feet square, at the full extent of which parallel lines are drawn one within the other, having sundry crosses and triangles described between them, close to which is formed the first or outer circle ; then, about half-a-foot within the same, a second circle is described, and within that another square correspondent to the first, the centre of which is the seat or spot where the master and associate are to be placed " The vacancies formed by the various lines and angles of the figure are filled up with the holy names of God, having crosses and triangles described between them. The reason assigned by magicians and others for the institution and use of circles, is, that so much ground being blessed and consecrated by such holy words and ceremonies as they make use of in forming it, hath a secret force to expel all evil spirits from the bounds thereof, and, being sprinkled with pure sanctified water, the ground is purified from all uncleanness ; besides, the holy names of God being written over every part of it, its force becomes so powerful that no evil spirit hath ability to break through it, or to get at the magician or his companion, by reason of the antipathy in nature they bear to these sacred names. And the reason given for the triangles is, that if the spirit be not easily brought to speak the truth, they may by the exorcist be conjured to enter the same, where, by virtue of the names of the essence and divinity of God, they can speak nothing but what is true and right. The circle, therefore, according to this account of it, is the principal fort and shield of the magician, from which he is not, at the peril of his life, to depart, till he has completely dismissed the spirit, particularly if he be of a fiery or infernal nature. Instances are recorded of many who perished by this means; particularly "Chiancungi," the famous Egyptian fortune-teller, who was so famous in England in the 17th century. He undertook for a wager, to raise up the spirit "Bokim," and having described the circle, he seated his sister Napula by him as his associate. After frequently repeating the forms of exorcism, and calling upon the spirit to appear, and nothing as yet answering his demand, they grew impatient of the business, and quitted the circle, but it cost them their lives; for they were instantaneously seized and crushed to death by that infernal spirit, who happened not to be sufficiently constrained till that moment, to manifest himself to human eyes."

There is a prescribed form of consecrating the magic circle, which we omit as unnecessary in a general illustration. The proper attire or "pontificalibus" of a magician, is an ephod made of fine white linen, over that a priestly robe of black bombazine, reaching to the ground, with the two seals of the earth drawn correctly upon virgin parchment, and affixed to the breast of his outer vestment. Round his waist is tied a broad consecrated girdle, with the names Ya, Ya,—Aie, Aaie,—Elibra,—Elchim,—Sadai, —Pah Adonai,—tuo robore,—Cinctus sum. Upon his shoes must be written Tetragrammaton, with crosses round about; upon his head a high-crowned cap of sable silk, and in his hand a Holy Bible, printed or written in pure Hebrew. Thus attired, and standing within the charmed circle, the magician repeats the awful form of exorcism; and presently, the infernal spirits make strange and frightful noises, howlings, tremblings, flashes, and most dreadful shrieks and yells, as the forerunner of their becoming visible. Their first appearance is generally in the form of fierce and terrible lions or tigers, vomiting forth fire, and roaring hideously about the circle; all which time the exorcist must not suffer any tremour of dismay; for, in that case, they will gain the ascendency, and the consequences may touch his life. On the contrary, he must summon up a share of resolution, and continue repeating all the forms of constriction and confinement, until they are drawn nearer to the influence of the triangle, when their forms will change to appearances less ferocious and frightful, and become more submissive and tractable. When the forms of conjuration have in this manner been sufficiently repeated, the spirits forsake their bestial shapes, and enter the human form, appearing like naked men of gentle countenance and behaviour, yet is the magician to be warily on his guard that they deceive him not by such mild gestures, for they are exceedingly fraudulent and deceitful in their dealings with those who constrain them to appear without compact, having nothing in view but to suborn his mind, or accomplish his destruction. With great care also must the spirit be discharged after the ceremony is finished, and he has answered all the demands made upon him. The magician must wait patiently till he has passed through all the terrible forms which announce his coming, and only when the last shriek has died away, and every trace of fire and brimstone has disappeared, may he leave the circle and depart home in safety. If the ghost of a deceased person is to be raised, the grave must be resorted to at midnight, and a different form of conjuration is necessary. Still another, is the infernal sacrament for "any corpse that hath hanged, drowned, or otherwise made away with itself;" and in this case the conjurations are performed over the body, which will at last arise, and standing upright, answer with a faint and hollow voice the questions that are put to it.

Eliphas Levi, in his *Ritual of Transcendent Magic* says that "evocations should always have a motive and a becoming end, otherwise they are works of darkness and folly, dangerous for health and reason." The permissible motive of an evocation may be either love or intelligence. Evoca-

tions of love require less apparatus and are in every respect easier. The procedure is as follows : "We must, in the first place, carefully collect the memorials of him (or her) whom we desire to behold, the articles he used, and on which his impression remains; we must also prepare an apartment in which the person lived, or otherwise one of a similar kind, and place his portrait veiled in white therein, surrounded with his favourite flowers, which must be renewed daily. A fixed date must then be observed, either the birthday of the person, or that day which was most fortunate for his and our own affection, one of which we may believe that his soul, however blessed elsewhere, cannot lose the remembrance; this must be the day for the evocation, and we must provide for it during the space of fourteen days. Throughout this period we must refrain from extending to anyone the same proofs of affection which we have the right to expect from the dead; we must observe strict chastity, live in retreat, and take only one modest and light collation daily. Every evening at the same hour we must shut ourselves in the chamber consecrated to the memory of the lamented person, using only one small light, such as that of a funeral lamp or taper. This light should be placed behind us, the portrait should be uncovered and we should remain before it for an hour, in silence; finally, we should fumigate the apartment with a little good incense, and go out backwards. On the morning of the day fixed for the evocation, we should adorn ourselves as if for a festival, not salute anyone first, make but a single repast of bread, wine, and roots, or fruits; the cloth should be white, two covers should be laid, and one portion of the bread broken should be set aside; a little wine should also be placed in the glass of the person we design to invoke. The meal must be eaten alone in the chamber of evocations, and in presence of the veiled portrait; it must be all cleared away at the end, except the glass belonging to the dead person, and his portion of bread, which must be placed before the portrait. In the evening, at the hour for the regular visit, we must repair in silence to the chamber, light a clear fire of cypress-wood, and cast incense seven times thereon, pronouncing the name of the person whom we desire to behold. The lamp must then be extinguished, and the fire permitted to die out. On this day the portrait must not be unveiled. When the flame is extinct, put more incense on the ashes, and invoke God according to the forms of the religion to which the dead person belonged, and according to the ideas which he himself possessed of God. While making this prayer we must identify ourselves with the evoked person, speak as he spoke, believe in a sense as he believed; then, after a silence of fifteen minutes, we must speak to him as if he were present, with affection and with faith, praying him to manifest to us. Renew this prayer mentally, covering the face with both hands; then call him thrice with a loud voice; tarry on our knees, the eyes closed and covered, for some minutes; then call again thrice upon him in a sweet and affectionate tone, and slowly open the eyes. Should nothing result, the same experiment must be renewed in the following year, and if necessary a third time, when it is certain that the desired apparition will be obtained, and the longer it has been delayed the more realistic and striking it will be.

"Evocations of knowledge and intelligence are made with more solemn ceremonies. If concerned with a celebrated personage, we must meditate for twenty-one days upon his life and writings, form an idea of his appearance, converse with him mentally, and imagine his answers; carry his portrait, or at least his name, about us; follow a vegetable diet for twenty-one days, and a severe fast during the last seven. We must next construct the magical oratory. This oratory must be invariably darkened; but if we operate in the daytime, we may leave a narrow aperture on the side where the sun will shine at the hour of the evocation, and place a triangular prism before the opening, and a crystal globe, filled with water, before the prism. If the operation be arranged for the night the magic lamp must be so placed that its single ray shall upon the altar smoke. The purpose of the preparations is to furnish the magic agent with elements of corporeal appearance, and to ease as much as possible the tension of imagination, which could not be exalted without danger into the absolute illusion of dream. For the rest, it will be easily understood that a beam of sunlight, or the ray of a lamp, coloured variously, and falling upon curling and irregular smoke, can in no way create a perfect image. The chafing-dish containing the sacred fire should be in the centre of the oratory, and the altar of perfumes close by. The operator must turn towards the east to pray, and the west to invoke ; he must be either alone or assisted by two persons preserving the strictest silence ; he must wear the magical vestments, which we have described in the seventh chapter, and must be crowned with vervain and gold. He should bathe before the operation, and all his under garments must be of the most intact and scrupulous cleanliness. The ceremony should begin with a prayer suited to the genius of the spirit about to be invoked and one which would be approved by himself if he still lived. For example, it would be impossible to evoke Voltaire by reciting prayers in the style of St. Bridget. For the great men of antiquity, we may see the hymns of Cleanthes or Orpheus, with the adjuration terminating the Golden Verses of Pythagoras. In our own evocation of Apollonius, we used the magical philosophy of Patricius for the ritual, containing the doctrines of Zoroaster and the writings of Hermes Trismegistus. We recited the Nuctemeron of Apollonius in Greek with a loud voice and added the following conjuration :—

" Vouchsafe to be present, O Father of All, and thou Thrice Mighty Hermes, Conductor of the Dead. Asclepius son of Hephaistus, Patron of the Healing Art ; and thou Osiris, Lord of strength and vigour, do thou thyself be present too. Arnebascenis, Patron of Philosophy, and yet again Asclepius, son of Imuthe, who presidest over poetry.

* * * *

" Apollonius, Apollonius, Apollonius, Thou teachest the Magic of Zoroaster, son of Oromasdes ; and this is the worship of the Gods."

For the evocation of spirits belonging to religions issued from Judaism, the following kabalistic invocation of Solomon should be used, either in Hebrew, or in any other tongue with which the spirit in question is known to have been familiar :—

" Powers of the Kingdom, be ye under my left foot and in my right hand ! Glory and Eternity, take me by the two shoulders, and direct me in the paths of victory ! Mercy and Justice, be ye the equilibrium and splendour of my life ! Intelligence and Wisdom, crown me ! Spirits of *Malchuth*, lead me betwixt the two pillars upon which rests the whole edifice of the temple ! Angels of *Netsah* and *Hod*, strengthen me upon the cubic stone of *Jesod* ! O *Gedulael* ! O *Geburael* ! O *Tiphereth* ! *Binael*, be thou my love ! *Ruach Hochmael*, be thou my light ! Be that which thou art and thou shalt be, O *Ketheriel* ! Tschim, assist me in the name of *Saddai* ! Cherubim, be my strength in the name of *Adonai* ! Beni-Elohim, be my brethren in the name of the Son, and by the power of *Zebaoth* ! Eloim, do battle for me in the name of *Tetragrammation* ! Malachim, protect me in the name of *Jod He Vau He* ! Seraphim, cleanse my love in the name of *Elvoh* ! Hasmalim, enlighten me with the splendours of *Eloi* and Shechinah ! Aralim, act ! Ophanim, revolve

and shine ! Hajoth a Kadosh, cry, speak, roar, bellow ! Kadosh, Kadosh, Kadosh, *Saddai*, *Adonai*, *Jotchavah*, *Eieazereie* : Hallelu-jah, Hallelu-jah, Hallelu-jah. Amen.'

It should be remembered above all, in conjurations, that the names of Satan, Beelzebub, Adramelek, and others do not designate spiritual unities, but legions of impure spirits.

" Our name is legion, for we are many," says the spirit of darkness in the Gospel. Number constitutes the law, and progress takes place inversely in hell—that is to say, the most advanced in Satanic development, and consequently the most degraded, are the least intelligent and feeblest. Thus, a fatal law drives the demons downward when they wish and believe themselves to be ascending. So also those who term themselves chiefs are the most impotent and despised of all. As to the horde of perverse spirits, they tremble before an unknown, invisible, incomprehensible, capricious, implacable chief, who never explains his law, whose arm is ever stretched out to strike those who fail to understand him. They give this phantom the names of Baal, Jupiter, and even others more venerable, which cannot, without profanation, be pronounced in hell. But this Phantom is only a shadow and remnant of God, disfigured by their wilful perversity, and persisting in their imagination like a vengeance of justice and a remorse of truth.

" When the evoked spirit of light manifests with dejected or irritated countenance, we must offer him a moral sacrifice, that is, be inwardly disposed to renounce whatever offends him ; and before leaving the oratory, we must dismiss him, saying : " May peace be with thee ! I have not wished to trouble thee ; do thou torment me not. I shall labour to improve myself as to anything that vexes thee. I pray, and will still pray, with thee and for thee. Pray thou also both with' and for me, and return to thy great slumber, expecting that day when we shall wake together. Silence and adieu ! "

Christian, in his *Historie de le magie* (Paris, 1871) says :— " The place chosen for the evocation is not an unimportant point. The most auspicious is undoubtedly that room which contains the last traces of the lamented person. If it be impossible to fulfil this condition, we must go in search of some isolated rural retreat which corresponds in orientation and aspect, as well as measurement, with the mortuary chamber.

" The window must be blocked with boards of olive wood, hermetically joined, so that no exterior light may penetrate. The ceiling, the four interior walls, and the floor must be draped with tapestry of emerald silk, which the operator must himself secure with copper nails, invoking no assistance from strange hands, because, from this moment, he alone may enter into this spot set apart from all, the arcane Oratory of the Magus. The furniture which belonged to the deceased, his favourite possessions and trinkets, the things on which his final glance may be supposed to have rested—all these must be assiduously collected and arranged in the order which they occupied at the time of his death. If none of these souvenirs can be obtained, a faithful likeness of the departed being must at least be procured, it must be full length, and must be depicted in the dress and colours which he wore during the last period of his life. This portrait must be set up on the eastern wall by means of copper fasteners, must be covered with a veil of white silk, and must be surmounted with a crown of those flowers which were most loved by the deceased.

" Before this portrait there must be erected an altar of white marble, supported by four columns which must terminate in bull's feet. A five-pointed star must be emblazoned on the slab of the altar, and must be composed of pure copper plates. The place in the centre of the star, between the plates, must be large enough to receive the pedestal of a cup-shaped copper chafing-dish, containing dessicated fragments of laurel wood and alder. By the side of the chafing-dish must be placed a censer full of incense. The skin of a white and spotless ram must be stretched beneath the alter, and on it must be emblazoned another pentagram drawn with parallel lines of azure blue, golden yellow, emerald green, and purple red.

" A copper tripod must be erected in the middle of the Oratory ; it must be perfectly triangular in form, it must be surmounted by another and similar chafing-dish, which must likewise contain a quantity of dried olive wood.

" A high candelabrum of copper must be placed by the wall on the southern side, and must contain a single taper of purest white wax, which must alone illuminate the mystery of the evocation.

" The white colour of the altar, of the ram's skin, and of the veil, is consecrated to Gabriel, the planetary archangel of the moon, and the Genius of mysteries ; the green of the copper and the tapestries is dedicated to the Genius of Venus.

" The altar and tripod must both be encompassed by a magnetized iron chain, and by three garlands composed of the foliage and blossoms of the myrtle, the olive, and the rose.

" Finally, facing the portrait, and on the eastern side, there must be a canopy, also draped with emerald silk, and supported by two triangular columns of olive wood, plated with purest copper. On the North and South sides, between each of these columns and the wall, the tapestry must fall in long folds to the ground, forming a kind of tabernacle ; which must be open on the eastern side. At the foot of each column there must be a sphinx of white marble, with a cavity in the top of the head to receive spices for burning. It is beneath this canopy that the apparitions will manifest, and it should be remembered that the Magus must turn to the east for prayer, and to the west for evocation.

" Before entering this little sanctuary, devoted to the religion of remembrance, the operator must be clothed in a vestment of azure, fastened by clasps of copper, enriched with a single emerald. He must wear upon his head a tiara surrounded by a floriated circle of twelve emeralds, and a crown of violets. On his breast must be the talisman of Venus depending from a ribbon of azure silk. On the annular finger of his left hand must be a copper ring containing a turquoise. His feet must be covered with shoes of azure silk, and he must be provided with a fan of swan's feathers to dissipate, if needful, the smoke of the perfumes.

" The Oratory and all its objects must be consecrated on a Friday, during the hours which are set apart to the Genius of Venus. This consecration is performed by burning violets and roses in a fire of olive wood. A shaft must be provided in the Oratory for the passage of the smoke, but care must be taken to prevent the admission of light through this channel.

" When these preparations are finished, the operator must impose on himself a retreat of one-and-twenty days, beginning on the anniversary of the death of the beloved being. During this period he must refrain from conferring on any one the least of those marks of affection which he was accustomed to bestow on the departed ; he must be absolutely chaste, alike in deed and thought ; he must take daily but one repast, consisting of bread, wine, roots, and fruits. These three conditions are indispensable to success in evocation, and their accomplishment requires complete isolation.

" Every day, shortly before mid-night, the Magus must assume his consecrated dress. On the stroke of the mystic hour, he must enter the Oratory, bearing a lighted candle in his right hand, and in the other an hour-glass. The candle must be fixed in the candelabra, and the hour-glass on the altar to register the flight of time. The operator must then proceed to replenish the garland and the floral crown. Then he shall unveil the portrait, and erect it immovable in front of the altar, being thus with his face to the East, he shall softly go over in his mind the cherished recollections he possesses of the beloved and departed being.

" When the upper reservoir of the hour-glass is empty the time of contemplation will be over. By the flame of the taper the operator must then kindle the laurel wood and alder in the chafing-dish which stands on the altar ; then, taking a pinch of incense from the censer, let him cast it thrice upon the fire, repeating the following words :— ' Glory be to the Father of life universal in the splendour of the infinite altitude, and peace in the twilight of the immeasurable depths to all Spirits of good will ! '

" Then he shall cover the portrait, and taking up his candle in his hand, shall depart from the Oratory, walking backward at a slow pace as far as the threshold. The same ceremony must be fulfilled at the same hour during every day of the retreat, and at each visit the crown which is above the portrait, and the garlands of the altar and tripod must be carefully renewed. The withered leaves and flowers must be burnt each evening in a room adjoining the Oratory.

" When the twenty-first day has arrived, the Magus must do his best to have no communication with any one, but if this be impossible, he must not be the first to speak, and he must postpone all business till the morrow. On the stroke of noon, he must arrange a small circular table in the Oratory, and cover it with a new napkin of unblemished whiteness. It must be garnished with two copper chalices, an entire loaf, and a crystal flagon of the purest wine. The bread must be broken and not cut, and the wine emptied in equal portions into the two cups. Half of this mystic communion, which must be his sole nourishment on this supreme day, shall be offered by the operator to the dead, and by the light of the one taper he must eat his own share, standing before the veiled portrait. Then he shall retire as before, walking backward as far as the threshold, and leaving the ghost's share of the bread and wine upon the table.

" When the solemn hour of the evening has at length arrived the Magus shall carry into the Oratory some well-dried cypress wood, which he shall set alight on the altar and the tripod. Three pinches of incense shall be cast on the altar flame in honour of the Supreme Potency which manifests itself by Ever Active Intelligence and by Absolute Wisdom. When the wood of the two chafing-dishes has been reduced to embers, he must renew the triple offering of incense on the altar, and must cast some seven times on the fire in the tripod ; at each evaporation of the consecrated perfume he must repeat the previous doxology, and then turning to the East, he must call upon God by the prayer of that religion which was professed by the person whom he desires to evoke.

" When the prayers are over he must reverse his position and with his face to the West, must enkindle the chafing-dishes on the head of each sphinx, and when the cypress is fully ablaze he must heap over it well-dried violets and roses. Then let him extinguish the candle which illuminates the Oratory, and falling on his knees before the canopy, between the two columns, let him mentally address the beloved person with a plenitude of faith and affection. Let him solemnly entreat it to appear and renew this interior adjuration seven times, under the auspices of the seven providential Genii, endeavouring during the whole of the time to exalt his soul above the natural weakness of humanity.

" Finally, the operator, with closed eyes, and with hands covering his face, must call the invoked person in a loud but gentle voice, pronouncing three times all the names which he bore.

" Some moments after the third appeal, he must extend his arms in the form of a cross, and lifting up his eyes, he will behold the beloved being, in a recognisable manner, in front of him. That is to say, he will perceive that ethereal substance separated from the perishable terrestrial body, the fluidic envelope of the soul, which Kabalistic initiates have termed the *Perispirit*. This substance preserves the human form but is emancipated from human infirmities, and is energised by the special characteristics whereby the imperishable individuality of our essence is manifested. Evoked and Evoker can then inter-communicate intelligibly by a mutual and mysterious thought-transmission.

" The departed soul will give counsel to the operator ; it will occasionally reveal secrets which may be beneficial to those whom it loved on earth, but it will answer no question which has reference to the desires of the flesh ; it will discover no buried treasures, nor will it unveil the secrets of a third person ; it is silent on the mysteries of the superior existence to which it has now attained. In certain cases, it will, however, declare itself either happy or in punishment. If it be the latter, it will ask for the prayer of the Magus, or for some religious observance, which we must unfailingly fulfil. Lastly, it will indicate the time when the evocation may be renewed.

" When it has disappeared, the operator must turn to the East, rekindle the fire on the altar, and make a final offering of incense. Then he must detach the crown and the garlands, take up his candle, and retire with his face to the West till he is out of the Oratory. His last duty is to burn the final remains of the flowers and leaves. Their ashes, united to those which have been collected during the time of retreat, must be mixed with myrtle seed, and secretly buried in a field at a depth which will secure it from disturbance of the ploughshare."

The last two examples are, of course, those of " white " *necromancy*. The procedure followed by savage tribes is of course totally different. Among certain Australian tribes the necromants are called Birraark. It is said that a Birraark was supposed to be initiated by the " mrarts " (ghosts) when they met him wandering in the bush. It was from the ghosts that he obtained replies to questions concerning events passing at a distance, or yet to happen, which might be of interest or moment to his tribe. An account of a spiritual séance in the bush is given in " Kamilaroi and Kurnai " (p. 254) : " The fires were let down ; the Birraark uttered the cry ' Coo-ee ' at intervals. At length a distant reply was heard, and shortly afterwards the sound as of persons jumping on the ground in succession. A voice was then heard in the gloom asking in a strange intonation ' What is wanted ? ' At the termination of the séance, the spirit voice said, ' We are going.' Finally, the Birraark was found in the top of an almost inaccessible tree, apparently asleep." (*See also* **New Zealand**.)

In Japan, ghosts can be raised in various ways. One mode is to " put into an andon " (a paper lantern in a frame), " a hundred rushlights, and repeat an incantation of a hundred lines. One of these rushlights is taken out at the end of each line, and the would-be ghost-seer then goes out in the dark with one light still burning, and blows it out, when the ghost ought to appear. Girls who have lost their lovers by death often try that sorcery."

The mode of procedure as practised in Scotland was thus. The haunted room was made ready. He, " who was to do the daring deed, about nightfall entered the room, bearing with him a table, a chair, a candle, a compass, a crucifix if one could be got, and a Bible. With the com-

pass he cast a circle on the middle of the floor, large enough to hold the chair and the table. He placed within the circle the chair and the table, and on the table he laid the Bible and the crucifix beside the lighted candle. If he had not a crucifix, then he drew the figure of a cross on the floor within the circle. When all this was done, he rested himself on the chair, opened the Bible, and waited for the coming of the spirit. Exactly at midnight the spirit came. Sometimes the door opened slowly, and there glided in noiselessly a lady sheeted in white, with a face of woe and told her story to the man on his asking her in the name of God what she wanted. What she wanted was done in the morning, and the spirit rested ever after. Sometimes the spirit rose from the floor, and sometimes came forth from the wall. One there was who burst into the room with a strong bound, danced wildly round the circle, and flourished a lnog whip round the man's head, but never dared to step within the circle. During a pause in his frantic dance he was asked, in God's name, what he wanted. He ceased his dance and told his wishes. His wishes were carried out, and the spirit was in peace."

In Wraxall's " Memoirs of the Courts of Berlin, Dresden, Warsaw, and Vienna " there is an amusing account of the raising of the ghost of the Chevalier de Saxe. Reports had been circulated that at his palace at Dresden there was secreted a large sum of money, and it was urged that if his spirit could be compelled to appear, interesting secrets might be extorted from him. Curiosity, combined with avarice, accordingly prompted his principal heir, Prince Charles, to try the experiment, and, on the appointed night, Schrepfer was the operator in raising the apparition. He commenced his proceedings by retiring into the corner of the gallery, where, kneeling down with many mysterious ceremonies, he invoked the spirit to appear. At length a loud clatter was heard at all the windows on the outside, resembling more the effect produced by a number of wet fingers drawn over the edge of glasses than anything else to which it could well be compared. This sound announced the arrival of the good spirits, and was shortly followed by a yell of a frightful and unusual nature, which indicated the presence of malignant spirits. Schrepfer continued his invocations, when " the door suddenly opened with violence, and something that resembled a black ball or globe rolled into the room. It was enveloped in smoke or cloud, in the midst of which appeared a human face, like the countenance of the Chevalier de Saxe, from which issued a loud and angry voice, exclaiming in German, " Carl, was wollte du mit mich ? "—" Charles, what would thou do with me ? " By reiterated exorcisms Schrepfer finally dismissed the apparition, and the terrified spectators dispersed fully convinced of his magical powers.

Neoplatonism : A mystical philosophic system initiated by Plotinus of Alexandria A.D. 233, which combined the philosophy of ancient Greece with more modern spiritual cravings. Although to some extent founded on the teaching of Plato, it was undoubtedly sophisticated by a deep mysticism, which in all probability emanated from the traditions of the land in which it originated. To a great extent it coloured the thought of mediæval mysticism and magic. Plotinus, its founder, commenced the study of philosophy in Alexandria at the age of 28. He early experienced an earnest desire to reach the truth concerning existence, and to that end made a deep study of the dialogues of Plato and the metaphysics of Aristotle. He practised the most severe austerities, and attempted to live what he called the " angelic " life, or the life of the disembodied in the body. He was greatly drawn to Apollonius of Tyana by reading his *Life* by Philostratus, and gave credence to many of the marvels recorded therein. The union of philosopher and priest in the character of

Apollonius fired the imagination of Plotinus, and in his Pythagorean teachings the young student discovered the elements of both Orientalism and Platonism,—for both Pythagoras and Plato strove to escape the sensuous, and to realise in contemplative abstraction that tranquility superior to desire and passion which made men approach the gods ; but in the hands of the later Pythagoreans and Platonists, the principles of the Hellenic masters degenerated into a species of theurgic freemasonry. Many of the Pythagoreans had joined the various Orphic associations, and indeed had sunk to be mere itinerant vendors of charms.

It is probable that at Alexandria Plotinus heard from Orientals the principles of eastern theosophy, which he did not find in Plato. But everywhere he found a growing indifference to religion as known to the more ancient Greeks and Egyptians. By this time, the Pantheons of Greece, Rome and Egypt, had become fused in the worship of Serapis, and this fusion had been forwarded by the works of Plutarch, Apuleius, and Lucian. The position of philosophy at this time was by no means a strong one. In fact speculation had given place to ethical teaching, and philosophy was regarded more as a branch of literature, or an elegant recreation. Plotinus persuaded himself that philosophy and religion should be one ; that speculation should be a search after God. It was at this time that he first heard of Ammonius Saccas, who shortly before had been a porter in the streets of Alexandria, and who lectured upon the possibilities of reconciling Plato and Aristotle. "Scepticism," said Ammonius, "was death." He recommended men to travel back across the past, and out of the whole bygone world of thought to construct a system greater than any of its parts. This teaching formed an epoch in the life of Plotinus, who was convinced that Platonism, exalted into a species of illuminism and drawing to itself like a magnet all the scattered truth of the bygone ages, could alone preserve mankind from scepticism. He occupied himself only with the most abstract questions concerning knowledge and being. "Truth," according to him, "is not the agreement of our comprehension of an external object with the object itself, but rather the agreement of the mind with itself. For the philosopher the objects we contemplate, and that which comtemplates are identical : both are thought." All truth is then easy. Reduce the soul to its most perfect simplicity, and we find it is capable of exploration into the infinite ; indeed it becomes one with the infinite. This is the condition of ecstasy, and to accomplish it a stoical austerity and asceticism was necessary. The Neoplatonists were thus ascetics and enthusiasts. Plato was neither. According to Plotinus, the mystic contemplates the divine perfection in himself ; all worldly things and logical distinctions vanish during the period of ecstasy. This, of course, is purely Oriental and not Platonic at all. Plotinus regards the individual existence as phenomenal and transitory, and subordinates reason to ecstasy where the Absolute is in question. It is only at the end of his chain of reasoning that he introduces the supernatural. He is first a rationalist, afterwards a mystic, and only a mystic when he finds that he cannot employ the machinery of reason. The letter of Plotinus, written about 260 A.D. well embodies his ideas on these heads, and is as follows :—

Plotinus to Flaccus.—I applaud your devotion to philosophy ; I rejoice to hear that your soul has set sail, like the returning Ulysses, for its native land—that glorious, that only real country—the world of unseen truth. To follow philosophy, the senator Rogatianus, one of the noblest of my disciples, gave up the other day all but the whole of his patrimony, set free his slaves, and surrendered all the honours of his station.

" Tidings have reached us that Valerian has been defeated and is now in the hands of Sapor. The threats of Franks and Allemanni, of Goths and Persians, are alike terrible by turns to our degenerate Rome. In days like these, crowded with incessant calamities, the inducements to a life of contemplation are more than ever strong. Even my quiet existence seems now to grow somewhat sensible of the advance of years. Age alone I am unable to debar from my retirement. I am weary already of this prison-house, the body, and calmly await the day when the divine nature within me shall be set free from matter.

" The Egyptian priests used to tell me that a single touch with the wing of their holy bird could charm the crocodile into torpor ; it is not thus speedily, my dear friend, that the pinions of your soul will have power to still the untamed body. The creature will yield only to watchful, strenuous constancy of habit. Purify your soul from all undue hope and fear about earthly things, mortify the body, deny self,—affections as well as appetites, and the inner eye will begin to exercise its clear and solemn vision.

" You ask me to tell you how we know, and what is our criterion of certainty. To write is always irksome to me. But for the continual solicitations of Porphyry, I should not have left a line to survive me. For your own sake, and for your father's, my reluctance shall be overcome.

" External objects present us only with appearances. Concerning them, therefore, we may be said to possess opinion rather than knowledge. The distinctions in the actual world of appearance are of import only to ordinary and practical men. Our question lies within the ideal reality which exists behind appearance. How does the mind perceive these ideas ? Are they without us, and is the reason, like sensation, occupied with objects external to itself ? What certainty could we then have, what assurance that our perception was infallible ? The object perceived would be a something different from the mind perceiving it. We should have then an image instead of reality. It would be monstrous to believe for a moment that the mind was unable to perceive ideal truth exactly as it is, and that we had not certainty and real knowledge concerning the world of intelligence. It follows, therefore, that this region of truth is not to be investigated as a thing external to us, and so only imperfectly known. It is *within* us. Here the objects we contemplate and that which contemplates are identical,—both are thought. The subject cannot surely *know* an object different from itself. The world of ideas lies within our intelligence. Truth, therefore, is not the agreement of our apprehension of an external object with the object itself. It is the agreement of the mind with itself. Consciousness, therefore, is the sole basis of certainty. The mind is its own witness. Reason sees in itself that which is above itself as its source ; and again, that which is below itself as still itself once more.

" Knowledge has three degrees—Opinion, Science, Illumination. The means or instrument of the first is sense ; of the second, dialectic ; of the third intuition. To the last I subordinate reason. It is absolute knowledge founded on the identity of the mind knowing with the object known.

" There is a raying out of all orders of existence, an external emanation from the ineffable One (prudos). There is again a returning impulse, drawing all upwards and inwards towards the centre from whence all came (epistrophe). Love, as Plato in the *Banquet* beautifully says, is the child of Poverty and Plenty. In the amorous quest of the soul after the Good, lies the painful sense of fall and deprivation. But that Love is blessing, is salvation, is our guardian genius ; without it the centrifugal law would overpower us, and sweep our souls out far from their source toward the cold extremities of the Material and the Manifold. The wise man recognises the idea of the Good within him. This he develops by withdrawal into the Holy Place of his own soul. He who does not understand how the soul contains the Beautiful within itself, seeks to realize beauty without, by laborious production. His aim should rather be to concentrate and simplify, and so to expand his being ; instead of going out into the Manifold, to forsake it for the One, and so to float upwards towards the divine fount of being whose stream flows within him.

" You ask, how can we know the Infinite ? I answer, not by reason. It is the office of reason to distinguish and define. The Infinite, therefore, cannot be ranked among its objects. You can only apprehend the Infinite by a faculty superior to reason, by entering into a state in which you are your finite self no longer, in which the Divine Essence is communicated to you. This is Ecstasy. It is the liberation of your mind from its finite consciousness. Like only can apprehend like ; when you thus cease to be finite, you become one with the Infinite. In the reduction of your soul to its simplest self (aplosis), its divine essence, you realize this Union, this Identity (enosin).

" But this sublime condition is not of permanent duration. It is only now and then that we can enjoy this elevation (mercifully made possible for us) above the limits of the body and the world. I myself have realized it but three times as yet, and Porphyry hitherto not once. All that tends to purify and elevate the mind will assist you in this attainment, and facilitate the approach and the recurrence of these happy intervals. There are, then, different roads by which this end may be reached. The love of beauty which exalts the poet ; that devotion to the One and that ascent of science which makes the ambition of the philosopher ; and that love and those prayers by which some devout and ardent soul tends in its moral purity towards perfection. These are the great highways conducting to that height above the actual and the particular where we stand in the immediate presence of the Infinite, who shines out as from the deeps of the soul."

Plotinus appears to have been greatly indebted to Numenius for some of the ideas peculiar to his system. Numenius attempted to harmonise Pythagoras and Plato, to elucidate and confirm the opinions of both by the religious dogmas of the Egyptians, the Magi and the Brahmans ; and he believed that Plato was indebted to the Hebrew as well as to the Egyptian theology for much of his wisdom. Like Plotinus he was puzzled that the immutable One could find it possible to create the Manifold without self-degradation, and he therefore posited a Being whom he calls the Demi-urge, or Artificer, who merely carried out the will of God in constructing the universe.

Taken in a nutshell, the mysticism of Plotinus is as follows : One cannot know God in any partial or finite manner ; to know him truly we must escape from the finite, from all that is earthly, from the very gifts of God to God Himself, and know him in the infinite way by receiving, or being received into him directly. To accomplish this, and to attain this identity, we must withdraw into our inmost selves, into our own essence, which alone is susceptible of blending with the Divine Essence. Hence the inmost is the highest, and as with all systems of mysticism introversion is ascension, and God is found within.

Porphyry entered the school of Plotinus when it had become an institution of some standing. At first he strongly opposed the teachings of his master, but soon became his most devoted scholar. He directed a fierce assault on Christianity, and at the same time launched strictures at Paganism ; but both forces were too strong

for him. The attempt of the school to combine religion and philosophy robbed the first of its only power, and the last of its only principle. Religion in the hands of the Neoplatonists lost all sanctity and authoritativeness, and philosophy all scientific precision, and the attempt to philosophise superstition ended in mere absurdity. But they succeeded in one thing, and that was in making philosophy superstitious—no very difficult task.

Porphyry modified the doctrine of Plotinus regarding ecstasy, by stating that in that condition the mind does not lose its consciousness of personality. He calls it a dream in which the soul, dead to the world, rises to a species of divine activity, to an elevation above reason, action and liberty. He believed in a certain order of evil genii, who took pleasure in hunting wild beasts, and others of whom hunted souls that had escaped from the fetters of the body ; so that to escape them, the soul must once more take refuge in the flesh. Porphyry's theosophic conceptions, based on those of Plotinus, were strongly and ably traversed by the theurgic mysteries of Iamblichus, to whom the priest was a prophet full of deity. Criticising Porphyry, Iamblichus says :—

" Often, at the moment of inspiration, or when the afflatus has subsided, a fiery Appearance is seen,—the entering or departing Power. Those who are skilled in this wisdom can tell by the character of this glory the rank of divinity who has seized for the time the reins of the mystic's soul, and guides it as he will. Sometimes the body of the man subject to this influence is violently agitated, sometimes it is rigid and motionless. In some instances sweet music is heard, in others, discordant and fearful sounds. The person of the subject has been known to dilate and tower to a superhuman height ; in other cases, it has been lifted up into the air. Frequently, not merely the ordinary exercise of reason, but sensation and animal life would appear to have been suspended ; and the subject of the afflatus has not felt the application of fire, has been pierced with spits, cut with knives, and been sensible of no pain. Yea, often, the more the body and the mind have been alike enfeebled by vigil and by fasts, the more ignorant or mentally imbecile a youth may be who is brought under this influence, the more freely and unmixedly will the divine power be made manifest. So clearly are these wonders the work, not of human skill or wisdom, but of supernatural agency ! Characteristics such as these I have mentioned, are the marks of the true inspiration.

" Now, there are, O Agathocles, four great orders of spiritual existence,—Gods, Dæmons, Heroes or Demi-gods, and Souls. You will naturally be desirous to learn how the apparition of a God or a Dæmon is distinguished from those of Angels, Principalities, or Souls. Know, then, that their appearance to man corresponds to their nature, and that they always manifest themselves to those who invoke them in a manner consonant with their rank in the hierarchy of spiritual natures. The appearances of Gods are uniform, those of Dæmons various. The Gods shine with a benign aspect. When a God manifests himself, he frequently appears to hide sun or moon, and seems as he descends too vast for earth to contain. Archangels are at once awful and mild ; Angels yet more gracious ; Dæmons terrible. Below the four leading classes I have mentioned are placed the malignant Dæmons, the Anti-gods.

" Each spiritual order has gifts of its own to bestow on the initiated who evoke them. The Gods confer health of body, power and purity of mind, and, in short, elevate and restore our natures to their proper principles. Angels and Archangels have at their command only subordinate bestowments. Dæmons, however, are hostile to the aspirant,—afflict both body and mind, and hinder our escape from the sensuous. Principalities, who govern the sublunary elements, confer temporal advantages. Those of a lower rank, who preside over matter, often display their bounty in material gifts. Souls that are pure are, like Angels, salutary in their influence. Their appearance encourages the soul in its upward efforts. Heroes stimulate to great actions. All these powers depend, in a descending chain, each species on that immediately above it. Good Dæmons are seen surrounded by the emblems of blessing, Dæmons who execute judgment appear with the instruments of punishment.

" There is nothing unworthy of belief in what you have been told concerning the sacred sleep, and divination by dreams. I explain it thus :—

" The soul has a two-fold life, a lower and a higher. In sleep that soul is freed from the constraint of the body, and enters, as one emancipated, on its divine life of intelligence. Then, as the noble faculty which beholds the objects that truly are—the objects in the world of intelligence—stirs within, and awakens to its power, who can be surprised that the mind, which contains in itself the principles of all that happens, should, in this its state of liberation, discern the future in those antecedent principles which will make that future what it is to be ? The nobler part of the soul is thus united by abstraction to higher natures, and becomes a participant in the wisdom and foreknowledge of the Gods.

" Recorded examples of this are numerous and well-authenticated ; instances occur, too, every day. Numbers of sick, by sleeping in the temple of Æsculapius, have had their cure revealed to them in dreams vouchsafed by the god. Would not Alexander's army have perished but for a dream in which Dionysius pointed out the means of safety ? Was not the siege of Aphutis raised through a dream sent by Jupiter Ammon to Lysander ? The night-time of the body is the day-time of the soul.''

We thus see how in the process of time the principles on which the system of Plotinus rested were surrendered little by little, while divination and evocation were practised with increasing frequency. Plotinus had declared the possibility of the absolute identification of the divine with human nature—the broadest possible basis for mysticism. Porphyry took up narrower ground and contended that in the union which takes place in ecstasy, we still retain consciousness of personality. Iamblichus diminished the real principle of mysticism still farther in theory, and denied that man has a faculty, eternally active and inaccessible, to passion : so that the intellectual ambition so lofty in Plotinus subsided among the followers of Iamblichus into magical practice.

Proclus was the last of the Greek Neoplatonists. He elaborated the Trinity of Plotinus into a succession of impalpable triads, and surpassed Iamblichus in his devotion to the practice of theurgy. With him, theurgy was the art which gives man the magical passwords that carry him through barrier after barrier, dividing species from species of the upper existences, till at the summit of the hierarchy he arrives at the highest. Above all being is God, the Non-Being, who is apprehended only by negation. When we are raised out of our weakness and on a level with God, it seems as though reason were silenced for then we are above reason. In short we become intoxicated with God. Proclus was an adept in the ritual of invocations among every people in the world, and a great magical figure. With the advance of Byzantinism, he represented the old world of Greek thought, and even those who wrote against him as a heathen show the influence he exercised on their doctrines. Thus Dionysius attempted to accommodate the philosophy of Proclus to Christianity, and greatly

admired his asceticism. The theology of the Neoplatonists was always in the first instance a mere matter of logic. They confounded Universals with Causes. The highest became with them merely the most comprehensive. As has been said *Neoplatonism* exercised great power among the scholiasts and magicians of the middle ages. In fact all that mediævalism knew of Plato was through the medium of the Neoplatonists. In Germany in the fourteenth century it became a vivifying principle ; for although its doctrine of emanation was abandoned, its allegorical explanation, its exaltation of the spirit above the letter was retained, and Platonism and mysticism together created a party in the church—the sworn foes of scholasticism and mere lifeless orthodoxy.

Neptesh : (*See* **Kabala.**)

Nervaura : (*See* **Aura.**)

Nervengeist : (*See* **Psychic Body** and **Spiritualism.**)

Neuhusens, Henrichus : (*See* **Rosicrucians.**)

Nevill, William : (*See* **England.**)

New Existence of Man upon the Earth : Spiritualistic Journal. (*See* **Spiritualism.**)

New Motor, The : A strange machine constructed in 1854 by John Murray Spear (q.v.) at the instigation of the " Association of Electricizers," one of the bands of spirits by whom he was controlled. It was to derive its motive power from the magnetic store of nature, and was therefore to be as independent of artificial sources of energy as was the human body. The machine was hailed as a god—the " Physical Saviour of the race," the " New Messiah "—and a certain lady, in obedience to a vision, went to the High Rock (Lynn, Mass.) whereon stood the *New Motor*, and for two hours suffered " birth-pangs," whereby she judged that the essence of her spiritual being was imparted to the machine. At the end of that time it was averred that pulsations were apparent in the *motor*. A. J. Davis expressed the belief that the design was the work of spirits of a mechanical turn of mind, but was of no practical value. The *New Motor* was finally smashed by the inhabitants of Randolph (N.Y.) whither it had been taken. In all it cost its builder some two thousand dollars. In common fairness to the Spiritualists it may be said that the majority had no sympathy whatever with such an absurd scheme.

Newstead Abbey : (*See* **Haunted Houses.**)

New Thought : A present-day religion which in some of its tenets is akin to Christian Science, or faith-healing. Unlike Christian Science, however, it does not affect entirely to dispense with all material aids, as drugs, the setting of broken bones, and so on. Nor does it give the whole credit for the cure to the imagination of the patient, as does hypnotism. But striking a point midway between the two it gives considerable prominence to the mind in the healing process, while not altogether despising the doctor. Mind is considered as highly refined matter, and therefore the " mind " cure is in a measure a material cure. It is clear that that part of the *New Thought* which deals with bodily healing has its roots in the Animal Magnetism and Mesmerism of bygone times. So much have they in common that it is needless to trace mental-healing further back than Dr. Phineas Parkhurst Quimby (1802–1866) the first to make use of the terms " mental-healing " and " Christian Science." Dr. Quimby was the son of a New Hampshire blacksmith, and was himself apprenticed to a clockmaker, having had but little education. At the age of thirty-six he attended a lecture on Mesmerism, and thereafter practised for himself. With the aid of a clairvoyant youth he cured diseases, and so successful was his treatment that he soon adopted magnetic healing as a profession. At length, however, he got a glimpse of the true reason for his success—the expectation of the patient. The diagnoses of his clairvoyant he attributed to the latter's telepathic reading of the patient's own thoughts, and he judged that the treatment prescribed depended for its efficacy on the confidence it inspired rather than on its intrinsic merits. From this point he gradually evolved his doctrine that disease was a mere delusion, a traditional error that had fixed itself in men's minds, which it behoved them to be rid of as soon as might be. The way to cure disease, therefore, was to destroy the error on which it rested. Besides Christian Science, Quimby called his doctrine the Science of Health, or the Science of Health and Happiness. He had many disciples, among whom were Mrs. Mary Baker G. Eddy, the founder of the Christian Science Church. Others whose influence was felt more in the direction of the *New Thought* movement were the Rev. W. F. Evans and Mr. and Mrs. Julius Dresser, whose son, Horatio W. Dresser, remains one of the ablest exponents of the *New Thought* As has been said, the method of healing practised by this school is not considered to be entirely immaterial. It is no longer believed, of course, that a fluid emanates from the finger-tips of the operator, or that he radiates a luminous odic force; but Mr. Dresser himself states that the communication is of a vibratory character, made up of ethereal undulations directed and concentrated by the thought of the healer. The power is equally efficacious at a distance and may be used without the patient's knowledge or even against his will. This belief in action at a distance is something of a bug-bear to the New Thinker, who fears the ascendency of an evil influence as the superstitious of the Middle Ages feared bewitchment. But there is a spiritual aspect of the *New Thought* as well as a physical one. The health of the soul is as fully considered as the health of the body. Spiritual sanity, then, is to be procured by lifting oneself to a higher plane of existence, by shutting out the things of the earth and living " in tune with the infinite." We must realise our own identity with the Infinite Spirit and open our lives to the Divine inflow. Ralph Waldo Trine, himself a New Thinker, says in an expressive metaphor, " To recognise our own divinity and our intimate relation to the Universal, is to attach the belt of our machinery to the power-house of the Universe." In short, we must have sufficient self-confidence to cast our fears aside and rise unfettered into the Infinite.

New Zealand : Maori superstitions. Amidst the mythological personages of *New Zealand* " the spirits of the dead " ever play a very prominent part, and our chief interest in noticing the Maoris, lies in the fact, that belief in, and open communion with these spirits, still exist. The priests or " Tohungas " are unmistakably " Mediums," in the modern sense of the term. Sometimes they are born with their gift, and sometimes they are devoted to the priestly office by their parents and acquire their power after the fashion of Eastern ecstatics, by prayer, fasting and contemplation. That good prophets exist amongst the Maoris has been abundantly proved. During the time when Great Britain busied herself in colonizing *New Zealand*, her officials frequently wrote home, that the Maori would never be conquered wholly; information of the parties sent out to attack them; the very colour of the boats, and the hour when they would arrive; the number of the enemy, and all particulars essential to their safety, being invariably communicated to the tribes beforehand by their prophets or Tohungas.

The best natural prophets and seers amongst the Maoris are of the female sex; and although the missionaries try to account for the marvellous powers they exhibit, above all for the sound of the Spirit voice, which is a common phase in their communion with the dead—on the hypothesis that the women who practise " the arts of sorcery," are ventriloquists—this attempted explanation rarely covers the ground of the intelligence which is received.

In his *Old New Zealand* General Cummings cites an interesting case of Tohungaism. A certain young chief had been appointed Registrar of births and deaths, when he suddenly came to a violent end. The book of registries was lost, and much inconvenience ensued. The man's relatives notified their intention of invoking his spirit, and invited General Cummings to be present at the ceremony, an invitation which he accepted. " The appointed time came. Fires were lit. The Tohunga repaired to the darkest corner of the room. All was silent, save the sobbing of the sisters of the deceased warrior-chief. There were thirty of us, sitting on the rush-strewn floor, the door shut and the fire now burning down to embers. Suddenly there came a voice out from the partial darkness, ' Salutation, salutation to my family, to my tribe, to you, pakeha, my friend !' Our feelings were taken by storm. The oldest sister screamed, and rushed with extended arms in the direction from whence the voice came. Her brother, seizing, restrained her by main force. Others exclaimed, ' Is it you ? Is it you ? Truly it is you ! aue ! aue !' and fell quite insensible upon the floor. The older women and some of the aged men were not moved in the slightest degree, though believing it to be the spirit of the chief.

" Whilst reflecting upon the novelty of the scene, the ' darkness visible ' and the deep interest manifest, the spirit spoke again, ' Speak to me my family; speak to me, my tribe : speak to me, the pakeha !' At last the silence gave way, and the brother spoke : ' How is it with you ? Is it well with you in that country ?' The answer came, though not in the voice of the Tohunga-medium, but in strange sepulchral sounds : ' It is well with me; my place is a good place. I have seen our friends; they are all with me !' A woman from another part of the room now anxiously cried out, ' Have you seen my sister ?' ' Yes, I have seen her; she is happy in our beautiful country.' ' Tell her my love so great for her will never cease.' ' Yes, I will bear the message.' Here the native woman burst into tears, and my own bosom swelled in sympathy.

" The spirit speaking again, giving directions about property and keepsakes, I thought I would more thoroughly test the genuineness of all this : and I said, ' We cannot find your book with the registered names; where have you concealed it ?' The answer came instantly, ' I concealed it between the tahuhu of my house, and the thatch; straight over you, as you go in at the door.' The brother rushed out to see. All was silence. In five minutes he came hurriedly back, with the book in his hand ! It astonished me.

" It was now late, and the spirit suddenly said, ' Farewell my family, farewell, my tribe; I go.' Those present breathed an impressive farewell, when the spirit cried out again, from high in the air, ' Farewell !'

" This, though seemingly tragical, is in every respect literally true. But what is that ? ventriloquism, the devil, or what ! . . ."

Mrs. Britten, in her *Nineteenth Century Miracles* says : " The author has herself had several proofs of the Mediumistic power possessed by these ' savages ' but as her experiences may be deemed of too personal a character, we shall select our examples from other sources. One of these is furnished by a Mr. Marsden, a person who was well-known in the early days of *New Zealand's* colonial history, as a miner, who grew rich ' through spiritual communications.' Mr. Marsden was a gentleman who had spent much time amongst the Maoris, and who still keeps a residence in ' the King country,' that is—the district of which they hold control. Mr. Marsden informed the author, that his success as a gold miner, was entirely due to a communication he had received through a native woman who claimed to have the power of bringing down spirits—the Maoris, be it remembered, always insisting that the spirits descend through the air to earth to visit mortals. Mr. Marsden had long been prospecting unsuccessfully in the gold regions. He had a friend in partnership with him, to whom he was much attached, but who had been accidentally killed by a fall from a cliff. The Spirit of this man came unsolicited, on an occasion when Mr. Marsden was consulting a native seeress, for the purpose of endeavouring to trace out what had become of a valuable watch which he had lost. The voice of the spirit was first heard in the air, apparently above the roof of the hut in which they sat, calling Mr. Marsden by his familiar name of ' Mars.' Greatly startled by these sounds, several times repeated, at the Medium's command, he remained perfectly still until the voice of his friend speaking in his well-remembered Scotch accent sounded close to his ear, whilst a column of grey misty substance reared itself by his side. This apparition was plainly visible in the subdued light of the hut, to which there was only one open entrance, but no window. Though he was much startled by what he saw and heard, Mr. Marsden had presence of mind enough to gently put his hand through the misty column which remained intact, as if its substance offered no resistance to the touch. Being admonished by an earnest whisper from the Maori woman, who had fallen on her knees before the apparition, to keep still, he obeyed, when a voice—seemingly from an immense distance off—yet speaking unmistakably in his friend's Scotch accents, advised him to let the watch alone—for it was irreparably gone—but to go to the stream on the banks of which they had last had a meal together trace it up for six miles and a half, and then, by following its course amidst the forest, he would come to a pile, which would make him rich, if he chose to remain so. Whilst he was waiting and listening breathlessly to hear more, Mr. Marsden was startled by a slight detonation at his side. Turning his head he observed that the column of mist was gone, and in its place, a quick flash, like the reflection of a candle, was all that he beheld. Here the séance ended, and the astonished miner left the hut, convinced that he had heard the Spirit of his friend talking to him. He added, that he followed the directions given implicitly, and came to a mass of surface gold lying on the stones at the bottom of the brook in the depth of the forest. This he gathered up, and though he prospected for several days in and about that spot, he never found another particle of this precious metal. That which he had secured he added, with a deep sigh, was indeed enough to have made him independent for life, had it not soon been squandered in fruitless speculations.''

So deeply has the Maori mind been saturated with ages of superstition that among the civilised, well-educated classes there may to-day be observed numerous expressions and actions which have their origin in an instinctive dread of the supernatural. Many degrees of superstition exist among the Maoris of the present day, says a writer in the *Pall Mall Gazette*. In the recesses of the Urewera country for example, diablerie has lost little of its early potency ; the *tohunga* there remains a power in the land. Among the more enlightened natives a precautionary policy is generally followed ; it is always wiser and safer, they say, to avoid conflict with the two mysterious powers *tapu* and *makuta*. Tapu is the less dangerous of the two ; a house, an individual, or an article may be rendered tapu, or sacred, and if the tapu be disregarded harm will befall someone. But makuta is a powerful evil spell cast for the deliberate purpose of accomplishing harm, generally to bring about death. The *tohunga* is understood to be in alliance with the spirits of the dead. The Maori dreads death, and he fears the dead. Places of burial are seldom approached during the day, never at

night. The spirits of the dead are believed to linger sometimes near places of burial. Without going to experts in Maori lore, who have many and varied theories to set forth, a preferable course is to discover what the average Maori of to-day thinks and believes respecting the strange powers and influences he deems are at work in the world around him.

A Maori of this type—who can read and write, is under forty years of age, and fairly intelligent—was drawn into a lengthy conversation with the writer. He believed, magistrates notwithstanding, that tohungas, somehow, had far more power than ordinary men. He did not think they got that power from the "tiapo" (the devil ?) ; they just were able to make themselves masters of men and of many things in the world. There are many degrees of Tohungaism. An ordinary man or woman was powerless against a *tohunga*, but one *tohunga* could overcome another. The speaker knew of an instance of one *tohunga* driving the tohunga power entirely out of a weaker rival. It was a fairly recent east coast occurrence. Three Maoris had accidentally permitted their pigs to trespass into the tohunga's potato paddock, and much damage and loss was the result. The *tohunga* was one of the dangerous type, and being very wroth, he *makutued* the three men, all of whom promptly died. Nobody was brave enough to charge the *tohunga* with causing the death of the men ; they were all afraid of this terrible *makuta*. At length another *tohunga* was heard of, one of very great power. This oracle was consulted, and he agreed to deal effectively with *tohunga* number one, and punish him for killing the owner of the pigs. So, following his instructions, the first-mentioned individual was seized, and much against his will, was conveyed to the home of the greater magician. Many Maoris, it should be known, stand in awe of hot water, they will not handle it, even for purposes connected with cooking or cleaning. Into a large tub of hot water the minor *tohunga* struggling frantically, was placed, then he was given a page torn from a Bible, which he was ordered to chew and swallow. The hot water treatment, combined with the small portion of the white man's sacred volume, did the expected work ; the man was no longer a *tohunga*, and fretting over his lost powers, he soon afterwards died.''

Spiritualism.—Amongst the earliest investigators in Dunedin, was a Mr. John Logan. Before he had become publicly identified with the cause of Spiritualism, an association had been formed, the members of which steadily pursued their investigations in private circles and semi-public gatherings. One of the most marked events in connection with the early development of Spiritualism in Dunedin, however, was the arraignment and church trial of Mr. Logan, the circumstances of which may be briefly summed up as follows. This gentleman, although holding a high position in the first Presbyterian church of the city, had attended circles and witnessed Spiritualistic phenomena and it was currently reported that one of his own near relatives was a very remarkable Medium. On the 19th of March, 1873, Mr. Logan was summoned to appear before a Church Convocation, to be held for the purpose of trying his case, and if necessary, dealing with his '' delinquency.'' Mr. Logan was in the event deprived of his church membership.

In many of the principal towns besides Dunedin, circles held at first in mere idle curiosity, have produced their usual fruit of mediumistic power, and this again has extended into associative action, and organisation into local societies. For over a year, the Spiritualists and Liberalists of Dunedin secured the services of Mr. Charles Bright as their lecturer. This gentleman had once been attached to the editorial staff of the *Melbourne Argus*, and had obtained a good reputation as a capable writer, and liberal thinker. Mr. Bright's lectures in Dunedin were highly appreciated, and by their scholarly style and attractive manner, served to band together the liberal element in the city. In Auckland, the principal town of the North Island, the same good service was rendered to the cause of religious thought, by the addresses of the Rev. Mr. Edgar, a clergyman whose Spiritualistic doctrines, had tended to sever him from sectarian organisations, and draw around him, the Spiritualists of the town. Besides the good work effected by these gentlemen, the occasional visits of Messrs. Peebles, Walker, J. Tyerman, and the effect of the many private circles held in every portion of the islands, tended to promote a general, though quiet, diffusion of Spiritual thought and doctrine, throughout *New Zealand.*

Ngai : (*See* **Magic.**)

Nganga : Members of the Ndembo Secret Society of the Lower Congo. *Nganga*—literally " the knowing ones "—is a term applied to those who have passed certain curious rites to distinguish them from the *Vanga* or uninitiated.

Ngembi : (*See* **Africa.**)

Nichusch : Prophetic indication. In accordance with the Kabalistic view that all events and natural happenings have a secret connection, and interact upon one another, it is believed that practically everything can become an object of soothsaying—the flight of birds, movement of clouds, cries of animals, events happening to man, and so on. Man himself may become *Nichusch* by saying that if such and such a thing takes place it will be a good or a bad omen.

Nick, or **Old Nick :** A well-known British appelation of the Devil. It seems probable that this name is derived from the Dutch *Nikken*, the devil, which again comes from the Anglo-Saxon *nœc-an*, to slay,—for as Wachter says the devil was " a murderer from the beginning." In northern countries there is a river spirit named " Neck," " Nikke," or " Nokke," of the same nature as the water Kelpie, and the Merman or Triton.

Nicolai, Christoph Friedrich : (1733–1811), A German author and bookseller of Berlin, is interesting from the occult point of view because of the peculiar experiences which befel him, and of which he treats in his personal account read before the Royal Society of Berlin. It would be impossible to present the circumstances of his case, which is one of the most celebrated in the annals of psychology, better than in his own words.

" In the first two months of the year 1791," he says, " I was much affected in my mind by several incidents of a very disagreeable nature ; and on the 24th of February a circumstance occurred which irritated me extremely. At ten o'clock in the forenoon my wife and another person came to console me ; I was in a violent perturbation of mind, owing to a series of incidents which had altogether wounded my moral feelings, and from which I saw no possibility of relief, when suddenly I observed at the distance of ten paces from me a figure—the figure of a deceased person. I pointed at it, and asked my wife whether she did not see it. She saw nothing, but being much alarmed, endeavoured to compose me, and sent for the physician The figure remained some seven or eight minutes, and at length I became a little more calm ; and as I was extremely exhausted, I soon afterwards fell into a troubled kind of slumber, which lasted for half an hour. The vision was ascribed to the great agitation of mind in which I had been, and it was supposed I should have nothing more to apprehend from that cause ; but the violent affection had put my nerves into some unnatural state. From this arose further consequences, which require a more detailed description.

" In the afternoon, a little after four o'clock, the figure which I had seen in the morning again appeared. I was alone when this happened, a circumstance which, as may be easily conceived, could not be very agreeable. I went therefore to the apartment of my wife, to whom I related it. But thither also the figure pursued me. Sometimes it was present, sometimes it vanished, but it was always the same standing figure. A little after six o'clock several stalking figures also appeared ; but they had no connection with the standing figure. I can assign no other cause for this apparition than that, though much more composed in my mind, I had not been able so soon entirely to forget the cause of such deep and distressing vexation, and had reflected on the consequences of it, in order, if possible, to avoid them ; and that this happened three hours after dinner, at the time when digestion just begins.

" At length I became more composed with respect to the disagreeable incident which had given rise to the first apparition ; but though I had used very excellent medicines and found myself in other respects perfectly well, yet the apparitions did not diminish, but on the contrary rather increased in number, and were transformed in the most extraordinary manner.

" The figure of the deceased person never appeared to me after the first dreadful day, but several other figures shewed themselves afterwards very distinctly, sometimes such as I knew, mostly, however, of persons I did not know, and amongst those known to me, were the semblance of both living and deceased persons, but mostly the former, and I made the observation, that acquaintance with whom I daily conversed never appeared to me as phantasms ; it was always such as were at a distance.

" It is also to be noted, that these figures appeared to me at all times, and under the most different circumstances, equally distinct and clear. Whether I was alone, or in company, by broad day-light equally as in the night-time, in my own as well as in my neighbour's house ; yet when I was at another person's house, they were less frequent, and when I walked the public street they very seldom appeared. When I shut my eyes, sometimes the figures disappeared, sometimes they remained even after I had closed them. If they vanished in the former case, on opening my eyes again, nearly the same figures appeared which I had seen before.

" I sometimes conversed with my physician and my wife concerning the phantasms which at the time hovered around me ; for in general the forms appeared oftener in motion than at rest. They did not always continue present—they frequently left me altogether, and again appeared for a short or longer space of time, singly or more at once ; but, in general, several appeared together. For the most part I saw human figures of both sexes ; they commonly passed to and fro as if they had no connection with each other, like people at a fair where all is bustle ; sometimes they appeared to have business with one another. Once or twice I saw amongst them persons on horseback, and dogs and birds ; these figures all appeared to me in their natural size, as distinctly as if they had existed in real life, with the several tints on the uncovered parts of the body, and with all the different kinds and colours of clothes. But I think, however, that the colours were somewhat *paler* than they are in nature.

" None of the figures had any distinguishing characteristic, they were neither terrible, ludicrous, nor repulsive ; most of them were ordinary in their appearance,—some were even agreeable.

" On the whole, the longer I continued in this state, the more did the number of the phantasms increase, and the apparitions became more frequent. About four weeks afterwards I began to hear them speak : sometimes the phantasms spoke with one another, but for the most part they addressed themselves to me, these speeches were in general short, and never contained anything disagreeable. Intelligent and respected friends often appeared to me, who endeavoured to console me in my grief, which still left deep traces on my mind. This speaking I heard most frequently when I was alone; though I sometimes heard it in company, intermixed with the conversation of real persons; frequently in single phrases only, but sometimes even in connected discourse.

"Though at this time I enjoyed rather a good state of health both in body and mind, and had become so very familiar with these phantasms, that at last they did not excite the least disagreeable emotion, but on the contrary afforded me frequent subjects for amusement and mirth; yet as the disorder sensibly increased, and the figures appeared to me for whole days together, and even during the night, if I happened to awake, I had recourse to several medicines."

He then recounts how the apparitions vanished upon blood being let.

"This was performed on the 20th of April, at eleven o'clock in the forenoon. I was alone with the surgeon; but during the operation, the room swarmed with human forms of every description, which crowded fast one on another. This continued till half-past four o'clock, exactly the time when the digestion commences. I then observed that the figures began to move more slowly; soon afterwards the colours became gradually paler; every seven minutes they lost more and more of their intensity, without any alteration in the distinct figure of the apparitions. At about half-past six o'clock all the figures were entirely white, and moved very little; yet the forms appeared perfectly distinct; by degrees they became visibly less plain, without decreasing in number, as had often formerly been the case. The figures did not move off, neither did they vanish, which also had usually happened on other occasions. In this instance they dissolved immediately into air; of some even whole pieces remained for a length of time, which also by degrees were lost to the eye. At about eight o'clock there did not remain a vestige of any of them, and I have never since experienced any appearance of the same kind. Twice or thrice since that time I have felt a propensity, if I may be allowed to express myself, or a sensation as if I saw something which in a moment again was gone. I was even surprised by this sensation whilst writing the present account, having, in order to render it more accurate, perused the papers of 1791, and recalled to my memory all the circumstances of that time. So little are we sometimes, even in the greatest composure of mind, masters of our imagination."

Nif : An Egyptian symbol in the form of a ship's sail widely spread, symbolizing breath.

Nifelheim : (*See* **Hell.**)

Night, Mystical, of the Sufis : It was believed by the *Sufis* that to attain to the coveted state of mystical contemplation, it was necessary to close the gateway of the physical senses, so that the inner or spiritual senses might operate more freely. This injunction was sometimes taken literally, as by the Brahmin Yogis, who carefully closed eyes, ears, nose and mouth, in order to attain to visionary ecstasy. The *Mystical Night* is thus a shutting out of all external sense-impressions, of hope, fear, consciousness of self, and every human emotion, so that the interior light may be more clearly perceived.

Nightmare : (Old English *night* and *mara*, a spectre). A disorder of the digestive functions during sleep, inducing the temporary belief that some animal or demon is sitting on the chest. Among savages and primitive people it is thought that the affection proceeds from the attentions of an evil spirit. Keysler in his very curious work, *Antiquitates*

selectae Septentrionales et Celticae, has collected many interesting particulars concerning the nightmare. *Nachtmar*, he says, is from *Mair*, an old woman, because the spectre which appears to press upon the breast and impede the action of the lungs is generally in that form. The English and Dutch words coincide with the German. The French *cochemar* is *Mulier incumbens* or *Incuba*. The Swedes use *Mara* alone, as we learn from the *Historia Seucorum Gothorumque* of Eric Olaus, where he states that Valender, the son of Suercher, succeeded to the throne of his father, who was suffocated by a dæmon in his sleep, of that kind which by the scribes is called *Mara*. Others, " we suppose Germans," continues Keysler, " call it *Hanon Tramp*. The French peasantry call it *Dianus* which is a corruption either of Diana or of *Dæmonium Meridianum* for it seems there is a belief (which Keysler, not improbably thinks may be derived from a false interpretation of an expression in the 91st Psalm ('the destruction that wasteth at noon-day') that persons are most exposed to such attacks at that time and, therefore, women in childbed are then never left alone. But though the *Dæmonium Meridianum* is often used for the Ephialtes, nevertheless it is more correctly any sudden and violent attack which deprives the patient of his senses. In some parts of Germany, the name given to this disorder is *den alp*, or *das Alp-dructen*, either from the 'mass' which appears to press on the sufferer or from *Alp* or *Alf* (elf). In Franconia it is *die Drud* or *das Druddructen*, from the Druid or Weird Women, and there is a belief that it may not only be chased away, but be made to appear on the morrow in a human shape, and lend something required of it by the following charm :—

> " Druid to-morrow
> So will I borrow."

These Druids, it seems, were not only in the habit of riding men, but horses also, and in order to keep them out of the stables, the salutary *pentalpha* (which bears the name of *Druden-fuss*, Druid's foot) should be written on the stable doors, in consecrated chalk, on the night of St. Walburgh. We must not omit that our English familiar appellation ' Trot ' is traced up to ' Druid ' " a decrepit old woman such as the Sagas might be," and the same may perhaps be said of a Scottish Saint, Triduana or Tredwin.

In Ihre's Glossary, a somewhat different account of the *Mara* is given. Here again, we find the ' witch-riding ' of horses, against which a stone amulet is provided by Aubrey, similar to one which we are about to notice immediately below.

Among the incantations by which the *nightmare* may be chased away, Reginald Scot has recorded the following in his *Discovery of Witchcraft*.

> " St. George, St. George, our lady's knight,
> He walked by day so did he by night :
> Until such times as he her found,
> He her beat and he her bound,
> Until her troth to him plight,
> He would not come to her that night."

" Item," continues the same ingenious author, " hang a stone over the afflicted person's bed, which stone hath naturally such a hole in it, as wherein a string may be put through it, and so be hanged over the diseased or bewitched party, be it man, woman, or horse."

Every reader of the above lines will be reminded of the similar charm which Shakespeare has put into the mouth of Edgar as Mad Tom in *King Lear*.

> " Saint Withold footed thrice the Wold ;
> He met the night-mare and her ninefold
> Bid her alight,
> And her troth plight
> And aroint thee, witch, aroint thee."

Another charm of earlier date occurs in Chaucer's *Miller's Tale*. When the simple Carpenter discovers the crafty Nicholas in his feigned abstraction, he thinks he may perhaps be hag-ridden, and addresses him thus :—

" I crouch the fro Elves and fro wikid wightes
And therewith the night-spell he seide arightes,
On four halvis of the house about,
And on the dreshfold of the dore without,
'Jesu Christ, and Seint Benedight,
Blesse this house from evrey wikid wight,
Fro the night's mare, the wite paternoster,
Where wennist thou Seint Peter's sister."

A more modern author has pointed to some other formularies, and has noticed that Asmodeus was the fiend of most evil repute on these occasions. In the *Otia Imperiala* of Gervase of Tilbury, some other protecting charms are said to exist. To turn to the medical history of the Incubus Pliny has recommended two remedies for this complaint ; one sufficiently simple, wild pæony seed. Another, which it would not be easy to discover in any modern pharmacopœia, is a decoction in wine and oil of the tongue, eyes, liver, and bowels of a dragon, wherewith, after it has been left to cool all night in the open air, the patient should be anointed every morning and evening.

Dr. Bond, a physician, who tells us that he himself was much afflicted with the *nightmare*, published an *Essay on the Incubus* in 1753. At the time at which he wrote, medical attention appears to have been very little called to the disease, and some of the opinions hazarded were sufficiently wild and inconclusive. Thus Dr. Willis said it was owing to some incongruous matter which is mixed with the nervous fluid in the cerebellum (*de Anima Brutorum*) ; and Bellini thought it imaginary, and to be attributed to the idea of some demon which existed in the mind the day before. Both of these writers might have known better if they would have turned to Fuchsius (with whom Dr. Bond appears to be equally acquainted) who in his work *de Curandi Ratione*, published as early as 1548, has an excellent chapter (I., 31) on the causes, symptoms, and cure of *nightmare*, in which he attributes it to repletion and indigestion, and recommends the customary discipline.

Nirvanic or **Atmic Plane :** (*See* **Spiritual World.**)

Norfolk, Duke of : (*See* **England.**)

Norton, Thomas : The exact date of this alchemist's birth is wrapped in mystery, while comparatively little is recorded about his life in general. But at least it is known that Bristol was his native place, and that, in the year 1436, he was elected to represent that town in Parliament. This points to his having been an upright and highly-esteemed person, and the conjecture is buttressed in some degree by the fact that Edward IV. made him a member of his privy council, and employed him repeatedly as an ambassador. At an early age *Norton* showed himself curious concerning alchemy and the like, demonstrating his predilection herein by attempting to make the personal acquaintance of George Ripley (q.v.), who, sometime Canon of Bridlington,

was reputed a man of extraordinary learning, and was author of numerous alchymical works. For many months *Norton* sought this person in vain, but at length the Canon, yielding to the other's importunity, wrote to him in the following manner :—" I shall not longer delay ; the time is come ; you shall receive this grace. Your honest desire and approved virtue, your love of truth, wisdom, and long perseverance, shall accomplish your sorrowful desires. It is necessary that, as soon as convenient, we speak together face to face, lest I should by writing betray my trust. I will make you my heir and brother in this art, as I am setting out to travel in foreign countries. Give thanks to God, Who next to His spiritual servants, honours the sons of this sacred science."

After receiving this very friendly and encouraging letter, *Norton* hurried straightway to Ripley's presence, and thereafter for upwards of a month the two were constantly together, the elder man taught the novice many things, while he even promised that, if he showed himself an apt and worthy pupil, he would impart to him the secret of the medicinal stone. And in due course this promise was fulfilled, yet it is reported that *Norton's* own chymical researches met with various signal disappointments. On one occasion, for instance, when he had almost perfected a certain tincture, his servant absconded with the crucible containing the precious fluid ; while at a later time, when the alchemist was at work on the same experiment, and thought he was just about to reach the goal, his entire paraphernalia was stolen by a Mayoress of Bristol. And this defeat must have been doubly galling to the unfortunate philosopher, for soon afterwards the Mayoress became very wealthy, presumably as a result of her theft.

Norton himself does not appear to have reaped pecuniary benefit at any time from his erudition, but to have been a comparatively poor man throughout the whole of his life ; and the fact is a little surprising, for his *Ordinall of Alchimy* was a popular work in the middle ages, and was repeatedly published. The original edition was anonymous, but the writer's identity has been determined because the initial syllables in the first six lines of the seventh chapter compose the following couplet :—

" *Thomas Norton* of Briseto
A parfet master you may him trow."

Norton died in 1477, and his predilections descended to one of his grandsons. This was Samuel Norton, who was born in 1548, studied science at St. John's College, Cambridge, and afterwards became a Justice of the Peace and Sheriff of Somersetshire. He died about 1604, and in 1630 a collection of his alchemistic tracts was published at Frankfort.

Noualli : Aztec magicians (*See* **Mexico and Central America.**)

Nuan : In Irish romance, the last of the sorceress-daughters of Conaran. Having put Finn under taboo to send his men in single combat against her as long as she wished, she was slain by Goll, her sister's slayer.

Numbers, Magical (*See* **Magic.**)

O

Oak Apples, as diviners. It is said that if one wishes to discover whether a child be bewitched, one may do so by following this procedure : drop three *oak apples* into a basin of water under the child's cradle, at the same time preserving the strictest silence ; if they float the child is not fascinated, but if they sink it is.

Oak Tree : The *oak*, from time immemorial, has held a high place as a sacred tree. The Druids worshipped the *oak*, and performed many of their rites under the shadow of its branches. When Augustine preached Christianity to the ancient Britons, he stood under an *oak tree*. The ancient

Hebrews evidently held the *oak* as a sacred tree. There is a tradition that Abraham received his heavenly visitors under an *oak*. Rebekah's nurse was buried under an *oak*, called afterwards the *oak* of weeping. Jacob buried the idols of Shechem under an *oak*. It was under the *oak* of Ophra, Gideon saw the angel sitting, who gave him instructions as to what he was to do to free Israel. When Joshua and Israel made a covenant to serve God, a great stone was set up in evidence under an *oak* that was by the sanctuary of the Lord. The prophet sent to prophesy against Jeroboam was found at Bethel sitting under an *oak*. Saul and his sons were buried under an *oak*, and, according to Isaiah, idols were made of *oak* wood. Abimelech was made king by the *oak* that was in Shechem. During the eighteenth century its influence in curing diseases was believed in. The toothache could be cured by boring with a nail the tooth or gum till blood came, and then driving the nail into an *oak tree*. A child with rupture could be cured by splitting an *oak* branch, and passing the child through the opening backwards three times ; if the splits grew together afterwards, the child would be cured.

Obambo, The : (*See* **Africa.**)

Obeah : (*See* **West Indian Islands.**)

Obercit, Johnan Hermann : Swiss Mystic and Alchemist, 1725–1798. Born in 1725 at Arbon, in Switzerland, *Johann Obercit* was the son of a scientist keenly interested in Hermetic philosophy, and no doubt the boy's own taste therefore developed the more speedily on account of the parental predilection. Very soon *Johann* became determined to discover the philosopher's stone, hoping thereby to resuscitate the fortunes of his family, which he found at a low ebb, presumably because the elder Obercit had expended large sums on his alchemistic pursuits ; and the young man worked strenuously to gain his ends, maintaining all along that whoso would triumph in this endeavour must not depend on scientific skill, but rather on constant communion with God. Notwithstanding this pious theory of his, he soon found himself under the ban of the civic authorities, who came to his laboratory, and forced him to forego futher operations, declaring that these constituted a danger to public health and safety. That, at least, they gave as their reason ; but the likelihood is that, in their ignorance, they looked askance upon all scientific researches. *Obercit*, bitterly incensed, appears to have left his native place, and to have lived for some time thereafter with one Lavater, a brother of the noted physiognomist of that name ; while it would seem that, at a later date, he renounced the civilised world altogether, and took up his abode in the lofty fastnesses of the Alps. No hermit's life did he live here, however ; for, according to his own recital, he took to himself as bride a seraphic shepherdess named Theantis, with whom he dwelt peacefully during a number of subsequent years. Whether children were born of this union between the terrestrial and the ethereal is not recorded, and the alchemist's account of the affair reads rather like Joe Smith's tale about receiving sacred books from an angel on the summit of a mountain overlooking Salt Lake City ; nor is there much to be said for two further works from *Obercit's* pen, the one entitled *Les Promenades de Gamaliel, juif Philosophe*, and the other *La Connexion Originaire des Esprits et des Corps, d'après les Principes de Newton* (Augsburg, 1776). Still, if our alchemist cannot be called an able writer, he must be hailed as a picturesque character ; and it is matter for regret that so little is known about his life, which extended to the year 1798.

Oberion : A spirit. (*See* **England.**)

Obsession and Possession : *Obsession*, from Latin *obsessionem —obsidere*, to besiege, is a form of insanity caused, according to traditional belief, by the persistent attack of an evil spirit without, this being the opposite of *possession*, control by an evil spirit from within, both meaning however the usurpation of the individuality and control of the body by a foreign and discarnate entity. This belief may be found in the earliest records of human history, and in the magical rites and formulæ of ancient religions, used as charms against and exorcism of these invading influences. Indian, Greek and Roman literature teem with instances, the Bible also furnishing many from the case of Saul " troubled with an evil spirit " only to be dispossessed by the music of David's harping, to the miracles of Jesus Christ who cast out legions of possessing spirits. Plato in his *Republic*

not only speaks of demons of various grades, but mentions a method of treating and providing for those obsessed by them. Sophocles and Euripides describe the possessed and mention of the subject is also to be found in Herodotus, Plutarch, Horace, and many others of the classics. Terrible and appalling episodes in the Middle Ages are to be traced to the unquestioned belief in the possibility of *possession* and *obsession* by the Devil and his legions. All madness was caused thereby, was indeed the visible manifestation of the Evil One, only to be exorcised by charms, averted by the observance of sacred rites, or later, to be burned and destroyed bodily for the good of the tortured soul within. The rites of Black Magic, in all ages and places, deliberately evoke this *possession* by the Devil and his demons for the communication and benefit of the infallible knowledge it was believed they conferred and its consequent power and control of man and his destinies.

Modern science with its patient and laborious researches into human psychology, has given the key to this baffling mystery, showing the human mind to be an incomparably delicate instrument, peculiarly at the mercy of the perceptions of the senses and their multitudinous impressions on the brain, its balance so easily shaken by a shock, a drug, a momentary excitement, oftener by prolonged and intense concentration upon single groups of ideas. It is to be noted that in the hallucinatory epidemics of all ages and countries there is to be found this unvarying characteristic : they are connected with some dominant cause, train of thought or religious sentiment prevalent at the time. In the Middle Ages when there flourished an intense belief in the positive apparitions of angels, saints and devils, the people's imagination was dominated and rendered intensely dramatic thereby. The transmigration of the human soul into animals was another popular belief and to this again can be traced the terrible superstition of Lycanthropy (q.v.) which possessed large numbers of people in France and Germany in the fourteenth and sixteenth centuries. The Flagellant mania took its rise at Perouse in the thirteenth century, caused by the panic attendant upon an outbreak of plague. These people maintained that there was no remission of sins without flagellation. This they preached with fanatical fervour and bands of them, gathering adherents everywhere, roamed through city and country, clad in scanty clothing on which were depicted skeletons and with frenzied movements publicly lashed themselves. It was to these exhibitions, the name of the " Dance of Death " was first applied. The Dancing mania, accompanied by aberration of mind and maniacal distortions of the body was very prevalent in Germany in the fourteenth century, and in the sixteenth century in Italy where it was termed " Tarantism " and as a variant in source, was ascribed to the bite of the Tarantula spider. The music and songs employed for the cure are still preserved. Edmund Parrish in his work *Hallucinations and Illusions* makes the following observations on this subject : " If not reckoned as true chorea, the epidemic of dancing which raged in Germany and the Netherlands in the Middle Ages comes under this head. Appearing in Aix it spread in a few months to Liège, Utrecht and the neighbouring towns, visited Metz, Cologne and Strasburg (1418) and after lingering into the sixteenth century gradually died out. This malady consisted in convulsions, contortions accompanying the dancing, hallucinations and so forth. The attack could be checked by bandaging the abdomen as well as by kicks and blows on that part of the body. Music had a great influence on the dancers, and for this reason it was played in the streets in order that the attacks might by this means reach a crisis and disappear the sooner. Quite trifling circumstances could bring on these seizures, the sight of pointed shoes for instance, and of the colour red which the dancers held in horror. In order to prevent such outbreaks the wearing of pointed shoes was forbidden by the authorities. During their dance many of the afflicted thought they waded in blood, or saw heavenly visions."

The same author remarks on other instances :—" To this category also belongs the history of demoniacal *possession*. The belief of being possessed by spirits, frequently met with in isolated cases, appeared at certain periods in epidemic form. Such an epidemic broke out in Brandenburg, and in Holland and Italy in the sixteenth century, especially in the convents. In 1350–60 it attacked the convent of St. Brigitta, in Xanthen, a convent near Cologne, and others. The nuns declared that they were visited by the Devil, and had carnal conversation with him. These and other ' possessed ' wretches were sometimes thrown into dungeons, sometimes burnt. The convent of the Ursulines at Aix was the scene of such a drama (1609–11) where two possessed nuns, tormented by all kinds of apparitions, accused a priest of witchcraft on which charge he was burnt to death (*See* **Grandier, Urbain**). The famous case of the nuns of Loudun (1632–39) led to a like tragic conclusion, as well as the Louvier case (1642) in which the two chief victims found their end in life-long imprisonment and the stake."

The widespread belief in and fear of magic and witchcraft operating on superstitious minds produced the most extraordinary hallucinations. Religious ecstasy partakes of the same character, the difference being that it is *possession* by and contact with so-called good spirits. The sacred books of all nations teem with instances of this and profane history can also furnish examples. The many familiar cases of ecstatic visions and revelations in the Old Testament may be cited, as well as those found in the legends of saints and martyrs, where they either appear as revelations from heaven or temptations of the Devil. In the latter case, a scientific authority, Krafft-Ebing, points out the close connection of religious ecstasy with sexual disturbances. That this condition of " ecstasy " was and is sought and induced the following passage amply proves :—" Among Eastern and primitive peoples such as Hindoos, American Indians, natives of Greenland, Kamtschatka and Yucatan, fetish-worshipping Negroes, and Polynesians, the ecstatic state accompanied with hallucinations is frequently observed, sometimes arising spontaneously, but more often artificially induced. It was known also among the nations of antiquity. The means most often employed to induce this state are beating of magic drums and blowing of trumpets, howlings and hour-long prayers, dancing, flagellation, convulsive movements and contortions, asceticism, fasting and sexual abstinence. Recourse is also had to narcotics to bring about the desired result. Thus the flyagaric is used in Western Siberia, in San Domingo the herb coca, tobacco by some tribes of American Indians, and in the East opium and hashish. The ancient Egyptians had their intoxicating drinks, and receipts for witch's salves and philtres have come down to us from mediæval times." In many countries this condition of *possession* is induced for religious and prophetic purposes, also for mere fortune-telling. The extent to which this belief in *obsession* and *possession* obtains at the present day is testified by Tylor in *Primitive Culture* :—" It is not too much to assert that the doctrine of demoniacal *possession* is kept up, substantially the same theory to account for substantially the same facts, by half the human race, who thus stand as consistent representatives of their forefathers back in primitive antiquity." In the cults of Modern Spiritualism and Theosophy it may be found as a leading tenet of their creeds. The obsessional theory is used to account for all forms of insanity and

crime. The following passage taken from the publication of a modern seer *Diakka and their Victims* by A. J. Davis indicates this modern belief :—" The country of the diakka is where the morally deficient and the affectionately unclean enter upon a strange probation. . . . . They are continually victimizing sensitive persons still in the flesh making sport of them and having a jolly laugh at the expense of really honest and sincere people. They (these demon-like spirits) teach that they would be elevated and made happy if only they could partake of whiskey and tobacco, or gratify their burning free-love propensities. . . . Being unprincipled intellectualities their play is nothing but pastime amusement at the expense of those beneath their influence." These creatures are also said to be of a malignant and blood-thirsty nature, inciting the beings they possess to murder, often of a terrible character.

Signs of Demoniac Possession.—Melanchthon, in one of his letters, says that though there may occasionally be some natural causes for a frenzy or mania, it is also quite certain that devils enter certain persons and there cause torment and fury with or without natural causes, just as one sees at times maladies cured with remedies which are not natural. Moreover, such spectacles are in the nature of wonders and forecasts of things to come. Twelve years before a woman of Saxony, who could neither read nor write, being controlled by a devil, spoke, after the torment was over, words in Greek and Latin to the effect that there would be great distress among the people.

Dr. Ese gives the following as possible signs of *possession* :—

   i. Imagining oneself possessed.
   ii. Leading an evil life.
   iii. Living alone.
   iv. Chronic ailments, unusual symptoms, a deep sleep, the vomiting of strange things.
   v. Blaspheming and frequent reference to the Devil.
   vi. Making a compact with the Devil.
   vii. Being controlled by spirits.
   viii. Having a face that inspires horror and fear.
   ix. Being tired of living and the giving up of hope.
   x. Being enraged and violent in action.
   xi. Making the cries and noises of a beast.

In an account of those possessed in Loudon, we find the questions put to the University of Montpellier by Santerre, priest and founder of the bishopric and diocese of Nimes touching on the signs and the judicial answers of this University.

Q.—Whether the bending and moving of the body, the head at times, touching the soles of the feet, with other contortions and strange positions are good signs of *possession* ?

A.—Mimics and acrobats make such strange movements, bending and twisting themselves in so many ways that one must conclude that there is no sort of position which men and women cannot take up, after long practice and application, even being able, with the ease of experience, to extend and spread out abnormally the legs and other parts of the body, by the extension of the nerves, muscles and tendon— such performances are not without the bounds of nature.

Q.—Whether the rapidity of the movement of the head backwards and forwards, touching the chest and the back, is an infallible sign of *possession* ?

A.—This movement is so natural that nothing need be added to what has been said about the movements of the other parts of the body.

Q.—Whether the sudden swelling of the tongue, the throat and the face, and the sudden changing of colour, are sure signs of *possession* ?

A.—The swelling and disturbance of the chest through interruption are the efforts of breathing or inspiration—

the normal actions in respiration—and *possession* cannot be inferred from them. The swelling of the throat may proceed from the retention of the breath and that of the other parts from the melancholic vapours which are often observed wandering through all parts of the body. Hence it follows that this sign of *possession* is inadmissible.

Q.—Whether a feeling, stupidly heedless, or the lack of feeling, to the point of being pricked or pinched without complaining or moving and not even changing colour are certain signs of *possession* ?

A.—The young Lacedemonian who allowed himself to be bitten by a fox which he had stolen without seeming to feel it, and those who flog themselves, even to death, before the altar of Diana, without turning a hair, they all show that, with resolution, pin-pricks can be endured without complaining. Moreover, it is certain that in the human body, small areas of skin are met with in some persons, which are insensitive, although the neighbouring parts may be quite sensitive, a condition which occurs the more frequently after some previous illness. Such a condition has, therefore, no bearing on *possession*.

Q.—Whether the total lack of bodily movement which, at the command of the exorciser, occurs in those supposedly possessed during, and in the middle of, their most violent actions, is an undeniable sign of a true diabolic *possession* ?

A.—The movements of the parts of the body being voluntary it is natural for well-disposed persons to move themselves or not at will, so that such a cessation of movement, if there is not entire lack of feeling, is not sufficient ground from which to infer a diabolic *possession*.

Q.—Whether the yelping or noise like that of a dog, which comes from the chest rather than from the throat, is a mark of *possession* ?

A.—Human skill adapts itself so easily to the counterfeiting of all kinds of expressions, that persons are met with every day who can give perfectly the expressions, cries and songs of all sorts of animals, and that with a practically imperceptible movement of the lips. Again, many are to be found who form their words in the stomach and they would seem to come from some other object rather than from the one who forms them. Such persons are called ventriloquists. However, such a condition is natural, as Pasquier shows, in Chap. 38 of his *Researches*, with one, Constantin, a jester, as an example.

Q.—Whether keeping the gaze fixed on some object without moving the eye, is a good sign of *possession* ?

A.—The movement of the eye is voluntary, like that of the other parts of the body, and it is natural to move it or keep it still—there is therefore, nothing of note in this.

Q.—Whether the answers, given in French, to questions put in Latin, to those supposedly possessed, are a mark of *possession* ?

A.—We assert that to understand and speak languages which one has not learnt is certainly supernatural, and would lead to the supposition that it occurred through the ministrations of the Devil or from some other cause beyond ; but merely to answer some questions suggests nothing more than long practice, or that one of the number is in league with them and able to contribute to such answers making it appear a fallacy to say that the devils hear the questions put to them in Latin and answer in French and in the tongue natural to the one who is to pass for the demoniac. If follows from this that such a result does not infer the occupation by a demon, more especially if the questions are of few words and not involved.

Q.—Whether the vomiting of such things as one has swallowed is a sign of *possession* ?

A.—Delrio, Bodin, and other authors say that by witchcraft, sorcerers sometimes manage to vomit nails, pins, and other strange things, by the work of the devil, who is able to do the same for the truly possessed. But to vomit things one has swallowed is natural, there being people with weak stomachs who keep down for several hours what they have swallowed and then return it as they have taken it ; also the lientery returns food through the bowel as it has been taken by the mouth.

Q.—Whether pricks with a lancet, in different parts of the body, without the drawing of blood, are a good sign of *possession* ?

A.—This is related to the composition of the melancholic temperament, in which the blood is so thick that it cannot issue from such small wounds and it is because of this that many when pricked by the surgeon's lancet, even in their very veins, do not bleed a drop, as is shown by experience. There is thus nothing extraordinary here.

Recorded Incidents of Possession.—Bouloese tells how twenty-six devils came out of the body of the possessed Nicoli, of Laon : " At two o'clock in the afternoon, the said Nicoli, being possessed of the Devil, was brought to the said church, where the said de Motta proceeded as before with the exorcism. In spite of all entreaty the said Beelzebub told them in a loud voice that he would not come out. Returning to their entreaties after dinner, the said de Motta asked him how many had come out, and he answered, ' twenty-six.' ' You and your followers,' then said de Motta, ' must now come out like the others.' ' No,' he replied, ' I will not come out here, but if you like to take me to Saint Restitute, we will come out there. It is sufficient for you that twenty-six are out.' Then the said de Motta asked for a convincing sign of how they had come out. For witness he told them to look in the garden of the treasury over the front gate, for they had taken and carried away three tufts (*i.e.* branches) from a green may-pole (a small fir) and three slates from above the church of Liesse, made into a cross, as others in France commonly, all of which was found true as shown by the Abbot of Saint-Vincent, M. de Velles, Master Robert de May, canon of the Church Notre-Dame of Laon, and others."

The same author gives an account of the contortions of the demoniac of Laon : he says :—" As often as the reverend father swung the sacred host before her eyes, saying, ' Begone, enemy of God,' so did she toss from side to side, twisting her face towards her feet, and making horrible noises. Her feet were reversed, with the toes in the position of the heel, and despite the restraining power of eight or the men, she stiffened herself and threw herself into the air a height of six feet, the stature of a man, so that the attendants, sometimes even carried with her into the air, perspired at their work. And although they bore down with all their might, still could they not restrain her, and torn away from the restraining hands, she freed herself without any appearance of being at all ruffled.

" The people, seeing and hearing such a horrible sight, one so monstrous, hideous and terrifying cried out, ' Jesus, have mercy on us ! ' Some hid themselves, not daring to look ; others, recognising the wild cruelty of such excessive and incredible torment, wept bitterly, reiterating piteously, ' Jesus, have mercy on us ! ' The reverend father then gave permission to those who wished to touch and handle the patient, disfigured, bent, and deformed, and with the rigidity of death. Chief among these were the would-be reformers, such men as Francois Santerre, Christofle, Pasquot, Gratian de la Roche, Masquette, Jean du Glas, and others well-known for their tendencies towards reform, all vigorous men. They all endeavoured, but in vain, to straighten her limbs, and bring them to a normal position, and to open her eyes and mouth—it was futile. Further, so stiff and rigid was she, that the limbs would have broken rather than give, as also the nose and ears. And then, as she said afterwards, she was possessed, declaring that she was enduring incredible pain. That is, by the soul torment, the devil makes the body become stone or marble.''

Jean Le Breton gives the following concerning those possessed in Louviers :—

" The fourth fact is that many times a day they show transports of rage and fury, during whch they call themselves demons, without, however, offending anyone or even hurting the fingers of the priests, which were put into their mouths at the height of their fury.

" The fifth is that during these furies they show strange convulsions and contortions, bending themselves back, among other things, in the form of a circle, without the use of the hands, and in such a way that their bodies are supported as much on the forehead as on the feet. The rest of the body is unsupported and remains so for a long time—the position being repeated seven or eight times. After such feats as this and many others, kept up sometimes for four hours, chiefly during the exorcism and during the warmest parts of the dog days, they are found on coming to, to be as normal, as fresh and with a pulse as even as if nothing had happened to them.

" The sixth is that some of them faint away at will during the exorcism and this condition occurs at a time when the face is the most suffused with blood and the pulse is the strongest. They come to of themselves and the recovery is more remarkable than the swooning—it begins as a movement of the toe, then of the foot and in their order, of the leg, thigh, abdomen, chest and throat, the movement of the, last three being one of wide dilation. The face, meanwhile is apparently devoid of expression, which finally returns with grimaces and shoutings, the spiritual element returning at the same time with its former disturbing contortions.''

Doctor Ese gives the following as the case of Sister Mary, of the Convent at Louviers :—

" The last was Sister Mary of St. Esprit, supposedly possessed by Dagon, a large woman, slender-waisted, and of good complexion, with no evidence of illness. She came into the refectory. . . . head erect and eyes wandering from side to side, singing, dancing and skipping. Still moving about and touching lightly those around her, she spoke with an elegance of language expressive of the good feeling and good nature which were his (usirg the person of the devil.) All this was done with movements and carriage alike haughty, following it up with a violence of blasphemy, then a reference to his dear little friend Magdalen, his darling and his favourite mistress. And then, without springing or using effort of any kind, she projected herself into a pane of glass and hanging on to a central bar of iron passed bodily through it, but on making an exit from the other side the command was given in Latin, ' est in nomine Jesu rediret non per aliam sed per eadem viam.' After some discussion and a definite refusal to return she, however, returned by the same route, whereupon the doctors examined her pulse and tongue, all of which she endured while laughing and discussing other things. They found no disturbance such as they had expected, nor any sign of the violence of her actions and words, her coming to being accompanied with some trivial remarks. The company then retired.''

Another writer on those possessed in Louviers gives the following astonishing fact :—

" Placed in the middle of the nave of this chapel was a vase of some kind of marble, some two feet in diameter and a little under a foot deep, with sides about three fingers' breadth in thickness. So heavy was it that three of the most robust persons would have had difficulty in raising it while on the ground, yet this girl, to all appearances of very low vitality, came into the chapel and grasping the vase merely by the ends of her fingers, raised it from the pedestal on which it was placed, turned it upside down and threw it on to the ground with as much ease as if it had been a piece of cardboard or paper. Such great strength in one so weak astonished all those present. Moreover, the girl, appearing wild and possessed, ran hither and thither with movements so abrupt and violent that it was difficult to stop her. One of the clerics present, having caught her by the arm, was surprised to find that it did not prevent the rest of her body from turning over and over as if the arm were fixed to the shoulder merely by a spring. This wholly unnatural performance was carried out some seven or eight times and that with an ease and speed difficult to imagine.''

The *Relation des Ursulines possedées d'Auxonne* contains the following :—

" M. de Chalons was no sooner at the altar (at midnight) than from the garden of the monastery and around the house was heard a confused noise, accompanied by unknown voices and some whistling ; at times loud cries with strange and indistinct sounds as from a crowd, all of which was rather terrifying among the shadows of the night. At the same time stones were thrown from different places against the windows of the choir where they were celebrating holy mass and this despite the fact that these windows were a good distance from the walls which enclosed the monastery which made it improbable that they came from without. The glass was broken in one place but the stone did not fall into the choir. This noise was heard by several persons, inside and out. The sentinel in the citadel on that side of the town took alarm at it as he said the next day, and at the altar the bishop of Chalons could not but feel a suspicion that something extraordinary was going on in the house and that demons or sorcerers were making some attempts at that moment which he repelled from where he was by secret imprecations and inward exorcisms.''

" The Franciscan nuns of the same town heard the noise and were terrified by it. They thought that the monastery shook beneath them and in this confusion and fear they were compelled to have recourse to prayer.''

" At the same time voices were heard in the garden, weak and moaning and as if asking for help. It was nearly an hour after midnight and very dark and stormy. Two clerics were sent out to see what was the matter and found Marguerite Constance and Denise Lamy in the monastery garden, the former up a tree and the latter seated at the foot of the stairway into the choir. They were at liberty and in the full possession of their senses, yet appeared distracted, especially the latter, and very weak and pale, though with blood on her face ; she was terrified and had difficulty in composing herself. The other had blood on her face also though she was not wounded. The doors of the house were tightly closed and the walls of the garden were some ten or twelve feet high.''

" In the afternoon of the same day the bishop of Chalons, with the intention of exorcising Denise Lamy, sent for her and when she was not found, he inwardly commanded her to come to him in the chapel of St. Anne where he was. It was striking to see the prompt obedience of the demon to this command, formulated merely in the mind, for in about a quarter of an hour a violent knocking was heard at the door of the chapel, as if by one hard pressed. On opening the door this girl entered the chapel abruptly, leaping and bounding, her face changed greatly and with high colour and sparkling eyes. So bold and violent was she that it was difficult to restrain her, nor would she allow the putting on of the stole which she seized and threw violently into the air despite the efforts of four or five clerics who did their best to stop her, so that finally it was proposed to bind, her, but this was deemed too difficult in the condition in which she was.''

" On another occasion, at the height of her frenzy. . . . .

the demon was ordered to stop the pulse in one of her arms, and it was immediately done, with less resistance and pain than before. Immediate response. was also made to the further order to make it return. The command being given to make the girl insensible to pain, she avowed that she was so, boldly offering her arm to be pierced and burnt as wished. The exorcist, fortified by his earlier experience, took a sufficiently long needle and drove it, full length, into the nail and flesh, at which she laughed aloud, saying that she felt nothing at all. Accordingly as he was ordered, blood was allowed to flow or not, and she herself took the needle and stuck it into different parts of her arm and hand. Further, one of the company took a pin and, having drawn out the skin a little above the wrist, passed it through and through so that the two ends were only visible, the rest of the pin being buried in the arm. Unless the order was given for some no blood issued, nor was there the least sign of feeling or pain."

The same account gives, as proofs of the *possession* of the Auxonne nuns, the following :—

" Violent agitation of the body only conceivable to those who have seen it. Beating of the head with all their might against the pavement or walls, done so often and so hard that it causes one to shudder on seeing it and yet they show no sign of pain, nor is there any blood, wound or contusion.

" The condition of the body in a position of extreme violence, where they support themselves on their knees with the head turned round an inclined towards the ground for a foot or so, which makes it appear as if broken. Their power of bearing, for hours together without moving, the head being lowered behind below the level of the waist ; their power of breathing in this condition ; the unruffled expression of the face which never alters during these disturbances ; the evenness of the pulse ; their coolness during these movements ; the tranquil state they are in when they suddenly return and the lack of any quickening in the respirations ; the turning back of the head, even to the ground, with marvellous rapidity. Sometimes the movement to and fro is done thirty or forty times running, the girl on her knees and with her arms crossed in front ; at other times, in the same position with the head turned about, the body is wound around into a sort of semicircle, with results apparently incompatible with nature."

" Fearful convulsions, affecting all the limbs and accompanied with shouts and cries. Sometimes fear at the sight of certain phantoms and spectres by which they say they are menaced, causes such a change in their facial expression that those present are terrified ; at other times there is a flood of tears beyond control and accompanied by groans and piercing cries. Again, the widely-opened mouth, eyes wild and showing nothing but the white, the pupil being turned up under cover of the lids—the whole returning to the normal at the mere command of the exorcist in conjunction with the sign of the cross.

" They have often been seen creeping and crawling on the ground without any help from the hands or feet ; the back of the head or the forehead may be touching the soles of the feet. Some lie on the ground, touching it with the pit of the stomach only, the rest of the body, head, feet and arms, being in the air for some length of time. Sometimes, bent back so that the top of the head and the soles of the feet touch the ground, the rest of the body being supported in the air like a table, they walk in this position without help from the hands. It is quite common for them, while on their knees to kiss the ground, with the face twisted to the back so that the top of the head touches the soles of the feet. In this position and with the arms crossed on the chest they make the sign of the cross on the pavement with their tongues.

" A marked difference is to be noticed between their condition when free and uncontrolled and that which they show when controlled and in the heat of their frenzy. By reason of their sex and delicate constitutions as much as from illness they may be weak, but when the demon enters them and the authority of the church compels them to appear they may become at times so violent that all the power of four or five men may be unable to stop them. Even their faces become so distorted and changed that they are no longer recognisable. What is more astonishing is that after these violent transports, lasting sometimes three or four hours ; after efforts which would make the strongest feel like resting for several days ; after continuous shrieking and heart-breaking cries ; when they become normal again—a momentary proceeding—they are unwearied and quiet, and the mind is as tranquil, the face as composed, the breathing as easy and the pulse as little changed as if they had not stirred out of a chair.

" It may be said, however, that among all the signs of *possession* which these girls have shown, one of the most surprising, and at the same time the most common, is the understanding of the thought and inward commands which are used every day by exorcists and priests, without there being any outward manifestation either by word or other sign. To be appreciated by them it is merely necessary to address them inwardly or mentally, a fact which has been verified by so many of the experiences during the stay of the bishop of Chalons and by any of the clergy, who wished to investigate, that one cannot reasonably doubt such particulars and many others, the details of which cannot be given here. "

A number of archbishops or bishops and doctors in Sorbonne made the following notification with regard to the condition at Auxonne.

" That among these differently-placed girls there are seculars, novices, postulants and professed nuns ; some are young, others old ; some from the town, others not ; some of high estate, others of lesser parentage ; some rich, others poor and of low degree. That it is ten years or more since the trouble began in this monastery ; that it is remarkable that a reign of deceit was able for so long to preserve the secret among girls in such numbers and conditions and interests so varied. That after research and a stricter enquiry, the said Bishop of Chalons has found nobody, either in the monastery or in the town, who could speak other than well of the innocence and integrity, alike of the girls and of the clergy who worked with him in the exorcisms, and, for himself, he finds them with the bearing of persons of uprightness and worth—evidence which he gives in the interest of truth and justice."

" Added to the above is the certificate of Morel, doctor and present at everything, who asserts that all these things exceed the bounds of nature and can only occur as the work of a demon ; in short, we consider that all the extraordinary findings with these girls are beyond the powers of human nature and can only be instigated by a demon possessing and controlling their bodies."

Goulart culls from Wier many stories of demoniacs.

" Antoine Benivenius in the eighth chapter of the *Livre des causes cachées des maladies* tells of having seen a girl of sixteen years whose hands contracted curiously whenever she was taken with a pain in the abdomen. With a cry of terror her abdomen would swell up so much that she had the appearance of being eight months pregnant—later the swelling went down and, not being able to lie still, she tossed about all over the bed, sometimes putting her feet above her head as if trying a somersault. This she kept up throughout the throes of her illness and until it had gone down by degrees. When asked what had happened to her, she denied any remembrance of it. But on seeking the causes of this affection we were of opinion that it arose from a choking of the womb and from the rising of malignant vapours affecting adversely the heart and brain. We were at length forced to relieve her with drugs but these were of no avail and becoming more violent and congested she at last began to throw up long iron nails all bent, brass needles stuck into wax, and bound up with hair and a part of her breakfast—a mass so large that a man would have had difficulty in swallowing it all. I was afraid, after seeing several of these vomitings, that she was possessed by an evil spirit, who deluded those present while he removed these things and afterwards we heard predictions and other things given which were entirely beyond human comprehension."

" Meiner Clath, a nobleman living in the castle of Boutenbrouch in the duchy of Juliers, had a valet named William who for fourteen years had had the torments of a *possession* by the devil, and when, at the instigation of the devil, he began to get ill, he asked for the curé of St. Gerard as confessor. . . . . who came to carry out his little part. . . . but failed entirely. Seeing him with a swollen throat and discoloured face and with the fear of his suffocating, Judith, wife of Clath and an upright woman, with all in the house, began to pray to God. Immediately there issued from William's mouth, among other odds and ends, the whole of the front part of the trousers of a shepherd, stones, some whole and other broken, small bundles of thread, a peruke such as women are accustomed to use, needles, a piece of the serge jacket of a little boy, and a peacock's feather which William had pulled from the bird's tail eight days before he became ill. Being asked the cause of his trouble he said that he had met a woman near Camphuse who had blown in his face and that his illness was the result of that and nothing else. Some time after he had recovered he contradicted what he had said and confessed that he had been instructed by the devil to say what he had. He added that all those curious things had not been in his stomach but had been put into his throat by the devil despite the fact that he was seen to vomit them. Satan deceives by illusions. The thought comes at times to kill oneself or to run away. One day, having got into a hog-shed and protected more carefully than usual he remained with his eyes so firmly closed that it was impossible to open them. At last Gertrude, the eldest daughter of Clath, eleven years old, came along and advised him to pray to God for the return of his sight, but he asked her to pray and the fact of her praying, to the great surprise of both, opened his eyes. The devil exhorted him often not to listen to his mistress or anyone else who bowed the head at the name of God, who could not help him as he had died once, a fact which was openly preached."

" He had once attempted rudely to touch a kitchenmaid and she had reproved him by name, when he answered in a voice of rage that his name was not William but Beelzebub, at which the mistress asked—' Do you think we fear you ? He Whom we serve is infinitely more powerful than you are.' Clath then read the eleventh chapter of St. Luke where mention is made of the casting out of the dumb devil by the power of the Saviour and also of Beelzebub, prince of devils. Finally William began to rest and slept till morning like a man in a swoon, then taking some broth and feeling much relieved he was sent home to his parents, after having thanked his master and mistress and asked God to reward them for the trouble they had been caused by his affliction. He married afterwards and had children, but was never again tormented by the devil."

On the 18th March, 1566, there occurred a memorable case in Amsterdam, Holland, on which the Chancellor of Gueldres, M. Adrian Nicolas, made a public speech, from which is the following :—" Two months or so ago thirty children of this town began to be strangely disturbed, as if frenzied or mad. At intervals they threw themselves on the ground and for half an hour or an hour at the most this torment lasted. Recovering, they remembered nothing, but thought they had had a sleep and the doctors, sorcerers, and exorcists were all equally unable to do any good. During the exorcism the children vomited a number of pins and needles, finger-stalls for sewing, bits of cloth, and of broken jugs and glass, hair and other things. The children didn't always recover from this but had recurrent attacks of it—the unusualness of such a condition causing great astonishment."

Jean Languis, a learned doctor, gives the following, in the first book of his *Epitres*, as having happened in 1539 in Fugenstall, a village in the bishopric of Eysteten and sworn to by a large number of witnesses :—

" Ulric Neusesser, a ploughman in this village, was greatly troubled by a pain in the side. On an incision being made into the skin by a surgeon an iron nail was removed, but this did not relieve the pain, rather did it increase so that, becoming desperate, the poor man finally committed suicide. Before burying him two surgeons opened his stomach, in front of a number of persons, and in it found some long round pieces of wood, four steel knives, some sharp and pointed, others notched like a saw, two iron rods each nine inches long and a large tuft of hair. One wondered how and by what means this mass of old iron could be collected together into the space of his stomach. There is no doubt that it was the work of the devil who is capable of anything which will maintain a dread of him."

" Antoine Lucquet, knight of the order of the Fleece, of high repute throughout Flanders, and privy counsellor of Brabant, had married in Bruges, and his wife, soon after the nuptials, began to show the torments of an evil spirit, so much so that at times, even in company, she was suddenly taken up and dragged through rooms and thrown from one corner to another, despite the efforts of those around to restrain and hold her. She was little conscious of her bodily welfare while in this frenzy and it was the general opinion that her condition had been induced by a former lover of her young and light-hearted husband. Meanwhile she became pregnant without a cessation in the evil torment and the time of her delivery being at hand the only woman present was sent for the midwife but instead, she came in and herself acted as midwife which disturbed the invalid so much that she fainted. She found, on recovering, that she had been delivered, yet to the astonishment of both there was no sign of a child. The next day on wakening up she found a child in swaddling clothes in the bed and she nursed it a couple of times. Falling asleep shortly afterwards the child was taken from her side and was never seen again. It was reported that notes with the hall-mark of magic had been found inside the door."

Goulart gives an account from Wier, of the multitude of terrible convulsions suffered by the nuns of the convent of Kentorp near Hammone, " Just before and during the attack their breath was fœtid and sometimes continued so for hours. While affected they did not lose their power of sound judgment nor of hearing and recognising those around them, despite the fact that owing to the spasm of the tongue and respiratory organs they could not speak during the attack. All were not equally affected but as soon as one was affected the others, though in different rooms, were immediately affected also. A soothsayer, who was sent for, said they had been poisoned by the cook, Else Kamense, and the devil taking advantage of the occasion increased their torment, making them bite and strike each other and throw each other down. After Else and her mother had been burnt some of the inhabitants of Hammone began to be tormented by an evil spirit. The minister of the Church took five of them home to warn them and strengthen them against the machinations of the enemy. They laughed at him and mentioned certain women of the place whom they would like to visit on their goats, which were to carry them there. Immediately one straddled a stool calling out that he was off, while another, squatting down, doubled himself up and rolled towards the door of the room which opened suddenly and through which he went falling to the bottom of the steps without hurting himself."

"The nuns of the Convent of Nazareth at Cologne (according to the same writer) were affected much the same as those of Kentorp. After being troubled for along time and in various ways by the devil they were more terribly affected in 1564 when they would lie out on the ground, with clothing disordered, as if for the companionship of man. During this their eyes would be closed and they would open them later with shame and feeling that they had endured some deep injury. A young girl of fourteen named Gertrude who had been shut up in this convent was subject to this misfortune. She had often been troubled by wild apparitions in bed as witness her mocking laughter, although she tried in vain to overcome it. A companion slept near her specially to protect her from the apparition but the poor girl was terrified at the noise from Gertrude's bed, the devil finally controlling the latter and putting her through a variety of contortions. . . . The beginning of all this trouble was in the acquaintance picked up with one or two of the nuns on a neighbouring tennis court by some dissolute young man who kept up their amours over the walls."

"The torments suffered by the nuns in Wertet in the county of Horne are also wonderful. The beginning is traced to a poor woman who borrowed from the nuns during Lent some three pounds of salt and returned double the amount before Easter. From that they began to find in their dormitory small white balls like sugar-plums, and salt to the taste, which they did not eat, nor did they know whence they came. Shortly after they heard a moaning as of a sick man, then warnings to rise and go to the help of a sick sister, which they would do but would find nothing. Sometimes in endeavouring to use a chamber it would be pulled away suddenly with a consequent soiling of the bed. At times they were pulled out by the feet, dragged some length, and tickled so much on the soles of the feet that they nearly died with laughter. Pieces of flesh were pulled out of some, while others had their legs, arms and heads twisted about. Thus tormented some would throw up a large quantity of black fluid, although for six weeks previously they had taken nothing but the juice of horse-radish without bread. This fluid was so bitter and so sharp that it blistered their mouths and one could evolve nothing which would give them an appetite for anything else. Some were raised into the air to the height of a man and as suddenly thrown to the ground again. When some thirty of their females visited this convent to congratulate those who seemed relieved and practically cured, some of them immediately fell backwards from the table they were at, losing the power of speech and of recognising anyone, while others were stretched out as if dead with arms and legs turned around. One of them was raised into the air against the restraining efforts of those present and then brought again to the ground so forcibly that she seemed dead. She rose, however, as if from a deep sleep and left the convent uninjured. Some moved about on the fronts of their legs as if lacking feet and as if dragged in a loose sack from behind. Others even climbed trees like cats and came down as easily. The Abbess told Margaret, Countess of Bure, that she cried aloud when pinched in the

leg ; it was as severe as if a piece had been pulled out, and that she was carried to bed at once and the place became black and blue, but she finally recovered. This derangement of the nuns was an open secret for three years but has been kept dark since."

"What we have just said applies equally to the early case of the Bridget nuns in their convent near Xanthus. Now, they gambol or bleat like sheep or make horrible noises. Sometimes they were pushed from their seats in church where their veils would be fastened above their heads. At other times their throats would be so stopped up that they could swallow no food, and this affliction lasted for ten years in some of them. It was said that the cause of all this was a young nun whose parents had refused to allow her to marry the young man she loved Further that the devil in the form of this young man had come to her at the height of her passion and had advised her to return to the convent which she did at once and when there she became frenzied and her actions were strange and terrible. The trouble spread like the plague through the other nuns, and the first one abandoned herself to her warder and had two children. Thus does Satan both within and without the convent, carry out his hateful schemes."

"Cardan relates that a ploughman. . . . often threw up glass, nails and hair and, on recovering, felt within a large quantity of broken glass which made a noise like that from a sackful of broken glass. This noise he said troubled him greatly and for some eighteen nights towards seven o'clock, although he had not observed the time and although he had felt cured for some eighteen years, he had felt blows in his heart to the number of hours which were to strike. All this he bore not without great agony."

"I have often seen," says Goulart, "a demoniac named George, who for thirty years on and off was tormented by an evil spirit and often I have seen her swell up, and become so heavy that eight strong men could not raise her from the ground. Then, exhorted and encouraged in the name of God and the hand of some good man extended to her, she would rise to her feet and return home, bent and groaning. She did harm to no one whether by day or night while in this condition, and she lived with a relative who had a number of children so used to her ways that when they saw her twisting her arms, striking her hands and her body swelling up in this strange way, they would gather in some part of the house and commend her to God and their prayers were never in vain. Finding her one day in another house of the village in which she lived I exhorted her to patience. . . She began to roar in a strange way and with a marvellous quickness shot out her left hand at me and enclosed in it my two hands, holding me as firmly as if I had been bound with stout cords. I tried, but in vain, to free myself, although I am of average strength. She interfered with me in no other way nor did she touch me with her right hand. I was held as long as it has taken to tell the incident and then she let me go suddenly, begging my pardon, and I commended her to God and led her quietly home. . . . Some days before her death being much tormented she went to bed with a low fever. The fury of the evil one was then so much curtailed that the patient, wonderfully strengthened inwardly, continued to praise God who had been so merciful to her in her affliction and comforting all who visited her. . . . I may add that Satan was overcome, and that she died peacefully, calling on her Saviour."

According to Goulart "there was, in the village of Leuensteet and duchy of Brunswick, a young girl of twenty years, Margaret Achels, who lived with her sister. Wishing to clean some shoes one day in June she took a knife some six inches long and sat down in a corner of the room for she was still weak from a fever of long standing, whereupon an old woman entered and inquired how she was and whether she still had the fever and then left without further words. After the shoes were cleaned she let the knife fall in her lap but subsequently could not find it despite a diligent search. The girl was frightened and still more so when she found a black dog under the table. She drove it out, hoping to find the knife, but the dog got angry, showed its teeth and growlingly made its way into the street and fled. The girl at once seemed to feel something indefinable which passed down her back like a chill and fainting suddenly she remained so for three days when she began to breathe better and to take a little food. When carefully questioned as to the cause of her illness she said that the knife which had fallen into her lap had entered her left side and that there she felt pain. Although her parents contradicted her, attributing her condition to a melancholic disposition, her long abstinence and other things, she did not cease to complain, to cry and to keep a continuous watch, so much so that her mind became deranged and sometimes for two days at a time she would take nothing even when kindly entreated to do so, so that sometimes force had to be used. Her attacks were more severe at times than others and her rest was broken by the continuous pains which beset her, being forced as she was to hold herself doubled over a stick. What increased her pain and lessened the chance of relief was her firm belief that the knife was buried in her body and the stubborn contradiction of the others who said it was impossible and thought it nothing but a phantom of the mind, since they saw nothing which would give them ground for believing her unless it were her continual complaints and tears. These were kept up for some months and until there appeared on her left side between the two false ribs a tumour as large as an egg which fluctuated in size with the changes in her own girth. Then the girl said to them : ' Up to the present you haven't wanted to believe that the knife was in my side, but you will soon see now that it is.' On the 30th June, that is after almost thirteen months of the trouble, the ulcer which developed on her side poured out so much material that the swelling began to go down and the point of the knife showed and the girl wanted to pull it out but her parents prevented her and sent for the surgeon of Duke Henry who was at the Castle of Walfbutel. This surgeon arrived on the 4th July and begged the curate to comfort, instruct and encourage the girl, and to take particular note of her answers since she was regarded as a demoniac. She agreed to be attended by the surgeon, not without the idea that a quick death would follow. The latter, seeing the point of the knife projecting, grasped it with his instruments and found that it was just like the other in the sheath and every much worn about the middle of the blade. The ulcer was finally cured.''

Goulart, quoting Melanchthon, says that '' there was a girl in the marquisate of Brandebourg who pulled some hairs off the clothing of some person and that these hairs were at once changed into coins of the realm which the girl chewed with a horrible cracking of the teeth. Some of these coins are kept still by persons who snatched them away from the girl and found them real. From time to time this girl was much tormented but after some months got quite well and has remained so since. Prayers, but nothing more, are often offered up for her.''

The same author also says : '' I have heard that there was in Italy a demented woman who when controlled by a devil and asked by Lazare Bonami for the best verse of Virgil, answered at once :

' Discite Justitiam Moniti et non temnere divos.'

' That,' she added, ' is the best and most-deserving verse that Virgil every wrote ; begone and don't come back here again to try me.' ''

Louise Maillat, a young demoniac who lived in 1598

lost the use of her limbs and was found to be possessed by five demons who called themselves, wolf, cat, dog, beauty and a griffin. At first two of these demons came out from her mouth in the form of balls the size of the fist, the first fire-red, the second, which was the cat, quite black ; the others left her with less violence. On leaving her they all made a few turns round the hearth and disappeared. Frances Secretain was known to have made this girl swallow these devils in a crust of bread the colour of manure.''

Od Force : (*See* **Emanations.**)

Odyle (also Od, Odic Force, Odyllic Force) : The term first used by Baron von Reichenbach to denote the subtle effluence which he supposed to emanate from every substance in the universe, particularly from the stars and planets, and from crystals, magnets and the human body. The *odyle* was perceptible only to sensitives, in whom it produced vague feelings of heat or cold, according to the substance from which it radiated ; or a sufficiently sensitive person might perceive the odyllic light, a clear flame of definite colour, issuing from the human finger-tips, the poles of the magnet, various metals, chemicals, etc., and hovering like a luminous cloud over new-made graves. The colours varied with each substance ; thus silver and gold had a white flame ; cobalt, a blue ; copper and iron, a red. The English mesmerists speedily applied Reichenbach's methods to their own sensitives, with results that passed their expectations. The thoroughness of Reichenbach's experiments, and the apparent soundness of his scientific methods, made a deep impression of the public mind. The objections of Braid, who at this time advanced his theory of suggestion, were ignored by the protagonists of *odyle*. In after years, when spiritualism had established itself in America, there remained a group of '' rational '' defenders of the movement, who attributed the phenomena of spiritualism as well as those of the poltergeist to the action of odylic force. Table-turning and rapping were also referred to this emanation by many who laughed to scorn Faraday's theory of unconscious muscular action. Others again, such as Mr. Guppy, regarded the so-called '' spirit '' intelligences producing the manifestations as being compounded of odylic vapours emanating from the medium, and probably connected with an all-pervading thought-atmosphere—an idea sufficiently like the '' cosmic fluid '' of the early magnetists.

Oil, Magical : (*See* **Magic.**)

Ointment, Witches' : It was believed in mediæval times that all the wonders performed by *witches*—i.e., changing themselves into animals, being transported through the air, etc.— were wrought by anointing themselves with a potent salve. As ointments are still used in Oriental countries as a means of inducing visions, it is possible that something of the kind may account for the hallucinations which the *witches* seem to have experienced. Lord Verulam says, '' The *ointment*, that *witches* use, is reported to be made of the *fat of children*, digged out of their *graves* ; of the *juices* of *smallage*, *wolfebane*, and *cinque foil*, mingled with the *meal* of fine *wheat* : but I suppose that the soporiferous medicines are likest to do it, which are *hen-bane*, *hemlock*, *mandrake*, *moonshade*, *tobacco*, *opium*, *saffron*, *poplar leaves*, etc.''

Okey Sisters : (*See* **Spiritualism.**)

Olcott, Colonel Henry Steel : The founder, together with Madame Blavatsky, of the movement known as Theosophy, and president of the Theosophical Society. Before he identified himself with this movement he was a well-known authority on matters connected with agriculture. In 1856 he founded in America an agricultural school on the Swiss model, was offered by the American Government the Chief Commissionership of Agriculture and by the Greek Government the Professorship of Agriculture at Athens. He was for a time agricultural editor of Horace Greeley's *New York*

Tribune, and published three works on agriculture. When the Civil War broke out he joined the Northerners, saw active service, and was invalided home. The government then made him Special Commissioner of the War Department. On the cessation of the war he retired into private life, and from 1875 till his death in 1906 taught the doctrines of Theosophy and neo-Buddhism. On the death of Madame Blavatsky he associated himself with Mrs. Annie Besant as the leader of Theosophy in India. (*See* **Theosophy.**)

Old Hat used for Raising the Devil : A popular mode of *raising the devil* in former times was to make a circle, place an *old hat* in the centre, and repeat the Lord's Prayer backwards. It was really a caricature of magical incantation.

Old man of the Mountain : (*See* **Assassins.**)

"Old Scratch" : One of the appellations given to the Evil One. It is supposed to have been derived from *Skrati*, an old Teutonic faun or Satyr, half-man and half-goat, and possessed of horns.

Olympian Spirits : (*See* **Seven Stewards of Heaven.**)

Olympic Spirits : (*See* **Arbatel.**)

Om : A Sanskrit word of peculiar sanctity in the Hindu religion. It is pronounced at the beginning and end of every lesson in the *Veda*, and is also the introductory word of the *Puranas*. It is said in the *Katha-Upanishad* : " Whoever knows this syllable obtains whatever he wishes." Various accounts are given of its origin ; one that it is the term of assent used by the gods, and probably an old contracted form of the Sanskrit word *evam* meaning " thus." The laws of the *Manu* say that the word was formed by Brahma himself, who extracted the letters *a u m* from the *Vedas*, one from each ; and they thus explain its mysterious power and sanctity. *Om* is also the name given by the Hindus to the spiritual sun, as opposed to " Sooruj " the natural sun.

Omar Khayyam : (*See* **Assassins.**)

Onimancy, or the observation of the angel Uriel, is thus performed. Upon the nails of the right hand of an unpolluted boy or a young virgin, or the palm of the hand, is put some oil of olives, or what is better, oil of walnuts mingled with tallow or blacking. If money or things hidden in the earth be sought, the face of the child must be turned towards the east. If crime be inquired into, or the knowledge of a person out of affection, towards the south ; for robbery towards the west, and for murder towards the south. Then the child must repeat the seventy-two verses of the Psalms, which the Hebrew kabalists collected for the Urim and Thummim. These will be found in the third book of Reuclin on the kabalistical art, and in a treatise *de verbo mirifico*. In each of these verses occurs the venerable name of four letters, and the three lettered name of the seventy-two angels, which are referred to the inquisitive name Schemhammaphoras, which was hidden in the folds of the lining of the tippet of the high priest. When the curious student has done this much, Saunders assures him that he " shall see wonders," but he omits to specify what these wonders are. Chiromancers give the name Onyomancy to the inspection of the natural signs on the nails.

Onion : The *Onion* was regarded as a symbol of the universe among the ancient Egyptians, and many curious beliefs were associated with it. It was believed by them that it attracted and absorbed infectious matters, and was usually hung up in rooms to prevent maladies. This belief in the absorptive virtue of the *onion* is prevalent even at the present day. " When a youth," says Napier, " I remember the following story being told, and implicitly believed by all. There was once a certain king or nobleman who was in want of a physician, and two celebrated doctors applied. As both could not obtain the situation, they agreed among

themselves that the one was to try to poison the other, and he who succeeded in overcoming the poison would thus be left free to fill the situation. They drew lots as to who should first take the poison. The first dose given was a stewed toad, but the party who took it immediately applied a poultice of peeled *onions* over his stomach, and thus abstracted all the poison of the toad. Two days after, the other doctor was given the *onions* to eat. He ate them, and died. It was generally believed that the poultice of peeled *onions* laid on the stomach, or underneath the arm-pits, would cure anyone who had taken poison."

Onomancy, it has been properly said, more correctly signifies divination by a donkey, than by a name ; and the latter science ought to be termed Onomamancy,or Onomatomancy. The notion that an analogy existed between men's names and their fortunes is supposed to have originated with the Pythagoreans ; it furnished some reveries to Plato, and has been the source of much small wit in Ausonius, which it may amuse the classical scholar to collate from his epigrams.

Two leading rules in the science of *Onomancy* were first, that an even number of vowels in a man's name signifies something amiss in his left side ; an uneven number a similar affection on the right ; so that, between the two, perfect sanity was little to be expected. Secondly, of two competitors, that one would prove successful the numeral letters in whose name when summed up exceeded the amount of those in the name of his rival ; and this was one of the reasons which enabled Achilles to triumph over Hector.

The Gothic King, Theodotus, is said, on the authority of Cælius Rhodiginus to have practised a peculiar species of *Onomancy* on the recommendation of a Jew. The diviner advised the prince, when on the eve of a war with Rome, to shut up thirty hogs in three different styes, having previously given some of them Roman and others Gothic names. On an appointed day, when the styes were opened, all the Romans were found alive, but with half their bristles fallen off—all the Goths, on the other hand, were dead ; and from this prognostic the onomantist foreboded that the Gothic army would be utterly destroyed by the Romans, who, at the same time, would lose half their own force.

Onychomancy : Divination by the finger-nails. It is practised by watching the reflection of the sun in the nails of a boy, and judging the future by the shape of the figures which show themselves on their surface.

Onyx : Its properties resemble those of Jasper, besides which it increases saliva in boys, and is said to bring terrible shapes to the dreamer. If applied to the eye it acts as if it were alive, by creeping about and removing anything noxious.

Ooscopy and Oomantia : Two methods of divination by eggs. An example under the former name is related by Suetonius, who says, that Livia, when she was anxious to know whether she should be the mother of a boy or girl, kept an egg in her bosom at the proper temperature, until a chick with a beautiful cockscomb came forth. The latter name denotes a method of divining the signs or characters appearing in eggs. The custom of pasche or paste eggs, which are stained with various colours, and given away at Easter, is well known, and is described at considerable length by Brand. The custom is most religiously observed in Russia, where it is derived from the Greek Church. Gilded or coloured eggs are mutually exchanged both by men and women, who kiss one another, and if any coolness existed previously become good friends again on these occasions. The egg is one of the most ancient and beautiful symbols of the new birth, and has been applied to natural philosophy as well as the spiritual creation of man.

Opal : Recreates the heart, preserves from contagion in the air, and dispels sadness ; it is also good for weak eyes. Pliny's description of this stone glows with enthusiasm, and he gives the preference to those which are shadowed as it were with the colour of wine. The name *poederos*, applied to the *opal*, is understood to indicate the beautiful complexion of youth.

Ophites : This gnostic sect seems to have dated from the second century. A full system of initiation was in vogue among the members, and they possessed symbols to represent purity, life, spirit and fire. The whole appears to have been of Egyptian origin. (*See* **Gnostics.**)

Oracles : Shrines where a god speaks to human beings through the mouths of priests or priestesses. The concept of the god become vocal in this manner was by no means confined to Greece or Egypt. Our object here is to deal with the most celebrated *oracles* of all nations as well as those of antiquity. Probably all the primitive gods—those, that is to say, of the fetish class, now under consideration—were consulted as *oracles* ; it is certain that they derived this character in a state of animism and that they transmitted it to gods of the most advanced type. In early times the great question was whether man would have food on the morrow or no ; perhaps the first *oracle* was the spirit which directed the hungry savage in his hunting and fishing expeditions. The Esquimaux still consult spirits for this purpose, and their wizards are as familiar with the art of giving ambiguous replies to their anxious clients as were the well-informed keepers of the *oracles* of Greece. As advancement proceeded, the direction of the gods was obtained in all the affairs of private and public life.

Greece.—The Oracle of Delphi. When Jupiter was once desirous to ascertain the central point of the earth, he despatched two eagles, or two crows, as they are named by Strabo. The messengers took flight in opposite courses, from sunrise and sunset ; and they met at Delphi, which place was thenceforward dignified with the title " The navel of the earth ; " an " umbilicus " being represented in white marble within its celebrated temple. Delphi thus became a place of great distinction, but it was not yet oracular, till the fumes which issued from a neighbouring cave were first discovered by a shepherd named Coretas. His attention was forcibly attracted to a spot round which whenever his goats were browsing they gambolled and bleated more than was their wont. Whether these fumes arose in consequence of an earthquake, or whether they were generated by demoniacal art is not to be ascertained ; but the latter hypothesis is thought by Clasen to be the more probable of the two. Coretas, on approaching the spot, was seized with ecstacy, and uttered words which were deemed inspired. It was not long before the danger arising in consequence of the excitement of curiosity among the neighbours, the deadly stupefaction often produced among those who inhaled the fumes without proper caution, and the inclination which it aroused in some to plunge themselves into the depths of the cavern below, occasioned the fissure to be covered by a sort of table, having a hole in the centre, and called a tripod, so that those who wished to try the experiment could resort there in safety. Eventually a young girl, of unsophisticated manners, became the chosen medium of the responses, now deemed oracular and called Pythian, as proceeding from Apollo, the slayer of Python, to whom Delphi was consecrated. A sylvan bower of laurel branches was erected over the spot, and at length the marble temple and the priesthood of Delphi arose where the Pythoness, seated on her throne, could be charged with

the divine " afflatus," and was thus rendered the vehicle of Apollo's dictation.

As the *oracle* became more celebrated, its prophetic machinery was constructed of more costly materials. The tripod was then formed of gold, but the lid, which was placed in its hollow rim, in order to afford the Pythoness a more secure seat, continued to be made of brass. She prepared herself by drinking out of a sacred fountain (Castalia), adjoining the crypt, the waters of which were reserved for her only, and in which she bathed her hair ; by chewing a laurel leaf, and by circling her brows with a laurel crown. The person who made inquiry from the *oracle*, first offered a victim, and then having written his question in a note-book, handed it to the Pythoness, before she ascended the tripod ; and he also as well as the priestess, wore a laurel crown. In early times the *oracle* spoke only in one month of the year, named " Byssus," in which it originated ; and at first only on the seventh day of that month, which was esteemed the birth-day of Apollo, and was called " Polyphonus."

Virginity was at first an indispensable requisite in the Pythoness ; on account, as Diodorus tells us, of the purity of that state and its relation to Diana ; moreover, because virgins were thought better adapted than others of their sex to keep oracular mysteries secret and inviolate. But an untoward accident having occurred to one of these consecrated damsels, the guardians of the temple, in order, as they imagined, to prevent its repetition for the future, permitted no one to fulfil the duties of the office till she had attained the mature age of fifty ; they still indulged her, however, with the use of a maiden's habit. The response was always delivered in Greek.

Oracle of Dodona. Another celebrated *oracle*, that of Jupiter, was at Dodona, in Epirus, from which Jupiter derived the name of Dodonus. It was situated at the foo of Mount Tomarus, in a wood of oaks ; and there the answers were given by an old woman under the name of Pelias. Pelias means dove in the Attic dialect, from which the fable arose, that the doves prophesied in the groves of Dodona. According to Herodotus, this legend contains the following incident, which gave rise to the *oracle* :—Two priestesses of Egyptian Thebes were carried away by Phœnician merchants ; one of them was conveyed to Libya, where she founded the *oracle* of Jupiter Ammon ; the other to Greece. The latter one remained in the Dodonian wood, which was much frequented on account of the acorns. There she had a temple built at the foot of an oak in honour of Jupiter, whose priestess she had been in Thebes ; and here afterwards a regular *oracle* was founded. He adds, that this priestess was called a dove, because her language could not be understood. The Dodonid and African *oracles* were certainly connected, and Herodotus distinctly states, that the manner of prophecy in Dodona was the same as that in Egyptian Thebes. Diana was worshipped in Dodona in conjunction with Zeus, and a female figure was associated with Amun in the Libyan Ammonium. Besides this, the dove was the bird of Aphrodite, the Diana of Zeus, or the Mosaic divine love, which saved mankind from complete destruction. According to other authors, there was a wondrous intoxicating spring at Dodona ; and in later times more material means were employed to produce the prophetic spirit.

Several copper bowls, namely, were placed upon a column, and the statue of a boy beside them. When the wind moved a rod or scourge having three bones attached to chains, it struck upon the metallic bowls, the sound of which was heard by the applicants. These Dodonian tones gave rise to a proverb : *æs Dodonæum*—an unceasing babbler.

The *oracle* at Dodona was dedicated to the Pelasgian

Zeus, who was worshipped here at the same time as the almighty ruler of the world, and as the friendly associate of mankind. In the course of the theogonic process, Diana was associated with him as his wife,—the mother of Aphrodite. The servants of Zeus were Selles, the priests of Diana, the so-called Peliades. According to Homer, the Selles inhabited the sanctum at Dodona, sleeping upon the earth, and with naked unwashed feet ; they served the Pelasgian Zeus. It is probable that they slept upon the earth on the hides of newly-sacrificed animals, to receive prophetic dreams, as was customary at other places, Calchos and Oropus, with many others.

As regards the mantic of Dodona, it was partly natural, from the excitement of the mind, partly artificial. Of the latter we may mention three modes—the ancient oak of Zeus, with its prophetic doves, the miraculous spring, and the celebrated Dodonian bowls of brass.

The far-spreading, speaking tree, the incredible wonder, as Æschylus calls it, was an oak, a lofty beautiful tree, with evergreen leaves and sweet edible acorns, which according to the belief of the Greeks and Romans, were the first sustenance of mankind. The Pelasgi regarded this tree as the tree of life. In this tree the god was supposed to reside, and the rustling of its leaves and the voices of birds showed his presence. When the questioners entered, the oak rustled, and the Peliades said, " Thus speaks Zeus." Incense was burned beneath it, which may be compared to the altar of Abraham under the oak Ogyges, which had stood there since the world's creation. According to the legend, sacred doves continually inhabited the tree, like the Marsoor *oracle* at Tiora Mattiene, where a sacred hawk foretells futurity from the top of a wooden pillar.

At the foot of the oak a cold spring gushes as it were from its roots, and from its murmur the inspired priestesses prophesied.

Of this miraculous fountain it is related, that lighted torches being thrust into it were extinguished, and that extinguished torches were re-lit ; it also rose and fell at various seasons. " That extinction and rekindling has," says Lassaulx, " perhaps the mystical signification that the usual sober life of the senses must be extinguished, that the prophetic spirit dormant in the soul may be aroused. The torch of human existence must expire, that a divine one may be lighted ; the human must die that the divine may be born ; the destruction of individuality is the awakening of God in the soul, or, as the mystics say, the setting of sense is the rising of truth."

The extinguishing of a burning light shows that the spring contained carbonic acid gas, which possesses stupifying and deadly properties, like all exhalations arising especially from minerals. The regular rising and sinking of the water is a frequent phenomenon, and has been observed from the earliest ages.

It appears that predictions were drawn from the tones of the Dodonian brass bowls, as well as from the rustling of the sacred oak and the murmuring of the sacred well.

The Dodonian columns, with that which stood upon them, appears to express the following :—The medium-sized brazen bowl was a hemisphere, and symbolised of heaven ; the boy-like male statue a figure of the Demiurgos, or constructor of the universe ; the bell-like notes a symbol of the harmony of the universe and music of the spheres. That the Demiurgos is represented as a boy is quite in the spirit of Egypto-Pelasgian theology as it reigned in Samothrace. The miraculous bell told all who came to Dodona to question the god that they were on holy ground, must inquire with pure hearts, and be silent when the god replied. It is easily imagined that these tones, independent and uninfluenced by human will, must have made a deep impression upon the minds of pilgrims. Those who questioned the god were also obliged to take a purificatory bath in the temple, similar to that by which the Delphian Pythia prepared herself for prophecy.

Besides this artificial soothsaying from signs, natural divination by the prophetic movements of the mind was practised. Where there are prophesying priestesses, there must also be ecstatic ones, similar to those in the magnetic state. Sophocles calls the Dodonean priestesses divinely inspired : Plato (Phædrus) says, more decidedly, that the prophetess at Delphi and the priestesses at Dodona had done much good in sacred madness, in private and public affairs, to their country, but in their senses little or nothing. We may see from this that the Delphian Pythia, as well as the Dodonian priestesses, did not give their oracles in the state of common waking consciousness, but in real ecstasy, to which the frequent incense—and drink—offerings would assist. Aristides states, still more clearly than the others, that the priestesses at Dodona neither knew, before being seized upon by the spirit, what would be said, nor remembered afterwards, when their natural consciousness returned, what they had uttered ; so that all others, rather than they, knew it.

Oracle of Jupiter Trophonius.—Trophonius, according to Pausanias, was the most skilful architect of his day. Concerning the origin of his *oracle* there are many opinions. Some say he was swallowed up by an earthquake in the cave which afterwards became prophetic ; others, that after having completed the Adytum of Apollo at Delphi (a very marvellous specimen of his workmanship, which Dr. Clarke thought might at some time be discovered on account of its singularity), he declined asking any specific pay, but modestly requested the god to grant him whatever was the greatest benefit a man could receive ; and in three days afterwards he was found dead. This *oracle* was discovered after two years of scarcity in its neighbourhood, when the Pythoness ordered the starving population, who applied to her, to consult Trophonius in Lebadæa. The deputation sent for that purpose could not discover any trace of such an *oracle*, till Saon, the oldest among them, obtained the desired information by following the flight of a swarm of bees. The responses were given by the genius of Trophonius to the inquirer, who was compelled to descend into a cave, of the nature of which Pausanias has left a very lively representation. The votary resided for a certain number of days in a sanctuary of good fortune, in which he underwent customary lustrations, abstained from hot baths, but dipped in the river Hercyna, and was plentifully supplied with meat from the victims which he sacrificed. Many, indeed, were the sacred personages whom he was bound to propitiate with blood ; among them were Trophonius himself and his sons, Apollo, Saturn, Jupiter, Vasileus, Juno Henioche, and Ceres Europa, who is affirmed to have been the nurse of Trophonius. From an inspection of the entrails, a soothsayer pronounced whether Trophonius was in fit humour for consultation. None of the " exta," however favourable they might have been, were of the slightest avail, unless a ram, immolated to Agamedes at the mouth of the cave on the very night of the descent, proved auspicious. When that propitious signal had been given ,the priests led the inquirer to the river Hercyna, where he was anointed and washed by two Lebadæan youths, thirteen years of age, named " Hermai." He was then carried farther to the two spring-heads of the stream, and there he drank first of Lethe, in order that he might forget all past events and present his mind to the *oracle* as a " tabula rasa " ; and secondly of Mnemosyne, that he might firmly retain remembrance of every occurrence which was about to happen within the cave. An image, reputed to be the workmanship of Dædalus, was then exhibited to him, and so great was its sanctity, that no other eyes but those of a person about to undertake the adventure of the cave were ever permitted to behold it. Next he was clad in a linen robe, girt with ribbons, and shod with sandals peculiar to the country. The entrance to the *oracle* was a very narrow aperture in a grove on the summit of a mountain, protected by a marble parapet about two cubits in height, and by brazen spikes above it. The upper part of the cave was artificial, like an oven, but no steps were cut in the rock, and the descent was made by a ladder brought to the spot on each occasion. On approaching the mouth of the adytum itself the adventurer lay flat, and holding in each hand some honeyed cakes, first inserted his feet into the aperture, then drew his knees and the remainder of his body after them, till he was caught by some hidden force, and carried downward as if by a whirlpool. The responses were given sometimes by a vision, sometimes by words; and a forcible exit was then made through the original entrance, and in like manner feet foremost. There was only a single instance on record of any person who had descended failing to return and that one deserved his fate; for his object was to discover treasure, not to consult the *oracle*. Immediately on issuing from the cavern, the inquirer was placed on a seat called that of Mnemosyne, not far from the entrance, and there the priests demanded a relation of everything which he had seen and heard; he was then carried once again to the sanctuary of good fortune, where he remained for some time overpowered by terror and lost in forgetfulness. By degrees his former powers of intellect returned, and, in contradiction to the received opinion, he recovered the power of smiling.

Dr. Clarke, in his visit to Lebadæa, found everything belonging to the hieron of Trophonius in its original state, excepting that the narrow entrance to the adytum was choked with rubbish. The Turkish governor was afraid of a popular commotion if he gave permission for cleansing this aperture. Mr. Cripps, however, introduced the whole length of his body into the cavity, and by thrusting a long pole before him found it utterly stopped. The waters of Lethe and Mnemosyne at present supply the washerwomen of Lebadæa.

Oracles of Delos and Branchus.—The *oracle* of "Delos," notwithstanding its high reputation, had few peculiarities: its virtue was derived from the nativity of Apollo and Diana in that island. At Dindyma, or Didyma, near Miletus, Apollo presided over the *oracle* of the "Branchidæ," so called from either one of his sons or of his favourites Branchus of Thessaly, whom he instructed in soothsaying while alive, and canonized after death. The responses were given by a priestess who bathed and fasted for three days before consultation, and then sat upon an axle or bar, with a charming-rod in her hand, and inhaling the steam from a hot spring. Offerings and ceremonies were necessary to render the inspiration effectual, including baths, fasting, and solitude, and Iamblichus censures those who despise them.

Oracle of the Clarian Apollo at Colophon.—Of the *oracle* of Apollo at Colophon, Iamblichus relates that it prophesied by drinking of water. "It is known that a subterranean spring exists there, from which the prophet drinks; after he has done so, and has performed many consecrations and sacred customs on certain nights, he predicts the future; but he is invisible to all who are present. That this water can induce prophecy is clear, but how it happens, no one knows, says the proverb." It might appear that the divine spirit pervades this water, but it is not so. God is in all things, and is reflected in this spring, thereby giving it the prophetic power. This inspiration of the water is not of an entirely divine nature, for it only prepares us

and purifies the light of the soul, so that we are fit to receive the divine spirit. There the divine presence is of such a nature that it punishes every one who is capable of receiving the god. The soothsayer uses this spirit like a work-tool over which he has no control. After the moment of prediction he does not always remember that which has passed; often he can scarcely collect his faculties. Long before the water-drinking, the soothsayer must abstain day and night from food, and observe religious customs, which are impossible to ordinary people, by which means he is made capable of receiving the god. It is only in this manner that he is able to hold the mirror of his soul to the radiance of free inspiration."

Oracle of Amphiaraus.—Another very celebrated *oracle* was that of Amphiaraus, who distinguished himself so much in the Theban war. He was venerated at Oropus, in Bœotia, as a seer. This *oracle* was consulted more in sickness than on any other occasion. The applicants had here, also, to lie upon the skin of a sacrificed ram, and during sleep had the remedies of their diseases revealed to them. Not only, however, were sacrifices and lustrations performed here, but the priests prescribed other preparations by which the minds of the sleepers were to be enlightened. They had to fast one day, and refrain from wine three. Amphilochus, as son of Amphiaraus, had a similar *oracle* at Mallos, in Cilicia, which Pausanias calls the most trustworthy and credible of the age. Plutarch speaks of the *oracles* of Amphilochus and Mopsus as being in a very flourishing state; and Lucian mentions that all those who wished to question the *oracle* had to lay down two oboles.

Egyptian Oracles.—The *oracles* of Ancient Egypt were as numerous as those of Greece. It must have been due to foreign influence that the *oracle*, that played so important a part in the Greek world at this time, was also thoroughly established on the banks of the Nile. Herodotus knew of no fewer than seven gods in Egypt who spake by *oracles*. Of these, the most reliable was considered to give an intimation of their intentions by means of remarkable events. These are carefully observed by the Egyptians, who write down what follows upon these prodigies. They also consider that the fate of a person is fixed by the day of his birth, for every day belongs to a special god. The *oracle* of Jupiter Ammon at the oasis of that name and the same deity at Thebes existed from the twentieth to the twenty-second Dynasty. He was consulted not only concerning the fate of empires but upon such trifling matters as the identification of a thief. In all serious matters, however, it was sought to ascertain his views. Those about to make their wills sought his *oracle*, and judgments were ratified by his word.

"According to the inscriptions, intercourse between king and god was arranged as follows :—The King present himself before the god and preferred a direct question, so framed as to admit of an answer by simple yes or no; in reply the god nodded an affirmative, or shook his head in negation. This has suggested the idea that the *oracles* were worked by manipulating statues of divinities mechanically set in motion by the priests. But as yet no such statues have been found in the Valley of the Nile, and contrivances of this kind could have had no other object than to deceive the people,—a supposition apparently excluded in this case by the fact that it was customary for the king to visit the god alone and in secret. Probably the king presented himself on such occasions before the sacred animal in which the god was incarnate, believing that the divine will would be manifested by its movements."

The Apis bull also possessed *oracles*. Bes, too, god of pleasure or of the senses, had an *oracle* at Abydos.

American Oracles.—Among the American races the *oracle* was frequently encountered. All the principal gods of aboriginal America universally act as *oracles*. With the ancient inhabitants of Peru, the *huillcas* partook of the nature of *oracles*. Many of these were serpents, trees, and rivers, the noises made by which appeared to the primitive Peruvians—as, indeed, they do to primitive folk all over the world—to be of the quality of articulate speech. Both the Huillcamayu and the Apurimac rivers at Cuzco were *huillca oracles* of this kind, as their names, " Huillca-river " and " Great Speaker," denote. These *oracles* often set the mandate of the Inca himself at defiance, occasionally supporting popular opinion against his policy.

The Peruvian Indians of the Andes range within recent generations continued to adhere to the superstitions they had inherited from their fathers. A rare and interesting account of these says that they " admit an evil being, the inhabitant of the centre of the earth, whom they consider as the author of their misfortunes, and at the mention of whose name they tremble. The most shrewd among them take advantage of this belief to obtain respect, and represent themselves as his delegates. Under the denomination of *mohanes*, or *agoreros*, they are consulted even on the most trivial occasions. They preside over the intrigues of love, the health of the community, and the taking of the field. Whatever repeatedly occurs to defeat their prognostics, falls on themselves ; and they are wont to pay for their deceptions very dearly. They chew a species of vegetable called *piripiri*, and throw it into the air, accompanying this act by certain recitals and incantations, to injure some, to benefit others, to procure rain and the inundation of rivers, or, on the other hand, to occasion settled weather, and a plentiful store of agricultural productions. Any such result, having been casually verified on a single occasion, suffices to confirm the Indians in their faith, although they may have been cheated a thousand times.

There is an instance on record of how the *huillca* could refuse on occasion to recognise even royalty itself. Manco, the Inca who had been given the kingly power by Pizarro, offered a sacrifice to one of these oracular shrines. The *oracle* refused to recognise him, through the medium of its guardian priest, stating that Manco was not the rightful Inca. Manco therefore caused the *oracle*, which was in the shape of a rock, to be thrown down, whereupon its guardian spirit emerged in the form of a parrot and flew away. It is probable that the bird thus liberated had been taught by the priests to answer to the questions of those who came to consult the shrine. But we learn that on Manco commanding that the parrot should be pursued it sought another rock, which opened to receive it, and the spirit of the *huillca* was transferred to this new abode.

Like the greater idols of Mexico, most of the principal huacas of Peru seem to have been also *oracles*. The guardians of the great speaking huacas appear to have exercised in virtue of their office an independent influence which was sometimes sufficiently powerful to resist the Apu-Ccapac-Inca himself. It was perhaps natural that they should be the exponents of the popular feeling which supported them, rather than of the policy of the sovereign chiefs, whose interest it was to suppress them : there was even a tradition that the Huillac-umu, a venerable huillac whom the rest acknowledged as their head, had in old times possessed jurisdiction over the supreme war-chiefs.

Many Indian tribes employ fetishes as *oracles*, and among the ancient Mexicans practically all the great gods were oracular.

Orbas : The name given by the French to a species of metallic electrum. According to Pliny a vessel of this substance has a certain magical property ; when it is filled with liquor is discovers poison by showing semi-circles like rainbows, while the fluid sparkles and hisses as if on the fire. The occult qualities of electrum are of a tell-tale nature.

Orchis, the Root of the : The *Root of the Satyrios Orchis* was believed to be a sure remedy against enchantment.

Ordinale of Alchemy, The : (*See* **Dalton, Thomas.**)

Orenda : A magical force. (*See* **American Indians.**)

Orleans, Duchess of : (*See* **France.**)

Orleans, Duke of : (*See* **France.**)

Ornithomancy is the Greek work for augury, the method of divination by the flight or the song of birds, which, with the Romans, became a part of their national religion, and had a distinct priesthood. For this reason it is treated in a separate article.

Oromase, Society : (*See* **Holland.**)

Orphic Magic : (*See* **Greece.**)

Orton : Alluded to by Froissart as the familiar of the Lord of Corasse, near Orthes. A clerk whom his lordship had wronged set this spirit the task of tormenting his superior, but by fair words the Lord of Corasse won him over to himself so that *Orton* became his familiar. Nightly *Orton* would shake his pillow and waken him to tell him the news of the world. Froissart says of their connection :—

" So *Orton* continued to serve the Lord of Corasse for a long time. I do not know whether he had more than one master, but, every week, at night, twice or thrice, he visited his master, and related to him the events which had happened in the different countries he had traversed, and the lord of Corasse wrote of them to the Count of Foix, who took a great pleasure in them, for he was the man in all the world who most willingly heard news of strange countries.

" Now it happened that the Lord of Corasse, as on other nights, was lying in his bed in his chamber by the side of his wife, who had become accustomed to listen to *Orton* without any alarm. *Orton* came, and drew away the lord's pillow, for he was fast asleep, and his lord awoke, and cried, ' Who is this ? ' He answered, ' It is I, *Orton*.' ' And whence comest thou ? ' ' I come from Prague, in Bohemia.' ' And how far from hence is this Prague, in Bohemia ? ' ' Why,' said he, ' about sixty days' journey.' ' And thou hast come so quickly ? ' ' Faith, I go as quickly as the wind, or even swifter.' ' And thou hast wings ? ' ' Faith, none.' ' How then canst thou fly so quickly ? ' *Orton* replied— ' It does not concern thee to know.' ' Nay,' said he, ' I shall be very glad to know what fashion and form thou art of,' *Orton* answered, ' It does not concern thee to know ; it is sufficient that I come hither, and bring thee sure and certain news.' ' By G—, *Orton*,' exclaimed the lord of Corasse, ' I should love thee better if I had seen thee.' ' Since you have so keen a desire to see me,' said *Orton* ' the first thing thou shalt see and encounter to-morrow morning, when you rise from your bed, shall be—I.' ' That is enough,' said the Lord of Corasse. ' Go, therefore ; I give thee leave for this night.'

" When the morrow came, the Lord of Corasse began to rise, but the lady was so affrighted that she fell sick and could not get up that morning, and she said to her lord, who did not wish her to keep her bed, ' See if thou seest *Orton*. By my faith, I neither wish, if it please God, to see nor encounter him.' ' But I do,' said the Lord of Corasse He leapt all nimbly from his bed, and seated himself upon the edge, and waited there to see *Orton*, but saw nothing. Then he went to the windows and threw them upon that he might see more clearly about the room, but he saw nothing, so that he could say, ' This is *Orton*.' The day passed, the night returned. When the Lord of Corasse was in his bed asleep, *Orton* came, and began speaking in his wonted manner. ' Go, go,' said his master, ' thou art a fibber : thou didst promise to show me to-day who thou wert, and thou hast not done so.' ' Nay,' said he, ' but I did.' ' Thou didst not.' ' And didst thou not see anything,' inquired *Orton*, ' when thou didst leap out of bed ? ' The Lord of Corasse thought a little while, and said—' Yes, while sitting on my bed, and thinking of thee, I saw two long straws upon the pavement, which turned towards each other and played about.' ' And that was I,' cried *Orton* ; ' I had assumed that form.' Said the Lord of Corasse : ' It does not content me : I pray thee change thyself into some other form, so that I may see and know thee.' *Orton* replied : ' You will act so that you will lose me.' ' Not so, 'said the Lord of Corasse : ' When I have once seen you, I shall not want to see you ever again.' ' Then,' said *Orton*, ' you shall see me to-morrow ; and remember that the first thing you shall see upon leaving your chamber, will be I.' ' Be it so,' replied the Lord of Corasse. ' Begone with you, therefore, now. I give thee leave, for I wish to sleep.'

" *Orton* departed. When the morrow came, and at the third hour, the Lord of Corasse was up and attired in his usual fashion, he went forth from his chamber into a gallery that looked upon the castle-court. He cast therein his glances, and the first thing he saw was the largest sow he had ever seen ; but she was so thin she seemed nothing but skin and bones, and she had great and long teats, pendant and quite attenuated, and a long and inflamed snout. The Sire de Corasse marvelled very much at this sow, and looked at her in anger, and exclaimed to his people, ' Go quickly, bring the dogs hither, and see that this Sow be well hunted.' The varlets ran nimbly, threw open the place where the dogs lay, and set them at the sow. The sow heaved a loud cry, and looked up at the Lord of Corasse, who supported himself upon a pillar buttress in front of his chamber. She was seen no more afterwards, for she vanished, nor did any one note what became of her. The Sire de Corrasse returned into his chamber pensively, and bethought himself of *Orton*, and said, ' I think that I have seen my familiar ; I repent me that I set my dogs upon him, for I doubt if I shall ever behold him again, since he has several times told me that as soon as I should provoke him I should lose him, and he would return no more.' He spoke truly ; never again did *Orton* return to the Lord of Corasse, and the knight died in the following year."

Ostiaks : (*See* **Siberia.**)

Oupnekhat, The : The *Oupnekhat* or *Oupnekhata* (Book of the Secret) written in Persian, gives the following instructions for the production of visions. " To produce the wise Maschqgui (vision), we must sit on a four-cornered base, namely the heels, and then close the gates of the body. The ears by the thumbs ; the eyes by the forefingers ; the nose by the middle ; the lips by the four other fingers. The lamp within the body will then be preserved from wind and movement, and the whole body will be full of light. Like the tortoise, man must withdraw every sense within himself ; the heart must be guarded, and then Brahma will enter into him, like fire and lightning. In the great fire in the cavity of the heart a small flame will be lit up, and in its centre is Atma (the soul) ; and he who destroys all worldly desires and wisdom will be like a hawk which has broken through the meshes of the net, and will have become one with the great being." Thus will he become Brahma-Atma (divine spirit), and will perceive by a light that far exceeds that of the sum. " Who, therefore, enters this path be Brahma must deny the world and its pleasures ; must only cover his nakedness, and staff in hand collect enough, but no more, alms to maintain life. The lesser ones only do this ; the greater throw aside pitcher and staff, and do not even read the *Oupnekhata*."

Owen, Robert : An early convert to spiritualism. He had been for many years an advanced socialist, and though at the time he embraced the spiritualistic doctrines—1853— he was already in his eighty-third year, he preached the new faith with undiminished vigour and with characteristic scorn of caution. Having first published his views in his periodical, the *Rational Quarterly Review*, he brought out, in 1854, the *New Existence of Man upon Earth*, at this period the only English paper devoted to the interests of spiritualism. Owen's view of the movement was that it was the inauguration of a sort of millennium, a social revolution, for which he had looked throughout his life.

P

Paigoels, The : The devils of Hindustan. Some of the Hindus believe that the Paigoels were originally created devils ; others that they were put out of heaven because of their great sin, and of all worlds that the earth is the only one with which they are allowed intercourse. Some of these devils have individual names, and are the tempters of men to special sins,—others again enter into the bodies of men and take possession of them. The Hindus also believe that the souls of wicked men go to join the number of the *paigoels*.

Palingenesy : A term employed by the philosophers of the seventeenth century to denote the " resurrection of plants," and the method of achieving their astral appearance after destruction. In very early times, we find philosophers inclined to doubt if apparitions might not be accounted for on natural principles, without supposing that a belief in them was either referable to hallucinations, to human imagination, or to impositions that might have been practised. At length Lucretius attacked the popular notion entertained of ghosts, by maintaining that they were not spirits returned from the mansions of the dead, but nothing more than thin films, pellicles, or membranes, cast off from the surface of all bodies like the exuviæ or sloughs of reptiles.

An opinion, by no means dissimilar to that of the Epicureans, was revived in Europe about the middle of the 17th century. It had its origin in *Palingenesy*, or the resurrec-tion of plants, a grand secret known to Digby, Kircher, Schot, Gafferel, Vallemont, and others. These philosophers performed the operation of Palingenesy after the following manner :—They took a plant, bruised it, burnt it, collected its ashes, and, in the process of calcination, extracted from it a salt. This salt they then put into a glass phial, and mixed with it some peculiar substance, which these chemists have not disclosed. When the compound was formed, it was pulverulent, and possessed a bluish colour. The powder was next submitted to a gentle heat, when its particles being instantly put into motion, there then, gradually arose, as from the midst of the ashes, a stem, leaves and flowers ; or, in other words, an apparition of the plant which had been submitted to combustion. But as soon as the heat was taken away, the form of the plant, which had been thus sublimed, was precipitated to the bottom of the vessel. Heat was then re-applied, and the vegetable phœnix was resusitated ; it was withdrawn, and the form once more became latent among the ashes. This notable experiment was said to have been performed before the Royal Society of England, and it satisfactorily proved to this learned body, that the presence of heat gave a sort of life to the vegetable apparition, and that the absence of caloric caused its death.

Cowley was quite delighted with the experiment of the rose and its ashes, and in conceiving that he had detected the same phenomenon in the letters written with the juice of lemons, which were revived on the application of heat, he celebrated the mystic power of caloric after the following manner :—

> Strange power of heat, thou yet dost show,
> Like winter earth, naked, or cloth'd with snow,
> But as the quick'ning sun approaching near,
> The plants arise up by degrees,
> A sudden paint adorns the trees,
> And all kind nature's characters appear.
>
> So nothing yet in thee is seen,
> But when a genial heat warms thee within,
> A new-born wood of various lines there grows ;
> Here buds an A, and there a B,
> Here sprouts a V, and there a T,
> And all the flourishing letters stand in rows.

The rationale of this famous experiment made on the ashes of roses was attempted by Kircher. He supposed that the seminal virtue of every known substance, and even its substantial form, resided in its salt. This salt was concealed in the ashes of the rose. Heat put it in motion. The particles of the salt were quickly sublimed, and being moved about in the phial like a vortex, at length arranged themselves in the same general form they had possessed from nature. It was evident, then, from the result of this experiment, that there was a tendency in the particles of the salt to observe the same order of position which they had in the living plant. Thus, for instance, each saline corpuscle, which in its prior state had held a place in the stem of the rose-slip, sympathetically fixed itself in a corresponding position when sublimed in the chemist's vial. Other particles were subject to a similar law, and accordingly, by a disposing affinity, resumed their proper position, either in the stalk, the leaves, or the flowers, and thus, at length, the entire apparition of a plant was generated.

The next object of these philosophers was to apply their doctrine to the explanation of the popular belief in ghosts. As it was incontestably proved that the substantial form of each body resided in a sort of volatile salt, it was perfectly evident in what manner superstitious notions must have arisen about ghosts haunting churchyards. When a dead body had been committed to the earth, the salts of it, during the heating process of fermentation, were exhaled. The saline particles then each resumed the same relative situation they had held in the living body, and thus a complete human form was induced, calculated to excite superstitious fear in the minds of all but Palingenesists.

It is thus evident that *Palingenesy* was nothing more Lucretius had made, with regard to the filmy substances than a chemical explanation of the discovery which that he had observed to arise from all bodies.

Yet, in order to prove that apparitions might be really explained on this principle, the *experimentum crucis* was still wanting. But this deficiency was soon supplied. Three alchemists had obtained a quantity of earth-mould from St. Innocent's Church, in Paris, supposing that this matter might contain the true philosopher's stone. They subjected it to a distillatory process. On a sudden they perceived in their vials forms of men produced, which immediately caused them to desist from their labours. This fact coming to the knowledge of the Institute of Paris, under the protection of Louis XIV., this learned body took up the business with much seriousness, and the result of their labours appears in the *Miscellania Curiosa*. Dr. Ferrier, in a volume of the *Manchester Philosophical Transactions*, went to the trouble of making an abstract of one of these French documents, which we prefer giving on account of its conciseness, rather than having rceourse to the original dissertation.

" A malefactor was executed, of whose body a grave physician got possession for the purpose of dissection. After disposing of the other parts of the body, he ordered his assistant to pulverize part of the cranium, which was a remedy at that time admitted in dispensatories. The powder was left in a paper on the table of the museum, where the assistant slept. About midnight he was awakened by a noise in the room, which obliged him to rise immediately. The noise continued about the table, without any visible agent ; and at length he traced it to the powder, in the midst of which he now beheld, to his unspeakable dismay, a small head with open eyes staring at him ; presently two branches appeared, which formed into arms and hands ; then the ribs became visible, which were soon clothed with muscles and integuments ; next the lower extremities sprouted out, and when they appeared perfect, the puppet (for his size was small) reared himself on his feet ; instantly his clothes came upon him, and he appeared in the very cloak he wore at his execution. The affrighted spectator, who stood hitherto mumbling his prayers with great application, now thought of nothing but making his escape from the revived ruffian ; but this was impossible, for the apparition planted himself in the way, and, after divers fierce looks and threatening gestures, opened the door and went out. No doubt the powder was missing next day."

But older analogous results are on record, indicating that the blood was the chief part of the human frame in which those saline particles resided, the arrangements of which gave rise to the popular notion of ghosts. Dr. Webster, in his book on witchcraft, relates an experiment, given on the authority of Dr. Flud, in which this very satisfactory conclusion was drawn.

" A certain chymical operator, by name La Pierre, near that place in Paris called Le Temple, received blood from the hands of a certain bishop to operate upon. Which he setting to work upon the Saturday, did continue it for a week with divers degrees of fire. But about midnight, the Friday following, this artificer, lying in a chamber next to his laboratory, betwixt sleeping and waking, heard a horrible noise, like unto the lowing of kine, or the roaring of a lion ; and continuing quiet, after the ceasing of the sound in the laboratory, the moon being at the full, and, by shining enlightening the chamber suddenly, betwixt himself and the window he saw a thick little cloud, condensed into an oval form, which, after, by little and little, did seem completely to put on the shape of a man, and making another and a sharp clamour, did suddenly vanish. And not only some noble persons in the next chambers, but also the host with his wife, lying in a lower room of the house, and also the neighbours dwelling in the opposite side of the street, did distinctly hear as well the bellowing as the voice ; and some of them were awaked with the vehemency thereof. But the artificer said, that in this he found solace, because the bishop, of whom he had it, did admonish him, that if any of them from whom the blood was extracted should die, in the time of its putrefaction, his spirit was wont often to appear to the sight of the artificer, with perturbation. Also forthwith, upon Saturday following, he took the retort from the furnace, and broke it with the light stroke of a little key, and there, in the remaining blood, found the perfect representation of an human head, agreeable in face, eyes, nostrils, mouth, and hairs, that were somewhat thin, and of a golden colour."

Regarding this narrative Webster adds :—" There were many ocular witnesses, as the noble person, Lord of Bourdalone, the chief secretary to the Duke of Guise ; and he (Flud) had this relation from the Lord of Menanton, living in that house at the same time, from a certain doctor of physic, from the owner of the house, and many others."

Palladino, Eusapia : The most famous physical medium of recent years, and one whose phenomena, investigated at length by some of the most distinguished scientists of Britain, France, and Italy, have led many to conclude that they are genuine manifestations from the spirit world, or that they illustrate the workings of some unknown force. *Eusapia* was a Neapolitan peasant woman who from her childhood had shown herself possessed of mediumistic powers. In 1892 a group of scientists—Professors Schiaparelli, Brofferio, Geroso, the well-known spiritualist M. Aksakoff, and others—held a series of sittings at Milan, with *Eusapia* as medium. Some of the séances were also attended by Professors Richet and Lombroso. The phenomena consisted of raps, materialisation of hands, levitation of the table and other furniture within a radius of three or four feet, and fluctuation of the medium's weight in the balance, to the extent °of some 17lbs. It was evident even then that *Eusapia* would not lose an opportunity of using fraud. Nevertheless Professor Richet was so impressed that in 1894 he organised a further series of sittings with the same medium at his house on the Ile Rouband, and on this occasion were present Professor—now Sir Oliver—Lodge, Mr. Myers, Dr. Ochorowicz, and at a later stage, Professor and Mrs. Sidgwick. The séances were held in darkness or semi-darkness, but the medium's hands and feet were controlled by the investigators. Mrs. Sidgwick, indeed, declared that *Eusapia* herself might easily have produced the phenomena, if she had the use of her hands, but Professor Lodge and others were inclined to attribute them to some external agency. In the following year further séances were held at Mr. Myer's house at Cambridge, and when it became evident that *Eusapia* frequently freed a foot or a hand Mr. Myer's own faith in the phenomena was temporarily—though only temporarily—destroyed. Professor Richet and Sir Oliver Lodge, however, retained their convictions unshaken. Dr. Hodgson, who had already suggested that *Eusapia* might use some such method, was also present at the Cambridge sittings. Besides those already mentioned, many prominent Continental scientists investigated *Eusapia's* manifestations among them being M. Camille Flammarion, Professor Morselli, and M. and Mme. Curie. The two last mentioned were members of a committee of the *Institut Général Psychologique of Paris*, which held an important series of sittings with the medium in 1905, 1906, and 1907. In 1908 and 1909 again, the Society for Psychical Research instituted a fresh enquiry into *Eusapia's* methods. On the whole, scientific opinion is still much divided as to the genuineness or otherwise of the phenomena. Some authorities, taking into consideration the many times the Italian medium has been caught cheating, and the absence of really conclusive tests, incline to the belief that *Eusapia* is merely a clever conjurer. Such were Dr. Hodgson, Mr. Podmore, Professor and Mrs. Sidgwick. Others, again, such as Professors Richet and Lombroso, M. Camille Flammarion and Sir Oliver Lodge, are of the opinion that the instances of fraud are mere incidents in the career of a true medium, whose performances plainly demonstrate the operation in the material world of strange, unknown forces.

Palladium : (*See* **Devil-worship.**)

Palladium, Order of : A masonic-diabolic order, also entitled the Sovereign-Council of Wisdom, founded in Paris on May 20th, 1737. It initiated women under the name of companions of Penelope. The fact that it existed is proved by the circumstance that Ragou, the Masonic antiquary, published its ritual.

Palmistry : The science of divination by means of lines and marks on the human hand. It is said to have been practised in very early times by the Brahmins of India, and to be known to Aristotle, who discovered a treatise on the subject written in letters of gold, which he presented to Alexander the Great, and which was afterwards translated into Latin by Hispanus. There is also extant a work on the subject by Melampus of Alexandria, and Hippocrates, Galen, and several Arabian commentators have also dealt with it. In the Middle Ages the science was represented by Hartlieb (circa 1448), and Cocles (circa 1054), and Fludd, Indigane, Rothmann, and many others wrote on cheiromancy. D'Arpentigny, Desbarolles, Carus, and others kept the science alive in the earlier half of the nineteenth century, since when a very large number of treatises upon it have been written. Since 1860, or thereabouts, *palmistry* has become very much more popular than ever before in these islands, and indeed is practised nearly all over the habitable globe.

Palmistry is sub-divided into three lesser arts—cheirognomy, cheirosophy and cheiromancy. The first is the art of recognising the type of intelligence from the form of the hands ; the second is the study of the comparative value of manual formations ; and the third is the art of divination from the form of the hand and fingers, and the lines and markings thereon. The palmist first of all studies the shape and general formation of the hand as a whole, afterwards regarding its parts and details,—the lines and markings being considered later. From cheirognomy and cheirosophy the general disposition and tendencies are ascertained, and future events are foretold from the reading of the lines and markings.

There are several types of hands : the elementary or large-palmed type ; the necessary with spatulated fingers ; the artistic with conical-shaped fingers ; the useful, the fingers of which are square-shaped ; the knotted or philosophical ; the pointed, or psychic ; and the mixed, in which the types are blended. The principal lines are : those which separate the hand from the forearm at the wrist, and which are known as the rascettes, or the lines of health, wealth and happiness. The line of life stretches from the centre of the palm around the base of the thumb almost to the wrist, and is joined for a considerable part of its course by the line of the head. The line of the heart runs across two-thirds of the palm, above the head line ; and the line of fate between it and the line of the head, nearly at right angles extending towards the wrist. The line of fortune runs from the base of the third finger towards the wrist parallel to the line of fate. If the lines are deep, firm and of narrow width the significance is good—excepting that a strong line of health shows constitutional weakness.

At the base of the fingers, beginning with the first, lie the mounts of Jupiter, Saturn, Apollo, and Mercury ; at the base of the thumb the mount of Venus ; and opposite to it, that of Luna. If well-proportioned they show certain virtues, but if exaggerated they indicate the vices which correspond to these. The first displays religion, reasonable ambition, or pride and superstition ; the second wisdom and prudence, or ignorance and failure ; the third when large makes for success and intelligence, when small for meanness or love of obscurity ; the fourth desire for knowledge and industry, or disinterestedness and laziness. The Lunar mount indicates sensitiveness, imagination, morality or otherwise ; and self-will : and the mount of Venus, charity and affection, or if exaggerated viciousness. The phalanges of the fingers are also indicative of certain faculties. For example, the first and second of the thumb, according to their length, indicate the value of the logical faculty and of the will ; those of the index finger in their order—materialism, law, and order ; of the middle finger—humanity, system, intelligence ; of the third finger—truth economy, energy ; and of the little finger goodness, prudence, reflectiveness. There are nearly a hundred other marks and signs, by which certain qualities, influences or events can be recognised. The line of life by its length indicates the length of existence of its owner. If it is short in both hands, the life will be a short one ; if broken in one hand and weak in the other, a serious illness is denoted. If broken in both hands, it means death. If it is much chained it means delicacy. If it has a second or sister line, it shows great vitality. A black spot on the line shows illness at the time marked. A cross indicates some fatality. The line of life coming out far into the palm is a sign of long life. The line of the head, if long and well-coloured, denotes intelligence and power. If descending to the mount of the Moon it shows that the head is much influenced by the imagination. Islands on the line denote mental troubles. The head line forked at the end indicates subtlety and a facility for seeing all sides of the question. A double line of the head is an indication of good fortune. The line of the heart should branch towards the mount of Jupiter. If it should pass over the mount of Jupiter to the edge of the hand and travel round the index finger, it is called " Solomon's ring " and indicates ideality and romance ; it is also a sign of occult power. Points or dots in this line may show illness if black, and if white love affairs ; while islands on the heart line indicate disease. The line of fate, or Saturn, if it rises from the Lunar mount and ascends towards the line of the heart is a sign of a rich marriage. If it extends into the third phalange of Saturn's finger it shows the sinister influence of that planet. A double line of fate is ominous.

In such an article as this it would be out of place to mention the very numerous lesser lines and marks which the hand contains, especially when so many excellent books of reference on the subject have recently been published. It but remains to say that practitioners of the science of *palmistry* are exceedingly numerous. Some of these work on strictly scientific lines, while others pick it up in a merely empirical way, and their forecasts of events to come are only so much " patter."

Papaloi : An Obeah priest : (*See* **West Indian Islands.**)

Papyri, Magical : (*See* **Egypt.**)

Para Brahm : Deity without form. The two indestructible principles from which all creation springs. (*See* **Kabala.**)

Paracelsus : In the history of alchemy there is not a more striking or picturesque figure than Aurœlus Philippus Theophrastus Paracelsus Bombast von Hohenheim, the illustrious physician and exponent of the hermetic philosophy who has chosen to go down to fame under the name of *Paracelsus.* He was born at Einsideln, near Zurich, in the year 1493. His father, the natural son of a prince, himself practised the " art of medicine," and was desirous that his only son should follow the same profession. To the fulfilment of that desire was directed the early training of *Paracelsus*—a training which fostered his imaginative rather than his practical tendencies, and which first cast his mind into the alchemical mould. It did not take him long to discover that the medical traditions of the time were but empty husks from which all substance had long since dried away. " I considered with myself," he says, " that if there were no teacher of medicine in the world, how would I set about to learn the art ? No otherwise than in the great open book of nature, written with the finger of God." Having thus freed himself from the constraining bonds of an outworn medical orthodoxy, whose chief resources were bleeding, purging, and emetics, he set about evolving a new system to replace the old, and in order that he might study the book of nature to better advantage he travelled extensively from 1513 to 1524, visiting almost every part of the known world, studying metallurgy, chemistry, and medicine, and consorting with vagabonds of every description. He was brought before the Cham of Tartary, conversed with the magicians of Egypt and Arabia,

and is said to have even reached India. At length his protracted wanderings came to a close, and in 1524 he settled in Basle, then a favourite resort of scholars and physicians, where he was appointed to fill the chair of medicine at the University. Never had Basle witnessed a more brilliant, erratic professor. His inflated language, his eccentric behaviour, the splendour of his conceptions flashing through a fog of obscurity, at once attracted and repelled, and gained for him friends and enemies. His antipathy to the Galenic school became ever more pronounced, and the crisis came when he publicly burned the works of Galen and Avicenna in a brazen vase into which he had cast nitre and sulphur. By such a proceeding he incurred the hatred of his more conservative brethren, and cut himself off for ever from the established school of medicine. He continued his triumphant career, however, till a conflict with the magistrates brought it to an abrupt close. He was forced to flee from Basle, and thereafter wandered from place to place, gaining a living as best he might. An element of mystery surrounds the manner of his death, which took place in 1541, but the best authenticated account states that he was poisoned at the instigation of the medical faculty.

But interesting as were the events of his life, it is to his work that most attention is due. Not only was he the founder of the modern science of medicine ; the magnetic theory of Mesmer, the " astral " theory of modern spiritualists, the philosophy of Descartes, were all foreshadowed in the fantastic, yet not always illogical, teaching of Paracelsus. He revived the " microcosmic " theory of ancient Greece, and sought to prove the human body analogous to the Solar System, by establishing a connection between the seven organs of the body and the seven planets. He preached the doctrines of the efficacy of will-power and the imagination in such words as these : " It is possible that my spirit, without the help of my body, and through an ardent will alone, and without a sword, can stab and wound others. It is also possible that I can bring the spirit of my adversary into an image and then fold him up or lame him at my pleasure." " Resolute imagination is the beginning of all magical operations." " Because men do not perfectly believe and imagine, the result is, that arts are uncertain when they might be wholly certain." The first principle of his doctrine is the extraction of the quintessence, or philosophic mercury, from every material body. He believed that if the quintessence were drawn from each animal, plant, and mineral, the combined result would equal the universal spirit, or " astral body " in man, and that a draught of the extract would renew his youth. He came at length to the conclusion that " astral bodies " exercised a mutual influence on each other, and declared that he himself had communicated with the dead, and with living persons at a considerable distance. He was the first to connect this influence with that of the magnet, and to use the word " magnetism " with its present application. It was on this foundation that Mesmer built his theory of magnetic influence. While *Paracelsus* busied himself with such problems, however, he did not neglect the study and practice of medicine. Indeed, astrology and the magnet entered largely into his treatment. When he was sought by a patient, his first care was to consult the planets, where the disease had its origin, and if the patient were a woman he took it for granted that the cause of her malady lay in the moon. His anticipation of the philosophy of Descartes, consisted in his theory that by bringing the various elements of the human body into harmony with the elements of nature—fire, light, earth, etc.—old age and death might be indefinitely postponed. His experiment in the extraction of its essential spirit from the poppy resulted in the production of laudanum, which he prescribed freely in the form of " three black pills." The recipes which he gives for the Philosopher's Stone, the Elixir of Life, and various universal remedies, are exceedingly obscure. He is deservedly celebrated as the first physici. n to use opium and mercury, and to recognise the value of sulphur. He applied himself also to the solution of a problem which still exercises the minds of scientific men—whether it is possible to produce life from inorganic matter. *Paracelsus* asserted that it was, and has, left on record a quaint recipe for a *homunculus*, or artificial man. By a peculiar treatment of certain " spagyric substances " —which he has unfortunately omitted to specify—he declared that he could produce a perfect human child in, miniature. Speculations such as these, medical, alchemical and philosophical, were scattered so profusely throughout his teaching that we are compelled to admit that here was a master-mind, a genius, who was a charlatan only incidently, by reason of training and temperament. Let it be remembered that he lived in an age when practically all scholars and physicians were wont to impose on popular ignorance, and we cannot but remark that *Paracelsus* displayed, under all his arrogant exterior, a curious singleness of purpose, and a real desire to penetrate the mysteries of science. He has left on record the principal points of the philosophy on which he founded his researches in his " *Archidoxa Medicinæ*." It contains the leading rules of the art of healing, as he practised and preached them. " I had resolved," he says, " to give ten books to the ' *Archidoxa*,' but I have reserved the tenth in my head. It is a treasure which men are not worthy to possess, and shall only be given to the world when they shall have abjured Aristotle, Avicenna, and Galen, and promised a perfect submission to *Paracelsus*." The world did not recant, but *Paracelsus* relented, and at the entreaty of his disciples published this tenth book, the key to the nine others, but a key which might pass for a lock, and for a lock which we cannot even pick. It is entitled the " *Tenth Book of the Arch-Doctrines* ; or, *On the Secret Mysteries of Nature*." A brief summary of it is as follows :—

He begins by supposing and ends by establishing that there is a universal spirit infused into the veins of man, forming within us a species of invisible body, of which our visible body, which it directs and governs at its will, is but the wrapping—the casket. This universal spirit is not simple—not more simple, for instance, than the number 100, which is a collection of units. Where, then, are the spiritual units of which our complex spirit is composed ? Scattered in plants and minerals, but principally in metals. There exists in these inferior productions of the earth a host of sub-spirits which sum themselves up in us, as the universe does in God. So the science of the philosopher has simply to unite them to the body—to disengage them from the grosser matter which clogs and confines them, to separate the pure from the impure.

To separate the pure from the impure is, in other words, to seize upon the soul of the heterogeneous bodies—to evolve their " predestined element," " the seminal essence of beings," " the first being, or quintessence."

To understand this latter word " quintessence," it is needful for the reader to know that every body, whatever it may be, is composed of four elements, and that the essence compounded of these elements forms a fifth, which is the soul of the mixed bodies, or, in other words, its " mercury," " I have shown," says *Paracelsus*, " in my book of ' Elements,' that the quintessence is the same thing as mercury. There is in mercury whatever wise men seek." That is, not the mercury of modern chemists, but a philosophical mercury of which every body has its own. " There are as many mercuries as there are things. The mercury of a vegetable, a mineral, or an animal of the same kind, although strongly resembling each other, does not precisely resemble another mercury, and it is for this reason that vegetables, minerals, and animals of the same species are not exactly alike. . . . The true mercury of philosophers is the radical humidity of each body, and its veritable *semen*, or essence."

Paracelsus now sought for a plant worthy of holding in the vegetable kingdom the same rank as gold in the metallic —a plant whose " predestined element " should unite in itself the virtues of nearly all the vegetable essences. Although this was not easy to distinguish, he recognised at a glance—we know not by what signs—the supremacy of excellence in the *melissa*, and first decreed to it that pharmaceutical crown which at a later period the Carmelites ought to have consecrated. How he obtained this new specific may be seen in the *Life of Paracelsus*, by Savarien :

" He took some balm-mint in flower, which he had taken care to collect before the rising of the sun. He pounded it in a mortar, reduced it to an impalpable dust, poured it into a long-necked vial which he sealed hermetically, and placed it to digest (or settle) for forty hours in a heap of horse-dung. This time expired, he opened the vial, and found there a matter which he reduced into a fluid by pressing it, separating it from its impurities by exposure to the slow heat of a *bain-marie*. The grosser parts sunk to the bottom, and he drew off the liqueur which floated on the top, filtering it through some cotton. This liqueur having been poured into a bottle he added to it the fixed salt, which he had drawn from the same plant when dried. There remained nothing more but to extract from this liqueur the first lief or being of the plant. For this purpose *Paracelsus* mixed the liqueur with so much ' water of salt ' (understand by this the mercurial element or radical humidity of the salt), put it in a matrass, exposed it for six weeks to the sun, and finally, at the expiration of this term, discovered a last residuum which was decidedly, according to him, the first life or supreme essence of the plant. But at all events, it is certain that what he found in his matrass was the genie or spirit he required ; and with the surplus, if there were any, we need not concern ourselves."

Those who may wish to know what this *genie* was like, are informed that it as exactly resembled, as two drops of water, the spirit of aromatic wine known to-day as *absinthe suisse*. It was a liquid green as emerald,—green, the bright colour of hope and spring-time. Unfortunately, it failed as a specific in the conditions indispensable for an elixir of immortality ; but it was a preparation more than half-celestial, which almost rendered old age impossible.

By means and manipulations as subtle and ingenious as those which he employed upon the melissa, *Paracelsus* did not draw, but learned to extract, the " predestined element " of plants which ranked much higher in the vegetable aristocracy,—the " first life " of the gilly-flower, the cinnamon, the myrrh, the scammony, the celandine. All these supreme essences, which, according to the 5th book of " *Archidoxa*," unite with a mass of " magisteries " as precious as they are rude, are the base of so many specifics, equally reparative and regenerative. This depends upon the relationship which exists between the temperament of a privileged plant and the temperament of the individual who asks of it his rejuvenescence.

However brilliant were the results of his discoveries, those he obtained or those he thought he might obtain, they were for *Paracelsus* but the a b c of Magic. To the eyes of so consummate an alchemist vegetable life is nothing ; it is the mineral—the metallic life—which is all. So we may assure ourselves that it was in his power to seize the first life-principle of the moon, the sun, Mars, or Saturn ; that is, of silver, gold, iron, or lead. It was equally facile for him to grasp the life of the precious stones, the bitumens, the sulphurs, and even that of animals.

Paracelsus sets forth several methods of obtaining this great arcanum. Here is the shortest and most simple as recorded by Incola Francus :—

" Take some mercury, or at least the element of mercury, separating the pure from the impure, and afterwards pounding it to perfect whiteness. Then you shall sublimate it with sal-ammoniac, and this so many times as may be necessary to resolve it into a fluid. Calcine it, coagulate it, and again dissolve it, and let it strain in a pelican during a philosophic month, until it thickens and assumes the form of a hard substance. Thereafter this form of stone is incombustible, and nothing can change or alter it ; the metallic bodies which it penetrates become fixed and incombustible, for this material is incombustible, and changes the imperfect metals into metal perfect. Although I have given the process in few words, the thing itself demands a long toil, and many difficult circumstances, which I have expressly omitted, not to weary the reader, who ought to be very diligent and intelligent if he wishes to arrive at the accomplishment of this great work."

Paracelsus himself tells us in his " *Archidoxa*," when explaining his own recipe for the completion of it, and profiting by the occasion to criticise his fellow-workers.

" I omit," he writes, " what I have said in different places on the theory of the stone ; I will say only that this *arcanum* does not consist in the blast (*rouille*) or flowers of antimony. It must be sought in the mercury of antimony, which, when it is carried to perfection, is nothing else than the *heaven* of metals ; for even as the heaven gives life to plants and minerals, so does the pure quintessence of antimony vitrify everything. This is why the Deluge was not able to deprive any substance of its virtue or properties, for the heaven being the life of all beings, there is nothing superior to it which can modify or destroy it.

" Take the antimony, purge it of its arsenical impurities in an iron vessel until the coagulated mercury of the antimony appears quite white, and is distinguishable by the star which appears in the superficies of the regulus, or semi-metal. But although this regulus, which is the element of mercury, has in itself a veritable hidden life, nevertheless these things are in virtue, and not actually.

" Therefore, if you wish to reduce the power to action, you must disengage the life which is concealed in it by a living fire like to itself, or with a metallic vinegar. To discover this fire many philosophers have proceeded differently, but agreeing to the foundations of the art, have arrived at the desired end. For some with great labour have drawn forth the quintessence of the thickened mercury of the regulus of antimony, and by this means have reduced to action the mercury of the antimony : others have considered that there was a uniform quintessence in the other minerals, as for example in the fixed sulphur of the vitriol, or the stone of the magnet, and having extracted the quintessence, have afterwards matured and exalted their *heaven* with it, and reduced it to action. Their process is good, and has had its result. Meanwhile this fire—this corporeal life—which they seek with toil, is found much more easily and in much greater perfection in the ordinary mercury, which appears through its perpetual fluidity—a proof that it possesses a very powerful fire and a celestial life similar to that which lies hidden in the regulus of the antimony. Therefore, he who would wish to exalt our *metallic heaven*, starred, to its greatest completeness, and to reduce into action its potential virtues, he must first extract from ordinary mercury its corporeal life, which is a celestial fire ; that is to say the quintessence of quicksilver, or, in other words, the metallic vinegar, that has resulted from its dissolution in the water

which originally produced it, and which is its own mother ; that is to say, he must dissolve it in the arcanum of the salt I have described, and mingle it with the ' stomach of Anthion,' which is the spirit of vinegar, and in this menstruum melt and filter and consistent mercury of the antimony, strain it in the said liquor, and finally reduce it into crystals of a yellowish green, of which we have spoken in our manual."

As regards the Philosopher's Stone, he gives the following formula :—

" Take," said he, " the electric mineral not yet mature (antimony), put it in its sphere, in the fire with the iron, to remove its ordures and other superfluities, and purge it as much as you can, following the rules of chymistry, so that it may not suffer by the aforesaid impurities. Make, in a word, the regulus with the mark. This done, cause it to dissolve in the ' stomach of the ostrich ' (vitriol), which springs from the earth and is fortified in its virtue by the ' sharpness of the eagle ' (the metallic vinegar or essence of mercury). As soon as the essence is perfected, and when after its dissolution it has taken the colour of the herb called *calendule*, do not forget to reduce it into a spiritual luminous essence, which resembles amber. After this, add to it of the ' spread eagle ' one half the weight of the election before its preparation, and frequently distil the ' stomach of the ostrich ' into the matter, and thus the election will become much more spiritualized. When the ' stomach of the ostrich ' is weakened by the labour of digestion, we must strengthen it and frequently distil it. Finally, when it has lost all its impurity, add as much tartarized quintessence as will rest upon your fingers, until it throws off its impurity and rises with it. Repeat this process until the preparation becomes white, and this will suffice ; for you shall see yourself as gradually it rises in the form of the ' exalted eagle,' and with little trouble converts itself in its form (like sublimated mercury) ; and that is what we are seeking.

" I tell you in truth that there is no greater remedy in medicine than that which lies in this election, and that there is nothing like it in the whole world. But not to digress from my purpose, and not to leave this work imperfect, observe the manner in which you ought to operate."

" The election then being destroyed, as I have said, to arrive at the desired end (which is, to make of it a universal medicine for human as well as metallic bodies), take your election, rendered light and volatile by the method above described.

" Take of it as much as you would wish to reduce it to its perfection, and put it in a philosophical egg of glass, and seal it very tightly, that nothing of it may respire ; put it into an athanor until of itself it resolves into a liquid, in such a manner that in the middle of this sea there may appear a small island, which daily diminishes, and finally, all shall be changed to a colour black as ink. This colour is the raven, or bird which flies at night without wings, and which, through the celestial dew, that rising continually falls back by a constant circulation, changes into what is called ' the head of the raven,' and afterwards resolves into ' the tail of the peacock,' then it assumes the hue of the ' tail of a peacock,' and afterwards the colour of the ' feathers of a swan ' ; finally acquiring an extreme redness, which marks its fiery nature, and in virtue of which it expels all kinds of impurities, and strengthens feeble members. This preparation, according to all philosophers, is made in a single vessel, over a single furnace, with an equal and continual fire, and this medicine, which is more than celestial, cures all kinds of infirmities, as well in human as metallic bodies ; wherefore no one can understand or attain such an arcanum without the help of God : for its virtue is ineffable and divine."

Paradise : From old Persian (Zeud) *pairedaèza* an enclosure, a walled-in place ; Old Persian *pairi*, around, *dig*, to mould, form, shape (hence to form a wall of earth).

Paradise has been sought for or located in many regions of the earth. In Tartary, Armenia, India, and China : on the banks of the Euphrates and of the Ganges ; in Mesopotamia, Syria, Persia, Arabia, Palestine, and Ethiopia, and near the mountains of Libanus and Anti-libanus. Perhaps the most noteworthy tradition is that which fixes its situation in the Island of Ceylon, the Serendib of the ancient Persians, and the Taprobane of the Greek geographers. " It is from the summit of Hamalleel or Adam's Peak," says Percival in his history of Ceylon, " that Adam took his last view of *Paradise* before he quitted it never to return. The spot on which his feet stood at the moment is still supposed to be found in an impression on the summit of the mountain, resembling the print of a man's foot, but more than double the ordinary size. After taking this farewell view, the father of mankind is said to have gone over to the continent of Judea, which was at that time joined to the island, but no sooner had he passed Adam's Bridge than the sea closed behind him, and cut off all hopes of return. This tradition, from whatever source it was derived, seems to be interwoven with the earliest notions of religion entertained by the Cingalese ; and it is difficult to conceive that it could have been engrafted on them without forming an original part. I have frequently had the curiosity to converse with black men of different castes concerning this tradition of Adam. All of them, with every appearance of belief, assured me that it was really true, and in support of it produced a variety of testimonies, old sayings, and prophecies, which have for ages been current among them. The origin of these traditions I do not pretend to trace ; but their connection with Scripture history is very evident, and they afford a new instance how universally the opinions with respect to the origin of man coincide." We are further informed by this writer that a large chair fixed in a rock near the summit of the mountain is said to be the workmanship of Adam. " It has the appearance of having been placed there at a very distant period, but who really placed it there, or for what purpose, it is impossible for any European to discover."

Paradise is a word of Persian origin, adopted by the Greeks, and literally denotes an inclosure or park planted with fruit-trees, and abounding with various animals. Eden is not termed *Paradise* in Genesis, but simply a garden planted eastwards in the country or district so called ; and it is this apparently indefinite locality which has caused so many conjectures as to its exact site. Some place it in Judea, where is now the sea of Galilee ; others in Armenia, near Mount Ararat ; and others in Syria, towards the sources of the Orontes, the Chrysorrhoas, and Barrady. Some think that by Eden is meant the whole earth, which was of surprising beauty and fertility before the Fall ; and it is curious that a notion prevailed to a great extent among the various nations, that the Old World was under a curse, and that the earth became very barren. We are also assured that the Hindoos and Chinese believe that all nature is contaminated, and that the earth labours undre some dreadful defilement—a sentiment which could only result from obscure traditions connected with the first human pair. Josephus gravely says that the Sacred Garden was watered by one river which ran round the whole earth, and was divided into four parts ; but he appears to think *Paradise* was merely a figurative or allegorical locality. Some of the natives of Hindostan have traditions of a place resembling *Paradise* on the banks of the Ganges ; but their accounts are so completely blended with their superstitions, and with their legends respecting the Deluge and the second peopling of the

world, as to be, to a certain extent, unintelligible. A writer who had diligently studied the Indian Puranas for many years, opened a new source of information, and placed Eden on the Imaus Mountains of India. " It appears from Scripture," he says, " that Adam and Eve lived in the countries to the eastward of Eden ; for at the eastern entrance of it God placed the angel with the flaming sword. This is also confirmed by the Puranics, who place the progenitor of mankind on the mountainous regions between Cabul and the Ganges, on the banks of which, in the hills, they show a place where he resorted occasionally for religious purposes. It is frequented by pilgrims. At the entrance of the passes leading to the place where I suppose was the Garden of Eden, and to the eastward of it, the Hindoos have placed a destroying angel, who appears, and it is generally represented like a cherub ; I mean Garudha, or the Eagle, upon whom Vishnu and Jupiter are represented riding. Garudha is represented generally like an eagle, but in his compound character somewhat like the cherub. He is represented like a young man, with the countenance, wings, and talons of the eagle. In Scripture the Deity is represented riding upon a cherub, and flying upon the wings of the wind. Garudha is called Vahan (literally the Vehicle) of Vishnu or Jupiter, and he thus answers to the cherub of Scripture ; for many commentators derive this word from the obsolete root c'harab, in the Chaldean language, a word implicitly synonymous with the Sanscrit Vahan." We may here add, that the Puranics considered the north-west part of India, about Cashmere, as the site of *Paradise*, and the original abode of the first human pair ; and that there, at the offering of a sacrifice Daksha was murdered by his jealous brother, who was in consequence doomed to become a fugitive on the earth.

In the fabled Meru of the Hindoo mythology, on the other hand, we have also a descriptive representation of the Mosaical Garden of Eden. Meru is a conical mountain, the exact locality of which is not fixed ; but as the Hindoo geographers considered the earth as a flat table, and the sacred mountain of Meru rising in the middle, it became at length their decided conviction that Meru was the North Pole, from their notion that the North Pole was the highest part of the world. So firmly we are told, was this tradition believed, that although some Hindoo writers admitted that Mount Meru must be situated in the central part of Asia, yet rather than relinquish their notion of and predilection for the North Pole as the real locality of their *Paradise*, they actually forced the sun out of the ecliptic, and placed the Pole on the elevated plains of the Lesser Bokhara. If we, however, examine the Hindoo description of this *Paradise*, we shall at once be able to trace its origin and its close analogy to the Mosaic account.

The summit of Meru is considered as a circular plain of vast extent, surrounded by a belt of hills—a celestial earth, the abode of immortals, and is designated Ida-Vratta, or the Circle of Ida. It is of four different colours towards the cardinal points, and is believed to be supported by four enormous buttresses of gold, silver, copper and iron. Yet doubts exist as to its real appearance, some alleging that its form is that of a square pyramid, others maintain that its shape is conical ; others that it resembles an inverted cone ; while others thought, that instead of a circular belt of mountains, Meru terminated in three lofty peaks. The Sawas assert that a vast river rises from the head of their deity Siva, and the Vaishnawas that it springs from beneath the feet of Vishnu, and, after passing through the circle of the moon, falls upon the summit of Meru, and divides itself into four streams, flowing towards the four cardinal points. Others believe that the four rivers of the sacred mountain spring from the roots of Jambri, a tree of immense size which, they say, conveys the most extensive and profound knowledge, and accomplishes the most desirable of human aspirations. The reader will recollect the Mosaical account of the Tree of Knowledge, which stood in the middle of the Garden, and of the river which went out of Eden to water it, dividing itself into four branches or streams of other rivers.

The river thus rising in Meru, the Hindoos further say, flows in four opposite directions to the four cardinal points and is supposed to issue from four rocks, carved in the shape of so many different animals, one of which is a cow ; and this, they allege, is the origin of the Ganges. Some among them, however, think that this river first flows round the sacred city of Brahma, and then discharges itself into a lake called Mansarovara, from which it issues through the rocky heads of four animals to the different divisions of the globe. The cow's head, from which issues the Ganges, they place towards the south ; and towards the north is the tiger, or lion's head. The horse's head is on the west, and on the east is that of the elephant.

The traditions of Cashmere represent that country as the original site of *Paradise*, and the abode of the first human pair ; and the Buddhists of Thibet hold opinion respecting the mountain Meru similar to those of the Hindoos. They locate the sacred Garden, however, at the foot of the mountain, near the source of the Ganges ; but the four holy rivers are made to issue through the heads of the same animals, which are believed to be the guardians of the divisions of the world. The tree of knowledge, or of life, they designate Zambri, which, they say, is a celestial tree, bearing immortal fruit, and flourishes near four vast rocks, from which issue the several rivers which water the world.

The Mussulmans inhabiting the adjacent countries have adopted the popular belief that *Paradise* was situated in Cashmere, adding that when the first man was driven from it, he and his wife wandered separately for some time. They met at a place called Bahlaka, or Balk, so called because they they mutually embraced each other after a long absence. Two gigantic statues, which they say, are yet to be seen between Bahlaka and Bamiyan, represent Adam and Eve, and a third of smaller dimensions is that of their son Seish or Seth, whose tomb, or its site, is pointed out near Bahlaka.

Some of the writers seriously maintained that *Paradise* was under the North Pole, arguing upon an idea of the ancient Babylonians and Egyptians, that the ecliptic or solar way was originally at right angles to the Equator, and so passed directly over the North Pole. The opinion generally entertained by the Mahomedans that it was in one of the seven heavens, is not more ridiculous than the preceding supposition. Dr. Clarke sums up the extravagant theories respecting the locality of *Paradise*. " Some place it as follows :—In the third heaven, others in the fourth, some within the orbit of the moon, others in the moon itself, some in the middle regions of the air, or beyond the earth's attraction, some on the earth, others under the earth, and others within the earth."

Before leaving the East, it may be observed that the Orientals generally reckon four sites of *Paradise* in Asia : the first Ceylon, already mentioned ; the second in Chaldea ; the third in a district of Persia, watered by a river called the Nilab ; and the fourth about Damascus in Syria, and near the springs of the Jordan. This last supposed site is not peculiar to the Oriental writers, as we find it maintained by some Europeans, especially Heidegger, Le Clerc, and Hardouin. The following are the traditions believed by the inhabitants of the city of Damascus—a city which the Emperor Julian the Apostate styled the Eye of all the East, the most sacred and most magnificent Damascus.

" I understand," says Lamartine," that Arabian traditions represent this city and its neighbourhood to form the site of the lost *Paradise*, and certainly I should think that no place upon earth was better calculated to answer one's ideas of Eden. The vast and fruitful plain, with the seven branches of the blue stream which irrigate it—the majestic framework of the mountains—the glittering lakes which reflect the heaven upon the earth—its geographical situation between the two seas—the perfection of the climate—every thing indicates that Damascus has at least been one of the first towns that were built by the children of men—one of the natural halts of fugitive humanity in primeval times. It is, in fact, one of those sites pointed out by the hand of God for a city—a site predestined to sustain a capital like Constantinople." According to the Orientals, Damascus stands on the site of the Sacred Garden, and without the city is the most beautiful meadow divided by the river Barrady, of the red earth of which Adam is alleged to have been formed. This field is designated Ager Damascenus by the Latins, and nearly in the centre of it a pillar formerly stood, intended to mark the precise spot where the Creator breathed into the first man the breath of life.

The numerous traditions which existed among ancient nations of the Garden of Eden doubtless originated those curious and magnificent gardens designed and planted by the Eastern princes, such as the Golden Garden of Aristobulus, King of the Jews, which was consecrated by Pompey to Jupiter Capitolinus. Nor is mythology deficient in similar legends. We have the Gardens of Jupiter, of Alcinous, and of the Fortunate Islands, but especially of the Hesperides, in which not only the primeval *Paradise*, but traditions of the Tree of Knowledge of good and evil, and of the original promise made to the woman, are prominently conspicuous. The Garden of the Hesperides produced golden fruit, guarded by a dangerous serpent—that this fierce reptile encircled with its folds a mysterious tree— and that Hercules procured the fruit by encountering and killing the serpent. The story of the constellation, as related by Eratosthenes, is applicable to the Garden of Eden, and the primeval history of mankind. " This serpent," says that ancient writer, alluding to the constellation, " is the same as that which guarded the golden apples, and was slain by Hercules. For, when the gods offered presents to Juno on her nuptials with Jupiter, the Earth also brought golden apples. Juno, admiring their beauty, commanded them to be planted in the garden of the gods ; but finding that they were continually plucked by the daughter of Atlas, she appointed a vast serpent to guard them. Hercules overcame and slew the monster. Hence, in this constellation the serpent is depicted rearing its head aloft, while Hercules, placed above it with one knee bent, tramples with his foot upon its head, and brandishes a club in his right hand." The Greeks placed the Garden of the Hesperides close to Mount Atlas, and then removed it far into the regions of Western Africa ; yet all knowledge of its Asiatic site was not erased from the classical mythologists, for Apollodorus tells us that certain writers situated it not in the Libyan Atlas, but in the Atlas of the Hyperboreans ; and he adds, that the serpent had the faculty of uttering articulate sounds.

Our Teutonic ancestors believed that the world was originally a *Paradise*, and its first inhabitants more than human, whose dwelling was a magnificent hall, glittering with fine gold, where love, and joy, and friendship presided. The most insignificant of their utensils were made of gold, and hence the appellation of the Golden age. But this happiness was soon overthrown by certain women from the country of the giants, to whose seductions the first mortals yielded, and their innocence and integrity were lost for ever. The transgression of Eve is the obvious prototype of the fatal curiosity of Pandora ; and the arrival of women from the country of the giants, and their intercourse with a distinct and purer line of mortals, can scarcely fail of bringing forcibly to our recollection the marriages of the sons of Seth with the daughters of Cain, with were the principal causes of the universal depravity of the Antediluvians.

The legends of Hindostan also supply us with accounts of the happiness of *Paradise* in the Golden Age of the classic mythology. " There can arise little doubt," says Maurice, " that by the Satya age, or Age of Perfection, the Brahmins obviously allude to the state of perfection and happiness enjoyed by man in *Paradise*. It is impossible to explain what the Indian writers assert concerning the universal purity of manners, and the luxurious and unbounded plenty prevailing in that primitive era, without this supposition. Justice, truth, philanthrophy, were then practised among all the orders and classes of mankind. There was then no extortion, no circumvention, no fraud, used in the dealings one with another. Perpetual oblations smoked on the altars of the Deity ; every tongue uttered praises, and every heart glowed with gratitude to the Supreme Creator. The gods, in token of their approbation of the conduct of mortals, condescended frequently to become incarnate, and to hold personal intercourse with the yet undepraved race, to instruct them in arts and sciences ; to unveil their own sublime functions and pure nature ; and to make them acquainted with the economy of those celestial regions into which they were to be immediately translated, when the period of their terrestial probation expired."

Parama-Hamsas : (*See* **India.**)

Paraskeva, Saint : A saint of the Russian Calendar, whose feast day is August 3rd. On that day pilgrims from all parts of Russia congregate in St. Petersburg for the purpose of casting out devils. A newspaper report of the proceedings as they occurred in 1913 is as follows :—

" Another *St. Paraskeva's* day has come and gone. The usual fanatical scenes have been enacted in the suburbs of St. Petersburg, and the ecclesiastical authorities have not protested, nor have the police intervened. Special trains have again been run to enable thousands of the lower classes to witness a spectacle, the toleration of which will only be appreciated by those acquainted with the writings of M. Pobiedonostzeff, the late Procurator of the Holy Synod. The Church of *St. Paraskeva* is situated in a factory district of the city. On the exterior side of one of the walls is an image of the Saint, to whom is attributed the power of driving out devils and curing epileptics, neurotics, and others by miraculous intervention. At the same time, the day is made a popular holiday, with games and amusements of all sorts, booths and lotteries, refreshment stalls and drinking bars. The newspapers publish detailed accounts of this year's proceedings without comment, and it is perhaps significant that the *Novoe Vremya*, a pillar of orthodoxy, ignores them altogether. Nor is this surprising when one reads of women clad in a single undergarment with bare arms being hoisted up by stalwart peasants to the level of the image in order to kiss it, and then having impure water and unclarified oil forced down their throats. The treatment of the first sick woman is typical of the rest. One young peasant lifted her in the air, two others held her arms fully extended, while a fourth seized her loosened hair, and, dragging her head from side to side and up and down, shouted " Kiss, kiss *St. Paraskeva*! " The woman's garment was soon in tatters. She began groaning. One of the men exclaimed : " Get out ! Satan ! Say where thou art lodged ! " The woman's head was pulled back by the hair, her mouth was forced open, and mud-coloured water (said to be holy water) was poured into it. She spat the water out, and was heard to

moan, " Oh, they are drowning me ! " The young man exultantly exclaimed, " So we've got you, devil, have we ? Leave her at once or we will drown you ! " He continued pouring water into the victim's mouth, and after that unclarified oil. Her lips were held closed, so that she was obliged to swallow it. The unfortunate woman was again raised and her face pressed against the image. " Kiss it ! kiss it ! " she was commanded, and she obeyed. She was asked who was the cause of her being " possessed." " Anna," was the whispered reply. Who was Anna ? What was her village ? In which cottage did she live ? A regular inquisition. The physical and mental sufferings of the first victim lasted about an hour, at the end of which she was handed over to her relatives, after a cross had been given to her, as it was found that she did not own one. According to accounts published by the *Retch, Molva*, etc., many other women were treated in the same fashion, the exercises lasting a whole day and night. The men " pilgrims " would seem to have been less severely handled. It is explained that the idea of unclothing the woman is that there should be no knot, bow, or fastening where the devil and his coadjutors could find a lodgment. And one is left with the picture of scores of women crawling around the church on their knees, invoking the aid of the Almighty for the future or His pardon for sins committed in the past."

The treatment of the " possessed " is analogous to that employed by many barbarous peoples for the casting out of devils, and notably among the Chams of Cambodia (q.v.) who force the possessed to eat garbage in order to disgust the fiend they harbour. (*See* also **Obsession.**)

Pasqually, Martinez de : (Kabalist and Mystic). [1715?–1779]. The date of *Martinez Pasqualis'* birth is not known definitely while even his nationality is a matter of uncertainty. It is commonly supposed, however, that he was born about 1715, somewhere in the south of France ; while several writers have maintained that his parents were Portuguese Jews, but this theory has frequently been contested. It is said that from the outset he evinced a predilection for mysticism in its various forms, while it is certain that, in 1754, he instituted a Kabalistic rite, which was gleaned from Hebraic studies, and whose espousers were styled *Cohens*, this being simply the Hebrew for priests. He propagated this rite in divers masonic lodges of France, notably those of Marseilles, Toulouse, Bordeaux and Paris ; while in 1768 we find him settled in the French capital, gathering round him many people addicted to mysticism, and impregnating them with his theories. His sojourn here was cut short eventually, nevertheless, for he heard that some property had been bequeathed to him in the island of St. Dominique, and he hastened thither with intent to assert his rights ; but he did not return to France, his death occurring in 1779 at Port-au-Prince, the principal town in the island aforesaid.

Pasqually is credited with having written a book, *La Réintégration*, but this was never published. As regards the philosophy which he promulgated, he appears to have believed partly in the inspiration of the Scriptures, the downfall of the angels, the theory of original sin, together with the doctrine of justification by faith ; but he seems to have held that man existed in an elemental state long before the creation detailed in Genesis, and was gradually evolved into his present form. In short, *Pasqually* was something of an anticipator of endless modern theorists ; nor did he fail to find a disciple who regarded him as a prophet and master, this being Louis Claude de St. Martin, a theosophist frequently styled in France " le philosophe inconnu," who founded the sect known as Martinistes. The reader will find some account of St. Martin in an article headed with his name.

Path, The : Is a term which represents an important theosophical teaching, and it is used in different senses to denote not only the *Path* itself but also the Probationary Path along which a man must journey before he can enter on the former. Impelled by profound longing for the highest, for service of God and his fellows, man first begins the journey and he must devote himself wholeheartedly to this service. At his entrance on the Probationary Path, he becomes the chela or disciple of one of the Masters or Perfected men who have all finished the great journey, and he devotes himself to the acquiring of four qualifications which are (1) knowledge of what only is real ; (2) rejection of what is unreal ; (3) the six mental attributes of control over thought, control over outward action, tolerance, endurance, faith and balance, these attributes though all necessary in some degree, not being necessary in perfect degree ; and (4) the desire to be one with God. During the period of his efforts to acquire these qualifications, the chela advances in many ways, for his Master imparts to him wise counsel ; he is taught by meditation to attain divine heights unthought of by ordinary man ; he constantly works for the betterment of his fellows, usually in the hours of sleep, and striving thus and in similar directions, he fits himself for the first initiation at the entrance to the *Path* proper, but it may be mentioned that he has the opportunity either during his probation or afterwards to forego the heavenly life which is his due and so to allow the world to benefit by the powers which he has gained, and which in ordinary course, he would utilise in the heavenly life. In this case, he remains in the astral world, from whence he makes frequent returns to the physical world. Of initiations there are four, each at the beginning of a new stage on the *Path*, manifesting the knowledge of that stage. On the first stage there are three obstacles or, as they are commonly termed, fetters, which must be cast aside and these are the illusion of self which must be realised to be only an illusion ; doubt which must be cleared away by knowledge ; and superstition which must be cleared away by the discovery of what in truth is real. This stage traversed, the second initiation follows, and after this comes the consciousness that earthly life will now be short, that only once again will physical death be experienced, and the man begins more and more to function in his mental body. After the third initiation, the man has two other fetters to unloose—desire and aversion ; and now his knowledge becomes keen and piercing and he can gaze deep into the heart of things. After the fourth initiation, he enters on the last stage and finally frees himself of what fetters remain—the desire for life whether bodily or not, and the sense of individual difference from his fellows. He has now reached the end of his journey, and is no longer trammelled with sin or with anything that can hinder him from entering the state of supreme bliss where he is reunited with the divine consciousness. (*See* **Theosophy.**)

Paulicians : (*See* **Gnostics.**)

Pauline Art : (*See* **Key of Solomon.**)

Pawang : (*See* **Malays.**)

Pazzani : (*See* **France.**)

Pearls : Occult properties of. Amongst the early Greeks and Romans, the wearing of gems as an amulet or talisman, was much in vogue. For this purpose *pearls* were often made into crowns. Rich says : " Pope Adrian, anxious to secure all the virtues in his favour, wore an amulet composed of a sunbaked toad, arsenic, tormentil, *pearl*, coral, hyacinth, smarag, and tragacanth."

It is also said that to dream of *pearls* means many tears. Their occult virtues are brought forth by being boiled in meat, when they heal the quartan ague : bruised and taken with milk, they are good for ulcers, and clear the voice. They also comfort the heart and render their possessor chaste.

Pedro de Valentia : (*See* **Spain.**)

Peliades : (*See* **Greece.**)

Pentagram : (*See* **Magical Diagram.**)

Perfect Sermon : A hermetic Book. (*See* **Hermes Trismegistus.**)

Pernety, Antoine Joseph : Author of the *Dictionnaire Mytho-Hermétique* and *Les Fables Egyptiennes et Grecques*. According to him the Golden Fleece, in the Jason Medea legend, is symbolical. The labours of Jason represent strivings towards perfection.

Persia : (*See* **Magi.**)

Peter of Apono : Born in 1250, at Apono, near Padua, a philosopher, mathematician, and astrologer of no mean skill. He practised physic in Paris with so great success that he soon became very rich, but his wealth and attainments were annulled by the accusation of sorcery which was brought against him. He was said to receive instruction in the seven liberal arts from seven spirits which he kept in crystal vessels. To him was ascribed also the curious and useful faculty of causing the money he spent to return to his own purse. His downfall was brought about by an act of revenge for which he was called to account by the Inquisition. A neighbour of his had been possessed of a spring of excellent water in his garden, from which he allowed *Peter of Apono* to drink at will. For some reason or another the permission was withdrawn, and *Peter*, with the assistance of the Devil, caused the water to leave the garden and flow uselessly in some distant street. Ere the trial was finished the unfortunate physician died, but so bitter were the inquisitors against him that they ordered his bones to be dug up and burned. This public indignity to his memory was averted by some of his friends, who, hearing of the vindictive sentence, secretly removed his remains from the burying-ground where they lay. The inquisitors thereupon satisfied their animosity by burning him in effigy.

Petetin : (*See* **Hypnotism.**)

Petra Philosophorum : (*See* **Fioravanti.**)

Phantasmagoria : An optical spectacle of the same class as the magic lantern ; dissolving views. These were formerly regarded by the ignorant as sorcery.

Philadelphian Society : (*See* **Visions.**)

Philalethes, Eirenæus : (circa, 1660) Alchemist. The life of this alchemist is wrapped in mystery, albeit a considerable mass of writing stands to his credit. The heading of this article is, of course, mere pseudonym, and, though some have tried hard to identify the writer who bore it with one Thomas Vaughan, a brother of Henry Vaughan, the " Silurist " poet, this theory is not supported by any very sound evidence. Others have striven to identify *Philalethes* with George Starkey, the quack doctor and author of *Liquor Alchahest* ; but then, Starkey died of the plague in London in 1665, whereas it is known that *Eirenæus* was living for some years after that date. He appears, also, to have been on intimate terms with Robert Boyle, and, though this points to his having spent a considerable time in England, it is certain on the other hand that he emigrated to America. Now Starkey, it will be remembered, was born in the Bermudas, and practised his spurious medical crafts in the English settlements in America, where, according to his contemporary biographers, he met *Eirenæus Philalethes*. This meeting, then, may have given rise to the identification at issue ; while it is probably Starkey to whom *Eirenæus* refers when, in a preface to one of his books, he tells of certain of his writings falling " into the hands of one who, I conceive, will never return them," for in 1654 Starkey issued a volume with the title, *The Marrow of Alchemy by Eirenæus Philoponus Philalethes*.

It is to these prefaces by *Philalethes* that we must chiefly look for any information about him, while in the thirteenth chapter of his *Introitus Apertus ad Occlusum Regis Palatium* (Amsterdam, 1667) he makes a few autobiographical avowals which illuminate his character and career. "For we are like Cain, driven from the pleasant society we formerly had," he writes, and this suggests that he was persecuted on account of his alchemistic predilections; while elsewhere he heaps scorn on most of the hermetic philosophers of his day, and elsewhere, again, he vituperates the popular worship of money-getting. "I disdain, loathe, and detest the idolizing of silver and gold," he declares, "by which the pomps and vanities of the world are celebrated. Ah! filthy, evil, ah! vain nothingness." That is vigorously written, and indeed nearly everything from the pen of *Philalethes*, whether in Latin or in English, proclaims him a writer of some care, skill and taste; while his scholarship was considerable also, and it is interesting to find that, in his preface to *Ripley Revived* (London, 1678), he gives some account of the authors to whom he felt himself chiefly indebted. "For my own part," he says, "I have cause to honour Bernard Trévisan, who is very ingenious, especially in the letter to Thomas of Boulogne, when I seriously confess I received the main light in the hidden secret. I do not remember that ever I learnt anything from Raymond Lully. . . . I know of none like Ripley, though Flamel be eminent."

Langlet du Fresnoy, in his *Histoire de la Philosophie Hermétique*, refers to numerous unpublished manuscripts by *Eirenæus Philalethes*, but nothing is known about these to-day, and in conclusion it behoves only to cite the more important of those things by the alchemist which were issued in book form: *Medulla Alchymiæ* (London, 1664), *Experimenta de Praeperatione Mercurii Sophici* (Amsterdam, 1668) and *Enarratio Methodica trium Gebri Medicinarum* (Amsterdam, 1668.)

Philosopher's Stone : A substance which enabled adepts in alchemy to compass the transmutation of metals. (*See* **Alchemy.**) It was imagined by the alchemists that some one definite substance was essential to the success of the transmutation of metals. By the application or admixture of this substance all metals might be transmuted into gold or silver. It was often designated the Powder of Projection. Zosimus, who lived at the commencement of the fifth century is one of the first who alludes to it. He says that the stone is a powder or liquor formed of diverse metals, infusioned under a favourable constellation. The *Philosopher's Stone* was supposed to contain the secret not only of transmutation, but of health and life, for through its agency could be distilled the Elixir of Life. It was the touchstone of existence. The author of a *Treatise on Philosophical and Hermetic Chemistry*, published in Paris in 1725 says: "Modern philosophers have extracted from the interior of mercury a fiery spirit, mineral, vegetable and mutliplicative, in a humid concavity in which is found the primitive mercury or the universal quintessence. In the midst of this spirit resides the spiritual fluid. . . . . This is the mercury of the philosophers, which is not solid like a metal, nor soft like quicksilver, but between the two. They have retained for a long time this secret, which is the commencement, the middle, and the end of their work. It is necessary then to proceed first to purge the mercury with salt and with ordinary salad vinegar, to sublime it with vitriol and saltpetre, to dissolve it in aqua-fortis, to sublime it again, to calcine it and fix it, to put away part of it in salad oil, to distill this liquor for the purpose of separating the spiritual water, air, and fire, to fix the mercurial body in the spiritual water or to distill the spirit of liquid mercury found in it, to putrefy all, and then to raise and exalt the spirit with non-odorous white sulphur—

that is to say, sal-ammoniac—to dissolve this sal-ammoniac in the spirit of liquid mercury which when distilled becomes the liquor known as the Vinegar of the Sages, to make it pass from gold to antimony three times and afterwards to reduce it by heat, lastly to steep this warm gold in very harsh vinegar and allow it to putrefy. On the surface of the vinegar it will raise itself in the form of fiery earth of the colour of oriental pearls. This is the first operation in the grand work. For the second operation; take in the name of God one part of gold and two parts of the spiritual water, charged with the sal-ammoniac, mix this noble confection in a vase of crystal of the shape of an egg: warm over a soft but continuous fire, and the fiery water will dissolve little by little the gold; this forms a liquor which is called by the sages "chaos" containing the elementary qualities—cold, dryness, heat and humidity. Allow this composition to putrefy until it becomes black; this blackness is known as the 'crow's head' and the 'darkness of the sages,' and makes known to the artist that he is on the right track. It was also known as the 'black earth.' It must be boiled once more in a vase as white as snow; this stage of the work is called the 'swan,' and from it arises the white liquor, which is divided into two parts—one white for the manufacture of silver, the other red for the manufacture of gold. Now you have accomplished the work, and you possess the *Philosopher's Stone*.

"In these diverse operations, one finds many by-products; among these is the 'green lion' which is called also 'azoph,' and which draws gold from the more ignoble elements; the 'red lion' which converts the metal into gold; the 'head of the crow,' called also the 'black veil of the ship of Theseus,' which appearing forty days before the end of the operation predicts its success; the white powder which transmutes the white metals to fine silver; the red elixir with which gold is made; the white elixir which also makes silver, and which procures long life—it is also called the 'white daughter of the philosophers.'"

In the lives of the various alchemists we find many notices of the Powder of Projection in connection with those adepts who were supposed to have arrived at the solution of the grand arcanum. Thus in the *Life of Alexander Seton* (q.v.), a Scotsman who came from Port Seton, near Edinburgh, we find that on his various travels on the continent he employed in his alchemical experiments a blackish powder, the application of which turned any metal given him into gold. Numerous instances are on record of Seton's projections, the majority of which are verified with great thoroughness. On one occasion whilst in Holland, he went with some friends from the house at which he was residing to undertake an alchemical experiment at another house near by. On the way thither a quantity of ordinary zinc was purchased, and this Seton succeeded in projecting into pure gold by the application of his powder. A like phenomenon was undertaken by him at Cologne, and elsewhere throughout Germany, and the extremest torture could not wring from him the secret of the quintessence he possessed. His pupil or assistant, Sendivogius, made great efforts to obtain the secret from him before he died, but all to no purpose. However, out of gratitude Seton bequeathed him what remained of his marvellous powder, which was employed by his Polish successor with the same results as had been achieved in his own case. The wretched Sendivogius fared badly, however, when the powder at last came to an end. He had used it chiefly in liquid form, and into this he had dipped silver coins which immediately had become the purest gold. Indeed it is on record that one coin, of which he had only immersed the half, remained for many years as a signal instance of the claims of alchemy in a museum or collection somewhere in South Germany. The half of this doubloon was gold, while the undipped portion had remained silver ; but the notice concerning it is scarcely of a satisfactory nature. When the powder gave out, Sendivogius was driven to the desperate expedient of gilding the coins, which, report says, he had heretofore transmuted by legitimate means, and this very naturally brought upon him the wrath of those who had trusted him. (See **Seton.**)

In the *Tale of the Anonymous Adept* we also find a powder in use, and indeed the powder seems to have been the favoured form of the transmuting agency. The term *Philosopher's Stone* probably arose from some Eastern talismanic legend. Yet we find in Egyptian alchemy— the oldest—the idea of the black powder—the detritus or oxide of all the metals mingled. (See **Egypt.**)

The *Philosopher's Stone* had a spiritual as well as a material conception attached to it, and indeed spiritual alchemy is practically identified with it ; but we do not find the first alchemists, nor those of mediæval times, possessed of any spiritual ideas ; their hope was to manufacture real gold, and it is only in later times that we find the altruistic idea creeping in, to the detriment of the physical one. Symbolic language was largely used by both schools, however, and we must not imagine that because an alchemical writer employs symbolical figures of speech that he is of the transcendental school, as his desire was merely to be understanded of his brother adepts, and to conserve his secret from the vulgar. (See **Alchemy.**)

Philosophic Summary, The : (See **Hamel.**)

Phreno-Magnet : Journal of Magnetism. (See **Spiritualism.**)

Phreno-Mesmerism (or Phrenopathy) : An application of the principles of *Mesmerism* to the science of phrenology. *Mesmerism* and phrenology had for some time been regarded by the English mesmerists as related sciences when it was discovered that a somnambule whose "bumps" were touched by the fingers of the operator would respond to the stimulus by exhibiting every symptom of the mental trait corresponding to the organ touched. Thus signs of joy, grief, destructiveness, combativeness, and friendship might be exhibited in rapid succession by the entranced patient. Among those who claimed to have discovered the new science were Dr. Collyer, a pupil of Dr. Elliotson's ; and the Rev. Laroy Sunderland, though the former afterwards repudiated it. As time went on enterprising phreno-mesmerists discovered many new cerebral organs as many as a hundred and fifty being found beside those already mapped out by Spurzheim and Gall. Among its supporters *phreno-mesmerism* numbered the distinguished hypnotist Braid, who expressed himself fully satisfied of its reality. He has recorded a number of cases in which the patient correctly indicated by his actions the organs touched, though demonstrably ignorant of phrenological laws, and inaccessible to outside information. Braid himself offers but a very halting and inadequate physiological explanation, and since he may be supposed to have been fully alive to the factors of suggestion and hyperæsthesia, it would seem advisable to admit the possibility of mental suggestion, or telepathy, by means of which the expectation of the operator, reproducing itself in the mind of the patient, would give rise to the corresponding reactions.

Phrygian Cap : Hargrave Jennings, in his *Rosicrucians. Their Rites and Mysteries*, says that the *Phrygian Cap*, the classic Mithraic Cap, sacrificial Cap, and mitre all derive from one common ancestor. The Mithraic or *Phrygian Cap* is the origin of the priestly mitre in all faiths. It was worn by the priest in sacrifice. When worn by a male, it had its crest, comb, or point, set jutting forward ; when worn by a female, it bore the same prominent part of the cap in reverse, or on the nape of the neck, as in the instance of the Amazon's helmet, displayed in all old scuplures, or

that of Pallas-Athene, as exhibited in the figures of Minerva. The peak, pic, or point, of caps or hats (the term "cocked hat" is a case in point) all refer to the same idea. This point had a sanctifying meaning afterwards attributed to it, when it was called the christa, crista, or crest, which signifies a triumphal top, or tuft. The "Grenadier Cap," and the loose black Hussar Cap, derive remotely from the same sacred, Mithraic, or emblematical bonnet, or high pyramidal cap. It, in this instance, changes to black, because it is devoted to the illustration of the "fireworkers" (grenadiers) who, among modern military, succeed the Vulcanists, Cyclopes, classic "smiths," or servants of Vulcan, or Mulciber, the artful worker among the metals in the fire, or amidst the forces of nature. This idea will be found by a reference to the high cap among the Persians, or Fire-worshippers ; and to the black cap among the Bohemians, and in the East. All travellers in Eastern lands will remember that the tops of the minarets reminded them of the high-pointed black caps of the Persians.

The *Phrygian Cap* is a most recondite antiquarian form ; the symbol comes from the highest antiquity. It is displayed on the head of the figure sacrificing in the celebrated sculpture, called the "Mithraic Sacrifice" (or the Mythical Sacrifice) in the British Museum. This loose cap, with the point protruding, gives the original form from which all helmets or defensive headpieces, whether Greek or Barbarian, deduce. As a *Phrygian Cap*, or Symbolising Cap, it is always sanguine in its colour. It then stands as the "Cap of Liberty" a revolutionary form ; also, in another way, it is even a civic or incorporated badge. It is always masculine in its meaning. It marks the "needle" of the obelisk, the crown or tip of the phallus, whether "human" or representative. It has its origin in the rite of circumcision—unaccountable as are both the symbol and the rite.

The real meaning of the bonnet rouge, or cap of liberty, has been involved from time immemorial in deep obscurity, notwithstanding that it has always been regarded as the most important hieroglyph or figure. It signifies the supernatural simultaneous "sacrifice" and "triumph." It has descended from the time of Abraham, and it is supposed to emblem the strange mythic rite of the "circumcisio preputii," The loose *Phrygian* bonnet conique, or "cap of liberty," may be accepted as figuring, or standing for, that detached integument or husk, separated from a certain point or knob, which has various names in different languages, and which supplies the central idea of this sacrificial rite—the spoil or refuse of which (absurd and unpleasant as it may seem) is borne aloft at once as a "trophy" and as the "cap of liberty." It is now a magic sign, and becomes a talisman of supposedly inexpressible power—from what particular dark reason it may be difficult to say. The whole is a sign of "initiation," and of baptism of a peculiar kind. The *Phrygian Cap*, ever after this first inauguration, has stood as the sign of the "Enlightened." The heroic figures in most Gnostic Gems, have caps of this kind. The sacrificer in the sculptured group of the "Mithraic Sacrifice," among the marbles in the British Museum, has a *Phrygian Cap* on his head, whilst in the act of striking the bull with the poniard— meaning the office of the immolating priest. The bonnet conique is the mitre of the Doge of Venice.

Cinteotl, a Mexican god of sacrifice, wears such a cap made from the thigh-skin of an immolated virgin. This head-dress is shaped like a cock's comb.

Besides the bonnet rouge, the Pope's mitre—nay, all mitres or conical head-coverings—have their name from the terms "Mithradic," or "Mithraic," The origin of the whole class of names is Mittra, or Mithra. The cap of the grenadier, the shape of which is alike all over Europe, is related to the Tartar lambskin caps, which are dyed black ; and it is black also from its associations with Vulcan and the " Fire-worshippers " (Smiths). The Scotch Glengarry cap will prove on examination to be only a " cocked " *Phrygian.* All the black conical caps, and the meaning of this strange symbol, came from the East. The loose black fur cap derives from the Tartars.

The " Cap of Liberty " (Bonnet Rouge), the Crista or Crest (Male), and the Female (Amazon) helmet, all mean the same idea ; in the instance of the female crest the knob is, however, depressed.

Phyllorhodomancy : Divination by rose-leaves. The Greeks clapped a rose-leaf on the hand, and judged from the resulting sound the success or otherwise of their desires.

Physical World : Formerly known as the Sthula Plane—is in the theosophic scheme of things the lowest of the seven worlds, the world in which ordinary man moves and is conscious under normal conditions. It is the limit of the ego's descent into matter, and the matter which composes the appropriate physical body, is the densest of any of these worlds. Physical matter has the seven divisions of solid, liquid, gas, ether, super-ether, sub-atom and atom, in common with the matter of the other worlds. Besides the physical body, familiar to ordinary vision, there is a finer body, the etheric double, which plays a very important part in collecting vitality from the sun for the use of the denser physical body, and reference is made to the articles on the Etheric Body, and Chaksams. At death, the physical body and the etheric double are cast aside and slowly resolve into their components. (*See* **Worlds, Planes** or **Spheres, Theosophy.**)

Pierart, Z. T. : French Spiritualist and editor of *La Revue Spiritualiste.* M. *Periart* was born in humble circumstances but managed to secure for himself an adequate education. He became in time professor at the College of Maubeuge, and afterwards secretary to Baron Du Potet. In 1858 he founded *La Revue Spiritualiste,* and led the French spirit-ualists, between whom and the spiritists under Allan Kardec there existed a certain rivalry. Until his death in 1878 he continued to devote his time and talents to the movement with which he had identified himself.

Pierre, La : (*See* Palingenesy.)

Pinto : Grand Master of Malta : (*See* **Cagliostro.**)

Piper, Mrs. : A famous trance medium, whose discourses and writings present the best evidence extant for the actuality of spirit communication. A native of America, it was there that *Mrs. Piper* first became entranced, while consulting a professional clairvoyant in 1884. Numerous spirits pur-ported to control her in these early days—Mrs. Siddons, Longfellow, Bach, to mention only the most celebrated—but in 1885, when she came under the observation of the Society for Psychical Research, her principal control was Dr. Phinuit. From that time forward her trance utterances and writings—for after 1890 the communications were generally in writing—were carefully recorded and analysed by members of the S.P.R., chiefly under the direction of Dr. Hodgson. In 1889–90 *Mrs. Piper* visited this country and gave many séances, most of which seemed to display supernormal powers in the medium. It is impossible in a limited space to detail her remarkable trance impersonations. On his death in 1905 Dr. Hodgson became one of her controls ; Mr. Myers and Mr. Gurney also controlled her. But perhaps the most life-like and convincing impersonation or spirit-manifestation—whichever it may have been—was that of George Pelham, a young American author and a friend of Dr. Hodgson, who had died suddenly in 1892. (*See* **Trance Personalities.**) The information given by this control, his recognition of friends, and so on, were so accurate as to convince many that it was indeed " G.P." who spoke.

From that time until 1896 the séances were especially productive, but in the latter year the medium underwent an operation. Phinuit, who often acted as a go-between for other controls and the sitter, now took his departure, and a band of other spirits, led by the " Imperator " of Stainton Moses, took control of *Mrs. Piper's* organism. The trance writings and utterances became fewer, and the spirits recommended that the number of sittings be cut down on account of the medium's health. Nevertheless some excellent tests were subsequently got with the Piper-Hodgson, Piper-Myers, and Piper-Gurney controls. *Mrs. Piper* was also one of those who took part in the " cross-correspondences " sittings held in 1906 and onwards, the other mediums being Mrs. Thompson, Mrs. Verrall, Miss Verrall, Mrs. Holland, Mrs. Forbes, etc. (*See* " **Spiritual-ism,** *and* **Cross-Correspondences.**) It seems clear that in *Mrs. Piper's* trance phenomena there are evidences of some supernormal faculty, at the best, of telepathy, though to the writer even that hypothesis seems to be inadequate. It would, for example, be a very complicated form of telepathy, that would enable some of these automatic " cross-correspondence " scripts to be written, in which, say, two scripts contain allusions unintelligible to the writers, and requiring a key provided by a third script to make them plain. Such a case inevitably suggests that one and the same intelligence directs all three mediums. *Mrs. Piper's* impersonation of George Pelham, again, calls for some explanation, since it would seem that all the information could hardly have been culled from the sitter's minds. (*See* **Spiritualism.**)

Planchette : An instrument designed for the purpose of communication with spirits. It consists of a thin-heart-shaped piece of wood, mounted on two small wheel-castors and carrying a pencil, point downwards, for the third support. The hand is placed on the wood and the pencil writes automatically, or presumably by spirit control operating through the psychic force of the medium.

In 1853, a well-known French spiritualist, M. Planchette, invented this instrument to which he gave his name. For quite fifteen years it was used exclusively by French spiritualists. Then in the year 1868 a firm of toy-makers in America took up the idea and flooded the booksellers' shops with great numbers of *planchettes.* It became a popular mania, and the instrument sold in thousands there and in Great Britain. It was, and is, largely used simply as a toy and any results obtained that may be arresting and seemingly inexplicable are explained by Animal Magnetism or traced to the power of subconscious thought.

Amongst spiritualists it has been used for spirit com-munication. Automatic writing has often been developed by use of the *planchette,* some mediums publishing books which, they claimed, were written wholly by their spirit-controls through the use of *planchettes.* Dr. Ashburnes, in his *Spiritualism Chemically Explained* says that the human body is a condensation of gases, which constantly exude from the skin in invisible vapour—otherwise electricity ; that the fingers coming in contact with the *planchette* transmit to it an " odic force," and thus set it in motion. He goes on to say that some people have phosphorous in excess in their system and the vapour " thus exuded forms a positively living, thinking, acting body, capable of directing a pencil." There are variations on the *planchette* form such as the *dial-planchette* which consists of a founda-tion of thick cardboard nine inches square on the face of which the alphabet is printed and also the numerals one to ten. There are the words " Yes," " No," " Goodbye " and " Don't know." These letters, words, and numerals are printed on the outer edge of a circle, the diameter of which is about seven inches. In the centre of this circle, and firmly affixed to the cardboard, is a block of wood three inches square. The upper surface of this block has a circular channel in it and in this run balls. Over the balls is placed a circular piece of hard wood, five inches in diameter, and attached to the outer edge of this a pointer. The upper piece of wood is attached to the lower by an ordinary screw, upon which the upper plate revolves when used for communication. Another form is the *Ouija* board on which in a convenient order the letters of the alphabet are printed and over which a pointer easily moves under the direction of the hand of the person or persons acting as mediums. It is stated that a form of this " mystic toy." was in use in the days of Pythagoras, about 540 B.C. In a French history of Pythagoras, the author describing his celebrated school of philosophy, asserts that the brotherhood held frequent séances or circles at which a mystic table, moving on wheels, moved towards signs inscribed on the surface of a stone slab on which the moving-table worked. The author states that probably Pythagoras, in his travels among the Eastern nations, observed some such apparatus in use amongst them and adapted his idea from them. Another trace of some such " communicating mechanism " is found in the legend told by the Scandinavian Blomsturvalla how the people of Jomsvikingia in the twelfth century had a high priest, one Völsunga, whose predictions were renowned for their accuracy throughout the length and breadth of the land. He had in his possession a little ivory doll that drew with " a pointed instrument " on parchment or " other substance," certain signs to which the priest had the key. The communications were in every case prophetic utterances, and it is said in every case came true. The writer who recounts the legend thought it probable that the priest had procured the doll in China. In the National Museum at Stockholm there is a doll of this description which is worked by mechanism, and when wound up walks round and round in circles and occasionally uses its right arm to make curious signs with a pointed instrument like a stylo which is held in the hand. Its origin and use have been connected with the legend recounted above.

Planet : (*See* **Planetary Chains.**)

Planetary Logos, or Ruler of Seven Chains, is, in the theosophic scheme, one of the grades in the hierarchy which assists in the work of creation and guidance. It is the supreme Logos who initiates this work, but in it he is helped by the " seven." They receive from him the inspiration and straightway each in his own Planetary Chain carries on the work, directed by him no doubt, yet in an individual fashion, through all the successive stages which go to compose a Scheme of Evolution. (*See* **Logos, Chains.**)

Planetary Spirits : In the theosophical scheme the number of these spirits is seven. They are emanations from the Absolute, and are the agents by which the Absolute effects all his changes in the Universe.

Planets : (*See* **Astrology.**)

Podovne Vile : (*See* **Slavs.**)

Poe, Edgar Allen : (*See* **Fiction, Occult English.**)

Poinandres : A hermetic book. (*See* **Hermes Trismegistus.**)

Polong : Malay familiar. (*See* **Malays.**)

Poltergeist : The name given to the supposed supernatural causes of outbreaks of rappings, inexplicable noises, and similar disturbances, which from time to time have mystified men of science as well as the general public. The term *poltergeist* (*i.e., Polter Geist,* rattling ghost) is sufficiently indicative of the character of these beings, whose manifestations are, at the best, puerile and purposeless tricks, and not infrequently display an openly mischievous and destructive tendency. The *poltergeist* is by no means indigenous to any one country, nor has he confined his attentions to any particular period. Lang mentions several cases belonging

to the Middle Ages, and one at least which dates so far back as 856 B.C. In both savage and civilised countries this peculiar form of haunting is well known, and it is a curious fact that the phenomena are almost identical in every case. The disturbances are always observed to be particularly active in the neighbourhood of one person, generally a child or a young woman, and preferably an epileptic or hysterical subject. According to the theory advanced by spiritualists, this centre of the disturbances is a natural medium, through whom the spirits desire to communicate with the world of living beings. In earlier times such a person was regarded as a witch, or the victim of a witch, whichever supposition was best fitted to the circumstances. The *poltergeist* is represented as a development from witchcraft, and the direct forerunner of modern spiritualism, and is, in fact, a link between the two.

Turning our attention first to some of the earlier records, we may consider briefly the case of the Drummer of Tedworth (1661), and the Epworth Case (1716). In both of these instances the manifestations witnessed were of the usual order. The spirits, if spirits they were, sought to attract attention by familiar childish tricks, and communicated by means of the same cumbrous process of knocking. The circumstances of the first-named instance are as follow : In 1661 a vagrant drummer was, at the instance of Mr. Mompesson of Tedworth, taken before a Justice of the Peace, and deprived of his drum, which instrument finally found a resting-place in the house of Mr. Mompesson, during that gentleman's absence from home. Immediately violent disturbances broke out in the house. Loud knockings and thumpings were heard, and the beating of an invisible drum. Articles flew recklessly about the rooms, and the bedsteads (particularly those in which the younger children lay) were violently shaken. After a time the drummer was transported, when the manifestations abruptly ceased, but a recurrence of the outbreak synchronised with his return. Contemporary opinion put the case down to witchcraft on the part of the drummer, but Mr. Podmore and other moderns incline to the belief that the " two little modest girls in the bed " had more than a little to do with the mysterious knockings and scratchings of the *poltergeist*. In the famous Epworth Case, where the phenomena is well attested by the whole Wesley family, and described in numerous contemporary letters, the disturbances comprised all the ordinary manifestations of levitations, loud and terrifying noises, and rappings, together with apparitions of rabbits, badgers, and so on. Podmore is of the opinion that one of the daughters, Hetty, was in some way implicated in the affair. She alone did not give an account of the manifestations, though she had promised to do so. The *poltergeist* showed a decided partiality for her company—a circumstance which, though not unobserved, does not seem to have held any special significance for her family. A more recent case in which a charge of witchcraft is involved, is the Cideville case, described by Mr. Lang in his *Cock Lane and Common Sense,* under the heading, " A Modern Trial for Witchcraft." In 1849 the Curé of Cideville, Seine Inférieure, was summoned to court by a shepherd named Thorel, who alleged that the Curé had denounced him for sorcery. In his defence the Curé stated that Thorel himself had confessed to having produced by means of sorcery certain mysterious manifestations which had disturbed the inmates of the Abbey. During the trial it transpired that the Curé, when visiting a sick parishioner, had driven from the bedside a man of notorious character, with an evil reputation for sorcery, who was about to treat the patient. The sorcerer retired, vowing vengeance on the Curé, and was shortly afterwards sent to prison. Later when two little boys, pupils of the Curé, were at an auction, they were approached by Thorel, who was known as a disciple of the sorcerer. He placed his hand on the head of one of the children, and muttered some strange words. When the boys returned to the Abbey the *poltergeist* performances commenced. Violent blows on the walls seemed about to demolish them, one of the children complained that he was followed by a man's shadow, and other witnesses declared that they had seen a grey hand and wreaths of smoke. Some of those who visited the Abbey were able to hold a conversation with the spirits by means of knocking. It was agreed that sharp-pointed irons should be driven into the walls, and on this being done, smoke and flames were seen to issue from the incisions. At last Thorel sought the Curé and confessed that the disturbances were the work of his master, the sorcerer. The plaintiff was non-suited, and the judge, in summing up, said that the cause of the "extraordinary facts" of this case "remained unknown." In February, 1851, the boys were removed from the Abbey, and the disturbances ceased.

Of those instances where a spiritualistic explanation has been offered perhaps the most outstanding is the case of the Cock Lane Ghost, almost too well-known to call for recapitulation. In 1761-2 raps and scratches were heard in a house in Cock Lane, generally occurring near the bed of the little daughter of the house, Elizabeth Parsons. Very soon the manifestations became so pronounced that people from all parts of the city were crowding to witness them. A code of raps was agreed upon, through which it was ascertained that the spirit was that of a lady named "Fanny," who declared that she had been poisoned by her deceased sister's husband, with whom she had lodged in the Cock Lane house some two years previously, and expressed a wish that he might be hanged. It is, indeed, quite a common thing for the *poltergeist* to reveal a crime, real or imaginary—and more often the latter, which is entirely in keeping with the character of the spirit. In the Cock Lane affair the manifestations followed the girl when she was removed to another house, and she trembled strongly, even in her sleep, on the approach of the ghost. The case which presents the most formidable array of evidence, however, is that of the Joller family in Switzerland. In 1860-2 serious disturbances broke out in Stans, in the home of M. Joller, a prominent lawyer, and a man of excellent character. Knocks were first heard by a servant-maid, who also averred that she was haunted by strange grey shapes, and the sound of sobbing. In the autumn of 1861, she was dismissed and another maid engaged. For a time there was peace, but in the summer of 1862 they commenced with redoubled vigour. The wife and seven children of M. Joller heard and saw many terrifying sights and sounds, but M. Joller himself remained sceptical. At length, however, even he was convinced that neither trickery nor imagination would suffice as an explanation of the phenomena. Meanwhile the manifestations became more and more outrageous, and continued in full view of the thousands of persons who were attracted by curiosity to the house, including the Land-Captain Zelger, the Director of Police Jaun, the President of the Court of Justice, and other prominent people, some of whom suggested that a commission be appointed to examine the house thoroughly. Three of the heads of police were deputed to conduct the enquiry. They demanded the withdrawal of M. Joller and his family, and remained in the house for six days without witnessing anything abnormal, and drew up a report to this effect. Directly the Joller family entered the house the interruptions were renewed. M. Joller became the butt of ridicule to all, even his political and personal friends, and was finally compelled to quit his ancestral home. This is undoubtedly one of the most striking cases of *poltergeist* haunting on record. Here, as

in almost every instance, there are children evidently and intimately bound up with the manifestations. It is his choice of a medium which has directed most suspicion to the *poltergeist*, and it on this that Mr. Podmore bases his assumption that all *poltergeist* visitations are traceable to the cunning tricks of "naughty little girls." He suggests that with the "medium" under careful control it is more than probable that the *poltergeist* will turn shy, and refuse to perform his traditional functions ! There is much to be said for this theory. The medium of the spiritualistic séance is frequently credited with the loftiest utterances, and the production of literary, musical, and artistic compositions. The *poltergeist* indulges in such futilities as the breaking of crockery, the throwing about of furniture, and the materialization of coal and carrots in the drawing-room. Why, if they are mature spirits, as they purport to be, should they practise such feats of mystification as would seem to be impelled either by the foolish vanity of a child, or the cunning impulses of a deranged mind ? Then there is often a curious hesitancy on the part of the medium, as in the case of Hetty Wesley, a trembling on the approach of the phenomena, and a tendency to such physical disturbances as epileptic and other fits. And sometimes the *poltergeist* confesses, as did the maid-servant Ann at Stockwell, to having manipulated the disturbing occurrences with the aid of wires and horsehair. But in such a case as that of the Joller family, the theory of "naughty little girls" is childishly inadequate. It is all but impossible to believe that children could produce the manifestations in full view of hundreds of people. It is still more difficult to understand how children and ignorant persons, with presumably no knowledge of previous instances, could fix upon exactly the same phenomena which has been produced by the *poltergeists* of every age and clime. And in the Joller case, there is the evidence of many spectators that the most violent disturbances were witnessed when the whole family were assembled outside the house and thus not in a position to assist the manifestations, which included the throwing open of all windows, doors, cupboards and drawers, the materialization of the "thin grey cloud," noises and apparitions. In short, it must be admitted that there is an element of mystery which calls for elucidation, and which the most scientific and critical minds have hitherto failed to make clear.

Polynesia : Magic in *Polynesia* is the preserve of the priestly and upper classes, although lesser sorcery is practised by individuals not of these castes. There is a prevailing belief in what is known as *mana*, or supernatural power, which is resident in certain individuals. The method of using this power is twofold. One of these is practised by a society known as the *Iniat*, where certain rites are carried out which are supposed to bring calamity upon the enemies of the tribe. The ability to exercise magic is known as *agagara*, and the magician or wizard is *tena agagara*. If the wizard desires to cast magic upon another man, he usually tries to secure something that that person has touched with his mouth, and to guard against this, the natives are careful to destroy all food-refuse that they do not consume, and they carefully gather up even a single drop of blood when they receive a cut or scratch, and burn it or throw it into the sea, so that the wizard may not obtain it. The wizard having obtained something belonging to the person whom he wishes to injure, buries it in a deep hole, together with leaves of poisonous plants and sharp-pointed pieces of bamboo, accompanying the action by suitable incantations. If he chances to be a member of the *Iniat* society, he will place on the top of the whole one of their sacred stones, as they believe that so long as the stone is pressing down the article which has been buried in the hole the man to whom it belonged will remain sick. Immediately a man falls sick, he sets enquiries on foot as to who has bewitched him, and there is always someone to acknowledge the soft impeachment. If he does not succeed in having the spell removed he will almost certainly succumb, but if he succeeds in having it taken away, he begins to recover almost immediately ; and the strange thing is that he evinces no enmity towards the person or persons who " bewitched " him,—indeed it is taken as a matter of course, and he quietly waits the time when he will be able to return the compliment !

These remarks apply for the most part to New Britain, and its system of magic is practically the same as that known in Fiji as *vakadraunikau* concerning which very little is known. In his work *Melanesians and Polynesians* the Rev. Dr. George Brown, the well-known pioneer missionary and explorer, gives an interesting account of the magical systems of these people, in which he incorporates several informative letters from brother missionaries, which are well worth quotation. For example, the Rev. W. E. Bromilow says that at Dobu in south-eastern New Guinea :—

" *Werabana* (evil spirits) are those which inhabit dark places, and wander in the night, and give witches their power to smite all round. *Barau* is the wizardry of men, who look with angry eyes out of dark places, and throw small stones, first spitting on them, at men, women, and even children, thus causing death. A tree falls, it is a witch who caused it to do so, though the tree may be quite rotten, or a gust of wind may break it off. A man meets with an accident, it is the *werabana*. He is getting better through the influence of the medicine-man, but has a relapse ; this is the *barau* at work, as we have ascertained from the terrified shouts of our workmen, as some sleeper has called out in a horrid dream. These medicine-men, too, have great power, and no wonder, when one of our girls gets a little dust in her eye, and the doctor takes a big stone out of it ; and when a chief has a pain in the chest, and *to obaoba* takes therefrom a two-inch nail.

" The people here will have it that all evil spirits are female. *Werabana* is the great word, but the term is applied to witches as well, who are called the *vesses* of the *werabana*, but more often the single word is used. I have the names of spirits inhabiting the glens and forests, but they are all women or enter into women, giving them terrible powers. Whenever any one is sick, it is the *werabana* who has caused the illness, and any old woman who happened to be at enmity with the sick person is set down as the cause. A child died the other day, and the friends were quite angry because the witches had not heeded the words of the *lotu*, i.e., the Christian religion *Taparoro*, and given up smiting the little ones. ' These are times of peace,' said they, ' why should the child die then ?' We, of course, took the opportunity and tried to teach them that sickness caused death without the influence of poor old women.

" Sorcerers are *barau*, men whose powers are more terrible than those of all the witches. I was talking to a *to obaoba*—medicine-man—the other day, and I asked him why his taking a stone out of a man's chest did not cure him. ' Oh,' said he, ' he must have been smitten by a *barau*.' A very logical statement this. Cases the *to obaoba* cannot cure are under the fell stroke of the *barau*, from which there is no escape, except by the sorcerer's own incantations.

" The Fijian sorcery of *drau-ni-kau* appears here in another form called *sumana* or rubbish. The sorcerer obtains possession of a small portion of his victim's hair, or skin, or food left after a meal, and carefully wraps it up in a parcel, which he sends off to as great a distance as is possible. In the meantime he very cunningly causes a report of the *sumana* to be made known to the man whom he wishes to kill, and the poor fellow is put into a great fright and dies."

The Rev. S. B. Fellows gives the following account of the beliefs of the people of Kiriwina (Trobiands group) :—

" The sorcerers, who are very numerous, are credited with the power of creating the wind and rain, of making the gardens to be either fruitful or barren, and of causing sickness which leads to death. Their methods of operation are legion. The great chief, who is also the principal sorcerer, claims the sole right to secure a bountiful harvest every year. This function is considered of transcendent importance by the people.

" Our big chief, Bulitara, was asking me one day if I had these occult powers. When I told him that I made no such claim, he said, ' Who makes the wind and the rain and the harvest in your land ?' I answered, ' God.' ' Ah,' said he, ' that's it. God does this work for your people, and I do it for our people. God and I are equal.' He delivered this dictum very quietly, and with the air of a man who had given a most satisfactory explanation.

" But the one great dread that darkens the life of every native is the fear of the *bogau*, the sorcerer who has the power to cause sickness and death, who, in the darkness of the night, steals to the house of his unsuspecting victim, and places near the doorstep a few leaves from a certain tree, containing the mystic power which he, by his evil arts, has imparted to them. The doomed man, on going out of his house next morning, unwittingly steps over the fatal leaves and is at once stricken down by a mortal sickness. Internal disease of every kind is set down to this agency. Bulitara told me the mode of his witchcraft. He boils his decoctions, containing numerous ingredients, in a special cooking-pot on a small fire, in the secret recesses of his own house, at the dead of night ; and while the pot is boiling he speaks into it an incantation known only to a few persons. The bunch of leaves dipped in this is at once ready for use. Passing through the villages the other day, I came across a woman, apparently middle-aged, who was evidently suffering from a wasting disease, she was so thin and worn. I asked if she had any pain, and her friends said ' No.' Then they explained that some *bogau* was sucking her blood. I said, ' How does he do it ?' ' Oh,' they said, ' that is known only to herself. He manages to get her blood which makes him strong, while she gets weaker every day, and if he goes on much longer she will die.'

" Deformities at birth, and being born dumb or blind, are attributed to the evil influence of disembodied spirits, who inhabit a lower region called *Tuma*. Once a year the spirits of the ancestors visit their native village in a body after the harvest is gathered. At this time the men perform special dances, the people openly display their valuables, spread out on platforms, and great feasts are made for the spirits. On a certain night, when the moon named *Namarama* is at the full, all the people—men, women and children—join in raising a great shout, and so drive the spirits back to *Tuma*.

" A peculiar custom prevails of wearing, as charms, various parts of the body of a deceased relative. On her breast, suspended by a piece of string round her neck, a widow wears her late husband's lower jaw, the full set of teeth looking ghastly and grim. The small bones of the arms and legs are taken out soon after death, and formed into spoons, which are used to put lime into the mouth when eating betel-nut. Only this week a chief died in a village three miles from us, and a leg and an arm, for the above purpose, were brought to our village by some relatives as their portion of their dead friend.

" An evidence of the passionate nature of this people is

seen in the comparatively frequent attempts at suicide. Their method is to climb into the top branches of a high tree, and, after tying the ankles together, to throw themselves down. During the last twelve months two attempts near our home were successful, and several others were prevented. In some cases the causes were trivial. One young man allowed his anger to master him because his wife had smoked a small piece of tobacco belonging to him ; he fell from the tree across a piece of root, which was above ground and broke his neck. A woman, middle-aged and childless, who had become jealous, climbed into a tree near her house, and calling out " Good-bye ' to her brother in the village, instantly threw herself down. Falling on her head she died in a few hours ; the thick skin on the scalp was cut, but so far as I could see the skull was not broken."

Some of the minor magical customs of *Polynesia* are worthy of note. Natives of the Duke of York group believe that by persistent calling upon a man whom they wish to get hold of he will by their call be drawn to them, even from a great distance. The natives will not eat or drink when at sea. In New Guinea and Fiji the custom prevails of cutting off a finger joint in token of mourning for a near relative, as do the bushmen of South Africa. (*See* **Magic, Prehistoric.**) They firmly believe in mermaids, tailed men and dwarfs ; and regarding these they are most positive in their assertions. The natives of the Duke of York group in fact declared to a missionary that they had caught a mermaid, who had married a certain native, and that the pair had several of a family ; " but unfortunately," says the relater of this story, " I could never get to see them." Like many other races, the Polynesians work themselves into a great state of terror whenever an eclipse takes place, and during the phenomenon they beat drums, shout and invoke their gods.

In Samoa magic is not practised to such an extent as in other Melanesian groups, although the sorcerer still exists. He is, however, much more sophisticated, and instead of asking merely for any trifling object connected with the person whom he desires to bewitch, he demands property, such as valuable mats and other things which are of use to him. His *modus operandi* was to get into communication with his god, who entered the sorcerer's body, which became violently contorted and convulsed. The assembled natives would then hear a voice speaking from behind a screen, probably a ventriloquial effort, which asserted the presence of the god invoked. Sickness was generally believed to be caused by the anger of some god, who could thus be concealed by the priest or wizard and duly placated. The " god " invariably required some present of substantial value, such as a piece of land, a canoe, or other property, and if the priest happens to know of a particularly valuable object belonging to the person who supposed himself bewitched, he stipulates that it shall be given up to him. This caste of priests is known as *taula-aitu*, and also act as medicine-men.

Polytrix : This is almost the only example of an inauspicious stone. It caused the hair to fall off the head of anyone who had it about his person.

Pontica : A blue stone with red stars, or drops and lines like blood. It compels the devil to answer questions, and puts him to flight.

Poppy Seeds : Divination by smoke was sometimes practised by magicians. A few jasmine or poppy seeds were flung upon burning coals, for this purpose ; if the smoke rose lightly and ascended straight into the heavens, it augured well ; but if it hung about it was regarded as a bad omen.

Pordage : (*See* **Visions.**)

Porka : (*See* **Slavs.**)

Port of Fortune : (*See* **Astrology.**)

Postel, Guillaume : A visionary of the sixteenth century,

born in the diocese of Avranches. He was so precocious that at fourteen years of age he was made master of a school. It is said that he was in the habit of reading the most profound works of the Jewish rabbis, and the vivacity of his imagination threw him into constant troubles, from which he had the greatest difficulty in extricating himself. He believed that he had been called by God to re-unite all men under one law, either by reason or the sword. The pope and the king of France were to be the civil and religious heads of his new republic. He was made Almoner to a hospital at Venice, where he came under the influence of a woman called Mère Jeanne, who had visions which had turned her head. Because of his heterodox preachings, *Postel* was denounced as a heretic, but latterly was regarded as merely mad. After having travelled somewhat extensively in the East, and having written several works in which he dealt with the visions of his coadjutor, he retired to the priory of St. Martin-des-Champs at Paris, where he died penitent in 1581.

Posthumous Letters : Many investigators of psychic science, members of the Society for Psychic Research and others, have left sealed letters, whose contents are known only to the writer. On the death of the writer, and before the letter shall have been opened, an attempt is made by a medium to reveal the contents. By this means it is hoped to prove the actuality or otherwise of spirit communication, for, since only the writer knows what the letter contains, it is presumed that on his death this knowledge can only be communicated through his discarnate spirit. This hypothesis certainly overlooks the fact that the information might be telepathically acquired during the writer's lifetime by a still living person, and so conveyed to the medium. As yet, however, hypotheses are premature, for no attempt of the kind has met with striking success.

Powder of Projection : A powder which assisted the alchemist in the transmutation of base metal into pure gold. (*See* **Seton.**)

Powder of Sympathy : A remedy which, by its application to the weapon which had caused a wound, was supposed to cure the hurt. This method was in vogue during the reigns of James I. and Charles I., and its chief exponent was a gentleman named Sir Kenelm Digby. An abstract of his theory, contained in an address given before an assembly of nobles and learned men at Montpellier in France, may be seen in Pettigrew's *Superstitions connected with Medicine and Surgery*. The following is the recipe for the powder :—" Take Roman vitriol six or eight ounces, beat it very small in a mortar, sift it through a fine sieve when the sun enters Leo ; keep it in the heat of the sun by day, and dry by night." This art has been treated by some authors with belief, and by others with unbelieving wit : Wrenfels says :—" If the superstitious person be wounded by any chance, he applies the salve, not to the wound, but, what is more effectual to the weapon by which he received it."

Pozenne Vile : (*See* **Slavs.**)

Pratyshara : One of the initial stages of yoga practice.

Precipitation of Matter : One of the phenomena of spiritualism which least admits of a rational explanation is that known as the " passing of solids through solids." The statement of the hypothetical fourth dimension of space is an attempt at a solution of the problem ; so also is the theory of " precipitation of matter." The latter suggests that before one solid body passes through another it is resolved into its component atoms, to be precipitated in its original form when the passage is accomplished. M. Camille Flammarion found a parallel to this process in the passage of a piece of ice—a solid—through a napkin. The ice passes through the napkin in the form of water, and may afterwards be re-frozen. This is matter passing through matter, a solid passing through a solid, after it has undergone a change of condition. And we are only carrying out M. Flammarion's inference in suggesting that it is something analogous to this process which occurs in all cases of solids passing through solids.

Prelati : *(See* **Gillis de Laval.***)*

Premonition : An impressional warning of a future event. Premonitions may range from vague feelings of disquiet, suggestive of impending disaster, to actual hallucinations, whether visual or auditory. Dreams are frequent vehicles of premonitions, either direct or symbolical, and there are countless instances of veridical dreams. In such cases it is hard to say whether the warning may have come from an external source, as spiritualists aver, or whether the portended catastrophe may have resulted, in part, at least, from auto-suggestion. The latter is plainly the explanation of another form of *premonition—i.e.,* the predictions made by patients in the magnetic or mediumistic trance with regard to their maladies. The magnetic subject who prophesied that his malady would reach a crisis on a certain date several weeks ahead, probably himself attended subconsciously to the fulfilling of his prophecy. Might not the same thing happen in " veridical" dreams and hallucinations ? We know that a subject obeying a post-hypnotic suggestion will weave his action quite naturally into the surrounding circumstances, though the very moment of its performance may have been fixed months before. That the dreamer and hallucinated subject also might suggest and fulfil their *premonitions,* either directly or by telepathic communication of the suggestion to another agent, does not seem very far-fetched or improbable. Then there is, of course, coincidence. It is impossible but that a certain proportion of verified *premonitions* should be the result of coincidence. Possibly, also, such impressions, whether they remain vague forebodings or are embodied in dreams or otherwise, must at times be subconscious inferences drawn from an actual, if obscure, perception of existing facts. As such, indeed, they are not to be lightly treated. Yet very frequently *premonitions* prove to be entirely groundless, even the most impressive ones, where the warning is emphasized by a ghostly visitant.

Prenestine Lots, The : or *Sortes Prenestinæ.* A method of divination by lots, in vogue in Italy. The letters of the alphabet were placed in an urn which was shaken, and the letters then turned out on the floor ; the words thus formed were received as omens. In the East this method of divination is still common.

Pretu (a departed ghost): The form which the Hindus believe the soul takes after death. This ghost inhabits a body of the size of a man's thumb, and remains in the keeping of Yumu, the judge of the dead. Punishment is inflicted on the *Pretu,* whose body is enlarged for this purpose and is strengthened to endure sorrow. At the end of a year the soul is delivered from this state by the performance of the Shraddhu, and is translated to the heaven of the Pitrees, where it is rewarded for its good deeds. Afterwards, in a different body, the soul enters its final abode. The performance of the Shraddhu is absolutely necessary to escape from the *Pretu* condition.

Prophecy : In an early state of society, the prophet and shaman were probably one and the same, as is still the case among primitive peoples. It is difficult to say whether the offices of the prophet are more truly religious or magical. He is usually a priest, but the ability to look into the future and read its portents can scarcely be called a religious attribute. In many instances *prophecy* is merely utterances in the ecstatic condition. We know that the pythonesses attached to the oracles of ancient Greece uttered prophetic words under the influences of natural gases or drugs ; and when the medicine-men of most savage tribes

attempt to peer into the future, they usually attain a condition of ecstasy by taking some drug, the action of which is well known to them. But this was not always the case ; the shaman often summoned a spirit to his aid to discover what portents and truths lie in the future ; but this cannot be called prophecy. Neither is divination *prophecy* in the true sense of the term, as artificial aids are employed, and it is merely by the appearance of certain objects that the augur can pretend to predict future events. We often find *prophecy* disassociated from the ecstatic condition, as for example among the prophets of Israel, who occupied themselves in great measure with the calm statement of future political events, or those priests of the Maya Indians of Central America known as *Chilan Balam,* who at stated intervals in the year made certain statements regarding the period which lay immediately before them. Is *prophecy* then to be regarded as a direct utterance of the deity, taking man as his mouthpiece, or the statement of one who seeks inspiration from the fountain of wisdom ? Technically, both are true of *prophecy,* for we find it stated in scripture that when the deity desired to communicate with man he chose certain persons as his mouthpieces. Again individuals (often the same as those chosen by God) applied to the deity for inspiration in critical moments. *Prophecy* then may be the utterances of God by the medium of the practically unconscious shaman or seer, or the inspired utterance of that person after inspiration has been sought from the deity.

In ancient Assyria the prophetic class were called *nabu,* meaning " to call " or " announce,"—a name probably adopted from that of the god, Na-bi-u, the speaker or proclaimer of destiny, the tablets of which he inscribed. Among the ancient Hebrews the prophet was called *nabhia,* a borrowed title probably adopted from the Canaanites. That is not to say, however, that the Hebrew *nabhiim* were indebted to the surrounding peoples for their prophetic system, which appears to have been of a much loftier type than that of the Canaanite peoples. Prophets appear to have swarmed in Palestine in biblical times, and we are told that four hundred prophets of Baal sat at Jezebel's table. The fact that they were prophets of this deity would almost go to prove that they were also priests. We find that the most celebrated prophets of Israel belonged to the northern portion of that country, which was more subject to the influence of the Canaanites. Later, distinct prophetic societies were formed,—the chief reason for whose existence appears to have been the preservation of nationality ; and this class appears to have absorbed the older castes of seers and magicians, and to some extent to have taken over their offices. Some of the later prophets,—Micah, for example—appear to have regarded some of these lesser seers as mere diviners, who were in reality not unlike the prophets of Baal. With Amos may be said to have commenced a new school of *prophecy*—the canonical prophets, who were also authors and historians, and who disclaimed all connection with mere professional prophets. The general idea in Hebrew Palestine was that Yahveh, or God, was in the closest possible touch with the prophets, and that he would do nothing without revealing it to them. The greatest importance was given to their utterances, which more than once determined the fate of the nation. Indeed no people has lent so close an ear to the utterance of their prophetic class as did the Jews of old times.

In ancient Greece, the prophetic class were generally found attached to the oracles, and in Rome were represented by the augurs. In Egypt the priests of Ra at Memphis acted as prophets, as, perhaps, did those of Hekt. Among the ancient Celts and Teutons, *prophecy* was frequent, the prophetic agent usually placing him or herself in the ecstatic condition. The Druids were famous practitioners of the prophetic art, and some of their utterances may be still extant in the so-called Prophecies of Merlin. In America, as has been stated, prophetic utterance took practically the same forms as in Europe and Asia. Captain Jonathan Carver, an early traveller in North America, cites a peculiar instance where the seers of a certain tribe stated that a famine would be ended by assistance being sent from another tribe at a certain hour on the following day. At the very moment mentioned by them a canoe rounded a headland, bringing news of relief. A strange story was told in the *Atlantic Monthly* some years ago by a traveller among the Plains tribes, who stated that an Indian medicine-man had prophesied the coming of himself and his companions to his tribe two days before their arrival among them.

Prophecy of Count Bombast : (*See* **Alary.**)

Prophetic Books : (*See* **Blake.**)

Prout, Dr. : (*See* **Alchemy.**)

Psychic : A sensitive, one susceptible to *psychic* influences. A *psychic* is not necessarily a medium, unless he is sufficiently sensitive to be controlled by disembodied spirits. The term *psychic* includes the somnambule, the magnetic or mesmeric subject, anyone who is in any degree sensitive. According to one view, all men are in some measure susceptible to spiritual influences, and to that extent deserve the name of *psychic*.

Psychic Body : A spiritualistic term variously applied to an impalpable body which clothes the soul on the "great dissolution," or to the soul itself. Sergeant Cox in his *Mechanism of Man* declares that the soul—quite distinct from mind, or intelligence, which is only a function of the brain—is composed of attenuated matter, and has the same form as the physical body, which it permeates in every part. From the soul radiates the psychic force, by means of which all the wonders of spiritualism are performed. Through its agency man becomes endowed with telekinetic and clairvoyant powers, and with its aid he can affect such natural forces as gravitation. When free of the body the soul can travel at a lightning speed, nor is it hindered by such material objects as stone walls or closed doors. The *psychic body* is also regarded as an intermediary between the physical body and the soul, a sort of envelope, more material than the soul itself, which encloses it at death. It is this envelope, the *psychic body* or *nervengeist*, which becomes visible at a materialisation by attracting to itself other and still more material particles. In time the *psychic body* decays just as did the physical, and leaves the soul free. During the trance the soul leaves the body, but the vital functions are continued by the *psychic body*.

Psychical Research : A term covering all scientific investigation into the obscure phenomena connected with the so-called "supernatural," undertaken with a view to their elucidation. Certain of these phenomena are known all over the world, and have remained practically unaltered almost since prehistoric times. Such are the phenomena of levitation, the fire-ordeal, crystal-gazing, thought-reading and apparitions, and whenever these were met with there was seldom lacking the critical enquiry of some psychical researcher, not borne away on the tide of popular credulity, but reserving some of his judgment for the impartial investigation of the manifestations. Thus Gaule, in his *Select Cases of Conscience touching Witches and Witchcraft* (London, 1646), says : " But the more prodigious or stupendous (of the feats mentioned in the witches' confessions) are effected meerly by the devill ; the witch all the while either in a rapt ecstasie, a charmed sleepe, or a melancholy dreame ; and the witches' imagination, phantasie, common sense, only deluded with what is now done, or pretended." And a few other writers of the same period arrived at a similar conclusion. The result of many of these

mediæval records was to confirm the genuineness of the phenomena witnessed, but here and there, even in those days, there were sceptics who refused to see in them any supernatural significance. Poltergeist disturbances, again, came in for a large share of attention and investigation, to which, indeed, they seemed to lend themselves. The case of the Drummer of Tedworth was examined by Joseph Glanvil, and the results set forth in his *Sadducisimus Triumphatus*, published in 1668. The Epworth Case, which occurred in the house of John Wesley's father, called forth many comments, as did also the Cock Lane Ghost, the Stockwell Poltergeist and many others. The Animal Magnetists and their successors the Mesmerists may, in a manner, be considered psychical researchers, since these variants of hypnosis were the fruits of prolonged investigation into the phenomena which indubitably existed in connection with the trance state. If their speculations were wild and their enquiries failed to elicit the truth of the matter, it was but natural, at that stage of scientific progress, that they should be so. And here and there even in the writings of Paracelsus and Mesmer we find that they had glimpses of scientific truths which were in advance of their age, foreshadowings of scientific discoveries which were to prove the triumph of future generations. The former, for example, states in his writings : " By the magic power of the will, a person on this side of the ocean may make a person on the other side hear what is said on this side. . . . . The ethereal body of a man may know what another man thinks at a distance of 100 miles and more." This reads uncommonly like an anticipation of telepathy, which has attained to such remarkable prominence in recent years, though it is not now generally attributed to " the ethereal body of a man." Such things as these would seem to entitle many of the mesmerists and the older mystics to the designation of " psychical researchers."

As knowledge increased and systematised methods came into use these enquiries became ever more searching and more fruitful in definite results. The introduction of modern spiritualism in 1848 undoubtedly gave a remarkable impetus to *psychical research*. The movement was so widespread, its effects so apparent, that it was inevitable but that some man of science should be drawn into an examination of the alleged phenomena. Thus we find engaged in the investigation of spiritualism Carpenter, Faraday and De Morgan, and on the Continent Count de Gasparin, M. Thury and Zöllner. One of the most important of individual investigators was undoubtedly Sir William Crookes, who worked independently for some time before the founding of the Society for *Psychical Research*.

However, although much good work was done by independent students of " psychic science," as it came to be called, and by such societies as the Dialectical Society (q.v.) and the Psychological Society (q.v.), it was not until 1882 that a concerted and carefully-organised attempt was made to elucidate those obscure problems which had so long puzzled the wits of learned and simple. In that year was founded the Society for *Psychical Research*, with the object of examining in a scientific and impartial spirit the realm of the supernatural. The following passage from the Society's original prospectus, quoted by Mr. Podmore in his *Naturalisation of the Supernatural*, indicates with sufficient clearness its aim and proposed methods.

" It has been widely felt that the present is an opportune time for making an organised and sytematic attempt to investigate that large group of debatable phenomena designated by such terms as mesmeric, psychical, and spiritualistic.

" From the recorded testimony of many competent witnesses, past and present, including observations recently made by scientific men of eminence in various countries, there appears to be, amid much delusion and deception, an important body of remarkable phenomena, which are *prima facie* inexplicable on any generally recognised hypothesis, and which, if incontestably established, would be of the highest possible value.

"The task of examining such residual phenomena has often been undertaken by individual effort, but never hitherto by a scientific society organised on a sufficiently broad basis."

The first president of the Society was Professor Henry Sidgwick, and among later presidents were Professor Balfour Stewart, Professor William James, Sir William Crookes, Mr. A. J. Balfour, Professor Richet and Sir Oliver Lodge, while prominent among the original members were Frank Podmore, F. W. H. Myers, Edmund Gurney, Professor Barrett, Rev. Stainton Moses and Mrs. Sidgwick. Lord Rayleigh and Andrew Lang were also early members of the Society. Good work was done in America in connection with the Society by Dr. Hodgson and Professor Hyslop. On the continent Lombroso, Maxwell, Camille Flammarion, and Professor Richet—all men of the highest standing in their respective branches of science—conducted exhaustive researches into the phenomena of spiritualism, chiefly in connection with the Italian medium Eusapia Palladino.

At first the members of the Society for *Psychical Research* found it convenient to work in concert, but as they became more conversant with the broad outlines of the subject, it was judged necessary for certain sections or individuals to specialise in various branches. The original plan sketched roughly in 1882 grouped the phenomena under five different heads, each of which was placed under the direction of a separate Committee.

1.—An examination of the nature and extent of any influence which may be exerted by one mind upon another, apart from any generally recognised mode of perception. (Hon. Sec. of Committee, Professor W. F. Barrett.)

2.—The study of hypnotism, and the forms of so-called mesmeric trance, with its alleged insensibility to pain; clairvoyance, and other allied-phenomena. (Hon. Sec. of Committee, Dr. G. Wyld.)

3.—A critical revision of Reichenbach's researches with certain organisations called "sensitive," and an inquiry whether such organisations possess any power of perception beyond a highly-exalted sensibility of the recognised sensory organs. (Hon. Sec. of Committee, Walter H. Coffin.)

4.—A careful investigation of any reports, resting on strong testimony, regarding apparitions at the moment of death, or otherwise, or regarding disturbances in houses reputed to be haunted. (Hon. Sec. of Committee, Hensleigh Wedgwood.)

5.—An enquiry into the various physical phenomena commonly called spiritualistic; with an attempt to discover their causes and general laws. (Hon. Sec., Dr. C. Lockhart Robertson.)

Besides these there was a Committee appointed to consider the literature of the subject, having as its honorary secretaries Edmund Gurney and Frederic W. H. Myers, who, with Mr. Podmore, collected a number of historic instances. Of the various heads, however, the first is now generally considered the most important, and is certainly that which has yielded the best results to investigators. In the case of hypnotism it is largely through the exertions of psychical researchers that it has been admitted to the sphere of legitimate physiology, whereas it was formerly classed among doubtful phenomena, even at the time the Society was founded. The examination of Reichenbach's claims to having discovered a new psychic fluid or force—

odyle (q.v.)—which issued like flame from the points of a magnet or the human finger-tips, was at length abandoned, nothing having been found to verify his conclusions which, however, previous to this had been largely accepted. The investigations in connection with apparitions and haunted houses, and with the spiritualistic phenomena, are still proceeding, though on the whole no definite conclusion has been arrived at. Though the members of the Society undertook to carry out their investigations in an entirely unbiased spirit, and though those members who joined the Society originally as avowed spiritualists soon dropped out, yet after prolonged and exhaustive research the opinion of the various investigators often showed marked divergence. So far from being pledged to accept a spirit, or any other hypothesis, it was expressly stated in a note appended to the prospectus that "Membership of this Society does not imply the acceptance of any particular explanation of the phenomena investigated, nor any belief as to the operation, in the physical world, of forces other than those recognised by Physical Science." Nevertheless Mr. Myers and Sir Oliver Lodge, to take two notable instances, found the evidence sufficient to convince them of the operation in the physical world of disembodied intelligences, who manifest themselves through the organism of the "medium" or "sensitive." Mr. Podmore, on the other hand, was the exponent of a telepathic theory. Any phase of the "manifestations" which was not explicable by means of such known physiological facts as suggestion and hyperæsthesia, the so-called "subconscious whispering," exaltation of memory and automatism, or the unfamiliar but presumably natural telepathy, must, according to him, fall under the grave suspicion of fraud. His theory of poltergeists, for example, by which he regards these uncanny disturbances as being the work of naughty children, does not admit the intervention of a mischievous disembodied spirit. In coincident hallucination, again, he considers telepathy a suitable explanation, as well as in all cases of "personation" by the medium. His view—one that was shared by Andrew Lang and others—was that if telepathy were once established the spirit hypothesis would not only be unnecessary, but impossible of proof.

The most important of telepathic experiments were those conducted by Professor and Mrs. Sidgwick in 1889–91. The percipients were hypnotised by Mr. G. A. Smith, who also acted as agent, and the matter to be transmitted consisted at first of numbers and later of mental pictures. The agent and percipient were generally separated by a screen, or were sometimes in different rooms, though the results in the latter case were perceptibly less satisfactory. On the whole, however, the percentage of correct guesses was far above that which the doctrine of chance warranted, and the experiments did much to encourage a belief that some hitherto unknown mode of communication existed. More recently the trance communication of Mrs. Piper would seem to point to some such theory, though Mr. Myers, Dr. Hodgson and Dr. Hyslop, who conducted a very profound investigation into those communications, were inclined to believe that the spirits of the dead were the agencies in this case. Telepathy cannot yet be considered as proved. At the best it is merely a surmise, which, if it could be established, would provide a natural explanation for much of the so-called occult phenomena. Even its most ardent protagonists admit that its action is extremely uncertain and experiment correspondingly difficult. Nevertheless, each year sees an increasing body of scientific and popular opinion favourable to the theory, so that we may hope that the surmised mode of communication may at last be within a reasonable distance of becoming an acknowledged fact. The machinery of telepathy is generally supposed to be in the form of ethereal vibrations, or "brain waves," acting in accordance with natural laws, though Mr. Gerald Balfour and others incline to an entirely metamorphosed theory, urging, *e.g.*, that the action does not conform to the law of inverse squares.

The subject of hallucinations, coincidental or otherwise, has also been largely investigated in recent years, and has been found to be closely connected with the question of telepathy. Apparitions were in former times regarded as the " doubles " or " ethereal bodies " of the persons they represented, but they are not now considered to be otherwise than subjective. Nevertheless the study of " coincidental hallucinations "—*i.e.*, hallucinatory apparitions which coincide with the death of the person represented, or with some other crises in his life—raises the question as to whether the agent may not produce such an hallucination in the mind of the percipient by the exercise of telepathic influence, which may be judged to be more powerful during an emotional crisis. Now hallucinations have been shown to be fairly common among sane people, about one person in ten having experienced one or more. But the chances that such an hallucination should coincide with the death of the person it represents are about, 1 in 19,000 ; that is, if no other factor than chance determines their ratio. With a view to ascertaining whether coincidental hallucinations did actually bear a higher proportion to the total number of hallucinations than chance would justify, the Society for *Psychical Research* took a census in 1889 and the three or four years immediately following. Professor Sidgwick and a committee of members of the Society conducted the investigations and printed forms were distributed among 410 accredited agents of the Society, including, besides its own members, many medical men and others belonging to the professional classes, all of whom gave their services without fee in the interests of science. In all some 17,000 persons were questioned, and negative as well as affirmative answers were sent in just as they were received, the agents being specially instructed to make no discrimination between the various replies. Out of 8372 men 655 had had an hallucination, and 1029 out of 8628 women—9.9 % of the total. When ample allowance had been made for defects of memory with regard to early hallucinations by multiplying the 322 recognised and definite cases by 4, it was found that 62 coincided with a death ; but, again making allowances, this number was reduced to 30. Thus we find 1 coincidental hallucination in 43 where, there being no causal connection we should expect 1 in 19,000. Clearly, then, if these figures be taken, there must be some causal connection between the death and the apparition, whether it be a spiritualistic or telepathic theory that may be used. Though it be true that memory plays strange tricks, yet is it difficult to understand how persons of education and standing could write down and attest minutes and dated records of events that never happened.

Apart from telepathy, which because it postulates the working of a hitherto unknown natural law, takes premier place, perhaps the most interesting field of research is that of automatism. Trance writings and utterances have been known since the earliest times, when they were attributed to demoniac possession, or, sometimes, angelic possession. By means of planchette, ouija, and such contrivances many people are able to write automatically and divulge information which they themselves were unaware of possessing. But here again the phenomena are purely subjective, and are the result of cerebral dissociation, such as may be induced in hypnosis. In this state exaltation of the memory may occur, and thus account for such phenomena as the speaking in foreign tongues with which the agent is but ill-acquainted. Or, conceivably, cerebral dissociation may produce a sensitiveness to telepathic influences, as would seem apparent in the case of

Mrs. Piper, whose automatic productions in writing and speaking have supplied investigators with plentiful material of recent years, and have done more, perhaps, than anything else to stimulate an interest in so-called spiritualistic phenomena. In connection with the " physical " phenomena—probably no less the result of automatism than the " subjective," though in a different direction—the Italian medium Eusapia Palladino has been carefully studied by many eminent investigators both in Great Britain and on the Continent, with the result that Camille Flammarion, Professor Richet, Sir Oliver Lodge—to mention only a few—have satisfied themselves with regard to the genuineness of some of her phenomena.

On the whole, even if *psychical research* has not succeeded in demonstrating such matters as the immortality of the soul or the possibility of communication between the living and the dead, it has done good work in widening the field of psychology and therapeutics and in gaining admission for that doctrine of suggestion which since the time of Bertrand and Braid had never been openly received and acknowledged by the medical profession. Many of the obscure phenomena attending mesmerism, magnetism, witchcraft, poltergeists, and kindred subjects have been brought into line with modern scientific knowledge. Little more than thirty years has elapsed since the Society for *Psychical Research* was founded, and probably in time to come it will accomplish still more, both in conducting experiments and investigations in connection with psychic phenomena, and in educating the public in the use of scientific methods and habits of thought in their dealings with the " supernatural."

Psychograph : An instrument to facilitate automatic writing. It is composed of a rotating disc, on which the medium's finger-tips are placed, thus carrying an index over the alphabet. A similar contrivance was used by Professor Hare in his spiritualistic experiments.

Psychography : Writing produced without human contact, and supposed to be the work of the spirits.

Psychological Society, The : The *Psychological Society* came into being in April, 1875, having as its founder and president Sergeant Cox, and numbering among its members the Rev. William Stainton Moses, Mr. Walter H. Coffin, and Mr. C. C. Massey. The avowed aim of the Society, as set forth in the president's inaugural address, was the elucidation of those spiritualistic and other problems now grouped under the term " psychical research," and to which the Society somewhat loosely attached the designation of psychology. To this end they proposed to collect and consider the available material bearing on psychic phenomena, but in reality they accomplished little of any practical value, as may be seen from their published *Proceedings* (London, 1878). The president himself had not the necessary scientific qualifications for an investigator of such phenomena. In November, 1879, on the death of its president, the Society came to an end. But though the *Psychological Society* regarded the psychic phenomena from a more or less popular standpoint, and conducted its investigations in a somewhat superficial manner, nevertheless it contained that germ of scientific enquiry into the domain of psychic science which, a few years later, in the Society for Psychical Research, was to raise the study to a level where it became worthy of the attention of philosopher and scientist. Hitherto those who were satisfied of the genuineness of the spiritualistic marvels had for the most part been content to accept the explanation of spirit intervention, but the *Psychological Society* was the crystallisation of a small body of " rationalist " opinion which had existed since the days of Mesmer. Sergeant Cox, in his work, *The Mechanism of Man* states that " spirit " is refined matter, or molecular matter split into its constituent atoms, which thus become imperceptible to our physical organism ; a view which was possibly shared by the *Psychological Society*.

Psychomancy : Divination by spirits or the art of evoking the dead. (*See* **Necromancy.**)

Psychometry : A term used by spiritualists to denote the faculty, supposed to be common among mediums, of reading the characters, surroundings, etc. of persons by holding in the hand small objects, such as a watch or ring, which they have had in their possession. The honour of having discovered the psychometric faculty belongs to Dr. J. R. Buchanan, who classed it among the sciences, and gave it the name it bears. His theory is based on the belief that everything that has ever existed, every object, scene, event, that has occurred since the beginning of the world, has left on the ether or astral light a trace of its being, indelible while the world endures ; and not only on the ether, but likewise on more palpable objects, trees and stones and all manner of things. Sounds also, and perfumes leave impressions on their surroundings. Just as a photograph may be taken on a plate and remain invisible till it has been developed, so may those psychometric " photographs " remain impalpable till the developing process has been applied. And that which is to bring them to light is— the mind of the medium. All mediums are said to possess the psychometric faculty in a greater or less degree. One authority, Professor William Denton, has declared that he found it in one man in every ten, and four women in ten. Dr. Buchanan's earliest experiments, with his own students, showed that some of them were able to distinguish the different metals merely by holding them in their hands. On medical substances being put into their hands they exhibited such symptoms as might have been occasioned if the substances were swallowed. Later he found that some among them could diagnose a patient's disease simply by holding his hand. Many persons of his acquaintance, on pressing a letter against their forehead, could tell the character and surroundings of the writer, the circumstances under which the letter was written and other particulars. Some very curious stories are told of fossilised bones and teeth revealing to the sensitives the animals they represent in the midst of their prehistoric surroundings. Professor Denton gave to his wife and mother-in-law meteoric fragments and other substances, wrapped in paper and thoroughly mixed to preclude the possibility of telepathy, which caused them to see the appropriate pictures. Many mediums who have since practised psychometry have become famous in their line. As has been said, the *modus* is to hold in the hand or place against the forehead some small object, such as a fragment of clothing, a letter, or a watch, when the appropriate visions are seen. Psychometrists may be entranced, but are generally in a condition scarcely varying from the normal. The psychometric pictures, printed presumably on the article to be psychometrised, have been likened to pictures borne in the memory, seemingly faded, yet ready to start into vividness when the right spring is touched. We may likewise suppose that the rehearsal of bygone tragedies so frequently witnessed in haunted houses, is really a psychometric picture which at the original occurrence impressed itself on the room. The same may be said of the sounds and perfumes which haunt certain houses.

Psylli : A class of persons in Ancient Italy who had the power of charming serpents. This name is given by other writers to the snake-charmers of Africa, and it is said that the serpents twist round the bodies of these *Psylli* without doing them any injury, although the reptiles have not had their fangs extracted or broken. In Kahira when a viper enters a house, the charmer is sent for, and he entices it out by the use of certain words. At other times music is used, and it is believed that the serpents understand what

is said to them by the snake-charmers, so obedient are they.

Purgatory of St. Patrick : (*See* **Ireland.**)

Purrah, The : A secret society of the Tulka-Susus, an African tribe who dwell between the Sierra Leone river and Cape mount. The Tulka consist of five small communities which together form a description of republic. Each group has its own chiefs and council, but all are under a controlling-power which is called the *Purrah*. Each of the five communities has also its own *purrah*, from which is formed the great or general *purrah*, which holds supreme sway over the five bodies. Before a native can join a district *purrah*, he must be thirty years of age, and ere he can be received into membership of the great *purrah*, he must have reached the age of fifty. Thus the oldest members of each district *purrah* are members of the head *purrah*. On desiring admittance to the examination for the district *purrah*, the relations of the candidate must swear to kill him if he does not stand the test, or if he reveals the mysteries and the secrets of the society. Froebenius says :—" In each district belonging to a *purrah* there is a sacred grove to which the candidate is conducted, and where he must stay in a place assigned to him, living for several months quite alone in a hut, whither masked persons bring him food. He must neither speak nor leave his appointed place of residence.

" Should he venture into the surrounding forest, he is as good as dead.

" After several months the candidate is admitted to stand his trial, which is said to be terrible. Recourse is had to all the elements in order to gain satisfaction as to his firmness and courage. We are even assured that at these mysteries use is made of fettered lions and leopards, that during the time of the tests and enrolment the sacred groves echo with fearful shrieks, that here great fires are seen at night, that formerly the fire flared up in these mysterious woods in all directions, that every outsider who through curiosity was tempted to stray into the woods was mercilessly sacrificed, that foolish people who would have penetrated into them disappeared and were never heard of again.

" If the candidate stands all the tests, he is admitted to the initiation. But he must first swear to keep all the secrets and without hesitation carry out the decisions of the *purrah* of his community and all the decrees of the great head *purrah*. If a member of the society betrays it or revolts against it, he is condemned to death, and the sentence is often carried out in the bosom of his family. When the criminal least expects it, a disguised, masked and armed warrior appears and says to him :—

" ' The great *purrah* sends thee death ! '

" At these words everybody stands back, no one dares to offer the least resistance, and the victim is murdered.

" The Court of each district *purrah* consists of twenty-five members, and from each of these separate courts five persons are chosen, who constitute the great *purrah*, or the High Court of the general association. Hence this also consists of twenty-five persons, who elect the head chief from their own body.

" The special *purrah* of each community investigates the offences committed in its district, sits in judgment on them, and sees that its sentences are carried out. It makes peace between the powerful families, and stops their wranglings.

" The great *purrah* meets only on special occasions, and pronounces judgment on those who betray the mysteries and secrets of the order, or on those who show themselves disobedient to its mandates. But usually it puts an end to the feuds that often break out between two communities belonging to the confederacy. When these begin to fight, after a few months of mutual hostilities, one or other of the parties, when they have inflicted sufficient injury on each other, usually wants peace. The commune repairs secretly to the great *purrah*, and invites it to become the mediator and put an end to the strife.

"Thereupon the great *purrah* meets in a neutral district, and when all are assembled announces to the communes at war that it cannot allow men who should live together as brothers, friends and good neighbours, to wage war, to waste each others' lands, to plunder and burn; that it is time to put an end to these disorders; that the great *purrah* will inquire into the cause of the strife; that it requires that this should cease and decrees that all hostilities be forthwith arrested.

"A main feature of this arrangement is that, as soon as the great *purrah* assembles to put a stop to the feud, and until its decision is given, all the belligerents of the two districts at war are forbidden to shed a drop of blood; this always carries with it the penalty of death. Hence everybody is careful not to infringe this decree, and abstains from all hostilities.

"The session of the High Court lasts one month, during which it collects all necessary information to ascertain which commune caused the provocation and the rupture. At the same time it summons as many of the society's fighting-men as may be required to carry out the decision. When all the necessary particulars are brought in, and everything is duly weighed, it settles the question by condemning the guilty commune to a four days' sack.

"The warriors who have to give effect to this decision are all chosen from the neutral districts; they set out by night from the place where the great *purrah* is assembled. All are disguised, the face being covered with an ugly mask, and armed with lighted torches and daggers. They divide into bands of forty, fifty, or sixty, and all meet unexpectedly before dawn in the district that they have to pillage, proclaiming with fearful shouts the decision of the High Court. On their approach men, women, children and old people, all take to flight, that is, take refuge in their houses, and should anyone be found in the fields, on the highway, or in any other place, he is either killed or carried off and no more is ever heard of him.

"The booty obtained by such plundering is divided into two parts, one of which is given to the injured commune, the other to the great *purrah*, which shares it with the warriors that have executed its decree. This is the reward for their zeal, their obedience and loyalty.

"If one of the families in a commune subject to the *purrah* becomes too powerful and too formidable, the great *purrah* meets, and nearly always condemns it to unexpected sack, which is carried out by night and, as usual, by masked and disguised men. Should the heads of such a dangerous family offer any resistance, they are killed, or carried off, and conveyed to the depths of a sacred and lonely grove where they are tried by the *purrah* for their insubordination; they are seldom heard of again.

"Such, in part, is the constitution of this extraordinary institution. Its existence is known; the display of its power is felt; it is dreaded; yet the veil covering its intentions, decisions and decrees is impenetrable, and not till he is about to be executed does the outlaw know that he has been condemned. The power and reputation of the *purrah* is immense, not only in the homeland, but also in the surrounding districts. It is reported to be in league with the spirits (instead of the devil).

"According to the general belief the number of armed men who are members and at the disposal of the *purrah* exceeds 6,000. Moreover, the rules, the secrets and the mysteries of this society are strictly obeyed and observed by its numerous associated members, who understand and recognise each other by words and signs."

Puysegur : (*See* **Hypnotism.**)

Pyromancy, or divining by fire, has been alluded to in **Extispicy.** The presage was good when the flame was vigorous and quickly consumed the sacrifice; when it was clear of all smoke, transparent, neither red-nor dark in colour; when it did not crackle, but burnt silently in a pyramidal form. On the contrary, if it was difficult to kindle, if the wind disturbed it, if it was slow to consume the victim, the presage was evil. Besides the sacrificial fire, the ancients divined by observing the flames of torches, and even by throwing powdered pitch into a fire; if it caught quickly, the omen was good. The flame of a torch was good if it formed one point, bad if it divided into two; but three was a better omen than one. Sickness for the healthy, and death for the sick, was presaged by the bending of the flame, and some frightful disaster by its sudden extinction. The vestals in the Temple of Minerva at Athens were charged to make particular observations on the light perpetually burning there.

Pythagoras : (*See* **Greece.**)

Pythia : (*See* **Greece.**)

Q

Quimby, Dr. Phineas : (*See* **New Thought.**)

Quindecem Viri : (*See* **Sibylline Books.**)

Quirardelli, Corneille : A Franciscan born at Boulogne towards the end of the sixteenth century. He studied

astrology, and was the author of several astrological and other works.

Quirinus, or Quirus, is described as "a juggling stone, found in the nest of the hoopoo." If laid on the breast of one sleeping, it forces him to discover his rogueries.

R

Races, Branch : (*See* **Planetary Chains.**)
Races, Root : (*See* **Planetary Chains.**)
Races, Sub : (*See* **Planetary Chains.**)
Rahat : (*See* **Adept.**)
Rahu : Whose name means "the tormenter," is one of the Hindoo devils. He is worshipped as a means of averting the attacks of evil spirits; and appears to be of a truly devilish character.
Rakshasa : An Indian demon. In one of the Indian folk-tales he appears black as soot, with hair yellow as the lightning, looking like a thunder-cloud. He had made himself a wreath of entrails; he wore a sacrificial cord of

hair; he was gnawing the flesh of a man's head and drinking blood out of a skull. In another story these Brahma *Rakshasas* have formidable tusks, flaming hair, and insatiable hunger. They wander about the forests catching animals and eating them. Mr. Campbell tells a Mahrata legend of a master who became a *Brahmaparusha* in order to teach grammar to a pupil. He haunted a house at Benares, and the pupil went to take lessons from him. He promised to teach him the whole science in a year on condition that he never left the house. One day the boy went out and learned that the house was haunted, and that he was being taught by a ghost. The boy returned and was ordered by the preceptor to take his bones to Gaya, and perform the necessary ceremonies for the emancipation of his soul. This he did, and the uneasy spirit of the learned man was laid.

Randolph, P. B. : (*See* **Spiritualism.**)

Raphael, the Angel : In the prophecy of Enoch it is said that : " Raphael presides over the spirits of men." In the Jewish rabbinical legend of the angelic hierarchies Raphael is the medium through which the power of Tsebaoth, or the Lord of hosts, passes into the sphere of the sun, giving motion, heat and brightness to it.

Rapping : Phenomena of knockings or *rappings* have always accompanied poltergeistic disturbances, even before the commencement of the modern spiritualistic movement. Thus they were observed in the case of the " Drummer of Tedworth " (q.v.), the " Cock Lane Ghost," and other disturbances of the kind, and also in the presence of various somnambules, such as the Seeress of Prevorst (q.v.). With the " Rochester Rappings "—the famous outbreak at Hydesville in 1848, to which may be directly traced the beginning of modern Spiritualism—the phenomenon took on a new importance, rapidly increased to an epidemic, remained throughout the earlier stages of the movements the chief mode of communication with the spirits. Though it was afterwards supplanted to some extent by more elaborate and complicated phenomena, it continued, and still continues, to occupy a place of some importance among the manifestations of the séance-room. It is apparent from descriptions furnished by witnesses that the raps varied considerably both in quality and intensity, being sometimes characterised as dull thuds, sometimes as clear sounds like an electric spark, and again as deep, vibrating tones. Doubtless the methods by which they are produced vary quite as much. It has been shown, in fact, that raps may be produced by the ankle-joints, knee-joints, shoulders, and other joints, one man—the Rev. Eli Noyes—claiming to have discovered seventeen different methods. There are also instances on record where specially constructed " medium " tables were responsible for the manifestations. Besides the frankly spiritualistic explanation and the frankly sceptical one of fraud, there have been other scientific or pseudo-scientific theories advanced, such as electricity, odyle, ectenic force, or magnetism.

Rapport : A mystical sympathetic or antipathetic connection between two persons. It was formerly believed that for a witch to harm her victims, the latter must first have become *in rapport* with her, either by contact with her person, or by contact with some garment she has worn. A certain witch, Florence Newton, was accused of establishing *rapport* between herself and those she sought to bewitch by kissing them, whereby she was able to compass their destruction. In the practice of animal magnetism it was considered that the only invariable and characteristic symptom of the genuine trance was the *rapport* between patient and operator. The former was deaf, dumb, blind, to all save his magnetizer, and those with whom his magnetizer placed him *in rapport*. This condition, however, still observed in hypnotism, is referable to a perfectly natural cause. (*See* **Hypnotism.**) The term is preserved at the present day in Spiritualism, when it signifies a spiritual sympathy between the " control " and the medium or any of the sitters. The medium—or, more properly, the control—may be placed *in rapport* with anyone who is absent or dead, merely by handling something which has belonged to them. It is for a similar reason that the crystal is held for a few moments prior to the inspection by the person on whose behalf the crystal-gazer is about to examine it.

Raymond : (*See* **Spiritualism.**)

Rector : Control of Rev. W. S. Moses. (*See* **Moses, William Stainton.**)

Red Cap : The witches of Ireland were wont to put on a magical red cap before flying through the air to their meeting-place.

Red Lion : (*See* **Philosopher's Stone.**)

Red Man : The demon of the tempests. He is supposed to be furious when the rash voyager intrudes on his solitude, and to show his anger in the winds and storms.

The French peasants believed that a mysterious little *red man* appeared to Napoleon to announce coming reverses.

Red Pigs : It was formerly believed that Irish witches could turn wisps of straw or hay into *red pigs*, which they sold at the market. But when the *pigs* were driven homeward by the buyers, they resumed their original shape on crossing running water.

Redcliff, Mrs. Ann : (*See* **Fiction, Occult English.**)

Regang : Malay system of Astrology. (*See* **Malays.**)

Regius MS. : (*See* **Freemasonry.**)

Reichenbach : (*See* **Hypnotism.**)

Reincarnation is an extremely important part of Theosophical theory, and, while it is commonly regarded as a succession of lives, the proper aspect in which to regard it is as one single, indivisible life, the various manifestations in the flesh being merely small portions of the whole. The Monad, the Divine Spark, the Ego—whose individuality remains the same throughout the whole course of *reincarnation*—is truly a denizen of the three higher worlds, the spiritual, the intuitional and the higher mental, but in order to further its growth and the widening of its experience and knowledge, it is necessary that it should descend into the worlds of denser matter, the lower mental, the actual and the physical, and take back with it to the higher worlds what it has learned in these. Since it is impossible to progress far during one manifestation, it must return again and again to the lower worlds. The theory which underlies *reincarnation* is entirely different from that of eternal reward and eternal punishment which underlies, say, the teachings of Christianity. Every individual will eventually attain perfection though some take longer to do so than others. The laws of his progress, the laws which govern *reincarnation*, are those of evolution and of karma. Evolution (q.v.) decrees that all shall attain perfection and that by developing to the utmost their latent powers and qualities, and each manifestation in the lower worlds is but one short journey nearer the goal. Those who realise this law shorten the journey by their own efforts while those who do not realise it and so assist its working, of course lengthen the journey. Karma (q.v.) decrees that effects good or bad, follow him who was their cause. Hence, what a man has done in one manifestation, he must be benefited by or suffer for in another. It may be impossible that his actions should be immediately effective, but each is stored up and sooner or later will bear fruit. It may be asked how one long life in the lower worlds should not suffice instead of a multitude of manifestations, but this is explicable by the fact that the dense matter which is the vehicle of these bodies, becomes after a time of progress, incapable of further alteration to suit the developing monad's needs and must accordingly be laid aside for a new body. After physical death, man passes first to the astral world, then to the heaven portion of the mental world, and in this latter world most of his time is spent except when he descends into the denser worlds to garner fresh experience and knowledge for his further development in preparation for passage into the still higher sphere. In the heaven world these experiences and this knowledge are woven together into the texture of his nature. In those who have not progressed far on the journey of evolution, the manifestations in the lower worlds are comparatively frequent, but with passage of time and development, these manifestations become rarer and more time is spent in the heaven world, till, at last, the great process of *reincarnation* draws to an end, and the pilgrims enter the Path which leads to perfection. (*See* **Theosophy, The Path,** and the articles on the various **Worlds.**)

Remie, Major J. : (*See* **Holland.**)

Reschith Hajalalim : The name of the ministering spirit in the Jewish rabbinical legend of the angelic hierarchies. To this angel, the pure and simple essence of the divinity flows through Hajoth Hakakos ; he guides the *primum mobile*, and bestows the gift of life on all.

Revue Spirite, La (Journal) : (*See* **France.**)

Revue Spiritualiste, La (Journal) : (*See* **France.**)

Rhabdomancy : From the Greek words meaning " a rod " and "divination," is thus alluded to by Sir Thomas Brown :—" As for the divination or decision from the staff, it is an augurial relic, and the practice thereof is accused by God himself : My people ask counsel of their stocks, and their staff declareth unto them. Of this kind was that practised by Nabuchadonosor in that Caldean miscellany delivered by Ezekiel." In *Brand's Antiquities* the following description is cited from a MS. Discourse on Witchcraft, written by Mr. John Bell, 1705, p. 41 ; it is derived from Theophylact :—" They set up two staffs, and having whispered some verses and incantations, the staffs fell by the operation of demons. Then they considered which way each of them fell, forward or backward, to the right or left hand, and agreeably gave responses, having made use of the fall of their staffs for their signs." This is the Grecian method of *Rhabdomancy*, and St. Jerome thinks it is the same that is alluded to in the above passage of Hosea, and in Ezekiel xxi. 21, 22, where it is rendered " arrows." Belomancy and *Rhabdomancy*, in fact, have been confounded in these two passages, and it is a question whether in one of the methods arrows and rods or stones were not used indifferently. The practice is said to have passed from the Chaldeans and Scythians to the German tribes, who used pieces from the branch of a fruit tree, which they marked with certain characters, and threw at hazard upon a white cloth. Something like this, according to one of the rabbis, was the practice of the Hebrews, only instead of characters, they peeled their rods on one side, and drew the presage from their manner of falling. The Scythians and the Alani used rods of the myrtle and sallow, and as the latter chose " fine straight wands " according to Herodotus, it may be inferred that their method was that of the Hebrews, or some modification of it.

Rhapsodomancy : Divination by means of opening the works of a poet at hazard and reading the verse which first presents itself oracularly.

Rhasis (or Rasi) : An Arabian alchemist whose real name was Mohammed-Ebn-Secharjah Aboubekr Arrasi. He was born at Ray, in Trâk, Khorassan, about 850. In his youth he devoted himself to music and the lighter pastimes, and it was not till he had passed his thirtieth year that he turned his attention to the healing art. But having done so, he studied it to good purpose, and speedily became a most skilful physician. His natural goodness of heart induced him to turn his knowledge and skill to account in order to benefit his poorer brethren. The study of philosophy also claimed his attention and he travelled to Syria, Egypt, and Spain in search of knowledge.

He was exceedingly fond of experimenting in medicine and chemistry, and was the first to mention borax, orpiment, realgar, and other chemical compounds. The authorship of two hundred and twenty-six treatises is ascribed to him, and some of these works influenced European medicine so late as the 17th century. He firmly believed in the

transmutation of metals, and wrote a glowing treatise on the subject which he presented to Emir Almansour, Prince of Khorassan. The Emir showed his gratitude in a practical fashion by giving *Rhasis* a thousand pieces of gold, at the same time desiring to be present during the working of some of the experiments with which the volume was plentifully illustrated. *Rhasis* consented, on condition that the prince supplied the necessary apparatus. No expense was spared in furnishing a laboratory for the alchemistical experiments, but unfortunately the boasted skill of the alchemist failed him and the performance ended miserably. *Rhasis*, who was now well advanced in years, was unmercifully beaten by the angry emir, who chose the unlucky treatise to belabour him with. This incident is said to have caused the blindness with which the alchemist was afterwards afflicted.

He died about 932 in the deepest poverty.

In his studies in chemistry he has left some results of real value, notwithstanding the time and trouble he spent in the pursuit of the philosopher's stone. Another theory which he held in common with Geber and others was that the planets influenced metallic formation under the earth's surface.

Richet, Professor : (*See* **Spiritualism.**)

Richter, Sigmund : (*See* **Rosicrucians.**)

Riko, A. J. : (*See* **Holland.**)

Rinaldo des Trois Echelles : A much-dreaded French sorcerer of the reign of Charles IX., who, at his execution, boasted before the king that he had in France three hundred thousand confederates, whom they could not thus commit to the flames—meaning, doubtless, the demons of the Sabbath.

Ripley, George : This alchemist was born about the middle of the fifteenth century at Ripley, in Yorkshire, in which county his kinsfolk appear to have been alike powerful and numerous. Espousing holy orders, he became an Augustinian, while subsequently he was appointed Canon of Bridlington in his native Yorkshire, a priory which had been founded in the time of Henry I. by Walter de Ghent. *Ripley's* sacerdotal office did not prevent him travelling, and he prosecuted empirical studies at various places on the continent, while he even penetrated so far afield as the island of Rhodes, where he is said to have made a large quantity of gold for the knights of St. John of Jerusalem. Going afterwards to Rome he was dignified by the Pope, the result being that, when he got back to Bridlington, he found his brethren there intensely jealous of him. It is reported, indeed, that he even resigned his position and retired to a priory at Boston, but this story is probably unfounded, the likelihood being that *Ripley* the alchemist has been confounded with George Ripley, a Carmelite friar who lived at Boston in the thirteenth century, and wrote a biography of St. Botolph.

Ripley died in England in 1490, but his fame did not die with him, and in fact his name continued to be familiar for many years after his decease. He had been among the first to popularise the chymical writings attributed to Raymond Lully, which first became known in England about 1445, at which time an interest in alchemy was increasing steadily among English scholars—the more so because the law against multiplying gold had lately been repealed ; while *Ripley* wrote a number of learned treatises himself, notably *Medulla Alchimiœ, The Treatise of Mercury* and *The Compound of Alchemie*, the last-named being dedicated to King Edward IV. A collected edition of his writings was issued at Cassel in Germany in 1649, while in 1678 an anonymous English writer published a strange volume in London, *Ripley Revived, or an Exposition upon George Ripley's Hermetico-Poetical Works.*

Ripley Revived : (*See* **Philalethes.**)

Rishi : (*See* **Adept** and **India.**)

Rita : (*See* **Materialisation** and **Spiritualism.**)

Robert the Devil was son of a Duke and Duchess of Normandy. He was endowed with marvellous physical strength, which he used only to minister to his evil passions. Explaining to him the cause of his wicked impulses, his mother told him that he had been born in answer to prayers addressed to the devil. He now sought religious advice, and was directed by the Pope to a hermit who ordered him to maintain complete silence, to take his food from the mouths of dogs, to feign madness and to provoke abuse from common people without attempting to retaliate. He became court fool to the Roman Emperor and three times delivered the city from Saracen invasions, having, in each case, been prompted to fight by a heavenly message. The emperor's dumb daughter was given speech in order to identify the saviour of the city with the court fool, but he refused his due recompense, as well as her hand in marriage, and went back to the hermit, his former confessor. The French Romance of Robert le Diable is one of the oldest forms of this legend.

Roberts, Mrs. : (*See* **Spiritualism.**)

Robes, Magical : (*See* **Magic.**)

Robsart, Amy : (*See* **Haunted Houses.**)

Rocail : Said to have been the younger brother of Seth, the son of Adam. The circumstances attending his history are picturesque and unique. A Dive, or giant of Mount Caucasus, finding himself in difficulties, applied for aid to the human race. *Rocail* offered his services to the giant, and so acceptable did these prove that the Dive made his benefactor grand vizier. For a long period he governed the giant's realm with entire success, and reached a position of dignity and honour. However, when he felt himself growing old he desired to leave behind him a more lasting monument than public respect, so he built a magnificent palace and sepulchre. The palace he peopled with statues, which, by the power of magic, he made to walk and talk, and act in all ways as though they were living men, as, indeed, all who beheld them judged them to be. (*See* D'Herbelot, *Bibliothèque Oriental.*)

Rochas d'Aiglun, Eugene-Auguste Albert de : French Officer and writer, born at Saint-Firmin in 1837. He is chiefly remembered as an exponent of the fluidic theory of magnetism. His works include *des Force non définies* (1887) ; *le Fluide des magnetiseurs* (1891) ; *les Etats profonds de l'hypnose* (1892) ; *l'Exterioration de la sensibilité* (1895) ; *l'Exterioration de la motricite* (1896) ; *Recueil de documents relatifs à la levitation du corps humain* (1897) ; *les Etats superficiels de l'hypnose* (1898) ; etc.

Rochester Rappings : The outbreak of rappings which occurred in Hydesville, near Rochester, N.Y., in 1848, and which is popularly known as the *Rochester Rappings*, is of peculiar importance, not because of its intrinsic superiority to any other poltergeistic disturbance, but because it inaugurates the movement of Modern Spiritualism. Hydesville is a small village in Arcadia, Wayne County, N.Y., and there, in 1848, there lived one John D. Fox, with his wife and two young daughters, Margaretta, aged fifteen, and Kate, aged twelve. Their house was a small wooden structure previously tenanted by one Michael Weekman, who afterwards avowed that he had frequently been disturbed by knockings and other strange sounds in the Hydesville house. Towards the end of March, 1848, the Fox family were much disturbed by mysterious rappings, and on the evening of the 31st they went to bed early, hoping to get some undisturbed sleep. But the rappings broke out even more vigorously than they had done on the previous occasions, and Mrs. Fox, much alarmed and excited when the raps manifested signs of intelligence, decided to call in her neighbours to witness the phenomenon. The neighbours heard the raps as distinctly as did the Foxes themselves. When the sounds had indicated that they were directed by some sort of intelligence it was no difficult matter to get into communication with the unseen. Questions were asked by the " sitters " of this informal " séance" and if the answer were in the affirmative, raps were heard, if in the negative, the silence remained unbroken. By this means the knocker indicated that he was a spirit, the spirit of a pedlar who had been murdered for his money by a former resident in the house. It also answered correctly other questions put to it, relating to the ages of those present and other particulars concerning persons who lived in the neighbourhood. In the few days immediately following hundreds of people made their way to Hydesville to witness the marvel. Fox's married son, David, who lived about two miles from his father's house, has left a statement to the effect that the Fox family, following the directions of the raps, which indicated that the pedlar was buried in the cellar, had begun to dig therein early in April, but were stopped by water. Later, however, hair, bones, and teeth were found in the cellar. Vague rumours were afloat that a pedlar had visited the village one winter, had been seen in the kitchen of the house afterwards tenanted by the Foxes, and had mysteriously disappeared, without fulfilling his promise to the villagers to return next day. But of real evidence there was not a scrap, whether for the murder or for the existence of the pedlar, particulars of whose life were furnished by the raps. Soon after these happenings Kate Fox went to Auburn, and Margaretta to Rochester, N.Y., where lived her married sister, Mrs. Fish (formerly Mrs. Underhill), and at both places outbreaks of rappings occurred. New mediums sprang up, circles were formed, and soon Spiritualism was fairly started on its career.

Rods, Magical : (*See* **Magic.**)

Rogers, Mr. Dawson : (*See* **British National Association of Spiritualists.**)

Rohan, Prince de : (*See* **Cagliostro.**)

Rome : Magical practice was rife amongst the Romans. Magic was the motive power of their worship which was simply an organized system of magical rites for communal ends. It was the basis of their mode of thought and outlook upon the world, it entered into every moment and action of their daily life, it affected their laws and customs. This ingrained tendency instead of diminishing, developed to an enormous extent, into a great system of superstition, and in the later years led to a frenzy for strange gods, borrowed from all countries. In times of misfortune and disaster the Romans were always ready to borrow a god if so be his favours promised more than those of their own deities. Though there was a strong conservative element in the native character, though the " custom of the elders " was strongly upheld by the priestly fraternity, yet this usually gave way before the will and temper of the people. Thus, as a rock shows its geological history by its differing strata, so the theogony of the Roman gods tells its tale of the race who conceived it. There are pre-historic nature deities, borrowed from the indigenous tribes, gods of the Sabines, from whom the young colony stole its wives ; gods of the Etruscans, of the Egyptians, Greeks and Persians. The temple of Jupiter on the Capitol contained the altar of a primitive deity, a stone-god, Terminus, the spirit of boundaries : in the temple of Diana of the Grove, a fountain nymph was worshipped. Instances of this description are numerous.

Spirits.—In addition to the *gods*, there were spirits to be propitiated. Indeed the objects offered to the Roman for adoration were numberless. Apuleius gives a description of this when he tells of a country road where one might meet an altar wreathed with flowers, a cave hung with garlands, an oak tree laden with horns of cattle, a hill marked by fences as sacred, a log rough-hewn into shape, an altar of turf smoking with libations or a stone anointed with oil. Every single action of man's daily life had a presiding spirit ; commerce and husbandry likewise. There was eating Ednea, drinking Potina ; there were spirits of departure, of journeying, of approaching and home-coming. In commerce there was Mercurius, the spirit of gain, of money, Pecunia ; in farming, the spirits of cutting, grinding, sowing and bee-keeping. A deity presided over streets and highways ; there was a goddess of the sewers, Cloacina ; a spirit of bad smells, Mephitis. Spirits of evil must also be propitiated by pacificatory rites, such as Robigo, the spirit of mildew ; in Rome there was an altar to Fever and Bad Fortune. From the country came Silvanus, god of farms and woods, and his Fauns and nymphs with Picus, the wood-pecker god who had fed the twins Romulus and Remus with berries—all these were possessed of influences and were approached with peculiar rites. The names of these spirits were inscribed on tablets, *indigitamenta*, which were in the charge of the pontiffs, who thus knew which spirit to evoke according to the need. Most of these spirits were animistic in origin.

The Roman Worship consisted of magical rites destined to propitiate the powers controlling mankind ; to bring man into touch with them, to renew his life and that which supported it, the land with its trees, corn and cattle, to stop that process of degeneration constantly set in motion by evil influences. Everything connected with it typified this restoration. *The Priests* who represented the life of the community, were therefore bound by strict observances from endangering it in any way. Rules as to attire, eating and touch were numerous. *Sacrifices* were systematised according to the end desired and the deity invoked. There were rules as to whether the victim must be young or full-grown, male or female ; oxen were to be offered to Jupiter and Mars ; swine to Juno, to Ceres the corn-goddess and to Silvanus. At one shrine a cow in calf was sacrificed and the ashes of the unborn young were of special magical efficacy. Human sacrifice existed within historical times. After the battle of Cannæ the Romans had sought to divert misfortune by burying two Greeks alive in the cattle-market while in the time of Julius Cæsar two men were put to death with sacrificial solemn-ities by the Pontiff and Flamen of Mars. Again, in the time of Cicero and Horace boys were killed for magical purposes. *Fire* possessed great virtue and was held sacred in the worship of Vesta, in early belief Vesta being the fire itself ; it presided over the family hearth ; it restored purity and conferred protection. *Blood* had the same quality and smeared on the face of the god symbolised and brought about the one-ness of the deity with the commun-ity. On great occasions the Statue of Jupiter was treated thus : the priests of Bellona made incisions in their shoul-ders and sprinkled the blood upon the image ; the face of a triumphant general was painted with vermilion to represent blood. *Kneeling* and prostration brought one into direct contact with the earth of the sacred place. *Music* was also used as a species of incantation, probably deriving its origin in sound made to drive away evil spirits. *Danc-ing* too was of magical efficacy. In *Rome* there were colleges of dancers for the purposes of religion, youths who danced in solemn measure about the altars, who, in the sacred month of Mars took part in the festivals and went throughout the city dancing and singing. One authority states four kinds of " holy solemnity " ; sacrifice, sacred banquets, public festivals and games. Theatrical per-formances also belonged to this category, in one instance being used as a means of diverting a pestilence. The *sacred banquets* were often decreed by the Senate as thanks-

giving to the gods. Tables were spread with a sumptuous repast in the public places and were first offered to the statues of the deities seated around. The *festivals* were numerous, all of a magical and symbolic nature. In the spring there was the *Parilia* when fires of straw were lighted, through which persons passed to be purified ; the *Cerealia*, celebrated with sacrifice and offerings to Ceres, the corn-goddess, and followed by banquets. The *Luper-calia*, the festival of Faunus, was held in February and symbolised the wakening of Spring and growth. Goats were slain as sacrifice and with their blood the Luperci, youths clad in skins, smeared their faces. They took thongs of the goat-skin and laughing wildly rushed through the city striking the crowd, Roman matrons believing that the blows thus received rendered them prolific. Juno, the goddess of marriage and childbirth also had her festival, the *Matronalia*, celebrated by the women of *Rome*. There were the *festivals of the dead* when the door leading to the other world was opened, the stone removed from its entrance in the Comitium, and the shades coming forth were appeased with offerings. On these days three times in the year, when the gods of gloom were abroad, complete cessation from all work was decreed, no battle could be fought nor ship set sail neither could a man marry. To the *Sacred Games* were taken the statues of the gods in gorgeous procession, chariots of silver, companies of priests, youths singing and dancing. The gods viewed the games reclining on couches. The *Chariot races* also par-took of the nature of rites. After the races in the Field of Mars came one of the most important Roman rites, the sacrifice of the October Horse. The right-hand horse of the victorious team was sacrificed to Mars, and the tail of the animal, running with blood, carried to the Altar of the Regia. The blood was stored in the temple of Vesta till the following spring and used in the sacrifice of the festival of Parilia. This sacrifice was essentially magical, all citizens present being looked upon as purified by the blood-sprinkling and lustral bonfire. The *Roman outlook upon life* was wholly coloured by magic. Bodily foes had their counterpart in the unseen world, wandering spirits of the dead, spirits of evil, the anger of innocently offended deities, the menace of the evil eye. *Portents* and *prodigies* were everywhere. In the heavens strange things might be seen. The sun had been known to double, even treble itself ; its light turn to blood, or a magical halo to appear round the orb. Thunder and lightning were always fraught with presage ; Jove was angered when he opened the heavens and hurled his bolts to earth. Phantoms, too, hovered amid the clouds ; a great fleet of ships had been seen sailing over the marshes. Upon the Campagna the gods were observed in conflict, and afterwards tracks of the combatants were visible across the plain. Unearthly voices were heard amid the mountains and groves ; cries of portent had sounded within the temples. Blood haunted the Roman imagination. Sometimes it was said to have covered the land as a mantle, the standing corn was dyed with blood, the rivers and fountains flowed with it, while walls and statues were covered with a bloody sweat. The *flight and song of birds* might be foretelling the decrees of Fate ; unappeased spirits of the dead were known to lurk near and steal away the souls of men and then they too were " dead." All these happenings were attributable to the gods and spirits, who, if the portent be one of menace, must be propitiated, if one of good fortune, thanked with offerings. Down to the later times this deep belief in the occurrence of prodigies persisted. When Otho set out for Italy, *Rome* rang with reports of a gigantic phantom rush-ing forth from the Temple of Juno ; of the Statue of Julius turning from east to west.

Augury.—*Divination* was connected with the Roman worship. There was a spot on the Capitol from which the augur with veiled head read the auspices in the flight of birds. Augurs also accompanied armies and fleets and read the omens before an engagement was entered upon. *Divination* was also practised by reading the intestines of animals, by dreams, by divine possession as in the case of the Oracles when prophecies were uttered. These had been gathered together in the Sibylline books (q.v.), and were consulted as oracles by the State. With the worship of Fortune were connected the *Lots of Præneste*. The questions put to the goddess were answered by means of oaken lots which a boy drew from a case made of sacred wood. The fortune-tellers also used a narrow-necked urn which, filled with water, only allowed one lot at a time to rise. *Astrologers* from Chaldea were also much sought after and were attached to the kingly and noble houses. Familiar things of everyday life were of magical import. *Words*, *Numbers*, odd ones specially for the Kalends, Nones and Ides were so arranged as to fall upon odd days ; *touch* was binding and so recognised in the law of *Rome*, as the grasp of a thing sold, from a slave to a turf of distant estate ; and *knotting* and twisting of thread was injurious so that women must never pass by cornfields twisting their spindles, they must not even be uncovered. There was a strange sympathy between the *trees* and mankind, and great honour was paid to the sacred trees of *Rome*. On the oak tree of Jupiter the triumphant general hung the shield and arms of his fallen foe ; while the hedges about the Temple of Diana at Nemi were covered with votive offerings. The trees also harboured the spirits of the dead who came forth as dreams to the souls of men. *Pliny* the elder says in this matter " Trees have a soul since nothing on earth lives without one. They are the temples of spirits and the simple countryside dedicates still a noble tree to some god. The various kinds of trees are sacred to their protecting spirits : the oak to Jupiter, the laurel to Apollo, olive to Minerva, myrtle to Venus, white poplar to Hercules." These trees therefore partook of the nature of their presiding spirits and it was desirable to bring about communion with their magical influence, as in the spring when laurel boughs were hung at the doors of the flamens and pontiffs and in the temple of Vesta where they remained hanging till the following year. Trees and their leaves were also possessed of healing and purifying value ; laurel was used for the latter quality as in the Roman triumphs the fasces of the commander, the spears and javelins of legionaries were wreathed with its branches to purify them from the blood of the enemy. *Man* himself had a presiding spirit, his genius, each woman her " juno " the Saturnalia was really a holiday for this " other self." The Roman kept his birthday in honour of his genius, offering frankincense, cakes and unmixed wine on an altar garlanded with flowers and making solemn prayers for the coming year. City and village had their genii, also bodies of men from the senate to the scullions.

Death was believed to be the life and soul enticed away by revengeful ghosts, hence death would never occur save by such agencies. The dead therefore must be appeased with offerings or else they wander abroad working evil among the living. This belief is present in Ovid's lines : " Once upon a time the great feast of the dead was not observed and the manes failed to receive the customary gifts, the fruit, the salt, the corn steeped in unmixed wine, the violets. The injured spirits revenged themselves on the living and the city was encircled with the funeral fires of their victims. The townsfolk heard their grandsires complaining in the quiet hours of the night, and told each other how the unsubstantial troop of monstrous spectres rising from their tombs, shrieked along the city streets and up and down the fields." *Beans* were used in the funeral feasts. They were supposed to harbour the souls of the dead, and the bean-blossom to be inscribed with characters of mourning.

Dreams were considered of great importance by the Romans ; many historical instances of prophetic dreams may be found. They were thought to be like birds, the " bronze-coloured " hawks ; they were also thought to be the souls of human beings visiting others in their sleep ; also the souls of the dead returning to earth. In Virgil much may be found on this subject ; Lucretius tried to find a scientific reason for them ; Cicero, though writing in a slighting manner of the prevalent belief in these manifestations of sleep, yet records dreams of his own, which events proved true.

Sorcery in all its forms, love-magic and death-magic was rife amongst all classes, besides necromantic practices. There were *charms and spells* for everything under the sun ; the rain-charm of the pontiffs consisting of the throwing of puppets into the Tiber ; the charm against thunder-bolts compounded of onions, hair and sprats ; the charm against an epidemic when the matrons of *Rome* swept the temple-floors with their hair ; and many more down to the simple love-charm strung round the neck of the country maiden.

Witches were prevalent. The poets often chose these sinister figures for their subjects, as when Horace describes the ghastly rites of two witches in the cemetery of the Esquiline. Under the light of the new moon they crawl about looking for poisonous herbs and bones ; they call the spectres to a banquet consisting of a black lamb torn to pieces with their teeth, and after, these phantoms must answer the questions of the sorceresses. They make images of their victims and pray to the infernal powers for help ; hounds and snakes glide over the ground, the moon turns to blood, and as the images are melted so the lives of the victims ebb away. Virgil gives a picture of a sorceress performing love-magic by means of a waxen image of the youth whose love she desired. Lucan in his Pharsalia treats of Thessaly, notorious in all ages for sorcery and draws a terrific figure—Erichtho, a sorceress of illimitable powers, one whom even the gods obeyed, to whom the forces of earth and heaven were bond-slaves ; and Fate waiting her least command. Both Nero and Agrippina his mother were reported to have had recourse to the infamous arts of sorcery ; while in the New Testament may be found testimony as to these practices in *Rome*. The attitude of the cultured class towards magic is illustrated by an illuminating passage to be found in the writings of Pliny the elder. He says " The art of magic has prevailed in most ages and in most parts of the globe. Let no one wonder that it has wielded very great authority inasmuch as it embraces three other sources of influence. No one doubts that it took its rise in medicine and sought to cloak itself in the garb of a science more profound and holy than the common run. It added to its tempting promises the force of religion, after which the human race is groping, especially at this time. Further it has brought in the arts of astrology and divination. For everyone desires to know what is to come to him and believes that certainty can be gained by consulting the stars. Having in this way taken captive the feelings of man by a triple chain it has reached such a pitch that it rules over all the world and in the East, governs the King of Kings." K. N.

Romer, Dr. C. : (*See* **Spiritualism.**)

Rose : From the earliest times the *rose* has been an emblem of silence. Eros, in the Greek mythology, presents a *rose* to the god of silence, and to this day sub rosa, or " under the *rose*," means the keeping of a secret. Roses were used in very early times as a potent ingredient in love philters.

In Greece it was customary to leave bequests for the maintenance of rose gardens, a custom which has come down to recent times. *Rose* gardens were common during the middle ages. According to Indian mythology, one of the wives of Vishnu was found in a *rose*. In Rome it was the custom to bless the *rose* on a certain Sunday, called Rose Sunday. The custom of blessing the golden rose came into vogue about the eleventh century. The golden rose thus consecrated was given to princes as a mark of the Roman Pontiffs' favour. In the east it is still believed that the first *rose* was generated by a tear of the prophet Mohammed, and it is further believed that on a certain day in the year the *rose* has a heart of gold. In the west of Scotland if a white *rose* bloomed in autumn it was a token of an early marriage. The red *rose*, it was said, would not bloom over a grave. If a young girl had several lovers, and wished to know which of them would be her husband, she would take a *rose* leaf for each of her sweethearts, and naming each leaf after the name of one of her lovers, she would watch them till one after another they sank, and the last to sink would be her future husband. Rose leaves thrown upon a fire gave good luck. If a rose bush were pruned on St. John's eve, it would bloom again in the autumn. Superstitions respecting the *rose* are more numerous in England than in Scotland.

Rosen, Paul : A sovereign Grand Inspector-General of the 33rd degree of the French rite of Masonry, who in 1888 decided that Masonry was diabolic in conception, and to prove his strictures published a work called *Satan et Cie.* The Satanism credited to Masonry by Rosen is social anarchy and the destruction of the Catholic religion.

Rosenberg, Count : (*See* **Dee.**)

Rosenkreuze, Christian : (*See* **Rosicrucians.**)

Rosicrucian Society of England : (*See* **Rosicrucians.**)

Rosicrucians : The idea of a Rosicrucian Brotherhood has probably aroused more interest in the popular mind than that of any other secret society of kindred nature : but that such a brotherhood ever existed is extremely doubtful. The very name of *Rosicrucian* seems to have exercised a spell upon people of an imaginative nature for nearly two hundred and fifty years, and a great deal of romantic fiction has clustered around the fraternity : such as for example Lord Lytton's romance of *Zanoni* ; Shelley's novel *St. Irvyne the Rosicrucian,* Harrison Ainsworth's *Auriol,* and similar works.

The name *Rosicrucian* is utilised by mystics to some extent as the equivalent of *magus,* but in its more specific application it was the title of a member of a suppositious society which arose in the late sixteenth century. There are several theories regarding the derivation of the name. The most commonly accepted appears to be that it was derived from the appellation of the supposed founder, Christian Rosenkreuze ; but as his history has been proved to be wholly fabulous, this theory must fall to the ground. Mosheim, the historian, gave it as his opinion that the name was formed from the Latin words *ros,* dew, *crux* a cross ; on the assumption that the alchemical dew of the philosophers was the most powerful dissolvent of gold, while the cross was equivalent to light. It is more probable that the name *Rosicrucian* is derived from *rosa* a rose, and *crux* a cross, and we find that the general symbol of the supposed order was a rose crucified in the centre of a cross. In an old *Rosicrucian* book of the last century, we further find the symbol of a red cross-marked heart in the centre of an open rose, which Mr. A. E. Waite believes to be a development of the monogram of Martin Luther, which was a cross-crowned heart rising from the centre of an open rose.

History of the Supposed Brotherhood.—Practically nothing definite was known concerning the Rosicrucian Brotherhood before the publication of Mr. Waite's work *The real History of the Rosicrucians* in 1887. Prior to that a great deal had been written concerning the fraternity, and shortly before Mr. Waite produced his well-known book another had made its appearance under the title of *The Rosicrucians, their Rites and Mysteries* by the late Mr. Hargrave Jennings. This book was merely a farrago of the wildest absurdities, rendered laughable by the ridiculous attitude of the author, who pretended to the guardianship of abysmal occult secrets. It was typical of most writings regarding the fraternity of the Rosy Cross, and as the *Westminster Review* wittily remarked in its notice of the volume, it deals with practically everything under the sun except the *Rosicrucians.* Mr. Waite's work, the result of arduous personal research, has gathered together all that can possibly be known regarding the *Rosicrucians,* and his facts are drawn from manuscripts, in some cases discovered by himself, and from skilful analogy. As it is the only authority on the subject worth speaking about, we shall attempt to outline its conclusions.

We find then that the name " Rosicrucian " was unknown previously to the year 1598. The history of the movement originates in Germany, where in the town of Cassel in the year 1614 the professors of magic and mysticism, the theosophists and alchemists, were surprised by the publication of a pamphlet bearing the title *The Fama of the Fraternity of the Meritorious Order of the Rosy Cross Addressed to the Learned in General and the Governors of Europe.* It purported to be a message from certain anonymous adepts who were deeply concerned for the condition of mankind, and who greatly desired its moral renewal and perfection. It proposed that all men of learning throughout the world should join forces for the establishment of a synthesis of science, through which would be discovered the perfect method of all the arts. The squabblings and quarrellings of the literati of the period were to be forgone, and the antiquated authorities of the elder world to be discredited. It pointed out that a reformation had taken place in religion, that the church had been cleansed, and that a similar new career was open to science. All this was to be brought about by the assistance of the illuminated Brotherhood,—the children of light who had been initiated in the mysteries of the Grand Orient, and would lead the age to perfection.

The fraternity kindly supplied an account of its history. The head and front of the movement was one C.R.C. of Teutonic race, a magical hierophant of the highest rank, who in the fifth year of his age had been placed in a convent, where he learned the Humanities. At the age of fifteen, he accompanied one, Brother P. A. L. on his travels to the Holy Land ; but the brother died at Cyprus to the great grief of C.R.C., who, however resolved to undertake the arduous journey himself. Arriving at Damascus, he there obtained knowledge of a secret circle of theosophists who dwelt in an unknown city of Arabia called Damcar, who were expert in all magical arts. Turning aside from his quest of the Holy Sepulchre, the lad made up his mind to trace these illuminati and sought out certain Arabians who carried him to the city of Damcar. There he arrived at the age of sixteen years, and was graciously welcomed by the magi, who intimated to him that they had long been expecting him, and relating to him several passages in his past life. They proceeded to initiate him into the mysteries of occult science, and he speedily became acquainted with Arabic, from which tongue he translated the divine book M into Latin. After three years of mystic instruction, he departed from the mysterious city for Egypt, whence he sailed to Fez as the wise men of Damcar had instructed him to do. There he fell in with other masters who taught him how to evoke the elemental spirits. After a further two years' sojourn at Fez, his period of initiation was over, and he proceeded to Spain to confer with the wisdom of that country, and convince its professors of the errors of their ways. Unhappily, the scholarhood of Spain turned its back upon him with loud laughter, and intimated to him that it had learned the principles and practice of the black art from a much higher authority, namely Satan himself, who had unveiled to them the secrets of necromancy within the walls of the university of Salamanca. With noble indignation he shook the dust of Spain from his feet, and turned his face to other countries only, alas, to find the same treatment within their boundaries. At last he sought his native land of Germany where he pored over the great truths he had learned in solitude and seclusion, and reduced his universal philosophy to writing. Five years of a hermit's life, however, only served to strengthen him in his opinions, and he could not but feel that one who had achieved the transmutation of metals and had manufactured the elixir of life was designed for a nobler purpose than rumination in solitude. Slowly and carefully he began to collect around him assistants who became the nucleus of the Rosircuian fraternity. When he had gathered four of these persons into the brotherhood they invented amongst them a magical language, a cipher writing of equal magical potency, and a large dictionary replete with occult wisdom. They erected a House of the Holy Ghost, healed the sick, and initiated further members, and then betook themselves as missionaries to the various countries of Europe to disseminate their wisdom. In course of time their founder, C.R.C., breathed his last, and for a hundred and twenty years the secret of his burial place was concealed. The original members also died one by one, and it was not until the third generation of adepts had arisen that the tomb of their illustrious founder was unearthed during the re-building of one of their secret dwellings. The vault in which this tomb was found was illuminated by the sun of the magi, and inscribed with magical characters. The body of the illustrious founder was discovered in perfect preservation, and a number of marvels were discovered buried beside him, which convinced the existing members of the fraternity that it was their duty to make these publicly known to the world. It was this discovery which immediately inspired the brotherhood to make its existence public in the circular above alluded to, and they invited all worthy persons to apply to them for initiation. They refused, however, to supply their names and addresses, and desired that those who wished for initiation could signify their intention by the publication of printed letters which they would be certain to notice. In conclusion they assured the public of the circumstance that they were believers in the reformed Church of Christ, and denounced in the most solemn manner all pseudo-occultists and alchemists.

This *Fama* created tremendous excitement among the occultists of Europe, and a large number of pamphlets were published criticising and defending the society and its manifesto, in which it was pointed out there were a number of discrepancies. To begin with no such city as Damcar existed within the bounds of Arabia. Where, it was asked, was the House of the Holy Ghost, which the *Rosicrucians* stated had been seen by 100,000 persons and was yet concealed from the world ? C.R.C., the founder, as a boy of fifteen must have achieved great occult skill to have astonished the magi of Damcar. But despite these objections considerable credit was given to the *Rosicrucian* publication. After a lapse of a year appeared the *Confession of the Rosicrucian Fraternity*, addressed to the learned in Europe. This offered initiation by gradual stages to selected applicants, and discovered its ultra-Protestant character by what an old Scots divine was wont

to call a " dig at the Pope," whom it publicly execrated, expressing the pious hope that his " asinine braying " would finally be put a stop to by tearing him to pieces with nails ! In the following year, 1616, *The Chymical Nuptials of Christian Rosencreutz* was published, purporting to be incidents in the life of the mysterious founder of the Brotherhood of the Rosy Cross. But the chymical marriage makes Christian Rosencreutz an old man when he achieved initiation, and this hardly squares with the original account of his life as given in the *Fama*. By this time a number of persons had applied for initiation, but had received no answer to their application. As many of these believed themselves to be alchemical and magical adepts, great irritation arose among the brotherhood, and it was generally considered that the whole business was a hoax. By 1620, the *Rosicrucians* and their publication had lapsed into absolute obscurity.

Numerous theories have been put forward as to the probable authorship of these manifestoes, and it has been generally considered that the theologian Andreæ produced them as a kind of laborious jest ; but this view is open to so many objections that it may be dismissed summarily. Their authorship has also been claimed for Taulerus, Joachim Jünge, and Ægidius Guttmann ; but the individual in whose imagination originated the Brotherhood of the Rosy Cross will probably for ever remain unknown. It is however, unlikely that the manifesto was of the nature of a hoax, because it bears upon its surface the marks of intense earnestness, and the desire for philosophical and spiritual reformation ; and it is not unlikely that it sprang from some mystic of the Lutheran school who desired the co-operation of like-minded persons. Mr. Waite thinks there is fair presumptive evidence to show that some corporate body such as the Rosicrucian Brotherhood did exist : but as he states that the documents which are the basis of this belief give evidence also that the association did not originate as it pretended, and was devoid of the powers which it claimed, this hypothesis seems in the highest degree unlikely. Such a document would more probably emanate from one individual, and it is almost impossible to conceive that a body of men professing such aims and objects as the manifesto lays claim to could possibly have lent themselves to such a farrago of absurdity as the history of C.R.C. A great many writers have credited the brotherhood with immense antiquity ; but as the publisher of the manifesto places its origin so late as the fifteenth century, there is little necessity to take these theories into consideration.

So far as can be gleaned from their publications, the *Rosicrucians*, or the person in whose imagination they existed, were believers in the doctrines of Paracelsus. They believed in alchemy, astrology and occult forces in nature and their credence in these is identical with the doctrines of the great master of modern magic. They were thus essentially modern in their theosophical beliefs, just as they were modern in their religious ideas. Mr. Waite thinks it possible that in Nuremburg in the year 1598 a Rosicrucian Society was founded by a mystic and alchemist named Simon Studion, under the title of *Militia Crucifera Evangelica*, which held periodical meetings in that city. Its proceedings are reported in an unprinted work of Studion's, and in opinions and objects it was identical with the supposed Rosicrucian Society. " Evidently," he says, " the Rosicrucian Society of 1614 was a transfiguration or development of the sect established by Simon Studion." But there is no good evidence for this statement. After a lapse of nearly a century, the *Rosicrucians* reappeared in Germany. In 1710, a certain Sincerus Racatus or Sigmund Richter, published *A Perfect and True Preparation of the Philosophical Stone according to the Secret Methods of the Brotherhood of the Golden and Rosy Cross*, and annexed to this treatise were the rules of the Rosicrucian Society for the initiation of new members. Mr. Waite is of opinion that these rules are equivalent to a proof of the society's existence at the period, and that they help to establish the important fact that it still held its meetings at Nuremburg, where it was originally established by Studion. In 1785, the publication of *The Secret Symbols of the Rosicrucians of the Sixteenth and Seventeenth Centuries* took place at Altona, showing in Mr. Waite's opinion that the mysterious brotherhood still existed ; but this was their last manifesto. These things are certainly of the nature of proof, but they are so scanty that any reasonable and workable hypothesis that such a society ever existed can scarcely be founded upon them. For all we know to the contrary they may be publications of enthusiastic and slightly unbalanced pseudo-mystics, and nothing definite can be gleaned from their existence.

In 1618 Henrichus Neuhuseus published a Latin pamphlet, which stated that the *Rosicrucian* adepts had migrated to India, and present-day Theosophists will have it that they exist now in the table-lands of Tibet. It is this sort of thing which altogether discredits occultism in the eyes of the public. Without the slightest shadow of proof of any kind, such statements are wildly disseminated ; and it has even been alleged that the *Rosicrucians* have developed into a Tibetan Brotherhood, and have exchanged Protestant Christianity for esoteric Buddhism ! Mr. Waite humorously states that he has not been able to trace the eastern progress of the Brotherhood further than the Isle of Mauritius, where it is related in a curious manuscript a certain Comte De Chazal initiated a Dr. Sigismund Bacstrom into the mysteries of the Rose Cross Order in 1794 ; but we know nothing about the Comte de Chazal or his character, and it is just possible that Dr. Bacstrom might have been one of those deluded persons who in all times and countries have been willing to purchase problematical honours. From the *Fama* and *Confessio*, we glean some definite ideas of the occult conceptions of the *Rosicrucians*. In these documents we find the doctrine of the Microcosmus (q.v.), which considers man as containing the potentialities of the whole universe. This is a distinctly Paracelsian belief. We also find the belief of the doctrine of Elemental Spirits (q.v.), which many people wrongly think originated with the *Rosicrucians*; but which was probably reintroduced by Paracelsus. We also find that the manifestoes contain the doctrine of the *Signatura Rerum*, which also is of Paracelsian origin. This is the magical writing referred to in the *Fama*; and the mystic characters of that book of nature, which, according to the *Confessio*, stand open for all eyes, but can be read or understood by only the very few. These characters are the seal of God imprinted on the wonderful work of creation, on the heavens and earth, and on all beasts. It would appear too, that some form of practical magic was known to the Brotherhood. They were also, according to themselves, alchemists, for they had achieved the transmutation of metals and the manufacture of the elixir of life.

In England the *Rosicrucian* idea was taken up by Fludd, who wrote a spirited defence of the Brotherhood ; by Vaughan who translated the *Fama* and the *Confessio*; and by John Heydon, who furnished a peculiarly quaint and interesting account of the *Rosicrucians* in *The Wise Man's Crown*; and further treatises regarding their alchemical skill and medical ability in *El Havarevna*, or *The English Physitian's Tutor*, and *A New Method of Rosie Crucian Physick*, London 1658. In France Rosicrucianism ran a like course. It has been stated by Buhle and others that there was much connection between the *Rosicrucians* and Freemasons.

A pseudo-Rosicrucian Society existed in England before the year 1836, and this was remodelled about the middle of last century under the title " The Rosicrucian Society of England." To join this it is necessary to be a Mason. The officers of the society consist of three magi, a master-general for the first and second orders, a deputy master-general, a treasurer, a secretary and seven ancients. The assisting officers number a precentor, organist, torchbearer, herald, and so forth. The society is composed of nine- grades or classes. It published a little quarterly magazine from 1868 to 1879, which in an early number stated that the society was " calculated to meet the requirements of those worthy masons who wished to study the science and antiquities of the craft, and trace it through its successive developments to the present time ; also to cull information from all the records extant from those mysterious societies which had their existence in the dark ages of the world, when might meant right." These objects were, however, fulfilled in a very perfunctory manner, if the magazine of the association is any criterion of its work. For this publication is filled with occult serial stories, reports of masonic meetings and verse. Mr. Waite states that the most notable circumstance connected with this society is the complete ignorance which seems to have prevailed among its members generally concerning everything connected with Rosicrucianism. The prime movers of the association were Robert Wentworth Little, Frederick Hockley, Kenneth Mackenzie and Hargrave Jennings, and in the year 1872 they seem to have become conscious that their society had not borne out its original intention. By this time the Yorkshire College and East of Scotland College at Edinburgh, had been founded—one does not know with what results. " This harmless association," says Mr. Waite, " deserves a mild sympathy at the hands of the student of occultism. Its character," he continues, " could hardly have deceived the most credulous of its postulants. Some of its members wrapped themselves in darkness and mystery, proclaimed themselves *Rosicrucians* with intent to deceive. These persons found a few—very few—believers and admirers. Others assert that the society is a cloak to something else— the last resource of cornered credulity and exposed imposture. There are similar associations in other parts of Europe, and also in America : *e.g.*, the *Societas Rosicruciana* of Boston." But in the concluding pages of Mr. Waite's book we find the following passage : " On the faith of a follower of Honnes, I can promise that nothing shall be held back from these true Sons of the Doctrine, the sincere seekers after light, who are empowered to preach the supreme Arcana of the psychic world with a clean heart and an earnest aim. True *Rosicrucians* and true alchemical adepts, if there be any in existence at this day, will not resent a new procedure when circumstances have been radically changed." Mr. Waite appeals to these students of occultism who are men of method as well of imagination to assist him in clearing away the dust and rubbish which have accumulated during centuries of oblivion in the silent sanctuaries of the transcendental sciences, that the traditional secrets of nature may shine forth in the darkness of doubt and uncertainty to illuminate the straight and narrow avenues which communicate between the seen and the unseen.

Rossetti, Dante Gabriel : English Author and Painter (1828 - 1882). *Gabriel Charles Dante Rossetti*, poet, painter and translator, and commonly known as *Dante Gabriel Rossetti*, was born in London in 1828, his father being an Italian who had settled in England. While yet a boy *Rossetti* manifested æsthetic leanings, and accordingly he was sent to study drawing under no less distinguished a preceptor than Cotman, while shortly afterwards he entered the

Royal Academy Schools. Then in 1848, feeling the need of still further tuition, he commenced working at the studio of Ford Madox Brown, a master who undoubtedly influenced him greatly ; and while under Brown's tuition he began to show himself a painter of distinct individuality, while simultaneously he made his first essays in translating Italian literature into English, and became known among his friends as a poet of rare promise. Meanwhile, however, *Rossetti* was really more interested in the brush than in the pen, and soon after finally quitting Brown's studio he brought about a memorable event in the history of English painting, this being the founding of the pre-Raphaelite brotherhood, a body consisting of seven members whose central aim was to render precisely and literally every separate object figured in their pictures.

Leaving his father's house in 1849, *Rossetti* went to live at Chatham Place, Blackfriars Bridge, and during the next ten years his activity as a painter was enormous ; while the year 1860 is a notable one in his career, marked as it is by his marriage to Eleanor Siddal. The love between the pair was of an exceptionally passionate order and from it sprang *Rossetti's* immortal sonnet-sequence called *The House of Life*, published in 1881 ; but Mrs. Rossetti died in 1862, and thereupon the poet, terribly cast down by his bereavement, went to live at a house in Chelsea with Swinburne and Meredith. Here he continued to write fitfully, while in 1871 he completed one of his most famous pictures, *Dante's Dream* ; yet the loss of his wife preyed upon him persistently, he was tortured by insomnia, and in consequence he began to take occasional doses of chloral. Gradually this practice developed into a habit, sapping alike the physical and mental strength of the poet ; and though he rallied for a while during a stay in Scotland, where he lived at Penkill Castle in Ayrshire, it soon became evident that his death was imminent unless he eschewed his drug. But he had not the strength of will necessary for this abjuration, he died in 1882 at Birchington, and his remains were interred in the cemetery there.

Rossetti had a marked bias for mysticism in various forms. William Bell Scott, in his *Autobiography*, tells how the poet became at one time much enamoured of table-turning and the like ; while waiving his somewhat childish taste herein, his temperament was undoubtedly a very religious one, and once towards the close of his life he declared that he had " seen and heard those that died long ago." Was it, then, a belief in the possibility of communicating with the dead which induced him, on his wife's death, to have some of his love poems enclosed in the coffin of the deceased ? while, be the answer to this question what it may, *Rossetti's* mysticism certainly bore good fruit in his art, his *Rose Mary* being among the most beautiful of English poems introducing the supernatural element. Nevertheless, it is by his painting rather than by his poetry that *Rossetti* holds a place as a great mystic ; for, despite his fondness for precise handling, all his pictures with the exception of *Found* are essentially of a mystical nature ; they are not concerned with the tangible and visible world, but body forth the scenes and incidents beheld in dreams, and do this with a mastery reflected by no other kindred works save those of Blake.

Round : (*See* **Planetary Chains.**)
Roustan : (*See* **France.**)
Rudolph II. : (*See* **Gustenhover.**)
Ruler of Seven Chains : (*See* **Planetary Logos.**)
Runes : (*See* **Teutons.**)
Rupa is the physical body, the most gross of the seven principles of which personality consists. (*See* **Seven Principles, Mayayi-rupa, Theosophy.**)
Rupecissa, Johannes de : This alchemist was an ancestor of Montfauçon, the distinguished archæologist, and his name

suggests that he was a man of gentle birth, while it is commonly supposed that he was a French monk of the order of St. Francis, and it is reported that in 1357, presumably on account of his alchemistic predilections, he was imprisoned by Pope Innocent VI. *Rupecissa* contributed four volumes to the literature of hermetic philosophy : *Coelum Philosophorum*, Paris 1543, *De Quinta Essentia Rerum Omniam*, Basle 1561, *De Secretis Alchemiæ*, Cologne 1579, *Livre de Lumière*, Paris, n.d. ; and these were admired by a number of the author's successors, but their value is really literary rather than scientific.

Rusalki : *Rusalki*, the lovely river nymph of Southern Russia seems to have been endowed with the beauty of person and the gentle characteristics of the Mermaids of Northern nations. Shy and benevolent, she lived on the small alluvial islands that stud the mighty rivers which drain this extensive and thinly-peopled country, or in the detached coppices that fringe their banks, in bowers woven of flowering reeds and green-willow-boughs ; her pastime and occupation being to aid in secret the poor fishermen in their laborious and precarious calling. Little is known of these beautiful creatures—as if the mystery and secrecy which was inculcated and enforced in all affairs of government in this country had been extended to its fairy faith. Even Keightley, so learned in fairy lore, knows little of *Rusalki*, and dismisses her with the following brief notice :—

" They are of a beautiful form, with long green hair, they swim and balance themselves on the branches of trees, bathe in the lakes and rivers, play on the surface of the water, and wring their locks on the green meads at the water's edge. It is chiefly at Whitsuntide that they appear ; and the people then, singing and dancing, weave garlands for them, which they cast into the stream."

Russia : (For early history of occult matters in Russia *see* **Slavs.**) Spiritualism was first introduced into Russia by persons who had become interested in the subject whilst abroad through witnessing manifestations of psychic phenomena and acquaintance with the works of Allan Kardec, the French exponent of Spiritualism. From the first the new doctrine found its followers chiefly among members of the professions and the aristocracy, finally including the reigning monarch of that time, Alexander II. with many of his family and entourage as devoted adherents. Because of the immense influence of such converts the progress of Spiritualism in Russia was made smoother than it otherwise would have been in a country where the laws of Church and State are nothing if not despotic and disposed to look upon anything new in matters religious, intellectual or merely of general interest as partaking of a revolutionary character. Even so, much of the spiritualistic propaganda, manifestations and publications were prosecuted under various ruses and subterfuges such as the circulation of a paper entitled " The Rebus," professedly devoted to innocent rebuses and charades and only incidentally mentioning Spiritualism the real object of its being. Chief amongst the distinguished devotees of the subject was Prince Wittgenstein, aide-de-camp and trusted friend of Alexander II., who not only avowed his beliefs openly but arranged for various mediums to give séances before the Emperor, one of these being the well-known D. D. Home. So impressed was the Czar that, it is said, from that time onwards he consulted mediums and their prophetic powers as to the advisability or otherwise of any contemplated change or step in his life; doubtless helped or driven to such dependence on mediums by the uncertain conditions under which occupants of the Russian throne seem to exist.

" Another Russian of high position socially and officially, M. Aksakof, interested himself in the matter in ways many and various, arranging séances to which he invited the scientific men of the University, editing a paper *Psychische Studien*, of necessity published abroad ; translating Swedenborg's works into Russian beside various French, American and English works on the same subject and thus becoming a leader in the movement. Later, with his friends, M. M. Boutlerof and Wagner, professors respectively of chemistry and zoology at the University of St. Petersburg, he specially commenced a series of séances for the investigation of the phenomena in an experimental manner and a scientific committee was formed under the leadership of Professor Mendleyef who afterwards issued an adverse report on the matter, accusing the mediums of trickery and their followers of easy credulity and the usual warfare proceeded between the scientific investigators and spiritual enthusiasts."

M. Aksakof's commission was reported upon unfavourably by M. Mendeleyef, but the former protested against the report.

At the other extreme of the Social scale among the peasantry and uneducated classes generally, the grossest superstition exists, an ineradicable belief in supernatural agencies and cases are often reported in the columns of Russian Papers of wonder-working, obsession and various miraculous happenings, all ascribed, according to their character, to demoniac or angelic influence, or in the districts where the inhabitants are still pagan to local deities and witchcraft.

Ruysbroeck or Ruysbrock : Flemish Mystic (1293–1381). It is probable that this mystic derived his name from the village of Ruysbreck, near Brussels, for it was there that he was born in the year 1293. Even as a child he showed distinct religious leanings, and before he was out of his teens he had steeped himself in a wealth of mystical literature. Naturally, then, he decided to espouse the clerical profession, and in 1317 he was duly ordained, while a little later he became vicar of St. Gudule, one of the parishes of Brussels. During his long term of acting in this capacity he became widely esteemed for his erudition, and for his personal piety ; while his sermons and even his letters were passed from hand to hand, and perused with great admiration by many of his fellow clerics. But he was never found guilty of courting fame or publicity of any kind, and at the age of sixty he retired to Groenendale, not far from the battlefield of Waterloo, where he founded a monastery. There he lived until his death in 1381, devoting himself chiefly to the study of mysticism, yet showing himself anything but averse to those charitable actions befitting a monk.

Ruysbroeck was known to his disciples as " the ecstatic teacher." As a thinker he was speculative and broadminded, and indeed he was one of those who prefigured the Reformation, the result being that, though he won the encomiums of many famous theologians in the age immediately succeeding his, an attempt to beatify him was sternly suppressed. He was a tolerably voluminous writer, and at Cologne, in 1552, one of his manuscripts found its way into book form with the title, *De Naptu svel de Ornatu Nupliarum Spiritualium ;* while since then a number of his further works have been published, notably *De Vera Contemplatione* and *De Septem Gradivus Amoris* (Hanover, 1848). The central tenet of his teaching is that " the soul finds God in its own depths," but, in contradistinction to many other mystics, he did not teach the fusion of the self in God, but held that at the summit of the ascent towards righteousness the soul still preserves its identity.

Ruysbroeck and his teaching begot many voluminous commentaries throughout the middle ages, and he has attracted a number of great writers, the Abbé Bossuet, for example, and at a later date Maurice Maeterlinck. In 1891 the latter published *L'Ornemant des Noces Spirituelles, de Ruysbroeck l'admirable,* and an English translation of this by J. T. Stoddart was issued in 1904. The reader desirous of further information should consult *Studies in Mystical Religion,* by Rufus M. Jones, 1909.

S

Saba : In Ossianic legend, wife of Finn and mother of Oisin. In the form of a fawn, she was captured by Finn in the chase, but noticing that his man-hounds would do her no hurt, he gave her shelter in his Dun of Allen. The next morning he found her transformed into a beautiful woman. She told him that an enchanter had compelled her to assume the shape of a fawn, but that her original form would be restored if she reached Dun Allen. Finn made her his wife, and ceased for a while from battle and the chase. Hearing one day, however, that the Northmen's warships were in the Bay of Dublin, he mustered his men and went to fight them. He returned victorious, but to find *Saba* gone. The enchanter, taking advantage of his absence, had appeared to her in the likeness of Finn with his hounds and so lured her from the dun, when she became a fawn again.

Sabbathi : To this angel, in the Jewish rabbinical legend of the celestial hierarchies, is assigned the sphere of Saturn. He receives the divine light of the Holy Spirit, and communicates it to the dwellers in his kingdom.

Sabellicus, Georgius : A magician who lived about the same time as Faustus of Wittenberg, about the end of the 15th century. His chief claims to fame as a sorcerer rest on his own wide and arrogant advertisement of his skill in necromancy. He styles himself, " The most accomplished *Georgius Sabellicus,* a second Faustus, the spring and centre of necromantic art, an astrologer, a magician, consummate in chiromancy, and in agromancy, pyromancy and hydromancy inferior to none that ever lived." Unfortunately, no proof is forthcoming that he ever substantiated these bombastic claims, or was ever regarded by anyone else as anything but a charlatan.

Sadhus : (*See* **India.**)

Sahu : The Egyptian name for the spiritual or incorruptible body. It is figured in the *Book of the Dead* as a lily springing from the Khat or corruptible body.

Saint Germain, Comte de : Born probably about 1710, one of the most celebrated mystic adventurers of modern times. Like Cagliostro and others of his kind almost nothing is known concerning his origin, but there is reason to believe that he was a Portuguese Jew. There are, however, hints that he was of royal birth, but these have never been substantiated. One thing is fairly certain, and that is that he was an accomplished spy, for he resided at many European Courts, spoke several languages fluently, and was even sent upon diplomatic missions by Louis XV. He had always abundance of funds at his command, and is alluded to by Grimm as the most capable and able man he had ever known. He pretended to have lived for centuries, to have known Solomon, the Queen of Sheba and many other persons of antiquity ; but although obviously a charlatan, the accomplishments upon which he based his reputation were in many ways real and considerable. Especially was this the case as regards chemistry, a science in which he was certainly an adept, and he pretended to have a secret for removing the flaws from diamonds, and to be able to transmute metals, and of course he possessed the secret of the elixir of life. He is mentioned by Horace Walpole as being in London about

1743, and as being arrested as a Jacobite spy, who was later released. Walpole writes of him : " He is called an Italian, a Spaniard, a Pole, a somebody who married a great fortune in Mexico and ran away with her jewels to Constantinople, a priest, a fiddler, a vast nobleman." Five years after his London experience, he attached himself to the court of Louis XV. where he exercised considerable influence, over that monarch, and was employed by him upon several secret missions. He was distinctly the fashion about this time, for Europe was greatly inclined to the pursuit of the occult at this epoch ; and as he combined mystical conversation with a pleasing character,and not a little flippancy, he was the rage. But he ruined his chances at the French court by interfering in a dispute between Austria and France, and was forced to remove himself to England. He resided in London for one or two years, but we trace him to St. Petersburg, 1762, where he is said to have assisted in the conspiracy which placed Catherine II. on the Russian throne. After this he travelled in Germany where he is said in the *Memoirs of Cagliostro* to have become the founder of freemasonry, and to have initiated Cagliostro into that rite. (*See* **Cagliostro**.) If Cagliostro's account can be credited, he set about the business with remarkable splendour, and not a little bombast, posing as a " deity," and behaving in a manner calculated to gladden pseudo-mystics of the age. He was nothing if not theatrical, and it is probably for this reason that he attracted the Land-grave Charles of Hesse, who set aside a residence for the study of the occult sciences. He died at Schleswig some-where between the years 1780 and 1785, but the exact date of his death and its circumstances are unknown. It would be a matter of real difficulty to say whether he possessed any genuine occult power whatsoever, and in all likelihood he was merely one of those charlatans in whom his age abounded. Against this view might be set the circum-stance that a great many really clever and able people of his own time thoroughly believed in him ; but we must remember the credulous nature of the age in which he flourished. It has been said that XVIII. century Europe was sceptical regarding everything save occultism and its professors, and it would appear to unbiassed minds that this circumstance could have no better illustration than the career of the *Comte de Saint Germain.*

A notable circumstance regarding him was that he possessed a magnificent collection of precious stones, which some consider to be artificial, but which others better able to judge believe to have been genuine. Thus he presented Louis XV. with a diamond worth 10,000 livres. All sorts of stories were in circulation concerning him. One old lady professed to have encountered him at Venice fifty years before, where he posed as a man of 60, and even his valet was supposed to have discovered the secret of immortality. On one occasion a visitor rallied this man upon his master being present at the marriage of Cana in Galilee, asking him if it were the case. " You forget, sir," was the reply, " I have only been in the Comte's service a century."

St. Irvyne, the Rosicrucian, by Wm. Godwin : (*See* **Fiction, Occult.**)

Saint Jacques, Albert de : A monk of the seventeenth cen-tury, who published a book entitled *Light to the Living by the Experiences of the Dead,* or divers apparitions of souls from purgatory in our century. The work was published at Lyons in 1675.

St. John's Crystal Gold : " In regard of the Ashes of Veget-ables," says Vaughan, " although their weaker exterior Elements expire by violence of the fire, yet their Earth cannot be destroyed, but is Vitrified. The Fusion and Transparency of this substance is occasioned by the Radicall moysture or Seminal water of the Compound.

This water resists the fury of the fire, and cannot possibly be vanquished. ' In hac Aquâ ' (saith the learned Sever-ine), ' Rosa latet in Hieme.' These two principles are never separated ; for Nature proceeds not so far in her Dissolutions. When death hath done her worst, there is a Union between these two, and out of them shall God raise us to the last day, and restore us to a spiritual constitution. I do not conceive there shall be a Resurrection of every Species, but rather their Terrestrial parts, together with the element of water (for ' there shall be no more sea' : Revela-tions), shall be united in one mixture with the Earth, and fixed to a pure Diaphanous substance. This is *St. John's Crystal Gold,* a fundamental of the New Jerusalem—so called, not in respect of Colour, but constitution. Their Spirits, I suppose, shall be reduced to their first Limbus, a sphere of pure, ethereal fire, like rich Eternal Tapestry spread under the throne of God."

St. John's Wort : *St. John's Wort.* In classical mythology the summer solstice was a day dedicated to the sun, and was believed to be a day on which witches held their festivities. *St. John's Wort* was their symbolical plant, and people were wont to judge from it whether their future would be lucky or unlucky ; as it grew they read in its progressive character their future lot. The Christians dedicated this festive period to *St. John's Wort* or root, and it became a talisman against evil. In one of the old romantic ballads a young lady falls in love with a demon, who tells her—

" Gin you wish to be leman mine
Lay aside the *St. John's Wort* and the vervain."

When hung up on St. John's day together with a cross over the doors of houses it kept out the devil and other evil spirits. To gather the root on St. John's day morning at sunrise, and retain it in the house, gave luck to the family in their undertakings, especially in those begun on that day.

St. Martin, Louis Claude de : French Mystic and Author, commonly known as " le philosophe inconnu." (1743–1803). The name of *Louis de St. Martin* is a familiar one, more familiar, perhaps, than that of almost any other French mystic ; and this is partly due to his having been a voluminous author, and partly to his being virtually the founder of a sect, " the Martinistes" ; while again, St. Beuve wrote about him in his *Causeries du Lundi,* and this has naturally brought him under wide notice.

Born in 1734 at Amboise, *St. Martin* came of a family of some wealth and of gentle birth. His mother died while he was a child, but this proved anything but unfortunate for him ; for his step-mother besides lavishing a wealth of affection on him, early discerned his rare intellectual gifts, and made every effort to nurture them. " C'est à elle," he wrote afterwards in manhood, " que je dois peut-être tout mon bonheur, puisque c'est elle que m'a donné les premiers éléments de cette education douce, attentive et pieuse, qui m'a fait aimer de Dieu et des hommes." The boy was educated at the Collège de Pontlevoy, where he read with interest numerous books of a mystical order, one which impressed him particularly being Abbadie's *Art de se connaître soi-même ;* and at first he intended to make law his profession, but he soon decided on a military career instead, and accordingly entered the army. A little before taking this step he had affiliated himself with the freemasons and, on his regiment being sent to garrison Bordeaux, he became intimate with certain new rites which the Portu-guese Jew, Martinez Pasqually (q.v.), had lately introduced into the masonic lodge there. For a while *St. Martin* was deeply interested, not just in the aforesaid but in the philosophy of Pasqually ; yet anon he declared that the latter's disciples were inclined to be too materialistic, and soon he was deep in the writings of Swedenborg, in whom he found a counsellor more to his taste. The inevitable result of studies of this nature was that he began to feel a great distaste for regimental life, and so, in 1771, he resigned his commission, determining to devote the rest of his life to philosophical speculations. He now began writing a book, *Des Erreurs et de la Vérité, ou les Hommes rappelés au Principe de la Science*, which was published in 1775, at Edinburgh, at this time on the eve of becoming a centre of literary activity of all sorts ; and it is worth recalling that this pristine effort by *St. Martin* was brought under the notice of Voltaire, the old cynic observing shrewdly that half a dozen folio volumes might well be devoted to the topic of *erreurs*, but that a page would suffice for the treatment of *vérité !*

The young author's next important step was to pay a visit to England, and thence in 1787 he went to Italy along with Prince Galitzin, with whom he had lately become friendly. They stayed together for some time at Rome, and then *St. Martin* left for Strassburg, his intention being to study German there, for he had recently grown interested in the teaching of Jacob Bœhme, and he was anxious to study the subject thoroughly. Very soon he had achieved this end, and at a later date, indeed, he translated a number of the German mystic's writings into French; but meanwhile returning to France, he found his outlook suddenly changed, the revolution breaking out in 1789, and a reign of terror setting in. No one was safe, and *St. Martin* was arrested at Paris, simply on account of his being a gentleman by birth ; but his affiliation with the freemasons stood him in good stead in this hour of need, and he was liberated by a decree of the ninth Thermidor. Accordingly he resumed activity with his pen, and in 1792 he issued a new book, *Nouvel Homme* ; while two years later he was commissioned to go to his native Amboise, inspect the archives and libraries of the monasteries in that region, and draw up occasional reports on the subject. Shortly afterwards he was appointed an *élève professeur* at the *École Normale* in Paris, in consequence of which he now made his home in that town ; and among others with whom he became acquainted there was Chateaubriand, of whose writing, he was an enthusiastic devotee, but who, on his parts appears to have received the mystic with his usual haughty coldness. *St. Martin* did not lack a large circle of admirers, however, and he continued to work hard, publishing in 1795 one of his most important books, *Lèttres à un Ami, ou Considérations politiques, philosophiques et réligieuses sur la Révolution*, which was succeeded in 1800 by two speculative treatises, *Ecce Homo* and *L'Esprit des Choses*. Then, in 1802, he issued yet another volume, *Ministère de l'Homme Esprit* ; but in the following year his labours were brought to an abrupt close, for while staying at Annay, not far from Paris, with a friend called Lenoir-Laroche, he succumbed to an apoplectic seizure. After his death it was found that he had left a considerable mass of manuscripts behind him, and some of these were issued by his executors in 1807, while in 1862 a collection of his letters appeared.

St. Martin was never married, but he appears to have exercised a most extraordinary fascination over women ; and in fact divers scandalous stories are told in this relation, some of them implicating various courtly dames of the French nobility of the Empire. As a philosopher *St. Martin* found a host of disciples among his contemporaries, these gradually forming themselves almost into a distinct sect, and, as observed before, acquiring the name of " Martinistes." What, then, was the teaching of their leader ? and what the nature of the tenets promulgated in his voluminous writings ? It is difficult to give an epitome in

so limited a space as that at disposal here, but turning to the author's *l'Homme du Désir* (1790), and again to his *Tableau natural des Rapports qui existent entre Die, et l'Homme et l'Univers* (1782), we find this pair tolerably representative of all his writing, and their key-note may certainly be defined as consisting in aspiration. Man is divine despite the fall recounted in the Scriptures, dormant within him lies a lofty quality of which he is too often scarcely conscious, and it is incumbent on him to develop this quality, striving thereafter without ceasing, and waiving the while everything pertaining to the category of materialism—such is the salient principle in *St. Martin's* teaching, a principle which seems literally trite nowadays, for it has been propounded by a host of modern mystics, notably A.E. in *The Hero in Man*. In writing in this wise, the French mystic undoubtedly owed a good deal to Swendenborg, while obligations to Bœhme are of course manifest throughout his later works ; and, while his debt to Martinez Pasqually has probably been exaggerated somewhat, there is no doubt that the Portuguese Jew influenced him greatly for a while, the latter's teaching coming to him at a time when he was still very young and susceptible, and fresh from readings of Abbadie.

Saintes Maries de la Mer : Ile de la Camarque, Church of. (*See* **Gypsies.**)

Sakta Cult : (*See* **India.**)

Salagrama, The : An Indian stone, credited with possessing magical properties, and worn as an amulet. This stone is black in colour, about the size of a billiard ball, and pierced with holes. It is said that it can only be found in the Gandaki, a river in Nepaul, which some believe rises at the foot of Vishnu, and others in the head of Siva. It is kept in a clean cloth, and often washed and perfumed by its fortunate owner. The water in which it has been dipped is supposed thereby to gain sin-expelling potency, and is therefore drunk and greatly valued. It possesses other occult powers, and is a necessary ingredient of the preparations of those about to die. The departing Hindu holds it in his hand, and believing in its powers has hope for the future, and dies peacefully.

Salamander's Feather : Otherwise known as Asbestos. A mineral of an incombustible nature, which resembles flax, being of fine fibrous texture. It was used by the Pagans to light their temples : when once it was lighted, they believed it could not be put out, even by rain and storms. Leonardus says : " Its fire is nourished by an inseparable unctuous Humid flowing from its substance ; therefore, being once kindled it preserves a constant light without feeding it with any moisture."

Sallow : A tree or shrub of the willow kind. Rods of this particular wood were much in use amongst the Scythians and the Alani for purposes of augurial divination. Fine straight wands were chosen, on which certain characters were written, and they were then thrown on a white cloth. From the way in which they fell the magician gained the desired information.

Salmael : (*See* **Astrology.**)

Salmesbury Hall : (*See* **Haunted Houses.**)

Salmonœus : (*See* **Astrology.**)

Samodivi : (*See* **Slavs.**)

Samothracian Mysteries : (*See* **Greece.**)

Samovile : (*See* **Slavs.**)

Samoyeds : (*See* **Siberia.**)

Samuel, Mother : (*See* **England.**)

San Domingo : (*See* **West Indian Islands.**)

Sannyasis : (*See* **India.**)

Sanyojanas are in the Theosphical scheme the obstacles which the traveller along the Path (q.v.) must surmount. The number of them is ten and they are :—

1.—Belief in the Ego as unchangeable.

2.—Lack of faith in higher effort.
3.—Reliance on ritual.
4.—Lust.
5.—Ill-will.
6.—Love of the world.
7.—Egotistic longing for a future life.
8.—Pride.
9.—Self-righteousness.
10.—Nescience.

Saphy : Perhaps from the Arabic *safi* " pure, select, excellent." Certain charms or amulets worn by the negroes as protection against thunderbolts and diseases, to procure them wives, and avert disasters of all kinds. They are composed of strips of paper on which sentences from the Koran are inscribed, sometimes intermixed with kabalistic signs. These strips are enclosed in silver tubes or silk bags, which are worn near the skin, and often fastened in the dress. Africans of both sexes and all religions are great believers in the occult properties of such talismans ; and Mungo Park resorted to the making of *Saphy,* or Grigris (as they are some times called), as a means of earning his living.

Sapphire : It is understood to make the melancholy cheerful and maintain the power or manly vigour of the body. The high priest of Egypt wore a *sapphire* upon his shoulder, and Aelian says that it was called truth. The Buddhists still ascribe a sacred magical power to it, and hold that it reconciles man to God. It is a good amulet against fear, promotes the flow of the animal spirits, hindereth ague and gout, promotes chastity, and prevents the eyes from being affected by small-pox.

Sara, St., of Egypt : (*See* **Gypsies.**)

Sardius : This gem resembles the cornelian, and is an antidote to the onyx. It prevents unpleasant dreams, makes its possessor wealthy, and sharpens the wit.

Sardou, Victorian : The famous French dramatist was a keen student of occultism, and studied spiritualism with Allan Kardec (q.v.). He achieved great facility as a medium for spirit drawings, and many of the examples by his hand are of great merit artistically as well as from an occult point of view. Some of them are reproduced in M. Camille Flammarion's book *Mysterious Psychic Forces.* (*See* **France.**)

Sat B'Hai : A Hindu society, the object of which was the study and development of Indian philosophy. It was so called after the bird *Malacocersis Grisis,* which always flies by sevens. It was introduced into England about the year 1872 by Major J. H. Lawrence Archer. It had seven descending degrees, each of seven disciples, and seven ascending degrees of perfection, Ekata or Unity. It ceased to be necessary on the establishment of the Theosophical Society.

Satan : (*See* **Devil.**)

Satanism : (*See* **Devil-worship.**)

Saul, Barnabas : (*See* **Dee.**)

Scandinavia : For the early history of occultism in *Scandinavia* (*see* article **Teutons.**)

Witchcraft.—In mediæval times Scandinavian examples of witchcraft are rare, but in 1669 and 1670 a great outbreak of fanaticism against it commenced in Sweden in the district of Elfdale.

The villages of Mohra and Elfdale are situated in the dales of the mountainous districts of the central parts of Sweden. In the first of the years above mentioned, a strange report went abroad that the children of the neighbourhood were carried away nightly to a place they called Blockula, where they were received by Satan in person ; and the children themselves, who were the authors of the report, pointed out to them numerous women, who, they said were witches and carried them thither. The alarm and terror in the district became so great that a report was at last made to the king, who nominated commissioners, partly clergy and partly laymen, to inquire into the extraordinary circumstances which had been brought under his notice, and these commissioners arrived in Mohra and announced their intentions of opening their proceedings on the 13th of August, 1670.

On the 12th of August, the commissioners met at the parsonage-house, and heard the complaints of the minister and several people of the better class, who told them of the miserable condition they were in, and prayed that by some means or other they might be delivered from the calamity. They gravely told the commissioners that by the help of witches some hundreds of their children had been drawn to Satan, who had been seen to go in a visible shape through the country, and to appear daily to the people ; the poorer sort of them, they said, he had seduced by feasting them with meat and drink.

The commissioners entered upon their duties on the next day with the utmost diligence, and the result of their misguided zeal formed one of the most remarkable examples of cruel and remorseless persecution that stains the annals of sorcery. No less than threescore and ten inhabitants of the village and district of Mohra, three-and-twenty of whom made confessions, were condemned and executed. One woman pleaded that she was with child, and the rest denied their guilt, and these were sent to Fahluna, where most of them were afterwards put to death. Fifteen children were among those who suffered death, and thirty-six more, of different ages between nine and sixteen, were forced to run the gauntlet, and be scourged on the hands at the church-door every Sunday for one year ; while twenty more, who had been drawn into these practices more unwillingly, and were very young, were condemned to be scourged with rods upon their hands for three successive Sundays at the church-door. The number of the children accused was about three hundred.

It appears that the commissioners began by taking the confessions of the children, and then they confronted them with the witches whom the children accused as their seducers. The latter, to use the words of the authorised report, having " most of them children with them, which they had either seduced or attempted to seduce, some seven years of age, nay, from four to sixteen years," now appeared before the commissioners. " Some of the children complained lamentably of the misery and mischief they were forced sometimes to suffer of the devil and the witches." Being asked, whether they were sure, that they were at any time carried away by the devil ? they all replied in the affirmative. " Hereupon the witches themselves were asked, whether the confessions of those children were true, and admonished to confess the truth, that they might turn away from the devil unto the living God. At first, most of them did very stiffly, and without shedding the least tear, deny it, though much against their will and inclination. After this the children were examined every one by themselves, to see whether their confessions did agree or no, and the commissioners found that all of them, except some very little ones, which could not tell all the circumstances, did punctually agree in their confessions of particulars. In the meanwhile, the commissioners that were of the clergy examined the witches, but could not bring them to any confession, all continuing steadfast in their denials, till at last some of them burst into tears, and their confession agreed with what the children said ; and these expressed their abhorrence of the fact, and begged pardon. Adding that the devil, whom they called Locyta, had stopped the mouths of some of them, so loath was he to part with his prey, and had stopped the ears of others. And being now gone from them, they could no longer conceal it; for they had now perceived his treachery." The witches asserted that, the journey to Blockula was not always made with the same kind of conveyance; they commonly used men, beasts, even spits and posts, according as they had opportunity. They preferred, however, riding upon goats, and if they had more children with them than the animal could conveniently carry, they elongated its back by means of a spit anointed with their magical ointment. It was further stated, that if the children did at any time name the names of those, either man or woman, that had been with them, and had carried them away, they were again carried by force, either to Blockula or the cross-way, and there beaten, insomuch that some of them died of it; "and this some of the witches confessed, and added, that now they were exceedingly troubled and tortured in their minds for it." One thing was wanting to confirm this circumstance of their confession. The marks of the whip could not be found on the persons of the victims, except on one boy, who had some wounds and holes in his back, that were given him with thorns; but the witches said they would quickly vanish.

The account they gave of Blockula was, that it was situated in a large meadow, like a plain sea, "wherein you can see no end." The house they met at had a great gate painted with many divers colours. Through this gate they went into a little meadow distinct from the other, and here they turned their animals to graze. When they had made use of men for their beasts of burden, they set them up against the wall in a state of helpless slumber, and there they remained till wanted for the homeward flight. In a very large room of this house, stood a long table, at which the witches sat down; and adjoining to this room was another chamber, where there were "lovely and delicate beds."

As soon as they arrived at Blockula, the visitors were required to deny their baptism, and devote themselves body and soul to Satan, whom they promised to serve faithfully. Hereupon he cut their fingers, and they wrote their name with blood in his book. He then caused them to be baptized anew, by priests appointed for that purpose. Upon this the devil gave them a purse, wherein there were filings of clocks, with a big stone tied to it, which they threw into the water, and said, "As these filings of the clock do never return to the clock, from which they were taken, so may my soul never return to heaven!" Another difficulty arose in verifying this statement, that few of the children had any marks on their fingers to show where they had been cut. But here again the story was helped by a girl who had her finger much hurt, and who declared, that because she would not stretch out her finger, the devil in anger had thus wounded it.

When these ceremonies were completed, the witches sat down at the table, those whom the fiend esteemed most being placed nearest to him; but the children were made to stand at the door, where he himself gave them meat and drink. Perhaps we may look for the origin of this part of the story in the pages of Pierre de Lancre. The food with which the visitors to Blockula were regaled, consisted of broth, with coleworts and bacon in it; oatmeal bread spread with butter, milk and cheese. Sometimes they said, it tasted very well, and sometimes very ill. After meals they went to dancing, and it was one peculiarity of these northern witches' sabbaths, that the dance was usually followed by fighting. Those of Elfdale confessed that the devil used to play upon a harp before them. Another peculiarity of these northern witches was, that children resulted from their intercourse with Satan, and these children having married together became the parents of toads and serpents.

The witches of Sweden appear to have been less noxious than those of most other countries, for, whatever they acknowledged themselves, there seems to have been no evidence of mischief done by them. They confessed that they were obliged to promise Satan that they would do all kinds of mischief, and that the devil taught them to milk, which was after this manner. They used to stick a knife in the wall, and hang a kind of label on it, which they drew and stroaked; and as long as this lasted, the persons they had power over were miserably plagued, and the beasts were milked that way, till sometimes they died of it. A woman confessed that the devil gave her a wooden knife, wherewith, going into houses, she had power to kill anything she touched with it; yet there were few that could confess that they had hurt any man or woman. Being asked whether they had murdered any children, they confessed that they had indeed tormented many, but did not know whether any of them died of these plagues, although they said that the devil had showed them several places where he had power to do mischief. The minister of Elfdale declared, that one night these witches were, to his thinking, on the crown of his head, and that from thence he had a long continued pain of the head. And upon this one of the witches confessed that the devil had sent her to torment that minister, and that she was ordered to use a nail, and strike it into his head, but his skull was so hard that the nail would not pentrate it, and merely produced that headache. The hard-headed minister said further, that one night he felt a pain as if he were torn with an instrument used for combing flax, and when he awoke he heard somebody scratching and scraping at the window, but could see nobody; and one of the witches confessed, that she was the person that had thus disturbed him. The minister of Mohra declared also, that one night one of these witches came into his house, and did so violently take him by the throat, that he thought he should have been choked, and awaking, he saw the person that did it, but could not know her; and that for some weeks he was not able to speak, or perform divine service. An old woman of Elfdale confessed that the devil had helped her to make a nail, which she stuck into a boy's knee, of which stroke the boy remained lame a long time. And she added, that, before she was burned or executed by the hand of justice, the boy would recover.

Another circumstance confessed by these witches was, that the devil gave them a beast, about the shape and bigness of a cat, which they called a carrier; and a bird as big as a raven, but white; and these they could send anywhere, and wherever they came they took away all sorts of victuals, such as butter, cheese, milk, bacon, and all sorts of seeds, and carried them to the witch. What the bird brought they kept for themselves, but what the carrier brought they took to Blockula, where the arch-fiend gave them as much of it as he thought good. The carriers, they said, filled themselves so full oftentimes, that they were forced to disgorge it by the way, and what they thus rendered fell to the ground, and is found in several gardens where coleworts grow, and far from the houses of the witches. It was of a yellow colour like gold, and was called witches' butter.

Such are the details, as far as they can now be obtained, of this extraordinary delusion, the only one of a similar kind that we know to have occurred in the northern part of Europe during the "age of witchcraft." In other countries we can generally trace some particular cause which gave rise to great persecutions of this kind, but here, as the story is told, we see none, for it is hardly likely that such a strange series of accusations should have been the mere involuntary creation of a party of little children. Suspicion is excited by the peculiar part which the two clergymen of Elfdale and Mohra acted in it, that they were not altogether strangers to the fabrication. They seem to have been weak superstitious men, and perhaps they had been reading the witchcraft books of the south till they imagined the country round them to be over-run with these noxious beings. The proceedings at Mohra caused so much alarm throughout Sweden, that prayers were ordered in all the churches for delivery from the snares of Satan, who was believed to have been let loose in that kingdom. On a sudden a new edict of the king put a stop to the whole process, and the matter was brought to a close rather mysteriously. It is said that the witch prosecution was increasing so much in intensity, that accusations began to be made against people of a higher class in society, and then a complaint was made to the king, and they were stopped.

Perhaps the two clergymen themselves became alarmed, but one thing seems certain, that the moment the commission was revoked, and the persecution ceased, no more witches were heard of.

Spiritualism.—In 1843 an epidemic of preaching occurred in Southern Sweden, which provides Ennemoser, with material for an interesting passage in his *History of Magic.* The manifestation of this was so similar in character to those described elsewhere, that it is unnecessary to allude to it in detail. A writer in the London *Medium and Daybreak* of 1878 says : " It is about a year and a half since I changed my abode from Stockholm to this place, and during that period it is wonderful how Spiritualism has gained ground in Sweden. The leading papers, that used in my time to refuse to publish any article on Spiritualism excepting such as ridiculed the doctrine, have of late thrown their columns wide open to the serious discussion of the matter. Many a Spiritualist in secret, has thus been encouraged to give publicity to his opinions without standing any longer in awe of that demon, public ridicule, which intimidates so many of our brethren. Several of Allan Kardec's works have been translated into Swedish, among which I may mention his *Evangile selon le Spiritisme* as particularly well-rendered in Swedish by Walter Jochnick. A spiritual Library was opened in Stockholm on the 1st of April last, which will no doubt greatly contribute to the spreading of the blessed doctrine. The visit of Mr. Eglinton to Stockholm was of the greatest benefit to the cause. Let us hope that the stay of Mrs. Esperance in the south of Sweden may have an equally beneficial effect. Notwithstanding all this progress of the cause in the neighbouring country, Spiritualism is looked upon here as something akin to madness, but even here there are thin, very thin rays, and very wide apart, struggling to pierce the darkness. In Norway, spiritualism as known to modern Europe, did not seem to have become existent until about 1880. A writer in a number of the *Dawn of Light* published in that year says : " Spiritualism is just commencing to give a sign of its existence here in Norway. The newspapers have begun to attack it as a delusion and the ' expose ' of Mrs. C., which recently took place at 38, Great Russell Street, London, has made the round through all the papers in *Scandinavia.* After all, it must sooner or later take root as in all other parts of the world. Mr. Eglinton, the English medium, has done a good work in Stockholm, showing some of the great savants a new world ; and a couple of years ago Mr. Slade visited Copenhagen. The works of Mr. Zollner, the great astronomer of Leipzig, have been mentioned in the papers and caused a good deal of sensation.

" Of mediums there are several here, but all, as yet, afraid to speak out. One writes with both hands ; a gentleman is developing as a drawing medium. A peasant, who died about five years ago, and lived not far from here, was an excellent healing medium ; his name was Knud, and the people had given him the nickname of Vise Knud (the wise

Knud) ; directly when he touched a patient he knew if the same could be cured or not, and often, in severe cases, the pains of the sick person went through his own body. He was also an auditive medium, startling the people many times by telling them what was going to happen in the future ; but the poor fellow suffered much from the ignorance and fanaticism around him, and was several times put in prison.

" I am doing all I can to make people acquainted with our grand cause."

A second and more hopeful letter of 1881, addressed to the editor of the *Revue Spirite*, is as follows :—

" My dear Brothers,—Here our science advances without noise. An excellent writing medium has been developed among us, one who writes simultaneously with both hands ; while we have music in a room where there are no musical instruments ; and where there is a piano it plays itself. At Bergen, where I have recently been, I found mediums, who in the dark, made sketches—were dessinateurs—using also both hands. I have seen, also, with pleasure that several men of letters and of science have begun to investigate our science spirite. The pastor Eckhoff, of Bergen, has for the second time preached against Spiritualism, ' this instrument of the devil, this psychographie ' ; and to give more of eclat to his sermon he has had the goodness to have it printed ; so we see that the spirits are working. The suit against the medium, Mme. F., in London, is going the rounds of the papers of Christiania ; these journals opening their columns, when occasion offers, to ridicule Spiritualism. We are, however, friends of the truth, but there are scabby sheep among us of a different temperament. From Stockholm they write me that a library of spiritual works has been opened there, and that they are to have a medium from Newcastle, with whom séances are to be held."

In the *London Spiritual Magazine* of May, 1885, is a long and interesting paper on Swedish Spiritualism, by William Howitt, in which he gives quite a notable collection of narratives concerning Phenomenal Spiritual Manifestations in Sweden, most of which were furnished by an eminent and learned Swedish gentleman—Count Piper. The public have become so thoroughly sated with tales of hauntings, apparitions, prevision, etc., that Count Piper's narrations would present few, if any features of interest, save in justification of one assertion, that Spiritualism is rife in human experience everywhere, even though it may not take the same form as a public movement, that it has done in America and England.

As early as 1864, a number of excellent leading articles commending the belief in Spiritual ministry, and the study of such phenomena as would promote communion between the " two worlds," appeared in the columns of the *Afton Blad*, one of the most popular journals circulated in Sweden.

Schroepfer : (*See* **Germany.**)

Scotland : (For early matter *see* the article **Celts.**)

Witchcraft.—Witchcraft and sorcery appear to have been practised in the earliest historical and traditional times. It is related that during the reign of Natholocus in the second century there dwelt in Iona a witch of great renown, and so celebrated for her marvellous power that the king sent one of his captains to consult her regarding the issue of a rebellion then troubling his kingdom. The witch declared that within a short period the king would be murdered, not by his open enemies but by one of his most favoured friends, in whom he had most especial trust. The messenger enquired the assassin's name. " Even by thine own hands as shall be well-known within these few dayes," replied the witch. So troubled was the captain on hearing these words that he railed bitterly against her, vowing that he would see her burnt before he would commit such a villainous crime. But after reviewing the matter carefully in his mind, he arrived at the conclusion that if he informed the king of the witch's prophecy, the king might for the sake of his personal safety have him put to death, so thereupon he decoyed Natholocus into his private chamber and falling upon him with a dagger slew him outright. About the year 388 the devil was so enraged at the piety of St. Patrick that he assailed the saint by the whole band of witches in *Scotland*. St. Patrick fled to the Clyde embarking in a small boat for Ireland. As witches cannot pursue their victims over running water, they flung a huge rock after the escaping saint, which however fell harmless to the ground, and which tradition says now forms Dumbarton Rock. The persecution of witches constitutes one of the blackest chapters of history. All classes, Catholic and Protestant alike, pursued the crusade with equal vigour, undoubtedly inspired by the passage in Exodus xxii., 18. While it is most probable that the majority of those who practised witchcraft and sorcery were of weak mind and enfeebled intellect, yet a large number adopted the supposed art for the purpose of intimidation and extortion from their neighbours. Witches were held to have sold themselves body and soul to the devil. The ceremony is said to consist of kneeling before the evil one, placing one hand on her head and the other under her feet, and dedicating all between to the service of the devil, and also renouncing baptism. The witch was thereafter deemed to be incapable of reformation. No minister of any denomination whatever would intercede or pray for her. On sealing the compact the devil proceeded to put his mark upon her. Writing on the "Witches' Mark" Mr. Bell, minister of Gladsmuir in 1705 says: "The witches' mark is sometimes like a blew spot, or a little tale, or reid spots, like fleabiting, sometimes the flesh is sunk in and hollow and this is put in secret places, as among the hair of the head, or eyebrows, within the lips, under the armpits, and even in the most secret parts of the body." Mr. Robert Kirk of Aberfoill in his *Secret Commonwealth* states: "A spot that I have seen, as a small mole, horny, and brown coloured, throw which mark when a large brass pin was thrust (both in buttock, nose, and rooff of the mouth) till it bowed (bent) and became crooked, the witches, both men and women, nather felt a pain nor did bleed, nor knew the precise time when this was doing to them (their eyes only being covered)."

In many cases the mark was invisible, and as it was considered that no pain accompanied the pricking of it, there arose a body of persons who pretending great skill therein constituted themselves as "witch prickers" and whose office was to discover and find out witches. The method employed was barbarous in the extreme. Having stripped and bound his victim the witch pricker proceeded to thrust his needles into every part of the body. When at last the victim worn out with exhaustion and agony remained silent, the witch pricker declared that he had discovered the mark. Another test for detection was trial by water. The suspects were tied hands and great toes together, wrapped in a sheet and flung into a deep pool. In cases where the body floated, the water of baptism was supposed to give up the accused, while those who sank to the bottom were absolved, but no attempt was made at rescue. When confession was demanded the most horrible of tortures were resorted to, burning with irons being generally the last torture applied. In some cases a diabolic contrivance called the "witches' bridle" was used. The "bridle" encircled the victim's head while an iron bit was thrust into the mouth from which prongs protruded piercing the tongue, palate and cheeks. In cases of execution, the victim was usually strangled and thereafter burned at the stake.

Witches were accused of a great variety of crimes. A common offence was to bewitch milch cattle by turning their milk sour, or curtailing the supply, raising storms, stealing children from their graves, and promoting various illnesses. A popular device was to make a waxen image of their victim, thrust pins into it and sear it with hot irons, all of which their victim felt and at length succumbed. Upon domestic animals they cast an evil eye, causing emaciation and refusal to take food till at length death ensued. To those who believed in them and acknowledged their power, witches were supposed to use their powers for good by curing disease and causing prosperity. Witches had a weekly meeting at which the devil presided, every Saturday commonly called "the witches' Sabbath," their meetings generally being held in desolate places or in ruined churches, to which they rode through the air mounted on broomsticks. If the devil was not present on their arrival, they evoked him by beating the earth with a fir-stick, and saying "Rise up foul thief." The witches appeared to see him in different guises; to some he appeared as a boy clothed in green, others saw him dressed in white, while to others he appeared mounted on a black horse. After delivering a mock sermon, he held a court at which the witches had to make a full statement of their doings during the week. Those who had not accomplished sufficient evil were beloboured with their own broomsticks, while those who had been more successful were rewarded with enchanted bones. The proceedings finished with a dance, the music to which the fiend played on his bagpipes. Robert Burns in his *Tale of Tam o' Shanter* gives a graphic description of this orgy. There were great annual gatherings at Candlemas, Beltane and Hallow-eve. These were of an international character at which the witch sisterhood of all nations assembled, those who had to cross the sea performing the journey in barges of egg-shell, while their aerial journeys were on goblin horses with enchanted bridles.

Witchcraft was first dealt with by law in *Scotland* when by a statute passed in 1563 in the Parliament of Queen Mary it was enacted: "That na maner of person nor persons of quhatsumever estaite, degree or condition they be of, take upon hand in onie times hereafter to use onie maner of witchcraft, sorcerie, or necromancie, under the paine of death, alsweil to be execute against the user, abuser, as the seeker of the response or consultation."

The great Reformer, John Knox, was accused by the Catholics of *Scotland* of being a renowned wizard and having by sorcery raised up saints in the churchyard of St. Andrews when Satan himself appeared and so terrified Knox's secretary that he became insane and died. Knox was also charged that by his magical arts in his old age he persuaded the beautiful young daughter of Lord Ochiltree to marry him. Nicol Burne bitterly denounces Knox for having secured the affections of "ane damosil of nobil blude, and he ane auld decrepit creatur of maist bais degree of onie that could be found in the country."

There were numerous trials for witchcraft in the Justiciary Court in Edinburgh and at the Circuit Courts, also session records preserved from churches all over *Scotland* show that numerous cases were dealt with by the local authorities and church officials.   A. J. B. G.

Rodgers, in his *Social Life in Scotland*, says: "From the year 1479 when the first capital sentence was carried out thirty thousand persons had on the charge of using enchantment been in Great Britain cruelly immolated; of these one fourth belonged to *Scotland*. No inconsiderable number of those who suffered on the charge of sorcery laid claim to necromantic acts with intents felonious or unworthy.

When James VI. of *Scotland*, in the year 1603, was

called upon to ascend the throne of Great Britain and Ireland, his own native kingdom was in rather a curious condition. James himself was a man of considerable learning, intimate with Latin and Theology, yet his book on Demonology marks him as distinctly superstitious; and, while education and even scholarship were comparatively common at this date in *Scotland*, more common in fact than they were in contemporary England, the great mass of Scottish people shared abundantly their sovereign's dread of witches and the like. The efforts of Knox and his doughty *confrères*, it is true, had brought about momentous changes in Scottish life, but if the Reformation ejected certain superstitions it undoubtedly tended to introduce others. For that stern Calvinistic faith, which now began to take root in Scotland, nourished the idea that sickness and accident are a mark of divine anger, nor did this theory cease to be common in the north till long after King James's day.

It is a pity that the royal author, in the curious treatise mentioned above, volunteers but few precise facts anent the practitioners of magic who throve in *Scotland* during his reign. But other sources of information indicate that these people were very numerous, and whereas, in Elizabethan England, it was customary to put a witch to death by the merciful process of hanging, in Jacobean *Scotland* it was usual to take stronger measures. In short, the victim was burnt at the stake; and it is interesting to note that on North Berwick Law, in the county of East Lothian, there is standing to this day a tall stone which, according to local tradition, was erstwhile used for the ghastly business in question. Yet it would be wrong to suppose that witches and sorcerers, though handled roughly now and then, were regarded with universal hatred; for in seventeenth century *Scotland* medicine and magic went hand in hand, and the man suffering from a physical malady, particularly one whose cause he could not understand, very seldom entrusted himself to a professional leech, and much preferred to consult one who claimed healing capacities derived from intercourse with the unseen world. Physicians of the latter kind, however, were generally experts in the art of poisoning; and, while a good many cures are credited to them, their triumphs in the opposite direction would seem to have been much more numerous. Thus we find that in July, 1702, a certain James Reid of Musselburgh was brought to trial, being charged not merely with achieving miraculous cures, but with contriving the murder of one David Libbertoun, a baker in Edinburgh. This David and his family, it transpires, were sworn enemies of a neighbouring household, Christie by name, and betimes their feud grew as fierce as that between the Montagues and Capulets; so the Christies swore they would bring things to a conclusion, and going to Reid they petitioned his nefarious aid. His first act was to bewitch nine stones, these to be cast on the fields of the offending baker with a view to destroying his crops; while Reid then proceeded to enchant a piece of raw flesh, and also to make a statuette of wax—the nature of the design is not recorded, but presumably Libbertoun himself was represented—and Mrs. Christie was enjoined to thrust the meat under her enemy's door, and then to go home and melt the waxwork before her own fire. These instructions she duly obeyed, and a little later the victim breathed his last; but Reid did not go unscathed, and after his trial the usual fate of burning alive was meted out to him.

A like sentence was passed in July 1605 on Patrick Lowrie, a native of Halic in Ayrshire, and known there as "Pat the Witch," who was found guilty of foregathering with endless sorceresses of the neighbourhood, and of assisting them in disinterring bodies which they afterwards

dismembered. Doubtless "Alloway's auld haunted Kirk," sacred to the memory of Burns, was among those ransacked for corpses by the band; yet if the crime was a gruesome one it was harmless withal, and assuredly Lowrie's ultimate fate was distinctly a hard one! On the other hand Isobel Griersone, a Prestonpans woman, received no more than justice when burnt to death on the Castle Rock, Edinburgh, in March 1607; for the record of her poisonings was a formidable one, rivalling that of Wainewright or that of Cellini himself, while it is even recorded that she contrived to put an end to several people simply by cursing them. Equally wonderful were the exploits of another sorceress, Belgis Todd of Longniddry, who is reported to have compassed the death of a man she hated just by enchanting his cat; but this picturesque *modus operandi* was scorned by a notorious Perthshire witch Janet Irwing, who about the year 1610 poisoned sundry members of the family of Erskine of Dun, in the county of Angus. The criminal was detected anon, and suffered the usual fate; while a few years later a long series of tortures, culminating in burning, were inflicted on Margaret Dein (née Barclay), whose accomplishments appear to have been of no commonplace nature. The wife of a burgess of Irvine, John Dein, this woman conceived a violent aversion for her brother-in-law, Archibald; and on one occasion, when the latter was setting out for France, Margaret hurled imprecations at his ship, vowing none of its crew or passengers would ever return to their native *Scotland*. Months went by, and no word of Archibald's arrival reached Irvine; while one day a pedlar named Stewart came to John Dein's house, and declared that the baneful prophecy had been duly fulfilled. The municipal authorities now heard of the affair, and arresting Stewart, whom they had long suspected of practising magic, they commenced to cross-examine him. At first he would tell nothing, but when torture had loosened his tongue he confessed how, along with Margaret Dein, he had made a clay model of the ill-starred barque, and thrown this into the sea on a particularly stormy night. His audience were horrified at the news, but they hastened to lay hands on the sorceress, whereupon they dealt with her as noted above.

No doubt this tale, and many others like it, have blossomed very considerably in the course of being handed down from generation to generation, and no doubt the witches of Jacobean *Scotland* are credited with triumphs far greater than they really achieved. At the same time, scanning the annals of sorcery, we find that a number of its practitioners avowed stoutly, when confronted by a terrible death, that they had been initiated in their craft by the foul fiend himself, or haply by a band of fairies; and thus, whatever capacities these bygone magicians really had, it is manifest that they possessed in abundance that confidence which is among the secrets of power, and is perhaps the very key to success in any line of action. Small wonder, then, that they were dreaded by the simple, illiterate folk of their day; and, musing on these facts, we feel less amazed at the credulity displayed by an erudite man like James VI.; we are less surprised at his declaring that all sorcerers "ought to be put to death according to the law of God, the civill and imperiale Law, and municipall Law of all Christian nations."

The last execution of a witch in *Scotland* took place in Sutherland in 1722. An old woman residing at Loth was charged amongst other crimes of having transformed her daughter into a pony and shod by the devil which caused the girl to turn lame both in hands and feet, a calamity which entailed upon her son. Sentence of death was pronounced by Captain David Ross, the Sheriff-substitute. Rodgers relates: "The poor creature when lead to the stake was unconscious of the stir made on her account, and warming her wrinkled hands at the fire kindled to consume her, said she was thankful for so good a blaze. For his rashness in pronouncing the sentence of death, the Sheriff was emphatically reproved."

The reign of ignorance and superstition was fast drawing to a close.

Witchcraft, if it can be so called nowadays, is dealt with under the laws pertaining to rogues, vagabonds, fortune-tellers, gamesters, and such like characters. (*See* **Fortune-telling.**)

Magic and Demonology.—Magic of the lower cultus, perhaps the detritus of Druidism, appears to have been common in *Scotland* until a late period. We find in the pages of Adamnan that the Druids were regarded by St. Columba and his priest as magicians, and that he met their sorcery with a superior celestial magic of his own. Thus does the religion of one race become magic in the eyes of another. Notices of sorcery in *Scotland* before the thirteenth century are scanty, if we except the tradition that Macbeth encountered three witches who prophesied his fate to him. We have no reason to believe that Thomas the Rhymer (who has been endowed by later superstition with adventures similar to those of Tannhauser) was other than a minstrel and maker of epigrams, or that Sir Michael Scot was other than a scholar and man of letters. Workers of sorcery were numerous but obscure, and although often of noble birth as Lady Glamis and Lady Fowlis, were probably very ignorant persons. We get a glimpse of Scottish demonology in the later middle ages in the rhymed fragment known as " The Cursing of Sir John Rowil," a priest of Corstorphine, near Edinburgh, which dates perhaps from the last quarter of the fifteenth century. It is an invective against certain persons who have rifled his poultry-yard, upon whom the priest calls down the divine vengeance. The demons who were to torment the evildoers are : Garog, Harog, Sym Skynar, Devetinus " the devill that maid the dyce," Firemouth, Cokadame, Tutivillus, Browny, and Syr Garnega, who may be the same as that Girnigo, to whom cross children are often likened by angry mothers of the Scottish working-classes, in such a phrase as " eh, ye're a wee girnigo," and the Scottish verb, to " girn," may find its origin in the name of a mediæval fiend, the last shadow of some Teutonic or Celtic deity of unlovable attributes. In Sym Skynar, we may have Skyrnir, a Norse giant in whose glove Thor found shelter from an earthquake, and who sadly fooled him and his companions. Skyrnir was, of course, one of the Jotunn or Norse Titans, and probably one of the powers of winter ; and he may have received the popular surname of " Sym " in the same manner as we speak of " Jack " Frost. A great deal has still to be done in unearthing the minor figures of Scottish mythology and demonology, and even the greater ones have not received the attention due to them. In Newhaven, a fishing district near Edinburgh, for example, we find the belief current in a fiend called Brounger, who is described as an old man who levies a toll of fish and oysters upon the local fisherman. If he is not placated with these, he wreaks vengeance on the persons who fail to supply him. He is also described as " a Flint and the son of a Flint," which proves conclusively that, like Thor and many other gods of Asia and America, he was a thunder or weather deity. In fact his name is probably a mere corruption of an ancient Scandinavian word meaning "to strike," which still survives in the Scottish expression to " make a breenge " at one. To return to instances of practical magic, a terrifying and picturesque legend tells how Sir Lewis Bellenden, a lord of session, and superior of the Barony of Broughton, near Edinburgh, succeeded by the aid of a sorcerer in raising the Devil in the backyard of his own house in the Canongate, somewhere about the end of the sixteenth century. Sir Lewis

was a notorious trafficker with witches, with whom his barony of Broughton was overrun. Being desirous of beholding his Satanic majesty in person, he secured the services of one Richard Graham. The results of the evocation were disastrous to the inquisitive judge, whose nerves were so shattered at the apparition of the Lord of Hades that he fell ill and shortly afterwards expired.

The case of Major Weir is one of the most interesting in the annals of Scottish sorcery. " It is certain," says Scott, " that no story of witchcraft or necromancy, so many of which occurred near and in Edinburgh, made such a lasting impression on the public mind as that of Major Weir. The remains of the house in which he and his sister lived are still shown at the head of the West Bow, which has a gloomy aspect, well suited for a necromancer. It was at different times a brazier's shop and a magazine for lint, and in my younger days was employed for the latter use ; but no family would inhabit the haunted walls as a residence ; and bold was the urchin from the High School who dared approach the gloomy ruin at the risk of seeing the Major's enchanted staff parading through the old apartments, or hearing the hum of the necromantic wheel, which procured for his sister such a character as a spinner.

" The case of this notorious wizard was remarkable chiefly from his being a man of some condition (the son of a gentleman, and his mother a lady of family in Clydesdale), which was seldom the case with' those that fell under similar accusations. It was also remarkable in his case that he had been a Covenanter, and peculiarly attached to that cause. In the years of the Commonwealth this man was trusted and employed by those who were then at the head of affairs, and was in 1649 commander of the City-Guard of Edinburgh, which procured him his title of Major. In this capacity he was understood, as was indeed implied in the duties of that officer at the period, to be very strict in executing severity upon such Royalists as fell under his military charge. It appears that the Major, with a maiden sister who had kept his house, was subject to fits of melancholic lunacy, an infirmity easily reconcilable with the formal pretences which he made to a high show of religious zeal. He was peculiar in his gift of prayer, and, as was the custom of the period, was often called to exercise his talent by the bedside of sick persons, until it came to be observed that, by some association, which it is more easy to conceive than to explain, he could not pray with the same warmth and fluency of expression unless when he had in his hand a stick of peculiar shape and appearance, which he generally walked with. It was noticed, in short, that when this stick was taken from him, his wit and talent appeared to forsake him. This Major Weir was seized by the magistrates on a strange whisper that became current respecting vile practices, which he seems to have admitted without either shame or contrition. The disgusting profligacies which he confessed were of such a character that it may be charitably hoped most of them were the fruits of a depraved imagination, though he appears to have been in many respects a wicked and criminal hypocrite. When he had completed his confession, he avowed solemnly that he had not confessed the hundredth part of the crimes which he had committed. From this time he would answer no interrogatory, nor would he have recourse to prayer, arguing that, as he had no hope whatever of escaping Satan, there was no need of incensing him by vain efforts at repentance. His witchcraft seems to have been taken for granted on his own confession, as his indictment was chiefly founded on the same document, in which he alleged he had never seen the devil, but any feeling he had of him was in the dark. He received sentence of death, which he suffered 12th April,

1670, at the Gallow-hill, between Leith and ˉEdinburgh. He died so stupidly sullen and impenitent as to justify the opinion that he was oppressed with a kind of melancholy frenzy, the consequence perhaps of remorse, but such as urged him not to repent, but to despair. It seems probable that he was burnt alive. His sister, with whom he was supposed to have had an incestuous connection, was condemned also to death, leaving a stronger and more explicit testimony of their mutual sins than could be extracted from the Major. She gave, as usual, some account of her connection with the queen of the fairies, and acknowledged the assistance she received from that sovereign in spinning an unusual quantity of yarn. Of her brother she said that one day a friend called upon them at noonday with a fiery chariot, and invited them to visit a friend at Dalkeith, and that while there her brother received information of the event of the battle of Worcester. No one saw the style of their equipage except themselves. On the scaffold this woman, determining, as she said, to die " with the greatest shame possible " was with difficulty prevented from throwing off her clothing before the people, and with scarce less trouble was she flung from the ladder by the executioner. Her last words were in the tone of the sect to which her brother had so long affected to belong : " Many," she said, " weep and lament for a poor old wretch like me ; but alas, few are weeping for a broken covenant."

Alchemy.—James IV. was attached to the science of alchemy. " Dunbar speaks of the patronage which the king bestowed upon certain adventurers, who had studied the mysteries of alchemy, and were ingenious in making ' quintiscence ' which should convert other metals into pure gold ; and in the Treasurer's Accounts there are numerous payments for the ' quinta essentia,' including wages to the persons employed, utensils of various kinds, coals and wood for the furnaces, and for a variety of other materials, such as quicksilver, aqua vitæ, litharge, auri, fine tin, burnt silver, alum, salt and eggs, saltpetre, etc. Considerable sums were also paid to several ' Potingairs ' for stuff of various kinds to the Quinta Essentia. Thus, on the 3rd of March, 1501, ' the king sent to Strivelin (Stirling) four Harry nobles in gold,'—a sum equal, as it is stated, to nine pounds Scots money—' for the leech to multiply.' On the 27th of May, 1502, the Treasurer paid to Robert Bartoun, one of the king's mariners, ' for certain droggis (drugs) brocht home by him to the French leich, £31 : 4 : 0.' On the 11th of February, 1503-4, we find twenty shillings given ' to the man suld mak *aurum potabile*, be the king's commands.' And on the 13th of October, 1507, the Treasurer paid six pounds for a puncheon of wine to the Abbot of Tungland, to ' mak Quinta Essentia.' The credulity and indiscriminate generosity of the Scottish monarch appear to have collected around him a multitude of quacks of all sorts, for, besides the Abbot, mention is made of ' the leech with the curland hair ' ; of ' the lang Dutch doctor,' of one Fullertone, who was believed to possess the secret of making precious stones ; of a Dr. Ogilvy who laboured hard at the transmutation of metals, and many other empirics, whom James not only supported in their experiments, but himself assisted in their laboratory. The most noted of these adventurers was the person who is variously styled in the Treasurer's Accounts ' the French Leich,' ' Maister John the French Leich,' ' Maister John the French Medicinar,' and ' French Maister John.' The real name of this empiric was John Damian ; and we learn from Dunbar that he was a native of Lombardy, and had practised surgery and other arts in France before his arrival in Scotland. His first appearance at the court of James was in the capacity of a French leech, and as he is mentioned among the persons who received ' leveray ' in

1501-2, there can be no doubt that he held an appointment as a physician in the royal household. He soon succeeded in ingratiating himself with the king, and it is probable that it was from him that James imbibed a strong passion for alchemy, as he about this time erected at Stirling a furnace for prosecuting such experiments, and continued during the rest of his reign to expend considerable sums of money in attempts to discover the philosopher's stone. ' Maister John,' says Bishop Lesley, ' caused the king believe, that he by multiplying and utheris his inventions sold make fine gold of uther metal, quhilk science he callit the Quintassence, whereupon the king made great cost, but all in vain.' There are numerous entries in the Treasurer's Accounts of sums paid for saltpetre, bellows, two great stillatours, brass mortars, coals, and numerous vessels of various shapes, sizes, and denominations, for the use of this foreign adept in his mystical studies. ' These, however, were not his sole occupations ; for after the mysterious labours of the day were concluded, Master John was wont to play at cards with the sovereign—a mode by which he probably transferred the contents of the royal exchequer into his own purse, as efficaciously as by his distillations.' We find that on the 4th of March, 1501, nine pounds five shillings were paid ' to the king and the French leich to play at cartis.' A few months later, on the occasion of a temporary visit which the empiric found it necessary to pay to France, James made him a present of his own horse and two hundred pounds. Early in the year 1504, the Abbot of Tungland, in Galloway, died, and the king, with a reckless disregard of the dictates of duty, and even of common decency, appointed this unprincipled adventurer to the vacant office. On the 11th March, the Treasurer paid ' to Gareoch Parsuivant fourteen shillings to pass to Tungland for the Abbacy to French Maister John.' On the 12th of the same month, ' by the king's command,' he paid ' to Bardus Altovite Lumbard twenty-five pounds for Maister John, the French Mediciner, new maid Abbot of Tungland, whilk he aucht (owed) to the said Bardus ; ' and a few days later on the 17th, there was given ' to Maister John the new maid Abbot of Tungland, seven pounds.' Three years after, in 1507, July 27, occurs the following entry : ' Item, lent, by the king's command to the Abbot of Tungland, and can nocht be gettin fra him £33 : 6 : 8.' An adventure which befel this dexterous impostor afforded great amusement to the Scottish court. On the occasion of an embassy setting out from Stirling to the court of France, he had the assurance to declare that by means of a pair of artificial wings which he had constructed, he would undertake to fly to Paris and arrive long before the ambassadors. ' This time,' says Bishop Lesley, ' there was an Italiane with the king, who was made Abbot of Tungland. This abbot tuke in hand to flie with wings, and to be in France before the said ambassadors ; and to that effect he caused make ane pair of wings of feathers, quhilk bein festinitt uponn him he flew off the castle-wall of Stirling ; but shortly he fell to the ground and broke his thie-bane ; but the wyte (blame) thereof he ascribed to their beand some hen feathers in the wings, quhilk yarnit, and coveted the myddin and not the skies.' This incident gave rise to Dunbar's satirical ballad entitled, ' Of the Fenyeit Friar of Tungland,' in which the poet exposes in the most sarcastic strain the pretensions of the luckless adventurer, and relates with great humour the result of his attempt to soar into the skies, when he was dragged to the earth by the low-minded propensities of the ' hen feathers,' which he had inadvertently admitted into the construction of his wings. The unsuccessful attempt of the abbot, though, according to Lesley, it subjected him to the ridicule of the whole kingdom, does not appear to have lost him the king's favour, for the Treasurer's books, from October, 1507, to

August, 1508, repeatedly mention him as having played at dice and cards with his majesty ; and on the 8th of September, 1508, ' Damiane, Abbot of Tungland,' obtained the royal permission to pursue his studies abroad during the space of five years. He must have returned to Scotland, however, before the death of James ; and the last notice given to this impostor is quite in character. On the 27th of March, 1513, the sum of twenty pounds was paid to him for his journey to the mine in Crawford Moor, where the king had at that time artisans at work searching for gold.'' From this reign to that of Mary no magician or alchemical practitioner of note appears to have existed in *Scotland*, and in the reign of James VI. too great severity was exhibited against such to permit of them avowing themselves publicly. In James's reign, however, lived the celebrated Alexander Seton (q.v.), of Port Seton near Edinburgh, known abroad as ' The Cosmopolite ' who is said to have succeeded in achieving the transmutation of metals.   L S.

Highlands.—Pagan *Scotland* appears to have been entirely devoid of benevolent deities. Those representatives of the spirit world who were on friendly terms with mankind were either held captive by magic spells, or had some sinister object in view which caused them to act with the most plausible duplicity. The chief demon or deity—one hesitates which to call her—was a one-eyed Hag who had tusks like a wild bear. She is referred to in folk tales as " the old wife " (Cailleach), " Grey Eyebrows " " the Yellow Muitearteach," etc., and reputed to be a great worker of spells. Apparently she figured in a lost creation myth, for fragmentary accounts survive of how she fashioned the hills, brought lochs into existence and caused whirlpools by vengeful operations in the sea. She is a lover of darkness, desolations and winter. With her hammer she alternately splinters mountains, prevents the growth of grass or raises storms. Numerous wild animals follow her, including deer, goats, wild boars. When one of her sons is thwarted in his love affairs by her, he transforms her into a mountain boulder " looking over the sea," a form she retains during the summer. She is liberated again on the approach of winter. During the Spring months the Hag drowns fishermen and preys on the food supply : she also steals children and roasts them in her cave. Her progeny includes a brood of monstrous giants each with several heads and arms. These are continually operating against mankind, throwing down houses, abducting women and destroying growing crops. Heroes who fight against them require the assistance of the witch who is called " Wise Woman," from whom they obtain magic wands. The witch of Scottish folk tales is the " friend of man," and her profession was evidently regarded in ancient times as a highly honourable one. Wizards also enjoyed high repute ; they were the witch-doctors, priests and magicians of the Scottish Pagans, and it was not until the sixteenth century that legal steps were taken to suppress them in the Highland districts. There was no sun-worship or moon-worship in *Scotland* ; neither sun nor moon were individualised in the Gælic language ; these bodies, however were reputed to exercise a magical influence. The moon especially was a " Magic Tank " from which supplies of power were drawn by those capable of performing requsite ceremonies. But although there were no lunar or solar spirits, there were numerous earth and water spirits. The " water wife," like the English " mere wife," was a greatly dreaded being who greedily devoured victims. She must not be confused with the Banshee, that Fate whose chief business it was to foretell disasters, either by washing blood-stained garments or knocking, knocking on a certain boulder beside a river, or in the locality where some great tragedy was impending. The water wife usually con-

fronted a late traveller at a ford. She claimed him as her own and if he disputed her claim, asked what weapons he had to use against her. The unwary one named each in turn, and when he did so the power to harm her passed away. One story of this character runs : " The wife rose up against the smith who rode his horse, and she said, " I have you : what have you against me ? " " My sword," the man answered. " I have that," she said, " what else ? " " My shield," the man said. " I have that and you are mine." " But," protested the man, " I have something else." " What is that ? " the water wife demanded. To this question the cautious smith answered, " I have the long, grey, sharp thing at my thigh." This was his dirk, and not having named it, he was able to make use of it. As he spoke he flung his plaid round the water wife and lifted her up on his horse behind him. Enclosed in the magic circle she was powerless to harm him, and he rode home with her, deaf to her entreaties and promises. He took her to his smithy and tied her to the anvil. That night her brood came to release her. They raised a tempest and tore the roof off the smithy, but the smith defied them. When day dawned they had to retreat. Then he bargained with the water wife, and she consented if he would release her that neither he nor any of his descendants should ever be drowned in any three rivers he might name. He named three and received her promise, but as she made her escape she reminded him of a fourth river. " It is mine still," she added. In that particular river the smith himself ultimately perished." To this day fishermen will not name either the fish they desire to procure or those that prey on their catches. Haddocks are " white bellies," salmon " red ones," and the dog-fish " the big black fellow." It is also regarded unlucky to name a minister, or refer to Sunday, in a fishing boat—a fact which suggests that in early Christian times fishermen might be pious churchmen on land but continued to practise paganism when they went to sea, like the Icelandic Norsemen who believed that Christ ruled their island, and Thor the ocean. Fairies must not be named on Fridays or at Hallowe'en, and Beltain (May Day) when charm fires were lit.

Earth worship, or rather the propitiation of earth spirits, was a prominent feature of Scottish paganism. There again magic played a leading role. Compacts were confirmed by swearing over a piece of turf, certain moors or mounds were set apart for ceremonial practices, and these were visited for the performance of child-procuring and other ceremonies which were performed at a standing stone. In cases of sickness a divination cake was baked and left at a sacred place ; if it disappeared during the night, the patient was supposed to recover ; if it remained untouched until the following morning it was believed that the patient would die. This practice is not yet obsolete. Offerings were constantly made to the earth spirits. In a witch trial recorded in Humbie Kirk Session Register (23rd September, 1649) one Agnes Gourlay is accused of having made offerings of milk, saying, " God betuch ws to ; they are wnder the yird that have as much need of it as they that are above the yird " ; *i.e.*, " God preserve us too ; they are under the earth that have as much need of it as they that are above the earth." The milk poured out upon the earth at magical ceremonies was supposed to go to the fairies. Gruagach stones have not yet entirely vanished in the Highlands. These are flat stones with deep " cup " marks. After a cow is milked, the milker pours into a hole the portion of milk required by the Gruagach, a long-haired spirit who is usually " dressed like a gentleman." If no offering is given to him, the cream will not rise on the milk, and, if it does the churning will be a failure. There are interesting records in the Presbytery records of Dingwall, Ross-shire, regarding the prevalence of milk pouring and other ceremonies during the seventeenth century. Among the "abominations" referred to are those for which Gairloch parish continued to be notorious—"frequent approaches to some ruinous chappels and circulateing them; and that future events in reference especiallie to lyfe and death, in takeing of Journeyes, was exspect to be manifested by a holl (hole) of a round stone quherein (wherein) they tryed the entering of their heade, which' (if they) could doe, to witt, be able to put in their heade, they exspect thair returning to that place, and failing they considered it ominous." Objection was also taken by the horrified Presbytery to "their adoring of wells and superstitious monuments and stones," and to the "sacrifice of bulls at a certaine tyme upon the 25 of August" and to "pouring milk upon hills as oblationes."

The seer was usually wrapped in the skin of a sacrificed bull and left lying all night beside a river. He was visited by supernatural beings in the darkness and obtained answers regarding future events. Another way to perform this divination ceremony was to roast a live cat. The cat was turned on a spit until the "Big Cat" (the devil) appeared and either granted the wish of the performer of the ceremony, or foretold what was to take place in answer to a query. At the present day there are many surviving beliefs regarding witchcraft, fairies, the evil eye, second sight and magical charms to cure or injure.

Individuals, domesticated animals and dwellings are charmed against witchcraft by iron and certain herbs or berries. The evil eye influence is dispelled by drinking "water of silver" from a wooden bowl or ladle. The water is taken from a river or well of high repute; silver is placed in it; then a charm is repeated, and when it has been passed over a fire, the victim is given to drink and what remains is sprinkled round the hearth-stone with ceremony which varies in districts. Curative charms are handed down in families from a male to a female and a female to a male. Blood-stopping charms are still regarded with great sanctity and the most persistent collectors have been unable to obtain them from those who are reported to be able to use these with effect. Accounts are still given of "blood-stopping" from a distance. Although the possessor of the power has usually a traditional charm, he or she rarely uses it without praying also. Some Highland doctors bear testimony in private to the wonderful effects of "blood-stopping" operations. A few years ago a medical officer of Inverness-shire stated in his official report to the County Council that he was watching with interest the operations of "King's Evil Curers" who still enjoy great repute in the Western Isles. These are usually "seventh sons." "Second-sight," like the power to cure and stop blood, runs in families. There is not a parish in the Scottish Highlands without its family in which one or more individuals are reputed to have occult powers. Some have visions either while awake or asleep. Others hear ominous sounds on occasions and are able to understand what they signify. Certain individuals confess, but with no appreciation of the faculty, that they are sometimes, not always, able to foretell that a person is likely to die ere long. Two instances of this kind may be given. A younger brother caught a chill. When an elder brother visited him he knew at once the young man would die soon, and communicated a statement to that effect to a mutual friend. According to medical opinion the patient who was not confined to bed, was in no danger, but three months afterwards he developed serious symptoms and died suddenly. When intelligence of the death was communicated to the elder brother he had a temporary illness. The same individual met a gentleman in a friend's house and had a similar experience: he "felt" he could not explain how, that this man was near death. On two

occasions within the following week he questioned the gentleman's daughter regarding her father's health and was informed that he was "as usual." The daughter was surprised at the inquiries. Two days after this meeting the gentleman in question expired suddenly while sitting in his chair. Again the individual, on hearing of the death, had a brief but distressing illness, with symptoms usually associated with shock. The mother of this man has a similar faculty. On several occasions she has seen lights. One day during the Boer War an officer passing her door bade her good-bye as he had been ordered to South Africa. She said, "He will either be slain or come back deformed," and turned ill immediately. A few months afterwards the officer was wounded in the lower jaw with a bullet and returned home with his face much deformed.

The "Second-sight" faculty manifests itself in various ways, as these instances show, and evidence that it is possessed by individuals may occur only once or twice in a lifetime. There are cases, however, in which it is constantly active. Those who are reputed to have the faculty are most reticent regarding it, and appear to dread it. At the close of the nineteenth century tow-charms to cure sprains and bruises were sold in a well-known Highland town by a woman who muttered a metrical spell over each magic knot she tied as the afflicted part was treated by her. She had numerous patients among all classes. Bone-setters still enjoy high repute in localities: not many years ago a public presentation was made to a Ross-shire bone-setter in recognition of his life-long services to the community. His faculty was inherited from his forbears.

Numerous instances may be gleaned in the Highlands of the appearance of the spirits of the living and the dead. The appearance of the spirit of a living person is said to be a sure indication of the approaching death of that individual. It is never seen by a member of the family, but appears to intimate friends. Sometimes it speaks and gives indication of the fate of some other mutual acquaintance.   DONALD MACKENZIE.

Scott, David and William Bell: These brothers, of whom *David* is by far the more important, certainly deserve a place in this volume. Born at Edinburgh in 1777, *David* lived a comparatively uneventful life, his lofty gifts being quite unrecognised by his contemporaries, and his death in 1849 being hastened in some degree by this persistent neglect. Nowadays, however, connoisseurs in Scotland are beginning to appreciate him, perceiving in his output technical merits far transcending those of Raeburn himself; while people who care for art dealing with the supernatural are coming to see, slowly but surely, that Scott's *Paracelsus* and *Vasco de Gama* are in the forefront of work of this kind; and that his beautiful drawings for *The Ancient Mariner* render the very spirit of Coleridge, the arch-mystic, render it with a skill unsurpassed in any previous or subsequent illustrations to the poem.

William Bell Scott was also a native of Edinburgh, being born there in 1811, and his career was very different from *David's*, for he won worldly success from the first, and ere his death in 1890 had received many laurels. Etching some of his brother's works, and painting a host of pictures, he was also a voluminous writer; and his *Autobiography* contains some really valuable comments on the mystic symbolism permeating the painting of the middle-ages, and embodies also a shrewd and interesting account of Rossetti's essays in table-turning and kindred practices. Moreover, *William Bell's* poems are almost all of a metaphysical order; and though it is extravagant to call him "the Scottish Blake," as many people have done, his mystical verse undoubtedly reflects a certain "meditative beauty," as Fiona Macleod once wrote on the subject.

Scott or Scot, Michael: Scottish Astrologer and Magician (1175–1234). Though *Michael Scott's* life is wrapped in obscurity his name is rather a familiar one, various causes having brought this about. In the first place, Dante refer to him in his *Inferno*, speaking of him as one singularly skilled in magical arts; while he is also mentioned by Boccaccio, who hails him as among the greatest masters of necromancy. Moreover, Coleridge projected a drama dealing with *Michael*, whom he asserted was a much more interesting personality than Faustus; and then there is a novel about him by Allan Cunningham, while, above all, he figures in *The Lay of the Last Minstrel*. And Sir Walter Scott, no very careful antiquarian, identifies the astrologer with one *Sir Michael Scott* of Balwearie, who, along with Sir David Wemyss of Wemyss, went to bring the Maid of Norway to Scotland in 1290; but this identification is manifestly wrong, for in a poem by Vincent de Beauvais published so early as 1235, *Michael* is mentioned as lately deceased. Of course this does not vitiate the idea that he emanated from the family of Balwearie, whose estates were situate near Kirkcaldy, in Fife; and it is almost certain indeed, that he was a man of gentle birth, it being recorded that he studied at Oxford university, where it is improbable he would have gone had his parents not been in comparatively affluent circumstances. When his Oxonian days were over *Michael* proceeded to the Sorbonne at Paris, where he acquired the title of *mathematicus*; and from the French capital he wandered on to Bologna, in those days famous as a seat of learning. He did not tarry here for long, however, but went to Palermo; while subsequently he settled for a while at Toledo, for he was anxious to study Arabic, and that town afforded good facilities therefor. He appears to have been successful with these studies, mastering the intricacies of the Arabic tongue thoroughly; yet there was nothing to induce him to continue in Spain, and accordingly he went to Sicily, where he became attached to the court of Ferdinand II., probably in the capacity of state-astrologer. At least, he is so designated in an early manuscript copy, now in the Bodleian Library, of his book on astronomy; yet it is clear that, at some time or other, *Michael* had espoused holy orders. For in 1223 the Pope, Honorius III., wrote to the Archbishop of Canterbury, urging him to procure an English benefice for *Scott*, while it appears that in the following year the Archbishopric of Cashel in Ireland was offered to him, and that he declined this on account of his total ignorance of the Erse language. This refusal to take a post for which he was unsuited reflects great credit on him, and it is patent that he was highly esteemed at the Vatican, for in 1227 Gregory IX., successor of Honorius, made further overtures to the English primate on behalf of *Michael*; and, whether these proved fruitful or not, according to Roger Bacon the necromancer came to England in 1230, bringing with him the works of Aristotle—at that date virtually unknown in this country—and contriving to give them a certain popularity amongst scholars.

It is reasonable to suppose that *Michael*, having come to England, also paid a visit to his native Scotland. And, though no documentary evidence is forthcoming to support this theory, local tradition at Melrose contends that the astrologer came to that town in his old age, and that he died there and was buried somewhere in the neighbourhood. Various other places in the Borders likewise claim this distinction, and Sir Walter Scott tells that, throughout the south of Scotland, " any great work of great labour or antiquity is ascribed either to Auld Michael, Sir William Wallace, or the Devil." One popular story about the necromancer maintains that he used to ride through the air on a demon horse, and another that he was wont to sail the seas on the back of some fabulous animal; while yet a further legend recounts that he went as Scottish envoy to the king of France, and that the first stamp of his black steed's horse rang the bells of Notre Dame, whereupon his most Christian majesty granted the messenger all he desired.

As regards the writings of *Michael*, he is credited with a translation of Aristotle's *De Animalibus*, but the ascription is not very well founded. However, it is almost certain that he wrote *Quæsto Curiosa de Natura Solis et Lunae*, which is included in the *Theatrum Chemicum*; while he was undoubtedly author of *Mensa Philosophica*, published at Frankfort in 1602; and also of *Liber Physiognomiæ Magistri Michaelis Scot*, a book which was reprinted nearly twenty times, and was translated into various languages. Reference has already been made to a manuscript in the Bodleian Library attributed to *Michael*, and it behoves to add here that at Corpus Christi College, Oxford, at the Vatican and at the Sorbonne, there are further documents purporting to have been penned by the astrologer himself, to have been written at his dictation, or to have been copied out by scribes soon after the actual author's decease.

Screech Owl: The cry of the *screech owl* at midnight is said to portend evil.

Sea Phantoms and Superstitions: Sailors as a class are invariably superstitious, while their predilection herein is shared in general by fishermen, and others who dwell by the marge of the great deep. The old songs of the outer Hebrides are full of wizardry, and this figures too in many a chanty composed by bygone seamen; while Captain Marryat, a writer who understood sailors as few others have done, testified repeatedly to their firm belief in the supernatural. Nor is he the only author who has dealt with this, for, not to mention less notable names, Coleridge touched on the matter in his poem of the Ancient Mariner; while turning from literature to painting, that exquisite Scottish master David Scott, in a memorable canvas now domiciled in the seaport town of Leith, shows Vasco de Gama and his henchmen gazing thunderstruck at an apparition rising from the waves. And it is scarcely surprising, after all, that credulity, in this relation should be a salient characteristic of sailors, the mere fact that they live in constant danger of sudden death constituting a good explanation and apology. In the duchy of Cornwall, so rich in romantic associations of all sorts, quite a number of stories concerning marine spectres have been handed down from generation to generation, and are current and even popular to this day. One of these stories relates how, on a winter's evening when a fierce gale was raging round the Cornish headlands, a fisherman chanced to see a ship in distress; and away the man hastened at once, calling on some of his fellows to come and aid him in the work of rescuing the perishing. In a few minutes a rowing boat had been manned, for Cornish fisherfolk are accustomed to go afloat in all weathers and to face the peril of drowning while very soon the gallant rescuers were almost within earshot of the distressed vessel, and could see her name clearly on the stern. They thought to jump on board, their idea being that, were the ship blest with a skilful pilot acquainted with the dangers of the coast, she might be steered safely into Falmouth harbour; but, just as one of the fishermen stood up in the prow of the boat with intent to throw a rope, the great vessel looming before him disappeared from sight altogether. She could not have sunk, for had that been her fate, some relics thereof must certainly have survived upon the seething foam and billows; and, vowing that the devil had conjured up a phantom to induce them to put out to sea, the rowers put their boat about speedily, and pulled for home with might and main. One and all, they were more afraid of the evil one's machinations than of the more genuine perils they were encountering; and an analogous, but more reasonable form of credulity on the part of the Cornish fisherfolk is instanced by another of their traditions, one associated with the village of Sennen Cove. This place is situate at the head of a bay flanked by two mighty capes. Sometimes a band of misty vapour stretches right across the bay, obscuring the villagers' outlook towards the sea beyond ; and whenever this occurs the fisherfolk regard it with awe, believing that it warns them not to put out in their boats. At one time, so it is recorded in the neighbourhood, Sennen Cove numbered among its inhabitants a group of doughty spirits who, wont to laugh at this superstition, were minded to demonstrate its absurdity ; and accordingly, when the warning band of vapour next made its appearance, they sailed off singing gaily. But their boat never returned, their fate remained a mystery ; and in fine they contrived to strengthen rather than weaken the belief they had ridiculed.

Scotland also has her stories of phantom barques. Near Ballachulish, on the west coast of Argyllshire, there is a rocky island on which the Macdonalds of Glencoe were wont to bury their honoured and laurelled dead ; and the lore of the district tells that once, some hundreds of years ago, a skiff bearing a beloved chieftain's corpse to this place of interment foundered ere reaching its destination. A horrible thing was this thought the Macdonalds, a horrible thing that the father of the clan should be swept from sea to sea, and be denied a resting-place beside his ancestors ; while anon it appeared as though the affair had verily been contrived by supernatural agency, for invariably, just before any misfortune overtook the tribe of Macdonald, the wrecked skiff was seen drifting about the sea, its dead oarsman clinging to it, and a coffin floating in its wake. Only too often this weird vision appeared, and it is said that, on the eve of the massacre of Glencoe, the spectre boat bore a crew of ghostly female mourners who sang a loud coronach, their wails reverberating far among the neighbouring mountains.

Another Highland story contends that a large ship, wrecked off the coast of Ross at the time of the first transportation of Celts to Canada, still rises occasionally from the waves which erstwhile claimed it as their prey, and, after sailing gallantly for a few minutes, suddenly lurches and sinks beneath the ocean ; while dwellers by the shores of the Solway tell how a certain craft, which went down there while conveying a gay bridal party towards Stranraer, is frequently seen driving at full speed before the gale, the bride and bridegroom clinging to the rigging as though in terror of immediate death by drowning. Nor is this the only phantom wherein the Solway rejoices, for that proverbially treacherous firth, round which Sir Walter Scott has cast so potent a halo of romance in *Redgauntlet*, witnessed once upon a time the foundering of two Scandinavian pirate-vessels, and these are said to rise periodically from the water, the fierce and murderous crew of each calling the while for the mercy which they themselves never accorded their victims.

Bidding adieu to British legends, and looking further afield, we find that religion plays a prominent part in stories of spectre ships. At Boulogne, for example, there is a tradition to the effect that on one occasion, at a remote date in the middle ages, the townspeople were desirous of building a church, for at this time they were without any public place of worship ; but, anxious as they were to choose a site which the Almighty would approve, they found it difficult to come to a decision on this head, everyone suggesting a different place. Finally, in despair, a body of them assembled on the beach, intending to offer up prayer for a solution to the problem ; and while they were engaged thus they happened to look out to sea, when lo ! a vessel was seen sailing towards them, the sacred Virgin herself on board. Standing erect in the bows, she pointed with her hand in a certain direction ; and the devout people realised at once that their petition had been answered whereupon the mysterious phantom vanished as quickly as it had come. Another French spectre-ship, however, was wont to remain in sight for longer periods, while its appearance invariably struck terror into the hearts of all who beheld it. Small wonder too, the vessel being manned by a crew of demons and great dogs—the perjured souls of men who had been guilty of fearful crimes ; yet the pious knew that in reality they had little to fear, the priests having told them that the repetition of a *paternoster* was adamantine proof against molestations from the hideous vision. Somewhat akin to this story is one associated with Venice, where, one stormy evening about the middle of the fourteenth century, a fisherman was requested to row three saints to a neighbouring village on the Adriatic ; and, after bending to his oars for a while, he suddenly stopped and gazed as though petrified, a galley filled with swarthy Saracens having risen beside his boat. The oarsman vowed he would put back with all speed, but his godly passengers bade him be of good cheer, and while they sang an *ave maria* the ominous galley was submerged by the hungry waves. So the fisherman rowed forward and reached his haven, the three saints rewarded him with a present of a gold ring, and that is why that article figures in the old coat-of-arms of the Venetian Republic.

Go where we will, to countries fringed or intersected by the sea, we find stories like this, or something like it. In Japan there are tales of phantom junks, and the Chinaman still paints a pair of great eyes on the prow of his craft, thinking that these will detect any monsters which chance to be prowling afloat ; while even on the coasts of America, usually considered so very prosaic a land, traditions anent spectral vessels prevail to this day. Kindred stories are known in the Ionian Islands, and the folk-lore of Shetland embodies a wealth of matter of this sort ; while round about the serried coast of Denmark, and the windswept fiords of Norway, many a phantom barque is supposed to hover ; and indeed it was on the North Sea that the most famous of all supernatural ships was wont to sail, the ship known to us as "The Flying Dutchman," and to the Germans as "Der Fliegende Holländer." A sailor, so goes the romance, had loved a maiden not wisely but too well, and having wronged her he grew weary of the *liaison*, left his sweetheart to languish, and put forth on the high seas where he committed many flagrant acts of piracy. But he was not to go unrequited, and the fates condemned him to sail wearily and everlastingly from shore to shore, this punishment to be endured till he should contrive to win the staunch affection of a virtuous woman and prove faithful to her. So the wayfarer's barque was driven hither and thither, the guilty man longed to tread solid ground once more ; but whenever he dared to put in to port, and commenced paying addresses to one whom he thought might be able to save him, the devil soon placed him on board ship again, and his interminable voyage commenced afresh. Century after century went past in this fashion, the ill-starred barque gradually becoming familiar to all who sailed upon the grey North Sea, or dwelt by its shores ; and the legend was not destined to dwindle away before the onslaughts of incoming cilivisation, for betimes a great artist arose to give a new and more genuine immortality to the story. Yes ! Richard Wagner evolved from it a mighty drama ; and sometimes, as we listen to his music—charged so abundantly with the weirdness, mystery and glamour of the surging ocean—we can verily picture the Dutchman's craft driving before a fearsome gale, and see the criminal sitting terror-struck and hopeless at his useless helm.

Seal of Solomon : (*See* **Magic.**)

Seance : A sitting held for the purpose of communicating with the dead, an essential requirement being that at least one member of the company be possessed of mediumistic powers. (*See* **Medium.**) Antiquity furnishes many examples of what may be called "séances"—*e.g.*, Saul's consultation with the Witch of Endor—but the term is generally used only in connection with modern spiritualism. When, in 1848, the Fox family at Hydesville called in their neighbours to listen to the mysterious sounds which have since become famous as the "Rochester Rappings," the gathering was too informal to be called a *séance*, though all the necessary elements were present ; but within the next two or three years the contagion spread throughout a large part of the eastern states, many "circles" (q.v.) were formed, and the phenomena which was in the first instance apparently spontaneous was now deliberately induced. In the early stages of the movement these *séances* were conducted by private mediums, who took no fee for their performances, but later professional mediums arose whose *séances* were open to the public on the payment of a fee. Both public and private *séances* continued, and still continue, to be an indispensable feature of spiritualism.

Besides the presence of a medium there are other conditions which must be observed if the *séance* is to be productive of phenomena. The chief of these is, perhaps, the darkness or semi-darkness of the séance-room, though this is by no means an invariable condition. The reason given by spiritualists is that light interferes with the manifestations of the spirits, though a less charitable construction is sometimes put upon the insistent demand for darkness. Sometimes the actual *séance* is preceded by playing or singing, a proceeding which one of Home's sitters states "always gave us a good *séance*." That this playing and singing was not without its purpose we may readily infer, for a state of expectancy and increased receptivity might easily be induced thereby, and it may be recalled, *en passant*, that D'Eslon and other disciples of Mesmer enjoined their patients to sing, or had some instrument played while the patients were seated around the *baquet*, or magnetic tub. To return to the *séance* ; the sitters take their places around a table and join hands, thus forming a "chain." The Baron de Guldenstubbé, in giving directions for the forming of a circle and the conducting of a *séance*, says : "In order to form a chain, the twelve persons each place their right hand on the table and their left hand on that of their neighbour, thus making a circle round the table. Observe that the medium or mediums, if there be more than one, are entirely isolated from those who form the chain." Dr. Lapponi, in his *Hypnotism and Spiritism*, says : "He (the medium) then invites some of his assistants to place their hands on the table in the following manner. The two thumbs of each person are to be touching each other, and each little finger is to be in communication with the little fingers of the persons on either side. He himself completes the *chain* with his two hands. The hands of all together rest on the edge of the table." Sometimes, again, as in the *séances* for table-turning and talking, the chain is formed simply by all the operators placing their finger-tips on the table. When the spirits have announced their presence by raps, tilting of the table, and so on, the chain may or may not be broken, but so long as it remains unbroken the sitters are entirely at the mercy of the spirits.

The phenomena which are thereafter witnessed are so diverse and varied that scarcely any account of a *séance* precisely matches another in detail, yet undoubtedly they all belong to certain well-defined classes. In the sphere of "physical" phenomena we have the movements of furniture, beginning with the table round which the members of the circle are seated, and affecting, perhaps, all the furniture in the room. These antics of inanimate objects in the séance-room are often practically identical with the spontaneous outbreaks of the poltergeist. Then there are the levitations (q.v.) both of the human body and of furniture and inanimate things. We are told of heavy wardrobes being raised to the ceiling without visible agency, and of several mediums floating upwards in like manner. Elongation (q.v.) is another phenomenon of the séance-room, an increase or apparent increase, of from a few inches to a foot taking place in the medium's height. Locked doors and cupboards are opened without keys, and without any trace of violence. Apports (q.v.) of small objects—flowers, fruit, jewels, anything, in fact—are brought from a distance through closed doors and barred windows, or abstracted in mysterious fashion from sealed boxes. Inanimate things show in their actions an almost human intelligence. Heavy objects become light enough to be raised by the touch of a finger, light articles become so weighty that the combined force of all present will not suffice to lift them. The medium can hold live coals in his hand, or in his handkerchief, without either being burned. Instruments are played upon when no visible hand is near them, or music is produced from the empty air without any instruments at all. Luminous hands and faces float in the air, sometimes recognised by the sitters as belonging to deceased friends and relatives, and touchings and caresses are felt. A breeze suddenly springs up in the séance-room—though the doors and windows are still closed—and curtains and the clothes of the sitters are inflated. If the *séance* is an especially successful one, complete spirit forms may be materialised. If the latter manifestation is to be asked for, a small cabinet is usually provided, into which the medium retires. Soon afterwards the filmy spirit form or forms are seen to issue from the cabinet, and in them the sitters frequently behold lost friends or relatives. The spirit forms will move about the room, allow themselves to be touched, and will, on occasion, even converse with their friends in the flesh, and give away locks of their hair and fragments of their clothing. Again, the materialisation may take place in the open, a small luminous cloud being first perceived, which gradually develops into a complete human figure ; or, as has been known to happen, the spirit may seem to issue from the medium's side, and remain united to him by a gossamer filament. In most cases the head and chin are shrouded in white draperies, only a portion of the face being visible. (*See* **Materialisation.**)

The automatic or "psychical" phenomena are of a different nature. Certain manifestations, such as table-tiltings (q.v.), rapping (q.v.), and slate-writing (q.v.), where the communication does not apparently come through the medium's organism, partake of the character of both "physical" and "psychical" phenomena. Purely "psychical" manifestations are the automatic writing and speaking of the medium. Sometimes the latter falls spontaneously into a trance, and delivers spirit messages while in that state, or the medium may remain to all appearances in a normal condition. Not only writings and utterances, but drawings and musical compositions may be produced automatically, and though automatism of this sort is by no means confined to the séance-room it still plays a large part therein, and is especially in favour with the more serious-minded spiritualists, to whom communications from the spirit-world are of greater importance than the tricks of household furniture.

A representative account of one of the *séances* of D. D. Home (q.v.), is given by H. D. Jencken in *Human Nature,* February, 1867, as follows :

"Mr. Home had passed into the trance still so often witnessed, rising from his seat, he laid hold of an armchair, which he held at arms' length, and was then lifted about three feet clear of the ground ; travelling thus suspended in space, he placed the chair next Lord Adare, and made a circuit round those in the room, being lowered and raised as he passed each of us. One of those present measured the elevation, and passed his leg and arm under Mr. Home's feet. The elevation lasted from four to five minutes. On resuming his seat, Mr. Home addressed Captain Wynne, communicating news to him of which the departed alone could have been cognisant.

"The spirit form that had been seen reclining on the sofa, now stepped up to Mr. Home and mesmerised him; a hand was then seen luminously visible over his head, about 18 inches in a vertical line from his head. The trance state of Mr. Home now assumed a different character; gently rising he spoke a few words to those present, and then opening the door proceeded into the corridor; a voice then said:—'He will go out of this window and come in at that window.' The only one who heard the voice was the Master of Lindsay, and a cold shudder seized upon him as he contemplated the possibility of this occurring, a feat which the great height of the third floor windows in Ashley Place rendered more than ordinarily perilous. The others present, however, having closely questioned him as to what he had heard, he at first replied, 'I dare not tell you,' when, to the amazement of all, a voice said, 'You must tell; tell directly.' The Master then said, 'Yes; yes, terrible to say, he will go out at that window and come in at this; do not be frightened, be quiet.' Mr. Home now re-entered the room, and opening the drawing-room window, was pushed out demi-horizontally into space, and carried from one window of the drawing-room to the farthermost window of the adjoining room. This feat being performed at a height of about sixty feet from the ground, naturally caused a shudder in all present. The body of Mr. Home, when it appeared at the window of the adjoining room, was shunted into the room feet foremost—the window being only 18 inches open. As soon as he had recovered his footing he laughed and said, 'I wonder what a policeman would have said had he seen me go round and round like a teetotum!' The scene was, however, too terrible—too strange, to elicit a smile; cold beads of perspiration stood on every brow, while a feeling pervaded all as if some great danger had passed; the nerves of those present had been kept in a state of tension that refused to respond to a joke. A change now passed over Mr. Home, one often observable during the trance states, indicative, no doubt, of some other power operating on his system. Lord Adare had in the meantime stepped up to the open window in the adjoining room to close it—the cold air, as it came pouring in, chilling the room; when, to his surprise, he only found the window 18 to 24 inches open! This puzzled him, for how could Mr. Home have passed outside through a window only 18 to 24 inches open. Mr. Home, however soon set his doubts at rest; stepping up to Lord Adare he said, 'No, no; I did not close the window; I passed thus into the air outside.' An invisible power then supported Mr. Home all but horizontally in space, and thrust his body into space through the open window, head-foremost, bringing him back again feet foremost into the room, shunted not unlike a shutter into a basement below. The circle round the table having re-formed, a cold current of air passed over those present, like the rushing of winds. This repeated itself several times. The cold blast of air, or electric fluid, or call it what you may, was accompanied by a loud whistle like a gust of wind on the mountain top, or through the leaves of the forest in late autumn; the sound was deep, sonorous, and powerful in the extreme, and a shudder kept passing over those present, who all heard and felt it. This rushing sound lasted quite ten minutes, in broken intervals of one or two minutes. All present were much surprised; and the interest became intensified by the unknown tongues in which Mr. Home now conversed. Passing from one language to another in rapid succes-

sion, he spoke for ten minutes in unknown languages.

"A spirit form now became distinctly visible; it stood next to the Master of Lindsay, clad, as seen on former occasions, in a long robe with a girdle, the feet scarcely touching the ground, the outline of the face only clear, and the tones of the voice, though sufficiently distinct to be understood, whispered rather than spoken. Other voices were now heard, and large globes of phosphorescent lights passed slowly through the room."

The following extract is taken from an account of a *séance* held by Professor Lombroso with the famous Italian medium, Eusapia Paladino.

"After a rather long wait the table began to move, slowly at first,—a matter explained by the scepticism, not to say the positively hostile spirit, of those who were this night in a *séance* circle for the first time. Then little by little, the movements increased in intensity. M. Lombroso proved the levitation of the table, and estimated at twelve or fifteen pounds the resistance to the pressure which he had to make with his hands in order to overcome that levitation.

"This phenomenon of a heavy body sustained in the air, off its centre of gravity and resisting a pressure of twelve or fifteen pounds, very much surprised and astonished the learned gentleman, who attributed it to the action of an unknown magnetic force.

"At my request, taps and scratchings were heard in the table. This was a new cause for astonishment, and led the gentlemen to themselves call for the putting out of the candles in order to ascertain whether the intensity of the noises would be increased, as had been stated. All remained seated and in contact.

"In a dim light which did not hinder the most careful surveillance, violent blows were first heard at the middle point of the table. Then a bell placed upon a round table, at a distance of a yard to the left of the medium (in such a way that she was placed behind and to the right of M. Lombroso), rose into the air, and went tinkling over the heads of the company, describing a circle around our table where it finally came to rest."

At this *séance* members of the company also felt themselves pinched and their clothes plucked, and experienced the touchings of invisible hands on their faces and fingers. The accuracy of the account—written by M. Ciolfi—was testified to by Professor Lombroso himself.   M. J.

Second Sight: The faculty of foreseeing future events which is supposed to belong to certain individuals in the Scottish Highlands. The belief in *second sight* dates back to a very early period in the history of these regions, and is still very far from being extinct, even in the more accessible parts. Saving the name, there is but little in *second sight* that is peculiar to the Celts of Scotland, for it is allied to the clairvoyance, prophetic vision, soothsaying, and so on, which have existed from time immemorial in practically every part of the world. Yet the *second sight* has certain distinctive features of its own. It may, for instance, be either congenital or acquired. In the former case it generally falls to the seventh son of a seventh son, by reason, probably, of the potency of the mystic number seven. Sometimes a Highlander may find himself suddenly endowed with the mysterious faculty. A person gifted with *second sight* is said to be "fey." Generally there is no apparent departure from the normal consciousness during the vision, though sometimes a seer may complain of a feeling of disquiet or uneasiness. A vision may be communicated from one person to another, usually by contact, but the secondary vision is dimmer than that of the original seer. A frequent vision is that of a funeral, indicating that a death will shortly take place in the community. This is an instance of the *second sight* taking a symbolical turn, and perhaps this is its usual form.

Occasionally the apparition of the doomed man will be seen—his wraith, or double—while he himself is far distant. Another form frequently taken by the *second sight* is that of " seeing lights." The lights, too, may indicate death, but they may likewise predict lesser happenings, or have no significance at all. Thus a light is seen by two persons to hover above the " Big House," then to travel swiftly in the direction of the gamekeeper's cottage, where it remains stationary for a while. On the morrow the gamekeeper is dead. Again a farmer returning from the market is preceded the whole of the way by a ball of fire, rolling along the road ahead of him. This time, however, the light portends no alarming occurrence, and the excitement of the glen quickly subsides. The lower animals also are said to possess *second sight*, which is especially frequent among dogs and horses. Two men were travelling from Easdale to Oban on a stormy night. In traversing a short cut through a wood one of them died from fatigue and exposure. That night more than one horse had to be carefully led past the spot by his driver, who as yet knew nothing of the tragedy. Indeed most Highlanders believe that the faculty is common to all the lower animals, else why should they whine and bristle when there is nothing visible to human eyes, nothing audible to human ears ? Notwithstanding that the march of civilisation has caused the Highlander partly to conceal his occult beliefs, at least from the unbelieving Sassenach, the writer can vouch for the fact that in certain districts *second sight* is almost a commonplace, believed in even by those who avow that they are not in the least " superstitious."
M. J.

Secret Commonwealth of Elves : (*See* **Scotland.**)

Secret Fire : Described by Philostratus as issuing from a basin in a well on the hill Athanor. A blue vapour rises from the well, changing into all the colours of the rainbow. The bottom is strewn with red arsenic ; on it is the basin full of fire, and from it rises flame without smell or smoke. Two stone reservoirs are beside it, one containing rain, the other wind.

Secret of Secrets : (*See* **Kabala.**)

Secret Tradition : It has long been an article of faith with students of occultism that the secret tenets of the various sciences embraced within it have been preserved to modern times by a series of adepts, who have handed them down from generation to generation in their entirety. There is no reason to doubt this belief, but that the adepts in question existed in one unbroken line, and that they all professed similar principles is somewhat improbable. But one thing is fairly certain, and that is, that proficiency in any one of the occult sciences requires tuition from a master of that branch. All serious writers on the subject are at one as regards this. It is likely that in neolithic times societies existed among our barbarian ancestors, similar in character to the Midiwiwin of the North-American Indians, the snake-dancers of the Hopi of New Mexico, or the numerous secret societies of aboriginal Australians. This is inferred from the certainty that totemism existed amongst neolithic peoples. Hierophantic castes would naturally hand down the tradition of the secret things of the Society from one generation to another. The early mysteries of Egypt, Eleusis, Samothrace, Cabiri, and so forth were merely the elaboration of such savage mysteries. There would appear to have been throughout the ages, what might be called, a fusion of occult beliefs : that when the hierophants of one system found themselves in juxtaposition, or even in conflict, with the professors of another, the systems in question appear to have received much from one another. It has been said that when the ancient mysteries are spoken about, it should be understood that one and the same series of sacred ceremonies is intended, one and the same initiatory processes and revelations, and

that what is true of one applies with equal certainty to all the others. Thus Strabo records that the strange orgies in honour of the mystic birth of Jupiter resembled those of Bacchus, Ceres and Cybele ; and the Orphic poems identified the orgies of Bacchus with those of Ceres, Rhea, Venus and Isis. Euripides also mentions that the rites of Cybele are celebrated in Asia Minor in an identical manner with the Grecians mysteries of Dionysius and the Cretan rites of the Cabiri. The Rev. Geo. Oliver in his *History of Initiation* affirms that the rites of the science which is now received under the appellation of Freemasonry were exercised in the antediluvian world, received by Noah after the Flood, practised by man at the building of Babel, conveniences for which were undoubtedly contained in that edifice, and at the dispersion spread with every settlement already deteriorated by the gradual innovations of the Cabiric priests, and moulded into a form, the great outlines of which are distinctly to be traced in the mysteries of every heathen nation, and exhibit shattered remains of the one true system, whence they were derived. This theory is of course totally mischievous, and although there may have been likenesses between the rites of certain societies, the idea that all sprang from one common source is absurd. One thing, however, is fairly certain : anthropology permits us to believe that the concepts of man, religious and mystical, are practically identical in whatever part of the world he may exist, and there is every possibility that the similarity between early mysteries results in this manner, and that it brought about a strong resemblance between the mystical systems of the older world. We have satisfactory evidence that the ancient mysteries were receptacles of a great deal of occult wisdom, symbolism, magical or semi-magical rite, and mystical practice in general ; and we are pretty well assured that when these fell into desuetude among the more intellectual classes of the various countries in which they obtained, they were taken up and practised in secret by the lesser ranks of society, even the lowest ranks, who are in all ages the most conservative, and who clung faithfully to the ancient systems, refusing to partake in the rites of the religions which had ousted them. The same can be posited of magical practice. The principles of magic are universal, and there can be no reason to doubt that these were handed on throughout the long centuries by hereditary castes of priests, shamans, medicinemen, magicians, sorcerers, and witches. But the same evidence does not exist with regard to the higher magic, concerning which much more difficult questions arise. Was this handed on by means of secret societies, occult schools or universities, or from adept to adept ? We speak not of the sorceries of empirics and savages, but of that spiritual magic which, taken in its best sense, shades into mysticism. The schools of Salamanca, the mystic colleges of Alexandria, could not impart the great truths of this science to their disciples : its nature is such that communication by lecture would be worse than useless. It is necessary to suppose then that it was imparted by one adept to another. But it is not likely that it arose at a very early period in the history of man. In his early psychological state he would not require it ; and we see no reason for belief that its professors came into existence at an earlier period than some three or four thousand years B.C. The undisturbed nature of Egyptian and Babylonian civilisation leads to the belief that these countries brought forth a long series of adepts in the higher magic. We know that Alexandria fell heir to the works of these men, but it is unlikely that their teachings were publicly disseminated in her public schools. Individuals of high magical standing would however be in possession of the occult knowledge of ancient Egypt, and that they imparted this to the Greeks of Alexandria is certain. Later Hellenic and Byzantine magical theory is distinctly Egyptian in character, and we know that its esoteric forms were disseminated in Europe at a comparatively early date, and that they placed all other native systems in the background, where they were pursued in the shadow by the aboriginal witch and sorcerer. We have thus outlined the genealogy of the higher magic from early Egyptian times to the European mediæval period. Regarding alchemy, the evidence from analogy is much more sure, and the same may be said as regards astrology. These are sciences in which it is peculiarly necessary to obtain the assistance of an adept if any excellence is to be gained in their practice ; and we know that the first originated in Egypt, and the second in ancient Babylon. We are not aware of the names of those early adepts who carried the sciences forward until the days of Alexandria, but subsequent to that period the identity of practically every alchemical and astrological practitioner of any note is fully known. In the history of no science is the sequence of its professors so clear as is the case in alchemy, and the same might almost be said as regards astrology, whose protagonists, if they have not been so famous, have at least been equally conscientious. We must pass over in our consideration of the manner in which occult science survived, the absurd legends which presume to state how such societies as the Freemasons existed from antediluvian times ; and will content ourselves with stating that the probabilities are that in the case of mystical brotherhoods a long line of these existed from early times, the traditions of which were practically similar. Many persons would be members of several of these, and would import the conceptions of one society into the heart of another, as we know Rosicrucian ideas were imported into Masonry. (*See* **Freemasonry.**) We seem to see in the mystic societies of the middle ages reflections of the older Egyptian and classical mysteries, and there is nothing absurd in the theory that the spirit and in some instances even the letter of these descended to mediæval and perhaps to present times. Such organisations die much harder than any credit is given them for doing. We know, for example, that Freemasonry was revolutionised at one part of its career, about the middle of the seventeenth century, by an influx of alchemists and astrologers, who crowded out the operative members, and who strengthened the mystical position of the brotherhood, and it is surely reasonable to suppose that on the fall or desuetude of the ancient mysteries, their disciples, looking eagerly for some method of saving their cults from entire extinction, would join the ranks of some similar society, or would keep alive the flame in secret ; but the fact remains that the occult idea was undoubtedly preserved through the ages, that it was the same in essence amongst the believers in all religions and all mysteries, and that to a great extent its trend was in the one direction, so that the fusion of the older mystical societies and their re-birth as a new brotherhood is by no means an unlikely hypothesis. In the article on the " Templars " for example, we have tried to show the possibility of that brotherhood having received its tenets from the East, where it sojourned for such a protracted period. It seems very likely from what we learn of its rites that they were oriental in origin, and we know that the occult systems of Europe owed much to the Templars, who, probably, after the fall of their own Order secretly formed others or joined existing societies. Masons have a hypothesis that through older origins they inherited from the Dionysian artificers, the artizans of Byzantium, and the building brotherhoods of Western Europe. To state this dogmatically as a fact would not be to gain so much credence for their theory as is due to that concerning the dissemination of occult lore by the Templars ; but it is much more feasible in every way than the absurd legend

concerning the rise of Freemasonry at the time of the building of the Temple. Secret societies of any description possess a strong attraction for a certain class of mind, or else a merely operative handicraft society, such as was mediæval Masonry, would not have been utilised so largely by the mystics of that time. One of the chief reasons that we know so little concerning these brotherhoods in mediæval times is that the charge of dabbling in the occult arts was a serious one in the eyes of the law and the church, therefore they found it necessary to carry on their practices in secret. But after the Reformation, a modern spirit took possession of Europe, and the protagonists of the occult sciences came forth from their caverns and practised in the open light of day. In England, for example, numerous persons avowed themselves alchemists ; in Germany the " Rosicrucians " sent out a manifesto ; in Scotland, Seton, a great master of the hermetic art, arose : never had occultism possessed such a heyday. But it was nearly a century later until further secret societies were formed, such as the Academy of the Ancients and of the Mysteries in 1767 ; the Knights of the True Light founded in Austria about 1780 ; the Knights and Brethren of Asia, which appeared in Germany in the same year ; the Order of Jerusalem which originated in America in 1791 ; the Society of the Universal Aurora established at Paris in 1783. Besides being masonic, these societies practised animal magnetism, astrology, Kabalism and even ceremonial magic. Others were political, such as the Illuminati, which came to such an inglorious end. But the individual tradition was kept up by an illustrious line of adepts, who were much more instrumental in keeping alive the flame of mysticism than even such societies as those we have mentioned. Mesmer, Swedenborg, St. Martin, Pasqually, Willermoz, all laboured to that end. We may regard all these as belonging to the school of Christian magicians, as apart from those who practised the rites of the grimoires or Jewish Kabalism. The line may be carried back through Lavater, Eckartshausen, and so on to the seventeenth century. These men were mystics besides being practitioners of theurgic magic, and they combined in themselves the knowledge of practically all the occult sciences.

With Mesmer began the revival of a science which cannot be altogether regarded as occult, when consideration is given to its modern developments, but which powerfully influenced the mystic life of his and many later days. The mesmerists of the first era are in direct line with the Martinists and the mystical magicians of the France of the late eighteenth century. Indeed in the persons of some English mystics, such as Greatrakes, mysticism and magnetism are one and the same thing. But upon " Hypnotism," to give it its modern name, becoming numbered with the more practical sciences, persons of a mystical cast of mind appear to have, to a great extent, deserted it. Hypnotism does not bear the same relation to mesmerism and magnetism as modern chemistry does to alchemy ; but the persons who practise it nowadays are as dissimilar to the older professors of the science as is the modern practitioner of chemistry to the mediæval alchemist. This is symptomatic of the occult sciences, that they despise that knowledge which is " exact " in the common sense of the term. Their practitioners do not delight in labouring upon a science, the laws of which are already known, cut and dried. The student of occultism, as a rule, possesses all the attributes of an explorer. The occult sciences have from time to time deeply enriched the exact sciences, but these enrichments have been acts of intellectual generosity. It is in effect as if the occultist made a present of them to the scientist, but did not desire to be troubled with their future development in any way. Occultism of the higher sort therefore does not to-day possess any great interest in hypnotism, and modern mystics of standing scarcely recognise it as a part of the hidden mysteries. But there is no question that the early mesmerists formed a link between the adepts of eighteenth-century France and those of the present day. The occultists of to-day, however, are harking farther back: they recognise that their forerunners of the seventeenth and eighteenth centuries drew their inspiration from older origins, and they feel that these may have had cognisance of records and traditions that we wot not of. The recovery of these is perhaps for the moment the great question of modern magic. But apart from this, modern magic of the highest type strains towards mysticism, and partakes more than ever of its character. It disdains and ignores ceremonial, and exalts psychic experience. That is not to say that numerous bodies do not exist throughout the world for the celebration of magical rite; but such fraternities have existed from time immemorial, and their protagonists cannot be placed on a higher footing than the hallucinated sorcerers of mediæval times.

Secret Words: Certain words relating to the Eucharist were communicated by Christ to Joseph of Arimathea and were committed orally from keeper to keeper of the Graal. In Robert de Borron's metrical romance, material power is added to their spiritual efficacy and whoever could acquire and retain them, had a mysterious power over all around him, could not suffer by evil judgments, could not suffer deprivation of his own rights, need not fear the result of battle, provided his cause were good. The words were the secret of the Graal were either incommunicable in writing or were written only in the Book of the Graal which, de Borron implies, was itself written by Joseph of Arimathea. These words are the chief mystery of the Lesser Holy Graal, as the prose version of de Borron's poem is called. They were most probably a form of eucharistic consecration, and there is evidence that the Celtic church, following the example of the Eastern Church used them in addition to the usual consecration as practised in the Latin Church, which is merely a repetition of the New Testament account of the Lord's Supper. The separate clause they are supposed to have formed is called Epiclesis and consisted of an invocation of the Holy Ghost.

Seik Kasso: Evil spirits inhabiting trees. (*See* **Burma.**)

Seiktha: An evil spirit. (*See* **Burma.**)

Semites, The: This article on the *Semites* applies to the more ancient divisions of the race, such as the Babylonians and Assyrians, and the Hebrews in Biblical times. For later Semitic occultism see **Kabala, Arabs,** etc. In ancient Babylon, and Chaldea, magic was of course a department of priestly activity, and in Mesopotamia we find a sect of priests, the Asipu, set apart for the practice of magic, which in their case probably consisted of hypnotism, the casting out of demons, the banning of troublesome spirits and so forth. The Baru again were augurs who consulted the oracles on the future by the inspection of the entrails of animals and the flight of birds, " the observation of oil in water, the secret of Anu, Bel, and Ea, the tablet of the gods, the sachet of leather of the oracles of the heavens and earth, the wand of cedar dear to the great gods." These priests of Baru and Asipu were clothed in vestments peculiar to their rank, which they changed frequently during the ceremonies in which they took part. In the tablets we find kings making frequent enquiry through these priestly castes; and in a tablet of Sippar, we find treated the installation of a Baru to the Sun-temple, and also Sennachrib seeking through the Baru the causes of his father's violent death. The Asipu again were exorcists, who removed *tabus* and laid ghosts. We find an Asipu's functions set forth in the following poem:—

" Incantation:—

(The man) of Ea am I,
(The man) of Damkina am I,
The messenger of Marduk am I,
My spell is the spell of Ea,
My incantation is the incantation of Marduk,
The circle of Ea is in my hand,
The tamarisk, the powerful weapon of Anu,
In my hand I hold,
The date-spathe, mighty in decision,
In my hand I hold."

" Incantation:

He that stilleth all to rest, that pacifieth all,
By whose incantation everything is at peace,
He is the great Lord Ea,
Stilling all to rest, and pacifying all,
By whose incantation everything is at peace.
When I draw nigh unto the sick man
All shall be assuaged.
I am the magician born of Eridu,
Begotten in Eridu and Subari.
When I draw nigh unto the sick man
May Ea, King of the Deep, safeguard me!"

" Incantation:—

O Ea, King of the Deep, to see . . . . .
I, the magician, am thy slave.
March thou on my right hand,
Assist (me) on my left;
Add thy pure spell to mine,
Add thy pure voice to mine,
Vouchsafe (to me) pure words,
Make fortunate the utterances of my mouth,
Ordain that my decisions be happy,
Let me be blessed where'er I tread,
Let the man whom I (now) touch be blessed.
Before me may lucky thoughts be spoken.
After me may a lucky finger be pointed.
Oh that thou wert my guardian genius,
And my guardian spirit!
O God that blesseth, Marduk,
Let me be blessed, where'er my path may be!
Thy power shall god and man proclaim;
This man shall do thy service,
And I too, the magician thy slave."

" Unto the house on entering . . . .
Samas is before me,
Sin (is) behind (me),
Nergal (is) at (my) right hand,
Ninib (is) at my left hand;
When I draw near unto the sick man,
When I lay my hand on the head of the sick man,
May a kindly Spirit, a kindly Guardian, stand
at my side."

The third caste was the Zammaru, who sang or chanted certain ceremonials.

The lower ranks of sorcery were represented by the Kassapu and Kassaptu, the wizard and witch, who, as elsewhere, practised black magic, and who are stoutly combated by the priest-magician caste. We find in the code of Hammurabi a stringent law against the professors of black magic:—" If a man has charged a man with sorcery and has not justified himself, he who is charged with sorcery shall go to the river, he shall plunge into the river, and if the river overcome him, he who accused him shall take to himself his house. If the river makes that man to be innocent, and he be saved, he who accused him shall be put to death. He who plunged into the river shall take to himself the house of him who accused him." This will recall the test for a witch, that if thrown into a pond, if she sinks she is innocent, but if she floats she is a witch indeed. Another series of tablets deals with the black magician and the witch who are represented as roaming the streets, entering houses, and prowling through towns, stealing the love of men, and withering the beauty of women. The exorcist goes on to say that he has made an image of the witch, and he calls upon the fire-god to burn it. He seizes the mouth, tongue, eyes, feet, and other members of the witch, and piously prays that Sin may cast her into an abyss of water and fire, and that her face may grow yellow and green. He fears that the witch is directing a like sorcery against himself, that she sits making spells against him in the shade of the wall, fashioning images of him. But he sends against her the *haltappan* plant and sesame to undo her spells and force back the words into her mouth. He devoutly trusts that the images she has fashioned will assume her own character, and that her spells may recoil upon herself. Another tablet expresses the desire that the god of night may smite the witch in her magic, that the three watches of the night may loose her evil sorcery, that her mouth may be fat and her tongue salt, that the words of evil that she hath spoken may be poured out like tallow, and that the magic she is working be crumbled like salt. The tablets abound in magical matter and in them we have the actual wizardry in vogue at the time they were written, which runs at least from the seventh century B.C. onwards until the time when the cuneiform ceased to be used. Chaldean magic was renowned throughout the world, particularly, however, its astrological side. Isaiah says "Let now the astrologers, star-gazers, monthly prognosticators, stand up and save thee from the things that shall come upon thee." In the book of Daniel, we find the magicians called Chaldeans, and up to the present time occultists have never tired of singing the praises of the Chaldean magi. Strabo and Ælian allude to their knowledge of astrology, as did Diodorus Siculus, and it is supposed to have been a Chaldean magician Œthanes who introduced his science into Greece, which he entered with Xerxes.

The great library of Assurbanipal, king of Assyria, who died in 626 B.C., affords us first-hand knowledge of Assyrian magic. He gathered together numerous volumes from the cities of Babylonia, and storing them in his great library at Nineveh, had them copied and translated. In fact letters have been discovered from Assurbanipal to some of his officials, giving instructions for the copying of certain incantations. Many grimoires too come from Babylonia, written during the later empire,—the best known of which are the series entitled *Maklu*, burning ; *Utukki limnuti*, evil spirits ; *Labartu*, hag-demon ; and *Nis kati*, raising of the hand. There are also available many ceremonial texts which throw considerable light on magical practice. The *Maklu* for example contains eight tablets of incantations and spells against wizards and witches—the general idea running through it being to instruct the bewitched person how to manufacture figures of his enemies, and thus destroy them. The series dealing with the exorcism of evil spirits enumerates demons, goblins and ghosts, and consists of at least sixteen tablets. They are for the use of the exorcist in driving out devils from possessed people, and this is to be accomplished by invoking the aid of the gods, so that the demons may be laid under a divine *tabu*. The demon who possesses the unfortunate victim must be described in the most minute manner. The series dealing with the *Labartu* or hag-demon, who is a kind of female devil who delights in attacking children, gives directions for making a figure of the *Labartu* and the incantations to be repeated over it. The magician and philosopher appear to have worked

together in Assyria, for we find medical men constantly using incantations to drive out demons, and incantations are often associated with prescriptions. Medical magic indeed appears to have been of much the same sort as we find amongst the American Indians and peoples in a like barbarian condition of existence.

We find the doctrine of the Incommunicable Name established among the early Semites, as among the Egyptians : the secret name of a god, which when discovered gave the speaker complete power over him by its mere utterance. The knowledge of the name, or description, of the person or demon the magician directs his charm against, is also essential to success. Drugs also, to which were originally ascribed the power vouchsafed by the gods for the welfare of mankind, were supposed to aid greatly in exorcism. In Assyrian sorcery, Ea and Marduk are the most powerful gods,—the latter being appealed to as intermediary between man and his father, Ea : indeed the legend of Marduk going to his father for advice was commonly repeated in incantations. When working against an individual too, it was necessary to have something belonging to him,—clippings of his hair, or nails if possible. The possessed person was usually washed, the principal of cleansing probably underlying this ceremony. An incantation called the Incantation of Eridu was often prescribed, and this must relate to some such cleansing, for Eridu is the Home of Ea, the Sea-god. A formula for exorcising or washing away a demon, Rabesu states that the patient is to be sprinkled with clean water twice seven times. Of all water none was so sacred as the Euphrates, and water from it was frequently used for charms and exorcisms. Fumigation with a censor was also employed by the Assyrians for exorcism, but the possessed person was often guarded from the attack of fiends by placing him in the middle of an enchanted circle of flour, through which it was thought no spirit could break. Wearing the glands from the mouth of a fish was also a charm against possession. In making a magic circle, the sorcerer usually formed seven little winged figures to set before the god Nergal, with a long spell, which states that he has completed the *usurtu* or magic circle with a sprinkling of lime. The wizard further prays that the incantation may be performed for his patient by the god. This would seem to be a prototype of the circle in use amongst magicians of mediæval times. Says Campbell Thompson in his *Semitic Magic* :—

" Armed with all these things—the word of power, the acquisition of some part of the enemy, the use of the magic circle and holy water, and the knowledge of the magical properties of substances—the ancient warlock was well fitted for his trade. He was then capable of defying hostile demons or summoning friendly spirits, of driving out disease or casting spells, of making amulets to guard the credulous who came to him. Furthermore, he had a certain stock-in-trade of tricks which were a steady source of revenus. Lovesick youths and maidens always hoped for some result from his philtres or love-charms ; at the demand of jealousy, he was ever ready to put hatred between husband and wife ; and for such as had not the pluck or skill even to use a dagger on a dark night, his little effigies, pierced with pins, would bring death to a rival. He was at once a physician and wonder-worker for such as would pay him fee."

"Among the more modern *Semites* magic is greatly in vogue in many forms, some of them quite familiar to Europeans : indeed we find in the *Arabian Nights* edited by Lane, a story of old women riding on a broom-stick. Among Mahommedans the wizard is thought to deserve death by reason of the fact that he is an unbeliever. Witches are fairly common in Arabic lore, and we usually find them figuring as sellers of potions and philtres. The European witch is usually supposed to be able to leave her dwelling at night by sprinkling some of the ashes of the hearth on the forehead of her husband, whereby he sleeps soundly till the morning. This is identical with French mediæval practice. In Arab folk tales the *moghrebi* is the sorcerer who has converse with demons, and we find many such in the Old and New Testaments, as well as diviners and other practitioners of the occult arts. In the *Sanhedrin*, Rabbi Akiba defines an enchanter as one who calculates the times and hours, and other rabbis state that " an enchanter is he who grows ill when his bread drops from his mouth, or if he drops the stick that supports him from his hand, or if his son calls after him, or a crow caws in his hearing, or a deer crosses his path, or he sees a serpent at his right hand, or a fox on his left." The Arabs believe that magic will not work while he that employs it is asleep. Besides it is possible to over-reach Satan himself, and many Arabic tales exist in which men of wisdom and cunning have succeeded in accomplishing this. 'Iblis once sent his son to an assembly of honourable people with a flint stone, and told him to have the flint stone woven. He came in and said, " My father sends his peace, and wishes to have this flint stone woven." A man with a goat-beard said, " Tell your father to have it spun, and then we will weave it." The son went back, and the Devil was very angry, and told his son never to put forth any suggestion when a goat-bearded man was present, " for he is more devilish than we." Curiously enough, Rabbi Joshua ben Hananiah makes a similar request in a contest against the wise men of Athens, who have required .him to sew together the fragments of a broken millstone. He asks in reply for a few threads made of the fibre of the stone. The good folk of Mosul, too, have ever prided themselves on a ready wit against the Devil. Time was, as my servant related to me, when Iblis came to Mosul and found a man planting onions. They fell to talking, and in their fellowship agreed to divide the produce of the garden. Then, on a day when the onions were ready, the partners went to their vegetable patch and the man said, " Master, wilt thou take as thy half that which is above ground or that which is below ? " Now the Devil saw the good green shoots of the onions sprouting high, and so carried these off as his share, leaving the gardener chuckling over his bargain. But when wheat time came round, and the man was sowing his glebe on a day, the Devil looked over the ditch and complained that he had made nothing out of the compact. " This time, quoth he, we will divide differently, and thou shalt take the tops " ; and so it fell out. They visited the tilth together and when the corn was ripe, and the fellah reaped the field and took away the ears, leaving the Devil stubbing up the roots. Presently, after he had been digging for a month, he began to find out his error, and went to the man, who was cheerily threshing his portion. " This is a paltry quibble," said Iblis, " thou hast cozened me this twice." " Nay," said the former, " I gave thee thy desire ; and furthermore, thou didst not thresh out thine onion-tops, as I am doing this." So it was a sanguine Devil that sent away to beat the dry onion-stalks, but in vain ; and he left Mosul sullenly, stalking away in dudgeon, and stopping once in a while to shake his hand against so crafty a town. " Cursed be he, ye tricksters ! who can outmatch devilry like yours ? "

" In modern times in the East," says Mr. Thompson, " from Morocco to Mesopotamia, books of magic are by no means rare, and manuscripts in Arabic, Hebrew, Gershuni, and Syriac can frequently be bought, all dealing with some form of magic or popular medicine. In Suakin in the Soudan I was offered a printed book of astrology in Arabic illustrated by the most grotesque and bizarre woodcuts of the signs of the Zodiac, the blocks for which seem to have

done duty in other places. Such books existed in manuscript in ancient days, as is vouched for by the story of the Sibylline books or the passage in Acts xix., 19 ; ' Not a few of them that practised curious arts brought their books together, and burned them in the sight of all.' "

It is curious to find the charm for raising hatred practically the same among the *Semites* as it is amongst the peoples of Hungary and the Balkan States : that is through the agency of the egg of a black hen. We find too, many minor sorceries the same among the Semites as among European races. To be invisible was another attainment much sought after, and it was thought that if one wore a ring of copper and iron engraved with certain magic signs this result would be secured, or the heart of a black cat, dried and steeped in honey. The article " **Solomon** " can be referred to for several instances of potent enchantments. Sympathetic magic is often resorted to by the Arabic witch and wizard, just as it was amongst the ancient Hebrews and Assyrians.

The great repertory of Semitic occultism is of course the Kabala, to which the reader is referred for later Hebrew mystical doctrine.

Sendivogius, Michael : (*See* **Seton.**)

Sensitive : One who is in any degree susceptible to the influence of spiritual beings. A medium is occasionally, and, according to some authorities, more correctly, termed a *sensitive*.

Sephiroth : (*See* **Kabala.**)

Serpent's Egg : (*See* **Amulets.**)

Sethos : A diviner, who was deprived of his sight by the Emperor Manuel because of his addiction to Magic. It is said that the Emperor Andronicus Comnenus obtained through him by hydromancy an answer to the question of who was to succeed him. The evil spirit gave the letters " S I " in reply ; and on being asked when, said before the Feast of the exaltation of the Cross. This prediction was fulfilled, for before the date mentioned Isaac Angelus had thrown Andronicus to be torn in pieces by the mob. When the devil spells, he spells backwards, so that " S I " may quite fairly be taken to represent Isaac according to the laws of magic !

Setna, Papyrus of : A papyrus of very ancient date, dealing with the personality of Prince Setna Kha-em-ust, son of Rameses II. of Egypt, and said to have been discovered by him under the head of a mummy in the Necropolis at Memphis. Says Wiedemann concerning it : The first text, which has been known to us since 1867, tells that this prince, being skilled and zealous in the practice of necromancy, was one day exhibiting his acquirements to the learned men of the court, when an old man told him of a magic book containing two spells written by the hand of Thoth himself, the god of wisdom. He who repeated the first spell bewitched thereby heaven and earth and the realm of night, the mountains and the depth of the sea ; he knew the fowls of the air and every creeping thing ; he saw the fishes, for a divine power brought them up out of the depth. He who read the second spell should have power to resume his earthly shape, even though he dwelt in the grave ; to see the sun rising in the sky with all the gods and the moon in the form wherein she displays herself. *Setna* inquired where this book was to be found, and learned that it was lying in the tomb of Nefer-ka-Ptah, a son of King Mer-neb-ptah (who is nowhere else named), and that any attempt to take away the book would certainly meet with obstinate resistance. These difficulties did not withhold *Setna* from the adventure. He entered the tomb of Nefer-ka-Ptah, where he found not only the dead man, but the Ka of his wife Ahuri and their son, though these latter had been buried in Koptos. But as in many other tales among many other peoples, success brought no blessing to the man who had disturbed the repose of the dead. *Setna* fell in love with the daughter of a priest at Memphis, who turned out to be a witch, and took advantage of his intimate connection with her to bring him to ignominy and wretchedness. At length the prince recognised and repented of the sacrilege he had committed in carrying off the book, and brought it back to Nefer-ka-Ptah. In the hope of atoning to some extent for his sin he journeyed to Koptos, and finding the graves of the wife and child of Nefer-ka-Ptah, he solemnly restored their mummies to the tomb of the father and husband, carefully closing the tomb he had so sacrilegiously disturbed. The second text, edited two years ago by Griffith from a London papyrus, is also genuinely Egyptian in its details. Three magic tales, interwoven one with another, are brought into connection with Saosiri, the supernaturally born son of *Setna.* In the first, Saosiri, who was greatly *Setna's* superior in the arts of magic, led his father down into the underworld. They penetrated into the judgment-hall of Osiris, where the sights they saw convinced *Setna* that a glorious future awaited the poor man who should cleave to righteousness, while he who led an evil life on earth, though rich and powerful, must expect a terrible doom. Saosiri next succeeded in saving his father, and with him all Egypt, from great difficulty by reading without breaking the seal of a closed letter brought by an Ethiopian magician, whom he thus forced to recognise the superior power of Egypt. The last part of the text tells of a powerful magician once dwelling in Ethiopia who modelled in wax a litter with four bearers to whom he gave his life. He sent them to Egypt, and at his command they sought out Pharaoh in his palace, carried him off to Ethiopia, and, after giving him five hundred blows with a cudgel, conveyed him during the same night back to Memphis. Next morning the king displayed the weals on his back to his courtiers, one of whom, Horus by name, was sufficiently skilled in the use of amulets to ward off by their means an immediate repetition of the outrage. Horus then set forth to bring from Hermopolis, the all-powerful magic book of the god Thoth, and by its aid he succeeded in treating the Ethiopian king as the Ethiopian sorcerer had treated Pharaoh. The foreign magician then hastened to Egypt to engage in a contest with Horus in magic tricks. His skill was shown to be inferior, and in the end he and his mother received permission to return to Ethiopia under a solemn promise not to set foot on Egyptian territory for a space of fifteen hundred years.

Seton (or Sethon) Alexander, was one of the very few alchemists who succeeded in the great experiment of the transmutation of metals. He took his name from the village of Seton, which is stated to have been in the vicinity of Edinburgh and close to the sea-shore, so that one may reasonably conclude that the little fishing community of Port Seton is meant, although Camden in his *Brittania* states that that was the name of his house. In the year 1601, the crew of a Dutch vessel had the misfortune to be wrecked on the coast near his dwelling, and *Seton* personally rescued several of them, lodged them in his house, and treated them with great kindness, ultimately sending them back to Holland at his own expense. In the following year he visited Holland, and renewed his acquaintance with at least one of the ship-wrecked crew, James Haussen, the pilot, who lived at Arksun. Haussen, determined on repaying him for the hospitality he had received in Scotland, entertained him for some time in his house, and to him *Seton* disclosed the information that he was a master of the art of alchemy, and proved his words by performing several transmutations. Haussen, full of the matter, confided it to one Venderlinden, a physician of Enkhuysen, to whom he showed a piece of gold which he had himself seen transmuted from lead.

This Venderlinden's grandson in turn, showed to the celebrated author, D. G. Morhoff, who wrote a letter concerning it to Langlet du Fresnoy, author of the *Histoire de la Philosophie Hermétique.*

Seton visited Amsterdam and Rotterdam, travelled by sea to Italy, and thence through Switzerland to Germany, accompanied by a professed sceptic of alchemy, one Wolfgang Dienheim, whom he convinced of the error of his views at Basle before several of its principal inhabitants. This person has described *Seton,* and from the pen picture he gives of him we can discern a typical Scot of the seventeenth century. " *Seton,*" he says, " was short but stout, and high-coloured, with a pointed beard, but despite his corpulence, his expression was spiritual and exalted." " He was," adds Dienheim, " a native of Molier, in an island of the ocean." One wonders if Molier is the German's corruption of Lothian.

Several experiments of importance were now demonstrated by *Seton.* In one of these the celebrated physician Zwinger himself brought the lead which was to be transmuted from his own house. A common crucible was obtained at a goldsmith's, and ordinary sulphur was bought on the road to the house where the experiment was to take place. *Seton* handled none of these materials and took no part in the operation except to give to those who followed his directions a small packet of powder which transformed the lead into the purest gold of exactly the same weight. Zwinger appears to have been absolutely convinced of the genuine nature of the experiment, for he wrote an account of it to his friend Dr. Schobinger, which appears in Lonig's *Ephemerides.* Shortly after this *Seton* left Basle, and changing his name went to Strasbourg, whence he travelled to Cologne, lodging with one Anton Bordemann, who was by way of being an alchemist. In this city he was sufficiently imprudent to blazon his knowledge far and wide,—on one occasion producing six ounces of gold through the application of one grain of his magical powder. The circumstance seems to have made an impression on at least one of the savants of the Cathedral City, for Theobald de Hoghelande in his *Historia Aliquot Transmutationis Mettalicæ,* which was published at Cologne in 1604, alludes to it.

Seton then went to Hamburg, whence he travelled south to Munich, where something more important than alchemy engaged his attention, for he eloped with the daughter of a citizen, whom he married. The young Elector of Saxony, Christian II. had heard of *Seton's* brilliant alchemical successes and invited him to his court, but *Seton,* loath to leave his young wife, sent his friend, William Hamilton, probably a brother-Scot, in his stead, with a supply of the transmuting agent. In the presence of the whole Court, Hamilton undertook and carried through an experiment with perfect success and the gold then manufactured resisted every known test. This naturally only whetted the Elector's desire to see and converse with the magus, and a pressing invitation, which amounted to a command, was dispatched to *Seton,* who, thus rendered unable to refuse, betook himself to the electoral court. He was received there with every mark of honour, but it soon became evident to him that Christian II. had only invited him thither for the purpose of extracting from him the nature of his grand secret, but *Seton,* as an adept in the mysteries of alchemy, remained true to his high calling, and flatly refused to gratify the Elector's greed. Promises of preferment and threats were alike indifferent to him, and in the end the Elector, in a passion, ordered him to be imprisoned in a tower, where he was guarded by forty soldiers. There he was subjected to every conceivable species of torture, but all to no purpose. The rack, the fire, and the scourge, failed to extort from him the methods by which he had achieved the grand arcanum. Quite as exhausted as his victim, the Elector at last forbore, and left the unfortunate Scot in peace.

At this juncture a Moravian chemist, Michael Sendivogius, who happened to be in Dresden heard of *Seton's* terrible experiences and possessed sufficient influence to obtain permission to visit him. Himself a searcher after the philosopher's stone, he sympathised deeply with the adept, and proposed to him that he should attempt to effect his rescue. To this *Seton* agreed, and promised that if he were fortunate enough to escape, he would reward Sendivogius with his secret. The Moravian travelled back to Cracow, where he resided, sold up his property, and returned to Dresden, where he lodged near *Seton's* place of confinement, entertaining the soldiers who guarded the alchemist, and judiciously bribing those who were directly concerned in his imprisonment. At last he judged that the time was ripe to attempt *Seton's* salvation. He feasted the guards in a manner so liberal that all of them were soon in a condition of tipsy carelessness. He then hastened to the tower in which *Seton* was imprisoned, but found him unable to walk, through the severity of his tortures. He therefore supported him to a carriage which stood waiting, and which they gained without being observed. They halted at *Seton's* house to take up his wife, who had in her possession some of the all-important powder, and whipping up the horses, sped as swiftly as possible to Cracow, which they reached in safety. When quietly settled in that city, Sendivogius reminded *Seton* of his promise to assist him in in his alchemical projects, but was met with a stern refusal, *Seton* explaining to him that it was impossible for him as an adept to reveal to his rescuer the terms of such an awful mystery. The health of the alchemist was, however, shattered by the dreadful torments through which he had passed, and which he survived only for about two years, presenting the remains of his magical precipitate to his preserver. The possession of this powder only made Sendivogius more eager than ever to penetrate the mysteries of the grand arcanum. He married *Seton's* widow, perhaps with the idea that she was in possession of her late husband's occult knowledge, but if so he was doomed to disappointment for she was absolutely ignorant of the matter. *Seton* had left behind him, however, a treatise entitled *The New Light of Alchymy*, which Sendivogius laid hands on and published as his own. In its pages he thought he saw a method of increasing the powder, but to his intense disappointment and disgust, he only succeeded in lessening it. With what remained, however, he posed as a successful projector of the grand mystery, and proceeded with much splendour from court to court in a sort of triumphal procession. In his own country of Moravia, he was imprisoned, but escaped. His powder, however, was rapidly diminishing, but he still continued his experiments. Borel in his work on French Antiquities mentions that he saw a crown piece which had been partially dipped into a mixture of the powder dissolved in spirits of wine, and that the part steeped in the elixir was of gold, was porous, and was not soldered or otherwise tampered with. The powder done, Sendivogius degenerated into a mere charlatan, pretending that he could manufacture gold, and receiving large sums on the strength of being able to do so. He survived until the year 1646 when he died at Parma at the age of 84. *Seton's New Light of Alchymy* would appear, from an examination of it, to deny that the philosopher's stone was to be achieved by the successful transmutation of metals. It says :—

"The extraction of the soul out of gold or silver, by what vulgar way of alchymy soever, is but a mere fancy, On the contrary, he which, in a philosophical way, can without any fraud, and colourable deceit, make it that it shall really tinge the basest metal, whether with gain or without gain, with the colour of gold or silver (abiding all requisite tryals whatever), hath the gates of Nature opened to him for the enquiring into further and higher secrets, and with the blessing of God to obtain them."

Seven Stewards of Heaven, by whom God governs the world. They are known in works on Magic as the Olympian Spirits, and they govern the Olympian spheres, which are composed of one hundred and ninety-six regions. Their names in the Olympian language are :—Arathron, the celestial spirit of Saturn, whose day is Saturday ; Bethor, the angel of Jupiter, whose day is Monday ; Phaleg, the prince of Mars, whose day is Tuesday ; Och, the master of the Sun, whose day is Sunday ; Hagith, the sovereign of Venus, whose day is Friday ; Ophiel, the spirit of Mercury, who must be invoked on Wednesday ; Phul, the administrator of affairs in the Moon, whose day is Monday. Each of these Seven Celestial Spirits may be invoked by magicians by the aid of ceremonies and preparations.

Sextus V., Pope, was one of the line of St. Peter accused of sorcery. De Thou says of him in his *Histoire Universelle* (tome XI.) " The Spaniards continued their vengeance against this Pontiff even after his death, and they forgot nothing in their anxiety to blacken his memory by the libels which they flung against him. *Sextus*, said they, who, by means of the magical art, was for a long time in confederacy with a demon, had made a compact with this enemy of humanity to give himself up to him, on condition he was made Pope, and allowed to reign six years. *Sextus* was raised to the chair of St. Peter, and during the five years he held sway in Rome he distinguished his pontificate by actions surpassing the feeble reach of the human intellect. Finally, at the end of this term, the *Pope* fell sick, and the devil arriving to keep him to his pact, *Sextus* inveighed strongly against his bad faith, reproaching him with the fact that the term they had agreed upon was not fulfilled, and that there still remained to him more than a twelve-month. But the devil reminded him that at the beginning of his pontificate he had condemned a man who, according to the laws, was too young by a year to suffer death, and that he had nevertheless caused him to be executed, saying that he would give him a year out of his own life ; that this year, added to the other five, completed the six years which had been promised to him, and that in consequence he did very wrong to complain. *Sextus*, confused and unable to make any answer, remained mute, and turning himself towards the *ruelle* of his bed, prepared for death in the midst of the terrible mental agitation caused by the remorse of his conscience. For the rest," adds De Thou, with amiable frankness, " I only mention this trait as a rumour spread by the Spaniards, and I should be very sorry to guarantee its truth."

Shaddai : One of the ten divine names given in the rabbinical legend of the angelic hierarchies. This essence influences the sphere of the moon : it causes increase and decrease, and rules the jinn and protecting spirits.

She-Goat : One of the branches of augury in ancient Rome dealt especially with the signs which might be derived from animals ; and it was believed that if a *she-goat* crossed the path of a man who was stepping out of his house it was a good omen, and he might proceed on his way rejoicing and " think upon Caranus."

Sheik Al Gebel : (*See* Assassins.)

Shekinah : Spiritualistic Journal. (*See* **Spiritualism.**)

Shelta Thari : An esoteric language spoken by the tinkers of Great Britain, and possibly a descendant of an " inner " language employed by the ancient Celtic Druids or bards. It was in 1876 that the first hint of the existence of *Shelta Thari* reached the ears of that prince of practical philologists, Charles Godfrey Leland. It seems strange that

George Borrow had never stumbled upon the language, and that fact may be taken as a strong proof of the jealousy with which the nomadic classes guarded it. Leland relates how he and Professor E. H. Palmer were wandering on the beach at Aberystwyth when they met a tramp, who heard them indulging in a conversation in Romany. Leland questioned the man as to how he gained a living, and he replied, " Shelkin gallopas." The words were foreign even to the master of dialect, and he inquired their import. " Why," said the man, " it means selling ferns. That is tinker's language or minklers' thari. I thought as you knew Romany, you might understand it. The right name for the tinkers' language is *Shelta*." " It was," says Leland, " with the feelings of Columbus the night before he discovered America that I heard the word *Shelta*, and I asked the fern-dealer if he could talk it." The man replied " A little," and on the spot the philologist collected a number of words and phrases from the fern-seller which gave him sufficient insight into the language to prove to him that it was absolutely different from Romany. The Celtic origin of the dialect soon began to commend itself to Leland, and he attempted to obtain from the man some verse or jingle in it, possibly for the purpose of observing its syntactical arrangement. But all he was able to drag from his informant were some rhymes of no philological value, and he found he had soon pumped the tramp dry. It was in America that Leland nearly terrified a tinker out of his wits by speaking to him in the lost dialect. The man, questioned as to whether he could speak *Shelta*, admitted the soft impeachment. He proved to be an Irishman, Owen Macdonald by name, and he furnished Leland with an invaluable list of several hundred words. But Leland could not be sure upon which of the Celtic languages the dialect was based. Owen Macdonald declared to him that it was a fourth language, which had nothing in common with old Irish, Welsh, or Gælic, and hazarded the information that it was the idiom of the " Ould Picts," but this appears to be rather too conjectural for the consumption of the philologist. *Shelta* is not a jargon, for it can be spoken grammatically without using English, as in the British form of Romany. Pictish in all probability was not a Celtic language, nor even an Aryan one, however intimately it may have been affected by Celtic speech in the later stages of its existence. Leland's discovery was greeted in some quarters with inextinguishable laughter. The *Saturday Review* jocosely suggested that he had been " sold," and that old Irish had been palmed off on him for a mysterious lingo. He put this view of the matter before his tinker friend, who replied with grave solemnity, " And what'd I be afther makin' two languages av thim for, if there was but wan av thim ? " Since Leland's day much has been done to reclaim this mysterious tongue, chiefly through the investigations of Mr. John Sampson and Professor Kuno Meyer. The basis of these investigations rested on the fact that the tinker caste of Great Britain and Ireland was a separate class—so separate indeed as almost to form a race by itself. For hundreds of years, possibly, this fraternity existed with nearly all its ancient characteristics, and on the general disuse of Celtic speech had conserved it as a secret dialect. The peculiar thing concerning *Shelta* is the extent of territory over which it is spoken. That it is known rather extensively in London itself was discovered by Leland, who heard it spoken by two small boys in the Euston Road. They were not Gypsies, and Leland found out that one of them spoke the language with great fluency. Since Leland's discoveries *Shelta* has been to some extent mapped out into dialects, one of the most important of which is that of Ulster. It would be difficult to explain in the course of such an article as this exactly how long the Ulster dialect of this strange and

ancient tongue differs from that in use in other parts of Great Britain and Ireland. But that it does so is certain. Nearly eighteen years ago Mr. John Sampson, of Liverpool, a worthy successor to Borrow and Leland, and a linguist of repute, collected a number of sayings and proverbs from two old Irish tinkers—John Barlow and Phil Murray—which he distinctly states are in the Ulster dialect of *Shelta*. Some of these may be quoted to provide the reader with specimens of the language :—Krish gyukera have muni Sheldru—Old beggars have good *Shelta*. Stimera dhi-ilsha, stimera aga dhi-ilsha—If you're a piper, have your own pipe. Mislo granhes thaber—The traveller knows the road. Thom Blorne mjesh Nip gloch—Every Protestant isn't an Orangeman. Nus a dhabjon dhuilsha—The blessing of God on you. Misli, gami gra dhi-il—Be off, and bad luck to you.

There seems to be considerable reason to believe that the tinker (or more properly " tinkler ") class of Great Britain sprang from the remnants of its ancient Celtic inhabitants, and differed as completely from the Gypsy, or Romany, race as one people can well differ from another. This is almost conclusively proved by the criterion of speech, for *Shelta* is a Celtic tongue and that Romany is a dialect of Northern Hindustan is not open to doubt. Those who now speak Romany habitually almost invariably make use of *Shelta* as well, but that only proves that the two nomadic races, having occupied the same territory for hundreds of years, had gained a knowledge of each other's languages. Who, then, were the original progenitors of the tinkers ? Whoever they were, they were a Celtic-speaking race, and probably a nomadic one. *Shelta* has been referred to as the language of the ancient bards of Ireland, the esoteric tongue of an Irish priesthood. Leland puts forward the hypothesis that the Shelta-speaking tinker is a descendant of a prehistoric guild of bronze-workers. This, he thinks, accounts in part for his secretiveness as regards his language. In Italy to this very day the tinker class is identified with the itinerant bronze workers. The tinker fraternity of Great Britain and Ireland existed with perhaps nearly all its ancient characteristics until the advent of railroads. But long before this it had probably amalgamated to a great extent with the Gypsy population, and the two languages had become common to the two peoples. This is the only explanation that can be given for the appearance of *Shelta*, a Celtic language, in the non-Celtic portions of Great Britain. That it originated in Ireland appears to be highly probable, for in no other part of these islands during the later Celtic period was there a state of civilisation sufficiently advanced to permit of the existence of a close corporation of metal-workers possessing a secret language. Moreover, the affinities of *Shelta* appear to be with old Irish more than with any other Celtic dialect. There is one other theory that presents itself in connection with the origin of *Shelta*, and that is, that it is the modern descendant of the language of the " Ould Picts " mentioned by Owen Macdonald, Leland's tinker friend. It has by no means been proved that Pictish was a non-Aryan language, and, despite the labours of Professor Rhys, we are as far off as ever from any definite knowledge concerning the idiom spoken by that mysterious people. But there are great difficulties in the way of accepting the hypothesis of the Pictish origin of *Shelta*, the chief among them being its obvious Irish origin. There were, it is known, Picts in the North of Ireland, but they were almost certainly a small and barbarous colony, and a very unlikely community to form a metal-working confraternity, possessing the luxury of a private dialect. It still remains for the Celtic student to classify *Shelta*. It may prove to be " Pictish," strongly influenced by the Gaelic of Ireland and Scotland. A comparison with Basque and the dialect of the Iberian tribes of Morocco might bring affinities to light, and thus establish the theory of its non-Aryan origin ; but its strong kinship with Erse seems undoubted. (*See Journal of the Gypsy Lore Society*, New Series.)

Shemhamphorash : In the *Talmud*, the external term representing the hidden word of power, by whose virtues it were possible to create a new world. But it is lost to man, though even sounds approximating to it have a magic power, and can give to him who pronounces them dominion in the spirit-world. Some of the Rabbis say that the word of power contains twelve letters, others, forty-two, and yet others seventy-two ; but these are the letters of the divine alphabet, which God created from certain luminous points made by the concentration of the primal universal Light. *Shemhamphorash* is, in fact, the *name* of this word.

Sheol : (*See* **Hell.**)

Ship of the Dead : Akin to the superstitious idea of the death-coach is the belief that at times a phantom barque carries away the souls of men. In the form of a cloud-ship, or wrapped in a driving mist, it sails over mountains and moors, and at sea it sails in despite of wind and tide. A story is told of a certain pirate, at whose death a spectral ship approached in a cloud. As it sailed over the roof the house was filled with a sound as of a stormy sea, and when the ship had passed by the soul of the pirate accompanied it.

Shorter, Thomas : (*See* **Spiritualism.**)

Siberia : The barbarian tribes of *Siberia* all more or less practise the art of Sorcery, and this has been from time immemorial in the hands of the shamanistic or medicine-man class. The Samoyeds who are idol-worshippers believe also in the existence of an order of invisible spirits which they call *tadebtsois*. These are ever circling through the atmosphere, and are a constant menace to the native, who is anxious to propitiate them. This can only be effected through the intervention of a *tadibe* or Necromancer, who, when his services are requisitioned, attires himself in magical costume of reindeer leather trimmed with red cloth, a mask of red cloth, and a breast-plate of polished metal. He then takes a drum of reindeer skin (*See* **Lapland**) ornamented with brass rings, and attended by an assistant, walks round in a circle invoking the presence of the spirits, shaking a large rattle the while. The noise grows louder, and as the spirits are supposed to draw near the sorcerer, he addresses them, beating his drum more gently, and pausing in his chant to listen to their answers. Gradually he works himself into a condition of frenzy, beats the drum with great violence, and appears to be possessed by the supernatural influence writhing and foaming at the mouth. All at once he stops, and oracularly pronounces the will of the spirits. The Tadibe's office is a hereditary one, but if a member of the tribe should exhibit special qualifications he is adopted into the priesthood, and by fasts, vigils, the use of narcotics and stimulants in the same manner as is employed by the N.A. Indians (q.v.), he comes to believe that he has been visited by the spirits. He is then adopted as a Tadibe with midnight ceremoinal, and is invested with a magic drum. A great many of the tricks of the priesthood are merely those of ordinary conjuring, such as the rope trick, but some of the illusions which these men secure are exceedingly striking. With their hands and feet tied together, they sit on a carpet of reindeer skin, and putting out the light, summon the assistance of the spirits. Peculiar noises herald their approach, snakes hiss, and bears growl, the lights are rekindled and the *tadibe* is seen released from his bonds. The Samoyeds sacrifice much to the dead, and perform various ceremonies in their honour, but they believe that only the souls of the *tadibes* enjoy immortality and hover through the air, demanding constant sacrifice.

Further to the east, inhabiting the more northerly part of *Siberia* dwell the Ostiaks, who have nominally adopted the rites of the Greek Church, but magic is rife amongst them. Many Ostiaks carry about with them a description of fetish, which they call *Schaitan*. Whether this name, like the Arabic *Sheitan*, is merely a corruption of that of Satan, it would be difficult to say. Larger images of this kind are part of the furniture of an Ostiak lodge, but they are attired in seven pearl embroidered garments, and suspended to the neck by a string of silver coins. In a strange sort of dualism they are placed in many of the huts cheek by jowl with the image of the Virgin Mary, and at meal-times their lips are smeared with the blood of raw game or fish.

It is this people, the Ostiaks, with whom the word "Shaman" originated. These Shamans are merely medicine-men.

The Mongols, who inhabit the more southern parts of the great waste of *Siberia* are also ancient practitioners in sorcery, and rely greatly on divination. In order to discover what description of weather will be prevalent for any length of time they employ a stone endowed with magic virtues called *yadeh-tash*. This is suspended over, or lies in a basin of water with sundry ceremonies, and appears to be the same kind of stone in use among the Turcomans as related by Ibn Mohalhal, an early Arab traveller.

The celebrated conqueror, Timur, in his Memoirs, records that the Jets resorted to incantations to produce heavy rains which hindered his cavalry from acting against them. A Yadachi, or weather-conjuror, was taken prisoner, and after he had been beheaded the storm ceased.

Babu refers to one of his early friends, Khwaja ka Mulai, as conspicuous for his skill in falconry and his knowledge of *Yadageri*, or the science of inducing rain and snow by means of enchantment. The Russians were much distressed by heavy rains in 1552, when besieging Kazan, and universally ascribed the unfavourable weather to the arts of the Tatar queen, who was an enchantress.

Early in the 18th century, the Chinese Emperor Shi-tsung issued a proclamation against rain-conjuring, addressed to the Eight Banners of Mongolia. " If," indignantly observes the Emperor, " if I, offering prayers in sincerity, have yet cause to fear that it may please heaven to leave *my* prayer unanswered, it is truly intolerable that mere common people wishing for rain should of their own fancy set up altars of earth ; and bring together a rabble of Hoshang (Buddhist Bonzes) and Taossi to conjure the spirits to gratify their wishes."

Sibylline Books : The manuscripts which embodied the secrets of human destiny, the work of the sibyls (q.v.) or prophetesses of the ancient world. According to Tacitus, these books were first preserved in the Capitol. When it was burnt down, the precious leaves of Fate were preserved, and removed to the temple of Apollo Palatinus. Their after-fate is enshrouded in mystery, but it would seem that the Cumean books existed until 339 A.D., when they were destroyed by Stilikon. Augustus sent three ambassadors—Paulus Gabinus, Marcus Otacillius, and Lucius Valerius—into Asia, Africa, and Italy, but especially to the Erythraean Sibyl, to collect whatever could be discovered of the Sibylline Oracles, to replace those which had been lost or burnt. The books are of two kinds ; namely, the books of the elder Sibyls, that is, of the earlier Greek and Roman times ; and the later, which were much falsified, and disfigured with numerous interpolations. Of the latter, eight books in Greek and Latin are still said to be extant. Those which are preserved in Rome had been collected from various places, at various times, and contained predictions of future events couched in the most mysterious of symbolic languages. At first they were permitted only to be read by descendants of Apollo, but later by the priests, until their care was entrusted to certain officials, who only replied to inquiries at the command of the Senate, in cases of extraordinary emergency. They were two at first, and named *duumviri :* these were appointed by Tarquinius Superbus. Two hundred and thirteen years afterwards, ten more were appointed to their guardianship (*decemviri*), and Sulla increased the number to fifteen (*quindecemviri.*)

Siderit : Another name for the magnet.

Signs, Planetary : (*See* **Astrology.**)

Silvester II., Pope, (Gerbert, died 1003) : One of a number of popes who from the tenth century onwards were regarded as sorcerers. It was said—and the story probably emanated from the Gnostics who had been proscribed by the Church—that Gerbert had evoked a demon who obtained for him the papacy, and who further promised him that he should die only after he had celebrated High Mass in Jerusalem. One day, while he was saying mass in a Church in Rome, he felt suddenly ill, and remembering that he was in the Church of the Holy Cross in Jerusalem, he knew that the demon had played him a trick. Before he died, the chronicler continues, he confessed to his cardinals his compact with the devil. However, as Gerbert had been preceptor of two monarchs, and a friend of others, it is more likely that he owed his preference to one of these. He was one of the most learned men of his day, a proficient in mathematics, astronomy, and mechanics. He it was who introduced clocks, and some writers credit him with the invention of arithmetic as we now have it. It is not at all improbable that his scientific pursuits seemed to the ignorant to savour of magic. The technical language employed in his various studies might well have a sinister significance to the ignorant. The brazen head which William of Malmesbury speaks of as belonging to *Silvester,* and which answered questions in an oracular manner probably had its origin in a similar misinterpretation of scientific apparatus. But however that may be, there is no lack of picturesque detail in some of the stories told of him. By the aid of sorcery he is said to have discovered buried treasure and to have visited a marvellous underground palace, whose riches and splendour vanished at a touch. His very tomb was believed to possess the powers of sorcery, and to shed tears when one of the succeeding popes was about to die.

Simon Ben Yohai : (*See* **Kabala.**)

Simon Magus : The sorcerer mentioned in the New Testament (Acts viii.) who bewitched the people of Samaria, and led them to believe that he was possessed of divine power. He was born in Samaria or Cyprus and was among the number of Samaritans who, moved by the preaching of Philip, came to him for baptism. Later, when Peter and John laid their hands on the new converts, so that they received the Holy Ghost, Simon offered the disciples money to procure a similar power. But Peter sternly rebuked him for seeking to buy the gift of God with money, and bade him pray that his evil thought might be forgiven, whereupon the already repentant *Simon* said, " Pray ye to the Lord for me, that none of these things which ye have spoken come upon me."

Though we are not told in detail what the sorceries were with which *Simon* bewitched the people of Samaria, certain early ecclesiastical writers have left a record of his doings. He could, they averred, make himself invisible when he pleased, assume the appearance of another person, or of the lower animals, pass unharmed through fire, cause statues to become alive, make furniture move without any visible means of imparting motion, and go through a long list of equally miraculous performances. In explanation of his desire to possess the apostles' power of working miracles

he is said to have affirmed that his sorceries took a great deal of time and trouble to perform, owing to the necessity for a multitude of magical rites and incantations, while the miracles of the apostles were accomplished easily, and successfully, by the mere utterance of a few words.

The adept from whom *Simon* learned the art of magic was one Dositheus, who pretended to be the Messiah foretold by the prophets, and who was contemporary with Christ. From this person he appears to have acquired a great store of occult erudition, and owed his power chiefly to the hysterical conditions into which he was capable of throwing himself. Through these he was enabled to make himself look either old or young, returning at will to childhood or old age. It is evident that he had not been initiated into Transcendental Magic, but was merely consumed by a thirst for power over humanity and the mysteries of nature. Repulsed by the Apostles, he is said to have undertaken pilgrimages, like them, in which he permitted himself to be worshipped by the mob. He declared that he himself was the manifestation of the Splendour of God, and that Helena, a Greek slave of his, was its reflection. Thus he imitated Christianity in the reverse sense, affirmed the eternal reign of evil and revolt, and was, in fact, an antichrist.

After a while he went to Rome, where he appeared before the Emperor Nero. He is said to have been decapitated by him, but his head was restored to his shoulders, and he was instituted by the tyrant as court sorcerer. Legend states that St. Peter, alarmed at the spread of the doctrine of *Simon* in Rome, repaired thither to combat it, that Nero was made aware of his arrival, and imagining Peter to be a rival sorcerer resolved to bring them together for his amusement. An account ascribed to St. Clement states that on the arrival of Peter, *Simon* flew gracefully through a window into the outside air. The Apostle gave vent to a vehement prayer, whereupon the magician, with a loud cry, crashed to the earth, and broke both his legs. Nero, greatly annoyed, immediately imprisoned the saint, and it is related that *Simon* died of his fall. He had, however, founded a distinct school headed by Merrander, which promised immortality of soul and body to its followers. As late as 1858 there existed in France and America a sect which credited the principles of this magician.

Siradz, Count of : (*See* **Dee.**)

Sixth Sense : A term used to denote the faculty of spiritual perception, which is distinct from, and higher than, the five physical senses. It is the possession of the medium, the psychic or sensitive, and in some measure of all hypnotic subjects. It is not properly a separate sense at all, but is compounded from the spiritual correlates of the physical senses.

Slade, Henry : An American medium, principally known in connection with his slate-writing exploits. He came to Britain in July, 1876, and was cordially received by the leading spiritualists. Very many people were impressed and completely mystified by the phenomena they witnessed at his séances, and Lord Rayleigh, at a meeting of the British Association in September, 1876, stated that he had attended a séance of *Slade's* in the company of a professional conjurer, and that the latter had failed entirely to find an explanation of the facts. A few days after this emphatic testimony was given, however, Professor Ray Lankester published in a letter to the Times the result of a séance at which he and Dr. Donkin were present. He had, he said, snatched the slate prematurely from " Dr." *Slade's* hand, and had found a message written thereon, though the sound of writing had not then been heard. The spiritualists maintained that the " exposure " was no exposure at all, since *Slade* declared that he had heard the spirits writing, and had mentioned the fact, but that his voice had been lost in the confusion. However, the medium's career in Britain was at an end. At the instance of Professor Lankester he was tried in a court of law, and sentenced to three months imprisonment with hard labour. He appealed, and the conviction was quashed because of a slight omission in the charge. A fresh summons was issued on the following day, but *Slade* had left the country, and did not thereafter return. In the years 1877–88 Professor Zöllner of Leipsic investigated the slate-writing and other phenomena occurring in the presence of *Slade*, mainly in the hope of establishing his theory of four-dimensional space. Knots were tied in endless cords, coins extracted from sealed boxes; but Professor Zöllner did not succeed in his attempt to have knots tied in a piece of bladder, or to have two rings of solid wood interlaced. In short, no really *conclusive* proof was obtained. In 1884 *Slade's* phenomena was investigated by a committee appointed by the University of Pennsylvania. The results of the latter investigation were, at the best, of a negative description. (*See also* **Slate-writing**.)

Slate-writing : A form of the so-called "direct" spirit writing, or autography, which has always been one of the most popular phenomena of the *séance*. The *modus operandi* is the same in the majority of cases. The medium and the sitter take their seats at opposite ends of a small table, each grasping a corner of an ordinary school slate, which they thus hold firmly pressed against the underside of the table. A small fragment of slate-pencil is first enclosed between slate and table, for the use of the supposed spirit-writer. Should the *séance* be successful, a scratching sound, as of someone writing on a slate, is heard at the end of a few moments, three loud raps indicate the conclusion of the message, and on the withdrawal of the slate, it is found to be partly covered with writing—either a general message from the spirit-world, or an answer to some question perviously written down by the sitter.

Among the mediums who were most successful in obtaining spirit writing in this manner were Dr. Slade and Mr. Eglinton. The former, an American medium, came to England in 1876, and succeeded in mystifying not a few men of education and of scientific attainments. His critics have attributed his success, in part at least, to his frank and engaging manner, which did much to disarm suspicious sitters. However, ere long Professor Ray Lankester exposed his trickery, though the exposure was regarded by many as inconclusive, and "Dr." Henry Slade was prosecuted. Though sentenced to three months' hard labour, the omission of certain words in the accusation made the conviction of no effect. But Dr. Slade found that England had become too hot for him, and speedily retired whence he had come. Many of the accounts of his *séances* in different countries are of interest, chiefly because of the discrepancy which exists between those of credulous spiritualists and those of trained investigators. Dr. Richard Hodgson, however, has pointed out that even in the latter class instances of mal-observation are the rule rather than the exception, particularly where sleight of hand plays a prominent part in the exhibition. A worthy successor to Slade was William Eglinton, who acted as medium for *slate-writing* manifestations, and attained to an extraordinary popularity, upwards of a hundred people testifying to his mediumistic powers in the spiritualist journal *Light*. Speaking of his performances, Mr. C. C. Massey said, "Many, of whom I am one, are of the opinion that the case for these phenomena generally, and for autography, in particular, is already complete." Eglinton's manifestations were produced in full light, and his séances were seldom blank, so it is hardly surprising that very many persons, ignorant of the lengths to which conjuring can be carried, and over-confident in their own ability to observe correctly, should see in *slate-writing* a phenomenon explicable only by a spiritualistic theory. But there was definite proof of fraud in several cases. Muslin and a false beard, part of the make-up of a "spirit" had been found in Eglinton's portmanteau, various persons averred that they had seen his messages written on prepared slates previous to the *séance*, and he had been concerned in other matters of an equally doubtful character. And though these detections also were disputed they left in the unbiassed mind but little doubt of the fraudulent nature of Eglinton's mediumship.

Spiritualists themselves admitted that fraud might occasionally be practised by genuine mediums, owing to the uncertainty of the "power." Particularly was this so in the case of professional mediums, who were obliged to produce *some* results, and who had to resort to trickery when other means failed them. Mr. S. J. Davey, an associate of the Society for Psychical Research who, having discovered the tricks of *slate-writing*, practised them himself, was claimed by certain spiritualists as a medium as well as a conjurer, and that notwithstanding his protestations to the contrary. This is undoubtedly a powerful argument against the good faith of *slate-writing*. If his sitters could mistake these sleight-of-hand tricks—which Mr. Davey practised with the express purpose of discrediting their professional mediums—for genuine spirit manifestations, might they not also be misled by the *legerdemain* of Slade and Eglinton, and other well-known mediums? It has been objected that even skilled conjurers such as "Professor" Hoffmann and Houdin professed themselves mystified by *slate-writing* performances, but the answer is fairly obvious, that quite a clever conjurer may be baffled by the performances of a brother-expert. The methods adopted by Mr. Davey were of a simple nature, requiring little or no apparatus. In the case of a long, general message, he would prepare a slate beforehand, and substitute it for the test slate. A shorter message, or a reply to a question, he would write on the reverse side of the slate, with a scrap of pencil fastened in a thimble, and so withdraw the slate that the side written on would be uppermost. There is reason to believe that like simple devices were used in other *séances*, for their very simplicity, and the absence of all apparatus, rendered them particularly difficult of detection. But where the sitters were more credulous, intricate furniture and appliances were used, and the most elaborate preparations made for the *séance*. (*See* **Pope John XXII.**)

Slavs : The Slavonic races have an extensive demonology, and in some measure their religious pantheon appears to have been in a stage between animism (q.v.) and polytheism, that is between god, and spirit-worship. Among them all witchcraft, fairy and folk-lore rest mainly in a belief in certain spirits of nature, which in some measure recall the pneumatology of Paracelsus and the Comte de Gabalis. "In the *vile*," says Dr. Krauss, "also known as *Samovile, Samodivi*, and *Vilivrjaci*, we have near relations to the forest and field spirits or the wood and moss-folk of Middle Germany, France and Bavaria the "wild people of Hesse, Eifel, Salzburg and the Tyrol, the wood-women and woodmen of Bohemia, the Tyrolese Fanggen, Fanken, Norkel and Happy Ladies, the Roumanish Orken, Euguane, and Dialen, the Danish Ellekoner, the Swedish Skogsnufvaz, and the Russian Ljesje, while in certain respects they have affinity with the Teutonic Valkyries." They are, however, more like divine beings, constantly watching over and controlling the destinies of men. They are prayed to or exorcised on all occasions. In short their origin is certainly Shamanistic. Says Leland : "We can still find the *vila* as set forth in old ballads, the incarnation of beauty and power, the benevolent friend of sufferers, the geniuses of heroes, the dwellers by rock and river and greenwood tree. But they are implacable in their wrath to all who deceive them, or who break a promise. Nay, they inflict terrible punishment even on those who disturb their rings, or the dances which they make by midsummer moonlight. Hence the proverb applied to any man who suddenly fell ill, ' he stepped on a fairy ring.' " (*See* **Circles.**)

There are three varieties of witches or spirits among the southern *Slavs*, the *Zracne vile*, or aerial spirits, evilly disposed to human beings, and inflicting serious injuries upon them, Will-'o-the-wisps, who lead people astray by nights ; the *Pozemne vile*, companionable spirits, who give sage counsel to mankind, and dwell in the earth ; and the *Podovne vile*, or water sprites, kindly to man on shore, but treacherous to a degree on their own element. Another water-spirit is the *Likho*, the Slavonic Polyphemus, a dread and terrible monster, the *Leshy* is a wood-demon, *Norka* is the frightful Lord of the Lower World, and *Koschei* is a description of ogre whose province is the abduction of princesses.

Witchcraft.—The witch is very frequently mentioned in Slavonic folk-tales, especially among the southern *Slavs*. She is called *vjestica*, (masculine *viestae*) meaning originally " the knowing " or " well-informed one," *Viedma* (Russian). In Dalmatia and elsewhere among the Southern *Slavs* the witch is called *Krstaca*, " the crossed " in allusion to the idea that she is of the hornèd race of Hell. It enrages the witches so much to be called by this word that when they hear that any one has used it they come to his house by night and tear him in four pieces, which they cast to the four winds of heaven, and drive away all his cattle and stock. Therefore the shrewd farmers of the country call the witch *hmana zena*, or " Common woman." There are many forms of Slavonic witch, however, and the *vjestica* differs from the *macionica* and the latter from the *Zlokobnica*, or " evil-meeter," one whom it is unlucky to encounter in the morning, or possesses the evil eye. A Serbian authority says : " I have often heard from old Hodzas and Kadijas that every female Wallach as soon as she is forty years old, abandons the " God be with us," and becomes a witch (*vjestica*) or at least a *zlokobnica* or *macionica*. A real witch has the mark of a cross under her nose, a *zlokobnica* has some hairs of a beard, and a *macionica* may be known by a forehead full of dark folds wtih blood-spots in her face."

In South Slavonian countries the peasants on St. George's Day adorn the horns of the cattle with garlands to protect them from witches. They attach great importance to a seventh or a twelfth child, who, they believe, are the great protectors of the world against witchcraft. But these are in great danger on St. John's Eve, for then the witches, having the most power, attack them with stakes or the stumps of saplings, for which reason the peasantry carefully remove everything of the kind from the ground in the autumn season. The *Krstnik*, or wizards, notoriously attract the *vila* ladies, who in most instances are desirous of becoming their mistresses, just as the womenkind of the salamanders desire to mate with men. (*See* the *Curiosa* of Heinrich Kornmann, 1666.) The man who gains the love of a *vila* is supposed to be extremely lucky. The *Slavs* believe that on St. George's Day the witches climb into the steeples of churches with the object of getting the grease from the axle of the bell, which, for some reason, they prize exceedingly. Transformation stories are fairly common, too, in Slavonic folklore, which proves that this was a form of magic employed by the witches of these countries. The belief in vampires is an outstanding superstition in Slavonic countries, and its connections are fully discussed in the article **Vampire.**

Slawensik Poltergeist : In the winter of 1806–7 Councillor Hahn and an officer named Charles Kern, living for the time in the Castle of Salwensik, Silesia, were disturbed by curious happenings which suggested that the Castle was haunted. Strange noises were heard, small objects were seen to rise from the table and fly through the room. The only account is by Councillor Hahn, and, as is generally the case in such circumstances, the most surprising occurrences were not witnessed by the recorder, but were told him by his friends. Thus Kern is said to have seen in the glass the apparition of a woman in white ; while Hahn was not present when a jug of beer was raised from the table by invisible hands, tilted, and its contents poured down an invisible throat.

Sleeping Preacher : Rachel Baker, known as the *Sleeping Preacher*, was born at Pelham, Massachusetts, in 1794. When she was nine years old her parents removed to Marcellus, N.Y. As a child she had a religious training, her parents being devout people, and she early manifested a strong conviction of her sinfulness. In 1811 she showed symptoms of somnambulism, in which she seemed stricken with horror and despondency. But gradually her mind became calmer, and delivered discourses of singular clearness, marked by a devout and solemn tone. These fits of somnambulism, or trance-speaking, seized her regularly every day, and soon became habitual. She began and concluded her devotional exercises with prayer, between which came the discourse. Then a state of apparent physical distress supervened, and sobs and groans shook her frame. At length the paroxysm passed, and she subsided into a natural sleep. Change of scene did not affect these exercises, but the administration of opium would interrupt them. Her trance discourses were afterwards published.

Smagorad, a magic book : (*See* **France.**)

Smith Helene : The *nom-de-guerre* of a trance medium who came under the observation of Professor Flournoy. Born about 1863, at the age of twenty-nine she joined a spiritualist circle and soon developed powerful mediumistic faculties. In 1894 M. Flournoy was admitted to the circle and thenceforward examined with much interest the clairvoyance and trance impersonations of *Hélène*. In the winter of 1894 she purported to have visited, during trance, the planet Mars, and many of her trance discourses after that date contain descriptions of Martian life—manners, dress, scenery. At length she claimed to have learned the language of the sister-planet, and this language she spoke with fluency and consistency. (*See* **Martian Language.**) Professor Flournoy however, found no evidence sufficient to justify any belief in a supernormal faculty, unless it be telepathy.

Smith, Joseph : (*See* **America, U.S. of.**)

Sneezing, Superstitions Relating to : It is said that the custom of blessing one who sneezes originated in Italy in the time of Gregory the Great, during a pestilence which proved mortal to those who sneezed. A still older date is given to this custom by some writers, who state that *sneezing* was fatal from the time of Adam to that of Jacob, when the latter begged that its fatal effects might be removed. On his request being granted, the people gratefully instituted the custom of saluting the sneezer. In some diseases *sneezing* was a bad, in others a good omen. *Sneezing* to the right was lucky, to the left, unlucky ; from noon to midnight good, from night to noon, bad. St. Austin says·that the ancients would return to bed if they sneezed while putting on a shoe.

Societas Rosicruciana of Boston : (*See* **Rosicrucians.**)

Societe Industrielle of Wiemar : (*See* **Alchemy.**)

Societe Industrielle of Wien : (*See* **Alchemy.**)

Societe Spiritual di Palermo : (*See* **Italy.**)

Societies of Harmony : Associations formed for the practice of magnetism by the pupils of F. A. Mesmer. The first

Société de l' Harmonie was formed at Paris, and its members seem to have acted in a manner that was anything but harmonious, for, after some quarrelling among themselves they at length broke their contract with Mesmer, whereby they promised before being admitted to his lectures, that they would not practice on their own account, or give away the secret of his methods, without his consent. Other *Societies of Harmony* soon sprang up, the most important being that of Strasbourg, founded in 1785 by de Puységur.

Society for Psychical Research : (*See* **Spiritualism, Psychic Research.)**

Solanot, Viscount : (*See* **Spain.**)

Solar Deity : (*See* **Theosophy.**)

Solar System : Theosophists have special doctrines as to the formation of *solar systems*. They start by postulating the existence of all pervading ether, or, as it is termed in occult chemistry (q.v.) *koilon*, an ether which is quite imperceptible to ordinary senses and indeed even to clairvoyants except the most highly-developed. It is, despite its diffusion, of extreme density. The Deity intending to create a universe invests this ether with his divine force, whereupon it becomes the constituent of matter in the shape of minute drops or bubbles, and of this the universe with its *solar systems* is formed. First a mass is aggregated by the appropriate agitation of these drops, and to this mass is imparted a rotatory motion. The mass thus formed, of course, contains the matter from which will be formed all the seven worlds, the existence of which Theosophy teaches, and it may be well here to observe that these worlds are not separate in the manner we usually conceive separate worlds to be, but inter-penetrate each other. The substance in its original form is of the texture of the first world, and in order to create the texture of the second—and lower—world the Deity sets up a vast number of rotatory agitations into each of which is collected 49 atoms arranged in a certain way, sufficient of the first atom having been left to form the first world. This process continues six times, the atoms of the succeeding lower worlds being formed from those of the world immediately higher and each time of a multiple of 49 atoms. Gradually and with the passing of long ages, the aggregation, which contains the atoms of all seven worlds completely intermingled, contracts and becomes more closely knit until it forms a nebula which eventually attains the flat, circular form familiar to students of astronomy. Towards the centre it is much more dense than at the fringes, and in the process of flattening and because of the initial revolving motion, rings are formed encircling the centre. From these rings the planets are formed, and after the further passing of ages, it is possible for human life to exist on them. The various worlds as has been said, penetrate each other substantially within the same bounds, the exceptions being the worlds of finer texture which extend beyond those relatively more dense. The names of the worlds are : the first which has not as yet been experienced by man—the Divine ; the second, the Monadic whence come the impulses that form man ; the third, the Spiritual, the highest world which man has as yet been able to experience ; the fourth, the Intuitional, the fifth, the Mental ; the sixth, the Emotional (Astral) world ; and the seventh is the world of matter as matter is familiar to us. Reference is made to the various articles dealing more fully with these worlds as follows :—

Adi	Plane, *See* **"Divine World and Solar System"**		
Annpadaka	,, ,, **Monadic**	,, ,, ,,
Atmic or Movanic	,, ,, **Spiritual**	,, ,, ,,
Buddhic	,, ,, **Inutitional**	,, ,, ,,
Astral	,, ,, **Emotional**	,, ,, ,,

Solomon : The connection of *Solomon*, son of David, the King of Israel, with magical practice, although it does not possess any Biblical authority, has yet a very considerable body of oriental tradition behind it. It is supposed, however, that the Jewish Solomon has in many cases been confounded with a still older and mythical figure. Then the Arabs and Persians have legends of a prehistoric race who were ruled by seventy-two monarchs of the name of Suleiman, of whom the last reigned one thousand years. " It does not seem," says Yarker, " that these Suleimans who are par excellence the rulers of all Djinn, Afreets and other elemental spirits, bear any relationship to the Israelite King." The name, he says, is found in that of a god of the Babylonians and the late Dr. Kenealy, the translator of Hafiz, says that the earliest Aryan teachers were named Mohn, Bodles or Solymi, and that Suleiman was an ancient title of royal power, synonymous with " Sultan " or " Pharaoh." A Persian legend states that in the mountains of Kaf, which can only be reached by the magic ring of *Solomon*, there is a gallery built by the giant Arzeak, where one kept the statues of a race who were ruled by the Suleiman or wise Kings of the East. There is a great chair or throne of *Solomon* hewn out of the solid rock, on the confines of the Afghanistan and India called the Takht-i-Suleiman or throne of *Solomon*, its ancient Aryan name being Shanker Acharga. It is to these older Suleiman's then, that we must probably look for a connection with the tradition of occultism, and it is not unlikely that the legend relating to *Solomon* and his temple have been confused with these, and that the protagonists of the antiquity of Freemasonry, who date their cult from the building of *Solomon's* Temple, have confounded some still older rite or mystery relating to the ancient dynasty of Suleiman with the circumstances of the masonic activities of the Hebrew monarch.

" God," says Josephus, " enabled *Solomon* to learn that skill which expels dæmons, which is a science useful and sanative to men. He composed such incantations, also, by which distempers are alleviated, and he left behind him the manner of using exorcisms, by which they drive away dæmons, so that they never return. And this method of cure is of great force unto this day ; for I have seen a certain man of my own country, whose name was Eleazar, releasing people that were dæmoniacal, in the presence of Vespasian and his sons, and his captains, and the whole multitude of his soldiers. The manner of the cure was this. He put a ring that had a root of one of these sorts mentioned by *Solomon* to the nostrils ; and when the man fell down immediately, he adjured him to return unto him no more, making still mention of *Solomon*, and reciting the incantations which he composed. And when Eleazar would persuade and demonstrate to the spectators that he had such a power, he set, a little way off, a cup, or basin full of water, and commanded the dæmon as he went out of the man, to overturn it, and thereby to let the spectators know that he had left the man." Some pretended fragments of these conjuring books of *Solomon* are noticed in the " Codex Pseudepigraphus " of Fabricius, and Josephus himself has described one of the antidæmoniacal roots, which must remind the reader of the perils attendant on gathering the " mandrake."

The Koran alleges that *Solomon* had power over the winds, and that he rode on his throne throughout the world during the day, and the wind brought it back every night to Jerusalem. This throne was placed on a carpet of green silk, of a prodigious length and breadth, and sufficient to afford standing-room to all *Solomon's* army, the men on his right hand and the Jinn on his left. An army of the most beatiful birds hovered near the throne, forming a kind of canopy over it, and the attendants, to screen the king and his soldiers from the sun. A certain number of evil spirits were also made subject to him, whose business it was to dive for pearls, and perform other work. We are also informed, on the same authority, that the devils, having received permission to tempt *Solomon*, in which they were not successful, conspired to ruin his character. They wrote several books of magic, and hid them under his throne ; and when he died they told the chief men among the Jews that if they wished to ascertain the manner in which *Solomon* obtained his absolute power over men, Genii, and the winds, they should dig under his throne. They did so and found the books, abounding with the most impious superstitions. The more learned and enlightened refused to participate in the practices described in those books, but they were willingly adopted by the common people. The Mahomedans assert that the Jewish priests published this scandalous story concerning *Solomon*, which was believed till Mahomet, by God's command, declared him to have been no idolater.

Solomon, it is further maintained by the Mahomedans, brought a thousand horses from Damascus and other cities he conquered, though some say they were left to him by his father David, who seized them from the Amalekites ; and others pretend that they came out of the Red Sea, and were provided with wings. The King wished to inspect his horses, and ordered them to be paraded before him ; and their symmetry and beauty so much occupied his attention that he gazed on them after sunset, and thus neglected evening prayers till it was too late. When sensible of his omission, he was so greatly concerned at it that he ordered all the horses to be killed as an offering to God, except a hundred of the best of them. This, we are informed, procured for him an ample recompense, as he received for the loss of his horses dominion over the winds.

The following tradition is narrated by the Mahomedan commentators relative to the building of the temple of Jerusalem. According to them, David laid the foundations of it, and when he died he left it to be finished by *Solomon*. That prince employed Jinn, and not men, in the work ; and this idea might probably originate from what is said in the First Book of Kings (vi., 7) that the Temple was " built of stone, made ready before it was brought thither, so that there was neither hammer, nor axe, nor any tool of iron, heard in the house while it was building " ; and the Rabbins notice a worm which, they pretend, assisted the workmen, the power of which was such as to cause the rocks and stones to separate in chiselled blocks. *Solomon*, while engaged in the erection of the Temple, found his end approaching, and he prayed that his death might be concealed from the Jinn till the building was finished. His request was granted. He died while in the act of praying, and leaning on his staff, which supported his body in that posture for a whole year, and the Jinn, who supposed him to be still alive, continued their work. At the expiration of the year the edifice was completed, when a worm which had entered the staff, ate it through, and to the amazement even of the Jinn the body fell to the ground, and the King was discovered to be dead.

The inhabitants of the valley of Lebanon believe that the celebrated city and temple of Baalbec were erected by the Jinn under *Solomon's* direction. The object of the erection of Baalbec is variously stated, one tradition affirming that it was intended to be a residence for the Egyptian princess whom *Solomon* married, and another that it was built for the Queen of Sheba.

Solomon Ibn Gabirol (1021–1058) : Spanish-Hebrew poet and mystic philosopher. He was a Neoplatonist, but at the same time subscribed to the mystical doctrine which states that the Deity can only be regarded as a negation of all attributes. This he considered essential to the preservation of the Jewish monotheism.

Solomon, Mirror of : The method of making the *Mirror of Solomon*, which is used for purposes of divination, is as follows : Take a shining and well-polished plate of fine steel, slightly concave, and with the blood of a white pigeon inscribe at the four corners the names—Jehovah, Eloym, Metatron, Adonay. Place the *mirror* in a clean and white cloth, and when you behold a new moon during the first hour after sunset, repeat a prayer that the angel Anaël may command and ordain his companions to act as they are instructed ; that is, to assist the operator in divining from the *mirror*. Then cast upon burning coals a suitable perfume, at the same time uttering a prayer. Repeat this thrice, then breathe upon the *mirror* and evoke the angel Anaël. The sign of the cross is then made upon the operator and upon the *mirror* for forty-five days in succession—at the end of which period Anaël appears in the form of a beautiful child to accomplish the operator's wishes. Sometimes he appears on the fourteenth day, according to the devotion and fervour of the operator. The perfume used in evoking him is saffron.

Solomon's Stables : (*See* **Subterranean Crypts.**)

Somnambulism : (Latin, *somnus*, sleep, and *ambulare*, to walk.) The condition in which walking, talking, and actions of a more complicated character are performed during sleep, without the agent's consciousness or after recollection. The somnambulist may have his eyes closed, and ears deaf to auditory impressions or sense impressions, without waking in him any gleam of consciousness. This may have some effect in rousing new trains of association and suggesting a new line of action. It is suggested that the sleep-walker may see only a mental picture of what he is doing—that is, a dream—and not the objective reality, and certain experimental tests have proved that this occurs in some cases at least. *Somnambulism* admits of many varying degrees. Its mildest form is typified in the inarticulate murmurings or vague gestures of a dreaming child, while in the most extreme cases where all the senses are active, and the actions apparently as purposive as in the normal waking state, it borders on the condition of spontaneous hypnotism. Indeed its affinity with hypnosis was early recognised, when the hypnotic subjects of the magnetists were designated *somnambules*. It is remarkable that somnambulists may walk in dangerous paths with perfect safety, but if they are suddenly awakened they are liable to fall. Spontaneous *somnambulism* generally indicates some morbid tendency of the nervous system, since, as a rule, only in some abnormal state could the dream ideas exercise so exciting an influence on the brain as to rouse to activity centres normally controlling voluntary movements.

Sorcery : (From Latin *sortiarius*, one who practices divination by lots.) The use of supposed supernatural power by the agency of evil spirits called forth by spells by a witch or black magician. (*See* **Magic.**)

Sorrel-leaf : A *sorrel-leaf* was sometimes used to bewitch people, as in the case of the Irish Witch mentioned in George Sinclair's *Satan's Invisible World Displayed*, who gave to a girl a leaf of *sorrel*, which the child put into her mouth. Great torture ensued for the child, such tortures being increased on the approach of the witch.

Sortilege, or divination by lots, is one of the most ancient and common superstitions. We find it used among the Oriental nations to detect a guilty person, as when Saul by this means discovered that Jonathan had disobeyed his command by taking food, and when the sailors by a similar process found Jonah to be the cause of the tempest by which they were overtaken. The methods of using the lot have been very numerous, such as Rhabdomancy, Clidomancy, the Sortes Sagittariæ, otherwise Belomancy, and the common casting of dice. The following are the more classical :—

Sortes Thriæcæ, or Thriæan lots, were chiefly used in Greece ; they were pebbles or counters distinguished by certain characters which were cast into an urn, and the first that came out was supposed to contain the right direction. This form of divination received its name from the Thriæ, three nymphs supposed to have nursed Apollo, and to have invented this mode of predicting futurity.

Sortes Viales, or street and road lots, were used both in Greece and Rome. The person that was desirous to learn his fortune carried with him a certain number of lots, distinguished by several characters or inscriptions, and walking to and fro in the public ways desired the first boy whom he met to draw, and the inscription on the lot thus drawn was received as an infallible prophecy. Plutarch declares that this form of divination was derived from the Egyptians, by whom the actions and words of boys were carefully observed as containing in them something prophetical. Another form of the Sortes Viales was exhibited by a boy, but sometimes by a man, who posted himself in a public place to give responses to all comers. He was provided with a tablet, on which certain fatidical verses were written ; when consulted, he cast dice on the tablet, and the verses on which they fell were supposed to contain the proper direction. Sometimes instead of tablets they had urns, in which the fatidical verses were thrown, written upon slips of parchment. The verse drawn out was received as a sure guide and direction. To this custom Tibullus alludes :—

Thrice in the streets the sacred lots she threw,
And thrice the boy a happy omen drew.

This form of divining was often practised with the Sibylline oracles, and was hence named Sortes Sibyllina.

Sortes Prenestinæ, or the Prenestine lots, were used in Italy ; the letters of the alphabet were placed in an urn and shaken ; they were then turned out upon the floor, and the words which they accidentally formed were received as omens. This superstitious use of letters is still common in Eastern nations. The Mussulmans have a divining table, which they say was invented by the prophet Edris or Enoch. It is divided into a hundred little squares, each of which contains a letter of the Arabic alphabet. The person who consults it repeats three times the opening chapter of the *Koran*, and the 57th verse of the 6th chapter : " With Him are the keys of the secret things ; none knoweth them but Him ; He knoweth whatever is on the dry ground, or in the sea : there falleth no leaf but He knoweth it ; neither is there a single grain in the dark parts of the earth, nor a green thing, nor a dry thing, but it is written in a perspicuous book." Having concluded this recitation, he averts his head from the table and places his finger upon it ; he then looks to see upon what letter his finger is placed, writes that letter ; the fifth following it ; the fifth following that again ; and so on until he comes back to the first he had touched : the letters thus collected form the answer.

Sortes Homericæ and Sortes Virgilianæ, divination by opening some poem at hazard, and accepting the passage which first turns up as an answer. This practice probably arose from the esteem which poets had among the ancients, by whom they were reputed divine and inspired persons. Homer's works among the Greeks had the most credit, but the tragedies of Euripides and other celebrated poems were occasionally used for the same purpose. The Latins chiefly consulted Virgil, and many curious coincidences are related by grave historians, between the prediction and the event ; thus, the elevation of Severus to the empire is supposed to have been foretold by his opening at this verse—

Remember, Roman, with imperial sway
to rule the nations.

It is said that Charles I. and Lord Falkland made trial of the Virgilian lots a little before the commencement of the great civil war. The former opened at that passage in the fourth book of the Æneid where Dido predicts the violent death of her faithless lover ; the latter at the lamentation of Evander over his son in the eleventh book ; if the story be true, the coincidences between the responses and events are among the most remarkable recorded.

Sortes Biblicæ, divination by the Bible, which the early Christians used instead of the profane poets. Nicephorus Gregoras recommends the Psalter as the fittest book for the purpose, but Cedrenus informs us that the New Testament was more commonly used. St. Augustine denounces this practice in temporal affairs, but declares in one of his letters that he had recourse to it in all cases of spiritual difficulty. Another form of the Biblical lots is to go to a place of worship, and take as an omen the first passage of Scripture read by the minister, or the text from which he preaches. This is no uncommon practice in modern times, and it is frequently vindicated by persons who ought to know better.

The Mussulmans consult the *Koran* in a similar manner, but they deduce their answer from the seventh line of the right-hand page. Others count how often the letters *kha* and *shin* occur in the page ; if *kha* (the first letter of *kheyr*, " good ") predominate, the answer is deemed favourable ; but if *shin* (the first letter of *shin* " evil ") be more frequent, the inference is that the projects of the inquirer are forbidden or dangerous.

It would be easy to multiply examples of these efforts to obtain guidance from blind chance ; they were once so frequent, that it was deemed necessary to denounce them from the pulpit as being clearly forbidden by the divine precept, " Thou shalt not tempt the Lord thy God."

South American Indians : (*See* **American Indians.**)

Sovereign Council of Wisdom : (*See* **Devil-worship.**)

Spain : *Witchcraft.*—From early times *Spain* was regarded as the special abode of superstition, and in the middle ages as the home of sorcery and magic, probably because of the immense notoriety given to the discoveries of the Moorish alchemists. (*See* **Moors.**) The Inquisition quickly took root in the country, and reaped a rich harvest among Jews, Moriscos, and superstitious Christians.

Alfonso de Spina, a Franciscan of Castille, where the Inquisition was not then established, wrote, about the year 1458 or 1460, a work especially directed against heretics and unbelievers, in which he gives a chapter on these articles of popular belief which were derived from the ancient heathendom of the people. Among these, witches, under the name of Xurguine (jurgina) or bruxe, held a prominent place.

He tells us that in his time these offenders abounded in Dauphiny and Gascony, where they assembled in great numbers by night on a wild table land, carrying candles with them, to worship Satan, who appeared in the form of a boar on a certain rock, popularly known by the name Elboch de Biterne, and that many of them had been taken by the inquisition of Toulouse and burnt. From that time we find, in Spanish history, the charge of witchcraft and sorcery not infrequently brought forward under different forms and circumstances, of which several remarkable examples are given by Llorente in his *History of the Inquisition in Spain.*

The first auto-da-fé against sorcery appears to have been that of Calahorra, in 1507, when thirty women, charged before the inquisition as witches, were burnt. In 1527, a great number of women were accused in Navarre of the practice of sorcery, through the information of two girls, one of eleven, the other only of nine years old, who confessed before the royal council of Navarre that they had been received into the sect of the jurginas, and promised on condition of being pardoned, to discover all the women who were implicated in these practices.

The moment the attention of the inquisition was thus drawn to the crime of sorcery, the prevalence of this superstition in the Basque provinces became notorious ; and Charles V., rightly judging that it was to be attributed more to the ignorance of the population of those districts than to any other cause, directed that preachers should be sent to instruct them.

The first treatise in the Spanish language on the subject of sorcery, by a Franciscan monk named Martin de Castanaga, was printed under approbation of the bishop of Calahorra in 1529. About this time the zeal of the inquisitors of Saragossa was excited by the appearance of many witches who were said to have come from Navarre, and to have been sent by their sect as missionaries to make disciples of the women of Arragon. This sudden witchpersecution in *Spain* appears to have had an influence on the fate of the witches of Italy. Pope Adrian IV., who was raised to the papal chair in 1522, was a Spanish bishop, and had held the office of inquisitor-general in *Spain*. In the time of Julius II., who ruled the papal world from 1503 to 1513, a sect of witches and sorcerers had been discovered in Lombardy, who were extremely numerous, and had their Sabbaths and all the other abominations of the continental witches. The proceedings against them appear to have been hindered by a dispute between the inquisitors and the ecclesiastical judges who claimed the jurisdiction in such cases. On the 20th July, 1523, pope Adrian issued a bull against the crime of sorcery, placing it in the sole jurisdiction of the inquisitors. This bull perhaps gave the new impulse to the prosecution of the witches in *Spain*.

Of the cases which followed during more than a century, the most remarkable was that of the auto-da-fé at Logrono on the 7th and 8th of November, 1610, which arose in some measure from the visitation of the French Basque province in the preceding year. The valley of Bastan is situated at the foot of the Pyrenees, on the French Frontier, and at no great distance from Labourd. It was within the jurisdiction of the inquisition established at Logrono in Castille. The mass of the population of this valley appear to have been sorcerers, and they held their meetings or Sabbaths at a place called Zugarramurdi.

A woman who was condemned implicated a number of other persons. All the persons arrested on this occasion agreed in their description of the Sabbath, and of the practices of the witches, which in their general features bore a close resemblance to those of the witches of Labourd. The usual place of meeting was known here, as in Labourd, by the popular name of Aquelarre, a Gascon word, signifying the meadow of the goat. Their ordinary meetings were held on the nights of Monday, Wednesday and Friday, every week, but they had grand feasts on the principal holidays of the church, such as Easter, Pentecost, Christmas, etc., All these feasts appear to have been fixed by the Christian teachers at the period of older pagan festivals.

The accounts of their Sabbaths are entirely similar to those given of such meetings elsewhere. They danced, sang took part in the most horrible orgies, and came into personal contact with Satan.

The auto-da-fé of Logrono, as far as it related to the sect of the sorcerers of Zugarramurdi, caused a great sensation, and brought the subject of witchcraft under the consideration of the Spanish theologians. These were so far more enlightened than the body of their contemporaries in other countries, that they generally leant to the opinion that witchcraft was a mere delusion, and that the details of

the confessions of the miserable creatures who were its victims were all creations of the imagination. They were punished because their belief was a heresy, contrary to the doctrines of the church. Llorente gives the abstract of a treatise on this subject by a Spanish ecclesiastic named Pedro de Valentia, addressed to the grand inquisitor in consequence of the trial at Logrono in 1610, and which remained in manuscript among the archives of the inquisition.

This writer adopts entirely the opinion that the acts confessed by the witches were imaginary ; he attributed them partly to the methods in which the examinations were carried on, and to the desire of the ignorant people examined to escape by saying what seemed to please their persecutors, and partly to the effects of the ointments and draughts which they had been taught to use, and which were composed of ingredients that produced sleep, and acted upon the imagination and the mental faculties.

Spiritualism.—A writer in the *Religious Philosophical Journal* says :—" The language that furnishes the largest number of periodicals devoted to the dissemination of the doctrine and philosophy of modern Spiritualism, is the Spanish. This statement will be somewhat surprising to many of our readers, for we have been accustomed to look upon the Spaniards as non-progressive and conservative in the extreme. *Spain*, until a few years, has always been intolerant of any religions except the Roman Catholic, and was the latest of European nations to yield to the spirit of religious progress. Protestantism has with the greatest difficulty obtained a foothold in that country within the last few years, but it has been attended with annoying restrictions and persecutions, while its progress has been exceedingly slow and discouraging.

Spiritualism in *Spain* commenced, as in many other lands, with a series of disturbances, which took place in a family residing in the outskirts of Cadiz. Stone-throwing, bellringing, and other preternatural annoyances were the first means of awakening attention to the subject, and as they occurred at the house of a Spanish gentleman who had just returned from the United States, full of the marvels of " the Rochester knockings," circles were at once formed, intelligent responses by rappings obtained, and a foot-hold gained, upon which the edifice of Spiritual progress was upreared. So rapidly did the interest thus awakened spread, that the first promulgators were soon lost sight of, and as early as 1854, a society was formed at Cadiz, which was organised for the sole purpose of publishing the communications received from " the Spirits " during two preceding years. From 1854 to 1860, Spiritualism spread through the principal towns and villages of *Spain* in the usual fashion. Circles were held in private families, and an endless number of " societies " were formed and dissolved, according to the exigencies of the time. One of the first public events of note in connection with Spanish Spiritualism, was of so remarkable a character, that it deserves special mention. This was no other than an Auto-da-fé, the only difference between the occasion under consideration and the fiery executions of olden times being, that the victims were formerly human beings, whereas in the present instance, they were all the books, pamphlets, and works of a Spiritualistic character that could be procured at that period of the movement. Amongst the pile thus offered up on the altar of religious enlightenment, were the writings of Kardec Dufau, Grand, and Guldenstubbé ; some copies of English and American Spiritual papers, and a large collection of tracts issued by the Spiritualists of *Spain*. This memorable scene occurred on the morning of the 9th of October, 1861, at the Esplanade Barcelona.

Among the well-know residents of Barcelona, was a

Señor Navarez, whose daughter, Rosa, had for many years been the subject of spasmodic attacks, called by the Catholic clergy " the obsession of demons "—by the medical faculty, an aggravated condition of epilepsy. Within two years after the Auto-da-fé, Rosa was pronounced entirely cured, by the magnetic passes of a gentleman who was the medium of the private circle held in the city. Shortly after this, Barcelona could boast of its well-approved Spiritual organs, numerous societies for investigation, and several mediums, who from their exclusive positions in private life, would object to their names being mentioned. The journal whs published by Señor Alcantara, and was warmly supported by the Viscount de Torres Solanot, and numbers of other leaders of science and literature in *Spain*. By this publication the opponents of Spiritualism were amazed to learn of the immense progress the cause was making, and the number of distinguished persons who assembled nightly in circles to promote investigation. A circular calling the attention of the Spanish public to the phenomena of Spiritualism was published in 1875 by Viscount Solanot. The authors of this circular, met with no response worthy of their fraternal intentions. It might have been difficult to define exactly what the Spanish brethren proposed to do or wished others to unite with them in doing ; certain it is, that no tangible results could be expected to follow from a very transcendental address to the scattered ranks of a movement, whose motto might well be Liberty, Inequality, and Disintegration : " Our Spanish friends mean well, but is it possible there can be unity enough amongst them to send a delegation to America ? " asked one of the shrewdest on perusing this grandiloquent circular. Nothing daunted by the impossibility of getting an international representation worthy of the cause at Philadelphia, the energetic Viscount Solanot again agitated the subject previous to the Paris Exposition of 1878. In the articles written for *El Criterio* on this proposition, the Viscount names amongst those societies of Spiritualists prepared to promote an International representation, " La Federation Espirita," of Belgium; " The British National Association of Spiritualists," England ; " La Sociedad Central Espirita," of the Republic of Mexico ; and " El Central General del Espiritismo." Notice is also taken, and with a hope of its ultimate success, of the attempt to form a national association and unite all the discordant elements under the one broad banner of simple Spiritualism.

Magnetism and Mediumistic Science.—In *Spain* as in Italy, a considerable amount of attention has been directed towards the unfoldment of Mediumistic power by means of Magnetism. Magnetic Societies abounded in *Spain* up to within the last few years, when many elements of internal discord prevailed in the ranks, and succeeded in dissolving the bonds which had united flourishing associations. Amongst the amateur mesmerists of *Spain* may be mentioned Don Juan Escudero, of Madrid, a gentleman who having witnessed some experiments in "animal magnetism " in California, tried its effect in his own family with success.

Among the numerous circles or " groups " formed in the different parts of *Spain* for the study of Spiritualism and its phenomena, was one of long standing at Tarragona called " The Christian Circle." Quite recently the President of this circle sent the following communication to the *Revue Spirite* of Paris :—" The convict prison here in Tarragona has 800 inmates sentenced to forced labour By some means, Spiritualistic books have been introduced among the prisoners. The circulation of these books among them has been the means of bringing seventy or eighty of them to be believers in our doctrine. These converts have ceased to regard their miserable position

from their old point of view ; they no longer entertain schemes of revolt against the authorities. They endure their lot with resignation under the influence of the teaching that this world is but a preliminary stage to another, where, if repentant of the ill they have done, and seeking the good of others, they will be better off than here. " Not long since one of these men died ; at his death he declined the established offices of the prison priest, on the ground that he was a Spiritualist and did not need them. The priest then discovered that Spiritualism was a subject of discussion with many of the prisoners. He made a representation of the matter to his bishop, who made formal complaint of it to the commandant of the prison, and the commandant made an investigation. In the end a particular prisoner was selected for punishment in the form of an additional weight of fetters. This coming to the knowledge of the Spiritualists of Tarragona, Barcelona, and Lerida, they had a meeting upon the subject and delegated one of their number, a man of position, to interview the commandant. The representations which he made, led the commandant to cancel his order as to the additional fetters. The bishop's censure against spiritualist books placed them under prohibition, which was maintained. It is known, however, that although never found by gaolers, the books are still there."

In April, 1881, the editor of the Madrid *El Criterio* says :— " that great progress has been made in the cause of Spiritualism ; that the hall of meeting of the Spiritual Society ' is completely full every Thursday evening,' and is not now large enough ' to hold the public who come to the sessions,' that Dr. Merschejewski has called the attention of the University of St. Petersburg to a psychometric phenomena of much importance ; to wit: A young man deemed from childhood to be an idiot, who will in some seconds solve any mathematical problem, while if a poem be read to him, even of many hundred verses, he will repeat the whole of it without failing in a single word." Señor Manuel Lopez in the same issue of *El Criterio* says, speaking of the progress of a society of Spiritualists in Madrid :—" We have received a mediumistic work of extraordinary merit, executed by a medium of the ' Society of Spiritualists ' of Zaragoza. It consists of a portrait of Isabel the Catholic, made with a pencil, and is a work truly admirable. It is said by intelligent persons who have examined it to be an exact copy of one preserved in the Royal Museum of Painters of this court. Many thanks are tendered to the Zaragozan Society for this highly appreciated present. It was about the end of the year 1880, that the Spiritualists of *Spain* sustained another series of attacks from the Church. The first of these was the refusal of the clergy to accord the customary rites of interment to the remains of two ladies, both of irreproachable character, and good standing in society, but both " guilty " of having believed in Spiritual manifestations. The second raid which the Church in *Spain* perpetrated about this time to the prejudice of the Spiritualists, was the suppression of a well-written Spiritual paper published at Lerida, entitled *El Buen Sentido*. The Bishop of Lerida had long threatened this step, and warned the editor to beware how he presumed to allow any writings reflecting upon clerical doings to appear in his columns. As some of the principal contributors were Madame Soler, Mdlle. Sans, Don Murillo, and others equally capable of arraigning the intolerant acts which Church policy seemed determined to push against the Spiritualists, it was scarcely likely that the Bishop's threats would produce much effect. The last article which seemed to inflame the clergy to retaliate was an indignant protest which appeared in the columns of this paper on the condemnation of a working man to three years' imprisonment, leaving a family of children destitute and all for speaking in public against the intolerance of the Church.

In a number of *El Criterio*, dated 1881, is a letter from Don Migueles, in which he gives a somewhat discouraging account of " the cause " as it recently existed in *Spain*. The editor says :—" Don Migueles visited many cities to examine into the state of affairs of a spiritual nature, but found many who were only to be enticed by physical phenomena, caring nothing for the esoteric beauties of our faith ; many who were convinced that they knew all there was to be known concerning it, and others who were timid fearing the disapproval of neighbours. In some places, however, excellent mediums were discovered. In Santiago, in Oviedo, in Corunna and Valladolid, an exceptional interest was manifest. Near Santiago, there was a young girl possessed of wonderful faculties. Two bars of magnetized iron held over her horizontally, half a metre distant, were sufficient to suspend her body in the air. " The proceedings of the Spanish Society, under the name of the *Sesiones de Controversio*, in the month of April last, are spoken of in the Critic as markedly impressive on account of the lofty sentiments maintained throughout the discussions, by the various speakers. ' In the past month were given also very interesting conferencias by our illustrious brothers, the Sres. Rebolledo and Huelbes.' The able engineer and inventor, belonging to the Society of Santiago de Chili and founder of that of Lima, D. R. Caruana y Berard, has just arrived in Madrid. The *Revista Espiritista* of Barcelona mentions the visit which its editor has made to the central societies of Spiritualists of Sabodell and Tarrasa, where a great number of brethren were assembled on the occasion, and which will result in great good to the doctrine." The Barcelona *Lux*, of date 1881, gives encouraging accounts of séances held at Cordova, Tarragona, Seville, and many other places. The editor, Madame Soler, also refers to the prohibition to Catholics, by an archbishop to have or to read the Spiritualistic work of Niram Aliv : of the " Society of Spiritualists " of Tarrasa ; of the circle of Santa Cruz of Tenerif ; of that of " Faith, Hope, and Charity," of Andujar, and of St. Vincent de Bogota.

Speal Bone, Divination by : A form of divination used in Scotland. A *speal bone*, or blade bone of a shoulder of mutton is used, but details of the method are wanting. A common soldier, accompanying Lord Loudon on his retreat to Skye, told the issue of the battle of Culloden at the very moment it was decided, pretending to have seen the event by looking through the *bone*.

Speers, Dr. : (*See* **Moses, William Stainton**.)

Spells : *Spells*, incantations, a written or spoken formula of words supposed to be capable of magical effects.

Anglo-saxon *spel*, a saying or story, hence a form of words ; Icelandic, *spjall*, a saying ; Gothic, *spill*, a fable.

The conception of *spells* appears to have arisen in the idea that there is some natural and intimate connection between words and the things signified by them. Thus if one repeats the name of a supernatural being the effect will be analogous to that produced by the being itself. It is assumed that all things are in sympathy, and act and react upon one another, things that have once been in contact continue to act on each other even after the contact has been removed. That certain names unknown to man, of gods, demi-gods, and demons, if discovered can be used against them by the discoverer, was believed in Ancient Egypt. *Spells* or enchantments can be divided into several classes as follows : (1) Protective *spells* ; (2) the curse or taboo ; (3) *Spells* by which a person, animal or object is to be injured or transformed ; (4) *Spells* to procure some minor end, or love-spells, the curing of persons and cattle, etc.

The power of the spoken word is implicitly believed in by all primitive peoples, especially if it emanates from a known professor of the art of magic, and if it be in a language or dialect unknown. Thus the magicians of Ancient Egypt employed foreign words for their incantations, such as Tharthar, thamara, thatha, mommon, thanabotha, opranu, brokhrex, abranazukhel," which occurs at the end of a *spell* the purpose of which is to bring dreams. The magicians and sorcerers of the middle ages likewise employed gibberish of a similar kind, as do the medicine men of the North American Indians at the present day. The reason for the *spell* being usually couched in a well-known formula, is probably because experience found that that and no other formula was efficacious. Thus in Ancient Egypt not only were the formulæ of *spells* well fixed, but the exact tone of voice in which they were to be pronounced was specially taught. The power of a *spell* remains until such time as it is broken by an antidote or exorcism. Therefore it is not a passing thing.

(1) The protective *spell*.—The commonest form of this is an incantation, usually rhymed, imploring the protection of certain gods, saints, or beneficent beings, who in waking or sleeping hours will guard the speaker from maleficent powers, such as :—

> " Matthew, Mark, Luke and John,
> Bless the bed that I lie on."

Of a deeper significance are these supposed to be spoken by the dead Egyptian on his journey through Amenti by which he wards off the evil beings who would hinder his way, and so the serpent who would bite the dead is addressed thus : " O serpent come not ! Geb and Shu stand against thee. Thou hast eaten mice. That is loathsome to the Gods. Thou hast gnawed the bones of a putrid cat." The Book of the Dead says, " Whoever readeth the *spells* daily over himself, he is whole- upon earth, he escapes from death, and never doth anything evil meet him," says Budge in *Egyptian Magic*, p. 128. " We learn how great was the confidence which the deceased placed in his words of power, and also that the sources from which they sprang were the gods of Thoth and Isis. It will be remembered the Thoth is called the " scribe of the gods," the " lord of writing," the " master of papyrus," the " maker of the palette and the ink-jar," the " lord of divine words," *i.e.*, the holy writings or scriptures, and as he was the lord of books and master of the power of speech, he was considered to be the possessor of all knowledge both human and divine. At the creation of the world it was he who reduced to words the will of the unseen and unknown creative Power, and who uttered them in such wise that the universe came into being and it was he who proved himself by the exercise of his knowledge to be the protector and the friend of Osiris, and of Isis, and of their son Horus. From the evidence of the texts we know that it was not by physical might that Thoth helped these three gods, but by giving them words of power and instructing them how to use them. We know that Osiris vanquished his foes, and that he re-constituted his body and became the king of the underworld and god of the dead, but he was only able to do these things by means of the words of power which Thoth had given to him, and which he had taught him to pronounce properly and in a proper tone of voice. It is this belief which makes the deceased cry out, " Hail, Thoth, who madest Osiris victorious over his enemies, make thou Ani to be victorious over his enemies in the presence of the great and sovereign princes who are in Tattu, or in any other place." Without the words of power given to him by Thoth, Osiris would have been powerless under the attacks of his foes, and similarly the dead man, who was always identified with Osiris, would have passed out of existence at his death but for the words of power provided by the writings that were buried with him. In the Judgment Scene it is Thoth who reports to the gods the result of the weighing of the heart in the balance, and who has supplied its owner with the words which he has uttered in his supplications, and whatever can be said in favour of the deceased he says to the gods, and whatever can be done for him he does. But apart from being the protector and friend of Osiris, Thoth was the refuge to which Isis fled in her trouble. The words of a hymn declare that she knew " how to turn aside evil hap," and that she was " strong of tongue and uttered the words of power which she knew with correct pronunciation, and halted not in her speech, and was perfect both in giving the command, and in saying the word," but this description only proves that she had been instructed by Thoth in the art of uttering words of power with effect, and to him, indeed, she owed more than this. *Spells* to keep away disease are of this class.

The amulets found upon Egyptian mummies, and the inscriptions on Gnostic gems are for the most part of a protective nature. (*See* **Egypt** and **Gnostics.**) The protective *spell* may be said to be an amulet in words, and is often found in connection with the amulet, on which it is inscribed.

(2) *The curse or taboo.*—(a) The word of blighting, the damaging word. (b) The word of prohibition or restriction.

(a) The curse is of the nature of a *spell*, even if it be not in the shape of a definite formula. Thus we have the Highland curses : " A bad meeting to you." " Bad understanding to you." " A down mouth be yours " which are certainly popular as formulæ.

Those who had seen old women, of the Madge Wildfire School, cursing and banning, say their manner is well-calculated to inspire terror. Some fifteen or twenty years ago, a party of tinkers quarrelled and fought, first among themselves, and then with some Tiree villagers. In the excitement a tinker wife threw off her cap and allowed her hair to fall over her shoulders in wild disorder. She then bared her knees, and falling on them to the ground, in a praying attitude, poured forth a torrent of wishes that struck awe into all who heard her. She imprecated " Drowning by sea and conflagration by land ; may you never see a son to follow your body to the graveyard, or a daughter to mourn your death. I have made my wish before this, and I will make it now, and there was not yet a day I did not see my wish fulfilled." Curses employed by witches usually inferred a blight upon the person cursed, their flocks, their herds and crops. Barrenness, too, was frequently called down upon women. A person under a curse or *spell* is believed in the Scottish Highlands " to become powerless over his own volition, is alive and awake but moves and acts as if asleep." Curses or *spells* which inferred death were frequently mentioned in works which deal with Mediæval Magic. (*See* Summons by accused.)

(b) The Taboo, the word of prohibition or restriction. This is found in the mystic expression " thou shalt not." Thus a number of the commandments are taboos, and the Book of Leviticus teems with them. The taboo is the " don't " applied to children—a curb on primitive desire. To break a taboo was to bring dire misfortune upon oneself, and often upon one's family.

Of injuring or transformation of a person, animal or object there are copious examples. These were nearly affected by a spell of a given formula. Thus no less than twelve chapters of the *Book of the Dead* (chapters LXXVII. to LXXXVIII) are devoted to providing the deceased with words of power, the recital of which was necessary to enable him to transform himself into various animal and human forms. The Rev. S. Baring Gould in his *Book of Folklore*, page 57, says, that in such cases the consequence of a *spell* being cast on an individual requiring him or her to become a beast or a monster with no escape except under conditions difficult of execution or of obtaining. To this

category belong a number of so-called fairy tales, that actually are folk-tales. And these do not all pertain to Aryan peoples for wherever magical arts are believed to be all-powerful, there one of its greatest achievements is the casting of a *spell* so as to alter completely the appearance of the person on whom it is cast, so that this individual becomes an animal. One need only recall the story in the *Arabian Nights* of the Calenders and the three noble ladies of Bagdad, in which the wicked sisters are transformed into bitches that have to be thrashed every day. Of this class are the stories of " Beauty and the Beast " and " The Frog Prince."

(4) *Spells* to procure some minor end, love-spells, etc., Love-spells were engraved on metal tables by the Gnostics, and the magicians of the middle ages. Instances of these are to be found in *The Book of the Sacred Magic* of Abraham the Jew (q.v.) *Spells* were often employed to imprison evil spirits.

The later Jews have many extravagant opinions and legends relating to this subject, which they appear to have derived in a great measure from the Babylonians. Josephus affirms that it was generally believed by his countrymen that Solomon left behind him many *spells*, which had the power of terrifying and expelling evil spirits. The Rabbins also almost uniformly describe Solomon as an accomplished magician. It is probable that the belief in the power of *spells* and incantations became general among the Jews during the captivity, and that the invention of them is attributed to Solomon, as a more creditable personage than the deities of the Assyrians. Those fictions acquired currency, not only among the Arabs, Persians, and other Mohammedan nations, but, in process of time, also in many Christian communities. They were first adopted by the Gnostics and similar sects, in whose creed heathenism preponderated over Christianity ; and, in the dark ages, they found their way among the Catholics ; principally by means of the Pseudo-gospels and fabulous legends of saints. An incident in the life of St. Margaret will suffice as a specimen. This holy virgin, having vanquished an evil spirit who assaulted her, demanded his name. " My name," replied the demon, " is Veltis, and I am one of those whom Solomon, by virtue of his spells, confined in a copper caldron at Babylon ; but when the Babylonians, in the hope of finding treasures, dug up the caldron and opened it, we all made our escape. Since that time, our efforts have been directed to the destruction of righteous persons ; and I have long been striving to turn thee from the course which thou hast embraced." The reader of the " Arabian Nights' Entertainments " will be immediately reminded of the story of the " Fisherman." The Oriental origin of many similar legends, e.g., of St. George of Cappadocia, is equally obvious.

Literature.—Grimm's *Deutsche Mythologie* ; Malleus Maleficarum ; Campbell's *Witchcraft and superstition in the Scottish Highlands* ; Budge's *Egyptian Magic* ; Henderson's, *Survivals in Belief among the Celts.*

Spider : As an amulet. This insect, baked, was sometimes worn round the neck as a charm. Elias Ashmole in his *Diary* says : " I took early in the morning a good dose of elixir, and hung three *spiders* about my neck, and they drove my ague away. Deo Gratias ! " *Spiders* and their webs were often recommended as a cure for this malady. Burton gives us the following tale : " Being in the country in the vacation time, not many years since, at Lindly in Leicestershire, my father's house, I first observed this amulet of a *spider* in a nut-shell, wrapped in silk, so applied for an ague by my mother...... This I thought most absurd and ridiculous, and I could see no warrant in it. . . . . till at length, rambling amongst authors, I found this very medicine in Dioscorides, approved by Matthiolus, repeated by Aldrovandus. . . . . I began to have a better opinion of it, and to give more credit to amulets, when I saw it in some parties answer to experience."

Spiegelschrift : Writing written *backwards*, from right to left, so as to be read in a mirror. Automatic writing is frequently done in this way, and it is said that the ability to produce *spiegelschrift* is often found where there is a natural tendency to automatism.

Spirit in Theosophy, is the monad after he has manifested himself in the Spiritual, Intuitional and Mental Worlds in the aspects of Will, Intuition and Intellect respectively, but the term is often used to denote the monad in the aspect of Will only. (*See* **Monad** and also the various articles on these Worlds.)

Spirit Messenger : Journal of Spiritualism. (*See* **Spiritualism.**)

Spirit Photography : The production of photographs on which alleged spirit-forms are visible. When the plate is developed there appears, in addition to the likeness of the sitter, a shape resembling more or less distinctly the human form, which at the moment of exposure was imperceptible to the normal vision. Spiritualists assert that there are photographs of spirits—the spirits of departed friends and relatives of the sitters—and that the presence of a medium is required to facilitate their production. Notwithstanding that on the recognition of the supposed spirit by the sitter and others rests the main evidence in favour of *spirit photography*, the "astral figure" is generally very vague and indistinct, with the head and shoulders enveloped in close-clinging draperies. The practice of *spirit photography* originated in America some fifty years ago, and has enjoyed a fitful existence to the present day. It was first introduced by Mumler, a Boston photographer, in 1862. Dr. Gardner, of the same city, was photographed by Mumler, and on the plate appeared an image which the sitter identified as his cousin, who had died twelve years before. Dr. Gardner published abroad his experience, and the new *photography* was at once adopted by spiritualists, who saw in it a means of proving their beliefs. In 1863, however, Dr. Gardner discovered that in at least two instances a living model had sat for Mumler's "spirit" pictures. Though he continued to believe that some of the photographs might be genuine, his exposure of Mumler's fraud effectively checked the movement for a time. After the lapse of six years Mumler appeared in New York, where the authorities endeavoured to prosecute him, but the evidence against him was insufficient to prove fraud, and he was acquitted. *Spirit photography* had flourished in America for some ten years before it became known in Britain. Mr. and Mrs. Guppy, the well-known spiritualistic mediums, endeavoured without success to produce spirit photographs in private, and at length called in the aid of a professional photographer, Mr. Hudson. A photograph of Mr. Guppy now revealed a dim, draped "spirit" form. Hudson speedily became popular, and his studio was as largely patronized as Mumler's had been. Mr. Thomas Slater, a London optician, made careful observations of his process without being able to detect any fraud. Mr. Beattie, a professional photographer, and something of a sceptic, made the following statement concerning Hudson's performances : "They were not made by double exposure, nor by figures projected in space in any way ; they were not the result of mirrors ; they were not produced by any machinery in the background, behind it, above it, or below it, nor by any contrivance connected with the bath, the camera, or the camera-slide." Mr. Traill Taylor, editor of the British Journal of Photography said that " at no time during the preparation, exposure, or development of the pictures was Mr. Hudsom within ten feet of the camera or dark room. Appearances of an abnormal kind did certainly appear on several plates." Such

testimonies as the above, from the lips of skilled and disinterested witnesses, would naturally seem to raise *spirit photography* to the level of a genuine psychic phenomenon. But a careful analysis of the evidence, such as is given by Mrs. Sidgwick in her article on *Spirit Photography* in the Psychical Research Society's Proceedings, vol. VII., will serve to show how even a trained investigator may be deceived by sleight-of-hand. And it is notable that Mr. Beattie himself afterwards pointed out instances of double exposure in Hudson's productions. In spite of this, Hudson continued to practise, and the various spiritualist magazines continued to lend him their support, with the exception of the *Spiritualist*, whose editor, himself a practical photographer, had aided Mr. Beattie in the denunciation of *spirit photography*. Another enthusiastic spiritualist, Mr. Enmore Jones, who at first professed to recognise a dead daughter in one of the pictured "spirits," afterwards admitted that he had been mistaken. Those who had pinned their faith to the genuineness of the photographic manifestations were naturally unwilling to relinquish their belief in what they considered a sure proof of the reality of the spirit-world, and ingenious explanations were offered to cover the circumstance of the apparent double exposure. The spirit aura, they said, differed from the natural atmosphere in its refracting power, and it was not to be wondered at that objects were sometimes duplicated. And so Hudson retained a considerable measure of popularity. Mr. Beattie himself afterwards attempted to produce spirit photographs, and succeeded in obtaining vague blotches and flaws on his pictures, some of them bearing a dim resemblance to a human figure. But there is reason to believe that a hired assistant, who provided studio and apparatus, was not entirely above suspicion. In 1874 Buguet (q.v.), a Paris photographer crossed over to London where he commenced the practice of *spirit photography*. Many of his pictures were recognized by his clients, and even when he had been tried by the French Government, and had admitted deception, there were those who refused to regard his confession as spontaneous, and inclined to the opinion that he had been bribed by the Jesuits to confess to fraud of which he was innocent ! Other spirit photographers were Parkes, a contemporary of Hudson, and Boursnell, who produced spirit pictures in London in more recent years. The principal evidence in favour of *spirit photography* is undoubtedly the recognition of the spirits by their friends and relatives, but the unreliable nature of such a test can be seen when we remember that time and again a single "spirit" has been claimed by several persons as a near relative —the sister of one, the grandfather of another, and so on. One of the most prominent defenders of the mediumistic photographers was the Rev. Stainton Moses (q.v.)—" M. A. Oxon "—who saw in them the best proof of the reality of spiritualism. The same view was shared by Mr. Alfred Russel Wallace (q.v.), who said in the *Arena*, January, 1891 : " It is that which furnishes, perhaps, the most unassailable demonstration it is possible to obtain of the objective reality of spiritual forms."

Spirit World : Spiritualistic Journal. (*See* **Spiritualism.**)

Spiritism : The name bestowed upon the French form of spiritualism, which was in the main founded on the doctrines of " Allan Kardec " (M. Rivail), (q.v.) *Spiritism* differed from spiritualism as expounded in Britain, America and elsewhere, chiefly in that it included among its tenets the doctrine of reincarnation. Allan Kardec, who prior to his adoption of spiritualistic creeds, about 1862 had been an exponent of animal magnetism and phrenology, based his new teachings on spirit revelations received through clairvoyants, and so popular were these teachings that they rapidly spread over the Continent. In Britain, however, spiritism obtained but little hold, its only exponent being Miss Anna Blackwell, who endeavoured without success to establish the doctrine of reincarnation in this country. *Spiritism* and spiritualism must not be confused. since the adherents of each section were opposed to the tenets of the other, and even in France, where *spiritism* obtained the most footing, there was a distinct spiritualistic party who looked askance at the doctrine of reincarnation. The word spiritist is sometimes applied to one who seeks only the physical phenomena, and neglects the religious and philosophic aspect of spiritualism.

Spiritualism : *Spiritualism* in its modern aspect has for its basic principles the belief in the continuance of life after death, and the possibility of communication between the dead and the living, through the agency of a *medium* or psychic, a person qualified in some unknown manner to be the mouthpiece of supernatural beings. On this foundation has been raised the belief known as *spiritualism*, variously regarded as a religion or a philosophy. Besides the speaking (or writing, drawing, etc.) indirectly through the agency of the medium, there are also *physical manifestations*, such as the materialisation of spirit forms, and "apports," (q.v.) the so-called " direct " writing, moving of inanimate objects without contact, and other phenomena of a like nature. The word " spiritism " used in France to denote *spiritualism*, is in this country only applied to the theories of Allen Kardec (q.v.) a well-known spiritualist who believed in re-incarnation, or to an inferior phase of *spiritualism*, in which only physical manifestations are sought, and the religious and ethical significance of the subject ignored.

Though the movement in its present form dates no further back than 1848, it is possible to trace its ancestry to witchcraft, demoniac possession, poltergeistic disturbances, and animal magnetism. In these all the phenomena of *spiritualism* may be found, though the disturbing influences were not in the earlier instances identified with the spirits of the deceased. Many famous outbreaks of an epidemic nature, such as that among the Tremblers of the Cevennes (q.v.) and the Convulsionaries of St. Medard (q.v.), which to the beholders showed clear indications of demonic possession, had in their symptoms considerable analogy with modern *spiritualism*. They were accompanied by spontaneous trance or ecstasy, utterance of long-winded discourses, and speaking in unknown tongues, all of which are to be found in the séance-room. The fluency of speech, especially of these ignorant peasants, has been equalled, if not surpassed, by the outpourings of the unlearned medium under the influence of her " control." In such cases the symptoms were generally referred either to angelic or diabolic possession, and most frequently to the latter. Witches also were supposed to hold converse with the Devil, and many aspects of witchcraft—and notably the part played in the persecution of suspects by young women and children—show an obvious relationship to those poltergeistic disturbances which were the connecting link between early forms of possession and modern *spiritualism*. Cases in which children of morbid tendencies pretend to be the victims of a witch are to be found in every record of witchcraft. It was the poltergeist (q.v.), however, who showed most affinity to the " control " of the mediumistic circle. For at least the past few centuries poltergeist disturbances have occurred from time to time, and the mischievous spirit's favourite modes of manifesting itself have been singularly akin to those adopted by the spirit control of our days. Again, both spirits require the agency of a medium for the production of their phenomena, and it is in the immediate presence of the medium that the phenomena generally make their appearance.

Magnetism.—Partly evolving from these phases of spirit-manifestation, and partly running parallel with them, was an extensive movement whose significance, from the spiritualist point of view, is very considerable. The doctrine of *animal magnetism* was, said to have originated with Paracelsus, and was much in favour with the old alchemists. The actual magnet was not greatly used, but was regarded as a symbol of the magnetic philosophy, which rested on the idea of a force or fluid radiating from the heavenly bodies, human beings, and indeed, from every substance, animate or in.nimate, by means of which all things interacted upon one another. While the mystics were engaged in formulating a magnetic philosophy, there were others, such as Valentine Greatrakes, who cured diseases, claiming their power as a divine gift, and not connecting it with the rationalist ideas of the alchemists. These two phases of magnetism united and came to a height in the work of Franz Antoine Mesmer, who in 1766 published his *De planetarum influxu*, a treatise on the influence of the planets on the human body. His ideas were essentially those of the magnetic philosophers, and his cures probably on a level with those of Valentine Greatrakes, but into both theory and practice he infused new life and won for himself the recognition, if not of the learned societies, at least of the general public. To him is due that application of the magnetic system which resulted in the discovery of the induced hypnotic trance, whose bearing on *spiritualism* is obvious and important. In 1784 a commission was appointed by the French Government to consider magnetism as practised by Mesmer and his followers but its report only served to cast discredit on the science, and exclude it from scientific discussion. Until the third decade of the nineteenth century the rationalist explanations of Mesmerism concerned themselves entirely with a fluid or force emanating from the person of the operator, and even visible to the clairvoyant eye, but in 1823 Alexandre Bertrand, a Paris physician, published a *Traité du Somnambulisme*, and in 1826 a treatise *Du Magnetisme Animal en France,* in which he established the relationship between ordinary sleep-walking, somnambulism associated with disease, and epidemic ecstasy, and advanced the doctrine now generally accepted—that of suggestion. Magnetism was by this time receiving a good deal of attention all over Europe. A second French Commission appointed in 1825 presented in 1831 a report which, though of no great value, contained a unanimous testimony to the actuality of the phenomena. In Germany also magnetism was practised to a considerable extent, and rationalist explanations found some acceptance. There was a class however, more numerous in Germany than elsewhere, who inclined towards a spiritualistic explanation of Mesmeric phenomena. Indeed, the belief in spirit-intercourse had grown up beside magnetism from its earliest conception, in opposition to the theory of a magnetic fluid. In the earlier phases of " miraculous " healing the cures were, as has been said, ascribed to the divine gift of the operator, who expelled the evil spirits from the patient. In epidemic cases in religious communities, as well as in individual instances, the spirits were questioned both on personal matters and on abstract theological questions. A detailed account of the trance utterances of an hypnotic subject was given in 1787 in the journals of the Swedish *Exegetical and Philanthropic Society.* The society naturally inclined to the doctrines of their countryman, Emanuel Swedenborg, who was the first to identify the " spirits " with the souls of deceased men and women. In Germany Dr. Kerner experimented with Frederica Hauffe, the " Seeress of Prevorst " (q.v.), in whose presence physical manifestations took place, and who described the conditions of the soul after death and the constitution of man—the physical body, the soul, spirit, and *nervengeist*, an ethereal body which clothes the soul after death—theories afterwards elaborated by spiritualists. Other German investigators, J. H. Jung (Jung-Stilling), Dr. C. Römer, and Dr. Heinreich Werner, recorded the phenomenon of clairvoyance in their somnambules. A French spiritualist, Alphonse Cahagnet, produced some of the best evidence which *spiritualism* can show, his accounts being as remarkable for their sincerity and good-faith as for the intelligence they display.

Magnetism received but little attention in England, till the third decade of the nineteenth century. Towards the end of the eighteenth century Dr. Bell, Loutherbourg, and others, practised the science in this country, but for about thirty years—from 1798 to 1828—it was quite neglected. In the latter year Richard Chenevix, an Irishman, gave mesmeric demonstrations. Dr. Elliotson, of University College Hospital, practised mesmerism with his somnambules, the sisters Okey, and though he first believed in the magnetic fluid, he afterwards became a spiritualist. In 1843 two journals dealing with the subject were founded—the *Zoist* and the *Phreno-magnet*. Most of the English magnetists of the time believed in a physical explanation of the phenomena. In 1845 Dr. Reichenbach published his researches, claiming to demonstrate the existence of an emanation (q.v.) which he called odylic or odic force, radiating from every substance. This effluence could be seen by clairvoyants, and had definite colours, and produced a feeling of heat or cold. Working on individual lines, Braid arrived at the same conclusions as Bertrand had done, and demonstrated the power of suggestion in " magnetic " experiments, but his theories were neglected as Bertrand's had been. By the medical profession, especially, the whole matter was freely ridiculed, and declared to be fraudulent. There is no doubt that their attitude would have changed—it had, indeed, already begun to do so—but for the wave of *spiritualism* that swept over America and Europe, and magnified the extravagant attendant phenomena of the trance state, and so obscured its true significance and scientific value.

It will thus be seen not only that magnetism contained the germs of spiritualistic phenomena, but that in many cases the phenomena were identical with those of *spiritualism* in its present stage of development. Trance-speaking was well-known, physical manifestations, though less frequently met with, were also witnessed, as in the case of Frau Hauffe ; and clairvoyance was regarded as a common adjunct of the trance. In later years, as has been seen, the so-called " magnetic " phenomena were largely attributed to the agency of the spirits of the deceased. For such an obviously supernormal faculty as clairvoyance—by means of which the subject professed himself able to see what was going on at a distance, or to distinguish objects carefully concealed from his normal sight—even such men as Bertrand and Braid do not seem to have offered an adequate explanation, nor have they refuted the evidence for it, though it was extensively practised both in France and England. Indeed, there sprang up in these countries a class who specialised in clairvoyance, and still further prepared the way for spiritualism.

Early American Spiritualism. — What is generally regarded as the birth of modern *spiritualism* took place in America in 1848. In that year an outbreak of rapping occurred in the home of the Fox family, at Hydesville, in Arcadia, Wayne County, N.Y. The household comprised John Fox, his wife, and their two young daughters, Margaretta and Kate, aged fifteen and twelve years respectively, and the house itself was a small wooden erection. On the 31st March, 1848, Mrs. Fox summoned her neighbours to hear the knockings, which had disturbed the family for a few days past. On being questioned the raps manifested signs of intelligence, and it was finally elicited that the

disturbing influence was the spirit of a pedlar, done to death by a former resident of the house at Hydesville for the sake of his money. It was afterwards said that in April of the same year the Foxes, while digging in their cellar at the instigation of the spirits, had discovered therein fragments of hair, teeth, and bones, supposed to be those of a human being, but the statement was not properly verified, and the evidence for the murder was but small. The neighbours of the Fox family, however, were deeply impressed by the " revelations," and, by way of a test, questioned the spirits on such matters as the ages of their acquaintances, questions which were answered, apparently, with some correctness. Soon afterwards Margaretta Fox visited her married sister, Mrs. Fish, at Rochester, New York, where the knockings broke out as vigorously as they had done at Hydesville. Her sister Catherine visited some friends at Auburn, and here, too, the rappings were heard. Many persons found themselves possessed of mediumistic powers, and the manifestations spread like an epidemic, till in a few years they were witnessed in most of the eastern states. Numerous circles were formed by private individuals, and professional mediums became ever more abundant. Mrs. Fox and her three daughters continued to hold the place of honour in the spiritualistic world, and gave exhibitions in many large towns. In 1850, while they were at Buffalo, some professors of the Buffalo University showed that the raps could be produced by the medium's joints, and shortly afterwards Mrs. Norman Culver, a relative by marriage of the Fox family, declared that Margaretta Fox had shown her how the rappings were obtained by means of the joints. She also alleged that Catherine Fox had told her that in a séance at Rochester where the medium's ankles were held to prevent fraud, a Dutch servant maid had rapped in the cellar on a signal from the medium. This latter statement was hotly denied by the spiritualists, but no refutation was attempted with regard to the other allegations. Many mediums confessed that they had resorted to trickery, but the tide of popular favour in America held to the actuality of the manifestations. These, as time went on, became more varied and complex. Table-turning and tilting (q.v.) in part replaced the simpler phenomena of raps. Playing on musical instruments by invisible hands, " direct " spirit writing, bell-ringing, levitation, and materialisation of spirit hands, are some of the phenomena which were witnessed and vouched for by such distinguished sitters as Judge Edmonds, the Hon N. P. Tallmadge, Governor of Wisconsin, and William Lloyd Garrison. We find the levitation of the medium Daniel D. Home (q.v.) recorded at an early stage in his career. Slate-writing (q.v.) and playing on musical instruments were also feats practised by the spirits who frequented Koon's " spirit-room " (q.v.) in Dover, Athens County, Ohio. At Keokuk, in Iowa, in 1854, two mediums spoke in tongues identified on somewhat insufficient data, as " Swiss," Latin, and Indian languages, and henceforward trance-speaking in their native language and in foreign tongues was much practised by mediums. The recognised foreign tongues included Latin and Greek, French, German, Spanish, Italian, Chinese and Gaelic, but generally the trance utterances, when they were not in English, were not recognised definitely as any known language, and frequently the " spirits " themselves interpreted the " tongue." The latter phenomena are evidently akin to the early outpourings of the " possessed " or the articulate but meaningless fluency of ecstatics during a religious epidemic. There have been cases, however, where persons in a state of exaltation have spoken fluently in a language of which they know but little in their normal state. Many of the " spirit " writings were signed with the names of great people—particularly Franklin, Swedenborg, Plato, Aristotle, St. John and St. Paul. Trance-lecturing before audiences was also practised, books of inspirational utterances were published, and poetry and drawings produced in abundance. These automatic productions had a character of their own—they were vague, high-sounding, incoherent, and distinctly reminiscent. In cases where they displayed even a fair amount of merit, as in the poems of T. L. Harris, it was pointed out that they were not beyond the capacity of the medium in his normal state. As a rule they had a superficial appearance of intelligence, but on analysis were found to be devoid of meaning. During the early years of spiritualism in America the movement was largely noticed by the press, and many periodicals devoted exclusively to *spiritualism* made their appearance. The *Spirit Messenger* was first published in 1849, *Heat and Light* in 1851, the *Shekinah* in 1852, *Spiritual Telegraph* in 1853, *Spirit World*, under the title of the *Spiritual Philosopher*, in 1850, under the editorship of Laroy Sunderland. From the beginning of the movement those who accepted the actuality of the phenomena ranged themselves into two separate schools, each represented by a considerable body of opinion. The theory of the first was frankly spiritualistic, the explanation of the second was that of Mesmer, now appearing under various guises, with a more or less definite flavour of contemporary scientific thought. These two schools, as we have seen, had their foundation in the early days of animal magnetism, when the rationalist ideas of the magnetists were ranged against the theories of angelic or diabolic possession. In America the suppositious "force" of the rationalists went by the name of "odylic force," "electro-magnetism," and so forth, and to it was attributed not only the subjective phenomena, but the physical manifestations as well. And poltergeistic disturbances occurring from time to time were ascribed either to spirits or odylic force, as in the case of the Ashtabula Poltergeist (q.v.). The Rev. Asa Mahan, one of the "rationalists," suggested that the medium read the thoughts of the sitter by means of odylic force. The protagonists of a magnetic theory attributed trance-speaking to the subject's own intelligence, but after the birth of American *spiritualism* in 1848 a spiritualistic interpretation was more commonly accepted. Notwithstanding these conflicting theories, of which some were certainly physical, practically nothing was done in the way of scientific investigation, with the exception of the experiments conducted by Dr. Hare, Professor of Chemistry in the University of Pennsylvania, though they hardly deserved the name of "scientific investigation." In 1857, when the experiments were made, Hare was already advanced in years, and seems to have been easily imposed upon. Very few exposures of fraud were made, partly because the majority of the sitters accepted the phenomena with unquestioning faith, and partly because the machinery with which such detection might be made was not forthcoming. The collaboration of skilful, trained, and disinterested investigators, such as have recently applied themselves to the elucidation of psychic problems, was entirely lacking in those days, and the public was left to form its own conclusions. *Spiritualism* in America was from the first intimately bound up with socialism. The cult of *spiritualism* was, in fact, the out-growth of the same state of things which produced socialistic communities, and occasioned the rise and fall of so many strange religions. Warren Chase, Horace Greeley, T. L. Harris, and other prominent spiritualists founded such communities, and the so-called "inspirational" writings frequently gave directions for their construction. It was characteristic of the nation and the time that the general trend of religious and philosophic speculation should run on democratic lines. The fixed standards of thought which obtained in Europe were not recognised in America; everyone thought for

himself, with but little educational training on which to base his ideas, and the result was that the vigour of his speculation frequently outran its discretion. As for the causes which made *spiritualism* more popular and more lasting than other strange doctrines of the time, they are probably to be found in the special conditions which prepared the way for *spiritualism*. Clairvoyants had made use of rapping prior to the mediumship of the Fox girls, the induced trance had only recently been brought to the notice of the American people by lecturers, the clergy and others, accustomed to departures from orthodoxy in every direction, found no difficulty in admitting the intervention of good or evil spirits in human affairs, while for those who refused to accept the spirit hypothesis a satisfactory explanation of the phenomena was found in electricity, electro-magnetism, or "odic force."

Spiritualism in England.—Though, as has been said, clairvoyants and somnambules were sufficiently common in England prior to the importation of *spiritualism* in its American form, the phenomena were, nevertheless, interpreted mainly on rationalist lines, and even when the spirit doctrine—which in those days had but a small following—became wide-spread and important, the theory of any rational explanation was still represented. In 1852, four years after the "Rochester Rappings," a medium named Mrs. Hayden was brought from America by a lecturer on "electro-biology." Soon afterwards another professional medium, Mrs. Roberts, crossed the Atlantic, and both ladies had a distinguished clientèle, and received substantial remuneration in the way of fees. Many of the most influential Journals published scornful comments on these performances, but a belief in the genuineness of the phenomena was expressed by one at least, *Chambers's Journal*, in an article by Robert Chambers himself. Professor de Morgan was another distinguished witness who testified to the actuality of the phenomena, and its supernormal character, and yet others were disposed to investigate. In 1853 an epidemic of table-turning (q.v.) spread from the Continent to Britain, and attained to immense popularity among all classes. So wide-spread did it become that such men as Braid, Faraday and Carpenter turned their attention to it, and showed it to result from unconscious muscular action. The "rationalist" explanation, be it said, was still well to the fore, with talk of odylic force, electricity, or magnetism. Faraday's experiments were ridiculed, and a pamphlet entitled *Table-turning by Animal Magnetism demonstrated* ran through more than a hundred editions in one year. Elliotson and the other protagonists of mesmerism found an illustration of their own views in table-turning. Those who inclined to a spiritualistic belief found a spirit agency at work in the same phenomena; while a band of clergymen, confessedly awaiting similar manifestations in fulfilment of Scriptural prophecy, concluded that Satanic agency was at the root of the matter, and had their conclusions supported by the "spirits" themselves, who confessed that they were fallen angels, or the spirits of evil-doers. Among the earliest converts to *spiritualism* were Sir Charles Isham, Dr. Ashburner, and the socialist Robert Owen, at that time already over eighty years of age, who published in 1854 the first number of *The New Existence of Man upon the Earth*, intended as the organ of a sort of millenium to be brought about by the spirits. Automatic writing is recorded at this period, one medium being a child of four, who wrote in Latin. In the autumn of 1853 Mrs. Hayden returned to America, and the practice of table-turning speedily declined. Until 1860 little more is heard of *spiritualism*, though a few journals were published in the interval. Owen continued to issue his *New Existence*, in which, however, *spiritualism* was only a secondary consideration. The *Yorkshire Spiritual*

Telegraph published at Keighley in 1855, ran till the end of 1859 (from 1857 under the name of the *British Spiritual Telegraph*). There were also a few other periodicals which did not enjoy so long a lease of life. But though the British books and papers dealing with the subject were but few, the lack was supplied by American productions, which were largely read in this country. Mediums, as well as literature, were imported from America, notable among them being Daniel Dunglas Home (q.v.) who crossed over to Britain in 1855 at the age of twenty-three, and who had already acted as a medium in America for some four years. Many of those who afterwards became prominent mediums were first coverted to *spiritualism* at Home's séances. In the autumn of 1855 Home returned to America, and in 1856 his place was taken by P. B. Randolph, who attended the meetings of the Charing Cross Circle. In 1859 came the Rev. T. L. Harris, deputed by the spirits to visit England. An English medium, named Mrs. Marshall, gave séances professionally, but much less successfully than did Home and the American mediums, though the phenomena were of a similar kind. English spiritualists, however, did not court publicity, but practised for the most part anonymously. The phenomena at these séances resemble those in America—playing of instruments without visible agency, materialisation of hands, table-turning, and so on—but on a much smaller scale. It was not so much these physical manifestations, however, which inspired the confidence or excited the credulity of early spiritualists, but rather the automatic writing and speaking which, rare at first, afterwards became a feature of mediumistic séances. So early as 1854 the trance utterances of a medium named Annie were recorded by a circle of Swedenborgians presided over by Elihu Rich. The importance given at this stage of the movement to subjective phenomena must be attributed to an imperfect understanding of unconscious cerebration. Such men as Mr. Thomas Shorter, editor of the *Spiritual Magazine*, failed to comprehend how the medium was able to reason while in the trance state, and to perform intelligent acts of which the normal consciousness knew nothing. Therefore they adopted the spirit hypothesis. Mrs. de Morgan and Mrs. Newton Crosland gave a ready credence to the automatic utterances of their friends. Symbolic drawings were a feature of Mrs. Crosland's circle, as was also the speaking in unknown tongues, which were translated by the spirit through another medium.

In 1860 a new spiritual era opened, and the whole subject came into more prominence than it had done heretofore. This was due to the increase in the number of British mediums and the emigration to Britain of many American mediums, including the Davenport Brothers (q.v.) and D. D. Home, who once more visited England in 1859. Home was treated respectfully, not to say generously, by the bulk of the press and by the public, and admitted to the highest grades of society. Another American medium who practised about the same time was J. R. M. Squire, whose manifestations were vouched for by Dr. Lockhart Robertson. Other mediums there were, however, such as Colchester and Foster, who practised trickery so openly that the spiritualists themselves exposed their fraud, though maintaining that at times the manifestations even of these mediums were genuine. After Home, the most famous American mediums were the brothers Davenport, who practised various forms of physical mediumship. They took their places in a small cabinet, bound hand and foot to the satisfaction of the sitters. When the lights were lowered, musical instruments were thrown about the room and played upon and other physical phenomena were apparent. When the séance was over and the lights once more raised, the brothers Davenport were found securely fastened in their cabinet. The manifestations were so

skilfully produced that many people hesitated whether to regard them as clever conjuring or spirit phenomena. At length, however, the Davenports were exposed through the agency of a secret knot called the " Tom Fool's knot," which they were unable to untie, and which rendered the necessary escape from their bonds impossible. Their career in Britain was at an end. Shortly afterwards the conjuring performances of Maskelyne and Cook, in emulation of the Davenport Brothers, drove the spiritualists to conclude that they also must be renegade mediums. Native mediumship developed much more slowly in England than that of the American spiritualists. Mrs. Marshall was for a time practically the only professional medium of standing in the country, though private mediums were less rare. Notable among the latter were Mrs. Everitt, Mr. Edward Child, and Miss Nichol, afterwards the second wife of Mr. Guppy, who became a famous medium. During this period poltergeistic disturbances were still recorded in which all the familiar phenomena reappeared, but they were explained on spiritualist lines. Crystal vision was practised and auras were commonly seen by the medium round the heads of his friends. Automatic writing, speaking, and drawing continued, and inspirational addresses, etc., were published. In 1869 a new impulse was given to *spiritualism* by the appearance of several public mediums, chief among them being F. Herne, who devoted his talents to the production of physical manifestations, and in connection with whom we first see the phenomenon of " elongation " (q.v.). Within a few years a number of other English mediums sprang up—Eglinton, Monck, Rita, and many more, while Dr. Slade, Annie Eva Fay, and Kate Fox (who afterwards married an English barrister named Jencken) came over from America. In 1870 the Rev. W. Stainton Moses (" M. A. Oxon,") destined to be one of the greatest of English mediums, devoted himself to private mediumship. In 1872 there was introduced into England, through the agency of the Guppys, the practice of Spirit Photography (q.v.), which had originated ten years earlier in America. To very many people a photograph containing, in addition to the sitter's portrait, a vague splotch of white, was conclusive evidence of the materialisation of spirits. After numerous exposures the craze for spirit photography declined and of late years little has been heard of it, though in spasmodic fashion it sometimes shows evidence of life. Slate-writing (q.v.) was a favourite mode of " direct " writing and one extensively practised. Sittings were generally held in the dark, and the sitters were enjoined to talk or sing, or perhaps a musical box was played. Most of the records of these earlier séances are singularly suggestive of fraud. In 1874 Mrs. Jencken (Kate Fox) was staying at Brighton with her baby, aged about six months, and it is related that the baby became a writing medium. A facsimile of its writing was published in the *Medium and Daybreak* of May 8th, 1874. In the same year came Mrs. Annie Eva Fay whose feats resembled those of the Davenports. Another celebrated medium was David Duguid, of Glasgow, who painted " under control." In 1876 Henry Slade came from America, and turned his attention chiefly to slate-writing. A few months after his appearance in Britain Professor Ray Lankester detected him in fraud, prosecuted him, and finally obliged him to leave the country. But the crowning manifestation, the climax of spiritual phenomena and apparently the most difficult of achievement, was materialisation (q.v.) It began with the materialisation of heads, hands, and arms, and proceeded to full materialisation. In 1872 Mrs. Guppy attempted this form of manifestation, but with no conspicuous success. The mediums Herne and Williams also included it in their repertory, but a new and successful medium made her appearance—Florence Cook, who

materialised the spirits of " John " and " Katie King."
When, during a séance, Miss Cook was seized by Mr.
Volckman while impersonating a spirit, the exposure drew
from Sir William Crookes several letters testifying to the
honesty of the medium, with whom he had experimented,
and rather helped the cause of *spiritualism* than otherwise.
Other private mediums also gave materialisation séances,
and from them the contagion spread to their professional
brethren, among whom the most successful was undoubtedly
William Eglinton. Miss Lottie Fowler also attained to
fame as a medium about the same time—the decade 1870–
80. These open séances offered a better opportunity to
the investigator, and though even in them some care was
doubtless exercised to prevent the intrusion of " adverse
influences," there were a good many instances where a
sceptic ventured to grasp the spirit, and when this occurred
spirit and medium were always fround to be one and the
same. By way of apology for these untoward happenings
the *Spiritualist* suggested that the spirit was composed of
emanations from the medium, and that when it was grasped
by the sitter spirit and medium would unite, the form
possessing most of the medium's force rejoining the other.
Another explanation, especially applicable to physical
manifestations, was that genuine mediums, giving professional séances, and forced to produce the phenomena on
all occasions, would sometimes resort to fraud when their
mediumistic powers temporarily failed them. This perfectly plausible excuse was always ready to meet a charge of
fraud. The subjective phenomena, as time advanced
became less in favour with investigators, who began really
to understand its subjective nature, but with spiritualists
it remained the most important form of manifestation
The trance utterances of Home (q.v.), Stainton Moses, and
Miss Lottie Fowler were highly valued. David Duguid,
the celebrated painting medium, was controlled by a new
spirit, Hafed, Prince of Persia, whose life and adventures
were delivered through the medium. Prominent inspirational speakers were Mrs. Emma Hardinge Britten, J. J.
Morse, and Mrs. Cora L. V. Tappan-Richmond. Among
English periodicals devoted to *spiritualism* were *Human
Nature*, first issued in 1867 ; the *Medium and Daybreak*,
founded a few years later ; the *Spiritual Magazine* ; and
the *Spiritualist* (1867), edited by Mr. W. H. Harrison, and
treating the subject in a scientific manner. A still more
recent paper, *Light*, dates from 1881, and still remains one
of the principal organs of the movement. One of the
earliest investigators was Sir William Crookes, whose
experiences with D. D. Home are not to be lightly passed
by. In 1863 Professor de Morgan, in a preface to Mrs. de
Morgan's book, *From Matter to Spirit*, suggests the agency
of some mysterious force, though he did not become a
spiritualist until afterwards. In 1868 Cromwell Varley,
the electrician, testified to the phenomena of Home. In
the following year the London Dialectical Society appointed
a Committee to enquire into the matter, whose members
included Alfred Russel Wallace (q.v.), Charles Bradlaugh,
and Sergeant Cox. The report of the committee stated
that the subject was " worthy of more serious and careful
investigation than it has hitherto received." Cromwell
Varley, and the Research Committee of the British National
Association of Spiritualists carried out various electrical
and other tests, but as these have since been proved to be
inadequate, it is not necessary to consider them in detail.
On the other hand Faraday and Tyndall, Huxley and
Carpenter, refused to have anything to do with the psychic
phenomena, and opposed the spiritualistic movement in a
spirit of intolerance which contrasted unfavourably with
the attitude of its scientific protagonists. Meanwhile the
old rationalist school of believers in magnetic or odylic
emanations still lingered and were represented by the

Psychological Society (founded in 1875, and came to an
end in 1879), the writings of its president, Sergeant Cox,
and those of the well-known spiritualist, Mr. Samuel
Guppy. One other scientific man of the period is deserving
of mention in this connection. In 1876 Professor Barrett
(now Sir William), lecturing before the British Association,
declared that hyperæsthesia and suggestion were not alone
capable of explaining the phenomena, and urged the
necessity for appointing a committee to investigate. However, his suggestion was not acted upon, and in 1882 he
called a conference to consider the question. The direct
result of this conference was the founding of the Society
for Psychical Research. Up to this point the English
movement differed from the American less in kind than in
degree, for it was altogether weaker and more restricted.
Indeed, the difference in the traditions of the two countries.
and in the general temper of their people, rendered it
impossible that the movement should spread here as rapidly
as it had done in America, or that it should be embraced
with such fervour. It was not—probably for the same
reason—inimical to Christianity in England, but rather
supplementary to it, and there were those who claimed to
be converted to Christianity through its means.

The Society for Psychical Research.—The history of the
criticism of occult phenomena in Great Britain from 1882
to the present time is intimately connected with the
Society for Psychical Research, and there is no development
worthy of record which its members have not investigated.
It was the first body to make a united and organised attempt
to deal with what was called, for want of a better name,
psychic phenomena, in a purely scientific and impartial
spirit, free from the bias of pre-conceived ideas on the
subject. It was, indeed, expressly stated in their prospectus that the members in no wise bound themselves to
accept any one explanation, or to recognise in the phenomena the working of any non-physical agency. The first
president of the Society was Professor Henry Sidgwick,
and the Council numbered among its members Edmund
Gurney, Frank Podmore, Frederic W. H. Myers, and
Professor Barrett ; and the Rev. W. Stainton Moses,
Morell Theobald, Dr. George Wild, and Dawson Rogers,
the latter four being spiritualists. It may be mentioned,
however, that the avowedly spiritualistic members of the
Society gradually dropped off. Other presidents of the
Society were, Professor Balfour Stewart, the Rt. Hon. A. J.
Balfour, Professor William James, Sir William Crookes,
Sir Oliver Lodge, and Professor Barrett, several of these
being among the original members. The scope of the
Psychical Research Society was defined by the appointment
of six committees, as follows :—(1) Committee on Thought
Transference ; (2) Committee on Hypnotism ; (3) Com-
mittee on Reichenbach's Experiments ; (4) Committee on
Apparitions ; (5) Committee on Physical (spiritualistic)
Phenomena ; and (6) a Committee to consider the history
and existing literature of the subject. The field of the
Society was thus a wide one, and it was still further enlarged in later years, when a committee, headed by Dr.
Richard Hodgson, conducted an enquiry into Theosophy
(q.v.). And the methods of psychic research were applied
to other matters also, which were outside of the Society's
original scope. In order to find an explanation for the
spiritualistic phenomena, its members journeyed into the
domain of psychology, and studied automatism, hallucinations, and thought transference, one or other of which has
been proved to have an important bearing on much of the
spiritualistic phenomena, if not on all. They were also
instrumental in detecting a great deal of fraud in connection with mediumistic performances, especially in such
phenomena as slate-writing (q.v.) and other " physical "
manifestations. The explanation of these, in fact, formed

one of the chief aims of the *Society*. Though at the time of its founding public mediumship seemed to have declined ; there was still more than enough phenomena for the Society to investigate, and the testimony of Sir William Crookes and others of standing and intellectual strength indicated that the matter was at least a fit subject for investigation. In connection with slate-writing, which many persons declared to be genuine and so simple that fraud was impossible, Mr. S. J. Davey, a member of the Society, gave a number of pseudo-séances. Having been himself deceived for a time by the performances in that line of the well-known medium, William Eglinton, and having at length discovered the *modus* of his slate-writing feats, Mr. Davey set himself to emulate the medium's "manifestations." In the interests of psychic research he undertook to give sittings, which were carefully recorded by Dr. Hodgson. So well were the devices of the professional mediums reproduced that none of the sitters were able to detect the *modus operandi* of Davey's performances, even though they were assured beforehand that it was simply a conjuring trick. Such a demonstration could not fail to do more than any amount of argument to expose the "phenomenon" of slate-writing. (*See* article on **Slate-writing.**) Excellent work was done by the Society in the collection of evidence relating to apparitions of the dead and the living, many of which are embodied in *Phantasms of the living*, by Messrs. Myers, Podmore and Gurney. A statistical enquiry on a large scale was undertaken by a Committee of the *Society* in 1889. Some 17,000 cases of apparitions were collected by the committee and its assistants. The main object in taking such a census was to obtain evidence for the working of telepathy in veridical or coincidental apparitions, and in order to make such evidence of scientific value, the utmost care was taken to insure the impartiality and responsible character of all who took part in the enquiry. The result was, that after every precaution had been taken the apparitions coinciding with a death or other crisis were found greatly to exceed the number which could be ascribed to chance alone. (*See also* **Psychical Research.**) But the most fruitful of the *Society's* researches were those concerning telepathy (q.v.), or thought-transference, and it was through the influence of its members that the doctrine of thought-transference, so long known to the vague speculations of the old magnetists and mesmerists, was first placed on a definite basis as a problem worthy of scientific enquiry. Investigations into this matter are still progressing, and trustworthy proof of such a mode of communication would affect the scientific view of spiritualism to a remarkable degree. Among the individual efforts of members of the *Society for Psychical Research* the most complete and the most successful were those conducted by Professor and Mrs. Sidgwick in 1889–91. (*See* **Telepathy.**) At the same time there was much to encourage the belief in some "supernormal" agency, especially in the last decade of the nineteenth century. The two mediums whose manifestations led many able men in this country, in America, and on the Continent, to conclude that the spirits of the dead were concerned in their phenomena were the Italian medium Eusapia Palladino (q.v.) and the American Mrs. Piper. In 1885 Professor James, of Harvard, studied the case of Mrs. Piper (q.v.), and a few years later Dr. Richard Hodgson of the American *Society for Psychical Research* also investigated her case, the latter commencing his investigations in an entirely sceptical spirit. Of all the trance mediums she offers the best evidence for a supernatural agency. Dr. Hodgson himself declared his belief that the spirits of the dead spoke through the lips of the medium, and among others who held that fraud alone would not account for the revelations given by Mrs. Piper in the trance state were

Professor James, Sir Oliver Lodge, Mr. Myers and Professor J. H. Hyslop. On the other hand, Mr. Podmore, while not admitting any supernormal agency, suggests that telepathy may help to explain the matter, probably aided by skilful observation and carefully-conducted enquiries concerning the affairs of prospective sitters. Mrs. Sidgwick, again, suggested that probably Mrs. Piper received telepathic communications from the spirits of the dead, which she reproduced in her automatic speaking and writing. The other medium was Eusapia Palladino, who, after attracting considerable attention from Professors Lombroso, Richet, Flammarion, and others on the Continent, came to Britain in 1895. Several English scientific men had already witnessed her telergic powers on the Continent, at the invitation of Professor Charles Richet—Sir Oliver Lodge, Mr. Myers, and others —and of these Sir Oliver Lodge, at least, had expressed himself as satisfied that no known agency was responsible for her remarkable manifestations. The English sittings were held at Cambridge, and as it was proved conclusively that the medium made use of fraud, the majority of the investigators ascribed her "manifestations" entirely to that. Later, however, in 1898, a further series of séances were held at Paris, and so successfully that Richet, Myers, and Sir O. Lodge once more declared themselves satisfied of the genuineness of the phenomena. A further account of this medium will be found under a separate heading. Perhaps the most convincing evidence for the working of some supernormal agency, however, is to be found in the famous cross-correspondence experiments conducted in recent years. Mr. Myers had suggested before he died that if a control were to give the same message to two or more mediums, it would go far to establish the independent existence of such control. On the death of Professor Sidgwick (in August, 1900) and of Mr. Myers (in January, 1901) it was thought that if mediums were controlled by these, some agreement might be looked for in the scripts. The first correspondences were found in the script of Mrs. Thomson and Miss Rawson, the former in London, the latter in the south of France. The Sidgwick control appeared for the first time to these ladies on the same day, January 11th, 1901. On the 8th of May, 1901 the Myers control appeared in the script of Mrs. Thompson and Mrs. Verrall, and later in that of Mrs. Piper and others. So remarkable were the correspondences obtained in some cases where there could not possibly be collusion between the mediums, that it is difficult to believe that some discarnate intelligence was not responsible for some, at least of the scripts. (*See also* **Cross-Correspondences.**)

See also the biographies of the various eminent spiritualists, mediums, and investigators dealt with in this work, and the articles on **Telepathy, Hallucination, Table-turning,** etc. Also the articles on the various countries of Europe.

M.J.

By far the most extraordinary experiments in connection with psychic phenomena were those undertaken by Sir William Crookes. Working under the most stringent conditions he and his fellow experimenters assured themselves that entrance or exit to the room in which their séances were held was impossible. Yet he succeeded by the aid of a medium in obtaining the best possible evidence of the presence of spirits or other entities in the apartment. These were of a tangible nature and were actually weighed by Sir William, who on one occasion even succeeded in obtaining a portion of the protoplasmic matter from which these entities were built up, which he kept in a box for several days. These entities emerged from the body of the medium or from that of one of the sitters, walked about, spoke, and even debated loudly and noisily with Sir William and the other sitters on many different topics over a prolonged space of time. They frequently vanished through the floor. Sir William found their average weight to be about one-third of that of a human being. These phenomena were witnessed by numerous persons of the highest intelligence and probity, among them, it is understood, some of exalted rank. A full statement regarding the phenomena in all their details may be found in Mr. Gambier Bolton's interesting little volume *Ghosts in Solid Form.*

No work of recent times furnishes the student of psychic research with such a masterly conspectus of the subject as Sir William F. Barrett's *On the Threshold of the Unseen* (1917). Expanded from an address on the phenomena of *spiritualism* delivered some twenty years ago, it covers the whole history of psychical research during that period and a notice of it may well serve to complete this article and furnish the reader with data concerning psychical research during the present century. The introductory chapter briefly reviews the work of eminent scientists and provides a frank statement of the present position of psychical research. Public opinion regarding the quest, and the conflicting objections of science and religion are briefly reviewed in chapters II. and III., and are followed by an essay on the physical phenomena of *spiritualism*, which contains little that is not noticed in the present article. Chapter VII., " On Certain more Disputable Phenomena of *Spiritualism*," deals with examples of the direct voice and direct writing, materialization and spirit photography, all of which phenomena have been termed *ectoplasms* by Professor Ochorowicz of Warsaw. " By Ectoplasy," says Sir William, " is meant the power of forming outside the body of the medium a concentration of vital energy or vitalized matter which operates temporarily in the same way as the body from which it is drawn, so that visible, audible or tangible human-like phenomena are produced. This is very much like the ' psychic force ' hypothesis under a new name. The chapter " On the Canons of Evidence in Psychical Research " includes a sentence which might well be taken to heart by the too sceptical : " It is utterly unphilosophical to ridicule or deny well-attested phenomena because they are inexplicable." Sir William shows how the critical examination of psychic phenomena has languished because of the lack of trained scientific observers, those devoting themselves to the subject being for the most part persons of more enthusiasm than judgment. The chapter on theories is eminently useful. " I have never yet," says the author, " met with anyone who has seriously studied the evidence or engaged in prolonged investigation of this subject who holds ' that all mediums are impostors.' " The theories examined to account for supernormal phenomena include those of hallucination, which is only partially admitted as a cause. Exo-neural action of the brain which is, however, a sub-conscious action, an effect of the subliminal self, but perhaps the most interesting of the hypotheses which account for these miraculous happenings is described as follows : " It may be that the intelligence operating at a séance is a thought-projection of ourselves—that each one of us has his simulacrum in the unseen ; that with the growth of our life and character here a ghostly image of oneself is growing up in the invisible world." *The Problem of Mediumship* is the subject of the tenth chapter. Objection is taken to the word " medium," not only because of its associations, but for more scientific reasons. A separate division of the book is occupied with the phenomenal evidence afforded by apparitions, automatic writing, supernormal messages, and the evidence of identity in the discarnate condition and of survival after death. The last portion of the volume brings the question of human personality up to date, especially as regards its higher aspects, the conclusion being

that only the barrier of our sense perceptions, a " threshold of sensibility," divides us from the world beyond our normal consciousness, just as " the organism of an oyster constitutes a threshold which shuts it out from the greater part of our sensible world." As regards the question of immortality it is concluded that " Life can exist in the unseen," but it does not follow that spirit communications teach us the necessary and inherent immortality of the soul. " If we accept the evidence for ' identity,' that some we have known on earth are still living and near us," we have still to remember that " entrance on a life after death does not necessarily mean immortality, that is eternal persistence of our personality, nor does it prove that survival after death extends to all. Obviously no experimental evidence can ever demonstrate either of these beliefs, though it may and does remove the objections raised as to the possibility of survival."

Towards the end of 1916 a great sensation was made not only in occult but in general circles by the publication by Sir Oliver Lodge of a memoir upon his son, the late Lieutenant Raymond Lodge, who was killed near Ypres in September, 1915. The book is divided into three parts, the first of which contains a history of the brief life of the subject of the memoir. The second part details numerous records of sittings both in the company of mediums and at the table by Sir Oliver Lodge and members of his family, and it is claimed that in these many evidences of the personal survival of his son were obtained, that the whole trend of the messages was eloquent of his personality and that although if the evidential matter were taken apart for examination single isolated proofs would not be deemed conclusive, yet when taken in a body it provides evidential material of an important nature. There is certainly ground for this contention and it must be admitted that proofs of identity are more valuable when experienced by those who were familiar with the subject during his earthly career. But to those who have not had this opportunity the balance of the evidence seems meagre and it is notable that in this especial case most of the tests of real value broke down when put into practice. The third part of the book deals with the scientific material relating to the life after death which is reviewed and summarized in a spirit of great fairness, although a natural bias towards belief in immortality is not a little obvious. In this the work differs from that by Sir William Barrett, with its wholly scientific attitude and its greater natural ability to discern dialectical weaknesses, but it is far from being unscientific in character. On the other hand Sir Oliver Lodge's work is inspired throughout by an enthusiasm which if not entirely absent in that of Sir William Barrett, is certainly not conspicuous in that writer's treatise. Sir Oliver's enthusiasm is, indeed, that of a Columbus or a Galileo. Throughout the centuries the pioneer and discoverer have been uplifted and assisted more by faith than by reason, and it is probably because of his abounding faith in human immortality that Sir Oliver Lodge will in future be regarded as perhaps the greatest pioneer in psychic science, not only of his own generation but of many generations. L. S.

Spiritualism as a Religion.—*Spiritualism* was, and is, regarded by its adherents as a religion, or a supplement to an existing religion, imposing certain moral obligations and offering new and far-reaching revelations on the conditions of existence beyond the grave. The continuity of life after death is, of course, one of its most important tenets, though not a distinctive one ; since on it depend most of the world's creeds and religions. But the spiritualist's ideas concerning the *nature* of the life of the freed soul are peculiar to his creed. The soul, or spirit, is composed of a sort of attenuated matter, inhabiting the body and resembling it in form. On the death of the body the soul withdraws itself, without however, undergoing any direct change, and for a longer or shorter period remains on the " earth plane." But the keynote of the spirit-world is *progress ;* so after a time the spirit proceeds to the lowest " discarnate plane," and from that to a higher and a higher, gradually evolving into a purer and nobler type, until at length it reaches the sphere of pure spirit. Another central belief of *spiritualism* is that the so-called " dead " can, and do, communicate with the living, through the agency of *mediums,* and can produce in the physical world certain phenomena depending for their operation on no known physical laws. To the earnest spiritualist, requiring no further proof of the reality of his creed, the subjective phenomena, as they are called, comprising trance-speaking, writing, etc., are of vastly greater importance than the physical manifestations, just as the latter are more in favour with psychical researchers, because of the better opportunities they offer for investigation. From the trance-speaking of the medium are gathered those particulars of the spirit world which to the outsider present one of the most unattractive pictures extant of that domain. The spirit life is, in fact, represented as a pale and attenuated reproduction of earthly life, conducted in a highly rarified atmosphere. Trance drawings, purporting to depict spirit scenes, afford a description no less flattering than the written picture. From their exalted spheres the spirits are cognisant of the doings of their fellow-men still on earth, and are at all times ready to aid and counsel the latter. This they can do only through the medium, who is a link between the seen and the unseen, perhaps through some quality of super-normal sensitiveness. There are those who maintain that those mediums who hold séances and become the direct mouthpieces of the spirits are only supereminently endowed with a faculty common to all humanity—that all men are mediums in a greater or less degree, and that all inspiration, whether good or bad, comes from the spirits. It is in connection with this idea of the universality of mediumship that the effect of *spiritualism* on the morals and daily life of its adherents is most clearly seen. For the spirits are naturally attracted to those mediums whose qualities resemble their own. Enlightened spirits from the highest spheres seek high-souled and earnest mediums through whom to express themselves, while mediums who use their divine gifts for a base end are sought by the lowest and wickedest human spirits, or by beings termed " elementals," who do not even reach the human standard of goodness. Indeed, it is stated that the lower spirits communicate with the living much more readily than do the higher, by reason of a certain gross or material quality which binds them to earth. The path of the medium is thus beset with many difficulties, and it is essential that he should be principled and sincere, a creature of pure life and high ideals, so that the circle of his " controls " be select. For not only do the tricky " elementals " deceive the sitters and the investigators with their lying ways, but they oft-times drive the medium himself to fraud, so that under their control he secretes " apports " about his person, and materialises false beards and dirty muslin. And as it is with the full-fledged medium, so with the normal individual. If he is to insure that the source of his inspiration be a high one he must live in such a way that only the best spirits will control him, and so his impulses shall be for his own good and the betterment of the race. It will thus be seen that *spiritualism* is in itself a complete religion ; but it also combines well with other religions and creeds. In America the spiritualistic and the socialistic elements mingled harmoniously and many of the socialistic communities were founded by spiritualists. Other sects there were which associated themselves with *spiritualism* during the early history of the movement in America, and rumour

—somewhat unfairly, it must be admitted—would have associated with it some less creditable ones, such as that which advocated free Love. But the many forms which *spiritualism* took in America were, as has been said, the product of the country and the time. In other lands the forms were different. In England, for instance, where wont and tradition were more happily settled, *spiritualism* was regarded as by no means incompatible with Christianity but rather as affording a fuller revelation of the Christian religion, a view which the trance utterances of the medium confirmed. In France, again, Allan Kardec's doctrine of re-incarnation blended happily with the doctrines of *spiritualism* to produce *spiritism.* Then we have the more modern example of theosophy (q.v.), a blending of *spiritualism* with oriental religions. But all these varied forms contain the central creed of *spiritualism* ; the belief in the continuance of life after the " great dissolution," or death of the body, and in continual progress ; and in the fact of communication between the freed spirit and living human beings. On the whole spiritualists have shown themselves rather tolerant than otherwise to those who were not of their band. On the one hand their mediums did not hesitate to claim kinship with the wizards, shamans and witch-doctors of savage lands, whom they hailed as natural mediums ; and on the other, there were many able and sincere spiritualists who joined forces with the Psychical Researcher, in the unflinching endeavour to expose fraud and get at the truth. M. J.

Spiritual Magazine : Spiritualistic Journal. (*See* **Spiritualism.**)

Spiritual Notes : (*See* **British National Association of Spiritualists.**)

Spiritual Philosopher : Spiritualistic Journal. (*See* **Spiritualism.**)

Spiritual Portraits : (*See* **Blake.**)

Spiritual Telegraph : Spiritualistic Journal. (*See* **Spiritualism.**)

Spiritualist : Spiritualistic Journal. (*See* **Spiritualism.**)

Spodomancy : Divination by means of the cinders from sacrificial fires.

Spunkie, The : A goblin of the same nature as the Scottish " Kelpie." He is popularly believed to be an agent of Satan, and travellers who have lost their way are his especial prey. He attracts his unfortunate victim by means of a light, which looks as if it were a reflection on a window, and is apparently not far away ; but as the man proceeds towards it, like the rainbow it recedes. However, he still follows its gleam, until the *Spunkie* has successfully lured him over a precipice or into a morass.

Squinting : An ill omen. In the book of Vairus it is said . " Let no servant ever hire himself to a *squinting* master."

Squire, J. R. M. : (*See* **Spiritualism.**)

Stapleton, William : (*See* **England.**)

Staus Poltergeist : The village of Staus, on the shores of Lake Lucerne, was in the years 1860–62 the scene of the most remarkable case of poltergeist-haunting to be found in modern records. The outbreak occurred in the house of M. Joller, a distinguished lawyer and a member of the Swiss national council, a man, moreover, whose character both in public and private life was beyond reproach. The household comprised M. Joller himself, his wife, seven children (four boys and three girls), and a servant-maid. One night in the autumn of 1860 the latter was disturbed by a loud rapping on her bedstead, which she regarded as a presage of death. M. Joller ascribed the sounds to the girl's imagination, and forbade her to speak of them. A few weeks later, returning after a short absence, he found his family much alarmed. The knocks had been repeated in the presence of his wife and daughter, and had even manifested signs of intelligence. When, a few days afterwards, they had news of the death of a friend, they imagined that this must have been what the raps portended. But again in June, 1861 the outbreak was renewed. This time it was one of the boys who fainted at the apparition of a white, indistinct figure. Other strange things began to be seen and heard by the children, and a few months later the maid complained that the kitchen was haunted by dim, grey shapes who followed her to her chamber, and sobbed all night in the lumber-room. In October of the same year the maid was replaced by another, the rappings ceased, and the disturbances seemed to be at an end. They were renewed, however, and with tenfold vigour, in August, 1862, during the absence on business of M. Joller, his wife, and their eldest son. So great was the annoyance that the children fled from the house into the garden, in spite of their father's threat to punish their credulity. But at length the *poltergeist* began to persecute M. Joller himself, pursuing him from room to room with loud knocks, and not all his efforts sufficed to elucidate the mystery. Things began to be thrown about by invisible hands, locked doors and fastened windows were flung wide, strange music and voices and the humming of spinning-wheels were heard. In spite of M. Joller's attempts to conceal these happenings, the news spread abroad, and hundreds, even thousands, of persons flocked to witness the phenomena. Finding no rational hypothesis to fit the circumstances M. Joller begged the Commissary Niederberger to come and investigate, but in the latter's absence Father Guardian visited the haunted house, blessed it, though without alleviating the disturbances, and suggested that an enquiry be made by men of authority. M. Joller privately called in several scientific men of his acquaintance, but they also were unable to find a solution, though various theories of electricity, galvanism, and magnetism were advanced. Other persons of authority, Land-Captain Zelger, the Director of Police Jann, Dr. Christen, the President of the Court of Justice, were present while Commissary Niederberger and Father Guardian made a careful examination of the house, without discovering any cause for the disturbances, which still continued unabated. At length M. Joller demanded of the police a formal examination, and three of the heads of the police were chosen to investigate. The Joller family were bidden to withdraw, and for six days the police remained in undisturbed possession. At the end of that period, having neither heard nor seen any sign of the *poltergeist*, they drew up a report to that effect, and took their departure. Immediately on the Jollers re-entering the house the phenomena began afresh. Ridicule was heaped upon the unfortunate member of council, even by those of his own party, and his house was in such an uproar that he found it impossible to go on with his business. Add to this the unwelcome curiosity of the crowds who flocked to witness the marvels, and it is not surprising that at length, in October, 1862, M. Joller left for ever his ancestral home. In the following spring he succeeded in finding a tenant for the house in *Staus*, but the *poltergeistic* outbreak was not renewed. It has been thought necessary to relate the above events somewhat fully, since they afford perhaps the best evidence extant for the hypothesis of discarnate intelligence operating in poltergeistic cases. The Joller case is exceedingly well-attested, not only by the curious crowds who saw the opening and shutting of windows, and so on, but also by men of responsibility, members of the national council, court of justice, and other institutions.

Stead, William Thomas : Journalist and Spiritualist, was born at Embleton, Northumberland, in 1849. On leaving school he was apprenticed in the office of a merchant, but soon drifted into journalism. In 1871 he was editor of the Darlington *Northern Echo*, and in 1883 of the *Pall Mall*

Gazette. In 1890 he founded the *Review of Reviews*, finding therein an outlet for his remarkable energy. His journalistic zeal led him to espouse many causes—he conducted a propaganda in favour of the peace movement, devoted himself to the interests of the Boers during the South African War, and issued cheap reprints of classical works. But not the latest of his activities was concerned with his advocacy of spiritualism. For four years—1893-97—he conducted a spiritualistic organ, the *Borderland*, and till his death gave the weight of his journalistic and personal influence to the movement. Notwithstanding that there was something of fanaticism in his zeal, and that his ardour sometimes carried him beyond prescribed limits, he was still a force to be reckoned with in the sphere of politics, and Cecil Rhodes, especially, was much influenced by his opinions. Mr. Stead perished with the sinking of the *Titanic* in April, 1912, since when many spiritualistic circles claim to have seen and spoken with him. His daughter, Miss Estelle Stead, has written his life.

Stevenson, R. L. : (*See* **Fiction, Occult English.**)

Sthulic Plane : (*See* **Physical World.**)

Stilling, Jung : (*See* **Germany.**)

Stoicheomancy : A method of divination which is practised by opening the works of Homer or Virgil, and reading as an oracular statement the first verse which presents itself. It is a branch of rhapsodomancy (q.v.).

Stoker, Bram : (*See* **Fiction, Occult English.**)

Stolisomancy : Divination from the manner in which a person dresses himself. Augustus believed that a military revolt was predicted on the morning of its occurrence by the fact that his valet had buckled his right sandal to his left foot.

Stomach, Seeing with the : A phenomenon frequently observed by the followers of Mesmer in their somnambules. The subject, in a cataleptic state closely resembling death, would show no signs of intelligence when questions were directed to his ears, but if the questions were addressed to the pit of the *stomach*, or sometimes to the finger-tips or toes, an answer would be immediately forthcoming. Several such cases are recorded by Dr. Pététin, of Lyons, who in 1808 published his *Electricité Animale*, and by other mesmerists. Not only hearing, but seeing, tasting and smelling were performed by the *stomach*, independent of the sensory organs. Pététin attributes the phenomenon to animal electricity and states that objects placed on the patient's *stomach* were not seen when they were wrapped in wax or silk—that is, non-conductors. The best way to communicate with a patient in the cataleptic state was for the operator to place his hand on the *stomach* of the subject, and address his question to the finger-tips of his own free hand. This trance phenomenon, as well as others, may now be referred to suggestion and hyperæsthesia.

Strange Story, A : by Bulwer Lytton. (*See* **Fiction, Occult English.**)

Strega : (*See* **Italy.**)

Strioporta : Frankish title for a witch. (*See* **France.**)

Stroking Stones and Images : It is related by Cotton Mather that an Irish-American witch produced pain and disease in others by merely wetting her finger with saliva, and *stroking* small *images*, or sometimes a long, slender *stone*.

Studion, Simon : *See* **Rosicrucians.**)

Subliminal Self : A term much used in psychical research to denote that part of the personality which is normally beneath the " threshold " (*limen*) separating consciousness from unconsciousness. The phrase owed its popularity largely to the late Mr. Myers, who made use of it to explain the psychic phenomena which he had observed. Mr. Myer's view was that only a fraction of the human personality, or soul, finds adequate expression through the ordinary cerebral processes, because of the fact that the brain and physical organism have not yet reached a very advanced stage of evolution. The soul, in short, is like an iceberg, with a fraction of its bulk above water, but having much the greater part submerged. The *subliminal self*, again according to Mr. Myers, was in touch with a reservoir of psychical energy, from which it drew forces which influenced the physical organism. Thus the inspiration of genius, the exaltation of the perceptive and intellectual faculties in hypnosis, and such exercises as automatic writing and talking and table-tilting, were referred to great influxes of these psychical forces rather than to any morbid tendencies in the agent. Indeed, abnormal manifestations were, and still are, regarded by some authorities as foreshadowing a new type in the progress of evolution whose faculties shall transcend those of man just as our human faculties transcend those of the lower animals. The soul, thus dependent for a very inadequate expression on a nervous system of limited scope, is at death freed from its limitations and comes into its heritage of full consciousness. These hypotheses have been pressed into service to explain telepathy and communication between the living and the dead, as well as hallucination, automatism, and all the hypnotic phenomena. But the two former, even if they could be demonstrated, would require to be explained on other grounds, while the others, whose existence is undisputed, are more generally regarded as resultant from cerebral dissociation—*i.e.*, the temporary dislocation of the connecting links between the various neural systems.

Subterranean Crypts and Temples : *Subterranean* resorts, crypts and places of worship, have ever exercised a deep fascination upon the mind of man. The mysteries of the Egyptian, and of other peoples were held in underground *crypts* possibly for the purposes of rendering these ceremonies still more secret and mysterious to the mob. But also, perhaps, because it was essential to the privacy they necessitated. The caves of Elephanta, the Catacombs and similar *subterranean* edifices will also recur to the mind of the reader. But the purpose of this article is to refer to several lesser and perhaps more interesting underground meeting-places and *temples* in various parts of the world.

Mr. Hargreave Jennings quoting Dr. Plot in his *History of Staffordshire*, written in the third quarter of the seventeenth century, gives an interesting account of a supposed Rosicrucian crypt in that county, which, however, cannot be found in the work alluded to. It is, however, given as an interesting imaginative effort. A countryman was employed, at the close of a certain dull summer's day, in digging a trench in a field in a valley, round which the country rose into sombre, silent woods, vocal only with the quaint cries of the infrequent magpies. It was some little time after the sun had sunk, and the countryman was just about giving over his labour for the day. In one or two of the last languid strokes of his pick, the rustic came upon something stony and hard, which struck a spark, clearly visible in the increasing gloom. At this surprise, he resumed his labour, and, curiously enough, found a large, flat stone in the centre of the field. This field was far away from any of the farms or " cotes," as they were called, with which the now almost twilight country was sparingly dotted. In a short time, he cleared the stone free of the grass and weeds which had grown over it ; and it proved to be a large, oblong slab, with an immense iron ring fixed at one end in a socket. For half an hour the countryman essayed to stir this stone in vain. At last he bethought himself of some yards of rope which he had lying near amongst his tools ; and these he converted, being an ingenious, inquisitive, inventive man, into a tackle—by means of which, and by passing the sling

round a bent tree in a line with the axis of the stone, he contrived, in the last of the light, and with much expenditure of toil to raise it. And then, greatly to his surprise, he saw a large, deep, hollow place, buried in the darkness, which, when his eyes grew accustomed a little to it, he discovered was the top-story to a stone staircase, seemingly of extraordinary depth, for he saw nothing below. The country-fellow had not the slightest idea of where this could lead to ; but being a man, though a rustic and a clown, of courage, and most probably urged by his idea that the stair-case led to some secret repository where treasure lay buried, he descended the first few steps cautiously, and tried to peer in vain down into the darkness. This seemed impenetrable, but there was one object at a vast, cold distance below. Looking up to the fresh air, and seeing the star Venus—the evening star—shining suddenly like a planet, in encouraging, unexpected brilliancy, although the sky had still some sunset-light in it, the puzzled man left the upper ground and descended silently a fair, though a somewhat broken stair-case. Here, at an angle, as near as he could judge, of a hundred feet underground, he came upon a square landing-place, with a niche in the wall ; and then he saw a further long stair-case, descending at right angles to the first stair-case, and still going down into deep, cold, darkness. The man cast a glance upwards, as if questioning the small segment of light from the upper world which shot down whether he should continue his search, or desist and return. All was stillest of the still about him but he saw no reason particularly to fear. So, imagining that he would in some way soon penetrate the mystery, and feeling in the darkness by his hands upon the wall, and by his toes first on each step, he resolutely descended, and he deliberately counted two hundred and twenty steps. He felt no difficulty in his breathing, except a certain sort of aromatic smell of distant incense, that he thought Egyptian, coming up now and then from below, as if from another though a subterranean world. " Possibly," thought he—for he had heard of them—" the world of the mining gnomes ; and I am breaking in upon their secrets, which is forbidden for man." The rustic, though courageous, was superstitious.

But, notwithstanding some fits of fear, the countryman went on, and at a much lower angle he met a wall in his face ; but, making a turn to the right, with a singular credit to his nerves, the explorer went down again. And now he saw at a vast distance below, at the foot of a deeper staircase of stone, a steady though a pale light. This was shining up as if from a star, or coming from the centre of the earth. Cheered by this light, though absolutely astounded—nay, frightened—at thus discovering light, whether natural or artificial, in the deep bowels of the earth, the man again descended, meeting a thin, humid trail of light, as it looked, mounting up the centre line of the shining though mouldering old stairs, which apparently had not been pressed by a human foot for very many ages. He thought now, although it was probable only the wind in some hidden recess, or creeping down some gallery, that he heard a murmur overhead, as if of the uncertain rumble of horses and of heavy wagons, or lumbering wains. Next moment, all subsided into total stillness ; but the distant light seemed to flicker, as if in answer to the strange sound. Half a dozen times he paused and turned as if he would remount—almost flee for his life upwards, as he thought ; for this might be the secret haunt of robbers, or the dreadful abode of evil spirits. What if, in a few moments, he should come upon some scene to affright, or alight in the midst of desperate ruffians, or be caught by murderers. He listened eagerly. He now almost bitterly repented his descent. Still the light streamed at a distance, but still there was no sound to interpret the meaning of the light, or to display the character of this mysterious place, in which the countryman himself was entangled hopelessly.

The discoverer by this time stood still in fear. But at last, summoning courage, and recommending himself devoutly to God, he determined to complete his discovery. Above, he had been working in no strange place: the field he knew well, the woods were very familiar to him, and his own hamlet and his family were only a few miles distant He now hastily, and more in fear than through courage, noisily with his feet descended the remainder of the stairs; and the light grew brighter as he approached, until at last, at another turn, he came upon a square chamber built up of large hewn stones. He stopped, silent and awestruck. Here was a flagged pavement and a somewhat lofty roof, gathering up into a centre; in the groins of which was a rose, carved exquisitely in some dark stone, or in marble. But what was this poor man's fright when, making another sudden turn, from between the jambs, and from under the large archivolt of a Gothic stone portal, light streamed out over him with inexpressible brilliancy, shining over every thing, and lighting up the place with brilliant radiance, like an intense golden sunset. He started back. Then his limbs shook and bent under him as he gazed with terror at the figure of a man, whose face was hidden, as he sat in a studious attitude in a stone chair, reading in a great book, with his elbow resting on a table like a rectangular altar, in the light of a large, ancient iron lamp, suspended by a thick chain to the middle of the roof. A cry of alarm, which he could not suppress, escaped from the scared discoverer, who involuntarily advanced one pace, beside himself with terror. He was now within the illuminated chamber. As his feet fell on the stone, the figure started bolt upright from his seated position as if in awful astonishment. He erected his hooded head, and showed himself as if in anger about to question the intruder. Doubtful if what he saw were a reality, or whether he was not in some terrific dream, the countryman advanced, without being aware of it, another audacious step. The hooded man now thrust out a long arm, as if in warning, and in a moment the discoverer perceived that his hand was armed with an iron bâton, and that he pointed it as if tremendously to forbid further approach. Now, however, the poor man, not being in a condition either to reason or to restrain himself, with a cry, and in a passion of fear, took a third fatal step; and as his foot descended on the groaning stone, which seemed to give way for a moment under him, the dreadful man, or image, raised his arm high like a machine, and with his truncheon struck a prodigious blow upon the lamp, shattering it into a thousand pieces, and leaving the place in utter darkness.

This was the end of this terrifying adventure. There was total silence now, far and near. Only a long, low roll of thunder, or a noise similar to thunder, seemed to begin from a distance, and then to move with snatches, as if making turns; and it then rumbled sullenly to sleep as if through unknown, inaccessible passages. What these were—if any passages—nobody ever found out. It was only suspected that this hidden place referred in some way to the Rosicrucians, and that the mysterious people of that famous order had there concealed some of their scientific secrets. The place in Staffordshire became afterwards famed as the sepulchre of one of the brotherhood, whom, for want of a more distinct recognition or name, the people chose to call "Rosicrucius," in general reference to his order; and from the circumstances of the lamp, and its sudden extinguishment by the figure that started up, it was supposed that some Rosicrucian had determined to inform posterity that he had penetrated to the secret of the making of the ever-burning lamps of the ancients,—though, at the moment that he displayed his knowledge, he took effectual means that no one should reap any advantage from it.

The Jesuit priests of the early eighteenth century have left descriptions of the well-known palace of Mitla in Central America, which leave no doubt that in their time it contained many subterranean chambers and one especially which appears to have surpassed all others in the dreadful uses to which it was put. Father Torquemada says of the place. "When some monks of my order, the Franciscan, passed, preaching and shriving through the province of Zapoteca, whose capital city is Tehuantepec, they came to a village which was called Mictlan, that is, underworld (hell). Besides mentioning the large number of people in the village they told of buildings which were prouder and more magnificent than any which they had hitherto seen in New Spain. Among them was the temple of the evil spirit and living rooms for his demoniacal servants, and among other fine things there was a hall with ornamented panels, which were constructed of stone in a variety of arabesques and other very remarkable designs. There were doorways there, each one of which was built of but three stones, two upright at the sides and one across them, in such a manner that, although these doorways were very high and broad, the stone sufficed for their entire construction. They were so thick and broad that we were assured there were few like them. There was another hall in these buildings, or rectangular temples, which was erected entirely on round stone pillars very high and very thick that two grown men could scarcely encircle them with their arms, nor could one of them reach the finger-tips of the other. These pillars were all in one piece and, it was said, the whole shaft of the pillar measured 5 ells from top to bottom, and they were very much like those of the church of Santa Maria Maggiore in Rome, very skillfully made and polished."

Father Burgoa is more explicit with regard to these *subterranean* chambers. He says, "There were four chambers above ground and four below. The latter were arranged according to their purpose in such a way that one front chamber served as chapel and sanctuary for the idols, which were placed on a great stone which served as an altar. And for the most important feasts which they celebrated with sacrifices, or at the burial of a king or great lord, the high priest instructed the lesser priests or the subordinate temple officials who served him to prepare the chapel and his vestments, and a large quantity of the incense used by them. And then he descended with a great retinue, which none of the common people saw him or dared to look in his face, convinced that if they did so they would fall dead to the earth as a punishment for their boldness. And when he entered the chapel they put on him a long white cotton garment made like an alb, and over that a garment shaped like a dalmatic, which was embroidered with pictures of wild beasts and birds; and they put a cap on his head, and on his feet a kind of shoe woven of many-colored feathers. And when he had put on these garments he walked with solemn mien and measured step to the altar, bowed low before the idols, renewed the incense, and then in quite unintelligible murmurs (muy entre dientes) he began to converse with these images, these depositories of infernal spirits, and continued in this sort of prayer with hideous grimaces and writhings, uttering inarticulate sounds, which filled all present with fear and terror, till he came out of that diabolical trance and told those standing around the lies and fabrications which the spirit had imparted to him or which he had invented himself. When human beings were sacrificed the ceremonies were multiplied, and the assistants of the high priest stretched the victim out upon a large stone, bareing his breast, which they tore open with a great stone knife, while the body writhed in fearful convulsions and they laid the heart bare, ripping it out, and with it the soul, which the devil took, while they carried the heart to the high priest that he might offer it to the idols by holding it to their mouths, among other ceremonies; and the body was thrown into the burial-place of their "blessed," as they called them. And if after the sacrifice he felt inclined to detain those who begged any favor he sent them word by the subordinate priests not to leave their houses till their gods were appeased, and he commanded them to do penance meanwhile, to fast and to speak with no woman, so that, until this father of sin had interceded for the absolution of the penitents and had declared the gods appeased they did not dare to cross their threshold.

"The second (underground) chamber was the burial place of these high priests, and third that of the kings of Theozapotlan, whom they brought thither richly dressed in their best attire, feathers, jewels, golden necklaces, and precious stones, placing a shield in their left hand and a javelin in the right, just as they used them in war. And at their burial rites great mourning prevailed; the instruments which were played made mournful sounds; and with loud wailing and continuous sobbing they chanted the life and exploits of their lord until they laid him on the structure which they had prepared for this purpose.

"The last (underground) chamber had a second door at the rear, which led to a dark and gruesome room. This was closed with a stone slab, which occupied the whole entrance. Through this door they threw the bodies of the victims and of the great lords and chieftains who had fallen in battle, and they brought them from the spot where they fell, even when it was very far off, to this burial place; and so great was the barbarous infatuation of these Indians that, in the belief of the happy life which awaited them, many who were oppressed by diseases or hardships begged this infamous priest to accept them as living sacrifices and allow them to enter through that portal and roam about in the dark interior of the mountains, to seek the great feasting-places of their forefathers. And when anyone obtained this favour the servants of the high priest led him thither with special ceremonies, and after they had allowed him to enter through the small door they rolled the stone before it again took leave of him, and the unhappy man, wandering in that abyss of darkness, died of hunger and thirst, beginning already in life the pain of his damnation; and on account of this horrible abyss they called this village Liyobaa, The Cavern of Death.

"When later there fell upon these people the light of the Gospel, its servants took much trouble to instruct them to find out whether this error, common to all these nations, still prevailed, and they learned from the stories which had been handed down that all were convinced that this damp cavern extended more than 30 leagues underground, and that its roof was supported by pillars. And there were people, zealous prelates anxious for knowledge, who, in order to convince these ignorant people of their terror, went into this cave accompanied by a large number of people bearing lighted torches and firebrands, and descended several large steps. And they soon came upon many buttresses which formed a kind of street. They had prudently brought a quantity of rope with them to use as a guiding line, that they might not lose themselves in this confusing labyrinth. And the putrefaction and the bad odour and the dampness of the earth were very great and there was also a cold wind which blew out their torches And after they had gone a short distance, fearing to be overpowered by the stench or to step on poisonous reptiles, of which some had been seen, they resolved to go out again

and to completely wall up this back door of hell. The four buildings above ground were the only ones which still remained open, and they had a court and chambers like those underground; and the ruins of these have lasted even to the present day."

The vast *subterranean* vaults under the temple hill at Jerusalem were probably used as a secret meeting-place by the Templars during their occupation of the Holy City, and it was perhaps there that the strange Eastern rites of Baphomet (q.v.) which they later affected were first celebrated. In his *Recent Discoveries on the Temple Hill* the Rev. James King says, "On the occasion of a visit to the Noble Sanctuary, the author had an opportunity of examining the ancient masonry inside the wall at the south-east corner, as well as the vast *subterranean* vaults popularly known as Solomon's stables. A small doorway, under a little dome at the south-east corner, admits by a flight of steps to a small chamber known as the Mosque of the Cradle of our Lord, from the existence of a hollowed stone which somewhat resembles a cradle, and a tradition that the Virgin Mary remained in this chamber for some time after her purification in the Temple. Passing through the chamber, the spacious vaults, which extend over an acre of ground, are reached. These *subterranean* substructures consist of one hundred square piers arranged in fifteen rows, each pier being five feet wide and composed of large marginal drafted stones, placed singly over each other. The rows are connected by semi-circular arches, the intercolumniations of which range from ten to twenty-three feet. The floor of these vaults is about forty-feet below the Haram Area, and more than a hundred feet above the great foundation corner-stone. They are called Solomon's Stables by the Franks. But the Moslems call the place, Al Masjed al Kadim, that is, The Old Mosque. These vaults were used as stables by the Frank kings and the Knights Templar, and holes in which rings were fastened can still be traced on some of the piers.

Since the floor of Solomon's Stables is upwards of a hundred feet above the foundation stone, it seems highly probable that there exists another system of vaults below, for the vast space from the rock upwards is not likely to be filled with solid earth.

Some allusion seems to be made to these vaults in the writings of Procopius, a Greek historian of the sixth century. He was born at Cæsarea, in Palestine, about 500 A.D., and as a young man went to Constantinople, where his eminent talents brought him under the notice of the Emperor Justinian. In 529 A.D. Justinian built a splendid church on the Temple Hill, in honour of the Virgin Mary, and in the writings of Procopius there is a full and detailed account of the edifice. The historian relates that the fourth part of the ground required for the building was wanting towards the south-east; the builders therefore laid their foundations on the sloping ground, and constructed a series of arched vaults, in order to raise the ground to the level of the other parts of the enclosure. This account is eminently descriptive of the *subterranean* vaults at the south-east portion of the Haram, and, according to Mr. Fergusson, the stone-work of these vaults certainly belongs to the age of Justinian.

Succubus: A demon who takes the shape of a woman. The Rabbi Elias says that it is mentioned in certain writings that Adam was visited during a hundred and thirty years by female demons, and had intercourse with demons, spirits, spectres, lemurs, and phantoms. Under the reign of Roger, king of Sicily, a young man, bathing by moonlight, with several others, thought he saw someone drowning, and hastened to the rescue. Having drawn from the water a beautiful woman, he became enamoured of her, married her, and had by her a child. Afterwards she disappeared mysteriously with her child, which made everyone believe that she was a *succubus*. Hector Boece, in his history of Scotland, relates that a very handsome young man was pursued by a female demon, who would pass through his closed door, and offer to marry him. He complained to his bishop, who enjoined him to fast, pray, and confess himself, when the infernal visitor ceased to trouble him. Delancre says that in Egypt, an honest maréchal-ferrant being occupied in forging during the night there appeared to him a demon under the shape of a beautiful woman. He threw a hot iron in the face of the demon, which at once took to flight.

Suflism : (*See* **Assassins.**)

Suggestion : The sensitiveness to *suggestion* of the entranced subject is the characteristic and invariable accompaniment of the hypnotic state, and is also a distinctive feature of hysteria. Indeed, many modern scientists give to hypnotism the name " Suggestion." An abnormal suggestibility implies some measure of cerebral dissociation. (*See* **Hypnotism.**) In this state every *suggestion* advanced by the operator, whether conveyed by word, gesture, or even unconscious glance, operates with abnormal force in the brain of the subject, as being relieved from the counter-excitement of other ideas. In the view of Professor Pierre Janet all suggestibility implies a departure from perfect sanity, but this, though perhaps true in the strictest sense, is somewhat misleading, since all are more or less amenable to *suggestion*. In hypnotism and hysteria, however, the normal suggestibility is greatly exaggerated, and the *suggestion*, meeting with no opposition from the recipient's critical or judicial faculties (because there are no other ideas with which to compare it) becomes for the time his dominant idea. The *suggestion* thus accepted has a powerful effect on both mind and body, hence the value of *suggestion* in certain complaints is incalculable. The " miracles " wrought by Christian Scientists, the efficacy of a pilgrimage to Lourdes, the feats of " healing mediums " all testify to its powerful effect. *Post-hypnotic suggestion* is the term applied to a *suggestion* made while the subject is entranced, but which is to be carried out after he awakes. Sometimes an interval of months may elapse between the utterance of a command and its fulfilment, but almost invariably at the stated time the *suggestion* is obeyed, the recipient is perhaps unaware of the source of his impulse, not finding adequate logical grounds for the action he performs, or perhaps automatically lapses into the hypnotic state. *Auto-suggestion* does not proceed from any extraneous source, but arises in one's own mind, either spontaneously or from a misconception of existing circumstances, as in the case of a person who drinks coloured water under the impression that it is poison, and exhibits every symptom of poisoning. Auto-suggestion may arise spontaneously in dream, the automatic obedience to such *suggestion* often giving rise to stories of " veridical" dreams. The outbreaks of religious frenzy or ecstasy which swept Europe in the Middle Ages were examples of the results of *mass-suggestion*—*i.e.*, *suggestion* made by a crowd, and much more potent than that made by an individual. Cases of so-called collective hallucination may be referred to the same cause. *Suggestion* is doubtless responsible to some extent for clairvoyant and mediumistic faculties, and on the whole enters largely into the study of psychic science.

Sukias : Central American witches. (*See* **American Indians.**)

Summa Perfectionis : (*See* **Arabs.**)

Summons by the Dying : It was formerly maintained by the theologians that if anyone who was unjustly accused or persecuted should summon, with his dying breath, his oppressor to appear before the supreme tribunal, a miracle would take place, and the person thus summoned would

die on the day fixed by his innocent victim. Thus the (Grand Master of the Templars) cited the pope and the king of France to appear before God on a certain date not very far ahead, and the story goes on to relate that both died at the appointed time. François I., Duke of Brittany, hired assassins to murder his brother, in 1450. The dying prince summoned his murderer before the highest of all courts, and François shortly expired. Yet another instance is that of Ferdinand IV., of Spain, who was summoned by two nobles whom he had condemned unjustly, and he also responded reluctantly at the end of thirty days.

Many more examples could be quoted to show how firmly-rooted was this belief in the power of the *dying* to avenge their death by supernatural means. Indeed, it would be safe to say that, by an inversion, of the usual order of cause and effect, the popular faith in the efficacy of the *summons* was responsible for such evidence as was forthcoming on its behalf. Fear, and possibly remorse, acting on the imagination of the guilty judge, might well cause him to expire at the stated time, and authenticated accounts of death caused by these agents are not unknown. This is further borne out by the fact that if the condemned man was guilty—that is, if the judge's conscience was clear—the summons had no effect. Sorcerers, especially, summoned their judges, but in vain. A story, is told of Gonzalvo of Cordova, who sentenced a soldier to death for sorcery. The soldier exclaimed that he was innocent, and summoned Gonzalvo to appear before God. " Go, then," said the judge, " and hasten the proceedings. My brother who is in heaven, will appear for me." Needless to say, Gonzalvo did not die, as he believed he had dealt justly and had no fear of the consequences of the *summons*.

Sunderland, Rev. Laroy : (*See* **Spiritualism.**)

Suth, Dr. Pietro : (*See* **Italy.**)

Swan, The : (*See* **Philosopher's Stone.**)

Swawm : Burmese Vampires : (*See* **Burma.**)

Swedenborg, Emanuel, 1688–1772 : One of the greatest mystics of all time, was born at Stockholm in Sweden on the 29th January. His father was a professor of theology at Upsala, and afterwards Bishop of Scara, and in his time was charged with possessing heterodox opinions. *Swedenborg* completed his education at the university of Upsala in 1710, after which he visited England, Holland, France and Germany. Five years later he returned to his native town, and devoted much time to the study of natural science and engineering, editing a paper entitled *Daedalus hyperboreus* which dealt chiefly with mechanical inventions. About 1716, Charles XII. appointed him to the Swedish Board of Mines. He appears at this time to have had many activities. He published various mathematical and mechanical works, and even took part in the siege of Friederickshall in an engineering capacity. Originally known as Swedberg, he was elevated to the rank of the nobility by Queen Ulrica and changed his name to *Swedenborg*. Sitting in the House of Nobles, his political utterances had great weight, but his tendencies were distinctly democratic. He busied himself privately in scientific gropings for the explanation of the universe, and published at least two works dealing with the origin of things which are of no great account, unless as foreshadowing many scientific facts and ventures of the future. Thus his theories regarding light, cosmic atoms, geology and physics, were distinctly in advance of his time, and had they been suitably disseminated could not but have influenced scientific Europe. He even sketched a flying-machine, and felt confident that although it was unsuitable to aerial navigation, if men of science applied themselves to the problem, it would speedily be solved. It was in 1734 that he published his *Prodomus Philosophiæ Ratiocinantrio de Infinite* which treats of the relation of the finite to the infinite and of the soul to the body. In this work he seeks to establish a definite connection between the two as a means of overcoming the difficulty of their relationship. The spiritual and the divine appear to him as the supreme study of man. He ransacked the countries of Europe in quest of the most eminent teachers and the best books dealing with anatomy, for he considered that in that science lay the germ of the knowledge of soul and spirit. Through his anatomical studies he anticipated certain modern views dealing with the functions of the brain, which are most remarkable.

About the age of fifty-five a profound change overtook the character of *Swedenborg*. Up to this time he had been a scientist, legislator, and man of affairs ; but now his enquiries into the region of spiritual things were to divorce him entirely from practical matters. His introduction into the spiritual world, his illumination, was commenced by dreams and extraordinary visions. He heard wonderful conversations and felt impelled to found a new church. He says that the eyes of his spirit were so opened that he could see heavens and hells, and converse with angels and spirits : but all his doctrines relating to the New Church came directly from God alone, while he was reading the gospels. He claimed that God revealed Himself to him and told him that He had chosen him to unveil the spiritual sense of the whole scriptures to man. From that moment worldly knowledge was eschewed by *Swedenborg* and he worked for spiritual ends alone. He resigned his several appointments and retired upon half pay. Refreshing his knowledge of the Hebrew tongue, he commenced his great works on the interpretation of the scriptures. After the year 1747 he lived in Sweden, Holland and London, in which city he died on the 29th of March 1772. He was buried in the Swedish Church in Prince's Square, in the parish of St. George's in the East, and in April, 1908 his bones were removed, at the request of the Swedish government, to Stockholm.

There can be no question as to the intrinsic honesty of *Swedenborg's* mind and character. He was neither presumptuous nor overbearing as regards his doctrines, but gentle and reasonable. A man of few wants, his life was simplicity itself—his food consisting for the most part of bread, milk and coffee. He was in the habit of lying in a trance for days together, and day and night had no distinctions for him. His mighty wrestlings with evil spirits at times so terrified his servants, that they would seek the most distant part of the house in refuge. But again he would converse with benignant angels in broad daylight. We are badly hampered regarding first-hand evidence of his spiritual life and adventures—most of our knowledge being gleaned from other than original sources.

So far from attempting to found a new church, or otherwise tamper or interfere with existing religious systems, *Swedenborg* was of the opinion that the members of all churches could belong to his New Church in a spiritual sense. His works may be divided into : expository volumes, notably *The Apocalypse Revealed, The Apocalypse Explained*, and *Arcana Celestia* ; books of spiritual philosophy, such as *Intercourse between the Soul and the Body Divine Providence*, and *Divine Love and Wisdom ;* books dealing with the hierarchy of supernatural spheres such as *Heaven and Hell* and *The Last Judgment* ; and those which are purely doctrinal, such as *The New Jerusalem, The True Christian Religion*, and *Canons of the New Church.* Of these his *Divine Love and Wisdom* is the volume which most succinctly presents his entire religious systems. God he regards as the Divine Man. Spiritually He consists of infinite love, and corporeally of infinite wisdom. From the divine love all things draw nourishment. The sun, as

we know it, is merely a microcosm of a spiritual sun which emanates from the Creator. This spiritual sun is the source of love and knowledge, and the natural sun is the source of nature ; but whereas the first is alive, the second is inanimate. There is no connection between the two worlds of nature and spirit unless in similarity of construction. Love, wisdom, use ; or end, cause and effect, are the three infinite and uncreated degrees of being in God and man respectively. The causes of all things exist in the spiritual sphere and their effects in the natural sphere, and the end of all creation is that man may become the image of his Creator, and of the cosmos as a whole. This is to be effected by a love of the degrees above enumerated. Man possesses two vessels or receptacles for the containment of God—the Will for divine love, and the Understanding for divine wisdom. Before the Fall, the flow of these virtues into the human spirit was perfect, but through the intervention of the forces of evil, and the sins of man himself, it was much interrupted. Seeking to restore the connection between Himself and man, God came into the world as Man ; for if He had ventured on earth in His unveiled splendour, he would have destroyed the hells through which he must proceed to redeem man, and this He did not wish to do, merely to conquer them. The unity of God is an essential of the Swedenborgian theology, and he thoroughly believes that God did not return to His own place without leaving behind Him a visible representative of Himself in the word of scripture, which is an eternal incarnation, in a three-fold sense—natural, spiritual and celestial. Of this *Swedenborg* is the apostle ; nothing was hidden from him ; he was aware of the appearance and conditions of other worlds, good and evil, heaven and hell, and of the planets. " The life of religion," he says, " is to accomplish good." " The kingdom of heaven is a kingdom of uses." One of the central ideas of his system is known as the Doctrine of Correspondences. Everything visible has belonging to it an appropriate spiritual reality. Regarding this Vaughan says : " The history of man is an acted parable ; the universe, a temple covered with hieroglyphics. Behmen, from the light which flashes on certain exalted moments, imagines that he receives the key to these hidden significances—that he can interpret the *Signatura Rerum*. But he does not see spirits, or talk with angels. According to him, such communications would be less reliable than the intuition he enjoyed. *Swedenborg* takes opposite ground. ' What I relate,' he would say, ' comes from no such mere inward persuasion. I recount the things I have seen. I do not labour to recall and to express the manifestation made me in some moment of ecstatic exaltation. I write you down a plain statement of journeys and conversations in the spiritual world, which have made the greater part of my daily history for many years together. I take my stand upon experience. I have proceeded by observation and induction as strict as that of any man of science among you. Only it has been given me to enjoy an experience reaching into two worlds—that of spirit, as well as that of matter.' . . . . .

" According to *Swedenborg*, all the mythology and the symbolisms of ancient times were so many refracted or fragmentary correspondences—relics of that better day when every outward object suggested to man's mind its appropriate divine truth. Such desultory and uncertain links between the seen and the unseen are so many imperfect attempts toward that harmony of the two worlds which he believed himself commissioned to reveal. The happy thoughts of the artist, the imaginative analogies of the poet, are exchanged with *Swedenborg* for an elaborate system. All the terms and objects in the natural and spiritual worlds are catalogued in pairs. This method appears so much formal pedantry. Our fancies will not work to order. The meaning and the life with which we continually inform outward objects—those suggestions from sight and sound, which make almost every man at times a poet—are our own creations, are determined by the mood of the hour, cannot be imposed from without, cannot be arranged like the nomenclature of a science. As regards the inner sense of scripture, at all events, *Swedenborg* introduces some such yoke. In that province, however, it is perhaps as well that those who are not satisfied with the obvious sense should find some restraint for their imagination, some method for their ingenuity, some guidance in a curiosity irresistible to a certain class of minds. If an objector say, ' I do not see why the ass should correspond to scientific truth, and the horse to intellectual truth,' *Swedenborg* will reply, ' This analogy rests on no fancy of mine, but on actual experience and observation in the spiritual world. I have always seen horses and asses present and circumstanced, when, and according as, those inward qualities were central.' But I do not believe that it was the design of *Swedenborg* rigidly to determine the relationships by which men are continually uniting the seen and unseen worlds. He probably conceived it his mission to disclose to men the divinely-ordered correspondences of scripture, the close relationship of man's several states of being, and to make mankind more fully aware that matter and spirit were associated, not only in the varying analogies of imagination, but by the deeper affinity of eternal law. In this way, he sought to impart an impulse rather than to prescribe a scheme. His consistent followers will acknowledge that had he lived to another age, and occupied a different social position, the forms under which the spiritual world presented itself in him would have been different. To a large extent, therefore, his *Memorable Relations* must be regarded as true for him only—for such a character, in such a day, though containing principles independent of personal peculiarity and local colouring. It would have been indeed inconsistent, had the Protestant who (as himself a Reformer) essayed to supply the defects and correct the errors of the Reformation—had he designed to prohibit all advance beyond his own position."

The style of *Swedenborg* is clear-cut and incisive. He is never overpowered by manifestations from the unseen. Whereas other mystics are seized by fear or joy by these and become incomprehensible, he is in his element, and when on the very pinnacles of ecstasy can observe the smallest details with a scientific eye. We know nowadays that a great many of his visions do not square with scientific probabilities. Thus those which detail his journeys among the planets and describe the flora and fauna, let us say, of Mars, can be totally disproved, as we are aware that such forms of life as he claims to have seen could not possibly exist upon that planet. The question arises : Did the vast amount of work accomplished by *Swedenborg* in the first half of his life lead to more or less serious mental derangement ? There have been numerous cases of similar injury through similar causes. But the scientific exactness and clarity of his mind survived to the last. So far as he knew science he applied it admirably and with minute exactness to his system ; but just as the science of Dante raises a smile, so we feel slightly intolerant of *Swedenborg's* scientific application to things spiritual. He was probably the only mystic with a real scientific training ; others had been adepts in chemistry and kindred studies, but no mystic ever experienced such a long and arduous scientific apprenticeship as *Swedenborg*. It colours the whole of his system. It would be exceedingly difficult to say whether he was more naturally a mystic or a scientist. In the first part of his life we do not find him greatly

exercised by spiritual affairs ; and it is only when he had passed the meridian of human days that he seriously began to consider matters supernatural. The change to the life of a mystic, if not rapid was certainly not prolonged : what then caused it ? We can only suspect that his whole tendency was essentially mystical from the first, and that he was a scientist by force of circumstance rather than because of any other reason. The spiritual was constantly simmering within his brain, but, as the world is ever with us, he found it difficult to throw off the superincumbent mass of affairs, which probably trammelled him for years. At length the fountains of his spirit welled up so fiercely that they could no longer be kept back ; and throwing aside his scientific oars, he leaped into the spiritual ocean which afterwards speedily engulfed him. There is perhaps no analogy to be found to his case in the biography of science. We cannot altogether unveil the springs of the man's spirituality, but we know that they existed deep down in him. It has often been said that he was a mere visionary, and not a mystic, in the proper sense of the word ; but the terms of his philosophy dispose of this contention ; although in many ways it does not square with the generally-accepted doctrines of mysticism, it is undoubtedly one of the most striking and pregnant contributions to it. He is the apostle of the divine humanity, and the '" Grand Man " is with him the beginning and end of the creative purpose. The originality of his system is marked, and the detail with which he surrounded it provides his followers of the present day with a greater body of teaching than that of probably any other mystical master.

The following extracts from *Swedenborg's* works will assist the reader in gaining some idea of his eschatology and general doctrine :—

" The universe is an image of God, and was made for use. Providence is the government of the Lord in heaven and on earth. It extends itself over all things, because there is only one fountain of life, namely, the Lord, whose power supports all that exists.

'' The influence of the Lord is according to a plan, and is invisible, as is Providence, by which men are not constrained to believe, and thus to lose their freedom. The influence of the Lord passes over from the spiritual to the natural, and from the inward to the outward. The Lord confers his influence on the good and the bad, but the latter converts the good into evil, and the true into the false ; for so is the creature of its will fashioned.

'' In order to comprehend the origin and progress of this influence, we must first know that that which proceeds from the Lord is the divine sphere which surrounds us, and fills the spiritual and natural world. All that proceeds from an object, and surrounds and clothes it, is called its sphere.

" As all that is spiritual knows neither time nor space, it therefore follows that the general sphere or the divine one has extended itself from the first moment of creation to the last. This divine emanation, which passed over from the spiritual to the natural, penetrates actively and rapidly through the whole created world, to the last grade of it, where it is yet to be found, and produces and maintains all that is animal, vegetable, and mineral. Man is continually surrounded by a sphere of his favourite propensities ; these unite themselves to the natural sphere of his body, so that together they form one. The natural sphere surrounds every body of nature, and all the objects of the three kingdoms. Thus it allies itself to the spiritual world. This is the foundation of sympathy and antipathy, of union and separation, according to which there are amongst spirits presence and absence.

'' The angel said to me that the sphere surrounded

men more lightly on the back than´on the breast, where it was thicker and stronger. This sphere of influence, peculiar to man, operates also in general and in particular around him by means of the will, the understanding, and the practice.

" The sphere proceeding from God, which surrounds man and constitutes his strength, while it thereby operates on his neighbour and on the whole creation, is a sphere of peace and innocence ; for the Lord is peace and innocence. Then only is man consequently able to make his influence effectual on his fellow man, when peace and innocence rule in his heart, and he himself is in union with heaven. This spiritual union is connected with the natural by a benevolent man through the touch and the laying on of hands, by which the influence of the inner man is quickened, prepared, and imparted. The body communicates with others which are about it through the body, and the spiritual influence diffuses itself chiefly through the hands, because these are the most outward or *ultimum* of man ; and through him, as in the whole of nature, the first is contained in the last, as the cause in the effect. The whole soul and the whole body are contained in the hands as a medium of influence. Thus our Lord healed the sick by laying on of hands, on which account so many were healed by the touch ; and thence from the remotest times the consecration of priests and of all holy things was effected by laying on of hand. According to the etymology of the word, hands denote power. Man believes that his thoughts and his will proceed from within him, whereas all this flows into him. If he considered things in their true form, he would ascribe evil to hell, and good to the Lord ; he would by the Lord's grace recognise good and evil within himself, and be happy. Pride alone has denied the influence of God, and destroyed the human race."

In his work *Heaven and Hell, Swedenborg* speaks of influence and reciprocities — Correspondences. The action of correspondence is perceptible in a man's counntenance. In a countenance that has not learned hypocrisy, all emotions are represented naturally according to their true form ; whence the face is called the mirror of the soul. In the same way, what belongs to the understanding is represented in the speech, and what belongs to the will in the movements. Every expression in the face, in the speech, in the movements, is called correspondence. By correspondence man communicates with the angels if he possess the science of correspondence by means of thought. In order that communication may exist between heaven and man, the word is composed of nothing but correspondences, for everything in the word is correspondent, the whole and the parts ; therefore he can learn secrets, of which he perceives nothing in the literal sense ; for in the word, there is, besides the literal meaning, a spiritual meaning—one of the world, the other of heaven. *Swedenborg* had his visions and communications with the angels and spirits by means of correspondence in the spiritual sense. " Angels speak from the spiritual word, according to inward thought; from wisdom, their speech flows in a tranquil stream, gently and uninterruptedly,—they speak only in vowels the heavenly angels in A and O, the spiritual ones in E and I, for the vowels give tone to the speech, and by the tone the emotion is expressed ; the interruptions, on the other hand, corresponds with creations of the mind ; therefore we prefer, if the subject is lofty, for instance of heaven or God, even in human speech, the vowels U and O, etc. Man, however, is united with heaven by means of the word, and forms thus the link between heaven and earth, between the divine and the natural."

" But when angels speak spiritually with me from heaven, they speak just as intelligently as the man by my side. But if they turn away from man, he hears nothing more whatever, even if they speak close to his ear. It is also remarkable that several angels can speak to a man ; they send down a spirit inclined to man, and he thus hears them united."

In another place he says :—" There are also spirits called natural or corporeal spirits ; these have no connection with thought, like the others, but they enter the body, possess all the senses, speak with the mouth, and act with the limbs, for they know not but that everything in that man is their own. These are the spirits by which men are possessed. They were, however, sent by the Lord to hell ; whence in our days there are no more such possessed ones in existence."

Swedenborg's further doctrines and visions of Harmonies, that is to say, of heaven with men, and with all objects of nature ; of the harmony and correspondence of all thing with each other ; of Heaven, of Hell, and of the world of spirits ; of the various states of man after death, etc.—are very characteristic, important, and powerful. " His contemplations of the enlightened inward eye refer less to everyday associations and objects of life (although he not unfrequently predicted future occurrences), because his mind was only directed to the highest spiritual subjects, in which indeed he had attained an uncommon degree of inward wakefulness, but is therefore not understood or known, because he described his sights so spiritually and unusually by language. His chapter on the immensity of heaven attracts more especially because it contains a conversation of spirits and angels about the planetary system. The planets are naturally inhabited as well as the planet Earth, but the inhabitants differ according to the various individual formation of the planets. These visions on the inhabitants of the planets agree most remarkably, and almost without exception with the indications of a clairvoyant whom I treated magnetically. I do not think that she knew *Swedenborg* ; to which, however, I attach little importance. The two seers perceived Mars in quite a different manner. The magnetic seer only found images of fright and horror. *Swedenborg,* on the other hand, describes them as the best of all spirits of the planetary system. Their gentle, tender, zephyr-like language, is more perfect, purer and richer in thought, and nearer to the language of the angels, than others. These people associate together, and judge each other by the physiognomy, which amongst them is always the expression of the thoughts. They honour the Lord as sole God, who appears sometimes on their earth."

" Of the inhabitants of Venus he says :—' They are of two kinds ; some are gentle and benevolent, others wild, cruel and of gigantic stature. The latter rob and plunder, and live by this means ; the former have so great a degree of gentleness and kindness that they are always beloved by the good ; thus they often see the Lord appear in their own form on their earth.' It is remarkable that this description of Venus agrees so well with the old fable, and with the opinions and experience we have of Venus.

" The inhabitants of the Moon are small, like children of six or seven years old ; at the same time they have the strength of men like ourselves. Their voice rolls like thunder, and the sound proceeds from the belly, because the moon is in quite a different atmosphere from the other planets."

Swedish Exegetical and Philanthropical Society : (*See* **Spiritualism.**)

Switzerland : For ancient matter see **Teutons.**

Spiritualism.—Two cases of spiritual visitation occurred in the Swiss Cantons during last century, of so startling a nature, as to attract the eyes of all Europe. The following brief summary of the Morzine epidemic is collated from the pages of the *Cornhill Magazine*, two or three of the London daily journals, the *Reveu Spirite*, and Mr. William Howitt's magazine article entitled, "The Devils of Morzine." The period of the occurrence was about 1860; the scene, the parish of Morzine, a beautiful valley of the Savoy, not more than half a day's journey from the Lake of Geneva. The place is quite, remote, and had been seldom visited by tourists before the period named above. Being moreover shut in by high mountains, and inhabited by a simple, industrious, and pious class of peasantry, Morzine might have appeared to a casual visitor the very centre of health, peace, and good order. The first appearance of an abnormal visitation was the conduct of a young girl, who, from being quiet, modest, and well-conducted, suddenly began to exhibit what her distressed family and friends supposed to be the symptoms of insanity. She ran about in the most singular and aimless way; climbed high trees, scaled walls, and was found perched on roofs and cornices, which it seemed impossible for any creature but a squirrel to reach. She soon became wholly intractable; was given to fits of hysteria, violent laughter, passionate weeping, and general aberration from her customary modest behaviour. Whilst her parents were anxiously seeking advice in this dilemma, another and still another of the young girl's ordinary companions were seized with the same malady. In the course of ten days the report prevailed, that over fifty females—ranging from seven years of age to fifty—had been seized, and were exhibiting symptoms of the most bewildering mental aberration. The crawling, climbing, leaping, wild singing, furious swearing, and frantic behaviour of these unfortunates, soon found crowds of imitators. Before the tidings of this frightful affliction, had passed beyond the district in which it originated several hundreds of women and children, and scores of young men, were writhing under the contagion. The seizures were sudden, like the attacks; they seldom lasted long, yet they never seemed to yield to any form of treatment, whether harsh or kind, medical, religious or persuasive. The first symptoms of this malady do not seem to have been noted with sufficient attention to justify one in giving details which could be considered accurate. It was only when the number of the possessed exceeded two thousand persons, and the case was attracting multitudes of curious enquirers from all parts of the Continent, that the medical men, priests, and journalists of the day, began to keep and publish constant records of the progress of the epidemic One of the strangest features of the case, and one which most constantly baffled the faculty, was the appearance of rugged health, and freedom from all physical disease, which distinguished this malady. As a general rule, the victims spoke in hoarse, rough tones unlike their own, used profane language, such as few of them could ever have heard, and imitated the actions of crawling, leaping, climbing animals with ghastly fidelity. Sometimes they would roll their bodies up into balls and distort their limbs beyond the power of the attendant physicians to account for, or disentangle. Many amongst them were levitated in the air, and in a few instances, the women spoke in foreign tongues, manifested high conditions of exaltation, described glorious visions, prophesied, gave clairvoyant descriptions of absent persons and distant places, sang hymns, and preached in strains of sublime inspiration. It must be added, that these instances were very rare, and were only noticeable in the earlier stages of the obsession. It is almost needless to say that the tidings of this horrible obsession attracted immense multitudes of witnesses, no less than the attention of the learned and philosophic. When the attempts of the medical faculty, the church, and the law, had been tried again and again, and all had utterly failed to modify the ever-increasing horrors of this malady, the Emperor of the French, the late Louis Napoleon, under whose protectorate Morzine was then governed, yielding to the representations of his advisers, actually sent out three military companies to Morzine, charged with strict orders to quell the disturbances " on the authority of the Emperor, or by force if necessary." The result of this high-handed policy was to increase tenfold the violence of the disease, and to augment the number of the afflicted, in the persons of many of the very soldiers who sank under the contagion which they were expected to quench. The next move of the baffled French Government, was a spiritual one; an army of priests, headed by a venerable Bishop, much beloved in his diocese, being despatched in the quality of exorcists, at the suggestion of the Archbishop of Paris. Unhappily this second experiment worked no better than the first. Respectable looking groups of well-dressed men, women, and children, would pass into the churches in reverent silence, and with all the appearance of health and piety—but no sooner was the sound of the priest's voice, or the notes of the organ heard, than shrieks, execrations, sobbings, and frenzied cries, resounded from different parts of the assembly. Anxious fathers and husbands were busy in carrying their distracted relatives into the open air, and whether in the church or the home, every attempt of a sacerdotal character, was sure to arouse the mania to heights of fury unknown before. The time came at length, when the good old Bishop thought of a coup de grace to achieve a general victory over the adversary. He commanded that as many as possible of the afflicted should be gathered together to hear high mass, when he trusted that the solemnity of the occasion would be sufficient to defeat what he evidently believed to be the combined forces of Satan.

According to the description cited by William Howitt in his paper on " The Devils of Morzine," the assemblage in question, including at least two thousand of the possessed, and a number of spectators, must have far more faithfully illustrated Milton's description of Pandemonium than any mortal scene before enacted. Children and women were leaping over the seats and benches; clambering up the pillars, and shrieking defiance from pinnacles which scarcely admitted of a foothold for a bird. The Bishop's letter contains but one remark which seems to offer a clue to these scenes of horror and madness. He says: " When in my distress and confusion I accidentally laid my hand on the heads of these unfortunates, I found that the paroxysm instantly subsided, and that however wild and clamorous they may have been before, the parties so touched generally sunk down as it were into a swoon, or deep sleep, and woke up most commonly restored to sanity, and a sense of propriety." The complete failure of episcopal influence threw the Government back on the help of medical science. Dr. Constans had, since his first visit, published a report, in which he held out hopes of cure if his advice were strictly followed. He was again commissioned to do what he could for Morzine. Armed with the powers of a dictator he returned there, and backed by a fresh detachment of sixty soldiers, a brigade of gendarmes and a fresh curé, he issued despotic decrees, and threatened lunatic asylums, and in any case deportation for the convulsed. He fined any person who accused others of magic, or in any way encouraged the prevalent idea of supernatural evil. He desired the curé to preach sermons against the possibility of demoniacal possession, but this order could not be carried out by even the most obedient priest. The persons affected with fits were dispersed in every direction. Some were sent to asylums and hospitals, and many were simply exiled from Chablais. They were not allowed to revisit except by very special favour. Mr. William Howitt, writing in the *London Spiritual Magazine* says: " We need not point to the salient facts of our narrative, or discuss the various theories that have been invented to account for them. . . . . It is impossible not to see the resemblance of the Morzine epidemic with the demonopathy of the sixteenth century, and the history of the Jansenist and Cevennes convulsionnaires. . . . . Some of the facts we have related were often observed in the state of hypnotism, or nervous sleep, with which physicians are familiar. The hallucinations of which we have given instances are too common to astonish us. But the likeness of this epidemic to others that have been observed does not account for its symptoms."

Sword, Magical : (*See* **Magic.**)

Sycomancy : Divination by the leaves of the fig tree. Questions or propositions on which one wished to be enlightened were written on these leaves. If the leaf dried quickly after the appeal to the diviner, it was an evil omen ; but a good augury if the leaf dried slowly.

Symbolism in Art : " It is in and through symbols," says Carlyle, " that man, consciously or unconsciously lives, works, and has his being " ; and his words apply very pertinently to art in all its branches, for every one of these represents, in the first place, an attempt to reincarnate something in nature, and this attempt cannot be made save with the assistance of some manner of symbolism. The author uses the arbitrary and sadly restricted symbol of language whereby to state his conception of life, the composer employs notes wherewith to body forth his impressions and emotions ; while the painter must needs be still more symbolical, his art consisting as it does in expressing distance on a flat surface, and in suggesting bulk by the practice known technically as modelling. The sculptor is also a symbolist, for, while he has at his disposal a third dimension not vouchsafed to the painter, he tries to delineate coloured things in a mono-chromatic material ; while again, it is impossible for him to convey motion or action as the writer can, and he can only suggest this by moulding a figure wherein an ephemeral gesture is perpetrated. Some kind of symbolism, then, is the technical basis of all the arts ; yet another kind of symbolic significance, a deeper and more mysterious one, transpires in them in many cases. As Coleridge observes, " An idea in the highest sense of the word, cannot be expressed but by a symbol " ; and from time immemorial painters and sculptors have realised this, and have tried to crystalise abstract ideas by the aid of certain signs, some of them having quite an obvious meaning, but others being cryptic. Among the Japanese masters of the Akiyoe school, Fuji-no-Yama was a favourite topic, one which many of them figured scores of times ; and to Occidental eyes a picture of this sort is just a picture of a mountain, but to the Japanese it meant something deeper, Fuji being almost sacred to them, and its representation in line and colour being a sort of symbol of patriotic devotion. Then Hokusai, commonly accounted the greatest master of the school aforesaid, loved to draw a pot-bellied man reclining at his ease against cushions ; and this too means little in the East but much in the West, for in reality it is more than a study in voluptuousness, it represents Hotei, the god of peace and plenty. And poor people in the Land of the Rising Sun would buy a copy of this picture—for those woodcuts which are so priceless now were mostly sold for a few pence originally, and were within the reach of the humblest. And they would hang it on the wall, trusting thus to win the favour of the deity it personified. Other Japanese, more religiously minded, preferred a picture of a curious male figure emanating from a plant, and this symbolised the legend that Buddha rose originally from a lotus ; while further, in many Japanese draperies and the like we find a strange decoration not unlike a *fleur-de-lys*, and this was originally a drawing of the foot of Buddha, a drawing which evolved

throughout the centuries into the form above-named.

The art of the Hindoos is likewise permeated with symbolism, much of it quite incomprehensible to Europeans ; while the ancient Greek masters also traded in symbols, one which occurs repeatedly in their output being the fig-leaf, which represented simply amorousness, and was a direct reference to the story of the fall of man as detailed in the book of Genesis. This same symbol is found occasionally in early Italian works of art and it is in these, really, that we find symbolism at its apogee ; for in Italy, more essentially than in any other country, art was long the handmaiden of the Church, and thus early Italian painting and sculpture is replete with emblems referring to the Christian faith. The frequent allusions in the Old Testament to the hand of God, as the instrument of his sovereign power, naturally inspired pristine artists to symbolise the deity's omnipotence by drawing a hand, sometimes with a cross behind it, sometimes emerging from clouds ; while equally common among the primitives was the practice of expressing the name of Christ by the first two letters of his name in Greek, and this emblem evolved betimes, assuming divine and intricate forms. Another familiar Christian symbol, figuring in numerous sarcophagi and mosaics, is a small picture of a fish ; and this refers indirectly to baptism but most directly to Christ, for those who first used this sign observed that the letters forming the word fish in Greek, IXOYE, when separated supplied the initials for the five words, Jesus Christ, Son of God, Saviour. Christ is also represented sometimes by a picture of a lion, this referring to the phrase in the Scriptures, " The lion of the tribe of Judah " ; while the Passion is frequently symbolised by a drawing of a pelican, tearing open her breast to feed her young. Then the Holy Ghost is invariably suggested by a presentment of a dove, while the phœnix and the peacock were both employed as symbols of the Resurrection ; nor does the symbolism in the art of Italy end here, for an early artist of that country, doing a picture of a saint, would usually add some sign having reference to an event in the subject's career, or to some particular predilection on his part. Thus, if the saint was famous as a devotee of pilgrimage, a shell was drawn at his feet ; or, if the doing of penance was his particular virtue, a skull was figured on some part of the picture ; while finally, if his life culminated in the glory of martyrdom, this was hinted at by a sketch of an axe, a lance or a club.

Mystic symbolism waned in Italy before the eleventh century was over. Some of the anonymous early Florentines had symbolised love by a great, flaring lamp ; but with the advent of Titian and Veronese all this sort of thing was discontinued, and amorous scenes were painted in realistic fashion. The great mediæval masters of religious art, moreover—men like Ghibert and Raphael, Pintunichio and Michelangelo—scorned to deal in mere emblems, and strove to depict biblical scenes with a ruthless veracity to nature, Ghibert going so far as to try and introduce a species of perspective into bas-relief. But meanwhile the practice of the fathers of Italian art had been taken up in France and in Spain, and more especially in Germany by Altdorfer and Albrecht Dürer ; while in England, too, symbolism of various kinds began to become very manifest in ecclesiastical architecture and craftsmanship. The beautiful Norman Church with its square tower gave place to a Gothic one with a spire, symbol of aspiration ; while the wood-work was garnished at places with emblems of the passion—three nails and a hammer, pincers, ladder, sponge, reed and spear. Besides, gargoyles commenced to appear on the outsides of Churches, the idea being that, when the building was consecrated, the devils took flight from the interior, and perched themselves on the roof, and this species of symbolism did not pass away with the middle ages, but was carried on for long afterwards, as also was the " rose window," symbol of the crown of thorns.

The churches' suzerainty over art was virtually dead by the end of the fifteenth century, and thenceforth, during fully a hundred years, painting found its chief patrons in various enlightened kings and noblemen. But symbolism was not altogether ousted accordingly, for the new patrons were hardly collectors in the usual sense of the term, they did not buy landscapes to decorate their dwellings—very few *bona fide* landscapes were done before the time of Claude, born in 1600—and it was mainly portraits of themselves and their families which they sought. So now, in consequence of this, a new form of symbolism became very manifest in painting, the artist being almost invariably charged to introduce his patron's coat-of-arms into some part of the canvas or panel; and, though this practice began to wane with the advent of the seventeenth century —when collecting in the real sense began painters still continued to trade in emblems of one kind and another. Even Antoine Watteau (born in 1684), doing a portrait of the divine Venetian pastellist, Rosalba Canicra, showed her with white roses in her lap ! and anon this rather obvious symbolism was deepened by the engraver Liotard, for beneath his print after Watteau he inscribed the beautiful if sentimental phrase, " La plus belle des fleurs ne dure qu'un matin." A practice akin to this lingered till the

close of the eighteenth century in engraving, the engraver of a portrait almost always thinking it necessary to surround his sitter with allegorical accessories ; and to choose a good example, in many prints of La Fontaine we find a scene from one of his fables introduced beneath the subject's visage. A few modern engravers have essayed something analogous, Mr. William Strange, for example, engraving a tiny portrait of a soldier in the corner of his familiar plate of Mr. Rudyard Kipling ; while reverting to painting many of the great English masters of portraiture saw fit to figure, almost in juxtaposition to the sitter, various items symbolising his tastes or action. Raeburn was among the last to do this, several of his pictures of great lawyers being only embellished with bundles of briefs tied up with red tape ; and, though this form of symbolism is practically dead now, the fact remains that most good portrait-painters still choose their *repoussoir* with a view to its aiding them in adumbrating more completely the sentiment of the subject in hand. Thus, doing a picture of a child, an artist will usually employ a high-pitched background, this being in some degree emblematic of youth ; while delineating an old man, he will almost certainly place him in sombre surroundings. And so we see again, as we saw at the outset, that all art is in a sense symbolical ; and that it is through symbols that it " Lives, works, and has its being." (*See* also **Magical Diagrams.**)

W. G. B. M.

Sympathetic Magic : (*See* **Magic.**)

T

Table-turning : A form of psychic phenomena in which a table is made to rotate, tilt, or rise completely off the ground by the mere contact of the operator's finger-tips, and without the conscious exercise of muscular force. The *modus operandi* is exceedingly simple. The sitters take their places round a table, on which they lightly rest their finger-tips, thus forming a " chain." In a few moments the table begins to rotate, and may even move about the room, seemingly carrying the experimenters with it. It was, and is, in high favour among spiritualists as a means of communicating with the spiritual world. The alphabet was slowly repeated, or a pencil was run down the printed alphabet, the table tilting at the letter which the spirits desired to indicate. Thus were dictated sermons, poems, information regarding the spirit-world, and answers to questions put by the sitters. *Table-turning*, in common with most spiritualistic phenomena, originated in America. It rapidly spread to Europe, and early in 1853 reached Britain, where it soon became immensely popular, and for the time replaced the earlier method of communication by means of raps. It commended itself to the public mainly because the services of an expensive professional medium were not required. In all parts of the country and in every grade of society the popular craze was practised with enthusiasm, and in this case as in others the results increased proportionately with the credibility of the sitters. In these earlier stages of the proceedings the gyrations of the table were attributed entirely to spirit agencies. So serious did matters become at last that men of science could no longer ignore the " manifestations," and were forced to turn the light of scientific knowledge on the phenomenon of *table-turning* and endeavour to explain it on rational grounds. Foremost among these distinguished investigators was the chemist Faraday, who showed by means of simple apparatus of his own devising that the movements of the table were due to unconscious muscular action on the part of the sitters, who were thus themselves the automatic authors of the messages purporting to come from the spirit world. Faraday's apparatus consisted of

two thin wooden boards with little glass rollers between, the whole bound together with rubber bands, and so contrived that the slightest lateral pressure on the upper board would cause it to slip a little way over the other. A haystalk or a scrap of paper served to indicate any motion of the upper board over the lower. The conclusion drawn from these experiments was that when the sitters believed themselves to be pressing *downwards*, they were really pressing obliquely, in the direction they expected the table to rotate. Other investigators also held that the expectation of the operators had a good deal to do with the motions of the table. Braid pointed out in the appendix to his *Hypnotic Therapeutics* that some one generally announced beforehand the direction in which the table would rotate, and so encouraged the expectation of the operators. Another authority, Dr. W. B. Carpenter, shared the same view, as did a committee of four medical men who published their experiences of *table-turning* in the *Medical Times and Gazette* Among the earliest investigators of the phenomena of *table-turning* were count de Gasparin and Professor Thury of Geneva, who held *séances*, and were satisfied that the movements resulted from a force radiating from the operators, to which they gave the name of " ectenic force." There were others, however, who were less rational in their attempts to explain the phenomenon. The public were on the whole indisposed to accept the conclusions of Faraday and the rest. They preferred the more popular spiritualistic explanations or the pseudo-scientific theories of such men as Dr. Koch, who believed that the " chain " of operators formed a sort of electric battery which supplied the table with vital energy or, as it was called, " electro-odyllic " force, and made it respond to the will as though it were a part of the human body. Other explanations offered were odic force, galvanism, animal magnetism, and, strangest notion of all, the rotation of the earth ! In an anonymous pamphlet published during the *table-turning* epidemic and entitled *Table-talking considered in connection with the dictates of reason and common sense*, the conclusions of Faraday are ridiculed, and an electrical theory advanced, in such a way, however, as to show that the writer is quite ignorant of his subject. Another pamphlet, also anonymous, entitled *Table-turning by Animal Magnetism demonstrated* ascribes the phenomenon to magnetism, and bases its suppositions on the results of some experiments in which the table was isolated by glass or gutta-percha. Dr. Elliotson and the other believers in a mesmeric " fluid " which would affect inanimate objects as well as living beings, saw in *table-turning* a support for their views. The Rev. G. Sandby and the Rev. C. H. Townshend, claimed to have experienced a feeling of fatigue after a *table-turning* séance as though they had been hypnotising someone. They also felt a tingling sensation in their finger-tips, and Townshend suggested that spirit rappings may be caused by a " disengagement of Zoogen from the System." Dr. Elliotson himself followed with an admission that the phenomenon was not explicable within the bounds of muscular force. There was another set, mainly composed of Evangelical clergymen, who credited the whole business to Satanic agency. The Rev. N. S. Godfrey, the Rev. E. Gillson, and others held *séances* in which the " spirits " confessed themeslves to be either the spirits of worthless persons of evil inclination, or devils, both of which confessions caused the reverend gentlemen to denounce the whole practice of *table-turning*. One of them remarks, apropos of Faraday's experiments, that the phenomena " appear to be whatever the investigator supposes them to be," a saying which aptly characterises their own attitude.

Camille Flammarion, whose exhaustive experiments and scientific attainments give to his opinion considerable weight, has offered an explanation of the various phases of *table-turning* phenomena. Simple rotation of the table he ascribes to an unconscious impulse given by the operators and other movements of the table while the fingers of the sitters rest upon it are ascribed to similar causes. The tilting of the table on the side furthest away from the operator can also be explained by muscular action. But vibrations in the wood of the table, or its levitation under the fingers, or, to a still greater extent, its rotation without contact of the operator's hands, he attributes to a force emanating from the body, and, in the latter case, capable of acting at a distance by means of ether-waves. This force, the result of a cerebral disturbance, is greater than that of the muscles, as is seen by the levitation of tables so weighted that the combined muscular strength of the operators would not suffice to lift it. To the dictating of messages and other intelligent manifestations he would also give an origin in this psychic force, which is perhaps identical with Thury's " ectenic " force, or " psychode," and which is obedient to the will and desires, or even, in some cases, the sub-conscious will of the operator. The hypothesis of spirits he does not consider necessary. It is possible, however, that fraud may have crept into the *séances* of M. Flammarion, as it has done in so many other cases. And there are those among the most profound students of psychic research who find in unconscious muscular action and deliberate fraud a satisfactory explanation of the phenomena.

Taboo, Tabu or Tapu : A Polynesian word meaning " prohibited " and signifying a prohibition enforced by religious or magical power, which has come to be applied to similar usages among savage peoples all over the world. *Taboo*, or prohibition is enforced in the cases of sacred things and unclean things. In the first instance, the *taboo* is placed on the object because of the possession by it of inherent mysterious power. But, *taboo* may be imposed by a chief or priest. It aims at the protection of important individuals ; the safeguarding of the weak, women, children and slaves from the magical influence of more highly-placed

individuals ; against danger incurred by handling or coming in contact with corpses ; or eating certain foods ; and the securing of human beings against the power of supernatural agencies, or the depredations of thieves. *Taboo* may also be sanctioned by social use or instinct. The violation of a *taboo* makes the offender himself *taboo*, for it is characteristic of the *taboo* that it is transmissible, but can be thrown off by magical or purificatory ceremonies. It may last for a short period, or be imposed in perpetuity. It may be said, generally speaking, that the practice of *taboo* was instituted through human instinct for human convenience. This applies of course merely to the most simple type of *taboo*. It is, for example, forbidden to reap or steal the patch of corn dedicated to an agricultural deity, for the simple reason that his wrath would be incurred by so doing. Similarly it is *taboo* to devour the flesh of the totem animal of the tribe, except in special circumstances with the object of achieving communion with him. It is *taboo* to interfere in any manner with the affairs of the shamans or medicine-men : this again is a type of the imposed *taboo* for the convenience of a certain caste. It is prohibited to marry a woman of the same totem as oneself, as all the members of a totemic band are supposed to be consanguineous, and such a union might incur the wrath of the patron deity. A very strict *taboo* is put upon the beholding of certain ritual instruments belonging to some barbarian tribes, but this only applies to women and uninitiated men : the reason for such *taboo* would be that it was considered degradation for women to behold sacred implements. *Taboo*, if it does not spring directly from the system known as totemism, was strongly influenced by it—that is, many intricate *taboos* arose from the totemic system. We have also the *taboo* of the sorcerer, which in effect is merely a spell placed upon a certain object, which makes it become useless to others. *Taboo*, or its remains, is still to be found in strong force even in the most civilised communities, and from its use the feeling of reverence for ancient institutions and those who represent them is undoubtedly derived.

Tadebtsois : Spirits believed in by the Samoyeds. (*See* **Siberia.**)

Tadibe : The name for a Samoyed magician. (*See* **Siberia.**)

Taigheirm : A magical sacrifice of cats to the infernal spirits, formerly practised in the Highlands and Islands of Scotland. It is believed to have been originally a ceremony of sacrifice to the subterranean gods, imported from more northern lands, which became in Christian times an invocation of infernal spirits. The word " Taigheirm " signifies either an armoury, or the cry of a cat, according to the sense in which it is used. A description of the ceremony, which must be performed with black cats, is given in Horst's Deuteroscopy : " After the cats were dedicated to all the devils, and put into a magico-sympathetic condition by the shameful things done to them, and the agony occasioned them, one of them was at once put upon the spit, and, amid terrific howlings, roasted before a slow fire. The moment that the howls of one tortured cat ceased in death, another was put upon the spit, for a minute of interval must not take place if they would control hell ; and this continued for the four entire days and nights. If the exorcist could hold it out still longer, and even till his physical powers were absolutely exhausted, he must do so." When the horrible rites had been continued for a time the demons began to appear in the shape of black cats, who mingled their dismal cries with those of the unfortunate sacrifices. At length a cat appeared of larger size and more frightful aspect than the others, and the time had come for the exorcist to make known his demands. Usually he asked for the gift of second sight, but other rewards might be asked for and received. The last *Taigheirm* was said to have been held in Mull about the middle of the seventeenth century. The exorcists were Allan Maclean and his assistant Lachlain Maclean, both of whom received the second sight. Of this particular ceremony Horst says : " The infernal spirits appeared some in the early progress of the sacrifices, in the shape of black cats. The first who appeared during the sacrifice, after they had cast a furious glance at the sacrifices, said— Lachlain Oer, that is, ' Injurer of Cats.' Allan, the chief operator, warned Lachlain, whatever he might see or hear, not to waver, but to keep the spit incessantly turning. At length the cat of monstrous size appeared ; and after it had set up a horrible howl, said to Lachlain Oer, that if he did not cease before their largest brother came he would never see the face of God. Lachlain answered that he would not cease till he had finished his work if all the devils in hell came. At the end of the fourth day, there sat on the end of the beam in the roof of the barn a black cat with fire-flaming eyes, and there was heard a terrific howl quite across the straits of Mull into Mowen." By this time the elder of the two men was quite exhausted, and sank down in a swoon, but the younger was sufficiently self-possessed to ask for wealth and prosperity, which both received throughout their life-time. Shortly before this, Cameron of Lochiel received at a *Taigheirm* a small silver shoe which, put on the foot of a new-born son of his family, would give courage and fortitude to the child. One boy, however, had at his birth, a foot too large for the shoe, a defect inherited from his mother, who was not a Cameron. His lack of the magically bestowed courage was apparent at Sheriffmuir, where he fled before the enemy.

Tales of Terror, by Matthew Lewis. (*See* **Fiction, Occult English**.)

Talisman : An inanimate object which is supposed to possess a supernatural capacity of conferring benefits or powers in contradistinction to the amulet (q.v.), the purpose of which is to ward off evil. It was usually a disc of metal or stone engraved with astrological or magical figures. *Talismans* were common in ancient Egypt and Babylon. The virtues of astrological *talismans* were as follows : The astrological figure of Mercury, engraven upon silver, which is the corresponding metal, and according to the prescribed rites, gave success in Merchandise ; that of Mars gave victory to the soldier ; that of Venus, beauty, and so of the rest. All such *talismans* likewise are more powerful in the hour of their planet's ascendency. There are three general varieties of these potent charms : 1. The astronomical, having the characters of the heavenly signs or constellations. 2. The magical, with extraordinary figures, superstitious words, or the names of angels. 3. The mixed, engraven with celestial signs and barbarous words. To these, Fosbrook, in his *Encyclopædia of Antiquities*, adds two others :—4. The *sigilla planetarum*, composed of Hebrew numeral letters, used by astrologers and fortune-tellers ; and 5. Hebrew names and characters. As an example of the most powerful of the latter, may be mentioned the sacred name of Jehovah. The famous tephillin or phylacteries, used in Jewish devotion, and which were bound on the head, the arm, and the hand, may be regarded as *talismans*, and they were the subject of many traditional ceremonies. We may also mention the mezuzoth or schedules for door-posts, and another article of this description mentioned in the following quotation from the *Talmud* :—" Whoever has the telphillin bound to his head and arm, and the tsitsith thrown over his garments, and the mezuza fixed on his door-post, is protected from sin."

Writing of *talismans* in his *Occult Sciences*, Mr. A. E. Waite says :

" I. The *Talisman* of the Sun must be composed of a pure and fine gold, fashioned into a circular plate, and well polished on either side. A serpentine circle, enclosed by a pentagram must be engraved on the obverse side with a diamond-pointed graving tool. The reverse must bear a human head in the centre of the six-pointed star of Solomon, which shall itself be surrounded with the name of the solar intelligence Pi-Rhé, written in the characters of the Magi. This *talisman* is supposed to insure to its bearer the goodwill of influential persons. It is a preservative against death by heart disease, syncope, aneurism, and epidemic complaints. It must be composed on a Sunday during the passage of the moon through Leo, and when that luminary is in a favourable aspect with Saturn and the Sun. The consecration consists in the exposure of the *talisman* to the smoke of a perfume composed of cinnamon, incense, saffron, and red sandal, burnt with laurel-wood, and twigs of dessicated heliotrope, in a new chafing-dish, which must be ground into powder and buried in an isolated spot, after the operation is finished. The *talisman* must be afterwards encased in a satchel of bright yellow silk, which must be fastened on the breast by an interlaced ribbon of the same material, tied in the form of a cross. In all cases the ceremony should be preceded by the conjuration of the Four, to which the reader has already been referred. The form of consecration, accompanied by sprinkling with holy water, may be rendered in the following manner :—

" In the name of Elohim, and by the spirit of the living waters, be thou unto me as a sign of light and a seal of will.

" Presenting it to the smoke of the perfumes :—By the brazen serpent before which fell the serpents of fire, be thou unto me as a sign of light and a seal of will.

" Breathing seven times upon the *talisman* :—By the firmament and the spirit of the voice, be thou unto me as a sign of light and a seal of will.

" Lastly, when placing some grains of purified earth or salt upon the pentacle :—In the name of the salt of the earth and by virtue of the life eternal, be thou unto me as a sign of light and a seal of will.

" II. The *Talisman* of the Moon should be composed of a circular and well-polished plate of the purest silver, being of the dimensions of an ordinary medal. The image of a crescent, enclosed in a pentagram, should be graven on the obverse side. On the reverse side, a chalice must be encircled by the duadic seal of Solomon, encompassed by the letters of the lunar genius Pi-Job. This *talisman* is considered a protection to travellers, and to sojourners in strange lands. It preserves from death by drowning, by epilepsy, by dropsy, by apoplexy, and madness. The dangers of a violent end which is predicted by Saturnian aspects in horoscopes of nativity, may be removed by its means. It should be composed on a Monday, when the moon is passing through the first ten degrees of Capricornus or Virgo, and is also well aspected with Saturn. Its consecration consists in exposure to a perfume composed of white sandal, camphor, aloes, amber, and pulverised seed of cucumber, burnt with dessicated stalks of mugwort, moonwort, and ranunculus, in a new earthen chafing-dish, which must be reduced, after the operation, into powder, and buried in a deserted spot. The *talisman* must be sewn up in a satchel of white silk, and fixed on the breast by a ribbon of the same colour, interlaced and tied in the form of a cross.

" III. The *Talisman* of Mars must be composed of a well-polished circular plate of the finest iron, and of the dimensions of an ordinary medal. The symbol of a sword in the centre of a pentagram must be engraved on the obverse side. A lion's head surrounded by a six-pointed star must appear on the reverse face, with the letters of the name Erotosi, the planetary genius of Mars, above the outer angles. This *talisman* passes as a preservative against all combinations of enemies. It averts the chance of death in brawls and battles, in epidemics and fevers, and by corroding ulcers. It also neutralizes the peril of a violent end as a punishment for crime when it is foretold in the horoscope of the nativity.

" This *talisman* must be composed on a Tuesday, during the passage of the moon through the ten first degrees of Aries or Sagittarius, and when, moreover, it is favourably aspected with Saturn and Mars. The consecration consists in its exposure to the smoke of a perfume composed of dried absinth and rue, burnt in an earthen vessel which has never been previously used, and which must be broken into powder, and buried in a secluded place, when the operation is completed. Finally, the *talisman* must be sewn up in a satchel of red silk, and fastened on the breast with ribbons of the same material folded and knotted in the form of a cross.

" IV. The *Talisman* of Mercury must be formed of a circular plate of fixed quicksilver, or according to another account of an amalgam of silver, mercury, and pewter, of the dimensions of an ordinary medal, well-polished on both sides. A winged caduceus, having two serpents twining about it, must be engraved in the centre of a pentagram on the obverse side. The other must bear a dog's head within the star of Solomon, the latter being surrounded with the name of the planetary genius, Pi-Hermes, written in the alphabet of the Magi. This *talisman* must be composed on a Wednesday, when the moon is passing through the ten first degrees of Gemini or Scorpio, and is well aspected with Saturn and Mercury. The consecration consists in its exposure to the smoke of a perfume composed of benzoin, macis, and storax, burnt with the dried stalks of the lily, the narcissus, fumitory, and marjolane, placed in a clay chafing-dish which has never been devoted to any other purpose, and which must, after the completion of the task, be reduced to powder and buried in an undisturbed place. The *Talisman* of Mercury is judged to be a defence in all species of commerce and business industry. Buried under the ground in a house of commerce, it will draw customers and prosperity. It preserves all who wear it from epilepsy and madness. It averts death by murder and poison ; it is a safeguard against the schemes of treason and it procures prophetic dreams when it is worn on the head during sleep. It is fastened on the breast by a ribbon of purple silk folded and tied in the form of a cross, and the *talisman* is itself enclosed in a satchel of the same material.

" V. The *Talisman* of Jupiter must be formed of a circular plate of the purest English pewter, having the dimensions of an ordinary medal, and being highly polished on either side. The image of a four-pointed crown in the centre of a pentagram must be engraved on the obverse side. On the other must be the head of an eagle in the centre of the six-pointed star of Solomon, which must be surrounded by the name of the planetary genius Pi-Zeous, written in the arcane alphabet.

" This *talisman* must be composed on a Thursday, during the passage of the moon through the first ten degrees of Libra, and when it is also in a favourable aspect with Saturn and Jupiter. The consecration consists in its exposure to the smoke of a perfume composed of incense, ambergris, balm, grain of Paradise, saffron, and macis, which is the second coat of the nutmeg. These must be burnt with wood of the oak, poplar, fig tree, and pomegranate, and placed in a new earthen dish, which must be ground into powder, and buried in a quiet spot, at the end of the ceremony. The *talisman* must be wrapped in a satchel of sky-blue silk, suspended on the breast by a ribbon of the same material, folded and fastened in the form of a cross.

" The *Talisman* of Jupiter is held to attract to the wearer the benevolence and sympathy of everyone. It averts anxieties, favours honourable enterprises, and augments well-being in proportion to social condition. It is a protection against unforeseen accidents, and the perils of a violent death when it is threatened by Saturn in the horoscope of nativity. It also preserves from death by affections of the liver, by inflammation of the lungs, and by that cruel affection of the spinal marrow, which is termed *tabes dorsalis* in medicine.

" VI. The *Talisman* of Venus must be formed of a circular plate of purified and well-polished copper. It must be of the ordinary dimensions of a medal, perfectly polished on both its sides. It must bear on the obverse face the letter G inscribed in the alphabet of the Magi, and enclosed in a pentagram. A dove must be engraved on the reverse, in the centre of the six-pointed star, which must be surrounded by the letters which compose the name of the planetary Genius Suroth. This *talisman* must be composed on a Friday, during the passage of the moon through the first ten degrees of Taurus or Virgo, and when that luminary is well aspected with Saturn and Venus. Its consecration consists in its exposure to the smoke of a perfume composed of violets and roses, burnt with olive wood in a new earthen chafing-dish, which must be ground into powder at the end of the operation and buried in a solitary spot. The *talisman* must, finally, be sewn up in a satchel of green or rose-coloured silk, which must be fastened on the breast by a band of the same material, folded and tied in the form of a cross.

The *Talisman* of Venus is accredited with extraordinary power in cementing the bonds of love and harmony between husbands and wives. It averts from those who wear it the spite and machinations of hatred. It preserves women from the terrible and fatal diseases which are known as cancer. It averts from both men and women all danger of death, to which they may be accidentally or purposely exposed. It counterbalances the unfortunate presages which may appear in the horoscope of nativity. Its last and most singular quality is its power to change the animosity of an enemy into a love and devotion which will be proof against every temptation, and it rests on the sole condition that such a person should be persuaded to partake of a liquid in which the *talisman* has been dipped.

" VII. The *Talisman* of Saturn must be composed of a circular plate of refined and purified lead, being of the dimensions of an ordinary medal, elaborately polished. On the obverse side must be engraven with the diamond-pointed tool which is requisite in all these talismanic operations, the image of a sickle enclosed in a pentagram. The reverse side must bear a bull's head, enclosed in the star of Solomon, and surrounded by the mysterious letters which compose, in the alphabet of the Magi, the name of the planetary Genius Tempha. The person who is intended to wear this *talisman* must engrave it himself, without witnesses, and without taking any one into his confidence.

" This *talisman* must be composed on a Saturday when the moon is passing through the first ten degrees of Taurus or Capricorn, and is favourably aspected with Saturn. It must be consecrated by exposure to the smoke of a perfume composed of alum, assa-fœtida, cammonée, and sulphur, which must be burnt with cypress, the wood of the ash tree, and sprays of black hellebore, in a new earthen chafing-dish, which must be reduced into powder at the end of the performance, and buried in a deserted place. The *talisman* must, finally, be sewn up in a satchel of black silk and fastened on the breast with a ribbon of the same material, folded and tied in the form of a cross. The *Talisman* of Saturn was affirmed to be a safeguard against death by apoplexy and cancer, decay in the bones, consumption, dropsy, paralysis, and decline ; it was also a preservative against the possibility of being entombed in a trance, against the danger of violent death by secret crime, poison, or ambush. If the head of the army in war-time were to bury the *Talisman* of Saturn in a place which it was feared might fall into the hands of the enemy, the limit assigned by the presence of the *talisman* could not be overstepped by the opposing host, which would speedily withdraw in discouragement, or in the face of a determined assault.'' (See **Ceremonial Magic.**)

Talmud, The : From the Hebrew *lamad*, to learn ; the name of the great code of Jewish civil and canonical law. It is divided into two portions—the *Mishna* and the *Gemara* ; the former constituted the text and the latter was a commentary and supplement. But besides being the basis of a legal code, it is also a collection of Jewish poetry and legend. The *Mishna* is a development of the laws contained in the Pentateuch. It is divided into six *sedarim* or orders, each containing a number of tractates, which are again divided into *peraqim* or chapters. The *sedarim* are : (1) *Zeraim*, which deals with agriculture ; (2) *Moed*, with festivals and sacrifices ; (3) *Nashim*, with the law regarding women ; (4) *Nezaqin*, with civil law ; (5) *Qodashim*, with the sacrificial law ; and (6) *Tohoroth* or *Tah*, with purifications. The *Mishna* was supposed to have been handed down by Ezra and to be in part the work of Joshua, David or Solomon, and originally communicated orally by the Deity in the time of Moses. There are two recensions,—the *Talmud* of Jerusalem, and the *Talmud* of Babylon ; which latter besides the *sedarim* mentioned contains seven additional treatises which are regarded as extra-canonical. The first is supposed to have been finally edited towards the close of the fourth century A.D., and the second by Rabbi Ashi, President of the Academy of Syro in Babylon, somewhere in the fourth century. Though revised from time to time before then, both versions have been greatly corrupted through the interpolation of gross traditions. The rabbinical decisions in the *Mishna* are entitled *helacoth* and the traditional narratives *haggadah*. The cosmogony of the *Talmud* assumes that the universe has been developed by means of a series of cataclysms : world after world was destroyed until the Creator made the present globe and saw that it was good. In the wonderful treatise on the subject by Deutsch which first appeared in the *Quarterly Review* in 1867, and is reprinted in his *Literary Remains*, the following passage appears :—

" The *how* of the creation was not mere matter of speculation. The co-operation of angels, whose existence was warranted by Scripture, and a whole hierarchy of whom had been built up under Persian influences, was distinctly denied. In a discussion about the day of their creation, it is agreed on all hands that there were no angels at first, lest men might say, ' Michael spanned out the firmament on the south, and Gabriel to the north.' There is a distinct foreshadowing of the Gnostic Demiurgos— that antique link between the Divine Spirit and the world of matter—to be found in the *Talmud*. What with Plato were the Ideas, with Philo the Logos, with the Kabalists the ' World of Aziluth,' what the Gnostics called more emphatically the wisdom (sophi), or power (dunamis), and Plotinus the nous, that the Talmudical authors call Metation. There is a good deal, in the post-captivity *Talmud*, about the Angels, borrowed from the Persian. The Archangels or Angelic princes are seven in number, and their Hebrew names and functions correspond almost exactly to those of their Persian prototypes. There are also hosts of ministering angels, the Persian *Yazatas*, whose functions, besides that of being messengers, were two-fold—

to praise God and to be guardians of man. In their first capacity they are daily created by God's breath out of a stream of fire that rolls its waves under the supernal throne. In their second, two of them accompany every man, and for every new good deed man acquires a new guardian angel, who always watches over his steps. When a righteous man died, three hosts of angels descend from the celestial battlements to meet him. One says (in the words of Scripture), ' He shall go in peace ' ; the second takes up the strain and says, ' Who has walked in righteousness ' ; and the third concludes, ' Let him come in peace and rest upon his bed.' In like manner, when the wicked man passes away, three hosts of wicked angels are ready to escort him, but their address is not couched in any spirit of consolation or encouragement.''

It would be impossible in this place to give a resumé of the traditional matter contained in the *Talmud*. Suffice it to say that it is of great extent. It has been considered by some authorities that a great many of the traditional tales have a magical basis, and that magical secrets are contained in them ; but this depends entirely upon the interpretation put upon them, and the subject is one which necessitates the closest possible study.

Tam o' Shanter : (See **Scotland.**)

Tannhauser : A mediæval German legend which relates how a minstrel and knight of that name, passing by the Hörselberg, or Hill of Venus, entered therein in answer to a call, and remained there with the enchantress, living an unholy life. After a time he grew weary of sin, and longing to return to clean living, he forswore the worship of Venus and left her. He then made a pilgrimage to Rome, to ask pardon of the Pope, but when he was told by Urban IV., himself that the papal staff would as soon blossom as such a sinner as *Tannhauser* be forgiven, he returned to Venus. Three days later, the Pope's staff did actually blossom, and he sent messengers into every country to find the despairing minstrel, but to no purpose, *Tannhäuser* had disappeared. The story has a mythological basis which has been laid over by mediæval Christian thought, and the original hero of which has been displaced by a more modern personage, just as the Venus of the existing legend is the mythological Venus only in name. She is really the Lady Holda, a German earth-goddess. *Tannhäuser* was a " minnesinger " or love-minstrel of the middle of the thirteenth century. He was very popular among the minnesingers of that time and the restless and intemperate life he led probably marked him out as the hero of such a legend as has been recounted. He was the author of many ballads of considerable excellence, which are published in the second part of the " Minnesinger " (Von der Hagen, Leipsic, 1838) and in the sixth volume of Haupt's *Zeitschrift fur deutsches Althertum*. The most authentic version of this legend is given in Uhland's *Alte hoch und niederdeutsche Volkslieder* (Stuttgart, 1845).

Tappan-Richmond, Mrs. Cora L. V. : Perhaps the best known of all the inspirational speakers who have appeared since the beginning of the spiritualistic movement. As a child Mrs. *Tappan-Richmond*—then Miss Scott—spent some time in the Hopedale Community (q.v.), so that she was early initiated into the mysteries of spiritualism. At the age of sixteen she went to New York, and became an " inspired " lecturer on spiritualism, in which capacity she soon became famous throughout America. Coming to Britain in 1873 she was warmly received by the spiritualists in this country, and for a number of years gave frequent trance discourses, characterised by their rhythm and fluency, and the comparative clarity of their ideas.

Tarot, or **Tarots,** is the French name for a species of playing-cards, originally used for the purpose of divination, and still employed by fortune-tellers. *Tarot* cards, however, form part of an ordinary pack in certain countries of southern Europe, whence the name of *tarocchi* given to an Italian game. The derivation of the word is uncertain. One suggestion is that these cards were so called because they were *tarotées* on the back; that is, marked with plain or dotted lines crossing diagonally. Confirmation of this theory may be found in the German form of the word; a *tarock-karte* being a card chequered on the back. Not improbably, however, there is here a confusion between cause and effect.

De l' Hoste Ranking, who dismisses as " obviously worthless " the explanations of Count de Gébelin, Vaillant and Mathers, refers the name to the Hungarian Gipsy *tar*, a pack of cards, and thence to the Hindustani *taru*. The figures on these cards are emblematic, and are believed by many to embody the esoteric religion of ancient Egypt and India; but on this subject there is much difference of opinion.

" The *tarot* pack most in use," observes Ranking, " consists of seventy-eight cards, of which twenty-two are more properly known as the *tarots*, and are considered as the ' keys ' of the *tarot*; these correspond with the twenty-two letters of the Hebrew alphabet, or, according to Falconnier and to Margiotta, with the ' alphabet of the Magi.' The suits are four: *wands, sceptres,* or *clubs,* answering to diamonds; *cups, chalices,* or *goblets,* answering to hearts; *swords,* answering to spades; *money, circles,* or *pentacles,* answering to clubs. Each suit consists of fourteen cards, the ace, and nine others, and four court cards: king, queen, knight, and knave. The four aces form the keys of their respective suits." As already indicated, the twenty-two " keys of the *tarot*," which consist of various emblematic figures, are assumed to be hieroglyphic symbols of the occult meanings of the letters of the Hebrew alphabet; or, alternatively, " the alphabet of the Magi." " Immense antiquity is claimed for these symbols," observes Ranking. " Alliette or (by transposition) Etteilla, a French mystic of the beginning of the nineteenth century, ascribed their origin to Hermes Trismegistus, under the name of *The Book of Thoth,* or *The Golden Book of Hermes.* Others have sought to identify the *tarot* with the sibylline leaves." Raymond Lully (1235-1315) is said to have based his great work, *Ars Generalis sive Magna,* on the application of the occult philosophy contained in the *tarot.*

The idea that the *tarot* was introduced into Europe by the Gypsies appears to have been first broached by Vaillant, who had lived for many years among the Gypsies, by whom he was instructed in their traditional lore. Much of the information thus obtained is incorporated in *Les Rômes, histoire vraie des vrais Bohémiens* (c. 1853), *La Bible des Bohémiens* (1860), and *La Clef Magique de la Fiction et du Fait* (1863). Vaillant's theory has been fully accepted by a French writer, " Papus," who published in 1889 *Le Tarot des Bohémiens: Le Plus Ancien Livre du Monde* ;describing it as " *la clef absolue de la science occulte.*" " The Gypsies possess a Bible," he asserts; " yes, this card game called the *Tarot* which the Gypsies possess is the Bible of Bibles. It is a marvellous book, as Count de Gébelin and especially Vaillant have realized. Under the names of *Tarot, Thora, Rota,* this game has formed successively the basis of the synthetic teaching of all the ancient peoples."

Although it may not be possible to accept this dictum in its entirety, it is of interest to note that Ranking concludes that these and all other playing-cards were introduced into Europe by the Gypsies. " I would submit,' he says, writing in 1908, " that from internal evidence we may deduce that the *tarots* were introduced by a race speaking an Indian dialect; that the form of the Pope (as portrayed in the *tarots*) shows they had been long in a

country where the orthodox Eastern Church predominated ; and the form of head-dress of the king, together with the shape of the eagle on the shield, shows that this was governed by Russian Grand Dukes, who had not yet assumed the Imperial insignia. This seems to me confirmatory of the widespread belief that it is to the Gypsies we are indebted for our knowledge of playing-cards." It will be seen that this conclusion is based upon independent judgment. As early, however, as 1865—two years after the appearance of Vaillant's last book—E. S. Taylor supported the same hypothesis in his *History of Playing Cards.* Willshire (*Descriptive Catalogues of Cards in the British Museum,* 1877) controverts Taylor's conclusion, on the ground that " whether the Zingari be of Egyptian or Indian origin, they did not appear in Europe before 1417, when cards had been known for some time." But this objection is nullified by the fact that the presence of Gypsies, in Europe is now placed at a date considerably anterior to 1417. There was, for example, a well-established *feudum Acinganorum,* or Gypsy barony, in the island of Corfu in the fourteenth century.

To examine in detail the various emblematic figures of the *tarot* would demand a disproportionate amount of space. Ranking's reference to the Pope and the King points to two of these twenty-two figures. The others are: the Female Pope, the Queen, Osiris Triumphant, The Wheel of Fortune, Justice, Prudence, Temperance, Strength, Marriage, The Philosopher, The Juggler, Death, The Devil, The Fool, The Lightning-struck Tower, The Sun, The Moon, The Star, The Universe, The Last Judgment. There is great diversity of opinion, even among " initiates," as to the meaning of these symbols. They are very fully discussed in the work of " Papus ". already cited ; to which the reader is specially referred. On the whole, there is much to be said in favour of the theory that the origin of the *tarot* is traceable to the esoteric philosophy of the schools of ancient Egypt and Chaldea, by whatever means it has found its way into Europe.

In addition to the works already cited, *see Le Monde Primitif,* by Count de Gébelin, Vol. VIII., Paris, 1781 ; *Les Origines des Cartes à Jouer,* by Merlin, Paris, 1869 ; *The Tarot,* by Mathers, London, 1888 ; *L'Art de Tirer les Cartes,* by Magus, Paris, 1895 ; *Le walladisme,* by Margistta, Grenoble, 1895 ; *Magie,* by Bourgeat, Paris, 1895 ; *Les XXII. Lames Hermétiques du Tarot,* by Falconnier, Paris, 1896 ; A. E. Waite, *Key to the Tarot,* 1910 ; and J. W. Brodie-Innes, *The Tarot Cards,* in the " Occult Review" for February, 1919.   DAVID MACRITCHIE.

Tatwic Yoga : meaning " The Science of Breath." The title of a little book translated from the Sanscrit some years ago by the Pandit Rama Prasad. The " breath " referred to is the life-giving breath of Brahman, and in it are contained the five elementary principles of nature, corresponding to the five senses of man. These principles are know as Tatwas, and of them the body is composed. The knowledge of the Tatwas is believed to confer wonderful power ; and to this end all undertakings must be commenced at times which are known to be propitious from the movements of the Tatwas in the body. An important method of *yoga* practice is given in the book, which will certainly assure marvellous results.

Taurabolmin : (*See* **Mithraic Mysteries.**)

Taxil, Leo : The pseudonum of M. Gabriel Jogaud-Pages, who in his works *The Brethren of the Three Points* and *Are there Women in Freemasonry ?* has accused the Masonic Fraternity of the practice of Satanism and sorcery. His assertions are of the most debatable description.

Tears on Shutters : It is mentioned in Pennant's *Tour* that in some parts of Scotland it was the custom, on the death of any person of distinction, to paint on the doors and window-shutters white tadpole-like shapes, on a black ground. These were intended to represent *tears*, and were a sign of general mourning.

Telekinesis : A term denoting the hypothetical faculty of moving material objects by thought alone. The movement of objects without contact—a frequent phenomenon of the séance-room, including in its wider sense rappings, table-tiltings, levitations, the conveyance of *apports*, practically all material phenomena, with the possible exception of materialisation—is exceeding difficult of explanation on rational grounds, and the attempt to explain it thus, without the intervention of discarnate spirits, has given rise to the telekinetic theory, which holds that all these varied feats are accomplished by the thoughts of medium and sitters, independent of muscular energy, whether direct or indirect. How thought can possibly act in this immediate way on inanimate matter is beyond comprehension in our present state of knowledge. The evidence for *telekinesis* is very much less than, say, that for telepathy. The telekinetic theory is akin to that offered by the magnetists, who regarded a fluidic or energetic emanation as the cause of the movements.

Telepathy : Of the various branches of psychic phenomena there is none which engages more serious attention at the present day than *telepathy* or thought transference. The idea of inter-communication between brain and brain, by other means than that of the ordinary sense-channels, is a theory deserving of the most careful consideration, not only in its simple aspect as a claimant for recognition as an important scientific fact, but also because there is practically no department of psychic phenomena on which it has not some bearing. To take one instance—a few decades ago the so-called " rationalist " view of ghosts was simply that supernatural phenomena did not exist, but now a telepathic explanation is offered, more or less tentatively, by an ever-increasing body of intelligent opinion. There are those who, while admitting the genuineness of psychic phenomena are yet satisfied that pure psychology provides a field sufficiently wide for their researches, and who are loath to extend its boundaries to include an unknown spirit-world where research becomes a hundred-fold more difficult. To such students the theory of *telepathy* affords an obvious way of escape from that element of the supernatural to which they are opposed, since it is generally agreed that in seeking an explanation of thought transference it is a physical process which must be looked for. In the words of Sir William Crookes : " It is known that the action of thought is accompanied by certain molecular movements in the brain, and here we have physical vibrations capable from their extreme minuteness of acting direct on individual molecules, while their rapidity approaches that of the internal and external movements of the atoms themselves."

There is therefore nothing to render the theory of thought-vibrations impossible, or even improbable, though the difficulty of proving it has yet to be overcome. We have, however, to contend with the fact that in many cases on record the most vivid impressions have been transmitted from a distance, thus showing that the distinctness of the impression does not necessarily decrease in proportion as the distance becomes greater. In this case we must either conclude that there are other factors to be taken into account, such as the varying intensity of the impression, and the varying degress of sensitiveness in the percipient, or we must conclude, as some authorities have done, that telepathic communication goes direct from one mind to another, irrespective of distance, just as thought can travel to the oppostie side of the globe with as much ease as it can pass to the next room. Other authorities claim that the transmission of thought is on a different plane from any

physical process, though, as the action of thought itself has a physical basis, it is difficult to understand why a supernatural explanation should be thought necessary in the case of *telepathy*. In the former connection it may be remarked that trivial circumstances can be transmitted to a percipient near at hand, while as a rule only the more intense and violent impressions are received from a distance. The question whether the telepathic principle is diffusive, and spreads equally in all directions, or whether it can be projected directly toward one individual, is still a vexed one. If it be in the form of ethereal vibrations, it would certainly seem easier to regard it as diffusive. On the other hand, practical experience has shown that in many instances, even when acting from a distance, it affects only one or two individuals. However, this might be explained naturally enough by the assumption that each transmitter requires a special receiver—*i.e.*, a mind in sympathy with itself. But as yet no explanation is forthcoming, and the most that can be done is to suspend judgment for the present, knowing that only the possibility, or, at most, the likelihood, of such a mode of communication has been proved, and that of its machinery nothing can be said beyond the vaguest surmise.

The theory of thought transference is no new one. Like gravitation, it is a daughter of the hoary science of astrology, but while gravitation is a full-grown fact, universally accepted of science, *telepathy*, in its scientific aspect, is as yet an infant, and a weakling at that. However, it is not difficult to understand how both should spring from astrology, nor to trace the connection between them. The wise men of ancient days supposed the stars to radiate an invisible influence which held them together in their course, and which affected men and events on our planet, receiving in their turns some subtle emanation from the earth and its inhabitants. From this idea it was but a step to assume that a radiant influence, whether magnetic or otherwise, passed from one human being to another. The doctrine of astral influence was shared by Paracelsus and his alchemistic successors until the epoch of Sir Isaac Newton, whose discovery of the law of gravitation brought the age of astrology to a close. To the conception of magnetic influence colour was lent by the practices of Mesmer, and his followers, who ascribed to the " magnetic fluid " the phenomena of hypnosis. The analogy between the mysterious and inexplicable force binding worlds together and the subtle influence joining mind with mind is sufficiently obvious, but the difficulty is that while gravitation may be readily demonstrated, and never fails to give certain definite results, experiments in *telepathy* reveal the phenomena only in the most spasmodic fashion and cannot be depended upon to succeed even under the most favourable conditions. Nevertheless such systematized experiments as have been conducted from time to time have more than justified the interest which has been displayed in *telepathy*. Science, which had so long held herself aloof from hypnosis, was not desirous of repeating her error in a new connection. In 1882 the Society for Psychical Research (q.v.) came into being, numbering among its members some of the most distinguished men in the country. It had for its object the elucidation of the so-called " supernatural " phenomena which were exciting so much popular interest and curiosity ; and foremost among these was the phenomenon of thought transference, or, as it has since been christened, *telepathy*. Viewing their subject in a purely scientific light, trained in the handling of evidence, and resolved to pursue truth with open and unbiassed minds, they did much to bring the study of psychic phenomena into a purer and more dignified atmosphere. They recognized the untrustworthiness of human nature in general, and the prevalence of fraud even where no object was to be gained but the gratification of a perverted vanity, and their experiments were conducted under the most rigid conditions, with every precaution taken against conscious or unconscious deception. Among the most valuable evidence obtained from experimental thought transference was that gleaned by Professor and Mrs. Sidgwick (q.v.) from their experiments at Brighton in 1889–91. In this series the percipients—clerks and shop assistants—were hypnotized. Sometimes they were asked to visualize, on a blank card, an image or picture chosen by the agent. At other times the agent would choose one of a bundle of cards numbered from 10 to 90, and the percipient was required to state the number on the picked card, which was done correctly in a surprising number of cases. We find, curiously enough, that the results varied in proportion as the agent and percipient were near or far apart, and were materially affected by the intervention of a door, or even a curtain, between the two, but this was ascribed to a lack of confidence on the part of the percipient, or to such physical causes as fatigue or ennui, rather than to the limited scope of the telepathic principle. On the whole we are justified in thinking that chance alone would not account for the number of correct replies given by the hypnotised subject.

Towards the end of the century a criticism was levelled at these experiments by Messrs. Hansen and Lehmann, of Copenhagen, whose belief it was that the phenomenon known as " subconscious whispering," together with hyperæsthesia on the part of the percipient, would suffice to produce the results obtained by the Sidgwicks. This suggested explanation, while it does not cover the entire ground has some right to our consideration. If hypnotism reveals so marvellous a refinement of the perceptions, may not some elements of hyperæsthesia linger in the sub-consciousness of the normal individual ? If dreams contain in the experience of almost everyone, such curious examples of deduction, may not the mental under-current follow in waking moments a process of reasoning of which the higher consciousness knows nothing ? It may, and it does. That " other self," which is never quite so much in the background as we imagine, sees and hears a thousand things of which we are unconscious, and which come to the surface in dreams, it may be long afterwards ; and there is no reason to suppose that it might not see and hear indications too slight to be perceived in a grosser sphere of consciousness, and thus account for some cases of " thought transference." On the other hand, we have evidences of *telepathy* acting at a distance where sub-conscious whisper-ing and hyperæsthesia are obviously out of the question. Though hyperæsthesia may be advanced as a plausible explanation in some—or, indeed, in many—instances of *telepathy*, it cannot be accepted as a complete explanation unless it covers *all* cases, and that it certainly does not. So we must look elsewhere for the explanation, though it is not without reluctance that we quit a theory so admir-ably adapted to known conditions that it scarcely requires a stretching of established physiological laws to make *telepathy* fit as naturally as wireless telegraphy into the scheme of things.

As has been earlier mentioned, practically every branch of psychic phenomena would be vitally affected by the scientific proof of *telepathy*. Coincident dreams might, in the majority of cases, be easily explained away. The visions of the crystal-gazer, the trance-utterances of the medium, could be accounted for in the same manner, to-gether with the occasional apparitions visiting the normal individual. Apparitions of the dead, however, do not so readily submit themselves to a telepathic explanation. If they are genuine apparitions, and not meaningless hallu-cinations, we must either admit that the impulse directing the impression comes from the surviving spirit of the deceased agent, or that it was transmitted while he was yet alive. In the latter case we are confronted with a difficulty—how to account for the time which may elapse between the death of the agent and the appearance of the vision. To bridge the gap thus formed Mr. Podmore (q.v.), in his work on *Telepathic Hallucinations*, has produced his theory of *latent impressions*, which successfully overcomes the difficulty. According to Mr. Podmore, impressions transmitted from one mind to another may remain latent for a considerable time awaiting a favourable opportunity for development. Thus the apparition of one who been dead for some time may result from an impression transmitted during his lifetime, which the percipient has retained, until a chance combination of ideas brings it into the upper stratum of consciousness in the form of a hallu-cination. Obviously the theory of latent impressions may bear on other phenomena than that of apparitions, and serve to fill in gaps which might otherwise remain blank.

It is interesting to compare the tone of criticisms pro-nounced on *telepathy* in the last quarter of the nineteenth century with that which characterises later utterances on the subject. Science is no longer ashamed to pursue her researches in psychic phenomena ; thought transference no longer appears to intellectual people as a doubtful by-path of psychology, and the change argues that at least a fair attempt will be made to reach the truth of the matter.

Literature. — Frank Podmore, *Telepathic Hallucina-tions ; The Naturalisation of the Supernatural ; Apparitions and Thought Transference* ; F. W. H. Myers, *Human Per-sonality* ; A. Lang, *Making of Religion* ; E. Parish, *Hallucinations and Illusions* ; E. Gurney, *Phantasms of the Living* ; Miss Goodrich Freer, *Essays in Psychical Research* ; *Proceedings* and *Journal* of the *Society for Psychical Research.* M. J.

Tellurism : A name applied by Kieser to Animal Magnetism (q.v.)

Temeraire, Charles A. : Duke of Burgundy. He disappeared after the battle of Morat ; and it was said by his chroniclers that he was carried off by the devil, like Roderick. Some maintained, however, that he had withdrawn to a remote spot and become a hermit.

Templars : The Knights *Templars* of the Temple of Solomon were a military order, founded by a Burgundian, Hugues de Payns, and Godeffroi de St. Omer, a French Knight, in 1119, for the purpose of protecting pilgrims journeying into the Holy Land. They were soon joined by other knights, and a religious chivalry speedily gathered around this nucleus. Baldwin I., King of Jerusalem, gave them as headquarters a portion of his palace, contiguous to a mosque which tradition asserted was part of the Temple of Solomon, and from this building they took their designa-tion. One of the purposes of the Society was to convert and render useful knights of evil life, and so many of these entered the order, as to bring it under the suspicion of the Church, but there is every reason to believe that its founders were instigated by motives of the deepest piety, and that they lived in a condition akin to poverty, notwithstanding the numerous gifts that were showered upon them, is the best proof of this. They had properly constituted officials, a Grand Master, knights, chaplains, sergeants, craftsmen, seneschals, marechals, and commanders. The order had its own clergy exempt from the jurisdiction of diocesan rule, and its chapters were held as a rule in secret. The dress of the brotherhood was a white mantle with a red cross for unmarried knights, and a black or brown mantle with a red cross for the others. The discipline was of the very strictest description and the food and clothing stipu-lated were rough and not abundant. By the middle of the twelfth century, the new order had got a footing in nearly all the Latin kingdoms of Christendom. Its power grew apace, and its organisation became widespread. It formed, as it were, a nucleus of the Christian effort against the paganism of the east, and its history may be said to be that of the crusades. Moreover it became a great trading corporation, the greatest commercial agency between the east and west, and as such amassed immense wealth. On the fall of the Latin kingdom in Palestine, the *Templars* had perforce to withdraw from that country, and although they continued to harass the Saracen power they made but little headway against it, and in reality appear to have undertaken commercial pursuits in preference to those of a more warlike character. When the Temple was at the apogee of its power, its success aroused the envy and avarice of Philip IV. of France, who commenced a series of attacks upon it. The election of Pope Clement V., who was devoted to his interests, and a denunciation of the order for heresy and immorality gave Philip his chance. For several generations before this time, strange stories had been circulating concerning the secret rites of the *Templars* which were assisted by the very strict privacy of these meetings, which were usually held at day-break with closely-guarded doors. It was alleged that the most horrible blasphemies and indecencies took place at these meetings, that the cross was trampled under foot and spat upon, and that an idol named Baphomet (q.v.) (*Baphe metios*, baptism of wisdom) was adored, or even the Devil in the shape of a black cat. Other tales told of the roasting of children, and the smearing of the idol with their burning fat, and other nonsense was wildly promulgated by the credulous and ignorant. A certain Esquian de Horian, pretended to betray the " secret " of the *Templars* to Philip, and they were denounced to the Inquisition ; and Jacques de Molay, the Grand Master, who had been called from Cyprus to France, was arrested with one hundred and forty of his brethren in Paris and thrown into prison. A universal arrest of the *Templars* throughout France followed. The wretched knights were tortured *en masse*, and as was usually the case, under such compulsion, confessed to the most grotesque crimes, and the most damning confession of all, was that of the Grand Master himself, who confessed that he had been guilty of denying Christ and spitting upon the Cross, but repudiated all charges of immorality in indignant terms.

The process dragged on slowly during more than three years, in consequence of the jealousies which arose among those who were more or less interested in its prosecution. The pope wished to bring it entirely under the jurisdiction of the church, and to have it decided at Rome. The king, on the other hand, mistrusting the pope, and resolved on the destruction of the order, and that none but himself should reap advantage of it, decided that it should be judged at Paris under his own personal influence. The prosecution was directed by his ministers, Nogaret, and Enguerrand de Marigny. The *Templars* asserted their innocence, and demanded a fair trial ; but they found few advocates who would undertake their defence, and they were subjected to hardships and tortures which forced many of them into confessions dictated to them by their persecutors. During this interval, the pope's orders were carried into other countries, ordering the arrest of the *Templars*, and the seizure of their goods, and everywhere the same charges were brought against them, and the same means adopted to procure their condemnation, although they were not everywhere subjected to the same severity as in France. At length, in the spring of 1316, the grand process was opened in Paris, and an immense number of *Templars*, brought from all parts of the kingdom, underwent a public examination. A long act of accusation was read, some of the heads of which were, that the *Templars*,

at their reception into the order, denied Christ (and sometimes they denied expressly all the saints) declaring that he was not God truly, but a false prophet, a man who had been punished for his crimes ; that they had no hope of salvation through him ; that they always, at their initiation into the order, spit upon the cross, and trod it under foot ; that they did this especially on Good Friday ; that they worshipped a certain cat, which sometimes appeared to them in their congregation ; that they did not believe in any of the sacraments of the church ; that they took secret oaths which they were bound not to reveal ; that the brother who officiated at the reception of a new brother kissed the naked body of the latter, often in a very unbecoming manner ; that each different province of the order had its idol, which was a head, having sometimes three faces, and at others only one ; or sometimes a human skull ; these idols they worshipped in their chapters and congregations, believing that they had the power of making them rich, and of causing the trees to flourish, and the earth to become fruitful ; that they girt themselves with cords, with which these idols had been superstitiously touched ; that those who betrayed the secrets of their order, or were disobedient, were thrown into prison, and often put to death ; that they held their chapters secretly and by night, and placed a watch to prevent them from any danger of interruption or discovery ; and that they believed the Grand Master alone had the power of absolving them from their sins. The publication of these charges, and the agitation which had been designedly got up, created such a horror throughout France, that the *Templars* who died during the process were treated as condemned heretics, and burial in consecrated ground was refused to their remains.

When we read over the numerous examinations of the *Templars*, in other countries, as well as in France, we cannot but feel convinced that some of these charges had a degree of foundation, though perhaps the circumstances on which they were founded were misunderstood. A very great number of knights agreed to the general points of the formula of initiation, and we cannot but believe that they did deny Christ, and that they spat and trod upon the cross. The words of the denial were, *Je reney Deu* or *Je reney Jhesu*, repeated thrice ; but most of those who confessed having gone through this ceremony, declared that they did it with repugnance, and that they spat beside the cross, and not on it. The reception took place in a secret room, with closed doors ; the candidate was compelled to take off part or all of his garments (very rarely the latter), and then he was kissed on various parts of the body. One of the knights examined, Guischard de Marzici, said he remembered the reception of Hugh de Marhaud, of the diocese of Lyons, whom he saw taken into a small room, which was closed up so that no one could see or hear what took place within ; but that when, after some time, he was let out, he was very pale, and looked as though he were troubled and amazed (*fuit valde pallidus et quasi turbatus et stupefactus.*) In conjunction, however, with these strange and revolting ceremonies, there were others that showed a reverence for the Christian church and its ordinances, a profound faith in Christ, and the consciousness that the partaker of them was entering into a holy vow.

M. Michelet, who has carefully investigated the materials relating to the trial of the *Templars*, has suggested at least an ingenious explanation of these anomalies. He imagines that the form of reception was borrowed from the figurative mysteries and rites of the early church. The candidate for admission into the order, according to this notion, was first presented as a sinner and renegade, in which character, after the example of St. Peter, he denied Christ. This denial was a sort of pantomime, in which the novice expressed his reprobate state by spitting on the cross. The candidate was then stripped of his profane clothing, received through the kiss of the order into a higher state of faith, and re-dressed with the garb of its holiness. Forms like these would, in the middle ages, be easily misunderstood, and their original meaning soon forgotten.

Another charge in the accusation of the *Templars* seems to have been to a great degree proved by the depositions of witnesses ; the idol or head which they were said to have worshipped, but the real character or meaning of which we are totally unable to explain. Many *Templars* confessed to having seen this idol, but as they described it differently, we must suppose that it was not in all cases represented under the same form. Some said it was a frightful head, with long beard and sparkling eyes ; others said it was a man's skull ; some described it as having three faces ; some said it was of wood, and others of metal ; one witness described it as a painting (*tabula picta*) representing the image of a man, (*imago hominis*), and said that when it was shown to him, he was ordered to " adore Christ his creator." According to some it was a gilt figure, either of wood or metal ; while others described it as painted black and white. According to another deposition, the idol had four feet—two before and two behind ; the one belonging to the order at Paris was said to be a silver head, with two faces and a beard. The novices of the order were told always to regard this idol as their saviour. Deodatus Jaffet, a knight from the south of France, who had been received at Pedenat, deposed that the person who in his case performed the ceremonies of reception, showed him a head or idol, which appeared to have three faces, and said, " You must adore this as your saviour, and the saviour of the order of the Temple," and that he was made to worship the idol, saying, " Blessed be he who shall save my soul." Cettus Ragonis, a knight received at Rome in a chamber of the palace of the Lateran, gave a somewhat similar account. Many other witnesses spoke of having seen these heads, which, however, were, perhaps, not shown to everybody, for the greatest number of those who spoke on this subject, said that they had heard speak of the head, but that they had never seen it themselves ; and many of them declared their disbelief in its existence. A friar minor deposed in England that an English *Templar* had assured him that in that country the order had four principal idols, one at London in the sacristy of the Temple, another at Bristelham, a third at Brueria (Bruern in Lincolnshire), and a fourth beyond the Humber.

Some of the knights from the south added another circumstance in their confessions relating to this head. A *Templar* of Florence declared that, in the secret meetings of the chapters, one brother said to the others, showing them the idol, " Adore this head. This head is your God, and your Mahomet." Another, Gauserand de Montpesant, said that the idol was made in the figure of Baffomet (*in figuram Baffometi*) ; and another Raymond Rubei, described it as a wooden head, on which was painted the figure of Baphomet, and he adds, " that he worshipped it by kissing its feet, and exclaiming, *Yalla*," which he describes as " a word of the Saracens" (*verbum Saracenorum*). This has been seized upon by some as a proof that the *Templars* had secretly embraced Mahometanism. As Baffomet or Baphomet is evidently a corruption of Mahomet ; but it must not be forgotten that the Christians of the West constantly used the word Mahomet in the mere signification of an idol, and that it was the desire of those who conducted the prosecution against the *Templars* to show their intimate intercourse with the Saracens. Others, especially Von Hammer, gave a Greek derivation of the word, and assumed it as a proof that Gnosticism was the secret doctrine of the Temple.

The confessions with regard to the mysterious cat were much rarer and more vague. Some Italian knights confessed that they had been present at a secret chapter of twelve knights held at Brindisi, at which a grey cat suddenly appeared amongst them, and that they worshipped it. At Nismes, some *Templars* declared that they had been present at a chapter at Montpellier, at which the demon appeared to them in the form of a cat, and promised them worldly prosperity ; and added, that they saw devils in the shape of women. Gilletus de Encreyo, a *Templar* of the diocese of Rheims, who disbelieved in the story of the cat, deposed that he had heard say, though he knew not by whom, that in some of their battles beyond sea, a cat had appeared to them. An English knight, who was examined at London, deposed, that in England they did not adore the cat or the idol to his knowledge, but he had heard it positively stated that they worshipped the cat and the idol in parts beyond sea. English witnesses deposed to other acts of " idolatry." It was of course the demon, who presented himself in the form of the cat. A lady, named Agnes Lovecote, examined in England, stated that she had heard that, at a chapter held in Dineslee (Dynnesley, in Hertfordshire), the devil appeared to the *Templars* in a monstrous form, having precious stones instead of eyes, which shone so bright that they illuminated the whole chapter ; the brethren, in succession, kissed him on the posteriors, and marked there the form of the cross. She was told that one young man, who refused to go through this ceremony, was thrown into a well, and a great stone cast upon him. Another witness, Robert de Folde, said that he had heard twenty years ago, that in the same place, the devil came to the chapter once a year, and flew away with one of the knights, whom he took as a sort of tribute. Two others deposed that certain *Templars* confessed to them that at a grand annual assembly in the county of York, the *Templars* worshipped a calf. All this is mere hearsay, but it shows the popular opinion of the conduct of the order. A *Templar* examined in Paris, named Jacques de Treces, who said that he had been informed that at secret chapters held at midnight, a head appeared to the assembled brethren, added, that one of them " had a private demon, by whose council he was wise and rich."

The aim of King Philippe was secured ; he seized upon the whole treasure of the temple in France, and became rich. Those who ventured to speak in defence of the order were browbeaten, and received little attention ; the torture was employed to force confessions ; fifty-four *Templars* who refused to confess were carried to the windmill of St. Antoine, in the suburbs of Paris, and there burnt ; and many others, among whom was the Grand Master himself, were subsequently brought to the stake. After having lasted two or three years, the process ended in the condemnation and suppression of the order, and its estates were given in some countries to the knights of St. John. It was in France that the persecution was most cruel ; in England, the order was suppressed, but no executions took place. Even in Italy, the severity of the judges was not everywhere the same ; in Lombardy and Tuscany, the *Templars* were condemned, while they were acquitted at Ravenna and Bologna. They were also pronounced innocent in Castile, while in Arragon they were reduced by force, only because they had attempted to resist by force of arms ; and both in Spain and in Portugal they only gave up their own order to be admitted into others. The pope was offended at the lenity shown towards them in England, Spain, and Germany. The order of the temple was finally dissolved and abolished, and its memory branded with disgrace. Some of the knights are said to have remained together, and formed secret societies. The result, in effect, was the same everywhere. Convicted of heresy, sorcery, and many other abominations, the wretched *Templars* were everywhere punished with death by fire, imprisonment, and their goods escheated to the various crowned heads of Europe, nearly all of whom followed the avaricious example of Philip of France. Jacques de Molay, the Grand Master, brought out on to a scaffold erected in front of Notre Dame in Paris, and asked to repeat his confession and receive sentence of perpetual imprisonment, flared into sudden anger, recanted all he had said, and protested his innocence. He was burnt, and summoned the Pope and the King with his dying breath, to meet him before the bar of Heaven. Both of these dignatories shortly afterwards died, and it remained in the public mind that the outcome of the Grand Master's summons had proved his innocence.

As has been said, there is every reason to believe that there was some foundation for the charges of heresy made against the *Templars*. Their intimate connection with the East, and the long establishment of the order therein had in all probability rendered their Christianity not quite so pure as that of Western Europe. Numerous treatises have been written for the purpose of proving and disproving the Temple heresy, to show that it followed the doctrines and rites of the Gnostic Ophites of Islam (Baphomet being merely a corruption of Mahomet), and it has been collated with various other eastern systems. Hans Prutz, in his *Geheimlehre* furthered the view of the rejection of Christianity in favour of a religion based on Gnostic dualism, and at once raised up a host of critics. But many defenders of the order followed, and it was proved in numerous instances the confessions wrung from the *Templars* were the result of extreme torture. In not a few cases were they acquitted, as in Castile, Aragon, Portugal, and at many German and Italian centres. It has also been shown that the answers of a number of the knights under torture were practically dictated to them. In England, out of eighty *Templars* examined, only four confessed to the charge of heresy, and of these two were apostates. The whole question may perhaps be summed up as follows. The *Templars*, through long association with the East, may have become more tolerant of paganism, more broadminded, in their outlook, than their bigoted stay-at-home countrymen. Expressions as regards the worthiness of Saracen nations, among whom the *Templars* had many friends, would be regarded askance in France, Spain and England, and habits acquired by residence in the East would probably add to the growing body of suspicion regarding the loyalty of the order to Christianity. It it even possible that the *Templars* introduced into their rites practices which savoured of Gnosticism or Mahomedanism, but that is unlikely. They were, in short, the victims of their own arrogance, their commercial success, and the superstitious ignorance of their contemporaries.

It has frequently been asserted that on the death of Jacques de Molay a conspiracy was entered into by the surviving *Templars* which had for its objects the destruction of papacy and the several kingdoms of Europe, and that this tradition was handed on through generations of initiates through such societies as the Illuminati and the Freemasons, who in the end brought about the French Revolution and the downfall of the French throne. Such a theory, however enticing to the pseudo-occultist, the defender of the theory that occult tradition has descended to us through a direct line of adepts, or the fictioneer, can receive no countenance here, and must be dismissed as a mere figment of enthusiasm or imagination.

Temple Church, London : Hargrave Jennings in his *Rosicrucians, their Rites and Mysteries*, says : The *Temple Church, London*, presents many mythic figures, which have a Rosicrucian expression. In the spandrels of the arches of the long church, besides the " Beauséant " which is repeated in many places, there are the armorial figures following ; " Argent, on a cross gules, the Agnus Dei, or Paschal Lamb, or, " Gules the Agnus Dei, displaying over the right shoulder the standard of the *Temple* ; or, a banner, triple cloven, bearing a cross gules ; " Azure, a cross prolonged potent issuant out of the crescent moon argent, horns, upwards, on either side of the cross, a star or." This latter figure signifies the Virgin Mary, and displays the cross as rising like the pole, or mast of a ship (argha) out of the midst of the crescent moon or navis biprora, curved at both ends ; " azure, semée de estoiles or." The staff of the Grand Master of the Templars displayed a curved cross of four splays, or blades, red upon white. The eight-pointed red Buddhist cross was also one of the Templar ensigns. The *Temple* arches abound with brandished estoiles, or stars, with wavy or crooked flames. The altar at the east end of the *Temple Church* has a cross flourie, with lower limb prolonged, or, on a field of estoiles, wavy ; to the right is the Decalogue, surmounted by the initials, A.O. (Alpha and Omega), on the left are the monograms of the Saviour, I. C., X. C. ; beneath, is the Lord's Prayer. The whole altar displays feminine colours and emblems, the *Temple Church* being dedicated to the Virgin Maria. The winged horse, or Pegasus, argent, in a field gules, is the badge of the Templars. The tombs of the Templars, disposed around the circular church in London, are of that early Norman shape called dos d'ane ; their tops are triangular ; the ridge-moulding passes through the temples and out of the mouth of a mask at the upper end, and issues out of the horned skull, apparently of some purposely trodden creature. The head at the top is shown in the " honour-point " of the cover of the tomb. There is an amount of unsuspected meaning in every curve of these Templar tombs.

Tempon-teloris—Ship of the Dead : Among the Dayaks of Borneo the *Ship of the Dead*, the vessel which carries the souls of the departed in search of the hereafter, is generally represented as being of the shape of a bird, the rhinoceroshornbill. Accompanying the souls on their journey through the fire-sea are all the stores which have been laid out at the trivah or feast of the dead, and all the slaves who have been killed for that purpose. After some vicissitudes in the fiery sea, the *Ship of the Dead*, with Tempon-telon at the helm, reaches the golden shores of the Blessed.

Temurah : (*See* **Gematria**.)

Tephillin : In the Hebrew tongue means " attachments." They were originally prayer thongs worn by the Jews at morning prayer—one on the left arm and another on the head. They came to be regarded as talismans and were used in many traditional ceremonies. The *Talmud* says : " Whoever has the *tephillin* bound to his head and arm . . . . is protected from sin."

Tephramancy : A mode of divination in which use is made of the ashes of the fire which had consumed the victims of a sacrifice.

Teraphim, The : Of the nature of oracles. The *teraphim* were taken away from Jacob by his daughter, Rachel, and this mention of them in the Bible is the earliest record we have of " magical " apparatus. Their form is not known, nor the exact use to which they were put ; but from an allusion to them in Hosea III., 4, they were evidently not idols. Spencer maintains that they were the same as the " Urim " of Mosaic ritual ; at any rate it seems likely that they were used as a means of divination.

Tetractas : (*See* **Alchemy**.)

Tetrad : (*See* **God**.)

Tetragram : (*See* **Alchemy**, **Magic**, and **Magical Diagram**.)

Teutons : The Teutonic or "Germanic" nations, embracing the peoples of High and Low German speech, Dutch, Danes, and Scandinavians, have always displayed and still display a marked leaning towards the study and consideration of the occult. We are, however, concerned here with their attitude towards the hidden sciences in more ancient times, and must refer the reader to the article on "Germany" and the other countries alluded to for information upon mediæval and modern occultism in them.

But little can be gleaned from the writings of classical authors upon the subject, and it is not until we approach the middle ages, the contemporary manuscripts concerning the traditions of an earlier day, and the works of usch writers as Snorre Sturluson and Sæmund (The *Eddas*) Saxo-Grammaticus, and such epics or pseudo-histories as *The Nibelungenlied* that we find any light thrown upon the dark places of Teutonic magical practice and belief. From the consideration of such authorities we arrive at several basic conclusions : (1) That magic with the *Teutons* was non-hierophantic, and was not in any respect the province of the priesthood, as with the Celtic Druids ; (2) That women were its chief conesrvators ; (3) That it principally resided in the study and elucidation of the runic script, in the same manner as in early Egypt it was part and parcel of the ability to decipher the hieroglyphic characters. Passing from the first conclusion, which is self-evident, as we discover all sorts and conditions of people dabbling in magical practice, we find that to a great extent sorcery—for efforts seem to have been confined mostly to black magic—was principally the province of women. This is to be explained, perhaps, by the circumstance that only those who could read the runes—that is, those who could read at all—were able to undertake the study of the occult, and that therefore the unlettered warrior, too restless for the repose of study, was barred from all advance in the subject. We find women in all ranks of life addicted to the practice of sorcery, from the queen on the throne to the wise-woman or witch dwelling apart from the community. Thus the mother-in-law of Siegfried bewitches him by a draught, and scores of similar instances could be adduced. At the same time the general type of ancient Teutonic magic is not very high, it is greatly hampered by human considerations, and is much at the mercy of the human element on which it acts, and the very human desires which call it forth. Indeed in many cases it is rendered nugatory by the mere cunning of the object upon which it is wreaked. In fine it does not rise very much above the type of sorcery in vogue among barbarian peoples at the present day. It is surprising, however, with all these weaknesses, how powerful a hold it contrived to get upon the popular imagination, which was literally drenched with the belief in supernatural science.

Runes.—(German, *rune* ; Anglo-Saxon *run* ; Icelandic *run*). The word is derived from an old Low German word *raunen* "to cut" or "to carve," and as the runes in more ancient times were invariably carved and not written, it latterly came to designate the characters themselves. As has been said, comparatively few were able to decipher them, and the elucidation was left to the curious, the ambitious among the female sex, and the leisured few in general, those perhaps including priests and lawmen. Consequently we find the power to decipher them an object of mysterious veneration among the ignorant and a belief that the ability to elucidate them meant the possession of magical powers. The possessors of this ability would in no wise minimise it, so that the belief in their prowess would flourish. Again, it is clear that a certain amount of patience and natural ability were necessary to the acquirement of such an intricate script.

The tradition that they were connected with sorcery has scarcely yet died out in some parts of Iceland. In later times the word runes came to be applied to all the alphabetical systems employed by the Teutonic peoples before the introduction of Christianity. Their origin is obscure, some authorities denying that it is Teutonic, and asserting that they are merely a transformation or adaptation of the Greek characters, and others that they have a Phœnician or even cuneiform ancestry. That they are of non-Teutonic origin is highly probable, as may be inferred from their strong resemblance to other scripts and from the circumstance that it is highly unlikely that they could have been separately evolved by the Teutonic race in the state of comparative barbarism in which it was when they first came into general use. They have been divided into three systems—English, German, and Scandinavian—but the difference between these is merely local. They were not employed in early times for literary purposes, but for inscriptions only, which are usually found on stone monuments, weapons, implements, and personal ornaments and furniture. In England runic inscriptions are found in the north only, where Scandinavian influence was strongest. The first symbols of the runic alphabet have the powers of the letters f, ú, th, ó, r, c, for which reason the order of the runic letters is called not an alphabet but a *futhorc*. The system is symbolic. Thus its first quantity or letter pictures the head and horns of an ox, and is called *feoh* after that animal, the second is called *ur*, after the word for "bull," the third *thoru*, a tree, the others following *os*, a door ; *rad*, a saddle,; *caen*, a torch, all because of some fancied resemblance to the objects, or, more properly speaking, because they were probably derived or evolved from a purely pictorial system in which the pictures of the animals or objects enumerated above stood for the letters of the alphabet. Since these were cut, some connection may be permitted between Anglo-Saxon *secgan*, to say, and Latin *secare*, to cut, especially when we find secret signatures made of old by merely cutting a chip from the bark manuscript. In spelling, for example, the old sense of "spell" was a thin chip or shaving. Tacitus mentions that in Teutonic divination a rod cut from a fruit-bearing tree was cut into slips, and the slips, having marks on them, were thrown confusedly on a white garment to be taken up with prayer to the gods and interpreted as they were taken. A special use of light cuttings for such fateful cross-readings or "Virgilian lots," may have given to "spells" their particular association with the words of the magician.

Belief in Nature Spirits.—The scope of this work is entirely without the consideration of mythology proper, that is to say that the greater deities of the many human religious systems receive no treatment save in several special circumstances. But the lesser figures of mythology, those who enter into direct contact with man and assist him, or are connected with him, in magical practice, receive special and separate notice. Thus the *duergar*, or dwarfs trolls, undines, nixies, and all the countless host of Teutonic folk-lore are alluded to under their separate headings, and we have here only to consider their general connection with Teutonic man in his magical aspect. His belief in them was distinctly of an animistic character. The dwarfs and trolls inhabited the recesses of the mountains, caves, and the underworld. The nixies and undines dwelt in the lakes, rivers, pools, and inlets of the sea. In general these were friendly to man, but objected to more than an occasional intercourse with him. Though not of the class of supernatural being who obey the behests of man in answer to magical summonses, these, especially the dwarfs, often acted as his instructors in art-magic, and many instances of this are to be met with in tales and romances of early Teutonic origin. The dwarfs were usually assisted by adventitious aids in their practice of magic, such as belts which endowed the wearer with strength, like that worn by King Laurin, shoes of swiftness, analogous to the seven-league boots of folk-tale, caps of invisibility, and so forth.

Witchcraft.—Witchcraft, with its accompaniment of diabolism was much more in favour among the northern *Teutons* than it was in Germany, and this circumstance has been attributed to their proximity to the Finns (q.v.), a race notorious for its magical propensities. In Norway, Orkney, and Shetland, we find the practice of sorcery almost exclusively in the hands of women of Finnish race, and there is little doubt that the Finns exercised upon the *Teutons* of Scandinavia the mythic influence of a conquered race, that is, they took full advantage of the terror inspired in their conquerors by an alien and unfamiliar religion and ritual, which partook largely of the magical. The principal machinery of Teutonic witchcraft was the raising of storms, the selling of pieces of knotted rope, each knot representing a wind, divination and prophecy, acquiring invisibility, and such magical practices as usually accompany a condition of semi-barbarism. In the North of Scotland the Teutonic and Celtic magical systems may be said to have met and fused, but not to have clashed, as their many points of resemblance outweighed their differences. As the sea was the element of the people, we find it the chief element of the witch of the northern *Teutons*. Thus we discover in the saga of *Frithjof*, the two sea-witches Heyde and Ham riding the storm and sent by Helgi to raise a tempest which would drown Frithjof, and taking the shape of a bear and a storm-eagle. In the saga of *Grettir the Strong* we find a witch-wife, Thurid, sending adrift a magic log which should come to Grettir's island, and which should lead to his undoing. Animal transformation plays a considerable part in Teutonic magic and witchcraft. In early Germany the witch (hexe) seems to have been also a vampire.

Second Sight.—It was, however, in prophecy and divination that the *Teutons* excelled, and this was more rife among the more northern branches of the people than the southern. Prophetic utterance was usually induced by ecstasy. But it was not the professional diviner alone who was capable of supernatural vision. Anyone under stress of excitement, and particularly if near death, might become " fey," that is prophetic, and great attention was invariably paid to utterances made whilst in this condition.

Literature.—Wilken, *Die Prosaische Edda*, Paderhorn, 1878 ; Grimm, *Teutonic Mythology* ; E. S. Bugge, *Studies in Northern Mythology*, 1884 ; *Home of the Eddic Poems*, 1899 ; H. A. Berger, *Nordische Mythologie*, 1834 ; E. H. Meyer, *Germanische Mythologie*, 1891 ; W. Goltha, *Religion und Mythen der Germanen*, 1909.

Thaumaturgy : (*See* **Magic.**)

Thau Weza : Burmese wizards, literally " wire-man who works in wire." (*See* **Burma.**)

Theobald, Morrell : (*See* **Spiritualism.**)

Theomancy : The part of the Jewish *Kabala* which studies the mysteries of the divine majesty and seeks the sacred names. He who possesses this science knows the future, commands nature, has full power over angels and demons, and can perform miracles. The Rabbis claimed that it was by this means that Moses performed so many marvels ; that Joshua was able to stop the sun ; that Elias caused fire to fall from heaven, and raised the dead ; that Daniel closed the mouths of the lions ; and that the three youths were not consumed in the furnace. However, although very expert in the divine names, the Jewish rabbis no longer perform any of the wonders done by their fathers.

Theosophical Society was founded in 1875 by Helena Petrovna Blavatsky and Henry Steele Olcott. They met in America in 1874 where Colonel Olcott was engaged in spiritualistic investigation at the house of the Eddy Brothers in Vermont. Madame Blavatsky was, of course, deeply read in every thing pertaining to the occult and similarity of tastes very naturally drew them together. Scientific materialism was then engaging general attention and making no little progress, and since theosophy is the antithesis of materialism of any kind, it was decided that some society should be formed to combat this movement. In May, 1875, a Miracle Club was formed, but it was a failure. Later in the same year, in the month of September, a fresh attempt was however, agreed on and this was made in November with Col. Olcott as president, and Madame Blavatsky as corresponding secretary, and a membership of twenty. This attempt seemed also to be doomed to failure, many members dropping off because no phenomena were manifested and indeed only Col. Olcott and Madame Blavatsky remained with two of the founders of the society and a few other members. Not discouraged by this, however, they decided to amalgamate with the Indian Society, but even this met with no more success, and it was not till by a happy inspiration the society was removed to India, that it began to attract attention and make headway. From that time its success was assured and, whatever opinions may be held of the soundness of *theosophical* teaching, no doubt can be entertained of the extent and influence of the society, which has numerous members in lands so far apart and so different in spirit as America and India, besides every other civilised country in the world. In accordance with the spirit of theosophy, no dogma is demanded of members save acceptance of the belief in the brotherhood of man, so that Christian and Mohammedan may meet on equal terms without any necessity of varying their peculiar religious beliefs. Its activities include study of everything germane to theosophy, religion, philosophy, laws of nature whether patent to all mankind as in the domain of science, or hidden as yet from all but those with special knowledge, as in the domain of the occult. (*See* **Theosophy.**)

Theosophical Society of Agrippa : Agrippa (q.v.) established in Paris and other centres a secret *theosophical society*, the rites of admission to which were of a peculiar character. The fraternity also possessed signs of recognition. Agrippa visited London in 1510, and whilst there he established a branch of the order in that city. A letter of Landulph's is extant in which he introduces to Agrippa a native of Nuremberg resident at Lyons, and whom he hopes " may be found worthy to become one of the brotherhood."

Theosophy : From the Greek *theos*, god, and *sophia*, wisdom ; a philosophical-religious system which claims absolute knowledge of the existence and nature of the deity, and is not to be confounded with the later system evolved by the founders of the Theosophical Society. This knowledge, it is claimed, may be obtained by special individual revelation, or through the operation of some higher faculty. It is the transcendent character of the godhead of theosophical systems which differentiates them from the philosophical systems of the speculative or absolute type, which usually proceed deductively from the idea of God. God is conceived in theosophical systems as the transcendent source of being, from whom man in his natural state is far removed. *Theosophy* is practically another name for speculative mysticism. Thus the Kabalistic and Neoplatonic conceptions of the divine emanations are in reality theosophical, as are the mystical systems of Boehme and Baader.

Theosophy has also come to signify the tenets and teachings of the founders of the Theosophical Society. This Society was founded in the United States in 1875 by Madame H. P. Blavatsky (q.v.), Col. H. S. Olcott (q.v.)

and others. Its objects were to establish a nucleus of the Universal Brotherhood of Humanity, to promote the study of comparative religion and philosophy and to investigate the mystic powers of life and matter. The conception of the Universal Brotherhood was based upon the oriental idea of One Life—that ultimate oneness which underlies all diversity, whether inward or outward. The study of comparative religion was materialised into a definite system of belief, the bounds of which were dogmatically fixed. It is set forth in the Theosophical system that all the great religions of the world originated from one supreme source and that they are merely expressions of a central " Wisdom Religion " vouchsafed to various races of the earth in such a manner as was best suited to time and geographical circumstances. Underlying these was a secret doctrine or esoteric teaching which it was stated, had been the possession for ages of certain *Mahatmas*, or adepts in mysticism and occultism. With these Madame Blavatsky claimed to be in direct communication, and she herself manifested occult phenomena, producing the ringing of astral bells, and so forth. On several occasions these efforts were unmasked as fraudulent, but that is no justification for believing that Madame Blavatsky was entirely a person of deceitful character. There can be very little doubt that she was one of those rare personalities who possess great natural psychic powers, which at times failing her, she was driven in self-protection to adopt fraudulent methods. The evidence for the existence of the " Great White Brotherhood " of Mahatmas, the existence of which she asserted, is unfortunately somewhat feeble. It rests, for the most part, on the statements of Madame Blavatsky, Col. Olcott, Mr. Sinnet, Mr. Leadbeater, and others, who claimed to have seen or communicated with them. With every desire to do justice to these upholders of the Theosophical argument, it is necessary to point out that it has been amply proved that in occult, or pseudo-occult experiences, the question of self-hallucination enters very largely (*See* **Witchcraft**), and the ecstatic condition may be answerable for subjective appearances which seem real enough to the visionary. Again the written communications of the Mahatmas give rise to some doubt. It is pointed out for instance that one of them employed the American system of spelling, and this was accounted for by the circumstance that his English had been sophisticated by reading American books.

The revelations of Madame Blavatsky were in reality no more than a *mélange* of Buddhistic, Brahministic and Kabalistic matter ; but the Theosophical Society has numbered within its members several persons of very high ability, whose statement and exegesis of their faith has placed it upon a much higher level and more definite foundation. If the system is intensely dogmatic, it is also constructed in a manner akin to genius, and evolved on most highly intricate lines. This system was to a great extent pieced together after the death of the original founder of the society, on which event a schism occurred in the Brotherhood through the claims to leadership of William Q. Judge, of New York, who died in 1896, and who was followed by Mrs. Katherine Tingley, the founder of the great theosophical community at Point Loma, California. Col. Olcott became the leader of the remaining part of the original Theosophical Society in America and India, being assisted in his work by Mrs. Annie Besant, but a more or less independent organisation was founded in England.

A brief outline of the tenets of *Theosophy* may be attempted. It posits absolute belief in its views instead of blind faith. It professes to be the religion which holds the germs of all others. It has also its aspect as a science— a science of life and of the soul. The facts which it was to lay before humanity are as follow :—" There are three truths which are absolute, and which cannot be lost, but yet may remain silent for lack of speech. The soul of man is immortal and its future is the future of the thing, whose growth and splendour has no limit. The principle which gives life dwells in us and without us, is undying and eternally beneficent, is not heard, or seen, or smelt, but is perceived by the man who desires perception. Each man is his own absolute law-giver, the dispenser of glory or gloom to himself, decreer of his life, his reward, his punishment."

Although *Theosophy* posits the existence of an Absolute, it does not pretend to knowledge of its attributes. In the Absolute are innumerable universes, and in each universe countless solar systems. Each solar system is the expression of a being called the *Logos*, the Word of God, or Solar Deity, who permeates it and exists above it and outside it. Below this Solar Deity are his seven ministers, called Planetary Spirits, whose relation to him is like that of the nerve centres to the brain, so that all his voluntary acts come through him to them. (*See* **Kabala**.) Under them are vast hosts or orders of spiritual beings called *devas*, or angels, who assist in many ways. This world is ruled by a great official who represents the Solar Deity, which is in absolute control of all the evolution that takes place upon this planet. When a new religion is to be founded, this being either comes himself or sends one of his pupils to institute it. In the earlier stages of the development of humanity, the great officials of the hierarchy are provided from more highly evolved parts of the system, but whenever men can be trained to the necessary level of power and wisdom these offices are held by them. They can only be filled by adepts, who in goodness, power and wisdom are immeasurably greater than ordinary men, and have attained the summit of human evolution. These advance until they themselves become of the nature of deities. There are many degrees and many lines of activity among these, but some of them always remain within touch of the earth and assist in the spiritual evolution of humanity. This body it is which is called the " Great White Brotherhood." Its members do not dwell together, but live separately apart from the world and are in constant communication with one another and with their head. Their knowledge of higher forces is so great that they have no necessity for meeting in the physical world, but each dwells in his own country, and their power remains unsuspected among those who live near them. These adepts are willing to take as apprentices those who have resolved to devote themselves utterly to the service of mankind, and anyone who will may attract their attention by showing himself worthy of their notice. Such an apprentice was Madame Blavatsky. One of these masters has said : " In order to succeed the pupil must leave his own world and come into ours."

The formation of a solar system and the cosmogonic operation of the theosophical conception has been treated in several separate articles ; as have the various planes on which the personality of a man dwells in its long journey from earth to the final goal of *Nirvana*. The theosophical conception of the constitution of man is that he is in essence a spark of the divine fire belonging to the Monadic world (q.v.). For the purposes of human evolution this monad manifests itself in lower worlds. Entering the Spiritual World it manifests itself there as the triple spirit having its three aspects, one of which always remains in the Spiritual Sphere. The second aspect manifests itself in the Intuitional World ; and the third in the Higher Mental World ; and these two are collated with intuition and intelligence. These three aspects combined make up the *ego* which is man during the human stage of evolution. The way or path towards enlightenment and emancipation is known as *karma*. The human personality is composed of a complex organisation consisting of seven principles which are united and interdependent, yet divided into certain groups, each capable of maintaining a kind of personality. Each of these principles is composed of its own form of matter and possesses its own laws of time, space and motion. The most gross of those, the physical body, is known as *rûpa*, which becomes more and more refined until we reach the universal self *âtmâ* ; but the circumstance which determines the individual's powers, tests and advantages, or in short his character, is his *karma*, which is the sum of his bodily, mental and spiritual growth and is spread over many lives past and future ; in short, as man soweth, so must he reap ; and if in one existence he is handicapped by any defect, mental or physical, it may be regarded as the outcome of past delinquencies. This doctrine is practically common to both Buddhism and Brahminism.

After this digression, which was entered into for the purpose of affording a fuller view of the theosophic conception of human personality, we return to the constitution of man. The *ego* existing in the Higher Mental World cannot enter the Physical World until it has drawn around itself a veil composed of the matter of these spheres : nor can it think in any but an abstract manner without them— its concrete ideas being due to them. Having assumed the astral and physical bodies, it is born as a human being ; and having lived out its earth-life sojourns for a time in the Astral World, until it can succeed in throwing off the shackles of the astral body. When that is achieved man finds himself living in his mental body. The stay in this sphere is usually a long one—the strength of the mental constitution depending upon the nature of the thoughts to which he has habituated himself. But he is not yet sufficiently developed to proceed to higher planes, and once more he descends into the denser physical sphere to again go through the same round. Although he come from on high into these lower worlds, it is only through that descent that a full recognition of the higher worlds is developed in him.

In the Higher Mental World, the permanent vehicle is a causal body, which consists of matter of the first, second and third sub-divisions of that world. As the *ego* unfolds his latent possibilities in the course of his evolution, this matter is greatly brought into action ; but it is only in the perfect man, or adept, that it is developed to its fullest extent. In the causal body none of the possibilities of the grosser bodies can manifest themselves.

The mental body is built up of matter of the four lower sub-divisions of the Mental World, and expresses man's concrete thoughts. Its size and shape are determined by those of the causal body.

While on earth the personality wears the physical, mental, and astral bodies all at once. It is the astral which connects him with the Astral World during sleep or trance (*See* **Astral Plane.**) It is easy to see how the doctrine of reincarnation arose from this idea. The *ego* must travel from existence to existence, physical, astral, mental, until it transcend the Mental World and enter the higher spheres.

We have in this sketch attempted as far as possible to eschew the oriental verbiage of the older theosophical teachers, which it is understood is now replaced by more modern terms, but this we have retained in some of the lesser articles dealing with *Theosophy*.

The theosophic path to the goal of *Nirvana* is practically derived from Buddhistic teaching, but there are also other elements in it,—Kabalistic and Greek. The path is the great work whereby the inner nature of the individual is consciously transformed and developed. A radical alteration must be made in the aims and motives of the ordinary mortal. The path is long and difficult, and as has been said extends over many existences. Morality alone is insufficient to the full awakening of the spiritual faculty, without which progress in the path is impossible. Something incomparably higher is necessary. The physical and spiritual exercises recommended by *Theosophy* are those formulated in the Hindu philosophical system known as *Raja Yoga*. The most strenuous efforts alone can impel the individual along the path, and thus to mount by the practice of *Vidyâ*, that higher wisdom which awakens the latent faculties and concentrates effort in the direction of union with the Absolute. The way is described as long and difficult, but as the disciple advances he becomes more convinced of his ultimate success, by the possession of transcendental faculties which greatly assist him to overcome difficulties. But these must not be sought for their own sake, as to gain knowledge of them for evil purposes is tantamount to the practice of Black Magic.

It is not pretended that in this brief sketch the whole of the theosophical doctrine has been set forth, and the reader who desires further information regarding it is recommended to the many and excellent handbooks on the subject which now abound.

Theot : (*See* **France.**)

Theurgia Goetia : (*See* **Key of Solomon the King.**)

Thian-ti-hwii—or Heaven and Earth League ; an ancient esoteric society in China, said to have still been in existence in 1674. The candidate before reception had to answer 333 questions. It professed to continue a system of brotherhood derived from ancient customs.

Thomas the Rhymer : Scottish Soothsayer (circa, 1220.) It is impossible to name the exact date which witnessed the advent of the Scottish soothsayer, *Thomas the Rhymer*, who is well known on account of his figuring in a fine old ballad, duly included in Sir Walter Scott's *Minstrelsy of the Scottish Border*. But *Thomas* is commonly supposed to have lived at the beginning of the thirteenth century, that period being assigned because the name, " Thomas Rimor de Ercildun," is appended as witness to a deed, whereby one " Petrus de Haga de Bemersyde " agrees to pay half a stone of wax annually to the Abbot of Melrose, and this " Petrus " has been identified with a person of that name known to have been living about 1220. Ercildun is simply the old way of spelling Earlston, a village in the extreme west of Berwickshire, hard by the line demarking that county from Roxburgh ; and it would seem that *Thomas* held estates in this region, for he is mentioned as a landed-proprietor by several early writers, most of whom add that he did not hold his lands from the Crown, but from the Earls of Dunbar. Be that as it may, *Thomas* probably spent the greater part of his life in and around Earlston, and a ruined tower there, singularly rich in ivy, is still pointed out as having been his home, and bears his name ; while in a wall of the village church there is a lichened stone with the inscription :—

" Auld Rhymour's Race
Lies in this Place."

and, according to local tradition, this stone was removed to its present resting place from one in a much older church, long since demolished. Nor are these things the only relics of the soothsayer, a lovely valley some miles to the west of Earlston being still known as " Rhymer's Glen " ; and it is interesting to recall that Turner painted a watercolour of this place, and no less interesting to remember that Sir Walter Scott, when buying the lands which eventually constituted his estate of Abbotsford, sought eagerly and at last successfully to acquire the glen in question. Naturally he loved it on account of its associations with the shadowy past, and Lockhart tells that many of the novelist's happiest times were spent in this romantic place ; while he relates how Maria Edgworth visited it in

1823, and that thenceforth Sir Walter used always to speak of a certain boulder in the glen as the " Edgworth stone," the lady writer whom he admired so keenly having rested here for a space. It seems probable, however, that the glen was so named by Scott himself.

It is thought that *Thomas* died about 1297, and it is clear that he had achieved a wide fame as a prophet, many references to his skill in this relation being found in writers who lived comparatively soon after him. A Harleian manuscript in the British Museum, known to have been written before 1320, discloses the significant phrase, " La Comtesse de Donbar demanda a *Thomas* de Essedoune quant la guere descoce prendreit fyn ; " but the lady in question was not a contemporary of the prophet. In Barbour's *Bruce*, composed early in the fourteenth century, we find the poet saying,

" Sikerly
I hop *Thomas* prophecy
Off Hersildoune sall weryfied be.''

Andro of Winton, in the *Originale Cronykil of Scotland*, also makes mention of *Thomas* as a redoubtable prophet ; while Walter Bower, the continuator of Fordun's *Scoticronicon*, recounts how once Rhymer was asked by the Earl of Dunbar what another day would bring forth, whereupon he foretold the death of the king, Alexander III., and the very next morning news of his majesty's decease was noised abroad. Blind Harry's *Wallace*, written midway through the fifteenth century, likewise contains an allusion to Thomas's prophesying capacities ; while coming to later times, Sir Thomas Gray, Constable of Norham, in his Norman-French *Scalacronica*, compiled during his captivity at Edinburgh Castle in 1555, speaks of the predictions of Merlin, which like those of " Banaster ou de Thomas de Ercildoune. . . . furount ditz en figure.''

A number of predictions attributed to *Thomas* the Rhymer are still current, for instance that weird verse which Sir Walter Scott made the motto of *The Bride of Lammermuir* ; and also a saying concerning a Border family with which, as we have seen, the soothsayer was at one time associated :

" Betide, betide, whate'er betide,
There'll aye be Haigs at Bemersyde.''

It will be observed that both the foregoing are couched in metre, yet there is really no sure proof that the soothsayer was a poet. It is usually supposed that he acquired the sobriquet of *Rhymer* because he was a popular minstrel in his day, but the fact remains that Rymour was long a comparatively common surname in Berwickshire, and, while it may have originated with *Thomas*, the assumption has but slight foundation. Again, the prophet of Earlston has been credited with a poem on the story of Sir Tristram, belonging to the Arthurian cycle of romance, and the Advocate's Library contains a manuscript copy of this, probably written as early as 1300. However, while Sir Walter Scott and other authorities believed in this ascription, it is quite likely that the poem is but a paraphrase from some French troubadour. For generations, however, the Scottish peasantry continued to be influenced by the sayings attributed to " True Thomas," as they named him, as is witnessed by the publication during comparatively modern times of books containing the prophecies which he is said to have uttered.

Thoth : (*See* **Hermes Trismegistus.**)

Thought-Reading : A term somewhat loosely applied to various forms of *apparent* thought-transference, even where the method employed is muscle-reading or actual fraud. It must not be confused with telepathy, for, though both terms are sometimes used synonymously, the latter implies the direct action of one mind on another, independent of the ordinary sense-channels, while no such restrictions are

contained in the term " thought-reading." In early times, when outbursts of ecstatic frenzy were ascribed to demoniac possession, we find the ecstatics credited with the power to read thoughts ; witches were supposed to be endowed with the same faculty ; Paracelsus and the early magnetists recognised its existence. The advent of spiritualism gave to *thought-reading* a new impetus. It was now the spirits who read the thoughts of the sitters and replied to them with raps and table-turnings. Until quite recently, however, *thought-reading* was attributed either to occultism or fraud. Not only was the " ethereal vibration " theory unthought of, but the phenomena of hyperæsthesia and " subconscious whispering " were very imperfectly understood in their bearing on *thought-reading*. Yet it is probable that these last offered a satisfactory explanation in many cases, especially when the subject was entranced. Professional thought-readers who performed on public platforms indulged largely in fraud. (*See* **Telepathy.**)

Thought Transference : (*See* **Telepathy.**)

Thought Vibrations, Theory of : (*See* **Telepathy.**)

Thrasyllus : (*See* **Astrology.**)

Tibet : In this country, the stronghold of Buddhism, all superstition circles around the national religion, which at the same time has absorbed into itself the aboriginal beliefs and demonology. Nowhere perhaps has such a vast amount of pure superstition crystallised around the kernel of Buddhism,—the pure doctrines of which were found by the Hindu conquerors of the Tibetans to be totally unsuited to the Hunnish aborigines of the country, who before the advent of Buddhism were in the aministic stage of religion. This was allowed to revive and rites and ceremonies, charms and incantations, of the very nature which Buddha had so strongly condemned, clustered quickly around his philosophy in *Tibet*. From this sprang the *tantra* system, which is almost a purely magical one. It was founded by Asanga, a monk of Peshawar, who composed its gospel, the *Yogachchara Bhumi Sastra* in the sixth century A.D. Basing his pantheon upon the debased system of Buddhism then prevalent, Asanga reconciled it to native requirements by placing a number of Saivite devil-gods and goddesses in the lower Buddhistic heavens. These he made subservient to the Buddha. His religion was speedily adopted by the barbarian tribes of *Tibet*, who sacrificed readily to the deities of this new religion. Very naturally they exaggerated the magical side of it, their main object being to obtain supernatural power by means of spoken spells and words of power. A very considerable literature sprang up in connection with the new faith, which has been scathingly commented upon by disciples of the purer Buddhism as being nothing more or less than mere barbarian sorcery. Of course the monkish class of lamas found it impossible altogether to ignore the tantra system, but Tsongkapa in the middle of the fourteenth century unhesitatingly condemned the whole system. The lamas had and have an esoteric form of Buddhism, which has but little in common with the tantra system of the people, but we find them at festivals and so on unbending so far as to represent the various devils and fiends of this faith. As literature, the tantras may be considered as a later development of the *puranas*, but they are without any poetic value. They are regarded as gospels by the Saktas, or worshippers of Kali, Durga or Purvati the wife of Siva, or some other creative agency. They abound in magical performances and mystic rites—a great many of which are of a quite unspeakable character. They usually take the form of a dialogue between Siva and his wife. There were originally sixty-four tantras, but as yet no satisfactory scholarly examination has been made of them.

Tii : A Polynesian Vampire . (*See* **Vampire.**)

Timæus of Locris : The earliest known writer on the doctrines of magic. The *Timæan* theory of God, the Universe, and the World-soul is thus set forth by Büsching : " God shaped the eternal unformed matter by imparting to it His being. The inseparable united itself with the separable ; the unvarying with the variable ; and, moreover, in the harmonic conditions of the Pythagorean system. To comprehend all things better, infinite space was imagined as divided into three portions, which are,—the centre, the circumference, and the intermediate space. The centre is most distant from the highest God, who inhabits the circumference ; the space between the two contains the celestial spheres. When God descended to impart His being, the emanations from Him penetrated the whole of heaven, and filled the same with imperishable bodies. Its power decreased with the distance from the source, and lost itself gradually in our world in minute portions, over which matter was still dominant. From this proceeds the continuous change of being and decay below the moon, where the power of matter predominates ; from this, also, arise the circular movements of the heaven and the earth, the various rapidities of the stars, and the peculiar motion of the planets. By the union of God with matter, a third being was created, namely, the world-soul, which vitalizes and regulates all things, and occupies the space between the centre and the circumference."

Tinkers' Talk : (*See* **Shelta Thari.**)

Tiromancy : Divination by means of cheese. It is practised in divers ways the details of which are not known.

Toltecs : (*See* **Mexico and Central America.**)

Tomga : Eskimo familiar spirits. (*See* **Eskimos.**)

Tongues, Speaking and Writing in : The *speaking and writing in foreign tongues*, or in unintelligible outpourings mistaken for such, is a very old form of psychic phenomenon. It was a frequent accompaniment of the epidemic ecstasy which was so common in mediæval Europe. Thus the Nuns of Loudon (q.v.) are declared to have understood and replied to questions put to them in Latin, Greek, Spanish, Turkish, and other even less-known languages. The Tremblers of the Cevennes (q.v.) spoke in excellent French, whereas French was to them a foreign language. And practically every epidemic of the kind was character-ised by the speaking in *tongues*, which seemed to be infec-tious, and spread rapidly through whole communities. In these early cases the phenomenon was ascribed to the power of supernatural agencies, whether demons or angels, who temporarily controlled the organism of the "possessed." But analogous instances are to be found in plenty in the annals of modern spiritualism, where they are of course regarded as manifestations of the spirits of the deceased through the material organism of the medium. Compara-tively early in the movement there are evidences of speaking and writing in Latin, Greek, French, Swiss, Spanish, and Red Indian languages. Judge Edmonds, the well-known American Spiritualist, testified to these faculties in his daughter and niece, who spoke Greek, Spanish, Polish, and Italian at various times, as well as Red Indian and other languages. Some of these cases are well attested. Two professional mediums (J. V. Mansfield and A. D. Ruggles) are known to have written automatically in many lan-guages, including Chinese and Gaelic, but whether or not they had any previous acquaintance with these languages remains at least a matter of doubt. In still more modern times speaking in *tongues* has been practised, notably by Hélène Smith, who invented the " Martian language." On the whole, we may take it that the so-called foreign *tongues* were generally no more than a meaningless jumble of articulate sounds, of which the spirits themselves some-times purported to offer a translation. Where there is good evidence to show that the writings were actually executed in a foreign language, as in the case of the pro-fessional mediums mentioned above, there is generally some reason to suppose a former acquaintance with the language, which the exaltation of memory incidental to the trance state might revive. When unknown *tongues* were written they were seldom found to correspond with any real language.

Toolemak : Eskimo familiar spirits. (*See* **Eskimos.**)

Totemism : (*See* **Fetishism.**)

Tower of London : The jewel-room of the *Tower of London* is reported to be haunted, and, in 1860, there was published in *Notes and Queries* by the late Edmund Lenthal Swifte, Keeper of the Crown Jewels the account of a spectral illusion witnessed by himself in the *Tower*. He says that in October, 1817, he was at supper with his wife, her sister, and his little boy, in the sitting-room of the jewel-house. To quote his own words : " I had offered a glass of wine and water to my wife, when, on putting it to her lips, she exclaimed, ' Good God ! what is that ? ' I looked up and saw a cylindrical figure like a glass tube, seemingly about the thickness of my arm, and hovering between the ceiling and the table ; its contents appeared to be a dense fluid, white and pale azure. This lasted about two minutes, when it began to move before my sister-in-law ; then, following the oblong side of the table, before my son and myself, passing behind my wife, it paused for a moment over her right shoulder. Instantly crouching down, and with both hands covering her shoulder, she shrieked out, ' O Christ ! it has seized me ! ' " " It was ascertained," adds Mr. Swifte, " that no optical action from the outside could have produced any manifestaion within, and hence the mystery has remained unsolved." Speaking of the *Tower*, we learn from the same source how " one of the night sentries at the jewel-house was alarmed by a figure like a huge bear issuing from underneath the jewel-room door. He thrust at it with his bayonet which stuck in the door. He dropped in a fit and was carried senseless to the guard-room. . . . In another day or two the brave and steady soldier died."

Tractatulus Alchimae : (*See* **Avicenna.**)

Trance : An abnormal state, either spontaneous or induced, bearing some analogy to the ordinary sleep-state, but differing from it in certain marked particulars. The term is loosely applied to many varied pathologic conditions— *e.g.*, hypnosis, ecstasy, catalepsy, somnambulism, certain forms of hysteria, and the mediumistic *trance*. Some-times, as in catalepsy, there is a partial suspension of the vital functions ; generally, there is insensibility to pain and to any stimulus applied to the sense-organs ; while the distinguishing feature of the *trance* is that the subject retains consciousness and gives evidence of intelligence, either his own normal intelligence or, as in cases of posses-sion and impersonation, some foreign intelligence. In hypnosis the subject, though indifferent to sensory stimuli applied to his own person, has been known to exhibit a curious sensitiveness to such stimuli applied to the person of the hypnotist. (*See* **Community of Sensation.**) In Ecstasy, which is frequently allied with hallucination, the subject remains in rapt contemplation of some transcen-dental vision, deaf and blind to the outside world. It was formerly considered to indicate that the soul of the ecstatic was viewing some great event distant in time or place or some person or scene from the celestial sphere. Now-a-days such a state is believed to be brought about by intense and sustained emotional concentration on some particular mental image, by means of which hallucination may be induced.

The mediumistic *trance* is recognised as having an affinity with hypnosis, for the hypnotic trance, frequently induced, may gradually become spontaneous, when it exhibits strong resemblances to the *trance* of the medium.

This latter is, among spiritualists, " The Trance " *par excellence*, and they object to the term being applied in any case where there is no sign of spirit " possession." The entranced medium—who seems able to produce this state at will—frequently displays an exaltation of memory (hypermesia), of the special senses (hyperæsthesia), and even of the intellectual faculties. Automatic writing and utterances are generally produced in the *trance* state, and often display knowledge of which the medium normally knows nothing, or which, according to some authorities, gives evidence of telepathy. Such are the *trance* utterances of Mrs. Piper, whose automatic phenomena have in recent years provided a wide field for research for many men of science both in Britain and on the Continent. Naturally these phenomena, and those of all *trance* mediums, are referred by spiritualists to the agency of disembodied intelligences—the spirits of the dead—acting through the medium's physical organism, a notion which is akin to the old idea of demoniac possession, to which spontaneous *trance* was referred. Moreover, the *trance* messages themselves purported to come from the spirits of deceased persons and there are many who see no reason to disbelieve the emphatic assertion of the " intelligence," especially when that assertion is supplemented by an exact representation of the voice, appearance, and known opinions of the deceased friend or relative whose spirit it claims to be. Such *trance* impersonations supply a large part of the evidence on which the structure of spiritualism rests. There is, however, nothing to show that the information concerning the deceased, thus reproduced, may not have been obtained by normal means, or, at the most, telepathically from the minds of the sitters.

Trance Personalities : Trance messages purporting to come from the medium's spirit control do not as a rule reveal a very definite personality. The control reflects the thoughts and opinions of the medium and the sitters, possesses little knowledge that they do not possess, and is in general a somewhat colourless creature. Yet not infrequently a trance medium is controlled by a spirit of distinct, not to say distinguished, personality, whose education and culture are on a much higher plane than the medium's own, and whose ideas and opinions are quite independent. Such spirits are generally given distinguishing names. They often control the medium alternately with other controls. On the other hand, the medium has generally a monopoly of one or more of these spirits, though sometimes one control may be shared by a number of mediums. Among those who may justly be regarded as the common property of the mediumistic fraternity are the spirits of certain great men—Virgil, Socrates, Shakespeare, Milton, Benjamin Franklin, Victor Hugo, Swedenborg, and so on. The messages delivered through their control seldom resemble anything they wrote during their lives. It would indeed be ludicrous to hold these great men responsible for the feeble outpourings delivered in their name. But these spirits come and go ; it is perhaps hardly accurate to call them *trance personalities* at all. Among the best known of the latter class are the spirits who purported to control the late Mr. Stainton Moses—Imperator, Rector, Mentor, Prudens, and others. What the real names of these controls may be is not known, for Mr. Moses only revealed the secret to a few of his most intimate friends. Imperator and Rector were among the controls of Mrs. Piper in still more recent years, and indeed much of her automatic discourse did not come directly from the communicating spirits, but was dictated by them to Rector. It is suggested, however, by Sir Oliver Lodge and other authorities, that the controls of Mrs. Piper are not identical with those of Stainton Moses, by whom were written through his hand the well-known *Spirit Teachings*, but are merely

masqueraders. But Mrs. Piper has several interesting *trance personalities* of her own, without borrowing from anybody. One of her earliest controls was Sebastian Bach, but ere long he gave place to a spirit calling himself " Dr. Phinuit," who held sway for a considerable time, but gave place in his turn to George Pelham—" G.P." Pelham was a young author and journalist who died suddenly in 1892. Soon after his death he purported to control Mrs. Piper, and gave many striking proofs of his identity. He constantly referred, with intimate knowledge, to the affairs of Pelham, recognised his friends, and gave to each his due meed of welcome. Not once, it is said, did he fail to recognise an acquaintance, or give a greeting to one whom he did not know. Many of Pelham's old friends did not hesitate to see in him that which he claimed to be. Only on one occasion, when asked for the names of two persons who had been associated with him in a certain enterprise, " G.P." refused, saying that as there was present one who knew the names, his mentioning them would be referred to telepathy ! Later, however, he gave the names—incorrectly. When " G.P." ceased to take the principle part in the control of Mrs. Piper, his place was taken by Rector and Imperator, as mentioned above. Another well-known medium, Mrs. Thompson, had as her chief control " Nelly," a daughter of hers who had died in infancy ; also a Mrs. Cartwright, and others. These controls of Mrs. Thomson are said not to have shown any very individual characteristics, but to resemble Mrs. Thomson herself very strongly both in voice and manner of speech, though Mrs. Verrall has stated that the impersonations gave an impression of separate identity to the sitter. Mrs. Thomson's early trance utterances were controlled by another band of spirits, with even less individuality than those mentioned. Frequently the mediums and investigators themselves, on reaching the discarnate plane, become controls in their turn. The late Mr. Myers, Mr. Gurney, Dr. Hodgson, and Professor Sidgwick purported to speak and write through many mediums, notably through Mrs. Piper and Mrs. Thompson, Mrs. Verrall and Mrs. Holland. Many of the statements made by these controls were correct, and some matters revealed which were apparently outside the scope of the medium's normal knowledge, but at the same time several fatal discrepancies were found to exist between the controls and those they were supposed to represent. Thus the script produced by Mrs. Holland contained grave warnings, purporting to come from Myers, against Eusapia Palladino and her physical phenomena, whereas Myers was known to hold in his lifetime opinions favourable to the physical manifestations. On the whole these *trance personalities* show themselves decidedly coloured by the personality of the medium. In cases where the latter was acquainted with the control the *trance personality* is proportionately strong, whereas when there was no personal acquaintance it is often of a neutral tint, and sometimes bad guesses are made, as when Mrs. Holland represented the Gurney control as of a brusque and almost discourteous temperament. But such instances must not be taken as impeaching the medium's good faith. Even where the *trance personality* is patently the product of the medium's own consciousness, there is no reason to suppose that there is any intentional deception. While in some of the most definite cases the evidence for the operation of a discarnate intelligence is very good indeed, and has proved satisfactory to many prominent investigators.

Transformation : (*See* **Spells.**)

Transmutation of Metals : (*See* **Alchemy.**)

Transmutation of the Body : This is indeed the end and aim of all Alchemy—to restore man to his primordial condition of grace, strength, perfection, beauty and physical immortality. With this in view the alchemists of all the ages have laboured to discover the secret of the Elixir of Life, which mystics believed would, literally, achieve this renewal of youth, and therefore immortality. Endless receipts for this medicine have been given, and some honestly believed they had attained it ; but all to no purpose, and the great secret still remains hidden from human eyes.

Tree Ghosts : Indian tree spirits. Says Mr. Crookes in his *Popular Religion of Northern India.* " These *tree ghoss* are, it is needless to say, very numerous. Hence most local shrines are constructed under trees ; and in one particular tree, the Bira, the jungle tribes of Mirzapur locate Bagheswar, the tiger godling, one of their most dreaded deities. In the Konkan, according to Mr. Campbell, the medium or Bhagat who becomes possessed is called *Jhad,* or ' tree,' apparently because he is a favourite dwelling-place for spirits. In the Dakkhin it is believed that the spirit of the pregnant woman of Churel lives in a tree, and the Abors and Padams of East Bengal believe that spirits in trees kidnap children. Many of these tree spirits appear in the folk-tales. Thus, Devadatta worshipped a tree which one day suddenly clave in two and a nymph appeared who introduced him inside the tree, where was a heavenly palace of jewels, in which, reclining on a couch, appeared Vidyatprabha, the maiden daughter of the king of the Yakshas ; in another story the mendicant hears inside a tree the Yaksha joking with his wife. So Daphne is turned into a tree to avoid the pursuit of her lover."

Tree of Life, The, and The Tree of the Knowledge of Good and Evil : Two of the trees planted by God in the Garden of Eden, which were believed by St. Ambrose to be of mystical significance. The former is understood to be the manifestation of God, and the latter of the worldly wisdom to which our human nature is too apt to incline.

Tremblers of the Cevennes : A Protestant caste of convulsonaires, who during the sixteenth century spread themselves from their centre in the Cevennes over almost the whole of Germany. They possessed many points of resemblance with cases of possession (q.v.), and are said to have been insensible to thrusts and blows with pointed sticks and iron bars, as well as to the oppression of great weights. They had visions, communicated with good and evil spirits, and are said to have performed many miraculous cures similar to the apostolic miracles. They made use of very peculiar modes of treatment called *grandes secours* or *secours meurtriers,* which are authenticated by the reports of eye-witnesses and by judicial documents. Although they were belaboured by the strongest men with heavy pieces of wood and bars of iron weighing at least thirty pounds, they complained of no injury, but of experiencing a sensation of pleasure. They also were covered with boards, on which as many as twenty men stood without its being painful to them. They even bore as many as 100 blows with a twenty-pounds weight, alternately applied to the breast and the stomach with such force that the room trembled, and they begged that the blows might be laid on harder, as light ones only increased their sufferings. Indeed only those who laid on the heaviest and most strenuous blows were thanked by their sick. It seemed that it was only when the power of these blows had penetrated to the most vital parts that they experienced real relief. Ennemoser explains this insensibility to pain by stating that in his experience " spasmodic convulsions maintain themselves against outward attempts, and even the greatest violence, with almost superhuman strength, without injury to the patient, as has often been observed in young girls and women, where anyone might have almost been induced to believe in supernatural influence. The tension of the muscles increases in power with the insensibility of the power, so that no outward

force is equal to it ; and when it is attempted to check the paroxysm with force, it gains in intensity, and according to some observers not less psychical than physical. . . . I have observed the same manifestations in children, in Catholics, Protestants and Jews, without the least variation, on which account I consider it to be nothing more than an immense abnormal and inharmonic *lusus naturæ.*"

Trevisan, Bernard : This Italian alchemist's life was a curious and intensely pathetic one. Bent on discovering the philosopher's stone, he began at an early age to lavish huge sums of money on the pursuit ; but again and again he was baffled, and it was only when old age was stealing upon him, and he had disbursed a veritable fortune, that his labours were crowned with some measure of success.

Bernard Trévisan, Comte de la Marche, was born in the year 1406 at Padua, a town whose inhabitants were famous for erudition throughout many centuries in the middle ages. His father was a doctor of medicine, so it is probable that *Bernard* received his initial training in science at home ; while ere he was out of his teens he began to devote himself seriously to alchemy, having been lured thereto by reading the works of the famous Eastern philosophers, Geber and Rhasis. *Bernard's* father was rich, and accordingly, whenever it was known that the young man was minded to dabble in gold-seeking, he found himself surrounded by charlatans offering counsel ; and his very first experiments resulted in his spending upwards of three thousand crowns, the bulk of which sum went into the pockets of the youth's fraudulent advisers. He was not discouraged, however ; and, finding new henchmen, and at the same time augmenting his learning by a close study of the writings of Sacrobosco and Rupecissa, he proceeded to make a new series of attempts. But these also proved futile, once more the alchemist did no more than enrich his assistants, and in consequence he vowed that henceforth he would prosecute his researches single-handed.

Bernard now engaged in a long course of sedulous reading, while he also began to give much time to prayer, thinking by this means to gain his desired end ; and anon he started fresh experiments, expending on these some six thousand crowns. But again his devotion and extravagance went unrewarded, year after year went by in this fashion, and betimes *Bernard* realised that he was past the prime of life, yet had achieved nothing whatsoever. His bitter disappointment engendered an illness, but scarcely was he restored to health ere he heard that one Henry, a German priest, had succeeded in creating the philosopher's stone ; and thereupon *Bernard* hastened to Germany, accompanied by various other alchemists. After some difficulty they made the acquaintance of the cleric in question, who told them he would disclose all would they but furnish a certain sum of money to procure the necessary tools and materials ; so they paid as desired, yet having devoted much time to watching the German at work they found themselves no nearer the goal than before.

This last piece of quackery opened *Bernard's* eyes, and he proclaimed his decision of eschewing hermetic philosophy altogether in the future—a decision which was warmly applauded by his relatives, for already his researches had cost a king's ransom. But it soon transpired that the alchemist was quite incapable of clinging to his resolution, and, growing more ardent than ever, he visited Spain and Great Britain, Holland and France, trying in each of these countries to enlarge his stock of learning, and to make the acquaintance of others who were searching like himself. Eventually he even penetrated to Egypt, Persia and Palestine, while subsequently he travelled in Greece, where he witnessed many alchemistic researches ; yet all proved vain, and ultimately *Bernard* found himself impoverished, and was forced to sell his parental estates.

Being thus without so much as a home, he retired to the Island of Rhodes, intending to live there quietly for the rest of his days ; but even here his old passion continued to govern him, and, chancing to make the acquaintance of a priest who knew something of science, the thwarted and ruined alchemist proposed that they should start fresh experiments together. The cleric professed himself willing to give all the help in his power, so the pair borrowed a large sum of money to admit of their purchasing the necessary paraphernalia ; and it was here, then, in this secluded island, and while in a literally bankrupt condition, that *Bernard* made the wonderful discovery with which he is traditionally credited. Doubtless the tradition has little foundation in fact, yet at least the philosopher deserved some reward for his indomitable if foolhardy perseverance, and it is pathetic to recall that his death occurred soon after the day of his triumph.

In contradistinction to the majority of his brother-alchemists, *Bernard* appears to have loved actual experiments much better than writing about them. It is probable however, that he was at least partly responsible for an octavo volume published in 1643, *Le Bernard d'Alchmague, cum Bernard Treveso* ; while he is commonly credited with another work also, *La Philosophic Naturelle des Metaux.* Herein he insists on the necessity of much meditation on the part of the scientist who would create the philosopher's stone, and this rather trite observation is followed by a voluminous alchemistic treatise, most of it sadly obscure, and demonstrating the author no great expert.

Triad : (*See* **God.**)

Triad Society : An ancient esoteric society of China. The candidate scantily clothed, is brought into a dark room by two members, who lead him to the President, before whom he kneels. He is given a living cock and a knife, and in this posture he takes a complicated oath to assist his brethren in any emergency, even at the risk of his life. He then cuts off the head of the cock, and mingles it with his own, the three assisting individuals adding some of their own blood. After being warned that death will be his portion should he divulge the secrets of the society, he is initiated into them, and is entrusted with the signs of recognition which are in triads. For example a member must lift any object with three fingers only. This society, originally altruistic, is now of a political character.

Triangle : (*See* **Magic.**)

Trident, Magical : (*See* **Magic.**)

Trine, Ralph Waldo : (*See* **New Thought.**)

Tripod : (*See* **Necromancy.**)

Trithemius : The son of a German vine-grower, named Heidenberg, received his Latinized appellation from Trittheim, a village in the electorate of Treves, where he was born in 1462. He might reasonably be included among those earnest and enthusiastic souls who have persevered in the pursuit of knowledge under difficulties ; for his mother, marrying a second time, had no love for the offspring of her first marriage. The young *Trithemius* was ill-fed, ill-clothed, and over-worked. All day he toiled in the vineyards ; but the nights he was able to devote to the acquisition of knowledge, and then he stole away from his miserable home, and perused what books he could beg or borrow, by the light of the moon. As his mind expanded he became sensible of the vast stores of learning to which his circumstances denied him access. He could not rest content with the few grains of sand he had picked up on the seashore. Extorting his small share of the patrimony bequeathed by his father, he wandered away to Treves, entered himself a student of its celebrated University, and assumed the name of *Trithemius.* His progress was now as rapid as might be inferred probable from the intensity of his aspirations and the keenness of his intellect. At the

age of twenty he had acquired the reputation of a scholar—a reputation which was of greater advantage in the 15th than it is in the 20th century. He was now desirous of once more seeing the mother whom he did not love the less because she had ill-used him, and in the winter of 1482 he quitted the cloistered shade of Treves on a solitary journey to Trittheim. It was a dark day, ending in a gloomy, fast-snowing night, and the good student, on his arrival near Spannheim, found the roads impassable. He sought refuge in a neighbouring monastery. There the weather imprisoned him for several days. The imprisonment proved so much to the liking of *Trithemius*, that he voluntarily took the monastic vows, and retired from the world. In the course of two years he was elected abbot, and devoting all his little fortune to the repair and improvement of the monastery, he gained the love and reverence of the brotherhood, whom he inspired with his own love of learning. But after a rule of one-and-twenty years, the monks forgot all his benefits, and remembered only the severity of his discipline. They broke out in revolt, and elected another abbot. The deposed *Trithemius* quitted Spannheim, and wandered from place to place, until finally elected Abbot of St. James of Wurzburg, where he died in 1516.

His fame as a magician rests on very innocent foundations He devised a species of short-hand called *steoganographia*, which the ignorant stigmatized as a cabalistical and necromantic writing, concealing the most fearful secrets. He wrote a treatise on the subject ; another upon the supposed administration of the world by its guardian angels—a revival of the good and evil geniuses of the Ancients—which William Lilly translated into English in 1647 ; a third upon Geomancy, or divination by means of lines and circles on the ground ; a fourth upon Sorcery ; and a fifth upon Alchemy. In his work upon Sorcery he makes the earliest mention of the popular story of Dr. Faustus, and records the torments he himself occasionally suffered from the malice of a spirit named Hudekin. He is said to have gratified the Emperor Maximilian with a vision of his deceased wife, the beautiful Mary of Burgundy, and was reputed to have defrayed the expenses of his monastic establishment at Spannheim by the resources which the Philosopher's Stone put at his disposal. His writings show him to have been an amiable and credulous enthusiast but his sincere and ardent passion for knowledge may well incline us to forgive the follies which he only shared with most of the scholars and wise men of his age.

Triumphal Chariot of Antimony : (*See* **Valentine, Basil.**)

Trivah : Among the natives of Borneo the *trivah*, or feast of the dead, is celebrated after a death has taken place. A panel containing a representation of Tempon-teloris' ship of the dead (q.v.) is generally set up at the *trivah*, and sacrifices of fowls are offered to it. Until the *trivah* has been celebrated the soul's soul is unable to reach the *Levu-liau.*

True Black Magic, Book of the : A Grimoire, which is simply an adapted version of the Key of Solomon (q.v.)

Tsithsith, The : An article of apparel, believed to be endowed with talismanic properties. A sentence in the *Talmud* runs thus : " Whoever has the tephillin bound to his head and arm, and the *tsithsith* thrown over his garments . . . . . is protected from sin."

Tumah : According to the *Kabala*, physical or moral uncleanness. The latter is divided into three main divisions—idolatry, murder, and immorality. Sin, says the same authority, not only rendered imperfect man himself, but also affected the whole of nature, even to the sphere of angels, and the Divinity himself. In physical uncleanness there is a coarser and a more subtle form. The latter causes a dimness in the soul which is most keenly felt by those who are nearest to sacred things. Organic things which come into contact with the human body are more liable to the *Tumah* than remoter things. The human corpse is more unclean than that of the lower animals, because its more complex nature involves a more repulsive decay. Thus the corpse of a holy man is most unclean of all.

Tunisa : Burmese diviners. (*See* **Burma**.)

Turcomans : (*See* **Siberia**.)

Turner, Ann : English witch. (*See* **England**.)

Turquoise : A good amulet for preventing accidents to

U

Ulysses : (*See* **Michael Maer**.)

Unguents : There are many kinds of *unguents*, each with its peculiar properties. It is known that the devil compounds them in order to harm the human race. One such *unguent* is composed of human fat, and is used by the witches to enable them to fly through the air to the Sabbath. Many old recipes exist for *unguents* to induce sleep, visions, etc., and these are compounded from various strange ingredients. (*See* Salverte " Les Science Occultes.")

Union Spirite Bordelaise (Journal) : (*See* **France**.)

Univercœlum, The : An American periodical having for its aim " the establishment of a universal System of Truth, the Reform and Reorganisation of Society." It made its first appearance in December, 1847, under the editorship of Andrew Jackson Davis (q.v.), and lived for about a year and a half. Its supporters and contributors looked for a new revelation to supplement those of the Old and New Testaments, Swedenborg and Fourier. Attention was given in its pages to prophecy, clairvoyance, somnambulism and trance phenomena generally, while it also taught " an interior and spiritual philosophy " whose central idea was that God was the infinitely intelligent Essence which pervaded all things—the Universal Soul, expressing itself in the material universe and the laws of nature as the human soul expresses itself through the material body. Though the Rochester Rappings broke out some time before the *Univercœlum* came to an end, the adherents of the paper did not seem to connect the disturbances with their propaganda. However, many of those who were associated with the *Univercœlum* afterwards became editors of spiritualistic papers. In July, 1849 the paper passed out of the hands of A. J. Davis, and became *The Present Age*, under the editorship of W. M. Channing.

Universal Balm : An elixir composed by the alchemists, which formed a sovereign remedy for every malady, and would even bring the dead to life.

Universities (Occult) : In many works on the occult sciences allusions are made to schools and *universities* for the instruction of those who were drawn to them. Thus we are told that Salamanca abounded in such schools ; that Jéchiel, a Jewish Rabbi of mediæval France, kept such a seminary ; and there is reason to believe that in all ages such institutions were by no means uncommon. Balzac alludes to one of them in a well-known novel *The Secret of Ruggier*, which he places at the time of Catherine de Medici. He says, " At this epoch the occult sciences were cultivated with an ardour which put to shame the incredulous spirit of our century. . . . The universal protection accorded to these sciences by the ruling sovereigns of the times was quite remarkable." He goes on to say that at the commencement of the sixteenth century Ruggier was the member of a secret university for the study of the occult sciences, where astrologers, alchemists, and others, studied several branches of hidden knowledge ; but he gives no details as to its locality, or as to the exact nature of its curriculum. There is no doubt that during the Middle Ages many extramural lecturers taught alchemy and kindred subjects at the

horsemen, and to prevent them wearying. It moves itself when any danger threatens its possessor.

Typtology : The science of communicating with the spirits by means of rapping, various codes being arranged for the purpose. Thus the sitters may read the alphabet aloud, or slowly pass a pencil down a printed alphabet, the rappings indicating the correct letters which, on being joined together, form a message or an answer to some question propounded. One rap may be made to mean " yes," two " no," and so on. (*See* **Rappings**.)

great *universities*. Thus Paracelsus lectured on alchemy at the University of Basel, and he was preceded and followed there and elsewhere by many illustrious professors of that and other occult arts. M. Figuier in his work *Alchemy and the Alchemists* (*See* **Alchemy**), alludes to a school in Paris frequented by alchemists, which he himself attended in the middle of the last century. The school—an ordinary chemical laboratory through the day—became in the evening a centre of the most elaborate alchemical study, where Figuier met many alchemical students, visionary and practical, with one of whom he had a prolonged argument, which we have outlined at considerable length in the article " Alchemy." Many professors of the occult sciences in early and later times drew around them considerable bands of students and assistants and formed distinct schools for the practice of magic and alchemy, principally the latter. The College of Augurs in Rome and the Calmecac of Ancient Mexico are distinct examples of institutions for the study of at least one branch of occult science, and in this connection the House of Wisdom of the Ismaelite sect at Cairo may be mentioned. It is likely that in ancient Egypt and Babylonia, institutions of the kind flourished more or less in secret. Mme. Blavatsky insisted to the last that a great " school " of illuminated occult adepts flourished in Tibet ; but as nobody except herself and her immediate friends ever saw them, or had any dealings with them ; and as all proof is against the existence of such a semi-divine brotherhood, her statements must be taken as being somewhat open to question. There is, however, no reason to doubt that bodies of men who study the higher occultism do exist in various Asiatic centres, whatever the nature of their powers, supernormal or otherwise, may be. Vague rumours reach students of occultism every now and again of schools or colleges on the continent of Europe, the purpose of which is to train aspirants in the occult arts ; but as definite information is seldom forthcoming regarding these, they can only be merely alluded to here. The " School for the Discovery of the Lost Secrets of Antiquity," which flourishes at Lotus-land, California, was founded by Catherine Tingley late in the nineteenth century, and is under theosophical régime. Numerous small bodies for the study of occultism exist in every town of considerable size in Europe and America ; but these cannot be dignified even by the name of " schools," as they are for the most part private affairs, the occultism of which is of an extremely amateurish and innocent character.

Ura : A spirit. (*See* **Babylonia**.)

Urgund : (*See* **Boehme**.)

Urim and Thummim : A means of divination employed by the ancient Hebrews, and which it was believed consisted of a species of casting lots. Their form and method of use is uncertain, but from passages in the Book of Samuel, it seems probable that (1) they were used to determine guilt and innocence, and (2) that this was done by means of categorical questions, to which the suspected person answered " Yes " or " No." They appear to have been the prerogative of the priesthood.

V

Valentine, Basil : This German adept in hermetic philosophy is commonly supposed to have been born at Mayence towards the close of the fourteenth century. As a young man he espoused holy orders, and it is recorded that he entered the Abbey of St. Peter, at Erfurt, and eventually became its Prior ; but otherwise very little is known concerning him, and even the date of his death is uncertain. He appears to have been a very modest person, for according to Olaus Borrichius, the author of *De Ortu et Progressu Chemiæ*, *Valentine* imprisoned all the manuscripts of his scientific writings inside one of the pillars of the Abbey Church ; and there they might have remained for an indefinite period, but a thunderstorm chanced ultimately to dislodge them from their curious hiding-place. It is possible, of course, that this incarceration was not altogether due to modesty on the writer's part, and arose rather from his dreading a visitation from the Inquisition in the event of their discovering his alchemistic proclivities ; but be that as it may, *Valentine's* works certainly mark him as a very shrewd man and a capable scientist. In contradistinction to most analogous mediæval literature, his treatises are not all couched in Latin, some of them being in high Dutch and others in the author's native German ; and prominent among those in the latter tongue is *The Triumphal Chariot of Antimony*, first published at Leipsic in 1624. Herein *Valentine* exalts antimony as an excellent medicine, while the volume likewise embodies a lengthy metrical treatise on the philosopher's stone, the writer contending that whoso would discover and use this must do charitable deeds, mortify the flesh, and pray without ceasing.

As regards the alchemist's further writings, it behoves to mention his *Apocalypsis Chymica, De Microcosmo degue Magno Mundi Mysterio et Medecina Hominis* and *Practica unà cum duodecim Clavibus et Appendice*. All these were originally published in Germany at the beginning of the seventeenth century, and divers passages in them demonstrate that the author understood the distillation of brandy, and was acquainted with the method of obtaining chlorohydric acid from salt-water ; while moreover, reverting to his faith in antimony, he has been credited with having been the first to extract this from sulphuret.

Vampire : (Russian *Vampir*, South Russian *upuir*, probably from the root *pi*, to drink, with the *prefix va*, or *av*.) A dead person who returns in spirit form from the grave for the purpose of destroying and sucking the blood of living persons, or a living sorcerer who takes a special form for the same purpose. The conception of the *vampire* is rifest among Slavonic peoples, and especially in the Balkan countries, and in Hungary, Bohemia, Moravia, and Silesia, and in these territories from 1730–35 there was a well-marked epidemic of vampirism, but it is by no means confined to them. In White Russia and the Ukraine it is believed that *vampires* are generally wizards or sorcerers, but in Bulgaria and Serbia it is thought that any corpse over which a cat or a dog jumps or over which a bird has flown is liable to become a *vampire*. In Greece (q.v.) a *vampire* is known as a *broncolaia* or *bourkabakos*, which has been identified with the Slavonic name for " werewolf " (q.v.), *vlkodlak*, or *vukodlak*. The *vampire*, too, is often supposed to steal the heart of his victim and to roast it over a slow fire, thus causing interminable amorous longings.

Marks of Vampirism.—Vampirism is epidemic in character. Where one instance is discovered it is almost invariably followed by several others. This is accounted for by the circumstance that it is believed that the victim of a *vampire* pines and dies and becomes in turn a *vampire* himself after death, and so duly infects others. On the disinterment of a suspected *vampire* various well-known signs are looked for by experienced persons. Thus, if several holes about the breadth of a man's finger, are observed in the soil above the grave the *vampire* character of its occupant may be suspected. On unearthing the corpse it is usually found with wide-open eyes, ruddy and life-like complexion and lips and a general appearance of freshness, and showing no signs of corruption. It may also be found that the hair and nails have grown as in life. On the throat two small livid marks may be looked for. The coffin is also very often full of blood, the body has a swollen and gorged appearance, and the shroud is frequently half-devoured. The blood contained in the veins of the corpse is found on examination to be in a fluid condition as in life, and the limbs are pliant and flexible and have none of the rigidity of death.

Examples of Vampirism.—Many well-authenticated examples of vampirism exist. Charles Ferdinand de Schertz in his work *Magia Posthuma* printed at Olmutz in 1706 relates several stories of apparitions of this sort, and particularises the mischief done by them. One, among others, is of a herdsman of the village of Blow near the town of Kadam in Bohemia, who appeared for a considerable length of time, and visited several persons, who all died within eight days. At last, the inhabitants of Blow dug up the herdsman's body, and fixed it in the ground with a stake driven through it. The man, even in this condition, laughed at the people that were employed about him, and told them they were very obliging to furnish him with a stick with which to defend himself from the dogs. The same night he extricated himself from the stake, frightened several persons by appearing to them, and occasioned the death of many more than he had hitherto done. He was then delivered into the hands of the hangman, who put him into a cart, in order to burn him without the town. As they went along, the carcass shrieked in the most hideous manner, and threw about its arms and legs, as if it had been alive ; and upon being again run through with a stake, it gave a loud cry, and a great quantity of fresh, florid blood issued from the wound. At last, the body was burned to ashes, and this execution put a final stop to the spectre's appearing and infecting the village.

Calmet in his *Dissertation on Vampires* appended to his *Dissertation upon Apparitions* (English translation, 1759), gives several well authenticated instances of vampirism as follows :—

" It is now about fifteen years since a soldier, who was quartered in the house of a Haidamack peasant, upon the frontiers of Hungary, saw, as he was at the table with his landlord, a stranger come in and sit down by them. The master of the house and the rest of the company were strangely terrified, but the soldier knew not what to make of it. The next day the peasant died, and, upon the soldier's enquiring into the meaning of it, he was told that it was his landlord's father, who had been dead and buried above ten years, that came and sat down at table, and gave his son notice of his death.

" The soldier soon propagated the story through his regiment, and by this means it reached the general officers, who commissioned the count de Cabreras, a captain in Alandetti's regiment of foot, to make an exact enquiry into the fact. The count, attended by several officers, a surgeon, and a notary, came to the house, and took the deposition of all the family, who unanimously swore that the spectre was the landlord's father, and that all the soldier had said was strictly true. The same was also attested by all the inhabitants of the village.

" In consequence of this the body of the spectre was dug up, and found to be in the same state as if it has been but just dead, the blood like that of a living person. The count de Cabreras ordered its head to be cut off, and the corpse to be buried again. He then proceeded to take depositions against other spectres of the same sort, and particularly against a man who had been dead above thirty years, and had made his appearance three several times in his own house at meal-time. At his first visit he had fastened upon the neck of his own brother, and sucked his blood ; at his second, he had treated one of his children in the same manner ; and the third time, he fastened upon a servant of the family, and all three died upon the spot.

" Upon this evidence, the count gave orders that he should be dug up, and being found, like the first, with his blood in a fluid state, as if he had been alive, a great nail was drove through his temples, and he was buried again. The count ordered a third to be burnt, who had been dead above sixteen years, and was found guilty of murdering two of his own children by sucking their blood. The commissioner then made his report to the general officers, who sent a deputation to the emperor's court for further directions ; and the emperor dispatched an order for a court, consisting of officers, lawyers, physicians, chirurgeons, and some divines, to go and enquire into the cause of these extraordinary events, upon the spot.

" The gentleman who acquainted me with all these particulars, had them from the count de Cabreras himself, at Fribourg in Brisgau, in the year 1730."

Other instances alluded to by Calmet are as follows :—

" In the part of Hungary, known in Latin by the name of *Oppida Heidonum*, on the other side of the Tibiscus, vulgarly called the Teyss ; that is, between that part of this river which waters the happy country of Tockay, and the frontiers of Transylvania, the people named *Heydukes* have a notion that there are dead persons, called by them *vampires*, which suck the blood of the living, so as to make them fall away visibly to skin and bones, while the carcasses themselves, like leeches, are filled with blood to such a degree that it comes out at all the apertures of their body. This notion has lately been confirmed by several facts, which I think we cannot doubt the truth of, considering the witnesses that attest them. Some of the most considerable of these facts I shall now relate.

" About five years ago, an Heyduke, named Arnold Paul, an inhabitant of Medreiga, was killed by a cart full of hay that fell upon him. About thirty days after his death, four persons died suddenly, with all the symptoms usually attending those who are killed by *vampires*. It was then remembered that this Arnold Paul had frequently told a story of his having been tormented by a Turkish *vampire*, in the neighbourhood of Cassova, upon the borders of Turkish Servia (for the notion is that those who have been passive *vampires* in their life-time become active ones after death ; or, in other words, that those who have had their blood sucked become suckers in their turn) but that he had been cured by eating some of the earth upon the *vampire's* grave, and by rubbing himself with his blood. This precaution, however, did not hinder him from being guilty himself after his death ; for, upon digging up his corpse forty days after his burial, he was found to have all the marks of an arch-vampire. His body was fresh and ruddy, his hair, beard, and nails were grown, and his veins were full of fluid blood, which ran from all parts of his body upon the shroud that he was buried in. The *hadnagy*, or bailiff of the village, who was present at the digging up of the corpse, and was very expert in the whole business of vampirism, ordered a sharp stake to be drove quite through the body of the deceased, and to let it pass through his heart, which was attended with a hideous cry from the

carcass, as if it had been alive. This ceremony being performed, they cut off the head, and burnt the body to ashes. After this, they proceeded in the same manner with the four other persons that died of vampirism, lest they also should be troublesome. But all these executions could not hinder this dreadful prodigy from appearing again last year, at the distance of five years from its first breaking out. In the space of three months, seventeen persons of different ages and sexes died of vampirism, some without any previous illness, and others after languishing two or three days. Among others, it was said, that a girl, named Stanoska, daughter of the Heyduke Jotuitzo, went to bed in perfect health, but awoke in the middle of the night, trembling, and crying out that the son of the Heyduke Millo, who died about nine weeks before, had almost strangled her while she was asleep. From that time she fell into a languishing state, and died at three days' end. Her evidence against Millo's son was looked upon as a proof of his being a *vampire*, and, upon digging up his body, he was found to be such.

" At a consultation of the principal inhabitants of the place, attended by physicians and chirurgeons, it was considered how it was possible that the plague of vampirism should break out afresh, after the precautions that had been taken some years before : and, at last, it was found out that the original offender, Arnold Paul, had not only destroyed the four persons mentioned above, but had killed several beasts, which the late *vampires*, and particularly the son of Millo, had fed upon. Upon this foundation a resolution was taken to dig up all the persons that had died within a certain time. Out of forty were found seventeen, with all the evident tokens of vampirism ; and they had all stakes drove through their hearts, their heads cut off, their bodies burnt, and their ashes thrown into the river.

" All these several enquiries and executions were carried on with all the forms of law, and attested by several officers who were in garrison in that country, by the chirurgeon-majors of the regiments, and by the principal inhabitants of the place. The original papers were all sent, in January last, to the Imperial council of war at Vienna, which had issued out a commission to several officers, to enquire into the truth of the fact."

Methods of Extirpation.—The commonest methods of the extirpation of *vampires* are—(a) beheading the suspected corpse ; (b) taking out the heart ; (c) impaling the corpse with a white-thorn stake (in Russia an aspen), and (d) burning it. Sometimes more than one or all of these precautions is taken. Instances are on record where the graves of as many as thirty or forty persons have been disturbed during the course of an epidemic of vampirism and their occupants impaled or beheaded. Persons who dread the visits or attacks of a *vampire* sleep with a wreath made of garlic round the neck, as that esculent is supposed to be especially obnoxious to the *vampire*. When impaled the *vampire* is usually said to emit a dreadful cry, but it has been pointed out that the gas from the intestines may be forced through the throat by the entry of the stake into the body, and that this may account for the sound. The method of discovering a *vampire's* grave in Serbia is to place a virgin boy upon a coal-black stallion which has never served a mare and marking the spot where he will not pass. An officer quartered in Wallachia wrote to Calmet as follows, giving him an instance of this method :—

" At the time when we were quartered at Temeswar in Wallachia, there died of this disorder two dragoons of the company in which I was cornet, and several more who had it would have died also, if the corporal of the company had not put a stop to it, by applying a remedy commonly made use of in that country. It is of a very singular kind, and, though infallibly to be depended on, I have never met with it in any Dispensatory.

" They pick out a boy, whom they judge to be too young to have lost his maidenhead, and mount him bare upon a coal-black stone-horse, which has never leaped a mare. This virgin-pair is led about the church-yard, and across all the graves, and wherever the animal stops, and refuses to go on, in spite of all the whipping they can give him, they conclude they have discovered a *vampire*. Upon opening the grave, they find a carcass as fleshy and fair as if the person were only in a slumber. The next step is to cut off his head with a spade, and there issues from the wound such a quantity of fresh and florid blood, that one would swear they had cut the throat of a man in full health and vigour. They then fill up the pit, and it may be depended on that the disorder will cease, and that all who were ill of it will gradually get strength, like people that recover slowly after a long illness. Accordingly this happened to our troopers, who were attacked with the distemper. I was at that time commanding officer of the troop, the captain and lieutenant being absent, and was extremely angry at the corporal for having made this experiment without me. It was with great difficulty that I prevailed with myself not to reward him with a good cudgel, a thing of which the officers of the emperor's service are usually very liberal. I would not, for the world, have been absent upon this occasion, but there was now no remedy."

A Bulgarian belief is that a wizard or sorcerer may entrap a *vampire* by placing in a bottle some food for which the *vampire* has a partiality, and on his entry in the shape of fluff or straw, sealing up the flask and throwing it into the fire.

Scientific Theories of Vampirism.—The English custom of piercing suicide's bodies with a stake would appear to be a survival of the belief in vampirism. Such demons are also to be seen in the Polynesian *tii*, the Malayan *hantu penyardin*, a dog-headed water-demon, and the *kephn* of the Karens, which under the form of a wizard's head and stomach devours human souls. Tylor considers *vampires* to be " causes conceived in spiritual form to account for specific facts of wasting disease." Afanasief regards them as thunder-gods and spirits of the storm who during winter slumber in their cloud-coffins to rise again in spring and draw moisture from the clouds. But this theory will scarcely recommend itself to anyone with even a slight knowledge of mythological science. Calmet's difficulty in believing in *vampires* was that he could not understand how a spirit could leave its grave and return thence with ponderable matter in the form of blood, leaving no traces showing that the surface of the earth above the grave had been stirred. But this view might be combated by the theory of the precipitation of matter.

Literature.—De Schertz, *Magia Posthuma*, Olmutz, 1706; Calmet, *A Dissertation on Apparitions* (Eng. trans.), 1759; Ennemoser, *History of Magic*; Herenberg, *Philosophicæ et Christianæ Cogitationes de Vampires*, 1733; *Mercure Galant*, 1693 and 1694; Ranfft, *De Masticatione Mortuorum in Tumulis*, Leipsic, 1728; Rehrius, *De Masticatione Mortuorum*, 1679; Herz, *Der Werwolf*, Stuttgart, 1862; Ralston, *Songs of the Russian People*, 1872, *Russian Folk Tales*, 1873; Mannhardt, *Ueber Vampirismus*, in Vol. IV. of *Zeitschrift fur Deutsche Mythologie.*

Van Calear, Elise : (*See* Holland.)

Van Herwerden, T. D. : (*See* Holland.)

Vana Vasin : (*See* India.)

Vanderdeken : (*See* Flying Dutchman.)

Vanga : The unenrolled members of the Ndembo Secret Society of the Lower Congo.

Varley, Cromwell : A distinguished electrician and fellow of the Royal Society, who on several occasions turned his

knowledge of electricity to account in devising tests for spiritualistic mediums. In March, 1874 he applied such a test to Miss Florence Cook, during a materialisation séance. The experiment, in common with many of these earlier tests, has since been proved inadequate. (*See* **Spiritualism.**)

Vassago : The spirit of the crystal, who is invoked by the crystal-gazer for the purposes of his art.

Vaudoux : (*See* **West Indian Islands.**)

Vaughan, Diana : Authoress of *Memories of an ex-Palladist* in which she states that she was a member of a Satanist association of Masonic origin in Charleston, U.S.A., presided over at one period by Albert Pike (q.v.). Her pretentions, which will scarcely bear a strict investigation, are that she was the chosen bride of Asmodeus and was on terms of intimacy with Lucifer, the deity worshipped by the Palladist confraternity.

Vaulderie : A connection with the Satanic powers, so called from Robinet de Vaulse, a hermit, one of the first persons accused of the crime. In 1453 the Prior of St. Germain-en-Laye, Guillaume de l'Allive, a doctor of theology, was accused of *Vaulderie*, and sentenced to perpetual imprisonment. Six years later there was burned at Lille a hermit named Alphonse, who preached heterodox doctrines. Such were the preludes of a persecution which, in the following year, the Vicar of the Inquisition, administrator of the Diocese of Arras, seconded by the Count d'Etampes, Governor of Artois, directed at first against loose women, but afterwards against citizens, magistrates, knights, and especially the wealthy. The procedures against the accused had almost always for their basis some accusation of sorcery. Most of the unhappy creatures confessed to have attended the " Witch's Sabbath," and the strange revelations wrung from them by torture, will give some idea of the ceremonies which according to the popular tradition, were enacted in the lurid festivals presided over by Satan. Here are some extracts from the judgment pronounced at Arras in 1460 upon five women, a painter, and a poet, nick-named " an abbé of little sense," and aged about seventy, and several others, who all perished in the flames kindled by a barbarous ignorance and fed by a cruel superstition.

" And the said Inquisition did say and declare, that those hereinunder named had been guilty of *Vaulderei* in manner following, that is to say :—' That when they wished to go to the said *Vaulderie*, they, with an ointment given to them by the devil, anointed a small wooden rod and their palms and their hands ; then they put the wand between their legs, and soon they flew wherever they wished to go, over fair cities, woods and streams ; and the devil carried them to the place where they should hold their assembly, and in this place they found others, and tables placed, loaded with wines and viands ; and there they found a demon in the form of a goat, a dog, an ape, or sometimes a man ; and they made their oblation and homage to the said demon, and adored him, and yielded up to him their souls, and all, or at least some portion, of their bodies ; then, with burning candles in their hands, they kissed the rear of the goat-devil. . . . . (Here the Inquisitor becomes untranslatable.) . . . . And this homage done, they trod and trampled upon the Cross, and befouled it with their spittle, in contempt of Jesus Christ, and the Holy Trinity, then turned their backs towards heaven and the firmament in contempt of God. And after they had all eaten and drunk well, they had carnal intercourse all together, and even the devil assumed the guise of man and woman, and had intercourse with both sexes. And many other crimes, most filthy and detestable, they committed, as much against God as against nature, which the said Inquisitor did not dare to name, that innocent ears might not be told of such villainous enormites.' "

The eagerness displayed by the Inquisitor and his acolytes so excited the public indignation, that at the close of the year 1460 the judges did not dare any longer to condemn to death the unfortunate wretches accused, it is said only for the purpose of depriving them of their property. As in the case of all great wrongs, a reaction set in—a re-action in favour of the right ; and thirty years later, when the county of Artois had been re-united to the Crown, the Parliament of Paris declared, on the 20th of May, 1491, these trials " abusive, void, and falsely made," and condemned the heirs of the duke of Burgundy and the principal judges to an amend of 500 Parisian livres, to be distributed as a reparation among the heirs of the victims.

Vecchia Religione, La : (*See* **Italy.**)

Vedanta Yoga : The higher branch of Hindu yoga practice.

Vehm-Gerichte : A secret tribunal which during the Middle Ages exercised a peculiar jurisdiction in Germany and especially in Westphalia. Its origin is quite uncertain. The sessions were often held in secret, and the uninitiated were forbidden to attend them on pain of death. The most absurd stories have been circulated concerning them,— that they met in underground chambers and so forth. These have been discounted by modern research. Far from dabbling in the occult, these courts frequently punished persons convicted of witchcraft and sorcery.

Veleda : A prophetess among the ancient Germans, of whom Tacitus says : " She exercises a great authority, for women have been held here from the most ancient times to be prophetic, and, by excessive superstition, as divine. The fame of *Veleda* stood on the very highest elevation, for she foretold to the Germans a prosperous issue, but to the legions their destruction ! *Veleda* dwelt upon a high tower, whence messengers were dispatched bearing her oracular counsels to those who sought them ; but she herself was rarely seen, and none was allowed to approach her. Cercalis is said to have secretly begged her to let the Romans have better success in war. The Romans, as well as those of her own race, set great store on her prophecies, and sent her valuable gifts. In the reign of the Emperor Vespasian she was honoured as a goddess."

Veltis : An evil spirit who assaulted St. Margaret but was overcome by her. On being asked by St. Margaret who he was and whence he came, he replied : " My name is *Veltis*, and I am one of those whom Solomon by virtue of his spells, confined in a copper cauldron at Babylon ; but when the Babylonians, in the hope of finding treasure dug up the cauldron and opened it, we all made our escape. Since that time our efforts have been directed to the destruction of righteous persons ; and I have long been striving to turn thee from the course thou hast embraced."

Verdelet : A demon of the second order, master of ceremonies at the infernal court. He is charged with the transport of witches to the Sabbath. He takes the names of Master Persil, Sante-Buisson, and other names of a pleasant sound, so as to entice women into his snares.

Veritas Society : (*See* **Holland.**)

Verite La (Journal) : (*See* **France.**)

Vervain : A sacred herb with which the altars of Jupiter were sprinkled. Water containing *vervain* was also sprinkled in houses to cast out evil spirits. Among the druids particularly it was employed in connection with many forms of superstition. They gathered it at day-break, before the sun had risen. Later sorcerers followed the same usage, and the demonologists believe that in order to evoke demons it is necessary to be crowned with *vervain*.

Vestments, Magical : (*See* **Magic.**)

Vidya in Theosophy is the knowledge by which man on the Path can discern the true from the false and so direct his efforts aright by means of the mental faculties which he has learnt to use. It is the antithesis of *Avidya*. (*See* **Path, Avidya,** and **Theosophy.**)

Viedma : Russian name for a witch. (*See* **Slavs.**)

Vila, The : Vili were nymphs who frequented the forests that clothe the bases of the Eastern Alps. They have been seen traversing glades, mounted on stags ; or driving from peak to peak on chariots of cloud. Serbian ballads tell how Marko the great hero of ancient Serbia, was joined in bond of " brotherhood " with a *Vila*, who showed to him the secrets of the future. At that period Serbia was a mighty nation, extending from the Alps to the Black Sea, from the Danube to the Adriatic—before her freedom was lost at the battle of Varna.

Vile : (*See* **Slavs.**)

Villorjaci : (*See* **Slavs.**)

Villanova, Arnold de : *Arnold de Villanova* was a physician by profession, and is reported to have been something of a theologian besides a skilled alchemist. His natal place has never been determined, but Catalonia, Milan and Montpellier have all been suggested ; while as to the precise date of his advent, this too is uncertain yet appears to have been about the middle of the thirteenth century. *Arnold* studied medicine for many years at the Sorbonne in Paris, which in mediæval times was the principal European nursery of physicians ; and thereafter he travelled for a long time in Italy, while subsequently he penetrated to Spain. Here, however, he heard that a friend of his was in the hands of the dreaded Inquisition ; and, fearing that he likewise might be trepanned by that body, he withdrew speedily to Italy. For a considerable period he lived at Naples, enjoying there the friendly patronage of the Neapolitan sovereign, and spending his time less in the actual practice of his profession than in the compilation of various scientific treatises ; while at a later date he was appointed physician in ordinary to Pope Clement V., so presumably the rest of his life was spent mainly at Rome, or possibly at Avignon. Meanwhile his interest in alchemy had become widely known, and indeed many people declared that his skill herein was derived from communications with the arch-fiend himself, and that the physician accordingly deserved nothing less than burning at the stake ; while he also elicited particular enmity from the clergy by sneering openly at the monastic *régime*, and by declaring boldly that works of charity are more acceptable to God than the repetition of *paternosters*. Thanks to Papal favour, nevertheless, *Arnold* went unscathed by his enemies ; but soon after his death, which occurred about the year 1310, the Inquisition decided that they had dealt too leniently with the deceased, and in consequence they signified their hatred of him, by ordering certain of his writings to be burned publicly at Tarragona.

Arnold was acquainted with the preparation of oil of turpentine and oil of rosemary, while the marcasite frequently mentioned by him is supposed to be identical with bismuth. His most important treatises are his *Thesaurus Thesaurorum, Rosarium Philosophorum, Speculam Alchemiæ* and *Perfectum Magisterum* ; while two others of some moment are his *Testamentum* and *Scientia Scientiæ*. A collected edition of his works was issued in 1520, while several writings from his pen are embodied in the *Bibliotheca Chemica Curiosa* of Mangetus, published in 1702.

Villars, l'Abbe de Montfaucon de : French Mystic (1635-1673.) This Churchman, author and mystic was what the French style " un méridional," being a native of southern Franch. He was born in 1635 at Toulouse, not very far from the seaport town of Bordeaux ; and at an early age he espoused holy orders, while in 1667 he left the south and came to Paris, eager to win fame as a preacher. Nor did this ambition of his go wholly ungratified, his eloquence in the pulpit winning him numerous admirers ; but he soon grew more interested in literature than in clerical affairs, and in 1670 he published his first and most important book, *Comte du Gabalis*. Ostensibly a novel, this volume is largely a veiled satire on the writings of La Calprenède, at this time very popular both in France and in England ; but the satirical element in *Villars'* paper is supplemented by a curious blend of history, philosophy and mysticism ; and, as much of the last-named is of a nature distinctly hostile to the dogmas of Rome, the author soon found himself in ill odour with his brother clerics. Probably it was for this reason that he renounced the pulpit, yet his literary activities were not vitiated by persecution ; and in 1671 he issued *De la Délicetesse*, a speculative treatise, couched in the form of dialogues, in which the author takes the part of one, a priest who had lately been writing in opposition to Port Royal doctrines. Like its predecessor this new book made a considerable stir, and *Villars* began to write voluminously, at the same time plunging deeply into the study of various kinds of mysticism ; but his activities were suddenly terminated in an unexpected fashion, for in 1673 he was murdered on the public high-road not far from Lyons, whither he was journeying from Paris. Presumably he had incurred the hatred of some one but the question is shrouded in mystery ; and, be the solution what it may, no attempt appears to have been made to frustrate the posthumous publication of divers works from *Villars'* pen. Within the first decade succeeding his death three such works appeared, *L'Amour sans Faiblesse, Anne de Bretague et Ailmanzaris*, and *Critique de la Bérénice de Racine et de Corneille*, the last-named subsequently winning the enconiums of a shrewd judge, Mme. de Sévigné ; while so late as 1715 a further production by *Villars* was issued, a sequel to the *Comte du Gabalis*, bearing the significant title of *Nouveaux Entretiens sur les Sciences secrètes*. This volume elicited ready and wide interest among thinkers in the eighteenth century, and it may be briefly defined as a treatise opposing the philosophical theories of Descartes, or rather, opposing the popular misapprehension and abuse of these.

Vintras, Eugene : A Norman peasant of great devoutness, who in the year 1839 was fixed upon by the Saviours of Louis XVII. (q.v.), as a fitting successor to their prophet Martin who had just died. They addressed a letter to the pretended Louis XVII. and arranged that it should fall into the hands of *Vintras*. It abounded in good promises for the reign to come and in mystical expressions calculated to inflame the brain of a person of weak and excitable character such as *Vintras* was. In a letter *Vintras* himself describes as follows the manner in which this communication reached him :—

" Towards nine o'clock I was occupied in writing, when there was a knock at the door of the room in which I sat, and supposing that it was a workman who came on business, I said rather brusquely, ' Come in.' Much to my astonishment, in place of the expected workman, I saw an old man in rags. I asked merely what he wanted. He answered with much tranquillity, ' Don't disturb yourself, Pierre Michel.' Now, these names are never used in addressing me, for I am known everywhere as *Eugène*, and even in signing documents I do not make use of my first names. I was conscious of a certain emotion at the old man's answer, and this increased when he said : ' I am utterly tired, and wherever I appear they treat me with disdain, or as a thief.' The words alarmed me considerably, though they were spoken in a saddened and even a woeful tone. I arose and placed a ten sous piece in his hand, saying, ' I do not take you for that, my good man,' and while speaking I made him understand that I wished to see him out. He received it in silence but turned his back with a pained air. No sooner had he set foot on the last step

than I shut the door and locked it. I did not hear him go down, so I called a workman and told him to come up to my room. Under some business pretext, I was wishing him to search with me all the possible places which might conceal my old man, whom I had not seen go out. The workman came accordingly. I left the room in his company, again locking my door. I hunted through all the nooks and corners, but saw nothing.

" I was about to enter the factory when I heard on a sudden the bell ringing for mass, and felt glad that, notwithstanding the disturbance, I could assist at the sacred ceremony. I ran back to my room to obtain a prayer book and, on the table where I had been writing, I found a letter addressed to Mme. de Generès in London ; it was written and signed by M. Paul de Montfleury of Caen, and embodied a refutation of heresy, together with a profession of orthodox faith. The address notwithstanding, this letter was intended to place before the Duke of Normandy the most important truths of our holy Catholic, Apostolic and Roman religion. On the document was laid the ten sous piece which I had given to the old man."

Vintras immediately concluded that the bringer of the letter was a messenger from heaven, and became devoted to the cause of Louis XVII. He became a Visionary. He had bloody sweats, he saw hearts painted with his own blood appear on hosts, accompanied by inscriptions in his own spelling. Many believed him a prophet and followed him, among them several priests, who alleged that they partook of his occult vision. Doctors analysed the fluid which flowed from the hosts and certified it to be human blood. His enemies referred these miracles to the Devil. *Vintras'* followers regarded him as a new Christ. But one of them, Gozzoli, published scandalous accounts of his doings, alleging that horrible obscenities and sacrilegious masses took place in their private chapel at Tilly-sur-seules. The unspeakable abominations alluded to are contained in a pamphlet entitled *Le Prophète Vintras* (1851). The sect was formally condemned by the Pope, and *Vintras* constituted himself sovereign Pontiff. He was arrested on a charge of exploiting his cult for money, was tried at Caen, and sentenced to five years' imprisonment. When freed in 1845 he went to England, and in London resumed the head-ship of his cult which seems to have flourished for some time afterwards.

Virgil, the Enchanter : (*See* **Italy.**)

Visions : (From Latin *visus*, p.p. of *videre*, to see.) The appearance to mortals of supernatural persons, or scenes. Of great frequency in early and mediæval times, and among savage or semi-civilised races, *visions* seem to have decreased proportionately with the advance of learning and enlightenment. Thus among the Greeks and Romans of the classic period they were comparatively rare, though *visions of* demons or gods were occasionally seen. On the other hand, among Oriental races the seeing of *visions* was a common occurrence, and these took more varied shapes. In mediæval Europe, again, *visions* were almost commonplaces, and directions were given by the Church to enable men to distinguish *visions* of divine origin from those false delusions which were the work of the Evil One. *Visions* may be roughly divided into two classes—those which are spontaneous, and those which are induced. But, indeed, the great majority belong to the latter class. Ennemoser enumerates the causes of such appearances thus : (1) Sensitive organism and delicate constitution ; (2) Religious education and ascetic life (fasting, penance, etc.) ; (3) Narcotics—opium, wine, incense, narcotic salves (witch-salves) ; (4) Delirium, monomania ; (5) Fear and expectation, preparatory words, songs, and prayers. Among the *visions* induced by prayer and fasting, and the severe self-discipline of the religious ascetic, must be included many historical or traditional instances—the *visions* of St. Francis of Assisi, St. Anthony, St. Bernard Ignatius, St. Catherine of Siena, St. Hildegarde, Joan of Arc. It may be noted that the convent has ever been the special haunt of religious *visions*, probably for the reasons above mentioned. But the most potent means for the inductions of visionary appearances are those made use of by the Orientals. Narcotics of all kinds—opium, haschish, and so on—are indulged in, and physical means used for this express purpose. Thus the Brahmins will gaze for hours at a time at the sun or moon, will remain for months in practically the some position, or will practise all manner of mortification of the body, so that they may fall at length into the visionary sleep (a species of catalepsy.) The narcotic salves with which they anoint themselves are said to be similar to the witch-salves used in the Middle Ages, which induced in the witch the hallucination that she was flying through the air on a goat or a broomstick. Opium also is said to produce a sensation of flying, as well as *visions* of celestial delight. Alcoholic intoxication induces *visions* of insects and small animals, as does also nitrogen. The vapours rising from the ground in some places, or those to be found in certain caverns, are said to exercise an effect similar to that of narcotics. The Indians of North America practise similar external methods of inducing *visions*—solitude, fasting, and the use of salves or ointments. The savages of Africa have dances which, by producing severe dizziness, help them towards the desired visionary ecstasy. The northern savages attain the same end by the use of drums and noisy music. Spontaneous *visions*, though less common, are yet sufficiently numerous to merit attention here. The difficulty is, of course, to know just how far " fear and expectation " may have operated to induce the *vision*. In many cases, as in that of Swedenborg, the *visions* may have commenced as " *visions* of the night," hardly to be distinguished from dreams, and so from *vision* of an " internal " nature to clearly externalised apparitions. Swedenborg himself declares that when seeing visions of the latter class he used his senses exactly as when awake, dwelling with the spirits as a spirit, but able to return to his body when he pleased. An interesting case of spontaneous *vision* is that of Benvenuto Cellini (q.v.). *Visions* are by no means confined to the sense of sight. Taste, hearing, smelling, touch, may all be experienced in a *vision*. Joan of Arc, for instance, heard voices encouraging her to be the deliverer of her country. Examples may be drawn from the Bible, as the case of the child Samuel in the Temple, and instances could be multiplied from all ages and all times. The *visions* of Pordage and the " Philadelphia Society,"—or, as they called themselves later, the " Angelic Brethren "—in 1651 are noteworthy in this respect because they include the taste of " brimstone, salt, and soot." In the presence of the " Angelic Brethren " pictures were drawn on the window-panes by invisible hands, and were seen to move about.

Physiological exlpanations of *visions* have from time to time been offered. Plato says : " The eye is the organ of a fire which does not burn but gives a mild light. The rays proceeding from the eye meet those of the outward light. With the departure of the outward light the inner also becomes less active ; all inward movements become calmer and less disturbed ; and should any more prominent influences have remained they become in various points where they congregate, so many pictures of the fancy."

Democritus held that *visions* and dreams are passing shapes, ideal forms proceeding from other beings. Of death-bed *visions* Plutarch says : " It is not probable that in death the soul gains new powers which it was not before possessed of when the heart was confined within the chains of the body ; but it is much more probable that these powers were always in being, though dimmed and clogged by the body ; and the soul is only then able to practise them when the corporeal bonds are loosened, and the drooping limbs and stagnating juices no longer oppress it." The spiritualistic theory of *visions* can hardly be called a physiological one, save in so far as spirit is regarded as refined matter. An old theory of visionary ecstasy on these lines was that the soul left the body and proceeded to celestial spheres, where it remained in contemplation of divine scenes and persons. Very similar to this is the doctrine of Swedenborg, whose spirit, he believed, could commune with discarnate spirits—the souls of the dead—as one of themselves. To this may be directly traced the doctrines of modern spiritualism, which thus regards *visions* as actual spirits or spirit scenes, visible to the ecstatic or entranced subject whose spirit was projected to discarnate planes. The question whether or no *visions* are contagious has been much disputed. It has been said that such appearances may be transferred from one person to another by the laying on of hands. In the case of the Scottish seers such a transference may take place even by accidental contact with the seer. The *vision* of the second person is, however, less distinct than that of the original seer. The same idea prevailed with regard to the visions of magnetised patients. In so far as these may be identified with the collective hallucinations of the hypnotic state, there is no definite scientific evidence to prove their existence.

Visions have by no means been confined to the ignorant or the superstitious. Many men of genius have been subject to visionary appearance. While Raphael was trying to paint the Madonna she appeared to him in a *vision*. The famous composition known as the " Devil's Sonata " was dictated to Tartini by the Evil One himself. Goethe also had *visions*. Blake's portraits of the Patriarchs were done from visionary beings which appeared to him in the night. And such instances might easily be multiplied.

Vitality, according to theosophists, comes from the sun. When a physical atom is transfused with *vitality*, it draws to itself six other atoms and thus makes an etheric element. The sum of their *vitality* is then divided among each of the atoms and in this state the element enters the physical body by means of one of the sense organs or *chaksams* of the etheric double—that situated opposite the spleen. Here the element is divided into its component parts and these are conveyed to the various parts of the physical body. It is on *vitality* that the latter depends, not only for life but for its well-being in life. A person sufficiently supplied with it enjoys good health and one insufficiently supplied is afflicted with poor health. In the case of a healthy person, however, more *vitality* is drawn in than is necessary for the vital purposes and the superfluous *vitality* acts beneficially on his neighbours, whether human or animal, while it can also be directed in certain definite channels to the healing of diseases and so forth. With unhealthy persons, the case is, of course, reversed, and they devitalise the more healthy, with whom they come in contact.

Vjestica, a Slav name for a witch : (*See* **Slavs.**)

Vukub-Came : (*See* **Hell.**)

W

Wafer : The sacred *wafer* is often used by devil-worshippers for purposes of profanation. (*See* **Devil-worship.**) There was found in the house of the notorious witch, Dame Alice Kyteler (q.v.), a *wafer* of sacramental bread, bearing thereon the name of the Devil.

Waldenses : The name of a Christian sect which arose in the south of France about 1170. They were much the same in origin and ethics as the Albigenses (q.v.), that is, their religious system rested upon that of Manichæism, which believed in dualism and severe asceticism. It undoubtedly arose from the desire of the bourgeois class to have changes made in the clerical discipline of the Roman Church. Its adherents called themselves *cathari* thus demonstrating the eastern origin of their system. There were two classes of these, *credentes* and *perfecti*, or neophytes and adepts,— the perfecti only being admitted to the esoteric doctrines of the Waldensian Church. Outwardly its aim and effort was rationalistic ; but the inner doctrine partook more of the occult. It was in 1170 that Peter Waldo, a rich merchant of Lyons, sold his goods and gave them to the poor, and from him the sect was named. The earliest account of Waldensian beliefs is that of an enemy, Sacconi, an inquisitor of the Holy Office, who wrote about the middle of the thirteenth century. He divides the Waldensians into two classes, those of Lombardy, and those north of the Alps. The latter believed that any layman might consecrate the sacrament of the altar, and that the Roman Church was not the Church of Christ ; while the Lombardian sect held that the Roman Church was the Scarlet Woman of the Apocalypse. They also believed that all men were priests. As their opinions became more widespread, persecution became more severe, and the Waldensians latterly withdrew themselves altogether from the Church of Rome, and chose ministers for themselves by election. Papal bulls were issued for their extermination, and a crusade was directed against them ; but they survived these attacks, and so late as the time of Cromwell were protected by him against the Duke of Savoy and the French king. Their ministers were later subsidised by the government of Queen Anne, and this subsidy was carried on until the time of Napoleon, when he granted them an equivalent. Latterly they have received much assistance from various Protestant countries of Europe, especially from England ; and at the present time number some 12,000 to 13,000 communicants.

During the Middle Ages, it was strongly held by the priesthood of the Roman Church that, like the Albigenses, the Waldensians had a diabolic element in their religion and they have been from time to time classed with the various secret societies that sprang up in mediæval Europe, such as the Knights Templar, the Rosicrucians, and so forth ; but although they possessed an esoteric doctrine of their own, there is no reason to believe that this was in any way magical, nor in any manner more " esoteric " than the inner doctrine of any other Christian sect.

Walder, Phileas : A Swiss, originally a Lutheran minister, a well-known occultist and spiritualist, and friend of Eliphas Levi (q.v.). He is represented by the pseudo-historians of " Satanism " as a right-hand man of Albert Pike (q.v.) in his alleged diabolic practices at Charleston, U.S.A. (*See* **Devil Worship**.) In reality *Walder* was an earnest mason and mystic.

Wallace, Alfred Russel : A distinguished British naturalist, who discovered the theory of evolution independent of Darwin. He was born at Usk, in Monmouthshire, on the 8th of January, 1823. His scientific studies included an enquiry into the phenomena of spiritualism, and he became a firm believer in the genuineness of these manifestations. *Dr. Wallace* had unique opportunities for studying these in connection with Mrs. Guppy, who, as Miss Nichols, lived for a time with his sister. Among his works was one entitled *Miracles and Modern Spiritualism*, published in 1881. *Dr. Wallace's* views on psychic phenomena remained unchanged until his death in 1903. His scientific position made him a tower of strength to the spiritualists.

Wallenstein, Albert Von, Duke of Friedland : (*See* **Astrology**.)

Wandering Jew, The : A mediæval German legend which has several forms. Through various writers, and differing in detail, the essential features of the narratives which have been handed down to us, are the same. The legend is that as Christ was dragged on his way to Calvary, he passed the house of a Jew, and stopping there, sought to rest a little, being weary under the weight of his cross. The Jew, however, inspired with the adverse enthusiasm of the mob, drove Him on, and would not allow Him to rest there. Jesus, looking at him, said, " I shall stand and rest, but thou shalt go till the last day." Ever afterwards the Jew was compelled to wander over the earth, till this prophecy should be fulfilled.

The legend of the *Wandering Jew* is to be regarded as the epic of the Semite people in the Middle Ages.

In some parts of Germany we find the *Wandering Jew* identified with the Wild Huntsman, whilst in several French districts that mythical character is regarded as the wind of the night. The blast in his horn, which, rushing through the valleys creates a hollow booming sound not unlike a great bugle. In this legend we have in all probability the clue to the mythological side of the story of the wandering *Jew*. Or perhaps the idea of the *Wandering Jew* has been fused with that of the conception of the wind. The resemblance between the two conceptions would be too strong to escape the popular mind. From a literary point of view this legend has been treated by Eugene Sué and Croly.

Wannein Nat : An evil spirit. (*See* **Burma**.)

War, Occult Phenomena during the : A surprising number of ideas regarding the supernatural have crystallized around the circumstances of the war. Perhaps the most striking of these was the alleged vision of angels at Mons. The first notice regarding this, or at least the most important and public record of the occurrence, was that contained in the *Evening News* for September 14th, 1915, in which Mr. Machen described the evidence as given to him by an officer who was in the retreat from Mons. This officer was a member of a well-known army family and was a person of great credibility, who stated that on August 26th, 1914, he was fighting in the battle of Le Cateau, from which his division retired in good order. " On the night of the 27th," he says, " I was riding along the column with two other officers. . . . As we rode along I became conscious of the fact that in the fields on both sides of the road along which we were marching I could see a very large body of horsemen. . . . the other two officers had stopped talking. At last one of them asked me if I saw anything in the fields. I told them what I had seen. The third officer confessed that he, too, had been watching these horsemen for the past twenty minutes. So convinced were we that they were really cavalry, that at the next halt one of the officers took a party of men out to reconnoitre and found no one there. The night then grew darker and we saw no more."

Mr. Harold Begbie in his book *On the Side of the Angels* states that a vision of angels was seen in the retreat from Mons and gives the narrative of a soldier, who states that an officer came up to him " in a state of great anxiety " and pointed out to him a " strange light which seemed to be quite distinctly outlined and was not a reflection of the moon, nor were there any clouds in the neighbourhood. The light became brighter and I could see quite distinctly three shapes, one in the centre having what looked like outspread wings. The other two were not so large, but were quite plainly distinct from the centre one. They appeared to have a long, loose-hanging garment of a golden tint and they were above the German line facing us. We stood watching them for about three-quarters of an hour." All the men in the battalion who saw this with the exception of five were killed. Mr. Begbie goes on to say that he was told by a nurse that a dying soldier spoke to her of the reluctance of the Germans to attack our line, " because of the thousands of troops behind us." This man had heard German prisoners say so and fully believed in the phantasmal nature of those supporting hosts.

In his monograph on the Bowmen at Mons, Mr. Machen put forward the idea that those seen before the retreat from Mons were the spirits of the English bowmen who had fought at Agincourt and this idea gained wide prevalence, an interesting monograph being written upon it by Mr. Ralph Shirley. Men from the front, too, have stated to interviewers that phantasms of the dead frequently appeared in the space between the German and British trenches called " No Man's Land."

Mr. Shirley has also written an excellent pamphlet on " Prophecies and Omens of the Great War " dealing with the various oracular utterances on the gigantic struggle, which may be referred to with confidence.

Stories, too, were current in the earlier times of the war regarding the appearance of saintly and protective figures resembling the patrons of the several allied countries. Thus the English were convinced that in certain engagements they had beheld the figure of Saint George mounted on a white charger and the French were equally sure that the figure in question was either Saint Denis or Joan of Arc. Wounded men in base hospitals asked for medallions or coins on which the likenesses of these saints were impressed in order to verify the statements they made.

Wayland Smith : A famous character in German mythological romance and father of Weltich, whom he trained in the art of warfare and sent to the Court of Dietrich in Bern. To him he gave the sword Miming and told him of a mermaid, his ancestress, to whom he was to apply when in difficulty. He is also referred to in the Sigfried story, being in company with a smith named Mimi, when Sigfried joins the smithy. His workmanship is praised in the Beowulf Saga and he is mentioned there and elsewhere as a maker of impregnable armour. He is the supernatural smith of the Teutonic peoples, and is comparable to Vulcan in Roman, and to Hephaistos in Greek mythology.

Weir, Major : (*See* Scotland.)

Weirtz : (*See* Hypnotism.)

Weishaupt : (*See* Illuminati.)

Werner, Dr. Heinrich : (*See* Spiritualism.)

Werwolf : A man temporarily or permanently transformed into a wolf, from the Anglo-Saxon *wer*, a man, and *wulf*, a wolf. It is a phase of Lycanthropy (q.v.), and in ancient and mediæval times was of very frequent occurrence. It was, of course, in Europe where the wolf was one of the largest carnivorous animals, that the superstition gained currency, similar tales in other countries usually introducing bears, tigers, and so forth.

The belief is probably a relic of early cannibalism. Communities of semi-civilised people would begin to shun those who devoured human flesh, and they would be ostracised and classed as wild beasts, the idea that they had something in common with these would grow, and the conception that they were able to transform themselves into veritable animals would be likely to arise therefrom.

There were two kinds of *werwolf*, voluntary and involuntary. The voluntary would be, as has been said, those persons who, because of their taste for human flesh, had withdrawn from intercourse with their fellows. These appeared to possess a certain amount of magical power, or at least sufficient of it to transform themselves into the animal shape at will. This they effected by merely disrobing, by the taking off a girdle made of human skin, or, putting on a similar belt of wolf-skin, obviously a substitute for an entire wolf-skin. But we also hear of their donning the entire skin. In other instances the body is rubbed with a magic ointment, or water is drunk out of a wolf's footprint. The brains of the animal are also eaten. Olaus Magnus says " that the *werwolves* of Livonia drained a cup of beer on initiation, and repeated certain magic words. In order to throw off the wolf shape the animal girdle was removed, or else the magician merely muttered a certain formula. In some instances the transformation was supposed to be the work of Satan.

The superstition regarding *werwolves* seems to have been exceedingly prevalent in France during the 16th century as is evidenced by numerous trials, in some of which it is clearly shown that murder and cannibalism took place. Self-hallucination, too, was accountable for some of these cases, the supposed *werwolves* fully admitting that they had transformed themselves and had slain numerous persons. But at the beginning of the 17th century, commonsense came to the rescue, and persons making such confessions were not credited. In Teutonic and Slavonic countries it was complained by men of learning that *werwolves* did more damage than the real criminals, and a regular " college " or institution for the practice of the art of animal transformation was attributed to them.

Involuntary *werwolves* were often persons transformed into an animal shape because of the commission of sin, and condemned to pass so many years in that form. Thus certain saints metamorphosed sinners into wolves. In Armenia it is thought that sinful women are condemned to pass seven years in the form of a wolf. To such a woman a demon appears, bringing a wolf-skin. He commands her to don it, from which moment she becomes a wolf with all the nature of a wild beast, devouring her own children and those of strangers, wandering forth at night, undeterred by locks, bolts, or bars, returning only with morning to resume her human form.

Romance, especially French romance, is full of *werwolves*, and one of the most remarkable instances of this is the Lay by Marie de France entitled *Bisclaveret*, the Lay of a *werwolf*.

Many *werwolves* were innocent persons suffering through the witchcraft of others. To regain their true form it was necessary for them to kneel in one spot for a hundred years, to lose three drops of blood, to be hailed as a *werwolf*, to have the sign of the cross made on their bodies, to be addressed thrice by their baptismal names, or to be struck thrice on the forehead with a knife.

According to Donat de Hautemer, quoted by Goulart, " there are some lycanthropes who are so dominated by their melancholy humour that they really believe themselves to be transformed into wolves. This malady, according to the testimony of Aetius in his sixth book, chapter XI., and Paulus in his third book, chapter XVI., and other moderns, is a sort of melancholy, of a black and dismal nature. Those who are attacked by it leave their homes in the months of February, imitate wolves in almost every particular, and wander all night long among the cemeteries and sepulchres, so that one may observe a marvellous change in the mind and disposition, and, above all in the depraved imagination, of the lycanthrope. The memory, however, is still vigorous, as I have remarked in one of this lycanthropic melancholiacs whom we call *werwolves*. For one who was well acquainted with me was one day seized with his affliction, and on meeting him I withdrew a little, fearing that he might injure me. He, having glanced at me for a moment, passed on followed by a crowd of people. On his shoulder he carried the entire leg and thigh of a corpse. Having received careful medical treatment, he was cured of this malady. On meeting me on another occasion he asked me if I had not been afraid when he met me at such and such a place, which made me think that his memory was not hurt by the vehemence of his disease, though his imagination was so greatly damaged."

" Guillaume de Brabant, in the narrative of Wier, repeated by Goulart, has written in his *History* that a certain man of sense and settled understanding was still so tormented by the evil spirit that at a particular season of the year he would think himself a ravening wolf, and would run here and there in the woods, caves and deserts, chasing little children. It was said that this man was often found running about in the deserts like a man out of his senses, and that at last by the grace of God he came to himself and was healed. There was also, as is related by Job Fincel in the second book *On Miracles* a villager near Paule in the year 1541, who believed himself to be a wolf, and assaulted several men in the fields, even killing some. Taken at last, though not without great difficulty, he stoutly affirmed that he was a wolf, and that the only way in which he differed from other wolves was that they wore their hairy coats on the outside, while he wore his between his skin and his flesh. Certain persons, more inhuman and wolfish than he, wished to test the truth of this story, and gashed his arms and legs severely. Then, learning their mistake, and the innocence of the melan-choliac, they passed him over to the consideration of the surgeons, in whose hands he died some days after. Those afflicted with this disease are pale, with dark and haggard eyes, seeing only with difficulty ; the tongue is dry, and the sufferer very thirsty. Pliny and others write that the brain of a bear excites such bestial imaginations. It is even said that one was given to a Spanish gentleman to eat in our times, which so disturbed his mind, that imagining himself to be transformed into a bear, he fled to the mountains and deserts."

" As for the lycanthropes, whose imagination was so damaged," says Goulart, " that by some Satanic efficacy they appeared wolves and not men to those who saw them running about and doing all manner of harm, Bodin maintains that the devil can change the shape of one body into that of another, in the great power that God gives him in this elementary world. He says, then, that there may be lycanthropes who have really been transformed into wolves, quoting various examples and histories to prove his contention. In short, after many disputes, he believes in Colt's forms of lycanthropy. And as for the latter, there is represented at the end of this chapter the summary of his proposition, to wit, that men are sometimes transformed into beasts, retaining in that form the human reason ; it may be that this comes about by the direct power of God, or it may be that he gives this power to Satan, who carries out his will, or rather his redoubtable judgments. And if we confess (he says) the truths of the sacred history in Daniel, concerning the transformation of Nebuchadnezzar, and the history of Lot's wife changed into motionless stone, the changing of men into an ox or a stone is certainly possible ; and consequently the transformation to other animals as well."

G. Peucer says in speaking of lycanthropy : " As for me I had formerly regarded as ridiculous and fabulous the stories I had often heard concerning the transformation of men into wolves ; but I have learnt from reliable sources, and from the testimony of trustworthy witnesses, that such things are not at all doubtful or incredible, since they tell of such transformations taking place twelve days after Christmas in Livonia and the adjacent countries ; as they have been proved to be true by the confessions of those who have been imprisoned and tortured for such crimes. Here is the manner in which it is done. Immediately after Christmas day is past, a lame boy goes round the country calling these slaves of the devil,

of which there are a great number, and enjoining them to follow him. If they procrastinate or go too slowly, there immediately appears a tall man with a whip whose thongs are made of iron chains, with which he urges them onwards, and sometimes lashes the poor wretches so cruelly, that the marks of the whip remain on their bodies till long afterwards, and cause them the greatest pain. As soon as they have set out on their road, they are all changed into wolves. . . . . They travel in thousands, having for their conductor the bearer of the whip, after whom they march. When they reach the fields, they rush upon the cattle they find there, tearing and carrying away all they can, and doing much other damage ; but they are not permitted to touch or wound persons. When they approach any rivers, their guide separates the waters with his whip, so that they seem to open up and leave a dry space by which to cross. At the end of twelve days the whole band scatters, and everyone returns to his home, having regained his own proper form. This transformation, they say, comes about in this wise. The victims fall suddenly on the ground as though they were taken with sudden illness, and remain motionless and extended like corpses, deprived of all feeling, for they neither stir, nor move from one place to another, nor are in any wise transformed into wolves, thus resembling carrion, for although they are rolled or shaken, they give no sign of life."

Bodin relates several cases of lycanthropy and of men changed into beasts.

" Pierre Mamot, in a little treatise he has written on sorcerers, says that he has observed this changing of men into wolves, he being in Savoy at the time. Henry of Cologne in his treatise *de Lamiis* regards the transformation as beyond doubt. And Ulrich in a little book dedicated to the emperor Sigismund, writes of the dispute before the emperor, and says that it was agreed, both on the ground of reason, and of the experience of innumerable examples, that such transformation was a fact ; and he adds that he himself had seen a lycanthrope at Constance, who was accused, convicted, condemned, and finally executed after his confession. And several books published in Germany say that one of the greatest kings of Christendom, who is not long dead, and who had the reputation of being one of the greatest sorcerers in the world, often changed into a wolf."

" I remember that the attorney-general of the King, Bourdin, has narrated to me another which was sent to him from the Low Countries, with the whole trial signed by the judge and the clerks, of a wolf, which was struck by an arrow on the thigh, and afterwards found himself in bed, with the arrow (which he had torn out), on regaining his human shape, and the arrow was recognised by him who had fired it—the time and place testified by the confession of the person."

" Garnier, tried and condemned by the parliament of Dole, being in the shape of a *werwolf*, caught a girl of ten or twelve years in a vineyard of Chastenoy, a quarter of a league from Dole, and having slain her with his teeth and claw-like hands, he ate part of her flesh and carried the rest to his wife. A month later, in the same form, he took another girl, and would have eaten her also, had he not, as he himself confessed, been prevented by three persons who happened to be passing by ; and a fortnight after he strangled a boy of ten in the vineyard of Gredisans, and ate his flesh ; and in the form of a man and not of a wolf, he killed another boy of twelve or thirteen years in a wood of the village of Porouse with the intention of eating him, but was again prevented. He was condemned to be burnt, and the sentence was executed."

" At the parliament of Bezançon, the accused were Pierre Burgot and Michel Verdun, who confessed to having renounced God, and sworn to serve the devil. And Michel Verdun led Burgot to the bord du Chastel Charlon where everyone carried a candle of green wax which shone with a blue flame. There they danced and offered sacrifices to the devil. Then after being anointed they were turned into wolves, running with incredible swiftness; then they were changed again into men, and suddenly transformed back to wolves, when they enjoyed the society of female wolves as much as they had done that of their wives. They confessed also that Burgot had killed a boy of seven years with his wolf-claws and teeth, intending to eat him, but the peasants gave chase, and prevented him. Burgot and Verdun had eaten four girls between them; and they had caused people to die by the touch of a certain powder.''

"Job Fincel, in the eleventh book of his *Marvels* wrote that there was at Padua a lycanthrope who was caught and his wolf-claws cut, and at the same instant he found his arms and feet cut. That is given to strengthen the case against the sorcerers of Vernon (1556) who assembled themselves in an old and ruined chateau under the shape of an infinite number of cats. There happened to arrive there one evening four or five men, who decided to spend the night in the place. They were awakened by a multitude of cats, who assaulted them, killed one of their number, and wounded others. The men, however, succeeded in wounding several of the cats, who found on recovering their human shape that they were badly hurt. And incredible as it may seem, the trial was not proceeded with.''

"But the five inquisitors who had experimented in these causes have left it in writing that there were three sorcerers in Strasbourg who, in the guise of three large cats, assaulted a labourer, and in defending himself he wounded and dispersed the cats, who found themselves, at the same moment, laid on sick-beds, in the form of women severely wounded. At the trial they accused him who had struck them, and he told the judges the hour and the place where he had been assaulted by the cats, and how he had wounded them.'' (*See* **Lycanthropy**.)

West Indian Islands: Magic and sorcery in the *West Indian Islands* are wholly the preserve of the negro population, who possess special magical cults called *Obeah* and *Vaudoux*, variants of West African fetishism. The root idea of Obeahism and Vaudoux is the worship and propitiation of, the snake-god Obi—a West African word typifying the Spirit of Evil. Vaudoux or Voodoo is a form of Obeah practised in Hayti, San Domingo, and the French West Indies. Its rites are always accompanied by the sacrifice of fowls and goats, and in only too many cases by the offering up of the " goat without horns "—the human sacrifice, usually a young girl or boy. The lonely groves and mountain caves where the devotees of Vaudoux enjoy the orgies of a Walpurgis night seldom give up their secrets. There are two sects of Vaudoux—the white and the red. The former, which only believes in the sacrifice of white fowls and goats, is tolerated by the laws of Hayti, and its rites are as commonly practised as those of the Catholic Church. But even the red sect, which openly stands for human sacrifice, is seldom interfered with. The authorities dare not suppress it, for their own policemen and soldiers stand in awe of the " Papaloi,'' and " Mamaloi ''—the priests and priestess of the snake-god. More than that, there have been Presidents of Hayti in recent years who believed in Vaudoux. Hippolyte was even a " Papaloi '' himself. He beat the black goatskin drum in the streets of the capital to call the faithful together to see him kill the *sen-sel* fowl. Another president, Geffard, tried to do his duty and stamp out the cult. A terrible revenge was taken upon him. His young daughter, Cora, was shot

dead as she knelt in prayer before the altar of a church in Port-au-Prince. To-day there is a temple of the red sect in the Haytian capital near a triumphal arch, which is inscribed with the unctuous words, " Liberty—education—progress.'' Under British government Obeahism perforce takes forms less dangerous to the social order than it does in Hayti; but it is none the less a constant public peril in Jamaica and the other British *West Indian Islands*. It is a bitter foe of religion, education and social advancement In olden days it worked by means of wholesale poisoning, and in quite recent days there have been not a few cases of Obeahmen seeking to do murder in the old way. A favourite method of the Obeahmen, both in Jamaica and Hayti, is to mix the infinitesimal hairs of the bamboo in the food of persons who refuse to bow the knee to them. This finally sets up malignant dysentery. If the afflicted one remains contumacious, he dies; if he makes his peace with the Obeahman, and gives him a handsome present, the slow process of poisoning ceases, and he lives. In all the crises and troubles of life the negro flies to the Obeahman. If he has to appear at the " Police Court he pays the Obeahman to go there also and " fix de eye '' of the magistrate, so that he will be discharged. Perhaps he has been turned out of his office of deacon in the Baptist Chapel by a white minister for immorality. In that case the Obeahman will arrange for a choice collection of the most powerful spells—such as dried lizards, fowls' bones, and graveyard earth—to be placed in the minister's Bible for him to stare upon when he looks up the text of his sermon. Then, if the Obeah works properly, the erring deacon will be received back to office. Even coloured men of education and official position are often tainted with Obeahism. They often make use of it for profit and to increase their power over the ignorant negroes. The mulatto chairman of a Parochial Board—the Jamaican equivalent of our County Council—was sent to goal for practising Obeah only a few years ago. A prominent member of the Kingston City Council was the leading Obeahman in the island—the pontiff of the cult. He was so clever that the police could never catch him, although he was supposed to make over £3,000 a year by his nefarious practices. Once some detectives raided his place, but he received timely warning and fled.

A writer to the press thus describes a " red " Vaudoux ceremony: " I had seen the ' white ' ritual several times in Port-au-Prince and elsewhere when at last I was permitted through the kindness of a mulatto general, to witness the ' red ' rite. I was informed that only cocks and goats would be sacrificed, and that turned out to be the fact. The General conducted me to a small wood about three miles from the town of Jacmel. By the light of kerosene oil flares I saw about forty men and women gathered round a rude stone altar, on which, twined around a *cocomacacque* stick, was the sacred green snake. The ' Mamaloi,' a tall, evil-looking negress, was dressed in a scarlet robe, with a red turban on her head. She was dancing a sinuous dance before the altar, and droning an ancient West African chant, which the onlookers repeated. Rapidly she worked herself up to a frantic pitch of excitement, pausing now and then to take a drink from one of the rum bottles which passed freely from hand to hand. At last she picked up a glittering *machete* from the altar, and with her other hand seized a black cock held by a bystander. She whirled the bird round her head violently until the feathers were flying in all directions, and then severed the head from the body with one swift stroke. The tense and horrible excitement had kept the worshippers silent, but they burst into a savage yell when the priestess pressed the bleeding neck of the slaughtered fowl to her lips. Afterwards she dipped her finger in the blood and made the sign of the cross on her forehead and pressed it to the forehead of some of her disciples."

The obeah man can always be easily recognised by one who has had much to do with negroes. He has an indescribably sinister appearance. He is unwashed, ragged, often half mad, usually diseased, and almost always has an ulcerated leg. This last, indeed, is a badge of the tribe. Often he is a very old negro who knew " slavery days " and more than half believes in his magical pretensions. But not all are of this disreputable type. Even some of the white planters themselves do not scorn to make use of obeah, although, of course, they have no belief in it. The theft of growing crops by the negroes is one of the greatest trials of their lives. Sometimes they adorn the trees round the edge of a " banana piece " or orange grove with miniature coffins, old bones, bottles of dirty water, and other obeah objects ; and then the negroes will not dare to enter and steal. An interesting report published in a Jamaican journal during 1908 gives particulars of an obeah case of possession or haunting as follows :

" The *cause célèbre* at Half-way Tree Court, Jamaica, recently, was the case of Rex v. Charles Donaldson for unlawfully practising obeah. Robert Robinson, who stated that he was a labourer living at Trench Pen, in the parish of St. Andrew, stated that on Tuesday, the 8th ult., he was sitting down outside the May Pen cemetery on the Spanish Town Road. He was on his way from work, and had a white handkerchief tied around his head. He was feeling sick, and that led him to sit down. While there sitting the prisoner came to him. He did not know the man before, but he began by asking him what was the matter. Witness replied, " I am well sick." The prisoner said, " No, you are not sick ; you have two ghosts on you—one creole and one coolie." Witness told the prisoner to go away and was left. He next saw prisoner on Wednesday 9th. He came to him at Bumper Hall, where he was working, and he said to him, " Man, how you find me here ? " " Oh," replied the prisoner, " if a man is in hell self I can find him ; I come for you to give me the job ? " Witness then inquired, " What job ? " and accused told him he wanted to " take off the two ghosts." He would do it for £25, and he " killed " for any sum from £25 to £50. He had worked for all classes—white, black, coolie, Chinese, etc. Witness said he did not give him any " good consent " at the time, but reported the matter after the accused left to Clark and Wright, two witnesses in the case. Clark told him he must not scare the man but go home. On Thursday, the 10th, the defendant came to him at his yard at French Pen. The accused told him he would come back to him to take off the ghost. He also told him to get a bottle of rum and 5s. He (witness) consented to the arrangement. The defendant began by taking off his jacket. He then opened his " brief bag " and took out a piece of chalk. The accused then made three marks on the table and took out a phial and a white stone. The phial contained some stuff which appeared like quicksilver. He arrayed his paraphernalia on the table. They consisted of a large whisky bottle with some yellow stuff, a candle, a pack of cards, a looking-glass, three cigarette pictures, a pocket knife, etc. The accused also took out a whistle which he sounded, and then placed the cards on the table. He then asked for the 5s. which was given to him. He placed the coins on the cards around a lighted candle. The pint of rum which he (witness) had brought was on the table and prisoner poured some of it into a pan. He went outside and sprinkled the rum at the four corners of the house. Accused came back in and said, " Papa ! papa ! your case is very bad ! There are two ghosts outside. The creole is bad, but the coolie is rather worse. But if he is made out of hell I will catch him."

The prisoner then began to blow his whistle in a very funny way—a way in which he had never heard a whistle blown before. He also began to speak in an unknown tongue and to call up the ghosts.

Mr. Lake—" Aren't there a lot of you people who believe that ghosts can harm and molest you ? "

Witness—" No, I am not one."

Mr. Lake—" Did you not tell him that a duppy struck you on your back and you heard voices calling you ? "

Witness—" He told me so." Continuing, witness said he had seen all sorts of ghosts at all different times and of different kinds also.

Mr. Lake—" Of all different sexes, man and woman ? "

Witness—" Yes ; any man who can see ghosts will know a man ghost from a woman ghost. Dem never walk straight."

Westcar Papyrus : An Egyptian *papyrus* dating from the eighteenth century B.C., devoted chiefly to tales of magic and enchantment. The commencement and ending are wanting, yet enough of the subject matter has survived to enable us to form a fairly correct idea of the whole. Wiedemann says concerning it (Popular Literature in Ancient Egypt) : " The *papyrus* tells how Kheops—the king whom notices of Greek writers have made universally famous as the builder of the Great Pyramid of Gizeh—commands stories of magic to be told to him. The first of these, of which the conclusion only remains, is supposed to have occurred in the reign of King T'eser of the Third Dynasty. The next, which is complete, belongs to the reign of Nebka, a somewhat earlier king. In those days it came to the ears of a great nobleman that his faithless wife was in the habit of meeting her lover by the side of a lake. Being skilled in magic he modelled a crocodile in wax and ordered one of his servants to cast it into the water. It was immediately transformed into a real crocodile and devoured the lover. Seven days later the king was walking by the lake with his friend the nobleman, when at the command of the latter the crocodile came to the shore and laid its victim at their feet. The king shuddered at the sight of the monster but at the touch of its maker it became once more a mere figure of wax. Then the whole astonishing story was told to the king, who thereupon granted the crocodile permission to take away that which was its own. The creature plunged into the depths of the lake and disappeared with the adulterer, while the guilty wife was burnt to death and her ashes were scattered in the stream.

A tale of enchantment follows, the scene of which is laid during the reign of King Sneferu, the predecessor of Kheops. The king was one day taking his pleasure on a lake in a boat rowed by twenty beautiful maidens, when one of the girls dropped a malachite ornament into the water. The king promised to give her another in its stead, but this did not content her, for she wanted her own jewel and no other. A magician was summoned who repeated a spell by the might of which he piled one half of the lake on the top of the other, so that the water, which at first was twelve ells deep in the middle of the lake, now stood twenty-four ells high. The jewel, found lying in the mud in the dry portion of the lake, was restored to its owner ; and the magician having once more mumbled his spell the water returned to its former place.

When Kheops had listened for some time with much interest to the accounts of the strange events that had transpired in the days of his predecessors, then stepped forward Prince Horduduf, who is really known to us from the song in the tomb-temple of King Antef as renowned for his wisdom. He told the king that all marvels were not things of the past but that even then there was living a magician named Deda, who was one hundred and ten years old, and consumed every day five hundred loaves, a side of beef, and a hundred jars of beer.

Kheops was so much interested that he sent the prince to escort the magician to his presence. Deda obeyed the royal summons and performed his chief feat before the king. This consisted in decapitating a goose, a duck, and an ox, and charming the heads back again on to the bodies so that the creatures lived and breathed as before. Kheops fell into talk with the magician, who told him that the wife of a priest in Sakhebu was awaiting the birth of three sons, children of the god Ra, who should one day sit on the throne of Egypt. Deda sought to allay the king's natural distress at this information by prophesying that only after the reigns of his son and grandson should the power fall into the hands of the descendants of the Sun-god. But Kheops was not to be consoled; he inquired into the details of the story and announced that he would himself travel to Sakhebu, no doubt with the ultimate intention of finding an opportunity to put out of the way the pretenders to his throne.

The scene of the sequel is laid in Sakhebu. The birth and infancy of the three children are described in detail, and all sorts of marvellous incidents are represented as influencing their fate. The gods cared for the safety of the little ones. A maid to whom the secret was known being enraged by a severe punishment inflicted upon her, threatened to betray all to Kheops. Her own brother beat her, and when she went down to the water she was carried off by a crocodile. Here the *papyrus* ceases, but it is possible to a certain extent to restore the conclusion. The names of the three children of Ra show that they stand for the first three kings of the Fifth Dynasty, the family that followed the house of Kheops. The *papyrus* must therefore have told how the boys escaped all the snares laid for their lives and in due time ascended the throne for which they were destined.''

Weza : Burmese sorcerers. (*See* **Burma.**)

Whistling : It is considered unlucky for sailors to whistle aboard ship. This is of the nature of sympathetic magic, as it might possibly raise a whistling wind.

White Daughter of the Philosophers : (*See* **Philosopher's Stone.**)

White Magic : (*See* **Magic.**)

Widdershins : (*See* **Magic.**)

Wier : (*See* **Demonology.**)

Wild-Women : A species of nature spirits believed in by the German peasantry. Says Keightley concerning them : "The *Wilde Frauen* or *Wild-women* of Germany bear a very strong resemblance to the Elle-maids of Scandinavia. Like them they are beautiful, have fine flowing hair, live within hills, and only appear singly or in the society of each other. They partake of the piety of character we find among the German Dwarfs.

"The celebrated Wunderberg, or Unaerberg, on the great moor near Salzburg, is the chief haunt of the *Wild-women*. The Wunderberg is said to be quite hollow, and supplied with stately palaces, churches, monasteries, gardens, and springs of gold and silver. Its inhabitants, besides the *Wild-women*, are little men, who have charge of the treasures it contains, and who at midnight repair to Salzburg to perform their devotions in the cathedral ; giants, who used to come to the church of Grodich and exhort the people to lead a godly and pious life ; and the great emperor Charles V., with golden crown and sceptre, attended by knights and lords. His grey beard has twice encompassed the table at which he sits, and when it has the third time grown round it, the end of the world and the appearance of the Antichrist will take place.

"The following is the only account we have of the *Wild-women*.

"The inhabitants of the village of Grodich and the peasantry of the neighbourhood assert that frequently, about the year 1753, the *Wild-women* used to come out of the Wunderburg to the boys and girls that were keeping the cattle near the hole within Glanegg, and give them bread to eat.

"The *Wild-women* used frequently to come to where the people were reaping. They came down eagerly in the morning, and in the evening, when the people left off work, they went back into the Wunderburg without partaking of the supper.

"It once fell out near this hill, that a little boy was sitting on a horse which his father had tethered on the headland of the field. Then came the *Wild-women* out of the hill and wanted to take away the boy by force. But the father, who was well acquainted with the secrets of this hill, and what used to occur there, without any dread hasted up to the women and took the boy from them, with these words : 'What makes you presume to come so often out of the hill, and now to take away my child with you ? What do you want to do with him ?' The *Wild-women* answered : 'He will be better with us, and have better care taken of him than at home. We shall be very fond of the boy, and he will meet with no injury' But the father would not let the boy out of his hands, and the *Wild-women* went away weeping bitterly.

"One time the *Wild-women* came out of the Wunderberg, near the place called the Kugel-mill, which is prettily situated on the side of this hill, and took away a boy who was keeping cattle. This boy, whom every one knew, was seen about a year after by some wood-cutters, in a green dress, and sitting on a rock of this hill. Next day they took his parents with them, intending to search the hill for him, but they all went about it to no purpose, for the boy never appeared any more."

Will is in theology, one of the aspects of the triplicity, of the Logos, and hence since the Monad is essentially a part of the Logos, it is also an aspect of the Monad, taken on when the latter commences his descent into matter by entering the Spiritual World and appearing as Spirit.

William Rufus : Son of William the Conqueror, and tyrant of England in the eleventh century ; a wicked and cruel prince. He was much disliked, particularly by the priests and monks, whom he reduced to the extremest poverty. One day when he was out hunting (in the year 1100, the forty-fourth year of his life, the thirtieth of his reign) he was killed by an arrow launched by an invisible hand. While he was drawing his last breath the comte de Comonailles, who had been separated from the hunt, saw a shaggy black goat carrying off a mangled human form, pierced by an arrow. The comte cried aloud to the goat to halt, and asked who he was, and where he was going. The goat responded that he was the devil, and was carrying off *William Rufus*, to present him before the great tribunal, where he would be condemned for his tyranny and forced to accompany him (the devil) to his abode.

Williams, Charles : An English medium who began to practice about 1870. In 1871 he went into partnership with the medium Herne. During the earlier years of their mediumship Mrs. Guppy, herself a well-known medium, was their patroness. The phenomena then produced were not of a very ambitous character, but consisted of lights, apports, movements of the furniture without contact, spirit voices, and the appearance of fiery letters in the air. One of the most curious feats of these early séances was the transit of Mrs. Guppy. (*See* **Levitation.**) Soon afterwards materialisation was attempted by Messrs. Herne and *Williams*, in emulation of the feats of Miss Florence Cook, who had been a sitter at their early séances. In 1878 *Williams's* was the mediumship chosen for investigation by the Research Committee of the British National Association of Spiritualists (q.v.). Notwithstanding the favourable report of the Committee, *Williams's* mediumship was not destined to last much longer. In company with a new partner, Rita, he had gone to Amsterdam, and there were found in their possession false beards, spirit draperies, and phosphorised oil. The exposure was entirely carried out and given to the public by indignant spiritualists.

Willow-tree : The *Willow*, as might be expected, had many superstitious notions connected with it, since, according to the authorized version of the English Bible, the Israelites are said to have hung their harps on *willow trees*. The weeping *willow* is said to have, ever since the time of the Jews' captivity in Babylon, drooped its branches, in sympathy with this circumstance. The common *willow* was held to be under the protection of the devil, and it was said that, if any were to cast a knot upon a young *willow*, and sit under it, and thereupon renounce his or her baptism, the devil would confer upon them supernatural power.

Windsor Castle : *Windsor Castle* is said to be the haunt of numerous spectres. Queen Elizabeth, Henry VIII., Charles I., and some of the Georges have all been reputed to haunt the *Castle*, while Herne the Hunter (q.v.) is also said to roam the Great Park. An officer of the Foot Guards, while on duty, was once sitting in the library reading in the gloaming when he declares he heard a rustle of silken dress, and, looking up, saw the ghost of Queen Elizabeth glide across the room. He buckled on his sword, and reported the matter. The story attracted the attention of the country for some weeks. Sir Richard Holmes and his assistants kept watch for many nights, but the ghost did not re-appear. Not long ago a housemaid in St. John's Tower thought she saw a ghost, and was so frightened that she became ill, and had to be sent home. In 1908 a sentry discharged five rounds of ball cartridge at a figure which he declared was a spectre which appeared on the terrace.

Winged Disk : (*See* **Horbehutet.**)

Wirdig's Magnetic Sympathy : The doctrine of magnetic attraction and repugnance formulated by *Tenzel Wirdig*, professor at Rostock, who published his *Tenzelius Wirdig, Nova medicina spirituum* in 1673. *Wirdig* believed that everything in the universe possessed a soul, and that the earth itself was merely a larger animal. Between the souls of things in accordance with each other there was a magnetic sympathy and a perpetual antipathy between those of an uncongenial nature. To this sympathy and antipathy *Wirdig* gave the name of magnetism. He says : " Out of this relationship of sympathy and antipathy arises a constant movement in the whole world, and in all its parts, and an uninterrupted communion between heaven and earth, which produces universal harmony. The stars whose emanations consist merely of fire and spirits, have an undeniable influence on earthly bodies ; and their influence on man demonstrates itself by life, movement, and warmth, those things without which he cannot live. The influence of the stars is the strongest at birth. The new-born child inhales this influence, and on whose first breath frequently his whole constitution depends, nay, even his whole life."

Wisconsin Phalanx : A spiritualistic community founded by Warren Chase in 1844. Chase had settled in Southport, Wisconsin, in 1838, and there, with his wife and child, he lived for a time in the deepest poverty. At length, however, their circumstances brightened, and Chase attained to a position of civic honour in Southport. Meanwhile he had studied mesmerism and socialism with the aid of a few periodicals—Laroy Sunderland's *Magnet* and the *New York Tribune*—and was filled with the idea of founding a community where his ideals of social order and harmony

might be carried out. With the aid of his friends such a community was formed, each member with a share of twenty-five dollars. The chosen settlement—near the town of Ripon—was christened Ceresco, in honour of Ceres. For six years the *Wisconsin Phalanx* flourished, having as its leader and ruling spirit Warren Chase himself. But at last dissensions arose, and in 1850 it was dissolved. When its affairs were wound up it was found that a considerable profit fell to the share of its members. In all, it was one of the most successful spiritualistic or socialistic communities of the time.

Wisdom Religion : (*See* **Theosophy.**)

Witchcraft : (From Saxen *Wicca*, a contraction of *witega*, a prophet or sorcerer.) The cult of persons who, by means of satanic assistance or the aid of evil spirits or familiars, are enabled to practise minor black magic. But the difference between the sorcerer and the witch is that the former has sold his soul to Satan for complete dominion over him for a stated period, whereas the witch usually appears as the devoted and often badly treated servant of the diabolic power. But she is often mistress of a familiar, her bounden slave, and among certain savage peoples her occult powers are self-evolved. The concept of *witchcraft* was perhaps brought into being by the mythic influence of conquered races. It closely resembles in ritual and practice the demonism of savage races, from which it probably sprang. (*See* **Devil Worship.**) That is, the non-Aryan peoples of Europe who preceded the Aryan population, carrying on the practice and traditions of their religions more or less in secret, awoke in the Aryan mind the idea that such practices were of a " magical " character. This idea they would not fail to assist, and would probably exaggerate such details as most strongly impressed the Aryan mind, to which their gods would appear as " devils," and their religious ritual as sorcery. This view has been combatted on the ground that the gap betwixt, say, the extinction of the pre-Aryan religion known as Druidism and the first notices of *witchcraft*, is too great to bridge. But Druidism continued to exist long after it was officially extinct, and British *witchcraft* is its lineal successor. The theory is further advanced that on the failure of the non-Aryan priesthood novices would be adopted from the invading race for the purpose of carrying on the old religion. It seems to the present writer that the circumstance that the greater number of the upholders of this ancient tradition were women points to the likelihood of an early custom of the adoption or marriage of Aryan women by a non-Aryan people who would prefer to recruit their novices and devotees from the more plastic sex, naturally distrusting the masculine portion of an alien people to fall in with their religious ideas, and that the almost exclusive employment of women in the cult (in Britain, at least) originated in this practice. Then individually all claimed to have been initiated. Says Gomme, " I am inclined to lay great stress upon the act of initiation. It emphasises the idea of a caste distinct from the general populace, and it postulates the existence of this caste anterior to the time when those who practice their supposed powers first come into notice. Carrying back this act of initiation age after age, as the dismal records of *witchcraft* enable us to do for some centuries, it is clear that the people from time to time thus introduced into the witch caste carried on the practices and assumed the functions of the caste even though they came to it as novices and strangers. We thus arrive at an artificial means of descent of a peculiar group of superstition, and it might be termed initiatory descent." This concept, thinks Gomme (*Folklore as an Historical Science*, p. 201 at seq.) was influenced in the Middle Ages by another.

" Traditional practices, traditional formulæ, and traditional beliefs are no doubt the elements of *witchcraft*, but it was not the force of tradition which produced the miserable doings of the Middle Ages, and of the seventeenth century against witches. These were due to a psychological force, partly generated by the newly acquired power of the people to read the Bible for themselves, and so to apply the witch stories of the Jews to neighbours of their own who possessed powers or peculiarities which they could not understand, and partly generated by the carrying on of traditional practices by certain families or groups of persons who could only acquire knowledge of such practices by initiation or family teaching. Lawyers, magistrates, judges, nobles and monarchs are concerned with *witchcraft*. These are not minds that have been crushed by civilisation, but minds which have misunderstood it or misused it."

Sabbath.—The mediæval criminal records abound in descriptions of a ceremony at which the rites of the witch cult were periodically celebrated. This was the witches' Sabbath. The Sabbath was generally held in some wild and solitary spot, often in the midst of forests or on the heights of mountains, at a great distance from the residence of most of the visitors. The circumstance connected with it most difficult of proof was the method of transport from one place to another. The witches nearly all agreed in the statement that they divested themselves of their clothes and anointed their bodies with an ointment made for that especial purpose. They then strode across a stick, or any similar article, and, muttering a charm, were carried through the air to the place of meeting in an incredibly short space of time. Sometimes the stick was to be anointed as well as their persons. They generally left the house by the window or by the chimney, which perhaps suggests survival of the custom of an earth-dwelling people. Sometimes the witch went out by the door, and there found a demon in the shape of a goat, or at times of some other animal, who carried her away on his back, and brought her home again after the meeting was dissolved. In the confessions extorted from them at their trials, the witches and sorcerers bore testimony to the truth of all these particulars ; but those who judged them, and who wrote upon the subject, asserted that they had many other independent proofs in corroboration.

We are told by Bodin that a man who lived at the little town of Loches having observed that his wife frequently absented herself from the house in the night, became suspicious of her conduct, and at last by his threats obliged her to confess that she was a witch, and that she attended the Sabbaths. To appease the anger of her husband, she agreed to gratify his curiosity by taking him with her to the next meeting, but she warned him on no account whatever to allow the name of God or of the Saviour to cross his lips. At the appointed time they stripped and anointed themselves, and, after uttering the necessary formula, they were suddenly transported to the *landes* of Bordeaux, at an immense distance from their own dwelling. The husband there found himself in the midst of a great assembly of both sexes in the same state of *deshabille* as himself and his wife, and in one part he saw the devil in a hideous form ; but in the first moment of his surprise he inadvertently uttered the exclamation, "*Mon Dieu !* ou sommes-nous ?" and all disappeared as suddenly from his view, leaving him cold and naked in the middle of the fields, where he wandered till morning, when the countrymen coming to their daily occupations told him where he was, and he made his way home in the best manner he could. But he lost no time in denouncing his wife, who was brought to her trial, confessed, and was burnt.

As the witches generally went from their beds at night to the meetings, leaving their husbands and family behind them, it may seem extraordinary that their absence was not more frequently perceived. They had, however, a method of providing against this danger, by casting a drowsiness over those who might be witnesses, and by placing in their bed an image which, to all outward appearance, bore an exact resemblance to themselves, although in reality was nothing more than a besom or some other similar article. But the belief was so inculcated that the witches did not always go in body to the Sabbath—that they were present only in spirit, whilst their body remained in bed. Some of the more rational writers on *witchcraft* taught that this was the only manner in which they were ever carried to the Sabbaths, and various instances are deposed to where that was manifestly the case. The president, Touretta told Bodin that he had examined a witch, who was subsequently burnt in the Dauphine, and who was carried to the Sabbath in this manner. Her master one night found her stretched on the floor before the fire in a state of insensibility and imagined her to be dead. In his attempt to arouse her, he first beat her body with great severity, and then applied fire to the more sensitive parts, which being without effect, he left her in the belief that she had died suddenly. His astonishment was great when in the morning he found her in her own bed, in an evident state of great suffering. When he asked what ailed her, her only answer was, " Ha ! mon maître, tant m'avez batue ! " When further pressed, however, she confessed that during the time her body lay in a state of insensibility, she had been herself to the witches' Sabbath, and upon this avowal she was committed to prison. Bodin further informs us that at Bordeaux, in 1571, an old woman, who was condemned to the fire for *witchcraft*, and confessed that she was transported to the Sabbath in this manner. One of her judges, who was personally known to Bodin, while she was under examination, pressed her to show him how she was effected, and released her from the fetters for that purpose. She rubbed herself in different parts of the body with " a certain grease," and immediately became stiff and insensible and, to all appearance, dead. She remained in this state about five hours, and then as quickly revived, and told her inquisitors a great number of extraordinary things, which showed that she must have been spiritually transported to far distant places.

The description of the Sabbath given by the witches differed only in slight particulars of detail ; for their examinations were all carried on upon one model and measure—a veritable bed of Procrustes, and equally fatal to those who were placed upon it. The Sabbath was, in general, an immense assemblage of witches and demons, sometimes from distant parts of the earth, at others only from the province or district in which it was held. On arriving, the visitors performed their homage to the evil one with unseemly ceremonies, and presented their new converts. They then gave an account of all the mischief they had done since the last meeting. Those who had neglected to do evil, or who had so far overlooked themselves as to do good, were treated with disdain, or severely punished. Several of the victims of the French courts in the latter part of this century confessed that, having been unwilling or unable to fulfil the commands of the evil one, when they appeared at the Sabbath he had beaten them in the most cruel manner. He took one woman, who had refused to bewitch her neighbour's daughter, and threatened to drown her in the Moselle. Others were plagued in their bodies, or by destruction of their property. Some were punished for their irregular attendance at the Sabbath ; and one or two, for slighter offences, were condemned to walk home from the Sabbath instead of being carried through the air. Those, on the other hand, who had exerted most their mischievous propensities were highly honoured at the Sabbath, and often rewarded with gifts of money. After this examination was passed, the demon distributed among his worshippers unguents, powders, and other articles for the perpetration of evil. A French witch, executed in 1580, confessed that some of her companions offered a sheep or a heifer; and another, executed the following year, stated that animals of a black colour were most acceptable. A third, executed at Gerbeville in 1585, declared that no one was exempt from this offering, and that the poorer sort offered a hen or a chicken, and some even a lock of their hair, a little bird, or any trifle, they could put their hands upon. Severe punishments followed the neglect of this ceremony. In many instances, according to the confessions of the witches, besides their direct worship of the devil, they were obliged to show their abhorrence of the faith they had deserted by trampling on the cross, and blaspheming the saints, and by other profanations.

Before the termination of the meeting, the new witches received their familiars, or imps, who they generally addressed as their "little masters," although they were bound to attend at the bidding of the witches, and execute their desires. These received names, generally of a popular character, such as were given to cats, and dogs, and other pet animals and the similarity these names bear to each other in different countries is very remarkable.

After all these preliminary ceremonies had been transacted, and a great banquet was laid out, and the whole company fell to eating and drinking and making merry. At times, every article of luxury was placed before them, and they feasted in the most sumptuous manner. Often, however, the meats served on the table were nothing but toads and rats, and other articles of a revolting nature. In general they had no salt, and seldom bread. But, even when best served, the money and the victuals furnished by the demons were of the most unsatisfactory character; a circumstance of which no rational explanation is given. The coin when brought forth by open daylight, was generally found to be nothing better than dried leaves or bits of dirt; and, however, greedily they may have eaten at the table, they commonly left the meeting in a state of exhaustion from hunger.

The tables were next removed, and feasting gave way to wild and uproarious dancing and revelry. The common dance, or carole, of the middle ages appears to have been performed by the persons taking each other's hand in a circle, alternately a man and a woman. This, probably the ordinary dance among the peasantry, was the one generally practised at the Sabbaths of the witches, with this peculiarity, that their backs instead of their faces were turned inwards. The old writers endeavour to account for this, by supposing that it was designed to prevent them from seeing and recognising each other. But this, it is clear, was not the only dance of the Sabbath; perhaps more fashionable ones were introduced for witches in better conditions in society; and moralists of the succeeding age maliciously insinuate that many dances of a not very decorous character invented by the devil himself to heat the imaginations of his victims, had subsequently been adopted in classes in society who did not frequent the Sabbath. It may be observed, as a curious circumstance that the modern waltz is first traced among the meetings of the witches and their imps! It was also confessed, in almost every case, that the dances at the Sabbaths produced much greater fatigue than commonly arose from such exercises. Many of the witches declared that, on their return home, they were usually unable to rise from their bed for two or three days.

Their music, also, was by no means of an ordinary character. The songs were generally obscene, or vulgar, or ridiculous. Of instruments there was considerable variety, but all partaking of the burlesque character of the proceedings. "Some played the flute upon a stick or bone; another was seen striking a horse's skull for a lyre; there you saw them beating the drum on the trunk of an oak, with a stick; here, others were blowing trumpets with the branches. The louder the instrument, the greater satisfaction it gave; and the dancing became wilder and wilder, until it merged into a vast scene of confusion, and ended in scenes over which, though minutely described in the old treatises on demonology, it will be better to throw a veil." The witches separated in time to reach their homes before cock-crow.

We then see that Satan had taken the place of the deities of the older and abandoned cults of the non-Aryans, whose obscene rites were attended by "initiated" or "adopted" neophytes of a race to the generality of which they were abominable, that witches often worked by means of familiars, whose shapes they were able to take, or by means of direct satanic agency. But there were probably mythological elements in *witchcraft* as well.

Powers of Witches.—In the eyes of the populace the powers of witches were numerous. The most peculiar of these were: The ability to blight by means of the evil eye (q.v.) the sale of winds to sailors, power over animals, and capacity to transform themselves into animal shapes. Thus, says Gomme—"The most usual transformations are into cats and hares, and less frequently into red deer, and these have taken the place of wolves. Thus, cat-transformations are found in Yorkshire, hare-transformations in Devonshire, Yorkshire and Wales, and Scotland, deer-transformations in Cumberland, raven-transformations in Scotland, cattle-transformations in Ireland. Indeed the connection between witches and the lower animals is a very close one, and hardly anywhere in Europe does it occur that this connection is relegated to a subordinate place. Story after story, custom after custom is recorded as appertaining to *witchcraft*, and animal transformation appears always.

Witches also possessed the power of making themselves invisible, by means of a magic ointment supplied to them by the devil, and of harming others by thrusting nails into a waxen image representing them.

Witchcraft among Savage People.—*Witchcraft* among savage people is, of course, allied to the various cults of demonism in vogue among barbarian folk all over the world. These are indicated in the various articles dealing with uncultured races. The name *witchcraft* is merely a convenient English label for such savage demon-cults, as is "witch-doctors" applied to those who "smell out" these practitioners of evil.

Evidence for Witchcraft.—The evidence for *witchcraft*, says Podmore (*Modern Spiritualism*) falls under four main heads: (a) the confessions of witches themselves; (b) the corroborative evidence of lycanthropy, apparitions, etc.; (c) the witch-marks; (d) the evidence of the evil effects produced upon the supposed victims.

"(a)—The confessions, as is notorious, were for the most part extracted by torture, or by lying promises of release. In England, where torture was not countenanced by the law, the ingenuity of Matthew Hopkins and other professional witch-finders could generally devise some equally efficient substitute, such as gradual starvation, enforced sleeplessness, or the maintenance for hours of a constrained and painful posture. But apart from these extorted confessions, there is evidence that in some cases the accused persons were actually driven by the accumulation of testimony against them, by the pressure of public opinion, and the singular circumstances in which they were placed, to believe and confess that they were witches indeed. Some of the women in Salem who had pleaded guilty to *witchcraft* explained afterwards, when the persecution had died down and they were released, that they had been

" consternated and affrighted even out of their reason " to confess that of which they were innocent. And there were not a few persons who voluntarily confessed to the practice of *witchcraft*, nocturnal rides, compacts with the devil, and all the rest of it." The most striking instances of this voluntary confession are afforded by children. For even among the earlier writers on *witchcraft* the opinion was not uncommonly held that the nocturnal rides and banquets with the devil were merely delusions, thought the guilt of the witch was not lessened thereby. And in the sixteenth centuries, at least in English-speaking countries this belief seems to have been generally alike by believers in *witchcraft* and their opponents. Thus Gaule: " But the more prodigious or stupendous (of the things narrated by witches in their confessions) are effected merely by the devil ; the witches all the while either in a rapt ecstasie, a charmed sleepe, or a melancholy dreame ; and the witches imagination, phantasie, common sense, only deluded with what is now done, or pretended. Even Antoinette Bourignon, observing her scholars eat " great pieces of bread and butter " at breakfast, pointed out to them that they could not have such good appetites if they had really fed on dainty meats at the devil's Sabbath the night before.

" (b)—But if the witch's own account of her marvellous feats may be explained as, at best, the vague remembrance of a nightmare, it is hardly necessary to go beyond this explanation to account for the prodigies reported by others. In most cases there is no need to suppose even so much foundation for the marvels, since the evidence (*e.g.*, for lycanthropy) is purely traditional. And when we get accounts at first hand, they are commonly concerned, not with such matters as levitation, or transformation of hares into old women, but merely with vague shapes seen in the dusk, or the unexplained appearance of a black dog. Even so the evidence comes almost exclusively from ignorant peasants, and is given years after the events."

" (c)—The evidence for " witch-marks " does not greatly concern us. The insensible patches on which Matthew Hopkins and other witch-finders relied may well have been genuine in some cases. Such insensible areas are known to occur in hysterical subjects, and the production of insensibility by means of suggestion is a commonplace in modern times. The supposed witches' teats, which the imps sucked, appear to have been found almost exclusively, like the imps themselves, in the English-speaking countries. Any wart, boil, or swelling would probably form a sufficient warrant for the accusation ; we read in Cotton Mather of a jury of women finding a preter-natural teat upon a witch's body, which could not be discovered when a second search was made three or four hours later, and of a witch's mark upon the finger of a small child, which took the form of " a deep red spot, about the bigness of a flea-bite." And the witch-mark which brought conviction to the mind of Increase Mather in the case of George Burroughs was his ability to hold a heavy gun at arm's length, and to carry a barrel of cider from the canoe to the shore."

" (d)—Of most of the evidence based upon the injuries suffered by the witches' supposed victims, it is difficult to speak seriously. If a man's cow ran dry, if his horse stumbled, his cart stuck in a gate, his pigs or fowls sickened, if his child had a fit, his wife or himself an unaccustomed pain, it was evidence acceptable in a court of law against any old woman who might be supposed within the last twelve months—or twelve years—to have conceived some cause of offence against him and his. Follies of this kind are too well known to need repetition.

But there is another feature of *witchcraft*, at any rate of the cases occurring in the sixteenth and seventeenth centuries in England and America, which is not so well recognised, and which has a more direct bearing upon our present inquiry—the predominant part played in the initial stages of witch persecution by malevolent or merely hysterical children and young women."

Symptoms of Bewitchment.—Mr. Podmore remarks : " The symptoms of the alleged bewitchment were, in all these cases monotonously alike. The victims would fall into fits or convulsions, of a kind which the physicians called in were unable to diagnose or to cure. In these fits the children would commonly call out on the old woman who was the imaginary cause of their ailment ; would profess, at times, to see her shape present in the room, and would even stab at it with a knife or other weapon. (In the most conclusive cases the record continues that the old woman, being straightway sought for, would be found attempting to conceal a corresponding wound on her person.) These fits, which sometimes lasted, with slight intermission, for weeks together would be increased in violence by the approach of the supposed witch ; or, as Hutchinson notes, by the presence of sympathetic spectators. The fits, as was also commonly noted by contemporary chroniclers, would diminish or altogether cease when the witch was imprisoned or condemned ; on the other hand, if the supposed witch were released the victim would continue to suffer horrible tortures, insomuch that at the Salem trials one old woman who had been acquitted by the jury was, because of the hideous outcry from the afflicted persons in court, straightway re-tried and condemned. The witch's touch would always provoke severe attacks, indeed, contact with the witch or the establishment of rapport between her and the victim by means of some garment worn by the latter, as in Mistress Faith Corbet's case, was generally regarded as an essential pre-requisite of the enchantment. Once this rapport established the mere look of the witch, or the direction of her evil will would suffice. The afflicted in Salem were, as the Mathers testify, much tortured in court by the malevolent glances of the poor wretches on trial ; and two ' visionary ' girls added greatly to the weight of the evidence by foretelling with singular accuracy, when such or such of the afflicted persons then present would feel the baneful influence, and howl for anguish. It should be added—though the evidence as we now understand the word, for the fact alleged is of course practically negligible—that it was commonly reported that the witch's victim could, although blindfolded, distinguish her tormentor by the touch alone from all other persons, and could even foresee her approach and discern her actions at a considerable distance.

" The effect of the convulsions and cataleptic attacks, which modern science would unhesitatingly dismiss as being simply the result of hysteria, was heightened in many cases by manifestations of a more material kind. It was a common feature for the victim to vomit pins, needles, wood, stubble, and other substances ; or for thorns or needles to be found embedded in her flesh. In a case recorded by Glanvil an hysterical servant girl, Mary Longdon, in addition to the usual fits, vomiting of pins, etc., was tormented by stones being continually flung at her, which stones when they fell to the ground straightway vanished. Her master bore witness in court to the falling of the stones and their miraculous disappearance. Moreover, the same Mary Longdon would frequently be transported by an invisible power to the top of the house, and there " laid on a board betwixt two Sollar beams," or would be put into a chest, or half suffocated between two feather-beds.

" Gross as these frauds appear to us, it is singular that for the most part they remained undetected, and even, it would seem, unsuspected, not merely by the ignorant peasants, for whose benefit the play was acted in the first instance, but in the larger theatre of a law court. But there are some notorious instances of confession or detection. Edmund Robinson, the boy on whose accusation the Lancashire witches were tried, subsequently confessed to imposture. Other youths were detected with blacklead in their mouths when foaming in sham epileptic fits, colouring their urine with ink, concealing crooked pins about their persons in order to vomit them later, scratching the bed posts with their toes, and surreptitiously eating to repletion during a pretended fast. But commonly the spectators were so convinced beforehand of the genuineness of such portents that they held it superfluous to examine the claims of any particular performance of this kind on their credence.

" It is difficult to know in such cases where self-deception ends and where malevolent trickery begins. Nor would the examination of these bygone outbreaks of hysteria trivial in themselves as terrible in their consequences—be of interest in the present connection, except for the fact that we find here the primitive form of those Poltergeist manifestations which gave the popular impetus in 1848 to the belief in Modern Spiritualism, and which are still appealed by those who maintain the genuineness of the physical manifestations of the séance room as instances of similar phenomena occurring spontaneously."

Difference between British and Continental Witchcraft.— The salient difference between British and Continental *witchcraft* systems seems to have been that whereas the former was an almost exclusively female system, the Continental one favoured the inclusion in the ranks of sorcerers (as foreign witches were called) of the male element ; this at least was the case in France and Germany, but there is evidence that in Hungary and the Slavonic countries, the female element was the more numerous. In Ireland we find women also pre-eminent ; this is probably to be accounted for by the circumstance before noted that the non-alien priesthoods in their decline became almost entirely dependent upon the offices of women. But the various forms of *witchcraft* are duly entered in the several articles dealing with European countries.

Growth of Belief in Witchcraft.—It is significant that in early times the supernatural side of *witchcraft* won little public credence. People believed in such things as magical poisoning and the raising of tempests by witches. but they refused to give credence to such superstitions as that the witch rode through the air. or had communion in any way with diabolic agency. As early as 800 A.D. an Irish synod pronounced the belief of flight through the air and vampirism, to be incompatible with Christian doctrine, and many early writers like Stephen of Hungary and Regino state that flight by night and kindred practices are merely a delusion. Indeed those who held these beliefs were actively punished by penance. In face of the later development of belief in *witchcraft*, this frank scepticism is almost amazing, and it is most strange that the tenth and eleventh centuries should have rejected superstitions embraced widely by the sixteenth and seventeenth.

From the thirteenth to the fifteenth centuries we find the conception of *witchcraft* and demonology greatly furthered and assisted by the writings of scholars and the institution of the Inquisition to deal with the rise of unbelief. A vast amount of literature was circulated dealing with questions relating to magic and sorcery, and regarding the habits and customs of witches, magicians and practitioners in " black magic," and many hairs were split. The Church gladly joined in this campaign against what it regarded as the forces of darkness, and indeed both accused and accusers seem to have lingered under the most dreadful delusions— delusions which were to cost society dear as a whole. The scholastic conception of demonology was that the witch was not a woman but a demon. Rationalism was at a

discount and the ingenuity of mediæval scholars disposed of all objections to the phenomena of *witchcraft*. The deities of pagan times were cited as practitioners of sorcery, and erudition, especially in ecclesiastical circles, ran riot on the subject. There also arose a class of judges or inquisitors like Bodin in France and Sprenger in Germany, who composed lengthy treatises upon the manner of discovering witches, of putting them to the test, and generally of presiding in *witchcraft* trials. The cold-blooded cruelty of these textbooks on current demonology can only be accounted for by the likelihood that their authors felt themselves justified in their composition through motives of fidelity to their church and religion. The awful terror disseminated especially among the intelligent by the possibility of a charge of *witchcraft* being brought against them at any moment brought about an intolerable condition of things. The intellectual might be arraigned at any time on a charge of *witchcraft* by any rascal who cared to make it. Position or learning were no safeguard against such a charge, and it is peculiar that the more thoughtful and serious part of the population should not have made some attempt to put a period to the dreadful condition of affairs brought about by ignorance and superstition. Of course the principal reason against their being able to do so was the fact that the whole system was countenanced by the Church, in whose hands the entire procedure of trials for *witchcraft* lay.

Strangely enough convents and monasteries were often the centres of demoniac possession. The conception of the incubi and succubi undoubtedly arose from the ascetic tortures of the monk and the nun. Wholesale trials, too, of wretched people who were alleged to attend Sabbatic orgies of the enemy of mankind on dreary heaths were gone through with an elaborateness which spread terror in the public mind. The tortures inflicted on those unfortunates were generally of the most fiendish description, but they were supposed to be for the good of the souls ot those who bore them. In France the majority of these trials took place in the fifteenth century ; whereas in England we find that most of them were current in the seventeenth century. Full details regarding these will be found in the articles **France** and **England.** The famous outburst of fanaticism in New England under Cotton Mather (*See* **America**) in 1691 to 1692 was by no means the last in an English-speaking country, for in 1712 a woman was convicted of *witchcraft* in England, and in Scotland the last trial and execution for sorcery took place in 1722. In Spain we find burnings by the Inquisition in 1781 ; in Germany as late as 1793, and as regards Latin South America a woman was burned in Peru so recently as 1888. The death of the belief in *witchcraft* was brought about by a more sane spirit of criticism than had before obtained. Even the dull wits of the inquisitorial and other courts began to see that the wretched creatures upon whom they passed sentence either confessed because of the extremity of torture they had to suffer, or else were under hallucination regarding the nature of their connection with the satanic power. Reginald Scot in his *Discovery of Witchcraft* (1584) proved that the belief on the part of the witch that she was a servant of the Devil was purely imaginary, and in consequence drew upon his work the wrath of the British Solomon, James I., who warmly replied to him in his *Demonologie*. But Friedrich von Spee's *Cautio Criminalis*, 1631, advanced considerations of still greater weight from the rationalistic point of view— considerations of such weight indeed that Bodin, the arch-demonologist, denounced him and demanded that he should be added to the long list of his victims.

Psychology of Witchcraft.—No doubt exists nowadays when the conditions of savage *witchcraft* have been closely examined and commented upon, that the witch and the sorcerer of the Middle Ages, like their prototypes among the native races of Africa, America, Asia and elsewhere, have a firmly-rooted belief in their own magical powers, and in their connection with unseen and generally diabolic agencies. It is a strange circumstance that in many instances the confessions wrung from two or more witches, when a number of them have been concerned in the same case, have tallied with one another in almost every detail. This would imply that these women suffered from collective hallucination, and actually believed that they had seen the supernatural beings with whom they confessed fellowship, and had gone through the rites and acts for which they suffered. A period arrived in the mediæval campaign against *witchcraft* when it was admitted that the whole system was one of hallucination; yet, said the demonologists, this was no palliation of the offence, for it was equally as evil to imagine such diabolic acts as actually to take part in them.

There is also evidence which would lead to the belief that the witch possessed certain minor powers of hypnotism and telepathy, which would give her real confidence in her belief that she wielded magical terrors. Again the phenomena of spiritualism and the large possibilities it offers for fraud suggest that some kindred system might have been in use amongst the more shrewd or the leaders in these Sabbatic meetings, which would thoroughly convince the ignorant among the sisterhood of the existence in their midst of diabolic powers. Trance and hysteria, drugs and salves, there is good reason to believe, were also used unsparingly, but the great source of witch-belief undoubtedly exists in auto-suggestion, fostered and fomented from ecclesiastical and scholastic sources, and by no means lessened by popular belief.

Since the above article was written an exhaustive examination of the phenomena of *witchcraft* has been made by Miss M. A. Murray, lecturer on Egyptology at University College, London. Basing her conclusions upon the suggestions of C. G. Leland, in his " Aradia, or the Witches of Italy," and those of other modern writers, she inclines to the hypothesis that witchcraft was in reality the modern and degraded descendant of an ancient nature-religion, the rites of which were actually carried out in deserted places and included child-sacrifice and other barbarous customs. In the Satanic presence at such gatherings she sees the attendance of a priest of the cult. In brief, her hypothesis tends to prove the actual reality of the witch-religion as against that of hallucination which, until recently, was the explanation accepted by students of the subject. Her remarks, too, upon the familiar, go to show that a large body of proof exists for the belief that this conception also rested upon actual occurrences. (*See* her papers in *Man* and elsewhere.)

Recent researches on the part of the writer have convinced him of the soundness of these views, but have added the conviction that witchcraft religion was, in some manner, possessed of an equestrian connection, the precise nature of which is still dark to him. The broomstick appears to be the magical equivalent of a horse, the witches occasionally rode to the Sabbath on horseback, and one of the tests for a witch was to see if her eye held the reflection or likeness of a horse. May it not be that the witch-religion was the remnant of a prehistoric horse-totem cult? But this is, after all, merely of the nature of surmise. The writer has also found good evidence for the existence of a witch-cult precisely similar to that of Europe in pre-Columbian Mexico, and has even encountered a picture of a naked witch with peaked cap riding on a broomstick in the native Mexican painting known as the Codex Fejèrvàry-Mayer, which seems to show that the witch-religion was in no sense limited to Europe, and was of most ancient origin.

Wolf, The : Amongst the ancient Romans, the wolf was a fruitful source of augury, and many are the tales in which he has figured as a good or evil omen. A *wolf* running to the right with his mouth full was a sign of great joy. If a *wolf*, after he had entered a Roman camp, escaped unhurt it was regarded as a sign of defeat ; and the terrible result of the second Punic war was said to have been augured from the carrying off of the sword of a sentinel in the camp by a *wolf*. Plutarch tells of a *wolf* who ate the landmarks of a proposed new settlement at Libya and thus stopped its colonisation ; but later another *wolf* which had stolen a burnt sacrifice led his pursuers to a place where they afterwards settled in. It is said that a *wolf* ran off with Hiero's slate when he was a schoolboy, and this was regarded as a sign of his future greatness. The peasants of Sweden do not dare to speak of a *wolf* by name but call him the " grey one " or " old grey " : they seem to regard the pronouncing of his name as unlucky.

Wonders of the Invisible World : (*See* **America, U.S. of.**)

World Period : (*See* **Planetary Chains.**)

Worlds, Planes, or Spheres : According to theosophists, these are seven in number and are as follows : The older Sanskrit names, which are now superseded, being given for reference :—Divine, or *Adi* ; Monadic or *Anutadaka*, Spiritual or *Nirvana*, Intuitional or *Buddhi*, Mental or *Manas*, Astral or *Kama*, and Physical or *Sthula*. These worlds are not physically separate in the manner which planets appear to be, but interpenetrate each other, and they depend for their differences, on the relative density of the matter which composes them, and the consequent difference in the rates at which the matter of each world vibrates.

Except for the physical world (the densest) our knowledge of them, so far as it extends, is dependent on clairvoyance, and the more exalted the vision of the clairvoyant the higher the world to which his vision can pierce. Each world has its appropriate inhabitants, clothed in appropriate bodies, and possessing appropriate states of consciousness. The two highest worlds, the Divine and the Monadic are at present incapable of attainment by human powers, the remaining five are in greater or less degree. The monad for the purpose of gathering experience and for development, finds it necessary to pass downwards into the material sphere, and, when it has taken possession of the spiritual, intuitional, and higher Mental Worlds, it may be looked on as an ego or soul embodying will, intuition and intellect, continuing eternally the same entity, never altering except by reason of increasing development, and hence being immortal. These Worlds, however, do not afford sufficient scope to the Monad and it presses s ill farther down into matter, through the lower Mental, into the Astral and Physical Worlds. The bodies with which it is there clothed form its personality and this personality suffers death and is renewed at each fresh incarnation. At the death of the physical body, the ego has merely cast aside a garment and thereafter continues to live in the next higher world, the Astral.

At the death of the Astral body in turn, another garment is cast aside, the ego is clear of all appendages and as it was before its descent into denser matter, having returned to the Mental World, the Heaven World. The ego finds itself somewhat strange to this owing to insufficient development, and it again descends into matter as before. This round is completed again and again, and each time the ego returns with a fresh store of experience and knowledge, which strengthens and perfects the mental body. When at last this process is complete, this body in turn is cast aside and the ego is clothed with its casual body. Again it finds itself strange and the round of descents into matters again begins and continues till the casual body has been fully developed. The two remaining worlds are but imperfectly known but the intuitional, as it's name indicates is that where the ego's vision is quickened to see things as they really are, and in the Spiritual World the divine and the human become unified and the divine purpose is fulfilled. (*See* the articles on the various Worlds and bodies **Theosophy, Monad, Evolution, Reincarnation.**)

Wraith : The apparition or " double " of a living person, generally supposed to be an omen of death. The wraith closely resembles its prototype in the flesh, even to details of dress. It is believed possible for people to see their own *wraiths,* and among those who have been warned of approaching dissolution in this wise are numbered Queen Elizabeth, Shelley, and Catherine of Russia, the latter of whom, seeing her " double " seated upon the throne, ordered her guards to fire upon it ! But *wraiths* of others may appear to one or more persons. Lord Balcarres saw the *wraith* of his friend " Bonnie Dundee " at the moment when the latter fell at Killiecrankie, while Ben Jonson saw

his eldest son's double when the original was dying of the plague. The belief flourishes also on the continent, and in different parts of Britain it goes under different names, such as " waff," " swarth," " task," " fye," etc. Variants of the *wraiths* are the Irish " fetch " (q.v.), and the Welsh " lledrith." In Scotland it was formerly believed that the *wraith* of one about to die might be seen wrapped in a winding-sheet. The higher the shroud reached the nearer was the approach of death. Something analogous to wraith-seeing comes within the scope of modern psychical science, and the apparition is explained in various ways, as a projection of the " astral body," an emanation from the person of its living prototype, or, more scientifically perhaps, on a telepathic basis. A well-known case in point is that of the Birkbeck Ghost, where three children witnessed the apparition of their mother shortly before her death. This instance, which is recorded in the " Proceedings " of the Psychical Research Society, is noteworthy because of the fact that Mrs. Birkbeck was conscious before she died of having spent the time with her children.

Wronski : (*See* **France.**)

X

Xibalba : the Kiche Hades. (*See* **Hell.**)

Xylomancy : Divination by means of wood, practised particularly in Slavonia. It is the art of reading omens from the position of small pieces of dry wood found in one's path. No less certain presages of future events may be

drawn from the arrangement of logs in the fire-place, from the manner in which they burn, etc. It is perhaps the survival of this mode of divination which makes the good people say, when a brand is disturbed, that " they are going to have a visitor."

Y

Y-Kim, Book of : A Chinese mystical book attributed to the Emperor Fo-Hi, and ascribed to the year, 3468 B.C. It consists of ten chapters, and is stated by Eliphas Levi in his *History of Magic* to be a complement and an appendix to the Kabalistic *Zohar,* or record of the utterances of Rabbi Simeon Ben Jochai. The *Zohar,* says Levi, explains universal equilibrium, and the *Y-Kim* is the hieroglyphic and ciphered demonstration thereof. The key to the *Y-Kim* is a pantacle known as the Trigrams of Fo-Hi. In the *Vay-Ky* of Leon-Tao-Yuen, composed in the Som dynasty (about eleventh century) it is recounted that the Emperor Fo-Hi was one day seated on the banks of a river, deep in meditation, when to him there appeared an animal having the parts of both a horse and a dragon. Its back was covered with scales, on each of which shone the mystic Trigrammic symbol. This animal initiated the just and righteous Fo-Hi into universal science. Numbering its scales, he combined the Trigrams in such a manner that there arose in his mind a synthesis of sciences compared and united with one another through the harmonies of nature. From this synthesis sprang the tables of the *Y-Kim.* The numbers of Fo-Hi are identical with those of the Kabala, and his pantacle is similar to that of Solomon. His tables are in correspondence with the subject-matter of the *Sephir Yetzirah* and the *Zohar.* The whole is a commentary upon the Absolute which is concealed from the profane, concludes Levi, but as he had little real acquaintance with the subject, these analogies must be taken as of small value.

Yadachi, or weather conjurer : (*See* **Siberia.**)

Yadageri : the science of inducing rain and snow by means of enchantment. (*See* **Siberia.**)

Yaksha or Jak : A species of Indian fiend or imp. Says Mr. Crookes : " The *Jak* is the modern representative of the *Yaksha,* who in better times was the attendant of Kuvera, the god of wealth, in which duty he was assisted by the Guhyaka. The character of the *Yaksha* is not very certain

He was called Punya-janas, " the good people," but he sometimes appears as an imp of evil. In the folk-tales, it must be admitted, the *Yakshas* have an equivocal reputation. In one story the female, or *Yakshini,* bewilders travellers at night, makes horns grow on their foreheads, and finally devours them ; in another the *Yakshas* have, like the *Churel,* feet turned the wrong way and squinting eyes ; in a third they separate the hero from the heroine because he failed to make due offerings to them on his wedding day. On the other hand, in a fourth tale the Yakshini is described as possessed of heavenly beauty ; she appears again when a sacrifice is made in a cemetery to get her into the hero's power, as a heavenly maiden beautifully adorned, seated in a chariot of gold surrounded by lovely girls ; and lastly, a Brahman meets some Buddhist ascetics, performs the *Uposhana* vow, and would have become a god, had it not been that a wicked man compelled him by force to take food in the evening, and so he was re-born as a *Guhyaka.*

" In the modern folk-lore of Kashmir, the *Yaksha* has turned into the *Yech* or *Yach,* a humorous, though powerful, sprite in the shape of a civet cat of a dark colour, with a white cap on his head. This small high cap is one of the marks of the Irish fairies, and the *Incubones* of Italy wear caps, ' the symbols of their hidden, secret natures.' The feet of the *Yech* are so small as to be almost invisible, and it squeaks in a feline way. It can assume any shape, and if its white cap can be secured, it becomes the servant of the possessor, and the white cap makes him invisible.

" In the *Vishnu Purana* we read that Vishnu created the *Yakshas* as beings emaciate with hunger, of hideous aspect, and with big beards, and that from their habit of crying for food they were so named. By the Buddhists they were regarded as benignant spirits. One of them acts as sort of chorus in the *Meghaduta* or ' Cloud Messenger ' of Kalidasa. Yet we read of the *Yaka Alawaka,* who, according to the Buddhist legend, used to live in a

Banyan tree, and slay any one who approached it ; while in Ceylon they are represented as demons whom Buddha destroyed. In later Hinduism they are generally of fair repute, and one of them was appointed by Indra to be the attendant of the Jaina Saint Mahavira.''

Yauhahu : A spirit. (See **American Indians.**)

Yeats, William Butler : Irish Author and Mystic. *William Butler Yeats* was born at Dublin in 1866, his father being John Yeats, a talented portrait-painter whose works include a fine likeness of Synge ; and during his boyhood the future author lived chiefly at his native town, and occasionally with his grandparents in County Sligo. At first he intended to make painting his life's work, and accordingly he entered the Dublin Art School ; but he soon left it, having realised that his true bent was for Literature ; and in 1887 he went to London, where he became intimate with Mr. Arthur Symons, and subsequently with Mr. George Moore. Prior to this Mr. Yeats had issued a little play, *Mosada* ; and now his gifts began to develop apace, the result being sundry volumes of beautiful poetry, notably *The Wanderings of Oisin* and *The Wind among the Reeds*. At this time, also, the author began to show himself an eminently thoughtful critic of literature ; while in 1870 he published a collection of Irish folk tales, and in the preface thereto he observed in relation to his compatriots that " a true literary consciousness—national to the centre—seems gradually to be forming out of all this disguising and prettyfing this penumbra of half-culture. We are preparing likely enough for a new Irish literary movement. . . . ." Nor was the prophecy unfulfilled, for, during the closing decade of the 19th century, the intellectuals of Ireland began to manifest a tense interest in their country's legendary lore, while simultaneously it transpired that the rising generation of writers in Ireland included many men of fine promise. Most of these last regarded *Mr. Yeats* as their leader, they rallied round him, he returned from London to Ireland, and anon he achieved the founding of the Irish Literary Theatre in Dublin, its *raison d'être* being the staging of plays by the new school of Hibernian authors.

This is not the place to detail the Irish artistic revival of the nineties of last century, and the reader may be referred to the monograph thereon by Mr. H. S. Krans, and more especially to Mr. George Moores' *Hail and Farewell*. Passing to speak of *Mr. Yeats'* contributions to the literature of Mysticism, these are mostly contained in a volume of collected essays, *Ideas of Good and Evil* ; and prominent among them are studies of the mystic element in Blake and Shelley, while another notable paper is one concerned with " The Body of the Father Christian Rosencrux.'' But still more important than these, perhaps, is a long study of " Magic,'' contained in the same volume, and here the author begins by bravely stating his creed : " I believe in

the practice and philosophy of what we have agreed to call magic, and what I must call the evocation of spirits, though I do not know what they are, in the power of creating magical illusions, in the visions of truth in the depths of the mind when the eyes are closed. . . . .''

After this declaration he tells how once an acquaintance of his, gathering together a small party in a darkened room, held a mace over " a tablet of many coloured squares, at the same time repeating " a form of words '' ; and straightway *Mr. Yeats* found that his " imagination began to move of itself, and to bring before me vivid images. . . . .'' He goes on to descant on these visions, while in the remainder of his essay he offers some details about superstitions in remote parts of Ireland ; and also furnishes sundry examples of thought-transmission and the like, most of them fresh and interesting.

But the author's interest in the supernatural does not transpire only in his prose, and, turning to his poems, one finds them permeated by a curious kind of mysticism which is perhaps essentially Celtic. For *Mr. Yeats*, it would seem, is only incidentally interested in holding communications with the dead, or with the spirit-world ; yet, like old bards of his native Ireland, he seems to find inanimate nature a living reality, he seems to have a strange intimacy therewith. A dreamer of dreams and a beholder of visions, he frequently crystalises these in his verse ; but the mystic element in his output consists pre-eminently in this, that he appears to hold actual converse with all those things which to ordinary men are no more than lifeless— with flowers and trees, with rivers, lakes and mountains.

W. G. B. M.

Yetziratic World : (See **Kabala.**)

Yoga, meaning " union,'' is applied in theosophy to assistance rendered to evolutionary process. The theosophical idea of evolution postulates a universal consciousness from which particular consciousness has come and to which each is returning along the path of evolution. The journey along this path can be quickened by the *Yoga*, the union of each particular with the universal consciousness. By the concentration of thought on any particular idea, that idea, in course of time becomes worked into the constitution of the thinker, so that, if the thought be good he will correspondingly help on the process of evolution. This general principle, applied in the light of past experience to the multifarious activities of the human mind, is of vast importance and influence in the moulding of the characters both of individuals and communities. (See **The Path, Karma, Theosophy.**)

Yogis : (See **India.**)

Yorkshire Spiritual Telegraph : Spiritualistic Journal. (See **Spiritualism.**)

Young, Brigham : (See **America U.S. of.**)

Z

Zabulon : A demon who possessed a lay sister of Loudon.

Zachaire, Denis : Alchemist. This French alchemist is chiefly remembered by his book, *Opuscule de la Philosophie de Metaux, traitant de l'Augmentation et Perfection de ceux*, and in the preface thereto he gives some account of his life, yet fails to state the precise date at which he was born. However, the event is commonly supposed to have taken place about 1510 ; while it is known that *Denis* was a native of La Guyenne, and that his parents were comfortably off, if not actually rich. As a young man he studied at Bordeaux, and subsequently at Toulouse, intending to become a lawyer ; yet he soon became more interested in alchemy than in legal affairs, and in 1535, on

his father's death putting him in possession of some money, he decided to try and multiply it by artificial means. Associating himself with an abbé who was reckoned a great adept in gold-making, *Denis* had soon disposed of the bulk of his patrimony ; but the charlatan's futile experiments, far from disillusioning him, served rather to nerve him to further endeavours, and in 1539 he went to Paris, where he made the acquaintance of many renowned alchemists. From one of them, so he declares, he imbibed the precious secret ; and thereupon he hastened to the court of the King of Navarre, Antoine d'Albert, grandfather of Henri IV., offering to make gold if the requisite materials were supplied. His majesty was deeply interested, and promised a reward of no less than four thousand crowns in the event of the researches proving fruitful ; but *Zachaires'* vaunted skill failed him in the hour of need, and he retired discomfited to Toulouse. Here he became friendly with a certain priest, who advised him strongly to renounce his quest, and study natural science instead ; so *Denis* went off to Paris once more, intending to act in accordance with his counsel. Ere a little while, nevertheless, he was deep in alchemy again, making actual experiments, and studying closely the writings of Raymond Lully and Arnold di Villanova ; while, according to his own account of his career, on Easter day in the year 1550 he succeeded in converting a large quantity of quicksilver into gold. Then, some time after this alleged triumph, he left France to travel in Switzerland, and lived for a while at Lausanne ; while later on he wandered to Germany, and there he died. It is probable that his closing years were spent in dire poverty, but this is not recorded definitely, nor has the exact date of the alchemist's demise ever been ascertained.

As regards the book by *Zachaire* cited above, it was published originally at Antwerp in 1567, it was repeatedly reprinted thereafter, and even won the honour of being translated into Latin ; while to this day, indeed, it is sought keenly by French philosphers with a taste for the curious.

Zacornu : A tree in the Mohamedan hell, which has for fruit the heads of devils.

Zadkiel : One of the angels in the Jewish rabbinical legend of the celestial hierarchies. He is the ruler of Jupiter, and through him pass grace, goodness, mercy, piety, and munificence, and he bestows clemency, benevolence and justice on all.

Zaebos : Grand count of the infernal regions. He appears in the shape of a handsome soldier mounted on a crocodile. His head is adorned with a ducal coronet. He is of a gentle disposition.

Zagam : Grand king and president of the infernal regions. He appears under the form of a bull with the wings of a griffin. He changes water into wine, blood into oil, the fool into a wise man, lead into silver, and copper into gold. Thirty legions obey him.

Zahuris or Zahories : French people who had travelled in Spain frequently had curious tales to tell concerning the *Zahuris* ; people who were so keen-sighted that they could see streams of water and veins of metal hidden in the earth, and could indicate the whereabouts of buried treasure and the bodies of murdered persons. Explanations have been offered on natural lines. It was said that these men knew where water was to be found by the vapours arising at such spots ; and that they were able to trace mines of gold and silver and copper by the particular herbs growing in their neighbourhood. But to the Spaniard such explanations are unsatisfactory ; they persist in believing that the *Zahuris* are gifted with supernatural faculties, that they are *en rapport* with the demons, and that, if they wished, they could, without any physical aid, read thoughts and discover secrets which were as a sealed book to the grosser senses of ordinary mortals. For the rest, the *Zahuris* have red eyes ; and in order that one should become a *Zahuri* it is necessary that he should have been born on Good Friday.

Zanoni, by Bulwer Lytton : (*See* **Fiction, Occult.**)

Zapan : According to Wierius, one of the Kings of Hell.

Zedekias : Notwithstanding the credulity of the French people in the reign of Pepin the Short, they refused to believe in the existence of elementary spirits. The Kabalist *Zedekias*, being minded to convince the world, thereupon commanded the sylphs to become visible to all men. According to the Abbé de Villars, the admirable creatures responded magnificently. They were beheld in human form, sometimes ranged in battle, whether marching in good order, or under arms, or camping in superb pavilions ; and, again, in aerial navies of marvellous structure, whose flying flotillas sailed through the air, at the will of the *Zephyrs.* But the ignorant generation to which they appeared failed entirely to understand the significance of the strange spectacle. They believed at first that the creatures were sorcerers who had betaken themselves to aerial regions for the purpose of exciting storms and sending down hail on the harvests. The sages and jurisconsuls were of the popular opinion. The emperors shared the same idea, which became so widespread that even the wise Charlemagne, and after him Louis the Debonnair, imposed heavy penalties on these supposed aerial tyrants. (*See* **Elementary Spirits and France.**)

Zeernebooch : A dark god, monarch of the empire of the dead among the ancient Germans.

Zepar : Grand duke of the infernal empire, who may be identical with Vepar, or Separ. Nevertheless, under the name of *Zepar* he has the form of a warrior. He casts men into the evil passions. Twenty-eight legions obey him.

Ziazaa : A black and white stone ; it renders its possessor litigious, and causes terrible visions.

Ziito : One of the most remarkable magicians of whom history has left any record. He was a sorcerer at the court of King Wenceslaus of Bohemia (afterwards Emperor of Germany) towards the end of the fourteenth century, and among his more famous exploits is one chronicled by Dulsavius, bishop of Olmutz, in his *History of Bohemia.* On the occasion of the marriage of Wenceslaus with Sophia, daughter of the elector Palatine of Bavaria, the elector, knowing his son-in-law's liking for juggling and magical exhibitions, brought in his train a number of morris-dancers, jugglers and such entertainers. When they came forward to give their exhibition *Ziito* remained unobtrusively among the spectators. He was not entirely unnoticed, however, for his remarkable appearance drew the attention of those about him. His oddest feature was his mouth, which actually stretched from ear to ear. After watching the magicians for some time in silence, *Ziito* appeared to become exasperated at the halting way in which the tricks were carried through, and going up to the principal magician he taunted him with incompetency. The rival professor hotly defended his performance, and a discussion ensued which was ended at last by *Ziito* swallowing his opponent, just as he stood, leaving only his shoes, which he said were dirty and unfit for consumption. After this extraordinary feat, he retired for a little while to a closet, from which he shortly emerged, leading the rival magician by the hand. He then gave a performance of his own which put the former exhibition entirely in the shade. He changed himself into many divers shapes, taking the form of first one person and then another, none of whom bore any resemblance either to himself or to each other. In a car drawn by barn-door fowls he kept pace with the King's carriage. When the guests were assembled at dinner, he played a multitude of elfish tricks on them, to their amusement or annoyance, as the case might be. Indeed, he was at all times an exceedingly mischievous creature as is shown by another story told of him. Feigning to be in want of money, and apparently casting about anxiously for the means of obtaining some, he at length took a handful of corn, and made it look like thirty fat hogs. These he took to Michael, a rich but very mean dealer. The latter purchased them after some haggling, but was warned not to let them drink at the river. But the warning was disregarded, and the hogs turned into grains of corn. The enraged dealer went in search of *Ziito*, whom he found at last in a vintner's shop. In vain Michael shouted and stamped, the magician took no notice, but seemed to be in a fit of abstraction. The dealer, beside himself, seized *Ziito's* foot and pulled it as hard as he could. To his dismay, the foot and leg came right off, while *Ziito* screamed lustily, and hauled Michael before the judge, where the two presented their complaints. What the decision was, history does not relate, but it is unlikely that the ingenious *Ziito* came off worse.

Zizis : The name which the modern Jews give to their phylacteries.

Zlokobinca : (Evil-meter.) Slavonic name for a witch. (*See* **Slavs.**)

Zoaphite : According to the *Journal des Voyages* of Jean Struys, a species of Cucumber which feeds on neighbouring plants. Its fruit has the form of a lamb, with the head, feet, and tail of that animal distinctly apparent, whence it it is called, in the language of the country, *Canaret*, or *Conarer*, signifying a lamb. Its skin is covered with a white down as delicate as silk. The Tartars think a great deal of it and most of them keep it carefully in their houses, where the author of the *Journal des Voyages* saw it several times. It grows on a stalk about three feet in height, to which it is attached by a sort of tendril. On this tendril it can move about, and turn and bend towards the herbs on which it feeds, and without which it soon drys up and withers. Wolves love it, and devour it with avidity, because it tastes like the flesh of 'amb. The author adds that he has been assured that it has bones, flesh, and blood, whence it is also known in its native country as *Zoaphite,* or animal plant.

Zodiac, Signs of the : (*See* **Astrology.**)

Zohar : (*See* **Kabala.**)

Zoist : Journal of Magnetism : (*See* **Spiritualism.**)

Zoroaster : (*See* **Persia.**)

Zracne Vile : (*See* **Slavs.**)

Zschocke : (*See* **Germany.**)

Zulu Witch-finders : (*See* **Africa.**)